Elementary and Middle School Mathematics

P9-AGT-064

Elementary and Middle School Mathematics

Mathematics

Teaching Developmentally

FIFTH EDITION

John A. Van de Walle

Virginia Commonwealth University

PEARSON

Boston | New York | San Francisco
Mexico City | Montreal | Toronto | London | Madrid | Munich | Paris
Hong Kong | Singapore | Tokyo | Cape Town | Sydney

L.C.C. SOUTH CAMPUS LIBRARY

Executive Editor: Steve Dragin
Series Editor: Traci Mueller
Development Editor: Sonny Regelman
Editorial Assistant: Krista E. Price
Senior Marketing Manager: Elizabeth Fogarty
Supplements Editor: Tom Jefferies
Permissions Coordinator: William Walsh
Permissions Research: Karyn Morrison
Composition and Prepress Buyer: Linda Cox
Manufacturing Buyer: Andrew Turso
Cover Administrator: Linda Knowles
Editorial-Production Service: Omegatype Typography, Inc.
Interior Designer: Carol Somberg
Cover Designer: Suzanne Harbison
Illustrations: Omegatype Typography, Inc.
Electronic Composition: Omegatype Typography, Inc.

For related titles and support materials, visit our online catalog at www.ablongman.com.

Copyright © 2004 Pearson Education, Inc.

All rights reserved. No part of the material protected by this copyright notice may be reproduced or utilized in any form or by any means, electronic or mechanical, including photocopying, recording, or by any information storage and retrieval system, without written permission from the copyright owner.

To obtain permission(s) to use material from this work, please submit a written request to Allyn and Bacon, Permissions Department, 75 Arlington Street, Boston, MA 02116, or fax your request to 617-848-7320.

Between the time Website information is gathered and then published, it is not unusual for some sites to have closed. Also, the transcription of URLs can result in typographical errors. The publisher would appreciate notification where these errors occur so that they may be corrected in subsequent editions.

QA
135.6
.V36
2004

Library of Congress Cataloging-in-Publication Data

Van de Walle, John A.
    Elementary and middle school mathematics : teaching developmentally / John A. Van de Walle.—5th ed.
        p. cm.
    Includes bibliographical references and index.
    ISBN 0-205-38689-X
        1. Mathematics—Study and teaching (Elementary) 2. Mathematics—Study and teaching (Middle school) I. Title.

    QA135.6.V36 2004
    510'.71'2—dc21

                                            2002043767

Printed in the United States of America

10 9 8 7 6 5 4 3   VH   09 08 07 06 05 04

NOV 0 9 2004

Brief Contents

Detailed Contents   vii

Preface   xix

SECTION I
Teaching Mathematics: Foundations and Perspectives   1

chapter 1
Teaching Mathematics in the Context of the Reform Movement   1

chapter 2
Exploring What It Means to Do Mathematics   12

chapter 3
Developing Understanding in Mathematics   22

chapter 4
Teaching Through Problem Solving   36

chapter 5
Building Assessment into Instruction   59

chapter 6
Planning in the Problem-Based Classroom   81

chapter 7
Teaching All Children Mathematics   91

chapter 8
Technology and School Mathematics   103

SECTION II
Development of Mathematical Concepts and Procedures   115

chapter 9
Developing Early Number Concepts and Number Sense   115

chapter 10
Developing Meanings for the Operations   135

chapter 11
Helping Children Master the Basic Facts   156

chapter 12
Whole-Number Place-Value Development   178

chapter 13
Strategies for Whole-Number Computation   201

chapter **14**

Computational Estimation with Whole Numbers   228

chapter **15**

Developing Fraction Concepts   242

chapter **16**

Computation with Fractions   264

chapter **17**

Decimal and Percent Concepts and
Decimal Computation   280

chapter **18**

Developing Concepts of Ratio and Proportion   298

chapter **19**

Developing Measurement Concepts   316

chapter **20**

Geometric Thinking and Geometric Concepts   345

chapter **21**

Exploring Concepts of Data Analysis
and Probability   386

chapter **22**

Algebraic Reasoning   417

chapter **23**

Exploring Functions   436

chapter **24**

Developing Concepts of Exponents,
Integers, and Real Numbers   453

appendix **A**

Principles and Standards for School Mathematics:
Content Standards and Grade Level Expectations   A-1

appendix **B**

Professional Standards for Teaching Mathematics:
Teaching Standards   B-1

appendix **C**

Guide to Blackline Masters   C-1

References   R-1

Index   I-1

Detailed Contents

Preface   xix

SECTION I
Teaching Mathematics: Foundations and Perspectives   1

The fundamental core of effective teaching of mathematics combines an understanding of how children learn, how to promote that learning by teaching through problem solving, and how to plan for and assess that learning on a daily basis. Introductory chapters in this section provide perspectives on trends in mathematics education and the process of doing mathematics and develop the core ideas of learning, teaching, assessment, and planning. Additional perspectives on mathematics for special children and the role of technology are also discussed.

chapter 1
Teaching Mathematics in the Context of the Reform Movement   1

An Era of Change   1
A Brief History of Reforms   1
Leadership Provided by NCTM   2

Principles and Standards for School Mathematics   2
Goals for Students   2
The Six Principles   3

A Pre-K-to-12 Perspective   4
The Five Content Standards   4
The Five Process Standards   4

The *Professional Standards for Teaching Mathematics*   6
Five Shifts in Classroom Environment   6
The Teaching Standards   6

The *Assessment Standards for School Mathematics*   6

Influences and Pressures on Reform   6
National and International Studies   7
State Standards   7
Curriculum   8

An Invitation to Learn and Grow   8

REFLECTIONS ON CHAPTER 1   9
Writing to Learn   9

For Discussion and Exploration   9
Recommendations for Further Reading   9
Reform Curricula   11

chapter 2
Exploring What It Means to Do Mathematics   12

Contrasting Perceptions of School Mathematics   12
Traditional Views of Mathematics   12
Mathematics as a Science of Pattern and Order   13

What Does It Mean to Do Mathematics?   13
The Verbs of Doing Mathematics   13
What Is Basic in Mathematics?   14
An Environment for Doing Mathematics   14

An Invitation to Do Mathematics   14
Let's Do Some Mathematics!   14
No Answer Book   19
Some More Explorations   19

Helping Students Do Mathematics   20

REFLECTIONS ON CHAPTER 2   20
Writing to Learn   20
For Discussion and Exploration   20
Recommendations for Further Reading   21

chapter 3

Developing Understanding in Mathematics   22

A Constructivist View of Learning   22
The Construction of Ideas   22
Understanding   24
Examples of Understanding   25
Benefits of Relational Understanding   26

Types of Mathematical Knowledge   27
Conceptual Knowledge of Mathematics   27
Procedural Knowledge of Mathematics   27
Procedural Knowledge and Doing Mathematics   28

The Role of Models in Developing Understanding   28
Models for Mathematical Concepts   28
Using Models in the Classroom   30
Incorrect Use of Models   31

Teaching Developmentally   31
Foundations of a Developmental Approach   31
Strategies for Effective Teaching   32

REFLECTIONS ON CHAPTER 3   34
Writing to Learn   34
For Discussion and Exploration   34
Recommendations for Further Reading   34

chapter 4

Teaching Through Problem Solving   36

Problem Solving as a Principal Instructional Strategy   36
An Illustration   36
Starting Where the Students Are: A Shift in Thinking About Mathematics Instruction   37
The Value of Teaching with Problems   37

Problems and Tasks for Learning Mathematics   38
A Description of Tasks or Problems   38
Examples of Problem-Based Tasks   38
Good Problems Have Multiple Entry Points   40

A Three-Part Lesson Format   41
Before, During, and After   41
Teacher Actions in the Before Phase   42
Teacher Actions in the During Phase   45
Teacher Actions in the After Phase   46

Designing and Selecting Effective Tasks   48
Your Textbook   48
Children's Literature   50
Other Resources   51
A Task Selection Guide   51

Teaching Tips and Questions   52
Promoting Discourse   52

Four Suggestions   52
How Much to Tell and Not to Tell   53
Frequently Asked Questions   53

Teaching About Problem Solving   54
Strategies and Processes   54
Metacognition   54
Disposition   55

Working Toward Problem-Solving Goals While Students Learn   55
Developing Problem-Solving Strategies   55
Plan-and-Carry-out Strategies   55
Developing Metacognitive Habits   56
Attending to Attitudinal Goals   56

REFLECTIONS ON CHAPTER 4   57
Writing to Learn   57
For Discussion and Exploration   57
Recommendations for Further Reading   57

chapter 5

Building Assessment into Instruction   59

Blurring the Line Between Instruction and Assessment   59
What Is Assessment?   59

The *Assessment Standards*   60
Purposes of Assessment   60

What Should Be Assessed?   61
Concepts and Procedures   61
Mathematical Processes   61
Disposition   62

Appropriate Assessment   62
Appropriate Assessment Tasks   62
Examples of Assessment Tasks   62
More Thoughts About Assessment Tasks   64

Rubrics and Performance Indicators   64
Simple Rubrics   64
Performance Indicators   64
Student Involvement with Rubrics   64
More Examples of Rubrics   64

Using Observation in Assessment   67
Anecdotal Notes   67
An Observation Rubric   67
Checklists or Forms for Individuals   68
Checklists for Full Classes   68

Writing and Journals   69
The Value of Writing   69
Journals   69
Writing Prompts and Ideas   70
Journals for Early Learners   70
Student Self-Assessment   71

Tests   72

Dealing with High-Stakes Testing   73
Teaching State-Mandated Standards   73
Improving Performance on High-Stakes Tests   73

Portfolios in the Assessment Plan   74
Portfolio Content Suggestions   74
Portfolio Management   76

Diagnostic Interviews   76
Reasons to Consider an Interview   76
Planning an Interview   76
Suggestions for Effective Interviews   77

Grading   77
Confronting the Myth   77
Grading Issues   78

REFLECTIONS ON CHAPTER 5   78
Writing to Learn   78
For Discussion and Exploration   79
Recommendations for Further Reading   79

chapter 6

Planning in the Problem-Based Classroom   81

Planning a Problem-Based Lesson   81
Variations of the Three-Part Lesson   83
Workstations and Games   83

Dealing with Diversity   84
Plan for Multiple Entry Points   84
Plan Differentiated Tasks   84
Use Heterogeneous Groupings   85
Listen Carefully to Students   85

Drill or Practice?   85
New Definitions of Drill and Practice   85
What Drill Provides   86
What Practice Provides   86
When Is Drill Appropriate?   86
Kids Who Don't Get It   87

Homework   87
Practice as Homework   87
Drill as Homework   88

The Role of the Textbook   88
How Are Textbooks Developed?   88
Teacher's Editions   88
Two-Page Lesson Format   88
Suggestions for Textbook Use   89

REFLECTIONS ON CHAPTER 6   89
Writing to Learn   89
For Discussion and Exploration   90
Recommendations for Further Reading   90

chapter 7

Teaching All Children Mathematics   91

Mathematics for All Children   91
Diversity in Today's Classroom   91
Challenging Traditional Beliefs   92

Children with Learning Problems   92

Specific Learning Disabilities   92
A Perspective on Learning Disabilities   93
Adaptations for Specific Learning Disabilities   93

Mental Disabilities   94
Modifications in Instruction   94
Modifications in Curriculum   95

Multicultural and Social Equity   95
A Question of Access   95
Expectations   95
Success for At-Risk Students   96

Culture, Language, and Mathematics   96
Cultural Diversity   96
Ethnomathematics   96
Teaching Second Language Learners   97

From Gender Bias to Gender Equity   98
Possible Causes of Gender Inequity   98
Working Toward Gender Equity: What Can Be Done?   98

Mathematics for the Gifted and Talented   99
Identification of Mathematically Promising Students   99
Acceleration, Enrichment, and Depth   99

REFLECTIONS ON CHAPTER 7   100
Writing to Learn   100
For Discussion and Exploration   101
Recommendations for Further Reading   101

chapter 8

Technology and School Mathematics   103

Calculators in the Mathematics Classroom   103
Benefits of Calculator Use   103
Addressing Myths and Fears About Using Calculators   104
Calculators for Every Student, Every Day   105

Graphing Calculators   105
What the Graphing Calculator Offers   105
Electronic Data Collection   106

The Computer as a Tool in Mathematics   107
Electronic Manipulatives for Numeration   107
Geometry Tools   108

Probability and Data Analysis Tools   109
Function Graphers   109

Instructional Software   109
Concept Instruction   109
Problem Solving   110
Drill   110

Guidelines for Selecting and Using Software   110
How to Select Software   110
Guidelines for Using Software   111

Mathematics Education Resources on the Internet   111
Professional Information   111
Teacher Resources   112
Applets   112

REFLECTIONS ON CHAPTER 8   113
Writing to Learn   113
For Discussion and Exploration   113
Recommendations for Further Reading   114

SECTION II

Development of Mathematical Concepts and Procedures   115

This section serves as the application of the core ideas of Section I. Here you will find chapters on every major area of content in the K–8 mathematics curriculum. Numerous problem-based activities to engage students are interwoven with a discussion of the mathematical content and how children develop their understanding of that content. At the outset of each chapter, you will find a listing of "Big Ideas," the mathematical umbrella for the chapter. Also included are ideas for incorporating children's literature, technology, and assessment. These chapters are designed to help you develop pedagogical strategies and to serve as a resource for your teaching.

chapter 9

Developing Early Number Concepts and Number Sense   115

■ **BIG IDEAS   115**
■ **CONTENT CONNECTIONS   115**

Number Development in Pre-K and Kindergarten   116
The Relationships of More, Less, and Same   116
Early Counting   116
Numeral Writing and Recognition   117

■ **Technology Note   118**
Counting On and Counting Back   118

Early Number Sense   119

Relationships Among Numbers 1 Through 10   119
A Collection of Number Relationships   119
Spatial Relationships: Patterned Set Recognition   120
One and Two More, One and Two Less   121
Anchoring Numbers to 5 and 10   122
Part-Part-Whole Relationships   123

■ **Technology Note   126**
Dot Card Activities   127

■ **Assessment Notes   127**

■ **INVESTIGATIONS IN NUMBER, DATA, AND SPACE:**
Grade K, *How Many in All?*   128

Relationships for Numbers 10 to 20   129
A Pre–Place-Value Relationship with 10   129
Extending More and Less Relationships   129
Double and Near-Double Relationships   129

Number Sense and the Real World   130
Estimation and Measurement   130
More Connections   130
Graphs   131

■ **Literature Connections   132**
Anno's Counting House   132
The Very Hungry Caterpillar   132
Two Ways to Count to Ten   132

Extensions to Early Mental Mathematics   132

■ **REFLECTIONS ON CHAPTER 9   133**
Writing to Learn   133
For Discussion and Exploration   134
Recommendations for Further Reading   134

chapter 10

Developing Meanings for the Operations   135

■ **BIG IDEAS   135**
■ **CONTENT CONNECTIONS   135**

Addition and Subtraction Problem Structures 135
Examples of Problems for Each Structure 136
Reflections on the Four Structures 137

Teaching Addition and Subtraction 138
Using Contextual Problems 138
Using Model-Based Problems 139
Comparison Models 140
The Order Property and the Zero Property 141

■ **INVESTIGATIONS IN NUMBER, DATA, AND SPACE:**
Grade 2, *Coins, Coupons, and Combinations* 142

■ **Technology Note 143**

**Problem Structures for Multiplication
and Division 143**
Examples of Problems for Each Structure 143
Reflections on the Multiplicative Structures 146

Teaching Multiplication and Division 146
Using Contextual Problems 147
Remainders 147
Using Models-Based Problems 147
Multiplication and Division Activities 148
Useful Multiplication and Division Properties 149

■ **Technology Note 150**

Solving Contextual Problems 150
Analyzing Context Problems 150
Two-Step Problems 152

■ **Assessment Notes 153**

■ **Literature Connections 153**
How Many Snails? 153
More Than One 153
Each Orange Had 8 Slices 153

REFLECTIONS ON CHAPTER 10 154
Writing to Learn 154
For Discussion and Exploration 154
Recommendations for Further Reading 154

CʜᴀᴘᴛᴇR **11**

Hᴇʟᴘiɴɢ Cʜiʟᴅʀᴇɴ Mᴀsᴛᴇʀ
ᴛʜᴇ Bᴀsic Fᴀcᴛs **156**

■ **BIG IDEAS 156**
■ **CONTENT CONNECTIONS 156**

A Three-Step Approach to Fact Mastery 156
The Role of Number and Operation Concepts 157
Development of Efficient Strategies 157
Drill of Efficient Methods and Strategy Selection 158
Overview of the Approach 158

Strategies for Addition Facts 159
One-More-Than and Two-More-Than Facts 160
Facts with Zero 161

Doubles 161
Near-Doubles 162
Make-Ten Facts 162
A Generic Task 163
Other Strategies and the Last Six Facts 164

Strategies for Subtraction Facts 165
Subtraction as Think-Addition 165
Subtraction Facts with Sums to 10 165
The 36 "Hard" Subtraction Facts: Sums
Greater Than 10 166

Strategies for Multiplication Facts 168
Doubles 169
Fives Facts 169
Zeros and Ones 170
Nifty Nines 170
Helping Facts 171

■ **INVESTIGATIONS IN NUMBER, DATA, AND SPACE:**
Grade 3, *Things That Come in Groups* 173

Division Facts and "Near Facts" 173

Effective Drill 174
When and How to Drill 174

■ **Technology Note 175**
What About Timed Tests? 175

**Fact Remediation with Upper-Grade
Students 176**

Facts: No Barrier to Good Mathematics 176

REFLECTIONS ON CHAPTER 11 177
Writing to Learn 177
For Discussion and Exploration 177
Recommendations for Further Reading 177

CʜᴀᴘᴛᴇR **12**

Wʜoʟᴇ-Nᴜᴍʙᴇʀ Pʟᴀcᴇ-Vᴀʟᴜᴇ
Dᴇᴠᴇʟoᴘᴍᴇɴᴛ **178**

■ **BIG IDEAS 178**
■ **CONTENT CONNECTIONS 178**

Pre-Base-Ten Concepts 178
Children's Pre–Base-Ten View of Number 179
Quantity Tied to Counts by Ones 179

Basic Ideas of Place Value 179
Integration with Base-Ten Groupings
with Counts by Ones 179
The Role of Counting in Constructing
Base-Ten Ideas 180
Integration of Groupings with Words 180
Integration of Groupings with Place-Value
Notation 180
Relational Understanding of Place Value 181

Models for Place Value 183
  Base-Ten Models and the Ten-Makes-One
    Relationship 183

■ **INVESTIGATIONS IN NUMBER, DATA, AND SPACE:**
  Grade 1, *Number Games and Story Problems* 182

▨ **Technology Note** 184
  Nonproportional Materials 184

Developing Place-Value Concepts and Procedures 184
  Grouping Activities 184

▨ **Technology Note** 187
  Oral Names for Numbers 188
  Written Symbols 190
  The Hundreds Chart 190

▨ **Technology Note** 193

Number Sense Development 193
  Relative Magnitude 193
  Connections to Real-World Ideas 194
  Approximate Numbers and Rounding 194

Numbers Beyond 1000 195
  Extending the Place-Value System 195
  Conceptualizing Large Numbers 196

▨ **Literature Connections** 197
  Moira's Birthday 197
  How to Count Like a Martian 197
  The King's Commissioners 197
  A Million Fish . . . More or Less 197

▨ **Assessment Notes** 198
  Ongoing Assessment 198
  Diagnosis of Place-Value Concepts 198

REFLECTIONS ON CHAPTER 12 199
  Writing to Learn 199
  For Discussion and Exploration 200
  Recommendations for Further Reading 200

ᴄʜᴀᴘᴛᴇʀ **13**

Sᴛʀᴀᴛᴇɢɪᴇs ꜰᴏʀ Wʜᴏʟᴇ-Nᴜᴍʙᴇʀ
Cᴏᴍᴘᴜᴛᴀᴛɪᴏɴ 201

■ **BIG IDEAS** 201
■ **CONTENT CONNECTIONS** 201

Toward Computational Fluency 202
  Direct Modeling 202
  Invented Strategies 203
  Contrasts with Traditional Algorithms 203
  Benefits of Invented Strategies 204
  Mental Computation 204
  Traditional Algorithms 204

Development of Invented Strategies: A General
  Approach 205

  Use Story Problems Frequently 205
  Use Three-Part Lesson Format 205
  Progression from Direct Modeling 205

Invented Strategies for Addition and Subtraction 205
  Adding and Subtracting Single Digits 206
  Adding and Subtracting Tens and Hundreds 206
  Adding Two-Digit Numbers 206
  Subtracting by Counting Up 207
  Take-Away Subtraction 207
  Extensions and Challenges 208

Activities for Flexible Thinking 208
  Working with Tens and Hundreds 209
  Thinking About Parts of Numbers 209

▨ **Assessment Notes** 211

Traditional Algorithms for Addition
  and Subtraction 211
  The Addition Algorithm 211
  The Subtraction Algorithm 213

Invented Strategies for Multiplication 214
  Useful Representations 214
  Multiplication by a Single-Digit Multiplier 215
  Using Multiples of 10 and 100 216
  Two-Digit Multipliers: The Area Model 216

■ **INVESTIGATIONS IN NUMBER, DATA, AND SPACE:**
  Grade 4, *Packages and Groups* 217

The Traditional Algorithm for Multiplication 217
  One-Digit Multipliers 217
  Two-Digit Multipliers 218

Invented Strategies for Division 220

The Traditional Algorithm for Division 220
  One-Digit Divisors 221
  Two-Digit Divisors 223

▨ **Technology Note** 224

▨ **Literature Connections** 224
  Cookies 224
  Is a Blue Whale the Biggest Thing There Is? 224

▨ **Assessment Notes** 224
  Ongoing Assessment 224
  Occasional Interviews 225

REFLECTIONS ON CHAPTER 13 225
  Writing to Learn 225
  For Discussion and Exploration 226
  Recommendations for Further Reading 226

ᴄʜᴀᴘᴛᴇʀ **14**

Cᴏᴍᴘᴜᴛᴀᴛɪᴏɴᴀʟ Esᴛɪᴍᴀᴛɪᴏɴ
ᴡɪᴛʜ Wʜᴏʟᴇ Nᴜᴍʙᴇʀs 228

■ **BIG IDEAS** 228
■ **CONTENT CONNECTIONS** 228

Introducing Computational Estimation   228
Understanding Computational Estimation   229
Choosing a Form of Computation   229
Suggestions for Estimation Instruction   229
Estimation Without Estimates   230

Estimations from Invented Strategies   231
Stop Before the Details   231
Cluster Problems   232

■ **INVESTIGATIONS IN NUMBER, DATA, AND SPACE:**
Grade 5, *Building on Numbers You Know*   233

Computational Estimation Strategies   233
Front-End Methods   234
Rounding Methods   234
Using Compatible Numbers   235

Estimation Exercises   237
Calculator Activities   237
More Estimation Activities   238

▨ Technology Note   238

Estimating with Fractions, Decimals,
and Percents   239

▨ Literature Connections   239
The Twelve Circus Rings   239
The 329th Friend   239

▨ Assessment Notes   240

REFLECTIONS ON CHAPTER 14   240
Writing to Learn   240
For Discussion and Exploration   240
Recommendations for Further Reading   240

chapter **15**

Developing Fraction Concepts   242

■ **BIG IDEAS**   242
■ **CONTENT CONNECTIONS**   242

Sharing and the Concept of Fractional Parts   243
Sharing Tasks   243
Sharing Tasks and Fraction Language   244

Models for Fractions   244
Region or Area Models   244
Length or Measurement Models   244
Set Models   246

From Fractional Parts to Fraction Symbols   246
Fractional Parts and Words   246
Understanding Fraction Symbols   247

Fraction Number Sense   251
Benchmarks of Zero, One-Half, and One   251
Thinking About Which Is More?   252

■ **INVESTIGATIONS IN NUMBER, DATA, AND SPACE:**
Grade 4, *Different Shapes, Equal Pieces*   255

▨ Technology Note   254
Estimation   256

Equivalent-Fraction Concepts   257
Concepts Versus Rules   257
Equivalent-Fraction Concepts   257
Developing an Equivalent-Fraction Algorithm   260

▨ Technology Note   261

▨ Literature Connections   261
The Doorbell Rang   262
Gator Pie   262

REFLECTIONS ON CHAPTER 15   262
Writing to Learn   262
For Discussion and Exploration   263
Recommendations for Further Reading   263

chapter **16**

Computation with Fractions   264

■ **BIG IDEAS**   264
■ **CONTENT CONNECTIONS**   264

Number Sense and Fraction Algorithms   264
The Dangerous Rush to Rules   265
A Problem-Based, Number Sense Approach   265

Addition and Subtraction   265
Informal Exploration   265
The Myth of Common Denominators   266
Developing the Algorithm   267
Estimation and Simple Methods   268

■ **CONNECTED MATHEMATICS:** Grade 6, *Bits and Pieces II*   269

Multiplication   270
Informal Exploration   270
Developing the Algorithm   272

Division   273
Informal Exploration: Partition Concept   274
Informal Exploration: Measurement Concept   275
Developing the Algorithms   277

▨ Technology Note   278

REFLECTIONS ON CHAPTER 16   278
Writing to Learn   278
For Discussion and Exploration   279
Recommendations for Further Reading   279

chapter **17**

Decimal and Percent Concepts
and Decimal Computation   280

■ **BIG IDEAS**   280
■ **CONTENT CONNECTIONS**   280

Connecting Two Different Representational Systems   280
Base-Ten Fractions   281
Extending the Place-Value System   282
Making the Fraction–Decimal Connection   284

Developing Decimal Number Sense   285
Familiar Fractions Connected to Decimals   285
Approximation with a Nice Fraction   286
Ordering Decimal Numbers   287

■ **Technology Note   288**
Other Fraction–Decimal Equivalents   288

Introducing Percents   288
A Third Operator System   288
Realistic Percent Problems   289

Computation with Decimals   292
The Role of Estimation   292
Addition and Subtraction   293
Multiplication   293
Division   294

■ **CONNECTED MATHEMATICS:** Grade 6, *Bits and Pieces II*   295

■ **Literature Connections   295**
The Phantom Tollbooth   296

■ **Assessment Notes   296**

REFLECTIONS ON CHAPTER 17   296
Writing to Learn   296
For Discussion and Exploration   297
Recommendations for Further Reading   297

CHAPTER 18

Developing Concepts of Ratio and Proportion   298

■ **BIG IDEAS   298**
■ **CONTENT CONNECTIONS   298**

Proportional Reasoning   298
Examples of Ratios in Different Contexts   299
Proportions   300
Proportional Reasoning and Children   300
Additive Versus Multiplicative Situations   300

Informal Activities to Develop Proportional Reasoning   301
Equivalent-Ratio Selections   301
Comparing Ratios   302
Scaling with Ratio Tables   303
Construction and Measurement Activities   305

■ **CONNECTED MATHEMATICS:** Grade 7, *Comparing and Scaling*   308

Solving Proportions   309
Within and Between Ratios   309

An Informal Approach   309
The Cross-Product Algorithm   310
Solve the Proportion   311
Activities Leading to Proportions   311
Percent Problems as Proportions   311

■ **Technology Note   313**

■ **Literature Connections   313**
If You Hopped Like a Frog   313
Counting on Frank   314
The Borrowers   314

■ **Assessment Notes   314**

REFLECTIONS ON CHAPTER 18   314
Writing to Learn   315
For Discussion and Exploration   315
Recommendations for Further Reading   315

CHAPTER 19

Developing Measurement Concepts   316

■ **BIG IDEAS   316**
■ **CONTENT CONNECTIONS   316**

The Meaning and Process of Measuring   317

Developing Measurement Concepts and Skills   318
A General Plan of Instruction   318
Informal Units and Standard Units: Reasons for Using Each   319
The Role of Estimation in Learning Measurement   319
The Approximate Nature of Measurement   319

Measuring Length   320
Comparison Activities   320
Using Units of Length   320
Two Units and Fractional Parts of Units   321
Making and Using Rulers   321

■ **INVESTIGATIONS IN NUMBER, DATA, AND SPACE:** Grade 3, *From Paces to Feet*   323

Measuring Area   323
Comparison Activities   323
Using Units of Area   325
Using Grids   326
Area and Perimeter   326

Measuring Volume and Capacity   327
Comparison Activities   327
Using Units of Volume   327
Making and Using Measuring Cups   327

Measuring Weight and Mass   328
Making Comparisons   328
Using Units of Weight or Mass   328
Making and Using a Scale   329

Measuring Angles   329
Comparing Angles   329
Making a Protractor   329

Introducing Standard Units   331
Instructional Goals   331
Important Standard Units   332

Estimating Measures   333
Techniques of Measurement Estimation   334
Tips for Teaching Estimation   334
Measurement Estimation Activities   335

Developing Formulas   335
Common Difficulties   335
The Area of Rectangles, Parallelograms, Triangles, and Trapezoids   336

■ **Technology Note   338**
Circle Formulas   338
Volumes of Common Solid Shapes   339

Measuring Time   341
Clock Reading   341
Related Concepts   342

■ **Assessment Notes   342**
Focus on Ideas   342
Standard Units   342
Formulas   342

■ **Literature Connections   343**
How Big Is a Foot?   343
Jim and the Beanstalk   343
Counting on Frank   343
8,000 Stones   343

REFLECTIONS ON CHAPTER 19   343
Writing to Learn   343
For Discussion and Exploration   344
Recommendations for Further Reading   344

chapter 20

Geometric Thinking and Geometric Concepts   345

■ **BIG IDEAS   345**
■ **CONTENT CONNECTIONS   345**

Three Exploratory Activities   346
Reflections on the Activities   346
Spatial Sense   347

The Development of Geometric Thinking   347
The van Hiele Levels of Geometric Thought   347
Characteristics of the van Hiele Levels   348

Instructional Goals: Thought and Content   349
Content Goals and Geometry   349
Goals of Geometric Thinking and Spatial Sense   349
Implications for Classroom Strategies   349
Task Selection and Levels of Thought   350

Activities for Level 0   350
Shapes and Properties   351

■ **INVESTIGATIONS IN NUMBER, DATA, AND SPACE:**
Grade 1, *Quilt Squares and Block Towns*   354

■ **Technology Note   356**
Location   358

■ **Technology Note   359**
Transformations   359
Visualization   361

■ **Technology Note   362**
Activities for Level 1   363
Shapes and Properties   363

■ **Technology Note   369**
Dynamic Geometry Software   369
Dynamic Geometry Examples   369
Location   370
Transformations   372

■ **Technology Note   375**
Visualization   375

Activities for Level 2   376
Shapes and Properties   376
Location   379
Transformations   380

■ **CONNECTED MATHEMATICS:** Grade 8,
Kaleidoscopes, Hubcaps, and Mirrors   381
Visualization   382

■ **Technology Note   382**

■ **Assessment Notes   383**
Clarifying Your Geometry Objectives   383

REFLECTIONS ON CHAPTER 20   384
Writing to Learn   384
For Discussion and Exploration   384
Recommendations for Further Reading   385

chapter 21

Exploring Concepts of Data Analysis and Probability   386

■ **BIG IDEAS   386**
■ **CONTENT CONNECTIONS   386**

Data Analysis and Probability in the Curriculum   387

Gathering Data to Answer Questions   387
Ideas for Questions and Data   387

■ **INVESTIGATIONS IN NUMBER, DATA, AND SPACE:**
Grade 5, *Data: Kids, Cats, and Ads*   388
The Shape of Data   389

Classification and Data Analysis   389
Attribute Materials   389
Activities with Attribute Materials   389

■ Technology Note   391

Graphical Representations   392
Bar Graphs   392
Stem-and-Leaf Plots   394
Continuous Data Graphs   395
Circle Graphs   396

Descriptive Statistics   397
Averages   397
Box-and-Whisker Plots   398
Understanding the Mean: Two Concepts   399

Scatter Plots and Relationships   402
Scatter Plots   402
Best-Fit Lines   402
Thinking About Functional Relationships   404

■ Technology Note   404

■ Assessment Notes   404
Choice   405
Interpretation   405

Introduction to Probability   405
Two Experiments   405
Theoretical Versus Experimental Probability   405
Implications for Instruction   406

Developing Probability Concepts   407
Early Concepts of Chance   407
Determining Probabilities for Simple Events   407
Experiments with Two or More Independent Events   408
Theoretical Probabilities with an Area Model   409
Exploring Dependent Events   410

Simulations   411

■ Technology Note   412
Probability Software   412
Probability with Calculators   413

■ Assessment Notes   414

■ Literature Connections   414
*Do You Wanna Bet? Your Chance to Find Out
    About Probability*   414
Frog and Toad Are Friends   414
Incredible Comparisons   414

REFLECTIONS ON CHAPTER 21   415
Writing to Learn   415
For Discussion and Exploration   415
Recommendations for Further Reading   415

ᴄʜᴀᴘᴛᴇʀ **22**

Aʟɢᴇʙʀᴀɪᴄ Rᴇᴀsᴏɴɪɴɢ   417
■ **BIG IDEAS   417**
■ **CONTENT CONNECTIONS   417**

Repeating Patterns   418
Using Materials in Patterning   418

Repeating-Pattern Activities   418

Growing Patterns   420
Searching for Relationships   421
Graphing the Patterns   423

■ **INVESTIGATIONS IN NUMBER, DATA, AND SPACE:**
Grade 5, *Patterns of Change*   424

Other Patterns to Explore   425
Patterns on the Hundreds Chart   425
Number Patterns   425
The Fibonacci Sequence   427

Variables and Equations   427
Variables   427
Equations and Inequalities   430

■ **Literature Connections   432**
Pattern   432
Anno's Mysterious Multiplying Jar   432
Anno's Magic Seeds   432

■ **Assessment Notes   433**

REFLECTIONS ON CHAPTER 22   433
Writing to Learn   433
For Discussion and Exploration   434
Recommendations for Further Reading   434

ᴄʜᴀᴘᴛᴇʀ **23**

Exᴘʟᴏʀɪɴɢ Fᴜɴᴄᴛɪᴏɴs   436
■ **BIG IDEAS   436**
■ **CONTENT CONNECTIONS   436**

Function Concepts and Representations   436
Contextual Representations of Functions   437
Table Representations of Functions   437
Language Expressions for Functions   437
Graphical Representations of Functions   438
Equations to Represent Functions   439

Developing Function Concepts in the Classroom   440
Begin with Meaningful Contexts   440
Connect Different Representations   440
Use Technology   440

Functions from Patterns   441

Functions from the Real World   442
Relationships Found in the Real World   442

■ **CONNECTED MATHEMATICS:** Grade 7, *Variables
and Patterns*   444

Proportional Situations   444
Functions from Formulas   445
Functions from Scatter Plot Data   446
Fun Experiments   448
Graphs Without Equations   448

■ **Assessment Notes   450**

REFLECTIONS ON CHAPTER 23   451
Writing to Learn   451
For Discussion and Exploration   451
Recommendations for Further Reading   451

cHapter **24**

Developing Concepts of Exponents, Integers, and Real Numbers   **453**

■ **BIG IDEAS   453**
■ **CONTENT CONNECTIONS   453**

Large Numbers, Small Numbers, and Exponents   453
Exponents   453
Calculators and Notation   454
Very Large Numbers   455
Representation of Large Numbers: Scientific Notation   455

■ **CONNECTED MATHEMATICS:** Grade 8, *Growing, Growing, Growing: Exponential Relationships*   456
Negative Exponents   457
Very Small Numbers   457

Integer Concepts   457
Intuitive Models of Signed Quantities   457
Mathematical Definition of Negative Numbers   458

Operations with Integers   458
Two Models for Integer Operations   458
Which Model to Use   459

A Problem-Solving Approach for Integers   459
Addition and Subtraction   460
Multiplication and Division   462

Rational Numbers   464
Fractions as Indicated Division   464
Fractions as Rational Numbers   464

Real Numbers   465
Introducing the Concept of Roots   465
Discussing Real Numbers   466

■ **Literature Connections   466**
The Phantom Tollbooth   466
In One Day   466
Math Curse   467

REFLECTIONS ON CHAPTER 24   467
Writing to Learn   467
For Discussion and Exploration   467
Recommendations for Further Reading   467

aPPeNdix **A:** *Principles and Standards for School Mathematics:* Content Standards and Grade Level Expectations   A-1

aPPeNdix **B:** *Professional Standards for Teaching Mathematics:* Teaching Standards   B-1

aPPeNdix **C:** Guide to Blackline Masters   C-1

References   R-1

Index   I-1

Preface

Learning is not the result of development; learning is development. It requires invention and self-organization on the part of the learner. Thus teachers need to allow learners to raise their own questions, generate their own hypotheses and models as possibilities, and test them for viability.

—Fosnot (1996, p. 29)

For several years, I have been saying that what is basic in mathematics is as simple as this: Math makes sense! Every child in his or her own way can come to believe this simple truth. More important, every child can come to believe that he or she is capable of making sense of mathematics. Every child should leave school confident in his or her ability to understand and do mathematics.

This is the goal of *Elementary and Middle School Mathematics*—to help both you and your students come to believe that math makes sense and that you are capable of making sense of it yourself. As the quotation from Catherine Fosnot suggests, students will have to develop this understanding themselves. Their understanding and, thus, their confidence will grow as a result of being engaged in the doing of mathematics. The subtitle of this book, *Teaching Developmentally*, refers to engaging students where you find them so that they can create or develop new ideas that they can use and understand—so they can see that math makes sense through their own eyes and can believe it because they can do it.

The same is true for you as the teacher of these children. When you believe that math makes sense and that you are capable of making sense of it, then you will be in the best position to help your students do mathematics with understanding and with confidence. This book is also aimed at helping you develop that personal understanding and confidence.

A continuing spirit of positive change has pervaded mathematics education for well over a decade. More and more teachers are working to adapt newer ways to help children learn. This book is written in a serious effort to reflect the best of that change and to help you become a part of it.

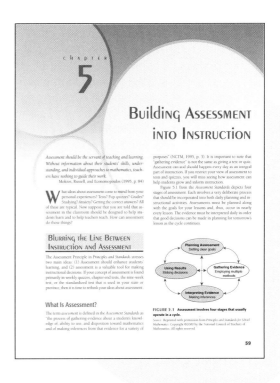

What You Will Find in This Book

This book has always been more than a textbook. It is a resource for teaching mathematics. If you are taking a course, you will almost certainly not "cover" the entire book. However, whether you are now in a course or are currently teaching, I think you will find—as many teachers have told me—that the book will be a well-used reference.

The chapters are separated into two distinct sections. The first section of eight chapters deals with important ideas that cross the boundaries of specific areas of content. The second section of 16 chapters offers teaching suggestions for every major topic in the K–8 curriculum.

Section I ■ Teaching Mathematics: Foundations and Perspectives

Consistently I find that the most effective teachers are those who have an understanding that children need to be mentally engaged in their learning and who are best at creating a problem-based atmosphere to promote that engagement. From this perspective, the two most important chapters in the book are Chapters 3 and 4. Here you will learn about a constructivist view of learning, how that is applied to the learning of mathematics, and how to teach mathematics through problem solving. Chapter 5 discusses the integration of assessment and instruction so that both planning and evaluation are conducted to best assist student learning. To complete these key ideas, Chapter 6 provides a practical perspective on planning lessons, on the value of drill and practice, and on homework and other issues.

This core of ideas represents the best thinking available about how to help children learn mathematics. I have worked hard to be sure that these ideas are reflected clearly and consistently throughout the second section of the book.

Surrounding these central ideas are four chapters offering perspective on the challenging task of helping children learn mathematics. It is important to know where mathematics is going and why so that you will know how to play a professional role in that endeavor. It is also important to have a feel for the discipline of mathematics—to know what it means to "do mathematics." The first two chapters address these issues.

In Chapter 7, you will read about working with children whose needs are special whether they are second language learners or gifted or have learning disabilities. Issues of gender and multiculturalism are also addressed.

Chapter 8 provides perspectives on the issues surrounding technology in the teaching of mathematics. A strong case is made for the use of calculators at all grade levels. Guidance is offered for the selection and use of computer software, and suggestions are made to help you find valuable resources on the Internet.

Section II ■ Development of Mathematical Concepts and Procedures

Chapters 9 through 24 focus on the specific mathematics topics found in grades K–8. Every major topic of the K–8 curriculum is addressed in depth. Each chapter provides a perspective of the mathematical content, how children best learn that content, and numerous suggestions for problem-based activities to engage children in the development of good mathematics.

School districts and classroom teachers commonly purchase this text for use as a resource book. Teachers tell me that the book gives them valuable assistance with content and how children learn that content. The problem-based tasks for students are integrated with the text; they are not added on. Reflecting on the activities as you read can help you think about the mathematics from the perspective of the child. Every activity requires that students be mentally engaged: to

figure something out, to search for a pattern, to explain a reason for an idea—to make sense of mathematics.

The activities are also there for you. Read them along with the text, not as an aside. After all, you are constructing new knowledge yourself—knowledge about teaching mathematics to children. Like children, become actively engaged in *your* learning *about children learning* mathematics. By actually doing the activities as you read through the book, you can get an idea of how children might react to or learn from each activity.

NEW TO THIS EDITION

New Features

■ Content Connections

■ NCTM Correlations

■ Stop and Reflect

■ *Investigations in Number, Data, and Space* and *Connected Mathematics*

Changes in Chapters

■ "Planning in the Problem-Based Classroom" (previously Chapter 22), "Teaching All Children Mathematics" (previously Chapter 23), and "Technology and School Mathematics" (previously Chapter 24) have been moved to Section I to emphasize their importance. They are Chapters 6, 7, and 8 in this fifth edition.

■ "Teaching All Children Mathematics" (Chapter 7) and "Technology and School Mathematics" (Chapter 8) have been substantially revised.

■ Chapter 20, "Geometric Thinking and Geometric Concepts" (previously Chapter 17), was completely rewritten to reflect the Geometry standard in *Principles and Standards for School Mathematics*.

For a further look at the new aspects of this book, see the "Changes in this Edition" section of this preface.

SPECIAL FEATURES OF THIS TEXT

This fifth edition of *Elementary and Middle School Mathematics* retains all of the features of the fourth edition plus a few additions that I think you will find useful. The intent of each is to make the book more informative and more useful as both a textbook and as a resource. Here are things to look for.

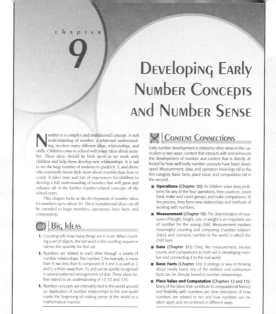

Big Ideas

Much of the literature espousing a student-centered approach suggests that teachers plan their instruction around "big ideas" rather than tiny skills or concepts. Identifying a big idea is not always easy. Near the start of each chapter in Section II you will find a list of the key mathematical ideas associated with the chapter. Teachers find these lists helpful for quickly getting a picture of the mathematics they are teaching.

Content Connections (NEW!)

One of the five process standards in the NCTM *Principles and Standards* document is Connections. "When students can connect mathematical ideas, their understanding is deeper and more lasting" (NCTM, 2000, p. 64). Following the Big Ideas lists in Section II are brief descriptions of other content areas in mathematics that are related to the content of the current chapter. It is offered to help you be more aware of the potential interaction of content as you plan lessons, diagnose students' difficulties, and learn more yourself about the mathematics you are teaching.

Activities

The numerous activities found in every chapter of Section II have always been an integral part of the book. Most of these are clearly framed in a box with a title. Other ideas are described directly in the text or in the illustrations. Every activity is a problem-based task as described in Chapter 4. Some new activities have been added, and some have been modified. Each one is designed to engage students in doing mathematics. The activities help to make this a resource as well as a textbook.

Stop and Reflect (NEW!)

Reflective thinking is the key to learning. To help you read more reflectively, I have chosen places throughout the book where I felt it would be good for you to pause and become truly engaged with an idea you have just read. These sections are indicated by a "stop" icon. With each pause you may be asked to do a small bit of mathematics or to reflect on a difficult idea. These stop and reflect sections do not signal every important concept, but I have tried to place them where it seemed natural for you to slow down a bit and think.

Investigations in Number, Data, ➤ *and Space* and *Connected Mathematics* Features (NEW!)

In every chapter of Section II you will find a feature describing an activity from the reform curriculum *Investigations in Number, Data, and Space* (an elementary reform curriculum) or *Connected Mathematics* (a middle school reform curriculum). The page includes a description of an activity in the program as well as the context of the unit in which it is found. The main purpose of this feature is to acquaint you with these materials that so clearly reflect the spirit of the NCTM *Standards* and the constructivist theory espoused in this book.

◄ NCTM Correlations (NEW!)

Throughout nearly every chapter, you will see an icon indicating a reference to NCTM's *Principles and Standards for School Mathematics*. Often the note consists simply of a quotation from the *Standards* document. At other times, I have tried to summarize what the *Standards* says about a particular topic or I have added a brief comment to the quotation. These notes point explicitly to the alignment of this book with the *Standards*. I hope that they encourage readers to go to the document—either in print or on the Web—turn to the page cited, and read more about what the authors of that important document have to say.

Assessment Notes ➤

Near the end of most chapters in Section II you will find a short Assessment Notes section. These sections are designed to point to special assessment ideas that build on the general themes of the full chapter on assessment, Chapter 5. These notes can assist you in making assessment an integral part of instruction.

Literature Connections ➤

Children's literature is one of the most inviting ways to get children actively involved in doing mathematics. Many of the chapters in Section II contain a Literature Connections section. In each of these sections, at least three children's literature titles are suggested with a brief description of how the mathematics of the chapter can be profitably built on the stories. Though certainly not a comprehensive listing of potential literature, these sections will get you started using this exciting vehicle for teaching mathematics.

Technology Notes ➤

In each chapter of Section II, you will find one or more Technology Note sections. When appropriate, these sections discuss how computers can be used profitably (or not) to help with the content just discussed. Descriptions are provided of specific software titles and (new in this edition) interactive applets available on the Internet. You should not think of these sections as a compendium of available software but as a pointer to the most useful types of programs that are available. Inclusion of any title in these notes should not be seen as an endorsement.

The computer icon will also be found with certain activities and with appropriate paragraphs throughout the text to indicate the use of computer technology.

◀ Calculators

Calculator activities are found in every appropriate chapter. They are identified with a small calculator icon. You will find frequent references to graphing calculators for middle school activities.

The calculator icon will also be found with appropriate paragraphs throughout the text to indicate the applicability of calculators with those topics.

Chapter End Matter

There are three headings at the end of every chapter.

Writing to Learn ➤

To help you focus on the important pedagogical ideas, a list of focusing questions is found at the end of every chapter under the heading "Reflections on Chapter X: Writing to Learn." These study questions are designed to help you reflect on the main points of the chapter. Actually writing out the answers to these questions in your own words is one of the best ways for you to develop your understanding of each chapter's main ideas.

For Discussion and Exploration ➤

Following the Writing to Learn list are a few additional questions that ask you to explore an issue, reflect on observations in a classroom, compare text ideas with those found in traditional curriculum materials, or perhaps take a position on a controversial issue. There are rarely "right" answers to these questions but I hope that they will stimulate thought and cause spirited conversations. Discuss these with your peer group or with teachers in the classroom.

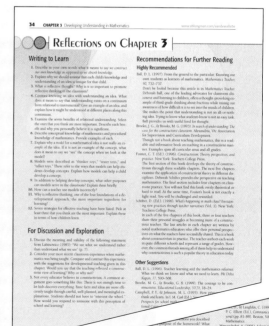

Recommendations for Further Reading ➤

The end of each chapter contains a bibliography of useful articles and books to augment the information found in the chapter. Usually these are taken from NCTM journals, yearbooks, and other professional resources that are targeted for the classroom teacher. Three or four of the readings I found especially important or useful are offered with a short annotation under the head "Highly Recommended." It would have been nice to annotate the whole list but space does not permit. (Note that all sources *cited within the text proper* appear in the References at the end of the book.)

NCTM *Standards* Appendixes ▶

NCTM's *Principles and Standards for School Mathematics* is described in depth in Chapter 1, pointed out periodically by the NCTM Correlations icon, and reflected in spirit throughout the book. In Appendix A, you will find a copy of the appendix to that document, listing all of the content standards and goals for each of the grade bands: pre-K–2, 3–5, 6–8, and 9–12.

As in the previous editions, Appendix B contains the six Standards for Teaching Mathematics from *Professional Standards for Teaching Mathematics*. Within Chapter 5, you will find the six Assessment Standards as well as the four Purposes of Assessment found in the *Assessment Standards for School Mathematics*.

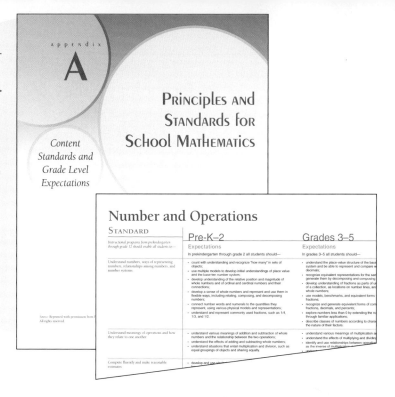

Changes in This Edition

"What's new in this edition?" This often-asked question is difficult to answer. It is easy to point to the new features—Content Connections, Stop and Reflect, *Investigations in Number, Data, and Space* and *Connected Mathematics* features, and NCTM Correlations—since these are quite obvious. But new features are not fundamental changes. What did *not* change at all with this edition is the basic philosophy of constructivism and the message of teaching through problem solving. However, I like to think of this book as being in a constant state of flux—morphing, as it were, from one edition to the next. Some changes are more drastic; for others you have to look closely. No chapter was left untouched. Let me try to highlight the larger changes.

Reorganization of Chapters

What used to be the last three chapters of the book (called Section III) are now Chapters 6, 7, and 8. The importance of these chapters is highlighted with the move. Besides the location, the chapters themselves underwent some change. Chapter 6, "Planning in a Problem-Based Classroom," begins with a detailed guide to help teachers think through the process of planning a lesson. Within that framework are suggestions for dealing with the diversity that is found in every classroom. Finally, a new distinction between drill and practice is offered, which I hope will prompt some serious thinking.

Chapter 7 is revised primarily thanks to the contributions of Thomasenia Lott Adams of the University of Florida. With her assistance, this chapter is not only up-to-date but also now includes thoughtful considerations of multicultural issues and problems of teaching children with limited or no English language skills.

Chapter 8 was similarly revised, in this case by the contributions of Jamar Pickreign of SUNY Fredonia. Jamar added thoughtful contributions to the chapter (and also to the Technology Notes throughout the book) and found numerous Web sites with applets for student use.

Geometry

Without question, the chapter most completely rewritten is the geometry chapter (Chapter 20). You will still find the emphasis on the first three levels of the van Hiele theory. However, within each level, the content is now organized in the same manner as the Geometry standard in *Principles and Standards for School Mathematics*. For each of the three van Hiele levels, you will find sections on Shapes and Properties, Location, Transformation, and Visualization. New activities have been added, and I think you will find a much clearer reflection of the van Hiele theory within the activities. It is possible to look at one of these content areas across the levels or to look at all four areas within any one level.

Other Changes

Although every chapter saw some change, a few specific areas may be worth noting.

● In the place-value chapter, more attention has been given to the hundreds chart (no longer a 0 to 99 chart).
● All aspects of whole-number computation except the discussion of computational estimation are now included in one chapter. Mental computation is more clearly seen as a variation of invented strategies. The number-sense activities that were in a separate chapter are now part of

the computation chapter. A full chapter is now devoted to computational estimation.

- Both the fraction chapter and the ratio and proportion chapter received some new material, much of which is reflective of the work of Susan Lamon. Her research and suggestions for instruction are at the forefront of thinking in this area.
- Data analysis and probability are still in one chapter, but the order of these topics has been reversed. This gives data analysis greater visibility and attention.

Finally, I feel I should comment on the use of the *Investigations in Number, Data, and Space* and the *Connected Mathematics Project* programs in the features described earlier. With three elementary and five middle school "reform" programs from which to choose (see Chapter 1), it is fair to ask, "Why only these two?" First, I believe that these two programs best reflect the philosophy of the book. The second reason is more practical. Both programs are published within the Pearson family of publishers, which includes Allyn & Bacon. Therefore, it was possible for me to have access and permission for their use. I hope you find these pages to be a useful addition.

Notes to the Instructor

No other book offers your students as much as this one does. Most important, it develops a strong theoretical perspective of children learning mathematics—not a casual overview. That perspective is reflected consistently throughout the book. Second, no other book of this type develops so clearly the strong position articulated by Hiebert et al. (1996, 1997) that the best approach to teaching mathematics is to teach with problem-based tasks. Third, teachers find the book to be a valuable resource that almost all carry into the classroom rather than sell back to the bookstore. Many school divisions, principals, and classroom teachers buy the book for the same purpose. It has become a standard reference for K–8 teachers. Teachers and supervisors continually tell me how readable and valuable they find the book.

It is a large book! It is not a book to "cover" but a book to use. I have never attempted to teach the content of the entire book in a single semester and would never expect you to. I've come to believe that fewer topics discussed in class but with time to develop the spirit of Chapters 3 and 4 is the best approach. As you explore the content topics you do select, allow your class to be a model of the instruction you want for all topics. Teaching with problem-based tasks and classroom discourse is a complete shift from the experiences of most teachers.

By providing your students with the detail and information found in this book, you send with them into the classroom the specifics you were unable to cover in class. And you can be assured that the spirit of what you do cover will also be evident in those chapters you skipped.

I am always amazed at how many different styles of methods courses are possible. All who have used this book

seem to find their own best strategies for their class. I am hesitant, therefore, to dictate a course, but I am proud to offer this text. I wish you and your teachers much success and excitement as you explore good mathematics with kids.

Acknowledgments

Many intelligent and talented people have contributed to the success of this book, and I am deeply grateful to all those who have assisted me along the way. These words of thanks must begin as they have in previous editions and as they will in any editions subsequent. Without the success of the first edition, there would certainly not have been a second, much less five editions. I will always be most sincerely indebted to Warren Crown (Rutgers), John Dossey (Illinois State University), Bob Gilbert (Florida International University), and Steven Willoughby (University of Arizona), who gave time and great care in offering detailed comments on the original manuscript. Few mathematics educators of their stature would take the time and effort that they gave to that endeavor.

A special word of gratitude is due to Thomasenia Lott Adams (University of Florida) and Jamar Pickreign (State University of New York at Fredonia). These contributors wrote manuscript for Chapters 7 and 8, respectively, offering their individual expertise in the areas of multicultural education and technology. These chapters and the technology notes throughout the book are much improved with their helpful input.

In preparing this fifth edition, I have received thoughtful input from the following educators who offered comments on the fourth edition and/or on the manuscript for the fifth:

Tom Bassarear, Keene State College
Janie M. Cates, State University of West Georgia
Kathleen Chamberlain, Lycoming College
Andrea Guillaume, California State University, Fullerton
William M. Hessmiller, Editors & Trainers Associates
William A. Jasper, Sam Houston State University
Art Johnson, Boston University
Jamar Pickreign, State University of New York at Fredonia
Donald Ploger, Florida Atlantic University
Mark A. Spikell, George Mason University
Sylvia R. Taube, Sam Houston State University
Timothy J. Touzel, Coastal Carolina University

Each review challenged me to think through important issues. Many specific suggestions have found their way into this book. These professionals each have my thanks.

Two special persons at Allyn & Bacon deserve my special thanks. My editor, Traci Mueller, is always there to answer questions and prod me on to the next task—all in a very friendly manner. My development editor, Sonny Regelman, has become a new friend, as together we got this manuscript in shape—our e-mails must number in the hundreds. Her editing has been superb! These two wonderful professionals have made it a real pleasure to belong to the Allyn & Bacon team. My sincere thanks to each of them.

I also extend my thanks to the production administrator, Donna Simons, at Allyn & Bacon, as well as everyone at Omegatype.

A Personal Note

As I've said, the many talented people have contributed in countless ways, many without even realizing it. However, the freely given help of one person towers above that of all others.

With each revision of this book, my wife, Sharon, has supported my efforts, patiently endured my anxieties, and gently encouraged me in every possible manner. This support she gives daily without complaint or reservation. Her love and friendship make the efforts worthwhile. I am truly blessed to be able to share my life and my work with this wonderful woman. I love you, Sharon.

On October 24, 2000, our daughter, Gretchen, brought into our world a beautiful ray of sunshine in the form of her very special daughter. This one's for you, Aidan!

John A. Van de Walle

Supplements

Instructor Supplements

■ Instructor's Manual

The Instructor's Manual for the fifth edition includes a wealth of resources designed to help instructors teach the course, including chapter notes, activity suggestions, suggested essay test questions, and instructor transparency masters. (These transparency masters may also be found at www.ablongman. com/ppt.)

■ Computerized Test Bank (NEW!)

The Computerized Test Bank contains hundreds of challenging questions in multiple-choice, true/false, fill-in-the-blank, and essay formats, along with an answer key. Instructors can choose from these questions and write their own to create custom exams.

■ PowerPoint™ Presentation— www.ablongman.com/ppt (NEW!)

Ideal for instructors to use for lecture presentations or student handouts, the PowerPoint presentation provides dozens of ready-to-use graphic and text images tied to the text. Also included are the transparency masters from the Instructor's Manual.

■ Dale Seymour *Developing Mathematical Ideas* Video Series: "Numbers and Operations," Part 1 and Part 2 (NEW!)

Available upon adoption of the fifth edition to qualified adopters, these professional development videos help preservice and in-service teachers think critically and get to the core of how children approach and understand mathematics.

Student Supplements

■ Field Experience Guide: Resources for Teachers of Elementary and Middle School Mathematics (includes Blackline Masters) (NEW!)

Intended for use in the elementary and middle school mathematics classroom, this practical guide features observation and assessment worksheets, reproducible activities with the lesson plans, and more than fifty Blackline Masters—all of those from the fourth edition along with several new ones. Utilizing the philosophy of this text, the Field Experience Guide is an invaluable resource for new classroom teachers.

■ Companion Web Site— www.ablongman.com/vandewalle5e (includes Blackline Masters)

Students who visit the Companion Web site for this edition will find an online study guide with practice tests, learning objectives, links to useful Web sites on the Internet, and the Blackline Masters from the fourth edition textbook, plus some new ones for the fifth edition.

■ Allyn and Bacon's Curriculum and Instruction SuperSite— www.ablongman.com/C&I

This password-protected comprehensive Web site features a wealth of information and practical resources for preservice and in-service teachers, including classroom activities and activities for all grade levels, teaching resources, subject-specific Web links, and information on related Allyn & Bacon professional titles. State Standards Correlations have also been integrated into the site for select states.

Elementary
and Middle School
Mathematics

1

Teaching Mathematics in the Context of the Reform Movement

In this changing world, those who understand and can do mathematics will have significantly enhanced opportunities and options for shaping their futures. Mathematical competence opens doors to productive futures. A lack of mathematical competence keeps those doors closed. . . . All students should have the opportunity and the support necessary to learn significant mathematics with depth and understanding. There is no conflict between equity and excellence.

NCTM (2000, p. 50)

Someday soon you will find yourself in front of a class of students, or perhaps you are already teaching. What general ideas will guide the way you will teach mathematics? Do children learn mathematics differently from other topics? How can you make it interesting and enjoyable? What does mathematics mean to you? What does it mean to "do mathematics"? If mathematics is not exactly your favorite subject, do you think that had anything to do with the way you were taught? How can you help children like the subject more than you do?

For the past 15 years, mathematics education has been undergoing slow but steady changes. Today, mathematics consists of much more than traditional computational skills. As content becomes more sophisticated, methods for teaching mathematics become more and more important. We now know that for children to learn mathematics in ways that make sense to them, they must be actively engaged in making sense of mathematics. Ultimately, it is you, the teacher, who will help to shape mathematics for the children you teach. How you answer the questions just posed will have a significant impact on how you approach teaching mathematics.

An Era of Change

There have been several notable shifts in the direction of mathematics education in our schools. It is useful to place these shifts and movements in the context of the forces that have shaped them.

A Brief History of Reforms

In April 2000, the National Council of Teachers of Mathematics (NCTM) released *Principles and Standards for School Mathematics*. The council presented *Principles and Standards* as an update of its original standards document released 11 years earlier in 1989. With this most important document, the council continues to guide a revolutionary reform movement in mathematics education, not just in the United States and Canada but also throughout the world.

The momentum for reform in mathematics education began in the early 1980s. Educators were responding to a "back to basics" cry, a reaction to the "new math" of the 1960s and 1970s. There was a growing interest in making problem solving a focus of the mathematics curriculum. The work of Piaget and other developmental psychologists was shifting the focus of mathematics educators from mathematics content to how children can best learn mathematics.

This momentum came to a head in 1989, when NCTM published *Curriculum and Evaluation Standards for School Mathematics*. Since then, we have been caught up in a revolution in mathematics education, a revolution that is more positive, more pervasive, and more widely accepted than any change previously experienced.

As we begin a new century, indeed a new millennium, it must be admitted that the vision of the 1989 *Curriculum*

Standards has still not been realized although much progress has been made. Change is visible, albeit slow and incremental. The political naysayers are becoming more and more influential in a bid to return again to "basics." But despite the slow pace of change in long-held beliefs about school mathematics, the revolution continues. This is not a pendulum that we can permit to swing backward.

Leadership Provided by NCTM

The National Council of Teachers of Mathematics is a professional, nonprofit organization. With over 125,000 members in the United States and Canada, it is the primary professional organization for teachers of mathematics in grades K through 12. NCTM provides leadership through its various journals for teachers, national and regional conferences, and numerous high-quality publications.

As noted, NCTM's release of the *Curriculum and Evaluation Standards for School Mathematics* in 1989 was a benchmark event in school mathematics. No other document has ever had such an enormous effect on school mathematics or on any other area of the curriculum. In 1991, NCTM published *Professional Standards for Teaching Mathematics*. The *Professional Standards* articulates a vision of teaching mathematics and builds on the notion found in the *Curriculum Standards* that good and significant mathematics is a vision for all children, not just a few. NCTM completed the package with the *Assessment Standards for School Mathematics* in 1995. The *Assessment Standards* shows clearly the necessity of integrating assessment with instruction and indicates the key role that assessment plays in implementing change. From 1989 to 2000, these three documents have guided the reform movement in mathematics education around the world. In fact, many countries have done a much better job of implementing the NCTM *Standards* than the United States has.

NCTM has always recognized the ongoing need to examine its standards and to make adjustments in light of new knowledge from research and practice, new demands of a changing society, and the continued impact of improved and more readily available technology.

PRINCIPLES AND STANDARDS FOR SCHOOL MATHEMATICS

Principles and Standards for School Mathematics is designed to provide guidance and direction for teachers and other leaders in mathematics education from pre-K to grade 12. Figure 1.1 outlines the general structure of *Principles and Standards* so that you can easily access it in ways that are most helpful to you. While it is important that teachers read and reflect on the *Standards* document, the next few pages will provide you some idea of what you will find there.

Principles and Standards for School Mathematics

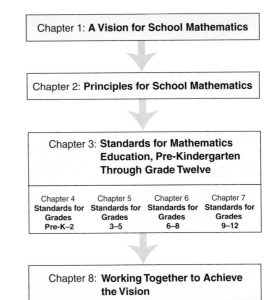

FIGURE 1.1 The structure of *Principles and Standards for School Mathematics* emphasizes the continuity of mathematics across all 14 years of school.

Goals for Students

Principles and Standards begins with an ambitious vision of a mathematics classroom, one we have barely begun to realize. At the heart of this vision are the same five goals set forth in the 1989 *Standards*. These goals state that *all* students should

1. Learn to value mathematics
2. Become confident in their ability to do mathematics
3. Become mathematical problem solvers
4. Learn to communicate mathematics
5. Learn to reason mathematically

Virtually every job in today's society requires mathematics and, more important, mathematical thinking and reasoning. Today's employers are searching for the ability as well as the confidence to solve problems that have never been encountered before. Children need to see themselves learning to reason and learning to solve problems, not just learning skills.

Taking pride in one's mathematical thinking power is all-important. It can no longer be fashionable to announce, "I never was any good at math." Children must, from the earliest grades and throughout their school experiences, be made to feel the importance of personal success in solving problems, figuring things out, and making sense of mathematics.

In the last chapter of *Principles and Standards,* the authors describe the necessary support required at every level to bring the vision of Chapter 1 to reality.

The Six Principles

One of the most important features of *Principles and Standards for School Mathematics* is the articulation of six principles fundamental to high-quality mathematics education:

- Equity
- Curriculum
- Teaching
- Learning
- Assessment
- Technology

According to *Principles and Standards,* these principles must be "deeply intertwined with school mathematics programs" (NCTM, 2000, p. 12). The principles make it clear that excellence in mathematics education involves much more than simply listing content objectives.

The Equity Principle

Excellence in mathematics education requires equity—high expectations and strong support for all students. (NCTM, 2000, p. 12)

The strong message of the Equity Principle is high expectations for all students. All students must have the opportunity and adequate support to learn mathematics "regardless of personal characteristics, backgrounds, or physical challenges" (p. 12). The message of high expectations for all is intertwined with every other principle and the document as a whole.

The Curriculum Principle

A curriculum is more than a collection of activities: it must be coherent, focused on important mathematics, and well articulated across the grades. (NCTM, 2000, p. 14)

Coherence speaks to the importance of building instruction around "big ideas" both in the curriculum and in daily classroom instruction. Students must be helped to see that mathematics is an integrated whole, not a list of isolated bits and pieces.

Mathematical ideas are "important" if they are useful in the development of other ideas, link ideas one to another, or serve to illustrate the discipline of mathematics as a human endeavor.

The Teaching Principle

Effective mathematics teaching requires understanding what students know and need to learn and then challenging and supporting them to learn it well. (NCTM, 2000, p. 16)

What students learn is almost entirely dependent on the experiences that teachers provide every day in the classroom. To provide high-quality mathematics education, teachers must (1) understand deeply the mathematics they are teaching; (2) understand how children learn mathematics, including a keen awareness of the individual mathematical development of their own students; and (3) select instructional tasks and strategies that will enhance learning. "Teachers' actions are what encourage students to think, question, solve problems, and discuss their ideas, strategies, and solutions" (p. 18).

The Learning Principle

Students must learn mathematics with understanding, actively building new knowledge from experience and prior knowledge. (NCTM, 2000, p. 20)

This principle is based on two fundamental ideas. First, learning mathematics with understanding is essential. Mathematics today requires not only computational skills but also the ability to think and reason mathematically in order to solve the new problems and learn the new ideas that students will face in the future.

Second, the principle states quite clearly that students *can* learn mathematics with understanding. Learning is enhanced in classrooms where students are required to evaluate their own ideas and those of others, are encouraged to make mathematical conjectures and test them, and develop their reasoning skills.

The Assessment Principle

Assessment should support the learning of important mathematics and furnish useful information to both teachers and students. (NCTM, 2000, p. 22)

In the authors' words, "Assessment should not merely be done *to* students, rather, it should also be done *for* students, to guide and enhance their learning" (p. 22). Ongoing assessment conveys to students what mathematics is important. Assessment that includes ongoing observation and student interaction encourages students to articulate and, thus, clarify their ideas. Feedback from daily assessment helps students establish goals and become more independent learners.

Assessment should also be a major factor in making instructional decisions. By continuously gathering information about student growth and understanding, teachers can better make the daily decisions that support student learning. For assessment to be effective, teachers must use a variety of assessment techniques, understand their mathematical goals deeply, and have a good idea of how their students may be thinking about the mathematics that is being developed.

The Technology Principle

Technology is essential in teaching and learning mathematics; it influences the mathematics that is taught and enhances students' learning. (NCTM, 2000, p. 24)

Calculators and computers should be seen as essential tools for doing and learning mathematics in the classroom. Technology permits students to focus on mathematical ideas, to reason, and to solve problems in ways that are often impossible without these tools. Technology enhances the learning of mathematics by allowing for increased exploration and enhanced representation of ideas. It extends the range of problems that can be accessed. It also allows students with special needs to bypass less important procedures so that important mathematics can be considered.

A Pre-K-to-12 Perspective

In addition to making the case for a coherent curriculum, the structure of *Principles and Standards* emphasizes the continuous growth of mathematics across all grades, pre-K to 12. The largest portion of *Principles and Standards* is built around 10 standards: five content standards and five process standards. Chapter 3 of the document helps the reader understand each of these standards from the perspective of the full pre-K–12 curriculum. This broad perspective is followed by chapters that take a closer look at each standard within each of four grade bands: pre-K–2, 3–5, 6–8, and 9–12.

The Five Content Standards

Principles and Standards describes five content standards or strands of mathematics:

- Number and Operations
- Algebra
- Geometry
- Measurement
- Data Analysis and Probability

Each content standard includes a small collection of goals that is applicable to all grade bands. Each grade-band chapter provides specific expectations for what students should know. These grade-band expectations are also concisely listed in the appendix to the *Standards* and in Appendix A of this book.

STOP Stop now and turn to Appendix A. Spend a few minutes with these expectations for the grade band in which you are most interested. How do these expectations compare with the mathematics you experienced in school?

Although the same five content standards apply across all grades, you should not infer that each strand has equal weight or emphasis in every grade band. Number and Operations is the largest strand from pre-K to grade 5 and continues to be important in the middle grades but has a lesser emphasis in grades 9–12. That emphasis is reflected in this book, with Chapters 9 through 18 addressing content found in the Number and Operations standard.

Algebra is clearly intended as a strand for all grades. This was almost certainly not the case when you were in school. Today, most states and provinces include algebra objectives at every grade level. In this book, Chapters 22, 23, and 24 address this strand.

Note that Geometry and Measurement are separate strands, suggesting the unique importance of each of these two areas to the elementary and middle grades curriculum.

The Five Process Standards

Following the five content standards, *Principles and Standards* lists five process standards:

- Problem Solving
- Reasoning and Proof
- Communication
- Connections
- Representation

The process standards refer to the mathematical process through which students should acquire and use mathematical knowledge. The statement of the five process standards can be found in Table 1.1 (p. 5).

The five process standards should not be regarded as separate content or strands in the mathematics curriculum. Rather, they direct the methods or processes of doing all mathematics and, therefore, should be seen as integral components of all mathematics learning and teaching.

To teach in a way that reflects these process standards is one of the best definitions of what it means to teach "according to the *Standards*."

Problem Solving

Problem solving is much more than finding answers to word problems and exercises labeled "problem solving." The Problem Solving standard says that all students should "build new mathematical knowledge through problem solving" (NCTM, 2000, p. 52). This statement clearly indicates that problem solving is to be viewed as the vehicle through which children develop mathematical ideas. Learning and doing mathematics *as you solve problems* is probably the most significant difference in what the *Standards* indicate and the way you most likely experienced mathematics.

Reasoning and Proof

If problem solving is the focus of mathematics, reasoning is the logical thinking that helps us decide if and why our answers make sense. Students need to develop the habit of providing an argument or a rationale as an integral part of every answer. Children can and do learn that the reasons for their answers are at least as important as the answers themselves. The habit of providing reasons for answers is best started in kindergarten. However, it is never too late to learn the satisfaction and the value of defending ideas through logical argument.

Communication

The Communication standard points to the importance of being able to talk about, write about, describe, and explain

TABLE 1.1

The Five Process Standards from *Principles and Standards for School Mathematics*

Problem Solving Standard
Instructional programs from prekindergarten through grade 12 should enable all students to—

- Build new mathematical knowledge through problem solving
- Solve problems that arise in mathematics and in other contexts
- Apply and adapt a variety of appropriate strategies to solve problems
- Monitor and reflect on the process of mathematical problem solving

Reasoning and Proof Standard
Instructional programs from prekindergarten through grade 12 should enable all students to—

- Recognize reasoning and proof as fundamental aspects of mathematics
- Make and investigate mathematical conjectures
- Develop and evaluate mathematical arguments and proofs
- Select and use various types of reasoning and methods of proof

Communication Standard
Instructional programs from prekindergarten through grade 12 should enable all students to—

- Organize and consolidate their mathematical thinking through communication
- Communicate their mathematical thinking coherently and clearly to peers, teachers, and others
- Analyze and evaluate the mathematical thinking and strategies of others
- Use the language of mathematics to express mathematical ideas precisely

Connections Standard
Instructional programs from prekindergarten through grade 12 should enable all students to—

- Recognize and use connections among mathematical ideas
- Understand how mathematical ideas interconnect and build on one another to produce a coherent whole
- Recognize and apply mathematics in contexts outside of mathematics

Representation Standard
Instructional programs from prekindergarten through grade 12 should enable all students to—

- Create and use representations to organize, record, and communicate mathematical ideas
- Select, apply, and translate among mathematical representations to solve problems
- Use representations to model and interpret physical, social, and mathematical phenomena

Source: Reprinted with permission from *Principles and Standards for School Mathematics.* Copyright © 2000 by the National Council of Teachers of Mathematics. All rights reserved.

mathematical ideas. Learning to communicate in mathematics fosters interaction and exploration of ideas in the classroom as students learn in an active, verbal environment. No better way exists for wrestling with an idea than to attempt to articulate it to others. Mathematical expression, therefore, is part of the process and not an end in itself.

Connections

The Connections standard has two separate thrusts. First, the standard refers to connections within and among mathematical ideas. For example, addition and subtraction are intimately related; fractional parts of a whole are connected to concepts of decimals and percents. Students should be helped to see how mathematical ideas build on one another in a useful network of connected ideas. Mathematics is not a laundry list of isolated rules and formulas.

Second, mathematics should be connected to the real world and to other disciplines. Children should see that mathematics plays a significant role in art, science, and social studies. This suggests that mathematics should frequently be integrated with other discipline areas and that applications of mathematics in the real world should be explored.

Representation

One of the reasons mathematics is so powerful is the way ideas can be expressed with symbols, charts, graphs, and diagrams.

Symbolism in mathematics, along with visual aids such as charts and graphs, should be understood by students as ways of communicating mathematical ideas to other people. Symbols, graphs, and charts, as well as physical representations such as counters or fraction "pie pieces," are also powerful learning tools. Moving from one representation to another is an important way to add understanding to an idea. As teachers help develop flexibility with a variety of representations for mathematical ideas, students not only add to their own understanding but also acquire skill in applying mathematical ideas to new areas and communicating ideas to others.

 NCTM Standards Throughout this book, this icon will alert you to specific information in *Principles and Standards* relative to the information you are reading. However, these notes and the brief descriptions you have just read should not be a substitute for reading the *Standards.* Fortunately, it is easy to access the *Standards* on the Web so that you can read relevant portions of the document as time permits. Visit the NCTM Web site at www.nctm.org. Click on NCTM Standards to find not only the full text of *Principles and Standards* but also the full text of each of the previous three standards documents.

The on-line version of the *Standards* is generally referred to as the *e-Standards.* The *e-Standards* also contains a number of electronic applets—interactive tools for learning about mathematical concepts. Many of these applets are referenced throughout this book. These applets are also free for your use with students.

On the NCTM Web site you can also find information about purchasing the *Standards* in print form or as a CD. The CD version, like the Web site, contains all of the applets and the full text of all of the four earlier standards texts.

The *Professional Standards* for *Teaching Mathematics*

Although *Principles and Standards* incorporates principles of teaching and assessment, the emphasis is curriculum. The *Professional Standards for Teaching Mathematics* focuses on teaching and is as important today as when it was released in 1991. The *Professional Standards* asserts that teachers are the key agents of change in the classroom. If the revolution is to continue, teachers must shift from a teacher-centered to a child-centered approach in their instruction. Through extended vignettes of real teachers, the document articulates the careful reflective work that must go into teaching. Effective teaching engages students in problem solving and promotes valuable reflective student discourse about important mathematical ideas.

Five Shifts in Classroom Environment

The introduction to the *Professional Standards* lists five major shifts in the environment of the mathematics classroom that are necessary to allow students to develop mathematical power. Teachers need to shift

- Toward classrooms as mathematics communities and away from classrooms as simply a collection of individuals
- Toward logic and mathematical evidence as verification and away from the teacher as the sole authority for right answers
- Toward mathematical reasoning and away from mere memorizing procedures
- Toward conjecturing, inventing, and problem solving and away from an emphasis on the mechanistic finding of answers
- Toward connecting mathematics, its ideas, and its applications and away from treating mathematics as a body of isolated concepts and procedures

The Teaching Standards

The *Professional Standards for Teaching Mathematics* contains chapters on teaching, the evaluation of teaching, professional development, and necessary support for teaching. The teaching section is extraordinarily useful. It offers six standards for the teaching of mathematics. These standards talk about the selection of tasks for learning and the nature of an interactive

classroom atmosphere in which students are engaged in the process of making sense of mathematics. This mathematical environment, in which students work as a community of learners on mathematical tasks, is an integral component of the approach to teaching mathematics described in this book. Reading the *Teaching Standards* is an excellent way to help you understand what this mathematical atmosphere is like.

✖ **STOP** The six teaching standards are located in Appendix B of this book. Take a moment now to look over this one-page listing. Select one or two of the standards that seem especially significant to you. Put a sticky note on the page to remind you to return to these important ideas from time to time as you work through this book.

The *Assessment Standards* for *School Mathematics*

The *Assessment Standards for School Mathematics* was published in 1995. It rounds out the trio of NCTM standards documents and is important reading for anyone interested in understanding the reform movement in mathematics education.

The *Assessment Standards* is not a how-to guide but a statement of philosophy and purpose, a book to provide guidance without prescription. It consists of six standards for assessment: Mathematics, Learning, Equity, Openness, Inferences, and Coherence. Further, it describes in some detail four purposes of assessment: to monitor the progress of students, to help make instructional decisions, to evaluate students' achievement, and to evaluate programs. All are aimed at the improvement of student learning.

The inescapable message of the *Assessment Standards* is that assessment and instruction are not separate activities but are intimately intertwined in improving the learning of mathematics. Chapter 5 of this book describes the six assessment standards and discusses the four purposes. There you will find suggestions for making assessment an integral component of instruction, an absolutely essential factor in being a *Standards*-oriented teacher.

Influences and Pressures on Reform

NCTM has provided the major leadership and vision for reform in mathematics education. However, no single factor controls the direction of change. National and international comparisons of student performances continue to make headlines, provoke public opinion, and pressure legislatures to call for tougher standards backed by testing. The pressures of testing policies exerted on schools and ultimately on teachers often have an impact on instruction that is different than the vision of the NCTM *Standards*. In addition to these pressures, there is also the strong influence of the textbook or curriculum materials that are provided to teachers, which are often not well aligned with state standards.

National and International Studies

Large studies that tell the American public how the nation's children are doing in mathematics receive a lot of attention. They influence political decisions as well as provide useful data for mathematics education researchers.

The National Assessment of Educational Progress

Since 1969, the National Assessment of Educational Progress (NAEP), a congressionally mandated program, has been assessing what students know and can do in various curriculum areas. To date, there have been eight mathematics assessments based on samples of students 9, 13, and 17 years of age or in grades 4, 8, and 12. The results are often published as "The Nation's Report Card." NAEP is a criterion-referenced study, telling us what percentages of American students know various mathematics concepts and skills. Much of the test is designed to reflect current curriculum.

NAEP provides us with both good and bad news. The good news is that on a small core of items that has been used consistently since 1973 to produce trend data, U.S. students clearly do things better now than in 1973 (Reese, Miller, Mazzeo, & Dossey, 1997; Silver & Kenney, 2000). This is in stark contrast to observers who contend that current mathematics reform is producing students who don't know "good old basic mathematics."

The bad news is that even though performance on these traditional items is increasing steadily, the overall performance of our students remains dismal. NAEP reports three levels of achievement: basic, proficient, and advanced. In 1996, only 21 percent of students at fourth grade, 24 percent at eighth grade, and 16 percent at twelfth grade were at or above the proficient level, a performance indicating "solid academic performance" (Reese et al., 1997). At fourth and eighth grades, 36 percent and 38 percent, respectively, were found to be below the basic level.

The Third International Mathematics and Science Study

In 1995 and 1996, 41 nations participated in the Third International Mathematics and Science Study (TIMSS), the largest study of mathematics and science education ever conducted. Data were gathered in grades 4, 8, and 12 from 500,000 students, and from teachers. A video study was conducted at the eighth grade. The most widely reported results are that U.S. fourth-grade students are above the average of the TIMSS countries, below the international average at the

eighth grade, and significantly below average at the twelfth grade (U.S. Department of Education, 1997a).

Even though the rank ordering for fourth grade places the United States above the average for 26 countries, seven countries (Singapore, Korea, Japan, Hong Kong, Netherlands, Czech Republic, and Austria) had significantly higher scores. Canada and Ireland were similar to the United States. Only 9 percent of U.S. fourth graders would fall in the top 10 percent of all students in the TIMSS study. This is in stark contrast with Japan (32 percent) and Singapore (39 percent) (U.S. Department of Education, 1997c).

A major finding of the TIMSS curriculum analysis is that U.S. curriculum is unfocused, contains many more topics than most countries, and involves much more repetition than is found in most countries. We attempt to do everything and as a consequence rarely do it in depth, making reteaching all too common (Schmidt, McKnight, & Raizen, 1996).

Many who advocate a return to "basics" point to the disappointing performance of American students. However, curriculum and instructional approaches in the United States are "less in line with cross-national commonalties than are the demanding curricula and classroom practices found in many high-achieving countries" (Babcock, 1998, p. 6). Furthermore, TIMSS does not support a number of other popular "basics" demands: more homework (U.S. students do more than students in most countries), less TV watching (Japanese students watch as much), and more time spent on mathematics (U.S. students have more hours of mathematics instruction than students in Japan or Germany). Tracking prior to high school, common in the United States, is not practiced in most TIMSS nations.

One of the most interesting components of TIMSS is the eighth-grade video study that was conducted in the United States, Germany, and Japan. The results indicate stark contrasts between instructional practices in Japan and the United States. "The typical goal of a U.S. eighth-grade mathematics teacher is to teach students how to do something. The typical goal of a Japanese teacher is to help students understand mathematical concepts" (U.S. Department of Education, 1997a, p. 33). In Japan, researchers found that 83 percent of the topics in eighth-grade lessons were developed rather than stated. By contrast, in the United States, only 22 percent of the topics were developed; 78 percent were stated (U.S. Department of Education, 1996). "The videotape study found that, in many ways, Japanese teaching resembled the recommendations of the U.S. reform movement more closely than did American teaching" (p. 47).

State Standards

The term *standards* was popularized by NCTM in 1989. Today it is used by nearly every state in the nation to refer to a grade-by-grade listing of very specific mathematics objectives. These state standards or objectives vary considerably from state to state in the degree to which they reflect the reform movement. Most states have had to be very cautious in embracing mathematics reform, especially in the current climate of antireform sentiment in the public sector. Cries for "accountability" and "basics" put serious pressure on states. Even for the states and local districts that encourage reform, the huge cost of teacher retraining and in-service with reform-oriented curricula has made change slow and difficult on any large scale.

Associated with every set of state standards is some form of testing program. Publicly reported test scores place pressure on superintendents, then on principals, and ultimately on teachers. Teachers feel enormous pressure to raise test scores at all costs (Schmidt et al., 1996). For a teacher who has little or no experience with the spirit of the *Standards,* it is very difficult to adopt the student-centered approach to mathematics and the teaching of mathematics espoused by reformers. Unfortunately for children, this often results in excessive drill, review, and practice tests.

Are these state standards incompatible with reform? In general, the answer is no. Reform is about helping children understand mathematics and become confident in their abilities to do mathematics and solve problems. There are many wonderful examples of teaching in the spirit of reform. Children in these classrooms achieve quite well, even on the most traditional of standardized tests. These stories need better publicity, and teachers need much more support than is often available. Basic skills can be taught with understanding—and they must be.

Curriculum

In most classrooms, the textbook is the single most influential factor in determining what actually gets taught and how. What is becoming increasingly complicated is how teachers and school systems attempt to blend the textbook or other curriculum materials with the mandated state standards and the professional directions of NCTM.

Though possibly an oversimplification, mathematics curriculum materials that are used in K–8 classrooms can be categorized as either traditional or reform. Traditional texts are usually developed by large commercial publishers. Reform programs have been initially developed with funding from the National Science Foundation (NSF) and other outside sources by teams of teachers, educational researchers, and mathematicians.

Traditional Curricula

The publishers of traditional textbooks employ author teams that always include excellent mathematics researchers and educators as well as teachers and supervisors. The tendency is to produce very large textbooks so that they can attend to the wide variety of state and professional agendas (Schmidt et al., 1996). Often publisher statements of compliance with NCTM standards are misleading. NCTM does not approve or sanction any commercial products, so publishers are free to make

whatever claims they feel they can support. You should remember that by its very nature, the publishing industry is market driven. The market—the individuals who make the decisions concerning which programs to purchase for the school systems—is composed largely of experienced teachers. Teachers are enormously pressured by state tests. Most of these decision makers have only a cursory understanding of the NCTM *Standards.* The result is that the market requires publishers to stick fairly close to the show-and-explain approach to teaching. Traditional books currently account for well over 80 percent of the textbooks used in schools.

Reform Curricula

At present, there are three elementary and five middle school programs commonly recognized as reform curricula.* Originally developed with NSF funds, each is now commercially available. A hallmark of these reform programs is student engagement. Children are challenged to make sense of new mathematical ideas through explorations and projects, often in real contexts. Written and oral communication is strongly encouraged. Most programs do not have textbooks but are supported with activity guides, teacher resources, and consumable materials for students. Teacher training is generally seen as important if not essential for districtwide implementation, a fact that adds to the already high cost of most reform programs.

Data concerning the effectiveness of reform curricula as measured by traditional testing programs continue to be gathered. It is safe to say that students in reform programs perform much better on problem-solving measures and at least as well on traditional skills as students in traditional programs (ARC Center, 2002; Bell, 1998; Boaler, 1998; Fuson, Carroll, & Drueck, 2000; Reys, Robinson, Sconiers, & Mark, 1999; Riordin & Noyce, 2001; Stein, Grover, & Henningsen, 1996; Stein & Lane, 1996; Wood & Sellers, 1996, 1997).

Comparing any of these with a corresponding traditional textbook would be an effective way to understand what reform or *Standards*-based mathematics is all about.

In each chapter of Section 2 you will find features describing activities from *Investigations in Number, Data, and Space* or *Connected Mathematics.* These features are included to offer you some insight into these nontraditional programs as well as to offer good ideas for instruction.

AN INVITATION TO LEARN AND GROW

The mathematics education described in the *Standards* is almost certainly not the same as the mathematics and the mathematics teaching you experienced in grades K through 8. Along the way, you may have had some excellent teachers

---

*A listing of the eight reform curricula—the developers, publishers, and Internet contacts—can be found at the end of this chapter.

who really did reflect the current reform spirit. Examples of good reform curriculum have been around since the early 1990s, and you may have benefited from one of those. But for the most part, with the reform movement well into its second decade, its goals have yet to be realized in the large majority of school districts in North America.

As a practicing or prospective teacher facing the challenge of the three *Standards* documents, this book may challenge you to confront some of your personal beliefs—about what it means to *do mathematics,* how one goes about *learning mathematics,* how to *teach mathematics through problem solving,* and what it means to *assess mathematics* integrated with instruction. The next four chapters of this book help you develop these four foundational ideas for teaching. Chapters 6, 7, and 8 discuss other topics that influence mathematics teaching across all strands and grade levels: planning and related classroom issues, reaching all children in mathematics, and the role of technology.

Section 2 of the book examines the teaching and learning of specific topics in mathematics. The chapters in the second section are designed not only as text material but also as a source of instructional tasks for your future or current teaching.

Teaching mathematics can be an exciting adventure. Perhaps the most exciting part is that you will grow and learn along with your students. Enjoy the journey!

REFLECTIONS ON CHAPTER 1

Writing to Learn

At the end of each chapter of this book, you will find a series of questions under this same heading. The questions are designed to help you reflect on the most important ideas of the chapter. Writing (or talking aloud with a peer) is an excellent way to explore new ideas and incorporate them into your own knowledge base. The writing (or discussion) will help make the ideas your own. After you have written your responses in your own words, return to the book to compare what you have written with the book. Make changes, if necessary, or discuss differences with your instructor.

1. What are the five goals for all students that were described originally in the 1989 *Curriculum Standards* and reflected again in the *Principles and Standards* document? Pick two of these goals that you think are the most important, and explain what they mean to you.
2. Give a brief description of each of the six principles in *Principles and Standards* (Equity, Curriculum, Teaching, Learning, Assessment, and Technology). Explain the importance of each principle to the teaching and learning of mathematics.
3. What are the five content strands (standards) defined by *Principles and Standards*?
4. What is meant by a *process* as referred to in the *Principles and Standards* process standards? Give a brief description of each of the five process standards.
5. Among the ideas in the *Professional Standards* are five shifts in the classroom environment, from traditional approaches to a *Standards*-oriented approach. Examine these five shifts, and describe in a few sentences what aspects of each shift seem most significant to you.
6. Describe at least two results derived from NAEP data. What are the implications?
7. Describe at least two results derived from TIMSS data. What are the implications?
8. Describe the influences of state-level standards on classroom mathematics education.
9. Discuss the difference between traditional textbooks and reform curricula.

For Discussion and Exploration

1. In recent years, the outcry for "basics" was again being heard from a loud and very political minority. The debate over reform or the basics is both important and interesting. For an engaging discussion of the reform movement in light of the "back to basics" outcry, read one or more of the first five articles in the February 1999 edition of the *Phi Delta Kappan.* Where do you stand on the issue of reform versus the basics?
2. Examine a traditional textbook at any grade level of your choice. If possible, use a teacher's edition. Page through any chapter, and look for signs of the five process standards. To what extent are children who are being taught from this book likely to be doing and learning mathematics in ways described by those processes? What would you have to do to change the general approach to this text?
3. Examine a unit from any one of the eight reform curriculum programs, and see how it reflects the NCTM vision of reform, especially the five process standards. How do these curriculum programs differ from traditional textbook programs?
4. Review the sample video from the eighth-grade TIMSS video study. It shows a geometry lesson and an algebra lesson from a typical eighth-grade classroom in each country. What elements of the reform movement do you see in each of these lessons? Caution: You will be very surprised at the U.S. lessons, especially in comparison to the others on the tape.

Recommendations for Further Reading

Highly Recommended

Ferrini-Mundy, J. (2000). The standards movement in mathematics education: Reflections and hopes. In M. J. Burke (Ed.), *Learning mathematics for a new century* (pp. 37–50). Reston, VA: National Council of Teachers of Mathematics.
　Joan Ferrini-Mundy chaired the writing group of *Principles and Standards.* In this article, written before the *Standards* was released,

she shares her unique and very well-informed view of this important publication, how it came to be, the impact of the earlier document, the political climate in which the *Standards* was released, and the intentions that the council had for the document. Of particular interest is the discussion of tensions between opposing, yet reasoned viewpoints that the authors of the *Standards* had to wrestle with. This article will provide an understanding of the *Standards* that is impossible to get from the document itself.

National Council of Teachers of Mathematics. (2000). *Principles and standards for school mathematics.* Reston, VA: Author.

This update to the 1989 document that signaled the beginning of the revolution in mathematics education is one of the most important books that you could read in order to understand the current directions in mathematics education. Every teacher and pre-service teacher should at a minimum read sections on Principles (Chapter 2), the K–12 overview (Chapter 3), and the standards for his or her grade band of interest. If possible, add *PSSM* to your professional library.

National Research Council. (1989). *Everybody counts: A report to the nation on the future of mathematics education.* Washington, DC: National Academy Press.

This little booklet, readable in a single evening, remains a "must read" more than 15 years since its publication. It provides a compelling rationale for reform in both the mathematics we teach and how it is taught. Here you will find the description of mathematics as "the science of pattern and order" used throughout this book. Myths concerning the nature of mathematics, how it is learned, and by whom are challenged from an angle that is difficult to dispute.

National Research Council. (2001). *Adding it up: Helping children learn mathematics.* J. Kilpatrick, J. Swafford, & B. Findell (Eds.). Mathematics Learning Study Committee, Center for Education, Division of Behavioral and Social Sciences and Education. Washington, DC: National Academy Press.

Perhaps the most important book since *Principles and Standards,* this work is the effort of a select committee representing mathematics educators, mathematicians, school administrators, and industry. The authors represent a balanced view of mathematics education in the United States. The book carefully describes the state of mathematics education and makes very specific recommendations about how to improve it. A hallmark of this book is the formulation of five strands of "mathematical proficiency": conceptual understanding, procedural fluency, strategic competence, adaptive reasoning, and productive disposition. Educators and policy makers will cite this book for many years to come.

Teppo, A. R. (Ed.). (1999). *Reflecting on practice in elementary school mathematics: Readings from NCTM's school-based journals and other publications.* Reston, VA: National Council of Teachers of Mathematics.

Frequently, NCTM publishes books of selected readings from its journals. In this instance, the more than 60 articles provide perspective on the reform movement both in general and organized according to major areas of the curriculum. For a teacher wanting to establish a beginning resource of short, easily read articles on a wide variety of topics, this is an excellent book with which to begin.

Other Suggestions

Battista, M. T. (1999). The mathematical miseducation of America's youth: Ignoring research and scientific study in education. *Phi Delta Kappan, 80,* 424–432.

Bay, J. M., Reys, B. J., & Reys, R. E. (1999). The top 10 elements that must be in place to implement standards-based mathematics curricula. *Phi Delta Kappan, 80,* 503–506.

Billstein, R. (1998). Middle grades math thematics: The STEM project—a look at developing a middle school mathematics curriculum. In L. Leutzinger (Ed.), *Mathematics in the middle* (pp. 93–106). Reston, VA: National Council of Teachers of Mathematics.

Boaler, J. (1998). Open and closed mathematics: Student experiences and understandings. *Journal for Research in Mathematics Education, 29,* 41–62.

Burrill, G. (1998). Changes in your classroom: From the past to the present to the future. *Teaching Children Mathematics, 5,* 202–209.

Curcio, F. R. (1999). Dispelling myths about reform in school mathematics. *Mathematics Teaching in the Middle School, 4,* 282–284.

Ferrini-Mundy, J., Graham, K., Johnson, L., & Mills, G. (Eds.) (1998). *Making change in mathematics education: Learning from the field.* Reston, VA: National Council of Teachers of Mathematics.

Fuson, K. C., Carroll, W. M., & Drueck, J. V. (2000). Achievement results for second and third graders using the *Standards*-based curriculum *Everyday Mathematics. Journal for Research in Mathematics Education, 31,* 277–295.

Goldsmith, L. T., & Mark, J. (1999). What is a standards-based mathematics curriculum? *Educational Leadership, 57*(3), 40–44.

Jones, M. G., Jones, B. D., Hardin, B., Chapman, L., Yarbrough, T., & Davis, M. (1999). The impact of high-stakes testing on teachers and students in North Carolina. *Phi Delta Kappan, 81,* 199–203.

Lappan, G. (1999). Revitalizing and refocusing our efforts. *Teaching Children Mathematics, 6,* 104–109.

Lappan, G., & Phillips, E. (1998). Teaching and learning in the Connected Mathematics Project. In L. Leutzinger (Ed.), *Mathematics in the middle* (pp. 83–92). Reston, VA: National Council of Teachers of Mathematics.

National Council of Teachers of Mathematics. (1991). *Professional standards for teaching mathematics.* Reston, VA: Author.

National Council of Teachers of Mathematics. (1995). *Assessment standards for school mathematics.* Reston, VA: Author.

National Council of Teachers of Mathematics. (2000). *Principles and standards for school mathematics.* Reston, VA: Author.

O'Brien, T. C. (1999). Parrot Math. *Phi Delta Kappan, 80,* 434–438.

Reys, B., Robinson, E., Sconiers, S., & Mark, J. (1999). Mathematics curricula based on rigorous national standards: What, why, and how? *Phi Delta Kappan, 80,* 454–457.

Reys, R. E., Reys, B. J., Barnes, D. E., Beem, J. K., Lapan, R. T., & Papick, I. J. (1998). Standards-based middle school mathematics curricula: What do students think? In L. Leutzinger (Ed.), *Mathematics in the middle* (pp. 153–157). Reston, VA: National Council of Teachers of Mathematics.

Riordin, J. E., & Noyce, P. E. (2001). The impact of two standards-based mathematics curricula on student achievement in Massachusetts. *Journal for Research in Mathematics Education, 32,* 368–398.

Schoen, H. L., Fey, J. T., Hirsch, C. R., & Coxford, A. F. (1999). Issues and options in the math wars. *Phi Delta Kappan, 80,* 444–453.

Stigler, J. W., & Hiebert, J. (1997). Understanding and improving classroom mathematics instruction: An overview of the TIMSS video study. *Phi Delta Kappan, 79*(1), 14–21.

Stigler, J. W., & Hiebert, J. (1999). *The teaching gap: Best ideas from the world's teachers for improving education in the classroom.* New York: The Free Press.

Van Boening, L. (1999). Growth through change. *Mathematics Teaching in the Middle School, 5,* 27–33.

Reform Curricula

Elementary Programs

Information about the elementary programs can be obtained from the ARC Center:
> E-mail: arccenter@mail.comap.com
> URL: www.arccenter.comap.com

UCSMP Elementary: Everyday Mathematics (K–6)
Developer: University of Chicago School Mathematics Project
Publisher: Everyday Learning
E-mail: aisaacs@midway.uchicago.edu
URL: http://everydaymath.uchicago.edu

Investigations in Number, Data, and Space (K–5)
Developer: TERC
Publisher: Scott Foresman
URL: www.terc.edu/investigations/index.html

Math Trailblazers: A Mathematical Journey Using Science and Language Arts (K–5)
Developer: Institute for Math and Science Education, University of Illinois, Chicago
Publisher: Kendall/Hunt
URL: www.math.uic.edu/IMSE

Middle School Programs

Information about the middle school programs can be obtained from the Show-Me Center:
> E-mail: Center@showme.missouri.edu
> URL: www.showmecenter.missouri.edu

Connected Mathematics (CMP) (6–8)
Developer: Michigan State University
Publisher: Prentice Hall
URL: www.msu.edu/cmp

Mathematics in Context (MIC) (5–8)
Developer: University of Wisconsin—Madison
Publisher: Encyclopaedia Britannica
URL: www.ebmic.com

MathScape (6–8)
Developer: Educational Development Center
Publisher: Creative Publications
URL: www.edc.org/mathscape

Middle School Mathematics Through Applications Project (MMAP) (6–8)
Developer: Institute for Research on Learning
Publisher: Voyager Expanded Learning
URL: www.imvoyager.com

Middle Grades Math Thematics (STEM) (6–8)
Developer: University of Montana
Publisher: McDougal/Littell
URL: www.mlmath.com

2

Exploring What It Means to Do Mathematics

As a practical matter, mathematics is a science of pattern and order. Its domain is not molecules or cells, but numbers, chance, form, algorithms, and change. As a science of abstract objects, mathematics relies on logic rather than on observation as its standard of truth, yet employs observation, simulation, and even experimentation as means of discovering truth.

Mathematical Sciences Education Board (1989, p. 31)

How would you describe what you are doing when you are *doing mathematics*? Stop for a moment and write a few sentences about what it means to know and do mathematics, based on your own experiences. Then put your paper aside until you have finished this chapter.

The description of doing mathematics you will read about here may not match your personal experiences. That's okay! It is okay to come to this point with whatever beliefs were developed in your previous mathematics experiences. However, it is *not* okay to accept outdated ideas about mathematics and expect to be a quality teacher. Your obligation and your challenge as you read this chapter and this book are to reconceptualize your own understanding of what it means to know and do mathematics so that the children with whom you work will have an exciting and accurate vision of mathematics.

CONTRASTING PERCEPTIONS OF SCHOOL MATHEMATICS

Much change has taken place since 1989 when NCTM set a vision for change in mathematics classrooms. More teachers are beginning to use what might be called a "*Standards* approach": more cooperative learning, more emphasis on concepts and problem solving, and a greater tolerance for and use of calculators. Often these changes are superficial and are not really changing the nature of what children do and how they think in the mathematics classroom. Furthermore, as noted in Chapter 1, the pressures of state test scores have a tendency to bring out "drill-and-kill" approaches even though such methods have consistently proved ineffective. Fortunately, wonderful exceptions are to be found everywhere.

Traditional Views of Mathematics

Most adults will acknowledge that mathematics is an important subject, but few understand what the discipline is about. For many, mathematics is a collection of rules to be mastered, arithmetic computations, mysterious algebraic equations, and geometric proofs. This perception is in stark contrast to a view of mathematics that involves making sense of mathematical objects such as data, form, change, or patterns. A substantial number of adults are almost proud to proclaim, "I was never any good at mathematics." How has this debilitating perspective of mathematics as a collection of arcane procedures and rules become so prevalent in our society? The best answer can be found in the traditional approaches to teaching mathematics. Traditional teaching, still the predominant instructional pattern, typically begins with an explanation of whatever idea is on the current page of the text followed by showing children how to do the assigned exercises. Even with a hands-on activity, the traditional teacher is guiding students, telling them exactly how to use the materials in a prescribed manner. The focus of the lesson is primarily on getting answers. Students rely on the teacher to determine if their answers are correct. Children emerge from these experiences with a view that mathematics is a series of arbitrary rules, handed down by the teacher, who in turn got them from some very smart source.

When children are neither asked nor required to understand rules or evaluate their own answers, they are being told loudly and clearly, "You are not capable of understanding these ideas." Children accept that every problem must have a predetermined solution, that there is only one way to solve any problem, and that they should not even expect to solve a problem unless they have been given a solution method ahead of time.

This follow-the-rules, computation-dominated, answer-oriented view of mathematics is a gross distortion of what mathematics is really about. It cannot be very exciting. A few children are good at learning rules and thrive on the ensuing good grades. But these are not necessarily the best thinkers in the room. The traditional system rewards the learning of rules but offers little opportunity actually to do mathematics.

Mathematics as a Science of Pattern and Order

Mathematics is the science of pattern and order. This wonderfully simple description of mathematics is found in the thought-provoking publication *Everybody Counts* (MSEB, 1989; see also Schoenfeld, 1992). This definition challenges the popular social view of mathematics as a discipline dominated by computation and rules without reasons. Science is a process of figuring things out or making sense of things. It begins with problem-based situations. Although you may never have thought of it in quite this way, mathematics is a science of things that have a pattern of regularity and logical order. Finding and exploring this regularity or order and then making sense of it is what doing mathematics is all about.

Even the youngest schoolchildren can and should be involved in the science of pattern and order. Have you ever noticed that 6 + 7 is the same as 5 + 8 and 4 + 9? What is the pattern? What are the relationships? When two odd numbers are multiplied, the result is also odd, but if the same numbers are added or subtracted, the result is even. There is a logic behind simple results such as these, an order, a pattern.

Consider the study of algebra. One can learn to graph the equation of a parabola by simply following rules and plotting points. Now calculators are readily available to do that as well and with a speed and precision we could never hope to achieve. But understanding why certain forms of equations always produce parabolic graphs involves a search for patterns in the way numbers behave. Discovering what types of real-world relationships are represented by parabolic graphs (for example, a pendulum swing related to the length of the pendulum) is even more interesting and scientific—and infinitely more valuable—than the ability to plot the curve when someone else provides the equation.

And pattern is not just in numbers and equations but also in everything around us. The world is full of pattern and order: in nature, in art, in buildings, in music. Pattern and order are found in commerce, science, medicine, manufacturing, and sociology. Mathematics discovers this order, makes sense of it, and uses it in a multitude of fascinating ways, improving our lives and expanding our knowledge. School must begin to help children with this process of discovery.

What Does It Mean to Do Mathematics?

Engaging in the science of pattern and order—in doing mathematics—is effortful and often takes time. There are lots of ideas to learn. Often these ideas show up on lists of "basic skills." For example, children should be able to count accurately, know their basic facts for addition and multiplication, have efficient methods of computing whole numbers, fractions, and decimals, know measurement facts such as the number of inches in a foot or quarts in a gallon, know the names of geometric shapes, and so on. But to master these bits and pieces is no more doing mathematics than playing scales on the piano is making music.

 NCTM Standards

The *Principles and Standards* document makes it very clear that there is a time and a place for drill but that drill should *never* come before understanding. Repetitive drill of the bits and pieces is not doing mathematics and will never result in understanding. Drill may produce short-term results on traditional tests, but the long-term effects have produced a nation of citizens happy to admit they can't do mathematics.

The Verbs of Doing Mathematics

Envision for a moment an elementary mathematics class where students are doing mathematics. What verbs would you use to describe the activity in this classroom? Stop for a moment and make a short list before reading further.

Children in traditional mathematics classes often describe mathematics as "work" or "getting answers." They talk about "plussing" and "doing times" (multiplication). In contrast, the following collection of verbs can be found in most of the literature describing the reform in mathematics education, and all are used in *Principles and Standards:*

explore	represent	explain
investigate	formulate	predict
conjecture	discover	develop
solve	construct	describe
justify	verify	use

These are science verbs indicating the process of "making sense" and "figuring out." When children are engaged in the kinds of activities suggested by this list, it is virtually impossible for them to be passive observers. They will necessarily be actively thinking about the mathematical ideas that are involved.

In classrooms where doing mathematics this way is a daily occurrence, the students are getting an empowering message: "You are capable of making sense of this—you are capable of *doing mathematics!*"

What Is Basic in Mathematics?

In a climate where "basics" are once again a matter of public discussion and there is an unrelenting pressure on teachers to raise test scores, it is useful to ask, "What is basic in mathematics?" The position of this text is as follows:

> The most basic idea in mathematics is that *mathematics makes sense!*
>
> ■ Every day students must experience that mathematics makes sense.
>
> ■ Students must come to believe that they are capable of making sense of mathematics.
>
> ■ Teachers must stop teaching by telling and start letting students make sense of the mathematics they are learning.
>
> ■ To this end, teachers must believe in their students—all of them!

Every idea introduced in the mathematics classroom can and should be completely understood by *every* child. *There are no exceptions!* There is absolutely no excuse for children learning any aspect of mathematics without completely understanding it. All children are capable of learning all of the mathematics we want them to learn, and they can learn it in a meaningful manner in a way that makes sense to them.

An Environment for Doing Mathematics

Look again at the verbs of doing mathematics. They are action verbs. They require reaching out, taking risks, placing ideas out where others can see. Contrast these with the verbs that might reflect the traditional mathematics classroom: *listen, copy, memorize, drill.* These are passive activities. They involve no risks and little initiative. Doing mathematics takes effort and initiative.

Though thinking, reasoning, and sense making can be fun, it can nevertheless be a bit frightening to stick out your neck when no one tells you exactly what to do. The classroom must be an environment where doing mathematics is not threatening and where every student is respected for his or her ideas. Students should feel comfortable taking risks, knowing that they will not be ridiculed if they are wrong.

The teacher's role is to create this spirit of inquiry, trust, and expectation. Within that environment, students are invited to do mathematics. Problems are posed; students wrestle toward solutions. The focus is on students actively figuring

things out, testing ideas and making conjectures, developing reasons and offering explanations. Students work in groups, in pairs, or individually, but they are always sharing and discussing. Reasoning is celebrated as students defend their methods and justify their solutions.

AN INVITATION TO DO MATHEMATICS

If you are to create a classroom environment where children are truly doing mathematics, it is important that you have a personal feel for doing mathematics in this manner. It is likely that your experiences in mathematics classes have been quite different. The purpose of this portion of the chapter is to provide you with opportunities to engage in the science of pattern and order—to do some mathematics. Although the tasks or problems are appropriate for students in the intermediate and middle grades, you should not be at all concerned now with how children might approach these problems. Rather, get personally involved in the problems as an adult and discover as much as you can in the process. If possible, find one or two friends to work with you. Get some paper to scribble ideas on. Try not to be shy about your ideas. Respect and listen to the ideas of your friends. You can and should challenge their ideas, but don't belittle them.

The book will provide hints and suggestions in a poor substitution for the interaction of a teacher. Don't read too much at once. Stop and do as much as you can until you and your group are stuck—really stuck; then read a bit more.

Let's Do Some Mathematics!

We will explore four different problems. Each is independent of the others. None requires any sophisticated mathematics, not even algebra. Don't be passive! Try your ideas out. Have fun!

START AND JUMP NUMBERS: SEARCHING FOR PATTERNS

You will need to make a list of numbers that begin with a "start number" and increase by a fixed amount we will call the "jump number." First try 3 as the start number and 5 as the jump number. Write the start number at the top of your list, then 8, 13, and so on, "jumping" by 5 each time until your list extends to about 130.

Your task is to examine this list of numbers and find as many patterns as you possibly can. Share your ideas with the group, and write down every pattern you agree really is a pattern.

 STOP Get to work before reading further. Keep looking for patterns until you simply cannot think of any more.

• For a jump number of 3, how is the ones-digit pattern related to the circle of numbers in Figure 2.1? Are there other circles of numbers for other jump numbers?

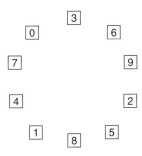

FIGURE 2.1 For jumps of 3, this cycle of digits will occur in the ones place. The start number determines where the cycle begins.

Looking Back. You may want to explore this idea even further—or perhaps you've had enough of jump numbers. There are more ideas than are suggested here.

A calculator can be used to make the list generation easy for young children or to work with big jump numbers, such as 25 or 36. Most simple calculators have an automatic constant feature that will add the same number successively. For example, if you press 3 ⊞ 5 ⊟ and then keep pressing ⊟, you will get the first sequence of numbers you wrote. (The calculator "stores" the last operation of +5 and repeats the operation on the display for each press of ⊟. This also works for the other three operations.)

TWO MACHINES, ONE JOB

Ron's Recycle Shop was started when Ron bought a used paper-shredding machine. Business was good, so Ron bought a new shredding machine. The old machine could shred a truckload of paper in 4 hours. The new machine could shred the same truckload in only 2 hours. How long will it take to shred a truckload of paper if Ron runs both shredders at the same time?

Get Started. Sometimes you just have to jump in and do something. Before reading any of the ideas that follow, go ahead and work on this until you either get an answer or get stuck. If you get an answer, try to decide how you can establish that it is correct. If you get stuck, be absolutely certain you are stuck. Write down everything you know, and examine every idea you have had.

  Work before reading on.

A Few Ideas. Here are some kinds of things you may already have thought of:

• There is at least one alternating pattern.
• Have you looked at odd and even numbers?
• What can you say about the number in the tens place? How did you think about the first two numbers with no tens-place digits? What happens when the numbers reach above 100? (There are two ways to think about that.)
• Have you tried doing any adding of numbers? Numbers in the list? Digits in the numbers?

  If there is an idea in this list you haven't tried, try that now.

Don't forget to think about what happens to your patterns after the numbers go over 100. How are you thinking about 113? One way is as 1 hundred, 1 ten, and 3 ones. But, of course, it could also be "eleventy-three," where the tens digit has gone from 9 to 10 to 11. How do these different perspectives affect your patterns? What would happen after 999?

When you added the *digits* in the numbers, the sums are 3, 8, 4, 9, 5, 10, 6, 11, 7, 12, 8, . . . Did you look at every other number in this string? And what is the sum for 113? Is it 5 or is it 14? (There is no "right" answer here. But it is interesting to consider different possibilities.)

Next Steps. Sometimes when you have discovered some patterns in mathematics, it is a good idea to make some changes and see how the changes affect the patterns. What changes might you make in this problem?

  Try some ideas now before going on.

Your changes may be even more interesting than the following suggestions. But here are some ideas that seem a bit more obvious than others:

• Change the start number but keep the jump number equal to 5. What is the same and what is different?
• Try keeping the start number the same, and examine different jump numbers. You will find out that changing jump numbers really "messes things up" a lot compared to changing the start numbers.
• If you have patterns for several different jump numbers, what can you figure out about how a jump number affects the patterns? For example, when the jump number was 5, the ones-digit pattern repeated every two numbers—it had a "pattern length" of two. But when the jump number is 3, the length of the ones-digit pattern is ten! Do other jump numbers create different lengths?

Stuck? Are you overlooking any assumptions made in the problem? Do the machines run simultaneously? The problem says "at the same time." Do they run just as fast when working together as when they work alone?

 STOP If this gives you an idea, pursue it before reading more.

Have you tried to predict approximately how much time you think it should take the two machines? Just make an estimate in round numbers. For example, will it be closer to 1 hour or closer to 4 hours? What causes you to answer as you have? Can you tell if your "guestimate" makes sense or is at least in the ballpark? Checking a guess in this way sometimes leads to a new insight.

Some people draw pictures to solve problems. Others like to use something they can move or change. For example, you might draw a rectangle or a line segment to stand for the truckload of paper, or you might get some counters (chips, plastic cubes, pennies) and make a collection that stands for the truckload.

 STOP Go back and try some more.

Consider Solutions of Others. Here are solutions of three elementary school teachers who worked on this problem. (The examples are adapted from Schifter & Fosnot, 1993, pp. 24–27.) Betsy teaches sixth grade. Here is Betsy's solution:

> Betsy holds up a bar of plastic cubes. "Let's say these 16 cubes are the truckload of paper. In 1 hour, the new machine shreds 8 cubes and the old machine 4 cubes." Betsy breaks off 8 cubes and then 4 cubes. "That leaves these 4 cubes. If the new machine did 8 cubes' worth in 1 hour, it can do 2 cubes' worth in 15 minutes. The old machine does half as much, or 1 cube." As she says this, she breaks off 3 more cubes. "That is 1 hour and 15 minutes, and we still

have 1 cube left." Long pause. "Well, the new machine did 2 cubes in 15 minutes, so it will do this cube in $7\frac{1}{2}$ minutes. Add that onto the 1 hour and 15 minutes. The total time will be 1 hour $22\frac{1}{2}$ minutes." (See Figure 2.2.)

Cora teaches fourth grade. She disagrees with Betsy. Here is Cora's proposal:

> "This rectangle [see Figure 2.3] stands for the whole truckload. In 1 hour, the new machine will do half of this." The rectangle is divided in half. "In 1 hour, the old machine could do $\frac{1}{4}$ of the paper." The rectangle is divided accordingly. "So in 1 hour, the two machines have done $\frac{3}{4}$ of the truck, and there is $\frac{1}{4}$ left. What is left is one-third as much as what they already did, so it should take the two machines one-third as long to do that part as it took to do the first part. One-third of an hour is 20 minutes. That means it takes 1 hour and 20 minutes to do it all."

Sylvia teaches third grade. She and her partner have these thoughts:

> At first, we solved the problem by averaging. We decided that it would take 3 hours because that's the average. Then Deborah asked how we knew to average. We thought we had a reason, but then Deborah asked how Ron would feel if his two machines together took longer than just the new one that could do the job in only 2 hours. So we can see that 3 hours doesn't make sense. So we still don't know whether it's 1 hour and 20 minutes or 1 hour and $22\frac{1}{2}$ minutes.

At the SummerMath institute where these teachers were participants, they were not told the solution to this problem. That in itself caused some disturbance. But there is little value in seeing a solution from a book or from a teacher. You end up feeling that the teacher is very smart and you are not so smart. No solution is provided here either.

If you have a solution, a good thing to do is see first why you think you are correct and try to articulate that. Then see if you can find a different way to solve the problem than the way you did it the first time. (What would be the value of two different solutions that both lead to the same answer?)

FIGURE 2.2 Betsy's solution to the paper-shredding problem.

New machine does this work in 1 hour. Old machine does this work in 1 hour. Both do this in 15 minutes. New machine does this in $7\frac{1}{2}$ minutes.

FIGURE 2.3 Cora's solution to the paper-shredding problem.

New machine in 1 hour. Old machine in 1 hour. Both machines together. 60 minutes. 20 minutes.

WHAT CAN YOU FIND OUT ABOUT THIS?

An excellent exploration for young children to help them begin to see how facts are related is to confront them with this observation:

When you make the first number 1 more and the second number 1 less, you get the same answer:

$$\begin{array}{cc}\Uparrow & \Downarrow\end{array}$$
$7 + 7 = 14$ is the same as $8 + 6 = 14$

It works for 5 + 5 too

$$\begin{array}{cc}\Uparrow & \Downarrow\end{array}$$
$5 + 5 = 10$ is the same as $6 + 4 = 10$

What can you find out about this?

Your task here is to examine *what happens when you change addition to multiplication in this exploration. What can you find out about that?* ($7 \times 7 = 49$ and $8 \times 6 = 48$)? *What other products should you examine?*

 Explore until you have developed some ideas. Write down whatever ideas you discover.

Try Using a Physical Model. You have probably found some interesting patterns. Can you tell why these patterns work? In the case of addition, it is fairly easy to see that when you take from one number and give to the other, the total stays the same. That is not exactly the way multiplication works. One way to explore this is to make rectangles for each product and see how they change when you adjust one factor up and the other down (see Figure 2.4a).

You may prefer to think of multiplication as equal sets. For example, 7×7 means seven sets with seven things in

each. You increase the number of sets and decrease the number in each set (or the other way around; see Figure 2.4b).

 Work with one or both of these approaches to see if you get any insights.

Things to Examine

There are a few different ways to go with this exploration. Here are a couple of suggestions. You may be pursuing something a bit different than these ideas. That is fine! The idea in this problem is to conduct your own exploration—to see what you can find out.

- Have you looked at how the first two numbers are related? For example, 7×7, 5×5, and 9×9 are all products with like factors. How do those results differ when the two factors are 1 apart (7×8 or 12×13)? What about when the factors differ by 2 or by 3?
- Maybe you have adjusted the factors up and down by 1. What if you go from 7×7 to 9×5? Try making adjustments by other numbers.
- Does it make any difference in the results if you use big numbers instead of small ones?
- What if *both* factors increase?

This exploration has lots of answers, but the questions to answer are the ones *you* ask. When the problem is really yours and it is not clear that the teacher already knows the answer, students feel more ownership and interest. Rather than asking "What do you want me to do?" problem ownership shifts the situation to "I think I am going to . . ." (Baker & Baker, 1990). The suggested questions offered here were presented as a list because this is a textbook. In a classroom, the teacher can select challenges and make suggestions when necessary. The teacher can also help students make their own conjectures and observations. Frequently, children will pursue a completely different tack than the one anticipated.

This is 7×7 as
7 rows of 7.

(a)

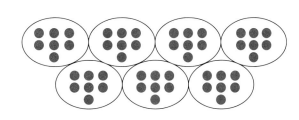

This is 7×7 as
7 sets of 7.

(b)

What happens when you change one of these to show 6×8?

FIGURE 2.4 Two physical ways to think about multiplication that might help in the exploration.

Scientists explore new ideas that strike them as interesting and promising rather than blindly following the direction of others. Mathematics is a science.

THE BEST CHANCE OF PURPLE

Three students are spinning to "get purple" with two spinners (either by spinning first red and then blue or first blue and then red; see Figure 2.5). They may choose to spin each spinner once or one of the spinners twice. Mary chooses to spin twice on spinner A; John chooses to spin twice on spinner B; and Susan chooses to spin first on spinner A and then on spinner B. Who has the best chance of getting a red and a blue (Lappan & Even, 1989, p. 17)?

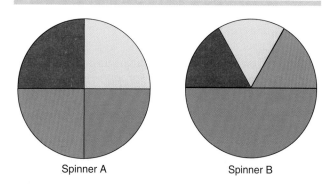

FIGURE 2.5 You may spin A twice, B twice, or A then B. Which option gives you the best chance of spinning a red and a blue?

 STOP   As with the other problems, first think about the problem and what you know and then try something that gives you some help. Before reading the suggestions, see what you can come up with.

Try It Out

Sometimes it is tough to get a feel for problems that seem too abstract to think about. In situations involving chance find a way to create the chance and see what happens. For this problem, you can easily make spinners using a freehand drawing on paper, a paper clip, and a pencil. Put your pencil point through the loop of the clip and on the center of your spinner. Now you can flip the paper clip "pointer." Try at least 20 pairs of spins for each choice, and keep track of what happens.

- For Susan's choice (A then B), would it matter if she spun B first and then A? Why or why not?
- Explain why you think purple is more or less likely in one of the three cases compared to the other two. It sometimes helps to talk through what you have observed to come up with a way to apply some more precise reasoning.

STOP   Try these suggestions before reading on.

Try Tree Diagrams

On spinner A, the four colors each have the same chance of coming up. You could make a tree diagram for A with four branches, and all the branches would have the same chance (see Figure 2.6). On spinner B, what is the relationship between the blue region and each of the others? How could you make a tree diagram for B with each branch having the same chance?

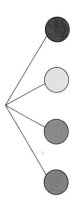

FIGURE 2.6 A tree diagram for spinner A in Figure 2.5.

How can you add to the diagram for spinner A so that it represents spinning A twice in succession? Why does your tree diagram make sense? What branches on your diagram represent getting purple?

How could you make tree diagrams for John's and Susan's choices? Why do they make sense?

Whatever idea you come up with on paper should be tested by actually spinning the spinner or spinners.

STOP   Tree diagrams are only one way to approach this. You may have a different way. As long as your way seems to be getting you somewhere, stick with that way. There is one more suggestion to follow, but don't read further if you have an idea to work on.

Using Grids

Suppose that you had a square that represented all the possible outcomes for spinner A and a similar square for spinner B. Although there are many ways to divide a square in four equal parts, if you use lines going all in the same direction, you can make comparisons of all the outcomes of one event (one whole square) with the outcomes of another event (drawn on a different square). When the second event (here the second spin) follows the first event, make the lines on the second square go the opposite way from the lines on the first. Make a tracing of one square in Figure 2.7 and place it on the other. You end up with 24 little sections.

Why are there six subdivisions for the spinner B square? What does each of the 24 little rectangles stand for? What sections would represent purple? In any other method you have been trying, did 24 come into play when you were looking at spinner A followed by B?

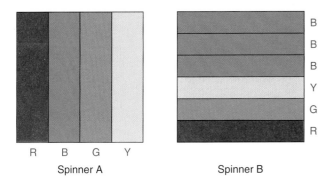

FIGURE 2.7 A square shows the chance of obtaining each color for the spinners in Figure 2.5.

No Answer Book

If you have worked hard on any or all of the four tasks just presented, you still may not have answers or found all of the patterns and ideas that someone else found. If you really gave it some effort and took some risks in sharing whatever ideas you had, you are on the right track. The science of pattern and order sometimes takes a little time and nearly always requires effort.

No answers or solutions are given in this text. How do you feel about that? What about the "right" answers? Are your answers correct? What makes the solution to any investigation "correct"?

In the classroom, the ready availability of the answer book or the teacher's providing the solution or verifying that an answer is correct sends a clear message to children about doing mathematics: "Your job is to find the answers that the teacher already has." In the real world of problem solving outside the classroom, there are no teachers with answers and no answer books. Doing mathematics includes deciding if an answer is correct and why.

Some More Explorations

Here are four more explorations. For these tasks, there are no hints or discussions, only the problems. The first two you could try with fourth- or fifth-grade children. All four would be useful in the middle grades. The main purpose of presenting them here is to give you an opportunity to do some more mathematics and to begin to experience what that means and feels like.

FOUR CONSECUTIVE NUMBERS

Some people say that to add four consecutive numbers, you add the first and the last numbers and multiply by 2. What can you find out about that?

Here is an example: 4, 5, 6, and 7 are four consecutive numbers. The sum is 22. Also 4 + 7 = 11 and 11 × 2 = 22.

The problem is taken from *Natural Learning and Mathematics* (Stoessiger & Edmunds, 1992). The authors use this task to provide a wonderful illustration of how 11- and 12-year-olds can generate ideas and make them grow. The book is highly recommended.

ACROBATS, GRANDMAS, AND IVAN

The problem is to use the information given to figure out who will win the third round of tug-of-war.

Round 1: On one side are four acrobats, each of equal strength. On the other side are five neighborhood grandmas, each of equal strength. The result is dead even.

Round 2: On one side is Ivan, a dog. Ivan is pitted against two of the grandmas and one acrobat. Again, it's a draw.

Round 3: Ivan and three of the grandmas are on one side, and the four acrobats are on the other.

Who will win the third round?

This problem was originally called "A Mathematical Tug-of-War" and is found in *Math for Smarty Pants* by Marilyn Burns (1982). For a discussion of how fifth graders approached the problem, see *50 Problem-Solving Lessons: Grades 1–6* (Burns, 1996). Silver, Smith, and Nelson (1995) discuss solutions offered by eighth graders.

PIZZAS: SMALL, MEDIUM, AND LARGE

Pizzas are often sold in small, medium, and large sizes—usually measured by the diameter of the circular pie. Of course, the prices are different for the three sizes. Do you think a large pizza is usually the best buy?

The Sole D'Italia Pizzeria sells small, medium, and large pies. The small pie is 9 inches in diameter, the medium pie is 12 inches in diameter, and the large pie is 15 inches in diameter. For a plain cheese small pizza, Sole D'Italia charges $6; for a medium pizza, it charges $9; for a large pizza, it charges $12. Are these fair prices?

- Which measures should be most closely related to the prices charged—circumference, area, radius, or diameter? Why?
- Use your results to write a report on the fairness of Sole D'Italia's pizza prices.

This problem (Lappan & Briars, 1995, p. 139) has a number of characteristics worth noting. First, it is contextual; it is a very realistic problem that might interest middle grade students. Second, the teacher can predict with some certainty what mathematics students will encounter in this problem (measurement and relationships in the geometry of circles). There are lots of ideas about circle measurement involved. This would be a good problem to use *before* the children have developed a collection of formulas. Students have many ways to get at the circle measures, including measuring some actual circles. Formulas are not necessary. There is also a nice opportunity to discuss rate as a type of ratio in this problem.

TRAPEZOIDS

A trapezoid is a four-sided figure with one pair of opposite sides parallel. Draw a trapezoid that has an area of 36.

If a teacher or a text gives you a formula for the area of a trapezoid, this is not a very interesting task. But there are some nice possibilities for discovering patterns and learning about area and perhaps even developing a formula that can come from this. One suggestion is to get some grid paper and draw some trapezoids.

Helping Students Do Mathematics

Assuming that you have worked on some of the problems in this chapter, you have most likely been trying to make sense of the situations or tasks that you confronted. You were involved in the science of pattern and order. You were *doing mathematics*.

In the best of situations, you did this science, this mathematics, with others. Perhaps you shared your ideas, right or wrong, and tried to defend them. You listened to your peers and tried to make sense of their ideas. Together you tried to come up with a solution. And then you had to decide if your answer was correct without looking in an answer book or asking the teacher.

When students do mathematics like this on a daily basis in an environment that encourages risk and expects participation, it becomes an exciting endeavor. Individuals who are uncomfortable in an answer-oriented, teacher-directed environment begin to develop confidence. Students talk more, share more ideas, offer suggestions, and challenge or defend the solutions of others.

Being the teacher responsible for creating this environment may sound overwhelming. You may have envisioned teaching mathematics as relatively easy—just demonstrate the rules and manage practice. Creating a classroom culture and environment in which children are doing mathematics is not easy. There is no reason to believe that you will be an expert from the start.

NCTM's *Professional Standards for Teaching Mathematics* (1991) offers important guidelines and examples of teachers making changes toward this vision of doing mathematics. As noted in Chapter 1, the first of the major shifts envisioned by the *Professional Standards* is "toward classrooms as mathematical communities" and "away from classrooms as simply a collection of individuals" (p. 3). So that you can create this mathematical community, you next need to understand how children develop mathematical ideas. That is what you will encounter in Chapter 3. In Chapter 4, we will build on the vision of what it means to do mathematics and an understanding of how children learn. There you will find strategies for teaching with tasks or problems. It is an exciting venture!

Reflections on Chapter 2

Writing to Learn

1. Explain what is meant by "Mathematics is a science of pattern and order." Contrast this view with traditional school mathematics.
2. How would you describe what it means to "do mathematics"?
3. Why is doing pencil-and-paper computation not "doing mathematics"?
4. What features of a classroom environment are important for students to be engaged in doing mathematics?
5. How can students come to believe that they are capable of making sense of mathematics?

For Discussion and Exploration

1. Explore the teacher's edition of any current basal textbook series for any grade level of your interest. Pick one chapter, and identify lessons or activities that promote doing mathematics as a science of pattern and order. In general, would you say that the flavor of the chapter you selected is in the spirit of mathematics as a science of pattern and order? Examine any of the reform curricula (see listing on p. 11). Is the approach there any closer to doing mathematics?

2. In the *Professional Standards,* read the first vignette (pp. 11–15), in which a sixth-grade teacher who has taught for 5 years confronts her own realization that she needs to change. In reaction to this vignette you might

a. Try her lesson with fifth- to seventh-grade children

b. Design a lesson on a topic of your own choice that would serve the same purpose of getting children actively involved in real mathematics

c. Take a lesson out of a fifth- to seventh-grade book and discuss how this teacher might now decide to teach the lesson

Recommendations for Further Reading

Highly Recommended

Lampert, M. (1990). When the problem is not the question and the solution is not the answer: Mathematical knowing and teaching. *American Educational Research Journal, 27,* 29–63.

Magdelene Lampert is one of mathematics education's most articulate voices for making shifts toward classrooms as communities where children do mathematics. In this article, she clearly articulates the spirit of the traditional classroom and how it adversely affects the concept of mathematics held by children and teachers.

Malloy, C. E. (1999). Developing mathematical reasoning in the middle grades. In L. V. Stiff (Ed.), *Developing mathematical reasoning in grades K–12* (pp. 13–21). Reston, VA: National Council of Teachers of Mathematics.

Russell, S. J. (1999). Mathematical reasoning in the elementary grades. In L. V. Stiff (Ed.), *Developing mathematical reasoning in grades K–12* (pp. 1–12). Reston, VA: National Council of Teachers of Mathematics.

These two articles are the lead chapters in the 1999 NCTM yearbook on reasoning. Both authors provide excellent perspectives on the importance of helping children engage in the logical solution of problems. Russell's chapter begins by stating: "Mathematical reasoning must stand at the center of mathematics learning." Malloy makes the point that even in a diverse classroom different reasoning styles can be engaged to make learning happen.

Mokros, J., Russell, S. J., & Economopoulos, K. (1995). *Beyond arithmetic: Changing mathematics in the elementary classroom.* Palo Alto, CA: Dale Seymour Publications.

These three author/researchers from TERC use numerous examples from the elementary classroom to develop a realistic image of teaching mathematics from a problem-solving perspective. In looking at teaching, curriculum, and assessment, the importance of problem solving as a way of learning mathematics is quite clear. For a realistic look at reform mathematics and children solving problems, consider this useful, easily read book.

Schifter, D., & Fosnot, C. T. (1993). *Reconstructing mathematics education: Stories of teachers meeting the challenge of reform.* New York: Teachers College Press.

The authors describe teachers who confront their own concept of mathematics by doing real mathematics themselves. There are also many insights into the classrooms to which these teachers return. Here Betsy and Cora solve the paper-shredder problem (the context was changed). If you feel a bit threatened by the call for change, this is a book that can give you some company.

Other Suggestions

Artzt, A. F., & Yaloz-Femia, S. (1999). Mathematical reasoning during small-group problem solving. In L. V. Stiff (Ed.), *Developing mathematical reasoning in grades K–12* (pp. 115–126). Reston, VA: National Council of Teachers of Mathematics.

Bosangue, M. V., Gannon, G. E., & Watson, K. L. (2000). The wonderful world of digital sums. *Teaching Children Mathematics, 6,* 310–313, 318–320.

Cantlon, D. (1998). Kids + conjecture = mathematics power. *Teaching Children Mathematics, 5,* 108–112.

Cobb, P., & Merkel, B. (1989). Thinking strategies: Teaching arithmetic through problem solving. In P. R. Trafton (Ed.), *New directions for elementary school mathematics* (pp. 70–81). Reston, VA: National Council of Teachers of Mathematics.

Curcio, F. R., & Schwartz, S. L. (1998). There are no algorithms for teaching algorithms. *Teaching Children Mathematics, 5,* 26–30.

Ginsburg, H. P., Inoue, N., & Seo, K. (1999). Young children doing mathematics: Observations of everyday activities. In J. V. Copley (Ed.), *Mathematics in the early years* (pp. 88–100). Reston, VA: National Council of Teachers of Mathematics.

Griffiths, R., & Clyne, M. (1994). *Math makes sense: Teaching and learning in context.* Portsmouth, NH: Heinemann.

Ma, L. (1999). *Knowing and teaching elementary mathematics: Teachers' understanding of fundamental mathematics in China and the United States.* Mahwah, NJ: Lawrence Erlbaum.

Malloy, C. E. (1999). Developing mathematical reasoning in the middle grades. In L. V. Stiff (Ed.), *Developing mathematical reasoning in grades K–12* (pp. 13–21). Reston, VA: National Council of Teachers of Mathematics.

Russell, S. J. (1999). Mathematical reasoning in the elementary grades. In L. V. Stiff (Ed.), *Developing mathematical reasoning in grades K–12* (pp. 1–12). Reston, VA: National Council of Teachers of Mathematics.

Steele, D. F. (2000). Enthusiastic voices from young mathematicians. *Teaching Children Mathematics, 6,* 464–468.

chapter 3

DEVELOPING UNDERSTANDING IN MATHEMATICS

If the creation of the conceptual networks that constitute each individual's map of reality—including her mathematical understanding—is the product of constructive and interpretive activity, then it follows that no matter how lucidly and patiently teachers explain to their students, they cannot understand for their students.

Schifter and Fosnot (1993, p. 9)

It is a commonly accepted goal among mathematics educators that students should understand mathematics (Hiebert & Carpenter, 1992). The most widely accepted theory, known as *constructivism*, suggests that children must be active participants in the development of their own understanding. Constructivism provides us with insights concerning how children learn mathematics and guides us to use instructional strategies that begin with children rather than with ourselves.

A CONSTRUCTIVIST VIEW OF LEARNING

Constructivism is firmly rooted in the cognitive school of psychology and the theories of Piaget dating back at least as far as 1960. Constructivism rejects the notion that children are blank slates. They do not absorb ideas as teachers present them. Rather, children are creators of their own knowledge.

The Construction of Ideas

The basic tenet of constructivism is simply this: *Children construct their own knowledge.* In fact, not just children, but all people, all of the time, construct or give meaning to things they perceive or think about. As you read these words, you are giving meaning to them. You are constructing ideas.

To construct or build something in the physical world requires tools, materials, and effort. How we construct ideas can be viewed in an analogous manner. The tools we use to build understanding are our existing ideas, the knowledge that we already possess. The materials we act on to build understanding may be things we see, hear, or touch—elements of our physical surroundings. Sometimes the materials are our own thoughts and ideas. The effort that must be supplied is active and reflective thought. If minds are not actively thinking, nothing happens.

The diagram in Figure 3.1 is meant as a metaphor for the construction of ideas. Consider the picture to be a small section of our cognitive makeup. The blue dots represent existing ideas. The lines joining the ideas represent our logical connections or relationships that have developed between and among ideas. The red dot is an emerging idea, one that is being constructed. Whatever existing ideas (dots) are used in the construction will necessarily be connected to the new idea because those were the ideas that gave meaning to it. If a potentially relevant idea that would add better meaning to the new idea is either not present in the learner's mind or is not actively engaged, then that potential connection to the new idea simply will not be made. Obviously, learners will vary in the number of connections between a new idea and existing ideas. Different learners will use different ideas to give meaning to the same new idea. What is significant is that the construction of an idea is almost certainly going to be different for every learner, even within the same environment or classroom.

Constructing knowledge is an extremely active endeavor on the part of the learner (Baroody, 1987; Cobb, 1988; Fosnot, 1996; von Glasersfeld, 1990, 1996). To construct and understand a new idea requires actively thinking about it.

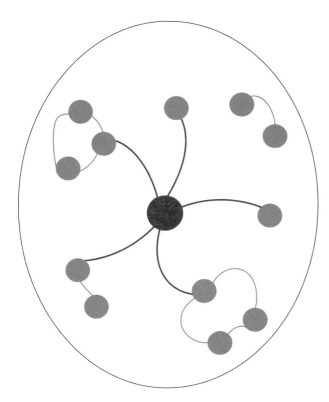

FIGURE 3.1 We use the ideas we already have (blue dots) to construct a new idea (red dot), developing in the process a network of connections between ideas. The more ideas used and the more connections made, the better we understand.

"How does this fit with what I already know?" "How can I understand this in the face of my current understanding of this idea?" Mathematical ideas cannot be "poured into" a passive learner. Children must be mentally active for learning to take place. In classrooms, children must be encouraged to wrestle with new ideas, to work at fitting them into existing networks, and to challenge their own ideas and those of others.

Put simply, constructing knowledge requires *reflective thought*, actively thinking about or mentally working on an idea. Reflective thought means sifting through existing ideas to find those that seem to be the most useful in giving meaning to the new idea.

Integrated networks, or *cognitive schemas,* are both the product of constructing knowledge and the tools with which additional new knowledge can be constructed. As learning occurs, the networks are rearranged, added to, or otherwise modified. When there is active, reflective thought, schemas are constantly being modified or changed so that ideas fit better with what is known.

The general principles of constructivism are based largely on Piaget's processes of assimilation and accommodation. *Assimilation* refers to the use of existing schema to give meaning to experiences. *Accommodation* is the process of altering existing ways of viewing things or ideas that contradict or do not fit into existing schema. Through reflective or purposeful thought, people may modify their existing schema to accommodate these ideas (Fosnot, 1996).

Examples of Constructed Learning

Consider the solution methods of two fourth-grade children who had been taught the meanings of the operations and had developed a good understanding of place-value concepts, some of the "dots" the children had at their disposal. Both children were from predominantly urban schools where a highly constructivist approach to mathematics had been in place for several years. They were asked to solve the following problem: "Four children had 3 bags of M&Ms. They decided to open all 3 bags of candy and share the M&Ms fairly. There were 52 M&M candies in each bag. How many M&M candies did each child get?" (Campbell & Johnson, 1995, pp. 35–36). Their solutions are shown in Figure 3.2.

Both children were able to determine the product 3 × 52 mentally. The two children used different cognitive tools to solve the problem of 156 ÷ 4. Marlena interpreted the task as

FIGURE 3.2 Two fourth-grade children construct unique solutions to a computation.

Source: Campbell & Johnson (1995). Used with permission.

Marlena's Solution

Darrell's Solution

"How many sets of 4 can be made from 156?" She first used facts that were either easy or available to her: 10×4 and 4×4. These totals she subtracted from 156 until she got to 100. This seemed to cue her to use 25 fours. Marlena made no hesitation in adding the number of sets of 4 that she found in 156 and knew the answer was 39 candies for each child.

Darrell's approach was more directly related to the sharing context of the problem. He formed four columns and distributed amounts to each, accumulating the amounts mentally and orally as he wrote the numbers. Like Marlena, Darrell used numbers that were either easy or available to him; first 20 to each, then 5, then 10, and then a series of ones. He added one of the columns without hesitation (Rowan, 1995).

If computational speed and proficiency were your goal, you might be tempted to argue that the children need further instruction. But both children clearly constructed ideas about the computation that had meaning to them. They demonstrated confidence, understanding, and a belief that they could solve the problem.

In contrast to these two children, consider a third-grade child in a traditional classroom. She has made a quite common error in subtraction, as shown in Figure 3.3. The problem appearing on a mathematics worksheet was subtraction, and the class had been doing subtraction with borrowing. This context narrowed the choices of ways to give meaning to the situation (the "dots" she would likely use). But this problem was a little different from the child's existing ideas about borrowing. The next column contained a 0. How could she take 1 from the 0? That part was different, creating a situation that for her was problem based. The child decided that "the next column" must mean the next one that has something in it. She, therefore, borrowed from the 6 and ignored the 0. This child used her existing ideas and gave her own meaning to the rule "borrow from the next column."

Children rarely give random responses (Ginsburg, 1977; Labinowicz, 1985). Their answers tend to make sense in terms of their personal perspective or in terms of the knowledge they are using to give meaning to the situation. In many instances, children's existing knowledge is incomplete or inaccurate, or perhaps the knowledge we assume to be there simply is not. In such situations, as in the present example, new knowledge may be constructed inaccurately.

$$\overset{5}{\overset{}{6}}\overset{13}{0\!\!\!/3}$$
$$-257$$
$$\overline{6}$$

There is nothing in this
next column, so I'll
borrow from the 6.

FIGURE 3.3 Children sometimes invent incorrect meanings by extending poorly understood rules.

Construction in Rote Learning

Constructivism is a theory about how we learn. If it is correct, then that is how *all* learning takes place, regardless of how we teach. We cannot choose to have children learn constructively on some days and not others. Even rote learning is a construction. But what tools or ideas are used for construction in rote learning? To what is rotely learned knowledge connected?

Children searching for a way to remember $7 \times 8 = 56$ might note that the numbers 5, 6 and 7, 8 go in order. Or they may connect the number 56 to that "hard fact" since 56 is unique in the multiplication table (but then so is 54). Repetition of a routine procedure may be connected to some mantra-type recitation of the rule, as in "Divide, multiply, subtract, and bring down." This sequence has even been related to the mnemonic "Dirty monkeys smell bad." New ideas learned like this are connected to things that can hardly be called mathematical. Nor are they part of networks of ideas. Each newly learned bit is essentially isolated. Rote knowledge will almost never contribute to a useful network of ideas. Rote learning can be thought of as a "weak construction" (Noddings, 1993).

When mathematical ideas are used to create new mathematical ideas, useful cognitive networks are formed. Returning to 7×8, imagine a class where children discuss and share clever ways to figure out the product. One child might think of 5 eights and then 2 more eights. Another may have learned 7×7 and noted that this is just one more seven. Still another might look at a list of 8 sevens and take half of them (4×7) and double that. This may lead to the notion that double 7 is 14, and double that is 28, and double that is 56. Not every child will construct 7×8 using all of these approaches. However, the class discussion brings to the fore a wide range of useful mathematical "dots" so that the potential is there for profitable constructions.

Understanding

It is possible to say that we know something or we do not. In other words, knowledge is something that we either have or don't have. Understanding is another matter. For example, how did you learn 7×8? If you learned it by rote, as most adults did, you may never have thought about the other ideas just discussed. Is your understanding of 7×8 just the same as that of a person who has connected some of these other ideas to that fact?

Understanding can be defined as a measure of the quality and quantity of connections that an idea has with existing ideas. Understanding depends on the existence of appropriate ideas and on the creation of new connections (Backhouse, Haggarty, Pirie, & Stratton, 1992; Davis, 1986; Hiebert & Carpenter, 1992; Janvier, 1987; Schroeder & Lester, 1989). Understanding is never an all-or-nothing proposition.

One way that we can think about an individual's understanding is that it exists along a continuum (see Figure 3.4). At one extreme is a very rich set of connections. The understood idea is associated with many other existing ideas in a meaningful network of concepts and procedures. Hiebert and

FIGURE 3.4 Understanding is a measure of the quality and quantity of connections that a new idea has with existing ideas. The greater the number of connections to a network of ideas, the better the understanding.

Carpenter (1992) refer to "webs" of interrelated ideas. Understanding at this rich interconnected end of the continuum will be referred to as *relational understanding*, borrowing a term made popular by Skemp (1978). At the other end of the continuum, ideas are completely isolated or nearly so. At this end, we have what we will call *instrumental understanding*, again borrowing from Skemp. Rotely learned knowledge is almost always understood instrumentally.

Examples of Understanding

If we accept the notion that understanding has both qualitative and quantitative differences, the question "Does she know it?" must be replaced with "How does she understand it? What ideas does she connect with it?" In the following examples, you will see how different children may well develop different ideas about the same knowledge and, thus, have different understandings.

Computation in Two Classrooms

Schifter and Fosnot (1993) describe a third-grade class where several children are discussing the problem of sharing 90 jelly beans among four children. They decide to use base-ten models (ones and tens). They share 2 tens to each group and trade a ten for 10 ones.

They next share 2 ones to each group. There is then a discussion of what to do with the 2 leftover ones and how to write down what they have done. One child suggests "$22\frac{1}{2}$" and another "22 R 2." They decide that the best answer for

any division depends on the situation and what you want to do with the leftovers.

In a more traditional class, another third grader was quite confident in her ability to do long divisions such as $24{,}682 \div 5$. When asked what the "R 2" meant when she computed $32 \div 5$, she could only identify 2 as the remainder. Asked to demonstrate $32 \div 5$ with blocks, she began but then decided it couldn't be done. The child was at a loss to explain "R 2" in terms of the leftover counters (Schifter & Fosnot, 1993). These children all have different understandings of division. Some are very rich understandings; some are very limited. All are different.

Connections with Early Number Concepts

Consider the concept of "seven" as constructed by a child in the first grade. Seven for a first grader is most likely connected to the counting procedure and the construct of "more than" and is probably understood as less than 10 and more than 2. What else will this child eventually connect to the concept of seven as it now exists? Seven is 1 more than 6; it is 2 less than 9; it is the combination of 3 and 4 or 2 and 5; it is odd; it is small compared to 73 and large compared to one-tenth; it is the number of days in a week; it is "lucky"; it is prime; and on and on. The web of potential ideas connected to a number can grow large and involved.

A Web of Ideas Involving Ratio

A clear example of the potential for rich relational understanding is found in the many ideas that can be associated with the concept of "ratio" (see Figure 3.5). Unfortunately,

FIGURE 3.5 Potential web of associations that could contribute to the understanding of "ratio."

Division: *The ratio 3 is to 4 is the same as 3 ÷ 4.*

Scale: *The scale on the map shows 1 inch per 50 miles.*

Trigonometry: *All trig functions are ratios.*

Slopes of lines (algebra) and slopes of roofs (carpentry): *The ratio of the rise to the run is $\frac{1}{8}$.*

Comparisons: *The ratio of sunny days to rainy days is greater in the South than in the North.*

RATIO

Geometry: *The ratio of circumference to diameter is always π or about 22 to 7. Any two similar figures have corresponding measurements that are proportional (in the same ratio).*

Unit prices: *12 oz. / $1.79 That's about 60¢ for 4 oz. or $2.40 for a pound.*

Business: *Profit and loss are figured as ratios of income to total cost.*

many children learn only meaningless rules connected with ratio, such as "given one ratio, how do you find an equivalent ratio?"

Benefits of Relational Understanding

To teach for a rich or relational understanding requires a lot of work and effort. Concepts and connections develop over time, not in a day. Tasks must be selected. Instructional materials must be made. The classroom must be organized for group work and maximum interaction with and among the children. The important benefits to be derived from relational understanding make the effort not only worthwhile but also essential.

It Is Intrinsically Rewarding

Nearly all people, and certainly children, enjoy learning. This is especially true when new information connects with ideas already possessed. The new knowledge makes sense; it fits; it feels good. Children who learn by rote must be motivated by external means: for the sake of a test, to please a parent, from fear of failure, or to receive some reward. Such learning is distasteful. Rewards of an extra recess or a star on a chart may be effective in the short run but do nothing to encourage a love of the subject when the rewards are removed.

It Enhances Memory

Memory is a process of retrieving information. When mathematics is learned relationally, there is much less chance that the information will deteriorate; connected information is simply more likely than disconnected information to be retained over time. Retrieval of the information is also easier. Connected information provides an entire web of ideas to reach for. If what you need to recall seems distant, reflecting on ideas that are related can usually lead you to the desired idea eventually. Retrieving disconnected information is more like finding a needle in a haystack.

A large portion of instructional time in American schools is devoted to reteaching and review. If ideas were learned relationally instead of instrumentally, much less time would need to be spent on review.

There Is Less to Remember

Traditional approaches have tended to fragment mathematics into seemingly endless lists of isolated skills, concepts, rules, and symbols. The lists are so lengthy that teachers and students become overwhelmed. Constructivists, for their part, talk about teaching "big ideas" (Brooks & Brooks, 1993; Hiebert et al., 1996; Schifter & Fosnot, 1993). Big ideas are really just large networks of interrelated concepts. Ideas are learned relationally when they are integrated into a larger web of information, a big idea. Frequently, the network is so well constructed that whole chunks of information are stored and retrieved as single entities rather than isolated bits. For example, knowledge of place value subsumes rules about lining up decimal points, ordering decimal numbers, moving decimal points to the right or left in decimal-percent conversions, rounding and estimating, and a host of other ideas. Similarly, knowledge of equivalent fractions ties together rules concerning common denominators, reducing fractions, and changing between mixed numbers and whole numbers.

It Helps with Learning New Concepts and Procedures

An idea fully understood in mathematics is more easily extended to learn a new idea. Number concepts and relationships help in the mastery of basic facts, fraction knowledge and place-value knowledge come together to make decimal learning easier, and decimal concepts directly enhance an understanding of percentage concepts and procedures. Many of the ideas of elementary arithmetic become the model for understanding ideas in algebra. Reducing fractions by finding common prime factors is the same thing as canceling out common factors.

Without these connections, children will need to learn each new piece of information they encounter as a separate, unrelated idea.

It Improves Problem-Solving Abilities

The solution of novel problems requires transferring ideas learned in one context to new situations. When concepts are embedded in a rich network, transferability is significantly enhanced and, thus, so is problem solving (Schoenfeld, 1992). NAEP data for 1990, 1992, and 1996 suggest a slow but significant growth each year in the percentage of U.S. students achieving at or above the basic and proficient levels (Reese, Miller, Mazzeo, & Dossey, 1997), reflecting the increased emphasis on understanding over that same period.

It Is Self-Generative

"Inventions that operate on understandings can generate new understandings, suggesting a kind of snowball effect. As networks grow and become more structured, they increase the potential for invention" (Hiebert & Carpenter, 1992, p. 74). Skemp (1978) noted that when gaining knowledge is found to be pleasurable, people who have had that experience of pleasure are likely to seek or invent new ideas on their own, especially when confronting problem-based situations.

It Improves Attitudes and Beliefs

Relational understanding has an affective effect as well as a cognitive effect. When learning relationally, the learner tends to develop a positive self-concept about his or her ability to learn and understand mathematics. There is a definite sense of "I can do this! I understand!" There is no reason to fear or to be in awe of knowledge learned relationally. Mathematics then makes sense. It is not some mysterious world that only "smart people" dare enter. At the other end of the continuum, instrumental understanding has the potential of producing mathematics anxiety, a real phenomenon that involves fear and avoidance behavior.

Relational understanding also promotes a positive view about mathematics itself. Sensing the connectedness and logic of mathematics, students are more likely to gravitate toward it or to describe the discipline in positive terms.

NCTM Standards The Learning Principle makes it very clear that learning with understanding is both essential and possible. That is, all children can and must learn mathematics with understanding. It is impossible to predict the kinds of problems that students will face in the future. The Learning Principle says that understanding is the only way to ensure that students will be able to cope with these unknown problems in the future.

Types of Mathematical Knowledge

All knowledge, mathematical or otherwise, consists of internal or mental representations of ideas that the mind has constructed. For some time now, mathematics educators have found it useful to distinguish between two types of mathematical knowledge: conceptual knowledge and procedural knowledge (Hiebert & Lindquist, 1990).

Conceptual Knowledge of Mathematics

Conceptual knowledge of mathematics consists of logical relationships constructed internally and existing in the mind as a part of a network of ideas. It is the type of knowledge Piaget referred to as logico-mathematical knowledge (Kamii, 1985, 1989; Labinowicz, 1985). By its very nature, conceptual knowledge is knowledge that is understood (Hiebert & Carpenter, 1992).

Ideas such as seven, rectangle, ones/tens/hundreds (as in place value), sum, product, equivalent, ratio, and negative are all examples of mathematical relationships or concepts.

Figure 3.6 shows three blocks commonly used to represent ones, tens, and hundreds. By the middle of second grade, most children have seen pictures of these or have used the actual blocks. It is quite common for these children to be able to identify the rod as the "ten" piece and the large square block as the "hundred" piece. Does this mean that they have constructed the concepts of ten and hundred? All that is known for sure is that they have learned the names for these objects, the conventional names of the blocks. The mathematical concept of a ten is that *a ten is the same as ten ones*. Ten is not a rod. The concept is the relationship between the rod and the small cube. It is not the rod or a bundle of ten sticks

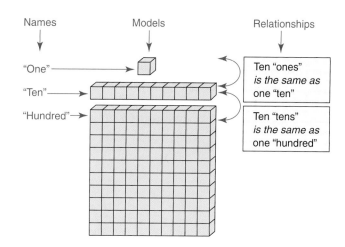

FIGURE 3.6 Objects and names of objects are not the same as relationships between objects.

or any other model of a ten. This relationship called "ten" must be created by children in their own minds.

In Figure 3.7, the shape labeled A is a rectangle. But if we call shape B "one" or a "whole," then we might refer to shape A as "one-half." The idea of "half" is the *relationship* between shapes A and B, a relationship that must be constructed in our mind. It is not in either rectangle. In fact, if we decide to call shape C the whole, shape A becomes "one-fourth." The physical rectangle did not change in any way. The concepts of "half" and "fourth" are not in rectangle A; we construct them in our mind. The rectangles help us "see" the relationships, but what we see are rectangles, not concepts.

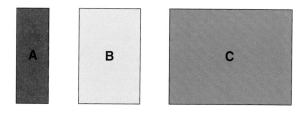

FIGURE 3.7 Three shapes, different relationships.

Procedural Knowledge of Mathematics

Procedural knowledge of mathematics is knowledge of the rules and the procedures that one uses in carrying out routine mathematical tasks and also the symbolism that is used to represent mathematics. Knowledge of mathematics consists of more than concepts. Step-by-step procedures exist for performing tasks such as multiplying 47×68. Concepts are represented by special words and mathematical symbols. These procedures and symbols can be connected to or supported by concepts, but very few cognitive relationships are needed to have knowledge of a procedure.

Procedures are the step-by-step routines learned to accomplish some task. "To add two three-digit numbers, first add the numbers in the right-hand column. If the answer is 10 or more, put the 1 above the second column, and write the other digit under the first column. Proceed in a similar manner for the next two columns in order." We can say that someone who can accomplish a task such as this has knowledge of that procedure. Again, the conceptual understanding that may or may not support the procedural knowledge can vary considerably from one student to the next.

Some procedures are very simple and may even be confused with conceptual knowledge. For example, seventh-grade children may be shown how to add the integers $^-7$ and $^+4$ by combining 7 red "negative" checkers with 4 yellow "positive" checkers. Pairs consisting of 1 red and 1 yellow checker are removed, and the result is noted. In this example, there would be 3 red negative checkers remaining, and the students would record $^-3$ as the sum. This might be called a manipulative or physical procedure. Notice that it is conceivable that a student could master a procedure such as this with very little understanding, or it could be integrated with a conceptual web related to integers and, thus, be well understood.

Symbolism includes expressions such as $(9 - 5) \times 2 = 8$, π, $<$, and $\neq$. What meaning is attached to this symbolic knowledge depends on how it is understood—what concepts and other ideas the individual connects to the symbols. Symbolism is part of procedural knowledge whether it is understood or not.

Procedural Knowledge and Doing Mathematics

Procedural knowledge of mathematics plays a very important role both in learning and in doing mathematics. Algorithmic procedures help us do routine tasks easily and, thus, free our minds to concentrate on more important tasks. Symbolism is a powerful mechanism for conveying mathematical ideas to others and for "doodling around" with an idea as we do mathematics. But even the most skillful use of a procedure will not help develop conceptual knowledge that is related to that procedure (Hiebert, 1990). Doing endless long-division exercises will not help a child understand what division means. In fact, students who are skillful with a particular procedure are very reluctant to attach meanings to it after the fact.

From the vantage of learning mathematics, the question of how procedures and conceptual ideas can be linked is much more important than the usefulness of the procedure itself (Hiebert & Carpenter, 1992). Recall the two children who used their own invented procedure to solve $156 \div 4$ (see Figure 3.2, p. 23). Clearly, there was an active and useful interaction between the procedures the children invented and the ideas they were constructing about division.

It is generally accepted that procedural rules should never be learned in the absence of a concept, although, unfortunately, that happens far too often.

The Role of Models in Developing Understanding

It has become a cliché that good teachers use a "hands-on approach" to teach mathematics. Manipulatives, or physical materials to model mathematical concepts, are certainly important tools available for helping children learn mathematics. But they are not the panacea that some educators seem to believe them to be. It is important that you have a good perspective on how manipulatives can help or fail to help children construct ideas.

Models for Mathematical Concepts

Return for a moment to the idea of a mathematical concept as a relationship, a logical idea. There are no physical examples of mathematical concepts in the physical world. The concept of "hundred," for example, is a quantity relationship that a group of 100 items has with a single item of the same type. We can talk of 100 people, 100 dollars, or 100 acts of kindness. None of those sets *is* a hundred. Hundred is only a relationship that the group has with one thing like those in the group. It is impossible to imagine "hundred" without first understanding "one."

A *model for a mathematical concept* refers to any object, picture, or drawing that represents the concept or onto which the relationship for that concept can be imposed. In this sense, any group of 100 objects can be a model of the concept "hundred" because we can impose the 100-to-1 relationship on the group and a single element of the group.

It is incorrect to say that a model "illustrates" a concept. To illustrate implies showing. That would mean that when you looked at the model, you would see an example of the concept. Technically, all that you actually see with your eyes is the physical object; only your mind can impose the mathematical relationship on the object (Thompson, 1994). For a person who does not yet have the relationship, the model does not illustrate the concept *for that person.*

Examples of Models

As noted, physical materials have become enormously popular as tools for teaching mathematics. They can run the gamut from common objects such as lima beans for counters to commercially produced materials such as wooden rods or plastic geometric shapes. Figure 3.8 shows six common examples of models for six different concepts.

✖ **STOP** Consider each of the concepts and the corresponding model. Try to separate the physical model from the relationship that you must impose on the model in order to "see" the concept. Try this before reading further.

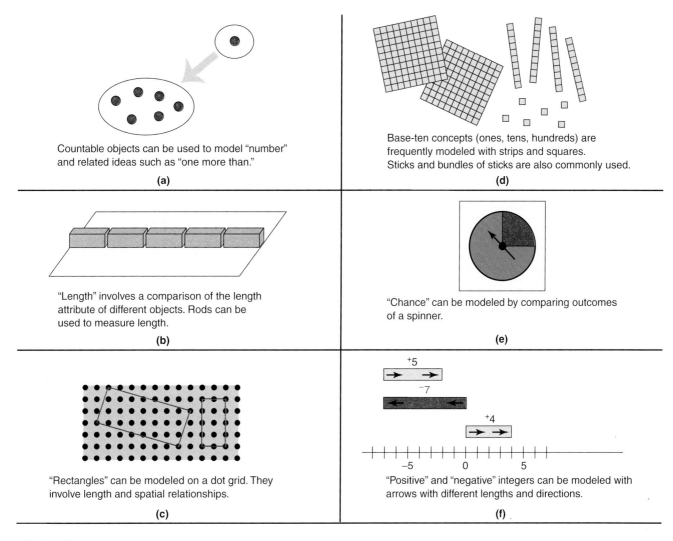

FIGURE 3.8 Examples of models to illustrate mathematics concepts.

For the examples in Figure 3.8:

(a) The concept of "six" is a relationship between sets that can be matched to the words *one, two, three, four, five, six*. Changing a set of counters by adding one changes the relationship. The difference between the set of 6 and the set of 7 is the relationship "one more than."

(b) The concept of "length" could not be developed without making comparisons of the length attribute of different objects. The length measure of an object is a comparison relationship of the length of the object to the length of the unit.

(c) The concept of "rectangle" is a combination of spatial and length relationships. By drawing on dot paper, the relationships of the opposite sides' being of equal length and parallel and the adjacent sides' meeting at right angles can be illustrated.

(d) The concept of "hundred" is not in the larger square but in the relationship of that square to the strip ("ten") and to the little square ("one").

(e) "Chance" is a relationship between the frequency of an event's happening compared with all possible outcomes. The spinner can be used to create relative frequencies. These can be predicted by observing relationships of sectors of the spinner. Note how chance and probability are integrated with ideas of fractions and ratio.

(f) The concept of a "negative integer" is based on the relationship "is the opposite of." Negative quantities exist only in relation to positive quantities. Arrows on the number line are not themselves negative quantities but model the "opposite of" relationship in terms of direction and size or magnitude relationship in terms of length.

Staying with integers for a moment, this concept is often modeled with counters in two colors, perhaps red for negative quantities and yellow for positive. The "opposite" aspect of integers can be imposed on the two colors. The "magnitude" aspect is found in the quantities of red and yellow counters. Although colored counters and arrows are physically very different, the same relationships can be imposed on each. Children must construct relationships in order to "see" positive and negative integers in either model.

It is important to include calculators in any list of common models. The calculator models a wide variety of numeric relationships by quickly and easily demonstrating the effects of these ideas. For example, if the calculator is made to count by increments of 0.01 (press ⊞ 0.01 ▤), the relationship of one-hundredth to one whole is illustrated. Press 3 ⊞ 0.01. How many presses of ▤ are required to get from 3 to 4? Doing the required 100 presses and observing how the display changes along the way is quite impressive. Especially note what happens after 3.19, 3.29, and so on.

Models and Constructing Mathematics

To "see" in a model the concept that it represents, you must already have that concept—that relationship—in your mind. If you did not, then you would have no relationship to impose on the model. This is precisely why models are often more meaningful to the teacher than to students. The teacher already has the concept and can see it in the model. A student without the concept sees only the physical object.

Thus, it seems that a child would need to know the relationship before imposing it on the model. If the concept does not come *from* the model—and it does not—how does the model help the child get it? The answer lies in the notion of an evolving idea.

Mathematical concepts that children are in the process of constructing are not the well-formed ideas conceived by adults. New ideas are formulated little by little over time. As children actively reflect on their new ideas, they test them out through as many different avenues as we might provide. For example, this is where the value of student discussions and group work comes in. Talking through an idea, arguing for a viewpoint, listening to others, and describing and explaining are all mentally active ways of testing an emerging idea against external reality. As this testing process goes on, the developing idea gets modified and elaborated and further integrated with existing ideas. When there is a good fit with external reality, the likelihood of a correct concept's having been formed is good.

Models can play this same role, that of a testing ground for emerging ideas. Models can be thought of as "thinker toys," "tester toys," and "talker toys."* It is difficult for students (of all ages) to talk about and test out abstract relationships using words alone. Models give learners something to think about, explore with, talk about, and reason with.

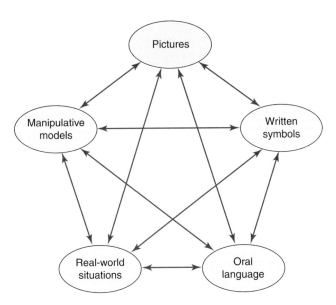

FIGURE 3.9 Five different representations of mathematical ideas. Translations between and within each can help develop new concepts.

Expanding the Idea of a Model

Lesh, Post, and Behr (1987) talk about five "representations" for concepts, two of which are manipulative models and pictures (see Figure 3.9). In their research, they also consider written symbolism, oral language, and real-world situations to be representations or models of concepts. Their research has found that children who have difficulty translating a concept from one representation to another are the same children who have difficulty solving problems and understanding computations. Strengthening the ability to move between and among these representations improves the growth of children's concepts.

The five representations illustrated in Figure 3.9 are simply an expansion of the model concept. The more ways that children are given to think about and test out an emerging idea, the better chance it has of being formed correctly and integrated into a rich web of ideas and relational understanding.

Using Models in the Classroom

If we think of models as thinker toys or talker toys, we can identify three related uses for them in a developmental approach to teaching:

1. To help children develop new concepts or relationships
2. To help children make connections between concepts and symbols
3. To assess children's understanding

Developing New Concepts

Models help children think and reflect on new ideas. To that end, they should always be accessible for students to select

---

*The term *thinker toy* is taken from Seymour Papert's book *Mindstorms* (1980), in which the inventor of the Logo computer language describes the computer as a powerful and flexible device that encourages learners to play with ideas and work through problems. "Tester toys" and "talker toys" were suggested in the current context by Laura Domalik, a first-grade teacher.

and use freely. A variety of models should be available to help with an important idea. Students should be encouraged to select and use materials to help them work through a problem or explain an idea to their group. They should select models that make sense to them. Do not force students to use a particular model.

You will undoubtedly encounter situations in which you use a model that you think clearly illustrates an idea but the child just doesn't get it. Remember that you already possess the well-formed concept, so you are able to impose it on the model. The child, however, is in the process of creating the concept and is using the model to test an emerging idea. Your job is to get children to think with models, to work actively at the test-revise-test-revise process until the new concept fits with the physical model you have offered. It is not possible to show mathematics with models. You can only provide models on which mathematical relationships or concepts can be imposed. When the child's concept fits the model, the child sees the concept. When the concept does not seem to fit, the child cannot see it in the model. The child's concept is different from the one that you can impose on the model and so must undergo further construction or revision.

Connecting Symbols and Concepts

Teachers will say, "But when they try to do it without manipulatives, they can't." Yet it is unrealistic to expect children automatically to transfer newly formed ideas to symbolic procedures without some guidance. Models can serve as a link between concepts and symbols as well as a means of developing concepts.

A general approach is to have students write down what they have done with models. "Write an equation to tell what you just did." "I see how you did that problem with the blocks. How would you go about recording what you did?" When children see written mathematics as expressions or recordings of ideas that they have already developed, the written or symbolic form is more likely to make sense.

Assessing Children's Understanding

When children in the classroom are using models in ways that make sense to them (rather than following your directions), how they use the physical models is a wonderful window into their minds. This allows classroom observation of your students to become a student-by-student assessment.

If you want more detailed information about the understanding children have constructed, a good suggestion is to have them explain ideas with manipulative materials. The models give the child something to talk with when their abstract ideas prove difficult for them to explain. This might be done in a diagnostic setting, where you sit down, one on one, with a child and try to find out what he or she is thinking. Remember that drawings are also models. When students write explanations for their answers or describe their ideas in writing, always encourage them to draw pictures to help them show what they are thinking. (Assessment is discussed in depth in Chapter 5.)

Incorrect Use of Models

The most widespread misuse of manipulative materials occurs when the teacher tells students, "Do as I do." There is a natural temptation to get out the materials and show children exactly how to use them. Children will blindly follow the teacher's directions, and it may even look as if they understand. It is just as possible to get students to move blocks around mindlessly as it is to teach them to "invert and multiply" mindlessly. Neither promotes thinking or aids in the development of concepts (Ball, 1992; Clements & Battista, 1990).

A natural result of overly directing the use of models is that children begin to use them as answer-getting devices rather than as thinker toys. When getting answers rather than solving problems becomes the focus of a lesson, children will gravitate to the easiest method available to get the answers. For example, if you have carefully shown and explained to children how to get an answer with a set of counters, then an imitation of that method is what they will most likely select. By strictly following your directions, little or no reflective thought will go into exploring the concepts involved. When an activity is not reflective, little real growth occurs, and little understanding is constructed.

TEACHING DEVELOPMENTALLY

Teaching involves decision making. Decisions are made as you plan lessons. *What is the best task to propose tomorrow? Considering what happened today, what will move the children forward?* And decisions are made minute to minute in the classroom. *How should I respond? Should they struggle some more, or should I intervene? Is progress being made? How can I help Suzy move in the correct direction without discouraging her?*

The ideas that have been discussed in this chapter provide a theoretical foundation for making those decisions.

Foundations of a Developmental Approach

Following is a summary of the major implications of the theory that has been discussed. A teacher who keeps these ideas in mind can be said to be basing his or her instruction on a constructivist view of learning or, in the terminology of this book, a *developmental approach*.

1. *Children construct their own knowledge and understanding; we cannot transmit ideas to passive learners.* Each child comes to us with a unique but rich collection of ideas. These ideas are the tools that will be used to construct new concepts and procedures as students wrestle with

ideas, discuss solutions, challenge their own and others' conjectures, explain their methods, and solve engaging problems. Ideas cannot be poured into children as if they were empty vessels.

2. *Knowledge and understanding are unique for each learner.* Each child's network of ideas is different from that of the next child. As new ideas are formed, they will be integrated into that web of ideas in a unique way as well. We should not try to make all children the same.

3. *Reflective thinking is the single most important ingredient for effective learning.* For children to create new ideas and to connect them in a rich web of interrelated ideas, children must be mentally engaged. They must find the relevant ideas they possess and bring them to bear on the development of new ideas and the solutions to new problems. Only by being mentally engaged with the task at hand can relational understanding of new ideas ever develop. "Passive learning" is an oxymoron!

4. *Effective teaching is a child-centered activity.* In a constructivist classroom, the emphasis is on learning rather than teaching. Students are given the task of learning. The role of the teacher is to engage the students by posing good problems and creating a classroom atmosphere of exploration and sense making. The source of mathematical truth is found in the reasoning carried out by the class. The teacher is not the arbiter of what is mathematically correct.

Strategies for Effective Teaching

How can we structure lessons to promote appropriate reflective thought? Purposeful mental engagement or reflective thought about the ideas we want students to develop is the single most important key to effective teaching. Without actively thinking about the important concepts of the lesson, learning will not happen. How can we make it happen? Here are seven suggestions based on the perspectives of this chapter. Perhaps you will be able to add to the list.

1. Create a mathematical environment.
2. Pose worthwhile mathematical tasks.
3. Use cooperative learning groups.
4. Use models and calculators as thinking tools.
5. Encourage discourse and writing.
6. Require justification of student responses.
7. Listen actively.

Creating a Mathematical Environment

In a mathematical environment, students feel comfortable trying out ideas, sharing insights, challenging others, seeking advice from other students and the teacher, explaining their thinking, and taking risks. No one is permitted to be a passive observer. An environment with these features is built around expectations, respect, and the belief that *all* children

can learn. Learning takes effort, and children need to know that as a class, their task is to work at doing mathematics. The interactions of a mathematical environment require students and teachers alike to respect one another, to listen attentively, and to learn to disagree without offending.

We cannot simply tell children how to think or what habits to acquire. Processes and habits of thought are developed over time within a community where such processes and thinking are the norm. In a community of mathematical discourse, students evaluate their own assumptions and those of others and argue about what is mathematically true (Corwin, 1996; Lampert, 1990). The goal is to let all students believe that they are the authors of mathematical ideas and logical arguments. In this environment, reasoning and mathematical argument—not the teacher—are the sources of an idea's legitimacy. "Doing mathematics is an act of sense-making" (Schoenfeld, 1994, p. 60). The classroom environment should be a place where figuring it out and "sense-making" are common practices, not just for individuals but for the class as a whole.

In an urban school in Montgomery County, Maryland, fourth graders were observed to raise their hands during a discussion and say, "I would like to add to what Marcel just said" or "I disagree with Tawanna." All students would face the speaker and listen attentively. In the same school, second-grade students raised their hands with the index finger pointing up to indicate "a point of interest," a polite way to disagree. In both classrooms, it was clear that teachers had spent time and effort developing this atmosphere of respect. "Creating contexts where students can safely express their own mathematical ideas is a central teaching task and a step toward developing students' mathematical power" (Smith, 1996, p. 397).

Posing Worthwhile Mathematical Tasks

The single most important principle for reform in mathematics is to allow students to make the subject of mathematics problematic (Hiebert et al., 1996). By problematic, these authors mean "allowing students to wonder why things are, to inquire, to search for solutions, and to resolve incongruities. It means that both curriculum and instruction should begin with problems, dilemmas, and questions for students" (p. 12). When students are actively looking for relationships, analyzing patterns, finding out which methods work and which don't, justifying results, or evaluating and challenging the thoughts of others, they are necessarily and optimally engaging in reflective thought about the ideas involved.

Tasks or problems must be designed to engage the students in the concepts of the curriculum. Tasks should be based on a knowledge of the mathematical content and an informed guess about the concepts the students in the class bring to the task (Fennema, Carpenter, Franke, & Carey, 1993; Simon, 1995). Time must be given to permit students to wrestle with these tasks individually or in groups and also to discuss solutions and strategies with the class as a whole.

The selection of good tasks requires that you listen each day to the way students are thinking about whatever mathematics is currently being discussed. The selection of the next day's task should be made in such a way as to help students reflect on the new ideas you want them to develop. Look for explorations that embody the big ideas of the chapter. As students wrestle with these problems, the tiny skills and ideas of the traditional curriculum will emerge. In a good task, students will "bump into" the important mathematics you have in mind for them to learn (Lappan & Briars, 1995).

Using Cooperative Learning Groups

Placing children in groups of three or four to work on a problem is an extremely useful strategy for encouraging the discourse and interaction envisioned in a mathematical community. A classroom arranged in small groups has many times more interaction and discussion going than can be accomplished in a full-class setting. Frequently, a simple pairing of students is all that is necessary. In groups or pairs, children are much more willing and able to speak out, explore ideas, explain things to their group, question and learn from one another, pose arguments, and have their own ideas challenged in a friendly atmosphere of learning. Children will take risks within a small group that they would never dream of taking in front of an entire class. Groups should usually be heterogeneous in ability so that all students are exposed to good thinking and reasoning.

While the groups are at work, the teacher has the opportunity to be an active listener to six or more different discussions. Time should always be allotted for full-class discussions so that group members can share their group's ideas and the teacher can focus attention on important ideas.

Using Models and Calculators as Thinking Tools

The use of models has already been thoroughly discussed. It is worth repeating that models help children explore ideas and make sense of them. Many good explorations are actually posed in terms of physical materials. For example, "Try to find different ways to make the number 437 using ones, tens, and hundreds pieces. What patterns can you find? What else do you notice about the ways you can make 437?" Here the model is the focus of the problem rather than a way of exploring a different task.

Manipulatives and calculators should always be readily available for student use as a regular part of your classroom environment. This is just as true for middle school classrooms as for the kindergarten.

Encouraging Discourse and Writing

To explain an idea orally or in written form forces us to wrestle with that idea until it is really ours and we personally understand it. The more we try to explain something or argue reasonably about something, the more connections we will search for and use in our explanation or in our argument. Talking gets the talker involved.

When children are asked to respond to and critique others, they are similarly forced to attend and to assimilate what is being said into personal mental schemas. Frequently, when we get involved verbally with an idea, we find ourselves changing or modifying the idea in midstream. The reflective thought required to make an explanation or argue a point is a true learning experience in itself (Corwin, 1996; Whitin & Wilde, 1995; Yackel, Cobb, Wood, Wheatley, & Merkel, 1990).

Writing can be a part of nearly every problem posed. Not only does it help children structure their thoughts, but writing also causes each student to commit to an idea and rehearse an explanation or defense in preparation for the class discussion. Of course, writing includes journals, formal essays, and reports. It is also a significant tool in assessment. Countryman (1992) states, "The writer reflects on, returns to, and builds upon what has gone before" (p. 59).

Requiring Justification of Student Responses

Requiring children to explain or defend their responses has a positive effect on how children view mathematics and their own mathematical abilities. Doing so also promotes confidence and self-worth. Justification of responses forces students to think reflectively. To defend or explain eliminates guessing or responses based on rote learning. Thus having children explain their answers is another excellent mechanism for getting the same benefits as from discourse and writing.

Requiring students to explain why, to tell how, and to detail their ideas communicates that mathematics is not mysterious or unfathomable. There is no need for the teacher to pose as the source of mathematical truth.

Listening Actively

To promote reflective thinking requires that teaching be child centered, not teacher centered. By placing attention on the children's thoughts instead of our own, we encourage children to do more thinking and, hence, to search for and strengthen more internal connections—in short, to develop understanding. When children respond to questions or make an observation in class, an interested but nonevaluative response is a way to ask for an elaboration: "Tell me more about that, Karen" or "I see. Why do you think that?" Even a simple "Um-hmm" followed by silence is very effective, permitting the child and others to continue their thinking.

Active listening requires that we believe in children's ideas. To wait 45 seconds, a minute, or even longer for a child to find a response or formulate even a simple idea is much easier when we believe that whatever the child says reflects a unique and valuable understanding. When you believe in children, children sense it and respond accordingly.

REFLECTIONS ON CHAPTER 3

Writing to Learn

1. Describe in your own words what it means to say *we construct our own knowledge* as opposed to *we absorb knowledge*.
2. Explain why we should assume that each child's knowledge and understanding of an idea is unique for that child.
3. What is reflective thought? Why is it so important to promote reflective thinking in the classroom?
4. Contrast knowing an idea with understanding an idea. What does it mean to say that understanding exists on a continuum from relational to instrumental? Give an example of an idea, and explain how it might be understood at different places along this continuum.
5. Examine the seven benefits of relational understanding. Select the ones that you think are most important. Describe each benefit and why you personally believe it is significant.
6. Describe conceptual knowledge of mathematics and procedural knowledge of mathematics. Provide examples of each.
7. Explain why a *model* for a mathematical idea is not really an *example* of the idea. If it is not an example of the concept, what does it mean to say we "see" the concept when we look at the model?
8. Models were described as "thinker toys," "tester toys," and "talker toys." These refer to the ways that models can help students develop concepts. Explain how models can help a child develop a concept.
9. In addition to helping develop concepts, what other purposes can models serve in the classroom? Explain these briefly.
10. How can a teacher use models incorrectly?
11. Why is reflective thinking, one of the four foundations of a developmental approach, the most important ingredient for learning?
12. Seven strategies for effective teaching have been listed. Pick at least three that you think are the most important. Explain these in terms of how children learn.

For Discussion and Exploration

1. Discuss the meaning and validity of the following statement from Labinowicz (1985): "We see what we understand rather than understand what we see" (p. 7).
2. Consider your most recent classroom experience when mathematics was being taught. Compare and contrast this experience with the suggestions for developmental teaching given in this chapter. Would you say that the teaching reflected a constructivist view of learning? Why or why not?
3. Not every educator believes in constructivism. A common argument goes something like this: There is not enough time to let kids discover everything. Basic facts and ideas are more efficiently taught through careful, well-planned, and meaningful explanations. Students should not have to "reinvent the wheel." How would you respond to someone with this perception of school and learning?

Recommendations for Further Reading

Highly Recommended

Ball, D. L. (1997). From the general to the particular: Knowing our own students as learners of mathematics. *Mathematics Teacher, 90,* 732–737.

Don't be fooled because this article is in *Mathematics Teacher.* Deborah Ball, one of the leading advocates for classroom discourse and listening to children, offers a thought-provoking example of third-grade thinking about fractions while raising our awareness of how difficult it is to see into the minds of children. She makes the point that understanding is not an all-or-nothing idea. Trying to know what students know is not an easy task. Ball provides us with useful food for thought.

Brooks, J. G., & Brooks, M. G. (1993). *In search of understanding: The case for the constructivist classroom.* Alexandria, VA: Association for Supervision and Curriculum Development.

Though not a book about teaching mathematics, this is a readable and informative book on teaching in a constructivist manner. Examples span all curricular areas and all grades.

Fosnot, C. T. (Ed.). (1996). *Constructivism: Theory, perspectives, and practice.* New York: Teachers College Press.

The first section of this book develops the theory of constructivism through three readable chapters. The next five chapters examine the application of constructivist theory in different disciplines. Deborah Schifter provides the perspective on teaching mathematics. The final section includes four chapters on classroom practice. You will not find this book overly theoretical or hard to read. At the same time, Fosnot's book is not exactly a light read. You will be challenged and rewarded.

Schifter, D. (Ed.). (1996). *What's happening in math class? Envisioning new practices through teacher narratives* (Vol. 1). New York: Teachers College Press.

In each of the five chapters of this book, three or four teachers share their personal struggles at becoming more of a constructivist teacher. The last articles in each chapter are written by noted mathematics educators who offer their personal perspectives on what the teachers have so candidly shared. This is a book about constructivism in practice. The teacher-authors each work in quite different schools and represent a range of grades. However, the common threads among all of them help us understand why constructivism is such a popular theory in education today.

Other Suggestions

Ball, D. L. (1996). Teacher learning and the mathematics reforms: What we think we know and what we need to learn. *Phi Delta Kapan, 77,* 500–508.

Brooks, M. G., & Brooks, G. B. (1999). The courage to be constructivist. *Educational Leadership, 57*(3), 18–24.

Campbell, P. F., & Johnson, M. L. (1995). How primary students think and learn. In I. M. Carl (Ed.), *Seventy-five years of progress: Prospects for school mathematics* (pp. 21–42). Reston, VA: National Council of Teachers of Mathematics.

Clements, D. H. (1997). (Mis?)constructing constructivism. *Teaching Children Mathematics, 4,* 198–200.

Cobb, P., & Bauersfeld, H. (Eds.). (1995). *The emergence of mathematical meaning: Interaction in classroom cultures.* Mahwah, NJ: Lawrence Erlbaum.

Fennema, E., Carpenter, T. P., Franke, M. L., & Carey, D. A. (1993). Learning to use children's mathematics thinking: A case study. In R. B. Davis & C. A. Maher, (Eds.), *School, mathematics, and the world of reality* (pp. 93–117). Needham Heights, MA: Allyn & Bacon.

Flores, A. (2001). How do children know that what they learn in mathematics is true? *Teaching Children Mathematics, 8,* 269–274.

Goldin, G., & Shteingold, N. (2001). Systems of representation and the development of mathematical concepts. In A. A. Cuoco (Ed.), *The roles of representation in school mathematics* (pp. 1–23). Reston, VA: National Council of Teachers of Mathematics.

Greenes, C. (1999). Ready to learn: Developing young children's mathematical powers. In J. V. Copley (Ed.), *Mathematics in the early years* (pp. 39–47). Reston, VA: National Council of Teachers of Mathematics.

Labinowicz, E. (1985). *Learning from children: New beginnings for teaching numerical thinking.* Menlo Park, CA: AWL Supplemental.

Russell, S. J., & Corwin, R. B. (1993). Talking mathematics: "Going slow" and "letting go." *Phi Delta Kappan, 74,* 555–558.

Schifter, D. (1996). A constructivist perspective on teaching and learning mathematics. *Phi Delta Kappan, 77,* 492–499.

Smith, J. P. III. (1996). Efficacy and teaching mathematics by telling: A challenge for reform. *Journal for Research in Mathematics Education, 27,* 387–402.

Sophian, C. (1999). Children's ways of knowing: Lessons from cognitive development research. In J. V. Copley (Ed.), *Mathematics in the early years* (pp. 11–20). Reston, VA: National Council of Teachers of Mathematics.

Whitenack, J., & Yackel, E. (2002). Making mathematical arguments in the primary grades: The importance of explaining and justifying ideas. *Teaching Children Mathematics, 8,* 524–527.

Teaching Through Problem Solving

We believe that if we want students to understand mathematics, it is more helpful to think of understanding as something that results from solving problems, rather than something we can teach directly.

Hiebert et al. (1997, p. 25)

There is no other decision that teachers make that has a greater impact on students' opportunity to learn and on their perceptions about what mathematics is than the selection or creation of the tasks with which the teacher engages the students in studying mathematics.

Lappan and Briars (1995, p. 138)

In 1989, the NCTM *Curriculum and Evaluation Standards* said that problem solving should be "a primary goal of all mathematics instruction and an integral part of all mathematical activity" (p. 23) and that students should "use problem-solving approaches to investigate and understand mathematical content" (p. 75). Over the next 10 years, evidence continued to mount that problem solving was a powerful and effective vehicle for learning. In 2000, NCTM's *Principles and Standards* document makes the case in even stronger language:

> Solving problems is not only a goal of learning mathematics but also a major means of doing so. . . . Problem solving is an integral part of all mathematics learning, and so it should not be an isolated part of the mathematics program. Problem solving in mathematics should involve all the five content areas described in these Standards. . . . Good problems will integrate multiple topics and will involve significant mathematics. (p. 52)

This vision is far from being realized. However, in classrooms where teachers have adopted this approach, teacher and student excitement is high and no one wants to return to traditional instruction.

Problem Solving as a Principal Instructional Strategy

The following statement is a major thesis of this chapter. It is a clear reflection of the *Principles and Standards* document as just noted and represents the current thinking of a wide segment of mathematics education researchers.

> **Most, if not all, important mathematics concepts and procedures can best be taught through problem solving.**

What the preceding statement means is that tasks or problems can and should be posed that engage students in thinking about and developing the important mathematics they need to learn. This proposition may strike some as extreme or unrealistic. Rather than accept it blindly or reject it, let's first consider why it may make sense.

An Illustration

Suppose that you are teaching fifth grade and the topic is comparison of fractions—given two fractions, tell which is greater. The teach-by-telling approach provides a rule: Get common denominators, and compare the numerators. You accompany the rule with a conceptual explanation and pictures so that students will see the concept. However, students are aware of the exercises to come and how to do them. The explanation is of little value since the rule is all that is necessary to get through the day. As your students find the common denominators and complete the exercises, they are doing little more than third-grade multiplication. They are not thinking about fraction concepts at all.

In contrast, at the 1999 NCTM annual conference, Marilyn Burns shared these two solutions given by fifth graders who were asked to compare $\frac{6}{8}$ and $\frac{4}{5}$. No rules or procedures had been provided.

> I know that $\frac{4}{5}$ is the same as $\frac{8}{10}$ and $\frac{8}{10}$ is two-tenths away from a whole. I know that $\frac{6}{8}$ is two-eighths away from a whole. And since tenths are smaller than eighths, $\frac{8}{10}$ must be closer to the whole and so $\frac{4}{5}$ is larger.

> I know that $\frac{6}{8}$ is the same as $\frac{12}{16}$ and $\frac{4}{5}$ is the same as $\frac{12}{15}$. Since fifteenths are bigger than sixteenths, $\frac{4}{5}$ must be larger.

STOP What ideas about fractions were these students using? Did the two students use different ideas? If they had been told, "To compare two fractions first find a common denominator and then choose the fraction with the larger new numerator," how would their thinking have been different?

These students were concentrating on the meaning of fractions and the size of fractional parts. The second student actually used a common *numerator* approach that is never taught in schools but is completely reasonable. These students and the others in their class almost certainly learned more than had they blindly followed rules. (In Chapter 15, you will learn more about ways students can compare fractions without recourse to rules.)

Starting Where the Students Are: A Shift in Thinking About Mathematics Instruction

Traditionally, the teacher taught the mathematics, the students practiced it for a while, and then they were expected to use the new skills or ideas in solving problems. This approach, strongly engrained in our culture, rarely works well. First, it begins where the teacher is rather than where the children are. It assumes that all children at that time possess the ideas required (the blue dots, the necessary schema) to make sense of the explanation in the manner the teacher thinks is best. This means that there is only one way for each student to "get it." It's the teacher's way or no way. However, it is unrealistic to expect the existence of a singular set of ideas across any typical class. Although a show-and-tell approach sometimes succeeds with some children, showing and telling depends on passive absorption of ideas and leaves most students believing that mathematics is mysterious and beyond understanding.

The second difficulty with the teach-then-solve paradigm is that problem solving is separated from the learning process. Children who have come to expect the teacher to tell them the rules are unlikely to solve problems for which solution methods have not been provided. By separating teaching from problem solving, learning mathematics is separated from doing mathematics. This simply does not make sense.

Effective lessons begin where the students are, not where we are. That is, teaching should begin with the ideas that children already have, the ideas they will use to create new ones. To engage students requires tasks or activities that are problem based and require thought. Students learn mathematics as a *result* of solving problems. Mathematical ideas are the *outcomes* of the problem-solving experience rather than elements that must be taught before problem solving (Hiebert et al., 1996, 1997). Furthermore, the process of solving problems is now completely interwoven with the learning; children are *learning* mathematics by *doing* mathematics!

The Value of Teaching with Problems

There is no doubt that teaching with problems is difficult. Tasks must be designed or selected each day, taking into consideration the current understanding of the students and the needs of the curriculum. It is often difficult to plan more than a few days in advance. If you have a traditional textbook, modifications will need to be made. There are good reasons to go to this effort.

- *Problem solving places the focus of the students' attention on ideas and sense making.* When solving problems, students are necessarily reflecting on the ideas that are inherent in the problems. Developing ideas are more likely to be integrated with existing ones, thereby improving understanding. By contrast, no matter how skillfully a teacher provides explanations and directions, students will be attending to "doing it right" or following the directions the teacher has provided.

- *Problem solving develops the belief in students that they are capable of doing mathematics and that mathematics makes sense.* Every time you pose a problem-based task and expect a solution, you say to students, "I believe you can do this." Every time the class solves a problem and students develop their understanding, confidence and self-worth are developed.

- *Problem solving provides ongoing assessment data that can be used to make instructional decisions, help students succeed, and inform parents.* Students engaging in problem solving will be discussing ideas, drawing pictures or using manipulatives, defending their solutions and evaluating others' solutions, and writing reports or explanations. This activity provides you with a steady stream of valuable information for planning the next lesson, helping individual students, evaluating their progress, and communicating with parents.

- *Problem solving develops "mathematical power."* Students solving problems in class will be engaged in all five of the process standards described by the *Principles and Standards* document: problem solving, reasoning, communication, connections, and representation. These are the processes of doing mathematics and go well beyond the content understanding that is developed.

- *Problem solving allows an entry point for a wide range of students.* Good problem-based tasks have multiple paths to the solution. Students may solve 42 − 26 by counting out a set of 42 counters and removing 26; by adding onto 26 in various ways; by subtracting 20 from 40 leaving 22, and then taking off 6 more; by counting forward (or backward) on a hundreds chart; or by using a standard computational method. Each student gets to make sense of the task using his or her own ideas. Furthermore, students expand on these ideas and grow in their understanding as they hear and reflect on the solution strategies of others. In contrast, the teacher-directed approach leaves only one option for each student.

- *A problem-based approach engages students so that there are fewer discipline problems.* Many discipline issues in a classroom are the result of students becoming bored, not understanding the teacher directions, or simply finding following directions to be tedious. Most students who are permitted to solve problems in ways that make sense to them find the process intrinsically rewarding. There is less reason to act out or to cause trouble. The task of learning is engaging.

- *It is a lot of fun!* Teachers who experience teaching in this manner never return to a teach-by-telling mode. The excitement of students' developing understanding through their own reasoning is worth all the effort. And, of course, it is fun for the students.

Problems and Tasks for Learning Mathematics

We have been talking about using problems to teach mathematics without having clearly defined what we mean by a problem. In the context of this discussion, the concept of "problem" is quite broad. The main point is that the problem, task, or activity engages students in making sense of the key ideas you want them to learn.

A Description of Tasks or Problems

A *problem* is defined here as any task or activity for which the students have no prescribed or memorized rules or methods, nor is there a perception by students that there is a specific "correct" solution method (Hiebert et al., 1997).

A problem for learning mathematics also has these features:

- *It must begin where the students are.* The design or selection of the task must take into consideration the current understanding of the students. They should have the appropriate ideas to engage and solve the problem and yet

still find it challenging and interesting. They should see the task as something to make sense of.

- *The problematic or engaging aspect of the problem must be due to the mathematics that the students are to learn.* In solving the problem or doing the activity, students should be concerned primarily with making sense of the mathematics involved and thereby developing their understanding of those ideas. Although it is acceptable and even desirable to have contexts or external conditions for problems that make them interesting, these aspects should not be the focus of the activity.

- *It must require justifications and explanations for answers and methods.* Students should understand that the responsibility for determining if answers are correct and why rests with them. Students should also expect to explain their solution methods.

Problems may be posed for individual students, pairs, or groups. They may involve hands-on materials or drawings. At other times, the work may involve pencil-and-paper tasks or be strictly mental work. Calculators may or may not be used.

It is important to understand that mathematics is to be taught *through* problem solving. That is, problem-based tasks or activities are the vehicle by which the desired curriculum is developed. The learning is an outcome of the problem-solving process.

Examples of Problem-Based Tasks

In Chapter 3, you saw that mathematical ideas could be categorized as conceptual or procedural. Students can learn both types of mathematics through problem-based activities. Here are some examples in each category.

Conceptual Mathematics

The following problem may be used for different purposes, depending on the students.

Think about the number 6 broken into two different amounts. Draw a picture to show a way that six things can be in two parts. Think up a story to go with your picture.

At the kindergarten or first-grade level, the teacher may want students simply to think about different parts of 6 and to connect these ideas into a context. In first or second grade, the teacher may challenge children to find all of the combinations rather than focus on the story or context. There is a nice relationship and pattern to be constructed. In a class discussion following work on the task, students are likely to develop an orderly process for listing all of the combinations: As one part grows from 0 to 6, the other part begins at 6 and shrinks by ones to 0. There are seven combinations for 6.

The following task might be used in grades 3–6 as part of the development of fraction concepts.

Place an X on the number line about where $\frac{11}{8}$ would be. Explain why you put your X where you did. Perhaps you will want to draw and label other points on the line to help explain your answer.

Note that the task includes a suggestion for how to respond but does not specify exactly what must be done. Students are able to use their own level of reasoning and understanding to justify their answers. In the follow-up discussion, the teacher may well expect to see a variety of justifications from which to help the class refine ideas about fractions that are greater than 1.

I used two identical shapes to make a rectangle. What might they have been? (Baker & Baker, 1991)

This task, appropriate for grades 3–8, is very open-ended. There is a good potential for students to learn about congruent shapes and rotations. (When two congruent shapes form a rectangle, one can be rotated around the center of the rectangle to match the other.) With this problem, everyone will be able to contribute some ideas and will be ready to reflect on the ideas of others.

Use your graphing calculator to find the intersection of the lines for $y = 3x - 6$ and $y = -2x + 4$. What do the coordinates of the point of intersection have to do with the two equations? Explain.

Students in an eighth-grade algebra class can use a variety of methods to find the point of intersection (graphing calculator, tables, graphs sketched on paper). They will find that the coordinates are solutions to both equations. This problem is a good example of a significant relationship that students can best understand by figuring it out on their own, rather than by having it explained to them in the text or by the teacher.

Procedures and Processes

Critics of the problem-solving approach often point to the need for students to learn basic skills, saying that these must be taught through direct instruction. In reality, students can develop procedures via a problem-solving approach. Imagine a class of second graders who had never been taught to add two-digit numbers in the conventional manner. They are challenged to find the sum of 48 and 25. In one second-

grade classroom, at least seven different solution methods were offered by the students. Two children employed two different counting techniques using a hundreds chart for assistance. Here are solutions of some of the others:

4$\boxed{8}$ + 2$\boxed{5}$ (Boxed digits help "hold" them.)
40 + 20 = 60
            $\boxed{3}$ (The 3 is left from the 5.)
8 + 2 = 10
60 + 10 = 70
70 + 3 = 73

---

40 + 20 = 60
60 + 8 = 68
68 + 5 = 73

---

48 + 20 = 68
68 + 2 ("from the 5") = 70
"Then I still have that 3 from the 5."
70 + 3 = 73

---

25 + 25 = 50 $\boxed{23}$
50 + 23 = 73
Teacher: Where does the 23 come from?
"It's sort of from the 48."
How did you split up the 48?
"20 and 20 and I split the 8 into 5 and 3."

---

48 – 3 = 45 $\boxed{3}$
45 + 25 = 70
70 + 3 = 73

In this class (reported by Russell, 1997), the students show a variety of levels of thinking and many interesting techniques. They had learned from each other the trick of placing numbers in "hold boxes," although not everyone used it. The children who are counting on the chart are showing that they may not yet have developed adequate place-value tools to understand these more sophisticated methods. Or the class discussion may help them activate those ideas or "dots" they simply had not considered. One question is this: Are these invented methods efficient or adequate? Regardless of how you feel about that, these children are at least minimally prepared to consider a variety of methods because they are developing meaningful ideas about the process. One option is to offer students an efficient way of adding two-digit numbers and asking the students to figure out why it works and to decide if it will work every time.

Imagine for yourself what might happen if fifth-grade students were asked to add 3.72 + 1.6 before having been told about lining up decimal points. Many students will do it incorrectly, perhaps aligning the 2 and 6 or the 3 and 1. The decimal may be placed in various places. But students attempting to defend their solutions will need to confront the size of the answer and the meaning of the digits in each position. A class of problem solvers will soon develop a good method for adding decimals.

Gary Tsuruda is a middle school teacher. His classes frequently work in small groups to solve problems. Figure 4.1 shows one example. Notice that the initial questions bring the requisite ideas needed for the task to the students' conscious level. Next they are asked to do some exploration and look for patterns. From these explorations the group must come up with a formula, test it, describe how it was developed, and illustrate its use.

TRAPEZOID AREA

GOAL: *Find an easy way to determine the area of any trapezoid.*

Be sure that you understand the answers to each of these questions:

1. What does "area" mean?
2. What is a trapezoid?
3. How do you find the area of other polygons? Show as many different ways as you can.

Now see if your group can find an easy way to determine the area of any trapezoid.

HINTS:

1. Draw several trapezoids on dot paper and find their areas. Look for patterns.
2. Consider how you find the area of other polygons. Are any of the key ideas similar?
3. You might try cutting out trapezoids and piecing them together.
4. If you find a way to determine the area, make sure it is as easy as you can make it and that it works for *any* trapezoid.

WRITE-UP:

1. Explain your answers to the first three questions in detail. Tell how your group reached agreement on the answers.
2. Tell what you did to get your formula for the area of any trapezoid. Did you use any of the hints? How did they help you?
3. Show your formula and give an illustration of how it works.

FIGURE 4.1 A middle school example in which students are required to construct a formula.

Source: From *Putting It Together: Middle School Math in Transition* (p. 7), by G. Tsuruda, 1994 Portsmouth, NH: Heinemann, a division of Reed Elsevier Inc. Reprinted by permission of Gary Tsuruda.

Tsuruda (1994) reports that every group was able to produce a formula. "Not all the formulas looked like the typical textbook formula, but they were all correct, and more important, each formula made sense according to the way the students in that group had constructed the knowledge from the data they themselves had generated" (p. 6).

In all of these examples, the students are very much engaged in the processes of doing mathematics—figuring out procedures, not accepting them blindly. What is abundantly clear is that the more problem solving that students do, the more willing they are to solve problems and the more methods they develop for attacking problems (Campbell, 1996; Lester, 1994; Rowan & Bourne, 1994; Schifter & Fosnot, 1993; Silver, Smith, & Nelson, 1995; Silver & Stein, 1996; Wood, Cobb, Yackel, & Dillon, 1993).

Good Problems Have Multiple Entry Points

As discussed earlier, one of the advantages of a problem-based approach is that it can help accommodate the diversity of learners in every classroom. A problem-based approach does not dictate how a child must think about a problem in order to solve it. When a task is posed, students are told, in essence, "Use the ideas *you* own to solve this problem." Because of the range of students' mental tools, concepts and ideas, many students in a class will have different ideas about the best way to complete a task. Thus, access to the problem by all students demands that there be multiple entry points—different places to "get on the ramp"—to reach solutions.

Once we stop thinking that there is only one way to solve a problem, it is not quite as difficult to develop good "ramp problems" or problems with multiple entry points. Although most problems have singular correct answers, there are often many ways to get there. The problems presented in this chapter nearly all have multiple entry points. Here are two more examples.

(For third or fourth grade) Find the area of the cover of your math book. That is, how many square tiles will fit on the cover of the book?

(For fifth or sixth grade) Clara has two whole pizzas and $\frac{1}{3}$ of another. All of the pizzas are the same size. If each of her friends will want to eat $\frac{1}{4}$ of a pizza, how many friends will she be able to feed with the $2\frac{1}{3}$ pizzas?

For these two problems or tasks, see if you can think of more than one path to the solution. Try to think of an approach that is near the bottom of the "ramp" (less sophisticated) and another that is closer to the middle or the top of the "ramp." Do this now before reading further.

The area problem can be solved with materials that directly attack the meaning of the problem. The cover of the book can be completely covered with tiles and then counted one at a time. Moving slightly up the ramp, a child may cover the book with tiles but count only the length of the row and the number of rows, multiplying to get the total. Another child may place tiles only along the edges of the book and multiply. Yet another child may use a ruler to measure the book edges, noting that the tiles are 1 inch on each side.

For the pizza task a direct approach is also possible. Plastic circular fraction pieces (or a drawing) can be used to represent $2\frac{1}{3}$ pizzas, and $\frac{1}{4}$ pieces can be placed on top of these until no more will fit. Another child may know that four fourths make a whole; therefore, two of the pizzas will feed eight friends. Children may or may not know how many fourths they can get from the $\frac{1}{3}$ piece and will have to tackle that part accordingly. A guess and check approach is possible, starting with perhaps six children, then seven, and so on until the pizza is gone. A few children may have learned a computational method for dividing $2\frac{1}{3}$ by $\frac{1}{4}$.

Having thought about these possible entry points, the teacher will be better prepared to suggest a hint that is appropriate for students who are "stuck" but who are likely different in what they bring to the task.

NCTM Standards The Equity Principle challenges teachers to believe that every student brings something of value to the tasks that they pose to their classes. The Teaching Principle calls for teachers to select tasks that "can be solved in more than one way, such as using an arithmetic counting approach, drawing a geometric diagram and enumerating possibilities, or using algebraic equations [so that tasks are] accessible to students with varied prior knowledge and experience" (p. 19).

A THREE-PART LESSON FORMAT

U.S. teachers typically spend a small portion of a lesson explaining or reviewing an idea and then go into "production mode," where students wade through a list of exercises. Lessons set up in this explain-then-practice pattern condition students to focus on procedures so that they can get through the exercises. Teachers find themselves going from desk to desk reteaching and explaining to individuals. This is in significant contrast to a lesson built around a single problem, an approach that is quite typical in Asian classrooms (see Figure 4.2). Much

---

> **The emphasis on understanding is evident in the steps typical of Japanese eighth-grade mathematics lessons:**
>
> - Teacher poses a complex thought-provoking problem.
> - Students struggle with the problem.
> - Various students present ideas or solutions to the class.
> - Class discusses the various solution methods.
> - The teacher summarizes the class's conclusions.
> - Students practice similar problems.
>
> **In contrast, the emphasis on skill acquisition is evident in the steps common to most U.S. and German math lessons:**
>
> - Teacher instructs students in a concept or skill.
> - Teacher solves example problems with class.
> - Students practice on their own while the teacher assists individual students.

FIGURE 4.2 Comparison of the steps typical of eighth-grade mathematics lessons in Japan, the United States, and Germany.
Source: Unpublished tabulations from the Third International Mathematics and Science Study, Videotape Classroom Study, University of California, Los Angeles, 1996. Used with permission.

more learning occurs and much more assessment information is available when a class works on a single problem and engages in discourse about the validity of the solution.

Before, During, and After

Teaching through problem solving does not mean simply providing a problem or task, sitting back, and waiting for magic to happen. The teacher is responsible for making the atmosphere and the lesson work. To this end, think of a lesson as consisting of three main parts: *before, during,* and *after.* Each portion carries specific agendas and requires specific teacher actions to make the lesson effective (see Figure 4.3).

- *Before.* The agenda in this part of the lesson is to get students mentally prepared to work on the problem and thinking about the kinds of ideas that will help them the most. You want to be sure they understand the task. You want to be sure they understand their responsibilities. At the end of this portion of the lesson, there should be no questions regarding the task or what is to be done. Students have already begun to think about the relevant ideas and are ready to go to work.

- *During.* The first agenda item here is to *let go!* Give students a chance to work without your constant guidance. Give them the opportunity to use *their* ideas and not simply follow directions. Have faith in their abilities. The second point is to *listen.* Find out how different children or groups are thinking, what ideas they are using, and how they are approaching the problem.

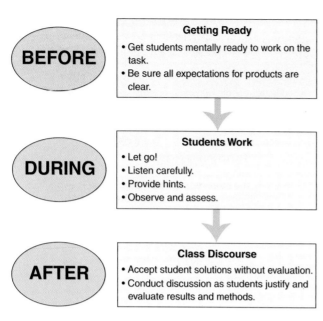

FIGURE 4.3 **Teaching through problem solving suggests a simple three-part structure for lessons.**

- *After.* In this portion of the lesson, you want to engage the class in productive discourse and help students begin to work as a community of learners. *Do not evaluate.* Students must learn to both contribute to and participate in these discussions. They must listen to others and help decide which approaches and solutions make the most sense and why. Thinking must not stop when the problem is solved. Now is the time to encourage reflection on solutions, methods, and extensions.

If you allot time for each before, during, and after segment, it is quite easy to devote a full period to one seemingly simple problem. As long as the problematic feature of the task is the mathematics you want students to learn, a lot of good learning will result from engaging students in only one problem. The same three-part structure can be applied to small tasks, resulting in a 10- to 20-minute minilesson (common in kindergarten). There are also times when the during and after portions extend into the next day or even longer.

Teacher Actions in the Before Phase

The kinds of things you do in the before phase of a lesson will vary with the task. Some tasks you can begin with immediately. For example, if your students are used to solving story problems and know they are expected to use words, pictures, and numbers to explain their solutions in writing, all that may be required is to read through the problem with them and be sure all understand it. The actual presentation of the task or problem may occur at the beginning or at the end of your "be-

fore actions." However, you will first engage students in some form of activity directly related to the problem in order to get them prepared. Consider the following "before actions."

Begin with a Simple Version of the Task

Suppose that you are interested in developing some ideas about area and perimeter in the fourth or fifth grade. This is the task you plan to present (Lappan & Even, 1989).

Assume that the edge of a square is 1 unit. Add squares to this shape so that it has a perimeter of 18.

Instead of beginning your lesson with this problem, you might consider one of the following simpler tasks:

- Draw a 3-by-5 rectangle of squares on the board, and let students tell things they know about the shape. (It's a rectangle. It has squares. There are 15 squares. There are three rows of five.) If no one mentions the words *area* and *perimeter,* you could write those two words on the board and ask if those words can be used in talking about this figure.
- Provide students with some square tiles or grid paper. "I want everyone to make a shape that has a perimeter of 12 units. After you make your shape, find out what its area is." After a short time, have several students share their shapes.

Each of these "warm-ups" gets the vocabulary you will need for your exploration out in the open. The second activity suggests the tiles as a possible model that students may choose to use. It has the added benefit of hinting that there are different figures with the same perimeter.

Dad says it is 503 miles to the beach. When we stopped for gas, we had gone 267 miles. How much farther do we have to drive?

This problem is designed to help children develop an add-on method of subtraction. Before presenting this problem, have students supply the missing part of 100 after you supply one part. Try numbers like 80 or 30 at first; then try

47 or 62. After presenting the actual task, you might ask students if the answer to the problem is more or less than 300.

Brainstorm

Often you can present a problem and have students suggest solutions or strategies. Their suggestions will not solve the problem for others because students must still work out the solution and an explanation. The following problem for middle school students is designed to address the ideas of ratio and proportion as well as data analysis. Since this is not a straightforward task, brainstorming will likely produce a variety of approaches, resulting in more profitable solutions by more students.

Enrollment data for the school provide information about the students and their families as shown here:

	School	*Class*
Siblings		
None	36	5
One	89	4
Two	134	17
More than two	93	3
Race		
African American	49	11
Asian American	12	0
White	219	15
Travel-to-school method		
Walk	157	10
Bus	182	19
Other	13	0

If someone asked you how typical your class was of the rest of the school, how would you answer? Write an explanation of your answer. Include one or more charts or graphs that you think would support your conclusion.

Estimate or Use Mental Computation

When the task is aimed at the development of a computational procedure, a useful before action is to have students actually do the computation mentally or suggest a ballpark answer. Have students independently think of an estimate or compute mentally, and then list these "pre-answers" on the board. You may even have students explain their reasoning. Again, this process will not spoil the problem for the class.

This technique would be useful with the earlier problem concerning how many miles to go to the beach. The following task is another example in which preliminary estimates or mental computations would be useful.

How many small squares (ones or units) will fit in a rectangle that is 54 units long and 36 units wide? Use base-ten pieces to help you with your solution.

Make a plan for figuring out the total number of pieces without doing too much counting. Explain how your plan would work on a rectangle that is 27 units by 42 units.

Prior to estimation or mental computation for this problem, several simpler problems will also help. For example, rectangles such as 30 by 8 or 40 by 60 could be explored, or these may have been problems from earlier days.

Be Sure the Task Is Understood

This action is not optional! You must always be sure that students understand the problem before setting them to work. Remember that their perspective is different from yours.

Consider the task of mastering the multiplication facts. The most difficult facts can each be connected or related to an easier fact already learned.

Use a fact you already know to help you solve each of these facts: 4×6, 6×8, 7×6, 3×8.

For this task, it is essential that students understand the idea of using a helping fact. They have most likely used helping facts in addition. You can build on this by asking, "When you were learning addition facts, how could knowing $6 + 6$ help you figure out $6 + 7$?" You may also need to help students understand what is meant by a fact they know—one they have mastered and know without counting.

When using a word problem, it is useful in the lower grades to ask a series of direct questions that can be answered just by looking at the problem.

The local candy store purchased candy in cartons holding 12 boxes per carton. The price paid for one carton was $42.50. Each box contained 8 candy bars that the store planned to sell individually. What was the candy store's cost for each candy bar?

"What did the candy store do? What is in a carton? What is in a box? What is the price of one carton? What does that mean when it says 'each box'?" The last question here is to identify vocabulary that may be misunderstood. It is also useful to be sure students can explain to you what the problem is asking. Rereading a problem does little good, but having students restate the problem in their own words forces them to think about what the problem is asking.

Establish Expectations

As with the previous action, this one is essential. Students need to be clearly told what is expected of them beyond an answer. It is always a good idea to have students write out an explanation for their solution. There is a significant difference between "Show how you got your answer" and "Explain why you think your answer is correct." With the former direction, students may simply record their steps ("First we did . . . , and then we . . . ") or present their work as self-evident. You can't expect students to explain their mental processes unless you ask for an explanation. In Figure 4.4 the work of two students illustrates the contrast.

When students are working in groups, only one written explanation should come from the group. All in the group must understand what is written, all should put their names on it, and any one in the group should be ready to make an oral presentation.

It is never too early to begin written explanations, even in kindergarten. There the writing may be in the form of drawings and numbers, but this early form of written com-

FIGURE 4.4 Betsy tells each step in her solution but provides no explanation. In contrast, Ryan's work includes reasons for his steps.

Kindergarten
How many ways can you show what 5 means?

FIGURE 4.5 A kindergarten student shows her thinking about ways to make 5.

munication is just as important. Figure 4.5 shows one student's solution for ways to make 5.

The written explanations may be in a journal or on a separate sheet of paper. Sometimes a group report can be prepared on a large sheet of newsprint. This is useful when students are going to make a presentation.

There may be occasions when you will not require written work. A very simple yet useful technique is to have students share their ideas with a partner and then between the two of them select the best approach to be presented. This causes students to defend their ideas to a peer and prepares them to talk to the class.

Students preparing to explain and defend their answers will spend time reflecting on the validity of their results and will often make revisions even before sharing them. They will have a greater interest in the class discussion because they will want to compare their solution with others' solutions. They will have "rehearsed" for the class discussion and be ready to participate. Even when students fail to solve a problem, they should be expected to show the ideas and the work that they have considered.

Teacher Actions in the During Phase

Once you are comfortable that students are ready to work on the task, it is time to let go. You must demonstrate confidence and respect for your students' abilities. Set them to work with the expectation that they will solve the problem. You *must* let go!

Students should get in the habit of working in groups so that there is no lost time in moving from the full-class discussion to the small groups. Groups of three or at most four work well, but pairs of students, especially at the K–2 level,

are often best. Your role now shifts to that of facilitator and active listener.

Listen Actively

This is one of two opportunities you will get in the lesson (the other is in the discussion portion of the lesson) to find out what your students know, how they think, and how they are approaching the task you have given them. You might sit down with a group and simply listen for a while, have the students explain what they are doing, or take notes. If you want further information, try saying, "Tell me what you are doing," or "I see you have started to multiply these numbers. Can you tell me why you are doing that?" You want to convey a genuine interest in what students are doing and thinking. This is *not* the time to evaluate or to tell students how to solve the problem.

Students may initially be timid when you sit down to join them, or they may change their minds as soon as you ask a question, taking it as a signal that they are wrong. However, soon they will accept that you are simply there to find out what they are doing. When they see that the more you learn about their reasoning and ideas the better you are able to help them, they will no longer be anxious when you are listening.

In Chapter 5, you will read about techniques for recording the information you find out during this time.

Provide Hints and Suggestions

How much help to give students is always going to be an issue. Should you let them stumble down the wrong path? How much direction should you provide? Do you correct errors you see?

If a group is searching for a place to begin, a hint may be appropriate. You might suggest that the students try using a particular manipulative or draw a picture if that seems appropriate.

In Fern's Furniture Store, Fern has priced all of her furniture at 20 percent over wholesale. In preparation for a sale, she tells her staff to cut all prices by 10 percent. Will Fern be making 10 percent profit, less than 10 percent profit, or more than 10 percent profit? Explain your answer.

For this problem, consider the following hints:

- Try drawing a picture or a diagram of something that shows what 10 percent off means.
- Try drawing a picture or a diagram that shows what 20 percent more means.
- Maybe you could pick a price of something and see what happens.
- Let's try a simpler problem. Suppose that you had 8 blocks and got 25 percent more. Then you lost 25 percent of the new collection.

Encourage Testing of Ideas

Students will look to you for approval of their results or ideas. Avoid being the source of "truth" or of right and wrong. When asked if a result or method is correct ask, "How can you decide?" or "Why do you think that might be right?" or "I see what you have done. How can you check that somehow?" Even if not asked for an opinion, asking, "How can we tell if that makes sense?" reminds students that answers without reasons are not acceptable.

Suggest Extensions or Generalizations

Lots of good problems are simple on the surface. It is the extensions that are excellent. The area and perimeter task is a case in point. Many students will quickly come up with one or two solutions. "I see you found one way to do this. Are there any other solutions? Are any of the solutions different or more interesting than others? Which of the shapes you found with a perimeter of 18 is the largest and which the smallest? Does the perimeter always change when you add another tile?"

What can you find out about that? This general question is at the very heart of mathematics as a science of pattern and order. It asks students to look for something interesting, to generalize. For example, in the area and perimeter problem, squares can be added to a shape in three situations: If a new square touches the old shape on only one side, the perimeter increases by 2. If it touches on two sides, there is no increase. If it fits into a "U" and touches on three sides, the perimeter actually decreases by 2.

Questions that begin "What if you tried . . . ?" or "Would that same idea work for . . . ?" are also ways to suggest different extensions. For example, "Suppose you tried to find all the shapes possible with a perimeter of 18. What could you find out about the areas?"

Find a Second Method

The value of students' solving a problem in more than one way cannot be overestimated. It shifts the value system in the classroom from answers to processes and thinking. It is a good way for students to make new and different connections.

For example, consider this sixth-grade problem.

The dress was originally priced at $90. If the sale price is 25 percent off, how much will it cost on sale?

This is an example of a straightforward problem with a single answer. Many students will solve it by multiplying by 0.25 and subtracting the result from $90. The suggestion to find another way may be all that is necessary. Others may re-quire specific directions: "How would you do it with fractions instead of decimals?" "Draw me a diagram that explains what you did." "How could this be done in just one step?" "Think of a way that you could do this mentally."

Second graders will frequently solve the next problem by counting or using addition.

Maxine had saved up $9. The next day, she received her allowance. Now she has $12. How much allowance did she get?

"How would you do that on a calculator?" and "Can you write an equation that tells what you did?" are ways of encouraging children to connect 9 plus ? = 12 with 12 − 9.

Solving a problem in a second way can help students who have made an error find their own mistake. Perhaps a student has used a symbolic method of her own invention and has made an error in reasoning. Suggesting only that she try to do the problem with physical models ("so that I can understand what you did") may be all that is necessary to have her make a self-correction.

Teacher Actions in the After Phase

Be certain to plan ample time for this portion of the lesson and then be certain to *save* the time. It is not necessary for every student to have finished. Often this is when the best learning will take place. Twenty minutes or more is not at all unreasonable for a good class discussion and sharing of ideas. This is not a time to check answers but for the class to share ideas. Over time, you will develop your class into a community of learners who together are involved in making sense of mathematics. This atmosphere will not develop easily or quickly. You must teach your students about your expectations for this time and how to interact with their peers.

Engage the Class in Discussion

You may want simply to list answers from all of the groups and put them on the board without comment. Following that, you can return to one or more students to get explanations for their solutions or to explain their processes. At other times, you may choose to call on groups or individuals that you noticed earlier doing something interesting or something of special value. This should not be restricted to correct solutions.

When there are different answers, the full class should be involved in the discourse concerning which answers are correct. Allow those responsible for the answers to defend them, and then open the discussion to the class. "Who has an idea about this? George, I noticed that you got a different answer than Tomeka. What do you think of her explanation?" Resist with every fiber in you the temptation to judge the correctness of an answer. Even when the class fails to come to a conclusion, rather than provide your solution, suggest that perhaps you will need to return to this later. Later will be when students have gained some additional insights to help them.

One of your functions is to make sure that all students participate, that all listen, and that all understand what is being said. Moving along too quickly cheats students who are not quite able to follow the faster explanations of the best children in the room. Encourage students to ask questions. "Pete, did you understand how they did that? Do you want to ask Mary a question?"

Use Praise Cautiously

Be an attentive listener to both good and not so good ideas. Support and praise effort and risk taking, but *expect* students to do good work. Praise offered for correct solutions or excitement over interesting ideas suggests that the students did something unusual or unexpected. This can be negative feedback for those who do not get praise. Comments such as "Good job!" and "Super work!" roll off the tongue easily. We use these statements to help children feel good about themselves. There is evidence to suggest that we should be cautious when using expressions of praise, especially with respect to student products and solutions (Schwartz, 1996). Praise not only supports students' feelings but also evaluates. "Good job!" says, "Yes, you did that correctly." "Nice work" can establish an expectation for others that products must be neat or beautiful in order to have value. This can make students who do excellent mathematical science hide their efforts if they appear sloppy or poorly presented.

In place of praise that is judgmental, Schwartz (1996) suggests comments of interest and extension: "I wonder what would happen if you tried . . . " or "Please tell me how you figured that out." Notice that these phrases express interest and value the child's thinking. They also can and should be used regardless of the validity of the responses.

Engage *All* Class Members

Teachers are finding a wider range of academic diversity in their classrooms. NCTM in its *Standards* documents is very clear in expressing the belief that all children can learn the mathematics of the regular curriculum. This view is supported by a number of prominent mathematics educators who have worked extensively with at-risk populations (Campbell, 1996; NCTM, 1989, 1991; Silver & Stein, 1996; Trafton & Claus, 1994).

But the needs and abilities of children are different, and it requires skill and practice to conduct a large group discus-

sion that is balanced and includes all children. Rowan and Bourne (1994) offer some excellent suggestions based on their work in an urban, multiracial, multiethnic, low-socioeconomic school district. They emphasize that the most important factor is to be clear about the purpose of group discussion—that is, to share and explore the variety of strategies, ideas, and solutions generated by the class and to learn to communicate these ideas in a rich mathematical discourse. Every class has a handful of students who are always ready to respond. Other children learn to be passive or do not participate. So rule number one is that the discussion is more important than hearing an answer.

A second suggestion is to begin discussions by calling first on the children who tend to be shy or lack the ability to express themselves well. Rowan and Bourne (1994) note that the more obvious ideas are generally given at the outset of a discussion. When asked to participate early and given sufficient time to formulate their thoughts, these reticent children can more easily participate and thus be valued.

Make it a habit to ask for explanations to accompany *all* answers. Soon the request for an explanation will not signal an incorrect response, as children initially believe. Many incorrect answers are the result of small errors in the context of otherwise excellent thinking. Likewise, many correct answers may not represent the insightful thinking you might have assumed. A child who has given an incorrect answer is very likely to see the error and correct it during the explanation. Try to support children's thinking without evaluating responses. "Does someone have a different idea or want to comment on what Daniel just said?" All children should hear the same teacher reactions that only the "smart kids" used to hear.

Many times a student will get stuck in the middle of an explanation. The silence can be difficult, and there is a temptation to call on someone else to "help out" or to suggest that the child get assistance from a classmate. Though well intentioned, the message this sends to the child is that he is not capable on his own. Children must learn that time will be given and that their classmates trust and believe in one another. This attitude conveys support and confidence and is usually all that is necessary to get a quality response.

There will, of course, be times when a response is simply not forthcoming. When this occurs, you might suggest taking some time to get thoughts together or to work out the idea with some materials. Promise to return to the child later, and then be *certain* to return to hear what was figured out.

Identify Rules, Hypotheses, and Future Problems

When you are satisfied with the discussion around the answer and the solution, summarize the main points of the discussion, and make sure that all students understand what has been agreed on. When a problem involves creating a procedure, the class may decide on one or more methods of solution, and these may be written on the board. For example, suppose that the task involved finding clever methods of adding when one of the addends is a 9 (e.g., 5 + 9 or 9 + 3). Some students may have devised a method of taking 1 off of the smaller number and putting it with the 9. This might be listed as Maggie's rule: *Shift 1 from the little number to make 10. 5 + 9 becomes 4 + 10.* Other students may have added 10 to the smaller number and subtracted 1. Yolanda's rule might be written: *Add 10 instead of 9 and then take 1 off. 5 + 9 is 5 + 10 − 1.* When students invent procedures for computation or measurement formulas, you may want to help them find a good way to write them, but do not change the students' basic ideas. No student should be required to use the ideas of others, but all students must try to understand them.

Often someone will make a generalization or an observation that he or she strongly believes in but cannot completely justify. These ideas should always be listened to with interest, even if they are incorrect. Untested ideas can be written up on the board as "Andrew's Hypothesis." Explain the meaning of *hypothesis* as an idea that may or may not be true. Testing the hypothesis may become the problem for another day, or the hypothesis may simply be kept on the board until additional evidence comes up that either supports or disproves it. For example, when comparing fractions, suppose that a group makes this generalization and you write it on the board: *When deciding which fraction is larger, the fraction in which the bottom number is closer to the top number is the larger fraction. Example:* $\frac{4}{7}$ *is not as big as* $\frac{7}{8}$ *because 7 is only 1 from 8 but 4 is 3 away from 7.* This is not an unusual conclusion, but it is not correct in all instances. A problem for a subsequent day would be to decide if the hypothesis is always right or to find fractions for which it is right (counterexamples).

Even when students have not suggested hypotheses, discussions will often turn up interesting questions that can profitably be used for tasks to help clarify an emerging idea.

Designing and Selecting Effective Tasks

A task is effective when it helps students learn the ideas you want them to learn. It must be the mathematics in the task that makes it problematic for the students so that it is the mathematical ideas that are their primary concern. Therefore, the first and most important consideration for selecting any task for your class must be the mathematics. That said, where do you look for tasks?

Your Textbook

Most teachers find their textbook to be the main guide to their day-to-day curriculum. However, when teachers let the text determine the next lesson, they assume that children learned from each page what was intended. Avoid the "myth of coverage": If we covered it, they must have learned it. Good teachers use their text as a resource and as a basic guide to

their curriculum. In the face of the current pressures from state-level standards, the state curriculum guide is also an important consideration.

Using Traditional Textbooks

Traditional textbooks are designed to be teacher directed, a contrast to the approach you have been reading about. But they should not be discarded. Much thought went into the content and the pedagogical ideas. Your book can still be used as a prime resource if you think about translating units and lessons to a problem-oriented approach.

Adopt a *unit perspective.* Avoid the idea that every lesson and idea in the unit requires attention. Examine a chapter or unit from beginning to end, and identify the two to four *big ideas,* the essential mathematics in the chapter. (Big ideas are listed at the start of each chapter in Section 2 of this book. These may be helpful as a reference.) Temporarily ignore the smaller subideas that often take up a full lesson.

With the big ideas of the unit in mind, you can now do two things: (1) adapt the best or most important lessons in the chapter to a problem-solving format and (2) create or find tasks in the text's teacher notes and other resources that address the big ideas. The combination will almost certainly provide you with an ample supply of tasks.

Adapting a Traditional Textbook Lesson

Figure 4.6 shows a page from a first-grade textbook. The lesson addresses an important idea: the connection of addition and subtraction. The approach on this page is fine: A bar of cubes in two colors is used to suggest an addition and a subtraction equation, thus connecting these concepts. However, as is typical of traditional K–2 texts, there are blanks to be filled in with very specific correct answers. Student attention turns almost immediately to how to get the right numbers in the blanks. Imagine for a moment how you might help students complete this page correctly. It is easy to slip into a how-to mode that focuses more on the blanks than on addition and subtraction. Let's convert this lesson to a problem-oriented task. How can children be challenged to wrestle with this idea? You might want to try this before reading on.

One thought is to provide a bar of cubes of one color and have students break the bar into two parts. The students' task is to write addition and subtraction equations that tell what they did with the bar. They should draw a picture to show how they broke the bar.

Another idea is to create a scenario where there are two amounts, such as toy cars, on two different shelves. *In the toy store, there were 11 cars, 4 on the top shelf and 7 on the next shelf.* Have the students create two story problems about the 11 cars, one that is an addition story and another that is a subtraction story.

In the first modification, the page was translated directly to a task. In the second, a similar task was designed that did not look the same but addressed exactly the same mathematics. In each case, the students will do only one or two ex-

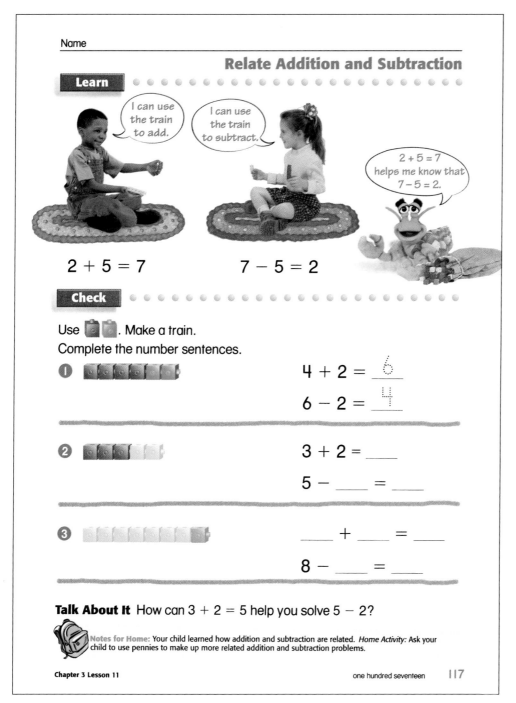

FIGURE 4.6 **A first-grade lesson from a traditional textbook.**

Source: From *Scott Foresman–Addison Wesley Math: Grade 1* (p. 117), by R. I. Charles et al., 1998, Glenview, IL: Scott Foresman–Addison Wesley. Copyright 1998 by Scott Foresman–Addison Wesley. Reprinted with permission.

amples rather than the eight that are on this page and on the other side. But in the during and after portions of either modified lesson, there will be a much greater opportunity for students to develop the connection between addition and subtraction. That concept will be the focus of the discussion, not filling in the blanks.

Figure 4.7 (p. 50) is a geometry lesson from a fifth-grade book. The content involves classification of triangles by relative side lengths and by the size of the angles, but notice how much of the lesson is simply providing definitions. The lesson is easily translated to a problematic task. Consider what *you* might do before reading on.

To make this a classification *task,* students need some triangles in all six categories, with two or three triangles per category. You might prepare a set of triangles, reproduce them, and have students cut them out, or geoboards could be used if they are available. (These and other ideas are discussed in Chapter 20.) Given a set of triangles, the task is to find two ways to sort the triangles into three separate piles. You could specify doing this first by sides and then by angles,

FIGURE 4.7 A fifth-grade lesson from a traditional textbook.

Source: From *Scott Foresman–Addison Wesley Math: Grade 5* (p. 272), by R. I. Charles et al., 1998, Glenview, IL: Scott Foresman–Addison Wesley. Copyright 1998 by Scott Foresman–Addison Wesley. Reprinted with permission.

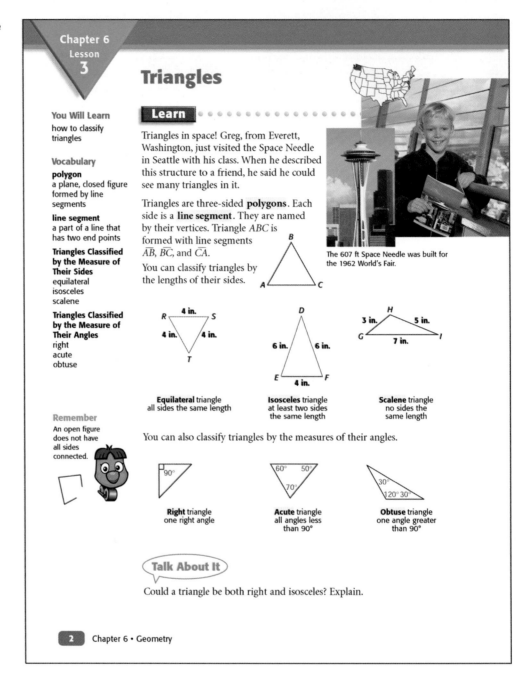

or let students develop their own classification schemes. In the during portion, you can provide hints that will help assure that some students create the categories you want. After students have created the categories, you can provide the appropriate vocabulary.

Using Reform Programs

If your school is using a "reform-oriented" textbook series (see p. 8), then you will likely find that most of the lessons are already geared to a problem-solving mode. Your main difficulty may be assuring yourself that all of the skills and concepts of your local curriculum are appropriately emphasized. Some

units may need additional activities or modifications based on the needs of your students, and others you may decide to skip. Some teachers use these programs as resource books, selecting only a few units or activities to augment their regular program.

Children's Literature

The use of children's literature is sufficiently important as a source of problems that it deserves some separate attention. Children's stories can be used in numerous ways to create reflective tasks at all grade levels, and there are many excellent books to help you in this area (Bresser, 1995; Burns, 2000; Sheffield, 1995; Theissen, Matthias, & Smith, 1998; Welchman-Tischler, 1992; Whitin & Wilde, 1992, 1995).

By way of example, a very popular children's book, *The Doorbell Rang* (Hutchins, 1986), can be used with different agendas at various grade levels. The story is a sequential tale of children sharing 12 cookies. On each page, more children come to the kitchen, and the 12 cookies must be redistributed. This simple yet engaging story can lead to exploring ways to make equal parts of almost any number for children at the K–2 level. It is a springboard for multiplication and division at the 3–4 level. It can also be used to explore fraction concepts at the 4–6 level.

Most of the chapters in Section 2 of this text include a section titled "Literature Connection" that suggests a few ideas for using literature to explore the mathematics of that chapter. Literature ideas are often found in the articles of NCTM's journals. It is an exciting approach to developing lessons.

Other Resources

You will never compile a perfect set of tasks for your class; every class is different. As already noted, your textbook is a good place to begin, and children's literature should always be considered. Here are some additional options to consider:

- Read the NCTM journals regularly: *Teaching Children Mathematics* (for grades K–6) or *Mathematics Teaching in the Middle School* (for grades 5–8). Copy and file articles to go with each chapter in your text or each section of your curriculum. Don't wait until you need an idea to begin flipping through journals.

- Begin to develop your personal professional library of resource books. Check out NCTM publications. The Addenda Series books are an excellent place to begin, but NCTM's catalog has lots of resources. Don't forget the book in your hands! Many teachers use it as their first resource. A number of commercial publishers and distributors specialize in materials for teaching mathematics, including resource books for teachers and activity books and manipulatives for students.

- Check out the reform curricula at your grade level, even if you don't use them regularly. Buy a single module to get your feet wet. Check out these implementation centers on the Web: for elementary school, Alternatives for Rebuilding Curricula at www.comap.com/arc; for middle school, Show-Me Center at http://showmecenter.missouri.edu.

- Surf the Web. There are lots of Web sites designed to offer help and teaching ideas for teachers. Many include complete lesson plans. One caution: Just because it's on the Web doesn't mean it's good. The things you will find range widely in quality. Good sites to get you started are noted in Chapter 8.

 "By analyzing and adapting a problem, anticipating the mathematical ideas that can be brought out by working on the problem, and anticipating students' questions, teachers can decide if particular problems will help to further their mathematical goals for the class" (p. 53).

A Task Selection Guide

Throughout this book, in every student textbook, and in every article you read or in-service workshop you attend, you will hear and read about suggestions for activities, problems, tasks, or explorations that someone believes are effective in helping children learn some aspect of mathematics. Selecting activities or tasks is, as Lappan and Briars (1995) contend, the most significant decision affecting your students' learning. The box below shows a four-step guide you can use when considering a new activity for your students.

Activity Evaluation and Selection Guide

STEP 1: How Is the Activity Done?

Actually do the activity. Try to get "inside" the task or activity to see how it is done and what thinking might go on.

How would *children* do the activity or solve the problem? (They don't know what you do!)

- What materials are needed?
- What is written down or recorded?

STEP 2: What Is the Purpose of the Activity?

What *mathematical ideas* will the activity develop?

- Are the ideas concepts or procedural skills?
- Will there be connections to other related ideas?

STEP 3: Will the Activity Accomplish Its Purpose?

What is *problematic* about the activity? Is the problematic aspect related to the mathematics you identified in the purpose?

What *must* children reflect on or think about to complete the activity? (Don't rely on wishful thinking.)

Is it possible to complete the activity without much reflective thought? If so, can it be modified so that students will be required to think about the mathematics?

STEP 4: What Must You Do?

What will you need to do in the *before* portion of your lesson?

- How will you prepare students for this task?
- What will be the students' responsibilities?

What difficulties might you anticipate seeing in the *during* portion of your lesson?

What will you want to focus on in the *after* portion of your lesson?

To evaluate the effectiveness of a task or activity you think may be good, begin by actually doing the activity yourself, trying to think of the ways children in your class might do it. Consider the information and skills *they* will bring to the activity.

The second step has you focus on what ideas and what mathematics the activity is likely to help children develop. Beware! The author's stated objective is not always an accurate indication of the mathematics in the task.

The third step is the most important point in determining if an activity will or will not accomplish its purpose. What is problematic about the activity? What will improve the chances that the children will be mentally active, reflecting on and constructing the ideas you identified in step 2? Try to predict what students will do with the activity. Think about how students might have difficulty with the task. Difficulties are usually the best opportunities for learning, but you would like to anticipate them if possible.

The fourth step in the guide focuses your attention on implementation issues. Consider possible before, during, and after actions of a lesson built on the task that will add to its effectiveness.

Practice using this guide with activities throughout this book. Work toward thinking about tasks or activities from the view of what is likely to happen inside children's minds, not just what they are doing with their hands. Good tasks are minds-on activities, not just hands-on activities.

STOP Suppose that your goal was for students to learn some of the harder multiplication facts that they had not yet mastered (grade 3 or 4). You pose the task on page 43 about finding a helping fact. Think about the questions in step 3 of the Activity Evaluation and Selection Guide. Do you think this will be an effective activity for your students? Why? Can you make it better? How?

TEACHING TIPS AND QUESTIONS

The ideas expressed here have been gathered from elementary and middle school teachers who have been working hard at developing a problem-solving approach in their classrooms and from the research literature on teaching via problem solving.

Promoting Discourse

The value of classroom discussion of ideas cannot be overemphasized. As students describe and evaluate solutions to tasks, share approaches, and make conjectures as members of a community of learners, learning will occur in ways that are impossible otherwise. Students begin to take ownership of ideas and develop a sense of power in making sense of mathematics.

Students should understand when given a task that one of their responsibilities is to prepare for discussion that will occur after they have had an opportunity to work on the problem. One fourth-grade teacher discovered that she was too involved in her class discussions. The students tended to wait for her questions rather than tell about their solutions. To help her students be more personally responsible, she devised three posters, inscribed as follows:

How did you solve the problem?

Why did you solve it this way?

Why do you think your solution is correct and makes sense?

In the beginning, students referred to the posters as they made presentations to the class, but soon that was not required. They continued to refer to the posters as they wrote up the solutions to problems in the during portion of lessons. Students began to prompt presenters: "You didn't answer the second question on the poster." One of the best results of these posters was that they helped remove the teacher from the content of the discussions. She was no longer in a position of asking questions that made it seem to students that she had a single "best" answer in mind.

Regardless of the exact structure or time frame for a lesson, an opportunity for discourse should always be built in. After students have played a game, worked in a learning center, completed a challenging worksheet, or engaged in a mental math activity with a full class, they can still discuss their activity: *What strategies worked well in the game? What did you find out in the learning center? What are different ways to do this exercise?*

Four Suggestions

1. *Predict! Don't hope.* When planning a task, it is not sufficient to think about how it will work if everything goes well. Think about your students—all of them. Predict their likely responses, and be prepared to deal with them. Things rarely go as you hope they will.

2. *Be clear in your own mind about the purpose of the task or activity.* Don't select problems simply because they are interesting. Always ask, "What *mathematics* will students be working with or develop by working on this task?" The purpose of an activity is not the same as what the students are asked to do. For example, students don't use blocks or graphing calculators to learn about blocks or graphing calculators.

3. *Recognize that there is much more to a problem than the answer.* Often the most learning occurs during the class discussion. Children's social interaction is at least as important as their independent reflection. Discussing various paths to the solution and, most important, deciding why an answer is right or wrong are learning opportu-

nities that should not be passed up. When children discover that they can determine the validity of answers, they learn that mathematics makes sense.

4. *Do not confuse open-ended problem solving with encouraging creativity.* Open-ended solutions are not the same as creative stories, artistic drawings, or students' supplying their own numbers for a problem. These latter approaches often detract from the mathematics of the task as students spend time coloring or writing stories. An "expensive" task is one in which students spend 50 percent or more of the time involved with context, materials, "cut and paste," and similar tasks with no mathematics being addressed.

How Much to Tell and Not to Tell

When teaching through problem solving, one of the most perplexing dilemmas is how much to tell. On one hand, telling diminishes student reflection. Students who sense that the teacher has a preferred method or approach are extremely reluctant to use their own strategies. Nor will students develop self-confidence and problem-solving abilities by following teacher directions. On the other hand, to tell too little can sometimes leave students floundering and waste precious class time.

Researchers connected with four different constructivist programs, while noting that there will never be a simple solution to this dilemma, offer the following guidance: Teachers should feel free to share relevant information as long as the mathematics in the task remains problematic for the students (Hiebert et al., 1997). That is, "information can and should be shared as long as it does not solve the problem [and] does not take away the need for students to reflect on the situation and develop solution methods they understand" (p. 36).

They go on to suggest three types of information that teachers should provide to their students:

- *Mathematical conventions.* The social conventions of symbolism and terminology that are important in mathematics will never be developed through reflective thought. For example, representing "three and five equals eight" as "3 + 5 = 8" is a convention. Definitions and labels are also conventions. What is important is to offer these symbols and words only when students need them or will find them useful. As a rule of thumb, symbolism and terminology should only be introduced *after* concepts have been developed and then specifically as a means of expressing or labeling ideas. They should rarely be presented solely as things to be memorized.
- *Alternative methods.* You can, with care, suggest to students an alternative method or approach for consideration. You may also suggest more efficient recording procedures for student-invented computational methods. A teacher must be cautious in not conveying to students that their ideas are second best. Nor should students ever be forced to adopt a teacher's suggestion over their own approach. The rule of thumb here is that the value of a procedure should always be a judgment of the students, not a dictate of the teacher. In this spirit, students can learn to appraise a teacher's suggestion without feeling obligated to use it.
- *Clarification of students' methods.* You should help students clarify or interpret their ideas and perhaps point out related ideas. A student may add 38 and 5 by noting that 38 and 2 more is 40 with 3 more making 43. This strategy can be related to the make-ten strategy used to add 8 + 3. The selection of 40 as a midpoint in this procedure is an important place-value concept. Such clarifications reinforce the students who have the ideas. Discussion or clarification of students' ideas focuses attention on ideas you want the class to learn. Care must be taken that attention to one student's ideas does not diminish those of other students. Nor should teacher attention to one method suggest that it is the preferred approach.

Frequently Asked Questions

The following are questions teachers have asked about this problem-based approach to teaching mathematics.

 Before reading the discussion that follows each of the following five questions, stop to consider your personal response. Then compare your thoughts with the ideas suggested.

1. *How can I teach all the basic skills I have to teach?* Many teachers, especially those feeling the current pressures of state testing programs, resort to rote drill and practice to teach "basic skills." There is a tendency to believe that mastery of the basics is incompatible with a problem-based approach. However, the evidence strongly suggests otherwise. First, drill-oriented approaches in U.S. classrooms have consistently produced poor results (Battista, 1999; Kamii & Dominick, 1998; O'Brien, 1999). Short-term gains on low-level skills may possibly result from drill, but even state testing programs require more. Both NAEP data (Kenney & Silver, 1997) and the TIMSS results (U.S. Department of Education, 1996, 1997b) suggest that drill is an inadequate answer.

Second, research data indicate that students in constructivist programs based on a problem-solving approach do as well or nearly as well as students in traditional programs on basic skills as measured by standardized tests (Campbell, 1995; Carpenter, Franke, Jacobs,

Fennema, & Empson, 1998; Hiebert & Wearne, 1996; Silver & Stein, 1996). Any deficit in skill development is more than outweighed by strength in concepts and problem solving.

Finally, traditional skills such as basic fact mastery and computation can be effectively taught in a problem-solving approach (for example, see Campbell, Rowan, & Suarez, 1998; Huinker, 1998).

2. *Why is it okay for students to "tell" or "explain" but not for me?* There are two answers to this question. First, students will question their peers when an explanation does not make sense to them, whereas explanations from the teacher are usually accepted without scrutiny (and, hence, without understanding). Second, when students are responsible for explaining, the class members develop a sense of pride and confidence that *they* can figure things out and make sense of mathematics. *They* have power and ability.

3. *Where can I find the time to cover everything?* Mathematics is much more connected and integrated than the itemized objectives like those found on many state "standards" lists would suggest. To deal with coverage, the first suggestion is to teach with a goal of developing the "big ideas," the main concepts in a unit or chapter. Most of the skills and ideas on your list of objectives will be addressed as you progress. If you focus separately on each item on the list, big ideas and connections, the essence of understanding, are unlikely to develop. Second, we spend far too much time reteaching because students don't retain ideas. Time spent up front to help students develop meaningful networks of ideas drastically reduces the need for reteaching, thus creating time in the long term.

4. *Is there any place for drill and practice?* Absolutely! The tragic error is to believe that drill is a method of developing ideas. Drill is only appropriate when (a) the desired concepts have been meaningfully developed, (b) flexible and useful procedures have been developed, *and* (c) speed and accuracy are needed. Watch children drilling basic facts who are counting on their fingers or using some other inefficient method. What they may be improving is their ability to count quickly. They are not learning their facts. Too many children are still counting in middle school because drill has not helped them develop efficient strategies. When you accept that drill does not produce understanding, you find there are really not many topics aside from basic fact mastery that should ever require drill.

5. *What do I do when a task bombs?* It will happen, although not as often as you think, that students just do not know what to do with a problem you pose no matter how many hints and suggestions you offer. Do not give in to the temptation to "tell 'em." Set it aside for the moment. Ask yourself why it bombed. Did the students have the ideas they needed? Was the task too advanced? Often we need to regroup and offer students a simpler related task

that gets them prepared for the one that proved difficult. When you sense that a task is not going anywhere, regroup! Don't spend days just hoping that something wonderful might happen. If you listen to your students, you will know where to go next.

TEACHING ABOUT PROBLEM SOLVING

The integration of problem solving and mathematics has obviously been a thrust of this chapter. But the standard on problem solving in *Principles and Standards* also speaks to the need to develop problem-solving *strategies and processes,* *metacognitive habits* of monitoring and regulating problem-solving activity, and a *positive disposition* toward mathematical problem solving. Each area suggests objectives or goals for the development of good problem solvers.

Strategies and Processes

Strategies for solving problems are identifiable methods of approaching a task that are completely independent of the specific topic or subject matter. Strategy goals play a part in all phases of problem solving: understanding the problem, solving the problem, and reflecting on the answer and solution.

Strategy and Process Goals

- *Develop problem analysis skills*—to improve students' ability to analyze an unfamiliar problem, identify wanted and needed information, ignore nonessential information, and clearly state the goal of the problem or task
- *Develop and select strategies*—to help students acquire a collection of problem-solving strategies that are useful in a variety of problem-solving settings and to select and use those strategies appropriately
- *Justify solutions*—to improve students' ability to assess the validity of answers
- *Extend or generalize problems*—to help students learn to go beyond the solution to problems; to consider results or processes applied in other situations or used to form rules or general procedures

Metacognition

Metacognition refers to conscious monitoring (being aware of how and why you are doing something) and regulation (choosing to do something or deciding to make changes) of your own thought process. Good problem solvers monitor their thinking regularly and automatically. They recognize when they are stuck or do not fully understand. They make conscious decisions to switch strategies, rethink the problem, search for related content knowledge that may help, or simply start afresh (Schoenfeld, 1992).

There is evidence that metacognitive behavior can be learned (Campione, Brown, & Connell, 1989; Garofalo, 1987; Lester, 1989). Further, students who learn to monitor and regulate their own problem-solving behaviors do show improvement in problem solving.

Metacognitive Goal

● *Monitor and regulate actions*—to help students develop the habit and ability to monitor and regulate their strategies and progress as they solve problems

Disposition

Disposition refers to the attitudes and beliefs that students possess about mathematics. Students' beliefs concerning their abilities to do mathematics and to understand the nature of mathematics have a significant effect on how they approach problems and ultimately on how well they succeed.

Students' attitudes (likes, dislikes, and preferences) about mathematics are nearly as important as their beliefs. Children who enjoy solving problems and feel satisfaction or pleasure at conquering a perplexing problem are much more likely to persevere, make second and third attempts, and even search out new problems. Negative attitudes have just the opposite effect.

Attitudinal Goals

● *Gain confidence and belief in abilities*—to develop students' confidence in their ability to do mathematics and to confront unfamiliar tasks
● *Be willing to try and to persevere*—to improve students' willingness to attempt unfamiliar problems and to develop their perseverance in solving problems without being discouraged by initial setbacks
● *Enjoy doing mathematics*—to help students learn to enjoy and sense personal reward in the process of thinking, searching for patterns, and solving problems

 NCTM Standards The first two goals of the problem-solving standard concern teaching through problem solving. The third and fourth goals refer to students learning problem-solving strategies and monitoring and reflecting on their own processes (metacognition). It would be beneficial to check these goals for the grade band that interests you most.

Working Toward Problem-Solving Goals While Students Learn

All of the goals of problem solving can and will be attained in classrooms that employ a problem-solving approach to the regular curriculum on a daily basis. A separate problem-solving strand is neither desirable nor necessary. It is important that the teacher be clearly aware of the goals of problem solving and focus attention on them regularly.

Developing Problem-Solving Strategies

Problem-solving strategies and processes are not so much taught as *modeled*. Your task as teacher is to suggest appropriate strategies and to point them out to students in class discussions as important ways of doing mathematics.

Strategies for Understanding the Problem

Your before actions provide a daily model of problem analysis skills. By entertaining a discussion of what is known, needed, and asked for or expected in the task, children will begin to understand that this is part of what solving problems is about. Soon you can say, "Before we get started, what should we do first?" Let students articulate good understanding strategies such as "Tell what we know" in their own language. Eventually, you can put students in groups and present problems or tasks without having to provide such explicit guidance. Give the responsibility to the students to do the things that you have modeled.

Plan-and-Carry-Out Strategies

The after phase of your lesson will inevitably include a discussion of methods that were used. When important or especially useful strategies crop up, they should be identified, highlighted, and discussed. Labeling a strategy provides a useful means for students to talk about their methods and for you to provide hints and suggestions. Hints or suggestions about a particular strategy may be appropriate in the before or during phases of your lesson.

The following strategies are most likely to appear in lessons where mathematical content is the main objective.

● *Draw a picture, act it out, use a model.* This is the strategy of using models as "thinker toys" as described in Chapter 3. "Act it out" extends models to a real interpretation of the problem situation.
● *Look for a pattern.* Pattern searching is at the heart of many activities, especially in the algebraic reasoning strand. Patterns in number and in operations play a huge role in helping students learn about and master basic facts and continues to be a major factor into the middle and high school years.
● *Make a table or chart.* Charts of data, function tables, tables for operations, and tables involving ratios or measurements are a major form of analysis and communication within mathematics. The use of a chart is often

combined with pattern searching as a means of solving problems or constructing new ideas.

- *Try a simpler form of the problem.* Here the general idea is to modify or simplify the quantities in a problem so that the resulting task is easier to understand and analyze. By solving the easier problem, the hope is to gain insights that can then be used to solve the original, more complex problem.
- *Guess and check.* This might be called "try and see what you can find out." A good way to work on a task that has you stumped is to *do something*. Make an attempt! Reflection even on a failed attempt can lead to a better idea. Another form of this strategy is to make an educated or reasoned guess at the solution and then see how the guess fits the conditions.
- *Make an organized list.* This strategy involves systematically accounting for all possible outcomes in a situation, either to find out how many possibilities there are or to be sure that all possible outcomes have been accounted for. One area where organized lists are very important is in probability.

Looking-Back Strategies

Looking-back strategies are the things that should always be done after a solution has been found: justify the answer, consider how the problem was solved, and look for possible extensions or generalizations. These are developed as you follow the teacher actions for the after portion of a lesson. Students in the upper grades should begin to accept responsibility for doing these things themselves without your leading every discussion. Help students understand that post-problem reflection is not just something that one does in school but also something that should be done whenever a problem is solved.

Developing Metacognitive Habits

We know that it is important to help students learn to monitor and control their own progress in problem solving. A simple formula that can be employed consists of three questions: *What* are you doing? *Why* are you doing it? *How* does it help you?

Though the exact form of the three questions is not significant, the idea is to be persistent with this reflective questioning as students work through problems or explorations. You can ask the questions as you sit down to listen to any group. By joining the group, you model questioning that you want the students eventually to do on their own. In the upper grades, each group will soon be able to designate a member to be the monitor. The monitor's job is to be the reflective questioner the same way you have modeled when working with the group.

Students can also be helped in developing self-monitoring habits after their problem-solving activity is over. A

brief discussion after a problem is over can focus on what types of things were done in solving the problem. "What did you do that helped you understand the problem? Did you find any numbers or information you didn't need? How did you decide what to do? Did you think about your answer after you got it? How did you decide your answer was right?"

Questioning similar to this tells students that all of these things are important. If they know you are going to be asking such questions, students will think about them ahead of time. Oral discussions with the class will be most helpful with younger children.

Attending to Attitudinal Goals

A classroom environment built on high expectations for all students and respect for each student's thoughts will go a long way toward achieving the attitudinal goals. Here are some additional ideas to help with these goals for all students.

- *Build in success.* In the beginning of the year, plan problems that you are confident your students can solve. Avoid creating a false success that depends on your showing the way at every step and curve.
- *Praise efforts and risk taking.* Students need to hear frequently that they are "good thinkers" capable of good, productive thought. When students volunteer ideas, listen carefully and actively to each idea, and give credit for the thinking and the risk that children take by venturing to speak out. Be careful to focus praise on the risk or effort and not the products of that effort, regardless of the quality of the ideas. Children whose weak or incorrect ideas are slighted or ignored develop a low sense of self-worth: "I'm no good. I can't think of good ideas." The same negative message comes through when praise is reserved only for the "best" ideas.
- *Listen to all students.* Avoid ending a discussion with the first correct answer. As you make nonevaluative responses, you will find many children repeating the same idea. Were they just copying a known leader? Perhaps, but more likely they were busy thinking and did not even hear what had already been said by those who were a bit faster. If ten hands go up, ten children may have been doing good thinking. Don't forget the suggestion made earlier to call on less secure students early in a discussion so that the most obvious ideas are not taken by the more aggressive students.
- *Provide special successes for special children.* Not all children will develop the same problem-solving abilities, but all have abilities and can contribute. This must be something you truly believe because it is difficult to fake. One way to provide success for students who are slower or not as strong is to involve them in groups with strong and supportive children. In group settings, all children can be made to feel the success of the group work.

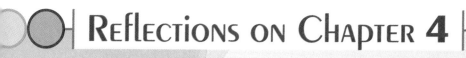

REFLECTIONS ON CHAPTER 4

Writing to Learn

1. Explain the difference between teaching that begins where the teacher is and teaching that begins where the students are.
2. Discuss each of the benefits of teaching with problems.
3. Describe what is meant by tasks or problems that can be used for teaching mathematics. Be sure to include the three important features that are required to make this method effective.
4. What is the teacher's purpose or agenda in each of the three parts of a lesson—before, during, and after?
5. Describe the kinds of actions or things that a teacher should be doing in each of the three parts of a lesson. (Note that not all of these would be done in every lesson.) Which actions should you use almost all of the time?
6. Select an activity from any chapter in Section 2 of this text. How can the activity be used as a problem or task for the purpose of instruction as described in this chapter? If you were using this activity in the classroom, what specifically would you do during the "before" section of the lesson?
7. The first of the four suggestions for teaching through problem solving is to predict rather than hope. Explain what this means. How should good predictions affect your lesson planning?
8. Goals for the development of good problem solving were separated under the headings of "Strategies and Processes," "Metacognition," and "Disposition." Describe what is meant by each of these types of goals.
9. For each category of problem-solving goals, describe how a teacher can help students develop these goals in the before, during, and after phases of a lesson.

For Discussion and Exploration

1. If you were to begin teaching a class of students who had never experienced learning mathematics in a problem-solving environment, they are likely not to know how to work at solving problems, work with a partner, or engage in a classroom discussion. How would you begin to deal with these and similar challenges so that students would develop an understanding of their role in such a classroom?
2. Find a traditional basal textbook for any grade level. Look through a chapter, and find at least one lesson that you could convert to a problem-solving lesson without drastically altering the lesson as it was written. Is there any content in the chapter, other than conventions, that you do not feel you could teach through problem solving?
3. Examine a lesson from one of the reform curricula. (See Chapter 1 for a list.) How does the general structure of the lesson you selected compare to the problem-solving approach to teaching described in this chapter?

Recommendations for Further Reading

Highly Recommended

Burns, M. (1996). *50 problem-solving lessons: Grades 1–6.* Sausalito, CA: Math Solutions Publications.

The 50 lessons are all in the spirit of teaching through problem solving. The content strands include number, geometry, mea-surement, statistics, probability, patterns and functions, algebra, and logic. Each is described in a few pages with ample examples of children's work, all in the spirit of this master teacher of mathematics. Not only a good resource but also a good model.

Hiebert, J., Carpenter, T. P., Fennema, E., Fuson, K., Wearne, D., Murray, H., Olivier, A., & Human, P. (1997). *Making sense: Teaching and learning mathematics with understanding.* Portsmouth, NH: Heinemann.

The authors of this highly readable and significant book are each connected to one of four problem-based, long-term research projects. They make one of the best cases currently in print for developing mathematics via problem-based tasks. After discussing features of the general approach and the supporting theory, a vignette from each project is discussed. *Making Sense* and the companion article by the same authors in the *Educational Researcher* (see the following list of readings) have guided the revision of Chapter 4 of this book.

Lester, F. K., & Charles, R. I. (Eds.) (in press). *Teaching mathematics through problem solving: Pre-K to 6.* Reston, VA: National Council of Teachers of Mathematics.

This is an important and valuable publication from the council. Topics include "Mathematics as Sense Making," "Designing and Selecting Tasks," "How to Problematize the Curriculum," "Listening to Children," "Problem Solving with Technology," and "Problem Posing." The 17 chapters, all written by top authors in the field, provide an in-depth examination of using a problem-based approach to teaching for understanding. The voices of teachers are also included in short reflections by those who have worked to make teaching through problem solving a success in their classrooms. (There is also a grade 6–12 volume.)

Reinhart, S. C. (2000). Never say anything a kid can say! *Mathematics Teaching in the Middle School, 5,* 478–483.

The author is an experienced middle school teacher who questioned his own "masterpiece" lessons after realizing that his students were often confused. The article is the result of the realization that he was doing the talking and explaining, and that was causing the confusion. Reinhart's suggestions for questioning techniques and involving students are superb!

Rowan, T. E., & Bourne, B. (1994). *Thinking like mathematicians: Putting the K–4 Standards into practice.* Portsmouth, NH: Heinemann.

A must read for any teacher in the K–5 range. Rowan and Bourne describe in 132 pages the spirit of the *Standards* as carried out by teachers in urban, multiethnic Montgomery County, Maryland, schools. The schools described were part of a project funded by the National Science Foundation to explore the effectiveness of a constructivist approach (see Campbell, P. F., 1996). The book contains practical suggestions and inspiring stories from teachers and from the classroom.

Thiessen, D., Matthias, M., & Smith, J. (1998). *The wonderful world of mathematics: A critically annotated list of children's books in mathematics* (2nd ed.). Reston, VA: National Council of Teachers of Mathematics.

In this second edition, Thiessen, Matthias, and Smith have compiled over 300 pages of children's books, each with annotation, rating, and suggested grade span. The book is structured by content area. A valuable resource for planning lessons around literature.

Other Suggestions

Ameis, J. A. (2001). Stories invite children to solve mathematical problems. *Teaching Children Mathematics, 8,* 260–264.

Arvold, B., Turner, P., & Cooney, T. J. (1996). Analyzing teaching and learning: The art of listening. *Mathematics Teacher, 89,* 326–329.

Ball, D. L. (1996). Connecting to mathematics as part of learning to teach. In D. Schifter (Ed.), *What's happening in math class? Reconstructing professional identities* (Vol. 2) (pp. 36–45). New York: Teachers College Press.

Brown, S. L., & Walter, M. I. (1990). *The art of problem posing,* 2nd ed. Mahwah, NJ: Lawrence Erlbaum.

Campbell, P. F. (1996). Empowering children and teacher in the elementary mathematics classrooms of urban schools. *Urban Education, 30,* 449–475.

Corwin, R. B. (1996). *Talking mathematics: Supporting children's voices.* Portsmouth, NH: Heinemann.

Dacey, L. S., & Eston, R. (1999). *Growing mathematical ideas in kindergarten.* Sausalito, CA: Math Solutions Publications.

English, L. D., Cudmore, D., & Tilley, D. (1998). Problem posing and critiquing: How it can happen in your classroom. *Mathematics Teaching in the Middle School, 4,* 124–129.

Heinz, K., Kinzel, M., Simon, M. A., & Tzur, R. (2000). Moving students through steps of mathematical knowing: An account of the practice of an elementary mathematics teacher in transition. *Journal of Mathematical Behavior, 19,* 64–83.

Henningsen, M., & Stein, M. K. (1997). Mathematical tasks and student cognition: Classroom-based factors that support and inhibit high-level mathematical thinking and reasoning. *Journal for Research in Mathematics Education, 28,* 524–549.

Hiebert, J., Carpenter, T. P., Fennema, E., Fuson, K., Human, P., Murray, H., Olivier, A., & Wearne, D. (1996). Problem solving as a basis for reform in curriculum and instruction: The case of mathematics. *Educational Researcher, 25* (May), 12–21.

Krech, B. (1998). *Special delivery: Putting math to work.* Orangeburg, NY: Cuisenaire.

Lappan, G., & Briars, D. (1995). How should mathematics be taught? In I. M. Carl (Ed.), *Seventy-five years of progress: Prospects for school mathematics* (pp. 115–156) Reston, VA: National Council of Teachers of Mathematics.

Lubienski, S. T. (1999). Problem-centered mathematics teaching. *Mathematics Teaching in the Middle School, 5,* 250–255.

Ma, L. (1999). *Knowing and teaching elementary mathematics: Teachers' understanding of fundamental mathematics in China and the United States.* Mahwah, NJ: Lawrence Erlbaum.

Manouchehri, A., & Enderson, M. C. (1999). Promoting mathematical discourse: Learning from classroom examples. *Mathematics Teaching in the Middle School, 4,* 216–222.

Mokros, J., Russell, S. J., & Economopoulos, K. (1995). *Beyond arithmetic: Changing mathematics in the elementary classroom.* White Plains, NY: Cuisenaire–Dale Seymour.

O'Connell, S. (2000). *Introduction to problem solving: Strategies for the elementary classroom.* Portsmouth, NH: Heinemann.

Romagnano, L. (1994). *Wrestling with change: The dilemmas of teaching real mathematics.* Portsmouth, NH: Heinemann.

Rowan, T. E., & Robles, J. (1998). Using questions to help children build mathematical power. *Teaching Children Mathematics, 4,* 504–509.

Sawada, D. (1997). Mathematics as reasoning—Episodes from Japan. *Mathematics Teaching in the Middle School, 2,* 416–421.

Sawada, D. (1999). Mathematics as problem solving: A Japanese way. *Teaching Children Mathematics, 6,* 54–58.

Schifter, D., & Fosnot, C. T. (1993). *Reconstructing mathematics education: Stories of teachers meeting the challenge of reform.* New York: Teachers College Press.

Sherin, M. G., Mendez, E. P., & Louis, D. A. (2000). Talking about math talk. In M. J. Burke (Ed.), *Learning mathematics for a new century* (pp. 188–196). Reston, VA: National Council of Teachers of Mathematics.

Silver, E. A., & Smith, M. S. (1996). Building discourse communities in mathematics classrooms: A worthwhile but challenging journey. In P. C. Elliott (Ed.), *Communication in mathematics, K–12 and beyond* (pp. 20–28). Reston, VA: National Council of Teachers of Mathematics.

Smith, M. S., & Stein, M. K. (1998). Selecting and creating mathematical tasks: From research to practice. *Mathematics Teaching in the Middle School, 3,* 344–350.

Stein, M. K., & Smith, M. S. (1998). Mathematical tasks as a framework for reflection: From research to practice. *Mathematics Teaching in the Middle School, 3,* 268–275.

Stigler, J. W., & Hiebert, J. (1999). *The teaching gap: Best ideas from the world's teachers for improving education in the classroom.* New York: Free Press.

Tsuruda, G. (1994). *Putting it together: Middle school math in transition.* Portsmouth, NH: Heinemann.

Wood, T. (1999). Creating a context for argument in mathematics class. *Journal for Research in Mathematics Education, 30,* 171–191.

5

Building Assessment into Instruction

Assessment should be the servant of teaching and learning. Without information about their students' skills, understanding, and individual approaches to mathematics, teachers have nothing to guide their work.

Mokros, Russell, and Economopoulos (1995, p. 84)

What ideas about assessment come to mind from your personal experiences? Tests? Pop quizzes? Grades? Studying? Anxiety? Getting the correct answers? All of these are typical. Now suppose that you are told that assessment in the classroom should be designed to help students learn and to help teachers teach. How can assessment do those things?

Blurring the Line Between Instruction and Assessment

The Assessment Principle in *Principles and Standards* stresses two main ideas: (1) Assessment should enhance students' learning, and (2) assessment is a valuable tool for making instructional decisions. If your concept of assessment is found primarily in weekly quizzes, chapter-end tests, the nine-week test, or the standardized test that is used in your state or province, then it is time to rethink your ideas about assessment.

What Is Assessment?

The term *assessment* is defined in the *Assessment Standards* as "the process of gathering evidence about a student's knowledge of, ability to use, and disposition toward mathematics and of making inferences from that evidence for a variety of

purposes" (NCTM, 1995, p. 3). It is important to note that "gathering evidence" is not the same as giving a test or quiz. Assessment can and should happen every day as an integral part of instruction. If you restrict your view of assessment to tests and quizzes, you will miss seeing how assessment can help students grow and inform instruction.

Figure 5.1 from the *Assessment Standards* depicts four stages of assessment. Each involves a very deliberate process that should be incorporated into both daily planning and instructional activities. Assessments must be planned along with the goals for your lessons and, thus, occur in nearly every lesson. The evidence must be interpreted daily in order that good decisions can be made in planning for tomorrow's lesson as the cycle continues.

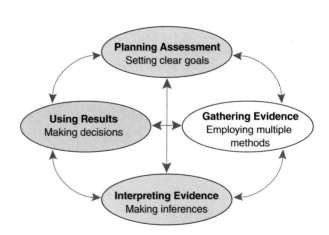

FIGURE 5.1 Assessment involves four stages that usually operate in a cycle.

Source: Reprinted with permission from *Principles and Standards for School Mathematics.* Copyright ©2000 by the National Council of Teachers of Mathematics. All rights reserved.

The Assessment Standards

Traditional testing has focused on what students *do not know* (how many wrong answers). In the 1989 *Curriculum Standards* the authors called for a shift toward assessing what students *do know* (what ideas they bring to a task, how they reason, what processes they use). This shift to finding out more about students is also a theme of the *Assessment Standards for School Mathematics* published by NCTM in 1995. The *Assessment Standards* contains six standards for assessment that are deserving of some reflection.

1. The Mathematics Standard

Assessment should reflect the mathematics that all students need to know and be able to do. (p. 11)

2. The Learning Standard

Assessment should enhance mathematics learning. (p. 13)

3. The Equity Standard

Assessment should promote equity. (p. 15)

4. The Openness Standard

Assessment should be an open process. (p. 17)

5. The Inferences Standard

Assessment should promote valid inferences about mathematics learning. (p. 19)

6. The Coherence Standard

Assessment should be a coherent process. (p. 21)

In nearly every school district, state or local standards will define in measurable terms the mathematical content students are to master. The danger is to focus on the tests and low-level skills. The Mathematics Standard indicates that assessment should reflect the mathematics that students *should* know, not just skills found on tests.

The Learning Standard speaks most clearly to the notion that assessment must be an integral part of instruction and not an interruption or a singular event at the end. Regular classroom instruction guides students' learning by informing them about what is important and what is valued. Assessment also aids students by aiding teachers in the design of instruction. Without listening thoughtfully to your students (assessing) on a daily basis, tomorrow's lesson can be based only on a guess at their needs.

The Equity Standard mandates that assessments respect the unique qualities, experiences, and expertise of every student. The Equity Principle in *Principles and Standards* echoes this standard when it calls for high expectations for all students while recognizing their individual needs.

The Openness Standard reminds us that students need to know what is expected of them and how they can demonstrate what they know. As we shift attention from answers to processes, we are telling students that their approach is valued and their reasoning will be listened to. Without this focus, students will learn that there is little more to mathematics than getting the answers by following rules.

In a system of ongoing, integrated assessment, the conclusions we draw are not as objective as when we simply count the number wrong and compute a percentage. The Inferences Standard requires that teachers reflect seriously and honestly on what students are revealing about what they know.

Finally, the Coherence Standard reminds us that our assessment techniques must reflect both the objectives of instruction as well as the methods of instruction. Students should be evaluated using the same methods, materials, and approaches they used for instruction. This will also ensure that assessments are a reflection of the content you want students to learn.

Purposes of Assessment

Even a cursory glance at the six assessment standards suggests a complete integration of assessment and instruction. The *Assessment Standards* outlines four specific purposes of assessment as depicted in Figure 5.2. With each purpose, the rectangle to the outside indicates a corresponding result.

Monitoring Student Progress

Assessment should provide both teacher and students with ongoing feedback concerning progress toward those goals. Assessment during instruction should inform each individual student and the teacher about growth toward mathematical power and problem-solving ability, not just mastery of procedural skills.

Making Instructional Decisions

Teachers planning tasks each day to develop student understanding must have daily information about how students are thinking and what ideas they are using and developing. Daily problem solving and discussion provide a much richer and more useful array of data than can ever be gathered from a chapter test. It comes at a time when you can formulate plans to help students develop ideas rather than remediate after the fact.

Evaluating Student Achievement

Evaluation is "the process of determining the worth of, or assigning a value to, something on the basis of careful examination and judgment" (NCTM, 1995, p. 3). Evaluation involves a teacher's judgment. It may include test data but should take into account a wide variety of sources and types of information gathered during the course of instruction. Most important, evaluation should reflect performance crite-

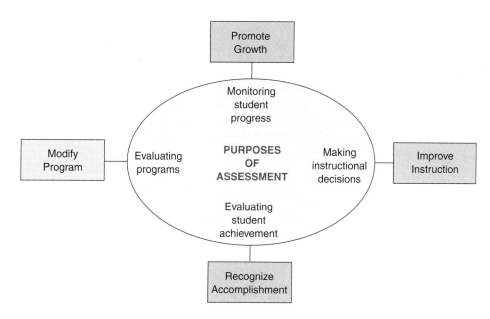

FIGURE 5.2 Four purposes of assessment and their results.
Source: Adapted from NCTM (1995, p. 25). Used with permission.

ria about what students know and understand; it should not be used to compare one student with another.

Evaluating Programs

Assessment data should be used as one component in answering the question "How well did this program work to achieve my goals?" In this context, *program* refers to any organized unit of study and need not be restricted to decisions such as which textbook should be adopted. For the classroom teacher, program includes such things as self-designed units of instruction or a chapter from a resource book or text.

What Should Be Assessed?

The broader view of assessment promoted here and by NCTM requires that appropriate assessment reflect the full range of mathematics: concepts and procedures, mathematical processes, and even students' disposition to mathematics.

Concepts and Procedures

A good assessment strategy will provide opportunity for students to demonstrate how they themselves understand the concepts under discussion. The traditional test generally targets only one way to know an idea, that determined by the test designer. If you collect information from students as they complete an activity, while it is being discussed, as results are justified—in short, while students are doing mathematics—you will gain information that provides insight into the nature of the students' understanding of that idea.

Procedural knowledge, including skill proficiency, should be included, although it should not be considered as more important than conceptual understanding. If a student can compute with fractions yet has no idea of why he needs a common denominator for addition but not for multiplication, then the rules that have been "mastered" are poorly connected to meaning. This would indicate only the tenuous presence of a skill. Whereas a routine skill can easily be checked with a traditional test, the desired conceptual connections require assessment of a different nature.

Mathematical Processes

Guidelines for defining the specifics of mathematical power can be found in the five process standards of *Principles and Standards*. Now, it is not reasonable to try to assess all of these processes, and certainly not every day. For each grade band, *Principles and Standards* describes what the process standards might look like at that level. Use these descriptions to craft statements about doing mathematics that your students can understand. Here are a few examples, but you should write your own or use those provided by your school system.

Problem Solving

- Works at understanding a problem before beginning work.
- Uses drawings, graphs, and physical models to help solve problems.
- Has and uses appropriate strategies for solving problems.
- Assesses the validity of answers.

Reasoning

- Justifies solution methods and results.
- Makes conjectures based on reasoning.
- Observes and uses patterns in mathematics.

Communication

- Explains ideas in writing.
- Communicates ideas clearly in class discussions.

These statements should be discussed with your students to help clarify them and to let students know that these are values to you. Periodically, use the statements to rate students' mathematical processes based on their individual work, group work, and participation in class discussions. If you use portfolios, work developed and collected over time, process assessment should almost certainly be considered. Processes must also be used in your grading or evaluation scheme, or students will not take them seriously.

Disposition

It is important to make occasional efforts to collect data on students' confidence and beliefs in their own mathematical abilities as well as their likes and dislikes about mathematics. This information is most easily obtained with self-reported checklists and journal writing. Information on perseverance and willingness to attempt problems is available to you every day in a problem-solving approach.

NCTM Standards "Assessment should not merely be done to students; rather, it should also be done for students" (p. 22). "Assessment should become a routine part of the ongoing classroom activity rather than an interruption" (p. 23). These thoughts lie at the heart of a well-thought-out assessment program in your classroom.

APPROPRIATE ASSESSMENT

An *appropriate assessment task* refers to a task or problem that allows students to demonstrate what they know. Both you and your students must see it as an integral part of the learning process.

If you take a problem-based approach to instruction but your assessments focus on recall and closed response items, you will not be successful. Recall and skill assessments tell students that what is valued is getting answers. They will not be willing to solve problems or engage in class discussions but rather will insist that you simply "show them how to get the answers."

The reverse situation—to engage in "traditional," teacher-directed instruction with open-ended, problem-solving tasks for assessment—asks students to demonstrate mathematical thinking and communication skills without ever having learned or experienced these important processes. Teachers who have tried various "alternative assessments" without significantly altering their instruction find them difficult or impossible for their students, and all involved become frustrated.

Appropriate Assessment Tasks

Recall from Chapter 4 that a problem was any task or activity for which the students have no prescribed or memorized rules or specific correct solution method. The same definition should be used for assessment tasks. Perhaps you have heard about *performance assessment tasks* or *alternative assessments*. These terms seem to refer to tasks that are in some way different from those used in instruction. They should not be different! An assessment task should be a performance task as should problem-based tasks for learning.

 STOP Recall that a problem for learning must (1) begin where the students are, (2) be problematic due to the mathematics we want students to learn, and (3) require justifications and explanations for answers and methods. Reflect on these three criteria for problem-based tasks. Do you think these same three task qualities should apply to assessments?

Good tasks should permit every student in the class, regardless of mathematical prowess, to demonstrate some knowledge, skill, or understanding. Lower-ability students should be encouraged to use the ideas they do possess to work on a problem even if these are not the same skills or strategies used by others in the room.

Often what are promoted as "alternative assessments" focus on the real-world or authentic contexts of the problems. Although contextual situations are often nice, how a student completes a task and justifies the solution should inform us about his or her understanding of the mathematics. That agenda should not be overshadowed because of difficulties that may arise from context.

The justifications for results, even those given orally, will almost certainly provide more information than the answers alone. Perhaps no better method exists for getting at student understanding.

There may be times when you do decide to use a task as a summative evaluation and, therefore, choose not to interact with students as they are working. In these instances, you will have already provided students with an opportunity to access and develop the content that is essential to the task. Using a task as a summative assessment simply changes the purpose and intent of the task. Taken out of this evaluative context, the task should still look exactly like a learning task.

Examples of Assessment Tasks

Each of the following tasks provides ample opportunity for students to learn. At the same time, it provides data for the teacher to use in assessment. Notice that these are not elaborate tasks and yet along with a discussion, each could engage students for most of a period. As you read each task, think about the following questions to decide what specific information might be assessed:

- What is the essential conceptual content in the task?
- What problem-solving processes might be observed?
- What opportunity might there be to observe communication skills?
- What about reasoning (if-then thinking)?

- Are there opportunities for students to connect the content with other content either in or outside of mathematics?
- Is the task accessible to a range of students in some way?

SHARES (GRADES K–3)

Leila has 6 gumdrops, Darlene has 2, and Melissa has 4. They want to share them equally. How will they do it? Draw a picture to help explain your answer.

At second or third grade, the numbers in Shares would probably be larger. What would happen if the problem were about cookies and the total number of cookies were 14?

SUBTRACTION (GRADES 1–2)

If you did not know the answer to 12 − 7, what are some ways you could find the answer?

HOW MUCH? (GRADES 1–2)

Gustavo has saved $15 to buy a game that he wants. The game costs $23. How much money does Gustavo still need?

These two problems are similar in that they involve subtraction and allow the teacher to see what strategies a student might use. In the second problem, the context increases the chances that students will use an "add-on" approach (15 and how much more to make 23?). Without context, you get a better chance to see what strategies students are using most regularly.

BROKEN KEYS (GRADES 2–4)

If the ⑤ key on your calculator were broken, how could you do this problem: 458 + 548 + 354? Is there more than one way? Which way do you like the best? Why?

Broken Keys is a good example of a task with many solutions. As students are working, you will be able to assess how easily students arrive at different approaches.

THE WHOLE SET (GRADES 3–5)

Mary counted 15 cupcakes left from the whole batch that Mother made for the picnic. "We've already eaten two-fifths," she noted. How many cupcakes did Mother bake?

This last problem could easily have been posed without any context. What is the value of context in tasks such as these?

In the following task, students are asked to judge the performance of other students. Analysis of student performance is a good way to create tasks.

DECIMALS (GRADES 4–6)

Alan tried to make a decimal number as close to 50 as he could using the digits 1, 4, 5, and 9. He arranged them in this order: 51.49. Jerry thinks he can arrange the same digits to get a number that is even closer to 50. Do you agree or disagree? Explain.

MENTAL MATH (GRADES 4–8)

Explain two different ways to multiply 4×276 in your head. Which way is easier to use? Would you use a different way to multiply 5×98? Explain why you would use the same or different methods.

Mental computation tasks should be done frequently at all grade levels beginning around grade 2. Other students pick up the methods that students share. The explanations also offer a lot of information about students' concepts and the types of strategies that they have already acquired. This information can be recorded with a variety of simple methods over time.

TWO TRIANGLES (GRADES 4–8)

Tell everything you can about these two triangles.

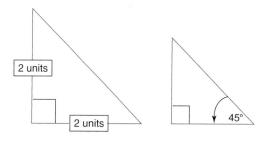

This task is a good example of a very open-ended assessment. Consider how much more valuable this task is than asking for the angle measure in the left-hand triangle.

ALGEBRA: GRAPHING (GRADES 7–8)

Does the graph of $y = x^2$ ever intersect the graph of $y = x^2 + 2$? What are some ways that you could test your idea?

Even with a graphing calculator, to prove that these two graphs will not intersect requires reasoning and an understanding of how graphs are related to equations and tables.

More Thoughts About Assessment Tasks

In some instances, the real value of the task or what can be learned about students will come only in the discussion that follows. For others, the information will be in the written report. In many of Marilyn Burns's books, you will see the phrase "We think the answer is . . . We think this because . . . ." Students must develop the habit of adding and listening to justifications. If explanations are not a regular practice in your room, do not expect students to offer good explanations in assessments, either written or oral.

Many activities have no written component and no "answer" or result. For example, students may be playing a game in which dice or dominoes are being used. A teacher who sits in on the game will see great differences in how children use numbers. Some will count every dot on the card or domino. Others will use a counting-on strategy. Some will recognize certain patterns without counting. Others may be unsure if 13 beats 11. This information significantly differentiates students relative to their understanding of number concepts. Data gathered from listening to a pair of children work on a simple activity or an extended project provide significantly greater insight into students' thinking than almost any written test we could devise. Data from student conversations and observations of student behavior can be recorded and used for the same purposes that written data can, including evaluation and grading. Especially in the case of grading, it is important to keep dated written notes that can be referred to later.

Much of the assessment literature has placed a significant value on situational problems or realistic problems and open-ended problems. These are often referred to as *authentic assessments*. There is no doubt that such problems have an important place in the mathematics classroom. But neither open-endedness nor real-world contexts are necessary for students to be meaningfully engaged in constructing mathematics. An open-ended, very realistic problem can be interesting and engaging and be mathematically trivial. For example, tasks involving spending money from a fast-food menu or a catalog are rarely more than glorified addition exercises. *Keep your focus on the mathematics.* The inclusion of real connections and open-ended tasks is possible without sacrificing the mathematics.

RUBRICS AND PERFORMANCE INDICATORS

Appropriate assessment tasks cannot be evaluated by simply counting correct answers. These tasks yield an enormous amount of information from students in both oral and written form. We need to find ways to manage this information and make it useful for the various purposes of assessment. One very useful tool is a rubric.

A *rubric* is a framework that can be designed or adapted by the teacher for a particular group of students or a particu-

lar mathematical task (Kulm, 1994). A rubric consists of a scale of three to six points that is used as a rating of performance rather than a count of how many items are correct or incorrect. The rating is applied by examining total performance on a task as opposed to counting the number of items correct.

Note that a rubric is a scale to judge performance on a single task, not a series of exercises.

Simple Rubrics

The following simple four-point rubric was developed by the New Standards Project and is used in the Pittsburgh Public School System:

4   Excellent: Full Accomplishment

3   Proficient: Substantial Accomplishment

2   Marginal: Partial Accomplishment

1   Unsatisfactory: Little Accomplishment

This simple rubric allows a teacher to rate performances using a double-sort technique as illustrated in Figure 5.3. The broad categories of the first sort are relatively easy to discern. The scale then allows you to separate each category into two levels as shown. Some teachers use a 4+ rating to note truly exceptional performance. A rating of 0 is given for no response or effort or for responses that are completely off task.

The advantage of the four-point scale is the relatively easy double sort that can be made. Others prefer a three-point rubric such as the following example:

3   Above and beyond—uses exemplary methods, shows creativity, goes beyond the requirements of the problem

2   On target—completes the task with no more than minor errors, uses expected approaches

1   Not there yet—makes significant errors or omissions, uses inappropriate approaches

These relatively simple scales are *general* rubrics. They label general categories of performance but do not define the specific criteria for a particular task. For any given task or process, it is usually helpful to create performance indicators for each level.

Performance Indicators

Performance indicators are task-specific statements that describe what performance looks like at each level of the rubric and in so doing establish criteria for acceptable performance (Ann Arbor Public Schools, 1993).

A rubric and its performance indicators should focus you and your students on your goals and away from the self-limiting question "How many can you miss and still get an A?" Like athletes who continually strive for better performances rather than "good enough," students should always see the possibility to excel. When you take into account the total per-

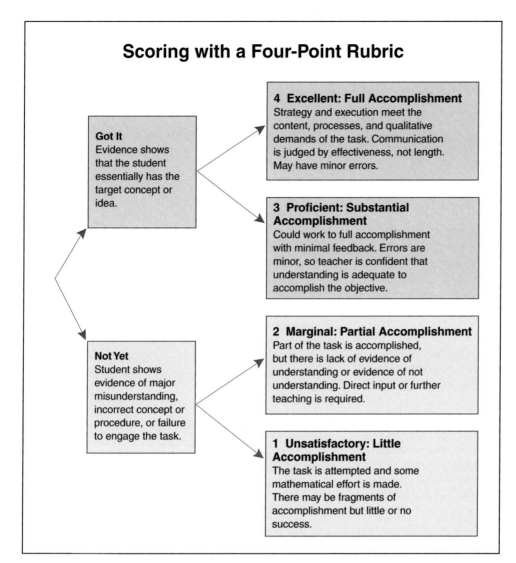

Scoring with a Four-Point Rubric

Got It
Evidence shows that the student essentially has the target concept or idea.

4 Excellent: Full Accomplishment
Strategy and execution meet the content, processes, and qualitative demands of the task. Communication is judged by effectiveness, not length. May have minor errors.

3 Proficient: Substantial Accomplishment
Could work to full accomplishment with minimal feedback. Errors are minor, so teacher is confident that understanding is adequate to accomplish the objective.

Not Yet
Student shows evidence of major misunderstanding, incorrect concept or procedure, or failure to engage the task.

2 Marginal: Partial Accomplishment
Part of the task is accomplished, but there is lack of evidence of understanding or evidence of not understanding. Direct input or further teaching is required.

1 Unsatisfactory: Little Accomplishment
The task is attempted and some mathematical effort is made. There may be fragments of accomplishment but little or no success.

FIGURE 5.3 With a four-point rubric, performances are first sorted into two categories. Each performance is then considered again and assigned to a point on the scale.

formance (processes, answers, justifications, extension, and so on), it is always possible to "go beyond."

What performance at different levels of your rubric will or should look like may be difficult to predict. Much depends on your experience with children at that grade level, your past experiences with students working on the same task, and your insights about the task itself and the ideas that it embodies or that children may use as they work on it.

If possible, it is good to write out indicators of "proficient" or "on target" performances before you use the task in class. This is an excellent self-check to be sure that the task is likely to accomplish the purpose you selected it for in the first place. Think about your process goals as well as your content goals. Think about how children are likely to approach the activity.

Remember that rubrics are applied to performance on a single task, although the task may have multiple components. If you find yourself writing performance indicators in terms of number of correct responses, you are most likely looking at drill exercises and not tasks for which a rubric is appropriate.

Consider the fraction problem titled "The Whole Set" on **STOP** page 63. Assume you are teaching fourth grade and wish to write performance indicators that you can share with your students. What would you use for indicators for level-3 and level-4 performances? Start with a level-3 performance, and then think about level 4. Try this before reading further.

Determining performance indicators is always a subjective process. Work from the ideas in the four-point rubric (Figure 5.3). Here is one possible set of indicators for "The Whole Set" task:

3 Determines the correct answer or uses an approach that would give a correct answer if not for minor errors. Reasons are either missing or incorrect. A correct result for the number eaten but not the total baked is also a level-3 performance.

4 Determines the total number baked and uses words and pictures to explain and justify the result and how it was obtained.

Indicators such as these can be shared ahead of time with students. Sharing indicators before working on a task clearly conveys what is valued. If you show students the indicators when you return papers, they can include the correct answers and some examples of drawings. This will help students understand how they may have done better. Often it is useful to show work from classmates (anonymously) or from a prior class. Students need to see models of what a top performance looks like.

What about level-1 and level-2 performances? Here are suggestions for the same task:

2 Uses some aspect of fractions appropriately (e.g., divides the 15 into 5 groups instead of 3) but fails to illustrate an understanding of how to determine the whole. The meanings of numerator and denominator are incorrect or confused.

1 Shows some effort but little or no understanding of a fractional part relative to the whole.

It does not seem necessary to share indicators for level-1 and level-2 level performances unless students or parents request further explanation. However, you often will be aided in your work if you articulate the differences between these performances.

Unexpected methods and solutions happen. Don't box students into demonstrating their understanding only as you thought or hoped they would when there is evidence that they are accomplishing your objectives in different ways.

Even if you have not written a performance indicator ahead of time, the double-sorting strategy described earlier (two categories, each then separated into two piles) is a useful approach to help you identify on-target performance. There will almost always be differences across your class, although you should make no attempt to have equal piles, and some categories may even have no students in them.

When you have finished your sorting process, use the results to write indicators for the task. Keep the descriptions as general as possible. These indicators can then be shared with students when you return the papers and kept in a file with the task for future use.

Student Involvement with Rubrics

In the beginning of the year, discuss your general rubric with the class. Post it prominently. Many teachers use the same rubric for all subjects; others prefer to use a special rubric for mathematics. In your discussion, let students know that as they do activities and solve problems in class, you will look at their work and listen to their explanations and provide them with feedback in terms of the rubric, rather than as a letter grade or a percentage.

When students start to understand what the rubric really means, begin to discuss performance on tasks in terms of the general rubric. You might have students rate their own work according to the general rubric and explain their reasons for

the rating. Older students can do this in written form, and you can respond in writing. For all students, you can have class discussions about a task that has been done and what might constitute good and exceptional performance.

More Examples of Rubrics

The four-point scale in Figure 5.3 is an example of a *holistic scale,* a single scale used to rate a complete task as a whole while possibly covering many subtopics and agendas. One rating on the scale summarizes the full performance.

However, suppose that you want to provide feedback to students concerning several particular aspects of their work. You may be interested in separating out one or more of the following: procedural skill, conceptual understanding, problem-solving processes, communication skills, or reasoning. It is never reasonable to rate any given task for every one of these features, but you may want to focus on two or three. It is possible to add several dimensions to your scale or rubric. A scale that rates a performance separately on each of two or more traits is known as an *analytic scale.*

The analytic scale in Figure 5.4 has become popular as a means of focusing on different aspects of students' problem-

---

Analytic Scoring Scale

Understanding the Problem	0 – Complete misunderstanding of the problem
	3 – Part of the problem misunderstood or misinterpreted
	6 – Complete understanding of the problem
Planning a Solution	0 – No attempt, or totally inappropriate plan
	3 – Partially correct plan based on correct interpretation of part of the problem
	6 – Plan could lead to a correct solution if implemented properly
Getting an Answer	0 – No answer, or wrong answer based on an inappropriate plan
	1 – Copying error, computational error, or partial answer for a problem with multiple answers
	2 – Incorrect answer although this answer follows logically from an incorrect plan
	3 – Correct answer and correct label for the answer

FIGURE 5.4 An analytic scale for problem solving with differential weightings.

Source: Adapted from *How to Evaluate Progress in Problem Solving,* by R. I. Charles, F. K. Lester Jr., & P. O'Daffer, 1987, Reston, VA: National Council of Teachers of Mathematics, as presented in "Cooperative Problem Solving: But What About Grades?" by D. L. Kroll, J. O. Masingila, & S. T. Mau, 1992, *Arithmetic Teacher, 39*(6), p. 18. Reprinted by permission of the National Council of Teachers of Mathematics.

solving skills. Generally, this scale is used to rate written performance on a problem-solving task. An interesting feature of the scale is the differential weighting used. Using this scale, a score of 3, 3, 6 would mean something quite different from a score of 6, 6, 0, although both scores total 12 points. The point total becomes a holistic rating based on an analytic process.

Using Observation in Assessment

All teachers learn useful bits of information about their students every day. When the three-part lesson format suggested in Chapter 4 is used, the flow of data increases dramatically, especially in the during and after portions of lessons. If you have a systematic plan for gathering this information while observing and listening to students, at least two very valuable things occur. First, you will likely gather a lot more information. Information that may have gone unnoticed is suddenly visible and important. Second, observation data gathered systematically can be added to other data and used in planning lessons, providing feedback to students, conducting parent conferences, and determining grades.

Depending on what information you may be trying to gather, a single observation scheme may require several days to two weeks before it has been observed. Long-term goals can be observed over a full marking period. Shorter periods of observation will focus on a particular cluster of concepts or skills. Over longer periods, you can note growth in various aspects of mathematical power, such as particular problem-solving skills or communication skills. To use ob-

servation effectively as a means of gathering assessment data from performance tasks, you should take seriously the following maxim: *Do not attempt to observe every student in a single class period.*

No single observation recording format will serve all purposes. Further, formats and methods of gathering observation data are going to be influenced by your individual teaching style and habits. Observation methods also vary with the purposes for which they are used.

Anecdotal Notes

A simple system for recording observations is to write short notes either during or immediately after a lesson in a brief narrative style. One possibility is to have a card for each student. Some teachers keep the cards on a clipboard with each taped at the top edge (see Figure 5.5). Each card can then be accessed quickly. Another option is to select cards for about five students a day, focusing your observations on those five. On another day, different students are selected. The students selected may be members of one or two cooperative groups. An alternative to cards is the use of large peel-off file labels, possibly preprinted with student names on your computer. The label notes are then moved to a more permanent notebook page for each student.

An Observation Rubric

Another possibility is to use your three- or four-point general rubric on a reusable form as in Figure 5.6. Include space for content-specific descriptors and another space to jot down names of students. A quick note or comment may be amended

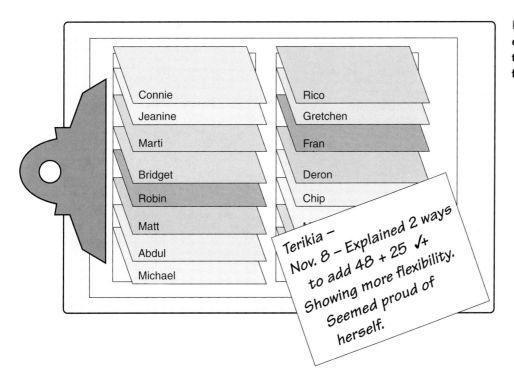

FIGURE 5.5 Cards for observation notes can be taped to a clipboard or folder for quick access.

Connie
Jeanine
Marti
Bridget
Robin
Matt
Abdul
Michael

Rico
Gretchen
Fran
Deron
Chip

Terikia –
Nov. 8 – Explained 2 ways
to add 48 + 25 ✓+
Showing more flexibility.
Seemed proud of
herself.

Making Whole Given Fraction Part	(3/17)
Super Clear understanding. Communicates concept in multiple representations. Shows evidence of using idea without prompting. *Fraction whole made from part in rods and in sets.* *Explains easily.*	Sally ✓ Latania ✓+ Greg Zal
On Target Understands or is developing well. Uses designated models. *Can make whole in either <u>rod</u> or <u>set</u> format (note). Hesitant. Needs prompt to get unit fraction.*	Lavant Tanisha Julie Lee George J.B. Maria John H.
Not Yet Some confusion or misunderstands. Only models idea with help. *Needs help to do activity. No confidence.*	John S. Mary

FIGURE 5.6 Record names in a rubric during an activity or for a single topic over several days.

FIGURE 5.7 A focused checklist and rubric can be printed for each student with the help of a computer.

NAME: *Sharon V.*	NOT YET	OK	SUPER	COMMENTS
FRACTIONS				
Understands numerator/denominator		✓		
Area models		✓		
Set models	✓			
Uses fractions in real contexts	✓			
Estimates fraction quantities		✓		*getting better*
PROBLEM SOLVING				
Understands problem before beginning work		✓		*this is good*
Is willing to take risks	✓			*problem area*
Justifies results				

to a name when appropriate. This method is especially useful for planning purposes.

Checklists or Forms for Individuals

To cut down on writing and to help focus your attention, a small form with several specific processes or content areas of interest can be devised and duplicated for each student (see Figure 5.7). Some teachers have found methods of printing these on their computer, perhaps on sticky labels. Once a computer format is worked out, it is easy to change the items on the checklist without retyping all the student names. Regardless of the checklist form, a place for comments should be included.

Checklists for Full Classes

Another format involves listing all students in a class on a single page or not more than three pages (see Figure 5.8). Across the top of the page are specific things to look for. Pluses and minuses, checks, or codes corresponding to your general rubric can be entered in the grid. A space left for comments is useful. A full-class checklist is more likely to be used for long-term objectives. Topics that might be appropriate for this format include problem-solving processes, communication skills, and such skills as basic facts or estimation. Dating entries or noting specific activities observed is also helpful.

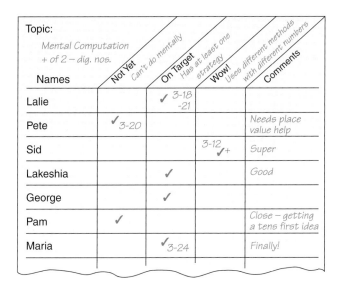

Topic: Mental Computation + of 2 – dig. nos. Names	Not Yet Can't do mentally	On Target Has at least one strategy	Wow! Uses different methods with different numbers	Comments
Lalie		✓ 3-18 -21		
Pete	✓ 3-20			Needs place value help
Sid			3-12 ✓+	Super
Lakeshia		✓		Good
George		✓		
Pam	✓			Close – getting a tens first idea
Maria		✓ 3-24		Finally!

FIGURE 5.8 **A full-class observation checklist can be used for longer-term objectives or for several days to cover a short-term objective.**

Writing and Journals

We have been emphasizing that instruction and assessment should overlap. No place is this more evident than in students' writing. Writing is both a learning and an assessment opportunity. Though some students initially have difficulty writing in mathematics, persistence pays off and students come to see writing as a natural part of the mathematics class.

The Value of Writing

When students write, they express their own ideas and use their own words and language. It is personal. In contrast, oral communication in the classroom is very public. Ideas "pop out" without editing or revision. Meaning is negotiated or elaborated on by the class as a whole. The individual reflective quality of writing as compared to classroom discourse is an important factor in considering the value of writing in mathematics.

> The process of writing requires gathering, organizing, and clarifying thoughts. It demands finding out what you know and don't know. It calls for thinking clearly. Similarly, doing mathematics depends on gathering, organizing, and clarifying thoughts, finding out what you know and don't know, and thinking clearly. Although the final representation of a mathematical pursuit looks very different from the final product of a writing effort, the mental journey is, at its base, the same—making sense of an idea and presenting it effectively. (Burns, 1995b, p. 3)

When students write, they are able to stop first and think. They can incorporate drawings and symbolism to help con-

vey their ideas. They can research an idea or look back on related work to help put ideas together. All of this is very powerful and deliberate reflective thinking.

As an assessment tool writing provides a unique window to students' thoughts and the way a student is thinking about an idea. Even a kindergarten child can express ideas in drawings or other markings on paper and begin to explain what he or she is thinking.

Oral communication, valuable as it may be, is gone at the end of the day. When you are able to sit down with students' writing, you can reflect on each person individually as well as on the class as a whole. You can use writing to target feedback and design special work for individual students. Written work helps you assess the progress you are making with the current unit. Finally, student writing is an excellent form of communication with parents during conferences. Writing shows students' thinking to their parents, telling them much more than any grade or test score.

When students write about their solutions to a task prior to the class discussion—that is, as part of the during portion of the lesson—the writing serves as a rehearsal for the discussion. Students who otherwise have difficulty thinking on their feet now have a script, so to speak, from which they can talk. This avoids having the few verbal students providing all of the input for the discussion. Call on these more reluctant talkers first so that their ideas are heard and valued. If they have written ahead of time, they will be ready to contribute.

Journals

Writing can, of course, be done on a single sheet of paper and turned in separately, but the use of a journal has real value. A journal may take the form of a composition booklet or, for K–1 children, folded writing paper stapled within a construction-paper cover. Binders and spiral notebooks are other options, but teachers find these bulky, and students are more likely to remove unwanted pages.

Journals are a way to make written communication a regular part of doing mathematics. Journals help you abandon the mistaken, counterproductive myth "If they write it, I must grade it." Journals are a place for students to write about such things as

- Their conceptual understandings and problem solving, including descriptions of ideas, solutions, and justifications of problems, graphs, charts, and observations
- Their questions concerning the current topic, an idea that they may need help with, or an area they don't quite understand
- Their feelings about aspects of mathematics, their confidence in their understanding, or their fears of being wrong

Even if you have students write in their journals nearly every day, be sure that these journals are special places for writing about mathematics. Drill, for example, should not be done in a journal. Lengthy projects done over several days should be separate from journals and given a special presentation. A performance task you plan to use primarily for evaluation purposes should probably not be in a journal. But the work for many of your performance tasks can and should go in the journal, communicating that the work is important and you do want to see it but you are not going to grade it.

To grade journal writing defeats its purpose. Graded journals would communicate that there is a specific "right" response you are seeking. It is essential, however, that you read and respond to journal writing. One form of response for a performance task would be to use the classroom's general rubric along with a helpful comment. This is another way to distinguish between rubrics and grades and still provide feedback.

On a regular basis, it is manageable to read and respond to about five journals a night. Following an especially interesting lesson, you might want to read the journal entry of every student in the class. Allow students to flag entries for which they want your special attention or response. If you do not read and respond to journals, students will quickly come to regard them as busywork and conclude that you do not value their efforts. Teachers whose students have learned to communicate honestly through their journals find them a key element in their assessment program, prized above all other sources of information to improve learning and instruction.

Writing Prompts and Ideas

Students should always have a clear, well-defined purpose for writing in their journals. They need to know exactly what to write about and who the audience is (you, an imaginary friend, a student in a lower grade, an adult, a Martian), and they should be given a definite time frame within which to write. Journal writing that is completely open-ended without goal or purpose will be a waste of time. Here are some suggestions for prompts to get you thinking; however, the possibilities are endless.

Concepts and Problem Solving

● "I think the answer is . . . I think this because. . . ." (The journal can be used to solve and explain any problem. Always be sure to include the problem. Some teachers duplicate the problem and have students tape it into the journal to save time and effort.)

● Write an explanation for other students (or for students in a lower grade) of why 4 × 7 is the same as 7 × 4 and why this works for 6 × 49 and 49 × 6.

● Explain to a student in grade X (or who was absent today) what you learned about decimals today.

● What about the work we did today was easy? What was hard? What do you still have questions about?

● If you got stuck today in solving a problem, where did you get stuck? Why do you think you had trouble there? If you did not get stuck, what idea helped you solve the problem?

● After you got the answer to today's problem, what did you do so that you were convinced your answer was correct? How sure are you that you got the correct answer?

● Write a story problem that goes with this picture (this graph, this diagram, this equation).

Affective Ideas

● "What I like most (or least) about mathematics is. . . ."

● Write a mathematics autobiography. Tell about your experiences in mathematics outside of school and how you feel about the subject.

● "Mathematics is like a . . . because. . . ."

● Write to an imaginary friend who is the same age as you, telling how you feel about what we did in mathematics this week.

Journals for Early Learners

If you are interested in working with K–1 children, the writing suggestions presented may have sounded discouraging because it is difficult for prewriters and beginning writers to express ideas like those suggested. There are specific techniques for journals in kindergarten and first grade that have been used successfully.

The Giant Journal

To begin the development of the writing-in-mathematics process, one kindergarten teacher uses a language experience approach. After an activity, she writes the heading "Giant Journal" and a topic or prompt on a large flipchart. Students respond to the prompt, and she writes their ideas, adding the contributor's name and even drawings when appropriate, as in Figure 5.9.

FIGURE 5.9   A journal in kindergarten may be a class product on a flipchart.

Drawings and Early Writing

All students can draw pictures of some sort to describe what they have done. Dots can represent counters or blocks. Shapes and special figures can be cut out from duplicated sheets and pasted onto the journal page.

It is important for the "writing" to be a record of something the student has just done and is comfortable with. Figure 5.10 shows problems solved in first and second grade. Do not be concerned about invented spellings to communicate ideas. Have students read their papers to you.

Brainstorming

Young children have difficulty translating what they say and think into written form. One way to help is to use discussion time to help children think about their journal entries. Record ideas on the board as they are contributed by students. For kindergartners and first graders, use very simple abbreviated versions of what they say. For children in grades 2 and 3, you may limit your recording to key phrases and special words. In this manner, the ideas that have been generated are now recorded

Grade 1
Read the problem. Think and use "stuff" to help you solve it.

There were 7 owls.
They found some mice in the woods to eat. Each owl got 5 mice.
How many mice did they find? How do you know?
Use pictures and words to show how you solved the problem.

Grade 2
The farmer saw five cows and four chickens. How many legs and tails in all did he see?

FIGURE 5.10 Journal entries of early-grades children.

for students to assemble into their own writing. When a student says, "I don't know what to write," have him tell you about his task or idea. Then have him write what he just told you.

Student Self-Assessment

Stenmark (1989) notes that "the capability and willingness to assess their own progress and learning is one of the greatest gifts students can develop. . . . Mathematical power comes with knowing how much we know and what to do to learn more" (p. 26).

In a self-assessment, students may tell you

- How well they think they understand a piece of content
- What they believe or how they feel about some aspect of mathematics, perhaps what you are covering right now

It is important to see that this is not your measure of their learning or disposition, but rather a record of how *they perceive* these things.

As you plan for a self-assessment, consider how you want the assessment to help you as a teacher. Tell your students why you are having them do this activity. Encourage them to be honest and candid. Though it may seem like fun to collect class information early in the year on a topic such as "Why I like mathematics," do not assign a self-assessment activity just to make yourself feel good about your students.

You can gather self-assessment data in several ways. A common method is to use some form of a questionnaire to which students respond. These can have open-ended questions, response choices (e.g., *seldom, sometimes, often; disagree, don't care, agree*), mind maps, drawings, and so on. Many such instruments appear in the literature, and many textbook publishers provide examples. Whenever you use a form or questionnaire that someone else has devised, be certain that it serves the purpose you intend. Often these forms are too long or include questions in which you have little interest. Modify them to suit your purposes. The fact that a form was professionally prepared or accompanies your text does not necessarily make it appropriate or useful to you.

An open-ended writing prompt such as was suggested for journals is another method of getting self-assessment data:

- How well do you think you understand the work we have been doing the last few days on fractions? If there is something that is causing you difficulty with fractions, please tell me what it is.
- Write one thing you liked and one thing you did not like about math class today (or this week).

You may find that a simple prompt can become familiar to students if you use it on a regular basis. For example, midway through a unit is a good time to listen to what students regard as things they know and do not know. As students learn that you will react in some way that is helpful to them, they will be more apt to provide you with candid, useful information.

Attitude Inventories

Students may find it difficult to write about attitudes and beliefs. An inventory where they can respond "yes," "maybe," or "no" to a series of statements is another approach. Encourage students to add comments under an item if they wish. Here are some items you could use to build such an inventory:

- I feel sure of myself when I get an answer to a problem.
- I sometimes just put down anything so I can get it over with.
- I like to work on really hard math problems.
- Math class makes me feel nervous.
- If I get stuck, I usually just quit or go to another problem.
- I am not as good in math as most of the other students in this class.
- Mathematics is my favorite subject.
- I do not like to work at problems that are hard to understand.
- Memorizing rules is the only way I know to learn mathematics.
- I will work a long time at a problem until I think I've solved it.

Another technique is to ask students to write a sentence at the end of any work they do in mathematics class saying how that activity made them feel. Young children can draw a face on each page to tell you about their feelings.

TESTS

Tests will always be a part of assessment and evaluation no matter how adept we become at blending assessment with instruction. However, a test need not be a collection of low-level skill exercises. Although simple tests of computational skills may have some role in your classroom, the use of such tests should be limited. Like all other forms of assessment, tests should reflect the goals of your instruction. Tests can be designed to find out what concepts students have and how their ideas are connected. Tests of procedural knowledge should go beyond just knowing how to perform an algorithm and should allow and require the student to demonstrate a conceptual basis for the process. The following examples will illustrate these ideas.

1. Write a multiplication problem that has an answer between the answers to these two problems:

$$\begin{array}{cc} 49 & 45 \\ \times\ 25 & \times\ 30 \end{array}$$

2. **a.** In this division exercise, what number tells how many tens were shared among the 6 sets?
   b. Instead of writing the remainder as "R 2," Elaine writes "$\frac{1}{3}$." Explain the difference between these two ways of handling the leftover part.

$$\begin{array}{cc} 49R2 & 49\frac{1}{3} \\ 6\overline{)296} & 6\overline{)296} \end{array}$$

3. On the grid, draw two figures with the same area but different perimeters. List the area and perimeter of each.
4. For each subtraction fact, write an addition fact that helps you think of the answer to the subtraction.

$$\begin{array}{cccc} 12 & 9 & 9 & 14 \\ -\ 3 & +\ 3 & -\ 4 & -\ 7 \\ \hline 9 & 12 & & \end{array}$$

5. Draw pictures of arrows to show why $^-3 + {^-4}$ is the same as $^-3 - {^+4}$.

If a test is well constructed, much more information can be found than simply the number of correct or incorrect answers. Here are some things to think about when constructing a test:

1. *Permit calculators all the time.* Except for tests of computational skills, the calculator allows students to focus on what you really want to test. It also communicates a positive attitude about calculator use to your students.
2. *Use manipulatives and drawings.* Students can use appropriate models to work on test questions when those same models have been used to develop concepts. (Note the use of drawings in Example 5 above.) Simple drawings can be used to represent counters, base-ten pieces, fraction pieces, and the like (see Figure 5.11). Be sure to provide examples in class of how to draw the models before you ask students to draw on a test.

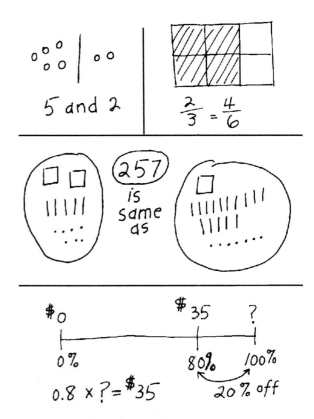

FIGURE 5.11 Students can use drawings to illustrate concepts on tests.

3. *Include opportunities for explanations.*
4. *Avoid always using "preanswered" tests.* These are tests in which questions have only one correct answer, whether it is a calculation, a multiple-choice, or a fill-in-the-blank question. Tests of this type tend to fragment what children have learned and hide most of what they know. Rather, construct tests that allow students the opportunity to show what they know.
5. *Assess affective factors on the test.* One idea is to have students rate their personal confidence level on each question as A (high), B (moderate), or C (low). Another idea is to have students draw a face showing how they feel about the question or the test in general. Ask students to complete a sentence that begins "I liked this test because . . . " or "I did not like this test because. . . ."

Dealing with High-Stakes Testing

In 2001, Congress passed the No Child Left Behind Act, which, among other things, mandates that every state test children in every grade beginning with grade 3. Testing is to begin no later than fall 2005. The method of testing and even the objectives to be tested are left up to the states. Most states are already testing students at some grade levels, and many districts test their students at every grade level.

Whatever the details of the testing program are in your particular state, these external tests (originating external to the classroom) impose significant pressures on school districts, which in turn put pressure on principals, who finally place pressures on teachers.

External testing that has consequences for students and teachers is typically referred to as "high-stakes testing." High stakes make the pressures of testing significant for both students (Will I pass? Will I have to go to summer school? Will my parents be upset?) and teachers (Will my class do as well as Mrs. Jones's next door? My scores have been below passing—I've got to get them up.). The pressures almost certainly have an effect on instruction.

Teaching State-Mandated Standards

In the context of accountability, the word *standard* is used differently than in the NCTM *Standards* documents. Whereas the standards discussed in *Principles and Standards* are broad statements applicable to 3-year grade bands, a state standard is generally a very specific objective or benchmark goal.

Teachers should be aware of the nature of the testing program for their state. If a norm-referenced test is used, the assumption is that the state standards will be reflected in the results even though not all standards are tested. Since norm-referenced tests are designed to spread performance rather than test all objectives, they are likely to include items not on the state standards list and omit many that are. It is always a

serious error for a teacher to "teach to the test," but this is especially true if the test is a norm-referenced exam.

Other states hire testing companies to design criterion-referenced tests, crafted to assess a specific list of objectives. The advantage for teachers is that the tests are supposed to reflect the objectives that they are under contract to teach. That still does not control for the difficulty of the test or the types of items included.

In 2000, the NCTM board of directors approved an official position statement on high-stakes testing.

> The National Council of Teachers of Mathematics believes that far-reaching and critical educational decisions should be made only on the basis of multiple measures. A well-conceived system of assessment and accountability must consist of a number of assessment components at various levels. (www.nctm.org/about/position_statements/highstakes.htm)

In the Rationale section, the council goes on to say that, "The movement toward high-stakes testing marks a major retreat from fairness, accuracy, and educational equity. When test use is inappropriate, especially in making high-stakes decisions about a child's future, it undermines the quality of education and equality of opportunity." You are encouraged to read the entire rationale and recommendations at the Web site. It offers a well-thought-out and reasoned perspective on this important issue in education.

Improving Performance on High-Stakes Tests

You will not be able to avoid the pressures of high-stakes testing. The question is, "How will you respond?"

Teaching to the Test

The advocates of high-stakes testing argue that teachers should simply teach the content that is in the standards and that, by so doing, students will do well on the tests. The difficulty with this argument is that typical state standards are not in the form of a curriculum. Rather, they are lists of objectives, usually stated in measurable (i.e., behavioral) terms. The result is that teachers work their way through a list of skills, often without attending to the underlying concepts that would connect one skill to another and make the skills meaningful. Students, especially those who have difficulty developing concepts on their own or with minimal assistance, begin to see mathematics as a collection of rules to be mastered. Inevitably, these rules become confused or forgotten. Teaching to the test, even if it means teaching to the required list of standards or objectives, is not in the best interest of students.

In many schools, especially where the scores have been consistently lower than acceptable, teachers are asked or required to give a series of practice tests. Those who advocate practice tests believe that teachers can use the test data to fill gaps in achievement and that the tests will prepare students for the real thing. Although an occasional test is important for a teacher to know where his or her students are, endless testing needlessly saps valuable time away from learning opportunities and can be defeating to students. You may not have control over such zealous approaches by those above you but, if possible, resist this approach to improving scores.

Teach Fundamental Concepts and Processes

Regardless of the state standards, the nature of the tests, or the consequences, the best advice is to teach to the big ideas in the mathematics curriculum. Students who have learned conceptual ideas in a relational manner and who have learned the processes of doing mathematics will always perform well on tests, regardless of the format or specific objectives.

This does not mean that you should ignore the standards you are under contract to teach. Rather, examine these lists of skills and objectives and identify the broader conceptual foundations on which they depend. Be certain that students have an opportunity to learn the content in the standards. At the start of each chapter of Section 2 of this book, you will find a short list of "Big Ideas" followed by a section called Content Connections. These will help you identify the broader ideas behind the objectives that you need to teach and help students deepen their understanding of connecting ideas and strands.

As pointed out in Chapter 1, there is ample evidence that students in the "reform" programs developed with NSF funding are doing well on standardized tests. In most cases these students significantly outperform comparable students in traditional programs on measures of problem solving, concepts, and reasoning. On measures of computational skills—what traditional programs teach best—the reform-program students tend to do as well or nearly as well as their counterparts in traditional programs. All of the reform programs have in common a focus on conceptual development, problem solving, reasoning, and classroom discussion. In short, a student-oriented, problem-based approach is the best course for raising scores.

Review and Practice

Short, regularly spaced reviews can have a positive effect as students develop skills for computation, mental computation, estimation, use of formulas, and other procedural ideas. Short reviews spread across the year will have a much more beneficial effect than a massive practice effort the week before the test. A blitz just before the test can only heighten anxieties and serve to confuse ideas.

Test-Taking Strategies

Another popular approach to raising test scores is to teach students to be test savvy—to teach them specific noncontent strategies useful for taking tests. With a healthy dose of caution, this approach may help some students. The cautions are these: First, if the students have not developed the concepts, the test strategies will be completely useless. Second, time teaching test strategies is best spent shortly before a test. Here are a few strategies that may have some positive effect.

● *Provide experience with different question formats.* If you have information about the types of formats the stan-

dardized test will employ, be sure to use these question formats regularly (not exclusively) in class.
● *Teach test-taking strategies.* Students are often not very efficient test takers, so helping them learn to take tests can have some benefits. Here are some teachable strategies:

* Read questions carefully. Practice identifying what questions are asking and what information is given to get the answer.

* Estimate the answer before spending time with computation. On multiple-choice tests, estimation and good number sense are often all that are needed to select the correct answer.

* Eliminate choices. Look at the available options. Some will almost certainly be unreasonable. Does a choice make sense? Can looking at the ones digit eliminate answers?

* Work backward from an answer.

Remember! Test-taking strategies require good concepts, skills, and number sense. Without good understanding, test strategies will do little good.

Portfolios in the Assessment Plan

A *portfolio* is an assemblage of many types of student work selected with both student and teacher input, designed to provide a holistic view of some aspect of mathematics that may not be evident from examination of any single entry. The portfolio should demonstrate and help students reflect on their mathematical power and what that really means. It may be used to focus on progress and growth, understandings, or problem-solving processes. The materials in the portfolio may include assignments, projects, reports, student writing, worksheets from texts or other sources, comments by teachers, observations from interviews, and self-evaluations of group and individual efforts. A portfolio should be more than a folder of student papers. It should tell a story that goes beyond the individual entries. The portfolio is an excellent form of communication between student and teacher, student and parent, and parent and teacher.

Portfolio Content Suggestions

Your own portfolio program should be carried out to serve the particular goals you have in mind and to communicate achievement of these goals to students and parents. These plans and goals should be discussed with your students from the outset and revisited periodically so that the students are fully involved in the process.

Table 5.1 is from a superb NCTM booklet, *Mathematics Assessment: Myths, Models, Good Questions, and Practical Suggestions* (Stenmark, 1991). It provides ideas for the types of entries that could be included to correspond to different goals. Any given portfolio will include only a sampling of these ideas and may contain only eight to ten entries.

TABLE 5.1

Goals and Suggested Portfolio Contents

Goal	Evidence, Examples, and Comments
Positive mathematical disposition Motivation Curiosity Perseverance Risk taking Flexibility Self-responsibility Self-confidence	• Journal entries depicting enthusiasm for mathematics • Photographs of large, colorful mathematics graphics by students • Problem solution with an added paragraph beginning with "On the other hand . . ." or "What if . . ." • Log of a week's or month's work showing a single important problem or investigation worked on over a period of time • Homework paper with a description of several approaches to a problem • Student-written planning calendar outlining work to be done • Mathematics autobiography
Growth in mathematical understanding Concept development Problem-solving skills Communication skills Construction of mathematics Reflection on approaches and solutions to problems or tasks	• Similar items collected at regular intervals from the beginning of the year • Written explanation of why an algorithm works • Diagram, table, or similar organized representation that clarifies a problem situation • Solution that defines assumptions, includes counterexamples • Photographs of a mathematics project • Journal entries delineating solution justifications and variations in strategies • Student identification of papers that need more work, with reasons • A paper that starts with "Today in math class I learned . . ." • Inclusion of drafts as well as finished work
Mathematical reasoning in a variety of mathematical topics Estimation, number sense, number operations, and computation Measurement, geometry, and spatial sense Statistics and probability Fractions and decimals Patterns and relationships	• Report on an investigation (e.g., number patterns in sums of sequential numbers) • Student-planned statistical survey, with accompanying graphic designs • Written report of a probability experiment and accompanying theoretical design • Response to an open-ended question regarding measurement of geometric shapes • Student explanation of what $\frac{1}{2}$ minus $\frac{1}{3}$ means • Diagram examples of multiplication using a number line, a rectangular array, and repeated groups of physical objects • Annotated drawing illustrating the Pythagorean theorem • Representation of an area model solution for a statistical problem

Mathematical connections
Connecting a mathematical idea to other
  mathematical topics, to other subject
  areas, and to real-world situations
	• Papers that show authentic use of mathematics in other curricular areas such as science or social studies
	• Student reflections on how mathematics is meaningful as it is used in the adult world
	• Examples from nature of occurrences of Pascal's triangle number patterns
	• A report on the relationship among arithmetic, algebra, and geometry with demonstrative examples on a coordinate grid
	• Student-constructed table of equivalent fractions, decimal numbers, and percents, with examples of where each type of number is used
	• Mathematical art project
	• Report about a person in history or personally known who contributed to mathematics

Group problem-solving Development of skills in working with others Communication	• A task design or plan • Group paper that includes the names of the members of the group and the tasks each did • Group self-assessment sheet • Videotape or audiotape of group working on problems or making oral reports • Group-work report of trying a second or third strategy applied when the first one didn't work
Use of tools Integration of technology—use of calculators and computers and so on Use of manipulatives	• Computer-generated statistical analysis of a problem • Frequent mention of use of calculators on open-ended problems • Diagrams representing use of manipulative material

Teacher and parent involvement
Communication between teacher and parent
  and between parent and student
Parental understanding of educational
  objectives and values
	• Consistency of program demonstrated by items from every grading period
	• Anecdotal report
	• Informal assessment sheet
	• Interview of student
	• Teacher- or parent-written comments
	• Assessment by teacher of student work
	• Student presentation of portfolio to parent during parent-teacher conference

Source: National Council of Teachers of Mathematics © 1991. In J. K. Stenmark (Ed.), *Mathematics Assessment.* Reprinted by permission.

Teachers who have used portfolios have noted that students begin to take more pride in their work and make extra efforts. Portfolios can add a sense of importance to daily work.

Portfolio Management

At first, the idea of keeping a portfolio for every child is a bit daunting. Included in this section are some ideas found in the Stenmark (1991) booklet.

A Working Portfolio

Set up folders for each student, and keep them where students can easily get to them. These folders serve as working portfolios and will hold students' potential portfolio entries. Encourage students to revise or correct work on special projects, but always keep the original versions to be able to track progress. The working portfolio is also the place where your observation notes or other items that originate with you can be kept. When groups turn in reports or projects, make copies for each group member's work portfolio.

Assembling the Portfolio

At the end of the unit or grading period, or whenever it is time to assemble the final portfolio, students select and clip together the items from the working portfolio that they want to be included in their final portfolio. Have a class discussion about how to select items and what the items should show. Encourage children to pick things that tell about themselves in mathematics: their strengths, weaknesses, points of pride, places they need help, and progress made over the period. Students should write a few sentences explaining each selection and why it was included. You should designate two or three items as "must include," usually the same ones for the whole class.

Students then review their portfolios and write a cover letter that discusses the content as a whole and gives their personal perspective on such things as problem-solving skills, confidence, attitudes, and growth in understanding, depending on the goals you and your class have established. This portfolio is now ready for evaluation and subsequent sharing with parents.

Portfolio Evaluation

You will probably have made comments on most or all of the materials as they were completed. Now you are looking at the portfolio as a whole. It is very important to provide feedback. It is an excellent way to encourage students and to build confidence and communicate perspective about mathematics. Your comments should be made with this in mind. If you plan to include the portfolio in your grading scheme, a rubric will be useful.

DIAGNOSTIC INTERVIEWS

An interview is simply a one-on-one discussion with a child to help you see how she is thinking about a particular subject, what processes she uses in solving problems, or what attitudes and beliefs she may have. A structured interview may be as short as 5 to 10 minutes. More open-ended or exploratory interviews may last as long as a half hour.

Many teachers avoid interviews because of time constraints. This is unfortunate because interviews have the potential to give you information that you simply cannot get in any other way. Think of interviews as a method to be used for only a few students at a time—not for every student in the class. You can interview a single student while the rest of the class is working on a task. Teachers in self-contained classrooms can find small bits of time throughout the day. Middle school teachers can find a few minutes during a regular class period or a study period, or even before or after school.

Reasons to Consider an Interview

There are at least two reasons why it may occasionally be well worth the time and effort to conduct interviews with a few selected students. The most obvious reason is that you need more information concerning a particular child and how he or she is constructing concepts or using a procedure. Remediation will almost always be more successful if you can pinpoint *why* a student is having difficulty before you try to fix the problem.

A second reason is to get information either to plan your instruction or to assess the effectiveness of your instruction. For example, are you sure that your students have a good understanding of equivalent fractions, or are they just doing the exercises according to rote rules? At the end of Chapter 12, a collection of tasks is suggested to get at students' understanding of place value. Concept tasks such as these might be used in interviews conducted at the beginning of a unit to see what ideas you need to work on.

Planning an Interview

There is no magic right way to plan or structure an interview. In fact, flexibility is a key ingredient. You should, however, have some overall game plan before you begin, and be prepared with key questions and materials. Begin an interview with questions that are easy or closest to what the child is likely to be able to do, usually some form of procedural exercise. For numeration or computation topics, for example, begin with a pencil-and-paper task such as a computation, writing or comparing numerals, or a simple translation problem. When the opening task has been completed, ask the child to explain what was done. "How would you explain this to a second grader (or your younger sister)?" "What does this (point to something on the paper) stand for?" "Tell me about why you do it that way." At this point, you may try a similar task but with a different feature; for example, after doing 372 − 54, try 403 − 37. The second problem has a zero in the tens place, a possible source of difficulty.

The next phase in the interview involves the use of models or drawings that the child can use to demonstrate understanding of the earlier procedural task. Computations can be done with base-ten materials, blocks or counters can be used, number lines explored, grid paper used for drawing, and so on. Be careful not to interject or teach. The temptation to do so is sometimes overwhelming. Watch and listen. Next, explore connections between what was done with models and what was done with pencil and paper. Many children will do the very same task and get two different answers. Does it matter to the children? How do they explain the discrepancy? Can they connect actions using models to what they wrote or explained earlier?

Alternative beginnings to an interview include making an estimate of the answer to either a computation or a word problem, doing a computation mentally, or trying to predict the solution to a given task. Notice that the interview does not generally proceed the way instruction does. That is, in an interview, the conceptual explanations and discussions in general come after the procedural activity. Your goal is not to use the interview to teach but rather to find out where the child is in terms of concepts and procedures at this time.

Suggestions for Effective Interviews

The following suggestions have been adapted from excellent discussions of interviewing children by Labinowicz (1985, 1987), Liedtke (1988), and Scheer (1980).

- *Be accepting and neutral as you listen to the child.* Smiles, frowns, or other body language can make the child think that the answer he or she gave is right or wrong. Develop neutral responses such as "Uh-huh," "I see," or even a silent nod of the head.
- *Avoid cuing or leading the child.* "Are you sure about that?" "Now look again closely at what you just did." "Wait. Is that what you mean?" These responses will indicate to children that they have made some mistake and cause them to change their responses. This can mask what they really think and understand. A similar form of leading is a series of easily answered questions that direct the student to a correct response. That is teaching, not interviewing.
- *Wait silently.* Give the student plenty of time before you ask a different question or probe. After the child makes a response, wait again! This second wait time is even more important because it allows and encourages the child to elaborate on the initial thought and provide you with more information. Wait even when the response is

correct. Waiting can also give you a bit more time to think about the direction you want the interview to take. Your wait time will almost never be as long as you imagine it is.
- *Do not interrupt.* Let children's thoughts flow freely. Encourage children to use their own words and ways of writing things down. Interjecting questions or correcting language can be distracting to the child's thinking.
- *Use imperatives rather than questions.* Say, "show me," "tell me," "do," or "try," rather than "Can you . . . ?" or "Will you . . . ?" In response to a question, the child can simply say no, leaving you in a vacuum.
- *Avoid confirming a request for validation.* Students frequently follow answers or actions with, "Is that right?" This query can easily be answered with a neutral, "That's fine," or "You're doing OK," regardless of whether the answer is right or wrong. Interviewing is not an easy thing to do well. Many teachers are timid about it and fail to take the time. But not much damage is possible, and the rewards of listening to children, both for you and your students, are so great that you really do not want to pass it up.

GRADING

Myth: A grade is an average of a series of scores on tests and quizzes. The accuracy of the grade is dependent primarily on the accuracy of the computational technique used to calculate the final numeric grade.

Reality: A grade is a statistic that is used to communicate to others the achievement level that a student has attained in a particular area of study. The accuracy or validity of the grade is dependent on the information that is used in preparing the grade, the professional judgment of the teacher, and the alignment of the assessments with the true goals and objectives of the course.

Confronting the Myth

Most experienced teachers will tell you that they know a great deal about their students in terms of what the students know, how they perform in different situations, their attitudes and beliefs, and their various levels of skill attainment. Good teachers have always been engaged in ongoing performance assessment, albeit informal and usually with no recording. However, even good teachers have relied on test scores to determine grades, essentially forcing themselves to ignore a wealth of information that reflected a truer picture of their children.

. The myth of grading by statistical number crunching is so firmly ingrained in schooling at all levels that you may find it hard to abandon. If one thing is clear from the discussions in this chapter, it should be that it is quite possible to gather a wide variety of rich information about students' understanding, problem-solving processes, and attitudes and beliefs. To ignore all of this information in favor of a handful of numbers based on tests, tests that usually focus on low-level skills, is unfair to students, to parents, and to you as the teacher.

Grading Issues

For effective use of the assessment information gathered from problems, tasks, and other appropriate methods to assign grades, some hard decisions are inevitable. Some are philosophical, some require school or district agreements about grades, and all require us to examine what we value and the objectives we communicate to students and parents.

Values

In contrast to the many myths of grading, one thing is undeniably true: *What gets graded is what gets valued.* Using rubric scales to provide feedback and to encourage a pursuit of excellence must also relate to grades. However, "converting four out of five to 80 percent or three out of four to a grade of C can destroy the entire purpose of alternative assessment and the use of scoring rubrics" (Kulm, 1994, p. 99). Kulm explains that directly translating rubrics to grades focuses attention on grades and away from the purpose of every good problem-solving activity, to strive for an excellent performance. When papers are returned with less than top ratings, the purpose is to help students know what is necessary to achieve at a higher level. Early on, there should be opportunities to improve based on feedback. When a grade of 75 percent or a C– is returned, all the student knows is that he or she did poorly. If, for example, a student's ability to justify her own answers and solutions has improved, should she be penalized in the averaging of numbers by a weaker performance early in the marking period?

What this means is that grading must be based on the performance tasks and other activities for which you assigned rubric ratings; otherwise, students will soon realize that these are not important scores. At the same time, they need not be added or averaged in any numeric manner. The grade at the end of the marking period should reflect a holistic view of where the student is now relative to your goals and your value system. That value system should be clearly reflected in your framework for rating tasks.

Alignment

The grades you assign should reflect all of your objectives. Procedural skills remain important but should be weighted in proportion to other goals in keeping with your value system. If you are restricted to assigning a single grade for mathematics, different factors probably have different weights or values in making up the grade. Student X may be fantastic at reasoning and truly love mathematics yet be weak in traditional skills. Student Y may be mediocre in problem solving but possess good communication skills. How much weight should you give to cooperation in groups, to written versus oral reports, to computational skills? There are no simple answers to these questions. However, they should be addressed at the beginning of the grading period and not the night you set out to assign grades.

A multidimensional reporting system is a big help. If you can assign several grades for mathematics and not just one, your report to parents is more meaningful. Even if the school's report card does not permit multiple grades, you can devise a supplement indicating several ratings for different objectives. A place for comments is also helpful. This form can be shared with students periodically during a grading period and can easily accompany a report card.

You can always involve students and parents in a discussion of a multidimensional approach to determining a grade based on rubric ratings for different components of your goals. Traditional test averaging has always done this. Not every test covers the same thing, and various scores (quizzes, homework, exams) are often assigned different weights. These are subjective, teacher-made decisions. The same subjective approach can be used with rubric scores without computing numeric averages.

REflEcTioNs oN ChApTER 5

Writing to Learn

1. How is assessment different from testing or evaluation?
2. Describe the four stages involved in integrating assessment with instruction.
3. The six assessment standards concern *mathematics, learning, equity, openness, inferences,* and *coherence.* For each, describe in your own words what the standard says and its importance for you as a teacher.
4. Describe the four purposes of assessment as outlined by the *Assessment Standards.* How do these purposes relate to you as a teacher?
5. What should we look for if we are trying to assess "mathematical power"?
6. In looking at procedural knowledge, what should be assessed in addition to skill proficiency? Why?

7. How can a learning task or problem be an assessment task? Why should these be the same thing?

8. Describe the essential features of a rubric. What are performance indicators? What is the difference between a rubric and a performance indicator? What is the difference between a holistic rubric and an analytic rubric?

9. How can students be involved in understanding and using rubrics to help with their learning?

10. How can you incorporate observational assessments into your daily lessons? What is at least one method of getting observations recorded? Do you have to observe every student?

11. Journals take many forms. What in your opinion is the best *use* of journals and the corresponding best *format* for journals?

12. How can children with limited writing skills "write" in mathematics?

13. Describe at least three of the six things that you might want to think about when constructing a test.

14. Why do you think teaching to the test is not a good method of raising scores on high-stakes tests? What is the best way to raise scores?

15. Describe what a portfolio is and why you might consider using one in your assessment plans.

16. What are two reasons you might consider conducting a diagnostic interview? What are a few of the things to keep in mind when conducting a diagnostic interview?

17. Why does a grade not have to be the average of a collection of scores? Explain.

For Discussion and Exploration

1. Examine a few chapter-end tests in various textbooks. How well do the tests reflect what is important in the chapter? Concepts and understanding? Mathematical power?

2. Select any good performance task for a grade level you are interested in. Try to answer the six questions on pages 62–63, just above the examples of problems for assessment. If possible, get some other people to do the same for the same task. Compare your ideas.

3. Pick a topic and a grade level. Try to write three good test questions for that topic.

4. How are teachers in your area responding to the pressures of state testing programs? Do you think that what they are doing is in the best interest of students? Is what they are doing the best thing to do in order to raise scores?

Recommendations for Further Reading

Highly Recommended

Bright, G. W., & Joyner, J. M. (Eds.). (1998). *Classroom assessment in mathematics: Views from a National Science Foundation working conference.* Lanham, MD: University Press of America.

In 1997, a conference was held in North Carolina on the topic of classroom assessment in mathematics. Participants were experts from around the country who shared their personal perspective and expertise on this issue. This book includes three position papers and 23 working papers presented at the conference, providing a wonderful resource for anyone looking for information on mathematics assessment practices.

Kulm, G. (1994). *Mathematics assessment: What works in the classroom.* San Francisco: Jossey-Bass.

Kulm has excellent credentials in the area of mathematics and science assessment. This book provides perspective, detailed guidance, and models that can be copied for direct use in the classroom. One of the best books on assessment in mathematics available.

Lambdin, D. V., Kehle, P. E., & Preston, R. V. (Eds.) (1996). *Emphasis on assessment: Readings from NCTM's school-based journals.* Reston, VA: National Council of Teachers of Mathematics.

An assembly of 30 articles on assessment taken from NCTM's various journals and organized in four categories: rationale for change, testing and grading, alternative assessment options, and evaluation of teacher effectiveness. At the end of the book are three annotated bibliographies for elementary and middle school teachers, secondary teachers, and a third from the *Journal for Research in Mathematics Education.*

Stenmark, J. K. (Ed.). (1991). *Mathematics assessment: Myths, models, good questions, and practical suggestions.* Reston, VA: National Council of Teachers of Mathematics.

Since its publication, this comprehensive look at new directions in assessment with examples, alternatives, ideas, and formats has been one of NCTM's most popular books. The author is associated with the EQUALS project and has written extensively on assessment. This remains a top-selling resource on this topic.

Other Suggestions

Billstein, R. (1998). Assessment: The STEM model. *Mathematics Teaching in the Middle School, 3,* 282–286, 294–296.

Brown-Herbst, K. (1999). So math isn't just answers. *Mathematics Teaching in the Middle School, 4,* 448–455.

Burns, M. (1995). *Writing in math class.* White Plains, NY: Cuisenaire Company of America (distributor).

Cai, J., Lane, S., & Jakabcsin, M. S. (1996). The role of open-ended tasks and holistic scoring rubrics: Assessing students' mathematical reasoning and communication. In P. C. Elliott (Ed.), *Communication in mathematics, K–12 and beyond* (pp. 137–145). Reston, VA: National Council of Teachers of Mathematics.

Cai, J., Magone, M. E., Wang, N., & Lane, S. (1996). Describing student performance qualitatively. *Mathematics Teaching in the Middle School, 1,* 828–835.

Cole, K. A. (1999). Walking around: Getting more from informal assessment. *Mathematics Teaching in the Middle School, 4,* 224–227.

Copley, J. V. (1999). Assessing the mathematical understanding of the young child. In J. V. Copley (Ed.), *Mathematics in the early years* (pp. 182–188). Reston, VA: National Council of Teachers of Mathematics.

Huinker, D., & Laughlin, C. (1996). Talk your way into writing. In P. C. Elliott (Ed.), *Communication in mathematics K–12 and beyond* (pp. 81–88). Reston, VA: National Council of Teachers of Mathematics.

Karp, K. S., & Huinker, D. (1997). Portfolios as agents of change. *Teaching Children Mathematics, 5,* 224–228.

Kuhs, T. M. (1997). *Measure for measure: Using portfolios in K–8 mathematics.* Portsmouth, NH: Heinemann.

McIntosh, M. E. (1997). 500+ writing formats. *Mathematics Teaching in the Middle School, 2,* 354–358.

Moon, J. (1997). *Developing judgement: Assessing children's work in mathematics.* Portsmouth, NH: Heinemann.

National Council of Teachers of Mathematics. (1995). *Assessment standards for school mathematics.* Reston, VA: The Council.

O'Brien, D. C. (1996). Math journals: First attempts in third grade. In D. Schifter (Ed.), *What's happening in math class? Reconstructing professional identities* (Vol. 2) (pp. 146–147). New York: Teachers College Press.

Popham, W. J. (1999). Why standardized tests don't measure educational quality. *Educational Leadership, 56*(6), 8–15.

Stylianou, D. A., Kenney, P. A., Silver, E. A., & Alacaci, C. (2000). Gaining insight into students' thinking through assessment tasks. *Mathematics Teaching in the Middle School, 6,* 136–144.

Whitin, D. J., & Wilde, S. (1995). *It's the story that counts: More children's books for mathematical learning, K–6.* Portsmouth, NH: Heinemann.

Williams, N. B., & Wynnem, B. D. (2000). Journal writing in the mathematics classroom: A beginner's approach. *The Mathematics Teacher, 93,* 132–135.

Zawojewski, J. S. (1996). Polishing a data task: Seeking better assessment. *Teaching Children Mathematics, 2,* 372–378.

Zazkis, R., & Hazzan, O. (1999). Interviewing in mathematics education research: Choosing the questions. *Journal of Mathematical Behavior, 17,* 429–439.

Planning in the Problem-Based Classroom

Natural learning . . . doesn't happen on a time schedule and often requires more time than schools are organized to provide. Problem-solving experiences take time. It's essential that teachers provide the time that's needed for children to work through activities on their own and that teachers not slip into teaching-by-telling for the sake of efficiency.

Burns (1992, p. 30)

The three-part lesson format described in Chapter 4 provided a basic structure for problem-based lessons. That basic framework resulted from the need for students to be engaged in problems followed by time for discussion and reflection. However, many of the practical details of working with students in this environment are not clear from this general paradigm for a lesson.

This chapter begins with a step-by-step guide for planning problem-based lessons. Also explored here are some variations of the three-part structure, tips for dealing with diversity in the classroom, cooperative learning techniques, issues of drill and practice, homework, textbooks, and grading. In short, this chapter discusses the "nuts and bolts" of effective teaching.

Planning a Problem-Based Lesson

Regardless of your experience, it is crucial that you give adequate thought to the planning of your lessons. There is no such thing as a "teacher-proof" curriculum—where you can simply teach every lesson as it is planned and in the order it appears. Every class is different. Choices of tasks and how they are presented to students must be made daily to best fit the needs of your students and the objectives you are hired to teach. The outline in Figure 6.1 illustrates the suggested

steps for planning a lesson. The first four steps are the most crucial. Decisions made here will define the content and the task that your students will work on. The next four steps are necessary to make sure that the lesson runs smoothly. Finally, you can write a concise lesson plan, knowing that you have thought it through thoroughly. Each step is discussed briefly next.

Step 1: Begin with the Math! Articulate clearly the *ideas* you want students to learn as a result of the lesson. Think in terms of mathematical concepts, not skills. Describe the mathematics, not the student behavior.

But what if a skill is the intended outcome? Perhaps you want students to master their subtraction facts or work on developing a method of multiplying two-digit numbers. For every skill there are underlying concepts and relationships. Identify these concepts at this step of your planning. The best tasks will get at skills through concepts.

Step 2: Consider Your Students. What do your students know or understand about this topic? Are they ready to tackle this bit of mathematics or are there some background ideas that they have not yet developed? Perhaps they already have some ideas that you have been working on and this lesson is aimed at expanding or refining these.

Be sure that the mathematics you identified in step 1 includes something new or at least slightly unfamiliar to your students. At the same time, be certain that your objectives are not out of reach. There is no sense in repeating old ideas. Nor is there any value in posing tasks that students cannot access without clear guidance from you. For real learning to take place, there must be some challenge, some new ideas—even if it is simply seeing an old idea in a new format or with a different model. Keep new ideas within the grasp of your students. If necessary, now is the time to revisit step 1 and make adjustments in your goals.

FIGURE 6.1 Planning steps for thinking through a problem-based lesson.

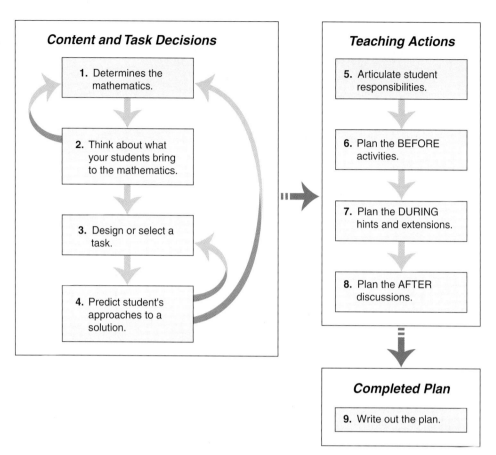

Step 3: Decide on a Task.
Keep it simple! Good tasks need not be elaborate. Often a simple story problem is all that is necessary as long as the solution involves children in the intended mathematics.

Chapter 4 gave examples of tasks and suggestions for creating or selecting them. This book is full of tasks. The more experience you have with the content in step 1 and the longer you have had to build a repertoire of task ideas from journals, resource books, conferences, and in-service, the easier this important step in planning will become.

Step 4: Predict What Will Happen.
You have made hypotheses about what your students know. Now use that information and think about *all* of the things your students are likely to do with this task. If you catch yourself saying, "Well, I hope that they will . . . ," then *stop*. Predict, don't hope!

Does every student in your class have a chance of engaging in this problem? Although students may each tackle the task differently, don't leave your struggling students to flounder. Perhaps you want to provide for modifications in the task for different students. (See the section on diversity later in this chapter.) This is also a good time to think about whether your students will work alone, in pairs, or in groups. Group work may be an assist to students in need of some extra help.

If your predictions are beginning to make you uneasy about your task, this is the time to revisit the task. Maybe it needs to be modified, or perhaps it is simply too easy or too difficult.

These first four decisions define the heart of your lesson. The next four decisions define how you will carry the plan out in your classroom.

Step 5: Articulate Student Responsibilities.
You always want more than answers. For nearly every task, you want students to be able to tell you

● What they did to get the answer
● Why they did it that way
● Why they think the solution is correct

You need to plan how students will supply this information. If responding in writing, will students write individually or prepare a group presentation? Will they write in their journals, on paper to be turned in, on a worksheet, on chart paper to present to the class, or on acetate to use on the overhead?

Of course, there is the option of no writing. You may want to have students simply report or discuss their ideas without writing. Although this option is often adequate, if used repeatedly or before students are accustomed to discussing mathematics, some form of written work that goes beyond the answer is strongly recommended. Remember, writing is a form of rehearsal for discussions.

Step 6: Plan the *Before* Portion of the Lesson.
Sometimes you can simply begin with the task and articulation of students' responsibilities. But, in many instances, you will want to prepare students by working quickly through an easier related task or some related warm-up exercise that orients students' thinking. After presenting the task, will you "let go" or do you want students to brainstorm solutions or estimate answers? (See Chapter 4 for discussion of the "before actions" in a lesson.)

Consider how you will present the task. Options include having it written on paper, taken from their texts, shown on the overhead, or written on the board or on chart paper. There are also times when it is adequate to simply present the problem orally. And don't forget to tell the students about their responsibilities (step 5).

Step 7: Think About the *During* Portion of the Lesson.
Look back at your predictions. What hints or assists can you plan in advance for students who may be stuck? Are there particular groups or individual students you wish to specially observe or assess in this lesson? Make a note to do so. Think of extensions or challenges you can pose to students who finish quickly.

Estimate how much time you think students should be given for the task. It is useful to tell students in advance. Some teachers set a timer that all students can see. Plan to be somewhat flexible, but do not use up your discussion period.

Step 8: Think About the *After* Portion of the Lesson.
How will you begin your discussion? One option is to simply list all of the different answers from groups or individuals, doing so without comment, and then returning to students or groups to explain their solutions and justify their answers. You may also begin with full explanations from each group or student before you get all the answers. If you accept oral reports, think about how you will record on the board what is being said.

Plan an adequate amount of time for your discussion. Five minutes is almost never sufficient. Aim for 20 minutes at least for rich problems. A good average is about 15 to 20 minutes.

Step 9: Write Your Lesson Plan.
If you have thought through these steps, a plan is simply a listing of the critical decisions you have already made. The outline shown here is a possible format:

- The mathematics or goals
- The task and expectations
- The *before* activities
- The *during* hints and extensions for early finishers
- The *after*-lesson discussion format
- Assessment notes (whom you want to assess and how)

Variations of the Three-Part Lesson

The basic lesson structure we have been discussing assumes that a class will be given a task or problem, allowed to work on it, and end with a discussion. Certainly, not every lesson is developed around a task given to a full class. However, the basic concept of tasks and discussions can be adapted to most any problem-based lesson.

Minilessons

Many tasks do not require the full period. The three-part format can be compressed to as little as 10 minutes. You might plan two or three cycles in a single lesson. For example, consider these tasks:

Grades K–1:   Make up two questions that we can answer using the information in our graph.

Grade 2–3:   Suppose you did not know the answer to problem 14. How could you start to figure it out?

Grades 4–5:   On your geoboard, make a figure that has line symmetry but not rotational symmetry. Make a second figure that has rotational symmetry but not line symmetry.

Grades 6–7:   Margie has this drawing of the first floor of her house. (Pass out drawing.) She wants to reduce it on the photocopy machine so that it will have a scale of 1 cm to the foot. By what percentage should she reduce it?

These are worthwhile tasks but probably would not require a full period to do and discuss.

A profitable strategy for short tasks is *think-pair-share*. Students are first directed to spend a minute developing their own thoughts and ideas on how to approach the task or even what they think may be a good solution. Then they pair with a classmate and discuss each other's ideas. This provides an opportunity to test out ideas and to practice articulating them. The last step is to share the idea with the rest of the class. The pair may actually have two ideas or can be told to come to a single decision. The entire process, including some discussion, may take less than 15 minutes.

Workstations and Games

It is often useful for students to work at different tasks or games at various locations around the room. Stations are a good way to manage materials without the need to distribute and collect them. They also help when it is unreasonable or impossible for all students to have access to the required materials for an activity. Good computer tasks do exist, especially on the Web. Computer stations make sense for these activities. Stations also allow you to differentiate tasks when your students are at different stages in developing the current concept.

You may want students to work at stations in small groups or individually. Therefore, for a given topic you might prepare from four to eight different activities. Not every station has to be different. Materials required for the activity or game, including any special recording sheets, are placed in a tub or folder to be quickly positioned at different locations in the classroom.

A good idea for younger children or for games and computer activities is to explain or teach the activity to the full class ahead of time. In this way students should not waste time when they get to the station and you will not have to run around the room explaining what to do.

Many station activities can be profitably repeated several times. For example, students might be replacing missing numbers on a hundreds chart or playing a "game" where one student covers part of a known number of counters and the other student names the covered part. The game "Fraction Track" in the NCTM *e-Standards* (E-example 5.1) can be played profitably several times.

STOP   Do these workstation activities or games fit the definition of a problem-based task as discussed in Chapter 4? Consider your answer before reading on.

A game or other repeatable activity may not look like a problem, but it can nonetheless be problem-based. The determining factor is this: Does the activity cause students to be reflective about new or developing mathematical relationships? Remember that it is reflective thought that causes growth. If the activity merely has students repeating a procedure without wrestling with an emerging idea, then it is not a problem-based experience. However, the few examples just mentioned and many others do have children thinking through ideas that they have not yet formulated well. In this sense, they fit the definition of a problem-based task.

The time during which students are working at stations is analogous to the *during* portion of a lesson. What kinds of things could you do for the *after* portion of the lesson? Discussions with students who have been working on a task are just as important for games and stations. However, these discussions will have to take place in small groups. You might sit down with students at a station and ask about what they have been doing, what strategies they have discovered, or how they have been going about the activity in general. Try to get at the reasoning behind what they are doing. Another possibility is to wait until all in the class have worked at the same game or station. Now you can have a full group discussion about the learning that came from that activity.

Just as with any task, some form of recording or writing should be included with stations whenever possible. Students solving a problem on a computer can write up what they did and explain what they learned. Students playing a game can keep records and then tell about how they played the game—what thinking or strategies they used.

Dealing with Diversity

Perhaps one of the most difficult challenges for teachers today is to reach all of the students in their increasingly diverse classrooms. Every teacher faces this dilemma because every classroom contains a range of student abilities and backgrounds.

Interestingly and perhaps surprisingly to some, the problem-based approach to teaching is the best way to teach mathematics and attend to the range of students. In the problem-based classroom, children are making sense of the mathematics in *their* way, bringing to the problems only the skills and ideas that they own. In contrast, in a traditional, highly directed lesson, it is assumed that all students will understand and use the same approach and the same ideas. Students not ready to understand the ideas presented by the teacher must focus their attention on following the teacher rules or directions in an instrumental manner. This, of course, leads to endless difficulties and leaves many students behind or in need of serious remediation.

In addition to using a problem-based approach, there are specific things you can do to help attend to the diversity of learners in your classroom.

- Be sure that problems have multiple entry points.
- Plan differentiated tasks.
- Use heterogeneous groupings.
- Listen carefully to students.

Plan for Multiple Entry Points

As suggested in the planning guidelines, when selecting a task it is important to think about how all of the students in the class are likely to approach it. Many tasks can be solved with a range of methods. This is especially true of computational tasks in classes where student-invented methods are encouraged and valued. (See Chapter 13.) For many tasks, the use or nonuse of manipulative models is all that is necessary to vary the entry point. Students should generally be permitted to use models with which they are familiar whenever they feel the need for them. Other students can be challenged to devise rules or to use methods that are less dependent on manipulatives or drawings.

Plan Differentiated Tasks

The idea here is to plan a task with multiple versions; some less difficult, others more so. There are several ways that you can make this happen.

For many problems involving computations, you can insert multiple sets of numbers. In the following problem students are permitted to select the first, second, or third number in each bracket.

Eduardo had {12, 60, 121} marbles. He gave Erica {5, 15, 46} marbles. How many marbles does Eduardo have now?

Students tend to select the numbers that provide them with the greatest challenge without being too difficult. In the discussions, all children benefit and feel as though they worked on the same task.

Another way to differentiate a task is to present a situation with related but different questions that can be asked. The situation might be data in a chart or graph, a measurement task, or a geometry task. Here is an example (adapted from Van de Walle, in press):

Students are given a collection of parallelograms including squares and rectangles as well as nonrectangular parallelograms. These questions can be posed:

- **Select a shape and draw at least three new shapes that are like it in some way. Tell how your new shapes are both similar to and different from the shape you selected.**
- **Draw diagonals in these shapes and measure them. See what relationships you can discover about the diagonals.**
- **Make a list of all of the properties that you can think of that every parallelogram in this set has.**

For this fifth- to eighth-grade task there is a challenge to engage nearly every student.

Still another method of differentiating the tasks in your classroom is by using workstations as described in the previous section. For example, if a fourth-grade class is working on equivalent fractions, a variety of equivalent fraction tasks can be designed all for the same concept. As you will experience in Chapter 15, not all such tasks are equally difficult. They are differentiated both by the kinds of materials that are used and the numbers involved. Stations can be assigned to students to best fit their needs and yet all will be working on the same concept.

Use Heterogeneous Groupings

Avoid ability grouping! Trying to split a class into ability groups is futile; every group will still have diversity. It is demeaning to those students not in the top groups. Students in the lower group will not experience the thinking and language of the top group, and top students will not hear the often unconventional but interesting approaches to tasks in the lower group. Furthermore, having two or more groups means that you must diminish the time you can spend with each group.

It is much more profitable to *capitalize* on the diversity in your room by using pairs or cooperative groups that are heterogeneous. Some teachers like to use random pairings or allow students to select the students they want to work with. These techniques may be fun occasionally, but it is advisable to think through carefully how you group your students. Try to pair students in need of help with capable students but also students who will be compatible and willing to assist. What all students will find is that everyone has ideas to contribute.

Listen Carefully to Students

Regardless of the classroom, it is always important to listen to your students. Try to find out how they are thinking, what ideas they have, how they are approaching problems causing difficulty, and in general develop as accurate an hypothesis about the ideas they have on the current topic as possible. Listening to children was mentioned as a strategy for effective teaching in Chapter 3 and as a means of assessing students in Chapter 5. This is not a new idea but an important one as you strive to help all children in your classroom. Every child is capable. By listening carefully you will be in a better position to put into practice the other suggestions in this section.

DRILL OR PRACTICE?

Drill and practice, if not a hallmark of American instructional methods in mathematics, is a strategy used regularly in nearly every classroom. Most lessons in traditional textbooks end with a section consisting of exercises, usually of a similar nature and always completely in line with the ideas that were just taught in the beginning of the lesson. This repetitive procedural work is supposed to cement the ideas just learned. On the surface, this idea seems to make sense. In addition to this common textbook approach, drill-and-practice workbooks and computer drill programs abound.

A question worth asking is, "What has all of this drill gotten us?" It has been an ever-present component of mathematics classes for decades and yet the adult population is replete with those who almost proudly proclaim "I was never any good at mathematics" and who understand little more about the subject than arithmetic. This section offers a different perspective.

New Definitions of Drill and Practice

The phrase "drill and practice" slips off the tongue so rapidly that the two words "drill" and "practice" appear to be synonyms—and, for the most part, they have been. In the interest of developing a new or different perspective on drill and practice, consider definitions that differentiate between these terms as different types of activities rather than link them together.

Practice **refers to different problem-based tasks or experiences, spread over numerous class periods, each addressing the same basic ideas.**

Drill **refers to repetitive, *non*-problem-based exercises designed to improve skills or procedures already acquired.**

STOP How are these two definitions different? Which is more in keeping with the view of drill and practice (as a singular term) with which you are familiar? The drill definition requires that skills are already acquired before they are drilled. What do you think about that?

Using these definitions as a point of departure, it is now useful to examine what benefits we can get from each and when each is appropriate.

What Drill Provides

Drill can provide students with the following:

- An increased facility with a strategy but *only* with a strategy already learned
- A focus on a singular method and an exclusion of flexible alternatives
- A false appearance of understanding
- A rule-oriented view of what mathematics is about

The popular belief is that somehow students learn through drill. In reality, drill can only help students get faster at what they already know. Students who count on their fingers to answer basic fact questions only get very good at counting on their fingers. Drill is not a reflective activity. The nature of drill asks students to do what they already know how to do, even if they just learned it. The focus of drill is on procedures with little or no encouragement for reflective thought.

For most school-level mathematics, including computation, there are numerous ways of doing things. For example, how many different mental methods can you think of to add 48 + 35? To find 25 percent of $84 you can divide by 4 and subtract rather than multiply by 0.25. What approach would you use to find 17 percent of $84? Similar examples of the value of flexible thinking are easily found. Drill has a tendency to narrow one's thinking rather than promote flexibility.

When students successfully complete a page of routine exercises, teachers (and even students) often believe that this is an indication that they've "got it." In fact, what they most often have is a very temporary ability to reproduce a procedure recently shown to them. The short-term memory required of a student to complete the exercises at the end of the traditional lesson is no indication of understanding. Superficially learned procedures are easily and quickly forgotten and confused.

When drill is such a prevalent component of the mathematics classroom, it is no wonder that so many students and adults dislike mathematics. Real mathematics is about sense making and reasoning—it is a science of pattern and order. Students cannot possibly obtain this view of the discipline when constantly being asked to repeat procedural skills over and over.

Finally, drill leaves students, even those good at rule learning, with little to like or enjoy. For many students there is much to fear and avoid. The pressures of getting it right coupled with minimal understanding are pressures that many students handle poorly.

What is most important to understand is this: Drill will *not* provide any new conceptual understanding or ideas. Drill will *not* provide any new skills or strategies. Drill focuses only on what is already known.

What Practice Provides

In essence, practice is what this book is about—providing students with ample and varied opportunities to reflect on or create new ideas through problem-based tasks. The following list of outcomes of practice should not be surprising:

- An increased opportunity to develop conceptual ideas and more elaborate and useful connections
- An opportunity to develop alternative and flexible strategies
- A greater chance for all students to understand, not just a few
- A clear message that mathematics is about figuring things out and making sense

Each of the preceding benefits has been explored in this or previous chapters and should require no further discussion. However, it is important to point out that practice can and does develop skills. The fear that without extensive drill students will not master "basic skills" is not supported by recent research on reform curriculum or practices (see Chapter 1). These programs include lots of practice as defined here and most include very minimal amounts of drill. Students in these programs perform about as well as students in traditional programs on computational skills and much better on nearly every other measure.

When Is Drill Appropriate?

Yes, there is a place for drill in mathematics but it need not occur nearly as frequently as most seem to believe.

Criteria for Using Drill

Consider these two proposed criteria for the profitable use of drill:

- An efficient strategy for the skill to be drilled is already in place
- Automaticity with the skill or strategy is a desired outcome

Is it possible to have a skill and still need to perfect it or to drill it? Clearly this happens outside of mathematics all the time with sports and music as good examples. We learn how to dribble a soccer ball or play the chords shown on a sheet of music. At the outset of instruction, we are given the necessary bits of information to perform these skills. Initially, the skills are weak and unperfected. They must be repeated in order to hone them to a state of efficiency. However, if the skill is not there to begin with, no amount of drill will create it.

Automaticity means that the skill can be performed quickly and mindlessly. Most adults have automaticity with basic facts and simple computation. They perform long division without thinking about the meaning behind the steps.

Stop and make a mental list of the things in K–8 mathematics with which you think students should have automaticity.

Probably your list includes how to count, read, and write numbers. It should include mastery of basic facts (e.g., 3 + 9 or 8 × 6). If you are like most people, you may have computation with whole numbers and even with fractions and decimals on your list. What may surprise you is that automaticity with computational skills is not nearly as important as it used to be. Certainly we want skills in computation but not necessarily with a singular or inflexible method. There are more items that are candidates for the list of desired automaticity but generally these will be small bits of mathematics, not big ideas. In fact, the list of things for which automaticity is truly required is actually quite short.

Automaticity with Flexible Strategies

Since flexible strategies have been mentioned as important, is it possible to develop automaticity with flexible strategies? At first blush this seems to be an oxymoron.

Flexibility is important in computation because the numbers and also the demands of the context suggest different approaches. Mental strategies vary widely for any operation depending on the numbers involved and the strategies that have been developed. Exact results are often not necessary and an estimation procedure can be employed. Even with something as simple as basic facts, we know that different students use different strategies. For example, to remember 9 + 5, some people think of 10 + 5 and take 1 off. Others take 1 from the 5 to make 10 + 4. And there are different strategies for different facts. Neither of the two ideas just mentioned is useful for mastering 5 + 6.

Developing flexible strategies requires adequate opportunity with varied numbers and contexts. Students need to learn how to sift through different methods of thinking. The development of different methods of thinking requires problem-based tasks. As more and more strategies are acquired, more opportunities to select from them and to get better at using them are required. There are elements of both practice (development of strategies) and drill (opportunities to select and use strategies) in becoming flexible with mathematical thinking. So perhaps this is a gray area between drill and practice. Or, perhaps as authors of most reform curricula seem to believe, flexible strategies are largely developed through practice in problem-based experiences. What is clear is that drill alone is not the answer.

Kids Who Don't Get It

As discussed earlier, the diversity in classrooms is a challenge for all teachers. For those students who don't pick up new ideas as quickly as most in the class, there is an overwhelming temptation to give in and "just drill 'em." Before committing to this

solution, ask yourself these two questions: *Has it worked before? What is this telling the child?* The child who has difficulties has certainly been drilled in the past. It is naive to believe that the drill you provide will be more beneficial than the endless drills this child has undoubtedly endured in the past. Although drill may provide some very short-term success, an honest reflection will suggest that it probably will have little effect in the long run. What these children learn from more drill is simple: "I'm no good at math. I don't like math. Math is rules."

The earlier section of this chapter, Dealing with Diversity, suggests strongly that a conceptual approach is the best way to help students who struggle. Drill is simply not the answer.

HOMEWORK

Data from the TIMSS suggest that U.S. fourth graders are assigned about as much homework as students in most other countries (U.S. Dept. of Education, 1997c). U.S. eighth graders are assigned more homework and spend more time in class talking about homework than do Japanese students who significantly outperform the U.S. students (U.S. Dept of Education, 1996). The real value of homework is unclear. Many parents expect to see homework and most teachers do assign homework.

But what should homework consist of? How do you deal with homework once it has been assigned? The distinction between drill and practice as described in the previous section provides a useful lens for looking at homework.

Practice as Homework

Traditionally, homework has consisted almost exclusively of drill. However, homework is a perfectly appropriate way to engage students in problem-based activities—in practice. A problem-based task similar to those described in Chapter 4 can profitably be assigned for homework provided that the difficulty of the task is within reach of most of the students. (Modifications such as those discussed earlier are also possible to accommodate diversity if needed.) The difference is that, when at home, students will be working alone rather than with a partner or group.

On the day following a practice or problem-based homework assignment, begin immediately with a discussion of the task—the after portion of a lesson. The before portion would have occurred at the time of assigning the task. Some form of written work must be required so that students are held responsible for the task and are prepared for the class discussion.

Homework built around problem-based tasks has another advantage beyond that of student growth. Homework of this nature communicates to parents the problem-based or sense-making nature of your classroom and can help them see the value in this approach. Parents want to see homework but few will have any concept of the type of instruction you have been reading about.

Drill as Homework

Remember the criteria for drill: The skill is present and automaticity is desired. Never assign drill for homework as a substitute for practice or before the requisite concepts have been developed. If you do assign drill for homework, here are some things to think about:

- Keep it short. Students don't like homework to begin with and drill is not particularly fun.
- Provide an answer key. At grade 3 and above, students are capable of checking their own work. They should not change their answers but should repeat the missed exercises and/or write a short note indicating where they had difficulty and what they do not understand. If you respond to these notes with assistance, students will begin to understand that homework drills are a way for them to receive help.
- Never grade homework based on correctness. Instead, grade only that it was or was not completed. Rather than penalize wrong answers, use wrong answers as an opportunity to assist students and promote growth. This suggestion applies equally well to practice homework.
- Do not waste valuable classroom time going over drill homework. Especially if the last two suggestions are followed, simply observing that it is complete is all that is required.

The Role of the Textbook

The textbook remains the most significant factor influencing instruction in the elementary and middle school classroom. To make decisions about the use of a textbook, it is good to have an objective view of textbooks and the role they can serve in instruction. When you realize that textbooks are not necessarily the best guide to instruction, you can make wiser choices in using them.

How Are Textbooks Developed?

It is worthwhile to remember that publishing textbooks is a business. If the very best ideas from mathematics educators were incorporated into a textbook that did not sell, those excellent books sitting in warehouses would be of no value to students and would cost the publisher millions of dollars.

Most publishers enlist as authors mathematics educators and teachers who are quite knowledgeable about teaching mathematics. They also do extensive market research to determine what will sell and what teachers think they want in a book. There is frequently a significant gap between what the authors think would be good and what the publisher thinks will sell. Compromise between author and market becomes the rule. Rather than be forward with new ideas for content or pedagogy, publishers make a serious attempt to offend no one. As a consequence, there is frequently a significant time lapse between state-of-the-art mathematics education and what appears in textbooks.

With exceptions found in occasional lessons, most traditional textbooks remain very close to a "teach by telling" model. It is simply not possible for the text to pose problems or tasks in the student books and not provide the solutions or explanations. Most teachers have not yet adapted the teaching-through-problem-solving approach described in this book. For most of the market, the textbook is expected to teach, not simply pose tasks. The mainstream textbook is designed for a teacher who believes that the best teaching is done by following the text and who values a high proportion of drill.

The reform curricula described in Chapter 1 are very different from traditional texts. The development was funded primarily by the National Science Foundation so that publishers did not have that expense. Authors were not bound by the market concerns. To use these texts, teachers must invest a significant amount of time reading the teacher material provided for them. Lessons are problem oriented and often involve extended explorations by students. Extensive drill is not a feature. The market for these programs is growing slowly; it is currently only around 15 percent at the K–5 level and less than that at the middle and high school levels. Traditional textbooks maintain a dominant presence in most classrooms.

Teacher's Editions

The teacher's editions give authors considerably more freedom. Many publishers now provide two extra teacher pages for each lesson as well as additional pages with ideas, explanations, and hints in the front and back of each chapter. The teacher's editions nearly always suggest alternative or additional activities completely separate from those presented on the student pages. Teachers should take advantage of this information. Too many teachers interpret the textbook curriculum as "getting students through the student pages" when in fact the real objectives require the much broader scope presented in the teacher's editions. Pupil pages are just one tool for instruction. Pupil pages are not the objective, nor are they the curriculum.

Two-Page Lesson Format

The typical textbook lesson in the pupil book is presented on two pages or, in the upper grades, occasionally four pages. An observable pattern to these lessons can be seen in almost all popular textbook series. A portion of the first page consists of pictures and illustrations that depict the concepts for that lesson. The teacher is to use this section of the page to discuss the concepts with the students. Next are well-explained examples for the students to follow or an exercise guided by the text. Finally, the lesson has a series of exercises or drill activities usually referred to as practice. Thus, many lessons move almost immediately from conceptual development to symbolic or procedural activities.

This three-part characterization of a textbook lesson is unfairly oversimplified. At the K–2 level, where the children write directly in consumable workbooks, what the student writes for all or most of the two pages may be closely tied to meaningful pictures or even simple hands-on models. The clear adherence to the two-page lesson is not always evident in seventh- and eighth-grade texts.

The two-page format sends a clear message to students that the pictures, concepts, and discussion part of a lesson can be ignored. They begin to tune out until the teacher explains how to do the exercises. Following page by page and assigning procedural exercises from every lesson can easily negate all other efforts to communicate the importance of reasoning, of making and testing conjectures, of justifying results—in short, of doing mathematics. Until the market (this includes you) demands a different approach, the show-and-tell method will dominate mainstream textbooks.

Suggestions for Textbook Use

Our task as teachers is to help children construct relationships and ideas, not to get them to "do pages." We should look on the textbook as simply one of a variety of teaching resources available in the classroom. The textbook is not the object of instruction.

If one considers the limitations of the print medium and understands that the authors and publishers had to make compromises, the textbook can be a source of ideas for designing lessons rather than prescriptions for what each lesson will be. Here are some suggestions:

- Teach to the big ideas or concepts, not the pages. Consider chapter objectives rather than lesson activities. The chapter or unit viewpoint will help focus on the big ideas rather than the activity required to complete a page.
- Consider the conceptual portions of lessons as ideas or inspirations for planning more problem-based activities.

The students do not actually have to do the page. Nor do they have to open the book if that will help present the task. (Chapter 4 provides two examples.)

- Let the pace of your lessons through a unit be determined by student performance and understanding rather than the artificial norm of two pages per day.
- Use the ideas in the teacher's edition.
- Remember that there is no law saying every page must be done or every exercise completed. Select activities that suit your instructional goals rather than designing instruction to suit the text. Feel free to omit pages and activities you believe to be inappropriate for the needs of your students and your instructional goals.
- If the general approach in the text for a particular unit is not the same as the approach you prefer, omit its use for that unit altogether, or select only exercises that provide appropriate drill after you have developed the concepts with your method.
- When drill is desired, look to the textbook as one source of such activity. Why write a drill if an acceptable one is there in the book?

The text is usually a good general guide for scope and sequence. There is no reason that you as a teacher should be required to be a curriculum designer. If tasks and activities are adapted from pages covering the objective you are teaching, you can be reasonably sure that they have been designed to work well for that objective. It is not easy to make up good tasks for every lesson. Take advantage of the text.

Textbooks and other supplementary materials (ancillaries) supplied by publishers usually include evaluation instruments that may be of use for diagnosis, for guiding the pace of your instruction, or for evaluation. At present, such tests are more likely to assess computational skills than conceptual understanding, problem solving, or other process objectives. However, there is a definite effort on the part of publishers to develop better assessments for these higher-order skills.

Reflections on Chapter 6

Writing to Learn

1. Review the steps for planning a lesson. For each of the first eight steps, describe in your own words the decisions that must be made.
2. Not every lesson will be built around a single task. What are other ways to structure problem-based activities in the class?
3. How can a game be considered a problem-based task?
4. How do you do the after portion of a lesson when students are working at stations?
5. Why is a problem-based approach a good way to reach all students in a diverse classroom?
6. Discuss what is meant by (a) tasks with multiple entry points and (b) differentiated tasks.
7. What sort of grouping should be used in a diverse classroom? Why?
8. This chapter suggests a possible distinction between drill and practice. Explain the difference and what each can provide.
9. When is it appropriate to use drill? Explain.

10. Is it ever appropriate to assign problem-based tasks for homework? Explain.
11. Describe the suggestions offered for drill homework.
12. What is the major difference between the instructional method described in this book and the predominant approach found in most mainstream textbooks? Describe briefly what is meant by the "two-page lesson format" that is often adhered to in traditional basal textbooks. What is a serious drawback of this form?

For Discussion and Exploration

1. Examine a textbook for any grade level. Look at a topic for a whole chapter, and determine the two or three main objectives or big ideas covered in the chapter. Restrict yourself to no more than three, and be sure that nearly all topics in the chapter can be built into these big ideas. Now look at the individual lessons. Are the lessons really aimed at the big ideas you have identified? Will the lessons effectively develop the big ideas for this chapter? Try to find two or three tasks or explorations related to the big ideas you have described. If students work on these explorations, how many of the individual lesson objectives will be met?

2. Select a lesson or a short series of lessons from a traditional textbook. Using the ideas on the student pages, go through the nine steps of planning a lesson. This will include designing or selecting a problem or task. Try to modify the instruction on the student page(s) or the ideas in the teacher notes to create a task. Were you able to create a full-period lesson (about 45 to 55 minutes) from a single task? Did your lesson adequately address the mathematics you described in step one?

3. What homework would you assign for the lessons you described in question 2? What is the purpose of the homework? What would you do with this homework on the following day when it was due?

Recommendations for Further Reading

Highly Recommended

Burns, M., & Silbey, R. (2000). *So you have to teach math? Sound advice for K–6 teachers.* Sausalito, CA: Math Solutions Publications.
This is a must read for new teachers and also for veteran teachers who are switching grades. Burns and Silbey offer practical advice on leading class discussions, using manipulatives, incorporating writing into your classroom, dealing with homework, dealing with parents, and more. Each topical chapter is organized by questions teachers typically ask. Almost certainly, your questions will be there also. Filled with practical tips, this will be a resource to come back to often.

Dacey, L. S., & Eston, R. (1999). *Growing mathematical ideas in kindergarten.* Sausalito, CA: Math Solutions Publications.
Kindergarten teachers often find it difficult to put the practices discussed in a mathematics methods class into the kindergarten context. Dacey and Eston make the kindergarten classroom come alive in practical ways that talk about many of the general themes you have read about here: choosing tasks, learning to talk and listen, assessment, and much more. This is a must-have book for any kindergarten teacher.

Litton, N. (1998). *Getting your math message out to parents: A K–6 resource.* Sausalito, CA: Math Solutions Publications.
Well-meaning parents who remember mathematics to be dominated by memorization and work sheets often challenge a constructivist, student-oriented approach to teaching. Litton is a classroom teacher who has practical suggestions for communicating with parents. The book includes chapters on parent conferences, newsletters, homework, and family math night.

Other Suggestions

Brownell, W. A., & Chazal, C. B. (1935). The effects of premature drill in third-grade arithmetic. *Journal of Educational Research, 29,* 17–28.

Buschman, L. (2001). Using student interviews to guide classroom instruction: An action research project. *Teaching Children Mathematics, 8,* 222–227.

Corwin, R. B. (with Storeygard, J., & Price, S. L.) (1996). *Talking mathematics: Supporting children's voices.* Portsmouth, NH: Heinemann.

Helton, S. M. (1995). I thik the citanre will hoder lase: Journal keeping in mathematics class. *Teaching Children Mathematics, 1,* 336–340.

Huinker, D., & Laughlin, C. (1996). Talk your way into writing. In P. C. Elliott (Ed.), *Communication in mathematics, K–12 and beyond* (pp. 81–88). Reston, VA: National Council of Teachers of Mathematics.

Manouchehri, A. (2001). A four-point instructional model. *Teaching Children Mathematics, 8,* 180–186.

McGrath, K. L. (1998). What is the score on scored discussions? *Mathematics Teaching in the Middle School, 4,* 50–58.

McNeal, B. (1995). Learning not to think in a textbook-based mathematics class. *The Journal of Mathematical Behavior, 14,* 205–234.

Mills, H., O'Keefe, T., & Whitin, D. (1996). *Mathematics in the making: Authoring ideas in primary classrooms.* Portsmouth, NH: Heinemann.

Mousley, J., & Sullivan, P. (Eds.). (1996). *Learning about teaching: An interactive tutorial program to facilitate the study of teaching.* The Australian Association of Mathematics Teachers (distributed by the National Council of Teachers of Mathematics).

Whitin, D. J., & Whitin, P. E. (1996). Fostering metaphorical thinking through children's literature. In P. C. Elliott (Ed.), *Communication in mathematics, K–12 and beyond* (pp. 60–65). Reston, VA: National Council of Teachers of Mathematics.

Whitin, D. J., & Whitin, P. (2000). Exploring mathematics through talking and writing. In M. J. Burke (Ed.), *Learning mathematics for a new century* (pp. 213–222). Reston, VA: National Council of Teachers of Mathematics.

TEACHING All ChildRen Mathematics

A society can claim success in eradicating the malady of mathematics illiteracy if and only if all its progeny are able to develop to their fullest potential. If its offspring can become employable workers, wisely choosing consumers, and autonomously thinking citizens who can be contributors in the super symbolic quantitative world they will inherit, then society can say, "Victory is ours!"

Elliott and Garnett (1994, p. 15)

In 1998 the NCTM board of directors adopted its "Every Child" statement, which states:

By "every child," we mean every child—no exception. We are particularly concerned about students who have been denied access to education opportunities for any reason, such as language, ethnicity, physical impairment, gender, socioeconomic status, and so on. We emphasize that "every child" includes:

- learners of English as a second language and speakers of English as a first language

- members of underrepresented ethnic groups and members of well-represented groups

- students who are physically challenged and those who are not

- females and males

- students who live in poverty and those who do not

- students who have not been successful and those who have been successful in school and in mathematics (p. 11)

MATHEMATICS for All ChildReN

❌ **STOP** Stop and think for a minute. Do you personally believe the "Every Child" statement? Children with disabilities, children from impoverished homes, minority children—can all of these children learn to think mathematically?

It is the responsibility of all who are concerned with children's mathematical learning to make that vision a reality.

Diversity in Today's Classroom

It is no longer reasonable to talk about "regular education" as if it were separate from addressing the needs of children who require specialized and specific academic services. It is even difficult to talk about the "average child." The range of abilities, disabilities, and socioeconomic circumstances in the regular classroom poses significant challenges to teachers. Addressing the needs of *all* children means providing opportunity for any or all of the following:

- *Students who are identified as having a specific learning disability*
- *Students from different cultural backgrounds*
- *Students who are at risk due to social inequities*
- *Students who are female*
- *Students who do not speak English*
- *Students who are mathematically promising*

In this chapter we will discuss working with children in each of these categories. There are no easy answers or solutions.

But it is our task to help all students learn mathematics. Children with special needs or difficulties to overcome cannot be excluded.

Challenging Traditional Beliefs

Meeting the needs of all children requires that we challenge and perhaps change many of our long-held assumptions about the mathematics curriculum and about how children learn mathematics.

Change Beliefs About the Mathematics Curriculum

Our concept of mathematics as a rule-driven, computation-dominated curriculum actually creates much of the difficulty we have in coping with the range of children's talents and abilities. When every child is required to master each algorithm and memorize every basic fact before being permitted to move on to the next procedure or rule, the more able children in the room quickly reach this objective and often become bored. Children at the other extreme begin to doubt that they have any mathematical ability. However, there is neither evidence nor any logical argument for the demands of computational proficiency as a prerequisite for meaningful mathematics. Furthermore, the computational curriculum of the past is no longer necessary for the daily lives of citizens once they leave school. What is critically important, however, is the ability to reason and solve problems.

Change Beliefs About How Children Learn Mathematics

There is no reason to believe that children with special needs, regardless of the nature of those needs, should learn any differently than other children (Carey, Fennema, Carpenter, & Franke, 1995; Gable & Hendrickson, 1997; Trafton & Claus, 1994). Inclusive education that simultaneously addresses the needs of regular and special-needs students in a single learning environment depends on the notion that appropriate instruction and equitable assessment can be designed to meet the needs of all students (Johnson, 1999). A well-planned mathematics lesson should always consider the varying abilities, interests, and needs of each child in the class. A problem-based approach will allow all children to access the tasks at their own level of ability. In contrast, as pointed out in Chapter 6, a top-down, show-and-tell approach allows each child only one interpretation, one avenue to success. Each child must be thinking in the same manner as the teacher.

Except in extreme circumstances, it is not necessary to separate or "pull out" children for alternative mathematics instruction.

When skills rather than problem solving and concepts dominate, teachers find it useful to form ability groups. The results of creating ability groups are usually not as good as teachers believe. Children in the lower groups are typically denied opportunities for interacting with their peers in situations involving higher-order thinking or reasoning. The mathematics in the bottom group is generally relegated to skill remedi-ation and isolated practice. Gamoran and Weinstein (1998) concluded from a study of 24 restructured schools that the need to implement ability grouping for teaching and learning mathematics to children with special needs is a perception rather than a reality. Teachers' conception (or misconception) arises from their belief that mathematics must be taught sequentially—with concept and skills approached on an "as mastered" basis. There is little or no evidence to support the homogeneous grouping of children within classrooms or the creation of special homogeneous classes (Davidson & Hammerman, 1993; Oakes, 1990; Usiskin, 1993).

Change Beliefs About Assessment of Mathematics

Appropriate assessment must consist of more than traditional testing methods that focus only on the number of correct answers. Although there may be some value in ascertaining such information, it sheds little light on what mathematics students know or do not know. A model of true assessment requires that students be given multiple ways to represent their knowledge because not all students learn in the same way and not all students can exhibit what they have learned in the same way. (See Chapter 5.)

Children with Learning Problems

The more a teacher knows about the nature of a child's learning difficulties, the better prepared that teacher will be to help.

As more and more children with special needs are included in regular classrooms, "the distinction between special and regular education will soon become obsolete" (Greenes, Garfunkel, & De Bussey, 1994, p. 133). The loud and clear message should be, "Become informed." Find out about how the special children in your classroom learn. Referral to the school's instructional support or consultation team should always be considered. However, the objective should be to secure assistance and, most important, information about the child.

Rather than be defeated by the reality of a diverse class of children, consider that inclusion helps special students develop good socialization skills and builds their self-esteem. Other benefits suggested by Borasi (1994) include the following:

- Regular students serve as learning models for students with special needs.
- Students with learning disabilities often offer unique alternative solutions to challenging problems.
- All students develop an awareness of and respect for individual differences.
- All students, not just the "regular" students, are exposed to good mathematics and challenging experiences.

Specific Learning Disabilities

The predominant instructional model for learning-disabled students has historically viewed the learner as passive, with the mastery of skills taking precedence over understanding

(Poplin, 1988a). It is this thinking that led to pull-out and self-contained classroom approaches. As noted, these skills-oriented models have produced very limited results.

Poplin's conclusion is that constructivist theory provides the best directions for teachers of special students. Nearly every author in NCTM's excellent book *Windows of Opportunity: Mathematics for Students with Special Needs* (Thornton & Bley, 1994) leaves the reader with this same conclusion. Put simply, there is no need to change the content of the curriculum for students with learning disabilities. What must be done is what all good teachers do—pay careful attention to the child and how he or she learns and design instruction (not content) that maximizes the strengths of the child while minimizing the impact of weaknesses.

A Perspective on Learning Disabilities

Students with learning disabilities have very specific problems with perceptual or cognitive processing. These problems may affect memory or the ability to speak or express ideas in writing, perceive auditory or written information, or integrate abstract ideas. It is insufficient simply to label a child "LD." The following insights offered by Borasi (1994) are an important point of departure for teachers who have children with learning disabilities in their classes:

- Students with learning disabilities are mentally capable; they are not slow or retarded.
- The classification of LD is not useful to the classroom teacher without a clear understanding of specific learning problems.
- Learning disabilities are not easily remediated and perhaps cannot be remediated.
- Learning disabilities should be compensated for by helping students use their strengths.
- Instructional modifications will be needed to accommodate children with specific learning disabilities.

Borasi suggests that teachers accept the fact that learning disabilities are real in the same sense that being blind or deaf is a real disability. You would not ask a blind person to "look more closely" or a deaf person to "listen more carefully." Hence, we should never ask a child with learning disabilities to do things that depend heavily on his or her area of deficit.

Adaptations for Specific Learning Difficulties

Note that deficits or disabilities may be present as auditory problems, visual problems, or sometimes both. If the child has already been evaluated by the school psychologist, test information will be available to help pinpoint specific weaknesses and also strengths. Working with the psychologist, you can find ways to adapt instructional strategies to avoid weaknesses and capitalize on strengths *without major modification of the curriculum.*

Adaptations for Perceptual Deficits

There are many variations of perceptual problems; some are visual and others auditory. All involve confusion of input in one way or another.

The entire area of perceptual problems is perhaps the clearest area in which the maxim "avoid weaknesses and capitalize on strengths" is best observed. The following are simply a few specific suggestions:

- Seat the child near you and the chalkboard.
- Keep the child's desk or workspace free of clutter.
- Maintain a moderate voice. Repeat main ideas.
- When using the overhead projector or other technology with the whole class, show only one main idea, problem, or exercise at a time.
- Maintain a classroom environment that values the importance of only one person talking at a time so that each child's voice is respected.
- Enunciate words clearly and attempt to face students when speaking to them.
- Design text or worksheet pages for the child. Provide templates to block out all but one problem or exercise at a time.
- Utilize methods for organizing written work. Have computations done on centimeter grid paper writing one number per square. Provide paper with columns or drawn templates for traditional algorithms.
- Use a tape recorder (headphones) with instructions explaining what may be difficult to discern from the visual materials.
- Provide real geometric models whenever possible instead of relying on pictures. Use geoboards and tiles such as pattern blocks for constructions to keep drawing to a minimum.
- Assign a buddy to help read, explain, or repeat directions.

Adaptations for Memory Deficits

Memory deficits can also be specifically visual or auditory. Children with *short-term memory* deficits can have trouble recalling things for even a few seconds, as when copying from the board or recalling information in a word problem. Children with *long-term memory* deficits may show no difficulty with material when presented but appear to have not learned at all a day or a week later. Mastery of basic facts is a hallmark problem for children with this disability.

You can diminish the load on short-term memory by breaking tasks and directions into small steps and providing a buddy to help with recall. Long-term memory problems require overlearning, frequent practice, and as many associations with other ideas as possible. The following additional specific suggestions may be useful:

- Rather than a series of instructions, provide only one at a time.
- After giving instructions, ask one or more students to state the instructions in their own words as a way to check for

broad understanding of the instructions and to allow other students to hear the instructions from a peer's perspective.

- When working on oral exercises or problems, allow students the option of using written versions as well.
- Exercise students' memory skills through games (e.g., matching games) related to mathematics content.
- For basic facts, use strategies and number relationships to promote memorization (see Chapter 11).
- Allow use of a calculator at all times.

Memory deficits tend to be exhibited in procedural work. Remember that no routine procedural knowledge, including mastery of basic facts, should prevent a student from progress in mathematical ideas. Exploration of new concepts is never dependent on mastery of skills.

Adaptations for Integrative Deficits

Children with integrative problems seem to have difficulty with abstract ideas and conceptualization. These children often have difficulty making the cognitive connections that others may find easy. Children with an integrative disorder may do quite well at rote procedures such as computational algorithms, but these are no longer the focus of the mathematics curriculum. A general principle for helping these children integrate concepts and develop understanding is to use experiences and ideas most familiar to them: their own invented procedures for solving problems, familiar models or personal drawings that make sense to them, and their own words in either written or oral form to express their ideas. The following more specific approaches may be helpful for children with integrative difficulties:

- Use familiar physical models for longer than the usual period of time.
- Have students verbalize what they do as often as possible. Use both written and oral expression.
- Frequently require explanations and justifications to heighten the children's awareness of new ideas and to assist them in making connections.
- Allow for repetition or practice of new conceptual ideas.
- Encourage students to restate word problems in their own words.
- Provide students with opportunities to teach a concept to a peer, hence organizing and reconceptualizing their own thoughts about the concept.
- Use multiple representations of abstract concepts (e.g., words, symbols, drawings, concrete objects, acting it out).

Adaptations for Attention Deficits

Many (not all) students with learning disabilities also are identified as having attention deficit disorder or attention deficit–hyperactivity disorder. These children have chronic difficulties with attention span, impulse control, and sometimes hyperactivity. Be careful to distinguish these true disorders from the behavior of children who have discipline problems for other reasons. The following strategies have proved useful:

- Establish clear routines, and discuss them with the child. Make expectations and consequences clear.
- Design learning activities that are active and involving rather than tedious or requiring lengthy periods of silent seatwork.
- Plan for the child to do independent work in an environment free of distractions.
- Use highlighters to attract attention to important key ideas in textual material.
- Keep assignments and exercise lists short. Plan smaller subtasks within larger explorations or projects.
- Assign a buddy, and impress on both that the agenda is to stay on task.
- Instead of placing the child in a cooperative group of three or four, use a buddy to form a separate group of two.

MENTAL DISABILITIES

All of us possess different mental capacities in addition to our individual strengths and weaknesses or learning styles. Children with mental disabilities (generally with IQ scores between 50 and 70) will be limited in the kind and degree of mathematical reasoning they can perform. Other children not as severely limited are sometimes in need of more time for learning than would be given under standard circumstances. Although severely disabled children are generally best served in a special classroom, a wide range of mental disabilities are likely to be present in the regular classroom.

Modifications in Instruction

Limited cognitive abilities do not in any way alter the way that children learn, but these limited abilities do alter the means by which children experience and acquire their learning. For example, a child with limited cognitive abilities can learn the part/whole concept of addition just as a child without limitations can. However, much more repetitiveness and use of concrete learning tools will likely be required. In general, these special children learn *much* more slowly than do their peers (Bley, 1994).

Though a fast-paced, highly interactive classroom may be somewhat overwhelming for children who need more time to learn, they can benefit from many of the same experiences as the rest of the class. They can and should participate in projects and hands-on activities with their peer group. They can participate in cooperative groups by taking on less demanding roles, such as materials organizer or encourager. They can learn to perform calculations on a calculator and can serve as the person in a group who performs this activity. Many such children are good at drawing or making graphs. These helping roles are consistent with the kinds of jobs they are likely to have in the adult world.

Partner the child with limited abilities with different students periodically, and have the partner help the child with the same task or idea. In this way, there is opportunity for needed repeated exposure or overlearning, and other students also will gain from serving as the explainer. It is important for all children in the room to involve children who need more time to learn in activities and projects. All children gain an appreciation for and acceptance of human differences.

Modifications in Curriculum

Since children with limited abilities need more time to learn than other children, it follows that less content can be learned during the years they are in school. It makes sense to focus the available instructional time on those areas that are going to be of the most value to these students as adults. Computational skill is the most obvious area where changes in curricular expectations should be made. There is no reason to be obsessive about fact mastery. Traditional computational algorithms should be eliminated from their curriculum altogether.

Students should have a calculator handy for all mathematics work. The child with limited abilities should be given careful instruction and lots of practice in using the calculator. A calculator with a printer is useful because it creates a printed record of work done.

Whereas calculations can be mastered via the calculator, the meanings of numbers in the real world cannot. Do not confuse number meaning with place-value concepts. What is important here is to realize that a bag of flour weighs 5 pounds, that $100 buys a pair of fancy shoes, or that it takes about 20 minutes to walk a mile. Numbers in the abstract will be of little use.

Multicultural and Social Equity

There is clear evidence that African American, Hispanic, and Native American children and children from homes with low socioeconomic status (SES) do poorly in mathematics (Hilliard, 1995; Anderson, 1990; Ladson-Billings, 1997). Do children in these groups not have the same mathematical or even general academic ability as their white, middle-class suburban counterparts? There is no evidence to support such a view, yet discrepancies in achievement levels in mathematics remain a fact.

A Question of Access

Students in at-risk populations (non-Asian ethnicities and low SES) are simply not getting the same access to quality teachers, to adequate resources and technology, or to quality curriculum as their middle- and upper-class suburban counterparts.

According to Oakes (1990, 1995), low-income and minority students are not being taught mathematics or science by high-quality teachers. The best teachers shy away from at-risk or disadvantaged school populations. Nearly all schools tend to place their least qualified teachers in low-ability classes.

The fact is that teachers can make a difference. You can help traditionally at-risk students achieve at the highest levels without any special "minority training," without special technology, and without special texts or materials.

> For some teachers, the surprising reality is that the low achievers change not because of the invention of some culturally specific exotic new method, but because many of them are exposed to regular high-quality instruction, to which many of the traditionally low performers had not been previously exposed. (Hilliard, 1995, p. 109)

The issue of resources is not an issue under teacher control. It is sad to note, however, that the areas where low-income and minority children attend schools are the areas where fewer dollars are spent on schools. Although money will never solve all problems, there is no doubt that it has an impact, if only in terms of teacher and student attitudes.

As for access to quality curriculum, evidence suggests that teachers in minority schools tend to place less emphasis on curricular goals such as inquiry and problem solving. It is within your power as a teacher to keep the emphasis in the classroom on higher-order thinking and engaging, meaningful tasks.

 The following statement is from the Equity Principle in the *Standards:* "All students, regardless of their personal characteristics, backgrounds, or physical challenges, must have opportunities to study—and support to learn—mathematics. Equity does not mean that every student should receive identical instruction; instead, it demands that reasonable and appropriate accommodations be made as needed to promote access and attainment for all students" (p. 12).

Expectations

It remains true that students will rise or fall to the level of our expectations. Two related factors seem to be working against minority and low-SES students: teachers' beliefs in their abilities and the effects of tracking or homogeneous grouping.

Teacher Expectations

Among teachers of at-risk children, there is a striking difference between those who believe in the abilities of their students and those who expect very little. The latter group of teachers have found it easy to blame the performance of their students on the myriad factors that exist outside the classroom. *It's the neighborhood. They don't have two parents making them work. The parents are not educated. These kids come from an environment infested with drugs.* Teachers who voice such laments are using real facts as excuses for not making a difference (Ladson-Billings, 1995). If the excuses were valid, no teachers would believe in their students—yet many do and achieve outstanding results.

Experts believe that one of the most important factors for success with disadvantaged or minority students is to develop in them a strong sense of self-esteem, helping children believe in themselves. This is an incredibly difficult task for the teacher whose expectations are low to begin with. Teachers must believe that all students are capable and willing to learn (Johnson, 1999).

Negative Effects of Tracking and Homogeneous Grouping

Teachers' assessments of students' abilities play a key role in deciding what types of educational experiences a student may receive. Once students are placed in a lower-level track or in a "slow" class, expectations decline accordingly. Students in low tracks are frequently denied access to challenging material and high-quality mathematics (Silver, Smith, & Nelson, 1995). The mathematics for the lower tracks or classes is almost totally oriented toward day after day of remedial drill with minimal success and no excitement. Teachers become reinforced in their low expectations because students are not encouraged to think, nor are they engaged in activities and interactions that would encourage thinking. Furthermore, tracking severely diminishes the potential for valuable interactions in the classroom. In heterogeneous classes, expectations are often turned upside down as children perceived as less able come to understand and work meaningfully with concepts to which they would never be exposed in a low-track homogeneous class. Exposing all students to higher-level thinking and quality mathematics avoids accentuating differences from year to year caused by low-track expectations.

Success for At-Risk Students

What we have learned over the years from massive federal programs that have failed is that narrow, skill-focused, highly prescriptive approaches do not work. We have also seen that programs that target disadvantaged kids by grouping them in special classrooms do not work. We *can* point to some recent examples of programs and the efforts of individual teachers that have worked exceptionally well with urban, minority, low-SES children. The common factors in these programs are not money, materials, technology, or tracking. What makes them succeed is a constructivist approach to instruction and a positive belief in the children.

Ms. Rossi is a veteran sixth-grade teacher in a low-SES, predominantly African American school. She is one of eight teachers studied by Ladson-Billings (1995) who are effective working with African American students. In one lesson, Rossi made a point of involving all students individually, assuring them that they were capable of mastering the problems. Students cheered one another and celebrated explanations. Students were pushed to explain "How do you know?" The textbook was generally not used. Rossi would help students see that what they had been doing was the same as what was in the text. The point was always that mathematics was not threatening and that the students were capable of good mathematics and quality thinking.

Based on her study of effective teachers, Ladson-Billings listed five guidelines or principles for the successful teaching of students who are traditionally at risk of failing:

1. *Have high expectations for all students, letting them know that you believe in them.* If you treat students as competent, they are likely to demonstrate competence.
2. *Use "instructional scaffolding."* Instead of worrying about what students do not know, work from what they do know toward what they do not know.
3. *Make instruction the focus of each class.* Avoid busywork. Confront restlessness with an adjustment in instruction rather than a focus on misbehavior.
4. *Extend students' thinking and abilities beyond what they already know.* Provide challenging mathematics for all students, rather than attempting to maintain low levels of performance.
5. *Work at gaining in-depth knowledge of your students as well as knowledge of the subject matter.* Develop a positive identification and relationship with all students.

Again you notice principles of constructivist teaching, belief in students, and challenging curriculum.

To examine two projects that have demonstrated the efficacy of quality teaching with at-risk children, see Campbell (1996) and Silver et al. (1995). Campbell's project IMPACT was a five-year program at the elementary level. Silver's QUASAR project focused on middle schools in economically disadvantaged communities. Both programs began with the belief that all children can learn mathematics. Both programs found this to be true.

CULTURE, LANGUAGE, AND MATHEMATICS

Because of the recent astonishing influx of peoples of myriad cultures and ethnicities to the United States, it is now the norm rather than the exception for a school to have students of multiple skin colors, languages, and ethnic heritages. These students are frequently new to the country and require our special attention even within the subject of mathematics.

Cultural Diversity

With the advent of students from diverse cultures in our classrooms, it is necessary to acknowledge, define, and act on the relationship between multicultural education and mathematics education. The terms *ethnomathematics* and *multicultural mathematics* are typically used to define the combination of these two areas of education.

Ethnomathematics

Ubiratan D'Ambrosio, a mathematics educator, introduced the term *ethnomathematics* in 1984. He suggests that ethnomathematics is based on the history of mathematics and cultural anthropology. D'Ambrosio (1985) defines ethnomathematics as "the mathematics which is practiced among identifiable cultural groups, such as national-tribal societies, labor groups, children of a certain age bracket, professional classes, and so on. Its identity depends largely on focuses of interest, on motivation, and on certain codes and jargons which do not belong to the realm of academic mathematics" (p. 45).

People invent terminology and ways of doing mathematics that are different from other people. Culture—peoples' beliefs, mores, traditions, practices, and so on—influences their mathematical activity as it would any other activity (Zaslavsky, 1996). Zaslavsky asserts that any school curriculum that proposes to represent multicultural mathematics in any form must include the following principles:

- All students can learn, and teachers must be willing to empower all students to learn by providing different ways for them to do so.
- The mathematics must be relevant to children in personal as well as in general ways. Any cultural content present in the curriculum must be realistic and engaging to students.
- The curriculum should be open-minded, focused on sharing knowledge, and respectful of the local and global cultural community.
- The curriculum should empower students through the acceptance of student differences, support of students' creativity, and recognition of students' varying abilities for doing mathematics.

STOP Reflect for a moment on the preceding list. How is it like the ideas you have learned about teaching through problem solving? How does this list add to those general principles of teaching?

The basic idea of multicultural mathematics is to provide a diverse perspective on how culture impacts the mathematics experience of students. Every student who enters the classroom represents a history and a culture. This can be a very powerful tool for enabling all students to connect to mathematics.

Addressing Cultural Issues

Teaching mathematics with respect to culture is one way to respect diversity within your classroom. Students can be personally engaged in mathematics by examining their own culture's impact on the ways they use, practice, and think about mathematics. A study of mathematics within other cultures provides an opportunity for students to "put faces" to mathematics instead of erroneously thinking that mathematics is a result of some mystical phenomenon.

There are many ways to approach mathematics from a cultural perspective (e.g., biographies of mathematicians, historical development of concepts, games, children's literature, and thematic units). Mathematics is the by-product of human ideas, creativity, problem solving, recreation, beliefs, values, and survival. Contributions to the field of mathematics come from diverse people all over the world.

Many topics are appropriate for the study of mathematics from a cultural approach via complete lessons, activities, thematic units, or small-group projects. The following topics suggest areas in which a cultural focus can be included:

- Abacus (Japanese and Chinese)
- Chinese calendar
- Counting words in various languages
- Egyptian numerals
- Native American arts and geometry
- Patterns and symmetry in art, fabrics, and architecture
- Place-value bases in various systems

In addition, there are numerous Web sites that support ethnomathematic or multicultural instruction. Here are just two:

International Study Group on Ethnomathematics
www.rpi.edu/~eglash/isgem.htm

Making Multicultural Connections Through Trade Books
www.mcps.k12.md.us/curriculum/socialstd/MBD/Lessons_index.html

Teaching Second Language Learners

As U.S. classrooms are increasingly populated with students from around the world, it is also true that many of these students are just learning English or perhaps speak no English. In some states, classroom teachers are mandated to have specific training related to teaching students whose first language is not English. Regardless of the law in your state, in your classroom the issue of students with limited English proficiency (LEP) cannot be ignored.

Children who are challenged by English for learning and doing mathematics require your patience, flexibility, and understanding. When students recognize that the teacher is willing to allow them time to process mathematics concepts in their own language and develop ways of expressing it in the English language, they are more likely to invest their effort and extend themselves in the mathematics process. No child likes to feel rushed or abandoned when they are having difficulty communicating. Children should feel supported to take risks with the English language, with mathematics language, and with doing mathematics.

Mather and Chiodo (1994) provide suggestions for teaching mathematics to LEP students as well as other students who may have difficulty with the English language. Their suggestions include the following:

- Stress understanding of mathematical concepts.
- Approach mathematics through the use of manipulatives and hands-on activities.
- Use cooperative groups and peer tutoring.
- Use appropriate methods of reinforcement and praise.

- Incorporate multicultural aspects into the curriculum.
- When possible use second language materials and texts.
- Monitor discourse to limit culturally based examples not generally understood.
- Use mathematics vocabulary in context.
- Become informed about how represented cultures teach mathematics.

Some say that mathematics is a universal language and is, therefore, easier for LEP students to understand. Regardless of your view on this issue, mathematics is a language. As a language, it shares many attributes (e.g., vocabulary) with standard spoken language. It is a language that must be learned by all students, regardless of their spoken language. Conversation about mathematics should be a regular part of every lesson as earlier chapters have emphasized. As with any language, children should be able to use mathematical terminology comfortably before they are required to use mathematical symbolism. In your assessments, be respectful of all students and their individual abilities with language (Wakefield, 2000).

 STOP Reflect on the suggestions you have just read. Which of these should apply to classrooms in which all students speak English?

From Gender Bias to Gender Equity

You would think that issues surrounding gender inequity would have disappeared by the end of the twentieth century. NAEP data from 1990, 1992, and 1996 assessments show that the gap between males and females has actually narrowed except at grade 4, where males significantly outperform females (Ansell & Doerr, 2000). Over that time, both male and female performance has improved. There persists in our society, however, a common belief that boys are better than girls at mathematics—what Damarin (1995) refers to as the "maleness of mathematics." And more males than females enter fields of study after high school that include heavy emphases on mathematics and science. It is important to be aware of gender inequity and make efforts to address it in your classroom.

Possible Causes of Gender Inequity

Although the achievement levels for females have improved substantially in the past decade, two facts remain. First, achievement differences among girls are significantly greater than differences among boys (Burton, 1995). To make conclusions based only on mean scores without considering medians and the spread of scores is misleading. Second, the perception that boys are better at mathematics than girls remains a seemingly intractable trait of our society. As Becker

and Jacobs (2001) point out, most of the research "is moving away from 'sex differences' to 'gender differences' in acknowledgment that gender is socially constructed and the differences are not biologically determined" (p. 2). We must look to the classroom for causes of gender inequity.

Teacher Interactions and Gender

Teachers may not consciously seek to stereotype students by gender; however, the gender-based biases of our society often affect teachers' interactions with students (Martin, Sexton, Wagner, & Gerlovich, 1997). For example, observations of teachers' gender-specific interactions in the classroom indicate that boys get more attention and different kinds of attention than girls do. Boys receive more criticism as well as more praise for correct answers. Boys also tend to be more involved in discipline-related attention and have their work monitored more carefully (Campbell, 1995; Leder, 1995). The increased attention, both positive and negative, that teachers unconsciously provide males contributes to the impression of mathematics as a male domain. Attention is interpreted as value, with a predictable effect on both sexes.

Research has found that teachers wait longer for responses from boys than from girls (Leder, 1995). In one study, females received more wait time on low-level questions concerning facts and procedures, whereas males received longer wait times on more difficult, more challenging, and higher-cognitive questions. Over time, these subtle but real differences suggest to girls that they are not perceived as capable of quality thinking, and they eventually adopt this belief themselves.

Belief Systems Related to Gender

The belief that mathematics is a male domain persists in our society and is held by both sexes. In adolescent years, when girls are significantly interested in and influenced by boys, many girls are afraid to act "too smart" for fear of alienating boys. Campbell (1995) points out that "unless boys as well as girls are convinced that 'real women do math,' efforts toward gender equity in mathematics will encounter obstacles based on stereotyped social roles" (p. 229).

Working Toward Gender Equity: What Can Be Done?

Campbell (1995) makes a compelling argument that we have tended to address gender inequity as a "girl problem." This places the focus of our solution efforts on girls—to make them somehow like mathematics more or take more courses in mathematics. This approach, she says, makes it seem that there really is something wrong with girls. "If you change a girl so that she 'loves math,' but then you put her back into the same environment and situations that caused her to hate mathematics in the first place, she will revert to hating mathematics" (p. 226). As already noted, the causes of girls' perceptions of themselves vis-à-vis mathematics are largely a function of the educational environment. That is where we should look for solutions.

Become Aware

As a teacher, you need to be aware whether you treat boys and girls differently. Work at ensuring equal treatment. As you interact with students, try to be aware of the interactions with both gender groups in relationship to the

- Number and type of questions you ask
- Amount of attention given to disturbances
- Kinds and topics of projects and activities assigned
- Praise given in response to students' participation
- Makeup of small groups

Being aware of your gender-specific actions is more difficult than it may sound. To receive feedback, try tape-recording a class or two on a periodic basis. Tally the number of questions asked of boys and girls. Also note which students ask questions and what kind of questions are being asked. At first, you will be surprised at how gender-biased your interaction is. Awareness takes effort.

Involve All Students

Find ways to involve all students in your class, not just those who seem eager. Girls tend to shy away from involvement and are not as quick to seek help. Perhaps the best suggestion for involving students is to follow the tenets of this book—use a problem-based approach to instruction. Mau and Leitze (2001) make the case that when teachers are in a show-and-tell mode, there is significantly more opportunity for the teacher to reinforce the more overt behaviors of boys and allow girls to be passive. In a classroom influenced by constructivist theory, all students are expected to both talk and listen. More mathematics is constructed with less teacher intervention. Authority resides in the students and in their arguments. The result is that girls are on an equal footing with the boys.

❌ **STOP** Stop for a moment and envision the directive teaching that most likely was the model you experienced. Can you see situations in which males are favored, encouraged, or assisted by the teacher—even without consciously being aware of any differential? How would these differentials possibly disappear in a problem-based, student-oriented environment?

Mathematics for the Gifted and Talented

Children who are typically known as "gifted" no doubt deserve consideration in the educational decisions required to provide all children with the best possible education. Considerable research is available on the education of the gifted but offers little consensus. Alternative views have typically focused

on two major questions: What does it mean to be gifted, and should the program for gifted children focus on acceleration or enrichment? In addition, there are practical considerations, not the least of which is how to deliver an appropriate program. Alternatives include pull-out designs, after-school models, and in-class programs. There are also questions of time, teachers, and materials.

Identification of Mathematically Promising Students

In 1995, NCTM convened the Task Force on the Mathematically Promising to prepare recommendations and draft a policy statement concerning the mathematically talented. The task force preferred to use the term *promising* rather than *gifted* or *talented* because under common definitions of the gifted and talented, many mathematically adept students have been overlooked or excluded. The task force explained that mathematical promise was a function of *ability, motivation, belief,* and *experience or opportunity.*

Many Americans tend to believe that children either "have it or they don't," that mathematical ability is a result of the roll of the genetic dice. In contrast, Asians generally believe that success in mathematics, as in any subject, is largely a function of individual effort.

The literature on mathematically promising students suggests that they may not be especially talented in other areas. Nor can mathematical promise be equated with general school achievement or facility with computational algorithms. Promising students generally have good verbal skills, curiosity, imagination, analytic thinking skills, and the ability to concentrate and work independently (House, 1999).

What all of this means for the identification of promising students is that simple criteria built on test scores, IQ, or high grades may exclude those who have a high probability of developing into exceptional mathematical students.

Acceleration, Enrichment, and Depth

For years, one of the primary debates related to the talented mathematics student was over the relative merits of enrichment versus acceleration. *Acceleration* occurs when students are either placed in a grade ahead of their normal age group or when the pace at which they progress through the regular curriculum is speeded up. *Enrichment* refers to the expansion of the regular curriculum to include additional topics.

Acceleration and Enrichment

Both merits and cautions are associated with acceleration and enrichment. Capable and promising students should be challenged to move at an appropriate pace through the curriculum and should be exposed to as much quality mathematics as time permits. The NCTM task force chose not to endorse either approach. Acceleration can have the effect of developing a large array of meaningless skills as students are pushed to learn more without exploring the ideas in a full conceptual manner. Without adequate time, the guidance of a skilled teacher, and the benefit of directed discourse and exploration, students in acceleration programs tend to focus on mechanical skills. This will often be the case as well when students are left to study independently.

Too often enrichment programs result in little more than "fun math time" with topics such as geometric puzzles, computer games, or the "problem of the day." Although good mathematics activities should be fun, they should accomplish much more. They should broaden students' mathematical horizons, require students to think deeply, make connections to earlier ideas and to real contexts, and challenge them to ask questions, make conjectures, and reason about important ideas.

The Addition of Depth

Recognizing the strengths and pitfalls of enrichment and acceleration, Sheffield (1999) argues for a three-dimensional approach: breadth (enrichment), rate (acceleration), and depth or complexity. That is, the benefits of both acceleration and enrichment should be coupled with the opportunity for studying the complexities of new mathematical ideas, both those in the regular curriculum and those that go beyond it. Sheffield writes that promising students should be introduced to the "joys and frustrations of thinking deeply about a wide range of original, open-ended, or complex problems that encourage them to respond creatively in ways that are original, fluent, flexible, and elegant" (p. 46).

In the regular classroom, teachers often "reward" highly capable students for finishing routine tasks quickly by having them do more exercises or more tedious exercises than those required of the rest of the class. For example, if the full class is working on the multiplication algorithm for multidigit

numbers, there is no redeeming value in having promising students who complete their work quickly do more exercises or exercises with more digits. However, they may be asked what would produce the largest or smallest products given four distinct digits to make two factors. Is there a general rule? Why does the rule work? What if there were five digits?

Even more interesting than the max/min task is that for some products, interchanging the digits in each two-digit factor produces the same result:

$$\begin{array}{cc} 24 & 42 \\ \times\,63 & \times\,36 \\ \hline 1512 & 1512 \end{array}$$

However, this is obviously not always the case, as a little experimentation will quickly show. When will this interchanging of the digits produce equal products and why? Students working on tasks such as these are engaged in a deeper exploration of the multiplication algorithm than simply understanding how it works and being able to use it.

There is no simple formula for adding depth to mathematical explorations, but some valuable insights may be learned from the Japanese. According to Hashimoto and Becker (1999), the Japanese approach to mathematical problem solving involves making the problem open in one of three ways: the process is open (multiple paths to a solution are explored), the end product is open (there are multiple correct answers to be discovered), or the formulation of new problems is open (students explore new problems related to the one solved).

These three approaches to open-ended problem solving are explored in depth in *The Open-Ended Approach: A New Proposal for Teaching Mathematics* (Becker & Shimada, 1997). Application of the open-ended methods is an excellent way to add depth to both acceleration and enrichment for special students.

REFLECTIONS ON CHAPTER 7

Writing to Learn

1. What traditional ideas about curriculum, teaching, and assessing children must be changed so that the NCTM vision of all children learning mathematics can be realized?
2. How would you argue for the values of a diverse class that includes children with learning problems?
3. Briefly describe each of the following specific learning disabilities, and give some indication of how the disability may affect mathematics learning or ability. For each disability, also list at

least two ideas that can be used by the classroom teacher to help the child.
   a. Perceptual deficits (figure-ground, discrimination, reversal, spatial)
   b. Memory deficits (short term and long term)
   c. Integrative deficits
   d. Attention deficits
4. For children with mental deficits and special learning needs, how should content and instruction each be modified?

5. Explain how teacher expectations and tracking have detrimental effects on minorities and low-SES children.
6. Describe in general terms one or more of the most significant ideas that should guide the teacher who is working with students from a cultural minority.
7. Describe ethnomathematics in your own words. Why is it important to consider culture in mathematics instruction?
8. What are some ways that cultural considerations can be included in the mathematics classroom?
9. Discuss at least two ideas that you think are most important in helping students who either do not speak English or who are just learning English.
10. What are some factors that contribute to gender inequity, and what are the long-term effects of that inequity?
11. How can teachers in the elementary or middle school work to erase gender inequity?
12. Describe what is meant by enrichment and by acceleration. What are the dangers of each for mathematically promising students?
13. In the context of providing for the mathematically promising, what is meant by depth? How can the Japanese open-ended approaches help provide depth?

For Discussion and Exploration

1. Two common threads in this chapter are the beliefs that all children will benefit from a developmental or constructivist approach to teaching and that there is real value in teaching children in diverse, heterogeneous classrooms. Some teachers may argue with this position, contending that it is best for the majority of children if "special needs" students are isolated. And besides, the argument continues, their special needs are best met by special teachers in classes with fewer students. Pick a position in this argument, and articulate it in writing or in a classroom discussion.
2. Develop your own philosophical statement for "all students" or "every child." Design a visual representation for your statement. Read the Equity Principle in *Principles and Standards* and see if your position is in accord with that principle.
3. What are some of the challenges faced by students whose first language is not English as they participate in mathematics learning? Talk to a teacher who has children with little or no English and find out how these children are being helped to participate in the classroom community of learners.
4. Develop a mathematics lesson plan that reflects a cultural approach to mathematics. What mathematics concepts does your lesson address?
5. What would you do if you found yourself teaching a class with one exceptionally talented child who had no equal in the room? Assume that acceleration to the next grade has been ruled out due to social adjustment factors.

Recommendations for Further Reading

Highly Recommended

Malloy, C. E., & Brader-Araje, L. (Eds.). (1998). *Challenges of the mathematics education of African American children: Proceedings of the Benjamin Banneker Association leadership conference.* Reston, VA: National Council of Teachers of Mathematics.

The Benjamin Banneker Association is an organization concerned with the mathematics education of African American children. These proceedings of a 1997 conference include six presentations by leaders in the field plus a number of other short papers. This is a short but useful collection of informed perspectives on a subject of great concern for all.

Robert, M. (2002). Problem solving and the at-risk students: Making "mathematics for all" a classroom reality. *Teaching Children Mathematics, 8,* 290–295.

This tale of a year in a fifth-grade classroom of seriously disadvantaged children, by a teacher who had spent two prior years in an affluent suburban school, will support and sustain teachers who think their class is simply too difficult. Robert tells about how she began with a complete failure and yet worked throughout the year to use a problem-based approach. Children began to catch on. This is an important story from a teacher for teachers.

Secada, W. G. (Series Ed.). (1999–2002). *Changing the faces of mathematics* (6 volumes). Reston, VA: National Council of Teachers of Mathematics.

These six books present perspectives on four categories of cultures: Asian Americans and Pacific Islanders, Native Americans, Latinos, and African Americans. The remaining two volumes address multiculturalism and gender equity. Each culture-specific volume explores curriculum, instruction, and assessment issues relevant to the culture for all grade levels. The authors stress pedagogical strategies, classroom environment, and positive practices that support the learning of students related to that particular culture. These are unique, excellent resources.

Sheffield, L. J. (Ed.) (1999). *Developing mathematically promising students.* Reston, VA: National Council of Teachers of Mathematics.

This book is the result of a recommendation to NCTM from the Task Force on Mathematically Promising Students. The book has a wealth of ideas and perspectives for working with our most talented students. Rather than the more simplistic approach of NCTM's earlier booklet on teaching the gifted, this book adds depth to any discussion of mathematics for the talented.

Thornton, C. A., & Bley, N. S. (Eds.). (1994). *Windows of opportunity: Mathematics for students with special needs.* Reston, VA: National Council of Teachers of Mathematics.

There are very few books that even attempt to address the issues of special-needs children and mathematics. Thornton and Bley have put together an excellent book that could be a methods text or a resource for the classroom teacher, consisting of seven chapters on issues, eight that address content through perspective and vignettes, and six that look at promising practices. This book will remain a valuable resource even after the next special needs book is published.

Other Suggestions

Adams, T. L. (1998). Pulling the plug on gender-related differences in mathematics. *Preventing School Failure, 42*(4), 176–180.

Ansell, E., & Doerr, H. M. (2000). NAEP findings regarding gender: Achievement, affect, and instructional experiences. In E. A. Silver & P. A. Kenney (Eds.), *Results from the seventh mathematics assessment of the National Assessment of Educational Progress* (pp. 73–106). Reston, VA: National Council of Teachers of Mathematics.

Bley, N. S. (1994). Accommodating special needs. In C. A. Thornton & N. S. Bley (Eds.), *Windows of opportunity: Mathematics for students with special needs* (pp. 137–163). Reston, VA: National Council of Teachers of Mathematics.

Bley, N. S., & Thornton, C. A. (1995). *Teaching mathematics to students with learning disabilities* (3rd ed.). Austin, TX: Pro-Ed.

Campbell, P. B. (1995). Redefining the "girl problem in mathematics." In W. G. Secada, E. Fennema, & L. B. Adajian (Eds.), *New directions for equity in mathematics education* (pp. 225–241). New York: Cambridge University Press.

Campbell, P. F. (1996). Empowering children and teachers in the elementary mathematics classrooms of urban schools. *Urban Education, 30*, 449–475.

Cole, K. (1999). Using assessments to improve equity in mathematics: Assessment that is open, explicit, and accessible helps all students achieve the goals of standards-based learning. *Educational Leadership, 56*(6), 56–58.

Davidson, E., & Hammerman, J. (1993). Homogenized is only better for milk. In G. Cuevas & M. Driscol (Eds.), *Reaching all students with mathematics* (pp. 197–212). Reston, VA: National Council of Teachers of Mathematics.

Davison, D. M. (1998). An ethnoscience approach to curriculum issues for American Indian students. *School Science and Mathematics, 98*, 250–265.

Education Development Center. (1995). *Equity in education series: Gender-fair math*. Newton, MA: Author.

Edwards, C. A. (1999). *Changing the faces of mathematics: Perspectives on Asian Americans and Pacific Islanders*. Reston, VA: National Council of Teachers of Mathematics.

Garrison, L. (1997). Making the NCTM's standards work for emergent English speakers. *Teaching Children Mathematics, 4*, 132–138.

Hilliard, A. G., III. (1995). Mathematics excellence for cultural "minority" students: What is the problem? In I. M. Carl (Ed.), *Seventy-five years of progress: Prospects for school mathematics* (pp. 99–114). Reston, VA: National Council of Teachers of Mathematics.

Karp, K., Allen, C., Allen, L. G., & Brown, E. T. (1998). Feisty females: Using children's literature with strong female characters. *Teaching Children Mathematics, 5*, 88–94.

Karp, K., Brown, E. T., Allen, L., & Allen, C. (1998). *Feisty females: Inspiring girls to think mathematically*. Portsmouth, NH: Heinemann.

Ladson-Billings, G. (1997). It doesn't add up: African-American students' mathematics achievement. *Journal for Research in Mathematics Education, 28*, 697–708.

Levi, L. (2000). Research into practice: Gender equity in mathematics education. *Teaching Children Mathematics, 7*, 101–105.

Lubienski, S. T. (2000). Problem solving as a means toward mathematics for all: An exploratory look through a class lens. *Journal for Research in Mathematics Education, 31*, 454–482.

Moldavan, C. (2001). Culture in the curriculum: Enriching numeration and number operations. *Teaching Children Mathematics, 8*, 238–243.

National Council of Teachers of Mathematics. (2001). Mathematics and culture [Focus Issue]. *Teaching Children Mathematics, 7*(6).

Rowser, J. F., & Koontz, T. Y. (1995). Inclusion of African-American students in mathematics classrooms: Issues of style, curriculum, and expectations. *Mathematics Teacher, 88*, 448–453.

Secada, W. G., Fennema, E., & Adajian, L. B. (Eds.). (1995). *New directions for equity in mathematics education*. New York: Cambridge University Press.

Silver, E. A., & Stein, M. K. (1996). The QUASAR Project: The "revolution of the possible" in mathematics instructional reform in urban middle schools. *Urban Education, 30*, 476–521.

Tate, W. F. (1997). Race-ethnicity, SES, gender, and language proficiency trends in mathematics achievement: An update. *Journal for Research in Mathematics Education, 28*, 652–679.

Toney, N. L. (1996). Facing racism in mathematics education. In D. Schifter (Ed.), *What's happening in math class? Reconstructing professional identities* (Vol. 2) (pp. 26–36). New York: Teachers College Press.

Trafton, P. R., & Claus, A. S. (1994). A changing curriculum for a changing age. In C. A. Thornton & N. S. Bley (Eds.), *Windows of opportunity: Mathematics for students with special needs* (pp. 19–39). Reston, VA: National Council of Teachers of Mathematics.

Trentacosta, J. (Ed.) (1997). *Multicultural and gender equity in the mathematics classroom: The gift of diversity*. Reston, VA: National Council of Teachers of Mathematics.

Weaver, L. R., & Gaines, C. (1999). What to do when they don't speak English: Teaching mathematics to English-language learners. In J. V. Copley (Ed.), *Mathematics in the early years* (pp. 198–204). Reston, VA: National Council of Teachers of Mathematics.

8

Technology and School Mathematics

Rapid developments in technology are changing (and ought to be changing) the way we teach mathematics both because they modify our goals for the mathematics education of people and because they provide new tools with which we can better achieve our goals.

Willoughby (1990, p. 60)

The term *technology* in the context of school mathematics refers primarily to calculators of all sorts and computers, including access to the Internet and the available resources. The most recent position statement on technology by NCTM, issued in 1998, states simply:

The appropriate use of instructional technology tools is integral to the learning and teaching of mathematics and to the assessment of mathematics learning at all levels. (www.nctm.org/about/position_statements/position_statement_13.htm)

In the rationale for this position, the council further states, "Technology is driving change in the content of mathematics programs, in methods for mathematics instruction, and in the ways that mathematics is learned and assessed." The short position statement includes a number of recommendations including access to an appropriate calculator for every student, access to computers and the Internet for every teacher, and computers in every classroom.

That technology is one of the six principles in the *Principles and Standards* document further highlights the importance that NCTM gives to technology (see Chapter 1).

Calculators and computer software (including Internet-based applications, or "applets") are highlighted throughout Section 2 of this text, with references to specific activities and programs where they are appropriate. The purpose of this chapter is to examine technology and the teaching of mathematics in a more general way so that you will be able to make informed judgments about the use of technology in your classroom.

Calculators in the Mathematics Classroom

Mathematics educators have long understood the value of calculators in the study of mathematics. Since 1976, NCTM has published numerous articles, books, and position statements, all advocating the regular use of calculators in the teaching of mathematics at all grade levels.

Unfortunately, the everyday use of calculators in society, coupled with professional support of calculators in schools, has had a muted impact on the mathematics classroom, especially at the elementary level. Resistance to the use of calculators has diminished but not disappeared. The vocal minority of detractors to the reform movement often assail the use of calculators as "dumbing down" the curriculum or as a "crutch." Their inflammatory rhetoric often resonates with parents, who want what is best for their children. Parents must be made aware of the fact that calculator use will in no way prevent children from learning mathematics; in fact, calculators used thoughtfully and appropriately can enhance the learning of mathematics. Furthermore, parents must learn that the use of both calculators and computers requires the student to be a "problem solver." Calculators always calculate according to the input information. So, if "garbage" is fed into the calculator, you can only expect to get "garbage" out. Calculators cannot substitute for understanding.

Benefits of Calculator Use

Rather than fearing potential damage that calculators might do, it is important to understand how calculators can contribute to the learning of mathematics. In this section, the focus is on simple calculators. A discussion of graphing calculators is reserved for later.

Calculators Can Be Used to Develop Concepts

The calculator can be much more than a device for calculation. It can be used effectively to develop concepts. *Adding It Up: Helping Children Learn Mathematics* (National Research Council, 2001) cites several long-term studies that have shown that students in grades 4–6 who used calculators improved their conceptual understanding. Activities for developing concepts with the calculator are suggested throughout the book, especially in the areas of numeration and computation. Here are two simple examples. On the calculator, $796 \div 42 = 18.95348$. Consider the task of using the calculator to determine the whole-number remainder. Another example is to use the calculator to find a number that when multiplied by itself will produce 43. In this situation, a student can press 6.1 ⨉ = to get the square of 6.1. For students who are just beginning to understand decimals, the activity will demonstrate that numbers such as 6.3 and 6.4 are between 6 and 7. Furthermore, 6.55 is between 6.5 and 6.6. For students who already understand decimals, the same activity serves as a meaningful and conceptual introduction to square roots.

Calculators Can Be Used for Drill

The calculator is an excellent drill device that requires no computer or software. For example, students who want to practice the multiples of 7 can press 7 ⨉ 3 and delay pressing the =. The challenge is to answer the fact to themselves before pressing the = key. Subsequent multiples of 7 can be checked by simply pressing the second factor and the =. In Chapters 13 and 14, activities with the calculator are suggested for developing mental computation and estimation skills.

A class can be split in half with one half required to use a calculator and the other required to do the computations mentally. For 3000 + 1765, the mental group wins every time. It will also win for simple facts and numerous problems that lend themselves to mental computation. Of course, there are many computations, such as 537×32, where the calculator is preferred and that side will win. Not only does this simple exercise provide practice with mental math, but it also demonstrates to students that it is not always appropriate to reach for the calculator. Studies have found that for average-ability learners, calculator use enhanced basic skills acquisition (NRC, 2001).

Calculators Enhance Problem Solving

Several research studies have found that calculator use improved the problem-solving abilities of learners at all ability levels for all grades (NRC, 2001). The mechanics of computation can often distract students' attention from the meaning of the problem they are working on. As students come to understand the meanings of the operations, they should be exposed to realistic problems with realistic numbers. The

numbers may be beyond their abilities to compute, but the calculator makes these realistic problems accessible.

Calculators Help Improve Student Attitudes

The overwhelming conclusion of numerous research studies is that students' attitudes toward mathematics are better in classrooms where calculators are used than where they are not (Hembree & Dessart, 1986; Reys & Reys, 1987; NRC, 2001). Students using calculators tend to be confident and persistent in solving problems. Although these studies are old, there is no reason to believe they are less valid today.

Calculators Save Time

By-hand computation is time consuming, especially for young students who have not developed a high degree of mastery. Why should time be wasted having students add numbers to find the perimeter of a polygon? Why compute averages, find percents, convert fractions to decimals, or solve problems of any sort with pencil-and-paper methods when computation skills are not the objective of the lesson?

Calculators Are Commonly Used in Society

Nowadays, almost everyone uses calculators in every facet of life that involves any sort of exact computation—everyone except schoolchildren. It is only logical that students be taught how to use this commonplace tool effectively. Many adults have not learned how to use the automatic constant feature of a calculator and are not practiced in recognizing gross errors that are often made on calculators. Effective use of calculators is an important skill that is best learned by using them regularly and meaningfully.

Addressing Myths and Fears About Using Calculators

The lingering opposition to calculators is largely based on misinformation. Myths and fears about students not learning because of using calculators still persist, even in the face of evidence to the contrary.

Myth: If Kids Use Calculators, They Won't Learn the "Basics"

Every advocate of calculator use must make it clear to parents that basic fact mastery and flexible computational skills, including mental computation, remain important goals of the curriculum. By and large, research has demonstrated that the availability of calculators has no negative effect on traditional skills (NRC, 2001). Although the eighth NAEP assessment data suggest a decrease in achievement for fourth graders who use calculators either weekly or every day, it is important to note that the same data also show that only 5 percent of teachers report everyday calculator use and only 21 percent report weekly use (http://nces.ed.gov/nationsreportcard/ mathematics/results). Moreover, evidence from a meta-analysis of calculator use shows a slight negative effect of calculators among fourth graders but not among students of any other grade (NRC, 2001). This may be an artifact of conditions specific to those studies of calculator use that included fourth graders. Most important, the performance of tedious by-hand computations does not involve thinking or reasoning or solving problems. Employers want employees who can think and solve novel problems.

Myth: Calculators Make Students Lazy

Almost no mathematical thinking is involved in doing routine computations by hand. People who use calculators when solving problems are, therefore, using their intellect in more important ways—reasoning, conjecturing, testing ideas, and solving problems. When used appropriately, calculators enhance learning; they do not get in the way of learning.

Myth: Students Should Learn the "Real Way" Before Using Calculators

Following rules for pencil-and-paper computation does little to help students understand the ideas behind them. A glaring example is the invert-and-multiply method for division of fractions. Few parents and elementary teachers can explain why this method makes sense. And yet they all had extensive practice with that technique. To one degree or another, the same is true of nearly all computational procedures.

It is essential to point out that by-hand techniques are not to be totally abandoned and that introductory explorations are often best done without a calculator. The teacher must play a role in setting the necessary explorations in the classroom. The calculator should never replace understanding!

Myth: Students Will Become Overly Dependent on Calculators

Calculators kept from students are like forbidden fruit. When finally allowed to use them, students often use them for the simplest of tasks. Teachers in the upper grades often complain that students are using their calculators all the time.

It is essential that mastery of basic facts, mental computation, and some attention to by-hand techniques continue to be requirements for all students. In lessons in which these skills are the objective, the calculator should simply be off limits. When students learn these essential noncalculator skills, they rarely use the calculator inappropriately. Further,

if the calculator is always available for appropriate uses, students learn when and how to use it wisely.

Calculators for Every Student, Every Day

> **Calculators should be in or on students' desks at all times from kindergarten through high school.**

 STOP This position may seem radical. Consider your own thoughts on this before reading further.

In addition to the benefits already described, here are a few arguments in favor of calculator access at all times:

- First and foremost, it does no harm. Any teacher can conduct an activity or pose tasks in which calculators are set off limits. Availability of calculators does not detract from the development of basic skills.
- Many excellent explorations that happen spontaneously in a problem-solving environment will be enhanced by the use of calculators. Students should not have to leave their desks or ask permission to use a calculator when solving a problem.
- When calculators are kept from students, they tend to be used for special "calculator lessons," promoting the student belief that calculators are not common tools for solving problems.
- Students must learn to make wise choices about when to use calculators—for tedious computations—and when to use mental math—for simple computations and estimations. They learn this only by making such choices independently and on a regular basis.

GRAPHING CALCULATORS

The graphing calculator, once thought useful only in high school, is so important to middle school mathematics that it deserves some special attention. Today, a graphing calculator makes sense for all middle school students. Cost is still a possible deterrent. Several models are available for under $75, less than the cost of a pair of sneakers or a few CDs. A calculator purchased in the sixth grade may be the only one the student will need through high school. A school can purchase a classroom set for less than the price of a single computer.

What the Graphing Calculator Offers

It is a mistake to think that graphing calculators are only for doing "high-powered" mathematics usually studied by honors students in high school. Here is a list of some features the graphing calculator offers, every one of which is useful within the standard middle school curriculum.

- The display window permits compound expressions such as 3 + 4(5 − 6/7) to be shown completely before being evaluated. Further, once evaluated, previous expressions can be recalled and modified. This promotes an understanding of notation and order of operations. The device is also a significant tool for exploring patterns and solving problems. Expressions can include exponents, absolute values, and negation signs, with no restrictions on the values used.

- Even without using function definition capability, students can insert values into expressions or formulas without having to enter the entire formula for each new value. The results can be entered into a list or table of values and stored directly on the calculator for further analysis.

- Variables can be used in expressions and then assigned different values to see the effect on expressions. This simple method helps with the idea of a variable as something that varies.

- The distinction between "negative" and "minus" is clear and very useful. A separate key is used to enter the negative of a quantity. The display shows the negative sign as a superscript. If $^-5$ is stored in the variable B, then the expression $^-2 - ^-B$ will be evaluated correctly as $^-7$. This feature is a significant aid in the study of integers and variables.

- Points can be plotted on a coordinate screen either by entering coordinates and seeing the result or by moving the cursor to a particular coordinate on the screen.

- Very large and very small numbers are managed without error. The calculator will quickly compute factorials, even for large numbers, as well as permutations and combinations. Graphing calculators use scientific notation so that large and small numbers do not result in error statements. For example, $23! = 1.033314797 \times 10^{40}$.

- Built-in statistical functions allow students to examine the means, medians, and standard deviations of large sets of realistic data without a computer. Data are easily entered, ordered, added to, or changed almost as easily as on a spreadsheet.

- Graphs for data analysis are available, including box-and-whisker plots, histograms, and, on some calculators, pie charts, bar graphs, and pictographs.

- Random number generators allow for the simulation of a variety of probability experiments that would be difficult without such a device.

- Scatter plots for ordered pairs of real data can be entered, plotted, and examined for trends. The calculator will calculate the equations of best-fit linear, quadratic, cubic, or logarithmic functions.

- Functions can be explored in three modes: equation, table, and graph. Because the calculator easily switches from one to the other and because of the trace feature, the connections between these modes become quite clear. Even sixth-grade students can explore a variety of types of functions along with their graphs and function tables.

There is no need to wait until high school to let students explore how the m and b in $y = mx + b$ affect the graph.

- The graphing calculator is programmable. Programs are very easily written and understood. For example, a program involving the Pythagorean theorem can be used to find the length of sides of right triangles.

- Data, programs, and functions can be shared from one graphing calculator to another and, thus, to the display calculator for the overhead or TV monitor. This permits students to share and discuss work with the rest of the class. Calculators also connect to computers to store data and programs and to print out anything that can be seen on the calculator screen.

Most of the ideas on this list are explored briefly in appropriate chapters in this book.

Arguments against graphing calculators are similar to those for other calculators—and are equally hollow and unsubstantiated. These amazing tools have the potential of significantly opening up real mathematics for students. It is time that graphing calculators became a regular tool in the middle grades.

Electronic Data Collection

In addition to the capabilities of the graphing calculator alone, electronic data collection devices make them even more remarkable. Texas Instruments calls its version the CBL (for *computer-based laboratory*), and such calculators are often referred to by that acronym. The current Texas Instruments version is the CBL-2. Casio's current version is called the EA-200 and is nearly identical in design. These devices accept a variety of data collection probes, such as temperature or light sensors and motion detectors, that can be used to gather real physical data. The data can be transferred to the graphing calculator, where they are stored in one or more lists. The calculator can then produce scatter plots or prepare other analyses. With appropriate software, the data can also be transferred to a computer.

A number of excellent resource books are available that describe experiments in detail. Most include disks with calculator programs that make the interface with the CBL quite easy. With a CBL, science and mathematics meet head-on.

The most popular probe for mathematics teachers is the motion detector. Texas Instruments has a special motion detector called a Ranger or CBR that connects directly to the calculator without requiring a CBL unit. Experiments with a motion detector include analysis of objects rolling down an incline, bouncing balls, or swinging pendulums. The motion actually determines the distance an object is from the sensor. When distance is plotted against time, the graph shows velocity. Students can plot their own motion walking toward or away from the detector. The concept of rate when interpreted as the slope of a distance-to-time curve can become quite dramatic.

Though not as widely used as calculators, personal digital assistants (PDAs) such as the PalmPilot or Handspring Visor have similar capabilities to the CBL. As with the CBL, PDAs can use software and available probes to collect and analyze data. The ImagiProbe from ImagiWorks (www.imagiworks.com)

connects to a PDA for distance and temperature data. The Technology Enhanced Elementary and Middle School Science site from the Concord Consortium (www.concord.org/teemss) offers strategies and ideas for using these devices.

Chapter 23 includes an example of a CBL activity. Further details on the use of these devices are beyond the scope of this text.

THE COMPUTER AS A TOOL IN MATHEMATICS

Tool software is a generic term for software that performs a function that makes doing something easier. The most common tool software is the word processor. Other popular tools include spreadsheets, databases, and presentation software such as PowerPoint. A number of powerful tools have been created for use in the mathematics classroom. These exist in two formats: as stand-alone programs that can be purchased from software publishers and as Internet-based applications or *applets* (for "little applications") accessible through Web browsers such as Netscape Navigator and Microsoft Internet Explorer. Applets are always much smaller, more targeted programs than commercial software. A significant advantage is that they are freely accessed on the Internet. Many can also be downloaded so that an Internet connection is not required for student use. Some of these applets are described briefly throughout this book. At the end of this chapter, sites are listed that collectively offer well over 100 applets. You are strongly urged to browse and play. Many of these are lots of fun!

In addition to applets on the Web, another excellent source is the CD-ROMs that come with every volume of the NCTM *Navigations* series. This newest collection of resources from NCTM is designed to help teachers translate *Principles and Standards for School Mathematics* into the classroom. As of 2003, grade-band books are available on the topics of Algebra, Geometry, and Number. More books are planned for the series.

A mathematical software tool is somewhat like a physical manipulative; by itself, it does not teach. However, the user of a well-designed tool software package has an electronic "thinker toy" with which to explore mathematical ideas.

Electronic Manipulatives for Numeration

Most tool software for grades K–4 falls in this category. In these programs, screen versions of popular manipulative models are available for students to work with freely without the computer posing problems, evaluating results, or telling the students what to do.

At the earliest level, there are programs that provide "counters" such as colored tiles, pictures of assorted objects, or in one specific case, Unifix cubes.* Typically, students can drag counters to any place on the screen, change the colors, and put them in groupings. Some programs have options that turn on counters for the screen or subsets of the screen. Nonmathematical programs such as *Kid Pix* (Learning Company, 1999) can also be used to "stamp" discrete objects on the screen.

Other models such as base-ten blocks (ones, tens, and hundreds models), assorted fraction pieces, and Cuisenaire Rods (centimeter rods) are available in some software packages. These include both pure tool programs and instructional software programs that attempt to teach or tutor. Some fraction models are more flexible than physical models. For example, a circular region might be subdivided into many more fractional parts than is reasonable with physical models. When the models are connected with on-screen counters, it is possible with some programs to have fraction or decimal representations shown so that connections between fractions and decimals can be illustrated. *Mighty Math: Number Heroes* (Edmark, 1996) does a nice job of connecting these types of representations for fractions with denominators as small as twelfths. Many of these commercial programs, however, are not completely open to student use without some constraints. For example, in *MathKeys: Unlocking Whole Numbers, Grades 3–5* (MECC, 1995b), pieces can be combined or taken apart only by adding or subtracting two quantities.

Web-based tools or applets exist that are designed so that students may manipulate them without constraint. For example, the Base Ten Block Applet (www.arcytech.org/java/b10blocks/b10blocks.html) allows children to collect as many flats, rods, and units as they wish, gluing together groups of ten, or breaking a flat into ten rods or a rod into ten units. Other than providing a description of the pieces, there is no attempt to teach or tutor.

The obvious question is, Why not simply use the actual physical models? When selecting these computer tools, there should always be some clear advantage to using the computer versions. The following are features or characteristics that may make these programs a worthwhile addition to your classroom. Not every program offers all of these features.

- *Freedom of manipulation.* Is it at least as easy to use the screen manipulative as it would be to use the physical version? Students should be allowed to use the models in their own way without undue guidance or feedback from the computer.
- *Connection with symbolism.* In what way are symbols attached to the models? Can the symbolism be turned on and off? Is there a variety of options?
- *Journal capability.* Many programs offer a space at the bottom of the screen where students can write about their work. Teachers may be able to use this same space to present problems that students then solve.
- *Print and save capabilities.* How easy is it for students to print a picture of their work? Can they easily save their work and return to it later? (This is unusual in most programs of this type.)

---

*Unifix® is the registered trademark for a set of plastic connecting cubes. The cubes are about 2 cm in width and snap easily into bars of any length. They are popular materials for grades K–2.

Geometry Tools

Computer tools for geometric exploration are much closer to pure tools than those just described for numeration. That is, students can use most of these tools without any constraints. They typically offer some significant advantages over physical models, although the computerized tools should never replace physical models in the classroom.

Blocks and Tiles

Programs that allow students to "stamp" geometric tiles or blocks on the screen are quite common. Typically, there is a palette of blocks, often the same as pattern blocks or tangrams, from which students can choose by clicking the mouse. Often the blocks can be made "magnetic" so that when they are released close to another block, the two will snap together, matching like sides. Blocks can usually be rotated, either freely or in set increments. Different programs offer different variations and features. Figure 8.1 shows a simple yet powerful applet that permits a student to slice any of the three shapes in any place and then manipulate any of the pieces. This is a good example of something a student can do with a computer that would be difficult or impossible with physical models. You may find the following:

- The ability to enlarge or reduce the size of blocks, usually by set increments
- The ability to "glue" blocks together to make new blocks
- The ability to reflect one or more blocks across a mirror line or to rotate them about a point
- Puzzle tasks built into the program
- The ability to measure area or perimeters
- The ability to select polygons with a variable number of sides
- The possibility of creating three-dimensional shapes and rotating them in space

In addition to these features, the presence of a journal or other space for writing is worth looking for, as with other tools. Print and save options are also important. With real blocks, the design is gone when the blocks are returned to the bucket. For students who have poor motor coordination or a physical disability that makes block manipulation difficult, the computer versions of blocks are a real plus. Colorful printouts can be displayed, discussed, and taken home.

Drawing Programs

For younger students, drawing shapes on a grid is much easier and more useful for geometric exploration than free-form drawing. Several programs offer electronic geoboards on which lines can be drawn between points on a grid. When a shape such as a triangle is formed, it can typically be altered just as you would a rubber band on a geoboard. For examples, check the NCTM e-Standards, e-Examples, or NCTM's Illuminations Web site. Addresses are at the end of this chapter. The electronic geoboard programs offer a larger grid on which to draw, ease of use, and the ability to save and print. Some include measuring capabilities as well as reflection and rotation of shapes, things that are difficult or impossible to do on a physical geoboard. An example of a good Internet applet for drawing is the Isometric Drawing Tool found at NCTM's Web site (see Figure 8.2).

Dynamic Geometry Software

Dynamic geometry programs are much more than simple drawing packages. These exciting programs allow students to create shapes on the computer screen and then manipulate and measure them by dragging vertices. Relationships between lines and shapes once created are always preserved. Originally designed for the high school, there is now good reason for these programs to be a part of the classroom as early as grade 4. More detailed discussion of these programs can be found in Chapter 20. Dynamic geometry software can dramatically both change and improve the teaching of geometry. The ability of students to explore geometric relationships with this software is unmatched with any noncomputer mode.

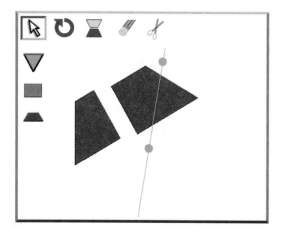

FIGURE 8.1 The "Cutting Shapes Tool."

Used with permission from the CD-ROM included with the NCTM pre-K–2 *Navigations* book for geometry by C. R. Findell, M. Small, M. Cavanagh, L. Dacey, C. E. Greenes, and L. J. Sheffield. Copyright © 2001 by the National Council of Teachers of Mathematics, Inc. All rights reserved. The presence of the screenshot from *Navigations* does not constitute or imply an endorsement by NCTM.

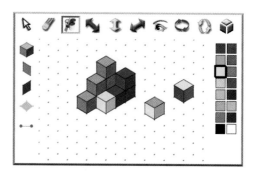

FIGURE 8.2 The "Isometric Drawing Tool" applet from NCTM's Illuminations Web site.

Used with permission from NCTM's Illuminations Web site. Copyright © 2003 by the National Council of Teachers of Mathematics, Inc. All rights reserved. The presence of the screenshot from Illuminations, http://illuminations.NCTM. org/mathlets/isometric/index.html, does not constitute or imply an endorsement by NCTM.

Probability and Data Analysis Tools

These computer tools allow for the entry of data and a wide choice of graphs made from the data. In addition, most will produce typical statistics such as mean, median, and range. Some programs are designed for students in the primary grades. Others are more sophisticated and can be used through the middle grades. These programs make it possible to change the emphasis in data analysis from "how to construct graphs" to "which graph best tells the story."

It should be noted that the spreadsheet and the graphing calculator provide much the same capabilities as dedicated data graphing software. Generally, the data programs, described in Chapter 21, offer more graphing options and easier use than a spreadsheet since they are designed to assist in the development of data analysis concepts.

Probability Tools

These programs, also described in Chapter 21, make it easy to conduct controlled probability experiments and see graphical representations of the results. The young student using these programs must accept that when the computer "flips a coin" or "spins a spinner," the results are just as random and have the same probabilities as if done with real coins or spinners. The value of these programs is found in the ease with which experiments can be designed and large numbers of trials conducted.

Spreadsheets

Spreadsheets are programs that can manipulate rows and columns of numeric data. Values taken from one position in the spreadsheet can be used in formulas to determine entries elsewhere in the spreadsheet. When an entry is changed, the spreadsheet updates all values immediately.

Because the spreadsheet is among the most popular pieces of standard tool software outside of schools, it is often available in integrated packages you may already have on your computer. There is a spreadsheet in *Microsoft Works, AppleWorks,* and *Microsoft Office.* The program *The Cruncher 2.0* (Sunburst, 1996) is an example of a slightly simplified spreadsheet designed for use by students in grades 3 and up. It includes colorful graphing capability, a clip-art component, and a place in each file where students can add notes in text form.

As an alternative to these commercial packages, the *Illuminations* Web site from NCTM offers a couple of very nice spreadsheet Internet applets, *Spreadsheet* and *Spreadsheet and Graphing Tool.* They can be used while connected to the Internet, or, if you have a slow Internet connection, they can be downloaded to your computer and then used without having to be online. And they are free!

Function Graphers

Function graphing software permits the user to create the graph of almost any function very quickly. Multiple functions can be plotted on the same axis. It is usually possible to trace along the path of a curve and view the coordinates at any point. The dimensions of the viewing area can be changed easily so that it is just as easy to look at a graph for x and y between -10 and $+10$ as it is to look at a portion of the graph thousands of units away from the origin. By "zooming in" on the intersection of two graphs, it is possible to find points of intersection without algebraic manipulation. Similarly, the point where a graph crosses the axis can be found to as many decimal places as is desired.

All of the features just described are available on all graphing calculators. What computer programs add is speed, color, visual clarity, and a variety of other interesting features to help students analyze functions.

INSTRUCTIONAL SOFTWARE

Instructional software is designed for student interaction in a manner similar to the textbook or a tutor. It is designed to teach. The distinction between tool and instructional software is not always clear since some packages include a tool-only component. Nor is it always clear how to categorize particular instructional programs. In the following discussion, the intent is to provide some perspective on the different kinds of input to your mathematics program that instructional software might offer.

Concept Instruction

A growing number of programs make an effort to offer conceptual instruction. Some, like the *Fizz & Martina's Math Adventures* series of programs (Tom Snyder Productions, 1998) and the *Prime Time Math* series (Tom Snyder Productions, 1999), rely on real-world contexts to illustrate mathematical ideas. These are problem-solving situations in which specific concepts are developed in a guided manner to solve the problem.

More common in this category is the use of a visual model and much more directed instruction. MECC's *MathKeys* programs (MECC, 1995a, 1995b, 1995c, 1996a, 1996b), *CampOS Math* (Pierian Spring Software, 1996), and the Tenth Planet series (1998a, 1998b) use this approach. In *MathKeys,* the models are set up in a noncontextual manner. *CampOS Math* and the Tenth Planet packages embed models into a contextual format, but these stop short of being real world.

What is most often missing is a way to make the mathematics problematic or to connect the conceptual activity with the symbolic techniques. Further, when students work on a computer, there is little opportunity for discourse, conjecture, or original ideas. Some software even presents concepts in such a fashion as to remove learners from thinking and constructing their own understanding. In some instances, the programs might be best used with the teacher controlling the program on a large display screen with the class. In this way, the teacher can pose questions and entertain discussion that is simply not possible with one student on a computer.

Problem Solving

With the current focus on problem solving, more software publishers purport to teach students to solve problems. The *Fizz & Martina* and *Prime Time Math* series can be included in the problem-solving category. Here the problems are not typical story problems awaiting a computation but more thoughtful stories set in real contexts. Another example is *The New Adventures of Jasper Woodbury* (Lawrence Erlbaum Associates, 1996). Designed for students in middle school, these video episodes are on videodisk. Bar codes included with the print material make it easy to jump to appropriate sections of the extended problems. A single unit may take as many as 5 days to complete.

At the other end of the spectrum are programs that offer little more than a large library of typical story problems. Usually, the teacher can control for problem difficulty and the operations to be used. These programs would be more valuable if they offered some conceptual assistance if the student gets the problems incorrect, but that is rarely the case.

Logic problem solving is another variant of problem-solving software. This category includes attribute activities, as in *The Zoombinis Logical Adventure* (Brøderbund, 1996b) and *Math Arena: Venn* (Sunburst), spatial reasoning, as in *Factory Deluxe* (Sunburst), and number patterns and operation sense, as in *Splish Splash Math* (Sunburst).

Drill

Drill programs give students practice with skills that are assumed to have been taught prior to using the programs. In general, a drill program poses questions that are answered directly or by selecting from a multiple-choice list. Many of these programs are set in arcade formats that make them exciting for students who like that sort of video game, but the format has nothing to do with the practice involved.

Drill programs evaluate responses immediately. How they respond to the first or second incorrect answer is one important distinguishing feature. At one extreme, the answer is simply recorded as wrong. There may be a second or third chance to correct it. At the other extreme, the program may branch to an explanation of the correct response. Others may provide a useful hint or supply a visual model to help with the task. Some programs offer record-keeping features for the teacher to keep track of individual students' progress.

Although computer drill is convenient, there is little evidence to suggest that it is any more effective than noncomputer drills. A major advantage is in the formats, which can add motivation to an otherwise boring drill.

Guidelines for Selecting and Using Software

There is so much software for mathematics today. Commercially published software is becoming increasingly expensive. Even though most Internet-based applets are free to use, schools still need to pay for Internet access and the appropriate hardware. In either case, it is important to make informed decisions when investing limited resources.

How to Select Software

The most important thing to do before purchasing software is to be well informed about the product and to evaluate its merits in an objective manner.

Gathering Information

One of the best sources of information concerning new software is the review section of the NCTM journals or other journals that you respect. Typically, two or three pieces of software are reviewed each issue, or approximately 20 titles per year. Search through 2 or 3 years of back issues to find software that appeals. Many Web sites offer reviews on both commercially available software and Internet-based applets. The Illuminations Web site by NCTM (http://illuminations.nctm.org) is one such site. Another is The Math Forum at Drexel University (formerly at Swarthmore) at http://mathforum.org. When selecting any computer-based tool or instructional software, it is important to evaluate it appropriately.

Next, try to get a preview copy or at least a demonstration version. The latter may not let you actually interact with the software but rather view a form of commercial on your computer. Many distributors will send their software to you for 30-day approval. If this option is available, take advantage of it. Before purchasing, try the software with kids in the grade that will be using it.

Catalogs are useful for finding prices and titles. They are of limited value for understanding how the software works or even what the content is. A title that says it treats "addition and subtraction" does not tell you if this is basic facts, concepts, contextual problems, or multidigit computation. Drill-and-practice software is rarely distinguished from concept software. Remember, it is the content you are interested in, not the game the students will be playing.

Criteria

Here are some things to think about as you review software before purchasing it or using it in your classroom:

- What does this do better than can be done without the computer? Don't select or use software just to put your students on the computer. Be sure to get past the clever graphics and the games. Focus on what students will be learning.
- How are students likely to be engaged with the *content* (not the bells and whistles)? Remember that student reflective thought is the most significant factor in effective instruction. Is the mathematics presented so that it is problematic for the student?
- How easy is the program to use? Students need not be able to learn the program on their own; you can teach

them to use it. But there should not be so much tedium in using the program that attention is diverted from the content or students become frustrated.

- What sort of conceptual information is provided? In drill programs, how are wrong answers handled? Are the models or explanations going to aid in student understanding?
- What controls are provided to the teacher? Are there options that can be turned on and off (e.g., sound, types of feedback or help, levels of difficulty)? Is there a provision for record keeping so that you will know what progress individual students have made?
- Is a manual or on-line instruction available? What is the quality of the manual or instructions? Minimally, the manual should make it clear how the program is to operate and provide assistance for troubleshooting.
- Is printable material available? What is the quality of this material? Many programs come with extensive off-computer activities, lesson plans, Blackline Masters, and suggestions for ways to use the program with your class.
- What is the nature of the licensing agreement? In the case of purchased software, is a site license or network license available? If you purchase a single-user package, it is not legal to install the software on multiple computers. Note also that many programs that come on a CD must have the CD in the computer to run the program. Many Internet applets require the computer to be connected to the Internet. Do these constraints fit with your school situation?

Guidelines for Using Software

How software is used in mathematics instruction will vary considerably with the topic, the grade level, and the software itself. The following are offered as considerations that you should keep in mind.

- Software should contribute to the objectives of the lesson or unit. It should not be used as an add-on or substitute for more accessible approaches. Its use should take advantage of what technology can do efficiently and well.
- For individualized or small group use, plan to provide specific instructions for how the software is used, and plan to provide time for students to freely explore or practice using the software.
- Combine software activities with off-computer activities (e.g., collect measurement data in the classroom to enter into a spreadsheet).
- Create a management plan for using the software. This could include a schedule for when the software is used (e.g., during centers, during small group work) and a way to assess the effectiveness of the software use. Although some software programs include a way to keep track of student performance, you may need to rely on

other assessment strategies to determine whether the software is being effective at meeting the objectives of the lesson or unit.

MATHEMATICS EDUCATION RESOURCES ON THE INTERNET

In addition to access to Internet-based software applications, or applets, the World Wide Web is a wellspring of information and resources for both teachers and students interested in mathematics and teaching mathematics.

Instead of using a standard search engine to find mathematics-related information, it is better to have some places to begin. Several good Web sites in different categories will usually provide you with more links to other sites than you will have time to search. One place to get good Web sites is from the NCTM's *News Bulletin*, a newsletter sent free to all members nine times each year. For several years, the *Bulletin* has featured information about useful Web sites. Make it a habit to check these out in each issue.

Professional Information

Most professional organizations have established Web sites on which they provide information about their organizations, conferences, current issues and events, publications, and other matters. Often these sites provide useful links to related resources or information. Periodic visits to these sites is a good way to stay current with what is going on. Here are some suggested sites.

National Council of Teachers of Mathematics
www.nctm.org

> The NCTM Web site is a must for every elementary teacher and teacher of mathematics. It includes specific information for teachers, parents, leaders, and researchers. The home page changes almost monthly, providing up-to-date information about conferences, publications, news, and more. Of particular interest is free access to the full electronic listing of the *Principles and Standards* document (the e-Standards). The e-Standards includes 22 e-examples (21 interactive applets and a video vignette), 17 of which are appropriate for grades K–8. The site provides a mechanism for joining the council, registering for conferences, purchasing publications and products, and linking to the Illuminations site (see below). Members can access their journals on-line, subscribe to a special electronic journal, and renew memberships. You can choose to be sent a monthly e-mail update informing you of recent additions to the Web site.

Eisenhower National Clearinghouse
www.enc.org

> This is a site of links. There are links to information about reform curriculum materials for K–12 mathematics and science, information and articles on reform issues, information about TIMSS, and ideas for classroom use.

American Association for the Advancement of Science
www.aaas.org

This is the association for *Project 2061,* a national science standards document. Access to this and other information concerning science education is available.

Association for Supervision and Curriculum Development
www.ascd.org

ASCD is an international nonprofit educational association that is committed to successful teaching and learning for all.

EQUALS and Family Math
http://equals.lhs.berkeley.edu

The EQUALS program is dedicated to equal opportunity for females in mathematics and science. It publishes *Family Math* and other valuable resources. For those interested in issues surrounding gender equity and parent involvement, this is a good place to begin.

Mathematically Sane
www.mathematicallysane.com

This is an important and unique Web site that provides evidence for and discussion of the success of reform initiatives in mathematics education. Its mission statement identifies the site as created by a "grassroots organization of teachers, administrators, teacher educators, parents, and mathematicians concerned about the future of mathematics education."

Teacher Resources

The Internet is a wonderful source of creative and useful lesson ideas. It is also a good way to find out about materials and software. The sites listed here were selected because of the quantity of information that is available on them and because the site addresses are not likely to change or disappear quickly. However, these few suggestions only scratch the surface. A large number of other resources are accessible through these sites.

NCTM Illuminations
http://illuminations.nctm.org

This is an incredible site developed by NCTM to provide Internet resources for teaching and learning intended to "illuminate" the *Principles and Standards for School Mathematics.* You can find resources from lesson ideas to "math-lets" (Internet-based applets designed to provide tools for developing understanding in mathematics). Also at this site are multimedia investigations for students and links to video vignettes designed to promote professional reflection.

The Math Forum
http://mathforum.org

Along with the NCTM sites, this may be your most important source of information and links to useful sites. The Forum has resources for both teachers and students. There are suggestions for lessons, puzzles, and activities, plus links to other sites with similar information. There are forums where teachers can talk with other teachers. Two pages accept questions about mathematics from students or teachers (Ask Dr. Math) and about teaching mathematics from teachers (Teacher 2 Teacher). Problems are regularly posted, and solutions can be entered via the Internet. Information is available about software, and some can be downloaded free.

MegaMath!
www.c3.lanl.gov/mega-math

This is a great site! A project of the Computer Research and Applications Group at Los Alamos National Laboratory, it is intended to bring unusual and important mathematical ideas to elementary classrooms.

Math Archives: K–12 Internet Sites
http://archives.math.utk.edu/k12.html

This page contains a very large collection of links to lessons, software, information (both public domain and commercial), and curriculum materials. Each of the hundreds of sites has a brief description. If you are looking for an Internet address for a mathematics resource, this may be a good place to look.

EdWeb Home Page
www.edwebproject.org

This site explores issues of educational reform and contains links to on-line resources around the world.

Home Page for New Math Teachers
http://people.clarityconnect.com/webpages/terri/terri.html

A veteran teacher, Terri Husted, offers advice on a list of subjects challenging the new teacher. In addition, she provides clever problems to pose to students, links to a huge number of useful sites, and much more.

Annenberg/CPB Projects
www.learner.org

The site lists free on-line learning activities, including information about all sorts of interesting uses of mathematics and science in the real world, resources for free and inexpensive materials from Annenberg, and information about funding opportunities. It is a tremendous resource.

Applets

Rather than attempt to select representative applets from the many that are available on the Internet, the following sites are recommended. Remember that all applets are not equal as all software is not equal. Applets vary considerably in the size or scope of the content they support. They vary in how much freedom they offer the student. Some can be considered pure tool software and others are closer to instructional devices. Some applets come packaged with detailed lessons or investigations and questions for students to answer. For all of the variability in applets, it is important to keep in mind the criteria for software that were listed earlier.

Some of the applets at these sites can be downloaded to your computer so that you do not need to be connected to the Web in order to use them. Even in an off-line mode, however, you will still need a current version of a Web browser such as Netscape Navigator or Microsoft Internet Explorer to run them.

In addition to the Web sites listed here, do not forget that each volume in NCTM's *Navigations* series of resource books contains a CD-ROM with applets appropriate for that volume.

National Council of Teachers of Mathematics e-Standards
http://standards.nctm.org/document/examples/index.htm

These applets are referenced in and directly support the text of *Principles and Standards for School Mathematics.* They are also available on the CD version of the *Standards.*

NCTM Illuminations
http://illuminations.nctm.org

Check both the i-Math Investigations (interactive math lessons, most built around applets) and Interactive Math-lets (a collection of applets). The Math-let applications cover the K–12 spectrum. They are ordered alphabetically, so be sure to check out the full list. This is a good collection of quality tools. The i-Math Investigations include all of the applets from the *e-Standards.*

The National Library for Virtual Manipulatives (NLVM)
http://matti.usu.edu/nlvm/nav/vlibrary.html

This NSF-funded site is located at Utah State University. It contains a huge collection of applets organized by the five content strands of the *Standards* and also by the same four grade bands. You may not find all of these applets equally interesting or usable but there is a lot more to like than not. Give the site a thorough look.

Arcytech
http://arcytech.org/java

At the time this was written this site included tool applets for base-ten blocks, pattern blocks, Cuisenaire rods, and fraction bars. There is also an extended interactive lesson developing the Pythagorean theorem.

Count On
www.mathsyear2000.org

This site is sponsored by the National Grid for Learning and contains all sorts of resources in addition to applets for mathematics. Click on the Explorer button to find a number of applets as well as other useful features such as a mathematics dictionary. Check out other areas of this site as well.

U.S. Census Data
www.census.gov

Copious statistical information by state, county, or voting district.

The World Fact Book
www.odci.gov/cia/publications/factbook/index.html

This page provides demographic information for every nation in the world, including population, age distributions, death and birth rates, and information on the economy, government, transportation, and geography. Maps are included as well.

REfLECTIONS ON CHAPTER **8**

Writing to Learn

1. Technology has affected the mathematics curriculum and how it is taught in three ways. Explain each, and give an example to support your explanation. Can you think of examples that are not included in this chapter?
2. Describe some of the benefits of using calculators regularly in the mathematics classroom. Which of these seem to you to be the most compelling? What are some of the arguments against using calculators? Answer each of the arguments against calculators as if you were giving a speech at your PTA meeting or arguing for regular use of calculators before your principal.
3. Aside from the special features of graphing calculators, what are some of the benefits that come simply from having a large display screen and the ability to recall prior statements?
4. What are at least three features of graphing calculators that truly improve the learning of mathematics in the middle grades?
5. Describe what is meant by tool software in mathematics. Describe several types.

6. Describe the three categories of computer instructional software. If you have seen or used examples from these categories, use those in your descriptions.
7. What are some criteria that seem most important to you when selecting software?
8. What kind of information can you expect to find on the Internet?

For Discussion and Exploration

1. Talk with some teachers about their use or nonuse of calculators in the classroom. How do the teachers who use them go about doing so? What are the main reasons for not using them? Read the Technology principle in *Principles and Standards for School Mathematics.* How do the reasons the teachers you talked with compare to the NCTM position?
2. Among the software kept at your school, find one example of drill software and one of some other form of instructional software for mathematics. Try each, and decide how it would be

used in your classroom (if at all). Be sure to check the documentation for suggested grade levels.

3. Check out at least three of the Web sites suggested for teacher resources. Be sure to follow some of the links to other sites. Share at least two good ideas with a friend. Get the friend to do the same.

4. Choose three or four applets from the National Library for Virtual Manipulatives (http://matti.usu.edu/nlvm/nav/vlibrary.html). Subject them to the criteria for selecting software. Which ones do you think measure up and which do not? Compare notes with a colleague.

Recommendations for Further Reading

Highly Recommended

Calvert, L. M. G. (1999). A dependence on technology and algorithms or a lack of number sense? *Teaching Children Mathematics, 6,* 6–7.

Calvert offers simple but convincing answers to those, including teachers, who believe that calculators stop children from thinking. This two-page article is well worth looking up.

Clements, D. H. (1999). The effective use of computers with young children. In J. V. Copley (Ed.), *Mathematics in the early years* (pp. 119–128). Reston, VA: National Council of Teachers of Mathematics.

Clements is a well-known researcher in the area of computer use for young children. In this article he offers guidance on the use of computers with young children, provides numerous examples of different types of programs for the young, and offers cautions about casually believing that all computer activities are good. There is an extensive bibliography.

Crown, W. D. (in press). Using technology to enhance a problem-based approach to teaching: What will and what won't work. In F. K. Lester & R. I. Charles (Eds.), *Teaching mathematics through problem solving: pre-K to 6.* Reston, VA: National Council of Teachers of Mathematics.

Crown offers an overview of both calculators and computers for problem-based mathematics. In his discussion of computers, he describes six categories of educational software. For each category, he explains why that particular type of software is or is not particularly useful in problem-based instruction. Crown's categories of software alone make it worth taking a look at this article.

National Council of Teachers of Mathematics. (2002). Learning and teaching mathematics with technology [Focus Issue]. *Teaching Children Mathematics, 8*(6).

In the practical manner of *TCM*, this special issue provides excellent articles on all aspects of technology in the classroom for young children.

Other Suggestions

Barron, A. E., & Hynes, M. C. (1996). Using technology to enhance communication in mathematics. In P. C. Elliott (Ed.), *Communication in mathematics, K–12 and beyond* (pp. 126–136). Reston, VA: National Council of Teachers of Mathematics.

Battista, M. T. (1998). *Shape makers: Developing geometric reasoning with the Geometer's Sketchpad.* Berkeley, CA: Key Curriculum Press.

Bitter, G. G., & Hatfield, M. M. (1998). The role of technology in the middle grades. In L. Leutzinger (Ed.), *Mathematics in the middle* (pp. 36–41). Reston, VA: National Council of Teachers of Mathematics.

Carlson, R. J., & Winter M. J. (1998). *Transforming functions to fit data: Mathematical explorations using probes, electronic data-collection devices, and graphing calculators.* Emeryville, CA: Key Curriculum Press.

Clements, D. H. (1999). The effective use of computers with young children. In J. V. Copley (Ed.), *Mathematics in the early years* (pp. 119–128). Reston, VA: National Council of Teachers of Mathematics.

Clements, D. H. (2000). From exercises and tasks to problems and projects: Unique contributions to computers to innovative mathematics education. *Journal of Mathematical Behavior, 19,* 9–48.

Clements, D. H., & McMillan, S. (1996). Rethinking "concrete" manipulatives. *Teaching Children Mathematics, 2,* 270–279.

Doyle, A. (1999). A practitioner's guide to snaring the net. *Educational Leadership, 56*(5), 12–15.

Drier, H. S., Dawson, K. M., & Garofalo, J. (1999). Not your typical math class. *Educational Leadership, 56*(5), 21–25.

Eisenhower National Clearinghouse for Mathematics and Science Education. (1999). Integrating technology in the classroom. [Theme Issue]. *ENC Focus: A Magazine for Classroom Innovators, 6*(3).

Huinker, D. (2002). Calculators as learning tools for young children's explorations of number. *Teaching Children Mathematics, 8,* 316–321.

Murray, M., Mokros, J., & Rubin, R. A. (1999). Mathematically rich, equitable game software. *Mathematics Teaching in the Middle School, 5,* 180–186.

Randall, J. (1998). *Sensor sensibility: Algebra explorations with a CBL, a TI-82 or TI-83, and Sensors.* Emeryville, CA: Key Curriculum Press.

Reys, Barbara J., & Arbaugh, Fran. (2001) Clearing up confusion over calculator use in grades K–5. *Teaching Children Mathematics, 8,* 90–94.

Russell, J. C. (1998). *Spreadsheet activities in middle school mathematics* (2nd ed.). Reston, VA: National Council of Teachers of Mathematics.

Schielack, J. F., & Chancellor, D. (1995). *Uncovering mathematics with manipulatives and calculators: Level 1.* Dallas, TX: Texas Instruments.

Schielack, J. F., & Chancellor, D. (1995). *Uncovering mathematics with manipulatives and calculators: Levels 2 & 3.* Dallas, TX: Texas Instruments.

St. John, D., & Lapp, D. A. (2000). Developing numbers and operations with affordable handheld technology. *Teaching Children Mathematics, 7,* 162–168.

Taylor, L. J. C., & Nichols, J. A. (1994). Graphing calculators aren't just for high school students. *Mathematics Teaching in the Middle School, 1,* 190–196.

Vonder Embse, C. (1992). Concept development and problem solving using graphing calculators in the middle school. In J. T. Fey (Ed.), *Calculators in mathematics education* (pp. 65–78). Reston, VA: National Council of Teachers of Mathematics.

Developing Early Number Concepts and Number Sense

Number is a complex and multifaceted concept. A rich understanding of number, a relational understanding, involves many different ideas, relationships, and skills. Children come to school with many ideas about number. These ideas should be built upon as we work with children and help them develop new relationships. It is sad to see the large number of students in grades 4, 5, and above who essentially know little more about number than how to count. It takes time and lots of experiences for children to develop a full understanding of number that will grow and enhance all of the further number-related concepts of the school years.

This chapter looks at the development of number ideas for numbers up to about 20. These foundational ideas can all be extended to larger numbers, operations, basic facts, and computation.

Big Ideas

1. Counting tells how many things are in a set. When counting a set of objects, the last word in the counting sequence names the quantity for that set.

2. Numbers are related to each other through a variety of number relationships. The number 7, for example, is more than 4, two less than 9, composed of 3 and 4 as well as 2 and 5, is three away from 10, and can be quickly recognized in several patterned arrangements of dots. These ideas further extend to an understanding of 17, 57, and 370.

3. Number concepts are intimately tied to the world around us. Application of number relationships to the real world marks the beginning of making sense of the world in a mathematical manner.

Content Connections

Early number development is related to other areas in the curriculum in two ways: content that interacts with and enhances the development of number and content that is directly affected by how well early number concepts have been developed. Measurement, data, and operation meanings fall in the first category. Basic facts, place value, and computation fall in the second.

■ **Operations** (Chapter 10): As children solve story problems for any of the four operations, they count on, count back, make and count groups, and make comparisons. In the process, they form new relationships and methods of working with numbers.

■ **Measurement** (Chapter 19): The determination of measures of length, height, size, or weight is an important use of number for the young child. Measurement involves meaningful counting and comparing (number relationships) and connects number to the world in which the child lives.

■ **Data** (Chapter 21): Data, like measurement, involve counts and comparisons to both aid in developing number and connecting it to the real world.

■ **Basic Facts** (Chapter 11): A strategy or way of thinking about nearly every one of the addition and subtraction facts can be directly traced to number relationships.

■ **Place Value and Computation** (Chapters 12 and 13): Many of the ideas that contribute to computational fluency and flexibility with numbers are clear extensions of how numbers are related to ten and how numbers can be taken apart and recombined in different ways.

NUMBER DEVELOPMENT IN PRE-K AND KINDERGARTEN

Parents help children count their fingers, toys, people at the table, and other small sets of objects. Questions concerning "who has more?" or "are there enough?" are part of the daily lives of children as young as 2 or 3 years of age. Considerable evidence indicates that these children have some understanding of the concepts of number and counting (Baroody, 1987; Fuson, 1988; Gelman & Gallistel, 1978; Gelman & Meck, 1986; Ginsburg, 1977).

The Relationships of More, Less, and Same

The concepts of "more," "less," and "same" are basic relationships contributing to the overall concept of number. Children begin to develop these ideas before they begin school. An entering kindergarten child can almost always choose the set that is *more* if presented with two sets that are quite obviously different in number. In fact, Baroody (1987) states, "A child unable to use 'more' in this intuitive manner is at considerable educational risk" (p. 29). Classroom activities should help children build on this basic notion and refine it.

Though the concept of less is logically equivalent to the concept of more (selecting the set with more is the same as *not* selecting the set with less), the word *less* proves to be more difficult for children than *more*. A possible explanation is that children have many opportunities to use the word *more* but have limited exposure to the word *less*. To help children with the concept of less, frequently pair it with the word *more* and make a conscious effort to ask "which is less?" questions as well as "which is more?" questions. For example, suppose that your class has correctly selected the set that has more from two that are given. Immediately follow with the question "Which is less?" In this way, the less familiar term and concept can be connected with the better-known idea.

For all three concepts (more, less, and same), children should construct sets using counters as well as make comparisons or choices between two given sets. The activities described here include both types. These activities should be conducted in a spirit of inquiry followed whenever possible with requests for explanations. "Why do you think this set has less?"

ACTIVITY 9.1

Make Sets of More/Less/Same

At a workstation or table, provide about eight cards with sets of 4 to 12 objects, a set of small counters or blocks, and some word cards labeled *More*, *Less*, and *Same*. Next to each card have students make three collections of counters: a set that is more, one that is less, and one that is the same. The appropriate labels are placed on the sets (see Figure 9.1).

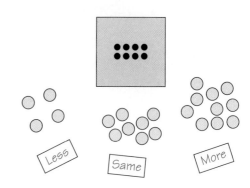

FIGURE 9.1 **Making sets that are more, less, and the same.**

In Activity 9.1, students create a set with counters, which gives them the opportunity to reflect on the sets and adjust them as they work. The next activity is done without counters. Although it addresses the same basic ideas, it provides a different problem situation.

ACTIVITY 9.2

Find the Same Amount

Give children a collection of cards with sets on them. Dot cards are one possibility (see the Blackline Masters). Have the children pick up any card in the collection and then find another card with the same amount to form a pair. Continue to find other pairs.

Activity 9.2 can be altered to have children find dot cards that are "less" or "more."

Observe children as they do this task. Children whose number ideas are completely tied to counting and nothing more will select cards at random and count each dot. Others will begin by selecting a card that appears to have about the same number of dots. This is a significantly higher level of understanding. Also observe how the dots are counted. Are the counts made accurately? Is each counted only once? A significant milestone for children occurs when they begin recognizing small patterned sets without counting.

STOP You have begun to see some of the early foundational ideas about number. Stop now and make a list of all of the important ideas that you think children should *know about 8* by the time they finish first grade. (The number 8 is used as an example. The list could be about any number from, say, 6 to 12.) Put your thoughts aside and we will revisit these ideas later.

Early Counting

Meaningful counting activities can begin in preschool. Generally, children at midyear in kindergarten should have a fair understanding of counting, but children must construct this idea.

It cannot be forced. Only the counting sequence is a rote procedure. The *meaning* attached to counting is the key conceptual idea on which all other number concepts are developed.

The Development of Counting Skills

Counting involves at least two separate skills. First, one must be able to produce the standard list of counting words in order: "One, two, three, four, ..." Second, one must be able to connect this sequence in a one-to-one manner with the items in the set being counted. Each item must get one and only one count.

Experience and guidance are the major factors in the development of these counting skills. Many children come to kindergarten able to count sets of ten or beyond. At the same time, children from impoverished backgrounds may require considerable practice to make up their experience deficit. The size of the set is also a factor related to success in counting. Obviously, longer number strings require more practice to learn. The first 12 counts involve no pattern or repetition, and many children do not recognize a pattern in the teens. Children still learning the skills of counting—that is, matching oral number words with objects—should be given sets of blocks or counters that they can move or pictures of sets that are arranged for easy counting.

Meaning Attached to Counting

Fosnot and Dolk (2001) make it very clear that an understanding of cardinality and the connection to counting is not a simple matter for 4-year-olds. Children will learn *how* to count (matching counting words with objects) before they understand that the last count word indicates the *amount* of the set or the *cardinality* of the set. Children who have made this connection are said to have the *cardinality principle,* which is a refinement of their early ideas about quantity. Most, but certainly not all, children by age $4\frac{1}{2}$ have made this connection (Fosnot & Dolk, 2001; Fuson & Hall, 1983).

To determine if young children have the cardinality rule, listen to how they respond when you discuss counting tasks with them. You ask, "How many are here?" The child counts correctly, and says, "Nine." Ask, "Are there nine?" Before developing cardinality, children may count again or will hesitate. Children with cardinality are apt to emphasize the last count, will explain that there are nine "Because I just counted them," and can use counting to find a matching set. Fosnot and Dolk discuss a class of 4-year-olds in which children who knew there were 17 children in the class were unsure how many milk cartons they should get so that each could have one.

To develop their understanding of counting, engage children in almost any game or activity that involves counts and comparisons. The following is a simple suggestion.

ACTIVITY 9.3

Fill the Chutes

Create a simple game board with four "chutes." Each consists of a column of about twelve 1-inch squares with a star at the top. Children take turns rolling a die and collecting the indicated number of counters. They then place these counters in one of the chutes. The object is to fill all of the chutes with counters. As an option, require that the chutes be filled exactly. A roll of 5 cannot be used to fill a chute with four spaces.

This "game" provides opportunities for you to talk with children about number and assess their thinking. Watch how the children count the dots on the die. Ask, "How do you know you have the right number of counters?" and "How many counters did you put in the chute? How many more do you need to fill the chute?"

Activities 9.1 and 9.2 also provide opportunities for diagnosis. Regular classroom activities, such as counting how many napkins are needed at snack time, are additional opportunities for children to learn about number and for teachers to listen to their students' ideas.

Numeral Writing and Recognition

Helping children read and write single-digit numerals is similar to teaching them to read and write letters of the alphabet. Neither has anything to do with number concepts. Traditionally, instruction has involved various forms of repetitious practice. Children trace over pages of numerals, repeatedly write the numbers from 0 to 10, make the numerals from clay, trace them in sand, write them on the chalkboard or in the air, and so on.

The calculator is a good instructional tool for numeral recognition. In addition to helping children with numerals, early activities can help develop familiarity with the calculator so that more complex activities are possible.

ACTIVITY 9.4

Find and Press

Every child should have a calculator. Always begin by having the children press the clear key. Then you say a number, and the children press that number on the calculator. If you have an overhead calculator, you can then show the children the correct key so that they can confirm their responses, or you can write the number on the board for children to check. Begin with single-digit numbers. Later, progress to two or three numbers called in succession. For example, call, "Three, seven, one." Children press the complete string of numbers as called.

Perhaps the most common kindergarten exercises have children match sets with numerals. Children are given pictured sets and asked to write or match the number that tells how many. Alternatively, they may be given a number and told to make or draw a set with that many objects. Many teacher resource books describe cute learning center activities where children put a numeral with the correct-sized set—numbered frogs on lily pads (with dots), for example. It is important to note that these frequently overworked activities involve only the skills of counting sets and numeral recognition or writing. When children are successful with these activities, little is gained by continuing to do them.

 ## Technology Note

Computer software that allows children to create sets on the screen with the click of a mouse is quite common. *Unifix Software* (Hickey, 1996) is an electronic version of the popular Unifix cubes, plastic cubes that snap together to make bars. The software allows the teacher to add features to counting activities that are not available with the cubes alone. In its most basic form, children can click to create as many single cubes as they wish. They can link cubes to make bars of cubes, break the bars, move them around, add sounds to each cube, and more. The teacher can choose to have a numeral appear on each bar showing the total. From one to four loops can be created, with the loop total another option. Not only can students count to specified numbers and have the numerals appear for reinforcement, but also they can informally begin to explore the idea that two quantities can form a larger amount.

Do not let these computer tools become toys. It is important to keep the task problem based. For example, in early kindergarten, students could make a set of single blocks in one loop that is just as many as (or more or less than) a bar the teacher has made in the first loop. (Files can be prepared ahead of time.) Later students can explore different combinations of two bars that would equal a third bar. ■

Counting On and Counting Back

Although the forward sequence of numbers is relatively familiar to most young children, counting on and counting back are difficult skills for many. Frequent short practice drills are recommended.

ACTIVITY 9.5

Up and Back Counting

Counting up to and back from a target number in a rhythmic fashion is an important counting exercise. For example, line up five children and five chairs in front of the class. As the whole class counts from 1 to 5, the children sit down one at a time. When the target number, 5, is reached, it is repeated; the child who sat on 5 now stands, and the count goes back to 1. As the count goes back, the children stand up one at a time, and so on, "1, 2, 3, 4, 5, 5, 4, 3, 2, 1, 1, 2, ..." Kindergarten and first-grade children find exercises such as this both fun and challenging. Any move-

---

ment (clapping, turning around, doing jumping jacks) can be used as the count goes up and back in a rhythmic manner.

The calculator provides an excellent counting exercise for young children because they see the numerals as they count.

ACTIVITY 9.6

Calculator Up and Back

Have each child press ⊞ 1 ⊟ ⊟ ⊟ ⊟ ⊟. The display will go from 1 to 5 with each ⊟ press. The count should also be made out loud in a rhythm as in the other exercises. To start over, press the clear key and repeat. Counting up and back is also possible, but the end numbers will not be repeated. The following illustrates the key presses and what the children would say in rhythm:

⊞ 1 ⊟ ⊟ ⊟ ⊟   ⊟   1 ⊟ ⊟ ⊟ ⊟   ⊞ 1 ⊟ ⊟ . . .

"1, 2, 3, 4, 5, minus 1, 4, 3, 2, 1, plus 1, 2, 3, . . . "

The last two activities are designed only to help students become fluent with the number words in both forward and reverse order and to begin counts with numbers other than 1. Although not at all easy for young students, these activities do not address counting on or counting back in a meaningful manner. Fosnot and Dolk (2001) describe the ability to count on as a "landmark" on the path to number sense. The next two activities are designed for that purpose.

ACTIVITY 9.7

Counting On with Counters

Give each child a collection of 10 or 12 small counters that the children line up left to right on their desks. Tell them to count four counters and push them under their left hands (see Figure 9.2). Then say, "Point to your hand. How many are there?" (Four.) "So let's count like this: f-o-u-r (pointing to their hand), five, six, ..." Repeat with other numbers under the hand.

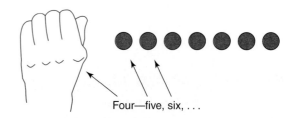

Four—five, six, . . .

FIGURE 9.2 Counting on: "Hide four. Count, starting from the number of counters hidden."

The following activity addresses the same concept in a bit more problem-based manner.

ACTIVITY 9.8

Real Counting On

This "game" for two children requires a deck of cards with numbers 1 to 7, a die, a paper cup, and some counters. The first player turns over the top number card and places the indicated number of counters in the cup. The card is placed next to the cup as a reminder of how many are there. The second child rolls the die and places that many counters next to the cup. (See Figure 9.3.) Together they decide how many counters in all. A record sheet with columns for "In the Cup," "On the Side," and "In All" is an option. The largest number in the card deck can be adjusted if needed.

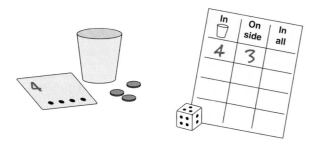

FIGURE 9.3   How many in all? How do children count to tell the total? Dump the counters? Count up from 1 without dumping the counters? Count on?

Watch how children determine the total amounts in this last activity. Children who are not yet counting on may want to dump the counters from the cup or will count up from one without dumping out the counters. Be sure to permit these strategies. As children continue to play, they will eventually count on as that strategy becomes meaningful and useful.

Early Number Sense

Number sense was a term that became popular in the late 1980s, even though terms such as this have somewhat vague definitions. Howden (1989) described number sense as a "good intuition about numbers and their relationships. It develops gradually as a result of exploring numbers, visualizing them in a variety of contexts, and relating them in ways that are not limited by traditional algorithms" (p. 11). This may still be the best definition.

In *Principles and Standards,* the term *number sense* is used freely throughout the Number and Operation standard. This example is from the K–2 level: "As students work with numbers, they gradually develop flexibility in thinking about numbers, which is a hallmark of number sense. . . . Number sense develops as students understand the size of numbers, develop multiple ways of thinking about and representing numbers, use numbers as referents, and develop accurate perceptions about the effects of operations on numbers" (p. 80).

The discussion of number sense begins in this book with the remainder of this chapter as we look at the kinds of relationships and connections children should be making about smaller numbers up to about 20. But "good intuition about numbers" does not end with these smaller whole numbers. Children continue to develop number sense as they begin to use numbers in operations, build an understanding of place value, and devise flexible methods of computing and making estimates involving large numbers. Flexible, intuitive thinking with numbers—number sense—should continue to be developed throughout the school years as fractions, decimals, and percents are added to students' repertoire of number ideas.

The early number ideas that have been discussed to this point in the chapter are the rudimentary aspects of number. Unfortunately, too many traditional programs move directly from these beginning ideas to addition and subtraction, leaving students with a very limited collection of ideas about number to bring to these new topics. The result is often that children continue to count by ones to solve simple story problems and have difficulty mastering basic facts. Early number sense development should demand significantly more attention than it is given in most traditional K–2 programs.

Relationships Among Numbers 1 Through 10

Once children have acquired a concept of cardinality and can meaningfully use their counting skills, little more is to be gained from the kinds of counting activities described so far. More relationships must be created for children to develop number sense, a flexible concept of number not completely tied to counting.

A Collection of Number Relationships

Figure 9.4 illustrates the four different types of relationships that children can and should develop with numbers:

- *Spatial relationships:* Children can learn to recognize sets of objects in patterned arrangements and tell how many without counting. For most numbers, there are several common patterns. Patterns can also be made up of two or more easier patterns for smaller numbers.
- *One and two more, one and two less:* The two-more-than and two-less-than relationships involve more than just the ability to count on two or count back two. Children should know that 7, for example, is 1 more than 6 and also 2 less than 9.

- *Anchors or "benchmarks" of 5 and 10:* Since 10 plays such a large role in our numeration system and because two fives make up 10, it is very useful to develop relationships for the numbers 1 to 10 to the important anchors of 5 and 10.
- *Part-part-whole relationships:* To conceptualize a number as being made up of two or more parts is the most important relationship that can be developed about numbers. For example, 7 can be thought of as a set of 3 and a set of 4 or a set of 2 and a set of 5.

The principal tool that children will use as they construct these relationships is the one number tool they possess: counting. Initially, then, you will notice a lot of counting, and you may wonder if you are making progress. Have patience! Counting will become less and less necessary as children construct these new relationships and begin to use the more powerful ideas.

Spatial Relationships: Patterned Set Recognition

Many children learn to recognize the dot arrangements on standard dice due to the many games they have played that use dice. Similar instant recognition can be developed for other patterns as well. The activities suggested here encourage reflective thinking about the patterns so that the relationships will be constructed. Quantities up to 10 can be known and named without the routine of counting. This can then aid in counting on (from a known patterned set) or learning combinations of numbers (seeing a pattern of two known smaller patterns).

A good set of materials to use in pattern recognition activities is a set of dot plates. These can be made using small paper plates and the peel-off dots commonly available in office supply stores. A reasonable collection of patterns is shown in Figure 9.5.

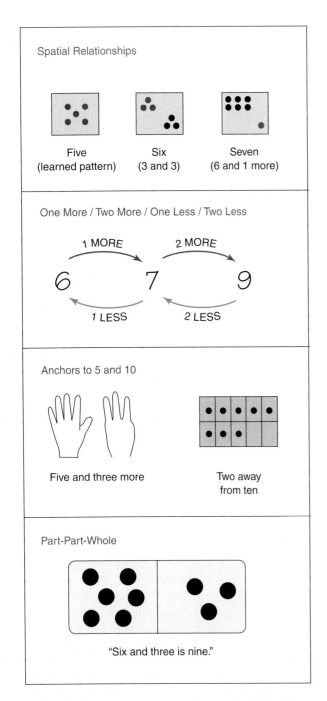

FIGURE 9.4 Four relationships to be developed involving small numbers.

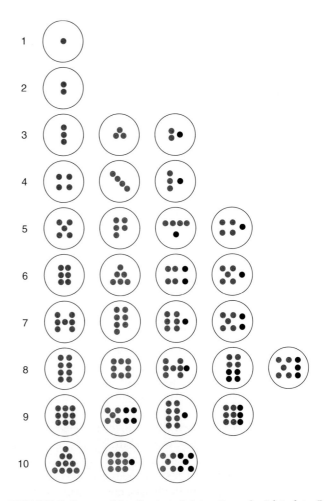

FIGURE 9.5 A useful collection of dot patterns for "dot plates."

Note that some patterns are combinations of two smaller patterns or a pattern with one or two additional dots. These should be made in two colors. Keep the patterns compact. If the dots are spread out, the patterns are hard to see.

ACTIVITY 9.9

Learning Patterns

To introduce the patterns, provide each student with about ten counters and a piece of construction paper as a mat. Hold up a dot plate for about 3 seconds. "Make the pattern you saw using the counters on the mat. How many dots did you see? How did you see them?" Spend some time discussing the configuration of the pattern and how many dots. Do this with a few new patterns each day.

ACTIVITY 9.10

Dot Plate Flash

Hold up a dot plate for only 1 to 3 seconds. "How many? How did you see it?" Children like to see how quickly they can recognize and say how many dots. Include lots of easy patterns and a few with more dots as you build their confidence. Students can also flash the dot plates to each other as a workstation activity.

ACTIVITY 9.11

Dominoes

Make a set of dominoes out of poster board and put a dot pattern on each end. The dominoes can be about 2 inches by 4 inches. The same patterns can appear on lots of dominoes with different pairs of patterns making up each one. Let the children play dominoes in the regular way, matching up the ends. As a speed activity, spread out all of the dominoes and see how fast the children play all of the dominoes or play until no more can be played. Regular dominoes could also be used, but there are not as many patterns.

The instant recognition activities with the plates are exciting and can be done in 5 minutes at any time of day or between lessons. There is value in using them at any primary grade level and at any time of year.

One and Two More, One and Two Less

When children count, they have no reason to reflect on the way one number is related to another. The goal is only to match number words with objects until they reach the end of the count. To learn that 6 and 8 are related by the twin relationships of "two more than" and "two less than" requires reflection on these ideas within tasks that permit counting. Counting on (or back) one or two counts is a useful tool in constructing these ideas.

ACTIVITY 9.12

One-Less-Than Dominoes

Use the dot-pattern dominoes or a standard set to play "one-less-than" dominoes. Play in the usual way, but instead of matching ends, a new domino can be added if it has an end that is one less than the end on the board. A similar game can be played for two less, one more, or two more.

The following activities can be done for any of the four relationships; each will be described for only one.

ACTIVITY 9.13

Make a Two-More-Than Set

Provide students with about six dot cards. Their task is to construct a set of counters that is two more than the set shown on the card. Similarly, spread out eight to ten dot cards, and find another card for each that is two less than the card shown. (Omit the 1 and 2 cards for two less than, and so on.)

In activities where children find a set or make a set, they can add a numeral card (a small card with a number written on it) to all of the sets involved. They can also be encouraged to take turns reading a number sentence to their partner. If, for example, a set has been made that is two more than a set of four, the child can read this by saying the number sentence, "Two more than four is six."

The calculator can be an exciting device to practice the relationships of one more than, two more than, one less than, and two less than.

ACTIVITY 9.14

A Calculator Two-More-Than Machine

Teach children how to make a two-more-than machine. Press 0 $\boxed{+}$ 2 $\boxed{=}$. This makes the calculator a two-more-than machine. Now press any number— for example, 5. Children hold their finger over the $\boxed{=}$ key and predict the number that is two more than 5. Then they press $\boxed{=}$ to confirm. If they do not press any of the operation keys (+, −, ×, ÷) the "machine" will continue to perform in this way.

What is really happening in the two-more-than machine is that the calculator "remembers" or stores the last operation, in this case "+2," and adds that to whatever number is in the window when the ▣ key is pressed. If the child continues to press ▣, the calculator will count by twos. At any time, a new number can be pressed followed by the equal key. To make a two-less-than machine, press 2 ▣ 2 ▣. (The first press of 2 is to avoid a negative number.) In the beginning, students forget and press operation keys, which change what their calculator is doing. Soon, however, they get the hang of using the calculator as a machine.

Anchoring Numbers to 5 and 10

Here again, we want to help children relate a given number to other numbers, specifically 5 and 10. These relationships are especially useful in thinking about various combinations of numbers. For example, in each of the following, consider how the knowledge of 8 as "5 and 3 more" and as "2 away from 10" can play a role: $5 + 3, 8 + 6, 8 - 2, 8 - 3, 8 - 4, 13 - 8$. (It may be worth stopping here to consider the role of 5 and 10 in each of these examples.) Later similar relationships can be used in the development of mental computation skills on larger numbers such as $68 + 7$.

The most common and perhaps most important model for this relationship is the ten-frame. Generally attributed to Robert Wirtz (1974), the ten-frame is simply a 2×5 array in which counters or dots are placed to illustrate numbers (see Figure 9.6). Ten-frames can be simply drawn on a full sheet of construction paper (or use the Blackline Master). Nothing fancy is required, and each child can have one. The ten-frame has been incorporated into a variety of activities in this book and is now popular in standard textbooks for children.

For children in kindergarten or early first grade who have not yet explored a ten-frame, it is a good idea to begin with a five-frame. This row of five sections is also drawn on a sheet of construction paper (or use the Blackline Master). Provide children with about ten counters that will fit in the five-frame sections, and conduct the following activity.

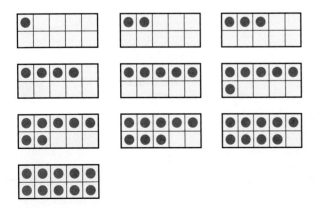

FIGURE 9.6 Ten-frames.

ACTIVITY 9.15

Five-Frame Tell-About

Explain that only one counter is permitted in each section of the five-frame. No other counters are allowed on the five-frame mat. Have the children show 3 on their five-frame. "What can you tell us about 3 from looking at your mat?" After hearing from several children, try other numbers from 0 to 5. Children may place their counters on the five-frame in any manner. What they observe will differ a great deal from child to child. For example, with four counters, a child with two on each end may say, "It has a space in the middle" or "It's two and two." There are no wrong answers. Focus attention on how many more counters are needed to make 5 or how far away from 5 a number is. Next try numbers between 5 and 10. The rule of one counter per section still holds. As shown in Figure 9.7, numbers greater than 5 are shown with a full five-frame and additional counters on the mat but not in the frame. In discussion, focus attention on these larger numbers as 5 and some more: "Eight is five and three more."

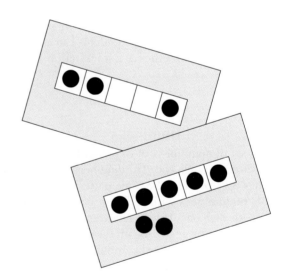

FIGURE 9.7 A five-frame focuses on the 5 anchor. Counters are placed one to a section, and students tell how they see their number in the frame.

Notice that the five-frame really focuses on the relationship to 5 as an anchor for numbers but does not anchor numbers to 10. When five-frames have been used for a week or so, introduce ten-frames. You may want to play a ten-frame version of a "Five-Frame Tell-About" but soon introduce the following rule for showing numbers on the ten-frame: *Always fill the top row first, starting on the left, the same way you read. When the top row is full, counters can be placed in the bottom row, also from the left.* This will produce the "standard" way to show numbers on the ten-frame as in Figure 9.6.

For a while, many children will count every counter on their ten-frame. Some will take all counters off and begin each number from a blank frame. Others will soon learn to adjust numbers by adding on or taking off only what is required, often capitalizing on a row of five without counting. Do not pressure students. With continued practice, all students will grow. How they are using the ten-frame provides insight into students' current number concept development.

ACTIVITY 9.16

Crazy Mixed-Up Numbers

This activity is adapted from *Mathematics Their Way* (Baratta-Lorton, 1976). All children make their ten-frame show the same number. The teacher then calls out random numbers between 0 and 10. After each number, the children change their ten-frames to show the new number. Children can play this game independently by preparing lists of about 15 "crazy mixed-up numbers." One child plays "teacher," and the rest use the ten-frames. Children like to make up their own number lists.

"Crazy Mixed-Up Numbers" is much more of a problem than it first appears. How do you decide how to change your ten-frame? Some children will wipe off the entire frame and start over with each number. Others will have learned what each number looks like. To add another dimension, have the children tell, *before changing their ten-frames,* how many more counters need to be added ("plus") or removed ("minus"). They then call out plus or minus whatever amount is appropriate. If, for example, the frames showed 6, and the teacher called out "four," the children would respond, "Minus two!" and then change their ten-frames accordingly. A discussion of how they know what to do is valuable.

Ten-frame flash cards are an important variation of ten-frames. Make cards from poster board about the size of a small index card, with a ten-frame on each and dots drawn in the frames. A set of 20 cards consists of a 0 card, a 10 card, and two each of the numbers 1 to 9. The cards allow for simple drill activities to reinforce the 5 and 10 anchors.

ACTIVITY 9.17

Ten-Frame Flash

Flash ten-frame cards to the class or group, and see how fast the children can tell how many dots are shown. This activity is fast-paced, takes only a few minutes, can be done at any time, and is a lot of fun if you encourage speed.

Important variations of "Ten-Frame Flash" include

- Saying the number of spaces on the card instead of the number of dots
- Saying one more than the number of dots (or two more, and also less than)
- Saying the "ten fact"—for example, "Six and four make ten"

Ten-frame tasks are surprisingly problematic for students. Students must reflect on the two rows of five, the spaces remaining, and how a particular number is more or less than 5 and how far away from 10. The early discussions of how numbers are seen on the five-frames or ten-frames are examples of brief "after" activities in which students learn from one another.

Part-Part-Whole Relationships

STOP   Before reading on, get some counters or coins. Count out a set of eight counters in front of you as if you were a first- or second-grade child counting them.

Any child who has learned how to count meaningfully can count out eight objects as you just did. What is significant about the experience is what it did *not* cause you to think about. Nothing in counting a set of eight objects will cause a child to focus on the fact that it could be made of two parts. For example, separate the counters you just set out into two piles and reflect on the combination. It might be 2 and 6 or 7 and 1 or 4 and 4. Make a change in your two piles of counters and say the new combination to yourself. Focusing on a quantity in terms of its parts has important implications for developing number sense. A noted researcher in children's number concepts, Lauren Resnick (1983) states:

> Probably the major conceptual achievement of the early school years is the interpretation of numbers in terms of part and whole relationships. With the application of a Part-Whole schema to quantity, it becomes possible for children to think about numbers as compositions of other numbers. This enrichment of number understanding permits forms of mathematical problem solving and interpretation that are not available to younger children. (p. 114)

A study of kindergarten children examined the effects of part-part-whole activities on number concepts (Fischer, 1990). With only 20 days of instruction to develop the part-part-whole structure, children showed significantly higher achievement than the control group on number concepts, word problems, and place-value concepts.

Basic Ingredients of Part-Part-Whole Activities

Most part-part-whole activities focus on a single number for the entire activity. Thus, a child or group of children working together might work on the number 7 throughout the activity. Either children build the designated quantity in two or more parts, using a wide variety of materials and formats, or else they start with the full amount and separate it into two or more parts. A group of two or three children may work on one number in one activity for 5 to 20 minutes. Kindergarten children will usually begin these activities working on the number 4 or 5. As concepts develop, the children can extend their work to numbers 6 to 12. It is not unusual to find children in the second grade who have not developed firm part-part-whole constructs for numbers in the 7-to-12 range.

When children do these activities, have them say or "read" the parts aloud or write them down on some form of recording sheet (or do both). Reading or writing the combinations serves as a means of encouraging reflective thought focused on the part-whole relationship. Writing can be in the form of drawings, numbers written in blanks (_____ and _____), or addition equations if these have been introduced (3 + 5 = 8). There is a clear connection between part-part-whole concepts and addition and subtraction ideas.

A special and important variation of part-part-whole activities is referred to as *missing-part* activities. In a missing-part activity, children know the whole amount and use their already developed knowledge of the parts of that whole to try to tell what the covered or hidden part is. If they do not know or are unsure, they simply uncover the unknown part and say the full combination as they would normally. Missing-part activities provide maximum reflection on the combinations for a number. They also serve as the forerunner to subtraction concepts. With a whole of 8 but with only 3 showing, the child can later learn to write "8 − 3 = 5."

Part-Part-Whole Activities

The following activity and its variations may be considered the "basic" part-part-whole activity.

ACTIVITY 9.18

Build It in Parts

Provide children with one type of material, such as connecting cubes or squares of colored paper. The task is to see how many different combinations for a particular number they can make using two parts. (If you wish, you can allow for more than two parts.) Each different combination can be displayed on a small mat, such as a quarter-sheet of construction paper. Here are just a few ideas, each of which is illustrated in Figure 9.8.

- Use two-color counters such as lima beans spray painted on one side (also available in plastic).
- Make bars of connecting cubes. Make each bar with two colors. Keep the colors together.
- Color rows of squares on 1-inch grid paper.
- Make combinations using two dot strips—strips of poster board about 1 inch wide with stick-on dots. (Make lots of strips with from one to four dots and fewer strips with from five to ten dots.)
- Make combinations of "two-column strips." These are cut from tagboard ruled in 1-inch squares. All pieces except the single squares are cut from two columns of the tagboard.

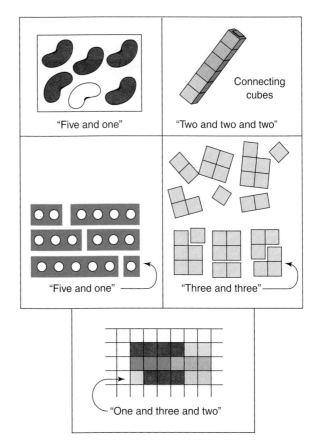

FIGURE 9.8 **Assorted materials for building parts of 6.**

As you observe children working on the "Build It in Parts" activity, ask them to "read" a number sentence to go with each of their designs. Encourage children to read their designs to each other. Two or three children working together with the same materials may have quite a large number of combinations including lots of repeats.

A note about the "two-column cards" mentioned in the activity and shown in Figure 9.8: In her unpublished research, Kuske (2001) makes the case that this two-column model for numbers is more valuable than dot patterns and ten-frames. Her reasoning is that the pieces are "additive." That is, the combination of any two of the pieces is another piece in the set, as can be seen in Figure 9.8. Of course, this is not true of dot patterns or ten-frames. In Kuske's research, sets of ten are given special importance and used as precursors to place value. For example, a 6 and a 7 piece make a 10 and 3 piece. Her research is quite interesting and, if nothing else, reinforces the importance of helping children think about numbers in terms of two parts.

In the "Build It in Parts" activity, the children are focusing on the combinations. To add some interest, vary the activity by adding a design component. Rather than create a two-part illustration for a number, they create an interesting design with an assigned number of elements. For each design, they are then challenged to see and read the design in two parts. Here are some ideas.

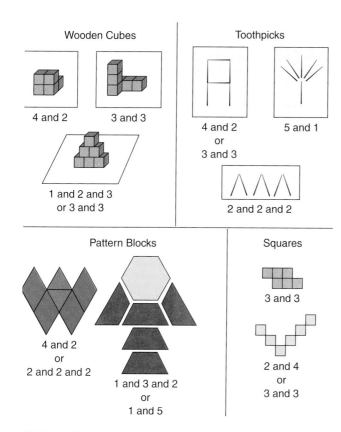

FIGURE 9.9 Designs for 6.

- Make arrangements of wooden cubes.
- Make designs with pattern blocks. It is a good idea to use only one or two shapes at a time.
- Make designs with flat toothpicks. These can be dipped in white glue and placed on small squares of construction paper to create a permanent record.
- Make designs with touching squares or triangles. Cut a large supply of small squares or triangles out of construction paper. These can also be pasted down.

It is both fun and useful to challenge children to see their designs in different ways, producing different number combinations. In Figure 9.9, decide how children look at the designs to get the combinations listed under each.

The following activity is strictly symbolic. However, children should use counters if they feel they need to.

ACTIVITY 9.19

Two out of Three

Make lists of three numbers, two of which total the whole that children are focusing on. Here is an example list for the number 5:

2—3—4
5—0—2
1—3—2

3—1—4
2—2—3
4—3—1

With the list on the board, overhead, or worksheet, children can take turns selecting the two numbers that make the whole. As with all problem-solving activities, children should be challenged to justify their answers.

Missing-Part Activities

Missing-part activities require some way for a part to be hidden or unknown. Usually this is done with two children working together or else in a teacher-directed manner with the class. Again, the focus of the activity remains on a single designated quantity as the whole. The next four activities illustrate variations of this important idea.

ACTIVITY 9.20

Covered Parts

A set of counters equal to the target amount is counted out, and the rest are put aside. One child places the counters under a margarine tub or piece of tagboard. The child then pulls some out into view. (This amount could be none, all, or any amount in between.) For example, if 6 is the whole and 4 are showing, the other child says, "Four and *two* is six." If there is hesitation or if the hidden part is unknown, the hidden part is immediately shown (see Figure 9.10).

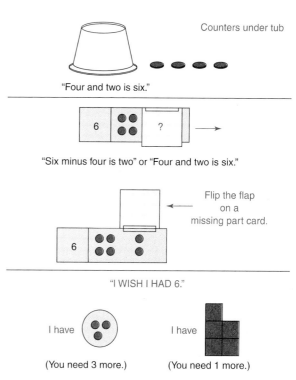

FIGURE 9.10 Missing-part activities.

ACTIVITY 9.21

Missing-Part Cards

For each number 4 to 10, make missing-part cards on strips of 3-by-9-inch tagboard. Each card has a numeral for the whole and two dot sets with one set covered by a flap. For the number 8, you need nine cards with the visible part ranging from 0 to 8 dots. Students use the cards as in "Covered Parts," saying, "Four and two is six" for a card showing four dots and hiding two (see Figure 9.10).

ACTIVITY 9.22

I Wish I Had

Hold out a bar of connecting cubes, a dot strip, a two-column strip, or a dot plate showing 6 or less. Say, "I wish I had six." The children respond with the part that is needed to make 6. Counting on can be used to check. The game can focus on a single whole, or the "I wish I had" number can change each time.

The following activity is completely symbolic.

ACTIVITY 9.23

Calculator Parts of 8 Machine

Make a parts of 8 machine by pressing 8 ⊟ 8 ⊒. Now if any number from 0 to 8 is pressed followed by ⊒, the display shows the other part. (The second part shows as a negative number. Tell students that is how they can tell it is the second part.) Children should try to say the other part before they press ⊒. Though this is basically a drill activity, a discussion with any child concerning his or her reasoning returns it to a problem orientation. Machines can be made for any number in the same way.

 TECHNOLOGY NOTE

There are lots of ways you can use computer software to create part-part-whole activities. All that is needed is a program that permits students to create sets of objects on the screen. *Unifix Software* (Hickey, 1996) is especially nice for this purpose. One approach has students create two-part bars to match a single bar that you specify. Here students could make many bars all for the same number. Alternatively, students could put counters in two set loops formed by the computer. As always, the computer should offer something beyond the

simple manipulative. In this instance, the advantage is your ability to control the type of feedback provided. Options include showing the total in a bar, the total in a loop, and the total of all blocks on the screen. For example, a student can make a bar of two and a bar of six with a numeral showing on each. When the bars are snapped together, the new bar total of eight appears.

Combining and Breaking Apart Numbers (Tenth Planet, 1998a) is specifically designed for part-part-whole activities. Although the early activities in this package are fairly passive and slow, the "Through" or last section makes the mathematics reasonably problematic. In various animated settings, children attempt to make a number either in two parts or by adding two groups and then removing one or two groups. This is an example of software that requires some teacher guidance to create good problems or else students will not stay engaged. The printed support material includes suggestions for corresponding off-line activities that make this a worthwhile program. ∎

 STOP　Remember the list you made earlier in the chapter about what children should know about the number 8? Get it out now and see if you would add to it or revise it based on what you have read to this point. Do this before reading on.

Here is a possible list of the kinds of things that children should know about the number 8 (or any number up to about 12) by the end of the first grade. Children should be able to:

- Count to eight (know the number words).
- Count eight objects and know that the last number word tells how many.
- Write the numeral 8.
- Recognize the numeral 8.

The preceding list represents the minimal skills of number. In the following list are the relationships students should have that contribute to number sense:

- More and less by 1 and 2: 8 is one more than 7, one less than 9, two more than 6, and two less than 10.
- Spatial patterns for 8 such as

● ● ● ●
● ● ● ●

- Anchors to 5 and 10: 8 is 5 and 3 more and 2 away from 10.
- Part-whole relationships: 8 is 5 and 3, 2 and 6, 7 and 1, and so on.
- Other relationships such as

　Doubles: double 4 is 8.

　Relationships to the real world: 8 is one more than the days of the week, my brother is 8 years old, my reading book is 8 inches wide.

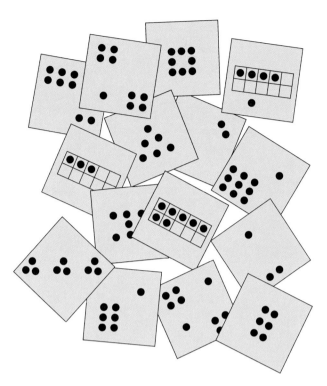

FIGURE 9.11   Dot cards can be made using the Blackline Masters.

Dot Card Activities

Many good number development activities involve more than one of the relationships discussed so far. As children learn about ten-frames, patterned sets, and other relationships, the dot cards in the Blackline Masters provide a wealth of activities (see Figure 9.11). The cards contain dot patterns, patterns that require counting, combinations of two and three simple patterns, and ten-frames with "standard" as well as unusual placements of dots. When children use these cards for almost any activity that involves number concepts, the cards make them think about numbers in many different ways. The dot cards add another dimension to many of the activities already described and can be used effectively in the following activities.

ACTIVITY 9.24
Double War

The game of "Double War" (Kamii, 1985) is played like war, but on each play, both players turn up two cards instead of one. The winner is the one with the larger total number. Children playing the game can use many different number relationships to determine the winner without actually finding the total number of dots.

ACTIVITY 9.25
Dot-Card Trains

Make a long row of dot cards from 0 up to 9, then go back again to 1, then up, and so on. Alternatively, begin with 0 or 1 and make a two-more/two-less train.

ACTIVITY 9.26
Difference War

Besides dealing out the cards to the two players as in regular "War," prepare a pile of about 50 counters. On each play, the players turn over their cards as usual. The player with the greater number of dots wins as many counters from the pile as the difference between the two cards. The players keep their cards. The game is over when the counter pile runs out. The player with the most counters wins the game.

ACTIVITY 9.27
Number Sandwiches

Select a number between 5 and 12, and find combinations of two cards that total that number. With the two cards students make a "sandwich" with the dot side out. When they have found at least ten sandwiches, the next challenge is to name the number on the other "slice" of the sandwich. The sandwich is turned over to confirm. The same pairs can then be used again to name the hidden part.

 ASSESSMENT NOTES

The four types of number relationships (spatial representations, one and two more or less than, 5 and 10 anchors, and part-whole relationships) provide an excellent reference for assessing where your students are relative to number concepts. If you have station activities for these relationships, careful observations alone will tell a lot about students' number concepts. For a more careful assessment, each relationship can be assessed separately in a one-on-one setting, taking only a few minutes.

With a set of dot plates and a set of ten-frame cards you can quickly check which dot patterns children recognize without counting and whether they recognize quantities on ten-frames. To check the one and two more or less than relationships, simply write a few numbers on a sheet of paper. Point to a number and have the child tell you the number that is "*two less than* this number," varying the specific request with different numbers. It is not necessary to check every possibility.

For part-whole relationships, use a missing-part assessment similar to Activity 9.20 ("Covered Parts") on p. 125. Begin

INVESTIGATIONS IN NUMBER, DATA, AND SPACE

Grade K, *How Many in All?*
Investigation 2: Six Tiles

Context

The activities in this investigation take place over one to two weeks near the end of the year but could be done earlier. The entire investigation focuses on the number 6. The authors explain that 6 is an amount most kindergarten children can count, even early in the year. Children need more than one hand to show 6. It provides enough two-part combinations to be interesting, and it is an amount that can be visually recalled and manipulated. Furthermore, most kindergarten children will turn 6 years old during the year.

Task Descriptions

In "Cover Up," the teacher draws an arrangement of six squares on a grid so that all can see. For example:

Students are told to look at the drawings and discuss different ways they could remember what they see. Then the picture is covered up and students try to describe the drawing. The discussion is focused on ideas that get at the parts of the picture, not just that there are six squares. "Cover Up" is repeated with several different drawings. "Six Tiles in All" is a follow-up activity in which students paste down six squares on grid paper in as many ways as they can find. Squares have to touch on a full side. The different arrangements are shared and the teacher helps students see number combinations for 6 as in the teacher

From *Investigations in Number, Data, and Space: Kindergarten* by Marlene Kliman et al. Copyright © 1998 by Dale Seymour Publications. Reprinted by permission of Pearson Education, Inc.

notes shown here. This investigation provides just one opportunity to naturally introduce the symbolism for addition as children say the combinations they see.

The authors point out that it is tempting to think that the activities in this unit could profitably be repeated for other numbers as well. Their experience, however, is that students get bored doing the same thing over and over. These ideas are important for other numbers, but students need different contexts and materials to maintain interest.

with a number you believe the child has "mastered," say, 5. Have the child count out that many counters into your open hand. Close your hand around the counters and confirm that she knows how many are hidden there. Then remove some and show them in the palm of your other hand. (See Figure 9.12.) Ask the child, "How many are hidden?" Repeat with different amounts removed, although it is only necessary to check three or four missing parts for each number. If the child responds quickly and correctly and is clearly not counting in any way, call that a "mastered number." If a number is mastered, repeat the entire process with the next higher number. Continue until the child begins to stumble. In early first grade you will find a range of mastered numbers from 4 to 7 or 8. By spring of the first grade, most children should have mastered numbers to 10. ∎

FIGURE 9.12 **A missing-part number assessment. Eight in all. "How many are hidden?"**

The *Investigations in Number, Data, and Space* curriculum for kindergarten integrates number development throughout most of the year. Four of seven units focus on the development of number, including the unit on data and measurement. The activity described in this excerpt provides some flavor of the *Investigations* program's early approach to number.

Relationships for Numbers 10 to 20

Even though kindergarten, first-, and second-grade children daily experience numbers up to 20 and beyond, it should not be assumed that they will automatically extend the set of relationships they have developed on smaller numbers to the numbers beyond 10. And yet these numbers play a big part in many simple counting activities, in basic facts, and in much of what we do with mental computation. Relationships with these numbers are just as important as relationships involving the numbers through 10.

A Pre–Place-Value Relationship with 10

A set of ten should play a major role in children's initial understanding of numbers between 10 and 20. When children see a set of six with a set of ten, they should know without counting that the total is 16. However, the numbers between 10 and 20 are not an appropriate place to discuss place-value concepts. That is, prior to a much more complete development of place-value concepts (appropriate for second grade and beyond), children should not be asked to explain the 1 in 16 as representing "one ten."

STOP Say to yourself, "One ten." Now think about that from the perspective of a child just learning to count to 20! What could *one* ten possibly mean when *ten* tells me how many fingers I have and is the number that comes after nine? How can it be one?

The concept of a single ten is just too strange for a kindergarten or early first-grade child to grasp. Some would say that it is not appropriate for grade 1 at all (Kamii, 1985). The inappropriateness of discussing "one ten and six ones" (what's a one?) does not mean that a set of ten should not figure prominently in the discussion of the teen numbers. The following activity illustrates this idea.

ACTIVITY 9.28
Ten and Some More
Use a simple two-part mat, and have children count out ten counters onto one side. Next have them put five counters on the other side. Together count all of the counters by ones. Chorus the combination: "Ten and five is fifteen." Turn the mat around: "Five and ten is fifteen." Repeat with other numbers in a random order but without changing the 10 side of the mat.

Activity 9.28 is designed to teach new number names and, thus, requires a certain amount of directed teaching. Following this activity, explore numbers to 20 in a more open-ended manner. Provide each child with two ten-frames drawn one under the other on a construction paper mat or use the Blackline Master provided. In random order, have children show numbers to 20 on their mats. There is no preferred way to do this as long as there are the correct number of counters. What is interesting is to discuss how the counters can be placed on the mat so that it is easy to see how many are there. Have children share their ideas. Not every child will use a full set of ten, but as this idea becomes more popular, the notion that ten and some more is a teen amount will soon be developed. Do not forget to include numbers less than ten as well. As you listen to your children, you may want to begin challenging them to find ways to show 26 counters or even more.

Extending More and Less Relationships

The relationships of one more than, two more than, one less than, and two less than are important for all numbers. However, these ideas are built on or connected to the same concepts for numbers less than 10. The fact that 17 is one less than 18 is connected to the idea that 7 is one less than 8. Children may need help in making this connection.

ACTIVITY 9.29
More and Less Extended
On the overhead, show 7 counters, and ask what is two more, or one less, and so on. Now add a filled ten-frame to the display (or 10 in any pattern), and repeat the questions. Pair up questions by covering and uncovering the ten-frame as illustrated in Figure 9.13.

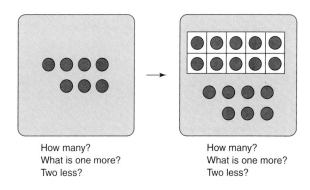

How many?
What is one more?
Two less?

How many?
What is one more?
Two less?

FIGURE 9.13 **Extending relationships to the teens.**

Double and Near-Double Relationships

The use of doubles (double 6 is 12) and near-doubles (13 is double 6 and 1 more) is generally considered a strategy for memorizing basic addition facts. There is no reason why children should not begin to develop these relationships long before they are concerned with memorizing basic facts. Doubles and near-doubles are simply special cases of the general part-part-whole construct.

Relate the doubles to special images. Thornton (1982) helped first graders connect doubles to these visual ideas:

Double 3 is the bug double: three legs on each side.

Double 4 is the spider double: four legs on each side.

Double 5 is the hand double: two hands.

Double 6 is the egg carton double: two rows of six eggs.

Double 7 is the two-week double: two weeks on the calendar.

Double 8 is the crayon double: two rows of eight crayons in a box.

Double 9 is the 18-wheeler double: two sides, nine wheels on each side.

Children can draw pictures or make posters that illustrate the doubles for each number. There is no reason that the images need be restricted to those listed here. Any images that are strong ideas for your children will be good for them.

Periodically conduct oral exercises in which students double the number you say. Ask children to explain how they knew a particular double. Many will not use the pictures.

ACTIVITY 9.30

The Double Maker

Make the calculator into a "double maker" by pressing 2 ⊠ ⊟. Now a press of any digit followed by ⊟ will produce the double of that number. Children can work in pairs or individually to try to beat the calculator.

As a related oral task, say a number, and ask students to tell what double it is. "What is fourteen?" (Double 7!) When students can do this well, use any number up to 20. "What is seventeen?" (Double 8 and 1 more.)

Number Sense and the Real World

Here we examine ways to broaden the early knowledge of numbers in a different way. Relationships of numbers to real-world quantities and measures and the use of numbers in simple estimations can help children develop the flexible, intuitive ideas about numbers that are most desired.

Estimation and Measurment

One of the best ways for children to think of real quantities is to associate numbers with measures of things. In the early grades, measures of length, weight, and time are good places to begin. Just measuring and recording results will not be very effective, however, since there is no reason for children to be interested in or think about the result. To help children think or reflect a bit on what number might tell how long the desk is or how heavy the book is, it would be good if they could

first write down or tell you an estimate. To produce an estimate is, however, a very difficult task for young children. They do not understand the concept of "estimate" or "about." For example, suppose that you have cut out of poster board an ample supply of very large footprints, say, about 18 inches long. All are exactly the same size. You would like to ask the class, "About how many footprints will it take to measure across the rug in our reading corner?" The key word here is *about*, and it is one that you will need to spend a lot of time helping children understand. To this end, the request of an estimate can be made in ways that help with the concept of "about" yet not require students to give a specific number.

The following estimation questions can be used with most early estimation activities:

- *More or less than* _____? Will it be more or less than 10 footprints? Will the apple weigh more or less than 20 wooden blocks? Are there more or less than 15 connecting cubes in this long bar?
- *Closer to* _____ *or to* _____? Will it be closer to 5 footprints or closer to 20 footprints? Will the apple weigh closer to 10 blocks or closer to 30 blocks? Does this bar have closer to 10 cubes or closer to 50 cubes?
- *About* _____. Use one of these numbers: 5, 10, 15, 20, 25, 30, 35, 40, ... About how many footprints? About how many blocks will the apple weigh? About how many cubes are in this bar?

Asking for estimates using these formats helps children learn what you mean by "about." Every child can make an estimate without having to pull a number out of the air.

To help with numbers and measures, estimate several things in succession using the same unit. For example, suppose that you are estimating and measuring "around things" using a string. To measure, the string is wrapped around the object and then measured in some unit such as craft sticks. After measuring the distance around Demetria's head, estimate the distance around the wastebasket or around the globe or around George's wrist. Each successive measure helps children with the new estimates. See Chapter 19 for a complete discussion of measurement.

More Connections

Here are some additional activities that can help children connect numbers to real situations.

ACTIVITY 9.31

Add a Unit to Your Number

Write a number on the board. Now suggest some units to go with it, and ask the children what they can think of that fits. For example, suppose the number is 9. "What do you think of when I say 9 *dollars*? 9 *hours*? 9 *cars*? 9 *kids*? 9 *meters*? 9 *o'clock*? 9 *hand spans*? 9 *gallons*?" Spend some time in discussion of each. Let children suggest units as well. Be prepared to explore some of the ideas either immediately or as projects or tasks to share with parents at home.

ACTIVITY 9.32

Is It Reasonable?

Select a number and a unit—for example, 15 feet. Could the teacher be 15 feet tall? Could your living room be 15 feet wide? Can a man jump 15 feet high? Could three children stretch their arms 15 feet? Pick any number, large or small, and a unit with which children are familiar. Then make up a series of these questions.

Once children are familiar with Activity 9.32, have them select the number and the unit or things (10 kids, 20 bananas, . . .), and see what kinds of questions children make up. When a difference of opinion develops, capitalize on the opportunity to explore and find out. Resist the temptation to supply your adult-level knowledge. Rather, say, "Well, how can we find out if it is or is not reasonable? Who has an idea about what we could do?"

These activities are problem-based in the truest sense. Not only are there no clear answers, but children can easily begin to pose their own questions and explore number in the part of the environment most interesting to them. Children will not have these real-world connections when you begin, and you may be disappointed in their limited ideas about number. Howden (1989) writes about a first-grade teacher of children from very impoverished backgrounds who told her, "They all have fingers, the school grounds are strewn with lots of pebbles and leaves, and pinto beans are cheap. So we count, sort, compare, and talk about such objects. We've measured and weighed almost everything in this room and almost everything the children can drag in" (p. 6). This teacher's children had produced a wonderfully rich and long list of responses to the question "What comes to your mind when I say twenty-four?" In another school in a professional community where test scores are high, the same question brought almost no response from a class of third graders. It can be a very rewarding effort to help children connect their number ideas to the real world.

Graphs

Graphing activities are another good way to connect children's worlds with number. Chapter 21 discusses ways to make graphs with children in grades K–2. Graphs can be quickly made of almost any data that can be gathered from the students: favorite ice cream, color, sports team, pet; number of sisters and brothers; kids who ride different buses; types of shoes; number of pets; and so on. Graphs can be connected to content in other areas. A unit on sea life might lead to a graph of favorite sea animals.

Once a simple bar graph is made, it is very important to take a few minutes to ask as many number questions as is appropriate for the graph. In the early stages of number development (grades K–1), the use of graphs for number relationships and for connecting numbers to real quantities in the children's environment is a more important reason for building graphs than the graphs themselves. The graphs focus attention on counts of realistic things. Equally important, bar graphs clearly exhibit comparisons between and among numbers that are rarely made when only one number or quantity is considered at a time. See Figure 9.14 for an example of a graph and questions that can be asked. At first, children will have trouble with the questions involving differences, but repeated exposure to these ideas in a bar graph format will

Class graph showing fruit brought for snack. Paper cutouts for bananas, oranges, apples, and cards for "others."

- — Which bar (or refer to what the graph represents) is most, least?
- — Which are more (less) than 7 (or some other number)?
- — Which is one less (more) than this bar?
- — How much more is _____ than _____? (Follow this question immediately by reversing the order and asking how much less.)
- — How much less is _____ than _____? (Reverse this question after receiving an answer.)
- — How much difference is there between _____ and _____ ?
- — Which two bars together are the same as _____ ?

FIGURE 9.14 Relationships and number sense in a bar graph.

improve their understanding. These comparison concepts add considerably to children's understanding of number.

NCTM Standards The *Standards* clearly recognizes the value of integrating number development with other areas of the curriculum. "Students' work with numbers should be connected to their work with other mathematics topics. For example, computational fluency . . . can both enable and be enabled by students' investigations of data; a knowledge of patterns supports the development of skip counting and algebraic thinking; and experiences with shape, space, and number help students develop estimation skills related to quantity and size" (p. 79).

LITERATURE CONNECTIONS

Children's literature abounds with wonderful counting books. Involving children with books in a variety of ways can serve to connect number to reality, make it a personal experience, and provide ample opportunities for problem solving. Be sure to go beyond simply reading a counting book or a number-related book and looking at the pictures. Find a way to extend the book into the children's world. Create problems related to the story. Have children write a similar story. Extend the numbers and see what happens. Create a mural, graphs, or posters. The ideas are as plentiful as the books. Here are a few ideas for making literature connections to number concepts and number sense.

Anno's Counting House
Anno, 1982

In the beautiful style of Anno, this book shows ten children in various parts of a house. As the pages are turned, the house front covers the children, and a few are visible through cutout windows. A second house is on the opposite page. As you move through the book, the children move one at a time to the second house, creating the potential for a 10–0, 9–1, 8–2, . . . , 0–10 pattern of pairs. But as each page shows part of the children through the window, there is an opportunity to discuss how many in the missing part. Have children use counters to model the story as you "read" it the second or third time.

What if the children moved in pairs instead of one at a time? What if there were three houses? What if there were more children? What else could be in the house to count? How many rooms, pictures, windows? What about your house? What about two classrooms or two buses instead of houses?

The Very Hungry Caterpillar
Carle, 1969

This is a predictable-progression counting book about a caterpillar who eats first one thing, then two, and so on. Children can create their own eating stories and illustrate them. What if more than one type of thing were eaten at each stop? What combinations for each number are there? Are seven little

things more or less than three very large things? What does all of this stuff weigh? How many things are eaten altogether?

Two Ways to Count to Ten
Dee, 1988

This Liberian folktale is about King Leopard in search of the best animal to marry his daughter. The task devised involves throwing a spear and counting to 10 before the spear lands. Many animals try and fail. Counting by ones proves too lengthy. Finally, the antelope succeeds by counting "2, 4, 6, 8, 10."

The story is a perfect lead-in to skip counting. Can you count to 10 by threes? How else can you count to 10? How many ways can you count to 48? What numbers can you reach if you count by fives? The size of the numbers you investigate is limited only by the children. A hundreds board or counters are useful thinker toys to help with these problems. Be sure to have children write about what they discover in their investigations.

Another fun book to use is *The King's Commissioners* (Friedman, 1994), a hilarious tale that also opens up opportunities to count by different groupings or skip counting. ∎

EXTENSIONS TO EARLY MENTAL MATHEMATICS

Teachers in the second and third grades can capitalize on some of the early number relationships and extend them to numbers up to 100. A useful set of materials to help with these relationships is the little ten-frames found in the Blackline Masters. Each child should have a set of 10 tens and a set of frames for each number 1 to 9 with an extra 5.

The following three ideas are illustrated with the little ten-frames in Figure 9.15. First are the relationships of one more than and one less than. If you understand that one more than 6 is 7, then in a similar manner, ten more than 60 is 70 (that is, one more ten). The second idea is really a look ahead to fact strategies. If a child has learned to think about adding on to 8 or 9 by first adding up to 10 and then adding the rest, the extension to similar two-digit numbers is quite simple; see Figure 9.15(b). Finally, the most powerful idea for small numbers is thinking of them in parts. It is a very useful idea (though not one found in textbooks) to take apart larger numbers to begin to develop some flexibility in the same way. Children can begin by thinking of ways to take apart a multiple of 10 such as 80. Once they do it with tens, the challenge can be to think of ways to take apart 80 when one part has a 5 in it, such as 25 or 35.

More will be said about early mental computation in Chapter 13. The point to be made here is that early number relationships have a greater impact on what children know than may be apparent at first. Even teachers in the upper grades may profitably consider the use of ten-frames and part-part-whole activities.

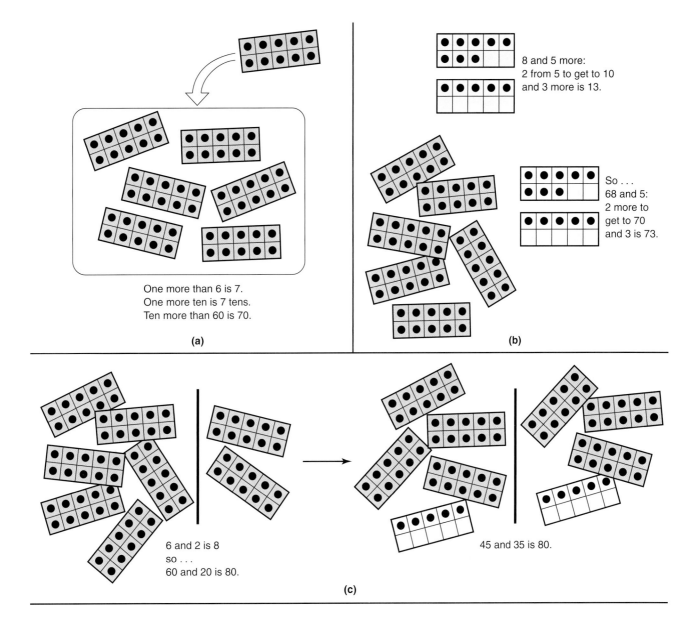

One more than 6 is 7.
One more ten is 7 tens.
Ten more than 60 is 70.

(a)

8 and 5 more:
2 from 5 to get to 10
and 3 more is 13.

So . . .
68 and 5:
2 more to
get to 70
and 3 is 73.

(b)

6 and 2 is 8
so . . .
60 and 20 is 80.

45 and 35 is 80.

(c)

FIGURE 9.15 Extending early number relationships to mental computation activities.

Reflections on Chapter 9

Writing to Learn

1. Describe an activity that deals with a basic concept of number that does not require an understanding of counting. Explain the purpose of this activity.

2. What things must a child be able to do in order to count a set accurately?

3. When does a child have the *cardinality principle*? How can you tell if this principle has been acquired?

4. Describe an activity that is a "set-to-numeral match" activity. What ideas must a child have to do these activities meaningfully and correctly?

5. How can "Real Counting On" (Activity 9.8, p. 119) be used as an assessment to determine if children understand counting on or are still in a transitional stage?

6. What are the four types of relationships that have been described for small numbers? Explain briefly what each of these means, and suggest at least one activity for each.

7. Describe a missing-part activity. What should happen if the child trying to give the missing part does not know it?

8. How can a teacher assess each of the four number relationships? Give special attention to part-whole ideas.

9. How can a calculator be used to develop early counting ideas connected with number? How can a calculator be used to help

a child practice number relationships such as part-part-whole or one less than?

10. For numbers between 10 and 20, describe how to develop each of these ideas:
    a. The idea of the teens as a set of 10 and some more
    b. Extension of the one-more/one-less concept to the teens
11. Describe briefly your own idea of what number sense is.
12. What are three ways that children can be helped to connect numbers to real-world ideas?
13. Give two examples of how early number relationships can be used to develop some early mental computation skills.

For Discussion and Exploration

1. Examine a textbook series for grades K–2. Compare the treatment of counting and number concept development with that presented in this chapter. What ideas are stressed? What ideas are missed altogether? If you were teaching in one of these grades, how would you plan your number concept development program? What part would the text play?
2. Many teachers in grades 3 and above find that their children do not possess the number relationships discussed in this chapter but rely heavily on counting. Given the pressures of other content at these grades, how much effort should be made to remediate these number concept deficiencies?

Recommendations for Further Reading

Highly Recommended

Burton, G. (1993). *Number sense and operations: Addenda series, grades K–6*. Reston, VA: National Council of Teachers of Mathematics.
Either this book or the *Number Sense and Operations* addenda series book for your grade level should be a must for developing number concepts. The activities are developed in sufficient detail to give you clear guidance and yet allow considerable flexibility.

Fuson, K. C., Grandau, L., & Sugiyama, P. A. (2001). Achievable numerical understandings for all young children. *Teaching Children Mathematics, 7,* 522–526.
Researchers who have long worked with the number development of young children, provide the reader with a concise overview of number development from ages 3 to 7. This practical reporting of their research is quite useful.

Van de Walle, J. A., & Watkins, K. B. (1993). Early development of number sense. In R. J. Jensen (Ed.), *Research ideas for the classroom: Early childhood mathematics* (pp. 127–150). Old Tappan, NJ: Macmillan.
This chapter includes a discussion of many of the K–2 topics covered in this text as well as a broader discussion of number sense, including mental computation and estimation. It pro-

vides a good mix of practical ideas with ample references to the research literature.

Other Suggestions

Baroody, A. J., & Wilkins, J. L. M. (1999). The development of informal counting, number, and arithmetic skills and concepts. In J. V. Copley (Ed.), *Mathematics in the early years* (pp. 48–65). Reston, VA: National Council of Teachers of Mathematics.

Bresser, R., & Holtzzman, C. (1999). *Developing number sense.* Sausalito, CA: Math Solutions Publications.

Clements, D. H. (1999). Subitizing: What is it? Why teach it? *Teaching Children Mathematics, 5,* 400–405.

Dacey, L. S., & Eston, R. (1999). *Growing mathematical ideas in kindergarten.* Sausalito, CA: Math Solutions Publications.

Fosnot, C. T., & Dolk, M. (2001). *Young mathematicians at work: Constructing number sense, addition, and subtraction.* Portsmouth, NH: Heinemann.

Fuson, K. C. (1989). *Children's counting and concepts of number.* New York: Springer-Verlag.

Kamii, C., Kirkland, L., & Lewis, B. (2001). Representation and abstraction in young children's numerical reasoning. In A. A. Cuoco (Ed.), *The roles of representation in school mathematics* (pp. 24–34). Reston, VA: National Council of Teachers of Mathematics.

Kouba, V. L., Zawojewski, J. S., & Strutchens, M. E. (1997). What do students know about numbers and operations? In P. A. Kenney, & E. A. Silver (Eds.), *Results from the sixth mathematics assessment of educational progress* (pp. 87–140). Reston, VA: National Council of Teachers of Mathematics.

McClain, K., & Cobb, P. (1999). Supporting students' ways of reasoning about patterns and partitions. In J. V. Copley (Ed.), *Mathematics in the early years* (pp. 112–118). Reston, VA: National Council of Teachers of Mathematics.

McIntosh, A., Reys, B., & Reys, B. (1997). *Number SENSE: Simple effective number sense experiences* [Grades 1–2]. White Plains, NY: Dale Seymour Publications.

Ritchhart, R. (1994). *Making numbers make sense: A sourcebook for developing numeracy.* Reading, MA: Addison-Wesley.

Weinberg, S. (1996). Going beyond ten black dots. *Teaching Children Mathematics, 2,* 432–435.

Whitin, D. J., Mills, H., & O'Keefe, T. (1994). Exploring subject areas with a counting book. *Teaching Children Mathematics, 1,* 170–174.

Whitin, D. J., & Wilde, S. (1995). *It's the story that counts: More children's books for mathematical learning, K–6.* Portsmouth, NH: Heinemann.

Wicket, M. S. (1997). Serving up number sense and problem solving: *Dinner at the Panda Palace. Teaching Children Mathematics, 3,* 476–480.

10

Developing Meanings for the Operations

This chapter is about helping children connect different meanings, interpretations, and relationships to the four operations of addition, subtraction, multiplication, and division so that they can effectively use these operations in real-world settings.

The main thrust of this chapter is helping children develop what might be termed *operation sense*, a highly integrated understanding of the four operations and the many different but related meanings these operations take on in real contexts.

Big Ideas

1. Addition and subtraction are connected. Addition names the whole in terms of the parts, and subtraction names a missing part.

2. Multiplication involves counting groups of like size and determining how many are in all (multiplicative thinking).

3. Multiplication and division are related. Division names a missing factor in terms of the known factor and the product.

4. Models can be used to solve contextual problems for all operations and to figure out what operation is involved in a problem regardless of the size of the numbers. Models also can be used to give meaning to number sentences.

Content Connections

The ideas in this chapter are most directly linked to concepts of numeration and the development of invented computation strategies.

■ **Number Development** (Chapter 9): As children learn to think about number in terms of parts and missing parts, they should be relating these ideas to addition and subtraction. Multiplication and division require students to

think about numbers as units: In 3 × 6 each of the three sixes is counted as a unit. In some sense, operations can be seen as simply a way to record ideas about numbers using symbols.

■ **Basic Facts** (Chapter 11): A good understanding of the operations can firmly connect addition and subtraction so that subtraction facts are a natural consequence of having learned addition. For example, 12 − 5 is 7 since 5 + 7 is 12. A firm connection between multiplication and division provides a similar benefit.

■ **Whole-Number Place Value and Computation** (Chapters 12 and 13): Students can work with and develop ideas about the base-ten number system as they solve story problems involving larger numbers. Although computational strategies have been traditionally taught separately from the meanings of the operations, it is reasonable to have children invent strategies for computing with two-digit numbers as they build their understanding of the operations.

■ **Fraction and Decimal Computation** (Chapters 16 and 17): These topics for the upper elementary and middle grades depend on a firm understanding of the operations.

■ **Algebraic Thinking** (Chapter 22): Representing contextual situations in equations is at the heart of algebraic thinking. This is exactly what students are doing as they learn to write equations to go with their solutions to story problems.

Addition and Subtraction Problem Structures

A significant method of developing meaning for the operations is to have children solve contextual problems or story problems.

FIGURE 10.1 **Four basic structures for addition and subtraction story problems. Each structure has three numbers. Any one of the three numbers can be the unknown in a story problem.**

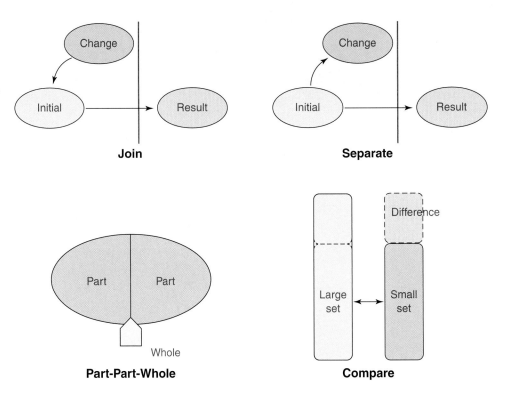

Researchers have separated addition and subtraction problems into categories based on the kinds of relationships involved. These include *join* problems, *separate* problems, *part-part-whole* problems, and *compare* problems (Carpenter & Moser, 1983; Gutstein & Romberg, 1995; Fennema, Carpenter, Levi, Franke, & Empson, 1997). The basic structure for each of these four types of problems is illustrated in Figure 10.1. Each structure involves a number "family" such as 3, 5, 8. A different problem results depending on which of the three quantities in the structure is unknown.

Examples of Problems for Each Structure

The number family 4, 8, 12 is used in each of the story problems that follow and can be connected to the structure in Figure 10.1. These drawings are not intended for children but to help you as a teacher consider the different structures. Also note that the problems are described in terms of their structure and not as addition or subtraction problems. Contrary to what you may have thought, a joining action does not always mean addition, nor does separate or remove always mean subtraction.

Join Problems

For the action of joining, there are three quantities involved: an initial amount, a change amount (the part being added or joined), and the resulting amount (the amount after the action is over).

JOIN: RESULT UNKNOWN

Sandra had 8 pennies. George gave her 4 more. How many pennies does Sandra have altogether?

JOIN: CHANGE UNKNOWN

Sandra had 8 pennies. George gave her some more. Now Sandra has 12 pennies. How many did George give her?

JOIN: INITIAL UNKNOWN

Sandra had some pennies. George gave her 4 more. Now Sandra has 12 pennies. How many pennies did Sandra have to begin with?

Separate Problems

Notice that in the separate problems, the initial amount is the whole or the largest amount, whereas in the join problems, the result was the whole. Again, refer to Figure 10.1 as you consider these problems. Be sure you can identify what quantities are the initial, change, and result amounts.

SEPARATE: RESULT UNKNOWN

Sandra had 12 pennies. She gave 4 pennies to George. How many pennies does Sandra have now?

SEPARATE: CHANGE UNKNOWN

Sandra had 12 pennies. She gave some to George. Now she has 8 pennies. How many did she give to George?

SEPARATE: INITIAL UNKNOWN

Sandra had some pennies. She gave 4 to George. Now Sandra has 8 pennies left. How many pennies did Sandra have to begin with?

Part-Part-Whole Problems

Part-part-whole problems involve two parts that are combined into one whole. The combining may be a physical action, or it may be a mental combination where the parts are not physically combined.

There is no meaningful distinction between the two parts in a part-part-whole situation, so there is no need to have a different problem for each part as the unknown. For each possibility (whole unknown and part unknown), two problems are given here. The first is a mental combination where there is no action. The second problem involves a physical action.

PART-PART-WHOLE: WHOLE UNKNOWN

George has 4 pennies and 8 nickels. How many coins does he have?

George has 4 pennies and Sandra has 8 pennies. They put their pennies into a piggy bank. How many pennies did they put into the bank?

PART-PART-WHOLE: PART UNKNOWN

George has 12 coins. Eight of his coins are pennies, and the rest are nickels. How many nickels does George have?

George and Sandra put 12 pennies into the piggy bank. George put in 4 pennies. How many pennies did Sandra put in?

Compare Problems

Compare problems involve the comparison of two quantities. The third amount does not actually exist but is the difference between the two amounts. There are three types of compare problems, corresponding to which quantity is unknown (smaller, larger, or difference). For each of these, two examples are given: one problem where the difference is stated in terms of more and another in terms of less.

COMPARE: DIFFERENCE UNKNOWN

George has 12 pennies and Sandra has 8 pennies. How many more pennies does George have than Sandra?

George has 12 pennies. Sandra has 8 pennies. How many fewer pennies does Sandra have than George?

COMPARE: LARGER UNKNOWN

George has 4 more pennies than Sandra. Sandra has 8 pennies. How many pennies does George have?

Sandra has 4 fewer pennies than George. Sandra has 8 pennies. How many pennies does George have?

COMPARE: SMALLER UNKNOWN

George has 4 more pennies than Sandra. George has 12 pennies. How many pennies does Sandra have?

Sandra has 4 fewer pennies than George. George has 12 pennies. How many pennies does Sandra have?

STOP   Go back through all of these problems and match the numbers in the problems with the components of the structures in Figure 10.1. For each problem, do two additional things. First, use a set of counters to model (solve) the problem as you think children in the primary grades might do. Second, for each problem, write either an addition or subtraction equation that you think best represents the problem as you did it with counters.

Reflections on the Four Structures

In most curricula, the overwhelming emphasis is on the easier join and separate problems with the result unknown. These become the de facto definitions of addition and subtraction: Addition is "put together" and subtraction is "take away." The fact is, these are *not* the definitions of addition and subtraction.

When students develop these limited put-together and take-away definitions for addition and subtraction, they often have difficulty later when addition or subtraction is called for but the structure is other than put together or take away. It is important that children be exposed to all forms within these structures.

Computational and Semantic Forms of Equations

If you wrote an equation for each of the problems as just suggested, you may have some equations where the unknown quantity is not isolated on one side of the equal sign. For example, a likely equation for the join problem with initial part unknown is $\boxed{8} + 4 = 12$. This is referred to as the *semantic* equation for the problem since the numbers are listed in the order that follows the meaning of the problem. When the semantic form does not isolate the unknown, an equivalent equation can be written for the same problem. In this case, the equation $12 - 4 = \boxed{8}$ is referred to as the *computational* form of the equation; it isolates the unknown. When the two forms are not the same, children must eventually come to see the equivalence of these equations.

Problem Difficulty

The various types of problems are not at all equal in difficulty for children (Thompson & Hendrickson, 1986). The change problems where the initial part is unknown are among the most difficult, probably because children modeling the problems directly do not know how many counters to put down to begin with. Problems where the change amounts are unknown are also difficult.

Many children will solve compare problems as part-part-whole problems without making separate sets of counters for the two amounts. The whole is used as the large amount, one part for the small amount and the second part for the difference. Which method did *you* use? There is absolutely no reason this should be discouraged as long as children are clear about what they are doing.

Teaching Addition and Subtraction

So far you have seen a variety of types of story problems for addition and subtraction and you probably have used some counters to help you understand how these problems can be solved by children. These two methods, contextual problems and models (counters, drawings, number lines), are the main teaching tools that you have to help students construct a rich understanding of these two operations. Let's examine how each approach can be used in the classroom.

Using Contextual Problems

There is more to think about than simply giving students problems to solve.

Context or Story Problems

In contrast with the rather sterile story problems in the previous section, consider the following problem.

Yesterday we were measuring how tall we were. You remember that we used the connecting cubes to make a big train that was as long as we were when we were lying down. Susan and Marcy were wondering how many cubes long they would be if they lay down head to foot. Susan had measured Marcy and she was 84 cubes long. Marcy measured Susan and she is 102 cubes long. Let's see if we can figure out how long they will be end to end, and then we can check by actually measuring them.

Fosnot and Dolk (2001) point out that in story problems, children tend to focus on getting the answer, probably in the way that the teacher wants. "Context problems, on the other hand, are connected as closely as possible to children's lives, rather than to 'school mathematics.' They are designed to anticipate and to develop children's mathematical modeling of the real world" (p. 24). Contextual problems might derive from recent experiences in the classroom, a field trip, a discussion you have been having in art or social studies, or from children's literature.

Lessons Built on Context or Story Problems

The tendency in the United States is to have students solve a lot of problems in a single class period. The focus of these lessons seems to be on how to get answers. In Japan, however, a complete lesson will often revolve around one or two problems and the related discussion (Reys & Reys, 1995).

What might a good lesson look like for second grade that is built around word problems? The answer comes more naturally if you think about students not just solving the problems but also using words, pictures, and numbers to explain how they went about solving the problem and why they think they are correct. Children should be allowed to use whatever physical materials they feel they need to help them, or they can simply draw pictures. Whatever they put on their paper should explain what they did well enough to allow someone else to understand it (allow at least a half page of space for a problem).

Choosing Numbers for Problems

Even kindergarten children should be expected to solve story problems. Their methods of solution will typically involve using counters in a very direct modeling of the problems. This is what makes the join and separate problems with the initial parts unknown so difficult. For these problems, children initially use a trial-and-error approach (Carpenter, Fennema, Franke, Levi, & Empson, 1999).

Although the structure of the problems will cause the difficulty to vary, the numbers in the problems should be in accord with the number development of the children. Kindergarten children can use numbers as large as they can count meaningfully, which is usually to about 10 or 12.

Second-grade children are also learning about two-digit numbers and are beginning to understand how our base-ten system works. Rather than wait until students have learned about place value and have developed techniques for computing numbers, word problems are a problem-based opportunity to learn about number and computation at the same time. For example, a problem involving the combination of 30 and 42 has the potential to help students focus on the sets of ten. As they begin to think of 42 as 40 and 2, it is not at all unreasonable to think that they will add 30 and 40 and then add 2 more. As you learn more about invented strategies for computation in Chapter 13, you will develop a better understanding of how to select numbers to aid in computational development.

NCTM Standards The *Standards* authors make clear the value of connecting addition and subtraction. "Teachers should ensure that students repeatedly encounter situations in which the same numbers appear in different contexts. For example, the numbers 3, 4, and 7 may appear in problem-solving situations that could be represented by 4 + 3, 3 + 4, or 7 − 3, or 7 − 4. . . . Recognizing the inverse relationship between addition and subtraction can allow students to be flexible in using strategies to solve problems" (p. 83).

Introducing Symbolism

Very young children have no need for the symbols +, −, and =. However, these symbolic conventions are important. When you feel your students are ready to use these symbols, introduce them in the discussion portion of a lesson where students have solved story problems. Say, "You had the whole number of 12 in your problem and the number 8 was one of the parts of 12. You found out that the part you did not know was 4. Here is a way we can write that: 12 − 8 = 4." The minus sign should be read as "minus" or "subtract" but not as "take away." The plus sign is easier since it is typically a substitute for "and."

Some care should be taken with the equal sign. The equal sign means "is the same as." However, most children come to think of it as a symbol that tells you that the "answer is coming up." It is interpreted in much the same way as the ⊡ on a calculator. That is, it is the key you press to get the answer.

An equation such as 4 + 8 = 3 + 9 has no "answer" and is still true because both sides stand for the same quantity. A good idea is to often use the phrase "is the same as" in place of or in conjunction with "equals" as you read equations with students.

Using Model-Based Problems

Many children will use counters or number lines (models) to solve story problems. The model is a thinking tool to help them both understand what is happening in the problem and a means of keeping track of the numbers and solving the problem. Problems can also be posed using models when there is no context involved. The part-part-whole concept as discussed in Chapter 9 is a good way to help students think about addition and subtraction when they are focused on models.

Addition

When the parts of a set are known, addition is used to name the whole in terms of the parts. This simple, albeit sterile, definition of addition serves both action situations (join and separate) and static or no-action situations.

Each of the part-part-whole models shown in Figure 10.2 is a model for 5 + 3 = 8. Some of these are the result of a definite put-together or joining action, and some are not. Notice that in every example, both of the parts are distinct, even after the parts are joined. If counters are used, the two parts should be kept in separate piles or in separate sections of a mat or should be two distinct colors. For children to see a relationship between the two parts and the whole, the image of the 5 and 3 must be kept as two separate sets. This helps children reflect on the action after it has taken place. "These red chips are the ones I started with. Then I added these five blue ones, and now I have eight altogether."

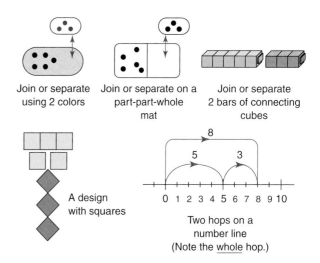

FIGURE 10.2 Part-part-whole models for 5 + 3 = 8 and 8 − 3 = 5.

A number line presents some real conceptual difficulties for first and second graders. Its use as a model at that level is generally not recommended. A number line measures distances from zero the same way a ruler does. In the early grades, children focus on the dots or numerals on a number line instead of the spaces. However, if arrows (hops) are drawn for each number in an exercise, the length concept is more clearly illustrated. To model the part-part-whole concept of 5 + 3, start by drawing an arrow from 0 to 5, indicating, "This much is five." Do not point to the dot for 5, saying "This is five."

ACTIVITY 10.1

Equations with Number Patterns

Recall Activity 9.18 (p. 124) called "Build It in Parts" and its variations, in which children made designs or built sets for a specific number. When children seem ready to deal with written symbolism, simply show them how to write a plus or addition number sentence (equation) for each design. In those initial activities, children said a combination, such as "Four and five is nine." Now they have a new symbolic way to match what they say.

Two children can work together, do something with a model, say the combination, and together write the equation. The children can vary the total amounts they construct each time—within appropriate limits, of course. Remember that what makes "Equations with Number Patterns" problem based is the challenge to find different combinations for a number.

Subtraction

In a part-part-whole model, when the whole and one of the parts are known, subtraction names the other part. This definition is in agreement with the drastically overused language of "take away." If you start with a whole set of 8 and remove a set of 3, the two sets that you know are the sets of 8 and 3. The expression 8 − 3, read "eight minus three," names the five remaining. Therefore, eight minus three is five. Notice that the models in Figure 10.2 are models for subtraction as well as addition (except for the action). Helping children see that they are using the same models or pictures aids in connecting the two operations.

ACTIVITY 10.2

Missing-Part Subtraction

A fixed number of counters is placed on a mat. One child separates the counters into two parts while the other child hides his or her eyes. The first child covers one of the two parts with a sheet of tagboard, revealing only the other part (see Figure 10.3). The second child says the subtraction sentence. For example, "Nine minus four [the visible part] is five [the

---

covered part]." The covered part can be revealed if necessary for the child to say how many are there. Both the subtraction equation and the addition equation can then be written.

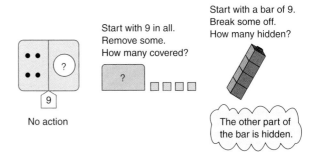

FIGURE 10.3 **Models for 9 − 4 as a missing-part problem.**

Subtraction as Think-Addition

Note that in Activity 10.2, the situation ends with two parts clearly distinct, even when there is a remove action. The removed part remains in the activity or on the mat as a model for an addition equation to be written after writing the subtraction equation. A discussion of how these two equations can be written for the same model situation is an important opportunity to connect addition and subtraction. This is significantly better than the traditional worksheet activity of "fact families" in which children are given a family of numbers such as 3, 5, and 8 and are told to write two plus equations and two minus equations. Very quickly this becomes a matter of dropping the numbers in the various slots.

Subtraction as "think-addition" is extremely significant for mastering subtraction facts. Because the counters for the remaining or unknown part are left hidden under the cover, when children do these activities, they are encouraged to think about the hidden part: "What goes with the part I see to make the whole?" For example, if the total or whole number of counters is 9, and 6 are removed from under the cover, the child is likely to think in terms of "6 and what makes 9?" or "What goes with 6 to make 9?" The mental activity is "think-addition" instead of a "count what's left" approach. Later, when working on subtraction facts, a subtraction fact such as 9 − 6 = □ should trigger the same thought pattern: "6 and what makes 9?"

Comparison Models

Comparison situations involve two distinct sets or quantities and the difference between them. Several ways of modeling the difference relationship are shown in Figure 10.4. The same kind of model can be used whether the difference or one of the two quantities is unknown.

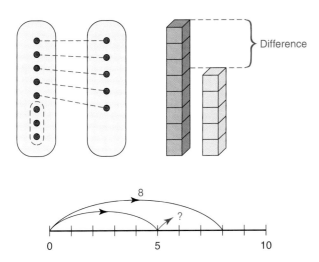

FIGURE 10.4 **Models for the difference between 8 and 5.**

Note that it is not immediately clear how you would associate either the addition or subtraction operations with a comparison situation. From an adult vantage point, you can see that if you match part of the larger amount with the smaller amount, the large set is now a part-part-whole model that can solve the problem. In fact, many children do model compare problems in just this manner. But that is a very difficult idea to show children if they do not construct the idea themselves.

Have children make two amounts, perhaps with two bars of connecting cubes. Discuss the difference between the two bars to generate the third number. For example, if the children make a bar of 10 and a bar of 6, the difference is 4. "What equations can we make with these three numbers?" Have children make up story problems that involve two amounts of 10 and 6. Discuss which equations go with the problems that are created.

The Order Property and the Zero Property

The *order* property (or *commutative* property) for addition says that it makes no difference in which order two numbers are added. Most children find little difficulty with this idea. Since it is quite useful in problem solving, mastering basic facts, and mental mathematics, there is value in spending some time helping children construct the relationship. The name of the property is not important, but the idea is.

To help children focus on the order property, pair problems that have the same addends but in different orders. The context for each problem should be different. For example:

Tania is on page 32 in her book. Tomorrow she hopes to read 15 more pages. What page will she be on if she reads that many pages?

The milk tray in the cafeteria was down to only 15 cartons. Before lunch, the delivery person brought in some more milk. She filled up the tray with 32 more cartons. How many cartons does the milk tray hold?

Ask if anyone notices how these problems are alike. If done as a pair, some (not all) students will see that having solved one they have essentially solved the other.

The following activity is also important and helps with the same idea.

ACTIVITY 10.3

More Than Two Addends

Give students six sums to find involving three or four addends. Prepare these on one page divided into six sections so that there is space to write beneath each sum. Within each, include at least one pair with a sum of ten or perhaps a double: $4 + 7 + 6, 5 + 9 + 9$, or $3 + 4 + 3 + 7$. Students should show how they added the numbers. Allow students to find the sums without any other directions.

Figure 10.5 illustrates how students might show what they did. As they share their solutions, almost certainly there will be students who added in different orders but got the same result. From this discussion you can help them conclude that you can add numbers in any order. You are also using the associative property but it is the order or commutative property that is more important. This is also an excellent number sense activity because many students will find combinations of ten in these sums or will use doubles (easy facts for many students). Learning to adjust strategies to fit the numbers is the beginning of the road to computational fluency.

Story problems involving zero and or using zeros in the three-addend sums is also a good method of helping students understand zero in addition or subtraction. Occasionally students feel that $6 + 0$ must be more than 6 or that $12 - 0$ must be 11 since "plus makes numbers bigger" or "minus makes numbers smaller." Instead of making arbitrary-sounding rules about adding and subtracting zero, build opportunities for discussing zero into the problem-solving routine.

The second-grade curriculum of *Investigations in Number, Data, and Space* places a significant emphasis on connecting

FIGURE 10.5 **Students show how they added.**

INVESTIGATIONS in NUMBER, DATA, and SPACE

Grade 2, *Coins, Coupons, and Combinations*

Investigation 3: Making Sense of Addition and Subtraction

Context

The *Coins, Coupons, and Combinations* unit occurs early in the second grade. It is one of two units in which the work on addition and subtraction is undertaken. In the first portion of the unit, the focus is on developing strategies for addition combinations (the ideas you will encounter in Chapter 11 of this book). Children are not only working with small addition "facts" but also are solving two-digit addition problems with invented strategies before they begin to work on story problems.

Task Description

As you can see from the problems shown here, *Investigations* has students explore addition and subtraction problems together. In the discussions surrounding these problems there is a definite effort to use the story problems to connect the concepts of addition and subtraction.

The problems on the page shown are duplicated and cut apart. Problems are put in six envelopes, one problem per envelope. Students may select any envelope, take a problem and paste it on their paper. In this manner, page format in no way suggests what is to be done or how much space is required for showing work. When one problem is complete, they can select another problem, and paste it on the page. Most students will complete from two to three problems on a sheet. The envelope technique is a useful way to attend to individual differences and pacing issues.

Students are to use whatever methods and materials they wish to solve the problems but are required to "show their solution so that someone else can understand it" (p. 104). In fact, for this lesson, children must show their solution to another student to check that what they wrote can be understood by someone else.

In this unit, all of the problems are *result unknown* (join and separate) or *part-whole* problems. In a later unit, *change unknown* problems are included.

---

1. Kira and Jake were eating peanuts. There were 39 peanuts in the bag. Kira ate 18 of them and Jake ate the rest. How many peanuts did Jake eat?

2. Kira and Jake were making snowballs. They both made 19 snowballs. How many did they make in all?

3. There were 47 students in the gym. One class of 23 students went back to their room. How many students were left in the gym?

4. The second grade class went on a trip to the zoo. There were 32 students and 12 adults on the trip. How many people went on the zoo trip?

5. Marcel and Shawn were counting pennies. Marcel had 33 pennies and Shawn had 36 pennies. How many pennies did they have in all?

6. Lin has 50 pennies in a cup. She spent 29 pennies at the store on a pencil. How much money does Lin have left?

7. Make up a problem to go with 30 – 13. Write about how you solved the problem. Use words, numbers, or pictures to show your thinking.

Page 163 from *The Number System: Coins, Coupons, and Combinations* by K. Economopoulos & S. J. Russell. *Investigations in Number, Data, and Space.* Copyright © 1998 by Dale Seymour Publications. Reprinted by permission of Pearson Education, Inc.

In a full-class session following this activity, students are given two story problems involving children getting on and off a bus. The first is a separate problem for 29 – 13 and the second is a part-whole problem for 16 + 13. After sharing how they would do these problems, students are asked if they see anything about the problems that is alike or how solving one might help them solve the other. They are also asked what equations they would write for each problem. This is a good example of how to focus on connecting the concepts of addition and subtraction.

---

addition and subtraction concepts. In the excerpt shown here, you can see an activity involving word problems for addition and subtraction and a discussion of this portion of the curriculum. Take special note of the envelope technique used.

This allows for all students to solve as many problems as their pace and time permit without having to face blank, incomplete work. The technique mixes the problems so that it will be possible to discuss all of the problems as a class.

Technology Note

The *Fizz & Martina* series (Tom Snyder Productions, 1998) embed problems in "real-life" adventures of Fizz and Martina. Available in videotape, videodisk, and CD formats, the stories require students to pay attention and take notes. A story is stopped when the problem is posed, and students work in groups without the video or computer. Printed support material is included. This model fits nicely with the before, during, and after format of a problem-solving lesson.

At present, few programs offer addition and subtraction word problems with the variety of problem types we have just explored. However, there are two other ways that you can take advantage of your classroom computers using almost any basic tool software you happen to have. First, you can provide problems yourself using your word processor or any program that allows shapes to be easily drawn and words to be typed. An example of the latter type is *Kid Pix* (Brøderbund, 1996a). Open a new file, and write a word problem in an appropriate space. Students open the file and use the drawing capabilities to record their solution. The students' work is either not saved or renamed so that your file remains as an activity.

Bridget Phipps, a first-grade teacher, notes that her children were much better at writing story problems on the computer than they were by hand, and she often had students write problems for pictures she created. Make a file with a drawing involving counters in two parts or with a whole specified and one part showing. Students write and solve a story problem on the computer to go with the drawing. *MathKeys: Unlocking Whole Numbers* (MECC, 1995b, 1996b) has a large variety of stamps to create counters and a readily available writing space beneath the pictures. ■

Problem Structures for Multiplication and Division

Like addition and subtraction, there are problem structures that will help you as the teacher in formulating and assigning multiplication and division tasks. As with the additive structures, these are for you, not for students.

Most researchers identify four different classes of multiplicative structures (Greer, 1992). Of these, the two described in Figure 10.6, *equal groups (repeated addition, rates)* and *multiplicative comparison,* are by far the most prevalent in the elementary school. Problems matching these structures can be modeled with sets of counters, number lines, or arrays. They represent a large percentage of the multiplicative problems in the real world. (The term *multiplicative* is used here to describe all problems that involve multiplication and division structure.)

The two other types of problems, *combinations (Cartesian products)* and *product-of-measures* problems (e.g., length times width equals area), are also important but receive much less attention in school. These problems will be described in terms of real-world contexts instead of a general structure.

Examples of Problems for Each Structure

In multiplicative problems one number or *factor* counts how many sets, groups, or parts of equal size are involved. The other factor tells the size of each set or part. These two factors have traditionally been referred to as the *multiplier* (number of parts) and the *multiplicand* (size of each part). These terms are not particularly useful to children and will not be

FIGURE 10.6 Two of the four basic structures for multiplication and division story problems. Each structure has three numbers. Any one of the three numbers can be the unknown in a story problem.

Equal Groups   **Multiplicative Comparison**

used here unless needed for clarity. The third number in each of these two structures is the *whole* or *product* and is the total of all of the parts. The parts and wholes terminology is useful in making the connection to addition.

Equal-Group Problems

When the number and size of groups are known, the problem is a multiplication situation. When either the number of sets or the size of sets is unknown, division results. But note that these latter two situations are not alike. Problems where the size of the sets is unknown are called *fair-sharing* or *partition* problems. The whole is shared or distributed among a known number of sets to determine the size of each. If the number of sets is unknown but the size of the equal sets is known, the problems are called *measurement* or sometimes *repeated-subtraction* problems. The whole is "measured off" in sets of the given size. These terms are used with the examples to follow. Keep in mind the structure in Figure 10.6 to see which numbers are given and which is unknown.

There is also a subtle difference between problems that might be termed *repeated-addition* problems (If 3 children have 4 apples each, how many apples are there?) and those that might be termed *rate* problems (If there are 4 apples per child, how many apples would 3 children have?). For each category, two examples of rate problems are provided.

EQUAL GROUPS: WHOLE UNKNOWN (MULTIPLICATION)

Mark has 4 bags of apples. There are 6 apples in each bag. How many apples does Mark have altogether?

If apples cost 7 cents each, how much did Jill have to pay for 5 apples? (*rate*)

Peter walked for 3 hours at 4 miles per hour. How far did he walk? (*rate*)

EQUAL GROUPS: SIZE OF GROUPS UNKNOWN (PARTITION DIVISION)

Mark has 24 apples. He wants to share them equally among his 4 friends. How many apples will each friend receive?

Jill paid 35 cents for 5 apples. What was the cost of 1 apple? (*rate*)

Peter walked 12 miles in 3 hours. How many miles per hour (how fast) did he walk? (*rate*)

EQUAL GROUPS: NUMBER OF GROUPS UNKNOWN (MEASUREMENT DIVISION)

Mark has 24 apples. He put them into bags containing 6 apples each. How many bags did Mark use?

Jill bought apples at 7 cents apiece. The total cost of her apples was 35 cents. How many apples did Jill buy? (*rate*)

Peter walked 12 miles at a rate of 4 miles per hour. How many hours did it take Peter to walk the 12 miles? (*rate*)

Multiplicative Comparison Problems

In multiplicative comparison problems, there are really two different sets, as there were with comparison situations for addition and subtraction. One set consists of multiple copies of the other. Two examples of each possibility are provided here. In the former, the comparison is an amount or quantity difference. In multiplicative situations, the comparison is based on one set's being a particular multiple of the other.

COMPARISON: PRODUCT UNKNOWN (MULTIPLICATION)

Jill picked 6 apples. Mark picked 4 times as many apples as Jill. How many apples did Mark pick?

This month Mark saved 5 times as much money as last month. Last month he saved $7. How much money did Mark save this month?

COMPARISON: SET SIZE UNKNOWN (PARTITION DIVISION)

Mark picked 24 apples. He picked 4 times as many apples as Jill. How many apples did Jill pick?

This month Mark saved 5 times as much money as he did last month. If he saved $35 this month, how much did he save last month?

COMPARISON: MULTIPLIER UNKNOWN (MEASUREMENT DIVISION)

Mark picked 24 apples, and Jill picked only 6. How many times as many apples did Mark pick as Jill did?

This month Mark saved $35. Last month he saved $7. How many times as much money did he save this month as last?

STOP What you just read is a lot to take in without reflection. Stop now and get a collection of counters—at least 35. Use the counters to solve each of the problems. Look first at the equal-group problems and do the "Mark problems" or the first problem in each set. Match the numbers with the structure model in Figure 10.6. How are these problems alike and how are they different, especially the two division problems? Repeat the exercise with the "Jill problems" and then the "Peter problems." Can you see how the problems in each group are alike and how the problems across groups are related?

When you are comfortable with the equal-group problems, repeat the same process with the multiplicative comparison problems. Again, start with the first problem in all three sets and then the second problem in all three sets. Reflect on the same questions posed earlier.

Combinations Problems

Combinations problems involve counting the number of possible pairings that can be made between two sets. The product consists of *pairs* of things, one member of each pair taken from each of the two given sets. The two factors in these problems each represent the size of a set, so there is no reason to distinguish between two division situations.

COMBINATIONS: PRODUCT UNKNOWN

Sam bought 4 pairs of pants and 3 jackets, and they all can be worn together. How many different outfits consisting of a pair of pants and a jacket does Sam have?

You want to make a set of attribute pieces that have 3 colors and 6 different shapes. If you want your set to have exactly one piece for every possible combination of shapes and colors, how many pieces will you need to make?

An experiment involves tossing a coin and rolling a die. How many different possible results or outcomes can this experiment have?

COMBINATIONS: SIZE OF A SET UNKNOWN

Sam bought some new pants and jackets. He has a total of 12 different outfits. If he bought 4 pairs of pants, how many jackets did Sam buy?

Your set of attribute materials consists of 18 different pieces. There are 3 colors, and each color comes in different shapes. How many different shapes are in the set?

In the experiment of tossing a coin and rolling a die, there are 12 possible outcomes. Of course, the coin has two sides. How many sides does the die have?

There are different ways to model these problems: indicate pairings using lines, model all pairs directly, or use an array. Figure 10.7 gives examples of all of these possibilities.

Combinations problems can have more than two quantities. For example, Sam may also have six different ties ($4 \times 3 \times 6$), the attribute pieces could include two sizes and have one,

2 × 5 pairs

Each line indicates a possible pair.

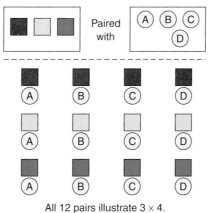

All 12 pairs illustrate 3 × 4.

FIGURE 10.7 **Models for combinations situations.**

Sugar   Cake   Waffle

	Sugar	Cake	Waffle
Vanilla			
Chocolate			
Strawberry			
Fudge ripple			
Orange sherbet			

5 × 3 possible ice cream cones

Each section is one combination of a flavor and a type of cone.

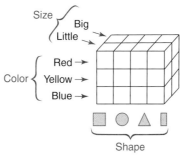

How many different pieces with these attributes?

(3×4) × 2 different pieces
(concept extended to 3 factors)

two, or three holes in each piece (3 × 6 × 2 × 3), and the experiment may include two coins instead of one (2 × 2 × 6). Modeling combinations from three or more sets is possible but quickly becomes tedious. The lower-right example in Figure 10.7 shows a three-dimensional array, although a line drawing or pairings could also have been used. In the upper grades, it is worthwhile exploring such combinations with small numbers to see that this concept of multiplication can be extended to any number of sets.

Product-of-Measures Problems

What distinguishes product-of-measures problems from the others is that the product is literally a different type of thing from the other two factors. In a rectangle, the product of two lengths (length × width) is an area, usually square units. Figure 10.8 illustrates how different the square units are from each of the two factors of length: 4 feet times 7 feet is not 28 feet but 28 *square* feet. The factors are each one-dimensional entities, but the product consists of *two*-dimensional things.

Two other fairly common examples in this category are number of workers × hours worked = worker-hours and kilowatts × hours = kilowatt-hours.

Reflections on the Multiplicative Structures

There is evidence that kindergarten and first-grade children are quite successful at solving multiplication and division problems, even division involving remainders (Carpenter, Ansell, Franke, Fennema, & Weisbeck, 1993; Carpenter, Carey, & Kouba, 1990; Fennema et al., 1997). Mulligan and Mitchelmore (1997), based on their own research and that of others, make a strong argument that students should be exposed to all four op-

erations from the first year of school and that multiplication and division should be much more closely linked in the curriculum.

TEACHING MULTIPLICATION AND DIVISION

Multiplication and division are taught separately in most traditional programs, with multiplication preceding division. It is important, however, to combine multiplication and division soon after multiplication has been introduced in order to help students see how they are related. In most curricula, these topics are a main focus of the third grade with continued development in the fourth and fifth grades.

One of the major conceptual hurdles of working with multiplicative structures is that of understanding groups of things as single entities while also understanding that a group contains a given number of objects (Clark & Kamii, 1996; Kouba, 1989; Steffe, 1988). Children can solve the problem *How many apples in 4 baskets of 8 apples each?* by counting out 4 sets of 8 counters and then counting all. To think multiplicatively about this problem as 4 *sets of eight* requires children to conceptualize each group of eight as a single item to be counted. Experiences with making and counting groups, especially in contextual situations, are extremely useful. (See the discussion of the book *Each Orange Had 8 Slices* at the end of this chapter.)

Using Contextual Problems

Many of the issues surrounding addition and subtraction also apply to multiplication and need not be discussed in depth again. It remains important to use contextual problems whenever reasonable instead of more sterile story problems. Just as with additive structures, it is a good idea to build lessons around only two or three problems. Students should solve problems using whatever techniques they wish. What is important is that they explain—preferably in writing—what they did and why it makes sense. Words, pictures, and numbers remain important.

Symbolism for Multiplication and Division

When students solve simple multiplication story problems before learning about multiplication symbolism, they will most likely write repeated-addition equations to represent what they did as an equation. This is your opportunity to introduce the multiplication sign and explain what the two factors mean.

The usual convention is that 4 × 8 refers to four sets of eight, not eight sets of four. There is absolutely no reason to be rigid about this convention. The important thing is that the students can tell you what each factor in *their* equations represents. In vertical form, it is usually the bottom factor that indicates the number of sets. Again, this distinction is not terribly important.

The quotient 24 divided by 6 is represented in three different ways: $24 \div 6$, $6\overline{)24}$, and $\frac{24}{6}$. The fraction notation becomes important at the middle school level. The computational form $6\overline{)24}$ would probably not exist if it were not for the standard pencil-and-paper procedure that utilizes it. Chil-

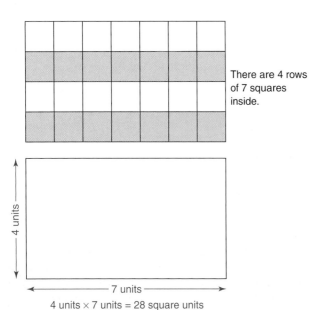

There are 4 rows of 7 squares inside.

4 units

7 units

4 units × 7 units = 28 square units

FIGURE 10.8 Length times length equals area.

dren have a tendency to read this as "6 divided by 24" due to the left-right order of the numerals. Generally this error does not match what they are thinking.

Compounding the difficulty of division notation is the unfortunate phrase, "six goes into twenty-four." This phrase carries little meaning about division, especially in connection with a fair-sharing or partitioning context. The "goes into" (or "guzinta") terminology is simply engrained in adult parlance and has not been in textbooks for years. If you tend to use that phrase, it is probably a good time to consciously abandon it.

Choosing Numbers for Problems

When selecting numbers for multiplicative story problems or activities, there is a tendency to think that large numbers pose a burden to students or that 3×4 is somehow easier to understand than 4×17. Conceptually, products or quotients are not affected by the size of numbers as long as the numbers are within the grasp of the students. Little is gained by restricting early explorations of multiplication to small numbers. Even in early third grade, students can work with larger numbers using whatever counting strategies they have at their disposal. A contextual problem involving 14×8 is not at all too large for third graders even before they have learned a computation technique. When given these challenges, children are likely to invent computational strategies.

Remainders

More often than not, division does not result in a simple whole number. For example, problems with 6 as a divisor will "come out even" only one time out of six. In the absence of a context, a remainder can be dealt with in only two ways: It can either remain a quantity left over or be partitioned into fractions. In Figure 10.9, the problem $11 \div 4$ is modeled to show fractions.

Partition $11 \div 4 = 2\frac{3}{4}$
$2\frac{3}{4}$ in each of the 4 sets
(each leftover divided in fourths)

Measurement $11 \div 4 = 2\frac{3}{4}$
$2\frac{3}{4}$ sets of 4
(2 full sets and $\frac{3}{4}$ of a set)

FIGURE 10.9 Remainders expressed as fractions.

In real contexts, remainders sometimes have three additional effects on answers:

The remainder is discarded, leaving a smaller whole-number answer.

The remainder can "force" the answer to the next highest whole number.

The answer is rounded to the nearest whole number for an approximate result.

The following problems illustrate all five possibilities.

You have 30 pieces of candy to share fairly with 7 children. How many pieces of candy will each child receive?
Answer: 4 pieces of candy and 2 left over. (left over)

Each jar holds 8 ounces of liquid. If there are 46 ounces in the pitcher, how many jars will that be?
Answer: 5 and $\frac{6}{8}$ jars. (partitioned as a fraction)

The rope is 25 feet long. How many 7-foot jump ropes can be made?
Answer: 3 jump ropes. (discarded)

The ferry can hold 8 cars. How many trips will it have to make to carry 25 cars across the river?
Answer: 4 trips. (forced to next whole number)

Six children are planning to share a bag of 50 pieces of bubble gum. About how many pieces will each child get?
Answer: About 8 pieces for each child. (rounded, approximate result)

Students should not just think of remainders as "R 3" or "left over." Remainders should be put in context and dealt with accordingly.

It is useful for you to make up problems in different contexts. **STOP** Include continuous quantities such as length, time, and volume. See if you can come up with problems in each division category for equal-group and comparison problems that would have remainders dealt with as fractions or as rounded-up or rounded-down results.

Using Models-Based Problems

In the beginning, children will be able to use the same models—sets and number lines—for all four operations. A model not generally used for addition but extremely important and widely used for multiplication and division is the array. An *array* is any arrangement of things in rows and columns, such as a rectangle of square tiles or blocks.

To make clear the connection to addition, early multiplication activities should also include writing an addition sentence for the same model. A variety of models are shown in Figure 10.10. Notice that the products are not included—only addition and multiplication "names" are written. This is another way to avoid the tedious counting of large sets. A similar

FIGURE 10.10
Models for equal-group multiplication.

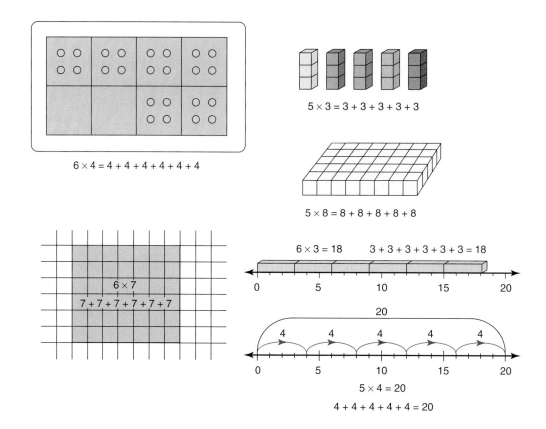

$6 \times 4 = 4 + 4 + 4 + 4 + 4 + 4$

$5 \times 3 = 3 + 3 + 3 + 3 + 3$

$5 \times 8 = 8 + 8 + 8 + 8 + 8$

6×7
$7 + 7 + 7 + 7 + 7 + 7$

$6 \times 3 = 18 \qquad 3 + 3 + 3 + 3 + 3 + 3 = 18$

$5 \times 4 = 20$
$4 + 4 + 4 + 4 + 4 = 20$

approach is to write one sentence that expresses both concepts at once, for example, $9 + 9 + 9 + 9 = 4 \times 9$.

Multiplication and Division Activities

As with additive problems, children can benefit from a few activities with models and no context. The purpose of such activities is to focus on the meaning of the operation and the associated symbolism. Activity 10.4 has a good problem-solving spirit. The language you use depends on what you have used with your children in the past.

ACTIVITY 10.4

Finding Factors

Start by assigning a number that has several factors—for example, 12, 18, 24, 30, or 36. Have students find multiplication expressions for their assigned number. With counters, students attempt to find a way to separate the counters into equal subsets. With arrays (perhaps made from square tiles or cubes or drawn on grid paper), students try to build rectangles that have the given number of squares. For each such arrangement of sets or appropriate rectangles, both an addition and a multiplication equation should be written.

Activity 10.4 can also include division concepts. When children have learned that 3 and 6 are factors of 18, they

can write the equations $18 \div 3 = 6$ and $18 \div 6 = 3$ along with $3 \times 6 = 18$ and $6 + 6 + 6 = 18$ (assuming that three sets of six were modeled). The following variation of the same activity focuses on division. Having children create word problems is another excellent elaboration of this activity. Require children to explain how their story problems fit with what they did with the counters.

ACTIVITY 10.5

Learning About Division

Provide children with an ample supply of counters and some way to place them into small groups. Small paper cups work well. Have children count out a number of counters to be the whole or total set. They record this number: "Start with 31." Next specify either the number of equal sets to be made or the size of the sets to be made: "Separate your counters into four equal-sized sets," or "Make as many sets of four as is possible." Next have the children write the corresponding multiplication equation for what their materials show; under that, have them write the division equation.

Be sure to include both types of exercises: number of equal sets and size of sets. Discuss with the class how these two are different, yet each is related to multiplication and each is written as a division equation. You can show both ways to write division equations at this time. Do Activity 10.5 several times. Start with whole quantities that are multiples of the divisor (no remainders) but soon include situations with remainders. (Note that it is technically incorrect to write 31 ÷ 4 = 7 R 3. However, in the beginning, that form may be the most appropriate to use.)

The activity can be varied by changing the model. Have children build arrays using square tiles or blocks or by having them draw arrays on centimeter grid paper. Present the exercises by specifying how many squares are to be in the array. You can then specify the number of rows that should be made (partition) or the length of each row (measurement). How could children model fractional answers using drawings of arrays on grid paper?

--- ACTIVITY 10.6 ---

The Broken Multiplication Key

The calculator is a good way to relate multiplication to addition. Students can be told to find various products on the calculator without using the ⊠ key. For example, 6 × 4 can be found by pressing ⊞ 4 ⊟ ⊟ ⊟ ⊟ ⊟ ⊟. (Successive presses of ⊟ add 4 to the display each time. You began with zero and added 4 six times.) Students can be challenged to demonstrate their result with sets of counters. But note that this same technique can be used to determine products such as 23 × 459 (⊞ 459 and then 23 presses of ⊟). Students will want to compare to the same product using the ⊠ key.

"The Broken Multiplication Key" can profitably be followed by "The Broken Division Key."

--- ACTIVITY 10.7 ---

The Broken Division Key

Have children work in groups to find methods of using the calculator to solve division exercises without using the divide key. The problems can be posed without a story context. "Find at least two ways to figure out 61 ÷ 14 without pressing the divide key." If the problem is put in a story context, one method may actually match the problem better than another. Good discussions may follow different solutions with the same answers. Are they both correct? Why or why not?

⊗ STOP There is no reason ever to show children how to do Activity 10.7. However, it would be a good idea for *you* to see if you can find *three* ways to solve 61 ÷ 14 on a calculator without using the divide key. For a hint, see the footnote.*

---

*There are two measurement approaches or two ways to find out how many 14s are in 61. A third way is essentially related to partitioning or finding 14 times what number is close to 61.

NCTM Standards "In grades 3–5, students should focus on the meanings of, and relationship between, multiplication and division. It is important that students understand what each number in a multiplication or division expression represents. . . . Modeling multiplication problems with pictures, diagrams, or concrete materials helps students learn what the factors and their product represent in various contexts" (p. 151).

Useful Multiplication and Division Properties

As with addition and subtraction, there are some multiplicative properties that are useful and, thus, worthy of attention. The emphasis should be on the ideas and not terminology or definitions.

The Order Property in Multiplication

It is not intuitively obvious that 3 × 8 is the same as 8 × 3 or that, in general, the order of the numbers makes no difference (the *order* or *commutative* property). A picture of 3 sets of 8 objects cannot immediately be seen as 8 piles of 3 objects. Eight hops of 3 land at 24, but it is not clear that 3 hops of 8 will land at the same point.

The array, by contrast, is quite powerful in illustrating the order property, as is shown in Figure 10.11. Children should draw or build arrays and use them to demonstrate why each array represents two different multiplications with the same product.

The Role of Zero and One in Multiplication

Zero and, to a lesser extent, 1 as factors often cause difficulty for children. In one recent third-grade text (Charles et al., 1998), a lesson on factors of 0 and 1 has children use a calculator to examine a wide range of products involving 0 or 1 (423 × 0, 0 × 28, 1536 × 1, etc.) and look for patterns. The pattern

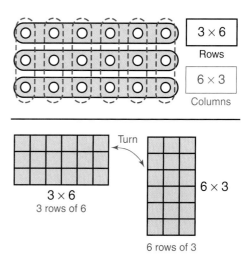

FIGURE 10.11 Two ways an array can be used to illustrate the order (commutative) property for multiplication.

suggests the rules for factors of 0 and 1 but not a reason. In the same lesson, a word problem asks how many grams of fat there are in 7 servings of celery with 0 grams of fat in each serving. This approach is far preferable to an arbitrary rule, since it asks students to reason. Make up interesting word problems involving 0 or 1, and discuss the results. Problems with 0 as a first factor are really strange. Note that on a number line, 5 hops of 0 land at 0 (5 × 0). What would 0 hops of 5 be? Another fun activity is to try to model 6 × 0 or 0 × 8 with an array. (Try it!) Arrays for factors of 1 are also worth investigating.

The Distributive Property

It may not be essential for young children to know the *distributive* property in the form $a \times (b + c) = (a \times b) + (a \times c)$. But the concept involved is very useful in relating one basic fact to another, and it is also involved in the development of two-digit computation. Figure 10.12 illustrates how the array model can be used to illustrate that a product can be broken up into two parts.

The next activity is designed to help children discover how to partition factors or, in other words, learn about the distributive property.

ACTIVITY 10.8

Slice It Up

Supply students with several sheets of centimeter grid paper. Assign each pair of students a product such as 6 × 8. (Products can vary across the class or all be the same.) The task is to find all of the different ways to make a single slice through the rectangle. For each slice students write an equation. For a slice of one row of 8, students would write 6 × 8 = 5 × 8 + 1 × 8. The individual products can be written in the arrays as was done in Figure 10.12.

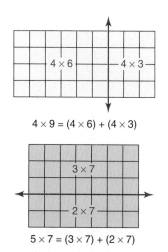

$$4 \times 9 = (4 \times 6) + (4 \times 3)$$

$$5 \times 7 = (3 \times 7) + (2 \times 7)$$

FIGURE 10.12 **Models for the distributive property.**

Why Not Division by Zero?

Some children are simply told "Division by zero is not allowed." To avoid an arbitrary rule, pose problems to be modeled that involve zero: "Take thirty counters. How many sets of zero can be made?" or "Put twelve blocks in zero equal groups. How many in each group?"

 ## Technology Note

The *Fizz & Martina* series (Tom Snyder Productions, 1998) was mentioned earlier as a vehicle for embedding story problems into real contexts. For the upper grades, the problems are both one- and two-step and involve a wider range of mathematical concepts than has been discussed here. Many teachers like the idea of a video format for its ease of use.

A few other programs have been found that use word problems. *Word Problem Square Off* (Gamco, 1994) and *Math for the Real World* (Kaplan/Knowledge Adventure) are two examples. Both are designed for grade 3 and higher, with *Square Off* available in three grade levels. Unless you find a value in the extrinsic motivation provided by the computer or by game formats that have nothing to do with the mathematics, the programs are little more than problem banks. Until something better is developed, you are almost certainly better off using problems in your textbook and making up your own. ■

Solving Contextual Problems

So far our focus has been on either additive or multiplicative problems. The purpose has been to help students learn about these operations and in the process to begin to develop some informal computational strategies.

In the upper grades (although not exclusively so) students see context or story problems and are at a loss for what to do. In this section you will learn some techniques for helping them.

Analyzing Context Problems

Consider the following problem:

In building the road through the subdivision, a low section in the land was filled in with dirt that was hauled in by trucks. The complete fill required 638 truckloads of dirt. The average truck carried $6\frac{1}{4}$ cubic yards of dirt, which weighed 17.3 tons. How many tons of dirt were used in the fill?

Typically, in fifth- to eighth-grade books, problems of this type are found as part of a series of problems revolving around a single context or theme. Data may be found in a graph or chart or perhaps a short news item or story. Most likely the problems will include all four of the operations. Students have difficulty deciding on the correct operation and even finding the appropriate data for the problem. Many students will find two numbers in the problem and guess at the correct operation. These children simply do not have any tools for analyzing problems. At least two strategies can be taught that are very helpful: Think about the answer before solving the problem, or solve a simpler problem that is just like this one.

Think About the Answer Before Solving the Problem

Poor problem solvers fail to spend adequate time thinking about the problem and what it is about. They rush in and begin doing calculations, believing that "number crunching" is what solves problems. That is simply not the case. Rather, students should spend time talking about (later, thinking about) what the answer might look like. For our sample problem, it might go as follows:

> *What is happening in this problem?* Some trucks were bringing dirt in to fill up a hole.
>
> *What will the answer tell us?* How many tons of dirt were needed in the fill.
>
> *Will that be a small number of tons or a large number of tons?* Well, there were 17.3 tons on a truck, but there were a lot of trucks, not just one. It's probably going to be a whole lot of tons.
>
> *About how many do you think it will be?* It's going to be really big. If there were just 100 trucks, it would be 1730 tons. It might be close to 10,000 tons. That's a lot of tons!

In this type of discussion, three things are happening. First, the students are asked to focus on the problem and the meaning of the answer instead of on numbers. The numbers are not important in thinking about the structure of the prob-

lem. Second, with a focus on the structure of the problem, students can identify the numbers that are important or data that they must look up in a table or graph as well as numbers that are not important to the problem. Third, the thinking leads to a rough estimate of the answer. Sometimes, for everyday things, this can simply be based on common sense. In any event, thinking about what the answer tells and about how large it might be is a useful first step.

Work a Simpler Problem

The reason that models are rarely used with problems such as the dirt problem is that the numbers are impossible to model easily. Dollars and cents, distances in thousands of miles, and time in minutes and seconds are all examples of data likely to be found in the upper grades, and all are difficult to model. The general problem-solving strategy of "try a simpler problem" can almost always be applied to problems with unwieldy numbers.

A simple strategy has the following steps:

1. Substitute small whole numbers for all relevant numbers in the problem.
2. Model the problem using the new numbers (counters, drawing, number line, array).
3. Write an equation that solves the small-number version of the problem.
4. Write the corresponding equation with the original numbers used where the small-number substitutes were.
5. Use a calculator to do the computation.
6. Write the answer in a complete sentence, and decide if it makes sense.

Figure 10.13 shows what might be done for the dirt problem. It also shows an alternative in which only one of the numbers is made smaller and the other number is illustrated symbolically. Both methods are effective.

FIGURE 10.13 Working a simpler problem: two possibilities.

Change all numbers:

Leave one number alone:

FIGURE 10.13 Working a simpler problem: two possibilities.

The idea is to provide a tool students can use to analyze a problem and not just guess at what computation to do. It is much more useful to have students do a few problems where they must use a model of a drawing to justify their solution than to give them a lot of problems where they guess at a solution but don't know if their guess is correct.

Caution: Avoid the Key Word Strategy!

It is often suggested that students should be taught to find "key words" in story problems. Some teachers even post lists of key words with their corresponding meanings. For example, "altogether" and "in all" mean you should add and "left" and "fewer" indicate you should subtract. The word "each" suggests multiplication. To some extent, teachers have been reinforced by the overly simple and formulaic story problems often found in textbooks. When problems are written in this way, it may appear that the key word strategy is effective.

In contrast with this belief, researchers and mathematics educators have long cautioned against the strategy of key words (e.g., Burns, 2000; Carpenter, 1985; Goldin, 1985; Kliman & Russell, 1998). Here are three arguments against the key word approach.

1. Key words are misleading. Often the key word or phrase in a problem suggests an operation that is incorrect. For example:

Maxine took the 28 stickers she no longer wanted and gave them to Zandra. Now Maxine has 73 stickers *left*. How many stickers did Maxine have to begin with?

If you look through the story problems in this chapter, you will find other examples of misleading key words.

2. Many problems have no key words. Especially when you get away from the overly simple problems found in primary textbooks, you will find that a large percentage of problems have no key words. A child who has been taught to rely on key words is left with no strategy. In both the additive and the multiplicative problems in this chapter, you will find numerous examples of problems with no key words. And this is from a collection of overly simple problems designed to help you with structure.

3. The key word strategy sends a terribly wrong message about doing mathematics. The most important approach to solving any contextual problem is to analyze its structure—to make sense of it. The key word approach encourages students to ignore the meaning and structure of the problem and look for an easy way out. Mathematics is about reasoning and making sense of situations. A sense-making strategy will *always* work.

Two-Step Problems

Students often have difficulty with multistep problems. If your students are going to work with multistep problems, be sure they can analyze one-step problems in the way that we have discussed. The following ideas, adapted from suggestions by Huinker (1994), are designed to help children see how two problems can be chained together.

1. Give students a one-step problem, and have them solve it. Before discussing the answer, have each student or group make up a second problem that uses the answer to the first problem. The rest of the class can then be asked to use the answer to the first problem to solve the second problem. Here is an example:

Given problem: It took $3\frac{1}{3}$ hours for the Joneses to drive the 195 miles to Washington. What was their average speed?

Second problem: The Jones children remember crossing the river at about 10:30, or 2 hours after they left home. About how far from home is the river?

---

2. Make a "hidden question." Repeat the first exercise by beginning with a one-step problem. You might give different problems to different groups. This time, have students write out both problems as before. Then write a single related problem that leaves out the question from the first problem. That question from the first problem is the "hidden question." Here is a simple example:

Given problem: Tony bought three dozen eggs for 89 cents a dozen. How much was the bill?

Second problem: How much change did Tony get back from $5?

Hidden-question problem: Tony bought three dozen eggs for 89 cents a dozen. How much change did Tony get back from $5?

Have other students identify the hidden question. Since all students are working on a similar task but with different problems (be sure to mix the operations), they will be more likely to understand what is meant by a hidden question.

3. Pose standard two-step problems, and have the students identify and answer the hidden question. Consider the following problem:

Willard Sales decides to add widgets to its line of sale items. To begin with, Willard bought 275 widgets wholesale for $3.69 each. In the first month, the com-

pany sold 205 widgets at $4.99 each. How much did Willard make or lose on the widgets? Do you think Willard Sales should continue to sell widgets?

Begin by considering the questions that were suggested earlier: "What's happening in this problem?" (Something is being bought and sold at two different prices.) "What will the answer tell us?" (How much profit or loss there was.) These questions will get you started. If students are stuck, you can ask, "Is there a hidden question in this problem?"

NCTM Standards

The value of student discussions to help develop meaning throughout mathematics including understanding the operations is quite evident in the *Standards*. At the K–2 level: "When students struggle to communicate ideas clearly, they develop a better understanding of their own thinking" (p. 129). At the 3–5 level: "The use of models and pictures provides a further opportunity for understanding and conversation. Having a concrete referent helps students develop understandings that are clearer and more easily shared" (p. 197).

ASSESSMENT NOTES

Simple one- and two-step word problems are excellent assessment tasks. Because similar tasks can be provided on different days, observation data can easily be gathered over time. The problems lend themselves to both group work and independent work. All children, even the youngest, can produce a written report of their work so that there is evidence to keep and also evidence of written communication skills.

Not only does using story problems make data gathering easy, but the problems also provide a wonderful opportunity to assess a wide range of information about your students. The obvious data are about conceptual understanding of the operations involved, connections between related operations, connections with operation symbolism (equations), and connections to real-world information.

Another area of conceptual knowledge and understanding is number sense. After students have decided what computation to do in a problem, it is useful to see how they go about doing it. Several programs, most notably *Cognitively Guided Instruction* (CGI) (Fennema et al., 1997; Hankes, 1996), rely almost entirely on solutions to word problems for the development of basic fact mastery and the invention of computational procedures. Regardless of how computational methods are developed in your class, children will exhibit their most spontaneous and personal approaches to computation when solving realistic story problems.

Finally, all aspects of problem solving, including the metacognitive and affective goals, can be observed as children work on simple story problems. ■

LITERATURE CONNECTIONS

Finding an exciting and fun way to use literature to develop or expand understanding of the operations is extremely easy. There are lots of books with stories or pictures concerning sets of things, buying things, measures, and so on, that can be used to pose problems or, better, to stimulate children to invent their own problems. Perhaps the most widely mentioned book in this context is *The Doorbell Rang* by Pat Hutchins (1986). You can check that one out yourself. Here are three additional suggestions.

How Many Snails?
Giganti, 1988

Appropriate for the K–2 set, this book includes a variety of pictures where the objects belonging to one collection have various subcollections (parts and wholes). For example, a sky full of clouds has various types of clouds. The text asks, "How many clouds are there? How many clouds are big and fluffy? How many clouds are big and fluffy and gray?" These pages lead directly to addition and subtraction situations matching the part-part-whole concepts. Of special note is the opportunity to have missing-part thinking for subtraction. Children can think of collections that they would like to draw so that subcollections have a variety of attributes. They can then pose their own questions about the drawing and add appropriate number sentences. In discussion, children could explain why they selected the particular equation and how it fits the picture.

More Than One
Hoban, 1981

The wonderful black-and-white photos of Tana Hoban are designed to introduce group words such as a *crowd* of people, a *herd* of elephants, or a *bundle* of wood. A discussion of group words (animal groups fit nicely with science—*flock, pride, covey,* etc.) beyond those that are in the book can be interesting in and of itself. Do different groups typically contain different numbers of things? Is it likely that there would be two elephants in a herd? Could there be 50? What is typical? These grouping words provide a real opportunity for children to develop *group* as a single entity but with separate things inside. Now suppose that there are many groups (herds, flocks, crowds). If we know the size of one, and we know how many herds, do we know how many elephants in all? Imagine a situation where that was always the case—all groups with group names have the same number of things. If there are 87 pieces of wood in 3 bundles, how many in a bundle? Clever one- and two-step multiplication and division stories can be generated.

Each Orange Had 8 Slices
Giganti, 1992

Each two-page spread shows objects grouped in three ways. For example, one spread has four trees, three bird's nests in each tree, and two eggs in each nest. The author asks three questions: "How many trees? How many nests? How many eggs?" The three questions with each picture extend multiplication to a three-factor product. In the case of the trees, nests, and eggs, the product is 4 × 3 × 2. After children get a handle on the predictable arrangement of the book's pictures, they can not only write multiplication stories that go with the pictures but also make up situations of their own. What similar situations can be found in the classroom? Perhaps desks, books, and pages or bookshelves, shelves, and books. There is no need to restrict the discussion to three nestings of objects. The same idea is present in measurements: yards, feet, inches or gallons, quarts, pints, cups, ounces. New problems can be posed that require division. What if there were some boxes with 6 cartons in each? Each carton has 4 widgets. If there are 72 widgets, how many boxes are there?

Reflections on Chapter 10

Writing to Learn

1. Make up a context for some story problems, and make up six different join and separate problems: three with a join action and three with a separate action. For all six problems, use the same number family: 9, 4, 13.
2. Make up a comparison word problem. Next change the problem to provide an example of all six different possibilities for comparison problems.
3. Why might a contextual problem be more effective than a simple story problem?
4. What considerations would you take into account when selecting numbers for addition and subtraction problems? Grade level will make a difference.
5. How can you use models in a problem-based way for addition and for subtraction?
6. Explain how missing-part activities prepare students for mastering subtraction facts.
7. Make up multiplication word problems to illustrate the difference between equal groups and multiplicative comparison. Can you create problems involving rates or continuous quantities?
8. Make up two different word problems for 36 ÷ 9. For one, the modeling should result in four sets of nine, and for the other, the modeling should result in nine sets of four. Which is which? Which of your problems is a measurement problem, and which is a partition problem?
9. Explain the meaning of the first and second factors in 3 × 8 = 24. What is 24 called in this equation?
10. Describe multiplication and division activities that begin with models rather than with word problems.
11. How would you help students learn these properties of multiplication: order or commutative property, distributive property, and property of zero? How would you help students discover that division by zero is not well defined and so is not really possible?
12. Make up realistic measurement and partition division problems where the remainder is dealt with in each of these three ways: (a) it is discarded (but not left over); (b) it is made into a fraction; (c) it forces the answer to the next whole number.
13. Explain how to help students analyze problems when the numbers are not small whole numbers but rather are large or are fractions or decimals that do not lend themselves to using counters.

14. Why is the use of key words not a good strategy to teach children?
15. Describe the sequence of steps suggested for helping children deal with two-step problems.

For Discussion and Exploration

1. *Cognitively Guided Instruction* is not a curriculum program but a professional development program in which teachers learn to use students' thinking to guide instruction. The predominant thrust of CGI is the use of story problems, not only for learning the operations but also for number and fact development and even for computation development with larger numbers. Select either basic fact mastery or computation development, and describe how you think these goals might be achieved primarily through story problems. If possible, view some of the CGI videotapes and the accompanying teacher's guide (Fennema et al., 1997) to compare your thoughts with theirs.
2. Examine a basal textbook at one or more grade levels. Identify how, and in what chapters, the meanings for the operations are developed. Discuss the relative focus on meanings of the operations with one-step story problems, use of models, mastery of basic facts, and where computation fits in.
3. See how many different types of story problems you can find in a basal textbook. In the primary grades, look for join, remove, part-part-whole, and compare problems. For grades 4 and up, look for the four multiplicative types. (Look in the multiplication and division chapters and also at special problem-solving lessons.) Are the various types of problems well represented?

Recommendations for Further Reading
Highly Recommended

Carpenter, T. P., Fennema, E., Franke, M. L., Levi, L., & Empson, S. (1999). *Children's mathematics: Cognitively guided instruction.* Portsmouth, NH: Heinemann. (Also published by NCTM)
 For teachers, this is the best book available for understanding the CGI approach to operations and the use of story problems to develop number, basic facts, and computational procedures. The classifications of word problems for all operations, as discussed in this chapter, are explained in detail along with methods for using these problems with students. With the book come two CDs,

one with classroom clips of CGI classrooms and the other showing children using the various strategies described in the book.

Gutstein, E., & Romberg, T. A. (1995). Teaching children to add and subtract. *Journal of Mathematical Behavior, 14*, 283–324.

A bit more research oriented than the Carpenter, Carey, and Kouba article and yet very worthwhile reading for a teacher who wants to have a clear understanding of how children develop addition and subtraction concepts. The article explores several research programs that have investigated different strategies for teaching addition and subtraction. It extends beyond operation meaning to the development of computational strategies.

Kouba, V. L., & Franklin, K. (1993). Multiplication and division: Sense making and meaning. In R. J. Jensen (Ed.), *Research ideas for the classroom: Early childhood mathematics* (pp. 103–126). Old Tappan, NJ: Macmillan.

This chapter, which seeks to help teachers understand the intricacies of multiplicative concepts, is complete and readable, providing teachers at the 3–4 level with a good perspective without being too technical.

Schifter, D., Bastable, V., & Russell, S. J. (1999b). *Developing mathematical understanding: Numbers and operations, Part 2, Making meaning for operations (Casebook)*. Parsippany, NJ: Dale Seymour Publications.

In this casebook, teachers in grades K–7 share their stories of working with children as they develop meanings for the four operations. The teachers discuss the kinds of actions and situations that students use as they come to understand the operations. This is a companion book to an extended in-service guide. There is also a video available to augment the series. However, the casebook is easily worthwhile by itself.

Other Suggestions

Baroody, A. J. (1999). Children's relational knowledge of addition and subtraction. *Cognition and Instruction, 17,* 137–175.

Bryant, P., Christie, C., & Rendu, A. (1999). Children's understanding of the relation between addition and subtraction: Inversion, identity, and decomposition. *Journal of Experimental Psychology, 74,* 194–212.

Burns, M. (2000). *About teaching mathematics: A K–8 resource* (2nd ed.). Sausalito, CA: Math Solutions Publications.

Burns, M. (1995). *Math by all means: Multiplication, grade 3.* Sausalito, CA: Math Solutions Publications.

Carroll, W. M., Fuson, K. C., & Diamond, A. (2000). Use of student-constructed number stories in a reform-based curriculum. *Journal of Mathematical Behavior, 19,* 49–62.

Clark, F. B., & Kamii, C. (1996). Identification of multiplicative thinking in children in grades 1–5. *Journal for Research in Mathematics Education, 27,* 41–51.

Hankes, J. E. (1996). An alternative to basic-skills remediation. *Teaching Children Mathematics, 2,* 452–457.

Kamii, C. (1994). Young children continue to reinvent arithmetic: 3rd grade. New York: Teachers College Press.

Ohanian, S., & Burns, M. (1995). *Math by all means: Division, grades 3–4.* Sausalito, CA: Marilyn Burns Education Associates.

Schifter, D. (1999). Reasoning about operations: Early algebraic thinking in grades K–6. In L. V. Stiff (Ed.), *Developing mathematical reasoning in grades K–12* (pp. 62–81). Reston, VA: National Council of Teachers of Mathematics.

11

Helping Children
Master the Basic Facts

Basic facts for addition and multiplication refer to combinations where both addends or both factors are less than 10. Subtraction and division facts correspond to addition and multiplication facts. Thus, $15 - 8 = 7$ is a subtraction fact because both parts are less than 10.

Mastery of a basic fact means that a child can give a quick response (in about 3 seconds) without resorting to nonefficient means, such as counting. Work toward mastery of addition and subtraction facts typically begins in the first grade. Most books include all addition and subtraction facts for mastery in the second grade, although much additional drill is usually required in grade 3 and even after. Multiplication and division facts are generally a target for mastery in the third grade, with more practice required in grades 4 and 5. Unfortunately, many children in grade 8 and above do not have a complete command of the basic facts.

All children are able to master the basic facts—including children with learning disabilities. Children simply need to construct efficient mental tools that will help them. This chapter is about helping children develop those tools.

Big Ideas

1. Number relationships provide the foundation for strategies that help students remember basic facts. For example, knowing how numbers are related to 5 and 10 helps students master facts such as $3 + 5$ (think of a ten-frame) and $8 + 6$ (since 8 is 2 away from 10, take 2 from 6 to make $10 + 4 = 14$).

2. "Think addition" is the most powerful way to think of subtraction facts. Rather than 13 "take away 6," which requires a lot of counting, students can think 6 and what makes 13. They might add up to 10 or they may think double 6 is 12 so it must be 13.

3. All of the facts are conceptually related. You can figure out new or unknown facts from those you already know. For example, 6×8 can be thought of as five 8s (40) and one more 8. It might also be three 8s doubled.

Content Connections

As should be clear from the Big Ideas, basic fact mastery is not really new mathematics; rather, it is the development of fluency with ideas that have already been learned.

■ **Number and Operations** (Chapters 9 and 10): Fact mastery relies significantly on how well students have constructed relationships on numbers and how well they understand the operations.

Fluency with basic facts allows for ease of computation, especially mental computations, and, therefore, aids in the ability to reason numerically in every number-related area. Although calculators and tedious counting are available for students who do not have command of the facts, reliance on these methods for simple number combinations is a serious handicap to mathematical growth.

A Three-Step Approach to Fact Mastery

Every teacher of grades 4 to 10 knows children who are still counting on their fingers, making marks in the margins to count on, or simply guessing at answers. These children have certainly been given more than adequate opportunity to drill their facts in years past. They have not mastered their facts because they have not developed efficient methods of producing a fact answer. Drill of inefficient methods does not produce mastery!

Fortunately, we know quite a bit about helping children develop fact mastery, and it has little to do with quantity of drill or drill techniques. Three components or steps to this end can be identified:

1. Help children develop a strong understanding of the operations and of number relationships.
2. Develop efficient strategies for fact retrieval through practice.
3. Then provide drill in the use and selection of those strategies once they have been developed.

The Role of Number and Operation Concepts

Number relationships play a significant role in fact mastery. The 8 + 6 example in the first Big Idea requires the relationship between 8 and 10 (8 is 2 away from 10), the part-part-whole knowledge of 6 (2 and 4 more makes 6), and the fact that 10 and 4 is 14. For 6 × 7, it is efficient to think "5 times 7 and 7 more." For many children, the efficiency of this approach is lost because they need to count on 7 to get from 35 to 42. With an extension of the number relationships just noted, it is possible to think "35 and 5 more is 40, and 2 more is 42." Every relationship discussed in Chapter 9 can contribute to fact mastery.

The meanings of the operations also play a role in the construction of efficient strategies. The ability to relate 6 × 7 to "5 times 7 and 7 more" is based on an understanding of the meanings of the first and second factors. To relate 13 − 7 to "7 and what makes 13" requires an understanding of how addition and subtraction are related. The commutative or "turnaround" properties for addition and multiplication reduce the number of addition and multiplication facts from 100 each to 55 each.

Teachers in the upper grades with students who have not mastered basic facts will do well to investigate what command of number relationships and operations the students have. Without these relationships and concepts, the strategies discussed throughout this chapter will necessarily be learned in an instrumental manner.

Development of Efficient Strategies

An efficient strategy is one that can be done mentally and quickly. The emphasis is on *efficient*. Counting is not efficient. If drill is undertaken when counting is the only strategy available, all you get is faster counting.

The use of strategies is not at all a new idea. Brownell and Chazal (1935) recognized that children use different thought processes with different facts. Since the mid-1970s, there has been a strong interest among mathematics educators in the idea of directly teaching strategies to children (e.g., Baroody, 1985; Bley & Thornton, 1995; Fuson, 1984, 1992; Isaacs & Caroll, 1999; Rathmell, 1978; Steinberg, 1985; Thornton & Noxon, 1977; Thornton & Toohey, 1984). Many of the ideas that appear in this chapter have been adapted from the work of these researchers.

What Is a Strategy?

We have already seen some efficient strategies: the use of building up through 10 in adding 8 + 6 and the use of the related fact 5 × 7 to help with 6 × 7.

 Consider for a moment how you think about 6 + 6. What about 9 + 5?

You may think that you just "know" these. What is more likely is that you used some ideas similar to double six (for 6 + 6) and 10 and 4 more (for 9 + 5). Your response may be so automatic by now that you are not reflecting on the use of these relationships or ideas. That is one of the features of efficient mental processes—they become automatic with use.

Many children have learned basic facts without being taught efficient strategies. They develop or learn many of these methods in spite of the drill they may have endured. The trouble is that far too many students do not develop strategies without instruction and far too many students in middle school continue to count on their fingers. The challenge for teachers is to devise lessons in which all children will develop strategies that are useful. A strategy is most useful to students when it is theirs, built on and connected to concepts and relationships they already own.

For your students to develop effective strategies, you yourself need to have a command of as many good strategies as possible, even if you have never used them. This will help you recognize your students' invented strategies and capitalize on those ideas.

Two Basic Approaches

Next you need to plan lessons in which specific strategies are likely to be developed. There are two basic types of lessons suggested for this purpose. The first is to use simple story problems designed in such a manner that students are most likely to develop a strategy as they solve it. In the discussion of these solution methods, you can focus attention on the methods that are most useful. You can have all students try the methods others have developed. Often a suggestion of an idea is all that is necessary. A second possible approach is a bit more direct. A lesson may revolve around a special collection of facts for which a particular type of strategy is appropriate. You can discuss how these facts might all be alike in some way, or you might suggest an approach and see if students are able to use it on similar facts.

There is a huge temptation simply to tell students about a strategy and then have them practice it. Though this can be effective for some students, many others will not personally relate to your ideas or may not be ready for them. Continue to discuss strategies invented in your class and plan lessons that encourage strategies.

Drill of Efficient Methods and Strategy Selection

If you have read the section entitled "Drill or Practice?" in Chapter 6 (p. 85), you will recall a distinction between what drill means and what practice means. In the context of fact mastery, "practice" applies to those lessons just discussed, that is, problem-based experiences in which students are encouraged to develop flexible and useful strategies that are personally meaningful.

Drill—repetitive non-problem-based activity—is appropriate for children who have a strategy that they understand, like, and know how to use but have not yet become facile with it. Drill with an in-place strategy focuses students' attention on that strategy and helps to make it more automatic.

Drill plays a significant role in fact mastery, and the use of old-fashioned methods such as flash cards and fact games can be effective if used wisely.

Avoid Premature Drill

It is critical that you do not introduce drill too soon. Suppose that a child does not know the 9 + 5 fact and has no way to deal with it other than to count fingers or use counters. These are inefficient methods. Premature drill introduces no new information and encourages no new connections. It is both a waste of time and a frustration to the child.

As you read through this chapter, you may feel that the strategies for some facts, especially the harder multiplication facts, do not seem to be efficient at all. However, as long as the strategy is completely mental and does not rely on a model, picture, or tedious counting, repeated use of the strategy will almost certainly render it automatic. The strategy provides a mental path from fact to answer. Soon the fact and answer are "connected" as the strategy becomes almost unconscious.

The discussion in this chapter focuses on one strategy at a time. It is not at all unreasonable for students to be engaged in drill activities with one strategy before they have developed (via practice or problem-based activity) strategies for other facts.

Many of the activities suggested in the chapter are simple drills—flash cards, matching games, dice, or spinner activities—in which the objective is quick response. Do not misinterpret these activities that are clearly drills as the way to introduce or develop strategies. Drill should only be used when an efficient strategy is in place.

Practice Strategy Selection or Strategy Retrieval

Strategy selection or *strategy retrieval* is the process of deciding what strategy is appropriate for a particular fact. If you don't think to use a strategy, you probably won't. Many teachers who have tried teaching fact strategies report that the method works well while the children are focused on whatever strategy they are working on. They acknowledge that children can learn and use strategies. But, they continue, when the facts are all mixed up or the child is not in "fact practice" mode, old counting habits return.

For example, suppose that your children have been practicing the near-doubles facts for addition: Use the better-known double, 7 + 7, to derive the unknown 8 + 7. Children become quite skilled at doubling the smaller number and adding 1. All of the facts they are practicing are selected to fit this model. On other days, they have learned and practiced other strategies. Later, on a worksheet or in a mental math exercise, the children are presented with a mixture of facts. In a single exercise, a child might see

$$\begin{array}{cccc} 7 & 4 & 2 & 8 \\ +6 & +9 & +6 & +5 \end{array}$$

There is no mind-set or reminder to use different processes for each. Especially if the children have previously been habituated to counting to get answers, they will very likely revert to counting and ignore the efficient methods that were the focus of recent drills. When they were drilling the strategy, there was no need to decide what strategy might be useful. All of the facts in the near-doubles practice were near-doubles, and the strategy worked. Later, however, there is no one to suggest the strategy.

A simple activity that is useful is to prepare a list of facts selected from two or more strategies and then, one fact at a time, ask children to name a strategy that would work for that fact. They should explain why they picked the strategy and demonstrate its use. This type of activity turns the attention to the features of a fact that lend it to this or that strategy.

Overview of the Approach

For each particular strategy, from development to eventual drill when the strategy is well understood, the general approach for instruction is very similar.

Make Strategies Explicit in the Classroom

As has been discussed, your students will develop strategies as they solve word problems or as they investigate a category of facts you present. When a student suggests a new strategy, be certain that everyone else in the room understands how it is used. Suppose that Aidan explains how she figured out 3 × 7 by starting with double 7 (14) and then adding 7 more. She knew that 6 more onto 14 is 20 and one more is 21. You can ask another student to explain what Aidan just shared. This requires students to attend to ideas that come from their classmates. Now explore with the class to see what other facts would work with Aidan's strategy. This discussion may go in a variety of directions. Some may notice that all of the facts with a 3 in them will work. Others may say that you can always add one more set on if you know the smaller fact. For example, for 6 × 8 you can start with 5 × 8 and add 8.

Don't expect to have a strategy introduced and understood with just one word problem or one exposure such as this. Try on several successive days problems in which the same type of strategy might be used. Children need lots of opportunities to make a strategy their own. Many children will simply not be ready to use an idea the first few days, and then all of a sudden something will click and a useful idea will be theirs.

It is a good idea to write new strategies on the board or make a poster of strategies students develop. Give the strategies names that make sense. (*Double and add one more set. Aidan's idea. Use with 3s.* Include an example.)

No student should be forced to adopt someone else's strategy, but every student should be required to understand strategies that are brought to the discussion.

Drill Established Strategies

When you are comfortable that children are able to use a strategy without recourse to physical models and that they are beginning to use it mentally, it is time to drill it. You might have as many as ten different activities for each strategy or group of facts. File folder or boxed activities can be used by children individually, in pairs, or even in small groups. With a large number of activities, children can work on strategies they understand and on the facts that they need the most.

Flash cards are among the most useful approaches to fact strategy practice. For each strategy, make several sets of flash cards using all of the facts that fit that strategy. On the cards, you can label the strategy or use drawings or cues to remind the children of the strategy. Examples appear throughout the chapter.

Other activities involve the use of special dice made from wooden cubes or foam rubber, teacher-made spinners, matching activities where a helping fact or a relationship is matched with the new fact being learned, and games of all sorts. A game or drill suggested for one strategy can usually be adapted to another. A child or group of children may even want to make their own flash cards or drill games to match their own newly invented ideas.

Individualize

To some extent, you want to individualize drills in such a way that students are using their preferred strategy in the drills. This is not as difficult as it may seem at first.

Different students will likely invent or adopt different strategies for the same collection of facts. For example, there are several methods or strategies that use 10 when adding 8 or 9. Therefore, a drill that includes all of the addition facts with an 8 or a 9 can accommodate any child who has a strategy for that collection. Two children can be playing a spinner drill game, each using different strategies.

It is imperative that you listen to your students. Keep track of what strategies different students are using. This will help you occasionally create groups of students that can all benefit from the same drills. This will also help you know which students have yet to develop an efficient strategy for one or more collection of facts. If you are not sure who knows what facts, gather small groups of students to take a diagnostic test, a simple fact test with facts mixed randomly. Explain that you want them to first answer only those facts that they "know" without any counting. Then they should go back and attempt the unknown facts. Listen to find out how they approach these strategies.

Practice Strategy Selection

After children have worked on two or three strategies, strategy selection drills are very important. These can be conducted quickly with the full class or a group, or independent games and activities can be prepared. Examples are described toward the end of the chapter.

 Critics of the reform movement in mathematics education often try to suggest that the *Standards* are "soft on the basics," especially mastery of facts. Nothing could be further from the truth. Among several similar statements that could be selected from the *Standards* document is this rather unambiguous quote: "Knowing the basic number combinations—single-digit addition and multiplication pairs and their counterparts for subtraction and division—is essential" (p. 32).

STRATEGIES FOR ADDITION FACTS

The strategies for addition facts are directly related to one or more number relationships. In Chapter 9, numerous activities were suggested to develop these relationships. When the class is working on addition facts, the number relationship activities can and should be included with those described here. The teaching task is to help children connect these number relationships to the basic facts.

One-More-Than and Two-More-Than Facts

Each of the 36 facts highlighted in the chart has at least one addend of 1 or 2. These facts are a direct application of the one-more-than and two-more-than relationships.

+	0	1	2	3	4	5	6	7	8	9
0		1	2							
1	1	2	3	4	5	6	7	8	9	10
2	2	3	4	5	6	7	8	9	10	11
3		4	5							
4		5	6							
5		6	7							
6		7	8							
7		8	9							
8		9	10							
9		10	11							

Join or part-part-whole problems in which one of the addends is a 1 or a 2 are easy to make up. For example, *When Tommy was at the circus, he saw 8 clowns come out in a little car. Then 2 more clowns came out on bicycles. How many clowns did Tommy see in all?* Ask different students to explain how they got the answer of 10. Some will count on from 8. Some may still need to count 8 and 2 and then count all. Others will say they knew that 2 more than 8 is 10. The last response gives you an opportunity to talk about facts where you can use the two-more-than idea.

The different responses will provide you with a lot of information about students' number sense. As students are ready to use the two-more-than idea without counting all, they can begin to practice with activities such as the following.

ACTIVITY 11.1

One-/Two-More-Than Dice

Make a die labeled +1, +2, +1, +2, "one more," and "two more." Use with another die labeled 4, 5, 6, 7, 8, and 9. After each roll of the dice, children should say the complete fact: "Four and two is six."

ACTIVITY 11.2

One-/Two-More-Than Match

In a matching activity, children can begin with a number, match that with the one that is two more, and then connect that with the corresponding basic fact.

ACTIVITY 11.3

Lotto for +1/+2

A lotto-type board can be made on a file folder. Small fact cards can be matched to the numbers on the board. The back of each fact card can have a small answer number to use as a check.

Figure 11.1 illustrates some of these activities and shows several possibilities for flash cards. Notice that activities such as the dice or spinner games and the lotto-type activity can be modified for almost all of the strategies in the chapter. These are not repeated for each strategy.

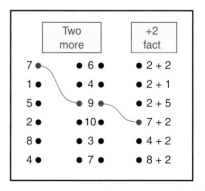

FIGURE 11.1 One-more and two-more facts.

Facts with Zero

Nineteen facts have zero as one of the addends. Though such problems are generally easy, some children overgeneralize the idea that answers to addition are bigger. Word problems involving zero will be especially helpful. In the discussion, use drawings that show two parts with one part empty.

+	0	1	2	3	4	5	6	7	8	9
0	0	1	2	3	4	5	6	7	8	9
1	1									
2	2									
3	3									
4	4									
5	5									
6	6									
7	7									
8	8									
9	9									

ACTIVITY 11.4

What's Alike? Zero Facts

Write about ten zero facts on the board, some with the zero first and some with the zero second. Discuss how all of these facts are alike. Have children use counters and a part-part-whole mat to model the facts at their seats.

Doubles

There are only ten doubles facts from 0 + 0 to 9 + 9, as shown here. These ten facts are relatively easy to learn and become a powerful way to learn the near-doubles (addends one apart). Some children use them as anchors for other facts as well.

+	0	1	2	3	4	5	6	7	8	9
0	0									
1		2								
2			4							
3				6						
4					8					
5						10				
6							12			
7								14		
8									16	
9										18

ACTIVITY 11.5

Double Images

Have students make picture cards for each of the doubles, and include the basic fact on the card as shown in Figure 11.2.

A simple "machine" can be drawn on the board or on a sheet of tagboard as shown in Figure 11.2. In this case the machine is labeled as the "Double" machine. Cards are made with an "input number" on one side and the double of the number on the reverse. A pair of students or a small group can use input/output machines, or you can lead the activity with a larger group.

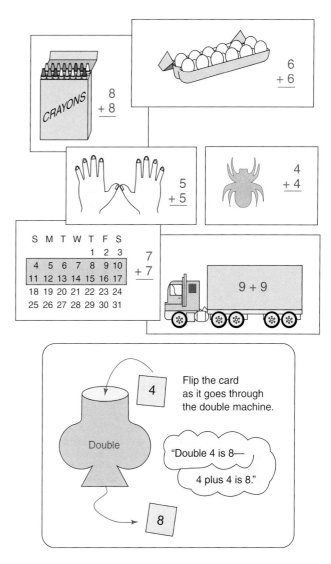

FIGURE 11.2 Doubles facts.

Word problems can focus on pairs of like addends. *Alex and Zack each found 7 seashells at the beach. How many did they find together?*

ACTIVITY 11.6

Calculator Doubles

Use the calculator and enter the "double maker" (2 $\times$ $=$). Let one child say, for example, "Seven plus seven." The child with the calculator should press 7, try to give the double (14), and then press $=$ to see the correct double on the display. (Note that the calculator is also a good way to practice +1 and +2 facts.)

Near-Doubles

Near-doubles are also called the "doubles-plus-one" facts and include all combinations where one addend is one more than the other. The strategy is to double the smaller number and add 1. Be sure students know the doubles before you focus on this strategy.

+	0	1	2	3	4	5	6	7	8	9
0		1								
1	1		3							
2		3		5						
3			5		7					
4				7		9				
5					9		11			
6						11		13		
7							13		15	
8								15		17
9									17	

To introduce the strategy to the class, write about ten near-doubles facts on the board. Use vertical and horizontal formats, and vary which addend is the smaller.

Have students work independently to write the answers. Then discuss their ideas for "good" (that is, efficient) methods of answering these facts. Some may double the smaller number and add one and others may double the larger and subtract. If no one uses a near-double strategy, write the corresponding doubles for some of the facts and ask how these facts could help.

Before using the following activity or the two shown in Figure 11.3, be sure to try word problems involving near-doubles. The discussion will give you a good idea of who is ready to drill this strategy.

ACTIVITY 11.7

Double Dice Plus One

Roll a single die with numerals or dot sets, and say the complete double-plus-one fact. That is, for 7, students should say, "Seven plus eight is fifteen."

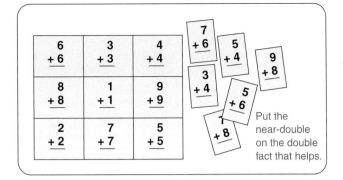

Put the near-double on the double fact that helps.

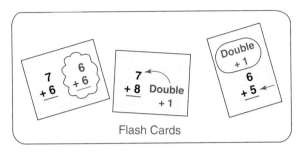

Flash Cards

FIGURE 11.3 **Near-doubles facts.**

Make-Ten Facts

These facts all have at least one addend of 8 or 9. One strategy for these facts is to build onto the 8 or 9 up to 10 and then add on the rest. For 6 + 8, start with 8, then 2 more makes 10, and that leaves 4 more for 14.

+	0	1	2	3	4	5	6	7	8	9
0										
1										10
2									10	11
3									11	12
4									12	13
5									13	14
6									14	15
7									15	16
8		10	11	12	13	14	15	16	17	
9	10	11	12	13	14	15	16	17	18	

Before using this strategy, be sure that children have learned to think of the numbers 11 to 18 as 10 and some more. Many second- and third-grade children have not constructed this relationship. (Refer to "Relationships for Numbers 10 to 20" in Chapter 9.)

The next activity is a good way to introduce the make-ten strategy.

ACTIVITY 11.8

Make 10 on the Ten-Frame

Give students a mat with two ten-frames (see Figure 11.4). Flash cards are placed next to the ten-frames, or a fact can be given orally. The students should first model each number in the two ten-frames and then decide on the easiest way to show (without counting) what the total is. The obvious (but not the only) choice is to move counters into the frame showing either 8 or 9. Get students to explain what they did. Focus especially on the idea that 1 (or 2) can be taken from the other number and put with the 9 (or 8) to make 10. Then you have 10 and whatever is left.

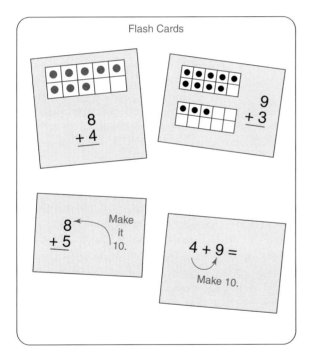

FIGURE 11.4 Make-ten facts.

Provide a lot of time with the make-ten activity. Encourage discussion and exploration of "easy ways" to think about adding two numbers when one of them is 8 or 9. Perhaps discuss why this is not a useful idea for a fact such as 6 + 5 where neither number is near 10.

Note that children will have many other ways of using 10 to add with 8 or 9. For example, with the fact 9 + 5, some will add 10 + 5 and subtract 1. This is a perfectly good strategy, and it uses 10. You may want to give efficient strategies unique names determined by the children and discuss which ones seem especially useful.

When children seem to have the make-ten idea or a similar strategy, try the same activity without counters. Use the little ten-frame cards found in the Blackline Masters. Make a transparency set for the overhead. Show an 8 (or 9) card on the overhead. Place other cards beneath it one at a time. Suggest *mentally* "moving" two dots into the 8 ten-frame. Have students say orally what they are doing. For 8 + 4, they might say, "Take 2 from the 4 and put it with 8 to make 10. Then 10 and 2 left over is 12." The activity can be done independently with the little ten-frame cards.

STOP As has been noted, there is more than one way to efficiently use 10 in a strategy for facts involving 8 or 9. Imagine two or three children who have on the table a small ten-frame card for 9 so that all can see. One at a time, other cards are turned up and the students are to name the total of the two cards. How many different efficient methods involving 10 can you think of that can be accommodated by this simple activity?

A Generic Task

So far the suggested activities each focus on a particular strategy. In contrast, the next activity can be thought of as a generic task that can be posed for any fact. Use it as a possible introduction to strategies for a new collection, or use it after several strategies for a collection of facts have already been introduced. This activity gives every student the message that their ideas are OK. For those students who do not think of a good strategy, they will benefit from the discussion.

ACTIVITY 11.9

If You Didn't Know

Pose the following task to the class: If you did not know the answer to 8 + 5 (or any fact that you want students to think about), what are some really good ways you can use to get the answer? Explain, that "really good" means that you don't have to count and you can do it in your head. Encourage students to come up with more than one way. Use a think-pair-share approach in which students discuss their ideas with a partner before they share them with the class.

In the event that no one comes up with a practical strategy you can offer one that a fictional friend shared with you—perhaps a student that you heard about in another school. You can also use this ploy to introduce a strategy that no one has thought about but which you think is possibly more efficient than those that have been suggested thus far. You are only offering ideas for consideration, not forcing them on students. You don't always have to rely on the students to come up with every strategy that they need.

Other Strategies and the Last Six Facts

To appreciate the power of strategies for fact learning, consider the following. We have discussed only five ideas or strategies (one or two more than, zeros, doubles, near-doubles, and make-ten), yet these ideas have covered 88 of the 100 addition facts! Further, these ideas are not really new but rather the application of important relationships. The 12 remaining facts are really only six facts and their respective turnarounds as shown on the chart.

+	0	1	2	3	4	5	6	7	8	9
0										
1										
2										
3						8	9	10		
4							10	11		
5				8				12		
6				9	10					
7				10	11	12				
8										
9										

Before trying to develop any particular strategies for these facts, spend several days with word problems where these facts are the addends. Listen carefully to the ideas that students use in figuring out the answers.

Doubles Plus Two, or Two-Apart Facts

Of the six remaining facts, three have addends that differ by 2: 3 + 5, 4 + 6, and 5 + 7. There are two possible relationships that might be useful here, each depending on knowledge of doubles. Some children find it easy to extend the idea of the near-doubles to double plus 2. For example, 4 + 6 is double 4 and 2 more. A different idea is to take 1 from the larger addend and give it to the smaller. Using this idea, the 5 + 3 fact is transformed into the double 4 fact—*double the number in between*.

Make-Ten Extended

Three of the six facts have 7 as one of the addends. The make-ten strategy is frequently extended to these facts as well. For 7 + 4, the idea is *7 and 3 more makes 10 and 1 left is 11*. You may decide to suggest this idea at the same time that you initially introduce the make-ten strategy. It is interesting to note that Japan, mainland China, Korea, and Taiwan all teach an addition strategy of building through 10 and do so in the first grade. Many U.S. second graders do not know what 10 plus any number is (Fuson, 1992).

Counting On

Counting on is the most widely promoted strategy. It is generally taught as a strategy for all facts that have 1, 2, or 3 as one of the addends and, thus, includes the one- and two-more-than facts. For the fact 3 + 8, the child starts with 8 and counts three counts: *9, 10, 11*. There are several reasons this approach is downplayed in this text. First, it is frequently applied to facts where it is not efficient, such as 8 + 5. It is difficult to explain

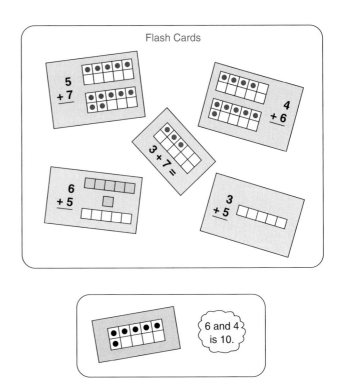

FIGURE 11.5 Ten-frame facts.

to young children that they should count for some facts but not others. Second, it is much more procedural than conceptual. Finally, if other strategies are used, it is not necessary.

Ten-Frame Facts

If you have been keeping track, all of the remaining six facts have been covered by the discussion so far, with a few being touched by two different thought patterns. The ten-frame model is so valuable in seeing certain number relationships that these ideas cannot be passed by in thinking about facts. The ten-frame helps children learn the combinations that make 10. Ten-frames immediately model all of the facts from 5 + 1 to 5 + 5 and the respective turnarounds. Even 5 + 6, 5 + 7, and 5 + 8 are quickly seen as two fives and some more when depicted with these powerful models (see Figure 11.5).

A good idea might be to group the facts shown in the chart here and practice them using one or two ten-frames as a cue to the thought process.

+	0	1	2	3	4	5	6	7	8	9
0						5				
1						6				10
2						7			10	
3						8		10		
4						9	10			
5	5	6	7	8	9	10	11	12	13	14
6					10	11				
7				10		12				
8			10			13				
9		10				14				

The next two activities are suggestive of the type of relationships that can be developed.

ACTIVITY 11.10

A Plus-Five Machine

Use the calculator to practice adding five. Enter ⊞ 5 ⊟. Next enter any number, and say the sum of that number plus 5 before pressing ⊟. Continue with other numbers. (The ⊞ 5 ⊟ need not be repeated.) If a ten-frame is present, the potential for strengthening the 5 and 10 relationships is heightened.

Obviously, the calculator can be made into a machine for adding any number and is a powerful drill device.

ACTIVITY 11.11

Say the Ten Fact

Hold up a ten-frame card, and have children say the "ten fact." For a card with 7 dots, the response is "seven and three is ten." Later, with a blank ten-frame drawn on the board, say a number less than 10. Children start with that number and complete the "ten fact." If you say, "four," they say, "four plus six is ten." Use the same activities in independent or small group modes.

STRATEGIES FOR SUBTRACTION FACTS

Subtraction facts prove to be more difficult than addition. This is especially true when children have been taught subtraction through a "count-count-count" approach; for 13 − 5, count 13, count off 5, count what's left. There is little evidence that anyone who has mastered subtraction facts has found this approach helpful. Unfortunately, many sixth, seventh, and eighth graders are still counting.

Subtraction as Think-Addition

In Figure 11.6, subtraction is modeled in such a way that students are encouraged to think, "What goes with this part to make the total?" When done in this *think-addition* manner, the child uses known addition facts to produce the unknown quantity or part. (You might want to revisit the discussion of missing-part activities in Chapter 9 and part-part-whole subtraction concepts in Chapter 10.) If this important relationship between

Connecting Subtraction to Addition Knowledge

1. Count out 13 and cover.

2. Count and remove 5. Keep these in view.

3. Think: "Five and what makes thirteen?" 8! 8 left. 13 minus 5 is 8.

4. Uncover.

8 and 5 is 13.

FIGURE 11.6 **Using a think-addition model for subtraction.**

parts and wholes—between addition and subtraction—can be made, subtraction facts will be much easier. When children see 9 − 4, you want them to think spontaneously, "Four and *what* makes nine?" By contrast, observe a third-grade child who struggles with this fact. The idea of thinking addition never occurs. Instead, the child will begin to count either back from 9 or up from 4. The value of think-addition cannot be overstated.

Word problems that promote think-addition are those that sound like addition but have a missing addend: *join, initial part unknown; join, change unknown;* and *part-part-whole, part unknown* (see Chapter 10). Consider this problem: *Janice had 5 fish in her aquarium. Grandma gave her some more fish. Then she had 12 fish. How many fish did Grandma give Janice?* Notice that the action is join and, thus, suggests addition. There is a high probability that students will think 5 *and how many more makes* 12. In the discussion in which you use problems such as this, your task is to connect this thought process with the subtraction fact, 12 − 5.

Subtraction Facts with Sums to 10

Think-addition is most immediately applicable to subtraction facts with sums of 10 or less. These are generally introduced with a goal of mastery in the first grade. Sixty-four of the 100 subtraction facts fall into this category.

If think-addition is to be used effectively, it is essential that addition facts be mastered first. Evidence suggests that children learn very few, if any, subtraction facts without first mastering the corresponding addition facts. In other words, mastery of 3 + 5 can be thought of as prerequisite knowledge for learning the facts 8 − 3 and 8 − 5.

Facts involving 0, 1, and 2 may be solved by different children in many different ways including think-addition.

These facts are closely related to important basic number relationships. If children experience difficulties with facts such as 8 − 0 or 7 − 2, it would be a good idea to investigate their number concepts. A child who says that 7 − 0 is 6 may have overgeneralized that subtraction makes the number smaller.

The 36 "Hard" Subtraction Facts: Sums Greater Than 10

STOP Before reading further, look at the three subtraction facts shown here, and try to reflect on what thought process you use to get the answers. Even if you "just know them," think about what a likely process might be.

$$\begin{array}{ccc} 14 & 12 & 15 \\ -\ 9 & -\ 6 & -\ 6 \end{array}$$

Many people will use a different strategy for each of these facts. For 14 − 9, it is easy to start with 9 and work up through 10: *9 and 1 more is 10, and 4 more makes 5.* For the 12 − 6 fact, it is quite common to hear "double 6," a think-addition approach. For the last fact, 15 − 6, 10 is used again but probably by working backward from 15—a take-away process: *Take away 5 to get 10, and 1 more leaves 9.* We could call these three approaches, respectively, build up through 10, think-addition, and back down through 10. Each of the remaining 36 facts with sums of 11 or more can be learned using one or more of these strategies. Figure 11.7 shows how these facts, in three overlapping groups, correspond to these three strategies. Keep in mind that these are not required

strategies. Some children may use a think-addition method for all. Others may have a completely different strategy for some or all of these. The three approaches suggested here are based on ideas already developed: the relationship between addition and subtraction and the power of 10 as a reference point.

Build Up Through 10

This group includes all facts where the part or subtracted number is either 8 or 9. Examples are 13 − 9 and 15 − 8.

ACTIVITY 11.12

Build Up Through the Ten-Frame

On the board or overhead, draw a ten-frame with 9 dots. Discuss how you can build numbers between 11 and 18, starting with 9 in the ten-frame. Stress the idea of *one more to get to 10* and then the rest of the number. Repeat for a ten-frame showing 8. Next, with either the 8 or 9 ten-frame in view, call out numbers from 11 to 18, and have students explain how they can figure out the difference between that number and the one on the ten-frame. Later, use the same approach, but show fact cards to connect this idea with the symbolic subtraction fact (see Figure 11.8).

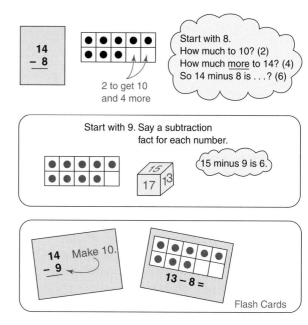

FIGURE 11.8 Build up through 10.

Back Down Through 10

Here is one strategy that is really take-away and not think-addition. It is useful for facts where the ones digit of the whole is close to the number being subtracted. For example, with 15 − 6, you start with the total of 15 and take off 5. That gets you down to 10. Then take off 1 more to get 9. For 14 − 6,

11	11	11	11	11	11	11	11
− 2	− 3	− 4	− 5	− 6	− 7	− 8	− 9

12	12	12	12	12	12	12
− 3	− 4	− 5	− 6	− 7	− 8	− 9

13	13	13	13	13	13
− 4	− 5	− 6	− 7	− 8	− 9

14	14	14	14	14
− 5	− 6	− 7	− 8	− 9

15	15	15	15
− 6	− 7	− 8	− 9

16	16	16
− 7	− 8	− 9

17	17
− 8	− 9

18
− 9

Build up through 10

Back down through 10

Think-addition (any fact)

FIGURE 11.7 The 36 "hard" subtraction facts.

just take off 4 and then take off 2 more to get 8. Here we are working backward with 10 as a "bridge."

ACTIVITY 11.13

Back Down Through the Ten-Frame

Start with two ten-frames on the overhead, one filled completely and the other partially filled as in Figure 11.9. For 13, for example, discuss what is the easiest way to think about taking off 4 counters or 5 counters. Repeat with other numbers between 11 and 18. Have students write or say the corresponding fact.

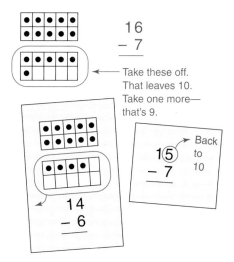

FIGURE 11.9 Back down through 10.

Extend Think-Addition

Think-addition remains one of the most powerful ways to think about subtraction facts. When the think-addition concept of subtraction is well developed, many children will use that approach for all subtraction facts. (Notice that virtually everyone uses a think-multiplication approach for division. Why?)

What may be most important is to listen to children's thinking as they attempt to answer subtraction facts that they have not yet mastered. If they are not using one of the three ideas suggested here, it is a good bet that they are counting—an inefficient method.

The activities that follow are all of the think-addition variety. There is of course no reason why these activities could not be used for all of the subtraction facts. They need not be limited to the "hard facts."

ACTIVITY 11.14

Missing-Number Cards

Show children, without explanation, families of numbers with the sum circled as in Figure 11.10(a). Ask why they think the numbers go together and why

---

one number is circled. When this number family idea is fairly well understood, show some families with one number replaced by a question mark, as in Figure 11.10(b), and ask what number is missing. When students understand this activity, explain that you have made some missing-number cards based on this idea. Each card has two of three numbers that go together in the same way. Sometimes the circled number is missing (the sum), and sometimes one of the other numbers is missing (a part). The cards can be made both vertically and horizontally with the sum appearing in different positions. The object is to name the missing number.

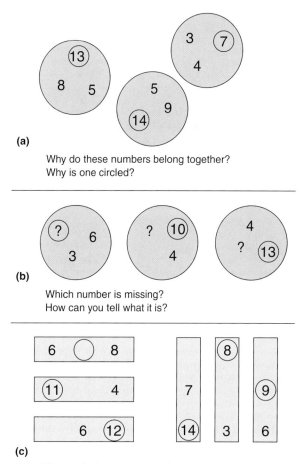

FIGURE 11.10 Introducing missing-number cards.

ACTIVITY 11.15

Missing-Number Worksheets

Make copies of the blank form found in the Blackline Masters to make a wide variety of drill exercises. In a row of 13 "cards," put all of the combinations from two families with different numbers missing, some parts and some wholes. Put blanks in different positions. An example is shown in Figure 11.11. After filling in numbers, run the sheet off, and have students fill in the missing numbers. Another idea is to group facts from one strategy or number relation or perhaps mix facts from two strategies on one page. Have students write an addition fact and a subtraction fact to go with each missing-number card. This is an important step because many children are able to give the missing part in a family but do not connect this knowledge with subtraction.

ACTIVITY 11.16

Find a Plus Fact to Help

Select a group of subtraction facts that you wish to practice. Divide a sheet of paper into small cards, about 10 or 12 to a sheet. For each subtraction fact, write the corresponding addition fact on one of the cards. Two subtraction facts can be related to each addition fact. Duplicate the sheet, and have students cut the cards apart. Now write one of the subtraction facts on the board. Rather than call out answers, students find the addition fact that helps with the subtraction fact. On your signal, each student holds up the appropriate fact. For 12 – 4 or 12 – 8, the students would select 4 + 8. The same activity can be made into a matching card game.

Teachers often ask when students should have mastered the addition and subtraction facts. According to the *Standards,* "By the end of grade 2, students should know the basic addition and subtraction combinations" (p. 35).

STRATEGIES FOR MULTIPLICATION FACTS

Multiplication facts can also be mastered by relating new facts to existing knowledge.

It is imperative that students completely understand the commutative property (go back and review Figure 10.11). For example, 2 × 8 is related to the addition fact double 8. But the same relationship also applies to 8 × 2 that many children think about as 2 + 2 + 2 + 2 + 2 + 2 + 2 + 2. Most of the fact strategies are more obvious with the factors in one order than in the other, but turnaround facts should always be learned together.

Of the five groups or strategies discussed next, the first four strategies are generally easier and cover 75 of the 100

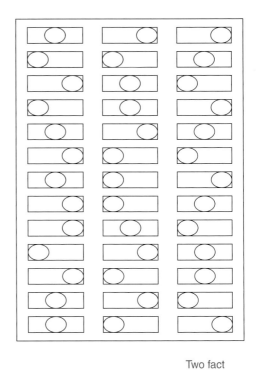

FIGURE 11.11 Missing-part worksheets. The blank version can be used to fill in any sets of facts you wish to emphasize (see Blackline Masters).

multiplication facts. You are continually reminded that these strategies are suggestions, not rules, and that the most general approach with children is to have them discuss ways that *they* can use to think of facts easily.

Doubles

Facts that have 2 as a factor are equivalent to the addition doubles and should already be known by students who know their addition facts. The major problem is to realize that not only is 2 × 7 double 7, but so is 7 × 2. Try word problems where 2 is the number of sets. Later use problems where 2 is the size of the sets.

×	0	1	2	3	4	5	6	7	8	9
0			0							
1			2							
2	0	2	4	6	8	10	12	14	16	18
3			6							
4			8							
5			10							
6			12							
7			14							
8			16							
9			18							

ACTIVITY 11.17

Calculator 2× Facts

Review the concept of doubles from addition. Play "Say the Double." You say a number, and the children say the double of that number. Use the calculator to practice doubles (press 2 ⊠ ⊟).

Make and use flash cards with the related addition fact or word *double* as a cue (see Figure 11.12).

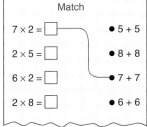

FIGURE 11.12 Multiplication doubles.

Fives Facts

This group consists of all facts with 5 as the first or second factor, as shown here.

×	0	1	2	3	4	5	6	7	8	9
0						0				
1						5				
2						10				
3						15				
4						20				
5	0	5	10	15	20	25	30	35	40	45
6						30				
7						35				
8						40				
9						45				

Practice counting by fives to at least 45. Connect counting by fives with rows of 5 dots. Point out that six rows is a model for 6 × 5, eight rows is 8 × 5, and so on.

ACTIVITY 11.18

Clock Facts

Focus on the minute hand of the clock. When it points to a number, how many minutes after the hour is it? Draw a large clock face, and point to numbers 1 to 9 in random order. Students respond with the minutes after. Now connect this idea to the multiplication facts with 5. Hold up a flash card, and then point to the number on the clock corresponding to the other factor. In this way, the fives facts become the "clock facts."

Include the clock idea on flash cards or to make matching activities (see Figure 11.13).

FIGURE 11.13 Fives facts.

Zeros and Ones

Thirty-six facts have at least one factor that is either 0 or 1. These facts, though apparently easy, tend to get confused with "rules" that some children learned for addition. The fact 6 + 0 stays the same, but 6 × 0 is always zero. The 1 + 4 fact is a one-more idea, but 1 × 4 stays the same. The concepts behind these facts can be developed best through story problems. Above all else, avoid rules that sound arbitrary and without reason such as "Any number multiplied by zero is zero."

×	0	1	2	3	4	5	6	7	8	9
0	0	0	0	0	0	0	0	0	0	0
1	0	1	2	3	4	5	6	7	8	9
2	0	2								
3	0	3								
4	0	4								
5	0	5								
6	0	6								
7	0	7								
8	0	8								
9	0	9								

Nifty Nines

Facts with a factor of 9 include the largest products but can be among the easiest to learn. The table of nines facts includes some nice patterns that are fun to discover. Two of these patterns are useful for mastering the nines: (1) The tens digit of the product is always one less than the "other" factor (the one other than 9), and (2) the sum of the two digits in the product is always 9. These two ideas can be used together to get any nine fact quickly. For 7 × 9, *1 less than 7 is 6, 6 and 3 make 9, so the answer is 63.*

×	0	1	2	3	4	5	6	7	8	9
0										0
1										9
2										18
3										27
4										36
5										45
6										54
7										63
8										72
9	0	9	18	27	36	45	54	63	72	81

Children are not likely to invent this strategy simply by solving word problems involving a factor of 9. Therefore, consider building a lesson around the following task.

ACTIVITY 11.19

Patterns in the Nines Facts

In column form, write the nines table on the board (9 × 1 = 9, 9 × 2 = 18, . . . , 9 × 9 = 81). The task is to find as many patterns as possible in the table. (Do not ask students to think of a strategy.) As you listen to the students work on this task, be sure that somewhere in the class the two patterns necessary for the strategy have been found. After discussing all the patterns, a follow-up task is to use the patterns to think of a clever way to figure out a nine fact if you didn't know it. (Note that even for students who know their nines facts, this remains a valid task.)

Once children have invented a strategy for the nines, practice activities such as those shown in Figure 11.14 are appropriate. Also consider word problems with a factor of 9 and check to see if the strategy is in use.

Warning: Although the nines strategy can be quite successful, it also can cause confusion. Because two separate rules are involved and a conceptual basis is not apparent, children may confuse the two rules or attempt to apply the idea to other facts. It is not, however, a "rule without reason." It is an idea based on a very interesting pattern that exists in the base-ten numeration system. One of the values of patterns in mathematics is that they help us do seemingly difficult things quite easily. The nifty-nine pattern illustrates clearly one of the values of pattern and regularity in mathematics.

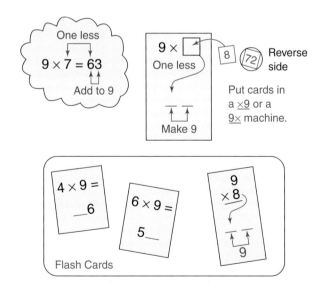

FIGURE 11.14 "Nifty nines" rule.

FIGURE 11.15 Another way to think of the nines.

An alternative strategy for the nines is almost as easy to use. Notice that 7 × 9 is the same as 7 × 10 less one set of 7, or 70 − 7. This can easily be modeled by displaying rows of 10 cubes, with the last one a different color, as in Figure 11.15. For students who can easily subtract 4 from 40, 5 from 50, and so on, this strategy may be preferable.

You might introduce this idea by showing a set of bars such as those in the figure with only the end cube a different color. After explaining that every bar has ten cubes, ask students if they can think of a good way to figure out how many are yellow.

Helping Facts

The chart shows the remaining 25 multiplication facts. It is worth pointing out to children that there are actually only 15 facts remaining to master because 20 of them consist of 10 pairs of turnarounds.

×	0	1	2	3	4	5	6	7	8	9
0										
1										
2										
3				9	12		18	21	24	
4				12	16		24	28	32	
5										
6				18	24		36	42	48	
7				21	28		42	49	56	
8				24	32		48	56	64	
9										

These 25 facts can be learned by relating each to an already known fact or *helping* fact. For example, 3 × 8 is connected to 2 × 8 (double 8 and 8 more). The 6 × 7 fact can be related to either 5 × 7 (5 sevens and 7 more) or to 3 × 7 (double 3 × 7). The helping fact must be known, and the ability to do the mental addition must also be there. For example, to go from 5 × 7 is 35 and then add 7 for 6 × 7, a student must be able to add 35 and 7. If you see finger counting

at that stage, the idea of make-ten can be extended: 35 and 5 more is 40 and 2 left makes 42.

How to find a helping fact that is useful varies with different facts and sometimes depends on which factor you focus on. Figure 11.16 illustrates models for four overlapping groups of facts and the thought process associated with each.

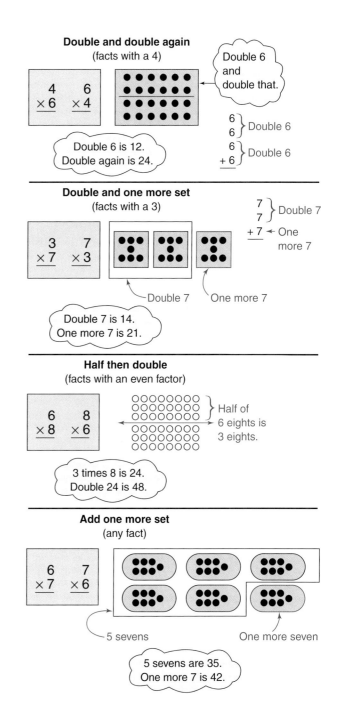

FIGURE 11.16 Finding a helping fact.

The *double and double again* approach is applicable to all facts with 4 as one of the factors. Remind children that the idea works when 4 is the second factor as well as when it is the first. For 4 × 8, double 16 is also a difficult fact. Help children with this by noting, for example, that 15 + 15 is 30, 16 + 16 is two more, or 32. Adding 16 + 16 on paper defeats the purpose.

Double and one more set is a way to think of facts with one factor of 3. With an array or a set picture, the double part can be circled, and it is clear that there is one more set. Two facts in this group involve difficult mental additions.

If either factor is even, a *half then double* approach can be used. Select the even factor, and cut it in half. If the smaller fact is known, that product is doubled to get the new fact. For 6 × 7, half of 6 is 3. 3 times 7 is 21. Double 21 is 42. For 8 × 7, the double of 28 may be hard, but it remains an effective approach to that traditionally hard fact. (Double 25 is 50 + 2 times 3 is 56.)

Many children prefer to go to a fact that is "close" and then *add one more set* to this known fact. For example, think of 6 × 7 as 6 sevens. Five sevens is close: That's 35. Six sevens is one more seven, or 42. When using 5 × 8 to help with 6 × 8, the set language "6 eights" is very helpful in remembering to add 8 more and not 6 more. Admittedly difficult, this approach is used by many children, and it becomes the best way to think of one or two particularly difficult facts. "What is seven times eight? Oh, that's 49 and 7 more—56." The process can become almost automatic.

The relationships between easy and hard facts are fertile ground for good problem-based tasks. Rather than tell students what helping facts to use and how to use them, select a fact from one of the strategies. Use the same formulation as in Activity 11.9, "If You Didn't Know" (p. 163). For example, "If you didn't know what 6 × 8 is, how could you figure it out by using something that you do know?" Students should be challenged to find as many as possible interesting and useful ways to answer a hard multiplication fact.

Go through each of the 20 "hard facts" and see how many of the strategies in Figure 11.16 you can use for each one. Many children will not think in terms of the arrays shown but rather will use a symbolic representation. For example, for 6 × 8 they might think of a vertical sum of six 8s or eight 6s. Try to see how this type of representation works for the ideas in Figure 11.16.

Since arrays are a powerful thinking tool for these strategies, provide students with copies of the ten-by-ten dot array (Figure 11.17, also in Blackline Masters). A tagboard *L* is used to outline specific product arrays. The lines in the array

FIGURE 11.17 **An array is a useful model for developing strategies for the hard multiplication facts. An array like this can be found in the Blackline Masters.**

make counting the dots easier and often suggest the use of the easier fives facts as helpers. For example, 7 × 7 is 5 × 7 plus double 7 ⟶ 35 + 14.

Don't forget to use word problems as a vehicle for developing these harder facts. Consider this problem: *Connie bundled up all of her old crayons into bags of 7 crayons each. She was able to make 8 bags with 3 crayons left over. How many crayons did she have?* As students work to get an answer, many of the strategies just discussed are possible. Plus there is the added benefit of the assessment value gained by listening to the methods different children bring to a situation that does not look like a fact drill.

Word problems can also be structured to prompt a strategy. *Carlos and Jose kept their baseball cards in albums with 6 cards on each page. Carlos had 4 pages filled, and Jose had 8 pages filled. How many cards did each boy have?* (Do you see the half-then-double strategy?)

It should be clear that the array plays a large part in helping students establish multiplication facts and relationships. In both third and fourth grades, the *Investigations in Number, Data, and Space* curriculum places a significant emphasis on arrays. They are used to help with multiplication facts, the relationship between multiplication and division, and in the development of computational procedures for multiplication. On page 173, several array activities from *Investigations* are described.

INVESTIGATIONS in NUMBER, DATA, and SPACE

Grade 3, *Things That Come in Groups*
Investigation 3: Arrays and Skip Counting

Context

This unit is scheduled for early in the third grade and is the main focus on multiplication and division for the grade. Prior to this investigation, students will have explored the idea of counting things in groups and will have considerable practice with skip counting using the hundreds chart. This investigation continues skip counting by counting rows and columns on an array. In this way skip counting is connected to groups of things, patterns on the hundreds chart, arrays, and later as a possible strategy for solving problems.

Page 49 from *Multiplication and Division: Things That Come in Groups* by C. Tierney, M. Berle-Carman, & J. Akers. *Investigations in Number, Data, and Space.* Copyright © 1998 by Dale Seymour Publications. Reprinted by permission of Pearson Education, Inc.

Task Description

The materials for this investigation consist of a collection of arrays made of half-inch grids, cut out by the students so that each child has a complete set. The set consists of 51 rectangles representing every product in the multiplication table from 1 × 2 to 12 × 12 with products between 2 and 50. For example, there is a 2 by 1, a 5 by 10, and a 12 by 4 rectangle but not a 7 by 8 or 9 by 6. On the grid side of the array or rectangle, students write the dimensions as a product (e.g., 3 × 7 and 7 × 3). On the blank side they write the product without the factors.

For the activity "Multiplication Pairs," two students spread out all of the array cards, some turned with the factors and grid side up and others showing the blank rectangle with the product. Students take turns selecting an array by placing their finger on it but not picking it up. Their task is to name either the factors or the product on the reverse side. When the grid side is down, the shape of the rectangle is a clue to the possible factors. When the grid side is up, the grid can aid students who are just learning the combinations. Students might skip count or use a related array product that they do know. Students are encouraged to keep track of the facts they "know" and "don't know yet" and keep this information in their folders.

At grade 4, the same game is played, however, the collection of arrays includes all of the products through 12 × 12.

Other activities with the arrays include building larger arrays from smaller arrays, skip counting with the arrays, and using the arrays in a compare game similar to "war."

DIVISION FACTS AND "NEAR FACTS"

 STOP What thought process do you use to recall facts such as 48 ÷ 6 or 36 ÷ 9?

If we are trying to think of 36 ÷ 9, we tend to think, "Nine times what is thirty-six?" For most, 42 ÷ 6 is not a separate fact but is closely tied to 6 × 7. (Would it not be wonderful if subtraction were so closely related to addition? It can be!)

An interesting question to ask is, "When children are working on a page of division facts, are they practicing division or multiplication?" There is undoubtedly some value in limited practice of division facts. However, mastery of multiplication facts and connections between multiplication and division are the key elements of division fact mastery. Word problems continue to be a key vehicle to create this connection.

Exercises such as 50 ÷ 6 might be called "near facts." Divisions that do not come out evenly are much more prevalent in computations and in real situations than division facts or division without remainders. To determine the answer to 50 ÷ 6, most people run through a short sequence of the multiplication facts, comparing each product to 50: "6 times 7 (low), 6 times 8 (close), 6 times 9 (high). Must be 8. That's 48 and 2 left over." This process can and should be drilled. That is, children should be able to do problems with one-digit divisors and one-digit answers plus remainders mentally and with reasonable speed.

ACTIVITY 11.20

How Close Can You Get?

To practice "near facts," try this exercise. As illustrated, the idea is to find the one-digit factor that makes the product as close as possible to the target without going over. Help children develop the process of going through the multiplication facts that was just described. This can be a drill with the full class by preparing a list for the overhead, or it can be a worksheet activity.

> Find the largest factor without going over the target number.

$4 \times \Box \longrightarrow 23, \Box$ left over
$7 \times \Box \longrightarrow 52, \Box$ left over
$6 \times \Box \longrightarrow 27, \Box$ left over
$9 \times \Box \longrightarrow 60, \Box$ left over

NCTM Standards

What does the *Standards* document tell us about multiplication and division facts? "Through skip-counting, using area models, and relating unknown combinations to known ones, students will learn and become fluent with unfamiliar combinations [multiplication facts]. . . . If by the end of the fourth grade, students are not able to use multiplication and division strategies efficiently, then they must either develop strategies so that they are fluent with these combinations or memorize the 'harder' combinations" (p. 153).

Effective Drill

There is little doubt that strategy development and general number sense (number relationships and operation meanings) are the best contributors to fact mastery. Drill in the absence of these factors has repeatedly been demonstrated as ineffective. However, the positive value of drill should not be completely ignored. Drill of nearly any mental activity strengthens memory and retrieval capabilities (Ashcraft & Christy, 1995).

When and How to Drill

Teachers and parents hold tenaciously to their belief in drill. Undoubtedly, far too much time is devoted to inefficient drill of basic facts, often with a negative impact on students' attitudes toward mathematics and beliefs in their abilities.

Avoid Inefficient Drill

Adopt this simple rule and stick with it: *Do not subject any student to fact drills unless the student has developed an efficient strategy for the facts included in the drill.* Drill can strengthen strategies with which students feel comfortable—ones they "own"—and will help to make these strategies increasingly automatic. Therefore, drill of strategies such as those discussed in this chapter will allow students to use them with increased efficiency, even to the point of recalling the fact without being conscious of using a strategy. Counting on fingers and making marks on paper can never result in automatic fact recall regardless of the amount of drill. Drill without an efficient strategy present offers no assistance. Short-term gains from inefficient drill are almost certain to be lost over time. Drill prior to development of efficient methods is simply a waste of precious instructional time.

It is worth mentioning that the preceding statement applies equally to students in the upper grades or middle school grades who have not yet mastered facts. Because the curriculum at these levels typically does not include strategy development, drill is often the only approach offered. Alternatives to this serious error are discussed later in the chapter.

Individualize Drill

It is unreasonable to expect every student in your class to develop and be comfortable with the same strategies. As you have seen, there are multiple paths to most facts. Different students will bring different number tools to the task and will develop strategies at different rates. This means that there are few drills that are likely to be efficient for a full class at any given time. That is why so many of the suggested activities are designed as flash cards, games, or simple repeatable worksheets. By creating a large number of drill activities promoting different strategies and addressing different collections of facts, it is not at all unreasonable to direct students to activities that are most useful for them.

By third grade, students can help you with this individualization process by keeping their own chart of facts mastered and facts yet to be mastered. If games and drill activities are well labeled, students can even select the activities they are ready to work on.

It is also important to listen carefully to the strategies different students are using. For example, if a student tends to solve multiplication facts with a 9 by multiplying by 10 and subtracting, it is not profitable to suggest the "nifty nine" strategy. A student who has not mastered addition facts is not ready for subtraction practice.

Drill for Strategy Retrieval

When a fact is presented without a reminder of a strategy, students need to select from their memory the mental method that works best for that fact. Drills can be devised that help students look at a fact and recall a strategy that works. The next two activities suggest how this might be done.

ACTIVITY 11.21

Circle the Strategy

On a worksheet, have students circle the facts that belong to a strategy they have been working on and answer only those facts. The same approach can be used with two or three strategies on one sheet.

ACTIVITY 11.22

Sort Them as You Do Them

Mix ordinary flash cards from two or more strategies into a single packet. Prepare simple pictures or labels for the strategies in the packet. Students first match a card with a strategy and then use the strategy to answer that fact.

Both of these activities can be tailored to match the strategies that an individual student is using and working on. Talk with the students, and have them help you put the activity together.

 TECHNOLOGY NOTE

There are literally hundreds of software programs that offer drill of basic facts. Nearly all fact programs offer games or exercises at various difficulty levels. Unfortunately, there do not seem to be any programs that organize facts the way they are organized in this chapter. It should be clear that computerized fact practice should be used only after students have developed some strategies.

A few representative programs are described here.

In *Math Munchers Deluxe* (The Learning Company, 1995), students move their muncher in a 3-D grid format. By answering questions, they can avoid six Troggles that chase the muncher and try to eat it. Like many programs, *Math Munchers* encourages speed and is highly motivating. It is aimed at grades 3 to 6 and could profitably be used through grade 8.

Math Blaster (Knowledge Adventure) promotes speed through an arcade format. There are children who are attracted to this approach and many who are not. For some, the formats in fancy, high-paced programs is a distraction to the mathematical thinking you want to promote. Like most programs, *Math Blaster* includes drills for more than just facts. It is not uncommon to see drill with multidigit computation, decimals, fractions, percents, estimation, and other topics, all in the same format.

One aspect of a program you should be aware of is how a student inputs answers. For fact practice, numbers are usually typed left to right. But in the same program, multidigit computation may be entered beginning with the ones place or right to left. In *Gold Medal Mathematics* (EdVenture Software, 1997), responses are always in multiple-choice format. This is not uncommon, especially for programs designed for younger children, but is less effective for basic facts.

Many commercial programs automatically keep performance records of individual students. There are numerous sites on the Internet that offer fact practice (for examples, see *Flashcards for Kids* at www.edu4kids.com/math, or *Arithm Attack* at www.dep.anl.gov/aattack.htm). Almost all provide immediate feedback and many provide options for the number of problems, the size of the numbers, and whether or not to time the student. ■

What About Timed Tests?

Consider the following:

> Teachers who use timed tests believe that the tests help children learn basic facts. This perspective makes no instructional sense. Children who perform well under time pressure display their skills. Children who have difficulty with skills or who work more slowly run the risk of reinforcing wrong practices under pressure. Also, they can become fearful about, and negative toward, their mathematics learning. (Burns, 1995a, p. 408)

Think about this quotation whenever you are tempted to give a timed test. Reasoning and pattern searching are never facilitated by restricting time. Some children simply cannot work well under pressure or in situations that provoke stress.

Although speed may encourage children to memorize facts, it is effective only for students who are goal oriented and who can perform in pressure situations. The pressure of speed can be debilitating and provides no positive benefits.

The value of speed drills or timed tests as a learning tool can be summed up as follows:

Timed tests

- Cannot promote reasoned approaches to fact mastery
- Will produce few long-lasting results
- Reward few
- Punish many
- Should generally be avoided

If there is any defensible purpose for a timed test of basic facts it may be for diagnosis—to determine which combinations are mastered and which remain to be learned. Even for diagnostic purposes there is little reason for a timed test more than once every couple of months.

Fact Remediation with Upper-Grade Students

Children who have not mastered their basic facts by the sixth or seventh grade are in need of something other than more drill. They have certainly seen and practiced facts countless times over the past several school years. There is no reason to believe that the drills *you* provide will somehow be more effective than last year's. These students need something better. The following key ideas can guide your efforts to help these older students.

1. *Recognize that more drill will not work.* Students' fact difficulties are due to a failure to develop or to connect concepts and relationships such as those that have been discussed in this chapter, not a lack of drill. At best, more drill will provide temporary results. At worst, it will cause negative attitudes about mathematics.

2. *Inventory the known and unknown facts for each student in need.* Find out from each student what facts are known quickly and comfortably and which are not. Middle grade students can do this diagnosis for you. Provide sheets of all facts for one operation in random order, and have the students circle the facts they are hesitant about and answer all others. Suggest that finger counting or making marks in the margin is not permitted.

3. *Diagnose strengths and weaknesses.* Find out what students do when they encounter one of their unknown facts. Do they count on their fingers? Add up numbers in the margins? Guess? Try to use a related fact? Write down times tables? Are they able to use any of the relationships that might be helpful as suggested in this chapter? Some of this you may be able to accomplish by having students write about how they approach two or three specific facts. More efficiently, you should conduct a 15-minute diagnostic interview with each student in need. Simply pose unknown facts and ask the student how he or she approaches them. Try an idea from this chapter, and see what connections are already there. Don't try to teach; just find out.

4. *Provide hope.* Children who have experienced difficulty with fact mastery often believe that they cannot learn facts or that they are doomed to finger counting forever. Let these children know that you will help them and that you will provide some new ideas that will help them as well. Take that burden on yourself, and spare them the prospect of more defeat.

5. *Build in success.* As you begin a well-designed fact program for a child who has experienced failure, be sure that successes come quickly and easily. Begin with easy strategies, and introduce only a few new facts at a time. Even with pure rote drill, repetitive exposure to five facts in three days will provide more success than introducing 15 facts in a week. Success builds success! With strategies as an added assist, success

comes even more quickly. Point out to children how one idea, one strategy, is all that is required to learn many facts. Use fact charts to show what set of facts you are working on. It is surprising how the chart quickly fills up with mastered facts. Keep reviewing newly learned facts and those that were already known. This is success. It feels good, and failures are not as apparent. Short practice exercises can be designed as homework. Explain strategies and build them into the exercises. At the end of the exercises, have students write about which ideas are helpful and which are not. Use this information to design the next exercise.

Your extra effort beyond class time can be a motivation to a student to make some personal effort on his or her own time. During class, these students should continue to work with all students on the regular curriculum. You must believe and communicate to these students that the reason they have not mastered basic facts is not a reflection of their ability. With efficient strategies and individual effort, success will come. Believe!

Facts: No Barrier to Good Mathematics

Students who have total command of basic facts do not necessarily *reason better* than those who, for whatever reason, have not yet mastered facts. Today, mathematics is not about computation, especially pencil-and-paper computation. Mathematics is about reasoning and patterns and making sense of things. Mathematics is problem solving. There is no reason that a child who has not yet mastered all basic facts should be excluded from real mathematical experiences.

The most obvious alternative is the calculator. It should be on the desk every day for all students. There is absolutely no evidence that the presence of a calculator will impede basic fact mastery. On the contrary, the more students use the calculator, the more proficient they will be with it. This will make many of the calculator fact drills more effective and provide students with ready access to electronic flash cards. In a classroom climate where most students do know their facts and where students help one another and share thinking strategies as has been suggested, very few students will rely on the calculator for any prolonged period.

Students who are relegated to drill of facts when the rest of the class is engaged in meaningful experiences will soon feel stupid and incapable of doing "real" mathematics. By contrast, when students who have not mastered facts are engaged in exciting and meaningful experiences, they have real motivation to learn facts and real opportunities to develop relationships that can aid in that endeavor. Do not allow students who are behind in fact mastery to fall behind in mathematics.

Reflections on Chapter **11**

Writing to Learn

1. Explain briefly each part of the three-step approach to fact mastery.
2. Explain how a teacher can use word problems as a means of helping students construct strategies for the basic facts. What type of word problem would you use for subtraction fact strategies? Explain.
3. For each addition fact strategy:
   a. List at least three facts for which the strategy can be used.
   b. Explain the thinking process or concepts that are involved in using the strategy. Use a specific fact as an illustration.
4. What is meant by subtraction as "think-addition"? How can you help children develop a think-addition thought pattern for subtraction?
5. For subtraction facts with sums greater than 10, it is reasonable that as many as three different thought patterns or strategies might be used. Describe each of those suggested in the text.
6. Why is the turnaround property (commutative property) more important in multiplication fact mastery than in addition?
7. For each multiplication strategy except "use a helping fact," answer the questions in item 3.
8. The "last 25" multiplication facts involve using a fact that has already been learned and working from that fact to the new or harder fact. Four different ways to make this connection with a helping fact were described. Some are applicable only to certain facts. Describe each of these approaches, and list the facts for which the approach is applicable.
9. Describe when it is appropriate to use drill and how it can help. What is "premature" drill?
10. Why not use speed drills to learn facts?
11. How do you help children who have been drilling their basic facts for years and still have not mastered them?

For Discussion and Exploration

1. Explore a computer software program that drills basic facts. What features does your program have that are good? Not so good? Explain. In general, do you think these programs are effective? How would you use such software in a classroom with only one or two available computers?
2. One view of thinking strategies is that they are little more than a collection of tricks for kids to memorize. Discuss the question, "Is teaching children thinking strategies for basic fact mastery in keeping with a constructivist view of teaching mathematics?" Carole Thornton (1990), a leading researcher in the area of basic-fact strategies, suggests a fairly direct approach to teaching strategies.
3. Examine a recently published second-, third-, or fourth-grade textbook to determine how thinking strategies for the basic facts have been developed. Compare what you find with the groupings of facts in this chapter. How would you use the text effectively in your program?

Recommendations for Further Reading

Highly Recommended

Fennema, E., & Carpenter, T. P. (with Levi, L., Franke, M. L., & Empson, S.) (1997). *Cognitively guided instruction: Professional development in primary mathematics.* Madison, WI: Wisconsin Center for Education Research.
   The CGI program believes that students develop their own strategies for mastering the basic facts. They are helped in this process by solving well-selected story problems. Teachers listen carefully to students' emerging processes and encourage increasingly efficient methods. This book provides detailed explanations. (See the annotation of this same book in Chapter 7.)

Hope, J. A., Leutzinger, L., Reys, B. J., & Reys, R. R. (1987). *Mental math in the primary grades.* Palo Alto, CA: Dale Seymour.
   This first book in a series of three on mental mathematics devotes roughly the first half of its pages to the development of basic facts using strategies similar to those found in this chapter. The lessons include transparency masters as well as activity sheets for children and encourage appropriate use of manipulatives such as ten-frames.

Rathmell, E. C., Leutzinger, L. P., & Gabriele, A. (2000). *Thinking with numbers.* Cedar Falls, IA: Thinking with Numbers, Inc.
   Rathmell was one of the first to write about the use of thinking strategies for basic facts. (See the 1978 NCTM Yearbook.) He and his colleagues have developed a large set of small cards, each with several simple story problems. The cards are organized by strategies for each of the operations. As children solve these problems (5 minutes per day), they invent their own strategies and share them with the class. The nature of the story problems encourages development of the strategies you have read about. This set of materials has been well tested in classrooms and supports the approach in this chapter.

Other Suggestions

Brownell, W. A., & Chazal, C. B. (1935). The effects of premature drill in third-grade arithmetic. *Journal of Educational Research, 29,* 17–28.

Burns, M. (1995). Timed tests. *Teaching Children Mathematics, 1,* 408–409.

Isaacs, A. C., & Carroll, W. M. (1999). Strategies for basic-facts instruction. *Teaching Children Mathematics, 5,* 508–515.

Kamii, C., Lewis, B. A., & Booker, B. M. (1998). Instead of teaching missing addends. *Teaching Children Mathematics, 4,* 458–461.

Leutzinger, L. P. (1999). Developing thinking strategies for addition facts. *Teaching Children Mathematics, 6,* 14–18.

Leutzinger, L. P. (1999). *Facts that last: A balanced approach to memorization* [separate books for each operation]. Mountain View, CA: Creative Publications.

Thornton, C. A. (1990). Strategies for the basic facts. In J. N. Payne (Ed.), *Mathematics for the young child* (pp. 133–151). Reston, VA: National Council of Teachers of Mathematics.

Thornton, C. A., & Jones, G. A. (1994). Computation sense. In C. A. Thornton & N. S. Bley (Eds.),*Windows of opportunity: Mathematics for students with special needs* (pp. 205–227). Reston, VA: National Council of Teachers of Mathematics.

12

WHOLE-NUMBER PLACE-VALUE DEVELOPMENT

A complete understanding of place value develops over the full K–6 grade span. In kindergarten, children begin learning to count to 100. By second grade, they are talking about tens and ones and are using these ideas in many ways. By fourth grade, students are working with numbers involving four or more digits. Numbers are experienced in computations, on calculators, in mental computations and estimations, and in connection with real-world quantities and measures. In fourth and fifth grades, the ideas of whole-number place value are extended to decimals.

Big Ideas

1. Sets of ten (and tens of tens) can be perceived as single entities. These sets can then be counted and used as a means of describing quantities. For example, three sets of ten and two singles is a base-ten method of describing 32 single objects. This is the major principle of base-ten numeration.

2. The positions of digits in numbers determine what they represent—which size group they count. This is the major principle of place-value numeration.

3. There are patterns to the way that numbers are formed. For example, each decade has a symbolic pattern reflective of the 1-to-9 sequence.

4. The groupings of ones, tens, and hundreds can be taken apart in different ways. For example, 256 can be 1 hundred, 14 tens, and 16 ones. Taking numbers apart and recombining them in flexible ways is a significant skill for computation.

5. "Really big" numbers are best understood in terms of familiar real-world referents. It is difficult to conceptualize quantities as large as 1000 or more. However, the number of people that will fill the local sports arena is, for example, a meaningful concept for those who have experienced that crowd.

CONTENT CONNECTIONS

The base-ten place-value system is the way that we communicate and represent anything that we do with whole numbers and later with decimals.

- **Whole-Number Computation and Number Sense (Chapters 13 and 14):** Flexible methods of computation including various mental methods, pencil-and-paper methods, estimation skills, and even effective use of calculators and computer computations depend completely on an understanding of place value. Computational strategies for addition and subtraction can and should be developed along with an understanding of place value.

- **Decimal and Percents (Chapter 15):** Whole-number place-value ideas are extended to allow for representation of the full range of rational numbers and approximations of irrational numbers.

- **Measurement (Chapter 19):** Problem-based tasks involving real measures can be used to help students structure ideas about grouping by tens. Through measures, people develop benchmarks and meaningful referents for numbers.

PRE-BASE-TEN CONCEPTS

Base-ten concepts are not at all trivial for children to develop. It is important for teachers to reflect on how these new and difficult concepts must be built on and connected to children's initial concepts of quantity.

It is tempting to think that children know a lot about numbers with two digits (10 to 99) even as early as kindergarten. After all, most kindergartners can and should learn to count to 100 and count out sets of things with as many as 20 or 30 objects. They do daily calendar activities, count children in the room, turn to specified page numbers in their books, and so on. However, their understanding is quite different from yours. It is based on a one-more-than or count-by-ones approach to quantity.

Children's Pre-Base-Ten View of Number

Ask first- or second-grade children to count out 53 tiles, and most will be able to do so or will make only careless errors. It is a tedious but not formidable task. If you watch closely, you will note that the children count out the tiles one at a time and put them into the pile with no use of any type of grouping. Have the children write the number that tells how many tiles they just counted. Most children will be able to write it. Some may write "35" instead of "53," a simple reversal.

So far, so good. Now ask the children to write the number that is 10 more than the number they just wrote. Most will begin to count, probably starting from 53. When counting on from 53, they find it necessary to keep track of the counts, probably on their fingers. Many, if not most, children in the first and early second grades will not be successful at this task, and almost none will know immediately that 10 more is 63. Asking for the number that is 10 less is even more problematic.

Finally, show a large collection of cards, each with a ten-frame drawn on it. Explain that the cards each have ten spaces and that each will hold ten tiles. Demonstrate putting tiles on the cards by filling up one of the ten-frames with tiles. Now ask, "How many cards like this do you think it will take if we want to put all of these tiles [the 53 counted out] on the cards?" A response of "53" is not unusual. Other children will say they do not know, and a few will try to put the tiles on the cards to figure it out.

Quantity Tied to Counts by Ones

The children just described know that there are 53 tiles "because I counted them." Writing the number and saying the number are usually done correctly, but their understanding of 53 derives from and is connected to the count by ones. Children do not easily or quickly develop a meaningful use of groups of ten to represent quantities.

With minimal instruction, children can tell you that in the numeral 53, the 5 is in the tens place or that there are "3 ones." However, it is likely that this is simply a naming of the positions with little understanding. If children have been exposed to base-ten materials, they may name a rod of ten as a "ten" and a small cube as a "one." These same children, however, may not be readily able to tell how many ones are required to make a ten. It is easy to attach words to both materials and groups without realizing what the materials or symbols represent.

Children do know that 53 is "a lot" and that it's more than 47 (because you count past 47 to get to 53). They think

of the "53" that they write as a single numeral. They do not know that the 5 represents five groups of ten things and the 3 three single things (Fuson et al., 1997; Ross, 1989). Fuson and her colleagues refer to children's pre-base-ten understanding of number as "unitary." That is, there are no groupings of ten, even though a two-digit number is associated with the quantity. They rely on unitary counts to understand quantities.

BASIC IDEAS OF PLACE VALUE

Place-value understanding requires an integration of new and difficult-to-construct concepts of grouping by tens (the base-ten concept) with procedural knowledge of how groups are recorded in our place-value scheme, how numbers are written, and how they are spoken.

Integration of Base-Ten Groupings with Counts by Ones

Recognizing that children can count out a set of 53, we want to help them see that making groupings of tens and leftovers is a way of counting that same quantity. Each of the groups in Figure 12.1 has 53 tiles. We want children to construct the idea that all of these are the same and that the sameness is clearly evident by virtue of the groupings of tens.

There is a subtle yet profound difference between two groups of children: those who know that group B is 53 because they understand the idea that 5 groups of 10 and 3 more

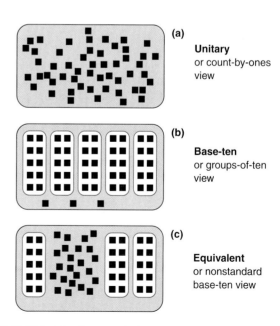

(a) **Unitary** or count-by-ones view

(b) **Base-ten** or groups-of-ten view

(c) **Equivalent** or nonstandard base-ten view

FIGURE 12.1 Three equivalent groupings of 53 objects. Group A is 53 because "I counted them (by ones)." Group B has 5 tens and 3 more. Group C is the same as B, but now some groups are broken into singles.

is the same amount as 53 counted by ones and those who simply say, "It's 53," because they have been told that when things are grouped this way, it's called 53. The latter children may not be sure how many they will get if they count the tiles in set B by ones or if the groups were "ungrouped" how many there would then be. The children who understand will see no need to count set B by ones. They understand the "fifty-threeness" of sets A and B to be the same.

> ✖ **STOP** The ideas in the preceding paragraph are important for you to understand so that the activities discussed later will make sense. Be sure you can talk about children who do and children who do not understand place value.

Recognition of the equivalence of groups B and C is another step in children's conceptual development. Groupings with fewer than the maximum number of tens can be referred to as *equivalent groupings* or *equivalent representations*. Understanding the equivalence of B and C indicates that grouping by tens is not just a rule that is followed but that any grouping by tens, including all or some of the singles, can help tell how many. Many computational techniques are based on equivalent representations of numbers.

The Role of Counting in Constructing Base-Ten Ideas

Counting plays a key role in constructing base-ten ideas about quantity and connecting these concepts to symbols and oral names for numbers.

Children can count sets such as those in Figure 12.1 in three different ways. Each way helps children think about the quantities in a different way (Thompson, 1990).

1. *Counting by ones.* This is the method children have to begin with. Initially, a count by ones is the only way they are able to name a quantity or "tell how many." All three of the sets in Figure 12.1 can be counted by ones. Before base-ten ideas develop, this is the only way children can be convinced that all three sets are the same.

2. *Counting by groups and singles.* In group B in Figure 12.1, counting by groups and singles would go like this: "One, two, three, four, five bunches of 10, and one, two, three singles." Consider how novel this method would be for a child who had never thought about counting a group of things as a single item. Also notice how this counting does not tell directly how many items there are. This counting must be coordinated with a count by ones before it can be a means of telling "how many."

3. *Counting by tens and ones.* This is the way adults would probably count group B and perhaps group C: "Ten, twenty, thirty, forty, fifty, fifty-one, fifty-two, fifty-three." While this count ends by saying the number that is there, it is not as explicit as the second method in counting the number of

groups. Nor will it convey a personal understanding of "how many" unless it is coordinated with the more meaningful count by ones.

Regardless of the specific activity that you may be doing with children, helping them integrate the grouping-by-tens concept with what they know about number from counting by ones should be your foremost objective. Children should frequently have the opportunity to count sets of objects in several ways. If first counted by ones, the question might be, "What will happen if we count these by groups and singles (or by tens and ones)?" If a set has been grouped into tens and singles and counted accordingly, "How can we be really certain that there are 53 things here?" or "What do you think we will get if we count by ones?" It is inadequate to *tell* children that these counts will all be the same. That is a relationship they must construct themselves through reflective thought, not because the teacher says it works that way.

Integration of Groupings with Words

The way we say a number such as "fifty-three" must also be connected with the grouping-by-tens concept. The counting methods provide a connecting mechanism. The count by tens and ones results in saying the number of groups and singles separately: "five tens and three." This is an acceptable, albeit nonstandard, way of naming this quantity. Saying the number of tens and singles separately in this fashion can be called *base-ten language* for a number. Children can associate the base-ten language with the usual language: "five tens and three—fifty-three."

Notice that there are several variations of the base-ten language for 53—5 tens and 3; 5 tens and 3 ones; 5 groups of 10 and 3 leftovers; 5 tens and 3 singles; and so on. Each may be used interchangeably with the standard name, "fifty-three."

It can easily be argued that base-ten language should be used throughout the second grade, even in preference to standard oral names.

Integration of Groupings with Place-Value Notation

In like manner, the symbolic scheme that we use for writing numbers (ones on the right, tens to the left of ones, and so on) must be coordinated with the grouping scheme. Activities can be designed so that children physically associate a tens and ones grouping with the correct recording of the individual digits, as Figure 12.2 indicates.

Language again plays a key role in making these connections. The explicit count by groups and singles matches the individual digits as the number is written in the usual left-to-right manner.

A similar coordination is necessary for hundreds.

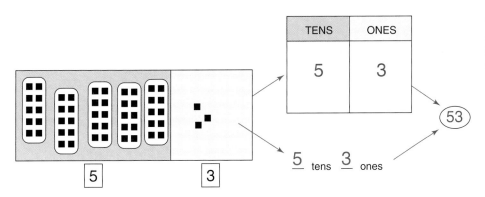

FIGURE 12.2 Groupings by 10 are matched with numerals, placed in labeled places, and eventually written in standard form.

 NCTM Standards "Making a transition from viewing 'ten' as simply the accumulation of 10 ones to seeing it both as 10 ones *and* as 1 ten is an important first step for students toward understanding the structure of the base-ten number system" (p. 33).

Relational Understanding of Place Value

Figure 12.3 summarizes the ideas that have been discussed so far.

- The conceptual knowledge of place value consists of the base-ten grouping ideas.

   When a collection of objects is grouped in sets of 10 and some leftover singles, counting the groups of ten and adding the singles tells how many are in the collection.

   There can be equivalent representations with fewer than the maximum groupings.

- The base-ten grouping ideas must be integrated with oral and written names for numbers.

- In addition to counting by ones, children use two other ways of counting: by groups and singles separately and by tens and ones. All three methods of counting are co-ordinated as the principal method of integrating the concepts, the written names, and the oral names.

Remember that these ideas are built on a count-by-ones understanding of number. The notion of sets of 10 as single entities must be constructed as a completely new way of thinking about number. Simply showing children groups of 10 and telling them that "10 ones is the same as 1 ten" will not construct that idea for them.

Think of Figure 12.3 as a triangle with the conceptual ideas **STOP** of place value at the top. The procedural ideas of how we say and write numbers are the other two corners. Counting is the main tool children use to help connect these ideas. Before moving further, be sure that you have a good feel for how these ideas are related. Remember that the conceptual ideas must first be built on the count-by-ones concept of quantity that children bring to this array of ideas.

In *Investigations in Number, Data, and Space,* first-grade students learn the oral sequence of numbers to 100, especially through the use of a hundreds chart. (See hundreds chart activities later in this chapter.) However, the authors are aware of the fact that most students rely on their counts by ones to understand quantity. The excerpt on page 182 illustrates how the *Investigations* curriculum nudges children gently to a more advanced understanding of counting.

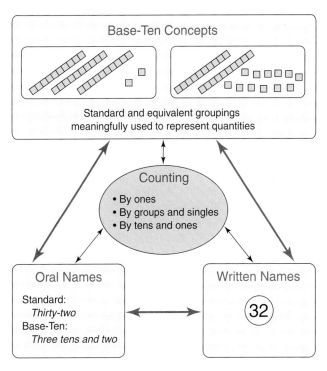

FIGURE 12.3 Relational understanding of place value integrates three components, shown as the corners of the triangle: base-ten concepts, oral names for numbers, and written names for numbers. Counting is a key activity by which children can construct and integrate these three ideas and connect them to the pre-place-value concepts of number that they have to begin with.

INVESTIGATIONS in NUMBER, DATA, and SPACE

Grade 1, *Number Games and Story Problems*

Investigation 2: Twos, Fives, and Tens

Context

In the introductory pages of this unit, the authors say, "By the end of the year, many students will have learned the oral counting sequence to 100, will recognize some patterns in the sequence of written numbers from 1 to 100, and will have a solid grasp of quantities up to about 25" (p. I-18). Within the unit, students learn to recognize numbers in groups and begin to skip count with the aid of the hundreds chart. The Number Games and Story Problems unit occurs in the latter half of the year.

Task Description

In a series of tasks called "How Many Squares?" students count the number of paper 1-inch squares prepared for them. One set has 8 single squares and 6 pairs (a strip of 2 squares). A second set has 7 single squares and 4 strips of 5 squares, and the third set has 5 single squares, 5 pairs, and 2 strips of 5.

Using the overhead to lead a discussion, the teacher encourages students to make an arrangement of the squares in the first set in order to count them in different ways. Initially students count each square one at a time and many continue in this manner regardless of how they arrange the squares. Some children will place the squares in sets of two or sets of three and either skip count or add up the squares as they go.

After the activity is introduced, children take a set of squares, arrange them in some manner for counting, record on paper how they arranged them, and show using words and/or numbers how they counted. The children's work shown here is taken from the assessment notes.

The child labeled (a) organizes her squares into groups of four and then puts the remainder in a row. She recognizes the sets of four as 4 but has difficulty when she attempts to skip count and eventually counts by ones. Child (b) makes several different groupings including the 2 fives to make 10. She records each group and then writes addition combinations to determine the totals. She is using known facts and there is some evidence that she uses 10 for small numbers. Students (c) and (d) are beginning to use the structure of place value. Child (d) counts the 5 twos by two and then "five, ten" for the fives.

It is interesting to note that no base-ten models are used at all in the *Investigations* program. In both the first and second grades, a lot of emphasis is placed on the hundreds chart in ways somewhat reflected in activities found in this book.

(a)

(b)

(c)

(d)

Pages 95–97 from *Addition and Subtraction: Number Games and Story Problems* by M. Kliman & S. J. Russell. *Investigations in Number, Data, and Space.* Copyright © 1998 by Dale Seymour Publications. Reprinted by permission of Pearson Education, Inc.

Models for Place Value

Physical models for base-ten concepts can play a key role in helping children develop the idea of "a ten" as both a single entity and as a set of 10 units. Remember, though, that the models do not "show" the concept to the children. The children must construct the concept and impose it on the model.

Base-Ten Models and the Ten-Makes-One Relationship

A good base-ten model for ones, tens, and hundreds is *proportional*. That is, a ten model is physically ten times larger than the model for a one, and a hundred model is ten times larger than the ten model. Base-ten models can be categorized as *groupable* and *pregrouped*.

Groupable Models

Models that most clearly reflect the relationships of ones, tens, and hundreds are those for which the ten can actually be made or grouped from the singles. When children bundle 10 Popsicle sticks, the bundle of 10 literally *is the same as* the 10 ones from which it was made. Examples of these groupable models are shown in Figure 12.4(a). These could also be called "put-together-take-apart" models.

Of the groupable models, beans or counters in cups are the cheapest and easiest for children to use. (Plastic portion cups can be purchased from stores specializing in paper supplies.) Plastic connecting cubes are attractive and provide a good transition to pregrouped tens sticks. Plastic chain links in ten-link chains are another popular model. Bundles of Popsicle sticks are perhaps the best-known base-ten model, but small hands have trouble with rubber bands and actually making the bundles. With most groupable materials, hundreds are possible but are generally not practical for most activities in the classroom.

As children become more and more familiar with these models, collections of tens can be made up in advance by the children and kept as ready-made tens. Lids can be purchased for the plastic portion cups, and the connecting cubes or the links can be left prebundled. This is a good transition into the pregrouped models described next.

Pregrouped or Trading Models

At some point, you will need to represent hundreds. Models that are pregrouped must be introduced. As with all base-ten models, the ten piece is physically equivalent to 10 ones and a hundred piece equivalent to 10 tens, as in Figure 12.4(b). However, children cannot actually take them apart or put them together. When 10 single pieces are accumulated, they must be exchanged or *traded* for a ten, and likewise, tens must be traded for hundreds.

The chief advantage of these models is their ease of use and the efficient way they model large numbers. Since they do not come apart, there are always readily available tens and hundreds. A significant disadvantage is the potential for

(a) Groupable Base-Ten Models

Counters and cups. Ten single counters are placed in a cup. Hundreds: ten cups in a margarine tub.

Interlocking cubes. Ten single cubes form a bar of 10. Hundreds: ten bars on cardboard backing.

Bundles of sticks (wooden craft sticks, coffee stirrers). (If bundles are left intact, these are a pregrouped model.) Hundreds: ten bundles in a big bundle.

(b) Pregrouped Base-Ten Models

Teacher-made strips and squares. Made from mount board and poster board. See Blackline Masters and Materials Construction Tips. Plastic versions are available.

Wooden or plastic units, longs, flats, and blocks. Also known as Dienes blocks or base-ten blocks. Expensive, durable, easily handled, the only model with 1000.

"Raft"

Bean sticks. Beans glued to craft sticks. Ten sticks in a raft is also made from cardboard.

See directions and alternatives in Blackline Masters and Materials Construction Tips.

FIGURE 12.4 Groupable and pregrouped base-ten models.

children to use them without reflecting on the ten-to-one relationships or without really understanding what they are doing. For example, if children are told to trade 10 ones for a ten, it is quite possible for them to make this exchange without attending to the "tenness" of the piece they call a ten. Similarly, children can learn to "make the number 42" by simply selecting 4 tens and 2 ones pieces without understanding that if the pieces all came apart there would be 42 ones pieces that could be counted by ones.

No model, including a groupable model, will guarantee that children are reflecting on the ten-to-one relationships in the materials. With pregrouped models we need to make an extra effort to see that children understand that a ten piece really is the same as 10 ones.

(See the Blackline Masters and Materials Construction Tips for making base-ten strips and squares and the bean sticks.)

Technology Note

The National Library of Virtual Manipulatives (NLVM) at Utah State University (http://matti.usu.edu/nlvm/nav/vlibrary.html) includes a base-ten block applet. The child can place units, rods, flats, or cubes on a place-value mat to create a model of any number through four digits. By clicking on ten of any one type of block, those blocks automatically "glue" together. When the child drags a rod, flat, or cube to a lower place column, the block is "broken" into its component pieces. Virtual tools similar to this are likely to become increasingly popular. Compared to real base-ten models, virtual blocks are cheap and are available in "endless" supply, even the thousands blocks. ■

Nonproportional Materials

In this text, colored counters, abacuses, and money are not considered to model base-ten ideas because the materials play no part in developing those relationships. With an abacus like the ones shown in Figure 12.5, ten beads in one column are exchanged for one bead in the next column to the left. There is nothing in the representation that illustrates the relationship between ten beads and the single bead to its left. By first grade, students do not need beads to understand numbers to 9. Nonproportional materials can keep track of numbers within a position but they do not illuminate an understanding of the relationship between positions as effectively as proportional materials.

Teachers and textbooks frequently use pennies, dimes, and dollars as a place-value model. If the relationship that a dime is worth 10 pennies and that a dollar is worth 10 dimes is part of the children's existing understanding, money will

model base-ten place value. But if the teacher must explain or impose this relationship, the trade rate between pennies and dimes is simply a "rule of the game" from the children's view. They can learn to obey the rule, but the model is not helping them see why 10 ones is the same as 1 ten. The relationship should be in the model. Once understood, money can be a useful aid in developing flexible approaches to computation. For example, if the sum of 76 and 28 is thought of in terms of quarters and pennies, the task is quite simple. However, money does not help in the early development of place value.

Developing Place-Value Concepts and Procedures

Now that you have a sense of the task of helping children develop place-value concepts, we can begin to focus on activities that can help with this task. This section focuses separately on the three corners of the triangle of ideas in Figure 12.3: base-ten concepts or grouping by tens, standard oral names for numbers, and written forms of numbers. The central idea of counting groups of ten to describe quantities is clearly the most important component to be developed. However, you should understand that the separation of the three goals in this section is to help you understand the objectives. In the classroom, the three corners of the triangle can and should be developed together.

Grouping Activities

Because children come to their development of base-ten concepts with a count-by-ones idea of number, you must begin there. You cannot arbitrarily impose grouping by 10 on children. The decision to use 10 as the base of our numeration system most likely stems from the fact that humans have ten fingers. And so we want children to experiment with showing amounts in groups of like size and perhaps to come to an agreement that 10 is a very useful size to use. The following activity could be done in late first grade or second grade and is designed as an example of a first effort at developing grouping concepts.

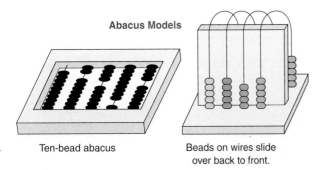

Ten-bead abacus　**Beads on wires slide over back to front.**

FIGURE 12.5 **Abacus models are nonproportional.**

ACTIVITY 12.1

Counting in Groups

Find a collection of things that children might be interested in counting—perhaps the number of eyes in the classroom or the number of shoes, a mystery jar of buttons or cubes, a long chain of plastic links, or the number of crayons in the crayon box. The quantity should be countable, somewhere between 25 and 100. Pose the question, "How could we count our shoes in some way that would be easier than counting by ones?" Whatever suggestions you get, try to implement them. After trying several methods, you can have a discussion of what worked well and what did not. If no one suggests counting by tens, you might casually suggest that as possibly another idea.

One teacher had her second-grade students find a good way to count all the connecting cubes being held by the children after each had been given a cube for each of their pockets. The first suggestion was to count by sevens. That was tried but did not work very well because none of the second graders could count by sevens. In search of a faster way, the next suggestion was to count by twos. This did not seem to be much better than counting by ones. Finally, they settled on counting by tens and realized that this was a pretty good method, although counting by fives worked pretty well also.

This and similar activities provide you with the opportunity to suggest that materials actually be arranged into groups of tens before the "fast" way of counting is begun. Remember that children may count "ten, twenty, thirty, thirty-one, thirty-two" but not fully realize the "thirty-two-ness" of the quantity. To connect the count-by-tens method with their understood method of counting by ones, the children need to count both ways and discuss why they get the same result.

The idea in the next activity is for children to make groupings of 10 and record or say the amounts. Number words are used so that children will not mechanically match tens and ones with individual digits. It is important that children confront the actual quantity in a manner meaningful to them.

ACTIVITY 12.2

Groups of 10

Prepare bags of counters of different types. Bags may have toothpicks, buttons, beans, plastic chips, connecting cubes, craft sticks, or other items. Children have a record sheet similar to the top example in Figure 12.6. The bags can be placed at stations around the room, or each pair of children can be given one. Children dump out and count the contents. The amount is recorded as a number word. Then the counters are grouped in as many tens as possible. The groupings are recorded on the form. Bags are traded, or children move to another station after returning all counters to the bag.

FIGURE 12.6 Number words and making groups of 10.

Number Words		
eleven	ten	one
twelve	twenty	two
thirteen	thirty	three
fourteen	forty	four
fifteen	fifty	five
sixteen	sixty	six
seventeen	seventy	seven
eighteen	eighty	eight
nineteen	ninety	nine

FIGURE 12.7 **A chart to help children write number words.**

If children have difficulty writing the number words, a chart can be displayed for students to copy from (see Figure 12.7).

Variations of the "Groups of 10" activity are suggested by the other record sheets in Figure 12.6. In "Get This Many," the children count the dots and then count out the corresponding number of counters. Small cups in which to put the groups of 10 should be provided. Notice that the activity requires students to address quantities in a way they understand, record the amount in words, and then make the groupings.

The activity starts where the students are and develops the idea of groups. "Fill the Tens" and "Loop This Many" begin with a verbal name (number word), and students must count the indicated amount and then make groups. As you watch children doing these activities, you will be able to learn a lot about their base-ten concept development. For example, how do children count out the objects? Do they make groupings of 10 as they go? Do they count to 10 and then start again at 1? Children who do that are already using the base-ten structure. But what you will more likely see early on is children counting a full set without any stopping at tens and without any effort to group the materials in piles. A second-grade teacher had her students count a jar of small beans. After they had recorded the number, they were to ask for plastic cups in which to make cups of 10. Several children, when asked how many cups they thought they might need, had no idea or made random guesses.

The following activity is another variant but includes an estimation component that adds interest, makes the activity more problem based, and contributes to number sense. It is helpful to add estimation to these early counting and grouping activities. Estimates encourage children to think about total quantities. Listening to students' estimates is also a useful assessment opportunity that tells you a lot about children's concepts of numbers in the range of your current activities.

ACTIVITY 12.3

Estimating Groups of Tens and Ones

Show students a length that they are going to measure—for example, the length of a student lying down or the distance around a sheet of newspaper. At one end of the length, line up 10 units (e.g., 10 cubes in a bar, 10 toothpicks, rods, or blocks). On a recording sheet (see Figure 12.8), students write down a guess of how many groups of 10 and leftovers they think will fit into the length. Next they find the actual measure, placing units along the full length. These are counted by ones and also grouped in tens. Both results are recorded.

Notice that all place-value components are included in Activity 12.3. Children can work in pairs to measure several lengths around the room. A similar estimation approach could be added to "Groups of 10" (Activity 12.2), where students first estimate the quantity in the bags. Estimation requires reflective thought concerning quantities expressed in groups.

FIGURE 12.8 **Record sheet for estimating groups of tens and ones.**

Technology Note

Unifix Software (Hickey, 1996) allows you to create useful grouping activities on the computer. As many as 100 individual cubes can be "stamped" onto the screen. The cubes are easily snapped into rods. With the "bar total" option on, the size of each rod is printed on the rod. A single cube shows "1." You could prepare a file with, say, 78 cubes and have students estimate how many tens. This could be done with or without displaying the total cubes on the screen. With both displays (rod and screen totals), students will note that the total does not change when cubes are made into bars of 10 or when bars are broken into singles. Another alternative is to have students show a specific number of bars (all totals turned off). Will students use bars of 10 to keep track of counts?

Grouping and Place Value (Tenth Planet, 1997) offers three animated grouping tasks: Balls are packed by a machine in groups of tens and then 10 tens form a hundred; a "space money" scenario has children match hundreds, tens, and ones "coins" to specified amounts; and children try to find which of four collections of objects matches a given number. Children have little control over the ball packing, but the animation is catchy. The money task involves more interaction but is symbolic. The last is perhaps the best. Children select a gadget that groups objects by twos, fives, or tens, thereby providing three grouping possibilities. After grouping, the counting is not done for the students as it is in the warm-up exercises. As with other Tenth Planet products, the print material offers excellent suggestions for using the software as well as related off-computer tasks. ■

The Strangeness of Ones, Tens, and Hundreds

Reflect for a moment on how strange it must sound to say "seven ones." Certainly children have never said they were "seven ones" years old. The use of the word *ten* as a singular group name is even more mysterious. Consider the phrase "Ten ones makes one ten." The first *ten* carries the usual meaning of 10 things, the amount that is 1 more than 9 things. But the other *ten* is a singular noun, a thing. How can something the child has known for years as the name for a lot of things suddenly become one thing? Bunches, bundles, cups, and groups of 10 make more sense in the beginning than "a ten."

As students begin to make groupings of 10, the language of these groupings must also be introduced. At the start, language such as "groups of 10 and leftovers" or "bunches of tens and singles" is most meaningful. For tens, use whatever terminology fits: bars of 10, cups of 10, bundles of 10. Eventually you can abbreviate this simply to "ten." There is no hurry to use the word "ones" for the leftovers. Language such as "four tens and seven" works very well.

The word *hundred* is equally strange and yet usually gets less attention. It must be understood in three ways: as 100 single objects, as 10 tens, and as a singular thing. These word names are not as simple as they seem!

Equivalent Representations

An important variation of the grouping activities is aimed at the equivalent representations of numbers. (See Figure 12.3.) For example, with children who have just completed the "Groups of 10" activity for a bag of counters, ask, "What is another way you can show your 42 besides 4 groups and 2 singles? Let's see how many ways you can find." Interestingly, most children will go next to 42 singles. The following activities are also directed to the idea of equivalent representations.

ACTIVITY 12.4
Odd Groupings

Show a collection of materials that are only partly grouped in sets of 10. For example, you may have 5 chains of 10 links and 17 additional links. Be sure the children understand that the groups each have 10 items. Count the number of groups, and also count the singles. Ask, "How many in all?" Record all responses, and discuss before you count. Let the children use whatever way they wish to count. Next change the groupings (make a ten from the singles, or break apart one of the tens) and repeat the questions and discussion. Do not change the total number from one time to the next. Once students begin to understand that the total does not change, ask in what other ways the items could be grouped if you use tens and singles.

The next activity is similar but is done using pregrouped materials.

ACTIVITY 12.5
Three Other Ways

Students work in groups or pairs. First they show "four hundred sixty-three" on their desks with strips and squares in the standard representation. Next they find and record at least three other ways of showing this number.

A variation of "Three Other Ways" is to challenge students to find a way to show an amount with a specific number of pieces. "Can you show 463 with 31 pieces?" (There is more than one way to do this.) Students in grades 4 or 5 can get quite involved with finding all the ways to show a three-digit number.

After children have had sufficient experiences with pregrouped materials, a "dot, stick, and square" notation can be

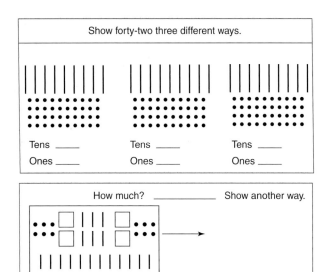

FIGURE 12.9 **Equivalent representation exercises using square-stick-dot pictures.**

used for recording ones, tens, and hundreds. By third grade, children can use small squares for hundreds, as shown in Figure 12.9. Use the drawings as a means of telling the children what pieces to get out of their own place-value kits and as a way for children to record results.

The next activity begins to incorporate oral language with equivalent representation ideas.

ACTIVITY 12.6

Base-Ten Riddles

Base-ten riddles can be presented orally or in written form. In either case, children should use base-ten materials to help solve them. The examples here illustrate a variety of possibilities with different levels of difficulty.

I have 23 ones and 4 tens. Who am I?

I have 4 hundreds, 12 tens, and 6 ones. Who am I?

I have 30 ones and 3 hundreds. Who am I?

I am 45. I have 25 ones. How many tens do I have?

I am 341. I have 22 tens. How many hundreds do I have?

I have 13 tens, 2 hundreds, and 21 ones. Who am I?

If you put 3 more tens with me, I would be 115. Who am I?

I have 17 ones. I am between 40 and 50. Who am I?

I have 17 ones. I am between 40 and 50. How many tens do I have?

"Four tens and seven ones—forty-seven"

FIGURE 12.10 **Mixed model of 47.**

Oral Names for Numbers

The standard name of the collection in Figure 12.10 is "forty-seven." A more explicit terminology in *base-ten language* is "four tens and seven ones." Base-ten language is rarely misunderstood by children working with base-ten materials and encourages thinking in terms of groups instead of a large pile of singles.

Two-Digit Number Names

In first and second grades, children need to connect the base-ten concepts with the oral number names they have used many times. They know the words but have not thought of them in terms of tens and ones.

Almost always use base-ten models while teaching oral names. Use base-ten language paired with standard language. Emphasize the teens as exceptions. Acknowledge that they are formed "backward" and do not fit the patterns.

ACTIVITY 12.7

Counting Rows of 10

Use a 10 × 10 array of dots on the overhead projector. Cover up all but two rows, as shown in Figure 12.11(a). "How many tens? (2.) Two tens is called *twenty*." Have the class repeat. "Sounds a little like *twin*." Show another row. "Three tens is called *thirty*. Four tens is *forty*. Five tens should have been *fivety* rather than *fifty*." The names *sixty, seventy, eighty,* and *ninety* all fit the pattern. Slide the cover up and down the array, asking how many tens and the name for that many.

Use the same 10 × 10 array to work on names for tens and ones. Show, for example, four full lines, "forty." Next expose one dot in the fifth row. "Four tens and one. Forty-one." Add more dots one at a time. "Four tens and two. Forty-two." "Four tens and three. Forty-three." This is shown in Figure 12.11(b). When that pattern is established, repeat with other decades from twenty through ninety.

(a)   "Two tens—twenty"

(b)   "Four tens—forty"
        "Four tens and three—forty-three"

FIGURE 12.11 **10 × 10 dot arrays are used to model sets of 10 and singles.**

Repeat this basic approach with other base-ten models. The next activity shows how this might be done.

ACTIVITY 12.8

Counting with Base-Ten Models

Show some tens pieces on the overhead. Ask how many tens. Ask for the usual name. Add a ten or remove a ten, and repeat the questions. Next add some ones. Always have children give the base-ten name and the standard name. Continue to make changes in the materials displayed by adding or removing 1 or 2 tens and by adding and removing ones. For this activity, show the tens and ones pieces in different arrangements rather than the standard left-to-right order for tens and ones. The idea is to connect the names to the materials, not the order they are in.

Reverse the activity by having children use base-ten pieces at their desks. For example, you say, "Make 63." The children make the number with the models and then give the base-ten name.

Note that Activities 12.7 and 12.8 will be much enhanced by discussion. Have children explain their thinking. If you don't require children to reflect on these responses, they soon learn how to give the response you want, matching number words to models, without actually thinking about the total quantities.

ACTIVITY 12.9

Tens, Ones, and Fingers

Ask your class, "How can you show 37 fingers?" (It is fun to precede this question by asking for different ways to show 6 fingers, 8 fingers, and other amounts less than 10.) Soon children will figure out that four children are required. Line up four children, and have three hold up 10 fingers and the last child 7 fingers. Have the class count the fingers by tens and ones. Ask for other children to show different numbers. Emphasize the number of sets of 10 fingers and the single fingers (base-ten language) and pair this with the standard language.

In the last three activities, it is important occasionally to count an entire representation by ones. Remember that the count by ones is the young child's principal linkage with the concept of quantity. For example, suppose you have just had children use connecting cubes to make 42. Try asking, "Do you think there really are 42 blocks there?" Many children are not convinced, and the count by ones is very significant.

Three-Digit Number Names

The approach to three-digit number names is essentially the same as for two-digit names. Show mixed arrangements of base-ten materials. Have children give the base-ten name and the standard name. Vary the arrangement from one example to the next by changing only one type of piece. That is, add or remove only ones or only tens or only hundreds.

Similarly, have children at their desks model numbers that you give to them orally using the standard names. By the time that children are ready for three-digit numbers, the two-digit number names, including the difficulties with the teens, have usually been mastered. The major difficulty is with numbers involving no tens, such as 702. As noted earlier, the use of base-ten language is quite helpful here. The zero-tens difficulty is more pronounced when writing numerals. Children frequently write 7002 for "seven hundred two." The emphasis on the meaning in the oral base-ten language form will be a significant help.

Written Symbols

The discussion so far has stressed the ideas of groups of 10 and the connection of these base-ten concepts to oral number names. No one would expect that written numbers are completely absent during this development. At the same time, it is correct to focus on the ideas of base-ten concepts before emphasizing the written numbers.

Place-Value Mats

Place-value mats are simple mats divided into two or three sections to hold ones and tens or ones, tens, and hundreds pieces as shown in Figure 12.12. You can suggest to your students that the mats are a good way to organize their materials when working with base-ten pieces. Explain that the standard way to use a place-value mat is with the space for the ones on the right and tens and hundreds places to the left.

Though there is no requirement to have anything printed on the mats, it is strongly recommended that two ten-frames be drawn in the ones place as shown. (See Blackline Masters and Materials Construction Tips for directions for making the mats.) That way, the amount of ones on the ten-frames is always clearly evident, eliminating the need for frequent and tedious counting (Thompson & Van de Walle, 1984). The ten-frame also makes it very clear how many additional counters would be needed to make the next set of 10. If children

are modeling two numbers at the same time, one ten-frame can be used for each number. Most illustrations of place-value mats in this book will show two ten-frames, even though that feature is not commonly seen in standard texts.

As children use their place-value mats, they can be shown how the left-to-right order of the pieces is also the way that numbers are written. The place-value mat becomes a link between the base-ten models and the written form of the numbers. Once again, be aware of how easy it would be for a child to show a number on a mat using tens and ones pieces and learn to write the number without any understanding of what the number represents. First- and second-grade textbooks often show a model and have children record numbers in this manner:

<u> 7 </u> tens and <u> 3 </u> ones is <u> 73 </u> in all.

It is all too easy to copy down the number of sticks and single blocks and rewrite these digits in a single number 73 and not confront what these symbols stand for.

The Hundreds Chart

The hundreds chart (Figure 12.13) is such an important tool in the development of place-value concepts that it deserves special attention. K–2 classrooms should have a hundreds chart displayed prominently.

An extremely useful version of the chart is made of transparent pockets into which each of the 100 numeral cards can be inserted. You can hide a number by inserting a blank card in front of a number in the pocket. You can insert colored pieces of paper in the slots to highlight various number patterns. And you can remove the number cards and have students replace them in their correct slots. A plastic desk-sized chart with removable number tiles is another good format for individual use.

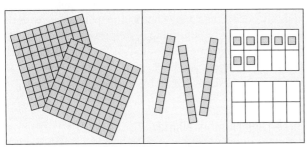

Strips and squares show
237 on three-place mat.

With two ten-frames,
cups and beans show 53.

FIGURE 12.12 Place-value mats with two ten-frames in the ones place to organize the counters and promote the concept of groups of 10.

1	2	3	4	5	6	7	8	9	10
11	12	13	14	15	16	17	18	19	20
21	22	23	24	25	26	27	28	29	30
31	32	33	34	35	36	37	38	39	40
41	42	43	44	45	46	47	48	49	50
51	52	53	54	55	56	57	58	59	60
61	62	63	64	65	66	67	68	69	70
71	72	73	74	75	76	77	78	79	80
81	82	83	84	85	86	87	88	89	90
91	92	93	94	95	96	97	98	99	100

FIGURE 12.13 A hundreds chart.

An overhead transparency of a hundreds chart is almost as flexible as the pocket chart version. Numbers can be hidden by placing opaque counters on them. Patterns can be marked with a pen or with transparent counters. A transparency of a blank 10 × 10 grid serves as an empty hundreds chart on which you can write numbers. These transparencies can be made from the Blackline Masters and are also available commercially. (A set of four smaller charts on one page is also available in the Blackline Masters and is useful for many student activities.)

At the kindergarten level, students can be helped to count and recognize two-digit numbers with the hundreds chart. There are many useful hundreds-chart activities for the K–2 level.

ACTIVITY 12.10

Patterns on the Hundreds Chart

Have children work in pairs to find patterns on the hundreds chart. Solicit ideas orally from the class. Have children explain patterns found by others to be sure that all understand the ideas that are being suggested.

There are many different patterns on the hundreds chart. In a discussion, different children will describe the same pattern in several ways. Accept all ideas. Here are some of the patterns they may point out:

- The numbers in a column all end with the same number, which is the same as the number at the top.
- In a row, one number "counts" (the ones digit goes 1, 2, 3, . . . , 9, 0); the "second" number goes up by ones, but the first number (tens digit) stays the same.
- In a column, the first number (tens digit) "counts" or goes up by ones.
- You can count by tens going down the right-hand column.
- The numbers under the 2 are all even numbers. (Every other number is even.)
- If you count by fives, you get two columns, the last column and the 5 column.

For children, these patterns are not at all obvious or trivial. For example, one child may notice the pattern in the column under the 4—every number ends in a 4. Two minutes later another child will "discover" the parallel pattern in the column headed by 7. That there is a pattern like this in every column may not be completely obvious.

Other patterns you might have students explore include numbers that have a 7 in them; numbers where the digits add up to four, and various skip-count patterns.

ACTIVITY 12.11

Skip-Count Patterns

As a full class activity, have students skip count by twos, threes, fours, and so on. After skip counting as a class, have students record a specific skip-count pattern on their own copy of the hundreds chart by coloring in each number they count. Every skip count produces an interesting pattern on the chart. You

should also discuss the patterns in the numbers. For example, when you skip count by fours, you only land on numbers that you get when you count by twos. Which counts make column patterns and which counts make diagonal patterns?

In the beginning, skip counting may be quite difficult for children. As they become more comfortable with skip counts, you can challenge students to skip count without the aid of the hundreds chart. Skip-counting skills show a readiness for multiplication combinations and also help children begin to look for interesting and useful patterns in numbers.

ACTIVITY 12.12

Missing Numbers

Provide students with a hundreds chart on which some of the number cards have been removed. (Use the classroom pocket chart or the plastic desktop charts.) The students' task is to replace the missing numbers in the chart. Beginning versions of this activity have only a random selection of individual numbers removed. Later, remove sequences of several numbers from three or four different rows. Finally, remove all but one or two rows or columns. Eventually, challenge children to replace all of the numbers in a blank chart.

Replacing the number cards or tiles from a blank chart is a good station activity for two students to work on together. By listening to how students go about finding the correct places for numbers you can learn a lot about how well they have constructed an understanding of the 1-to-100 sequence.

ACTIVITY 12.13

More and Less on the Hundreds Chart

In a similar manner to "Missing Numbers," begin with a blank or nearly blank chart. Circle a particular missing number. Students are to fill in the designated number and its "neighbors," the numbers to the left, right, above, and below. This can be done with the full class on the overhead projector, or worksheets can be prepared using a blank hundreds chart or 10 × 10 grid. After students become comfortable naming the neighbors of a number, ask what they notice about the neighbor numbers. The numbers to the left and right are one more and one less than the given number. Those above and below are ten less and ten more, respectively. By discussing these relationships on the chart, students begin to see how the sequence of numbers is related to the numeric relationships in the numbers.

Notice that children will first use the hundreds chart to learn about the patterns in the sequence of numbers. Many students, especially at the K or 1 level, will not understand the corresponding numeric relationships such as those discussed in the last activity. In the following activity, number relationships on the chart are made more explicit by including the use of base-ten models.

ACTIVITY 12.14
Models with the Hundreds Chart

This activity has several variations that can be conducted with the full class or can be made into an activity in which two students work together to explore an idea and write about what they have discovered. Use any physical model for two-digit numbers with which the students are familiar.

- Give children one or more numbers to first make with the models and then find on the chart. Use groups of two or three numbers either in the same row or the same column.
- Have students make all of the numbers in a row or in a column. How are the numbers in the row (or column) alike? How are they different? What happens at the end of the row?
- Indicate a number on the chart. What would you have to change to make each of its neighbors (the numbers to the left, right, above, and below)?

It is becoming more and more popular to have a chart that extends to 200, even in the first grade. Perhaps a more powerful idea is to extend the hundreds chart to 1000, even at the second or third grade.

ACTIVITY 12.15
The Thousands Chart

Provide students with several sheets of the blank hundreds charts from the Blackline Masters. Assign groups of three or four students the task of creating a 1-to-1000 chart. The chart is to be made by taping ten charts together in a long strip. Students should decide how they are going to divide up the task with different students taking different parts of the chart.

The thousands chart should be discussed as a class to examine how numbers change as you count from one hundred to the next, what the patterns are, and so on. In fact, the earlier hundreds chart activities can all be extended to a thousands chart. You may want to make a blank thousands chart (clearly indicating each 100-square). Use the students' charts for other discussions.

 The *Standards* points to another method of developing place-value concepts that is reflected in the reform programs but only minimally in traditional programs. "It is not necessary to wait for

students to fully develop place-value understandings before giving them opportunities to solve problems with two- and three-digit numbers. When such problems arise in interesting contexts, students can often invent ways to solve them that incorporate and deepen their understanding of place value, especially when students have the opportunities to discuss and explain their invented strategies and approaches" (p. 82).

More Connections with Numbers

The next three activities are designed to help children make connections among all three representations: models, oral language, and written forms. They can be done with two- or three-digit numbers in grades 1–4.

ACTIVITY 12.16
Say It/Press It

Display some ones and tens (and hundreds) so that the class can see. (Use the overhead projector or simply draw on the board using the square-stick-dot method.) Arrange the materials in a mixed design, not in the standard left-to-right format. Students say the amount shown in base-ten language ("four hundreds, one ten, and five") and then in standard language ("four hundred fifteen"), and finally they enter it on their calculators. Have someone share his or her display and defend it. Make a change in the materials and repeat.

"Say It/Press It" is especially good for helping with teens (note the example in the activity description) and for three-digit numbers with zero tens. If you show 7 hundreds and 4 ones, the class says "seven hundreds, zero tens, and four—seven hundred (*slight pause*) four." The pause and the base-ten language suggest the correct three-digit number to press or write. Many students have trouble with this example and write "7004," writing exactly what they hear in the standard name. Similarly, first- and second-grade children often write "504" for fifty-four. This activity will help. The next activity simply changes the representation that is presented first to the students.

ACTIVITY 12.17
Show It/Press It

Say the standard name for a number (with either two or three digits). At their desks, students use their own base-ten models to show that number and press it on their calculators (or write it). Again, pay special attention to the teens and the case of zero tens.

The following activity has been popular for decades and remains a useful challenge for students in the early stages of place-value development.

ACTIVITY 12.18

Digit Change

Have students enter a specific two- or three-digit number on the calculator. The task is to then change one of the digits in the number without simply entering the new number. For example, change 48 to 78. Change 315 to 305 or to 295. Changes can be made by adding or subtracting an appropriate amount. Students should write or discuss explanations for their solutions.

 TECHNOLOGY NOTE

Several software packages include hundreds charts that allow students to explore patterns. Many of these offer little advantage over a physical chart. *Learning About Number Relationships* is an e-example from NCTM's *e-Standards* that has a calculator and hundreds chart and allows for a fairly open exploration. Patterns are colored on the chart as students skip count with the calculator. Students can skip count by any number and also begin their counts at any number. Any two patterns can be overlapped using two colors. Patterns are easily cleared to try another. The chart also extends to 1000. The *Number Patterns* applet from the NLVM (http://matti.usu.edu/nlvm/nav/vlibrary.html) presents students with number patterns to complete. ■

NUMBER SENSE DEVELOPMENT

The discussion so far has addressed the three main components of place-value understanding: the integration of base-ten groupings, oral names, and written names. But students need to expand these ideas beyond basic numeration concepts and reading and writing numerals in order to develop number sense. These activities should be an ongoing feature of your instruction.

Relative Magnitude

Relative magnitude refers to the size relationship one number has with another—is it much larger, much smaller, close, or about the same? There are several quick activities that can be done with a number line sketched on the board. The number line can help children see how one number is related to another.

ACTIVITY 12.19

Who Am I?

Sketch a line labeled 0 and 100 at opposite ends. Mark a point with a ? that corresponds to your secret number. (Estimate the position the best you can.) Students try to guess your secret number. For each guess, place and label a mark on the line.

Continue marking each guess until your secret number is discovered. As a variation, the endpoints can be other than 0 and 100. For example, try 0 and 1000, 200 and 300, or 500 and 800.

ACTIVITY 12.20

Who Could They Be?

Label two points on a number line (not necessarily the ends).

Ask students what numbers they think different points labeled with letters might be and why they think that. In the example shown here, B and C are less than 100 but probably more than 60. E could be about 180. You can also ask where 75 might be or where 400 is. About how far apart are A and D? Why do you think D is more than 100?

In the next activity, some of the same ideas are discussed without benefit of a number line.

ACTIVITY 12.21

Close, Far, and in Between

Put any three numbers on the board. If appropriate, use two-digit numbers.

With these three numbers as referents, ask questions such as the following, and encourage discussion of all responses:

Which two are closest? Why?

Which is closest to 300? To 250?

Name a number between 457 and 364.

Name a multiple of 25 between 219 and 364.

Name a number that is more than all of these.

About how far apart are 219 and 500? 219 and 5000?

If these are "big numbers," what are some small numbers? Numbers about the same? Numbers that make these seem small?

Connections to Real-World Ideas

We should not permit children to study place-value concepts without encouraging them to see number in the world about them. You do not need a prescribed activity to bring real numbers into the classroom.

Children in the second grade should be thinking about numbers under 100 first and, soon after, numbers up to 1000. Quantities larger than that are difficult to think about. Where are numbers like this? Around your school: the number of children in each class, the numbers on the school buses, the number of minutes devoted to mathematics each day and then each week, the number of cartons of chocolate and plain milk served in the cafeteria each day, the numbers on the calendar (days in a week, month, year), the number of days since school has started. And then there are measurements, numbers at home, numbers on a field trip, and so on.

What do you do with these numbers? Turn them into interesting graphs, write stories using them, make up problems, devise contests.

As children get a bit older, the interest in numbers can expand beyond the school and classroom. All sorts of things can and should be measured to create graphs, draw inferences, and make comparisons. For example, what numbers are associated with the "average" fifth grader? Height, weight, arm span, age in months, number of siblings, number of grandparents, distance from home to school, length of standing broad jump, number of pets, hours spent watching TV in a week. How can you find the average for these or other numbers that may be of interest to the students in your room? Is anyone really average?

The particular way you bring number and the real world together in your class is up to you. But do not underestimate the value of connecting the real world to the classroom.

Approximate Numbers and Rounding

In our number system, some numbers are "nice." They are easy to think about and work with. What makes a nice number is sort of fuzzy. However, numbers such as 100, 500, and 750 are easier to use than 94, 517, and 762. Multiples of 100 are very nice, and multiples of 10 are not bad either. Multiples of 25 (50, 75, 425, 675, etc.) are nice because they combine into 100s and 50s rather easily, and we can mentally place those between multiples of 100s. Multiples of 5 are a little easier to work with than other numbers.

Flexible thought with numbers and many estimation skills are related to the ability to substitute a nice number for one that is not so nice. The substitution may be to make a mental computation easier, to compare it to a familiar reference, or simply to store the number in memory more easily.

In the past, students were taught rules for rounding numbers to the nearest 10 or nearest 100. Unfortunately, the emphasis was placed on applying the rule correctly. (If the next digit is 5 or more, round up; otherwise, leave the number alone.) A context to suggest why they may want to round numbers was usually a lesser consideration.

The activities here are designed to help students recognize what nice numbers are and to identify a nice-number substitute. (*Author note:* The term *nice number* is not found in standard textbooks. It is an invention of mine. There is no commonly accepted definition.)

ACTIVITY 12.22

Nice-Number Skip Counts

Count by 5s, 10s, 25s, and 50s with your students. The 5s and 10s are fairly easy, but the skill is certainly worth practicing. Counts by 25s or 50s may be hesitant at first. Students can use a calculator to assist with their counting and connect the counts with numerals (press ⊞ 25 ⊟ ⊟ ⊟ . . .). At first, start all counts at zero. Later, start at some multiple of your skip amount. For example, begin at 275 and count by 25s. Counts by 10s should also begin at numbers ending in 5 as well as multiples of 10. Also count backward by these same amounts (press 650 ⊟ 50 ⊟ ⊟ ⊟ . . .).

Counting Money

Too often children are expected to count coins without any preparation or background. It is not that money is hard for children but rather that skip counting by different amounts is difficult. The next activity extends "Nice-Number Skip Counts" in preparation for counting money by shifting from one skip count to another.

ACTIVITY 12.23

Money Counts

Explain to the students that they will start counting by one number and at your signal they will shift to a count by a different number. Begin with only two different amounts, say, 25 and 10. Write these numbers on the board. Point to the larger number (25), and have students begin to count. After three or more counts, raise your hand to indicate a pause in the counting. Then lower your hand and point to the smaller number (10). Children continue the count from where they left off but now count by 10s. Use any two of these numbers: 100, 50, 25, 10, 5, 1. Always start with the larger. Later, try three numbers, still in descending order.

Note that the counts in "Money Counts" are the same as are used when counting coins or money. These skills can be applied to bills and coins. Plastic money is available for use on the overhead and is an effective substitute.

Rounding

To round a number simply means to substitute a nice number that is close so that some computation can be done more eas-

FIGURE 12.14 A blank number line can be labeled in different ways to help students with near and nice numbers.

ily. The close number can be any nice number and need not be a multiple of 10 or 100, as has been traditional. It should be whatever makes the computation or estimation easier or simplifies numbers sufficiently in a story, chart, or conversation. You might say, "Last night it took me 57 minutes to do my homework" or "Last night it took me about one hour to do my homework." The first expression is more precise; the second substitutes a rounded number for better communication.

A number line with nice numbers highlighted can be useful in helping children select near nice numbers. An unlabeled number line like the one shown in Figure 12.14 can be made using three strips of poster board taped end to end. Labels are written above the line on the chalkboard. The ends can be labeled 0 and 100, 100 and 200, . . . , 900 and 1000. The other markings then show multiples of 25, 10, and 5. Indicate a number above the line that you want to round. Discuss the marks (nice numbers) that are close.

Numbers Beyond 1000

For children to have good concepts of numbers beyond 1000, the conceptual ideas that have been carefully developed must be extended. This is sometimes difficult to do because physical models for thousands are not commonly available. At the same time, number sense ideas must also be developed. In many ways, it is these informal ideas about very large numbers that are the most important.

Extending the Place-Value System

Two important ideas developed for three-digit numbers should be carefully extended to larger numbers. First, the grouping idea should be generalized. That is, 10 in any position makes a single thing (group) in the next position, and vice versa. Second, the oral and written patterns for numbers in three digits are duplicated in a clever way for every three digits to the left. These two related ideas are not as easy for children to understand as adults seem to believe. Because models for large numbers are so difficult to have or picture, textbooks must deal with these ideas in a predominantly symbolic manner. That is not sufficient!

ACTIVITY 12.24

What Comes Next?

Have a "What Comes Next?" discussion with the use of base-ten strips and squares. The unit or ones piece is a 1 centimeter (cm) square. The tens piece is a 10 × 1 strip. The hundreds piece is a square, 10 cm × 10 cm. What is next? Ten hundreds is called a thousand. What shape? It could be a strip made of 10 hundreds squares. Tape 10 hundreds together. What is next? (Reinforce the idea of "ten makes one" that has progressed to this point.) Ten one-thousand strips would make a square measuring 1 meter (m) on a side. Once the class has figured out the shape of the thousand piece, the problem-based task is "What comes next?" Let small groups work on the dimensions of a ten-thousand piece.

If your students become interested in seeing the big pieces from "What Comes Next?" engage them in measuring them out on paper. Ten ten-thousand squares (100,000) go together to make a huge strip. Draw this strip on a long sheet of butcher paper, and mark off the 10 squares that make it up. You will have to go out in the hall.

How far you want to extend this square, strip, square, strip sequence depends on your class. The idea that 10 in one place makes 1 in the next can be brought home dramatically. It is quite possible with older children to make the next 10 m × 10 m square using chalk lines on the playground. The next strip is 100 m × 10 m. This can be measured out on a large playground with kids marking the corners. By this point, the payoff includes an appreciation of the increase in size of each successive amount as well as the ten-makes-one progression. The 100 m × 10 m strip is the model for 10 million, and the 10 m × 10 m square models 1 million. The difference between 1 million and 10 million is dramatic. Even the concept of 1 million tiny centimeter squares is dramatic.

The three-dimensional wooden or plastic base-ten materials are all available with a model for thousands, which is a 10-cm cube. These models are expensive, but having at least one large cube to show and talk about is a good idea.

Try the "What Comes Next?" discussion in the context of these three-dimensional models. The first three shapes are distinct: a *cube*, a *long*, and a *flat*. What comes next? Stack 10 flats and they make a cube, same shape as the first one only 1000 times larger. What comes next? (See Figure 12.15.) Ten

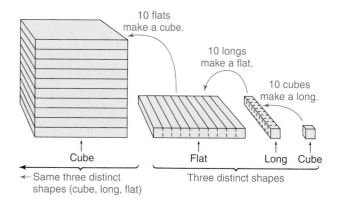

FIGURE 12.15 With every three places, the shapes repeat. Each cube represents a 1, each long represents a 10, and each flat represents a 100.

FIGURE 12.16 **The triples system for naming large numbers.**

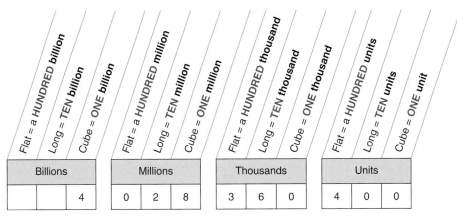

"Four billion, twenty-eight million, three hundred sixty thousand, four hundred."

cubes make another *long*. What comes next? Ten big *longs* make a big *flat*. The first three shapes have now repeated! Ten big flats will make an even bigger cube, and the triplet of shapes begins again.

Each cube has a name. The first one is the *unit* cube, the next is a *thousand*, the next a *million*, then a *billion*, and so on. Each long is 10 cubes: 10 units, 10 thousands, 10 millions. Similarly, each flat shape is 100 cubes.

To read a number, first mark it off in triples from the right. The triples are then read, stopping at the end of each to name the unit (or cube shape) for that triple (see Figure 12.16). Leading zeros in each triple are ignored. If students can learn to read numbers like 059 (fifty-nine) or 009 (nine), they should be able to read any number. To write a number, use the same scheme. If first mastered orally, the system is quite easy.

It is important for children to realize that the system does have a logical structure, is not totally arbitrary, and can be understood.

Conceptualizing Large Numbers

The ideas just discussed are only partially helpful in thinking about the actual quantities involved in very large numbers. For example, in extending the square, strip, square, strip sequence, some appreciation for the quantities of 1000 or of 100,000 is included. But it is hard for anyone to translate quantities of small squares into quantities of other items, distances, or time.

 STOP How do you think about 1000 or 100,000? Do you have any real concept of a million?

Creating References for Special Big Numbers

In these activities, numbers like 1000, 10,000, or even 1 million are translated literally or imaginatively into something that is easy or fun to think about. Interesting quantities become

lasting reference points or benchmarks for large numbers and thereby add meaning to numbers encountered in real life.

ACTIVITY 12.25

Collecting 10,000

Collections. As a class or grade-level project, collect some type of object with the objective of reaching some specific quantity—for example, 1000 or 10,000 buttons, walnuts, old pencils, jar lids, or pieces of junk mail. If you begin aiming for 100,000 or 1 million, be sure to think it through. One teacher spent nearly 10 years with her classes before amassing a million bottle caps. It takes a small dump truck to hold that many!

ACTIVITY 12.26

Showing 10,000

Illustrations. Sometimes it is easier to create large amounts. For example, start a project where students draw 100 or 200 or even 500 dots on a sheet of paper. Each week, different students contribute a specified number. Another idea is to cut up newspaper into pieces the same size as dollar bills to see what a large quantity would look like. Paper chain links can be constructed over time and hung down the hallways with special numbers marked. Let the school be aware of the ultimate goal.

ACTIVITY 12.27

How Long?/How Far?

Real and imagined distances. How long is a million baby steps? Other ideas that address length: toothpicks, dollar bills, or candy bars end to end; children holding hands in a line; blocks or bricks stacked up; children lying down head to toe. Real measures can also be used: feet, centimeters, meters.

ACTIVITY 12.28
A Long Time

Time. How long is 1000 seconds? How long is a million seconds? A billion? How long would it take to count to 10,000 or 1 million? (To make the counts all the same, use your calculator to do the counting. Just press the ☐.) How long would it take to do some task like buttoning a button 1000 times?

Estimating Large Quantities

Activities 12.25 through 12.28 focus on a specific number. The reverse idea is to select a large quantity and find some way to measure, count, or estimate how many.

ACTIVITY 12.29
Really Large Quantities

Ask how many

> Candy bars would cover the floor of your room
>
> Steps an ant would take to walk around the school building
>
> Grains of rice would fill a cup or a gallon jug
>
> Quarters could be stacked in one stack floor to ceiling
>
> Pennies can be laid side by side down an entire block
>
> Pieces of notebook paper would cover the gym floor
>
> Seconds you have lived

Big-number projects need not take up large amounts of class time. They can be explored over several weeks as take-home projects or group projects or, perhaps best of all, be translated into great schoolwide estimation contests.

NCTM Standards The *Standards* document also recognizes the need for relating large numbers to the real world. "A third-grade class might explore the size of 1000 by skip-counting to 1000, building a model of 1000 using ten hundred charts, gathering 1000 items such as paper clips and developing efficient ways to count them, or using strips that are 10 or 100 centimeters long to show the length of 1000 centimeters" (p. 149).

 LITERATURE CONNECTIONS

Books that emphasize groups of things, even simple counting books, are a good beginning to the notion of 10 things in a single group. Many books have wonderful explorations of large quantities and how they can be combined and separated.

Moira's Birthday
Munsch, 1987

As Moira plans her birthday party, she invites more and more children until she has invited all the children in the kindergarten, first, second, third, fourth, fifth, and sixth grades. Then she needs to order food. She orders 200 cakes and 200 pizzas. Wonderful bedlam ensues as the food and the children all arrive at the party. A second-grade teacher, Diane Oppedal (1995), used this story as a background for the question "How can you show 200 things in different ways?" As children work on this or similar projects, they can be encouraged to use some form of groups to keep track of their collections.

The same book can also be used to motivate a variety of computation situations that could be used prior to structured computation instruction. "How many children are in three classrooms?" "What if everyone at the party got two pieces of pizza?" "If Moira gave 37 of her 94 presents back to the children who helped her clean up, how many presents did she have left?"

How to Count Like a Martian
St. John, 1975

This book explores number systems from different ancient cultures (Chinese, Roman, Egyptian, etc.) and so has a culture connection as well as a mathematics connection. The contrast of the different systems, most of which are not place-value systems, can be a good way for children in the fourth and fifth grades to appreciate and discuss the base-ten place-value system. Most other numeration systems do not have a zero, for example. Several numeration systems use the same symbol repeatedly to express multiples of a certain quantity. Children could write numbers in different systems, try to compute in another system, or discuss how they might make up a system of their own. Why is it that most of the world has adopted the system we use?

The King's Commissioners
Friedman, 1994

The king has so many commissioners, he can't keep track of how many there are. In a hilarious tale, the commissioners are marched into the throne room to be counted. One person tries to count them by twos and another by fives. The princess convinces the king that there are many other excellent ways to count. The story is a natural background for place-value concepts, including grouping and different counting methods, large numbers, and informal early computation challenges. Stephanie Sheffield (1995) offers specific suggestions for using this story with children at about the second-grade level.

A Million Fish . . . More or Less
McKissack, 1992

This story, which takes place in lower Louisiana, is a tall tale of a boy who catches three fish . . . and then a million more.

The story is full of exaggerations such as a turkey that weighs 500 pounds and a jump-rope contest (using a snake) where the story's hero wins with 5553 jumps. "Could these things really be? How long would it take to jump 5553 times? Could Hugh put a million fish in his wagon? How do you write half of a million?" Rusty Bresser (1995) suggests a number of excellent ways this tale can be used to investigate large numbers and how they are written. The connections to real things and real ideas is just the ticket to add number sense to an upper-grade unit on place value.

Many other excellent books investigate very large numbers in interesting contexts. *How Much Is a Million?* (1985) and *If You Made a Million* (1989), both by David Schwartz, have become very popular. Wanda Gag's *Millions of Cats* (1928) is a classic that is still worth the time to investigate. Just one more of many possibilities is *Six Dogs, Twenty-Three Cats, Forty-Five Mice, and One Hundred Sixteen Spiders* (Chalmers, 1986). The imagination that these books inspire can lead children into fascinating investigations of large numbers, and with a bit of guidance, good place-value concepts can be visited along the way. ■

Assessment Notes

Ongoing Assessment

Most of the activities suggested in this chapter serve as opportunities to find out what children know and understand about place value. They are performance tasks. A lot of the assessment information you will need can come from watching and listening as children do these tasks.

● How do children count or estimate quantities? Do they spontaneously use sets of tens?

● When materials are already arranged in groups of 10 (counters in cups, dots in ten-frames) or in groups of 100, do the children use these structures to tell how many?

● How flexible are children with their thinking about numbers? Can they take them apart and combine them in ways that reflect an understanding of ones, tens, and hundreds?

● How well are they able to relate numbers appropriate for their age to real quantities, measures, and events?

The following activity is frequently used in interviews with individual students but could easily be a task posed to the whole class or a small group for discussion. As you listen to how children solve these problems, you will realize that there is a lot more information to be found out about their thinking beyond simply getting the answer correct.

┌─────────────────────────────────────┐
│ **ACTIVITY 12.30** │
└─────────────────────────────────────┘

Mystery Mats

First, show a mat or board with some base-ten pieces covered and some showing. Tell the child how many pieces are hidden under the cover, and ask him or her to figure out how much is on the board altogether, as in Figure 12.17(a).

After that, show a board partially covered as before. Tell the child how many pieces are on the board altogether, and ask how many are hidden, as in Figure 12.17(b).

(a)   "How many on the board altogether?"

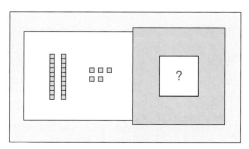

(b)   "There are 62 on the whole board. How many are covered?"

FIGURE 12.17 **Two useful assessment activities.**

Activity 12.30 could also involve hundreds. The amounts that you tell the child could be given in written form instead of orally. ■

Diagnosis of Place-Value Concepts

Much information can be had from observation and discussion. However, you may still be curious to know exactly what level of understanding a few particular children may have about place-value concepts. Children are often able to disguise their lack of understanding in this area by following directions, using the tens and ones pieces in prescribed ways, and using the language of place value.

Another reason for a short diagnostic interview with a few students may be to confirm that the assessments you have made through observation are in fact valid.

The diagnostic tasks presented here are designed to help you look more closely at children's understanding of place value. They are not suggested as definitive tests but as means of obtaining information for the thoughtful teacher. These tasks have been used by several researchers and are adapted primarily from Labinowicz (1985) and Ross (1986). The tasks are designed for one-on-one settings. They should not be used as instructional activities.

Counting Skills

A variety of oral counting tasks provide insight into the counting sequence.

- Count forward for me, starting at 77.
- Count backward, starting at 55.
- Count by tens.
- Count by tens, starting at 34.
- Count backward by tens, starting at 130.

In the tasks that follow, the manner in which the child responds is as important as the answers.

One More and Ten More, One Less and Ten Less

Write the number 342. Have the child read the number. Then have the child write the number that is 1 more than the number. Next ask for the number that is 10 more than the number. You may wish to explore further with models. One less and 10 less can be checked the same way.

Digit Correspondence

Dump out 36 blocks. Ask the child to count the blocks, and then have the child write the number that tells how many there are. Circle the 6 in 36 and ask, "Does this part of your 36 have anything to do with how many blocks there are?" Then circle the 3 and repeat the question exactly. Do not give clues. Based on responses to the task, Ross (1989) has identified five distinct levels of understanding of place value:

1. *Single numeral.* The child writes 36 but views it as a single numeral. The individual digits 3 and 6 have no meaning by themselves.
2. *Position names.* The child identifies correctly the tens and ones positions but still makes no connections between the individual digits and the blocks.
3. *Face value.* The child matches 6 blocks with the 6 and 3 blocks with the 3.
4. *Transition to place value.* The 6 is matched with 6 blocks and the 3 with the remaining 30 blocks but not as 3 groups of 10.
5. *Full understanding.* The 3 is correlated with 3 groups of 10 blocks and the 6 with 6 single blocks.

Using Tens

Dump out 47 counters, and have the child count them. Next show the child at least ten cards, each with a ten-frame drawn on it. Ask, "If we wanted to put these counters in the spaces on these cards, how many cards could we fill up?" (If the ten-frame has been used in class to model sets of 10, use a different frame such as a 10-pin arrangement of circles. Be sure the child knows there are 10 spaces on each card.)

Using Groups of 10

Prepare cards with beans or other counters glued to the cards in an obvious arrangement of 10. Supply at least ten cards and a large supply of the beans. After you are sure that the child has counted several cards of beans and knows there are 10 on each, say, "Show me 34 beans." (Does the child count individual beans or use the cards of 10?) The activity can also be done with hundreds.

O┤Reflections on Chapter **12**├

Writing to Learn

1. Explain how a child who has not yet developed base-ten concepts understands quantities as large as, say, 85. Contrast this with a child who understands these same quantities in terms of base-ten groupings.

2. What is meant by *equivalent representations*?

3. Explain the three ways one can count a set of objects and how these methods of counting can be used to coordinate concepts and oral and written names for numbers.

4. Describe the two types of physical models for base-ten concepts. What is the significance of the difference between these two types of models? Why is an abacus not considered a model for place value?

5. Describe an activity for developing base-ten grouping concepts, and reflect on how the activity encourages children to construct base-ten concepts.

6. How do children learn to write two- and three-digit numbers in a way that is connected to the base-ten meanings of ones and tens or ones, tens, and hundreds?

7. How would you describe good place-value number sense? There are a variety of aspects to number sense with large numbers. Describe activities that are designed to help develop these different features of good number sense with larger numbers.

8. What are two different ideas that you would want children to know about very large numbers (beyond 1000)? Describe one or two activities for each.

For Discussion and Exploration

1. Based on the suggestions toward the end of this chapter and on the content of a standard basal textbook, design a diagnostic interview for a child at a particular grade level, and conduct the interview. It is a good idea to take a friend to act as an observer or to use a tape recorder or video recorder to keep track of how the interview went.

2. A popular collection of activities, sometimes referred to as "trading activities," are done with base-ten models. In all of these activities, children have a place-value mat on which they accumulate materials or from which they remove materials. The activities generally take a game format. Perhaps a die is rolled and the die tells the child how many ones are to be placed on the mat or how many may be removed. Whenever 10 pieces in one section are accumulated, a trade is made for a single piece in the next place: 10 ones for a ten, 10 tens for a hundred. Similarly, in the process of removing pieces, trades are made in the reverse manner: 1 ten for 10 ones.

   Do these trading activities contribute any new connections or ideas to place-value understanding? If so, what are they? Are trading activities problem based? Are there any activities in this chapter that get at the same ideas?

Recommendations for Further Reading

Highly Recommended

Burns, M. (1994). *Math by all means: Place value, grade 2*. Sausalito, CA: Math Solutions Publications.

Burns provides 25 days of very detailed lessons in place value for second-grade children. In her usual style, there are ample examples of children's written work and descriptions of interactions that took place in the classroom. It is possible to take issue with the claims the author makes for the complete development resulting from these lessons, but that does not detract from the value of most of the activities. Perhaps most important is the way that Burns brings you into the classroom to get a feel for how these activities will work with children.

Jones, G. A., Thornton, C. A., Putt, I. J., Hill, K. M., Mogill, A. T., Rich, B. S., & Van Zoest, L. R. (1996). Multidigit number sense: A framework for instruction and assessment. *Journal for Research in Mathematics Education, 27,* 310–336.

Based on a two-year study of first- and second-grade children, this research refined an earlier framework for place-value development. It consists of four constructs: counting, partitioning, grouping, and number relationships. Within each, five levels of understanding were identified. Although in a research journal, there is ample practical information for the first- through third-grade teacher, for both instructional purposes and for assessment.

Richardson, K. (1990). *A look at children's thinking: Video II and study guide*. Norman, OK: Educational Enrichment, Inc.

This tape showing diagnostic interviews is must viewing for anyone interested in how children develop number concepts and place value in particular. Richardson uses the same series of questions with several children at different stages of development. Her commentary clearly describes why the questions are asked, what she is looking for, and an analysis of the students' responses. You cannot watch this tape and not fully appreciate the complexity of place-value concepts and the difficulty children have developing them.

Schifter, D., Bastable, V., & Russell, S. J. (1999a). *Developing mathematical understanding: Numbers and operations, Part 1, Building a system of tens (Casebook)*. Parsippany, NJ: Dale Seymour Publications.

Schifter and her colleagues at TERC have compiled in this book a wonderful collection of cases, each written by a classroom teacher, in which the complexities of place-value development truly come to light. Although this is a companion book to an in-service program, the cases by themselves are worth reading. They will provide useful insights into children's thinking and useful points of discussion. The book includes 29 different cases from grades 1 to 6 and covers situations involving invented computations and decimals as well as whole number meanings.

Other Suggestions

Auriemma, A. (1999). How huge is a hundred? *Teaching Children Mathematics, 6,* 154–159.

Cotter, J. A. (2000). Using language and visualization to teach place value. *Teaching Children Mathematics, 7,* 108–114.

Fuson, K. C., Wearne, D., Hiebert, J. C., Murray, H. G., Human, P. G., Olivier, A. I., Carpenter, T. P., & Fennema, E. (1997). Children's conceptual structures for multidigit numbers and methods of multidigit addition and subtraction. *Journal for Research in Mathematics Education, 28,* 130–162.

Kouba, V. L., & Wearne, D. (2000). Whole number properties and operations. In E. A. Silver & P. A. Kenney (Eds.), *Results from the seventh mathematics assessment of the National Assessment of Educational Progress* (pp. 141–162). Reston, VA: National Council of Teachers of Mathematics.

Labinowicz, E. (1985). *Learning from children: New beginnings for teaching numerical thinking*. Menlo Park, CA: AWL Supplemental.

Larsen, N. (1996). Making cents. *Teaching Children Mathematics, 2,* 520–522.

Little, C. (1999). Counting grass. *Mathematics Teaching in the Middle School, 5,* 7–10.

Nagel, N. G., & Swingen, C. C. (1998). Students' explanations of place value in addition and subtraction. *Teaching Children Mathematics, 5,* 164–170.

Payne, J. N., & Huinker, D. M. (1993). Early number and numeration. In R. J. Jensen (Ed.), *Research ideas for the classroom: Early childhood mathematics* (pp. 43–71). Old Tappan, NJ: Macmillan.

Reys, B. J. (1991). *Developing number sense in the middle grades: Addenda series, grades 5–8*. Reston, VA: National Council of Teachers of Mathematics.

Ritchhart, R. (1994). *Making numbers make sense: A sourcebook for developing numeracy*. Reading, MA: Addison-Wesley.

Ross, S. H. (1989). Parts, wholes, and place value: A developmental perspective. *Arithmetic Teacher, 36*(6), 47–51.

Whitin, D. J. (1995). Connecting literature and mathematics. In P. A. House (Ed.), *Connecting mathematics across the curriculum* (pp. 134–141). Reston, VA: National Council of Teachers of Mathematics.

STRATEGIES FOR WHOLE-NUMBER COMPUTATION

Much of the public sees computational skill as the hallmark of what it means to know mathematics at the elementary school level. Although this is far from the truth, the issue of computational skills with whole numbers is, in fact, a very important part of the elementary curriculum, especially in grades 2 to 6.

Rather than a single method of subtracting (or any operation), the most appropriate method can and should change flexibly as the numbers and the context change. In the spirit of the *Standards*, the issue is no longer a matter of "knows how to subtract three-digit numbers"; rather it is the development over time of an assortment of flexible skills that will best serve students in the real world.

It is quite possible that you do not have these skills, but you can acquire them. Work at them as you learn about them. Equip yourself with a flexible array of computational strategies.

Big Ideas

1. Flexible methods of computation involve taking apart and combining numbers in a wide variety of ways. Most of the partitions of numbers are based on place value or "compatible" numbers—number pairs that work easily together, such as 25 and 75.

2. Invented strategies are flexible methods of computing that vary with the numbers and the situation. Successful use of the strategies requires that they be understood by the one who is using them—hence, the term *invented*. Strategies may be invented by a peer or the class as a whole; they may even be suggested by the teacher. However, they must be constructed by the student.

3. Flexible methods for computation require a good understanding of the operations and properties of the operations, especially the turnaround property and the

distributive property for multiplication. How the operations are related—addition to subtraction, addition to multiplication, and multiplication to division—is also an important ingredient.

4. The traditional algorithms are clever strategies for computing that have been developed over time. Each is based on performing the operation on one place value at a time with transitions to an adjacent position (trades, regrouping, "borrows," or "carries"). Traditional algorithms tend to make us think in terms of digits rather than the composite number that the digits make up. These algorithms work for all numbers but are often far from the most efficient or useful methods of computing.

CONTENT CONNECTIONS

Flexible computation is built on the ideas found in the preceding three chapters. Flexible methods for computing, especially mental methods, allow one to reason much more effectively in every area of mathematics involving numbers.

■ **Operation Meanings and Fact Mastery** (Chapters 10 and 11): The need for understanding the ideas in these chapters is evident. Children can and should explore contextual problems involving multidigit numbers as they develop their understanding of the operations. Without basic facts, students will be severely disadvantaged in any computational endeavor.

■ **Place Value** (Chapter 12): Place value is not only a basis for computation; students can also develop place value understanding as a *result* of finding their own methods of computing. In the process of making sense of different computational methods, students explore and develop place-value concepts.

- **Computational Estimation** (Chapter 14): Computational estimation involves substituting "nice" numbers in a computation so that the new computation can be done mentally or at least with minimal effort. Without good computational skills—especially methods other than the traditional algorithms—estimation is nearly impossible.

Toward Computational Fluency

With today's technology the need for doing tedious computations by hand has essentially disappeared. At the same time, we now know that there are numerous methods of computing that can be handled either mentally or with pencil-and-paper support. In most everyday instances, these alternative strategies for computing are easier and faster, can often be done mentally, and contribute to our overall number sense. The traditional algorithms (procedures for computing) do not have these benefits.

Consider the following problem.

Mary had 114 spaces in her photo album. So far she has 89 photos in the album. How many more photos can she put in before the album is full?

 Try solving the photo album problem using some method other than the one you were taught in school. If you want to begin with the 9 and the 4, try a different approach. Can you do it mentally? Can you do it in more than one way? Work on this before reading further.

Here are just four of many methods that have been used by students in the primary grades to solve the computation in the photo album problem:

89 + 11 is 100. 11 + 14 is 25.

90 + 10 is 100 and 14 more is 24 plus 1 (for 89, not 90) is 25.

Take away 14 and then take away 11 more or 25 in all.

89, 99, 109 (that's 20). 110, 111, 112, 113, 114 (keeping track on fingers) is 25.

Strategies such as these can be done mentally, are generally faster than the traditional algorithms, and make sense to the person using them. Every day, students and adults resort to error-prone, traditional strategies when other, more meaningful methods would be faster and less susceptible to error. Flexibility with a variety of computational strategies is an important tool for successful daily living. It is time to broaden our perspective of what it means to compute.

FIGURE 13.1 Three types of computational strategies.

Figure 13.1 lists three general types of computing. The initial, inefficient direct modeling methods can, with guidance, develop into an assortment of invented strategies that are flexible and useful. As noted in the diagram, many of these methods can be handled mentally, although no special methods are designed specifically for mental computation. The traditional pencil-and-paper algorithms remain in the mainstream curricula. However, the attention given to them should, at the very least, be debated.

NCTM Standards "Equally essential [with basic facts] is computational fluency—having and using efficient and accurate methods for computing. Fluency might be manifested in using a combination of mental strategies and jottings on paper or using an algorithm with paper and pencil, particularly when the numbers are large, to produce accurate results quickly. Regardless of the particular methods used, students should be able to explain their method, understand that many methods exist, and see the usefulness of methods that are efficient, accurate, and general" (p. 32).

Direct Modeling

The developmental step that usually precedes invented strategies is called *direct modeling*: the use of manipulatives or drawings along with counting to represent directly the meaning of an operation or story problem. Figure 13.2 provides an example using base-ten materials, but often students use simple counters and count by ones.

Students who consistently count by ones most likely have not developed base-ten grouping concepts. That does

FIGURE 13.2 A possible direct modeling of 36 × 7 using base-ten models.

not mean that they should not continue to solve problems involving two-digit numbers. As you work with these children, suggest (don't force) that they group counters by tens as they count. Perhaps instead of making large piles, they might make bars of ten from connecting cubes or organize counters in cups of ten. Some students will use the ten-stick as a counting device to keep track of counts of ten, even though they are counting each segment of the stick by ones.

If you feel students are capable of more sophisticated strategies, perhaps the counters should mysteriously "disappear" for a few days, or you might challenge students to find a more clever way to solve a problem.

When children have plenty of experience with base-ten concepts and models, they begin to use these ideas in the direct modeling of the problems. Even when students use base-ten materials, they will find many different ways to solve problems.

Invented Strategies

Carpenter, Franke, Jacobs, Fennnema, and Empson (1998) refer to any strategy other than the traditional algorithm and that does not involve the use of physical materials or counting by ones an *invented strategy*. We will use this term also, although *personal and flexible strategies* might be equally appropriate. At times, invented strategies are done mentally. For example, 75 + 19 can be done mentally (75 + 20 is 95, less 1 is 94). For 847 + 256, some students may write down intermediate steps to aid in memory as they work through the problem. (Try that one yourself.) In the classroom, some written support is often encouraged as strategies develop. Written records of thinking are more easily shared and help students focus on the ideas. The distinction between written, partially written, and mental is not important, especially in the development period.

Over the past two decades, a number of research projects have focused attention on how children handle computational situations when they have not been taught a specific algorithm

or strategy.* The three elementary reform curricula each base the development of computational methods on student-invented strategies. "There is mounting evidence that children both in and out of school can construct methods for adding and subtracting multi-digit numbers without explicit instruction" (Carpenter et al., 1998, p. 4). Data supporting students' construction of useful methods for multiplication and division have also been gathered (Baek, 1998; Fosnot & Dolk, 2001; Kamii & Dominick, 1997; Schifter, Bastable, & Russell, 1999b).

Not all students invent their own strategies. Strategies invented by class members are shared, explored, and tried out by others. However, no student should be permitted to use any strategy without understanding it (Campbell, Rowan, & Suarez, 1998).

Contrasts with Traditional Algorithms

There are significant differences between invented strategies and the traditional algorithms.

1. *Invented strategies are number oriented rather than digit oriented.* For example, an invented strategy for 68 × 7 begins 7 × 60 is 420 and 56 more is 476. The first product is 7 times *sixty*, not the digit 6, as would be the case in the traditional algorithm. Using the traditional algorithm for 45 + 32, children never think of 40 and 30 but rather 4 + 3. Kamii, long a crusader against standard algorithms, claims that they "unteach" place value (Kamii & Dominick, 1998).

2. *Invented strategies are left-handed rather than right-handed.* Invented strategies begin with the largest parts of numbers, those represented by the leftmost digits. For 26 × 47, invented strategies will begin with 20 × 40 is 800, providing some sense of the size of the eventual answer in just one step. The traditional algorithm begins with 7 × 6 is 42. By beginning on the right with a digit orientation, traditional methods hide the result until the end. Long division is an exception.

3. *Invented strategies are flexible rather than rigid.* Invented strategies tend to change with the numbers involved in order to make the computation easier. Try each of these mentally: 465 + 230 and 526 + 98. Did you use the same method? The traditional algorithm suggests using the same tool on all problems. The traditional algorithm for 7000 − 25 typically leads to student errors, yet a mental strategy is relatively simple (Carroll & Porter, 1997).

---

*The Cognitively Guided Instruction (CGI) project , directed by Carpenter, Fennema, and Franke at the University of Wisconsin; the Conceptually Based Instruction (CBI) project, directed by Hiebert and Wearne at the University of Delaware; the Problem Centered Mathematics Project (PCMP), directed by Human, Murray, and Olivier at the University of Stellenbosch, South Africa; the Supporting Ten-Structured Thinking (STST) project, directed by Fuson at Northwestern University; and ongoing research by Kamii at the University of Alabama are all examples of efforts that have informed thinking about invented strategies for computation.

Benefits of Invented Strategies

The development of invented strategies delivers more than computational facility. Both the development of these strategies and their regular use have positive benefits that are difficult to ignore.

- *Base-ten concepts are enhanced.* There is a definite interaction between the development of base-ten concepts and the process of inventing computational strategies (Carpenter et al., 1998). "Invented strategies demonstrate a hallmark characteristic of understanding" (p. 16). The development of invented strategies should be integrated with the development of base-ten concepts, even as early as first grade.
- *Invented strategies are built on student understanding.* Students rarely use an invented strategy they do not understand. In contrast, students are frequently seen to use traditional algorithms without being able to explain why they work (Carroll & Porter, 1997).
- *Students make fewer errors with invented strategies.* Data collected by Kamii and Dominick (1997) provide some hard evidence for this claim. With traditional algorithms, students tend to develop systematic errors or "buggy algorithms" that they use again and again. Careless errors often result from confusion with carried digits or column alignment. Systematic errors are not typical of invented strategies.
- *Invented strategies serve students at least as well on standard tests.* Evidence from the reform programs suggests that students not taught traditional algorithms fare about as well in computation on standardized tests as students in traditional programs (Campbell, 1996; Carroll, 1996, 1997; Chambers, 1996). As an added bonus, students tend to do quite well with word problems, since they are the principal vehicle for developing invented strategies. The pressures of external testing do not dictate a focus on the traditional algorithms.

Mental Computation

A mental computation strategy is simply any invented strategy that is done mentally. What may be a mental strategy for one student may require written support by another. Initially, students should not be asked to do computations mentally, as this may threaten students who have not yet developed a reasonable invented strategy or who are still at the direct modeling stage. At the same time, you may be quite amazed at the ability of students (and at your own ability) to do computations mentally.

Try your own hand with this example:

$$342 + 153 + 481$$

❌ **STOP** For the addition task just shown, try this method: Begin by adding the hundreds, saying the totals as you go—*3 hundred, 4 hundred, 8 hundred*. Then add on to this the tens in successive manner and finally the ones. Do it now.

When the computations are a bit more complicated, the challenge is more interesting and generally there are more alternatives. Here is an example taken from the grades 3–5 chapter of the *Standards* (p. 152).

$$7 \times 28$$

The *Standards* lists three paths to a solution but there are at least two more (NCTM, 2000, p. 152). How many ways can you find to do this one?

As your students become more adept, they can and should be challenged from time to time to do appropriate computations mentally. Do not expect the same skills of all students.

Traditional Algorithms

In everyday life, the need for a traditional algorithm generally increases as the number of digits or complexity of a necessary computation increases. It is difficult to compute 486×372 without a digit-oriented algorithm. Similar statements are true of division. For addition and subtraction, one can easily argue that well-understood and practiced invented strategies are more than adequate. Since we have grown up with the traditional algorithms, abandoning them is difficult to imagine.

Delay! Delay! Delay!

Students almost certainly are not going to invent the traditional algorithms. You will need to introduce and explain each algorithm to them and help them understand how and why they work. No matter how carefully you introduce these algorithms into your classroom as simply another alternative, students are likely to sense that "this is the real way" or the "right way" to compute. "This is the way the teacher taught us to do it and it is the way my mom and dad compute." Once having begun with traditional methods, it is extremely difficult to suggest to students that they learn other methods. Notice how difficult it is for you to begin computations by working from the left rather than the right and to think in terms of whole numbers rather than digits. These habits, once established, are difficult to break.

Can the traditional algorithms be taught meaningfully? Absolutely! Meaningful approaches for teaching each algorithm will be discussed. If you plan to teach the traditional algorithms, you are well advised to first spend a significant time with invented strategies. Do not feel that you must rush to the traditional methods. Delay! Spend most of your effort on invented methods. The understanding children gain from working with invented strategies will make it much easier for you to teach the traditional methods.

Traditional Algorithms Will Happen

You probably cannot keep the traditional algorithms out of your classroom. Children pick up the traditional algorithms from older siblings, last year's teacher, well-meaning parents ("My dad showed me an easy way"). Traditional algorithms are in no way evil, and so to forbid their use is somewhat arbitrary. However, students who latch on to a traditional method often resist the invention of more flexible strategies. What do you do then?

First and foremost, apply the same rule to traditional algorithms as to all strategies: *If you use it, you must understand why it works and be able to explain it.* In an atmosphere that says, "Let's figure out why this works," students can profit from making sense of these algorithms just like any other. But the responsibility should be theirs, not yours.

Accept a traditional algorithm (once it is understood) as one more strategy to put in the class "tool box" of methods. But reinforce the idea that like the other strategies, it may be more useful in some instances than in others. Pose problems where a mental strategy is much more useful, such as 504 − 498 or 75 × 4. Discuss which method seemed best. Point out that for a problem such as 4568 + 12,813, the traditional algorithm has some advantages. But in the real world, most people do those computations on a calculator.

Development of Invented Strategies: A General Approach

Students do not spontaneously invent wonderful computational methods while the teacher sits back and watches. Among different experimental programs, students tended to develop or gravitate toward different strategies suggesting that teachers and the programs do have an effect on what methods students develop (Fuson et al., 1997). This section discusses general pedagogical methods for helping children develop invented strategies.

Use Story Problems Frequently

When computational tasks are embedded in simple contexts, students seem to be more engaged than they are with bare computations. Furthermore, the choice of story problems influences the strategies students use to solve them. Consider these problems:

Max had already saved 68 cents when Mom gave him some money for running an errand. Now Max has 93 cents. How much did Max earn for his errand?

George took 93 cents to the store. He spent 68 cents. How much does he have left?

The computation 93 − 68 solves both problems, but the first is more likely than the second to be solved by an add-on method. In a similar manner, fair-share division problems are more likely to encourage a share strategy than a measurement or repeated subtraction problem.

Not every task need be a story problem. Especially when students are engaged in figuring out a new strategy, bare arithmetic problems are quite adequate.

Use the Three-Part Lesson Format

The three-part lesson format described in Chapter 4 is a good structure for an invented-strategy lesson. The task can be one or two story problems or even a bare computation but always with the expectation that the method of solution will be discussed. Sometimes you can provide variations with different numbers to different groups to adjust for difficulty.

Allow plenty of time to solve a problem. Listen to the different strategies students are using, but do not interject your own. Challenge able students to find a second method, solve a problem without models, or improve on a written explanation. Allow children who are not ready for thinking with tens to use simple counting methods. Students who finish quickly may share their methods with others before sharing with the class.

The most important portion of the lesson comes when students explain their solution methods. Help students write their explanations on the board or overhead. Encourage students to ask questions of their classmates. Occasionally have the class try a particular method with different numbers to see how it works. When students find a particular idea worthwhile, record it on a "strategies chart." Remember, not every student will invent strategies. However, students can and will try strategies that they have seen and that make sense to them. Make a firm rule that *no one may use a strategy that he or she does not understand.*

Progression from Direct Modeling

Direct modeling involving tens and ones can and will lead eventually to invented strategies. However, students may need to be encouraged to move away from the direct modeling process. Here are some ideas:

- Record students' verbal explanations on the board in ways that they and others can model. Have the class follow the recorded method using different numbers.
- Ask students who have just solved a problem with models to see if they can do it in their heads.
- Pose a problem to the class, and ask students to solve it mentally if they are able.
- Ask children to make a written numeric record of what they did when they solved the problem with models. Explain that they are then going to try to use the same method on a new problem.

Invented Strategies for Addition and Subtraction

Research has demonstrated that children will invent a lot of different strategies for addition and subtraction. Your goal might be that each of your children has at least one or two methods that are reasonably efficient, mathematically correct, and useful with lots of different numbers. Expect different children to settle on different strategies.

It is not at all unreasonable for students to be able to add and subtract two-digit numbers mentally by third grade.

However, daily recording of strategies on the board not only helps communicate ideas but also helps children who need the short-term memory assistance of recording intermediate steps.

Adding and Subtracting Single Digits

Children can easily extend addition and subtraction facts to higher decades.

Tommy was on page 47 of his book. Then he read 8 more pages. How many pages did Tommy read in all?

If students are simply counting on by ones, the following activity may be useful. It is an extension of the make-ten strategy for addition facts.

ACTIVITY 13.1

Ten-Frame Adding and Subtracting

Quickly review the make-ten idea from addition facts using two ten-frames. (Add on to get up to ten and then add the rest.) Challenge children to use the same idea to add on to a two-digit number as shown in Figure 13.3. Two students can work together. First, they make a specified two-digit number with the little ten-frame cards. They then stack up all of the less-than-ten cards and turn them over one at a time. Together they talk about how to get the total quickly.

The same approach is used for subtraction. For instance, for 53 – 7, take off 3 to get to 50, then 4 more is 46.

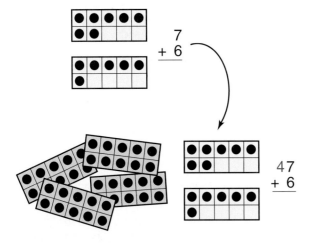

FIGURE 13.3 Little ten-frame cards can help children extend the make-ten idea to larger numbers.

Adding and Subtracting Tens and Hundreds

Sums and differences involving multiples of 10 or 100 are easily computed mentally. Write a problem such as the following on the board:

$$300 + 500 + 20$$

Challenge children to solve it mentally. Ask students to share how they did it. Look for use of place-value words: "3 *hundred* and 5 *hundred* is 8 *hundred,* and 20 is 820."

Use base-ten models to help children begin to think in terms of tens and hundreds. Early examples should not include any trades. The exercise 420 + 300 involves no trades, whereas 70 + 80 may be more difficult.

Adding Two-Digit Numbers

For the examples that follow, a possible recording method is offered. These are intended to be suggestions, not prescriptions. Children have difficulty inventing recording techniques. If you record their ideas on the board as they explain their ideas, you are helping them develop written techniques. You may even discuss recording methods with individuals or with the class to decide on a form that seems to work well. Horizontal formats encourage students to think in terms of numbers instead of digits. A horizontal format is also less likely to encourage use of the traditional algorithms.

Students will often use a counting-by-tens-and-ones technique for some of these methods. That is, instead of "46 + 30 is 76," they may count "46 ⟶ 56, 66, 76." These counts can be written down as they are said to help students keep track.

Figure 13.4 illustrates four different strategies for addition of two two-digit numbers. The following story problem is a suggestion.

The two Scout troops went on a field trip. There were 46 Girl Scouts and 38 Boy Scouts. How many Scouts went on the trip?

The *move to make ten* and *compensation* strategies are useful when one of the numbers ends in 8 or 9. To promote that strategy, present problems with addends like 39 or 58. Note that it is only necessary to adjust one of the two numbers.

 Try adding 367 + 155 in as many different ways as you can. How many of your ways are like those in Figure 13.4?

Invented Strategies for Addition with Two-Digit Numbers

Add Tens, Add Ones, Then Combine

46 + 38

40 and 30 is 70.
6 and 8 is 14.
70 and 14 is 84.

$$\begin{array}{r} 46 \\ +38 \\ \hline 70 \\ 14 \\ \hline 84 \end{array}$$

Add On Tens, Then Add Ones

46 + 38

46 and 30 more is 76.
Then I added on the other 8.
76 and 4 is 80 and 4 is 84.

$46 + 38 \rightarrow$
$76 + 8 \rightarrow 80, 84$

Move Some to Make Tens

46 + 38

Take 2 from the 46 and put
it with the 38 to make 40.
Now you have 44 and 40
more is 84.

$$\overset{2}{4\!\!6 + 3\!\!8}$$
$$44 + 40$$
$$84$$

Use a Nice Number and Compensate

46 + 38

46 and 40 is 86.
That's 2 extra, so it's 84.

$46 + 38$
$46 + 40 \rightarrow$
$86 - 2 \rightarrow 84$

FIGURE 13.4 Four different invented strategies for adding two two-digit numbers.

Subtracting by Counting Up

This is an amazingly powerful way to subtract. Students working on the *think-addition* strategy for their basic facts can also be solving problems with larger numbers. The concept is the same. It is important to use *join with change unknown* problems or *missing-part* problems to encourage the counting-up strategy. Here is an example of each.

Sam had 46 baseball cards. He went to a card show and got some more cards for his collection. Now he has 73 cards. How many cards did Sam buy at the card show?

Juanita counted all of her crayons. Some were broken and some not. She had 73 crayons in all. 46 crayons were not broken. How many were broken?

The numbers in these problems are used in the strategies illustrated in Figure 13.5.

Take-Away Subtraction

Using take-away is considerably more difficult to do mentally. However, take-away strategies are common, probably because traditional textbooks emphasize take-away as the

---

Invented Strategies for Subtraction by Counting Up

Add Tens to Get Close, Then Ones

73 − 46

46 and 20 is 66.
(30 more is too much.)
Then 4 more is 70 and 3 is 73.
That's 20 and 7 or 27.

$$\begin{array}{r} 46 > 20 \\ 66 > 4 \\ 70 > 3 \\ 73 \hline \\ 27 \end{array}$$

Add Tens to Overshoot, Then Come Back

73 − 46

46 and 30 is 76.
That's 3 too much,
so it's 27.

73 − 46
$46 + 30 \rightarrow 76 - 3 \rightarrow 73$
$30 - 3 = 27$

Add Ones to Make a Ten, Then Tens and Ones

73 − 46

46 and 4 is 50.
50 and 20 is 70 and 3
more is 73. The 4 and 3
is 7 and 20 is 27.

$$\begin{array}{r} 73 - 46 \\ 46 + 4 \rightarrow 50 \\ + 20 \rightarrow 70 \\ + 3 \rightarrow 73 \\ \hline 27 \end{array}$$

Similarly,
46 and 4 is 50.
50 and 23 is 73.
23 and 4 is 27.

$46 + 4 \rightarrow 50$
$50 + 23 \rightarrow 73$
$23 + 4 = 27$

FIGURE 13.5 Subtraction by counting up is a powerful method.

FIGURE 13.6 Take-away strategies work reasonably well for two-digit problems. They are a bit more difficult with three digits.

Invented Strategies for Take-Away Subtraction

Take Tens from the Tens, Then Subtract Ones

73 – 46

70 minus 40 is 30.
Take away 6 more
is 24.
Now add in the
3 ones → 27.

$70 - 40 \rightarrow 30 - 6 \rightarrow$
$24 + 3 \rightarrow 27$

Or

70 minus 40 is 30.
I can take those 3 away,
but I need 3 more
from the 30 to make 27.

73
– 46
30
– 3
27

Take Away Tens, Then Ones

73 – 46

73 minus 40 is 33.
Then take away 6:
3 makes 30 and
3 more is 27.

$73 - 40 \rightarrow 33 - 3$
$30 - 3 \rightarrow 27$

Take Extra Tens, Then Add Back

73 – 46

73 take away 50 is 23.
That's 4 too many.
23 and 4 is 27.

$73 - 50 \rightarrow 23 + 4$
27

Add to the Whole If Necessary

73 – 46

Give 3 to 73 to make 76.
76 take away 46 is 30.
Now give 3 back → 27.

+3
73 – 46
$76 - 46 \rightarrow 30$
$- 3 \rightarrow 27$

---

meaning of subtraction. Four different strategies are shown in Figure 13.6.

There were 73 children on the playground. The 46 second-grade students came in first. How many children were still outside?

The two methods that begin by taking tens from tens are reflective of what most students do with base-ten pieces (Madell, 1985). The other two methods leave one of the numbers intact and subtract from it. Try 83 – 29 in your head by first taking away 30 and adding 1 back. This is a good mental method when subtracting a number that is close to a multiple of ten.

Sometimes we need to be reminded of what comes naturally to children. Campbell (1997) tested over 2000 students in Baltimore who had not been taught the traditional algorithm for subtraction. Not one student began with the ones place!

 Try computing 82 – 57. Use both take-away and counting up methods. Can you use all of the strategies in Figure 13.5 and 13.6 without looking?

Extensions and Challenges

Each of the examples in the preceding sections involved sums less than 100 and all involved *bridging a ten*; that is, if done with a traditional algorithm, they require carrying or bor-

rowing. Bridging, the size of the numbers, and the potential for doing problems mentally are all issues to consider.

Bridging

For most of the strategies, it is easier to add or subtract when bridging is not required. Try each strategy with 34 + 52 or 68 – 24 to see how it works. Easier problems instill confidence. They also permit you to challenge your students with a "harder one." There is also the issue of bridging 100 or 1000. Try 58 + 67 with different strategies. Bridging across 100 is also an issue for subtraction. Problems such as 128 – 50 or 128 – 45 are more difficult than ones that do not bridge 100.

Larger Numbers

Most curricula will expect third graders to add and subtract three-digit numbers. Your state standards may even require work with four-digit numbers. Try seeing how *you* would do these without using the traditional algorithms: 487 + 235 and 623 – 247. For subtraction, a counting-up strategy is usually the easiest. Occasionally, other strategies appear with larger numbers. For example, "chunking off" multiples of 50 or 25 is often a useful method. For 462 + 257, pull out 450 and 250 to make 700. That leaves 12 and 7 more ⟶ 719.

Activities for Flexible Thinking

In addition to the ideas from the preceding section, students also need experiences to help them develop flexibility with numbers so that they can and will create those flexible approaches. This section offers some ideas.

Working with Tens and Hundreds

In the discussion of place value (Chapter 12), considerable attention was given to the hundreds chart. Activities with the hundreds chart should continue as children develop computational strategies. The row structure of the hundreds chart emphasizes each decade. Many invented strategies involve bridging but do not involve regrouping. The chart helps to develop methods involving adding up to the next ten.

Many of the skills of invented strategies appear in the next activity, which combines symbolism with base-ten representations. In all of these activities, class discussion should have children explain how they did the exercises or tell how they thought about them.

ACTIVITY 13.2

Numbers, Squares, Sticks, and Dots

As illustrated in Figure 13.7, prepare a worksheet or overhead transparency on which a numeral and some base-ten pieces are shown. Use small squares, sticks, and dots for base-ten pieces to keep drawing simple. Students write the totals that they compute mentally.

Figure 13.8 is a take-away version of the same activity. As shown, the amount removed can be either the numeral or the squares and sticks. Try it both ways.

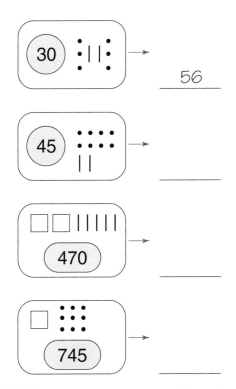

FIGURE 13.7 **Flexible counting on or addition using both models and numerals.**

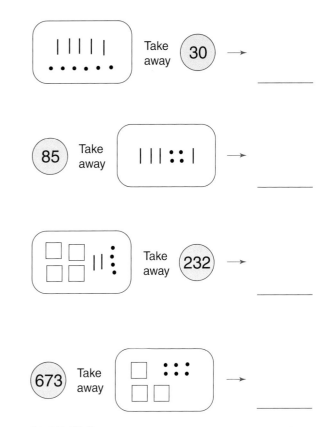

FIGURE 13.8 **Counting back or subtraction using both models and numerals.**

Thinking About Parts of Numbers

Another important focus involves thinking about a number in terms of two parts, especially thinking about a missing part, which is the agenda of the next several activities.

Often in computations it is useful to recognize that a number can be made up of a "nice" number and some more. The nice part (maybe a multiple of 50 or 100) is dealt with first and then the smaller leftover piece can be considered.

ACTIVITY 13.3

50 and Some More

Say a number between 50 and 100. Students respond with "50 and _____." For 63, the response is "50 and 13." Use other numbers that end in 50 such as "450 and some more."

Nice numbers also are often broken apart in computations. The next two activities are extremely useful for developing the thinking required for counting-up approaches to subtraction.

Introduce these activities to the full class using the overhead projector. Have students share their thinking strategies.

ACTIVITY 13.4

The Other Part of 100

Two students work together with a set of little ten-frame cards. One student makes a two-digit number. Then both students work mentally to determine what goes with the ten-frame amount to make 100. They write their solutions on paper and then check by making the other part with the cards to see if the total is 100. Students take turns making the original number. Figure 13.9 shows three different thought processes that students might use.

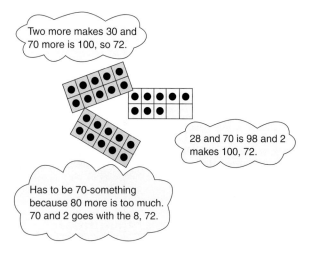

FIGURE 13.9 Using little ten-frames to help think about the "other part of 100."

Being able to give the other part of 100 is so useful in invented strategies that students should get quite good at it.

If your students are adept at parts of 100, you can change the whole from 100 to another number. At first try other multiples of 10 such as 70 or 80. Then extend the whole to any number less than 100.

⊗ **STOP** Suppose that the whole is 83. Sketch four little ten-frame cards showing 36. Looking at your "cards," what goes with 36 to make 83? How did you think about it?

What you just did in finding the other part of 83 was subtract 36 from 83. You did not borrow or regroup. Most likely you did it in your head. With more practice you (and students as early as the third grade) can do this without the aid of the cards.

Compatible numbers for addition and subtraction are numbers that go together easily to make nice numbers. Num-

bers that make tens or hundreds are the most common examples. Compatible sums also include numbers that end in 5, 25, 50, or 75, since these numbers are easy to work with as well. The teaching task is to get students accustomed to looking for combinations that work together and then looking for these combinations in computational situations.

ACTIVITY 13.5

Compatible Pairs

Searching for compatible pairs can be done as a worksheet activity or with the full class using the overhead projector. Prepare a transparency, or duplicate a page with a search task. Five possibilities of different difficulty levels are shown in Figure 13.10. Students call out or connect the compatible pairs as they see them.

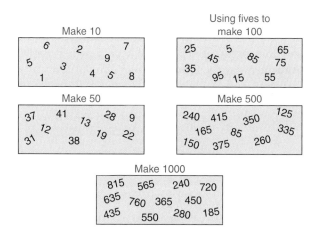

FIGURE 13.10 Compatible-pair searches.

Here are two more activities that combine some of the ideas we have been exploring.

ACTIVITY 13.6

Calculator Challenge Counting

Students press any number on the calculator (e.g., 17), then ⊞ 8. They say the sum before they press ⊟. Then they continue to add 8 mentally, challenging themselves to say the number before they press ⊟. They should see how far they can go before making a mistake.

The constant addend in "Challenge Counting" can be any number, even a two- or three-digit number. Try 20 or 25. Try 40 and then 48. As an added challenge, after a student has progressed eight or ten counts, have the student reverse the process by pressing ⊟ followed by the same number and then ⊟, ⊟, ... Discuss patterns that appear.

ACTIVITY 13.7

Little Ten-Frame Addition and Subtraction

Provide a set of little ten-frame cards for each of two students. Each student makes a number with his or her cards. When both have their number ready, they place it out so both can see. Then they try to be the first to tell the total. For the subtraction version, one student makes a number greater than 50 and the other writes a number on paper that is less than 50. The written number is to be subtracted from the modeled number. Students should be encouraged to share strategies to see how fast they can get.

Although activities like those in this section can be done independently or in pairs, it is good to occasionally do them with the full class so that strategies can be discussed.

 ## Assessment Notes

Students who exhibit difficulty with any of these activities will also have difficulty with almost any type of invented computation. For example, how do students go about the exercises in Activity 13.2, "Numbers, Squares, Sticks, and Dots"? This activity demands that children have sufficient understanding of base-ten concepts that they can use them in meaningful counts. If students are counting by ones, perhaps on their fingers, then more practice with these activities may be misplaced. Consider additional counting and grouping activities (Chapter 12) where students have the opportunity to see the value of groups of ten. ■

NCTM Standards A reading of the Number and Operation standard in both the pre-K–2 and 3–5 chapters will clearly demonstrate that the *Standards* are supportive of the approaches described in this chapter. For example, "When students compute with strategies they invent or choose because they are meaningful, their learning tends to be robust—they are able to remember and apply their knowledge. Children with specific learning disabilities can actively invent and transfer strategies if given well-designed tasks that are developmentally appropriate" (p. 86).

 # Traditional Algorithms for Addition and Subtraction

The traditional algorithms require an understanding of *regrouping*, exchanging 10 in one place-value position for 1 in the position to the left—or the reverse, exchanging 1 for 10 in the position to the right. The corresponding terms *carry-ing* and *borrowing* are obsolete and conceptually misleading. The word *regroup* also has little meaning for young children. A preferable term is *trade*. Ten ones are *traded* for a ten. A hundred is *traded* for 10 tens.

It is a serious error to work for mastery of nonregrouping problems before tackling regrouping. To keep these problems separate has been the documented source of many error patterns. Teaching nonregrouping problems first causes bad habits that children must later unlearn.

If you develop traditional algorithms in a problem-solving manner, there is no reason why your students should not be expected to understand them!

The Addition Algorithm

Explain to the students that they are going to learn a method of adding that most "big people" learned when they were in school. It is not the only way or even the best way; it is just a method you want them to learn.

Begin with Models Only

In the beginning, avoid any written work except for the possible recording of an answer. Provide children with place-value mats and base-ten models. The mat with two ten-frames in the ones place (Blackline Masters) is suggested.

Have students make one number at the top of the mat and a second beneath it as shown in the top portion of Figure 13.11.

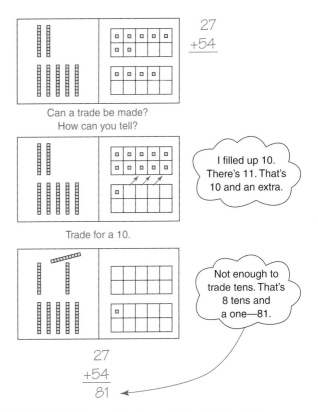

FIGURE 13.11 **Working from right to left in addition.**

If children are still developing base-ten concepts, a groupable model such as counters in cups is most helpful.

Explain this one rule: *You begin in the ones column.* "This is a way people came up with a long time ago, and it worked for them." Let students solve the problem on their own. Provide plenty of time, and then have students explain what they did and why. Let students use overhead models or magnetic pieces to help with their explanations.

One or two problems in a lesson with lots of discussion is much more productive than a lot of problems based on rules children don't understand.

Develop the Written Record

Reproduce pages with simple place-value charts similar to those shown in Figure 13.12. The charts will help young children record numerals in columns. The general idea is to have children record on these pages each step of the procedure they

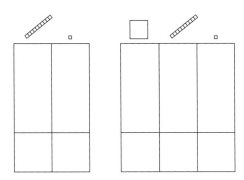

FIGURE 13.12 Blank recording charts are helpful (see Blackline Masters).

do with the base-ten models *as it is done*. The first few times you do this, guide each step carefully, as illustrated in Figure 13.13. A similar approach would be used for three-digit problems.

FIGURE 13.13 Help students record on paper each step they do on their mats as they do it.

Group ones.

How much is in the ones column? (14)

Will you need to make a trade? (yes)

How many tens will you make? (1) How many ones will be left? (4)

Good! Make the trade now.

Trade for a ten.

Let's stop now and record exactly what we have done. You had 14 ones, and you made 1 ten and 4. Write a small "1" at the top of the tens column to show the ten you put there and a "4" in the answer space of the ones column for the 4 ones left.

Look at the tens column on your mat. You have 1 ten on top, 3 from the 36, and 4 more from the 48. See how your paper shows the same thing?

Group tens.

Now add all the tens together. Write how many tens that is in the answer space for the tens column.

FIGURE 13.14 An alternative recording scheme for addition. Notice that this can be used from left to right as well as from right to left.

A suggestion is to have children work in pairs. One child is responsible for the models and the other for recording the steps. Children reverse roles with each problem.

Figure 13.14 shows a variation of the traditional recording scheme that is quite reasonable, at least for up to three digits. It avoids the little "carried ones" and focuses attention on the value of the digits. If students were permitted to start adding on the left as they are inclined to do, this recording procedure is the same as that shown for the invented strategy "Add tens, add ones, then combine" (Figure 13.4, p. 207).

The Subtraction Algorithm

The general approach to developing the subtraction algorithm is the same as for addition. When the procedure is completely understood with models, a do-and-write approach connects it with a written form.

Begin with Models Only

Start by having children model the top number in a subtraction problem on the top half of their place-value mats. For the amount to be subtracted, have children write each digit on a small piece of paper and place these pieces near the bottom of their mats in the respective columns, as in Figure 13.15. To avoid inadvertent errors, suggest making all trades first. That way, the full amount on the paper slip can be taken off at once. Also explain to children that they are to begin working with the ones column first, as they did with addition.

Anticipate Difficulties with Zeros

Exercises in which zeros are involved anywhere in the problem tend to cause special difficulties. Give extra attention to these cases while still using models.

The very common error of "borrowing across zero" is best addressed at the modeling stage. For example, in 403 − 138,

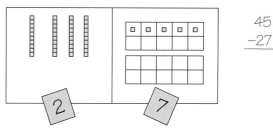

Not enough ones to take off 7.
Trade a ten for 10 ones.

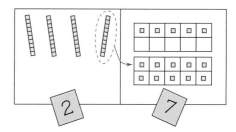

Now there are 15 ones.
I can take 7 off easily.

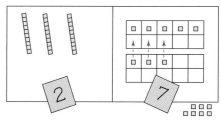

It does not matter which ones come off. Put the leftovers together.

And now I can take off 2 tens.

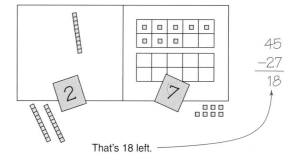

That's 18 left.

FIGURE 13.15 Two-place subtraction with models.

children must make a double trade, exchanging a hundreds piece for 10 tens and then one of the tens for 10 ones.

Develop the Written Record

The process of recording each step as it is done is the same as was suggested for addition. The same recording sheets (Figure 13.12) are also recommended.

When children can explain symbolism, that is a signal for moving children on to a completely symbolic level. Again, be attentive to problems with zeros.

$$\begin{array}{r}
{\scriptstyle 13\ \ 14} \\
7\cancel{3}\cancel{4} \\
-275 \\
\hline
\cancel{5}00 \\
4\cancel{6}0 \\
59 \\
\hline
459
\end{array}$$

FIGURE 13.16 A left-hand recording scheme for subtraction. Other methods can also be devised.

If students are permitted to follow their natural instincts and begin with the big pieces (from the left instead of the right), recording schemes similar to that shown in Figure 13.16 are possible. The trades are made from the pieces remaining *after* the subtraction in the column to the left has been done. A "borrow across zero" difficulty will still occur, but in problems like this: 462 − 168. Try it.

Invented Strategies for Multiplication

Computation strategies for multiplication are considerably more complex than for addition and subtraction. Often, but by no means always, the strategies that students invent are very similar to the traditional algorithm. The big difference is that students think about numbers, not digits. They always begin with the large or left-hand numbers.

For multiplication, the ability to break numbers apart in flexible ways is even more important than in addition or subtraction. The distributive property is another concept that is important in multiplication computation. For example, to multiply 43 × 5, one might think about breaking 43 into 40 and 3, multiplying each by 5, and then adding the results. Children require ample opportunities to develop these concepts by making sense of their own ideas and those of their classmates.

Useful Representations

The problem 34 × 6 may be represented in a number of ways, as illustrated in Figure 13.17. Often the choice of a model is influenced by a story problem. To determine how many Easter eggs 34 children need if each colors 6 eggs, children may model 6 sets of 34 (or possibly 34 sets of 6). If the problem is about the area of a rectangle that is 34 cm by 6 cm, then some

form of an array is likely. But each representation is appropriate for thinking about 34 × 6 regardless of the context, and students should get to a point where they select ways to think about multiplication that are meaningful to them.

How children represent a product interacts with their methods for determining answers. The groups of 34 might suggest repeated additions—perhaps taking the sets two at a time. Double 34 is 68 and there are three of those, so 68 + 68 + 68. From there a variety of methods are possible.

The six sets of base-ten pieces might suggest breaking the numbers into tens and ones: 6 times 3 tens or 6 × 30 and 6 × 4. Some children use the tens individually: 6 tens make 60. So that's 60 and 60 and 60 (180). Then add on the 24 to make 204.

It is not uncommon to arrange the base-ten pieces in a nice array, even if the story problem does not suggest it. The area model is very much like an arrangement of the base-ten pieces.

All of these ideas should be part of students' repertoire of models for multidigit multiplication. Introduce different

FIGURE 13.17 Different ways to model 34 × 6 may support different computational strategies.

representations (one at a time) as ways to explore multiplication until you are comfortable that the class has a collection of useful ideas. At the same time, do not force students who reason very well without drawings to use models when they are not needed.

Multiplication by a Single-Digit Multiplier

As with addition and subtraction, it is helpful to place multiplication tasks in contextual story problems. Let students model the problems in ways that make sense to them. Do not be concerned about mixing of factors (6 sets of 34 or 34 sets of 6). Nor should you be timid about the numbers you use. The problem 3 × 24 may be easier than 7 × 65, but the latter provides challenge. The types of strategies that students use for multiplication are much more varied than for addition and subtraction. However, the following three categories can be identified from the research to date.

Complete-Number Strategies

Children who are not yet comfortable breaking numbers into parts using tens and ones will approach the numbers in the sets as single groups. For students who think this way, Figure 13.18 illustrates two methods they may use. These children will benefit from listening to children who use base-ten models. They may also need more work with base-ten grouping activities where they take numbers apart in different ways.

Partitioning Strategies

Children break numbers up in a variety of ways that reflect an understanding of base-ten concepts, at least four of which

FIGURE 13.18 **Children who use a complete-number strategy do not break numbers apart into decades or tens and ones.**

are illustrated in Figure 13.19. The "By Decades" approach is the same as the standard algorithm except that students always begin with the large values. It extends easily to three digits and is very powerful as a mental math strategy. Another valuable strategy for mental methods is found in the "Other Partitions" example. It is easy to compute mentally with multiples of 25 and 50 and then add or subtract a small adjustment. All partition strategies rely on the distributive property.

Compensation Strategies

Children look for ways to manipulate numbers so that the calculations are easy. In Figure 13.20, the problem 27 × 4 is changed to an easier one, and then an adjustment or compensation is made. In the second example, one factor is cut in half and the other doubled. This is often used when a 5 or

FIGURE 13.19 **Numbers can be broken apart in different ways to make easier partial products, which are then combined. Partitioning by decades is useful for mental computation and is very close to the standard algorithm.**

Compensation Strategies for Multiplication

27×4

$27 + 3 \rightarrow 30 \times 4 \longrightarrow 120$
$3 \times 4 = 12 \longrightarrow -12$
$\overline{108}$

250×5

I can split 250 in half
and multiply by 10.
$125 \times 10 = 1250$

17×70

3×70

$20 \times 70 \longrightarrow 1400 - 210 \longrightarrow 1190$

FIGURE 13.20 Compensation methods use a product related to the original. A compensation is made in the answer, or one factor is changed to compensate for a change in the other factor.

a 50 is involved. Because these strategies are so dependent on the numbers involved, they can't be used for all computations. However, they are powerful strategies, especially for mental math and estimation.

Using Multiples of 10 and 100

There is a value in exposing students early to products involving multiples of 10 and 100.

The Scout troop wanted to package up 400 fire starter kits as a fund-raising project. If each pack will have 12 fire starters, how many fire starters are the Scouts going to need?

Children will use $4 \times 12 = 48$ to figure out that 400×12 is 4800. There will be discussion around how to say and write "forty-eight hundred." Be aware of students who simply tack on zeros without understanding why. Try problems such as 30×60 or 210×40 where tens are multiplied by tens.

Two-Digit Multipliers: The Area Model

A problem such as this one can be solved in many different ways:

The parade had 23 clowns. Each clown carried 18 balloons. How many balloons were there altogether?

Some children look for smaller products such as 6×23 and then add that result three times. Another method is to do 20×23 and then subtract 2×23. Others will calculate four separate partial products: $10 \times 20 = 200$, $8 \times 20 = 160$,

$10 \times 3 = 30$, and $8 \times 3 = 24$. And still others may add up a string of 23s. Two-digit multiplication is both complex and challenging. But children can solve these problems in a variety of interesting ways, many of which will contribute to the development of the traditional algorithm or one that is just as efficient. Time devoted to working on these tasks in the fourth through sixth grades is well spent.

A valuable exploration is to prepare large rectangles for each group of two or three students. The rectangles should be measured carefully, with dimensions between 25 cm and 60 cm, and drawn accurately with square corners. (Use the corner of a piece of poster board for a guide.) The students' task is to determine how many small ones pieces (base-ten materials) will fit inside. Wooden or plastic base-ten pieces are best, but cardboard strips and squares are adequate. Alternatively, rectangles can be drawn on base-ten grid paper (see Blackline Masters), or students can simply be given the task verbally: *What is the area of a rectangle that is 47 cm by 36 cm?*

Most children will fill the rectangle first with as many hundreds pieces as possible. One obvious approach is to put the 12 hundreds in one corner. This will leave narrow regions on two sides that can be filled with tens pieces and a final small rectangle that will hold ones. Especially if students have had earlier experiences with finding products in arrays, figuring out the size of each subrectangle is not terribly difficult. The sketch in Figure 13.21 shows the four regions.

STOP If you did not already know the algorithm, how would you determine the size of the rectangle? Use your method (not the standard algorithm) on a rectangle that measures 68 cm × 24 cm. Make a sketch to show and explain your work.

As you will see in the discussion of the traditional algorithm, the area model leads to a fairly reasonable approach to multiplying numbers, even if you never have students "carry," which is a source of many errors.

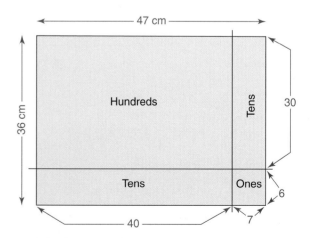

FIGURE 13.21 Ones, tens, and hundreds pieces fit exactly into the four sections of this 47 × 36 rectangle. Figure the size of each section to determine the size of the whole rectangle.

INVESTIGATIONS in NUMBER, DATA, and SPACE

Grade 4, *Packages and Groups*
Investigation 2: Double-Digit Multiplication

Context

This unit occurs in the latter half of the fourth grade. Earlier in the same grade, children are introduced to the general approach of cluster problems, which is the topic of the task described here. In the earlier unit, students explored ways to multiply two-digit numbers by one-digit numbers. Here they are working on more difficult tasks. The same approach is used later for division.

Task Description

Cluster problems are a major feature of this unit and are found in quite a few of the investigations. This rather unique approach to the topic encourages students to use facts and combinations they know in order to figure out complex computations. For example, the following cluster is used in an introductory lesson in the unit: $3 \times 7, 5 \times 7, 10 \times 7, 50 \times 7$, and 53×7. The goal is to figure out the last product. Students solve all of the problems and explain what problems were helpful in solving the last problem. Not every problem in the clusters needs to be used to solve the final problem.

The figure here is taken from the teacher notes showing how a student completed one of the cluster problem worksheets. Notice how students draw lines to show connections and add new problems.

Here are two cluster problems taken from a worksheet found later in the unit:

$3 \times 50, \quad 10 \times 50, \quad 34 \times 25, \quad 30 \times 50, \quad \mathbf{34 \times 50}$

$60 \times 20, \quad 62 \times 10, \quad 62 \times 3, \quad \mathbf{62 \times 23}$

Students are asked to make an estimate of the last problem before they solve the cluster problems including the

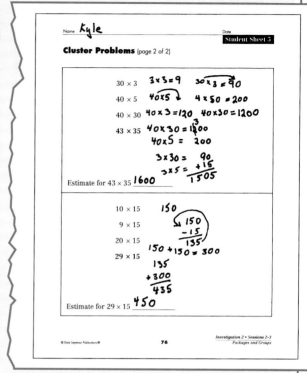

Page 76 from *Multiplication and Division: Packages and Groups* by K. Economopoulos, S. J. Russell, & C. Tierney. *Investigations in Number, Data, and Space.* Copyright © 1998 by Dale Seymour Publications, Inc. Reprinted by permission of Pearson Education, Inc.

last problem. Students are encouraged to add their own helping problems to the clusters if they wish. Later, students make up their own cluster problems for a given problem. That is essentially solving the problems without any assistance—using easier related problems is a general strategy for invented approaches to multiplication.

In the fourth and fifth grades of *Investigations in Number, Data, and Space,* one approach to multidigit multiplication is called "cluster problems." The excerpt on this page explains the approach and shows an example. This method could easily be incorporated into any program.

The Traditional Algorithm for Multiplication

The traditional multiplication algorithm is probably the most difficult of the four algorithms if students have not had plenty of opportunities to explore their own strategies. The multiplication algorithm can be meaningfully developed using either a repeated addition model or an area model. For single-digit multipliers, the difference is minimal. When you move to two-digit multipliers, the area model has some advantages. For that reason, the discussion here will use the area model.

One-Digit Multipliers

As with the other algorithms, as much time as possible should be devoted to the conceptual development of the algorithm with the recording or written part coming later.

Begin with Models

Give students a drawing of a rectangle 47 cm by 6 cm. *How many small square centimeter pieces will fit in the rectangle?*

FIGURE 13.22 **A rectangle filled with base-ten pieces is a useful model for two-digit-by-one-digit multiplication.**

6 times 40 is 240.

or

6 ones times 4 tens is 24 tens, or 240.

6 ones times 7 ones is 42 ones.

(What is the area of the rectangle in square centimeters?) Let students solve the problem in groups before discussing it as a class.

As shown in Figure 13.22, the rectangle can be "sliced" or separated into two parts so that one part will be 6 ones by 7 ones, or 42 ones, and the other will be 6 ones by 4 tens, or 24 tens. Notice that the base-ten language "6 ones times 4 tens is 24 tens" tells how many *pieces* (sticks of ten) are in the big section. To say "6 times 40 is 240" is also correct and tells how many units or square centimeters are in the section. Each section is referred to as a *partial product*. By adding the two partial products, you get the total product or area of the rectangle.

To avoid the tedium of drawing large rectangles and arranging base-ten pieces, use the base-ten grid paper found in the Blackline Masters. On the grid paper, students can easily draw accurate rectangles showing all of the pieces. Check to be sure students understand that for a product such as 74 × 8, there are two partial products, 70 × 8 = 560 and 4 × 8 = 32, and the sum of these is the product. Do not force any recording technique on students until they understand how to use the two dimensions of a rectangle to get a product.

Develop the Written Record

To help with a recording scheme, provide sheets with base-ten columns on which students can record problems. When the two partial products are written separately as in Figure 13.23(a), there is little new to learn. Students simply record the products and add them together. As illustrated, it is possible to teach students how to write the first product with a carried digit so that the combined product is written on one line. This traditional recording scheme is known to be problematic. The little carried digit is often the source of difficulty—it gets added in before the second multiplication or is forgotten.

There is absolutely no practical reason why students can't be allowed to record both partial products and avoid the errors related to the carried digit. When you accept that, it makes no difference in which order the products are written. Why not simply permit students to do written multiplication as shown in Figure 13.23? When the factors are in a word

problem, chart, or other format, all that is really necessary is to write down all the partial products and add. Furthermore, that is precisely how this is done mentally.

Most standard curricula progress from two digits to three digits with a single-digit multiplier. Students can make this progression easily. They still should be permitted to write all three partial products separately and not have to bother with carrying.

Two-Digit Multipliers

With the area model, the progression to a two-digit multiplier is relatively straightforward. Rectangles can be drawn on base-ten grid paper, or full-sized rectangles can be filled in with base-ten pieces. There will be four partial products, corresponding to four different sections of the rectangle.

Several variations in language might be used. Consider the product 47 × 36 as illustrated in Figure 13.24. In the partial product 40 × 30, if base-ten language is used—*4 tens times 3 tens is 12 hundreds*—the result tells how many hundreds pieces are in that section. Verbally, the product "forty

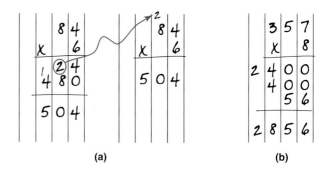

(a)   (b)

FIGURE 13.23 **(a) In the standard form, the product of ones is recorded first. The tens digit of this first product can be written as a "carried" digit above the tens column. (b) It is quite reasonable to abandon the carried digit and permit the partial products to be recorded in any order.**

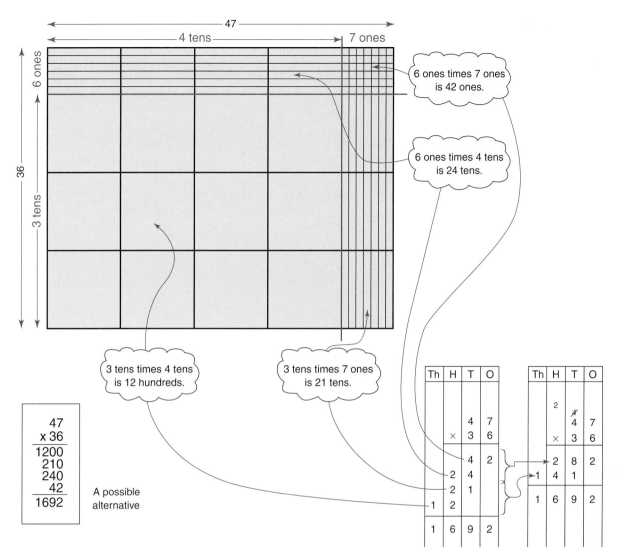

FIGURE 13.24 **47 × 36 rectangle filled with base-ten pieces. Base-ten language connects the four partial products to the traditional written format. Note the possibility of recording the products in some other order.**

times thirty" is formidable. Try to avoid "four times three," which promotes thinking about digits rather than numbers. It is well worth stressing the idea that in all cases, a product of *tens times tens is hundreds.*

Figure 13.24 also shows the recording of four partial products in the traditional order and how these can be collapsed to two lines if carried digits are used. Here the second "carry" technically belongs in the hundreds column but it rarely is written there. Often it gets confused with the first and is thus an additional source of errors. The lower left of the figure shows the same computation with all four products written in a different order. This is quite an acceptable algorithm. In the rare instance when someone multiplies numbers such as 538 × 29 with pencil and paper, there would be six par-

tial products. But far fewer errors would occur, requiring less instructional time and much less remediation.

NCTM Standards

"As students move from third to fifth grade, they should consolidate and practice a small number of computational algorithms for addition, subtraction, multiplication and division that they understand well and can use routinely. . . . Having access to more than one method for each operation allows students to choose an approach that best fits the numbers in a particular problem. For example, 298 × 42 can be thought of as (300 × 42) − (2 × 42), whereas 41 × 16 can be computed by multiplying 41 × 8 to get 328 and then doubling 328 to get 656" (p. 155).

Invented Strategies for Division

Even though many adults think division is the most onerous of the computational operations, it can be considerably easier than multiplication. It is appropriate to begin thinking about division computation in the third and fourth grades.

Recall that there are two concepts of division. First there is the partition or fair-sharing idea, illustrated by this story problem:

The bag has 783 jelly beans, and Aidan and her four friends want to share them equally. How many jelly beans will Aidan and each of her friends get?

Then there is the measurement or repeated subtraction concept:

Jumbo the elephant loves peanuts. His trainer has 625 peanuts. If he gives Jumbo 20 peanuts each day, how many days will the peanuts last?

Students should be challenged to solve both types of problems. However, the fair-share problems are often easier to solve with base-ten pieces. Furthermore, the traditional algorithm is built on this idea. Eventually, students will develop strategies that they will apply to both types of problem, even when the process does not match the action of the story.

Figure 13.25 shows some strategies that fourth-grade children have used to solve division problems. The first example illustrates 92 ÷ 4 using base-ten pieces and a sharing process. A ten is traded when no more tens can be passed out. Then the 12 ones are distributed, resulting in 23 in each set. This direct modeling approach with base-ten pieces is quite easy even for third-grade students to understand and use.

In the second example, the student sets out the base-ten pieces and draws a "bar graph" with six columns. After noting that there are not enough hundreds for each kid, he splits the 3 hundreds in half, putting 50 in each column. That leaves him with 1 hundred, 5 tens, and 3 ones. After trading the hundred for tens (now 15 tens), he gives 20 to each, recording 2 tens in each bar. Now he is left with 3 tens and 3 ones, or 33. He knows that 5 × 6 is 30, so he gives each kid 5, leaving him with 3. These he splits in half and writes ½ in each column.

The child in the third example is solving a sharing problem but tries to do it as a measurement process. She wants to find out how many 8s are in 143. Initially she guesses. By multiplying 8 first by 10, then by 20, and then by 14, she knows the answer is more than 14 and less than 20. After some more work (not shown), she rethinks the problem as how many 8s in 100 and how many in 40.

(a)
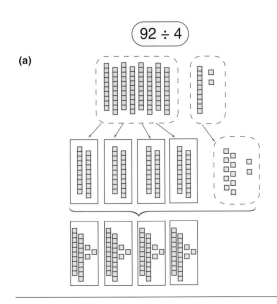

(b)   453 ÷ 6
(share with 6 kids)

(c)   143 jelly beans shared with 8 kids

Try 14 × 8 → 112
12 groups of 8 is 96.
12 groups in 100 leaves 4.
 5 groups of 8 is 40.
And 3 more left over.
12 + 5 is 17 with 7 left.

FIGURE 13.25 Students use both models and symbols to solve division tasks.

Source: Adapted from *Developing Mathematical Ideas: Numbers and Operations, Part I: Building a System of Tens Casebook,* by D. Schifter, V. Bastable, & S. J. Russell. Copyright © 1999 by the Educational Development Center, Inc. Published by Dale Seymour Publications, an imprint of Pearson Learning. Used by permission.

The Traditional Algorithm for Division

Long division is the one traditional algorithm that starts with the left-hand or big pieces. The conceptual basis for the algorithm most often taught in textbooks is the partition or fair-share method.

The task is to share these 5 hundreds, 8 tens, and 3 ones among these four sets so that each set gets the same amount.

I'll begin with the hundreds pieces. There are enough so that each set can get 1 hundred. That leaves 1 hundred left that cannot be shared.

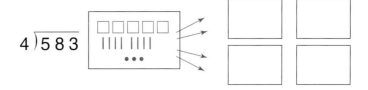

I can trade the hundred for 10 tens. That gives me a total of 18 tens. With 18 I can put 4 tens in each of the four sets and have 2 tens left. Two is not enough to go around to all four sets.

I can trade the 2 tens for 10 ones each or a total of 20 ones. With the 3 ones I already had, that gives me 23 ones. I can put 5 ones in each of the four sets. That leaves me with only 3 ones left over as a remainder.

Each set got 145. I record that on the top of the problem in the right place-value columns. The answer tells how much went to each set.

If I added up how much they got altogether, that would be 4 × 145 or 580. The remainder of 3 makes the 583 I started with.

FIGURE 13.26 **Sharing pieces within each place value and trading leftovers for the next smaller place is the entire conceptual basis for the long-division algorithm.**

One-Digit Divisors

Typically, the division algorithm with one-digit divisors is introduced in the third grade. If done well, it should not have to be retaught, and it should provide the basis for two-digit divisors. Students in the upper grades who are having difficulty with the division algorithm can also benefit from a conceptual development.

Begin with Models

Traditionally, if we were to do a problem such as $4\overline{)583}$, we might say "4 goes into 5 one time." This is quite mysterious to children. How can you just ignore the "83" and keep changing the problem? Preferably, you want students to think of the 583 as 5 hundreds, 8 tens, and 3 ones, not as the independent digits 5, 8, and 3. One idea is to use a context such as candy bundled in boxes of ten with 10 boxes to a carton. Then the problem becomes *We have 5 boxes, 8 cartons, and 3 pieces of candy to share between 4 schools evenly.* In this context,

it is reasonable to share the cartons first until no more can be shared. Those remaining are "unpacked," and the boxes shared, and so on. Money ($100, $10, and $1) can be used in a similar manner.

 Figure 13.26 shows the process in detail. Try this yourself using base-ten pieces and the problem 524 ÷ 3. Try to talk through the process without using "goes into." Think sharing.

Develop the Written Record

The recording scheme for the long-division algorithm is not completely intuitive. You will need to be quite directive in helping children learn to record the fair sharing with models. There are essentially four steps:

1. *Share* and record the number of pieces put in each group.
2. *Record* the number of pieces shared in all. Multiply to find this number.

3. *Record* the number of pieces remaining. Subtract to find this number.

4. *Trade* (if necessary) for smaller pieces, and combine with any that are there already. Record the new total number in the next column.

When students model problems with a one-digit divisor, steps 2 and 3 seem unnecessary. Explain that these steps really help when you don't have the pieces there to count.

Record Explicit Trades

Figure 13.27 details each step of the recording process just described. On the left, you see the traditional algorithm. To the right is a suggestion that matches the actual action with the models by explicitly recording the trades. Instead of the somewhat mysterious "bring-down" procedure, the traded pieces are crossed out, as is the number of existing pieces in the next column. The combined number of pieces is written in this col-

FIGURE 13.27 The traditional and explicit-trade methods are connected to each step of the division process. Every step can and should make sense.

FIGURE 13.28 **Using lines to mark place-value columns can help avoid forgetting to record zeros.**

umn using a two-digit number. In the example, 2 hundreds are traded for 20 tens, combined with the 6 that were there for a total of 26 tens. The 26 is therefore written in the tens column.

Students who are required to make sense of the long-division procedure find the explicit-trade method easier to follow. Blank division charts with wide place-value columns are highly recommended. These can be found in the Blackline Masters. Without the charts, it is important to spread out the digits in the dividend when writing down the problem. (The explicit-trade method is an invention of mine. It has been used successfully in grades 3 to 8. You will not find it in textbooks.)

Both the explicit-trade method and the use of place-value columns will help with the problem of leaving out a middle zero in a problem (see Figure 13.28).

Two-Digit Divisors

There is almost no justification for having children master division with two-digit divisors. A large chunk of the fourth, fifth, and sometimes sixth grade is frequently spent on this outdated skill. The cost in terms of time and students' attitudes toward mathematics is enormous. Only a few times in any adult's life will an exact result to such a computation be required and a calculator not be available. If you can possibly influence the removal of this outdated skill from your school's curriculum, you are encouraged to speak up.

With a two-digit divisor, it is hard to come up with the right amount to share at each step. A guess too high or too low means you have to erase and start all over.

An Intuitive Idea

Suppose that you were sharing a large pile of candies with 36 friends. Instead of passing them out one at a time, you conservatively estimate that each person could get at least 6 pieces. So you give 6 to each of your friends. Now you find there are more than 36 pieces left. Do you have everyone give back the 6 pieces so you can then give them 7 or 8? That would be silly! You simply pass out more.

The candy example gives us two good ideas for sharing in long division. First, always underestimate how much can be shared. You can always pass out some more. Second, if there is enough left to share some more, just do it! To avoid ever overestimating, always pretend there are more sets among which to share than there really are. For example, if you are dividing 312

by 43 (sharing among 43 sets or "friends"), pretend you have 50 sets instead. Round *up* to the next multiple of 10. You can easily determine that 6 pieces can be shared among 50 sets because 6 × 50 is an easy product. Therefore, since there are really only 43 sets, clearly you can give *at least* 6 to each. Always consider a larger divisor; *always round up*. If your underestimate leaves you with more to share, simply pass out some more.

Using the Idea Symbolically

These ideas are used in Figure 13.29. Both the traditional method and the explicit-trade method of recording are illustrated. The rounded-up divisor, 70, is written in a little "think bubble" above the real divisor. Rounding up has another advantage: It is easy to run through the multiples of 70 and compare them to 374. Think about sharing base-ten pieces (thousands, hundreds, tens, and ones). Work through the problem one step at a time, saying exactly what each recorded step stands for.

This approach has proved successful with children in the fourth grade learning division for the first time and with children in the sixth to eighth grades in need of remediation. It reduces the mental strain of making choices and essentially eliminates the need to erase. If an estimate is too low, that's okay. And if you always round up, the estimate will never be too high. Nor is there any reason ever to change to the more familiar approach. It is just as good for adults as for children. The same is true of the explicit-trade notation. It is certainly an idea to consider.

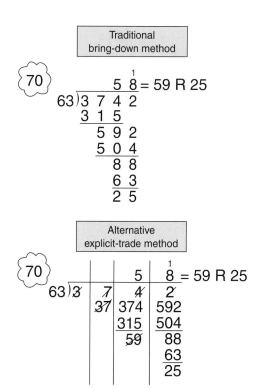

FIGURE 13.29 **Round the divisor up to 70 to think with, but multiply what you share by 63. In the ones column, share 8 with each set. Oops! 88 left over. Just give 1 more to each set.**

The following comes from the 3–5 chapter of the *Standards*: "Although the expectation is that students develop fluency in computing with whole numbers, frequently they should use calculators to solve complex computations involving large numbers or as part of an extended problem" (p. 155).

TECHNOLOGY NOTE

Most software programs that provide drill of any sort will also provide drill in multidigit computation. Most simply provide problems at different levels and evaluate answers. These programs have limited advantages for the teacher. In *Gold Medal Mathematics* (EdVenture Software, 1997), for example, students are first "warmed up" with fact practice. Then, in a practice setting, students continue to solve problems until they complete ten in a row correctly. The challenge round encourages speed. Somewhat unusual is the fact that all answers are in multiple-choice format. This permits students to use any strategy, encourages mental computation, and may be good practice for standardized tests. The program includes two-digit addition and subtraction as well as multiplication and division.

Some programs provide base-ten blocks on the screen that students can manipulate to help solve problems. Before purchasing these programs or using Internet applets, see how much freedom is provided, and ask what the computer program does that could not be accomplished at least as well with physical materials. *MathKeys* (MECC, 1995a, 1996b), for example, includes very attractive screen graphics that permit modeling numbers into the thousands. However, the computer forces trading and always updates totals. There is no problem-solving spirit to this program.

On the other hand, the applet at www.arcytech.org/java/b10blocks allows much more experimentation with base-ten blocks and does not force regrouping. It also has an option for associating numerals with the blocks as they change on the screen. There are links at this site connecting to activities and lesson ideas. Some textbook publishers (see, for example, Scott Foresman) have tools with similar features. These more flexible tools offer more advantages than those that are constrained. ∎

LITERATURE CONNECTIONS

Children's literature can play a very useful role in helping you develop problems for your invented strategies and mental computation lessons. Your simple story problems every day may be great, but children deserve a change. Turn to children's books. There are a great many fascinating books that involve large numbers and opportunities to compute. Some are about real data, and others are fictional.

Cookies
Jaspersohn, 1993

This is the true story of Wally Amos and his Famous Amos Chocolate Chip Cookies. (Are you interested already?) The text includes a large number of color and black-and-white photos that show the production and distribution of Famous Amos cookies. Because it is filled with facts about the cookies—numbers sold, number the average person eats in a year, and so on—you can easily pose questions that require computation and that children will find interesting. Although actual computations can be done on a calculator, this context clearly suggests that estimates and round numbers make more sense. As you discuss ideas generated by the book, some computations can be done mentally to determine exact answers. Other computations will be estimates. Students can extend the story to a project to research cookie consumption in their home, data from grocery stores about other cookies, or the number of trucks or miles required to get cookies to market. The possibilities are endless. During these projects, suggest that students pay attention to where an estimate makes more sense than an exact computation. Find out if there are places as they are working on their project where they made a quick mental estimate or did a mental computation.

Is a Blue Whale the Biggest Thing There Is?
Wells, 1993

This is one of the most intriguing books you will find about large things and large distances. Blue whales look small next to Mount Everest, which in turn looks small next to the earth. The data in the book allow children to make other comparisons, such as the number of fourth graders that would have the same weight or volume as a blue whale or would fill the gymnasium. As with the Famous Amos data, these comparisons are the perfect place for estimations and discussions about how much accuracy is necessary to make a meaningful comparison. Bresser (1995) provides excellent insights into the use of this story with fourth-, fifth-, and sixth-grade students. ∎

ASSESSMENT NOTES

Parents are perhaps more interested in their children's computational skills than in any other area. It is quite easy to give a test of computation like those provided in traditional textbooks. When students do well on these tests, parents are pleased. But what do you know when students do not do well? At best you can make inferences based on the papers turned in. You can look for basic-fact errors and carelessness or perhaps find a systematic error in an algorithm. What you do not know is how children are solving these problems and what ideas and strategies they have developed that are useful or need further development.

Ongoing Assessment

When computational strategies and algorithms are developed in the manner suggested in this chapter, every day you are presented with a wealth of assessment data. The important thing is to gather, record, and use these data for individual children the same as you would for tests and quizzes. A sim-

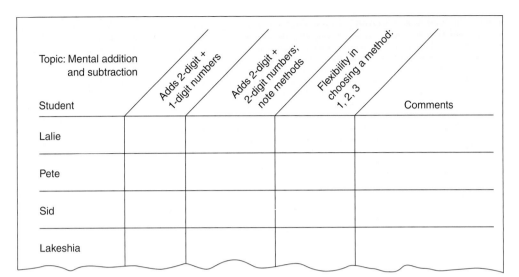

FIGURE 13.30
A checklist with space for comments or notes lets you record daily observations of students' direct modeling and invented strategies.

ple chart something like the one in Figure 13.30 may be all you need. Note that the third column includes a minirubric or a three-point scale. Students' names can be arranged in groups, by how they sit in the room, or alphabetically—any way that makes them easy to find.

As you walk around in the during portion of your lessons, and also in the after portion when children explain their computation strategies and reasoning, you can make notes on the chart. Make a new chart each week, but keep the old ones to provide evidence of growth over time. These charts can be useful for grading and for parent conferences. There is no harm in giving an occasional quiz or test of computational skills. But avoid giving more value to tests simply because they are objective. Compare the results with the information you have gathered through observation. Did you get any new information? Were the results consistent? If not, why not?

Occasional Interviews

It is not always easy to tell what concepts or thought processes individual students are using. For example, some students may get overly attached to a particular approach and not be flexible enough to switch to a more efficient method when the numbers call for it. Some children do not provide as much in-formation in class as you need because they are shy or not very verbal. You may need to find out more about underlying conceptual understanding of base-ten concepts. For these and many other reasons, it is often useful to stop and listen more carefully to a single child. A little interview may take 5 to 10 minutes. Perhaps you can do it while others are working on a problem you have posed, or maybe you will find a time outside of the lesson.

The interview format is similar to the lessons that have been described. Pose a word problem or computation, and ask the student to "think out loud" while she works. Explain that you want to find out how she is thinking. Avoid any teaching at this time. Do not make evaluative comments. Show your interest in the student's thinking. Ask questions to clarify thinking that may not be clear. If a child is making errors with symbolic techniques, ask if he can show you how to do the same task with counters or base-ten models. Similarly, a student who seems to rely heavily on physical models can be challenged in an interview to try a problem without models.

Some children will give you a much clearer picture of their abilities and understanding in an interview than when they feel pressured by talking in a full-class setting. ∎

REFLECTIONS ON CHAPTER 13

Writing to Learn

1. What is the difference between solving a problem with direct modeling and solving a problem with an invented strategy? What is a traditional algorithm?
2. How are traditional algorithms different from invented strategies? Explain the benefits of invented strategies over traditional algorithms.
3. When a problem has been solved, how do you manage all of the different methods that students may propose, and what should you do about students who propose no ideas of their own?
4. What do you do when someone brings a traditional algorithm into the classroom before you have introduced it? What if you never plan to teach the traditional algorithm but students want to use it anyway?

5. Explain how strategies for problems such as 58 + 6 or 72 − 5 are similar to the make-ten strategies for basic facts. How can you help children extend their basic fact strategies to these larger numbers?

6. Illustrate three different strategies for adding 46 + 39. Which ones are easy to do mentally? Is there a strategy that is easier because 39 is close to 40? What strategies work well for sums such as 538 + 243? For each strategy you work with, think about how you could record it on the board so that other students will be able to follow what is being done.

7. Use two different adding-up strategies for 93 − 27 and for 545 − 267. Make up a story problem that would encourage an adding-up strategy.

8. Describe how you would go about developing the traditional algorithms for addition and subtraction. How would you deal with the issue of beginning on the right with the ones place when students' natural tendency is to begin on the left? Use 385 + 128 to illustrate a reasonable written algorithm that begins on the left instead of the right. Do the same for 453 − 278.

9. Draw pictures showing how 57 × 4 could be modeled: with counters, with base-ten pieces, with rectangles or arrays on base-ten grids.

10. How might you help a student who is using a complete-number strategy for multiplication?

11. Try to develop some skill using an invented strategy for multiplying by single-digit numbers. Can you do 327 × 6 mentally? How would you record the steps on the chalkboard if a student gave them to you the way you did it?

12. Use a compensation strategy for these: 68 × 20, 5 × 46, 25 × 480.

13. Draw a rectangle for 28 × 57, and explain how it could be used to compute the product.

14. Which division concept, measurement or partition, is easier for direct modeling and is also the one used to develop the usual long-division algorithm? Make up an appropriate word story with that concept to go with 735 ÷ 6.

15. Use the traditional algorithm for 735 ÷ 6, and then repeat the process using the text's suggestion of recording trades explicitly. With the two algorithms side by side, explain every recorded number in terms of what it stands for when sharing base-ten pieces.

16. To avoid erasures in long division, a rounded-up divisor can be used to make estimates of the quotient in each place value. Show how this method works and avoids erasures using the problem 4589 ÷ 62.

For Discussion and Exploration

1. Examine any or all of these three books on mental computation (or similar resource books on the same topic):

   Mental Math in the Primary Grades (Hope, Leutzinger, Reys, & Reys, 1988)

   Mental Math in the Middle Grades (Hope, Reys, & Reys, 1987)

   Mental Math in the Junior High School (Hope, Reys, & Reys, 1988)

   Although the ideas suggested in these books are excellent, you will notice that the instructional strategy is considerably more guided than that described in this chapter. Would you use these books or their equivalent in your computational program?

Would you use this approach instead of the one suggested here, or should methods such as these be integrated into a problem-solving approach?

2. Select any grade between 2 and 6, and discuss what you feel is an appropriate skill level for whole-number computation at that grade. Should these skills be taught at that grade or earlier? How do your views compare with the treatment given whole-number computation in a traditional textbook for that grade level? How does the textbook treatment compare with the general position offered in this chapter?

3. Examine one of the three reform curricula (see Chapter 1, p. 8) for the elementary grades. How is whole-number computation developed?

Recommendations for Further Reading

Highly Recommended

Campbell, P. F., & Johnson, M. L. (1995). How primary students think and learn. In I. M. Carl (Ed.), *Prospects for school mathematics* (pp. 21–42). Reston, VA: National Council of Teachers of Mathematics.

   Campbell and Johnson describe a project in an urban school system that is completely based in a constructivist paradigm. The purpose of the chapter is to describe how children are able to construct their own ideas. Interestingly, most of the examples provided surround computation and student-invented methods. Absolutely worth reading.

Fosnot, C. T., & Dolk, M. (2001). *Young mathematicians at work: Constructing multiplication and division.* Portsmouth, NH: Heinemann.

Fosnot, C. T., & Dolk, M. (2001). *Young mathematicians at work: Constructing number sense, addition, and subtraction.* Portsmouth, NH: Heinemann.

   These are two in a series of three books that are the product of Fosnot (a U.S. mathematics educator and expert in constructivism) and Dolk (a mathematics educator at the Freudenthal Institute in the Netherlands). The books are products of a collaborative effort begun in 1988, of working with teachers, examining how children learn, and how to support that learning. They show children constructing ideas about number, operations, and computation in ways not found elsewhere. The authors talk about the "landscape of learning" and ideas "on the horizon"—the places where children are working and the ideas they are working toward. Refreshing, thoughtful, and informative. (Their third book is on fractions and decimals.)

Morrow, L. (Ed.). (1998). *The teaching and learning of algorithms in school mathematics.* Reston, VA: National Council of Teachers of Mathematics.

   Mastery of algorithms is and always has been a topic that anti-reformers choose to attack, usually because they believe that reform means stop teaching computation. In this NCTM yearbook we find well-articulated perspectives on the issue. More important, there are numerous articles with practical teaching suggestions at the elementary, middle, and secondary levels.

Russell, S. J. (2000). Developing computational fluency with whole numbers. *Teaching Children Mathematics, 7,* 155–158.

   In just four pages, Russell provides an articulate view of what *Principles and Standards* means by computational fluency. Russell accompanies each of her points with examples from children.

She talks about connecting understanding with procedures and how to assess computational fluency. She ends this little article by explaining that teaching for fluency is a complex task requiring the teacher's understanding of the mathematics, selecting appropriate tasks, and recognizing when to capitalize on students' ideas.

Schifter, D., Bastable, V., & Russell, S. J. (1999a). *Developing mathematical understanding: Numbers and operations, Part 1, Building a system of tens (Casebook).* Parsippany, NJ: Dale Seymour Publications. The cases in this book clearly demonstrate the interaction between children's place-value understanding and their invented strategies for computation. It is from this book and its companion in-service guide that much of the information in this chapter regarding invented strategies was derived. For any teacher seriously interested in the development of student-invented methods of computation, this book provides practical insights.

Other Suggestions

Baek, J. (1998). Children's invented algorithms for multidigit multiplication problems. In L. J. Morrow (Ed.), *The teaching and learning of algorithms in school mathematics* (pp. 151–160). Reston, VA: National Council of Teachers of Mathematics.

Bresser, R., & Holtzman, C. (1999). *Developing number sense: Grades 3–6.* Sausalito, CA: Math Solutions Publications.

Campbell, P. F., Rowan, T. E., & Suarez, A. R. (1998). What criteria for student-invented algorithms? In L. J. Morrow (Ed.), *The teaching and learning of algorithms in school mathematics* (pp. 49–55). Reston, VA: National Council of Teachers of Mathematics.

Carroll, W. M., & Porter, D. (1997). Invented strategies can develop meaningful mathematical procedures. *Teaching Children Mathematics, 3,* 370–374.

Chambers, D. (1996). Direct modeling and invented procedures: Building on students' informal strategies. *Teaching Children Mathematics, 3,* 92–95.

Creative Publications. (1996). *Smart arithmetic* [video]. Mountain View, CA: Author.

Hope, J. A., Leutzinger, L. P., Reys, B. J., & Reys, R. E. (1988). *Mental math in the primary grades.* Palo Alto, CA: Dale Seymour.

Hope, J. A., Reys, B. J., & Reys, R. E. (1987). *Mental math in the middle grades.* Palo Alto, CA: Dale Seymour.

Hope, J. A., Reys, B. J., & Reys, R. E. (1988). *Mental math in the junior high school.* Palo Alto, CA: Dale Seymour.

Kamii, C. (1994). *Young children continue to reinvent arithmetic: 3rd grade.* New York: Teachers College Press.

Kamii, C., & Dominick, A. (1997). To teach or not to teach algorithms. *Journal of Mathematical Behavior, 16,* 51–61.

Kamii, C., & Lewis, B. A. (1993). The harmful effects of algorithms in primary arithmetic. *Teaching K–8, 23*(5), 36–38.

Kouba, V. L., & Wearne, D. (2000). Whole number properties and operations. In E. A. Silver & P. A. Kenney (Eds.), *Results from the seventh mathematics assessment of the National Assessment of Educational Progress* (pp. 141–162). Reston, VA: National Council of Teachers of Mathematics.

Li, Y., & Silver, E. (2000). Can younger students succeed where older students fail? An examination of third graders' solutions of a division-with-remainder (DWR) problem. *Journal of Mathematical Behavior, 9,* 233–246.

Ma, L. (1999). *Knowing and teaching elementary mathematics: Teachers' understanding of fundamental mathematics in China and the United States.* Mahwah, NJ: Lawrence Erlbaum.

Reys, B. J., & Reys, R. E. (1998). Computation in the elementary curriculum: Shifting the emphasis. *Teaching Children Mathematics, 5,* 236–241.

Reys, R. E., Reys, B. J., Nohda, N., & Emori, H. (1995). Mental computation performance and strategy use of Japanese students in grades 2, 4, 6, and 8. *Journal for Research in Mathematics Education, 26,* 304–326.

Rubenstein, R. N. (2001). Mental mathematics beyond the middle school: Why? What? Where? *Mathematics Teacher, 94,* 442–446.

Schneider, S. B., & Thompson, C. S. (2000). Incredible equations develop incredible number sense. *Teaching Children Mathematics, 7,* 146–148, 165–168.

Skinner, P. (1999). *It all adds up! Engaging 8-to-12-year-olds in math investigations.* Sausalito, CA: Math Solutions Publications.

Trafton, P. R., & Hartman, C. L. (1997). Developing number sense and computational strategies in problem-centered classrooms. *Teaching Children Mathematics, 4,* 230–233.

Whitenack, J. W., Knipping, N., Novinger, S., & Underwood, G. (2001). Second graders circumvent addition on subtraction difficulties. *Teaching Children Mathematics, 8,* 228–232.

Wickett, M., & Burns, M. (2001). *Teaching arithmetic: Lessons for extending multiplication, grades 4–5.* Suasalito, CA: Math Solutions Publications.

14

Computational Estimation with Whole Numbers

Recall that *Principles and Standards* defined computational fluency as "having and using efficient and accurate methods for computing" (NCTM, 2000, p. 32). Computational estimation skills round out a full development of flexible and fluent thinking with whole numbers. Estimation skills with whole numbers also form the foundation for most estimation skills with fractions, decimals, and percents.

Mental computation and computational estimation are highly related yet quite different skills. Estimates are made using mental computations with numbers that are easier to work with than the actual numbers involved. Thus, estimation depends on students' mental computational skills. However, because of the importance of estimation—both in the real world and in much of mathematics—and because the strategies for computational estimation are quite different from those discussed in the preceding chapter, it makes sense to address this topic separately.

Big Ideas

1. Multidigit numbers can be built up or taken apart in a wide variety of ways. When the parts of numbers are easier to work with, these parts can be used to create estimates in calculations rather than using the exact numbers involved. For example, 36 is 30 and 6 or 25 and 10 and 1. 483 can be thought of as 500 − 20 + 3.

2. Nearly all computational estimations involve using easier-to-handle parts of numbers or substituting difficult-to-handle numbers with close "nice" numbers so that the resulting computations can be done mentally.

Content Connections

Estimation skills once developed are a tool for everyday living as well as a tool for sense making in other areas of mathematics.

- **Operations, Place Value, and Whole-Number Computation** (Chapters 10, 12, and 13): Many of the skills of estimation grow directly out of invented strategies for computation. For example, to estimate 708 ÷ 27 you might compute 20 × 27 (540) and then 5 × 27 (135, for a total of 675). Thus, the quotient is a little more than 25. To compute these two products requires an understanding of place value. To understand how multiplication can help with the division estimate requires an understanding of how multiplication and division are related.

- **Estimation with Fractions, Decimals, and Percents** (Chapters 16 and 17): Once students have an understanding of what an estimate is and have developed strategies for whole-number estimation, few new strategies are required for estimation with other types of numbers. To estimate 3.45 + 24.06 − 0.0057 requires no new estimation skills, only a good conceptual understanding of the decimals involved. Similar statements are true of fractions and percents.

Introducing Computational Estimation

The long-term goal of computational estimation is to be able quickly to produce an approximate result for a computation that will be adequate for the situation. In everyday life, estimation skills are valuable time savers. Many situations do not require an exact answer, so reaching for a calculator or a pencil is not necessary if one has good estimation skills.

Good estimators tend to employ a variety of computational strategies they have developed over time. Teaching these strategies to children has become a regular part of the curriculum. Beginning about grade 3, we can help children develop an understanding of what it means to estimate a computation and start to develop some early strategies that may be useful. From then on through middle school, children should continue to develop and add to their estimation strategies and skills.

Understanding Computational Estimation

By itself, the term *estimate* refers to a number that is a suitable approximation for an exact number given the particular context. This concept of an estimate is applied not only to computation—the topic of this chapter—but also to measures and quantities.

Three Types of Estimation

The term *estimation* in the K–8 mathematics curriculum refers to three quite different ideas and it is worthwhile to understand the differences. To estimate a measure—*measurement estimation*—means to determine an approximate measure without making an exact measurement. For example, we can estimate the length of a room or the weight of a watermelon in the grocery store. To estimate a quantity—*quantity estimation*—means to approximate the number of items in a collection. For example, we might estimate the number of students in the auditorium or jelly beans in the "guessing jar." To estimate a computation—*computational estimation*—means determining a number that is an approximation of a computation that we cannot or do not wish to determine exactly. For example, we might want to know the approximate gas mileage in our car if we travel 326 miles on 16 gallons of gas ($326 \div 16$). In some instances, it is sufficient to know that a computation is either more or less than a given number. Do I have enough money to buy six boxes at $3.29 each? We have 28 dozen donuts. Are there enough for the 117 students to have two each?

Estimate or Guess

Many children confuse the idea of estimation with guessing. None of the three types of estimation involves outright guessing. Each involves some form of reasoning. Computational estimation involves some computation; it is not a guess at all. Since it is based on computation, how can there be different answers to estimates? The answer, of course, is that any particular estimate depends on the strategy used and the kinds of adjustments in the numbers that might be made. Estimates also tend to vary with the need for the estimate. Estimating your gas mileage is quite different from trying to decide if your last $5 will cover the three items you need at the Fast Mart. These are new and difficult ideas for young students.

Choosing a Form of Computation

Whenever we are faced with a computation in real life or even in school, we have a variety of choices to make concerning how we will handle the computation. As pointed out in the 1989 *Standards* document, the first decision is: "Do we need an exact answer or will an approximate answer be okay?" If an exact answer is called for, we can use an invented or mental strategy, a pencil-and-paper algorithm, a calculator, or even a computer. A computer is called for when there are many repetitive computations that lend themselves to spreadsheet formats. Often, however, we do not need an exact answer and so we can use an estimate. How good an estimate—how close it must be to the actual computation—is a matter of context, as was the original decision to be satisfied with an estimate.

 NCTM Standards "Teachers should help students learn how to decide when an exact answer or an estimate would be more appropriate, how to choose the computational methods that would be best to use, and how to evaluate the reasonableness of answers to computations. Most calculations should arise as students solve problems in context" (p. 220).

Suggestions for Estimation Instruction

Here are some general principles that are worth keeping in mind as you help your students develop estimation skills.

Find Real Examples of Estimation

Discuss situations in which computational estimations are used in real life. Some simple examples include dealing with grocery store situations (doing comparative shopping, determining if there is enough to pay the bill), adding up distances in planning a trip, determining approximate yearly or monthly totals of all sorts of things (school supplies, haircuts, lawnmowing income, time watching TV), and figuring the cost of going to a sporting event or show including transportation, tickets, and snacks. Discuss why exact answers are not necessary in some instances and why they are necessary in others. Look in a newspaper or magazine to find where numbers are the result of estimation and where they are the result of exact computations.

Use the Language of Estimation

Words and phrases such as *about, close, just about, a little more* (or *less*) *than,* and *between* are part of the language of estimation. Students should understand that they are trying to get as close as possible using quick and easy methods, but there is no correct estimate. Language can help convey that idea.

Connect to the Real World

A real-world number sense also plays a role in estimation. For thirty 69-cent soft drinks, is $2.10, $21, or $210 most reasonable? It is much easier to focus on 7 × 3 and use a result that makes sense than to compute 0.69 × 30 and try to place the decimal correctly. Similar assists come from knowing if the cost of a car would likely be $950 or $9500. Could attendance at the school play be 30 or 300 or 3000? A simple computation can provide the important digits, with number sense providing the rest.

Accept a Range of Estimates

What estimate would you give for 27 × 325? If you use 20 × 300, you might say 6000. Or you might use 25 for the 27, noting that four 25s make 100. Since 325 ÷ 4 is about 81, that would make 8100. If you use 30 × 300, your estimate is 9000, and 30 × 320 gives an estimate of 9600. Is one of these "right"?

By listing the estimates of many students and letting students discuss how and why different estimates resulted, they can begin to see that estimates generally fall in a range around the exact answer. Different approaches provide different results. And don't forget the context. Some situations call for more careful estimates than others.

Focus on Flexible Methods, Not Answers

Remember that your primary concern is to help students develop strategies for making estimates. It is, therefore, reflection on the strategies that will lead to strategy development. Class discussion of strategies for estimation is just as important as it was for the development of invented methods of computation. For any given estimation, there are often several very good but different methods of estimation. Students will learn strategies from each other.

The discussion of different strategies will also help students understand that there is no "right" estimate. Different strategies produce different estimates.

STOP ⊗ Estimate this product: 438 × 62. Use the first idea that comes to your head and write down the result. Then return to the task and try a different approach, perhaps using different numbers in your approach to the estimate.

Sometimes different strategies produce the same estimates. For 438 × 62, you might have thought about using 450 × 60 as a first step. Then suppose you think 10 × 450 is 4500. Double 4500 is 9000 and 3 × 9000 is 27,000. You might also have thought 6 × 45 is 240 + 30 or 270. But this is not 6 × 45 but 60 times 450 so you add two more zeros—27,000. Here two good strategies produce the same result.

Alternatively, you could have used 400 × 60 and gotten 24,000 and then recognized that you rounded both numbers down. You lost at least 38 sets of 62 or about 40 × 60. So add 2400 to the 24,000 to get 26,400.

If just a "ballpark" estimate were OK, you might have thought 500 × 60 is 30,000 and realized that it was a bit high. But the exact answer is also at least 400 × 60 or 24,000. So its between 24 and 30 thousand.

You've just seen four of many possible estimation strategies for one computation. The more strategies you experience, the more you will learn. The more strategies you have, the better you can select one to use for the situation at hand. Students will learn like this as well. In contrast, if you tell students to use a given strategy (e.g., round each number to one significant digit and multiply), everyone will get the same answer or they will be "wrong." Different strategies are useful to learn. Different strategies often give different estimates.

Estimation Without Estimates

Consider the threat a third-grade student perceives when you ask for an estimate of the sum $349.29 + $85.99 + $175.25. The requirement is to come up with *a number.* Even textbooks, in an attempt to teach a particular estimation strategy, will lead students through a series of rounding and adding and come up with a singular answer. This is contrary to the idea of what an estimate really is: producing answers that are "good enough" for the purposes. The purposes often determine what we need to know. For the three prices, the question "About how much?" is quite different from "Is it more than $600?" How would you answer each of those questions?

Each activity that follows suggests a format for estimation in which a specific numeric response is not required.

─── **ACTIVITY 14.1** ───

Over or Under?

Prepare several estimation exercises on a transparency. With each, provide an "over or under number." In Figure 14.1, each is either over or under $1.50, but the number need not be the same for each task.

FIGURE 14.1 *"Over or Under?"* is a good beginning estimation activity.

The last activity need not be very elaborate. Here are some more "over/under" examples:

37 + 75	over/under 100
712 − 458	over/under 300
17 × 38	over/under 400
319 ÷ 45	over/under 6

Simple, noncontextual tasks such as these can be prepared quickly. After presenting each, have students select their choice and then discuss their reasoning. The next activity is similar. It is adapted from an activity in the *Investigations in Number, Data, and Space* fifth-grade materials.

ACTIVITY 14.2

High or Low?

Display a computation and three or more possible computations that might be used to create an estimate. The students' task is to decide if the estimation will be higher or lower than the actual computation. For example, present the computation 736 × 18. For each of the following, decide if the result will be higher or lower than the exact result and explain why you think so.

$$750 \times 10 \qquad 730 \times 15$$
$$700 \times 20 \qquad 750 \times 20$$

ACTIVITY 14.3

Best Choice

For any single estimation task, offer three or four possible estimates.

About how much in all?

65¢ 79¢ 39¢

How close the choices are will determine the difficulty of the task. Sometimes it is a good idea to use multiples of ten, such as $21, $210, and $2100.

With all of these tasks, the three-part lesson format remains useful. Present the exercise, have students quickly write their choice on paper (this commits them to an answer), and then discuss why the choice was made. All three parts may take only 10 minutes. In the discussion, a wide variety of estimates and estimation methods will be shared. This will help students see that estimates fall in a range and that there is no single correct estimate or method.

ESTIMATIONS FROM INVENTED STRATEGIES

Suppose that you were asked to compute the sum of 64 and 28. You might begin by adding 60 and 20 or 64 and 30. For each of these beginnings, you would need to make one or two additional computations before arriving at the answer. However, each of these beginnings is actually a reasonable estimate.

Stop Before the Details

Often it is the first step or two in an invented computation that is good enough for the estimate. In the 64 + 28 example, even a third grader would probably continue to the exact answer. But estimations are generally called for because an exact answer is too tedious or not necessary. When students have a good repertoire of invented strategies, one approach to an estimate is to simply begin to compute until you've gotten close enough to the result.

ACTIVITY 14.4

That's Good Enough

Present students with a computation that is reasonably difficult for their skills. For example: *T-shirts with the school logo cost $6 wholesale. The Pep Club has saved $257. How many shirts can they buy for their fund-raiser?* The task is to describe the steps they would take to get an exact answer but not do them.

Share students' ideas. Next, have students actually do as many of the steps as they can in their heads. When it begins to get too tough, stop and see if that is a good estimate or if it can be used for an estimate. Complete the steps using paper and pencil to help. Compare the various estimates with the exact amount.

The example in "That's Good Enough" may have seemed difficult to you. Try the same idea with a sum of four to six numbers: 47 + 29 + 74 + 55. Try it with a nasty difference: 7021 − 4583. Try it with a product: 86 × 29. The methods that students will come up with will be based on the ideas that they have learned for computing. In most instances, the beginnings of these computations are good estimates. By completing the steps, students are also improving their understanding of invented strategies and computations. For older students, use computations in this task that typically they would use a calculator to do. For younger students (grades 3 or 4), the tasks need not be terribly difficult. It is fun to see if you can do tough calculations without a standard algorithm or a calculator.

Cluster Problems

In the preceding chapter, the excerpt from *Investigations in Number, Data, and Space* illustrated the use of cluster problems. (See p. 217.) The idea is that students solve a collection of problems that is somewhat easier but related to the target problem. Then students use some or all of the easier problems to solve the harder problem. They may want to add additional problems to solve the target problem. An important aspect of the cluster problem approach is that students first make (and write down) an estimate of the target computation.

⚅ **STOP** What follows are some cluster problems for each of the operations. The last problem is the target problem. Give these a try. Don't forget to first make an estimate of the target. Then solve all of the problems in the cluster. Use any of the cluster problems and any additional problems to solve the target. Indicate how you solved the target problem. No traditional methods allowed!

4 + 5 + 6	600 − 300
400 + 500 + 600	600 − 400
400 + 600	85 + 15
60 + 30 + 100	15 + 13
60 + 20 + 90	85 − 13
467 + 528 + 693	613 − 385

$10 \div 7$	6×7
$70 \div 7$	6×8
7×11	70×7
7×12	60×7
$87 \div 7$	68×7

40×20	5×20
50×4	5×22
48×2	5×10
48×4	22×10
50×20	2×22
48×24	$147 \div 22$

There are many possible paths to the results. Notice how in your own work, however, the cluster problems (not the target) are actually good problems to use in making estimates.

Once students have gotten comfortable with cluster problems, try the following task.

ACTIVITY 14.5

Make a Little Cluster

Give students a target problem for a cluster. It can be any operation that you are working on. The task is to create a cluster of no more than two problems that will help produce a reasonable estimate. Once students have made the little cluster, they should use their problems to estimate the target.

The excerpt from *Investigations in Number, Data, and Space* on page 233 shows another activity in the same spirit as those just discussed. In the activity, students continue to solve the problems to get exact answers. However, the activity is designed to help students choose places to begin when making an estimate.

INVESTIGATIONS in Number, Data, and Space

Grade 5, *Building on Numbers You Know*

Investigation 3: Ways to Multiply and Divide

Context

In this investigation, cluster problems are used for both multiplication and division targets. The students are always encouraged to make an estimate of the target computation before beginning the cluster problems. The task described here follows the work with cluster problems. The unit is designed for about midway in the year.

Task Description

To introduce an activity called "Solving a Problem with the First Step Given," the teacher puts the problem 133 ÷ 6 on the board. Instead of students solving the problem using their own methods, the teacher explains that she wants them to start in a certain way. "Suppose someone said that when she solved this problem, the first thing she did was solve 6 × 10. Think about it: How could solving 6 × 10 have helped her? What's one thing she could have done next?" (p. 92). Students discuss ways to approach the problem with this beginning and solve it accordingly. In a similar manner, they consider starting the same problem with 12 ÷ 6. Students are also asked to suggest other possible first steps.

There are several first-step worksheets to follow this introduction. The one shown here is the second of five that are available for both in-class work and for homework. The pages show three to five possible first steps toward a solution. The students are to select two of the first steps and show how they could solve the problem with those first steps.

Note that this activity remains quite flexible. If students do not know how to begin with one of the given steps, they may solve the problem in a way that makes sense for them. Solutions are discussed in class. There is often more than one path to a solution from a given first step.

Name _____ Date _____

Student Sheet 27

How Did I Solve It? (page 2 of 3)

For each problem, choose **two** first steps to complete.

3. 22 × 37 =

  a. Start by solving 22 × 10 =

  b. Start by solving 37 × 10 =

  c. Start by solving 20 × 30 =

4. 754 ÷ 30 =

  a. Start by solving 30 × 10 =

  b. Start by solving 30 × 2 =

  c. Start by solving 300 ÷ 30 =

  d. Start by solving 25 × 30 =

  e. Start by solving 75 ÷ 3 =

© Dale Seymour Publications®　　　**187**　　　*Investigation 3 • Sessions 7–9*
Building on Numbers You Know

Page 187 from *Computation and Estimation Strategies: Building on Numbers You Know* by M. Kliman, S. J. Russell, C. Tierney, and M. Murray. *Investigations in Number, Data, and Space.* Copyright © 1998 by Dale Seymour Publications, Inc. Reprinted by permission of Pearson Education, Inc.

In a later activity, students are given a problem and are asked to suggest two first steps on their own and to solve the problem using each first step.

COMPUTATIONAL ESTIMATION STRATEGIES

Estimation strategies are specific algorithms that produce approximate results rather than exact results. The strategies discussed in this section are the ones good estimators use.

As you work through the strategies in this section, you should recognize many of the same approaches that students are likely to have developed from their invented methods. However, it is also likely that many of the strategies in this section will not have been developed. You should feel free to suggest these to your students as additional alternatives to estimation. Be very clear whenever you suggest a strategy that the intention is to create a good full "basket" of strategies. Those that you introduce are no more correct or important than ideas that they have devised. After introducing a strategy, you can have students practice it so that it is clearly understood.

When students have seen a variety of strategies, stop specifying which strategy to use. Rather, provide a task, and let students come up with an estimate using whatever strategy makes sense to them. Even in groups of three or four, students can each make an estimate and then compare both estimates and strategies. This helps in the selection of a strategy as well as in allowing for a range of answers.

Front-End Methods

Front-end methods focus on the leading or leftmost digits in numbers, ignoring the rest. After an estimate is made on the basis of only these front-end digits, an adjustment can be made by noticing how much has been ignored.

Front-End Addition and Subtraction

Front end is a good beginning strategy for addition or subtraction. This approach is reasonable when all or most of the numbers have the same number of digits. Figure 14.2 illustrates the idea. Notice that when a number has fewer digits than the rest, that number is ignored completely.

After adding or subtracting the front digits, an adjustment is made to correct for the digits or numbers that were ignored. Making an adjustment is actually a separate skill. For young children, practice first just using the front digits. Pay special attention to numbers of uneven length when not in a column format.

The leading-digit strategy is easy to use and easy to teach because it does not require rounding or changing numbers. The numbers used are there and visible, so children can see what they are working with. It is a good first strategy for children as early as the third grade.

Front-End Multiplication and Division

For multiplication and division, the front-end method uses the first digit in each factor. The computation is then done us-

ing zeros in the other positions. For example, a front-end estimation of 48×7 is 40 times 7, or 280. When both numbers have more than one digit, the front ends of both are used. For 452×23, consider 400×20, or 8000.

For division, the best approach to estimation is to think multiplication. Avoid presenting problems using the computational form $(7)\overline{3482}$ because this tends to suggest a computation rather than an estimate and encourages a "goes into" approach. Present problems in context or using the algebraic form: $3482 \div 7$. For this problem the front-end digit is determined by first getting the correct position. (100×7 is too low. 1000×7 is too high. It's in the hundreds.) There are 34 hundreds in the dividend, so since $34 \div 7$ is between 4 and 5, the front-end estimate is 400. In this example, since $34 \div 7$ is almost 5, a closer estimate is 500.

Rounding Methods

Rounding is the most familiar form of estimation. Estimation based on rounding is a way of changing the problem to one that is easier to work with mentally. Good estimators follow their mental computation with an adjustment to compensate for the rounding. To be useful in estimation, rounding should be flexible and well understood conceptually.

Rounding in Addition and Subtraction

When a lot of numbers are to be added, it is usually a good idea to round them to the same place value. Keep a running sum as you round each number. In Figure 14.3, the same total is estimated two ways using rounding. A combination of the two is also possible.

In subtraction situations, there are only two numbers to deal with. For subtraction and for additions involving only two addends, it is generally necessary to round only one of the two numbers. For subtraction, round only the subtracted number. In $6724 - 1863$, round 1863 to 2000. Then it is easy: $6724 - 2000$ is 4724. Now adjust. You took away a big-

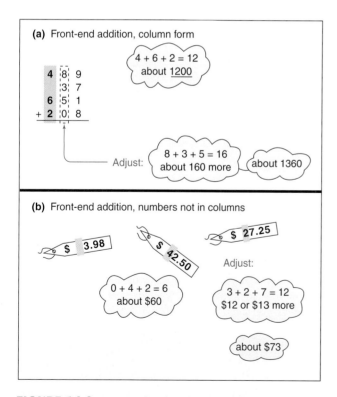

FIGURE 14.2 Front-end estimation in addition.

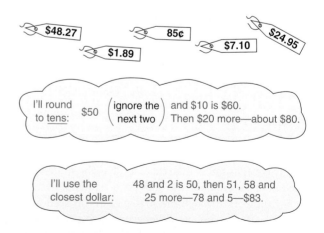

FIGURE 14.3 Rounding in addition.

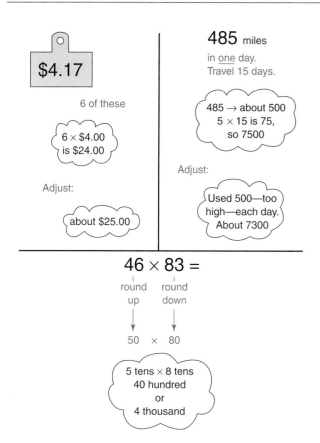

FIGURE 14.4 **Rounding in multiplication.**

ger number, so the result must be too small. Adjust to about 4800. For 627 + 385, you might round 627 to 625 because multiples of 25 are almost as easy to work with as multiples of 10 or 100. After substituting 625 for 627, you may or may not want to round 385 to 375 or 400. The point is that there are no rigid rules. Choices depend on the relationships held by the estimator, on how quickly the estimate is needed, and on how accurate an estimate is required.

Rounding in Multiplication and Division

The rounding strategy for multiplication is no different from that for other operations. However, the error involved can be significant, especially when both factors are rounded. In Figure 14.4, several multiplication situations are illustrated, and rounding is used to estimate each.

If one number can be rounded to 10, 100, or 1000, the resulting product is easy to determine without adjusting the other factor.

When one factor is a single digit, examine the other factor. Consider the product 7 × 836. If 836 is rounded to 800, the estimate is relatively easy and is low by 7 × 36. If a more accurate result is required, round 836 to 840, and add two partial products. Then the estimate is 5600 plus 280, or 5880 (7 × 800 and 7 × 40).

If possible, round only one factor—select the larger one if it is significantly larger. (Why?) For example, in 47 × 7821, 47 × 8000 is 376,000, but 50 × 8000 is 400,000.

Another good rule of thumb with multiplication is to round one factor up and the other down (even if that is not the closest round number). When estimating 86 × 28, 86 is between 80 and 90, but 28 is very close to 30. Try rounding 86 down to 80 and 28 up to 30. The actual product is 2408, only 8 off from the 80 × 30 estimate. If both numbers were rounded to the nearest 10, the estimate would be based on 90 × 30, with an error of nearly 300.

With one-digit divisors, it is almost always best to search for a compatible dividend rather than to round off. For example, 4325 ÷ 7 can be estimated by using the close compatible number, 4200, to yield an estimate of 600. Rounding would suggest a dividend of 4000 or 4300, neither of which is very helpful.

Using Compatible Numbers

When adding a long list of numbers, it is sometimes useful to look for two or three numbers that can be grouped to make 10 or 100. If numbers in the list can be adjusted slightly to produce these groups, that will make finding an estimate easier. This approach is illustrated in Figure 14.5.

FIGURE 14.5 **Compatibles used in addition.**

FIGURE 14.6 Compatibles can mean an adjustment that produces an easy difference.

In subtraction, it is often possible to adjust only one number to produce an easily observed difference, as illustrated in Figure 14.6.

Frequently in the real world, an estimate is needed for a large list of addends that are relatively close. This might happen with a series of prices of similar items, attendance at a series of events in the same arena, cars passing a point on successive days, or other similar data. In these cases, as illustrated in Figure 14.7, a nice number can be selected as representative of each, and multiplication can be used to determine the total. This is more of an *averaging technique* than a compatible-numbers strategy.

One of the best uses of the compatible-numbers strategy is in division. The two exercises shown in Figure 14.8 illustrate adjusting the divisor or dividend (or both) to create a division that comes out even and is, therefore, easy to do mentally. Many percent, fraction, and rate situations involve division, and the compatible-numbers strategy is quite useful, as shown in Figure 14.9.

FIGURE 14.8 Adjusting to simplify division.

Source: From *GUESS* (*Guide to Using Estimation Skills and Strategies*) (box II, cards 2 and 3), by B. J. Reys and R. E. Reys, 1983, White Plains, NY: Dale Seymour Publications. Copyright 1983 by Dale Seymour Publications. Reprinted by permission of Dale Seymour Publications.

Cookies Sold Troop 124	
1. Marcie	___ 68
2. Sally	___ 42
3. Chris	___ 81
4. Yvonne	___ 35
5. Yolanda	___ 57
6. Andrea	___ 60
7. Meggan	___ 71
8. Jo Ann	___ 63

FIGURE 14.7 Estimating sums using averaging.

 You have seen two approaches to helping students develop **STOP** estimation strategies. In the first case, the students make estimates based on ideas they have developed for computation. In the second approach, if the students have not developed particular strategies, the teacher suggests them and students practice them. Later, they are left to devise estimates using whatever strategies they wish. Which approach seems better to you? Why? Can you use them both?

NCTM Standards In partial response to the question just posed, here is a statement that suggests the perspective found in the *Standards*. "Instructional attention and frequent modeling by the teacher can help students develop a range of computational estimation strategies including flexible rounding, the use of benchmarks, and front-end strategies. Students should be encouraged to frequently explain their thinking as they estimate" (p. 156).

73% of our 132 eighth graders watch more than 2 hours of TV per day.

73% → about 75% or $\frac{3}{4}$.

If I use 120, one-fourth is 30 and three-fourths is 90. (That's probably a little low. I used a bigger percentage but fewer students.) About 90 to 95.

The chances of getting a winning lottery ticket are about 1 in 8. Zeke bought 60 tickets. About how many "winners" is reasonable?

$\frac{1}{8}$ of 60 → $\frac{1}{8}$ of 64 is 8.

About 7 or 8 winners.

A box of 36 thank-you cards is $6.95. How much is that per card?

36 × 2 is 72 → or 36 × 20 is 720.

$6.95 is close to $7.20. So these cards cost a little less than 20¢ each.

FIGURE 14.9 Using compatible numbers in division.

ESTIMATION EXERCISES

The examples presented here are not designed to teach estimation strategies but offer useful formats to provide your students with practice using skills as they are being developed. These will be a good addition to any estimation program.

Calculator Activities

The calculator is not only a good source of estimation activities but also one of the reasons estimation is so important. In the real world, we frequently hit a wrong key, leave off a zero or a decimal, or simply enter numbers incorrectly. An estimate of the expected result alerts us to these errors. The calculator as an estimation-teaching tool lets students work independently or in pairs in a challenging, fun way without fear of embarrassment. With a calculator for the overhead

projector, some of the activities described here work very well with a full class.

ACTIVITY 14.6

The Range Game

This is an estimation game for any of the four operations. First pick a start number and an operation. The start number and operation are stored in the calculator. Students then take turns entering a number and pressing = to try to make the result land in the target range. The following example for multiplication illustrates the activity: Suppose that a start number of 17 and a range of 800 to 830 are chosen. Press 17 × = to store 17 as a factor. Press a number and then =. Perhaps you try 25. (Press 25 =.) The result is 425. That is about half the target. Try 50. The result is 850—maybe 2 or 3 too high. Try 48. The result is 816—in the target range! Figure 14.10 gives examples for all four operations. Prepare a list of start numbers and target ranges. Let students play in pairs to see who can hit the most targets on the list (Wheatley & Hersberger, 1986).

After entering the setup with the start # as shown, players take turns pressing a number, then = to try to get a result in the target range.

Addition: Press: 0 + (start #) =

START	TARGET
153	790 → 800
216	400 → 410
53	215 → 220

Subtraction: Press: 0 − (start #) =

START	TARGET
18	25 → 30
41	630 → 635
129	475 → 485

Multiplication: Press: (start #) × 0 =

START	TARGET
67	1100 → 1200
143	3500 → 3600
39	1600 → 1700

Division: Press: 0 ÷ (start #) =

START	TARGET
20	25 → 30
39	50 → 60
123	15 → 20

FIGURE 14.10 "The Range Game"—a calculator game.

"The Range Game" can be played with an overhead calculator with the whole class, by an individual, or by two or three children with calculators who can race one another. The speed element is important. The width of the range and the type of numbers used can all be adjusted to suit the level of the class.

ACTIVITY 14.7

The Range Game: Sequential Versions

Select a target range as before. Next enter the starting number in the calculator, and hand it to the first player. For addition and subtraction, the first player then presses either ⊞ or ⊟, followed by a number, and then ⊜. The next player begins his or her turn by entering ⊞ or ⊟ and an appropriate number, operating on the previous result. If the target is 423 to 425, a sequence of turns might go like this:

Start with 119.

⊞ 350 ⊜ ⟶ 469 (too high)

⊟ 42 ⊜ ⟶ 427 (a little over)

⊟ 3 ⊜ ⟶ 424 (success)

For multiplication or division, only one operation is used through the whole game. After the first or second turn, decimal factors are usually required. This variation provides excellent understanding of multiplication or division by decimals. A sequence for a target of 262 to 265 might be like this:

Start with 63.

⊠ 5 ⊜ ⟶ 315 (too high)

⊠ 0.7 ⊜ ⟶ 220.5 (too low)

⊠ 1.3 ⊜ ⟶ 286.65 (too high)

⊠ 0.9 ⊜ ⟶ 257.985 (too low)

⊠ 1.03 ⊜ ⟶ 265.72455 (very close!)

(What would you press next?)

Try a target of 76 to 80, begin with 495, and use only division.

More Estimation Activities

Most of the discussion in this chapter has had students focus on their strategies for estimating. The following game adapted from the *Investigations in Number, Data, and Space* curriculum challenges students to make estimates that are as close as possible to the actual computation.

ACTIVITY 14.8

How Close?

Decide which type of problem (the operation and the number of digits) you want students to practice and create a "structure page." For example, if you want students to practice estimations of two-digit by two-digit products, the structure would be __ __ × __ __. Draw this on a sheet of paper. The game is played in groups of three to six students. One student leads a round by drawing numbers one at a time from a set of 1 to 9 numeral cards or tiles. These numbers are placed into the structure from left to right. The students then have 30 seconds (use an egg timer or other timer controlled by the leader) to come up with an estimate. Players are required to work mentally without paper but must write down their estimate before the 30 seconds is up. Next, the exact answer is computed with a calculator. Students record both their estimate and the exact answer and subtract the smaller from the larger to determine their score for that round. After three rounds, scores are totaled. The goal is to have the smallest score.

The following activity works well on the overhead projector as do many full-class estimation activities. This activity is also good for engaging students in discussions of estimation strategies.

ACTIVITY 14.9

What Was Your Method?

Select a problem with an estimation given. For example, 139 × 43 might be estimated as 6000. Ask questions concerning this estimate: "How do you think that estimate was arrived at? Was that a good approach? How should it be adjusted? Why might someone select 150 instead of 140 as a substitute for 139?" Almost every estimate can involve different choices and methods. Alternatives make good discussions, helping students see different methods and learn that there is no single correct estimate.

 ## Technology Note

Estimation skills are often embedded in software drill-and-practice packages, although very few are designed for estimation skills alone. *Math Blaster* (Knowledge Adventure) and *CornerStone ATS 3.2: Mathematics* (The Learning Company) are a couple of examples. The estimation activities in *Math Blaster* are in an arcade format. This adds the useful element of speed but may be a turn-off for students who do not care for the format. *CornerStone ATS 3.2: Mathematics* has test-generating materials that are useful for evaluation and practice in test taking.

The *Blue Falls Elementary* title in *Fizz & Martina's Math Adventures* (Tom Snyder Productions, 1998) includes three estimation problems in each of the four episodes. (The *Fizz & Martina* programs are each built around adventure stories with group problem solving in a realistic context.) Students are encouraged to estimate and then explain the strategy they have used. At least one strategy is provided. ■

Estimating with Fractions, Decimals, and Percents

It might be argued that much of the estimation in the real world involves fractions, decimals, and percents. A few examples are suggested here:

SALE! $51.99. Marked one-fourth off. What was the original price?

About 62 percent of the 834 students bought their lunch last Wednesday. How many bought lunch?

Tickets sold for $1.25. If attendance was 3124, about how much was the total gate?

I drove 337 miles on 12.35 gallons of gas. How many miles per gallon did my car get?

STOP Suppose you were to make estimates in each of the previous situations. Without actually getting an estimate, decide what numbers you would use in each case. For instance, in the first example you would not use 51.99 but perhaps 50 or 52. What about the fractions, decimals, and percents in the other problems? Think about that now before reading on.

The first example asks for an estimate of $\frac{3}{4}$ of $51.99. To get $\frac{3}{4}$ of a quantity requires dividing by 4 and multiplying by 3. Those are whole-number computations, but they require an understanding of fraction multiplication.

In the next example, the problem is finding a way to deal with 62 percent. Well, that's close to 60 percent, which is $\frac{3}{5}$ or equivalently, 6 times 10 percent. In either case, the required computations involve whole numbers. The translation of 62 percent requires an understanding of percents.

In the third example, an understanding of decimals and fractions converts the problem to $1\frac{1}{4}$ of 3125. The computations involve dividing 3125 (perhaps 3200) by 4 and adding that to 3125—all whole-number computations. Similarly, the final example requires an understanding of decimals followed by whole-number computations.

The point is that when fractions, decimals, and percents are involved, an understanding of numeration is often the first thing required to make an estimate. That understanding often translates the situation into one involving only whole-number computations.

Of course, this is not always the case for fractions and decimals. Consider what is required to make estimates for the following:

$$2\frac{3}{8} + 4\frac{1}{9} - \frac{1}{12}$$

$$4.0178 + 73.4$$

A reasonable estimate in each case relies almost entirely on an understanding of the numbers involved. There are very few new estimation skills required.

In any good curriculum, computational estimation will be coupled with computational skill development. Therefore, when computation involving fractions, decimals, and percents is discussed, estimation should certainly be a part of that development (as it will be in this book). Most if not all of the computational skills required involve whole-number strategies as discussed in this chapter.

 Literature Connections

Interesting literature often provides a diversionary context in which the mathematics may be a bit more fun and possibly more realistic. Even if realism in these two books is a bit stretched, the context makes a welcome change of pace.

The Twelve Circus Rings
Chwast, 1993

Based on the same pattern as "The Twelve Days of Christmas," the 12 circus rings each contain more animals or more acts: "six acrobats, five dogs a-barking, four aerialists zooming, three monkeys playing, two elephants, and a daredevil on high wire." The colorful illustrations add to the excitement of the circus and the growing number of performers. After 12 days, how many aerialists are zooming? Remember that there are four aerialists not only in ring 4 but also in rings 5 through 12. The story lends itself to some early estimation but can easily be extended to create some fun questions. "About how much do the bows cost for all the dogs a-barking if each bow costs $1.29?" Both you and your students can make up estimation questions that challenge the skills you've been developing. In addition to the potential for both estimation and mental computation, the author also considers patterns as another extension.

The 329th Friend
Sharmat, 1979

This book not only offers the opportunity to examine mental math strategies and practice in the context of the story but is also about friendship and the need to be liked. The story is about Emery Raccoon, who has no friends. Because he is lonely, Emery invites 328 strangers to lunch to make new friends. There are considerations about the number of dishes, knives, forks, and spoons that suggest multiplying 329 by small numbers and different ways of doing this. The story is easily expanded into other similar number questions. At the end, Emery discovers that although his guests ignored him, there was one friend that was there all along—himself. ■

ASSESSMENT NOTES

Since estimation involves a certain element of speed, teachers often wonder how they can test it so that students are not computing on paper and then rounding the answer to look like an estimate. One method is to prepare a short list of about three estimation exercises on a transparency. The cards in the GUESS boxes (Reys & Reys, 1983) are a ready source for these, or you can simply write bare computations. Students have their paper ready as you very briefly show one exercise at a time on the overhead, perhaps for 20 seconds, depending on the task. Students write their estimate immediately and indicate if they think their estimate is "low" or "high"—that is, lower or higher than the exact computation. They are not to do any written computation. Continue until you are finished. Then show all the exercises, and have students write down how they did each estimate. They should also indicate if they think the estimate was a good estimate or not so good and why. By only doing a few estimates but having the students reflect on them in this way, you actually receive more information than you would with just the answers to a longer list. ■

⟨○○⟩─Reflections on Chapter **14**├

Writing to Learn

1. How is computational estimation different from other types of estimation?
2. Why might the idea of an estimate for a computation be strange to students?
3. Describe each of the general strategies that were offered for conducting estimation activities.
4. Young children often find it difficult to come up with an estimate. What are the suggested techniques where students are required to estimate but not to actually produce an estimate?
5. Describe in general terms how estimation can grow out of the development of invented strategies.
6. What is a cluster problem and how is it used for developing both invented strategies and estimation skills? Make up cluster problems for 72 × 16 and for 342 ÷ 13.
7. Describe each of these estimation strategies. Be able to make up a good example and use it in your explanation.
   a. Front-end addition and subtraction.
   b. Front-end multiplication.
   c. Rounding in addition.
   d. Rounding in subtraction.
   e. Rounding in multiplication.
   f. Compatible numbers in addition and subtraction.
   g. Compatible numbers in division.
8. How can the calculator be used to practice estimation strategies?
9. Describe an estimation practice activity that you think is especially useful. Why do you think it is good?

For Discussion and Exploration

1. In the past, the computation curriculum focused only on the traditional algorithms. There was only one way to compute. In the K–8 curriculum today, how much emphasis should be given to each of the forms of computation that have been discussed (invented strategies both with pencil and paper and mental, traditional algorithms and variations, and finally estimation)? Try to support your argument on the basis of real-world use.

2. Do the curriculum standards for your state require computational estimation? Mental computation? For "straightforward computation," is there any requirement that a particular algorithm or method of computation be used? How does your state's computational guidelines influence what computation methods are taught in school? Do you agree with what is required?

Recommendations for Further Reading

Highly Recommended

Bresser, R., & Holtzman, C. (1999). *Developing number sense: Grades 3–6.* Sausalito, CA: Math Solutions Publications.

Bresser and Holtzman are classroom teachers who have compiled 13 worthwhile number-sense activities covering a range of topics including mental computation, number meanings, and estimation. With each activity the authors provide pages of extensions, practical suggestions, and answers to questions concerning using the activity in the classroom. Most activities include examples of students' work.

Reys, R. E., & Nohda, N. (Eds.). (1994). *Computational alternatives for the twenty-first century: Cross-cultural perspectives from Japan and the United States.* Reston, VA: National Council of Teachers of Mathematics.

This book addresses similarities and differences between computation in the United States and Japan. Divided into three sections, the articles discuss mental computation, estimation, and the use of calculators in the two countries. Respected researchers from both countries have contributed to this work. Although not designed as a resource book, the thoughtful teacher will certainly find practical ideas as well as interesting perspectives.

Reys, R. E., & Reys, B. J. (1983). *Guide to using estimation skills and strategies (GUESS) Boxes I & II.* Palo Alto, CA: Dale Seymour.

Still among the best materials for teaching computational estimation strategies, these two hefty boxes of cards provide the fourth- through eighth-grade teacher with a complete program. Two of the cards are shown in Figure 14.8. Use them as transparencies, in small groups, or as independent work.

Other Suggestions

Auriemma, S. H. (1999). How huge is a hundred? *Teaching Children Mathematics, 6,* 154–159.

Hunting, R. P. (1999). Rational-number learning in the early years: What is possible? In J. V. Copley (Ed.), *Mathematics in the early years* (pp. 80–87). Reston, VA: National Council of Teachers of Mathematics.

McIntosh, A., Reys, B., & Reys, R. (1997a). *Number SENSE: Simple effective number sense experiences, grades 3–4* (also, *grades 4–6,* and *grades 6–8*). White Plains, NY: Dale Seymour Publications.

Reys, R. E. (1998). Computation versus number sense. *Mathematics Teaching in the Middle School, 4,* 110–112.

Reys, R. E., Trafton, P. R., Reys, B. J., & Zawojewski, J. (1987). *Computational estimation (Grades 6, 7, 8).* Palo Alto, CA: Dale Seymour.

Sowder, J. T., & Kelin, J. (1993). Number sense and related topics. In D. T. Owens (Ed.), *Research ideas for the classroom: Middle grades mathematics* (pp. 41–57). Old Tappan, NJ: Macmillan.

Thornton, C. A., Jones, G. A., & Neal, J. L. (1995). The 100s chart: A stepping stone to mental mathematics. *Teaching Children Mathematics, 1,* 480–483.

Van de Walle, J. A., & Watkins, K. B. (1993). Early development of number sense. In R. J. Jensen (Ed.), *Research ideas for the classroom: Early childhood mathematics* (pp. 127–150). Old Tappan, NJ: Macmillan.

C H A P T E R

15

Developing Fraction Concepts

Fractions have always represented a considerable challenge for students, even into the middle grades. Results of NAEP testing have consistently shown that students have a very weak understanding of fraction concepts (Wearne & Kouba, 2001). This lack of understanding is then translated into untold difficulties with fraction computation, decimal and percent concepts, the use of fractions in measurement, and ratio and proportion concepts.

Big Ideas

1. Fractional parts are equal shares or equal-sized portions of a whole or unit. A unit can be an object or a collection of things. More abstractly, the unit is counted as 1. On the number line, the distance from 0 to 1 is the unit.

2. Fractional parts have special names that tell how many parts of that size are needed to make the whole. For example, *thirds* require three parts to make a whole.

3. The more fractional parts used to make a whole, the smaller the parts. For example, eighths are smaller than fifths.

4. The denominator of a fraction indicates by what number the whole has been divided in order to produce the type of part under consideration. Thus, the denominator is a divisor. In practical terms, the denominator names the kind of fractional part that is under consideration. The numerator of a fraction counts or tells how many of the fractional parts (of the type indicated by the denominator) are under consideration. Therefore, the numerator is a multiplier—it indicates a multiple of the given fractional part.

5. Two equivalent fractions are two ways of describing the same amount by using different-sized fractional parts. For

example, in the fraction $\frac{6}{8}$, if the eighths are taken in twos, then each pair of eighths is a fourth. The six-eighths then can be seen to be three-fourths.

Content Connections

What students bring to the topic of fractions is an understanding of fair sharing. So there is a minimal connection to division of whole numbers. Other whole-number ideas actually interfere in early fraction development. However, fraction concepts are intimately connected to other areas of the curriculum.

■ **Fraction Computation** (Chapter 16): Without a firm conceptual understanding of fractions, computation with fractions is relegated to rules without reasons.

■ **Decimals and Percents** (Chapter 17): A key idea for students is that decimal notation and percent notation are simply two other methods of representing fractions. By making the connections between these three representations, the load of new ideas to be learned is significantly reduced.

■ **Ratio and Proportion** (Chapter 18): A part-to-whole concept of a fraction is just one form of ratio. However, because the same fraction notation is often used for other ratios (e.g., the ratio of boys to girls in the room is 3 to 5 or $\frac{3}{5}$), it is important to understand what a fraction is so that concepts are not confused. Equivalent ratio concepts are very similar to equivalent fraction ideas.

In addition to the clear content connections just listed, fractions are used frequently in measurement (Chapter 19) and in probability (Chapter 21).

SHARING AND THE CONCEPT of FRACTIONAL PARTS

The first goal in the development of fractions should be to help children construct the idea of *fractional parts of the whole*— the parts that result when the whole or unit has been partitioned into *equal-sized portions* or *fair shares*.

Children seem to understand the idea of separating a quantity into two or more parts to be shared fairly among friends. They eventually make connections between the idea of fair shares and fractional parts. Sharing tasks are, therefore, good places to begin the development of fractions.

Sharing Tasks

Considerable research has been done with children from first through eighth grades to determine how they go about the process of forming fair shares and how the tasks posed to students influence their responses (e.g., Empson, 2002; Lamon, 1996; Mack, 2001; Pothier & Sawada, 1983).

Sharing tasks are generally posed in the form of a simple story problem. *Suppose there are four square brownies to be shared among three children so that each child gets the same amount. How much (or show how much) will each child get?* Task difficulty changes with the numbers involved, the types of things to be shared (regions such as brownies, discrete objects such as pieces of chewing gum), and the presence or use of a model.

Students initially perform sharing tasks (division) by distributing items one at a time. When this process leaves leftover pieces, it is much easier to think of sharing them fairly if the items can be subdivided. Typical "regions" to share are brownies (rectangles), sandwiches, pizzas, crackers, cake, candy bars, and so on. The problems and variations that follow are adapted from Empson (2002).

Four children are sharing 10 brownies so that each one will get the same amount. How much can each child have?

Problem difficulty is determined by the relationship between the number of things to be shared and the number of sharers. Because children's initial strategies for sharing involve halving, a good place to begin is with two, four, or even eight sharers. For ten brownies and four sharers, many children will deal out two to each child and then halve each of the remaining brownies. (See Figure 15.1.)

Consider these variations in numbers:

5 brownies shared with 2 children

2 brownies shared with 4 children

5 brownies shared with 4 children

4 brownies shared with 8 children

3 brownies shared with 4 children

 STOP Try drawing pictures for each of the preceding sharing tasks. Which do you think is most difficult? Which of these represent essentially the same degree of difficulty? What other tasks involving two, four, or eight sharers would you consider as similar, easier, or more difficult than these?

When the numbers allow for some items to be distributed whole (five shared with two), some students will first share whole items and then cut up the leftovers. Others will slice every piece in half and then distribute the halves. When there are more sharers than items, some partitioning must happen at the beginning of the solution process.

When students who are still using a halving strategy try to share five things among four children, they will eventually get down to two halves to give to four children. For some, the solution is to cut each half in half; that is, "each child gets a whole (or two halves) and a half of a half."

It is a progression to move to three or six sharers because this will force children to confront their halving strategies.

 STOP Try solving the following variations using drawings. Can you do them in different ways?

4 pizzas shared with 6 children

7 pizzas shared with 6 children

5 pizzas shared with 3 children

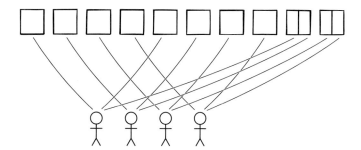

FIGURE 15.1 Ten brownies shared with four children.

(a) Four candy bars shared with six children:

Cut all the bars in half.
Cut the last two halves into three parts.
Each child gets a half and sixth.

(b) Four pizzas shared with three children:

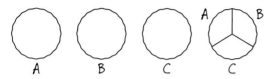

Pass out whole pizzas.
Cut the last pizza in three parts.
Each child gets 1 whole and one-third.

(c) Five sandwiches shared with three children:

Cut each sandwich in three parts (thirds).
Each child gets five parts—five-thirds.

FIGURE 15.2 Three different sharing processes.

To subdivide a region into a number of parts other than a power of two (four, eight, etc.) requires an odd subdivision at some point. This is difficult for young children.

Several types of sharing solutions might be observed. Figure 15.2 shows some different approaches.

Use a variety of representations for these problems. The items to be shared can be drawn on worksheets as rectangles or circles along with a statement of the problem. Another possibility is to cut out construction paper circles or squares. Some students may need to cut and physically distribute the pieces. Students can use connecting cubes to make bars that they can separate into pieces. Or they can use more traditional fraction models such as circular "pie" pieces.

Sharing Tasks and Fraction Language

During the discussions of students' solutions (and discussions are essential!) is a good time to introduce the vocabulary of fractional parts. This can be quite casual and, at least for younger children, should not involve any fraction symbolism. When a brownie or other region has been broken into equal shares, simply say, "We call these *fourths*. The whole is cut into four parts. All of the parts are the same size—fourths."

Children need to be aware of two aspects or components of fractional parts: (1) the number of parts and (2) the equality of the parts (in size, not necessarily in shape). Emphasize that the number of parts that make up a whole determines the name of the fractional parts or shares. They will be familiar with halves but should quickly learn to describe thirds, fourths, fifths, and so on.

Models for Fractions

There is substantial evidence to suggest that the use of models in fraction tasks is important (Cramer & Henry, 2002). Unfortunately, many teachers in the upper grades, where manipulative materials are not as common, fail to use models for fraction development. Models can help students clarify ideas that are often confused in a purely symbolic mode. Sometimes it is useful to do the same activity with two quite different models; from the viewpoint of the students, the activity is quite different. In this chapter we will distinguish among three types of models: area or region models, length models, and set models.

Region or Area Models

In the discussion of sharing, all of the tasks involved sharing something that could be cut into smaller parts. The fractions are based on parts of an area or region. This is a good place to begin and is almost essential when doing sharing tasks. There are many good region models, as shown in Figure 15.3.

Circular "pie" piece models are by far the most commonly used area model. (See the Blackline Masters for masters of pie models.) The main advantage of the circular region is that it emphasizes the amount that is remaining to make up a whole. The other models in Figure 15.3 are more flexible and allow for different-sized units or wholes. Paper grids, several of which can be found in the Blackline Masters, are especially flexible and do not require management of materials.

Length or Measurement Models

With measurement models, lengths are compared instead of areas. Either lines are drawn and subdivided, or physical materials are compared on the basis of length, as shown in Figure 15.4. Manipulative versions provide more opportunity for trial and error and for exploration.

Fraction strips are a teacher-made version of Cuisenaire rods. Both the strips and the rods have pieces that are in lengths of 1 to 10 measured in terms of the smallest strip or rod. Each length is a different color for ease of identification.

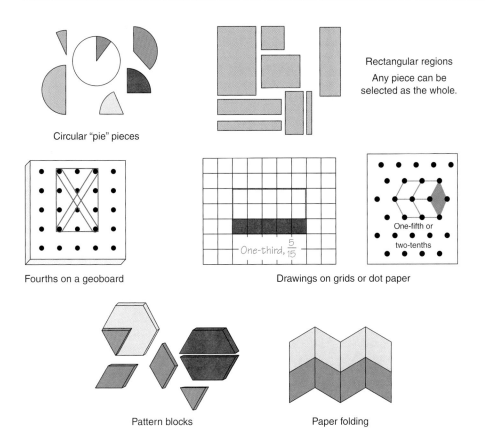

FIGURE 15.3 **Area or region models for fractions.**

FIGURE 15.4 **Length or measurement models for fractions.**

Strips of construction paper or adding-machine tape can be folded to produce equal-sized subparts.

The rod or strip model provides the most flexibility while still having separate pieces for comparisons. To make fraction strips, cut 11 different colors of poster board into strips 2 cm wide. Cut the smallest strips into 2-cm squares. Other strips are then 4, 6, 8, . . . , 20 cm, producing lengths 1 to 10 in terms of the smallest strip. Cut the last color into strips 24 cm long to produce a 12 strip. If you are using Cuisenaire rods, tape a red 2 rod to an orange 10 rod to make a 12 rod. In this chapter's illustrations, the colors of the strips will be the same as the corresponding lengths of the Cuisenaire rods:

1 White	7 Black
2 Red	8 Brown
3 Light green	9 Blue
4 Purple	10 Orange
5 Yellow	12 Pink or red-orange
6 Dark green	

The number line is a significantly more sophisticated measurement model (Bright, Behr, Post, & Wachsmuth, 1988). From a child's vantage point, there is a real difference between putting a number on a number line and comparing

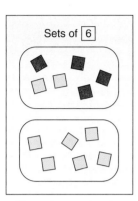

Sets of 6

Two-color counters in
loops drawn on paper.
Shows $1\frac{2}{6}$.

Two-color counters in arrays.
Rows and columns help show
parts. Each array makes a
whole. Here $\frac{3}{5} = \frac{9}{15}$.

Drawings using
Xs and Os.
Shows $\frac{2}{3} = \frac{10}{15}$.

FIGURE 15.5 Set models for fractions.

one length to another. Each number on a line denotes the distance of the labeled point from zero.

Set Models

In set models, the whole is understood to be a set of objects, and subsets of the whole make up fractional parts. For example, three objects are one-fourth of a set of 12 objects. The set of 12, in this example, represents the whole or 1. It is the idea of referring to a collection of counters as a single entity that makes set models difficult for primary school children. However, the set model helps establish important connections with many real-world uses of fractions and with ratio concepts. Figure 15.5 illustrates several set models for fractions.

Counters in two colors on opposite sides are frequently used. They can easily be flipped to change their color to model various fractional parts of a whole set.

FROM FRACTIONAL PARTS TO FRACTION SYMBOLS

As already discussed, one of the best ways to introduce the concept of fractional parts is through sharing tasks. However, the idea of fractional parts is so fundamental to a strong development of fraction concepts that it should be explored further with additional tasks.

Fractional Parts and Words

In addition to helping children use the words *halves, thirds, fourths, fifths,* and so on, be sure to make regular comparison of fractional parts to the whole. Make it a point to use the terms *whole,* or *one whole,* or simply *one* so that students have a language that they can use regardless of the model involved.

The following activity is a simple extension of the sharing tasks. It is important that students can tell when a region has been separated into a particular type of fractional part.

ACTIVITY 15.1

Correct Shares

As in Figure 15.6, show examples and nonexamples of specified fractional parts. Have students identify the wholes that are correctly divided into requested fractional parts and those that are not. For each response, have students explain their reasoning. The activity should be done with a variety of models, including length and set models.

In the "Correct Shares" activity, the most important part is the discussion of the nonexamples. The wholes are already partitioned either correctly or incorrectly, and the children were not involved in the partitioning. It is also useful for children to create designated equal shares given a whole, as they are asked to do in the next activity.

FIGURE 15.6 Find correct examples of fourths. Why are the nonexamples wrong?

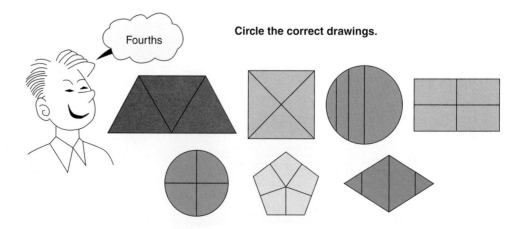

ACTIVITY 15.2

Finding Fair Shares

Give students models, and have them find fifths or eighths or other fractional parts using the models. (The models should never have fractions written on them.) The activity is especially interesting when different wholes can be designated in the same model. That way, a given fractional part does not get identified with a special shape or color but with the relationship of the part to the designated whole. Some ideas are suggested in Figure 15.7.

Notice when partitioning sets that children frequently confuse the number of counters in a share with the name of the share. In the example in Figure 15.7, the 12 counters are partitioned into four sets—*fourths*. Each share or part has three counters, but it is the number of shares that makes the partition show *fourths*.

Understanding Fraction Symbols

Fraction symbolism represents a fairly complex convention that is often misleading to children. It is well worth your time to help students develop a strong understanding of what the top and bottom numbers of a fraction tell us.

Fractional-Parts Counting

Counting fractional parts to see how multiple parts compare to the whole creates a foundation for the two parts of a fraction. Students should come to think of counting fractional parts in much the same way as they might count apples or any other objects. If you know the kind of part you are counting, you can tell when you get to one, when you get to two, and so on. Students who understand factional parts should not need to arrange pie pieces into a circle to know that four fourths make a whole.

Display some pie-piece fraction parts in groups as shown in Figure 15.8. For each collection, tell students what type of piece is being shown and simply count them together: "*one-*fourth, *two-*fourths, *three-*fourths, *four-*fourths, *five-*fourths." Ask, "If we have five-fourths, is that more than one whole, less than one whole, or the same as one whole?"

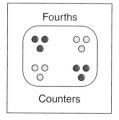

FIGURE 15.7 Given a whole, find fractional parts.

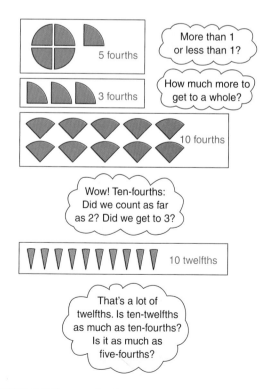

FIGURE 15.8 Counting fractional parts.

As students count each collection of parts, discuss the relationship to one whole. Make informal comparisons between different collections. "Why did we get almost two wholes with seven-fourths, and yet we don't even have one whole with ten-twelfths?"

Also take this opportunity to lay verbal groundwork for mixed fractions. "What is another way that we could say seven-thirds?" (Two wholes and one more third or one whole and four-thirds.)

With this introduction, students are ready for the following task.

ACTIVITY 15.3

More, Less, or Equal to One Whole

Give students a collection of fractional parts (all the same type) and indicate the kind of fractional part they have. Parts can be drawn on a worksheet or physical models can be placed in plastic baggies with an identifying card. For example, if done with Cuisenaire rods or fraction strips, the collection might have seven light green rods/strips with a caption or note indicating "these are eighths." The task is to decide if the collection is less than one whole, equal to one whole, or more than one whole. Students must draw pictures and/or use numbers to explain their answer. They can also tell how close the set is to a complete whole. Several collections constitute a reasonable task.

Try Activity 15.3 with several different fraction models (although pie pieces are too much of a giveaway). Pattern blocks make a good manipulative format and are also easily drawn with a template. The same is true of Cuisenaire rods. A set model may cause students some initial difficulty but it is especially important, even if they have been successful with region or length models. For example, show a collection of 15 counters (dots or actual counters) and indicate that a set of 5 counters is one-fourth. How much is the set of 15 counters?

Top and Bottom Numbers

The way that we write fractions with a top and a bottom number and a bar between is a convention—an arbitrary agreement for how to represent fractions. (By the way, always write fractions with a horizontal bar, not a slanted one. Write $\frac{3}{4}$, not 3/4.) As a convention, it falls in the category of things that you simply tell students. However, a good idea is to make the convention so clear by way of demonstration that students will tell *you* what the top and bottom numbers stand for. The following procedure is recommended even if your students have been "using" symbolic fractions for several years.

Display several collections of fractional parts in a manner similar to those in Figure 15.8. Have students count the parts together. After each count, write the correct fraction, indicating that this is how it is written as a symbol. Include sets that are more than one, but write them as simple or "improper" fractions and not as mixed numbers. Include at least two pairs of sets with the same top numbers such as $\frac{4}{8}$ and $\frac{4}{3}$. Likewise, include sets with the same bottom numbers. After the class has counted and you have written the fraction for at least six sets of fractional parts, pose the following questions:

What does the bottom number in a fraction tell us?

What does the top number in a fraction tell us?

STOP Before reading further, answer these two questions in your own words. Don't rely on formulations you've heard before. Think in terms of what we have been talking about—namely, fractional parts and counting fractional parts. Imagine counting a set of 5 eighths and a set of 5 fourths and writing the fractions for these sets. Use children's language in your formulations and try to come up with a way to explain these meanings that has nothing to do with the type of model involved.

Here are some reasonable explanations for the top and bottom numbers.

● *Top number:* This is the counting number. It tells how many shares or parts we have. It tells how many have been counted. It tells how many parts we are talking about. It counts the parts or shares.

● *Bottom number:* This tells what is being counted. It tells what fractional part is being counted. If it is a 4, it means we are counting *fourths;* if it is a 6, we are counting *sixths;* and so on.

This formulation of the meanings of the top and bottom numbers may seem unusual to you. It is often said that the top number tells "how many" (this phrase seems unfinished) and the bottom tells "how many parts it takes to make a whole." This may be correct but can be misleading. For example, a $\frac{1}{6}$ piece is often cut from a cake without making any slices in the remaining $\frac{5}{6}$ of the cake. That the cake is only in two pieces does not change the fact that the piece taken is $\frac{1}{6}$. Or if a pizza is cut in 12 pieces, two pieces still make $\frac{1}{6}$ of the pizza. In neither of these instances does the bottom number tell how many pieces make a whole.

There is evidence that an iterative notion of fractions, one that views a fraction such as $\frac{3}{4}$ as a count of three things called *fourths,* is an important idea for children to develop (Post, Wachsmuth, Lesh, & Behr, 1985; Tzur, 1999). The iterative concept is most clear when focusing on these two ideas about fraction symbols:

● The top number *counts.*
● The bottom number tells *what is being counted.*

The *what* of fractions are the fractional parts. They can be counted. Fraction symbols are just a shorthand for saying *how many* and *what*.

Smith (2002) points out a slightly more "mathematical" definition of the top and bottom numbers that is completely in accord with the one we've just discussed. For Smith, it is important to see the bottom number as the divisor and the top as the multiplier. That is, $\frac{3}{4}$ is three *times* what you get when you *divide* a whole into four parts. This multiplier and divisor idea is especially useful when students are asked later to think of fractions as an indicated division; that is, $\frac{3}{4}$ also means $3 \div 4$.

The *Standards* supports a strong conceptual development of fractions in grades 3 to 5 but suggests that computation be primarily a middle school topic. "During grades 3–5, students should build their understanding of fractions as parts of a whole and as division. They will need to see and explore a variety of models of fractions, focusing primarily on fractions such as halves, thirds, fourths, fifths, sixths, eighths, and tenths" (p. 150).

Numerator and *Denominator*

To count a set is to *enumerate* it. *Enumeration* is the process of counting. The common name for the top number in a fraction is the *numerator.*

A $1 bill, a $5 bill, and a $10 bill are said to be bills of different denominations. Similarly, the word *denomination* is used to differentiate among branches of religions (such as Baptists, Presbyterians, Episcopalians, and Catholics). A denomination is the name of a class or type of thing. The common name for the bottom number in a fraction is the *denominator.*

The words *numerator* and *denominator* have no common reference for children. Whether these words are used or not, the words themselves will not help young children understand the meanings.

Mixed Numbers and Improper Fractions

In the fourth National Assessment of Educational Progress, about 80 percent of seventh graders could change a mixed number to an improper fraction, but fewer than half knew that $5\frac{1}{4}$ was the same as $5 + \frac{1}{4}$ (Kouba et al., 1988a). The result indicates that many children are using a mindless rule that is in fact relatively easy to construct.

If you have counted fractional parts beyond a whole, your students already know how to write $\frac{13}{6}$ or $\frac{11}{3}$. Ask, "What is another way that you could say 13 *sixths?*" Students may suggest "two wholes and one-sixth more," or "two plus one-sixth." Explain that these are correct and that $2 + \frac{1}{6}$ is usually written as $2\frac{1}{6}$ and is called a *mixed number.* Note that this is a symbolism convention and must be explained to children. What is not at all necessary is to teach a rule for converting mixed numbers to common fractions and the reverse. Rather, consider the following task.

ACTIVITY 15.4

Mixed-Number Names

Give students a mixed number such as $3\frac{2}{5}$. Their task is to find a single fraction that names the same amount. They may use any familiar materials or make drawings, but they must be able to give an explanation for their result. Similarly, have students start with a fraction greater than 1, such as $\frac{17}{4}$, and have them determine the mixed number and provide a justification for their result.

Repeat the "Mixed-Number Names" task several times with different fractions. After a while, challenge students to figure out the new fraction name without the use of models. A good explanation for $3\frac{1}{4}$ might be that there are 4 fourths in one whole, so there are 8 fourths in two wholes and 12 fourths in three wholes. The extra fourth makes 13 fourths in all, or $\frac{13}{4}$. (Note the iteration concept playing a role.)

There is absolutely no reason ever to provide a rule about multiplying the whole number by the bottom number and adding the top number. Nor should students need a rule about dividing the bottom number into the top to convert fractions to mixed numbers. These rules will readily be developed by the students but in their own words and with complete understanding.

ACTIVITY 15.5

Calculator Fraction Counting

Calculators that permit fraction entries and displays are now quite common in schools. The TI-Math Explorer Plus and the Casio FX-55 are two examples. If these are available, they can be quite effective in helping children understand fraction symbolism. Counting by fourths, for example, can be done by pressing ⊞ 1 ⧸ 4 ⊟ ᴏᴘ₁ to store adding $\frac{1}{4}$ in the operation key. Then press ᴏᴘ₁. The display will show 1/4. Students should have models for fourths to manipulate as they count. When they add successive fourths to the pile, they press ᴏᴘ₁ for each piece. At four-fourths, the calculator shows 4/4. Continued presses simply add on to the numerator. To see the corresponding mixed number, press the ᴀᵦ/c key. The mixed number for $\frac{6}{4}$ is shown as 1_2/4. Since the calculator will not reduce the fraction automatically, the count agrees with the physical models.

Fraction calculators provide a powerful way to help children develop fractional symbolism. A variation on Activity 15.5 is to show children a mixed number such as $3\frac{1}{8}$ and ask how many counts of $\frac{1}{8}$ on the calculator it will take to count that high. The students should try to stop at the correct number ($\frac{25}{8}$) before pressing Ab/c the key.

Parts-and-Whole Tasks

The exercises presented here can help children develop their understanding of fractional parts as well as the meanings of the top and bottom numbers in a fraction. Models are used to represent wholes and parts of wholes. Written or oral fraction names represent the relationship between the parts and wholes. Given any two of these—whole, part, and fraction—the students can use their models to determine the third.

Any type of model can be used as long as different sizes can represent the whole. Traditional pie pieces do not work because the whole is always the circle, and all the pieces are *unit fractions*. (A *unit fraction* is a single fractional part. The fractions $\frac{1}{3}$ and $\frac{1}{8}$ are unit fractions.)

Examples of each type of exercise are provided in Figure 15.9, Figure 15.10, and Figure 15.11. Each figure includes examples with a region model (freely drawn rectangles), a length model (Cuisenaire rods or fraction strips), and set models.

🛑 **STOP** It would be a good idea to work through these exercises before reading on. For the rectangle models, simply sketch a similar rectangle on paper. For the rod or strip models, use Cuisenaire rods or make fraction strips. The colors used correspond to the actual rod colors. Lengths are not given in the figures so that you will not be tempted to use an adult-type numeric approach. If you do not have access to rods or strips, just draw lines on paper. The process you use with lines will correspond to what is done with rods.

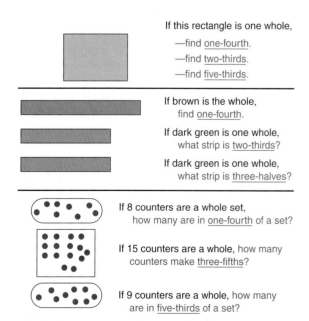

FIGURE 15.9 **Given the whole and the fraction, find the part.**

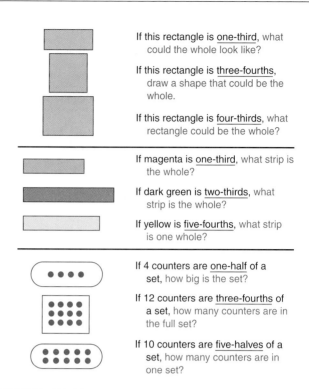

FIGURE 15.10 **Given the part and the fraction, find the whole.**

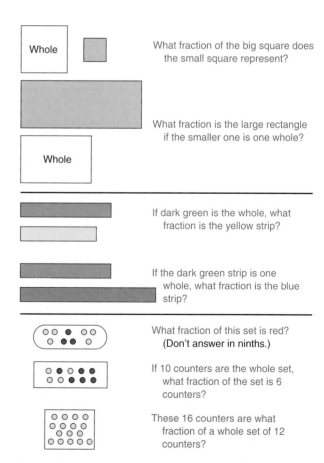

FIGURE 15.11 **Given the whole and the part, find the fraction.**

The questions that ask for the fraction when given the whole and part require a lot of trial and error and can frustrate young students. Be sure that appropriate fractional parts are available for the region and length versions of these questions.

Two or three challenging parts-and-whole questions can make an excellent lesson. The tasks should be presented to the class in just the same form as in the figures. Physical models are often the best way to present the tasks so that students can use a trial-and-error approach to determine their results. As with all tasks, it should be clear that an explanation is required to justify each answer. For each task, let several students supply answers and explanations.

Sometimes it is a good idea to create simple story problems that ask the same questions.

Mr. Samuels has finished $\frac{3}{4}$ of his patio. It looks like this:

Draw a picture that might be the shape of the finished patio.

The problems can also involve numbers instead of models:

If the swim team sold 400 raffle tickets, it would have enough money to pay for new team shirts. So far the swimmers have $\frac{5}{8}$ of the necessary raffle tickets sold. How many more tickets do they need to sell?

With some models, it is necessary to be certain that the answer exists within the model. For example, if you were using fraction strips, you could ask, "If the blue strip (9) is the whole, what strip is two-thirds?" The answer is the 6 strip, or dark green. You could not ask students to find "three-fourths of the blue strip" because each fourth of 9 would be $2\frac{1}{4}$ units, and no strip has that length. Similar caution must be taken with rectangular pieces.

Questions involving unit fractions are generally the easiest. The hardest questions usually involve fractions greater than 1. For example, *If 15 chips are five-thirds of one whole set, how many chips are in a whole?* However, in every question, the unit fraction plays a significant role. If you have $\frac{5}{3}$ and want the whole, you first need to find $\frac{1}{3}$.

Avoid being the answer book for your students. Make students responsible for determining the validity of their own answers. In these exercises, the results can always be confirmed in terms of what is given.

FRACTION NUMBER SENSE

The focus on fractional parts is an important beginning. But number sense with fractions demands more—it requires that students have some intuitive feel for fractions. They should know "about" how big a particular fraction is and be able to tell easily which of two fractions is larger.

Benchmarks of Zero, One-Half, and One

The most important reference points or benchmarks for fractions are 0, $\frac{1}{2}$, and 1. For fractions less than 1, simply comparing them to these three numbers gives quite a lot of information. For example, $\frac{3}{20}$ is small, close to 0, whereas $\frac{3}{4}$ is between $\frac{1}{2}$ and 1. The fraction $\frac{9}{10}$ is quite close to 1. Since any fraction greater than 1 is a whole number plus an amount less than 1, the same reference points are just as helpful: $3\frac{3}{7}$ is almost $3\frac{1}{2}$.

ACTIVITY 15.6

Zero, One-Half, or One

On the board or overhead, write a collection of 10 to 15 fractions. A few should be greater than 1 ($\frac{9}{8}$ or $\frac{11}{10}$), with the others ranging from 0 to 1. Let students sort the fractions into three groups: those close to 0, close to $\frac{1}{2}$, and close to 1. For those close to $\frac{1}{2}$, have them decide if the fraction is more or less than $\frac{1}{2}$. The difficulty of this task largely depends on the fractions. The first time you try this, use fractions such as $\frac{1}{20}$, $\frac{53}{100}$, or $\frac{9}{10}$ that are very close to the three benchmarks. On subsequent days, use fractions with most of the denominators less than 20. You might include one or two fractions such as $\frac{2}{8}$ or $\frac{3}{4}$ that are exactly in between the benchmarks. As usual, require explanations for each fraction.

The next activity is also aimed at developing the same three reference points for fractions. In "Close Fractions," however, the students must come up with the fractions rather than sort them.

ACTIVITY 15.7

Close Fractions

Have your students name a fraction that is close to 1 but not more than 1. Next have them name another fraction that is even closer to 1 than that. For the second response, they have to explain why they believe the fraction is closer to 1 than the previous fraction. Continue for several fractions in the same manner, each one being closer to 1 than the previous fraction. Similarly, try close to 0 or close to $\frac{1}{2}$ (either under or over). The first several times you try this activity, let the students use models to help with their thinking. Later, see how well their explanations work when they cannot use models or drawings. Focus discussions on the relative size of fractional parts.

Understanding why a fraction is close to 0, $\frac{1}{2}$, or 1 is a good beginning for fraction number sense. It begins to focus on the size of fractions in an important yet simple manner. The next activity also helps students reflect on fraction size.

ACTIVITY 15.8
About How Much?
Draw a picture like one of those in Figure 15.12 (or prepare some ahead of time for the overhead). Have each student write down a fraction that he or she thinks is a good estimate of the amount shown (or the indicated mark on the number line). Listen without judgment to the ideas of several students, and discuss with them why any particular estimate might be a good one. There is no single correct answer, but estimates should be "in the ballpark." If children have difficulty coming up with an estimate, ask if they think the amount is closer to 0, $\frac{1}{2}$, or 1.

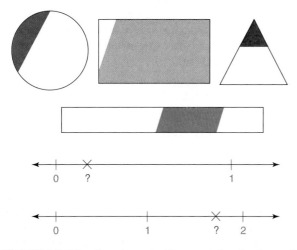

FIGURE 15.12 **About how much? Name a fraction for each drawing, and explain why you chose that fraction.**

Thinking About Which Is More

The ability to tell which of two fractions is greater is another aspect of number sense with fractions. That ability is built around concepts of fractions, not on an algorithmic skill or symbolic tricks.

Concepts, Not Rules
Children have a tremendously strong mind-set about numbers that causes them difficulties with the relative size of fractions. In their experience, larger numbers mean "more." The tendency is to transfer this whole-number concept to fractions: Seven is more than four, so sevenths should be bigger than fourths (Mack, 1995). The inverse relationship between number of parts and size of parts cannot be told but must be a creation of each student's own thought process.

ACTIVITY 15.9
Ordering Unit Fractions
List a set of unit fractions such as $\frac{1}{3}$, $\frac{1}{8}$, $\frac{1}{5}$, and $\frac{1}{10}$. Ask children to put the fractions in order from least to most. Challenge children to defend the way they ordered the fractions. The first few times you do this activity, have them explain their ideas by using models.

This idea is so basic to the understanding of fractions that arbitrary rules ("Larger bottom numbers mean smaller fractions") are not only inappropriate but dangerous. Come back to this basic idea periodically. Children will seem to understand one day and revert to their more comfortable ideas about big numbers a day or two later.

You have probably learned rules or algorithms for comparing two fractions. The usual approaches are finding common denominators and using cross-multiplication. These rules can be effective in getting correct answers but require no thought about the size of the fractions. This is especially true of the cross-multiplication procedure. If children are taught these rules before they have had the opportunity to think about the relative size of various fractions, there is little chance that they will develop any familiarity with or number sense about fraction size. Comparison activities (which fraction is more?) can play a significant role in helping children develop concepts of relative fraction sizes. But keep in mind that reflective thought is the goal, not an algorithmic method of choosing the correct answer.

Before reading further, try the following exercise. Assume for a moment that you know nothing about equivalent fractions or common denominators or cross-multiplication. Assume that you are a fourth- or fifth-grade student who was never taught these procedures. Now examine the pairs of fractions in Figure 15.13 and select the larger of each pair. Write down or explain one or more reasons for your choice in each case.

Which fraction in each pair is greater?
Give one or more reasons. Try not to use drawings or models.
<u>Do</u> not <u>use</u> common denominators or cross-multiplication.
Rely on concepts.

A. $\frac{4}{5}$ or $\frac{4}{9}$ G. $\frac{7}{12}$ or $\frac{5}{12}$

B. $\frac{4}{7}$ or $\frac{5}{7}$ H. $\frac{3}{5}$ or $\frac{3}{7}$

C. $\frac{3}{8}$ or $\frac{4}{10}$ I. $\frac{5}{8}$ or $\frac{6}{10}$

D. $\frac{5}{3}$ or $\frac{5}{8}$ J. $\frac{9}{8}$ or $\frac{4}{3}$

E. $\frac{3}{4}$ or $\frac{9}{10}$ K. $\frac{4}{6}$ or $\frac{7}{12}$

F. $\frac{3}{8}$ or $\frac{4}{7}$ L. $\frac{8}{9}$ or $\frac{7}{8}$

FIGURE 15.13 Comparing fractions using concepts.

Conceptual Thought Patterns for Comparison

The first two comparison schemes listed here rely on the meanings of the top and bottom numbers in fractions and on the relative sizes of unit fractional parts. The third and fourth ideas use the additional ideas of 0, $\frac{1}{2}$, and 1 as convenient anchors or benchmarks for thinking about the size of fractions.

1. *More of the same-size parts.* To compare $\frac{3}{8}$ and $\frac{5}{8}$, it is easy to think about having 3 of something and also 5 of the same thing. It is common for children to choose $\frac{5}{8}$ as larger simply because 5 is more than 3 and the other numbers are the same. Right choice, wrong reason. Comparing $\frac{3}{8}$ and $\frac{5}{8}$ should be like comparing 3 apples and 5 apples.

2. *Same number of parts but parts of different sizes.* Consider the case of $\frac{3}{4}$ and $\frac{3}{7}$. If a whole is divided into 7 parts, the parts will certainly be smaller than if divided into only 4 parts. Many children will select $\frac{3}{7}$ as larger because 7 is more than 4 and the top numbers are the same. That approach yields correct choices when the parts are the same size, but it causes problems in this case. This is like comparing 3 apples with 3 melons. You have the same number of things, but melons are larger.

3. *More and less than one-half or one whole.* The fraction pairs $\frac{3}{7}$ versus $\frac{5}{8}$ and $\frac{5}{4}$ versus $\frac{7}{8}$ do not lend themselves to either of the previous thought processes. In the first pair,

$\frac{3}{7}$ is less than half of the number of sevenths needed to make a whole, and so $\frac{3}{7}$ is less than a half. Similarly, $\frac{5}{8}$ is more than a half. Therefore, $\frac{5}{8}$ is the larger fraction. The second pair is determined by noting that one fraction is less than 1 and the other is greater than 1.

4. *Distance from one-half or one whole.* Why is $\frac{9}{10}$ greater than $\frac{3}{4}$? Not because the 9 and 10 are big numbers, although you will find that to be a common student response. Each is one fractional part away from one whole, and tenths are smaller than fourths. Similarly, notice that $\frac{5}{8}$ is smaller than $\frac{4}{6}$ because it is only one-eighth more than a half, while $\frac{4}{6}$ is a sixth more than a half. Can you use this basic idea to compare $\frac{3}{5}$ and $\frac{5}{9}$? (*Hint:* Each is half of a fractional part more than $\frac{1}{2}$.) Also try $\frac{5}{7}$ and $\frac{7}{9}$.

How did your reasons for choosing fractions in Figure 15.13 compare to these ideas? It is important that you are comfortable with these informal comparison strategies as a major component of your own number sense as well as for helping children develop theirs.

Tasks you design for your students should assist them in developing these and possibly other methods of comparing two fractions. It is important that the ideas come from your students and their discussions. To teach "the four ways to compare fractions" would be adding four more mysterious rules and would be defeating for many students.

ACTIVITY 15.10

Choose, Explain, Test

Present two or three pairs of fractions to students. The students' task is to decide which fraction is greater (choose), to explain why they think this is so (explain), and then to test their choice using any model that they wish to use. They should write a description of how they made their test and whether or not it agreed with their choice. If their choice was incorrect, they should try to say what they would change in their thinking. In the student explanations, rule out drawing as an option. Explain to students that drawings are sometimes inaccurate and can lead to faulty conclusions.

Rather than directly teach the different possible methods for comparing fractions, select pairs that will likely elicit desired comparison strategies. On one day, for example, you might have two pairs with the same denominators and one with the same numerators. On another day, you might pick fraction pairs in which each fraction is exactly one part away from a whole. Try to build strategies over several days by the appropriate choice of fraction pairs.

The use of a model in Activity 15.10 is an important part of students' development of strategies as long as the model is helping students create the strategy. However, after several experiences, change the activity so that the testing portion with a model is omitted. Place greater emphasis on students' reasoning. If class discussions yield different choices, allow students to use their own arguments for their choices in order to make a decision about which fraction is greater.

The next activity extends the comparison task a bit more.

ACTIVITY 15.11

Line 'Em Up

Select four or five fractions for students to put in order from least to most. Have them indicate approximately where each fraction belongs on a number line labeled only with the points 0, $\frac{1}{2}$, and 1. Students should include a description of how they decided on the order for the fractions. To place the fractions on the number line, students must also make estimates of fraction size in addition to simply ordering the fractions.

Including Equivalent Fractions

The discussion to this point has somewhat artificially ignored the idea that students might use equivalent fraction concepts in making comparisons. Equivalent fraction concepts are such an important idea that a separate section is devoted to the development of that idea. However, equivalent fraction concepts need not be put off until last and certainly should be allowed in the discussions of which fraction is more.

Smith (2002) thinks that it is essential that the comparison question is asked as follows: "Which of the following two (or more) fractions is greater, *or are they equal*?" (p. 9, emphasis added). He points out that this question leaves open the possibility that two fractions that may look different can, in fact, be equal.

In addition to this point, with equivalent fraction concepts, students can adjust how a fraction looks so that they can use ideas that make sense to them. Burns (1999) told of fifth graders who were comparing $\frac{6}{8}$ to $\frac{4}{5}$. (You might want to stop for a moment and think how you would compare these two.) One child changed the $\frac{4}{5}$ to $\frac{8}{10}$ so that both fractions would be two parts away from the whole and he reasoned from there. Another changed both fractions to a common *numerator* of 12.

Be absolutely certain to revisit the comparison activities and include pairs such as $\frac{8}{12}$ and $\frac{2}{3}$ in which the fractions are equal but do not appear to be. Also include fractions that are not in lowest terms.

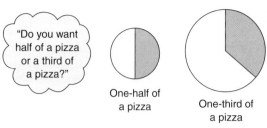

What assumption is made when answering this question?

FIGURE 15.14 **The "pizza fallacy."**

Only One Size for the Whole

A key idea about fractions that students must come to understand is that a fraction does not say anything about the size of the whole or the size of the parts. A fraction tells us only about the *relationship between* the part and the whole. Consider the following situation.

Mark is offered the choice of a third of a pizza or a half of a pizza. Since he is hungry and likes pizza, he chooses the half. His friend Jane gets a third of a pizza but ends up with more than Mark. How can that be? Figure 15.14 illustrates how Mark got misdirected in his choice. The point of the "pizza fallacy" is that whenever two or more fractions are discussed in the same context, the correct assumption (the one Mark made in choosing a half of the pizza) is that the fractions are all parts of the same size whole.

Comparisons with any model can be made only if both fractions are parts of the same whole. For example, $\frac{2}{3}$ of a light green strip cannot be compared to $\frac{2}{5}$ of an orange strip.

In the fourth grade of the *Investigations in Number, Data, and Space* program, many of the same ideas just discussed are developed very carefully. The excerpt on page 255 is an example.

 TECHNOLOGY NOTE

Representing Fractions (Tenth Planet, 1998d) is software that offers a range of challenges for fraction development. In two of the four activities, students build given fractions using models of unit fractions. Though not open-ended, these activities may reinforce the iterative concept of fractions. The computer orally counts to the fraction target when a solution is offered: "One-fourth, two-fourths, three-fourths." Another task area requires students to build a whole based on a given fractional part. This activity is similar to building a whole with fraction strips, given the fraction and the part as described earlier in this chapter.

"Open-Ended Build and Play" is a component of *Representing Fractions* in which the user can slice up squares, circles, or triangles by connecting equally spaced dots on the

INVESTIGATIONS in NUMBER, DATA, and SPACE

Grade 4, *Different Shapes, Equal Pieces*

Investigation 2: Parts of Rectangles: Thirds, Sixths, and Twelfths

Context

In the first three sessions of this investigation, students work with 5 × 7 dot grids (4 squares by 6 squares) to show different ways to make thirds, sixths, and twelfths. In the previous investigation, they explored halves, fourths, eighths, and sixteenths—building on students' propensity for halving. Ordering or comparing fractions and an informal development of equivalent fractions are the focus of the investigation that follows this one.

Task Description

This session or class period is entitled "Working with $\frac{2}{3}$, $\frac{3}{4}$, $\frac{5}{6}$, and $\frac{7}{8}$." Notice that each of these fractions is one part away from a whole. The session begins with a class discussion of these two squares. Students are asked, "How much is colored and how much is not colored?"

After this introductory discussion, students are told to color four squares of their own, one showing $\frac{3}{4}$ colored, one showing $\frac{2}{3}$, one showing $\frac{5}{6}$, and one showing $\frac{7}{8}$. For their drawings students use squares with either six or eight equal spaces marked on the edges. They are told that the colored parts need not be all connected. Given prior experiences, students will likely color their fractions in many different ways. They do not label the squares.

Next, they exchange their drawings with other students. With their exchanged designs, they work in pairs to determine what fraction is shown on each square. To this

Page 74 from *Fractions and Area: Different Shapes, Equal Pieces* by C. Tierney, M. Ogonowski, A. Rubin, & S. J. Russell. *Investigations in Number, Data, and Space.* Copyright © 1998 by Dale Seymour Publications, Inc. Reprinted by permission of Pearson Education, Inc.

point no comparisons have been involved. The squares are collected and posted under the names of the four fractions.

The coloring of squares is followed with the worksheet shown here. After completing this, there is a class discussion of students' reasoning. Notice how this entire lesson focuses on the idea of one part missing, yet never directly tells this to students. The last question on the sheet is a review.

edges. Parts can then be cut into even smaller pieces. The individual pieces can be painted different colors and dragged to any part of the screen. This open-ended model provides teachers or students with a tool that is more flexible than any physical model. Note that this is a pure model or tool. No

fraction symbols are provided, nor are any problems posed. The computer does no evaluation. The teacher can pose tasks and let students use the program to work on solutions. Alternatively, students can devise their own challenges for each other using the drawing tool. As with all Tenth Planet activities, a journal permits students to copy a picture of their work, write about it, and even record a short message.

Fizz & Martina's Math Adventures: Lights, Camera, Fractions (Tom Snyder Productions, 1998) is software supposedly designed for grades 5 and 6. However, the concepts and presentation are closer to grade 4. Fraction problems are embedded in an elaborate cartoon video involving Fizz and Martina. The software is designed to be shown to a full class and stopped at appropriate times to let students work in groups to solve the problem and write on the journal sheets provided. Multiple-solution strategies are encouraged. The problems are good, but the story line is a bit corny and very time intensive. Most tasks involve finding fractional parts of amounts ($\frac{1}{4}$ of 120 words, $\frac{2}{3}$ of $180). The ideas and the support material are good, and the program is designed in the same spirit as the three-part lesson format described in this book. Since each episode involves only a few problems, the program is somewhat limited in its use. ■

Estimation

A frequently quoted result from the Second National Assessment (Post, 1981) concerns the following item:

Estimate the answer to $\frac{12}{13} + \frac{7}{8}$. You will not have time to solve the problem using paper and pencil.

Here is how 13-year-olds answered:

Response	Percent of 13-Year-Olds
1	7
2	24
19	28
21	27
Don't know	14

A more recent study of sixth- and eighth-grade Taiwanese students included this same item. The results were nearly identical to those in the NAEP study (Reys, 1998). In the Taiwanese study, a significantly higher percentage of students (61 percent and 63 percent) was able to correctly compute the sum, a process that requires finding the common denominator of thirteenths and eighths! Notice that to estimate this sum requires no skill whatsoever with computation—only a feeling for the size of the two fractions.

The development of fraction number sense should most certainly include estimation of fraction sums and differences—even before computational strategies are introduced. The following activity can be done regularly as a short full-class warm-up for any fraction lesson.

ACTIVITY 15.12

First Estimates

Tell students that they are going to estimate a sum or difference of two fractions. They are to decide only if the exact answer is more or less than one. On the overhead projector show, for no more than about 10 seconds, a fraction addition or subtraction problem involving two proper fractions. Students write down on paper their choice of more or less than one. Do several problems in a row. Then return to each problem and discuss how students decided on their estimate.

Restricting Activity 15.12 to proper fractions keeps the difficulty to a minimum. When students are ready for a tougher challenge, choose from the following variations:

- Use fractions that are less than one. Estimate to the nearest half (0, $\frac{1}{2}$, 1, $1\frac{1}{2}$, 2).
- Use both proper and mixed fractions. Estimate to the nearest half.
- Use proper and mixed fractions. Estimate the best answer you can.

In the discussions following these estimation exercises, ask students if they think that the exact answer is more or less than the estimate that they gave. What is their reasoning?

Figure 15.15 shows six sample sums and differences that might be used in a "First Estimates" activity.

STOP Test your own estimation skills with the sample problems in Figure 15.15. Look at each computation for only about 10 seconds and write down an estimate. After writing down all six of your estimates, look at the problems and decide if your estimate is higher or lower than the actual computation. Don't guess! Have a good reason.

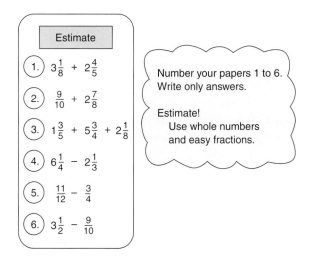

FIGURE 15.15 **Fraction estimation drill.**

In most cases students' estimates should not be much more than $\frac{1}{2}$ away from the exact sum or difference.

NCTM Standards "The development of rational-number concepts is a major goal for grades 3–5, which should lead to informal methods for calculating with fractions. For example, a problem such as $\frac{1}{4} + \frac{1}{2}$ should be solved mentally with ease because students can picture $\frac{1}{2}$ and $\frac{1}{4}$ or can use decomposition strategies, such as $\frac{1}{4} + \frac{1}{2} = \frac{1}{4} + (\frac{1}{4} + \frac{1}{4})$" (p. 35).

EQUIVALENT-FRACTION CONCEPTS

 STOP How do you know that $\frac{4}{6} = \frac{2}{3}$? Before reading further, think of at least two different explanations.

Concepts Versus Rules

Here are some possible answers to the question just posed:

1. They are the same because you can reduce $\frac{4}{6}$ and get $\frac{2}{3}$.
2. If you have a set of 6 things and you take 4 of them, that would be $\frac{4}{6}$. But you can make the 6 into groups of 2. So then there would be 3 groups, and the 4 would be 2 groups out of the 3 groups. That means it's $\frac{2}{3}$.

3. If you start with $\frac{2}{3}$, you can multiply the top and the bottom numbers by 2, and that will give you $\frac{4}{6}$, so they are equal.
4. If you had a square cut into 3 parts and you shaded 2, that would be $\frac{2}{3}$ shaded. If you cut all 3 of these parts in half, that would be 4 parts shaded and 6 parts in all. That's $\frac{4}{6}$, and it would be the same amount.

All of these answers are correct. But let's think about what they tell us. Responses 2 and 4 are very conceptual, although not very efficient. The procedural responses, 1 and 3, are quite efficient but indicate no conceptual knowledge. All students should eventually be able to write an equivalent fraction for a given fraction. At the same time, the rules should

never be taught or used until the students understand what the result means. Consider how different the algorithm and the concept appear to be.

> *Concept:* Two fractions are equivalent if they are representations for the same amount or quantity—if they are the same number.
>
> *Algorithm:* To get an equivalent fraction, multiply (or divide) the top and bottom numbers by the same nonzero number.

In a problem-based classroom, students can develop an understanding of equivalent fractions and also develop from that understanding a conceptually based algorithm. As with most algorithms, a serious instructional error is to rush too quickly to the rule. Be patient! Intuitive methods are always best at first.

Equivalent-Fraction Concepts

The general approach to helping students create an understanding of equivalent fractions is to have them use models to find different names for a fraction. Consider that this is the first time in their experience that a fixed quantity can have multiple names (actually an infinite number). The following activities are possible starting places.

ACTIVITY 15.13

Different Fillers

Using an area model for fractions that is familiar to your students, prepare a worksheet with two or at most three outlines of different fractions. Do not limit yourself to unit fractions. For example, if the model is circular pie pieces, you might draw an outline for $\frac{2}{3}$, $\frac{1}{2}$, and $\frac{3}{4}$. The students' task is to use their own fraction pieces to find as many single-fraction names for the region as possible. After completing the three examples, have students write about the ideas or patterns they may have noticed in finding the names. Follow the activity with a class discussion.

In the class discussion following the "Different Filler" activity, a good question to ask involves what names could be found if students had any size pieces that they wanted. For example, ask students "What names could you find if we had sixteenths in our fraction kit? What names could you find if you could have any piece at all?" The idea is to push beyond filling in the region in a pure trial-and-error approach.

The following activity is just a variation of "Different Fillers." Instead of a manipulative model, the task is constructed on dot paper.

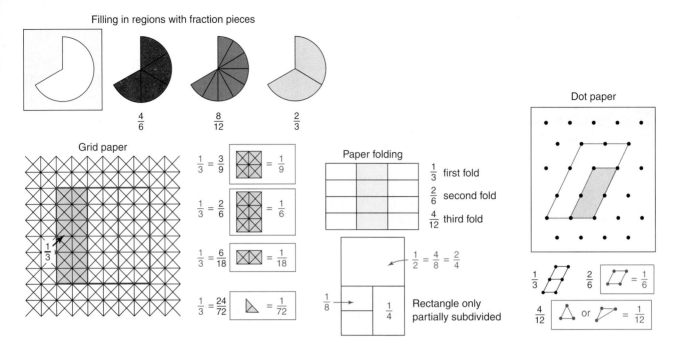

FIGURE 15.16   Area models for equivalent fractions.

Dot Paper Equivalencies

Create a worksheet using a portion of either isometric or rectangular dot grid paper. (These can be found in the Blackline Masters.) On the grid, draw the outline of a region and designate it as one whole. Draw a part of the region within the whole. The task is to use different parts of the whole determined by the grid to find names for the part. Figure 15.16 includes an example drawn on an isometric grid. Students should draw a picture of the unit fractional part that they use for each fraction name. The larger the size of the whole, the more names the activity will generate.

The "Dot Paper Equivalencies" activity is a form of what Lamon (2002) calls "unitizing," that is, given a quantity, finding different ways to chunk the quantity into parts in order to name it. She points out that this is a key ability related not only to equivalent fractions but also to proportional reasoning, especially in the comparison of ratios. (See also Lamon, 1999 a, b.)

Length models can be used to create activities similar to the "Different Fillers" task. For example, as shown in Figure 15.17, rods or strips can be used to designate both a whole and a part. Students use smaller rods to find fraction names for the

given part. To have larger wholes and, thus, more possible parts, use a train of two or three rods for the whole and the part. Folding paper strips is another method of creating fraction names. In the example shown in Figure 15.17, one half is subdivided by successive folding in half. Other folds would produce other names and these possibilities should be discussed if no one tries to fold the strip in an odd number of parts.

The following activity is also a unitizing activity in which students look for different units or chunks of the whole in or-

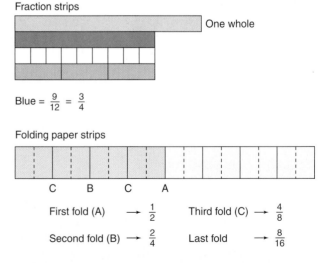

FIGURE 15.17   Length models for equivalent fractions.

der to name a part of the whole in different ways. This activity is significant because it utilizes a set model.

ACTIVITY 15.15

Group the Counters, Find the Names

Have students set out a specific number of counters in two colors—for example, 24 counters, 16 of them red and 8 yellow. The 24 make up the whole. The task is to group the counters into different fractional parts of the whole and use the parts to create fraction names for the red and the yellow counters. In Figure 15.18, 24 counters are arranged in different array patterns. You might want to suggest arrays or allow students to arrange them in any way they wish. Students should record their different groupings and explain how they found the fraction names. They can simply use Xs and Os for the counters.

In Lamon's version of the last activity, she prompts students with questions such as, "If we make groups of four, what part of the set is red?" With these prompts you can suggest fraction names that students are unlikely to think of. For our example in Figure 15.18, if we make groups of one-half counters, what would the yellow set be called? Suppose we

made groups of six? (Groups of six result in a fractional numerator. Why not?)

In the activities so far, there has only been a hint of a rule for finding equivalent fractions. The following activity moves a bit closer but should still be done before development of a rule.

ACTIVITY 15.16

Missing-Number Equivalencies

Give students an equation expressing an equivalence between two fractions but with one of the numbers missing. Here are four different examples:

$$\frac{5}{3} = \frac{\square}{6} \qquad \frac{2}{3} = \frac{6}{\square} \qquad \frac{8}{12} = \frac{\square}{3} \qquad \frac{9}{12} = \frac{3}{\square}$$

The missing number can be either a numerator or a denominator. Furthermore, the missing number can either be larger or smaller than the corresponding part of the equivalent fraction. (All four of these possibilities are represented in the examples.) The task is to find the missing number and to explain your solution.

When doing "Missing-Number Equivalencies" you may want to specify a particular model, such as sets or pie pieces.

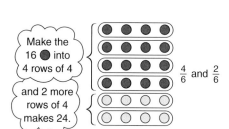

FIGURE 15.18 **Set models for equivalent fractions.**

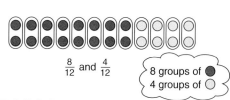

Alternatively, you can allow students to select whatever methods they wish to solve these problems. One or two equivalencies followed by a discussion is sufficient for a good lesson. This activity is surprisingly challenging, especially if students are required to use a set model.

Before continuing with development of an algorithm for equivalent fractions with your class, you should revisit the comparison tasks as children begin to realize that they can change the names of fractions in order to help reason about which fraction is greater.

Developing an Equivalent-Fraction Algorithm

Kamii and Clark (1995) argue that undue reliance on physical models does not help children construct equivalence schemes. When children understand that fractions can have different names, they should be challenged to develop a method for finding equivalent names. It might also be argued that students who are experienced at looking for patterns and developing schemes for doing things can invent an algorithm for equivalent fractions without further assistance. However, the following approach will certainly improve the chances of that happening.

An Area Model Approach

Your goal is to help students see that if they multiply both the top and bottom numbers by the same number, they will always get an equivalent fraction. The approach suggested here is to look for a pattern in the way that the fractional parts in both the part as well as the whole are counted. Activity 15.17 is a good beginning, but a good class discussion following the activity will also be required.

ACTIVITY 15.17

Slicing Squares

Give students a worksheet with four squares in a row, each approximately 3 cm on a side. Have them shade in the same fraction in each square using vertical dividing lines. For example, slice each square in fourths and shade three-fourths as in Figure 15.19. Next, tell students to slice each square into an equal number of horizontal slices. Each square is sliced with a different number of slices, using anywhere from one to eight slices. For each sliced square, they should write an equation showing the equivalent fraction. Have them examine their four equations and the drawings and challenge them to discover any patterns in what they have done. You may want them to repeat this with four more squares and a different fraction.

Start with each square showing $\frac{3}{4}$.

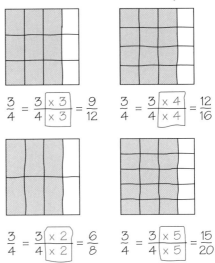

$$\frac{3}{4} = \frac{3}{4}\boxed{\begin{array}{c}\times\,3\\\times\,3\end{array}} = \frac{9}{12} \qquad \frac{3}{4} = \frac{3}{4}\boxed{\begin{array}{c}\times\,4\\\times\,4\end{array}} = \frac{12}{16}$$

$$\frac{3}{4} = \frac{3}{4}\boxed{\begin{array}{c}\times\,2\\\times\,2\end{array}} = \frac{6}{8} \qquad \frac{3}{4} = \frac{3}{4}\boxed{\begin{array}{c}\times\,5\\\times\,5\end{array}} = \frac{15}{20}$$

What <u>product</u> tells how many parts are shaded?

What <u>product</u> tells how many parts in the whole?

Notice that the same factor is used for both part and whole.

FIGURE 15.19 A model for the equivalent-fraction algorithm.

Following this activity, write on the board the equations for four or five different fraction names found by the students. Discuss any patterns they found. To focus the discussion, show on the overhead a square illustrating $\frac{4}{5}$ made with vertical slices as in Figure 15.20. Turn off the overhead and slice the square into six parts in the opposite direction. Cover all but two edges of the square as shown in the figure. Ask, "What is the new name for my $\frac{4}{5}$?"

The reason for this exercise is that many students simply count the small regions and never think to use multiplication. With the covered square, students can see that there are four columns and six rows to the shaded part, so there must be 4×6 parts shaded. Similarly, there must be 5×6 parts in the whole. Therefore, the new name for $\frac{4}{5}$ is $\frac{4 \times 6}{5 \times 6}$.

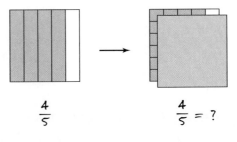

$$\frac{4}{5} \qquad\qquad \frac{4}{5} = ?$$

FIGURE 15.20 How can you count the fractional parts if you cannot see them all?

Using this idea, have students return to the fractions on their worksheet to see if the pattern works for other fractions.

Examine examples of equivalent fractions that have been generated with other models, and see if the rule of multiplying top and bottom numbers by the same number holds there also. If the rule is correct, how can $\frac{6}{8}$ and $\frac{9}{12}$ be equivalent? What about fractions like $2\frac{1}{4}$? How could it be demonstrated that $\frac{9}{4}$ is the same as $\frac{27}{12}$?

Writing Fractions in Simplest Terms

The multiplication scheme for equivalent fractions produces fractions with larger denominators. To write a fraction in *simplest terms* means to write it so that numerator and denominator have no common whole number factors. (Some texts use the name *lowest terms* instead of *simplest terms*.) One meaningful approach to this task of finding simplest terms is to reverse the earlier process, as illustrated in Figure 15.21. Try to devise a problem-based task that will help students develop this reverse idea.

Of course, finding and eliminating a common factor is the same as dividing both top and bottom by the same number. The search for a common factor keeps the process of writing an equivalent fraction to one rule: Top and bottom numbers of a fraction can be multiplied by the same nonzero number. There is no need for a different rule for rewriting fractions in lowest terms.

Two additional notes:

1. Notice that the phrase *reducing fractions* was not used. This unfortunate terminology implies making a fraction smaller and is rarely used anymore in textbooks.

2. Many teachers seem to believe that fraction answers are incorrect if not in simplest or lowest terms. This is also unfortunate. When students add $\frac{1}{6} + \frac{1}{2}$ and get $\frac{4}{6}$, they have added correctly and have found the answer. Rewriting $\frac{4}{6}$ as $\frac{2}{3}$ is a separate issue.

Multiplying by One

Many middle school textbooks use a strictly symbolic approach to equivalent fractions. It is based on the multiplicative property that says that any number multiplied by 1 remains unchanged. Any fraction of the form $\frac{n}{n}$ can be used as the identity element. Therefore, $\frac{3}{4} = \frac{3}{4} \times 1 = \frac{3}{4} \times \frac{2}{2} = \frac{6}{8}$.

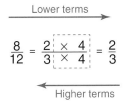

$$\frac{8}{12} = \frac{2}{3} \frac{\times\ 4}{\times\ 4} = \frac{2}{3}$$

FIGURE 15.21 **Using the equivalent-fraction algorithm to write fractions in simplest terms.**

Furthermore, the numerator and denominator of the identity element can also be fractions. In this way, $\frac{6}{12} = \frac{6}{12} \times \left(\frac{1/6}{1/6}\right) = \frac{1}{2}$.

This explanation relies on an understanding of the multiplicative identity property, which most students in grades 4 to 6 do not fully appreciate. It also relies on the procedure for multiplying two fractions. Finally, the argument uses solely deductive reasoning based on an axiom of the rational number system. It does not lend itself to intuitive modeling. A reasonable conclusion is to delay this important explanation until at least seventh or eighth grade in an appropriate prealgebra context and not as a method or a rationale for producing equivalent fractions.

 ## Technology Note

In the NCTM e-examples (www.nctm.org), there is a very nice fraction game for two players (*Applet 5.1, Communicating About Mathematics Using Games*). The game uses a number-line model, and knowledge of equivalent fractions plays a significant role.

The NLVM Web site (http://matti.usu.edu/nlvm/nav/vlibrary.html) has a limited applet tool for exploring equivalent fractions, *Fractions—Equivalent*. Proper fractions are presented randomly in either square or circular formats. Students can slice the model in as many parts as they wish to see which slicings create equivalent fractions. For squares, the new slices go in the same direction as the original slices. For circles, it is a bit hard to distinguish new slices from old. Students enter an equivalent fraction and then click a button to check their response.

A lot of computer software seems to be better at providing a high-tech model to illustrate equivalent fractions than it is at creating a problem-solving mode where students can think through an equivalent fraction task. *MathKeys: Unlocking Fractions and Decimals, Grades 3–5* (MECC, 1996a) provides a counter model, a bar model, and a circle model for fractions. In circles, two fractions can be modeled side by side, subdivided, and shaded in up to 16 sections. However, the symbolic fractions are never in lowest terms, and the symbols for each model are always present with the relation symbol ($<$, $>$, $=$) placed between them. The graphics are easy to manipulate and are quite good. However, this software is an example of students being able to use a model without reflective thought to solve a problem. Programs such as this may be best used as a class demonstration tool. ■

 ## Literature Connections

Fractions in textbooks and even in the activities in this chapter lack context. Context takes children away from rules and encourages them to explore ideas in a more open and informal manner. The way that children approach fraction concepts in these contexts may surprise you.

The Doorbell Rang
Hutchins, 1986

Often used to investigate whole-number operations of multiplication and division, this book is also an excellent early introduction to fractions. The story is a simple tale of two children preparing to share a plate of 12 cookies. Just as they have figured out how to share the cookies, the doorbell rings and more children arrive. This continues to happen until there are more children than cookies. Grandma saves the day. By changing the number of children to create an uneven division, children have to figure out how to divide the remaining cookies fairly. If given drawings of circles for cookies, investigations of situations such as four cookies for six children provide a variety of ways to solve fraction problems and discuss the need for fractional parts consisting of equal shares.

Gator Pie
Mathews, 1979

Appropriate even for grades 5 and 6, this delightful book has Alvin, Alice, and other alligators sharing a pie they find in the woods. As more and more gators arrive, the need for cutting the pie into more and more pieces is evident, finally ending in hundredths, making a nice connection between decimals and fractions. An interesting exploration involves cutting a pie (or a rectangle) into halves or thirds and then deciding how to share it among a larger number once already cut. To go from halves to sixths is reasonably easy but may surprise you. What if the pie is cut in thirds and then we want to share it in tenths?

The Man Who Counted: A Collection of Mathematical Adventures
Tahan, 1993

This book contains a story, "Beasts of Burden," about a wise mathematician, Beremiz, and the narrator, who are traveling together on one camel. They are asked by three brothers to solve an argument. Their father has left them 35 camels to divide among them: half to one brother, one-third to another, and one-ninth to the third. The story provides an excellent context for discussing fractional parts of sets and how fractional parts change as the whole changes. However, if the whole is changed from 35 to, say, 36 or 34, the problem of the indicated shares remains unresolved. The sum of $\frac{1}{2}$, $\frac{1}{3}$, and $\frac{1}{9}$ will never be one whole, no matter how many camels are involved. Bresser (1995) describes three full days of wonderful discussions with his fifth graders, who proposed a wide range of solutions. Bresser's suggestions are worth considering. ■

Reflections on Chapter 15

Writing to Learn

1. Describe what is meant by sharing activities. What is the goal of these activities? When would you use them? Distinguish between early and later sharing activities. What makes them different?
2. Give examples of three categories of fraction models. Why are set models more difficult for younger children?
3. Describe fractional parts. What are the two distinct requirements of fractional parts? Explain how children's concepts of partitioning need to be refined to produce a concept of fractional parts.
4. What are children learning in activities in which you count fractional parts? How can this type of activity help children learn to write fractions meaningfully?
5. Give a fourth-grade explanation of the meaning of the top number and the bottom number in a fraction.
6. Using a length model, make up part-and-whole questions for each of the following cases:
   a. Given a part and a nonunit fraction less than 1, find the whole.
   b. Given a part and a nonunit fraction greater than 1, find the whole.
   c. Given a whole and a nonunit fraction less than 1, find the part.
   d. Given a whole and a nonunit fraction greater than 1, find the part.
   Try your questions with a friend. Then change each question so that it is in terms of sets. With sets, be sure that a unit fraction is never a single counter. That is, if the question is about fourths, use whole sets of size 8 or 12 or more. What is the main purpose of these activities?
7. Describe several types of ideas for number sense with fractions and an activity for each.
8. Make up pairs of fractions that can be compared ("select the larger") without using an algorithm. See if you can make up examples that use the four different ideas that were suggested for comparing fractions. How do these activities change as students begin to use equivalent fractions?
9. Explain the difference between understanding the concept of equivalent fractions and knowing the algorithm for writing an equivalent fraction.
10. Describe some activities that will help children develop the equivalent-fraction concept.
11. How can you help children develop the algorithm for equivalent fractions?

For Discussion and Exploration

1. A common error that children make is to write $\frac{3}{5}$ for the fraction represented here:

Why do you think that they do this? In this chapter, the notation of fractional parts and counting by unit fractions were introduced before any symbols. How could this help avoid the type of thinking that is involved in this common error?

2. Experiment with rods made of connecting cubes as a model for fractions. For example, if a bar of 12 cubes is a whole, then bars of 3 cubes would be fourths. Since the bars can be taken apart and put together and since the individual cubes can be counted, there are some significant differences between this model and those suggested in the text. Is this a length model or a set model?

3. In an editorial in *Mathematics Teaching in the Middle School*, Patrick Groff (1996) questions the importance of teaching fractions in the upper-elementary and middle grades. His arguments are based in part on the difficulty of learning fraction ideas at this level, the decreased use of fractions in everyday life, and the press for space in the curriculum from other topics that have recently been introduced. His opinion is rebutted in the "Readers Write" section of the September–October 1996 issue by a former physicist and by a current teacher. The discussion has merit. Which side of this argument makes more sense? Why?

Recommendations for Further Reading

Highly Recommended

Burns, M. (2001). *Teaching arithmetic: Lessons for introducing fractions, grades 4–5.* Sausalito, CA: Math Solutions Publications.
Typical of Marilyn Burns, this book offers well-designed lessons with lots of details, sample student dialogue, and Blackline Masters. These are introductory ideas for fraction concepts. Five lessons cover one-half as a benchmark. Assessments are also included.

Reys, B. J., Kim, O., & Bay, J. M. (1999). Establishing fraction benchmarks. *Mathematics Teaching in the Middle School, 4,* 530–532.
This short article describes a simple three-question interview administered to 20 fifth-grade students. The results are both sad and surprising. A significant conclusion is that the teaching of benchmarks for fractions, specifically 0, $\frac{1}{2}$, and 1, is generally neglected in the standard curriculum. The questions used in the interview can profitably be used with children in grades 4 to 7.

Tzur, R. (1999). An integrated study of children's construction of improper fractions and the teacher's role in promoting learning. *Journal for Research in Mathematics Education, 30,* 390–416.
Don't shy away from this research article. Tzur's teaching experiment is described in detail, providing the reader with a real understanding of the construction of fraction concepts at the fourth-grade level.

Watanabe, T. (1996). Ben's understanding of one-half. *Teaching Children Mathematics, 2,* 460–464.

This provocative article examines three very interesting tasks that were presented to a second-grade child. Even if you are interested in the upper grades, this is a worthwhile article. Not only are the tasks or variations of them quite interesting for all children, but the implications are also worth considering. Listening carefully to children informs us best.

Other Suggestions

Empson, S. B. (2002). Organizing diversity in early fraction thinking. In B. Litwiller (Ed.), *Making sense of fractions, ratios, and proportions* (pp. 29–40). Reston, VA: National Council of Teachers of Mathematics.

Fosnot, C. T., & Dolk, M. (2002). *Young mathematicians at work: Constructing fractions, decimals, and percents.* Portsmouth, NH: Heinemann.

Groff, P. (1996). It is time to question fraction teaching. *Mathematics Teaching in the Middle School, 1,* 604–607.

Lamon, S. J. (1999). *More: In-depth discussion of the reasoning activities in "Teaching fractions and ratios for understanding."* Mahwah, NJ: Lawrence Erlbaum.

Lamon, S. J. (1999). *Teaching fractions and ratios for understanding: Essential content knowledge and instructional strategies for teachers.* Mahwah, NJ: Lawrence Erlbaum.

Lamon, S. (2001). Presenting and representing: From fractions to rational numbers. In A. A. Cuoco (Ed.), *The roles of representation in school mathematics* (pp. 146–165). Reston, VA: National Council of Teachers of Mathematics.

Lamon, S. (2002). Part-whole comparison with unitizing. In B. Litwiller (Ed.), *Making sense of fractions, ratios, and proportions* (pp. 79–86). Reston, VA: National Council of Teachers of Mathematics.

Mack, N. K. (1995). Confounding whole-number and fraction concepts when building on informal knowledge. *Journal for Research in Mathematics Education, 26,* 422–441.

Middleton, J. A., van den Heuvel-Panhuizen, M., & Shew, J. A. (1997). Using bar representations as a model for connecting concepts of rational number. *Mathematics Teaching in the Middle School, 3,* 302–312.

Moskal, B. M., & Magone, M. E. (2002). Making explicit what students know about representing fractions. In B. Litwiller (Ed.), *Making sense of fractions, ratios, and proportions* (pp. 121–129). Reston, VA: National Council of Teachers of Mathematics.

Moss, J., & Case, R. (1999). Developing children's understanding of the rational numbers: A new model and an experimental curriculum. *Journal for Research in Mathematics Education, 30,* 122–147.

Schifter, D., Bastable, V., & Russell, S. J. (1999b). *Developing mathematical understanding: Numbers and operations, Part 2, Making meaning for operations (Casebook).* Parsippany, NJ: Dale Seymour Publications.

Smith, J. P. III. (2002). The development of students' knowledge of fractions and ratios. In B. Litwiller (Ed.), *Making sense of fractions, ratios, and proportions* (pp. 3–17). Reston, VA: National Council of Teachers of Mathematics.

Tzur, R. (1999). An integrated study of children's construction of improper fractions and the teacher's role in promoting that learning. *Journal for Research in Mathematics Education, 30,* 390–416.

Wearne, D. (2000). Rational numbers. In E. A. Silver & P. A. Kenney (Eds.), *Results from the seventh mathematics assessment of the National Assessment of Educational Progress* (pp. 163–192). Reston, VA: National Council of Teachers of Mathematics.

16

COMPUTATION with FRACTIONS

A fifth-grade student asks, "Why is it when we times 29 times two-ninths that the answer goes down?" (Taber, 2002, p. 67). Although generalizations from whole numbers can confuse students, you should realize that their ideas about the operations were developed with whole numbers. Students need to build on their ideas of whole-number operations. This is where students are. We can use their understanding of what the operations mean to give meaning to fraction computation.

However, as you will discover in this chapter, a firm understanding of fractions is the most critical foundation for fraction computation. Without this foundation, your students will almost certainly be learning rules without reasons, an unacceptable goal.

 ## Big Ideas

1. The meanings of each operation on fractions are the same as the meanings for the operations on whole numbers. Operations with fractions should begin by applying these same meanings to fractional parts.
   - For addition and subtraction, it is critical to understand that the numerator tells the number of parts and the denominator the type of part.
   - For multiplication by a fraction, it is useful to recall that the denominator is a divisor. This idea allows us to find parts of the other factor. (See Chapter 15, p. 249.)
   - For division by a fraction, the two ways of thinking about the operation—partition and measurement—are extremely important. The partition or fair-sharing concept of division will lead to a very different division procedure than will the measurement or repeated subtraction concept.

2. Estimation of fraction computations is tied almost entirely to concepts of the operations and of fractions. A compu-

tation algorithm is not required for making estimates. Estimation should be an integral part of computation development to keep students' attention on the meanings of the operations and the expected size of the results.

 ## CONTENT CONNECTIONS

Computation with fractions is built on an understanding of the operations and on fraction sense. The ability to compute and estimate with fractions will serve the user well whenever these skills are required. However, understanding fraction computation has a special connection in two areas.

- **Decimals and Percents (Chapter 17):** Because decimals and percents are alternative representations for fractions, they can often help with computational fluency, especially in the area of estimation. For example, 2.452×0.513 is about $2\frac{1}{2} \times \frac{1}{2}$ or $1\frac{1}{4} = 1.25$. Twenty-five percent off of the $132 list price is easily computed as $\frac{1}{4}$ of 132.

- **Proportional Reasoning (Chapter 18):** Fraction multiplication helps us to think about fractions as operators. This in turn is connected to the concepts of ratio and proportion, especially the ideas of scaling and scale factors.

NUMBER SENSE AND FRACTION ALGORITHMS

Today it is important to be able to compute with fractions, primarily for the purpose of making estimates, for understanding computations done with technology, and for relatively simple calculations. Even standardized testing reflects an emphasis on less-tedious computations with fractions.

The Dangerous Rush to Rules

It is important to give students ample opportunity to develop fraction number sense as described in the previous chapter and not immediately to start talking about common denominators and other rules of computation.

Premature attention to rules for fraction computation has a number of serious drawbacks. None of the rules helps students think about the operations and what they mean. Armed only with rules, students have no means of assessing their results to see if they make sense. Surface mastery of rules in the short term is quickly lost. When mixed together, the myriad rules of fraction computation soon become a meaningless jumble. Students ask, "Do I need a common denominator, or do you just add the bottom numbers like in multiplication?" "Which one do you invert, the first or the second number?" The algorithm rules do not immediately apply to mixed numbers. More rules! And perhaps most important is that this approach to mathematics is immensely defeating to the child.

Principles and Standards suggests that the main focus on fractions and decimals in grades 3–5 should be on the development of number sense and informal approaches to addition and subtraction. In grades 6–8, students should expand their skills to include all operations with fractions, decimals, and percents.

A Problem-Based, Number Sense Approach

Even if your curriculum guidelines call for teaching all four of the operations with fractions in the fifth grade, you are still advised to delay a rush to algorithmic procedures until it becomes clear that students are ready. (Very few states call for multiplication and division of fractions before the fifth grade.) Students can become adequately proficient using informal, student-invented methods that they understand.

The following guidelines should be kept in mind when developing computational strategies for fractions:

1. *Begin with simple contextual tasks.* Huinker (1998) makes an excellent case for the use of contextual problems and for letting students develop their own methods of computation with fractions. Problems or contexts need not be elaborate. What you want is a context for both the meaning of the operation and the fractions involved.

2. *Connect the meaning of fraction computation with whole-number computation.* To consider what $2\frac{1}{2} \times \frac{3}{4}$ might mean, we should ask, "What does 2×3 mean?" The concepts of each operation are the same, and benefits can be had by connecting these ideas.

3. *Let estimation and informal methods play a big role in the development of strategies.* "Should $2\frac{1}{2} \times \frac{3}{4}$ be more or less

than 1? More or less than 3?" Estimation keeps the focus on the meanings of the numbers and the operations, encourages reflective thinking, and helps build informal number sense with fractions.

4. *Explore each of the operations using models.* Use a variety of models. Have students defend their solutions using the models. You will find that sometimes it is possible to get answers with models that do not seem to help with pencil-and-paper approaches. That's fine! The ideas will help children learn to think about the fractions and the operations, contribute to mental methods, and provide a useful background when you eventually do get to the standard algorithms.

In the discussions that follow, informal exploration is encouraged for each operation. There is also a guided development of each traditional algorithm.

Addition and Subtraction

The idea of developing invented strategies for fractions beginning with contextual problems is similar to the approach described in Chapter 13 for whole-number computation. As with whole numbers, expect that students will use a variety of methods and that the methods will vary widely with the fractions encountered in the problems.

No attempt is made in this chapter to describe all of the solution strategies that students might develop. Students will continue to find ways to solve problems with fractions, and their informal approaches will contribute to the development of more standard methods (Huinker, 1998; Lappan & Mouck, 1998; Schifter, Bastable, & Russell, 1999c).

Informal Exploration

Consider the following simple context:

Paul and his brother were each eating the same kind of candy bar. Paul had $\frac{3}{4}$ of his candy bar. His brother still had $\frac{7}{8}$ of a candy bar. How much candy did the two boys have together?

This is an example of the type of task you can pose to students from the very beginning of their exploration with fraction computation.

Using nothing other than simple drawings, how would you solve this problem without setting it up in the usual manner and finding common denominators? Can you think of two different methods?

FIGURE 16.1 How could you combine these two quantities to determine the sum?

Most students will draw a simple rectangle for the two candy bars as in Figure 16.1. The drawing of $\frac{7}{8}$ suggests that if you had one more eighth it would be a whole. So it is the same as $1\frac{3}{4}$ with $\frac{1}{8}$ taken off. Or, the drawing might suggest taking a fourth from the $\frac{7}{8}$ and putting it with the $\frac{3}{4}$ to make a whole. That would leave $\frac{5}{8}$.

Drawings are not always as helpful as physical models because students draw conclusions based on inaccurate drawings. Sometimes there is a value in specifying that a particular model be used. Suppose that you ask students to solve the following problem by using fraction strips.

Jack and Jill ordered two identical-sized pizzas, one cheese and one pepperoni. Jack ate $\frac{5}{6}$ of a pizza and Jill ate $\frac{1}{2}$ of a pizza. How much pizza did they eat together?

The first decision that must be made is what strip to use as the whole. That decision is not required with a circular model. The whole must be the same for both fractions although there is a tendency to use the easiest whole for each fraction. Again, this issue does not arise with circles. In this case, the smallest strip that will work is the 6 strip or the dark green strip. Figure 16.2 illustrates a solution. The thinking required in this task helps pave the way for a common denominator approach.

Subtraction of two fractions with models is a similar process, as shown in Figure 16.3. Notice that it is sometimes possible to find the sum or difference of two fractions without splitting pieces into smaller parts. Often the answer is determined by looking at the part left over.

Most of your problems should involve simple fractions with "friendly" denominators no greater than 12. There is no need to add fifths and sevenths or even fifths and twelfths. The results involve numbers that cannot be handled with any model or drawing. Those numbers are rarely found in real problems. At the same time, do not be afraid of including mixed numbers and unlike denominators.

The Myth of Common Denominators

Teachers commonly tell students, "In order to add or subtract fractions, you must first get common denominators." The explanation usually goes something like, "After all, you can't add apples and oranges." This well-intentioned statement is

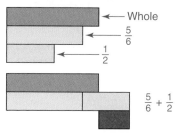

Find a strip for a whole that allows both fractions to be modeled.

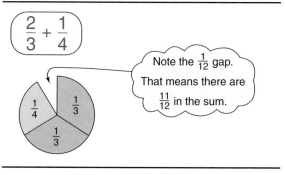

The sum is 1 whole and a red rod more than a whole. A red is $\frac{1}{3}$ of a dark green. So $\frac{5}{6} + \frac{1}{2} = 1\frac{1}{3}$.

Note the $\frac{1}{12}$ gap. That means there are $\frac{11}{12}$ in the sum.

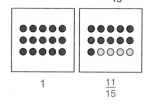

What set size can be used for the whole? The smallest is a set of 15.

$\frac{2}{5}$ $\frac{4}{3}$

Combine (add) the fractions. $\frac{2}{5}$ is 6 counters, and $\frac{4}{3}$ is 20 counters. In sets of 15, that is $\frac{26}{15}$, or $1\frac{11}{15}$.

1 $\frac{11}{15}$

FIGURE 16.2 Using models to add fractions.

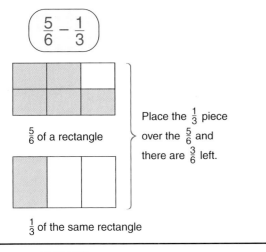

$$\frac{5}{6} - \frac{1}{3}$$

$\frac{5}{6}$ of a rectangle

$\frac{1}{3}$ of the same rectangle

Place the $\frac{1}{3}$ piece over the $\frac{5}{6}$ and there are $\frac{3}{6}$ left.

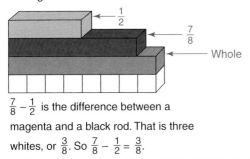

$$\frac{7}{8} - \frac{1}{2}$$

Find a rod that can be broken into eighths and halves: brown.

$\frac{1}{2}$

$\frac{7}{8}$

Whole

$\frac{7}{8} - \frac{1}{2}$ is the difference between a magenta and a black rod. That is three whites, or $\frac{3}{8}$. So $\frac{7}{8} - \frac{1}{2} = \frac{3}{8}$.

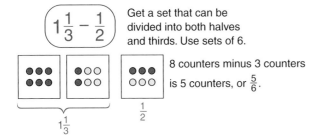

$$1\frac{1}{3} - \frac{1}{2}$$

Get a set that can be divided into both halves and thirds. Use sets of 6.

8 counters minus 3 counters is 5 counters, or $\frac{5}{6}$.

$1\frac{1}{3}$

$\frac{1}{2}$

FIGURE 16.3 Using models to subtract fractions.

essentially false. A correct statement might be, "In order *to use the standard algorithm* to add or subtract fractions, you must first get common denominators." And the explanation is then, "The algorithm is designed to work only with common denominators."

Using their own invented strategies, students will see that many correct solutions are found without ever getting a common denominator. Consider these sums and differences:

$$\frac{3}{4} + \frac{1}{8} \qquad \frac{1}{2} - \frac{1}{8} \qquad \frac{2}{3} + \frac{1}{2} \qquad 1\frac{1}{2} - \frac{3}{4} \qquad 1\frac{2}{3} + \frac{3}{4}$$

Working with the ways different fractional parts are related one to another often provides solutions without common denominators. For example, halves, fourths, and eighths are easily related. Also, picture three thirds making up a whole in a circle. Have you ever noticed that one-half of the whole is a third and a half of a third or a sixth? Similarly, the difference between a third and a fourth is a twelfth. With relationships such as these, many fraction computations can be solved without first getting common denominators.

Developing the Algorithm

The foregoing notwithstanding, it is important to develop an algorithm for addition and subtraction, and children will likely need some guidance in doing so. At the same time, they can easily build on their informal explorations and see that the common-denominator approach is meaningful.

Like Denominators

Most lists of objectives first specify addition and subtraction with like denominators. This is both unfortunate and unnecessary! If students have a good foundation with fraction concepts, they should be able to add or subtract like fractions immediately. Students who are not confident solving problems such as $\frac{3}{4} + \frac{2}{4}$ or $3\frac{7}{8} - 1\frac{3}{8}$ almost certainly do not have good fraction concepts and will be lost in any further development. The idea that the top number counts and the bottom number tells what is counted makes addition and subtraction of like fractions the same as adding and subtracting whole numbers.

Unlike Denominators

To get students to move to common denominators, consider a task such as $\frac{5}{8} + \frac{2}{4}$. Let students use pie pieces to get the result of $1\frac{1}{8}$ using any approach. Many will note that the models for the two fractions make one whole and there is $\frac{1}{8}$ extra. The key question to ask at this point is, "How can we change this problem into one that is just like the easy ones where the parts are the same?" For this example, it is relatively easy to see that fourths could be changed into eighths. Have students use models to show the original problem and also the converted problem. The main idea is to see that $\frac{5}{8} + \frac{2}{4}$ is exactly the same problem as $\frac{5}{8} + \frac{4}{8}$.

Next try some examples where both fractions need to be changed—for example, $\frac{2}{3} + \frac{1}{4}$. Again, focus attention on *rewriting the problem* in a form that is like "adding apples and apples," where the parts of both fractions are the same. As students discuss solutions, be sure they understand clearly that the new form of the problem is the same problem. This can and should be demonstrated with models. However, if your students express any doubt about the equivalence of the two problems ("Is $\frac{11}{12}$ really the answer to $\frac{2}{3} + \frac{1}{4}$?"), that should be a clue that the concept of equivalent fractions is not well understood.

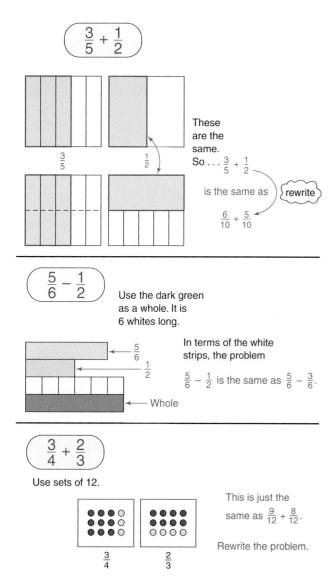

FIGURE 16.4   **Rewriting addition and subtraction problems involving fractions.**

As a result of modeling and rewriting fractions to make the problems easy, students will come to understand that the process of getting a common denominator is really one of looking for a way to change the *statement* of the problem without changing the problem itself. These ideas are illustrated in Figure 16.4.

Subtraction of two simple fractions follows exactly the same approach.

Common Multiples

Many students have trouble with finding common denominators because they are not able to come up with common multiples of the denominators quickly. That is a skill that can be drilled. It also depends on having a good command of the basic facts for multiplication. Here is an activity aimed at the skill of finding least common multiples or common denominators.

ACTIVITY 16.1

LCM Flash Cards

Make flash cards with pairs of numbers that are potential denominators. Most should be less than 16, as before. For each card, students try to give the least common multiple (LCM; see Figure 16.5). Be sure to include pairs that are prime, such as 9 and 5; pairs in which one is a multiple of the other, such as 2 and 8; and pairs that have a common divisor, such as 8 and 12.

FIGURE 16.5   **Least common multiple (LCM) flash cards.**

Mixed Numbers

A separate algorithm for mixed numbers in addition and subtraction is not necessary even though mixed numbers are often treated as separate topics in traditional textbooks and in some lists of objectives. Avoid layering fractions with yet another rule. Include mixed numbers in all of your activities with addition and subtraction, and let students solve these problems in ways that make sense to them. Furthermore, it is almost certain that students will add the whole numbers first and then deal with the fractions using the algorithm or whatever method makes sense.

For subtraction, dealing with the whole numbers first still makes sense. Consider this problem: $5\frac{1}{8} - 3\frac{5}{8}$. After subtracting 3 from 5, students will need to deal with the $\frac{5}{8}$. Some will take $\frac{5}{8}$ from the whole part, 2, leaving $1\frac{3}{8}$, and then $\frac{1}{8}$ more is $1\frac{4}{8}$. Others may take away the $\frac{1}{8}$ that is there and then $\frac{4}{8}$ from the remaining 2. A third but unlikely method is to trade one of the wholes for $\frac{8}{8}$, add it to the $\frac{1}{8}$, and then take $\frac{5}{8}$ from the resulting $\frac{9}{8}$. This last method is the same as the traditional algorithm.

Estimation and Simple Methods

With denominators of 16 or less, estimation using "nice" fractions like halves and fourths is usually possible and should be encouraged. Estimation also leads to informal methods that are often easier than traditional algorithms for getting exact answers.

CONNECTED MATHEMATICS

MIDDLE GRADES

Grade 6, *Bits and Pieces II*
Investigation 4: Adding and Subtracting Fractions

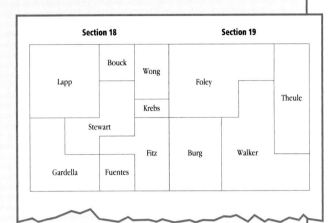

Context

Bits and Pieces II is the second full unit of the sixth grade that explores fractions. In the earlier unit, the emphasis is placed on fraction meanings and connections to decimals and percents. In this unit, strategies for all four of the operations are explored as well as computations with decimals and percents.

Task Description

This problem builds on students' understanding of fractions as part of a region. Two sections of land are shown on the map, each section being 640 acres (1 square mile). The problem is in two parts. First, students are to determine what fraction of a section (one square) each person owns. As a follow-up they also find the number of acres each person owns, an early application of a fraction times a whole number.

The second part of the problem includes a small logic task, as well as addition of fractions, involving owners of some parcels sold to other landowners. Students are given clues about the transactions. Their task is to redraw the map, find out how much land each of the remaining four owners has, and to explain their reasoning. Here are the transaction clues:

Clue 1: When all the sales are completed, four people—Theule, Fuentes, Wong, and Gardella—own all of the land in the two sections.

Clue 2: Theule bought from one person and now owns land equivalent to $\frac{1}{2}$ of one section.

Clue 3: Fuentes bought from three people and now owns the equivalent of $\frac{13}{32}$ of one section.

Clue 4: Gardella now owns the equivalent of $\frac{1}{2}$ of a section.

From *Connected Mathematics: Bits and Pieces II: Using Rational Numbers.* © 2002 by Michigan State University, Glenda Lappan, James T. Fey, William M. Fitzgerald, Susan N. Friel, and Elizabeth Difanis Phillips. Published by Prentice Hall. Used by permission of Prentice Hall, Inc.

Clue 5: Wong now owns all of the rest of the land in the two sections.

Clue 6: Each of the four owners can walk around all of their land without having to cross onto another person's land.

According to the manual, most students end up subdividing each section with an 8 × 8 grid and use this to determine the fractional part of each parcel. In the discussion, students are encouraged not only to use their drawings but also to use addition of fractions to justify their conclusions from the clues.

The logical reasoning component and the contextual setting for this problem make it engaging for sixth graders. In the next lesson, students are challenged to design at least one algorithm for adding fractions and one for subtracting fractions. Notice how the land problem can help students see a value in a common denominator and prepare them for designing their own procedures.

Consider $7\frac{1}{8} - 2\frac{3}{4}$. A first estimate might be 5, ignoring the fractions. Will it be more or less than 5? Others may begin by thinking $7\frac{1}{8}$ is close to 7 and $2\frac{3}{4}$ is close to 3 $\longrightarrow$ about 4, maybe a little more. Once students begin to think in these terms, a meaningful method for an exact answer is often possible without using an algorithm.

Examine the fraction exercises for addition and subtraction in a middle grades textbook. See how many of them

you can do without pencil and paper. Challenge students to do the same.

At the sixth grade, the *Connected Mathematics* program does not spend a great deal of time with addition and subtraction of fractions. However, it pays considerable attention to connecting fractions, decimals, and percents. The activity described on this page involves an open-ended approach to fraction addition appropriate at that grade level.

Multiplication

When working with whole numbers, we would say that 3 × 5 means "3 sets of 5." The first factor tells how much of the second factor you have or want. This is a good place to begin. Simple story problems are a significant help in this development.

Informal Exploration

The story problems that you use to pose multiplication tasks to children need not be elaborate, but it is important to think about the numbers that you use in the problems. A possible progression of problem difficulty is developed in the sections that follow.

Beginning Concepts

Consider these two problems as good starting tasks:

There are 15 cars in Michael's toy car collection. Two-thirds of the cars are red. How many red cars does Michael have?

Suzanne has 11 cookies. She wants to share them with her three friends. How many cookies will Suzanne and each of her friends get?

Finding the fractional part of a whole number, which is the task in both problems, is not unlike the task of finding a fractional part of a whole. In Michael's car problem, think of the 15 cars as the whole and you want $\frac{2}{3}$ of the whole. First, find thirds by dividing 15 by 3. Multiplying by thirds, regardless of how many thirds, involves dividing by 3. The denominator is a divisor.

Suzanne's cookie problem is the same as the sharing problems discussed in the last chapter. Dividing by 4 is the same as multiplication by $\frac{1}{4}$. Or think of the 11 cookies as the whole. How many in one-fourth? Cookies are used so that the items can be subdivided. The many ways that students solve these sharing problems were discussed in Chapter 15.

Problems in which the first factor or multiplier is a whole number are also important.

Wayne filled 5 glasses with $\frac{2}{3}$ liter of soda in each glass. How much soda did Wayne use?

This problem may be solved in different ways. Some children will put the thirds together, making wholes as they go. Others will count all of the thirds and then find out how many whole liters are in 10 thirds.

Unit Parts Without Subdivisions

To expand on the ideas just presented, consider these three problems:

You have $\frac{3}{4}$ of a pizza left. If you give $\frac{1}{3}$ of the leftover pizza to your brother, how much of a whole pizza will your brother get?

Someone ate $\frac{1}{10}$ of the cake, leaving only $\frac{9}{10}$. If you eat $\frac{2}{3}$ of the cake that is left, how much of a whole cake will you have eaten?

Gloria used $2\frac{1}{2}$ tubes of blue paint to paint the sky in her picture. Each tube holds $\frac{4}{5}$ ounce of paint. How many ounces of blue paint did Gloria use?

Notice that the units or fractional parts in these problems do not need to be subdivided further. The first problem is $\frac{1}{3}$ of three things, the second is $\frac{2}{3}$ of nine things, and the last is $2\frac{1}{2}$ of four things. The focus remains on the number of unit parts in all, and then the size of the parts determines the number of wholes. Figure 16.6 shows how problems of this type might be modeled. However, it is very important to let students model and solve these problems in their own way, using whatever models or drawings they choose. Require only that they be able to explain their reasoning.

Subdividing the Unit Parts

When the pieces must be subdivided into smaller unit parts, the problems become more challenging.

Zack had $\frac{2}{3}$ of the lawn left to cut. After lunch, he cut $\frac{3}{4}$ of the grass he had left. How much of the whole lawn did Zack cut after lunch?

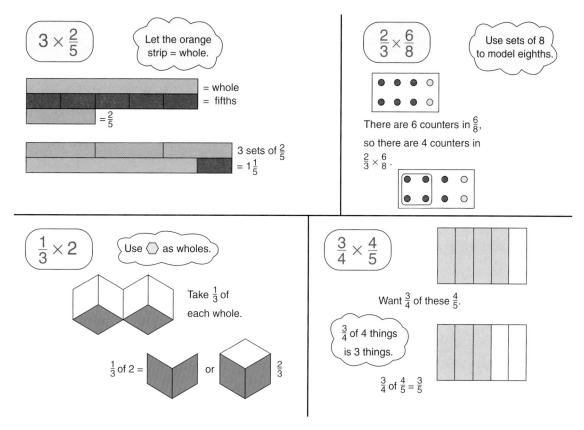

FIGURE 16.6 **Modeling multiplication problems in which the unit pieces do not require further subdivision.**

The zookeeper had a huge bottle of the animals' favorite liquid treat, Zoo Cola. The monkey drank $\frac{1}{5}$ of the bottle. The zebra drank $\frac{2}{3}$ of what was left. How much of the bottle of Zoo Cola did the zebra drink?

> ✕ **STOP** Stop for a moment and figure out how you would solve each of these problems. Draw pictures to help you, but do not use a computational algorithm.

In Zack's lawn problem, it is necessary to find fourths of two things, the 2 *thirds* of the grass left to cut. In the Zoo Cola problem, you need thirds of four things, the 4 *fifths* of the cola that remain. Again, the concepts of the top number counting and the bottom number naming what is counted play an important role. Figure 16.7 shows two possible solutions for Zack's lawn problem. Similar approaches can be used for the Zoo Cola problem. You may have used different drawings, but the ideas should be the same.

How much is $\frac{3}{4}$ of $\frac{2}{3}$?

Cut each third in half, and take 3 parts.
Half of a third is a sixth, so it's $\frac{3}{6}$.

Cut all 3 thirds into 4 parts. Each part is $\frac{1}{12}$.
Three-fourths of the 8 twelfths of the grass left to cut is $\frac{6}{12}$.

FIGURE 16.7 **Solutions to fraction products when the unit parts must be subdivided.**

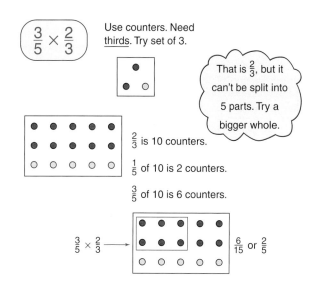

FIGURE 16.8 Modeling multiplication of fractions with counters.

If students use counters to model problems where the units require subdivision, an added difficulty arises. Figure 16.8 illustrates what might happen solving the problem $\frac{3}{5} \times \frac{2}{3}$. (*Three-fifths of $\frac{2}{3}$ of a whole is how much of a whole?*) Here the representation of a whole must be changed so that the thirds can be subdivided. Do not discourage students from using counters, but be prepared to help them find ways to show thirds using larger sets.

The problem in Figure 16.8 offers another possible twist worth mentioning. Since there is no context to the problem, why not use the commutative property—turn the factors around and consider $\frac{2}{3}$ of $\frac{3}{5}$. Wow! Do you see that the answer is $\frac{2}{5}$ almost immediately?

Developing the Algorithm

If you have spent adequate time with your students exploring multiplication of fractions as just described, the traditional multiplication algorithm will be relatively simple to develop. Shift from contextual problems to a straight computation. Have students use a square or a rectangle as the model.

A Beginning Task

To make the development problem based for students, provide them with a drawing of $\frac{3}{4}$ of a square as shown in Figure 16.9. The task is to use the drawing to determine the product $\frac{3}{5} \times \frac{3}{4}$ (three-fifths of three-fourths of a whole) and explain the result. Remember, you want to find a fractional part of the shaded part. The *unit*, however, the way the parts are measured, must remain the whole.

Drawn as shown, the easiest way to get $\frac{3}{4}$ of the shaded region is to divide it into fourths using lines in the opposite direction. Then the problem is to determine what types of unit pieces these are. Although students may not think of it, an easy method of doing this is to extend the lines, subdividing the entire whole into fourths. Then the product of the

FIGURE 16.9 Development of the algorithm for multiplication of fractions.

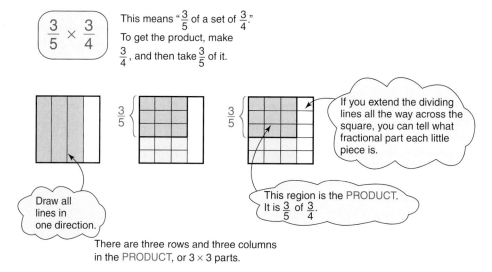

denominators tells how many pieces are in the whole (the kind of unit), and the product of the numerators tells the number of pieces in the product.

Avoid pushing students to formalize the rule or algorithm of multiplying tops and bottoms. Many students will simply count each small part in the drawings and not notice that the numbers of rows and columns are actually the two numerators and the two denominators, respectively. You might steer students in this direction by posing a problem with the initial sketch but asking them to determine the product without additional drawing. Try this with $\frac{7}{8} \times \frac{4}{5}$, where the numbers make it almost mandatory that you multiply.

A cautionary note: Many texts make this sliced-square approach so mechanical that it actually becomes a meaningless algorithm in itself. Students are told to shade a square one way for the first factor and the opposite way for the second factor. Without rationale, they are told that the product is the region that is double-shaded. You might as well give students the rule and forget about explanations.

Factors Greater Than One

Once students have explored products with both factors less than 1, it may be challenging to have them see if they can use a similar type of drawing to explain products with either or both factors greater than 1. Figure 16.10 shows how this might look when both factors are mixed numbers. Keep the task problem based. This can be a significant and worthwhile challenge. There is no need to explain how to do this.

Mental Techniques and Estimation

In the real world, there are many instances when the product of a whole number times a fraction occurs, and a mental estimate or even an exact answer is quite useful. For example, sale items are frequently listed as "$\frac{1}{4}$ off," or we read of a "$\frac{1}{3}$ increase" in the number of registered voters. Fractions are excellent substitutes for percents, as you will see in the next chapter. To get an estimate of 60 percent of $36.69, it is useful to think of 60 percent as $\frac{3}{5}$ or as a little less than $\frac{2}{3}$.

These products of fractions with large whole numbers can be calculated mentally by thinking of the meanings of the top and bottom numbers. For example, $\frac{3}{5}$ is 3 one-fifths. So if you want $\frac{3}{5}$ of 350, for example, first think about one-fifth of 350, or 70. If one-fifth is 70, then three-fifths is 3 × 70, or 210. Although this example has very accommodating numbers, it illustrates a process for mentally multiplying a large number by a fraction: First determine the unit fractional part, and then multiply by the number of parts you want.

When numbers are not so nice, encourage students to use compatible numbers. To estimate $\frac{3}{5}$ of $36.69, a useful compatible is $35. One-fifth of 35 is 7, so three-fifths is 3 × 7, or 21. Now adjust a bit—perhaps add an additional 50 cents, for an estimate of $21.50.

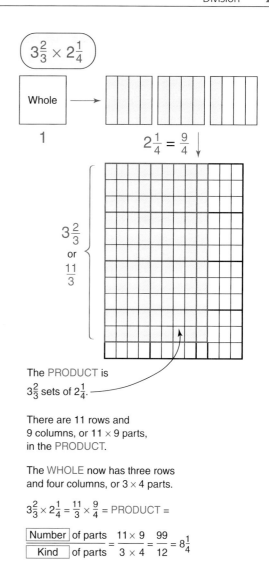

The PRODUCT is $3\frac{2}{3}$ sets of $2\frac{1}{4}$.

There are 11 rows and 9 columns, or 11 × 9 parts, in the PRODUCT.

The WHOLE now has three rows and four columns, or 3 × 4 parts.

$$3\frac{2}{3} \times 2\frac{1}{4} = \frac{11}{3} \times \frac{9}{4} = \text{PRODUCT} =$$

$$\frac{\boxed{\text{Number}} \text{ of parts}}{\boxed{\text{Kind}} \text{ of parts}} = \frac{11 \times 9}{3 \times 4} = \frac{99}{12} = 8\frac{1}{4}$$

FIGURE 16.10 The same approach used to develop the algorithm for fractions less than 1 can be expanded to mixed numbers.

Students should practice estimating fractions times whole numbers in lots of real contexts: $3\frac{1}{4}$ gallons of paint at $14.95 per gallon or $\frac{7}{8}$ of the 476 students who attended Friday's football game. When working with decimals and percents, these skills will be revisited, and once again mathematics will seem more connected than disconnected.

Division

Invert the divisor and multiply is probably one of the most mysterious rules in elementary mathematics. We want to avoid this mystery at all costs. However, first it makes sense to examine division with fractions from a more familiar perspective.

As with the other operations, go back to the meaning of division with whole numbers. Recall that there are two meanings of division: partition and measurement. We will review each briefly and look at some story problems that involve fractions. (Can you make up a word problem right now that would go with the computation $2\frac{1}{2} \div \frac{1}{4}$?)

You should have students explore both measurement and partition problems. Here we will discuss each type of problem separately for the purpose of clarity. In the classroom, the types of problems should probably be mixed. As with multiplication, how the numbers relate to each other in the problems tends to affect the difficulty.

Informal Exploration: Partition Concept

Too often we think of the partition problems strictly as sharing problems: 24 apples to be shared with 4 friends. How many will each friend get? Recall from Chapter 10, however, that this same sharing structure applies to rate problems: If you walk 12 miles in 3 hours, how many miles do you walk per hour? Both of these problems, in fact, all partition problems, ask the questions, "How much is one?" "How much is the amount for one friend?" "How many miles are walked in one hour?" The 24 is the amount for the 4 friends. The 12 miles is the amount for the 3 hours.

Whole-Number Divisors

Having the total amount be a fraction with the divisor a whole number is not really a big leap. These problems still are easy

to think of as sharing situations. However, as you work through these questions, notice that you are answering the question, "How much is the whole?" or "How much for one?"

Cassie has $5\frac{1}{4}$ yards of ribbon to make three bows for birthday packages. How much ribbon should she use for each bow if she wants to use the same length of ribbon for each?

When the $5\frac{1}{4}$ is thought of as fractional parts, there are 21 fourths to share, or 7 fourths for each ribbon. Alternatively, one might think of first allotting 1 yard per bow, leaving $2\frac{1}{4}$ yards, or 9 fourths. These 9 fourths are then shared, 3 fourths per bow, for a total of $1\frac{3}{4}$ yards for each bow. Regardless of the particular process, the unit parts required no further subdivision in order to do the division. In the following problem, the parts must be split into smaller parts.

Mark has $1\frac{1}{4}$ hours to finish his three household chores. If he divides his time evenly, how many hours can he give to each?

Note that the question is, "How much for one chore?" The 5 fourths of an hour that Mark has do not split neatly into three parts. So some or all of the parts must be subdivided. Figure 16.11 shows three different models for figuring this out. In each case, all of the fourths are subdivided into three

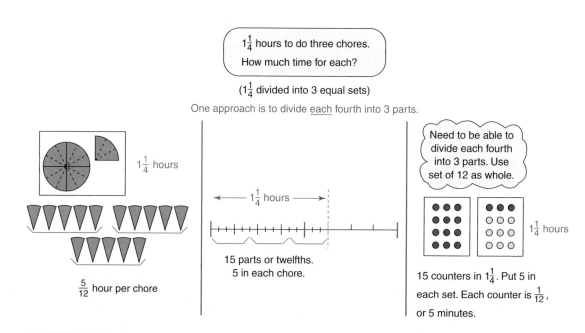

FIGURE 16.11 **Three models of partition division with a whole-number divisor.**

equal parts, producing twelfths. There are a total of 15 twelfths, or $\frac{5}{12}$ hour for each chore. (Test this answer against the solution in minutes: $1\frac{1}{4}$ hours is 75 minutes, which divided among 3 chores is 25 minutes per chore.)

Fractional Divisors

The sharing concept appears to break down when the divisor is a fraction. However, it is enormously helpful to keep in mind that for partition and rate problems the fundamental question is, "How much is one?" Interestingly, this is exactly the second type of question in the parts-and-whole tasks from Chapter 15: Given the part, find the whole—how much is one? For example, if a set of 18 counters is $2\frac{1}{4}$, how much is a whole set? In solving these problems, the first task is to find the number in *one*-fourth and then multiply by 4 to get four-fourths or one. Let's see if we can see the same process in the following problem:

Elizabeth bought $3\frac{1}{3}$ pounds of tomatoes for $2.50. How much did she pay per pound?

🛑 **STOP** The given amount of $2.50 is (distributed across) $3\frac{1}{3}$ pounds. How much is (distributed across) 1 pound? Solve the problem the same way as you would a parts-and-whole problem. Try it now before reading on.

In $3\frac{1}{3}$ there are 10 thirds. Since the $2.50 covers (or is distributed across) ten-thirds, one third is covered by one-tenth of the $2.50 or 25 cents. There are three thirds in one. Therefore, 75 cents must cover 1 pound, or 75 cents per pound.

Try the following problems using a similar strategy.

Dan paid $2.40 for a $\frac{3}{4}$-pound box of candy. How much is that per pound?

Aidan found out that if she walks really fast during her morning exercise, she can cover $2\frac{1}{2}$ miles in $\frac{3}{4}$ of an hour. She wonders how fast she is walking in miles per hour.

With both problems, first find the amount of one-fourth and then the value of one whole. Aidan's walking problem is a bit harder because the $2\frac{1}{2}$ miles, or 5 half-miles, do not neatly divide into three parts. If this was difficult for you, try dividing each half into three parts. Draw pictures or use models if that will help.

Informal Exploration: Measurement Concept

Almost all division explorations with fractions found in the elementary and middle school curriculum involve the measurement concept. To review, $13 \div 3$ with this concept means "How many sets of 3 are in 13?" Here is a contextual setting: *If you have 13 quarts of lemonade, how many canteens holding 3 quarts each can you fill?* A key idea to get from this example involves how to deal with that last quart after filling the first four canteens. If you continue to fill a fifth canteen, it will get only one quart. It will be only one-third full. So one answer is $4\frac{1}{3}$ *canteens.*

Since this is the concept of division that is almost always seen in textbooks and will be used to develop an algorithm for dividing fractions, it is important for students to explore this idea in contextual situations.

Whole-Number Results

Students readily understand problems such as the following:

You are going to a birthday party. From Ben and Jerry's ice cream factory, you order 6 pints of ice cream. If you serve $\frac{3}{4}$ of a pint of ice cream to each guest, how many guests can be served? (Schifter, Bastable, & Russell, 1999b, p. 120)

Students typically draw pictures of six things divided into fourths and count out how many sets of $\frac{3}{4}$ can be found. The difficulty is in seeing this as $6 \div \frac{3}{4}$, and that part will require some direct guidance on your part. One idea is to compare the problem to one involving whole numbers (6 pints, 2 per guest) and make a comparison.

Here is a slightly more complex problem:

Farmer Brown found that he had $2\frac{1}{4}$ gallons of liquid fertilizer concentrate. It takes $\frac{3}{4}$ gallon to make a tank of mixed fertilizer. How many tankfuls can he mix?

Try solving this problem yourself. Use any model or drawing you wish to help explain what you are doing. Notice that you are trying to find out *How many sets of 3 fourths are in a set of 9 fourths?* Your answer should be 3 tankfuls (not 3 fourths). Here is another problem to try:

Linda has $4\frac{2}{3}$ yards of material. She is making baby clothes for the bazaar. Each dress pattern requires $1\frac{1}{6}$ yards of material. How many dresses will she be able to make from the material she has?

$$4\tfrac{2}{3} \div 1\tfrac{1}{6}$$

I broke the 2 thirds into 4 sixths. Then I used 1 whole and 1 sixth for each piece. There were four pieces.

I broke it all up into sixths. That made 24 (from the 4) and 4 more from the $\tfrac{2}{3}$. That's 28 in all. Then $1\tfrac{1}{6}$ is $\tfrac{7}{6}$, so I divided the 28 by 7 and got 4.

FIGURE 16.12 Two solutions to the problem: *How many lengths of $1\tfrac{1}{6}$ yards can be cut from $4\tfrac{2}{3}$ yards of cloth?*

What makes this problem a bit different is that the given quantity is in thirds and the divisor is in sixths. Since you want to measure off "sets" of $1\tfrac{1}{6}$, someplace in the solution, sixths will need to be used. Two ideas are shown in Figure 16.12.

Answers That Are Not Whole Numbers

If Linda had 5 yards of material, she could still make only four dresses because a part of a dress does not make sense. But suppose that Farmer Brown began with 4 gallons of concentrate. After making five tanks of mix, he would have used $\tfrac{15}{4}$, or $3\tfrac{3}{4}$ gallons, of the concentrate. With the $\tfrac{1}{4}$ gallon remaining he could make a *partial* tank of mix. He could make $\tfrac{1}{3}$ of a tank of mix, since it takes 3 fourths to make a whole, and he has *1* fourth of a gallon.

Here is another problem to try:

> John is building a patio. Each section requires $\tfrac{2}{3}$ of a cubic yard of concrete. The concrete truck holds $2\tfrac{1}{4}$ cubic yards of concrete. If there is not enough for a full section at the end, John can put in a divider and make a partial section. How many sections can John make with the concrete in the truck?

 STOP You should first try to solve this problem in some way that makes sense to *you*. Stop and do this now.

After you have solved it your way, try this method. Change all of the numbers to the same unit (twelfths). Then the problem becomes: *How many sets of 8 twelfths are in a set of 27 twelfths?* Figure 16.13 shows two noncontextual problems solved in this same way, each with a different model. That is, both the dividend or given quantity and the divisor are expressed in the same type of fractional parts. This results

FIGURE 16.13 Models for the measurement concept of fraction division.

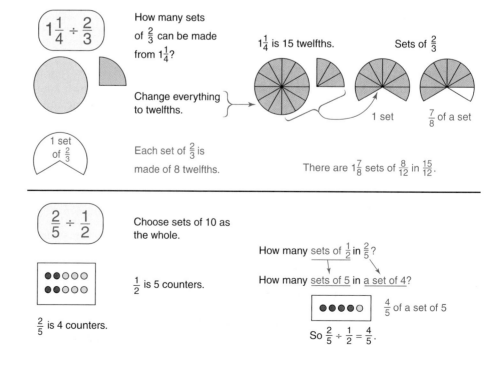

in a whole-number division problem. (In the concrete problem, the answer is the same as $27 \div 8$.) In the classroom, after students have solved problems such as this using their own methods, suggest this common-unit approach.

Developing the Algorithms

There are two different algorithms for division of fractions. Methods of teaching both algorithms are discussed here.

The Common-Denominator Algorithm

The common-denominator algorithm relies on the measurement or repeated subtraction concept of division. Consider the problem $\frac{3}{5} \div \frac{1}{2}$. As shown in Figure 16.14, once each number is expressed in terms of the same fractional part, the answer is exactly the same as the whole-number problem $10 \div 3$. The name of the fractional part (the denominator) is no longer im-

portant, and the problem is one of dividing the numerators. The resulting rule or algorithm, therefore, is as follows: *To divide fractions, first get common denominators, and then divide numerators.* For example, $\frac{5}{3} \div \frac{1}{4} = \frac{20}{12} \div \frac{3}{12} = 20 \div 3 = \frac{20}{3} = 6\frac{2}{3}$.

Try using pie pieces, fraction strips, and then sets of counters to model $1\frac{2}{3} \div \frac{3}{4}$ and $\frac{5}{8} \div \frac{1}{2}$ to help yourself develop this algorithm.

The Invert-and-Multiply Algorithm

To invert the divisor and multiply may be one of the most poorly understood procedures in the K–8 curriculum. (Do you know why invert-and-multiply works?) Interestingly, in a much discussed study of Chinese and U.S. teachers, Liping Ma (1999) found that most Chinese teachers not only use and teach this algorithm, but they also understand why it works. U.S. teachers were found to be sadly lacking in their understanding of fraction division.

If you return to the few partition problems that were discussed, you will find that solving these problems almost immediately gives rise to the invert-and-multiply algorithm. Let's look at one more example in which both the dividend and the divisor are proper fractions.

A small pail can be filled to $\frac{7}{8}$ full using $\frac{2}{3}$ of a gallon of water. How much will the pail hold if filled completely?

Ignore temporarily that the amount is $\frac{2}{3}$ of a gallon of water. Draw a simple picture like the one in Figure 16.15. Again, recall the parts-and-whole problems in which the task was to find the whole. That is what is done here—find the *whole* pail if the given water is $\frac{7}{8}$ of the whole. A full pail is $\frac{8}{8}$. Because the water in the pail is seven of the eight parts needed to fill the pail, dividing the water by 7 and multiplying that amount by 8 solves the problem. Therefore, take the $\frac{2}{3}$, divide by 7, and multiply by 8.

Now recall the meanings of the denominator and numerator. The denominator in a fraction divides the whole into parts, thus indicating the type of part. The denominator is a divisor. The numerator tells us the number of those parts. The numerator is a multiplier. In the problem we divided the $\frac{2}{3}$ by 7 and multiplied by 8. Therefore, we multiplied the $\frac{2}{3}$ by $\frac{8}{7}$.

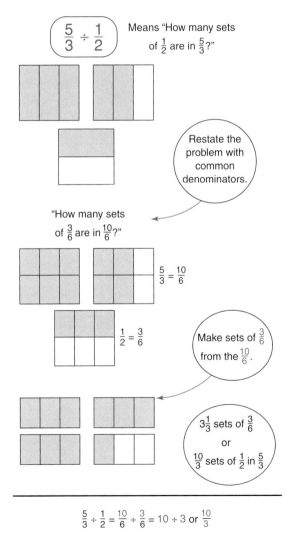

$$\frac{5}{3} \div \frac{1}{2} = \frac{10}{6} \div \frac{3}{6} = 10 \div 3 \text{ or } \frac{10}{3}$$

FIGURE 16.14　Models for the common-denominator method for fraction division.

FIGURE 16.15　The pail is $\frac{7}{8}$ full. One-eighth of the water times 8 will be how much it takes to fill the entire pail.

$$\frac{3}{4} \div \frac{5}{6} = \boxed{}$$

Write the equation in an equivalent form as a product with a missing factor.

$$\frac{3}{4} = \boxed{} \times \frac{5}{6}$$

Multiply both sides by $\frac{6}{5}$. ($\frac{6}{5}$ is the inverse of $\frac{5}{6}$.)

$$\frac{3}{4} \times \frac{6}{5} = \boxed{} \times \left(\frac{5}{6} \times \frac{6}{5}\right)$$

$$\frac{3}{4} \times \frac{6}{5} = \boxed{} \times 1$$

$$\frac{3}{4} \times \frac{6}{5} = \boxed{}$$

But $\frac{3}{4} \div \frac{5}{6} = \boxed{}$ also.

Therefore,

$$\frac{3}{4} \div \frac{5}{6} = \frac{3}{4} \times \frac{6}{5} = \boxed{}$$

In general,

$$\frac{a}{b} \div \frac{c}{d} = \frac{a}{b} \times \frac{d}{c}$$

FIGURE 16.16 **To divide, invert the divisor and multiply.**

In many middle school textbooks, a more symbolic justification for the invert-and-multiply procedure is offered. That explanation goes something like the one shown in Figure 16.16.

STOP Read through the explanation in Figure 16.16. Is that rationale more or less meaningful to you than the one based on the problem with the pail of water? Given your choice, which algorithm—common denominator or invert-and-multiply—would you select to teach to your students?

Curricular Decisions

Your answers to the questions just posed may have an influence on how you teach division of fractions. It matters very little *how* students do operations, only that they can do them meaningfully and accurately in a reasonably efficient manner. Each of the algorithms has value. Regardless of which algorithm is your goal, you are strongly advised to build on informal work with story problems. Most textbook story problems for fraction division seem to be measurement problems. This is not the case

in China. In the United States, very little research has been done to explore the partition approach to invert-and-multiply.

 ## TECHNOLOGY NOTE

Very few software programs adequately address the four operations with fractions. Tenth Planet's *Fraction Operations* (1998b) is one of the better programs in this arena. All Tenth Planet packages have three sections called "Into," "Through," and "Beyond." In *Fraction Operations*, the "Through" section focuses entirely on finding common denominators. Students will see that common denominators are the same as common subdivisions. The software cleverly helps find them in a visual manner. However, as is true with this entire program, there is nothing in the presentation that will help students develop an independent or symbolic method of finding common denominators. The program finds a common subdivision but does not relate this to a common multiple of the denominators.

The "Beyond" section has four components, one for each of the four operations. In each, a contextual setting remains fixed, with different problems randomly generated for that context.

With each of the four operations, the concept is very nicely and correctly illustrated. The development of the harder concepts of multiplication and division (measurement concept) are especially well designed. The downside is that there is nothing in the program to promote reflective thinking or problem solving. The clever graphics and audio information provide all the directions. The measurement tools even make finding the common denominators and fractional parts nearly mechanical.

How can these programs be used profitably? One idea is to use them to pose problems to the class. Even with numbers randomly generated, it is easy to flip through problems until you find one you would like students to solve. The essential parts of the graphics are easy to sketch on paper. Students can solve the problems themselves, pose solutions, and discuss as usual. Student solutions and methods can then be compared with the computer solutions.

Students who need special help with the concept can work with the program on their own. ■

REFLECTIONS ON CHAPTER 16

Writing to Learn

1. Make up an example, and use pie pieces (or draw pictures) to show how two fractions with unlike denominators can be added without first getting a common denominator. In your example, did you get your answer by either looking at the part that was more than a whole or at the missing part that was just less than a whole? Explain both of these ideas.

2. Suppose that you got pie pieces out to show $\frac{2}{3} + \frac{1}{2}$ and by some informal means your students are now convinced that the sum is $1\frac{1}{6}$. Now suppose that you substitute $\frac{16}{24}$ for the $\frac{2}{3}$ and $\frac{7}{14}$ for the $\frac{1}{2}$. "What is this sum ($\frac{16}{24} + \frac{7}{14}$)?" Explain why you would want students to say *immediately* that the sum was $1\frac{1}{6}$. Why is this idea important to the use of common denominators in addition and subtraction?

3. Explain why it is obvious that $\frac{3}{4} \times \frac{8}{5} = \frac{6}{5}$ without using the algorithm and without first getting $\frac{24}{20}$.

4. Draw pictures of squares for the whole to illustrate these products and explain each:

$$3 \times \frac{2}{5} \qquad \frac{3}{4} \times \frac{2}{3} \qquad 2\frac{1}{2} \times \frac{2}{3}$$

5. Explain at least one mental method (estimation or mental computation) for each of these:

$$\frac{3}{4} \times 5\frac{1}{2} \qquad 1\frac{1}{8} \text{ of } 679$$

6. Make up a word problem with a fraction as a divisor. Is your problem a measurement problem or a partition problem? Make up a second word problem with fractions of the other type (measurement or partition).

7. Draw pictures to explain each of these divisions using a measurement approach:

$$\frac{2}{4} \div \frac{1}{4} \qquad 2\frac{1}{3} \div \frac{2}{3} \qquad \frac{3}{4} \div \frac{1}{8} \qquad 2\frac{3}{4} \div \frac{2}{3}$$

In the second and fourth examples, the answer is not a whole number. To help you explain the fractional part of the answer, use a set of counters to explain why $13 \div 5 = 2\frac{3}{5}$ also using a measurement approach. (That is, how many sets of 5 are in a set of 13?)

8. Use the same problems you modeled in item 7 to explain a common-denominator algorithm for division. Use the same rationale to explain why $\frac{13}{79} \div \frac{5}{79} = 13 \div 5 = \frac{13}{5}$.

9. What is one strong reason for not teaching "invert and multiply"?

For Discussion and Exploration

1. Give two reasons why the following argument is flawed:

$$\frac{1}{2} \qquad\qquad \frac{1}{3}$$

● ○ ● ○ ○

add

● ● ○ ○ ○

Therefore, $\frac{1}{2} + \frac{1}{3} = \frac{2}{5}$.

Add tops and bottoms.

2. Examine a textbook series, and see where each fraction algorithm is first introduced. Does the preparation for the algorithm seem appropriate? How guided is the development? Will students develop an understanding of the rule or simply apply it to the exercises?

3. Several calculators are now available that do computations in fractional form as well as in decimal form. Some of these automatically give results in simplest terms. If you have access to such a calculator, discuss how it might be used in teaching fractions and especially fraction computation. If such calculators become commonplace, should we continue to teach fraction computation?

Recommendations for Further Reading

Highly Recommended

Huinker, D. (1998). Letting fraction algorithms emerge through problem solving. In L. J. Morrow (Ed.), *The teaching and learning of algorithms in school mathematics* (pp. 170–182). Reston, VA: National Council of Teachers of Mathematics.

Huinker takes the idea of students inventing algorithms as described for whole numbers in Chapter 10 and applies it to problems involving fractions. With examples of children's work, this article makes a good case for avoiding rules and letting students work with ideas that make sense. As always, Huinker is worth reading.

Kamii, C., & Warrington, M. A. (1999). Teaching fractions: Fostering children's own reasoning. In L. V. Stiff (Ed.), *Developing mathematical reasoning in grades K–12* (pp. 82–92). Reston, VA: National Council of Teachers of Mathematics.

Kamii begins with a quick review of Piagetian constructivism but quickly moves to apply this theory to the development of fraction operations. As always, Kamii avoids the use of models and relies on carefully selected word problems. All four operations are discussed.

Kieren, T., Davis, B., & Mason, R. (1996). Fraction flags: Learning from children to help children learn. *Mathematics Teaching in the Middle School, 2,* 14–19.

The authors began with a simple area model involving rectangular pieces cut from a standard sheet of paper. When smaller pieces were placed on larger pieces with spaces in between, the results looked like flags and presented interesting problem-based tasks for the students. These researchers have a long history of work with fractions and this article offers useful insights as well as a suggestion for an easily made model.

Other Suggestions

Flores, A. (2002). Profound understanding of division of fractions. In B. Litwiller (Ed.), *Making sense of fractions, ratios, and proportions* (pp. 237–246). Reston, VA: National Council of Teachers of Mathematics.

Huinker, D. (2002). Examining dimensions of fraction operation sense. In B. Litwiller (Ed.), *Making sense of fractions, ratios, and proportions* (pp. 72–78). Reston, VA: National Council of Teachers of Mathematics.

Langrall, C. W., & Swafford, J. (2000). Three balloons for two dollars. *Mathematics Teaching in the Middle School, 6,* 254–261.

Ma, L. (1999). *Knowing and teaching elementary mathematics: Teachers' understanding of fundamental mathematics in China and the United States.* Mahwah, NJ: Lawrence Erlbaum.

Mack, N. (1998). Building a foundation for understanding the multiplication of fractions. *Teaching Children Mathematics, 5,* 34–38.

Mack, N. K. (2001). Building on informal knowledge through instruction in a complex content domain: Partitioning, units, and understanding multiplication of fractions. *Journal for Research in Mathematics Education, 32,* 267–295.

Steencken, E., & Maher, C. A. (2002). Young children's growing understanding of fraction ideas. In B. Litwiller (Ed.), *Making sense of fractions, ratios, and proportions* (pp. 49–60). Reston, VA: National Council of Teachers of Mathematics.

Taber, S. B. (2002). Go ask Alice about multiplication of fractions. In B. Litwiller (Ed.), *Making sense of fractions, ratios, and proportions* (pp. 61–71). Reston, VA: National Council of Teachers of Mathematics.

Warrington, M. A., & Kamii, C. (1998). Multiplication with fractions: A Piagetian, constructivist approach. *Mathematics Teaching in the Middle School, 3,* 339–343.

Wu, Z. (2001). Multiplying fractions. *Teaching Children Mathematics, 8,* 174–177.

17

DECIMAL AND PERCENT CONCEPTS AND DECIMAL COMPUTATION

I n the U.S. curriculum, decimals are typically introduced in the fourth grade and most of the computation work with decimals occurs in the fifth grade and is repeated later in grades 6 and 7. This fractions-first, decimals-later sequence is arguably the best approach. However, the unfortunate fact is that the topics of fractions and decimals are too often developed separately. Linking the ideas of fractions to decimals can be extremely useful, both from a pedagogical view as well as a practical, social view. Most of this chapter focuses on that connection.

Big Ideas

1. Decimal numbers are simply another way of writing fractions. Both notations have value. Maximum flexibility is gained by understanding how the two symbol systems are related.

2. The base-ten place-value system extends infinitely in two directions: to tiny values as well as to large values. Between any two place values, the ten-to-one ratio remains the same.

3. The decimal point is a convention that has been developed to indicate the units position. The position to the left of the decimal point is the unit that is being counted as singles or ones.

4. Percents are simply hundredths and as such are a third way of writing both fractions and decimals.

5. Addition and subtraction with decimals are based on the fundamental concept of adding and subtracting the numbers in like position values—a simple extension from whole numbers.

6. Multiplication and division of two numbers will produce the same digits, regardless of the positions of the decimal point. As a result, for most practical purposes, there is no reason to develop new rules for decimal multiplication and division. Rather, the computations can be performed as whole numbers with the decimal placed by way of estimation.

CONTENT CONNECTIONS

The most important connections for decimals are built within this chapter—between decimal numbers and the concepts of fractions.

■ **Fraction Concepts** (Chapter 15): Both decimal and fraction symbolism represents the same ideas—the rational numbers.

■ **Measurement** (Chapter 19): The metric system is modeled after the base-ten system, and all metric measures are expressed in decimals rather than fractions. Conversion from one metric measure to another is quite simple, given an understanding of the decimal system.

■ **Real Number System** (Chapter 24): Decimal numeration is helpful in characterizing and understanding the density of the rational numbers and also for approximating irrational numbers.

CONNECTING TWO DIFFERENT REPRESENTATIONAL SYSTEMS

The symbols 3.75 and $3\frac{3}{4}$ represent the same quantity, yet on the surface the two appear quite different. For children especially, the world of fractions and the world of decimals are very distinct. Even adults tend to think of fractions as sets or regions (three-fourths *of* something), whereas we think of decimals as being more like numbers. When we tell children that 0.75 is the same as $\frac{3}{4}$, this can be especially confusing. Even though different ways of writing the numbers have been invented, the numbers themselves are not different. A significant goal of instruction in decimal and fraction numeration should be to help students see that both systems represent the same concepts.

To help students see the connection between fractions and decimals, we can do three things. First, we can use familiar fraction concepts and models to explore rational numbers that are easily represented by decimals: tenths, hundredths, and thousandths. Second, we can help them see how the base-ten system can be extended to include numbers less than 1 as well as large numbers. Third, we can help children use models to make meaningful translations between fractions and decimals. These three components are discussed in turn.

Base-Ten Fractions

Fractions that have denominators of 10, 100, 1000, and so on will be referred to in this chapter as *base-ten fractions*. This is simply a convenient label and is not one commonly found in the literature. Fractions such as $\frac{7}{10}$ or $\frac{63}{100}$ are examples of base-ten fractions.

Base-Ten Fraction Models

Most of the common models for fractions are somewhat limited for the purpose of depicting base-ten fractions. Generally, the familiar fraction models cannot show hundredths or thousandths. It is important to provide models for these fractions using the same conceptual approaches that were used for fractions such as thirds and fourths.

Two very important region models can be used to model base-ten fractions. First, to model tenths and hundredths, circular disks such as the one shown in Figure 17.1 can be printed on tagboard (see Blackline Masters). Each disk is marked with 100 equal intervals around the edge and is cut along one radius. Two disks of different colors, slipped together as shown, can be used to model any fraction less than 1. Fractions modeled on this hundredths disk can be read as base-ten fractions by noting the spaces around the edge but are still reminiscent of the traditional pie model.

The most common model for base-ten fractions is a 10 × 10 square. These squares can be run off on paper for students to shade in various fractions (see Figure 17.2 and Blackline Masters). Another important variation is to use base-ten place-value strips and squares. As a fraction model, the 10-cm square that was used as the hundreds model for whole numbers is taken as the whole or 1. Each strip is then 1 tenth, and each small square is 1 hundredth. In the Black-

10 × 10 squares on paper. Each square is one whole. Students shade fractional parts.

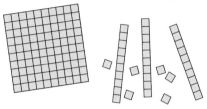

Base-ten strips and squares can be used to model base-ten fractions. Instead of shading in the large square, strips and small squares are placed on it to show a fractional part.

FIGURE 17.2 **10 × 10 squares model base-ten fractions.**

line Masters you will find a large square that is subdivided into 10,000 tiny squares. When shown on an overhead projector, individual squares or ten-thousandths can easily be identified and shaded in with a pen on the transparency.

One of the best length models is a meter stick. Each decimeter is one-tenth of the whole stick, each centimeter is one-hundredth, and each millimeter is one-thousandth. Any number-line model broken into 100 subparts is likewise a useful model for hundredths.

Many teachers use money as a model for decimals, and to some extent this is helpful. However, for children, money is almost exclusively a two-place system: Numbers like 3.2 or 12.1389 do not relate to money. Children's initial contact with decimals should be more flexible, and so money is not recommended as a decimal model. Money is certainly an important *application* of decimal numeration.

Multiple Names and Formats

Early work with base-ten fractions is designed primarily to acquaint students with the models, to help them begin to think of quantities in terms of tenths and hundredths, and to learn to read and write base-ten fractions in different ways.

FIGURE 17.1 **A hundredths disk for modeling base-ten fractions.**

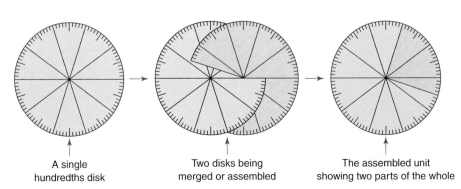

A single
hundredths disk

Two disks being
merged or assembled

The assembled unit
showing two parts of the whole

Have students show a base-ten fraction using any base-ten fraction model. Once a fraction, say, $\frac{65}{100}$, is modeled, the following things can be explored:

- Is this fraction more or less than $\frac{1}{2}$? Than $\frac{2}{3}$? Than $\frac{3}{4}$? Some familiarity with these fractions can be developed by comparison with fractions that are easy to think about.
- What are some different ways to say this fraction using tenths and hundredths? ("6 tenths and 5 hundredths," "65 hundredths") Include thousandths when appropriate.
- Show two ways to write this fraction ($\frac{65}{100}$ or $\frac{6}{10} + \frac{5}{100}$).

The last two questions are very important. When base-ten fractions are later written as decimals, they are usually read as a single fraction. That is, 0.65 is read "sixty-five hundredths." But to understand them in terms of place value, the same number must be thought of as 6 tenths and 5 hundredths. A mixed number such as $5\frac{13}{100}$ is usually read the same way as a decimal: 5.13 is "five and thirteen-hundredths." For purposes of place value, it should also be understood as $5 + \frac{1}{10} + \frac{3}{100}$.

The expanded forms will be helpful in translating these fractions to decimals. Exercises at this introductory level should include all possible connections between models, various oral forms, and various written forms. Given a model or a written or oral fraction, students should be able to give the other two forms of the fraction, including equivalent forms where appropriate.

Extending the Place-Value System

Before considering decimal numerals with students, it is advisable to review some ideas of whole-number place value.

One of the most basic of these ideas is the 10-to-1 relationship between the value of any two adjacent positions. In terms of a base-ten model such as strips and squares, 10 of any one piece will make 1 of the next larger, and vice versa.

A Two-Way Relationship

The 10-makes-1 rule continues indefinitely to larger and larger pieces or positional values. This concept is fun to explore in terms of how large the strips and squares will actually be if you move six or eight places out.

If you are using the strip-and-square model, for example, the strip and square shapes alternate in an infinite progression as they get larger and larger. Having established the progression to larger pieces, focus on the idea that each piece to the right in this string gets smaller by one-tenth. The critical question becomes "Is there ever a smallest piece?" In the students' experience, the smallest piece is the centimeter square or unit piece. But couldn't even that piece be divided into 10 small strips? And couldn't these small strips be divided into 10 very small squares, and so on? In the mind's eye, there is no smallest strip or smallest square.

The goal of this discussion is to help students see that a 10-to-1 relationship can extend *infinitely in two directions.* There is no smallest piece and no largest piece. The relationship between adjacent pieces is the same regardless of which two adjacent pieces are being considered. Figure 17.3 illustrates this idea.

The Role of the Decimal Point

An important idea to be realized in this discussion is that there is no built-in reason why any one position should naturally

FIGURE 17.3 Theoretically, the strips and squares extend infinitely in both directions.

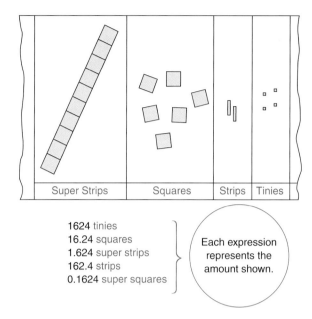

1624 tinies
16.24 squares
1.624 super strips
162.4 strips
0.1624 super squares

Each expression
represents the
amount shown.

FIGURE 17.4 **The decimal point indicates which position is the units.**

be chosen to be the unit or ones position. In terms of strips and squares, for example, which piece is the ones piece? The small centimeter square? Why? Why not a larger or a smaller square? Why not a strip? *Any piece could effectively be chosen as the ones piece.*

As shown in Figure 17.4, a given quantity can be written in different ways, depending on the choice of the unit or what piece is used to count the entire collection. The decimal point is placed between two positions with the convention that the position to the left of the decimal is the units or ones position. Thus, the role of the decimal point is *to designate the units position,* and it does so by sitting just to the right of that position.

A fitting caricature of the decimal is shown in Figure 17.5. The "eyes" of the decimal always focus up toward the name of the units or ones. A tagboard disk of this decimal-point face can be used between adjacent base-ten models or on a place-value chart (found with the hundredths disk in the Blackline Masters). If such a decimal point were placed between the squares and strips in Figure 17.4, the squares would then be designated as the units, and 16.24 would be the correct written form for the model.

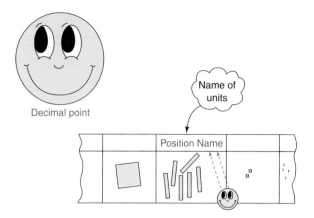

FIGURE 17.5 **The decimal point always "looks up at" the name of the units position.**

ACTIVITY 17.1

The Decimal Names the Unit

Have students display a certain number of base-ten pieces on their desks. For example, put out 3 squares, 7 strips, and 4 tinies. Refer to the pieces as "squares," "strips," and "tinies," and reach an agreement on names for the theoretical pieces both smaller and larger. To the right of tinies can be "tiny strips" and "tiny squares." To the left of squares can be "super strips" and "super squares." Each student should also have a tagboard smiley decimal point. Now ask students to write and say how many squares they have, how many super strips, and so on, as in Figure 17.4. The students position their decimal point accordingly and both write and say the amounts.

Activity 17.1 illustrates vividly that the decimal indicates the named unit and that the unit can change without changing the quantity.

The Decimal with Measurement and Monetary Units

The notion that the decimal "looks at the units place" is useful in a variety of contexts. For example, in the metric system, seven place values have names. As shown in Figure 17.6, the decimal can be used to designate any of these places as the

kilometer	hectometer	dekameter	meter	decimeter	centimeter	millimeter	
		4	3	8	5		

4 dekameters, 3 meters, 8 decimeters, and 5 centimeters =

43.85	meters
43850	millimeters
0.04385	kilometers
4385	centimeters

Unit names

FIGURE 17.6 **In the metric system, each place-value position has a name. The decimal point can be placed to designate which length is the unit length.**

unit without changing the actual measure. Our monetary system is also a decimal system. In the amount $172.95, the decimal point designates the dollars position as the unit. There are 1 hundred (of dollars), 7 tens, 2 singles, 9 dimes, and 5 pennies or cents in this amount of money regardless of how it is written. If pennies were the designated unit, the same amount would be written as 17,295 cents or 17,295.0 cents. It could just as correctly be 0.17295 thousands of dollars or 1729.5 dimes.

In the case of actual measures such as metric lengths or weights or the U.S. monetary system, the name of the unit is written after the number rather than above the digit as on a place-value chart. You may be 1.62 meters tall, but it does not make sense to say you are "1.62 tall." In the paper, we may read about Congress spending $7.3 billion. Here the units are billions of dollars, not dollars. A city may have a population of 2.4 million people. That is the same as 2,400,000 individuals.

Making the Fraction–Decimal Connection

To connect the two numeration systems, fractions and decimals, students should make concept-oriented translations. The purpose of such activities has less to do with the skill of converting a fraction to a decimal than with construction of the concept that both systems express the same ideas.

ACTIVITY 17.2

Base-Ten Fractions to Decimals

For this activity, have students use their place-value strips and squares. Agree that the large square represents one. Have students cover a base-ten fractional amount of the square using their strips and tinies. For example, have them cover $2\frac{35}{100}$ of the square. Whole numbers require additional squares. The task is to decide how to write this fraction as a decimal and demonstrate the connection using their physical models.

For the last activity, a typical (and correct) reason why $2\frac{35}{100}$ is the same as 2.35 is that there are 2 wholes, 3 tenths, and 5 hundredths. It is important to see this physically. The exact same materials that are used to represent $2\frac{35}{100}$ of the square can be rearranged or placed on an imaginary place-value chart with a paper decimal point used to designate the units position as shown in Figure 17.7.

The reverse of this activity is also worthwhile. Give students a decimal number such as 1.68 and have them show it with base-ten pieces. Their task is to write it as a fraction and show it as a fractional part of a square.

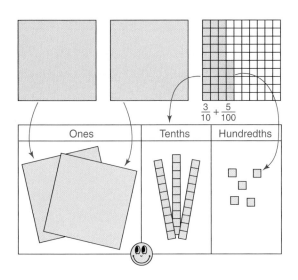

$2\frac{35}{100}$ = 2.35 = "two and thirty-five hundredths"

FIGURE 17.7 **Translation of a base-ten fraction to a decimal.**

Although these translations between decimals and base-ten fractions are rather simple, the main agenda is for students to learn from the beginning that decimals are simply fractions.

The calculator can also play a significant role in decimal concept development.

ACTIVITY 17.3

Calculator Decimal Counting

Recall how to make the calculator "count" by pressing ⊞ 1 ⊟ ⊟ . . . Now have students press ⊞ 0.1 ⊟ ⊟ . . . When the display shows 0.9, stop and discuss what this means and what the display will look like with the next press. Many students will predict 0.10 (thinking that 10 comes after 9). This prediction is even more interesting if, with each press, the students have been accumulating base-ten strips as models for tenths. One more press would mean one more strip, or 10 strips. Why should the calculator not show 0.10? When the tenth press produces a display of 1 (calculators never display trailing zeros to the right of the decimal), the discussion should revolve around trading 10 strips for a square. Continue to count to 4 or 5 by tenths. How many presses to get from one whole number to the next? Try counting by 0.01 or by 0.001. These counts illustrate dramatically how small one-hundredth and one-thousandth really are. It requires 10 counts by 0.001 to get to 0.01 and 1000 counts to reach 1.

The fact that the calculator counts 0.8, 0.9, 1, 1.1 instead of 0.8, 0.9, 0.10, 0.11 should give rise to the question "Does this make sense? If so, why?"

Calculators that permit entry of fractions also have a fraction–decimal conversion key. On some calculators a decimal such as 0.25 will convert to the base-ten fraction $\frac{25}{100}$ and allow for either manual or automatic simplification. Graphing calculators can be set so that the conversion is either with or without simplification. The ability of fraction calculators to go back and forth between fractions and decimals makes them a valuable tool as students begin to connect fraction and decimal symbolism.

Developing Decimal Number Sense

So far, the discussion has revolved around the connection of decimals with base-ten fractions. Number sense implies more. It means having intuition about or a friendly understanding of numbers. To this end, it is useful to connect decimals to the fractions with which children are familiar, to be able to compare and order decimals readily, and to approximate decimals with useful familiar numbers.

Familiar Fractions Connected to Decimals

Chapter 15 showed how to help students develop a conceptual familiarity with simple fractions, especially halves, thirds, fourths, fifths, and eighths. We should extend this familiarity to the same concepts expressed as decimals. One way to do this is to have students translate familiar fractions to decimals by means of a base-ten model.

The following two activities have the same purpose—to help students think of decimals in terms of familiar fraction equivalents and to make this connection in a conceptual manner.

ACTIVITY 17.4
Friendly Fractions to Decimals
Students are given a "friendly" fraction to convert to a decimal. They first model the fraction using either a 10 × 10 grid or the base-ten strips and squares. With the model as a guide, they then write and draw an explanation for the decimal equivalent. If strips and squares are used, be sure that students draw pictures as part of their explanations.

A good sequence is to start with halves and fifths, then fourths, and possibly eighths. Thirds are best done as a special activity.

Figure 17.8 shows how translations in the last activity might go with a 10 × 10 grid. For fourths, students will of-

$$\frac{1}{4} = \frac{25}{100} = .25 \qquad \frac{3}{8} = \frac{37}{100} + \frac{5}{1000} = .375$$

$$\frac{3}{5} = \frac{6}{10} = .6$$

FIGURE 17.8 Familiar fractions converted to decimals using a 10 × 10 square.

ten shade a 5 × 5 section (half of a half). The question then becomes how to translate this to decimals. Ask these students how they would cover $\frac{1}{4}$ with strips and squares if they were only permitted to use nine or fewer tinies. The fraction $\frac{3}{8}$ represents a wonderful challenge. A hint might be to find $\frac{1}{4}$ first and then notice that $\frac{1}{8}$ is half of a fourth. Remember that the next smaller pieces are tenths of the little squares. Therefore, a half of a square is $\frac{5}{1000}$.

Because the circular model carries such a strong mental link to fractions, it is well worth the time to do some fraction-to-decimal conversions with the hundredths disk.

ACTIVITY 17.5
Estimate, Then Verify
With the blank side of the disk facing them, have students adjust the disk to show a particular friendly fraction, for example, $\frac{3}{4}$. Next they turn the disk over and record how many hundredths were in the section they estimated (note that the color reverses when the disk is turned over). Finally, they should make an argument for the correct number of hundredths and the corresponding decimal equivalent.

The estimation component of the last activity adds interest, and the visual "feeling" for fractions is greater than with strips and squares. In one fifth-grade class that was having difficulty finding a decimal equivalent for their hundredths disk fraction, the teacher cut up some extra disks into tenths and hundredths so that these parts of the fraction could be placed on a chart. (See Figure 17.9.)

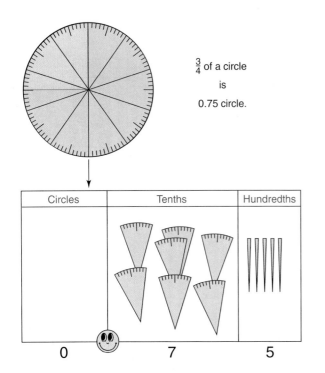

$\frac{3}{4}$ of a circle

is

0.75 circle.

FIGURE 17.9 **Fraction models could be decimal models.**

should be only fourths, only thirds, or only fifths but without labels. The students' task is to locate each of the decimal numbers on the number line and to provide the fraction equivalent for each.

Results of National Assessment of Educational Progress (NAEP) examinations consistently reveal that students have difficulties with the fraction–decimal relationship. Kouba et al. (1988a) note that students could express proper fractions as decimals but only 40 percent of seventh graders could give a decimal equivalent for a mixed number. In the sixth NAEP, students had difficulty placing decimals on a number line where the subdivisions were fractions (Kouba, Zawojewski, & Strutchens, 1997). In the seventh NAEP, only 39 percent of eighth graders correctly placed decimal numbers on a number line when the increments were multiples of 0.1—not even in fraction increments (Wearne & Kouba, 2000). Division of the numerator by the denominator may be a means of converting fractions to decimals, but it contributes nothing to understanding the resulting equivalence. Note that this method has not been and will not be suggested in this chapter.

The exploration of modeling $\frac{1}{3}$ as a decimal is a good introduction to the concept of an infinitely repeating decimal. Try to partition the whole square into 3 parts using strips and squares. Each part receives 3 strips with 1 left over. To divide the leftover strip, each part gets 3 small squares with 1 left over. To divide the small square, each part gets 3 tiny strips with 1 left over. (Recall that with base-ten pieces, each smaller piece must be $\frac{1}{10}$ of the preceding size piece.) Each of the 3 parts will get 3 tiny strips with 1 left over. It becomes obvious that this process is never-ending. As a result, $\frac{1}{3}$ is the same as 0.333333 . . . or 0.$\overline{3}$. For practical purposes, $\frac{1}{3}$ is about 0.333. Similarly, $\frac{2}{3}$ is a repeating string of sixes, or about 0.667. Later, students will discover that many fractions cannot be represented by a finite decimal.

The number line is another good connecting model. Students are more apt to think of decimals as numbers that appear on the number line than they are to think of fractions in that way. The following activity continues the development of fraction–decimal equivalences.

Approximation with a Nice Fraction

In the real world, decimal numbers are rarely those with exact equivalents to nice fractions. What fraction would you say approximates the decimal 0.52? In the sixth NAEP exam, only 51 percent of eighth graders selected $\frac{1}{2}$. The other choices were $\frac{1}{50}$ (29 percent), $\frac{1}{5}$ (11 percent), $\frac{1}{4}$ (6 percent), and $\frac{1}{3}$ (4 percent) (Kouba et al., 1997). Again, the most plausible explanation for this performance is a reliance on rules. Students need to wrestle with the size of decimal numbers and begin to develop a sense of familiarity with them.

As with fractions, the first benchmarks that should be developed are 0, $\frac{1}{2}$, and 1. For example, is 7.3962 closer to 7 or 8? Why? (Would you accept this response: "Closer to 7 because 3 is less than 5"?) Is it closer to 7 or $7\frac{1}{2}$? Often the 0, $\frac{1}{2}$, or 1 benchmarks are good enough to make sense of a situation. If a closer approximation is required, students should be encouraged to consider the other friendly fractions (thirds, fourths, fifths, and eighths). In this example, 7.3962 is close to 7.4, which is $7\frac{2}{5}$. A good number sense with decimals would imply the ability to think quickly of a meaningful fraction that is a close substitute for almost any number.

To develop this type of familiarity with decimals, children do not need new concepts or skills. They do need the opportunity to apply and discuss the related concepts of fractions, place value, and decimals in activities such as the following.

ACTIVITY 17.6

Decimals on a Friendly Fraction Line

Give students five decimal numbers that have friendly fraction equivalents. Keep the numbers between two consecutive whole numbers. For example, use 3.5, 3.125, 3.4, 3.75, and 3.66. On a worksheet, show a number line encompassing the same whole numbers. The subdivisions on the number line

---

ACTIVITY 17.7

Close to a Friendly Fraction

Make a list of about five decimals that are close to but not exactly equal to a nice or friendly fraction equivalent. For example, use 24.8025, 6.59, 0.9003, 124.356, and 7.7.

The students' task is to decide on a decimal number that is close to each of these decimals and that also has a friendly fraction equivalent that they know. For example, 6.59 is close to 6.6, which is $6\frac{3}{5}$. They should write an explanation for their choices. Different students may select different equivalent fractions providing for a discussion of which is closer.

ACTIVITY 17.8

Best Match

On the board, list a scattered arrangement of five familiar fractions and at least five decimals that are close to the fractions but not exact. Students are to pair each fraction with the decimal that best matches it. Figure 17.10 is an example. The difficulty is determined by how close the various fractions are to one another.

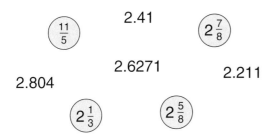

FIGURE 17.10 **Match the decimal numbers with the closest fraction expression.**

In Activities 17.7 and 17.8, students will have a variety of reasons for their answers. Sharing their thinking with the class provides a valuable opportunity for all to learn. Do not focus on the answers but on the rationales.

Ordering Decimal Numbers

Putting a list of decimal numbers in order from least to most is a skill closely related to the one just discussed. In the fourth NAEP (Kouba et al., 1988a), only about 50 percent of seventh graders could identify the largest number in the following list: 0.36, 0.058, 0.375, and 0.4. The most common error is to select the number with more digits, which is an incorrect application of whole-number ideas. Some students later pick up the idea that digits far to the right represent very small numbers. They then incorrectly identify numbers with more digits as smaller. Both errors reflect a lack of conceptual understanding of how decimal numbers are constructed. The following activities can help promote discussion about the relative size of decimal numbers.

ACTIVITY 17.9

Line 'Em Up

Prepare a list of four or five decimal numbers that students might have difficulty putting in order. They should all be between the same two consecutive whole numbers. Have students first predict the order of the numbers, from least to most. Next have them place each number on a number line with 100 subdivisions, as in Figure 17.11. As an alternative, have students shade in the fractional part of each number on a separate 10×10 grid using estimates for the thousandths and ten-thousandths. In either case, it quickly becomes obvious which digits contribute the most to the size of a decimal.

ACTIVITY 17.10

Close "Nice" Numbers

Write a four-digit decimal on the board—3.0917, for example. Start with the whole numbers: "Is it closer to 3 or 4?" Then go to the tenths: "Is it closer to 3.0 or 3.1?" Repeat with hundredths and thousandths. At each answer, challenge students to defend their choices with the use of a model or other conceptual explanation. A large number line without numerals, shown in Figure 17.11, is useful.

FIGURE 17.11 **A decimal number line.**

Cut four strips of poster board measuring 6 × 28 inches. Tape end to end. Place on chalk tray.

Write on board above. Endpoints can be any interval of 1, $\frac{1}{10}$, $\frac{1}{100}$.

Too often, the process of rounding numbers is taught as an algorithm without any reflection on why the algorithm makes sense. Children come to believe that to "round" a number means to do something to it or change it in some way. In reality, to *round* a number means that you *substitute* a "nice" number as an approximation for the cumbersome original number. In this sense, we can also round decimal numbers to "nice fractions" and not just to tenths and hundredths. For example, instead of rounding 6.73 to the nearest tenth, a number sense perspective might suggest rounding it to the nearest quarter (6.75 or $6\frac{3}{4}$) or to the nearest third (6.67 or $6\frac{2}{3}$).

 ## Technology Note

The drill program *Math Munchers Deluxe* (The Learning Company) provides useful drill of decimal–fraction equivalence in a format students seem to like. An array of 25 fractions, decimals, fraction region models, percents, and ratios is presented. The student is to find all instances that are equivalent to a given decimal number. The game can also be played with less than or greater than rather than equivalent. The 17 levels of difficulty provide ample challenge. This is a good example of worthwhile drill. However, it must come after conceptual ideas are well developed. The program offers no feedback or conceptual assistance. ■

Other Fraction–Decimal Equivalents

Recall that the denominator is a divisor and the numerator is a multiplier. For example, $\frac{3}{4}$, therefore, means the same as $3 \times (1 \div 4) = 3 \div 4$. So how would you express $\frac{3}{4}$ on a simple four-function calculator? Simply enter $3 \div 4$. The display will read 0.75.

Too often students think that dividing the denominator into the numerator is simply an algorithm for converting fractions to decimals, and they have no understanding of why this might work. Use the opportunity to help students develop the idea that in general $a/b = a \div b$. (See Chapter 15, p. 249, and Chapter 24, p. 464.)

Finding the decimal equivalents with a calculator can produce some interesting patterns and observations. For example, here are some questions to explore:

- Which fractions have decimal equivalents that terminate? Is the answer based on the numerator, the denominator, or both?
- For a given fraction, how can you tell the maximum length of the repeating part of the decimal? Try dividing by 7 and 11 and 13 to reach an answer.
- Explore all of the ninths—$\frac{1}{9}$, $\frac{2}{9}$, $\frac{3}{9}$, . . . $\frac{8}{9}$. Remember that $\frac{1}{3}$ is $\frac{3}{9}$ and $\frac{2}{3}$ is $\frac{6}{9}$. Use only the pattern you discover to predict what $\frac{9}{9}$ should be. But doesn't $\frac{9}{9} = 1$?
- How can you find what fraction produced this repeating decimal: 3.454545 . . . ?

The final task in this list can be generalized for any repeating decimal, illustrating that every repeating decimal is a rational number. It is not at all useful for students to become skillful at this.

 Much of what was discussed in this section is recommended by the *Standards*. "Students in [grades 3 to 5] should use models and other strategies to represent and study decimal numbers. For example, they should count by tenths (one-tenth, two-tenths, three-tenths, . . .) verbally or use a calculator to link and relate whole numbers with decimal numbers. . . . They should also investigate the relationship between fractions and decimals, focusing on equivalence" (p. 150).

Introducing Percents

Textbooks have traditionally treated percents as a separate topic from fractions and decimals or stuck them in a chapter on ratios. The connection of percents to fraction and decimal concepts is so strong that it also makes sense to discuss percents as students begin to have a good grasp of the fraction–decimal relationships.

A Third Operator System

The results of the NAEP tests and numerous other studies have consistently shown that students have difficulty with problems involving percents (Wearne & Kouba, 2000). For example, on the seventh NAEP, only 35 percent of eighth graders could determine an amount following a given percent of increase. Almost half selected the answer obtained by adding the percent itself to the original amount. That is, for a 7 percent increase, they selected the answer that was 7 more than the original amount. A good reason for this continual dismal performance is a failure to develop percent concepts meaningfully. In this book we explore percentages twice. Here we will connect them to fractions and decimals. In the next chapter we will revisit percent as a ratio as part of the study of proportional reasoning. It can be argued that the connection to fractions is more important for daily understanding.

Another Name for Hundredths

The term *percent* is simply another name for *hundredths*. If students can express common fractions and simple decimals as hundredths, the term *percent* can be substituted for the term *hundredth*. Consider the fraction $\frac{3}{4}$. As a fraction expressed in hundredths, it is $\frac{75}{100}$. When $\frac{3}{4}$ is written in decimal form, it is 0.75. Both 0.75 and $\frac{75}{100}$ are read in exactly the same way, "seventy-five hundredths." When used as operators, $\frac{3}{4}$ of

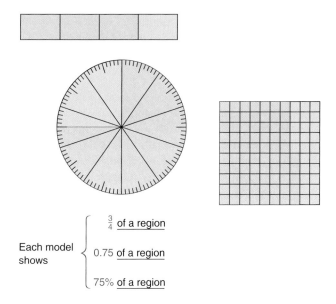

Each model shows
$\begin{cases} \dfrac{3}{4} \text{ of a region} \\[4pt] 0.75 \text{ of a region} \\[4pt] 75\% \text{ of a region} \end{cases}$

FIGURE 17.12 **Models connect three different notations.**

something is the same as 0.75 or 75 percent of that same thing. Thus, percent is merely a new notation and terminology, not a new concept.

Models provide the main link among fractions, decimals, and percents, as shown in Figure 17.12. Base-ten fraction models are suitable for fractions, decimals, and percents, since they all represent the same idea.

Another helpful approach to the terminology of percent is through the role of the decimal point. Recall that the decimal identifies the units. When the unit is ones, a number such as 0.659 means a little more than 6 tenths of 1. The word *ones* is understood (6 tenths of 1 *one*). But 0.659 is also 6.59 tenths and 65.9 hundredths and 659 thousandths. In each case, the name of the unit must be explicitly identified, or else the unit ones would be assumed. Since *percent* is another name for *hundredths,* when the decimal identifies the hundredths position as the units, the word *percent* can be specified as a synonym for *hundredths.* Thus, 0.659 (of some whole or 1) is 65.9 hundredths or 65.9 percent of that same whole. As illustrated in Figure 17.13, the notion of placing the dec-

Ones	Tenths	Percent	
		Hundredths	Thousandths
	3	6	5

0.365 (of 1) = 36.5 percent (of 1)

FIGURE 17.13 **Hundredths are also known as percents.**

imal point *to identify the percent position* is conceptually more meaningful than the apparently arbitrary rule: "To change a decimal to a percent, move the decimal two places to the right." A better idea is to equate hundredths with percent both orally and in notation.

Using Percent with Familiar Fractions

Students should use base-ten models for percents in much the same way as for decimals. The disk with 100 markings around the edge is now a model for percents as well as a fraction model for hundredths. The same is true of a 10 × 10 square. Each tiny square inside is 1 percent of the square. Each row or strip of 10 squares is not only a tenth but also 10 percent of the square.

Similarly, the familiar fractions (halves, thirds, fourths, fifths, and eighths) should become familiar in terms of percents as well as decimals. Three-fifths, for example, is 60 percent as well as 0.6. One-third of an amount is frequently expressed as $33\frac{1}{3}$ percent instead of 33.3333 . . . percent. Likewise, $\frac{1}{8}$ of a quantity is $12\frac{1}{2}$ percent or 12.5 percent of the quantity. These ideas should be explored with base-ten models and not as rules about moving decimal points.

Realistic Percent Problems

The Three Percent Problems

Junior high school teachers talk about "the three percent problems." The sentence "_____ is _____ percent of _____" has three spaces for numbers; for example, "20 is 25 percent of 80." The classic three percent problems come from this sterile expression; two of the numbers are given, and the students are asked to produce the third. Students learn very quickly that you either multiply or divide the two given numbers, and sometimes you have to move a decimal point. But they have no way of determining when to do what, which numbers to divide, or which way to shift the decimal. As a result, performance on percentage problems is very poor. Furthermore, commonly encountered expressions using percent terminology, such as sales figures, taxes, census data, political information, and trends in economics, are almost never in the "_____ is _____ percent of _____" format. So when asked to solve a realistic percent problem, students are frequently at a loss.

Chapter 15 explored three types of exercises with fractions, in which one element—part, whole, or fraction—was unknown. Students used models and simple fraction relationships in those exercises. Those three types of exercises are precisely the same as the three percent problems. Developmentally, then, it makes sense to help students make the connection between the exercises done with fractions and those done with percents. How? Use the same types of models and the same terminology of parts, wholes, and fractions.

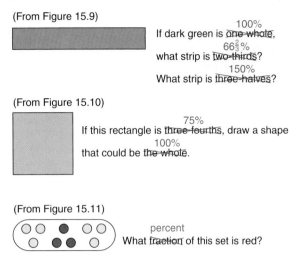

FIGURE 17.14 **Part-whole-fraction exercises can be translated into percent exercises.**

The only thing that is different is that the word *percent* is used instead of *fraction*. In Figure 17.14, three exercises from Chapter 15 have been changed to the corresponding percent terminology. A good idea for early work with percents would be to review (or explore for the first time) all three types of exercises in terms of percents. The same three types of models can be used (refer to Figures 15.9, 15.10, and 15.11 on p. 250).

Realistic Percent Problems and Nice Numbers

Though students must have some experience with the non-contextual situations in Figure 17.14, it is important to have them explore these relationships in real contexts. Find or make up percent problems, and present them in the same way that they appear in newspapers, on television, and in other real contexts. In addition to realistic problems and formats, follow these maxims for your unit on percents:

- Limit the percents to familiar fractions (halves, thirds, fourths, fifths, and eighths) or easy percents ($\frac{1}{10}, \frac{1}{100}$), and use numbers compatible with these fractions. The focus of these exercises is the relationships involved, not complex computational skills.
- Do not suggest any rules or procedures for different types of problems. Do not categorize or label problem types.
- Use the terms *part, whole,* and *percent* (or *fraction*). *Fraction* and *percent* are interchangeable. Help students see these percent exercises as the same types of exercises they did with simple fractions.
- Require students to use models or drawings to explain their solutions. It is better to assign three problems requiring a drawing and an explanation than to give 15

problems requiring only computation and answers. Remember that the purpose is the exploration of relationships, not computational skill.
- Encourage mental computation.

The following sample problems meet these criteria for easy fractions and numbers. Try working each problem, identifying each number as a part, a whole, or a fraction. Draw length or area models to explain or work through your thought process. Examples of this informal reasoning are illustrated with additional problems in Figure 17.15.

1. **The PTA reported that 75 percent of the total number of families were represented at the meeting last night. If children from 320 families go to the school, how many were represented at the meeting?**
2. **The baseball team won 80 percent of the 25 games it played this year. How many games were lost?**
3. **In Mrs. Carter's class, 20 students, or $66\frac{2}{3}$ percent, were on the honor roll. How many students are in her class?**
4. **George bought his new computer at a $12\frac{1}{2}$ percent discount. He paid $700. How many dollars did he save by buying it at a discount?**
5. **If Joyce has read 60 of the 180 pages in her library book, what percent of the book has she read so far?**
6. **The hardware store bought widgets at 80 cents each and sold them for $1 each. What percent did the store mark up the price of each widget?**

⊗ **STOP**   Examine the examples in Figure 17.15. Notice how each problem is solved with simple fractions and mental math. Then try each of the six problems just listed. Each can be done easily and mentally using friendly fraction equivalents.

Estimation in Percent Problems

Of course, not all real percent problems have nice numbers. Frequently in real life an approximation or estimate in percent situations is all that is required or is enough to help one think through the situation. Even if a calculator will be used to get an exact answer, an estimate based on an understanding of the relationship can confirm that a correct operation was performed or that the decimal was positioned correctly.

To help students with estimation in percent situations, two ideas that have already been discussed can be applied. First, when the percent is not a "nice" one, substitute a close percent that is easy to work with. Second, select numbers that are compatible with the percent involved, to make the calculation easy to do mentally. In essence, convert the not-nice percent problem into one that is nice. Here are some examples.

FIGURE 17.15 Real percent problems with nice numbers. Simple drawings help with reasoning.

1. The 83,000-seat stadium was 73 percent full. How many people were at the game?
2. The treasurer reported that 68.3 percent of the dues had been collected, for a total of $385. How much more money could the club expect to collect if all dues are paid?
3. Max McStrike had 217 hits in 842 at-bats. What was his batting average?

 Use friendly fractions and compatible numbers to solve each of these last three problems. Do this before reading on.

Possible Estimates

1. (Use $\frac{3}{4}$ and 80,000) $\longrightarrow$ about 60,000
2. (Use $\frac{2}{3}$ and $380; will collect $\frac{1}{3}$ more) $\longrightarrow$ about $190
3. (4 × 217 > 842; $\frac{1}{4}$ is 25 percent, or 0.250) $\longrightarrow$ a bit more than 0.250

The following activity is also useful in helping students with estimation in percent situations.

ACTIVITY 17.11

Estimate with Nice Fractions

Provide students with realistically stated percent problems. For percentages in the problems, use values that are close to but not the same as the nice percents or friendly fractions. Choose the other numbers in the problems so that they are compatible with the close friendly fraction. The students' task is to make estimates of the answers using easy computations or mental mathematics. As always, they should write down their procedures and rationale. Do not expect that every student will estimate in the same manner.

Here are three percent problems with two sets of numbers. The first set involves nice numbers that allow the problem to be worked mentally using fraction equivalents. The second set of numbers requires that the numbers be substituted with approximations allowing for an estimate as in the last activity.

1. The school enrolls {480, 547} students. Yesterday {$12\frac{1}{2}$ percent, 13 percent} of the students were absent. How many came to school?
2. Mr. Carver sold his lawn mower for {$45, $89}. This was {60 percent, 62 percent} of the price he paid for it new. What did the mower cost when it was new?
3. When the box fell off the shelf {90, 63} of the {720, 500} widgets broke. What percentage was lost in the breakage?

The first problem asks for a part (whole and fraction given), the second asks for a whole (part and fraction given), and the third asks for a fraction (part and whole given). Notice again that these are exactly the same as the three parts-and-whole questions found in Chapter 15.

It is also convenient at times to use simple base-ten equivalents: 1 percent and 10 percent and multiples of these (including halves). For example, we often use 10 percent plus half of that much to compute a 15 percent tip at a restaurant. To find 0.5 percent we can think of half of 1 percent. Some adults (and also students) get so used to the strategies related to these base-ten fractions that they never think to use other fraction equivalents that might produce more accurate results. A focus on these base-ten percentages is not as likely to help students conceive of percents as fractions.

COMPUTATION WITH DECIMALS

Certainly, students should develop some computational fluency with decimal numbers. In the past, decimal computation was dominated by the following rules: Line up the decimal points (addition and subtraction), count the decimal places (multiplication), and shift the decimal point in the divisor and dividend so that the divisor is a whole number (division). Traditional textbooks continue to emphasize these rules. The position taken in this book and in some of the reform curricula is that specific rules for decimal computation are not really necessary, especially if computation is built on a firm understanding of place value and a connection between decimals and fractions.

NCTM Standards

At the 3–5 level, the *Standards* says that students should "develop and use strategies to estimate computations involving fractions and decimals in situations relevant to students' experience" (p. 148). At the 6–8 level, students are to "select appropriate methods and tools for computing with fractions and decimals from among mental computation, estimation, calculators or computers, and paper and pencil, depending on the situation" (p. 214).

The Role of Estimation

Contrary to the traditional curriculum, students should become adept at estimating decimal computations well before they learn to compute with pencil and paper. For many decimal computations, rough estimates can be made easily by rounding the numbers to nice whole numbers or simple base-ten fractions. A minimum goal for your students should be to have the estimate contain the correct number of digits to the left of the decimal—the whole-number part. Select problems for which estimates are not terribly difficult.

 STOP Before going on, try making easy whole-number estimates of the following computations. Do not spend time with fine adjustments in your estimates.

1. 4.907 + 123.01 + 56.1234
2. 459.8 − 12.345
3. 24.67 × 1.84
4. 514.67 ÷ 3.59

Your estimates might be similar to the following:

1. Between 175 and 200
2. More than 400, or about 425 to 450
3. More than 25, closer to 50 (1.84 is more than 1 and close to 2)
4. More than 125, less than 200 (500 ÷ 4 = 125 and 600 ÷ 3 = 200)

In these examples, an understanding of decimal numeration and some simple whole-number estimation skills can produce rough estimates. When estimating, thinking focuses on the meaning of the numbers and the operations and not on counting decimal places. However, students who are taught to focus on the pencil-and-paper rules for decimal computation do not even consider the actual values of the number much less estimate.

Therefore, a good *place* to begin decimal computation is with estimation. Not only is it a highly practical skill, but it also helps children look at answers in ballpark terms and can form a check on calculator computation.

A good *time* to begin computation with decimals is as soon as a conceptual background in decimal numeration has been developed. Learning the rules for decimal computation will do little or nothing to help students understand decimal numeration and will interfere with a more robust development of number sense.

Addition and Subtraction

Consider this problem:

Max and Moe each timed his own quarter-mile run with a stopwatch. Max says that he ran the quarter in 74.5 seconds. Moe was more accurate. He reported his run as 81.34 seconds. How many seconds faster did Max run than Moe?

Students who understand decimal numeration should first of all be able to tell approximately what the difference is—close to 7 seconds. With an estimate as a beginning, students should then be challenged to figure out the exact difference. The estimate will help them avoid the typical error of lining up the 5 under the 4. A variety of student strategies are possible. For example, students might note that 74.5 and 7 is 81.5 and then figure out how much extra that is. Others may count on from 74.5 by adding 0.5 and then 6 more seconds to get to 81 seconds and then add on the remaining 0.34 second. These and other strategies will eventually confront the difference between the one-place decimal (.5) and the two-place decimal (.34). Students can resolve this issue by returning to their understanding of place value. Similar story problems for addition and subtraction, some involving different numbers of decimal places, will help develop students' understanding of these two operations. Always request an estimate prior to computation.

After students have had several opportunities to solve addition and subtraction story problems, the following activity is reasonable.

The earlier estimation practice will focus students' attention on the meanings of the numbers. It is reasonable to expect that students will develop an algorithm that is essentially the same as aligning the decimal points.

Multiplication

Estimation should play a significant role in developing an algorithm for multiplication. As a beginning point, consider this problem:

The farmer fills each jug with 3.7 liters of cider. If you buy 4 jugs, how many liters of cider is that?

Begin with an estimate. It is more than 12 liters. What is the most it could be? Could it be 16 liters? Once an estimate of the result is decided on, let students use their own methods for determining an exact answer. Many will use repeated addition: 3.7 + 3.7 + 3.7 + 3.7. Others may begin by multiplying 3 × 4 and then adding up 0.7 four times. Eventually, students will agree on the exact result of 14.8 liters. Explore other problems involving whole-number multipliers. Multipliers such as 3.5 or 8.25 that involve nice fractional parts—here, one-half and one-fourth—are also reasonable.

As a next step, have students compare a decimal product with one involving the same digits but no decimal. For example, how are 23.4 × 6.5 and 234 × 65 alike? Interestingly, both products have exactly the same digits: 15210. (The zero may be missing from the decimal product.) Using a calculator, have students explore other products that are alike except for the decimals involved. The digits in the answer are always alike.

ACTIVITY 17.12

Exact Sums and Differences

Give students a sum involving different numbers of decimal places. For example: 73.46 + 6.2 + 0.582. The first task is to make an estimate and explain the way the estimate was made. The second task is to compute the exact answer and explain how that was done (no calculators). In the third and final task students devise a method for adding and subtracting decimal numbers that they can use with any two numbers.

When students have completed these three tasks, have students share their strategies for computation and test them on a new computation that you provide.

The same task can be repeated for subtraction.

ACTIVITY 17.13

Where Does the Decimal Go?: Multiplication

Have students compute the following product: 24 × 63. Using only the result of this computation and estimation, have them give the exact answer to each of the following:

0.24 × 6.3   24 × 0.63   2.4 × 63   0.24 × 0.63

For each computation they should write a rationale for their answers. They can check their results with a calculator. Any errors must be acknowledged, and the rationale that produced the error adjusted.

STOP   The product of 24 × 63 is 1512. Use this information to give the answer to each of the products in the previous activity. Do *not* count decimal places. Remember your fractional equivalents.

The method of placing the decimal point in a product by way of estimation is more difficult as the product gets smaller. For example, knowing that 54 × 83 is 4482 does not make it easy to place the decimal in the product 0.0054 × 0.00083. Even the product 0.054 × 0.83 is hard. The practical question is this: Can you think of any situation outside of school in which someone might require an exact answer to a product such as one of these but would not have access to a calculator? When precision is important, technology makes sense and is always available. Yes, there is a conceptual rationale for counting the decimal places. Even if learned, it focuses attention on the smallest part of the product and provides absolutely no practice with estimation. It is a non-number-sense method that need not be used today.

Division

Division can be approached in a manner exactly parallel to multiplication. In fact, the best approach to a division estimate generally comes from thinking about multiplication rather than division. Consider the following problem:

> The trip to Washington was 282.5 miles. It took exactly $4\frac{1}{2}$ hours or 4.5 hours to drive. What was the average miles per hour?

To make an estimate of this quotient, think about what times 4 or 5 is close to 280. You might think 60 × 4.5 = 240 + 30 = 270. So maybe about 61 or 62 miles per hour.

Here is a second example without context. Make an estimate of 45.7 ÷ 1.83. Think only of what times $1\frac{8}{10}$ is close to 45.

STOP   Will the answer be more or less than 45? Why? Will it be more or less than 20? Now think about 1.8 being close to 2. What times 2 is close to 46? Use this to produce an estimate.

Since 1.83 is close to 2, the estimate is near 22. And since 1.83 is less than 2 the answer must be greater than 22—say 25 or 26. (The actual answer is 24.972677.)

Okay, so estimation can produce a reasonable result, but you may still require a pencil-and-paper algorithm to produce the digits the way it was done for multiplication. Figure 17.16 shows division by a whole number and how that can be carried out to as many places as you wish. (The explicit-trade

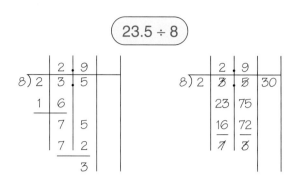

Trade 2 tens for 20 ones, making 23 ones.
Put 2 ones in each group, or 16 in all.
That leaves 7 ones.

Trade 7 ones for 70 tenths, making 75 tenths.
Put 9 tenths in each group, or 72 in all.

Trade the 3 tenths for 30 hundredths.

(Continue trading for smaller pieces as long as you wish.)

FIGURE 17.16 Extension of the division algorithm.

method described in Chapter 13 is shown on the right.) It is not necessary to move the decimal point up into the quotient. Leave that to estimation.

ACTIVITY 17.14

Where Does the Decimal Go?: Division

Provide a quotient such as 146 ÷ 7 = 20857 correct to five digits but without the decimal point. The task is to use only this information and estimation to give a fairly precise answer to each of the following:

  146 ÷ 0.7   1.46 ÷ 7   14.6 ÷ 0.7   1460 ÷ 70

For each computation students should write a rationale for their answers and then check their results with a calculator. Any errors should be acknowledged, and the rationale that produced the error adjusted.

   Give the answer to each of the products in the previous activity.

A reasonable algorithm for division is parallel to that for multiplication: *Ignore the decimal points, and do the computation as if all numbers were whole numbers. When finished, place the decimal by estimation.* This is reasonable for divisors with no more than two significant digits. If students have a method for dividing by 45, they can divide by 0.45 and 4.5 and even 0.045.

CONNECTED MATHEMATICS

Grade 6, *Bits and Pieces II*
Investigation 6: Computing with Decimals

Context

"Computing with Decimals" is the only place in the whole *Connected Mathematics* program in which decimal computation is explicitly addressed. The investigation is scheduled for approximately five days. Prior to this, students have worked at computation with fractions. The first two lessons in the investigation develop the addition and subtraction algorithm. The lesson just prior to the activity described here explores patterns in products with factors of 0.1, 0.01, 0.001, and 0.0001.

Task Description

Rather than begin with the factors, this activity begins with the product and has students explore the factors. In a full-class discussion, students find pairs of numbers with a product of 1560. This is based on earlier work with prime factorization. Given a list of four pairs with a product of 1560, the students are asked to find a pair with a product of 156.0 and a pair with a product of 1.560. Students use calculators to work on these tasks and find that the factors involve the exact same digits as for the whole-number product. For example, 2.4×0.65, 0.024×65, 0.39×4, and so on, all have a product of 1.560. With this introduction, students are given the task shown here.

The teaching notes suggest that part B of the task is more difficult because students have no specific number to begin with. Each student in a group is encouraged to come up with different factors so that as a group there will be a variety of examples. Once there are numbers that satisfy part

> **Problem 6.4**
>
> **A.** 1. Find two numbers with a product of 1344.
> 2. Find two numbers with a product of 134.4.
> 3. Find two numbers with a product of 1.344.
> 4. Find two numbers with a product of 0.1344.
> 5. Explain how you got your answers and why you think they are correct.
>
> **B.** 1. Find two numbers with a product between 2000 and 3000.
> 2. By moving decimal points, change the value of each of the numbers you found in part 1 so that their product is between 200 and 300.
> 3. By moving decimal points, change the value of each of the numbers you found in part 1 so that their product is between 20 and 30.
> 4. By moving decimal points, change the value of each of the numbers you found in part 1 so that their product is between 2 and 3.
> 5. Explain what you did to get your answers and why you think they are correct.

From *Connected Mathematics: Bits and Pieces II: Using Rational Numbers.* © 2002 by Michigan State University, Glenda Lappan, James T. Fey, William M. Fitzgerald, Susan N. Friel, and Elizabeth Difanis Phillips. Published by Prentice Hall. Used by permission of Pearson Education, Inc.

B1, the task is about how to adjust these numbers to get products in different ranges. Notice that there is no direct discussion in this task of how to multiply decimal numbers.

The last lesson of the unit is built on a contextual problem about fencing a rectangular pen for a dog. Students must determine the amount of fence, the number of posts, and the number of staples needed. Unit prices are given, and a 7 percent sales tax must also be computed. The problem involves addition and multiplication of decimal numbers in context. Calculators are permitted.

It is interesting to notice how different programs deal with computation beyond whole numbers. *Investigations in Number, Data, and Space,* a K–5 program, does not mention computation with decimals but works hard to connect decimal numeration to fractions and percents. Traditional programs develop addition and subtraction skills in the fifth grade, all four operations in the sixth grade, and review them again in the seventh. The *Connected Mathematics* program provides five or six days of development work on the addition, subtraction, and multiplication with decimals in the sixth grade but no division. No further work with these skills is found in the seventh and eighth grades. This page shows an interesting multiplication activity from *Connected Mathematics*.

LITERATURE CONNECTIONS

Few interesting stories inspire exploration of decimals and percents for children in the fifth grade and higher. One notable exception is *The Phantom Tollbooth,* a story that should not be missed regardless of its mathematical significance.

In the daily paper and weekly magazines, you will find decimal and percent situations with endless real-world connections. One issue with percents in news stories is the frequent omission of the base amount or the whole on which the percent is determined. "March sales of widgets were reported to be up 3.6 percent." Does that mean an increase over February or over

March of the previous year? Increase and decrease by percents are interesting to project over several years. If the consumer price index rises 3 percent a year, how much will a $50 basket of groceries cost by the time your students are 21 years old?

The Phantom Tollbooth
Juster, 1961

References to mathematical ideas abound throughout this book. Milo enters a world of crazy places and imaginative creatures after driving his toy car through a model of a turnpike tollbooth. Several chapters involve adventures in Digitopolis, where everything is number-oriented. In Digitopolis, Milo meets a boy who is only half of a boy, appearing in the drawing to be the left half of a boy cut top to bottom. As it turns out, the boy is actually 0.58 since he is a member of the average family: a mother, father, and 2.58 children. The boy is the 0.58. One advantage, he explains, is that he is the only one who can drive the $\frac{3}{10}$ of a car, the average family owning 1.3 cars. This section of the tale involves a great discussion of averages that come out in decimal numbers.

An obvious extension of the story is to explore averages of things that are interesting to the students (average number of siblings, average arm span, etc.) and see where these odd decimal parts come from. In the case of measures of length, for example, an average length can be a real length even if no one has it. But an average number of something like cars or sisters can be very humorous as discussed in the story. Where else are fractions and decimals used in this way? ■

 ## ASSESSMENT NOTES

The real danger in teaching the topics discussed in this chapter is in emphasizing skills instead of the concepts and big ideas. Traditional tests will focus on children's ability to round numbers, order decimals, compute with pencil and paper, and solve sterile percent problems. These assessments are far too skill-oriented.

The activities described in this chapter will involve discussions and explanations. For example, Activity 17.7, "Close to a Friendly Fraction" (p. 287), will very likely produce an array of answers as your students select a "nice" decimal and fractional equivalent. How did they make that choice? Which seems "best"? Is there always a best answer? When students use a 10 × 10 square to find a decimal equivalent for $\frac{3}{8}$ or $\frac{2}{3}$, there will be lots of discussion if you are not overly directive. From these discussions, you can gather data about your students' understanding of concepts.

So as not to rely totally on listening to discussions, you can and should have students write out explanations and draw pictures to support their answers to many of the activities. Here are two questions that could serve as assessments or as instructional tasks:

1. Consider these two computations: $3\frac{1}{2} \times 2\frac{1}{4}$ and 2.276×3.18. Without doing the calculations, which do you think is larger? Provide a reason for your answer that can be understood by someone else in this class.
2. How much larger is 0.76×5 than 0.75×5? How can you tell without doing the computation? (Kulm, 1994)

Realistic percent problems are still the best way to assess a student's understanding of percent. Assign one or two, and have students explain why they think their answer makes sense. You might take a realistic percent problem and substitute fractions for percents (e.g., use $\frac{1}{8}$ instead of 12.5 percent) to see how students handle these problems with fractions compared to decimal numbers.

If your focus is on reasons and justifications rather than number of problems correct, you will be able to collect all the information you need. ■

REFLECTIONS ON CHAPTER 17

Writing to Learn

1. Describe three different base-ten models for fractions and decimals, and use each to illustrate how base-ten fractions can easily be represented.
2. Explain why the place-value system extends infinitely in two directions. How can this idea be developed with students in the fifth or sixth grade?
3. Use an example involving base-ten pieces to explain the role of the decimal point in identifying the units position. Relate this idea to changing units of measurement as in money or metric measures.

4. What are the suggested "familiar fractions"? How can these fractions be connected to their decimal equivalents in a conceptual manner?
5. What should be emphasized if you want children to have good number sense with decimals?
6. Describe one or two ways in which a calculator can be used to develop number ideas with decimals.
7. What does rounding mean? What type of rounding can we do that is different from rounding to the nearest tenth or hundredth? Explain how a number line can be used in rounding.
8. Make up three realistic percent problems in which the percents are actually nice fractions and the numbers involved are com-

patible with the fractions. One problem should ask for the part, given the whole and the percent. One should ask for the percent, given the whole and the part. The third should ask for the whole, given the part and the percent. Model each, and show how each can be solved using fraction ideas.

9. For addition and subtraction, the line-up-the-decimals rule can be reasonably taught without much trouble. Explain.

10. Why does the multiplication procedure of counting decimal places to determine decimal-point placement not help with number sense? What are the contrasting values of using the estimation approach described in the chapter?

11. Give an example explaining how, in most problems, multiplication and division with decimals can be replaced with estimation and whole-number methods.

For Discussion and Exploration

1. For each of the four operations, discuss what computational skill with decimals is necessary for children to have. For example, if you believe that division with decimal numbers is important, what is the most tedious problem you would consider having students master? What alternatives to traditional pencil-and-paper computation do you think should be included in the curriculum?

2. One way to order a series of decimal numbers is to annex zeros to each number so that all numbers have the same number of decimal places. For example, rewrite

0.34		0.3400
0.3004	as	0.3004
0.059		0.0590

Now ignore the decimal points and any leading zeros, and order the resulting whole numbers. Discuss the merits of teaching this approach to children.

3. Talk individually with some seventh- or eighth-grade students. First find out if they can do simple fraction exercises that ask for the part, the whole, or the fraction given the other two (as in Chapter 15). Encourage them to make drawings and give explanations. Next ask them to solve simple percent word problems that require the same type of reasoning using simple fractions and compatible numbers. Compare students' abilities with these mathematically identical problems.

Recommendations for Further Reading

Highly Recommended

Bennett, A. B., & Nelson, L. T. (1994). A conceptual model for solving percent problems. *Mathematics Teaching in the Middle School, 1,* 20–25.

This article introduces a useful twist on using the 10 × 10 grid to understand percents. The authors provide a series of increasingly difficult tasks that can easily be used in a construc-

tivist environment to challenge a range of students. Realistic percent problems are used throughout.

McIntosh, A., Reys, B., Reys, R., & Hope, J. (1997). *Number SENSE: Simple effective number sense experiences [Grades 3–4, Grades 4–6, Grades 6–8].* White Plains, NY: Cuisenaire–Dale Seymour.

These three activity resource books provide blackline masters that are designed to help students develop a wide range of useful number relationships. Of special note are activities that use benchmarks of 0, $\frac{1}{2}$, and 1 for fractions and for decimals. There are also good activities for connecting fractions and decimals. The pages can be used with a full class as overhead transparencies or for individual use.

Moss, J., & Case, R. (1999). Developing children's understanding of the rational numbers: A new model and an experimental curriculum. *Journal for Research in Mathematics Education, 30,* 122–147.

These authors devised and taught a fourth-grade sequence that began with percents, moved on to decimals, and covered fractions last—the exact opposite of the sequence suggested in this text. A linear model was the main representation used. Although quite nontraditional, much can be learned from this study by two thoughtful researchers who have done considerable work in the area of fraction and decimal conceptual development.

Owens, D. T., & Super, D. B. (1993). Teaching and learning decimal fractions. In D. T. Owens (Ed.), *Research ideas for the classroom: Middle grades mathematics* (pp. 137–158). Old Tappan, NJ: Macmillan.

Owens and Super offer useful insights from research on how children develop decimal concepts and the difficulties involved. The chapter also provides a variety of useful activities for decimal concept development. The authors have also included results of NAEP testing that give some perspective on what is typical student development.

Other Suggestions

Chappell, M. F., & Thompson, D. R. (1999). Modifying our questions to assess students' thinking. *Mathematics Teaching in the Middle School, 4,* 470–474.

Irwin, K. C. (2001). Using everyday knowledge of decimals to enhance understanding. *Journal for Research in Mathematics Education, 32,* 399–420.

Oppenheimer, L., & Hunting R. P. (1999). Relating fractions and decimals: Listening to students talk. *Mathematics Teaching in the Middle School, 4,* 318–321.

Reys, B. J. (1991). *Developing number sense in the middle grades: Addenda series, grades 5–8.* Reston, VA: National Council of Teachers of Mathematics.

Thompson, C. S., & Walker, V. (1996). Connecting decimals and other mathematical content. *Teaching Children Mathematics, 2,* 496–502.

Williams, S. E., & Copley, J. V. (1994). Promoting classroom dialogue: Using calculators to discover patterns in dividing decimals. *Mathematics Teaching in the Middle School, 1,* 72–75.

18

DEVELOPING CONCEPTS OF RATIO AND PROPORTION

P roportional reasoning has been referred to as the capstone of the elementary curriculum and the cornerstone of algebra and beyond (Lesh, Post, & Behr, 1987). The ability to reason proportionally was a hallmark of Piaget's distinction between concrete levels of thought and formal operational thought. It represents the ability to begin to understand multiplicative relationships where most arithmetic concepts are additive in nature.

Big Ideas

1. A ratio is a comparison of any two quantities. A key developmental milestone is the ability of a student to begin to think of a ratio as a distinct entity, different from the two measures that made it up.

2. Proportions involve multiplicative rather than additive comparisons. Equal ratios result from multiplication or division, not from addition or subtraction.

3. Proportional thinking is developed through activities involving comparing and determining the equivalence of ratios and solving proportions in a wide variety of problem-based contexts and situations without recourse to rules or formulas.

CONTENT CONNECTIONS

Proportional reasoning is indeed the cornerstone of a wide variety of topics in the middle and high school curriculum.

■ **Fractions** (Chapter 15): Equivalent fractions are found through a multiplicative process; numerators and denominators are multiplied or divided by the same number. Equivalent ratios can be found in the same manner.

In fact, part-whole relationships (fractions) are an example of ratio.

■ **Similarity** (Chapter 20): When two figures are the same shape but different sizes (i.e., similar), they constitute a visual example of a proportion. The ratios of linear measures in one figure will be equal to the corresponding ratios in the other.

■ **Data Graphs** (Chapter 21): A relative frequency histogram shows the frequencies of different related events compared to all outcomes (visual part-to-whole ratios). A box-and-whisker plot shows the relative distribution of data along a number line and can be used to compare distributions of populations of very different sizes.

■ **Probability** (Chapter 21): A probability is a ratio that compares the number of outcomes in an event to the total possible outcomes. Proportional reasoning helps students understand these ratios, especially in comparing large and small sample sizes.

■ **Algebra** (Chapters 23 and 24): Much of algebra concerns a study of change and, hence, rates of change (ratios) are particularly important. In this chapter you will see that the graphs of equivalent ratios are straight lines passing through the origin. The slope of the line is the unit ratio. Slope itself is a rate of change and is an important component in understanding algebraic representations of related quantities.

PROPORTIONAL REASONING

So that the reading of this chapter is based on common ground, several exercises are provided for your exploration. Each typifies the relationships that make up the concepts of ratio and proportion. It does not matter what your personal mathematical acquaintance with ratio actually is. Try each of the following problems. You may wish to discuss and explore the exercises in a group or with a friend.

LAPS

Yesterday, Mary counted the number of laps she ran and recorded the amount of time it took. Today she ran fewer laps in more time than yesterday. Did she run faster, slower, or at about the same speed today—or can't you tell? What if she had run more laps in more time?

SIMILAR SHAPES

Place a piece of paper over the dot grid in Figure 18.1. Using the dots as a guide, draw a shape that is *like* the one shown but larger. How many different shapes that are like the given shape can you draw and still stay within the grid provided?

FIGURE 18.1 Draw some shapes just like this, only larger.

TOMATOES

At the farmers' market, Jones sells tomatoes at 5 pounds for $7 whereas Smith sells his tomatoes at 4 pounds for $6. Which farmer sells his tomatoes at a cheaper price?

SHORT AND TALL

Mr. Green sells trophies on the basis of height. A short trophy measures 6 paper clips tall, as shown in Figure 18.2. According to his price chart, this short trophy sells for $4.00. Mr. Green has a taller trophy that is worth $6.00 according to the same scale. How many paper clips tall is the $6.00 trophy?

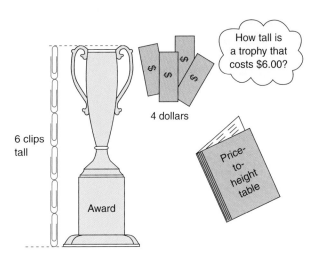

FIGURE 18.2 The "Short and Tall" trophy problem.

Examples of Ratios in Different Contexts

A *ratio* is an ordered pair of numbers or measurements that expresses a comparison between the numbers or measures. To students, ratios in different settings or contexts may present very different ideas and different difficulties.

Part-to-Whole Ratios

Ratios can express comparisons of a part to a whole, for example, the ratio of girls to all students in the class. Because fractions are also part-whole ratios, it follows that every fraction is also a ratio. In the same way, percentages are ratios, and in fact, percentages are sometimes used to express ratios. Probabilities are ratios of a part of the sample space to the whole sample space.

Part-to-Part Ratios

A ratio can also express one part of a whole to another part of the same whole. For example, the number of girls in the class can be compared to the number of boys. For other examples, consider Democrats to Republicans or peanuts to cashews. Although the probability of an event is a part-to-whole ratio, the *odds* of an event happening is a ratio of the number of ways an event can happen to the number of ways it cannot happen—a part-to-part ratio.

Rates as Ratios

Both part-to-whole and part-to-part ratios compare two measures of the same type of thing. A ratio can also be a *rate*. A rate is a comparison of the measures of two different things or quantities; the measuring unit is different for each value.

In the "Short and Tall" exercise, the comparison between paper clips and money is a ratio that is a rate—in this case, dollars per paper clip. All prices are rates and are, therefore, ratios: 69 cents each, 3 for a dollar, 12 ounces for $1.39.

The "Laps" exercise involves comparisons of time to distance, another example of rate. In that example the reasoning is qualitative rather than quantitative, but the ratio concept is basically the same. All rates of speed are comparisons of time and distance: for example, driving at 55 miles per hour (time to distance) or jogging at 9 minutes per mile (distance to time).

Miles per gallon, square yards of coverage per gallon of paint, passengers per busload, and roses per bouquet are all rates. Relationships between two units of measure are also rates or ratios, for example, inches per foot, milliliters per liter, and centimeters per inch.

Other Examples of Ratio

In geometry, the ratios of corresponding parts of similar geometric figures are always the same, as in the "Similar Shapes" exercise. The diagonal of a square is always $\sqrt{2}$ times a side. π (pi) is the ratio of the circumference of a circle to the diameter. The trigonometric functions can be developed from ratios of sides of right triangles. The slope of a line or of a roof is a ratio of rise for each unit of horizontal distance or run.

In nature, the ratio known as the *golden ratio* is found in many spirals, from nautilus shells to the swirls of a pinecone or a pineapple. Artists and architects have used the same ratio in creating shapes that are naturally pleasing to the eye.

Proportions

As students begin to reflect on a variety of examples of ratios, they will also begin to see two or more comparisons that are in the *same ratio*. In the "Similar Shapes" exercise, the ratio of any two sides of a small shape is the same as the ratio of the corresponding sides of a larger but similar shape. The "Tomatoes" problem also involved two ratios. Here the task was to compare the ratios to decide which was greater. The comparison of ratios forms an important category of tasks for students in developing proportional reasoning.

A *proportion* is a statement of equality between two ratios. Different notations for proportions can be used, for example:

$$3 : 9 = 4 : 12 \qquad \text{or} \qquad \frac{3}{9} = \frac{4}{12}$$

These might be read "3 is to 9 as 4 is to 12" or "3 and 9 are in the same ratio as 4 and 12."

A ratio that is a rate usually includes the units of measure when written, for example:

$$\frac{\$12.50}{1 \text{ gallon}} = \frac{\$37.50}{3 \text{ gallons}}$$

In the "Short and Tall" problem, you completed a proportion, or "solved" it, by completing the second ratio. Find-

ing one number in a proportion when given the other three is called *solving* a proportion.

Proportional Reasoning and Children

Proportional reasoning is difficult to define in a simple sentence or two. Proportional reasoning is not something that you either can or cannot do. It is, as the example problems show, both a qualitative and quantitative process. According to Lamon (1999), the following are a few of the characteristics of proportional thinkers:

● Proportional thinkers have a sense of covariation. That is, they understand relationships in which two quantities vary together and are able to see how the variation in one coincides with the variation in another.
● Proportional thinkers recognize proportional relationships as distinct from nonproportional relationships in real-world contexts.
● Proportional thinkers develop a wide variety of strategies for solving proportions or comparing ratios, most of which are based on informal strategies rather than prescribed algorithms.
● Proportional thinkers understand ratios as distinct entities representing a relationship different from the quantities they compare.

It is estimated that more than half of the adult population cannot be viewed as proportional thinkers (Lamon, 1999). That means that we do not acquire the habits and skills of proportional reasoning simply by getting older. On the other hand, Lamon's research and that of others indicate that instruction can have an effect, especially if rules and algorithms for fraction computation, for comparing ratios, and for solving proportions are delayed. Students may need as much as three years' worth of opportunities to reason in multiplicative situations in order to adequately develop proportional reasoning skills. Premature use of rules encourages students to apply rules without thinking and, thus, the ability to reason proportionally often does not develop.

Additive Versus Multiplicative Situations

Consider the following problem adapted from the book *Adding It Up* (National Research Council, 2001).

Two weeks ago, two flowers were measured at 8 inches and 12 inches, respectively. Today they are 11 inches and 15 inches tall. Did the 8-inch or 12-inch flower grow more?

STOP Before reading further, find and defend two different answers to this problem.

One answer is that they both grew the same amount—3 inches. This correct response is based on additive reasoning. That is, a single quantity was added to each measure to result in the two new measures. A second way to look at the problem is to compare the amount of growth to the original height of the flower. The first flower grew $\frac{3}{8}$ of its height while the second grew $\frac{3}{12}$. Based on this multiplicative view ($\frac{3}{8}$ *times as much* more), the first flower grew more. This is a proportional view of this change situation. An ability to understand the difference between these situations is an indication of proportional reasoning.

Considerable research has been conducted to determine how children reason in various proportionality tasks and to determine if developmental or instructional factors are related to proportional reasoning (for example, see Karplus, Pulos, & Stage, 1983; Lamon, 1993; Lo & Watanabe, 1997; Noelting, 1980; and Post, Behr, & Lesh, 1988).

The research provides direction for how to help children develop proportional thought processes. Some of these ideas are outlined here.

1. Provide ratio and proportion tasks in a wide range of contexts. These might include situations involving measurements, prices, geometric and other visual contexts, and rates of all sorts.
2. Encourage discussion and experimentation in predicting and comparing ratios. Help children distinguish between proportional and nonproportional comparisons by providing examples of each and discussing the differences.
3. Help children relate proportional reasoning to existing processes. The concept of unit fractions is very similar to unit rates. Research indicates that the use of a unit rate for comparing ratios and solving proportions is the most common approach among junior high students even when cross-product methods have been taught. (This approach is explained later.)
4. Recognize that symbolic or mechanical methods, such as the cross-product algorithm, for solving proportions do not develop proportional reasoning and should not be introduced until students have had many experiences with intuitive and conceptual methods.

 NCTM Standards In 1989, the *Curriculum Standards* noted that proportional reasoning "was of such great importance that it merits whatever time and effort must be expended to assure its careful development" (NCTM, 1989, p. 82). The emphasis on proportional reasoning is similarly reflected in the 2000 *Standards*. The *Prin-*

ciples and Standards authors have focused on the need for an integrative approach, one that involves "percent, similarity, scaling, linear equations, slope, relative frequency histograms, and probability" (NCTM, 2000, p. 212).

INFORMAL ACTIVITIES TO DEVELOP PROPORTIONAL REASONING

Four categories of informal activities are suggested here: selection of equivalent ratios, comparison of ratios, scaling with ratio tables, and construction and measurement activities. Each provides a different opportunity for the development of proportional reasoning. The activities are not in any definitive sequence, nor are they designed to teach specific methods for solving proportions.

Equivalent-Ratio Selections

In selection activities, a ratio is presented, and students select an equivalent ratio from others presented. The focus should be on an intuitive rationale for why the pairs selected are in the same ratio. Sometimes numeric values will play a part to help students develop numeric methods to explain their reasoning. In later activities, students will be asked to construct an equivalent ratio without choices being provided.

It is extremely useful in these activities to include pairs of ratios that are not proportional but have a common difference. For example, $\frac{5}{8}$ and $\frac{9}{12}$ are not equivalent ratios, but the corresponding differences are the same: $8 - 5 = 12 - 9$. Students who focus on this additive relationship are not seeing the multiplicative relationship of proportionality.

ACTIVITY 18.1

Look-Alike Rectangles

Draw a collection of 13 rectangles on one sheet of paper. Use a sheet of centimeter grid paper, and trace the rectangles using whole-number measures for at least one dimension of each rectangle. Make four rectangles with sides in the ratio of 1 to 4, four in the ratio 2 to 5, four in the ratio 5 to 8, and one square about midsize to the other 12 rectangles. Label the rectangles A to M in a mixed order.

The task is to group the rectangles into three sets of four that "look alike" with one "oddball." When they have decided on their groupings, stop and discuss reasons they classified the rectangles as they did. Be prepared for some students to try to match sides or look for rectangles that have the same amount of difference between them. Do not evaluate any rationale offered. Next have them measure and record the sides of each rectangle to the nearest half-centimeter and calculate the ratios of the short to long sides for each. You may want to prepare a little worksheet as shown in Figure 18.3. Discuss these results, and ask students to offer explanations. If the groups are formed of proportional (similar) rectangles, the ratios within each group will all be the same.

Look-Alike Rectangles

Group 1

Rectangle	Short Side	Long Side	Short ÷ Long
_____	_____	_____	_____
_____	_____	_____	_____
_____	_____	_____	_____
_____	_____	_____	_____

Group 2

Rectangle	Short Side	Long Side	Short ÷ Long
_____	_____	_____	_____
_____	_____	_____	_____

FIGURE 18.3 A recording sheet for "Look-Alike Rectangles."

From a geometric standpoint, "Look-Alike Rectangles" is an activity about similarity. The two concepts—proportionality and similarity—are closely connected. However, if the activity were done with figures other than rectangles, the congruent angles of similar figures would defeat the purpose.

Another feature of proportional rectangles can be observed by stacking like rectangles aligned at one corner, as in Figure 18.4. Place a straightedge across the diagonals, and you will see that opposite corners also line up. If the rectangles are placed on a coordinate axis with the common corner at the origin, the slope of the line joining the corners is the ratio of the sides. Here is a connection between proportional reasoning and algebra.

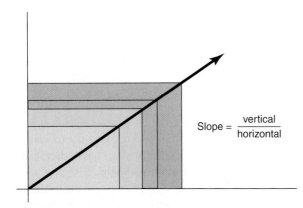

$$\text{Slope} = \frac{\text{vertical}}{\text{horizontal}}$$

FIGURE 18.4 The slope of a line through a stack of proportional rectangles is equal to the ratio of the two sides.

ACTIVITY 18.2

Different Objects, Same Ratios

Prepare cards with distinctly different objects, as shown in Figure 18.5. Given one card, students are to select a card on which the ratio of the two types of objects is the same. This task moves students to a numeric approach rather than a visual one and introduces the notion of ratios as rates. A unit rate is depicted on a card that shows exactly one of either of the two types of objects. For example, the card with three boxes and one truck provides one unit rate. A unit rate for the other ratio is not shown. What would it be? Objects paired with coins or bills is a way to introduce price as a ratio.

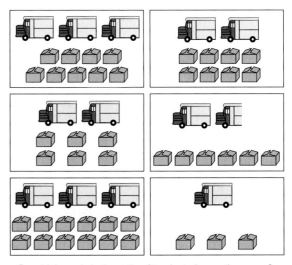

On which cards is the ratio of trucks to boxes the same? Also, compare trucks to trucks and boxes to boxes.

FIGURE 18.5 Rate cards: Match cards with the same rate of boxes per truck.

Comparing Ratios

An understanding of proportional situations includes being able to distinguish between two ratios as well as to identify those ratios that are equivalent. Consider the following problem:

Two camps of Scouts are having pizza parties. The Bear Camp ordered enough so that every 3 campers will have 2 pizzas. The leader of the Raccoons ordered enough so that there would be 3 pizzas for every 5 campers. Did the Bear campers or the Raccoon campers have more pizza to eat?

STOP Get some scrap paper and solve this problem without using any numeric algorithms such as cross-products. You may want to draw pictures or use counters, but there is no prescribed method to use.

(a)

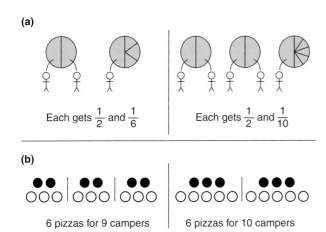

Each gets $\frac{1}{2}$ and $\frac{1}{6}$ Each gets $\frac{1}{2}$ and $\frac{1}{10}$

(b)

6 pizzas for 9 campers   6 pizzas for 10 campers

FIGURE 18.6 Two informal methods for comparing two ratios.

Figure 18.6 shows two different possibilities for informal methods.

When the pizzas are sliced up into fractional parts (Figure 18.6a), the approach is to look for a unit rate—pizzas per camper. A sharing approach has been used for each ratio just as described for fractions in Chapter 15. But notice that this problem does not say that the camps have only 3 and 5 campers, respectively. Any multiples of 2 to 3 and 3 to 5 can be used to make the appropriate comparison. This is the approach used in Figure 18.6b. Three "clones" of the 2-to-3 ratio and two clones of the 3-to-5 ratio are made so that the number of campers getting a like number of pizzas can be compared. From a vantage of fractions, this is like getting common numerators. Because there are more campers in the Raccoon ratio (larger denominator), there is less pizza for each camper.

The following activity suggests some similar comparison tasks.

ACTIVITY 18.3
Comparing Ratios

Pose problems to students that are similar to the following. Allow them to solve the problems in any manner they wish as long as they can explain why their answers make sense. Do not allow any algorithms that the students cannot defend in the context of the problem.

a. Terry can run 4 laps in 12 minutes. Susan can run 2 laps in 5 minutes. Who is the faster runner?
b. Jack and Jill were picking strawberries at the Pick Your Own Berry Patch. Jack "sampled" 5 berries every 25 minutes. Jill ate 3 berries every 10 minutes. If they both pick at about the same speed, who will bring home more berries?
c. Some of the hens in Farmer Brown's chicken farm lay brown eggs and the others lay white eggs. Farmer Brown noticed that in the large hen house he collected about 4 brown eggs for every 10 white ones. In the smaller hen house the ratio of brown to white was 1 to 3. In which hen house do the hens lay more brown eggs?
d. Talks-A-Lot phone company charges 70¢ for every 15 minutes. Reaching Out phone company charges $1.00 for 20 minutes. Which company is offering the cheaper rate?
e. Which rectangle is "fatter": a 3 × 5 rectangle or an 8 × 14 rectangle?

The suggested problems in Activity 18.3 are simply to provide you with some ideas. You can easily make up your own. You can also change the numbers to make the tasks easier or harder.

Scaling with Ratio Tables

Ratio tables or charts that show how two variable quantities are related are often good ways to organize information. Consider the following table:

Acres	5	10	15	20	25	
Pine trees	75	150	225			

If the task were to find the number of trees for 65 acres of land or the number of acres needed for 750 trees, students can easily proceed by using addition. That is, they can add 5's along the top row and 75's along the bottom row until the problems are solved. Although this is efficient and orderly, it is an additive procedure and does little as a task to promote proportional reasoning. As illustrated in the next activity, the instructional "trick" is to select numbers that require some form of multiplicative thinking.

ACTIVITY 18.4
Using Ratio Tables

Given a situation like one of the following, the task is to build a ratio table and use it to answer the question. Tasks are adapted from Lamon (1999, p. 183).

a. A person who weighs 160 pounds on Earth will weigh 416 pounds on the planet Jupiter. How much will a person weigh on Jupiter who weighs 120 pounds on earth?
b. At the local college, 5 out of every 8 seniors live in apartments. How many of the 30 senior math majors are likely to live in an apartment?
c. The tax on a purchase of $20 is $1.12. How much tax will there be on a purchase of $45.50?
d. When in Australia you can exchange $4.50 in U.S. dollars for $6 Australian. How much is $17.50 Australian in U.S. dollars?

(a)

(b)

(c)

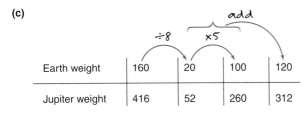

FIGURE 18.7 **160 pounds on Earth is 416 pounds on Jupiter. If something weighs 120 pounds on Earth, how many pounds would it weigh on Jupiter? Three solutions using ratio tables.**

	Pounds	Cost	Notes
A	1	4.25	Given
B	10	42.50	A × 10
C	2	8.50	A × 2
D	0.1	0.425	A ÷ 10
E	12.1	51.425	B + C + D
F	0.01	0.0425	D ÷ 10
G	0.03	0.1275	F × 3
H	12.13	51.5525	E + G

FIGURE 18.8 **A more structured ratio table. The notes column shows what was done in each step. The task is to find the cost of 12.13 pounds.**

The tasks in this activity are typical "solve the proportion" tasks. One ratio and part of a second are given with the task being to find the fourth number. However, tasks such as these should come long before any formal approach is suggested. Further note that in no case is it easy to simply add or subtract to get to the desired entry. Rather, the student should use a ratio table to solve the problem. Figure 18.7 shows three different ways to solve the Jupiter weight task using ratio tables.

The format of these ratio tables is not at all important. Some students may not use a table format at all and simply draw arrows and explain in words how they got from one ratio to another. You may find value in a more structured format. The following problem and the table in Figure 18.8 are taken from Lamon (1999, p. 233). Notice that the numbers are not "nice" at all.

Cheese is $4.25 per pound. How much will 12.13 pounds cost?

The format in Figure 18.8 allows for easier tracing of what was done at each step. The format is just that—a format. It is not the same as an algorithm. For any problem there are likely to be several different reasonable ratio tables. In applying this technique, students are using multiplicative relationships to transform a given ratio into an equivalent ratio. As Lamon points out, the process is not at all random. Students should mentally devise a plan for getting from one number to another. Consider the following problem:

How many pounds of grass seed can be purchased for $18 if you can buy 28 pounds for $35?

⊗ **STOP** Before reading further, write down a plan for moving from 35 to 18. Then create a ratio table using your plan to solve the problem. Compare your strategy with someone else's, or try to find another one yourself.

One possible plan for getting from 35 to 18 as follows: 35 ÷ 5 is 7; 7 × 2 is 14. (Now you need 4 more.) Go back to 7: 7 ÷ 7 is 1; 1 × 4 is 4. Now add 4 and 14 to make 18. When these same steps are applied to 28, the foregoing problem is solved.

The tasks suggested in Activity 18.4 have quite reasonable numbers. However, as you can see from the cheese example, it is quite possible to use this technique with almost any numbers. By using easy multiples and divisors, often the arithmetic can be done mentally.

Any ratio table, even a quite simple one such as you might find in textbooks, provides data that can be graphed. Make each axis correspond to one of the quantities in the table. This idea is developed in the next activity.

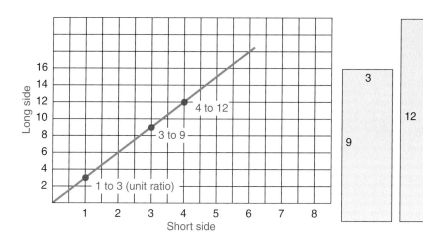

FIGURE 18.9 **Graphs show ratios of sides in similar rectangles.**

Graphs Showing Ratios

Have students make a graph of the data from a collection of equal ratios that they have scaled or discussed. The graph in Figure 18.9 is of the ratios of two sides of similar rectangles. If only a few ratios have actually been computed, the graph can be drawn carefully and then used to determine other equivalent ratios. This is especially interesting when there is a physical model to coincide with the ratio. In the rectangle example, students can draw rectangles with sides determined by the graphs and compare them to the original rectangles. A unit ratio can be found by locating the point on the line that is directly above or to the right of the number 1 on the graph. (There are actually two unit ratios for every ratio. Why?) Students can then use the unit ratio to scale up to other values and check to see

that they are on the graph as well. Note that the slope of any line through the origin is a ratio.

Graphs provide another way of thinking about proportions, and they connect proportional thought to algebraic interpretations. All graphs of equivalent ratios fall along straight lines that pass through the origin. If the equation of one of these lines is written in the form $y = mx$, the slope m is always one of the equivalent ratios. Figure 18.10 shows the graph of the prices of widgets.

Construction and Measurement Activities

In these activities, students make measurements or construct physical or visual models of equivalent ratios in order to provide a tangible example of a proportion as well as look at numeric relationships.

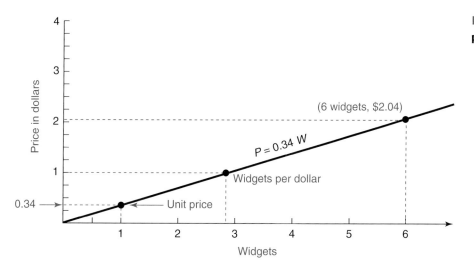

FIGURE 18.10 **Graph of price-to-item ratios.**

ACTIVITY 18.6

Different Units, Equal Ratios

Cut strips of adding machine tape all the same length, and give one strip to each group in your class. Each group is to measure the strip using a different unit. Possible units include different Cuisenaire rods, a piece of chalk, a pencil, the edge of a book or index card, or standard units such as inches or centimeters. When every group has measured the strip, ask for the measure of one of the groups, and display the unit of measure. Next, hold up the unit of measure used by another group, and have the class compare it with the first unit. See if the class can estimate the measurement that the second group found. The ratio of the measuring units should be the inverse of the measurements made with those units. For example, if two units are in a ratio of 2 to 3, the respective measures will be in a ratio of 3 to 2. Examine measurements made with other units. Finally, present a unit that no group has used, and see if the class can predict the measurement when made with that unit.

Activity 18.6 can be profitably extended by providing each group with an identical set of four strips of quite different lengths. Good lengths might be 20, 50, 80, and 120 cm. As before, each group measures the strips using a different unit.

This time, have each group enter data into a common spreadsheet. (Alternatively, share group data so that all groups can enter data on their own spreadsheets.) Figure 18.11 shows what a spreadsheet might look like for three groups.

A template can be prepared ahead of time, or students can create their own spreadsheets. Almost all spreadsheets will offer a variety of graphing options. In this activity, bar graphs show the actual measurements for each group and circle graphs show each measure in ratio to the sum of the measures (i.e., a percentage of total measures.)

Once the graphs are completed, there are numerous opportunities to observe and explore proportions. The bar graphs, though different, all look "alike." Since the circle graphs illustrate the ratios rather than the actual measurements, they will be identical or nearly so. Within ratios (for a set of strips) and between ratios (one unit to another) are easily calculated with the spreadsheet. (Within and between ratios are discussed later in the chapter.)

Continue the exploration by introducing a new strip. If you know its measure with any one of the units, what will its measure be with the other units? Similarly, if a new unit of measure is introduced, how can the measures of the strips be determined? Can this be done by comparing the new unit with an old one? If a known strip is measured with the new unit, can all other measures and ratios be determined?

Bar graphs and circle plots are also easily made with a TI-73 graphing calculator. If technology is not available, this same activity can be done by hand. To make circle graphs, use the hundredths disk in the Blackline Masters.

The connection between proportional reasoning and the geometric concept of similarity is very important. Similar figures provide a visual representation of proportions, and proportional thinking enhances the understanding of similarity. Whenever similarity is discussed, ratios in the figures should almost certainly be explored. The next two activities are aimed at this connection.

FIGURE 18.11

A spreadsheet can be used to record data, create tables of interesting ratios, and produce bar and circle graphs.

Source: Screen reprinted with permission from Apple Computer, Inc.

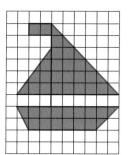

Use a metric ruler
- Choose two lengths on one boat and form a ratio (use a calculator). Compare to the ratio of the same parts of the other boats.
- Choose two boats. Measure the same part of each boat, and form a ratio. Compare with the ratios of another part.
- Compare the areas of the big sails with the lengths of the bottom sides.

FIGURE 18.12 **Comparing similar figures drawn on grids.**

ACTIVITY 18.7

Scale Drawings

On grid or dot paper (see the Blackline Masters), have students draw a simple shape using straight lines with vertices on the dots. After one shape is complete, have them draw a larger or smaller shape that is the same as or similar to the first. This can be done on a grid of the same size or a different size, as shown in Figure 18.12. After completing two or three pictures of different sizes, the ratios of the lengths of different sides can be compared.

Corresponding sides from one figure to the next should all be in the same ratio. The ratio of two sides within one figure should be the same as the ratio of the corresponding two sides in another figure.

ACTIVITY 18.8

Length, Surface, and Volume Ratios

A three-dimensional version of Activity 18.7 can be done with blocks, as shown in Figure 18.13. Using 1-inch or 2-cm wooden cubes, make a simple "building." Then make a similar but larger building, and compare measures. A different size can also be made

using different-sized blocks. To measure buildings made with different blocks, use a common unit such as centimeters.

Activities 18.7 and 18.8 involve area and volume as well as length. Comparisons of corresponding lengths, areas, and volumes in proportional figures lead to some interesting ratios. If two figures are proportional (similar), any two linear dimensions you measure will be in the same ratio on each, say, 1 to k. Corresponding areas, however, will be in the ratio of 1 to k^2, and corresponding volumes in the ratio of 1 to k^3. Try this with some constructions of your own.

As a means of contrasting proportional situations with additive ones, try starting with a figure on a grid or a building made with blocks and adding two units to every dimension in the figure. The result will be larger but will not look at all the same. Try this with a simple rectangle that is 1 cm by 15 cm. The new rectangle is twice as "thick" (2 cm) but

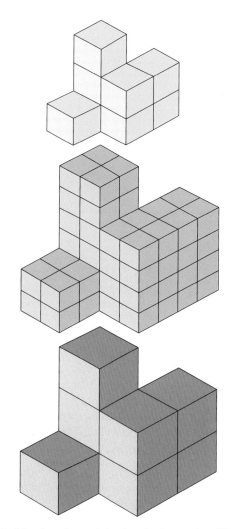

Similar "buildings" can be made by changing the number of blocks in each dimension (factor of change) or by using different-sized blocks.

FIGURE 18.13 **Similar constructions.**

CONNECTED MATHEMATICS

MIDDLE GRADES

Grade 7, *Comparing and Scaling*
Investigation 3: Comparing and Using Ratios

Context

This investigation occurs in the second week of the unit on ratio and proportions. In earlier activities, students explored ratios and percents to compare survey data from large populations with similar data gathered from their own class. Students used fractions, decimals, and percents to express ratios, and they compared ratios using their own strategies.

Task Description

The problem shown here is introduced in the context of students deciding on the best mix of juice for a camping trip.

Within the same investigation are two similar problems that are paraphrased here:

1a. A can of tomatoes will make sauce for 5 to 6 campers. How many cans should be purchased to make spaghetti for 240 campers? Five cans cost $4. How much will the cans of tomatoes cost?

2a. If pizzas are shared evenly, will a camper get more pizza sharing 4 pizzas with 10 campers or 3 pizzas with 8 campers?

2b. The ratio of 10-seat tables to 8-seat tables is 8 to 5. If there are just enough tables for all 240 campers, how many of each type are there?

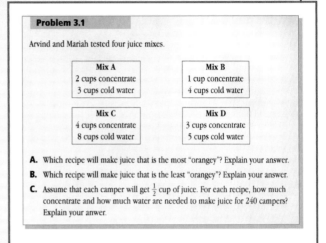

Problem 3.1

Arvind and Mariah tested four juice mixes.

Mix A
2 cups concentrate
3 cups cold water

Mix B
1 cup concentrate
4 cups cold water

Mix C
4 cups concentrate
8 cups cold water

Mix D
3 cups concentrate
5 cups cold water

A. Which recipe will make juice that is the most "orangey"? Explain your answer.

B. Which recipe will make juice that is the least "orangey"? Explain your answer.

C. Assume that each camper will get $\frac{1}{2}$ cup of juice. For each recipe, how much concentrate and how much water are needed to make juice for 240 campers? Explain your anwer.

From *Connected Mathematics: Comparing and Scaling: Ratio, Proportion, and Percent.* © 2002 by Michigan State University, Glenda Lappan, James T. Fey, William M. Fitzgerald, Susan N. Friel, and Elizabeth Difanis Phillips. Published by Prentice Hall. Used by permission of Pearson Education, Inc.

The full unit contains six investigations, each with numerous real contexts. Scaling, the use of unit rates, and percentages are suggested techniques. However, no particular method is forced on the students.

---

only a bit longer. It will not appear to be the same shape as the original.

    Dynamic geometry software such as *The Geometer's Sketchpad* (Key Curriculum Press) offers a very effective method of exploring the idea of ratio. In Figure 18.14, two lengths are drawn on a grid using the "snap-to-grid" option. The lengths are measured, and two ratios are computed. As the length of either line is changed, the measures and ratios are updated instantly. A screen similar to this could be used to discuss ratios of lengths as well as inverse ratios with your full class. In this example, notice that the second pair of lines has the same difference but that the ratios are not the same. A similar drawing could be prepared for the overhead on a transparency of a centimeter dot grid if software was not available.

The *Connected Mathematics* program places the main emphasis on proportional reasoning in the seventh grade. In the eighth grade, the proportional concepts are applied throughout the curriculum. The sample activity on this page is similar to the comparing ratio ideas you have read about earlier.

FIGURE 18.14 Dynamic geometry software or just a centimeter grid can be used to discuss ratios of two lengths.

NCTM Standards

"Attention to developing flexibility in working with rational numbers contributes to students' understanding of, and facility with, proportionality. Facility with proportionality involves much more than setting two ratios equal and solving for a missing term. It involves recognizing quantities that are related proportionally and using numbers, tables, graphs, and equations to think about the quantities and their relationship" (p. 217).

Solving Proportions

The activities to this point have been designed to lead students to an intuitive concept of ratio and proportion to help in the development of proportional reasoning.

One practical value of proportional reasoning is to use observed proportions to find unknown values. Knowledge of one ratio can often be used to find a value in the other. Comparison pricing, using scales on maps, and solving percentage problems are just a few everyday instances where solving proportions is required. Students need to learn to set up proportions symbolically and to solve them.

Within and Between Ratios

When examining two ratios, it is sometimes useful to think of them as being either *within* ratios or *between* ratios. A ratio of two measures in the same setting is a *within* ratio. For example, in the case of similar rectangles, the ratio of length to width for any one rectangle is a within ratio, that is, it is "within" the context of that rectangle. For all similar rectangles, corresponding within ratios will be equal.

A *between* ratio is a ratio of two corresponding measures in different situations. In the case of similar rectangles, the ratio of the length of one rectangle to the length of another is a between ratio; that is, it is "between" the two rectangles. For two similar rectangles, all of the between ratios will be equal. However, the between ratios for each pair of similar rectangles will be different.

STOP Consider three rectangles *A*, *B*, and *C*. *A* measures 2 × 6, *B* measures 3 × 9, and *C* measures 8 × 24. Find the within ratio for each rectangle. This should convince you that the rectangles are similar. Now examine the between ratios for *A* and *B*, and for *A* and *C*. Why are these ratios different?

Figure 18.5 (p. 302) shows six pictures of trucks and boxes. The within ratios are trucks to boxes (within one picture). The between ratios are from trucks to trucks and boxes to boxes. Be sure that you can distinguish within and between ratios in that figure.

The simple drawing in Figure 18.15 is a nice generic way of looking at two ratios and determining if a ratio is between

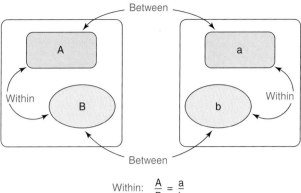

Within: $\dfrac{A}{B} = \dfrac{a}{b}$

Between: $\dfrac{A}{a} = \dfrac{B}{b}$

FIGURE 18.15 Given a proportional situation, the two between ratios and the two within ratios will be the same.

or within. A drawing similar to this will be very helpful to students in setting up proportions. Pick any two equivalent truck and box pictures and place the numbers in this figure.

An Informal Approach

Traditional textbooks show students how to set up an equation of two ratios involving an unknown, "cross-multiply," and solve for the unknown. This can be a very mechanical approach and will almost certainly lead to confusion and error. Although you may wish eventually to cover the cross-product algorithm, it is well worth the time for students to find ways to solve proportions using their own ideas first. If you have been exploring proportions informally, students will have a good foundation on which to build their own approaches.

To illustrate some intuitive approaches for solving proportions, consider the following tasks:

Tammy bought 3 widgets for \$2.40. At the same price, how much would 10 widgets cost?

Tammy bought 4 widgets for \$3.75. How much would a dozen widgets cost?

STOP Before reading further, solve these two problems using an approach for each that seems most reasonable to you.

In the first situation, it is perhaps easiest to determine the cost of one widget—the unit rate or unit price. This can be found by dividing the price of three widgets by 3. Multiplying this unit rate of $0.80 per widget by 10 will produce the answer. This approach is referred to as a *unit-rate* method of solving proportions. Notice that the unit rate is a within ratio.

In the second problem, a unit-rate approach could be used, but the division does not appear to be easy. Since 12 is a multiple of 4, it is easier to notice that the cost of a dozen is 3 times the cost of 4. This is called a *factor-of-change* method. It could have been used on the first problem but would have been awkward. The factor of change between 3 and 10 is $3\frac{1}{3}$. Multiplying $2.40 by $3\frac{1}{3}$ will produce the correct answer. Although the factor-of-change method is a useful way to think about proportions, it is most frequently used when the numbers are compatible. Students should be given problems in which the numbers lend themselves to both approaches so that they will explore both methods. The factor of change is a between ratio.

For each of the following two problems, place the numbers in a little drawing of two ratios in Figure 18.15. Solve each problem. Think about within or between ratios matching up. Do not use cross-multiplication.

At the Office Super Store, you can buy plain #2 pencils, four for 59 cents. The store also sells the same pencils in a large box of 5 dozen pencils for $7.79. How much do you save by buying the large box?

The price of a box of 2 dozen candy bars is $4.80. Bridget wants to buy 5 candy bars. What will she have to pay?

To solve the pencil problem, you might notice that the between ratio of pencils to pencils is 4 to 60, or 1 to 15. If you multiply the 59 cents by 15, the factor of change, you will get the price of the box of 60 if the pencils were sold at the same price. In the candy problem, the within ratio of 24 to $4.80 is easy to use to get the unit rate of 20 cents per candy bar. But what do you do if the numbers don't "come out nicely" like they do in these problems?

Try solving the same problems with new numbers that do not work out so easily. If you are having difficulty with the new problems, discuss them with a friend.

❌ **STOP** Try the following problem. Make a little sketch as before, and use a technique you have figured out yourself. (Do this now before reading on.)

Brian can run 5 km in 18.4 minutes. If he keeps on running at the same speed, how far can he run in 23 minutes?

The first situation for your sketch is Brian's 5-km run (5 km and 18.4 minutes). The second situation is the unknown distance and 23 minutes. There are at least two things you might consider, and one is no easier than the other. You could look at the between ratios of minutes to minutes in order to find a factor of change. That is, what do you multiply 18.4 by to get 23? On the calculator, compute 23 ÷ 18.4 to get 1.25, the factor of change. Now 5 km × 1.25 is 6.25 km.

The second possibility is to get a unit rate for the 5 km and multiply by 23. That would mean divide both the 5 and the 18.4 by 18.4 (like simplifying a fraction to a denominator of 1). The calculator yields 0.2717391, or about 0.27 km per minute. Multiply this unit rate by 23 minutes and you get 6.2499993 km. In both cases, the longer distance is 6.25 km.

What is important here is to see how to use multiplication to solve the proportional situation. Further, notice that the calculations are based on ideas already developed. The sketch of the two ratios helps keep things straight and avoids any ambiguous cross-multiplying.

The Cross-Product Algorithm

The methods just described come close to being well-defined algorithms, though they are a bit more flexible than cross-product methods. The reality is that the computations involved are exactly the same as in cross-multiplication. Yet some teachers may still want to teach cross-multiplication.

Draw a Simple Model

Given a ratio word problem, the greatest difficulty students have is setting up a correct proportion or equation of two ratios, one of which includes the missing value. "Which fractions do I make? Where does the *x* go?"

Rather than drill and drill in the hope that they will somehow eventually get it, show students how to sketch a simple picture that will help them determine what parts are related. In Figure 18.16, a simple model is drawn for a typical rate or price problem. The two equations in the figure come from setting up within and between ratios.

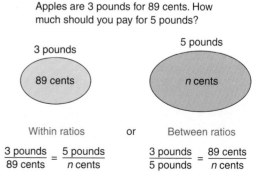

Apples are 3 pounds for 89 cents. How much should you pay for 5 pounds?

3 pounds — 89 cents   5 pounds — *n* cents

Within ratios   or   Between ratios

$$\frac{3 \text{ pounds}}{89 \text{ cents}} = \frac{5 \text{ pounds}}{n \text{ cents}}$$ $$\frac{3 \text{ pounds}}{5 \text{ pounds}} = \frac{89 \text{ cents}}{n \text{ cents}}$$

FIGURE 18.16 A simple drawing helps in a price-to-ratio problem.

Solve the Proportion

Examine the left (within) ratios in the same way as for Brian's 5-km race: Find out what to multiply the left fraction by to get the right. To do this, we would divide 5 by 3 and then multiply that result by 89:

$$\frac{5}{3} \times 89$$

Looking at the same left equation in Figure 18.16, we could also determine the unit price or the price for 1 pound by dividing the 89 cents by 3 and then multiplying this result by 5 to determine the price of 5 pounds:

$$\frac{89}{3} \times 5$$

Now look what happens if we cross-multiply in the original equation:

$$3n = 5 \times 89$$

$$n = \frac{5 \times 89}{3}$$

This equation can be solved by dividing the 5 by 3 and multiplying by 89 or dividing 89 by 3 and multiplying by 5. These are exactly the two devices we employed in our more intuitive approach. If you cross-multiply the between ratios, you get exactly the same result. Furthermore, you get the same result if you had written the two ratios inverted, that is, with the reciprocals of each fraction. Try it!

So if you want to develop a cross-product algorithm, it is not unreasonable to do problems like these while encouraging students to use their own methods. If you write out the computations involved, a very small amount of direct teaching can develop the cross-product approach. But why hurry?

In Figure 18.17, a problem involving rates of speed is modeled with simple lines representing the two distances. The distance and the time for each run are modeled with the same line. You cannot see time, but it fits into the distance covered. All equal-rates-of-speed problems can be modeled this way. There really is no significant difference from the

drawing used for the apples. Again, it is just as acceptable to write between ratios as within ratios, and students need not worry about which one goes on top as long as the ratios are written in the same order. The model helps with this difficulty.

Activities Leading to Proportions

In the preceding discussion, simple rate problems were used to help students develop a technique for solving proportions. The next two activities illustrate other common uses of proportional reasoning.

ACTIVITY 18.9

Scale Drawings
Provide students with a drawing of a simple geometric figure, including its dimensions. The task is to create a new drawing that is either larger or smaller than the given one. One dimension of the new drawing is specified (see Figure 18.18 for an example). Students can set up between or within ratios and determine the other dimensions by solving the proportion.

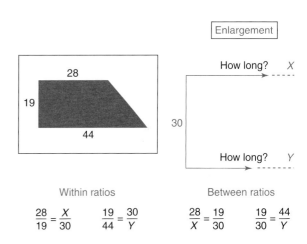

FIGURE 18.18 **Pictures help in establishing equal ratios.**

This scale drawing activity is somewhat simplistic, but it provides students with the essential ideas for setting up proportions. Here are some more interesting situations to consider:

● If you wanted to make a scale model of the solar system and use a Ping-Pong ball for the earth, how far away should the sun be? How large a ball would you need?
● What scale should be used to draw a scale map of your city (or some interesting region) so that it will nicely fit onto a standard piece of poster board?
● Use the scale on a map to estimate the distance and travel time between two points of interest.
● Roll a toy car down a ramp, timing the trip with a stopwatch. How fast was the car traveling in miles per hour? If the speed is proportional to the size of the car, how fast would this have been for a real car?

FIGURE 18.17 **Line segments can be used to model both time and distance.**

- Your little sister wants a table and chair for her doll. Her doll is 14 inches tall. How big should you make the table?
- Determine the various distances that a ten-speed bike travels in one turn of the pedals. You will need to count the sprocket teeth on the front and back gears.

Have you ever wondered how scientists estimate the number of bass in a lake or the number of monarch butterflies that migrate each year to Mexico? One method often used is a capture-recapture technique modeled in the next activity.

ACTIVITY 18.10

Capture-Recapture

Prepare a shoebox full of some uniform small object such as centicubes or plastic chips. You could also use a larger box filled with Styrofoam packing "peanuts." If the box is your lake and the objects are the fish you want to count, how can you estimate the number without actually counting them? Remember, if they were fish, you couldn't even see them! Have a student reach into the box and "capture" a representative sample of the "fish." For a large box, you may want to capture more than a handful. "Tag" each fish by marking it in some way—marking pen or sticky dot. Count and record the number tagged, and then return them to the box. The assumption of the scientist is that tagged animals will mix uniformly with the larger population, so mix them thoroughly. Next, have five to ten students make a recapture of fish from the box. Each counts the total captured and the number in the capture that are tagged. Accumulate these data.

 Now the task is to use all of the information to estimate the number of fish in the lake. The recapture data provide an estimated ratio of tagged to untagged fish. The number tagged to the total population should be in the same ratio. After solving the proportion, have students count the actual items in the box to see how close their estimate is.

For a more detailed description of the "Capture-Recapture" activity, see the NCTM Addenda Series book *Understanding Rational Numbers and Proportions* (Curcio & Bezuk, 1994).

Percent Problems as Proportions

Percent has traditionally been included as a topic with ratio and proportion because percent is one form of ratio, a part-to-whole ratio. In Chapter 17, it was shown that percent problems can be connected to fraction concepts. Here the same part-to-whole fraction concept of percent will be extended to ratio and proportion concepts. Ideally, all of these ideas (fractions, decimals, ratio, proportion, and percent) should be conceptually integrated. The better that students

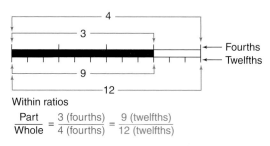

FIGURE 18.19 Equivalent fractions as proportions.

connect these ideas, the more flexible and useful their reasoning and problem-solving skills will be.

Equivalent Fractions as Proportions

First consider how equivalent fractions can be interpreted as a proportion using the same simple models already used. In Figure 18.19, a line segment is partitioned in two different ways: in fourths on one side and in twelfths on the other. In the previous examples, proportions were established based on two amounts of apples, two different distances or runs, and two different sizes of drawings. Here only one thing is measured—the part of a whole—but it is measured or partitioned two ways: in fourths and in twelfths.

The within ratios are ratios of part to whole within each measurement. Within ratios result in the usual equivalent fraction equation, $\frac{3}{4} = \frac{9}{12}$ (3 fourths are to 4 fourths as 9 twelfths are to 12 twelfths). The between proportion equates a part-to-part ratio with a whole-to-whole ratio, or $\frac{3}{9} = \frac{4}{12}$ (3 fourths are to 9 twelfths as 4 fourths are to 12 twelfths).

A simple line segment drawing similar to the one in Figure 18.19 could be drawn to set up a proportion to solve any equivalent-fraction problem, even ones that do not result in whole-number numerators or denominators. An example is shown in Figure 18.20.

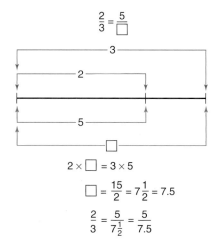

Can you interpret these fractions?

FIGURE 18.20 Solving equivalent-fraction problems as equivalent ratios using cross-products.

Percent Problems

All percent problems are exactly the same as the equivalent-fraction examples. They involve a part and a whole measured in some unit and the same part and whole measured in hundredths—that is, in percents. A simple line segment drawing can be used for each of the three types of percent problems. Using this model as a guide, a proportion can be written and solved by the cross-product algorithm. Examples of each type of problem are shown in Figure 18.21.

It is tempting to teach all percent problems in this one way. Developmentally, such an approach is not recommended. Even though the approach is conceptual, it does not

translate easily to intuitive ideas, mental arithmetic, or estimation as discussed in Chapter 17. The modeling and proportion approach of Figure 18.21 is suggested only as a way to help students analyze problems that may verbally present some difficulty. The approach of Chapter 17, which relates percent to part-whole fraction concepts, should probably receive more emphasis.

TECHNOLOGY NOTE

You have already seen how spreadsheets can be used to create tables and compute ratios. Dynamic geometry programs allow figures to be scaled to larger or smaller sizes by using either a specified ratio or the dilation feature. This provides an excellent connection between the concepts of similarity and proportion.

Very few computer programs specifically address the issue of proportionality. *CampOS Math* (Pierian Spring Software, 1996) has an activity called the Color Mixer in which the concept of ratio is applied to the mixing of red, green, and blue light to create new colors. By way of example, the student may be asked to set the color mixer so that the blue light is at 30 percent intensity and R:G (the ratio of red to green) = 5:9. There is some potential confusion between types of ratios. The program provides a somewhat realistic use of ratio and some minimal problem solving. ■

LITERATURE CONNECTIONS

Literature brings an exciting dimension to the exploration of proportional reasoning. Many books and stories discuss comparative sizes; concepts of scale as in maps; giants and miniature people who are proportional to regular people; comparative rates, especially rates of speed; and so on. A book may not appear to explore proportions, and the author may not have had that in mind at all, but comparisons are the stuff of many excellent stories and are at the heart of proportional ideas. The suggestions here are intended to give you an idea of what you might look for.

If You Hopped Like a Frog
Schwartz, 1999

David Schwartz, the author of *How Much Is a Million?* and *If You Made a Million*, has found some wonderful mathematics in nature with this new book. Here Schwartz uses proportional reasoning to determine what it would be like if we had the powers or dimensions of familiar animals. "If you hopped like a frog, you could jump from home plate to first base in one mighty leap." This short picture book contains 12 of these fascinating proportions: if you were as strong as an ant . . . , if you flicked your tongue like a chameleon . . . , and so on. At the end of the book, Schwartz provides some factual data on which the proportions are based. The book could be read at least twice at the start of a lesson, and students

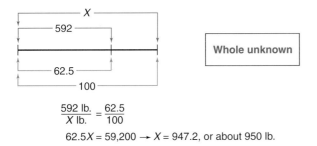

FIGURE 18.21 The three percentage problems solved by setting up a proportion using a simple line segment model.

could find their own comparisons to calculate. This is a wonderful connection to science. There is no reason the comparisons need be between animals and humans as in this book. The toy-car to real-car ratio is an example of comparisons students could be encouraged to explore using this delightful book as a springboard.

Counting on Frank
Clement, 1991

We will refer to this wonderful book again when we discuss measurement in Chapter 19. It is hard to imagine that more mathematics could spring from 24 pages mostly covered with pictures. But the ideas appeal to all ages, and the potential for good investigations is clearly there for older children. The narrator and his pet dog, Frank, estimate, figure, and ponder interesting facts, usually about large numbers in odd settings (enough green peas to be level with the kitchen tabletop). But three spreads of the book are wonderful fantasies of proportions that could easily inspire an entire unit of proportional reasoning projects.

> "If I had grown at the same speed as the tree—6 feet per year—I'd now be almost 50 feet tall!" How fast do we grow? What if we kept growing at the same rate? How old is the narrator? How old would he be when he is 75 feet tall?

> If the mosquito that bothers him were 4 million times bigger . . . What would any common object be like if it were a million times bigger?

> If the toaster that shoots toast 3 feet in the air were as big as the house . . .

The Borrowers
Norton, 1953

This is the classic tale of little folk living in the walls of a house. The furnishings and implements are created from odds and ends from the full-size human world. The potential to make scale comparisons is endless.

A similar tale unfolds in Shel Silverstein's poem "One Inch Tall" (1974), in which you are invited to imagine being 1 inch tall.

At the other extreme are stories about giants and dinosaurs, but the concepts of scale are similar. Suppose that a giant were 18 feet tall, or three times the height of a tall man. All linear dimensions (arm span, foot length, etc.) would also be three times that of the man. But the surface area would be 3^2 or 9 times as large, and the giant's volume and hence his weight would be 3^3 or 27 times as much as the man's. That would make the giant weigh about 5400 pounds. With a cross-sectional area of the bones only 9 times more, the bones would not be able to hold the weight. This is one reason there are no real giants. ■

 ## ASSESSMENT NOTES

As you work with your students in solving proportional reasoning tasks, it will be useful for you to think about the type of reasoning that students are using.

● Do they distinguish between proportional situations and additive or nonproportional ones?

● Are they flexible in the way that they attempt to solve proportions? A nonflexible or algorithmic approach, even if correct, may signal that a student is simply following rules.

● Are there differences in thinking about different types of proportional situations? For example, discrete (countable) items in a proportion are sometimes easier to deal with than continuous quantities such as time, distance, or volume.

● Do students seem to understand rates (miles per hour, inches per yard, dollars per pound) as ratios? How students deal with these ideas reflects the development of their proportional thinking.

Keep in mind that proportional reasoning develops slowly over the middle school years. A first unit of two or three weeks' duration in the sixth grade will not be enough for most children to develop true proportional thought. It will be useful to collect anecdotal evidence related to the questions just listed. If most of your students seem to be at the beginning levels of proportional thought, activities involving selection of equal ratios, constructions, and scaling will be more useful than harder proportion problems. Using numbers that lend themselves to easy relationships will also make it easier for students to describe different methods for solving proportion tasks. ■

REFLECTIONS ON CHAPTER 18

Writing to Learn

1. Describe the idea of a ratio in your own words. Explain how your idea fits with each of the following statements:
   a. A fraction is a ratio.
   b. Ratios can compare things that are not at all alike.
   c. Ratios can compare two parts of the same whole.
   d. Rates such as prices or speeds are ratios.

2. What is a proportion? For each of the statements in item 1, give an example of a proportion. Also give an example of a comparison that is additive rather than proportional.

3. Much of this chapter is about activities that help students observe ratios and develop proportional reasoning abilities. These activities were grouped into four categories:
   a. Selection of equivalent ratios
   b. Comparisons of ratios
   c. Scaling activities using ratio tables
   d. Construction and measurement
   For each of these four categories, pick one activity presented in the book that you did not do as part of your class experiences. Do the activity and briefly describe how you think the activity would contribute to students' proportional reasoning.
4. What can you say about the graph of a collection of equivalent ratios?
5. Make up a realistic proportional situation that can be solved by a factor-of-change approach and another that can be solved by a unit-rate approach. Explain each.
6. Consider this problem: If 50 gallons of fuel oil cost $56.95, how much can be purchased for $100? Draw a sketch to illustrate the proportion, and set up the equation in two different ways. One equation should equate within ratios and the other between ratios.
7. Make up a realistic percentage problem, and set up a proportion. Draw a model to help explain why the proportion makes sense. Illustrate how this method could be used for any of the three types of percentage problems.

For Discussion and Exploration

1. Examine a teacher's edition of a basal textbook for the sixth, seventh, or eighth grade. How is the topic of ratio developed? What is the emphasis? Select one lesson, and write a lesson plan that extends the ideas found on the student pages and actively involves the students.
2. In Chapter 17, the three percent problems were developed around the theme of which element was missing—the part, the whole, or the fraction that related the two. In this chapter, percent is related to proportions, an equality of two ratios with one of these ratios a comparison to 100. How are these two approaches alike? Do you prefer one or the other?

Recommendations for Further Reading

Highly Recommended

Lamon, S. J. (1999). *Teaching fractions and ratios for understanding: Essential content knowledge and instructional strategies for teachers.* Mahwah, NJ: Lawrence Erlbaum.

Lamon is one of the most prolific researchers and writers on the subject of fractions, ratios, and proportional reasoning. Her work is full of specific practical examples of activities and is freely illustrated with children's work. At the same time this is a serious, research-based, and thought-provoking book. Many of the ideas found in this chapter are adapted from this book and other works by Lamon. Anyone seriously interested in the development of proportional reasoning needs to have this book. There is a companion volume with additional examples to elaborate the ideas found here. (See the other suggested readings that follow.)

Langrall, C. W., & Swafford, J. (2000). Three balloons for two dollars. *Mathematics Teaching in the Middle School, 6,* 254–261.

If you cannot find the Lamon book just mentioned and would like to see an overview of her ideas in a short article, then try this one. The authors describe and give examples of four levels of proportional reasoning using examples from the classroom. A good article on a difficult topic.

Miller, J. L., & Fey, J. T. (2000). Proportional reasoning. *Mathematics Teaching in the Middle School, 5,* 310–313.

This short article describes three proportionality tasks with a total of seven questions that were posed to middle school students. The results compared students in a reform curriculum with those in a traditional curriculum. The interesting tasks are quite reproducible. The discussion is also valuable.

Other Suggestions

Alcaro, P., Alston, A., & Katims, N. (2000). Fractions attack! Children thinking and talking mathematically. *Teaching Children Mathematics, 6,* 562–565.

Ben-Chaim, D., Fey, J. T., Fitzgerald, W. M., Benedetto, C., & Miller, J. (1998). Proportional reasoning among 7th grade students with different curricular experiences. *Educational Studies in Mathematics, 36,* 247–273.

Cai, J., & Sun, W. (2002). Developing students' proportional reasoning: A Chinese perspective. In B. Litwiller (Ed.), *Making sense of fractions, ratios, and proportions* (pp. 195–205). Reston, VA: National Council of Teachers of Mathematics.

Cramer, K., Post, T. R., & Currier, S. (1993). Learning and teaching ratio and proportion: Research implications. In D. T. Owens (Ed.), *Research ideas for the classroom: Middle grades mathematics* (pp. 159–178). Old Tappan, NJ: Macmillan.

Kenney, P. A., Lindquist, M. M., & Heffernan, C. L. (2002). Butterflies and caterpillars: Multiplicative and proportional reasoning in the early grades. In B. Litwiller (Ed.), *Making sense of fractions, ratios, and proportions* (pp. 87–99). Reston, VA: National Council of Teachers of Mathematics.

Lamon, S. J. (1999). *More: In-depth discussion of the reasoning activities in "Teaching fractions and ratios for understanding."* Mahwah, NJ: Lawrence Erlbaum.

Lamon, S. J. (2002). Part-whole comparisons with unitizing. In Litwiller, B. (Ed.), *Making sense of fractions, ratios, and proportions* (pp. 79–86). Reston, VA: National Council of Teachers of Mathematics.

Lappan, G., Fitzgerald, W., Winter, M. J., & Phillips, E. (1986). *Middle grades mathematics project: Similarity and equivalent fractions.* Menlo Park, CA: AWL Supplemental.

Lo, J., & Watanabe, T. (1997). Developing ratio and proportion schemes: A story of a fifth grader. *Journal for Research in Mathematics Education, 28,* 216–236.

Middleton, J. A., & Van den Heuvel-Panhuizen, M. (1995). The ratio table. *Mathematics Teaching in the Middle School, 1,* 283–287.

Moss, J. (2002). Percents and proportion at the center: Altering the teaching sequence for rational number. In B. Litwiller (Ed.), *Making sense of fractions, ratios, and proportions* (pp. 109–120). Reston, VA: National Council of Teachers of Mathematics.

Smith, J. P. III. (2002). The development of students' knowledge of fractions and ratios. In B. Litwiller (Ed.), *Making sense of fractions, ratios, and proportions* (pp. 3–17). Reston, VA: National Council of Teachers of Mathematics.

Thompson, D. R., Austin, R. A., & Beckmann, C. E. (2002). Using literature as a vehicle to explore proportional reasoning. In B. Litwiller (Ed.), *Making sense of fractions, ratios, and proportions* (pp. 130–137). Reston, VA: National Council of Teachers of Mathematics.

CHAPTER

19

DEVELOPING MEASUREMENT CONCEPTS

That measurement was given its own standard in *Principles and Standards* points to the complexity of the subject. Between kindergarten and eighth grade, students must learn the attributes that they will be measuring (length, weight, capacity, and so on); what it means to measure, including an understanding of units of measure and how unit size affects measures; the selection and use of measurement instruments; systems of measurement (metric and customary); and formulas that can be used for determining measurements. Measurement is far more complex than we often realize.

Big Ideas

1. Measurement involves a comparison of an attribute of an item or situation with a unit that has the same attribute. Lengths are compared to units of length, areas to units of area, time to units of time, and so on. Before anything can be measured meaningfully, it is necessary to understand the attribute to be measured.

2. Meaningful measurement and estimation of measurements depend on a personal familiarity with the unit of measure being used.

3. Estimation of measures and the development of personal benchmarks for frequently used units of measure help students increase their familiarity with units, prevent errors in measurements, and aid in the meaningful use of measurement.

4. Measurement instruments are devices that replace the need for actual measurement units. It is important to understand how measurement instruments work so that they can be used correctly and meaningfully.

5. Area and volume formulas provide a method of measuring these attributes by using only measures of length.

6. Area, perimeter, and volume are related to each other, although not precisely or by formula. For example, as the shapes of regions or three-dimensional objects change but maintain the same areas or volumes, there is a predictable effect on the perimeters and surface areas.

CONTENT CONNECTIONS

Measurement has traditionally been paired in the curriculum with geometry. However, measurement is actually more closely connected to other mathematical topics.

- **Number** (Chapter 9): Early measurement activities are a very meaningful context for counting. Measurement of important objects in the familiar environment connects ideas of number to the real world, enhancing number sense.

- **Place Value** (Chapter 10): Multiples of ten are profitably used by young children in counting informal measures such as the height of the door in terms of connecting cubes. The metric system of measurement is built on the base-ten system of numeration. An understanding of each topic enhances the use of and understanding of the other.

- **Proportional Reasoning** (Chapter 18): The use of benchmarks in estimating measures (e.g., a door is about 3 feet wide so the room is about seven "doors" or 21 feet) promotes multiplicative thinking, a fundamental aspect of proportional reasoning. Measures are used in scale drawings. Proportions are used to find unknown measures of similar figures.

- **Fractions** (Chapter 15): The need for increased precision leads to fractional parts of units.

- **Geometry** (Chapter 20): The development and understanding of perimeter, area, and volume formulas require an understanding of the shapes and relationships involved.

Measures help to describe shapes, and angular measures play a significant role in the properties of shapes.

- **Algebra** (Chapter 23): Functions are used to study and describe the relationships between various phenomena, especially things that are measured. Measurement formulas are themselves functions.

- **Data** (Chapter 21): Statistics and graphs are used to describe our world and help us answer questions about it. Often this description is in terms of measures. Graphing and measurement are easily blended into the same units or activities.

The Meaning and Process of Measuring

Suppose that you were asked to measure an empty bucket. The first thing you would need to know is *what* about the bucket is to be measured. You might measure the height or depth, diameter (distance across), or circumference (distance around). All of these are length measures. The surface area of the side could be determined. A bucket also has volume and weight. Each of these *aspects that can be measured* is an *attribute* of the bucket.

Once you determine the attribute to be measured, you can choose a unit of measure. The unit must have the attribute that is being measured. Length is measured with units that have length, volume with units that have volume, and so on.

Technically, a *measurement* is a number that indicates a comparison between the attribute of the object (or situation, or event) being measured and the same attribute of a given unit of measure. We commonly use small units of measure to determine in some way a numeric relationship (the measurement) between what is measured and the unit. For example, to measure a length, the comparison can be done by lining up copies of the unit directly against the length being measured. To measure weight, which is a pull of gravity or a force, the weight of the object might first be applied to a spring. Then the comparison is made by finding out how many units of weight produce the same effect on the spring. In either case, the number of units is the measure of the object.

For most of the attributes that are measured in schools, we can say that *to measure* means that the attribute being measured is "filled" or "covered" or "matched" with a unit of measure with the same attribute (as illustrated in Figure 19.1). This concept of measurement will adequately serve the purposes of this chapter and is a good way to discuss with children what a measurement is. It is appropriate with this understanding, then, to say that the measure of an attribute is a count of how many units are needed to fill, cover, or match the attribute of the object being measured.

In summary, to measure something, one must perform three steps:

1. Decide on the attribute to be measured.
2. Select a unit that has that attribute.
3. Compare the units, by filling, covering, matching, or some other method, with the attribute of the object being measured.

Measuring instruments such as rulers, scales, protractors, and clocks are devices that make the filling, covering, or matching process easier. A ruler lines up the units of length and numbers them. A protractor lines up the unit angles and numbers them. A clock lines up units of time and marks them off.

FIGURE 19.1 Measuring different attributes of a bucket.

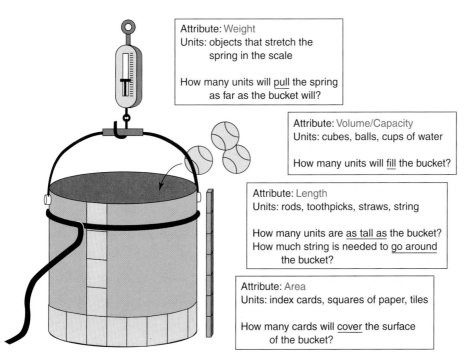

Attribute: Weight
Units: objects that stretch the
spring in the scale

How many units will pull the spring
as far as the bucket will?

Attribute: Volume/Capacity
Units: cubes, balls, cups of water

How many units will fill the bucket?

Attribute: Length
Units: rods, toothpicks, straws, string

How many units are as tall as the bucket?
How much string is needed to go around
the bucket?

Attribute: Area
Units: index cards, squares of paper, tiles

How many cards will cover the surface
of the bucket?

Developing Measurement Concepts and Skills

A typical group of first graders measures the length of their classroom by laying strips 1 meter long end to end. But the strips sometimes overlap, and the line weaves in a snakelike fashion around the desks. Do they understand the concept of length as an attribute of the classroom? Do they understand that each strip of 1 meter has this attribute of length? Do they understand that their task is to fill smaller units of length into the longer one? What they most likely understand is that they are supposed to be making a line of strips stretching from wall to wall (and from their vantage point, they are doing quite well). They are performing a procedure instrumentally, without a conceptual basis.

A General Plan of Instruction

A basic understanding of measurement suggests how to help children develop a conceptual knowledge of measuring. These are summarized in Table 19.1.

Let's briefly discuss each of these three instructional components described in the table.

Making Comparisons

When students compare objects on the basis of some measurable attribute, that attribute becomes the focus of the activity. For example, is the capacity of one box more than, less

TABLE 19.1
Plan for Measurement Instruction

Step One
Goal: Students will understand the attribute to be measured.
Type of Activity: Make comparisons based on the attribute. For example, longer/shorter, heavier/lighter. Use direct comparisons whenever possible.
Notes: When it is clear that the attribute is understood, there is no further need for comparison activities.

Step Two
Goal: Students will understand how filling, covering, matching, or making other comparisons of an attribute with measuring units produces a number called a measure.
Type of Activity: Use physical models of measuring units to fill, cover, match, or make the desired comparison of the attribute with the unit.
Notes: In most instances it is appropriate to begin with informal units. Progress to the direct use of standard units when appropriate and certainly before using formulas or measuring tools.

Step Three
Goal: Students will use common measuring tools with understanding and flexibility.
Type of Activity: Make measuring instruments and use them in comparison with the actual unit models to see how the measurement tool is performing the same function as the individual units. Be certain to make direct comparisons between the student-made tools and the standard tools.
Notes: Student-made tools are usually best made with informal units. Without a careful comparison with the standard tools, much of the value in making the tools can be lost.

than, or about the same as the capacity of another? No measurement is required, but some manner of comparing one volume to the other must be devised. The attribute of "capacity" (how much a container can hold) is inescapable.

Many attributes can be compared directly, such as placing one length directly in line with another. In the case of volume or capacity, some indirect method is probably required, such as filling one box with beans and then pouring the beans into the other box. Using a string to compare the height of a wastebasket to the distance around is another example of an indirect comparison. The string is the intermediary. It is impossible to compare these two lengths directly.

Constructing or making something that is the same in terms of a measurable attribute is another type of comparison activity—for example, "Cut the straw to be just as long as this piece of chalk" or "Draw a rectangle that is about the same size (has the same area) as this triangle."

Using Models of Units

For most attributes that are measured in elementary schools, it is possible to have physical models of the units of measure. Time and temperature are exceptions. (Many other attributes not commonly measured in school also do not have physical units of measure. Light intensity, speed, loudness, viscosity, and radioactivity are just a few examples.) Unit models can be found for both informal units and standard units. For length, for example, drinking straws (informal) or tagboard strips 1 foot long (standard) might be used as units.

The most easily understood use of unit models is actually to use as many copies of the unit as are needed to fill or match the attribute measured. To measure the area of the desktop with an index card unit, you can literally cover the entire desk with index cards. Somewhat more difficult, especially for younger children, is to use a single copy of the unit with an iteration process. The same desktop area can be measured with a single index card by moving it from position to position and keeping track of which areas the card has covered.

It is useful to measure the same object with different-sized units. Results should be predicted in advance and discussed afterward. This will help students understand that the unit used is as important as the attribute being measured. The fact that smaller units produce larger numeric measures, and vice versa, is hard for young children to understand. This inverse relationship can only be constructed by reflecting on measurements with varying-sized units. Predictions and discussions of results add to the reflective nature of the activities.

Making and Using Measuring Instruments

In the sixth National Assessment of Educational Progress (Kenney & Kouba, 1997), only 24 percent of fourth-grade students and 62 percent of eighth-grade students could give the correct measure of an object not aligned with the end of a ruler, as in Figure 19.2. These results point to the difference between using a measuring device and understanding how it works. Students also experienced difficulty when the increments on a measuring device were other than one unit.

FIGURE 19.2 *"How long is this segment?"*

If students actually make simple measuring instruments using unit models with which they are familiar, it is more likely that they will understand how an instrument measures. A ruler is a good example. If students line up physical units along a strip of tagboard and mark them off, they can see that it is the *spaces* on rulers and not the marks or numbers that are important. It is essential that the measurement with actual unit models be compared with the measurement using an instrument. Without this comparison, students may not understand that these two methods are really two means to the same end. Always have students explain how the ruler, scale, or other device compares to using actual units.

A discussion of student-made measuring instruments for each attribute is provided in the text that follows. Of course, children should also use standard, ready-made instruments such as rulers and scales and should compare the use of these devices with the use of the corresponding unit models.

Informal Units and Standard Units: Reasons for Using Each

It is common in primary grades to use nonstandard or informal units to measure length and sometimes area. Unfortunately, measurement activities in the upper grades, where other attributes are measured, often do not begin with informal units. The use of informal units for beginning measurement activities is beneficial at all grade levels.

- Informal units make it easier to focus directly on the attribute being measured. For example, in a discussion of how to measure the area of an irregular shape, units such as lima beans, square tiles, or circular counters may be suggested. Each unit covers area and each will give a different result. The discussion focuses on what it means to measure area.
- By selecting units carefully, the size of the numbers in early measurements can be kept reasonable. The measures of length for first-grade students can be kept less than 20 even when measuring long distances.
- The use of informal units can avoid conflicting objectives in the same beginning lesson. Is your lesson about what it means to measure area or about understanding square centimeters?
- Informal units provide a good rationale for standard units. A discussion of the need for a standard unit can have more meaning after groups in your class have measured the same objects with their own units and arrived at different answers.
- Using informal units can be fun.

The use of standard units is also important in your measurement program at any grade level.

- Knowledge of standard units is a valid objective of a measurement program and must be addressed. Students must not only develop a familiarity with standard units but must also learn appropriate relationships between them.
- Once a measuring concept is fairly well developed, it is frequently just as easy to use standard units. If there is no good instructional reason for using informal units, why not use standard units and provide the exposure?

There is no simple rule for when to use standard or informal units. Children's initial measurement of any attribute should probably begin with informal units and progress over time to the use of standard units and standard measuring tools. The amount of time that should be spent using informal unit models varies with the age of the children and the attributes being measured. First-grade children need a lot of experience with a variety of informal units of length, weight, and capacity. Informal units might be used at this level all year. Conversely, the benefits of nonstandard measuring units may last only a day or two for measurements of angles at the middle school level.

The Role of Estimation in Learning Measurement

It is very important to have students estimate a measurement before they make it. This is true with both informal and standard units. There are at least four good reasons for including estimation in measurement activities:

- Estimation helps students focus on the attribute being measured and the measuring process. Think how you would estimate the area of the front of this book with standard playing cards as the unit. To do so, you have to think about what area is and how the units might be fitted into the book cover.
- Estimation provides intrinsic motivation to measurement activities. It is fun to see how close you can come in your estimate or if your team can make a better estimate than the other teams in the room.
- When standard units are used, estimation helps develop familiarity with the unit. If you estimate the height of the door in meters before measuring, you have to devise some way to think about the size of a meter.
- As noted in the Content Connections, the use of a benchmark to make an estimate promotes multiplicative reasoning. The width of the building is about one-fourth of the length of a football field—perhaps 25 yards.

The Approximate Nature of Measurement

In all measuring activities, emphasize the use of approximate language. The desk is *about* 15 orange rods long. The chair is *a little less than* 4 straws high. The use of approximate language is very useful for younger children because many measurements do not come out even. Older children will begin to search for smaller units or will use fractional units to try to measure exactly. Here is an opportunity to develop the idea that all measurements include some error. Each smaller unit or subdivision does produce a greater degree of *precision*. For example, a length measure can never be more than one-half unit in error. And yet, since there is mathematically no "smallest unit," there is always some error involved.

In the following sections, the attributes of length, area, volume or capacity, weight or mass, and angle size are each discussed separately. Within each section you will see the progression from comparisons, to informal units, and finally to measurement tools. There are separate discussions of standard units, estimation, and the development of formulas.

NCTM Standards The Measurement Standard in *Principles and Standards* has two main parts. The first emphasizes the need for students to understand the attributes of things they will be measuring and the process of using units to create measures. The second part focuses on the use of measurement tools and the use of formulas. The *Standards* authors stress that students should have ample opportunities to use informal units and similar meaningful experiences with measurement—regardless of grade level—before focusing on tools and formulas.

MEASURING LENGTH

Length is usually the first attribute students learn to measure. Be aware, however, that length measurement is not immediately understood by young children.

Comparison Activities

At the kindergarten level, children should begin with direct comparisons of two or more lengths.

ACTIVITY 19.1

Longer, Shorter, Same

Make a sorting-by-length station at which students sort objects as longer, shorter, or about the same as a specified object. It is easy to have several such stations in your room. The reference object can be changed occasionally to produce different sorts. A similar task is to put objects in order from shortest to longest.

ACTIVITY 19.2

Length (or Unit) Hunt

Give pairs of students a strip of tagboard, a stick, a length of rope, or some other object with an obvious length dimension. The task on one day might be to find five things in the room that are shorter than,

longer than, or about the same length as their object. They can draw pictures or write the names of the things they find.

By making the target length a standard unit (e.g., a meter stick or a 1-meter length of rope), the activity can be repeated to provide familiarity with important standard units.

It is important to compare lengths that are not in straight lines. One way to do this is with string or rope. Students can wrap string around objects in a search for things that are, for example, as long around as the distance from the floor to their belly button or as long as the distance around one's head or waist. Body measures are always fun.

Indirect comparisons are used in the next activity.

ACTIVITY 19.3

Crooked Paths

Make some crooked or curvy paths on the floor with masking tape. The task is to determine which path is longest, next longest, and so on. The students should find a way to make straight paths that are just as long as the crooked paths so that they can be compared easily. (You may or may not wish to offer this suggestion.) Provide pairs of students with a long piece of rope. The task is easier if the rope is longer than the crooked paths. The students can draw their straight paths on the board, mark them with tape on the floor, or use some other method that you devise. Have students explain how they solved the problem. (This is a good outdoor activity also.)

Using Units of Length

Students can use a variety of informal units to begin measuring length, for example:

Giant footprints: Make about 20 copies of a large footprint about $1\frac{1}{2}$ to 2 feet long cut out of poster board.

Measuring ropes: Cut cotton clothesline into lengths of 1 m. These are useful for measuring curved lines and the circumference of large objects such as the teacher's desk.

Plastic straws: Drinking straws are inexpensive and provide large quantities of a useful unit. Straws are easily cut into smaller units. You can link straw units together with a long string. The string of straws is an excellent bridge to a ruler or measuring tape.

Short units: Toothpicks, connecting cubes, wooden cubes, and paper clips are all useful units for measuring shorter lengths. Cuisenaire rods are one of the nicest sets of units because they come in ten different lengths, are easily placed end to end, and can be related to each other. Paper clips can readily be made into chains as can plastic chain links, available from suppliers of manipulatives.

Young children often will place units in a snake-like fashion and/or overlap the units. Rather than correcting these inappropriate techniques the first time, consider using the opportunity that will undoubtedly arise when students obtain different measures to discuss why some measures are different. As a result, the need for aligning units end to end and in a straight path is more likely to be understood rather than seen as just another rule to follow.

ACTIVITY 19.4

Guess and Measure

Make lists of things in the room to measure (see Figure 19.3). For younger children, run a piece of masking tape along the dimension of each object to be measured. On the list, designate the units to be used. Do not forget to include curves or other distances that are not straight lines. Include estimates before the measures. Young children will not be very good at estimating distances at first.

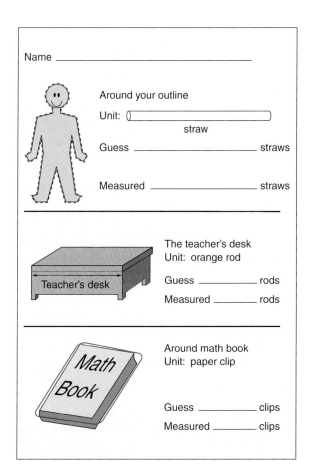

FIGURE 19.3 Record sheet for measuring with informal length units.

ACTIVITY 19.5

Changing Units

Have students measure a distance with one unit; then provide them with a different unit and see if they can predict the measure with the new unit. Students should write down their predictions and explanations of how they were made. Then have them make the actual measurement. In the class discussions that follow, the predictions and explanations will be the most educational part of the activity. The first few times you do this activity, the larger unit should be a simple multiple of the smaller unit. If the two units are not related by a whole-number multiple, the task becomes numerically difficult.

Two Units and Fractional Parts of Units

Children are sometimes perplexed when their measurements do not come out evenly. One suggestion you might make to younger students is to use a smaller unit to fill in the remaining gap as in Figure 19.4. Another idea is to suggest that fractions be used. Both ideas are used in standard measurements. In the metric system, units are rarely mixed, and fractional units are expressed in decimal form (e.g., 3.2 m). In the customary system, both approaches are used. A measurement of 4 feet 3 inches is sometimes reported as 51 inches or as $4\frac{1}{4}$ feet. The use of fractional units is a good readiness for subdivision marks on a ruler.

Making and Using Rulers

Ruler construction should be directly related to a measuring experience with a unit that is small but not less than 5 cm. It is important that students have used the actual unit models before making the rulers. Rulers can be made on long strips of tagboard about 5 cm wide. If you precut narrow strips of construction paper, students can cut these into shorter pieces using their unit model as a guide. Discuss how the paper strips could be used for measuring just as well as the actual units. Next, students can paste the paper units along the edge

Width = 5 orange and 4 red

FIGURE 19.4 Using two units to measure length.

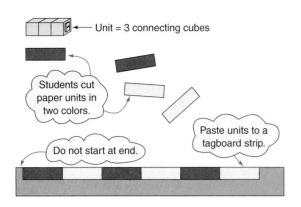

FIGURE 19.5 **Making a simple ruler.**

of the tagboard. Use two contrasting colors, and alternate them as shown in Figure 19.5.

Pasting down copies of the units on a ruler maximizes the connection between the spaces on a ruler and the actual units. Older children can make rulers by using a real unit to make marks along a tagboard strip and then coloring in the spaces. Children should not be encouraged to use the end of a ruler as a starting point; many real rulers are not made that way. If the first unit on a ruler does not coincide with the end of the ruler, the student is forced to attend to aligning the units on the ruler with the object measured.

Students should eventually put numbers on their home-made rulers, as shown in Figure 19.6. For young children, numbers can be written in the center of each unit to make it clear that the numbers are a way of precounting the units. When numbers are written in the standard way, at the ends of the units, the ruler becomes a number line. This format is more sophisticated and should be carefully discussed with children.

Assessment Note

Although Figure 19.6 illustrates a developmental progression, children should be encouraged to number their rulers

First rulers: Students count units.

Second rulers: Numbers help to count.
Numbers in center of units.

Standard rulers: Numbers are at ends of
units. Notice where 0 is.

FIGURE 19.6 **Give meaning to numbers on rulers.**

in ways that make sense to them. By having students make their own rulers and by having them explain the measures obtained by using their rulers, you receive an enormous amount of assessment data about how well students understand the measurement process. By contrast, if you carefully direct how children should construct and use their rulers, they may very well use the rulers mechanically, without understanding what they are doing.

Putting measurement tasks into problem-solving exercises increases your information flow. For example, how could you explain in a letter to a class in another state just how large your classroom is or the size of the model of a blue whale you have been building? Let different groups decide how to do this and make the measurements. Then compare results and see if each solution actually conveys the meaning.

Using Rulers and Tape Measures

It is important to use the rulers students have made. In addition to the estimate-and-measure activities mentioned earlier, have teams measure items once with a ruler and a second time with actual unit models. Although the results should be the same, inaccuracies or incorrect use of the ruler may produce differences that are important to discuss. Also, use the ruler to measure lengths that are longer than the ruler.

ACTIVITY 19.6

More Than One Way

Challenge students to find different ways to measure the same length with one ruler. (Start from either end; start at a point not at the end; measure different parts of the object and add the results.)

After working with simple rulers and tapes, have students make rulers with subunits or fractional units.

Much of the value of student-made rulers can be lost if you do not transfer this knowledge to standard rulers. Give children a standard ruler, and discuss how it is like and how it differs from the ones they have made. What are the units? Could you make a ruler with paper units the same as this? Could you make some cardboard units and measure the same way as with the ruler? What do the numbers mean? What are the other marks for? Where do the units begin?

In contrast with many traditional texts, the *Investigations in Number, Data, and Space* curriculum has first-grade children exploring a variety of attributes (length, weight, capacity, and area), but in the second and third grade the entire measurement units are devoted to length. See the excerpt from the third grade on p. 323.

NCTM Standards In the Pre-K–2 section of the *Standards*, it is suggested that students become familiar with the attributes of length, volume, area, and time. However, the authors stress that "linear measurements are the main emphasis" of the primary years

INVESTIGATIONS in NumbER, Data, and SpacE

Grade 3, *From Paces to Feet*
Investigation 2: Measuring Centers

Context

The activities described here occur roughly halfway through a unit of at least three weeks that focuses on linear measurement including estimation, the use of standard and nonstandard units (customary and metric), and rulers. In addition, students graph their measurement data as they develop graphing techniques and examine the "shape" of data.

Task Description

In this investigation, students spend roughly one day working through four centers and another session developing a graph of the data from one of the centers. The centers are described briefly here.

> *Measure and Compare.* Students complete the sheet shown here and a second that is similar to it.
> *Body Benchmarks.* With another worksheet for guidance, students find personal references on their bodies for lengths of 1, 6, and 12 inches.
> *How Far Can a Third Grader Jump?* Students each complete a standing jump, measure the distance, and record measurements on a line plot posted on the wall. Students make decisions about how to measure their jumps and other details such as number of trial jumps.
> *How Far Can You Blow a Pattern Block?* Students blow a pattern block on a flat table surface, again determining their own rules and gathering class data.

Students select their own methods of measurement and make their own decisions concerning precision (e.g., half units or "about"). The entire measurement unit is nicely integrated with learning about data representation.

Page 90 from *Measuring Data: From Paces to Feet* by K. Economopoulos, J. Mokros, & S. J. Russell. *Investigations in Number, Data, and Space.* Copyright © 1998 by Dale Seymour Publications. Reprinted by permission of Pearson Education, Inc.

Real measurements collected by students offer numeric data that are graphed on a line plot. The concept of median is also explored. A final investigation in the unit offers two activities involving early concepts of scale and proportion in a measurement context.

(p. 103). "Teachers cannot assume that students understand measurement fully even when they are able to tell how long an object is when it is aligned with a ruler" (p. 106).

MEASURING AREA

Data from the seventh National Assessment of Educational Progress suggest that fourth- and eighth-grade students have an incomplete understanding of area (Martin & Strutchens, 2000).

Comparison Activities

One of the purposes of early comparison activities with areas is to help students distinguish between size (or area) and shape, length, and other dimensions. A long, skinny rectangle may have less area than a triangle with shorter sides. This is an especially difficult concept for young children to understand. Piagetian experiments indicate that many 8- or 9-year-olds do not understand that rearranging areas into different shapes does not affect the amount of area.

Direct comparison of two areas is nearly always impossible except when the shapes involved have some common dimension or property. For example, two rectangles with the same width can be compared directly, as can any two circles. Comparison of these special shapes, however, fails to deal with the attribute of area. Instead, activities in which one area is rearranged are suggested. Cutting a shape into two parts and reassembling it in a different shape can show that the before and after shapes have the same area, even though they are different shapes. This idea is not at all obvious to children in the K–2 grade range.

ACTIVITY 19.7

Two-Piece Shapes

Give children a rectangle of construction paper, and have them fold and cut it on the diagonal, making two identical triangles. Next, have them rearrange the triangles into different shapes, including the original rectangle. The rule is that only sides of the same length can be matched up and must be matched exactly. Have each group find all the shapes that can be made this way, pasting the triangles on paper as a record of each shape (see Figure 19.7). Discuss the size and shape of the different results. Is one shape bigger than the rest? How is it bigger? Did one take more paper to make, or do they all have the same amount of paper? Help children conclude that although each figure is a different shape, all the figures have the same *area*. (*Size* in this context is a useful substitute for *area* with very young children, although it does not mean exactly the same thing.)

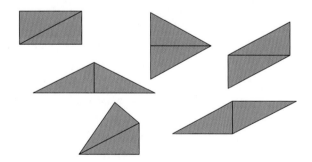

FIGURE 19.7 Different shapes, same size.

Tangrams, a very old and popular set of puzzle shapes, can be used in a similar way. The standard set of seven tangram pieces is cut from a square, as shown in Figure 19.8. The two small triangles can be used to make the parallelogram, the square, and the medium triangle. Four small triangles will make the large triangle. This permits a similar discussion about the pieces having the same size (area) but different shapes (Seymour, 1971). (Tangram pieces can be found in the Blackline Masters.)

The following activities suggest methods for comparing areas without measuring.

 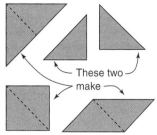

7 tangram shapes

The 2 small triangles make each of the medium shapes.

These two make

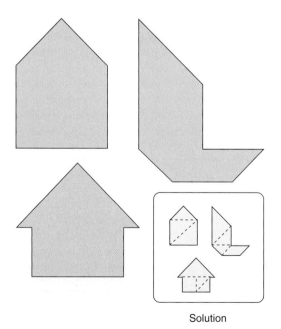

Two small triangles with any of the medium pieces will make the large triangle.

FIGURE 19.8 Tangrams provide a nice opportunity to investigate size and shape concepts.

ACTIVITY 19.8

Tangram Areas

Draw the outline of several shapes made with tangram pieces, as in Figure 19.9. Let students use tangrams to decide which shapes are the same size, which are larger, and which are smaller. Shapes can be duplicated on paper, and children can work in groups. Let students explain how they came to their conclusions. There are several different approaches to this task, and it is best if students determine their own solutions rather than blindly follow your directions.

Solution

FIGURE 19.9 Compare shapes made of tangram pieces.

You might stop here, get a set of tangrams, and make the area comparisons suggested in Figure 19.9.

STOP

ACTIVITY 19.9

Fill and Compare

Draw two or three shapes on a piece of paper and duplicate them. The shapes can be irregular blobs or more familiar shapes such as triangles, circles, or rectangles. In pairs or small groups, have students decide simply by observation which of the shapes is largest and which smallest. Then have them find a way to determine if their original estimates are correct. You can suggest methods of comparison, or you can leave the methods completely to the students' invention.

Activity 19.9 allows you to observe what kinds of ideas your children bring to the concept of area. In a completely open approach, you might suggest a wide variety of "tools" from which they may choose, or they can decide on their own methods of determining which shape is largest. For example, you could provide scissors, 1-inch plastic squares (such as Color Tiles), lima beans, centimeter grid paper, tangrams, or any other type of counter or tile. By not prescribing the method of comparison, you will be able to see children's current understanding of the area concept.

Methods of comparison include filling one shape with counters and then moving these same counters to a second shape to see if it takes more or fewer counters to fill its interior. Another possibility is to cut out the shapes and place one on top of the other. Some children may think of cutting a shape into two or more pieces so that it can be rearranged to compare with another. Shapes may be traced onto grid paper to count the squares that are inside. String is not really useful for comparing areas.

Using Units of Area

Although squares are very nice units of area (and the most commonly used), any tile that conveniently fills up a plane region can be used. Even filling a region with uniform circles or lima beans provides a useful idea of what it means to measure areas. Here are some suggestions for area units that are easy to gather or make in the large quantities you will need.

> Cut squares or triangles (diagonals of squares) from cardboard. Large squares or triangles (about 20 cm on a side) work well for large areas. Smaller units should be about 5 to 10 cm on a side.
>
> Sheets of newspaper make excellent units for very large areas.
>
> Pattern blocks provide six different units. The hexagon, trapezoid, large diamond, and triangle can be related to each other in a manner similar to the tangrams.
>
> Index cards or old business cards make good medium-sized units.
>
> Round plastic chips, pennies, or lima beans can be used. It is not necessary at a beginning stage that the area units fit with no gaps.

Children can use units to measure surfaces in the room such as desktops, bulletin boards, or books. Large regions can be outlined with masking tape on the floor. Small regions can be duplicated on paper so that students can work at their desks. Odd shapes and curved surfaces provide more challenge and interest. The surfaces of a watermelon or of the side of the wastebasket provide useful challenges.

In area measurements, there may be lots of units that only partially fit. You may wish to begin with shapes in which the units fit. Build a shape with units, and draw the outline. By third or fourth grade, students should begin to wrestle with partial units and mentally put together two or more partial units to count as one (see Figure 19.10).

FIGURE 19.10 Measuring the area of a large shape drawn with tape on the floor. Units are pieces of tagboard all cut to the same shape.

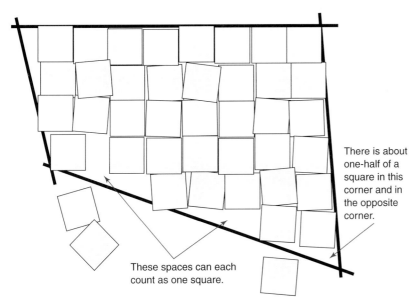

There is about one-half of a square in this corner and in the opposite corner.

These spaces can each count as one square.

Your objective in the beginning is to develop the idea that area is a *measure of covering*. Do not introduce formulas. Simply have the students fill the shapes and count the units. Be sure to include estimation before measuring (this is significantly more difficult than for length), use approximate language, and relate precision to the size of the units in the same manner as with length. Groups are very likely to come up with different measures for the same region. Discuss these differences with the children, and point to the difficulties involved in making estimates around the edges. Avoid the idea that there is a "right" answer.

The following activity is similar to Activity 19.9, "Fill and Compare." What is different is that you are now asking students not only to make comparisons but also to use a measurement of some sort to order the shapes by size.

ACTIVITY 19.10

Smaller to Larger

Present a series of quite different shapes with only slightly different areas. Students first predict the order of the shapes from the smallest to largest and record their prediction. The task is then to determine the correct order using any methods and units they wish. The determination of the "correct" order is left to the students. This can lead to a profitable class discussion about different methods.

It is important to stress that filling areas with units to determine a measure has almost no impact on students' understanding of formulas such as $L \times W$ for determining area. The filling process does not help them focus on the dimensions or on multiplying as a means of counting units. The only goal of these activities is to understand the meaning of measurement.

Using Grids

With the exception of computer drafting equipment, there really are no instruments designed for measuring area. However, grids of various types can be thought of as a kind of "area ruler." A grid of squares for area does exactly what a ruler does for length. It lays out the units for you. Square grids are available in the Blackline Masters. Note that triangular grids can also be used. Make transparencies of any grid paper. Have students place the grid over a region to be measured and count the units inside. An alternative method is to trace around a region on a paper grid.

Area and Perimeter

Area and perimeter (the distance around a region) are continually a source of confusion for students. Perhaps it is because both involve regions to be measured or because students are taught formulas for both concepts and tend to get formulas confused. Whatever the reason, expect that students even in the fifth and sixth grades will confuse these two

ideas. Several good books are available that address this confusion. (See Rectanus, 1997; Shroyer & Fitzgerald, 1986.)

An interesting approach to alleviating this confusion is to contrast the two ideas as in the next activities.

ACTIVITY 19.11

Fixed Areas

Give students 16 square tiles such as Color Tiles. The task is to create different shapes and explore how the perimeters change or stay the same. The shapes must be made using all 16 tiles. Each tile must share at least one full edge with another tile. Obviously, all shapes will have the same area because all are made of the same number of tiles. Each shape made can be recorded by sketching it on square grid paper. Students should check the perimeter of each new shape they make and see how many different perimeters they can find for areas of 16 square units.

ACTIVITY 19.12

Fixed Perimeters

Give students a loop of string that is exactly 24 units long. (Use a nonstretchy string. Double the string and make a mark 1 foot from the loop. Tie a knot just beyond the marks so that the resulting loop is 24 inches.) The task is to decide what different-sized rectangles can be made with a perimeter of 24 inches. Students may want to use a 1-inch grid to place their strings on. Each different rectangle can be recorded on grid paper with the area noted.

An alternative to the string loop is to simply use centimeter grid paper and ask students to find rectangles with a perimeter of 24.

❌ **STOP** Before reading further, think about the two previous activities. For "Fixed Areas," will all of the perimeters be the same? If not, what can you say about the shapes with longer or shorter perimeters? For "Fixed Perimeters," will the areas remain the same? Why or why not?

You may have been surprised to find out that two rectangles having the same area do not necessarily have the same perimeter. Similarly, two shapes with the same perimeter do not always have the same area. And, of course, this fact is not restricted to rectangles.

There is a relationship of sorts that is fairly interesting. If you have explored the last two activities, you may have noticed that, when the area is fixed, the shape with the smallest perimeter is a square. For a fixed perimeter, the rectangle with the largest area is also a square. If you allow for any shapes whatsoever, the shape with the smallest perimeter and a fixed area is a circle. That is, the "fatter" a shape, the smaller its perimeter and the skinnier a shape, the larger its perimeter, assuming the areas are the same. (A corresponding result is true in three dimensions. Replace perimeter with surface area and area with volume.)

Measuring Volume and Capacity

Volume and *capacity* are both terms for measures of the "size" of three-dimensional regions. Standard units of volume are expressed in terms of length units, such as cubic inches or cubic centimeters. Capacity units are generally applied to liquids or the containers that hold liquids. Standard capacity units include quarts and gallons, liters and milliliters.

Comparison Activities

Most solid shapes and containers must be compared indirectly. By far the easiest comparisons are made between containers that can be filled with something that is then poured into another container.

Young children should have lots of experiences directly comparing the capacities of different containers. Collect a large assortment of cans, small boxes, and plastic containers. Gather as many different shapes as possible. Also gather some plastic scoops. Cut a plastic 2-liter bottle in half, and use the top portion as a funnel. Rice or dried beans are good fillers to use. Sand and water are both considerably messier.

ACTIVITY 19.13
Capacity Sort

Provide a collection of labeled containers, with one marked as the "target." The students' task is to sort the collection into those that hold more than, less than, or about the same amount as the target container. Provide a recording sheet on which each container is listed and a place to circle "holds more," "holds less," and "holds about the same." List the choices twice for each container. The first choice is to record a guess made by observation. The second is to record "what was found." Provide a filler (such as beans or rice), scoops, and funnels. Avoid explicit directions, but later discuss students' ideas for solving the task.

ACTIVITY 19.14
Capacity Lineup

Given a series of five or six labeled containers of different sizes and shapes, the task is to order them from least volume to most. This can be quite challenging. Do not provide answers. Let students work in groups to come up with a solution and also explain how they arrived at it.

Solids such as a rock, a ball, a block, or an apple can also be compared in terms of volume, but it is a bit more difficult. Some method of displacement must be used. One approach is to use a container that will hold each of the items. Place an object in the container and fill with rice to a level that will be above all of the objects. Mark this level on the container. Then remove the object and mark the new level. Each new object should be put in the container and buried with rice to the same initial level. The problem-solving nature of the activity is enhanced if students are challenged to devise their own methods.

Using Units of Volume

Two types of units can be used to measure volume and capacity: solid units and containers. Solid units are things like wooden cubes or old tennis balls that can be used to fill the container being measured. The other type of unit model is a small container that is filled and poured repeatedly into the container being measured. The following are a few examples of units that you might want to collect.

Plastic caps and liquid medicine cups are all good for very small units.

Plastic jars and containers of almost any size can serve as a unit.

Wooden cubic blocks or blocks of any shape can be units as long as you have a lot of the same size.

Styrofoam packing peanuts can be used. Even though they do not pack perfectly, they still produce conceptual measures of volume.

Measuring activities for volume and capacity are similar to those for length and area. Estimation of volumes is a lot more fun because it is much more difficult. Finding ways to measure containers such as a large cardboard carton in terms of a relatively small container-type unit can be an excellent challenge for groups of fourth or fifth graders. This can be done long before volume formulas are developed.

When measuring with solid units such as cubes or balls, it is difficult to use only one and iterate it, as can be done with length or area. However, a worthwhile challenge is to determine the volumes of containers given only enough units to cover the bottom. Do not forget very large volumes such as your room. How many cubic meters will the room hold? Be sure to make these projects where groups devise their methods and provide written explanations and drawings.

Making and Using Measuring Cups

Instruments for measuring capacity are generally used for small amounts of liquids or pourable materials such as rice or water. These tools are commonly found in kitchens and laboratories. As with other instruments, if children make their own, they are likely to develop a better understanding of the units and the approach to the measuring process.

A measuring cup can be made by using a small container as a unit. Select a large, transparent container for the cup and a small container for a unit. Fill the unit with beans or rice, empty it into the large container, and make a mark indicating the level. Repeat until the cup is nearly full. If the unit is small, marks may only be necessary after every 5 units. Numbers need not be written on the container for every marking. Students frequently have difficulty reading scales in which not every mark is labeled or where each mark represents more than one unit. This is an opportunity to help them understand how to interpret lines on a real measuring cup.

Students should use their measuring cups and compare the measures with those made by directly filling the container from the unit. The cup is likely to produce errors due to inaccurate markings. This is an opportunity to point out that measuring instruments themselves can be a source of error in measurement. The more accurately made the instrument, and the finer the calibration, the less the error from that source.

Measuring Weight and Mass

Weight is a measure of the pull or force of gravity on an object. *Mass* is the amount of matter in an object and a measure of the force needed to accelerate it. On the moon, where gravity is much less than on earth, an object has a smaller weight but the identical mass as on earth. For practical purposes, on the earth, the measures of mass and weight will be about the same. In this discussion, the terms *weight* and *mass* will be used interchangeably.

Making Comparisons

The most conceptual way to compare the weights of two objects is to hold one in each hand, extend your arms, and experience the relative downward pull on each—effectively communicating to a young child what "heavier" or "weighs more" means. This personal experience can then be transferred to one of two basic types of scales—balances and spring scales. Figure 19.11 shows a homemade version of each. Simple scales of each type are available through school-supply catalogs.

Children should first use their hands to estimate which of two objects is heavier. When they then place the objects in the two pans of a balance, the pan that goes down can be understood to hold the heavier object. Even a relatively simple balance will detect small differences. If two objects are placed one at a time in a spring scale, the heavier object pulls the pan down farther. Both balances and spring scales have real value in the classroom. (Technically, spring scales measure weight and balance scales measure mass. Why?)

With either scale, sorting and ordering tasks are possible with very young children. For older children, comparison activities for weight are not necessary. (Why?)

Two-pan balance

Rubber-band (spring) scales
Marks show where different objects
pulled the scale.

Eraser
Block
Apple

FIGURE 19.11 Two simple scales.

Using Units of Weight or Mass

Any collection of uniform objects with the same mass can serve as weight units. For very light objects, wooden or plastic cubes work well. Large metal washers found in hardware stores are effective for weighing slightly heavier objects. You will need to rely on standard weights to weigh things as heavy as a kilogram or more.

In a balance scale, place an object in one pan and weights in the other until the two pans balance. In a spring scale, first place the object in and mark the position of the pan on a piece of paper taped behind the pan. Remove the object and place just enough weights in the pan to pull it down to the same level. Discuss how equal weights will pull the spring or rubber band with the same force.

While the concept of heavier and lighter is learned rather early, the notion of units of weight or mass is a bit more mysterious. At any grade level, even a brief experience with informal unit weights is good preparation for standard units and scales.

Making and Using a Scale

Most scales that we use in our daily lives produce a number when an object is placed on or in it. There are no visible unit weights. How does the scale produce the right number? By making a scale that gives a numeric result without recourse to units, children can see how scales work.

Students can use informal weight units and calibrate a simple rubber-band scale like the one in Figure 19.11. Mount the scale with a piece of paper behind it, and place weights in the pan. After every five weights, make a mark on the paper. The resulting marks correspond to the markings around the dial of a standard scale. The pan serves as the pointer. In the dial scale, the downward movement of the pan mechanically causes the dial to turn. The value of this activity is seeing how scales are made. Even digital readout scales are based on the same principle.

MEASURING ANGLES

Angle measurement causes difficulty for two reasons: The attribute of angle size is often misunderstood, and protractors are introduced and used without understanding how they work.

Comparing Angles

The attribute of angle size might be called the "spread of the angle's rays." Angles are composed of two rays that are infinite in length with a common vertex. The only difference in their size is how widely or narrowly the two rays are spread apart.

Some authors have students think of how much one ray has rotated away from the other. Two rulers held together near the ends can be used to demonstrate this idea. As one ruler is rotated, the size of the angle is seen to get larger. However, when we see angles, the rays have already been spread—there is no rotation. Do you think of the angles in a triangle as one side being rotated away from the other?

To help children conceptualize the attribute of the spread of the rays, two angles can be directly compared by tracing one and placing it over the other, as in Figure 19.12. Be sure to have students compare angles with sides of different lengths. A wide angle with short sides may seem smaller than a narrow angle with long sides. This is a common misconception among students. As soon as students can tell the difference between a large angle and a small one, regardless of the length of the sides, you can move on to measuring angles.

Using Units of Angular Measure

A unit for measuring an angle must be an angle. Nothing else has the same attribute of spread that we want to measure. (Contrary to popular opinion, you do not need to use degrees to measure angles.)

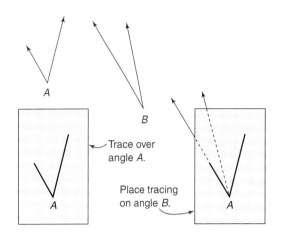

FIGURE 19.12 Which angle is larger? Use tracings to compare.

──────── ACTIVITY 19.15 ────────

A Unit Angle

Give each student an index card or a small piece of tagboard. Have students draw a narrow angle on the tagboard using a straightedge and then cut it out. The resulting wedge can then be used as a unit of angular measure by counting the number that will fit in a given angle. Pass out a worksheet with assorted angles on it, and have students use their unit to measure them. Because students made their own unit angles, the results will differ and can be discussed in terms of unit size.

Activity 19.15 illustrates that measuring an angle is the same as measuring length or area. Unit angles are used to fill or cover the spread of an angle just as unit lengths fill or cover a length. Once this concept is well understood, you can move on to the use of measuring instruments.

Making a Protractor

The protractor is one of the most poorly understood measuring instruments found in schools. Part of the difficulty arises because the units (degrees) are so very small. It would be physically impossible to cut out a single degree and use it in, say, Activity 19.15. Another problem is that there are no visible angles showing; there are only little marks around the outside edge of the protractor. Finally, the numbering that appears on most protractors runs both clockwise and counterclockwise along the marked edges. "Which numbers do I use?" By making a protractor with a large unit angle, all of these mysterious features can be understood. A careful comparison with a standard protractor will then permit that instrument to be used with understanding.

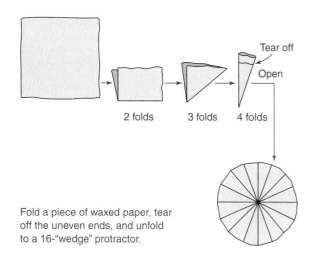

Fold a piece of waxed paper, tear off the uneven ends, and unfold to a 16-"wedge" protractor.

FIGURE 19.13 **Making a waxed-paper protractor.**

Tear off about a foot of ordinary waxed paper for each student. Have the students fold the paper in half and crease the fold tightly. Fold in half again so that the folded edges match. Repeat this two more times, each time bringing the folded edges together and creasing tightly. Cut or tear off the resulting wedge shape about 4 or 5 inches from the vertex and unfold. If done correctly, there will be 16 angles surrounding the center, as in Figure 19.13. This serves as an excellent protractor with a unit angle that is one-eighth of a straight angle. It is sufficiently transparent that it can be placed over an angle on paper, on the blackboard, or on the overhead projector to measure angles, as shown in Figure 19.14. Reasonable estimates of angle measures can be made with a waxed-paper protractor as small as the one in Figure 19.14. In that figure, one angle of a free-form polygon is measured for you. Use a waxed-paper protractor to measure the other four angles in this polygon as carefully as possible. Use fractional estimates. Your sum for all five interior angles should

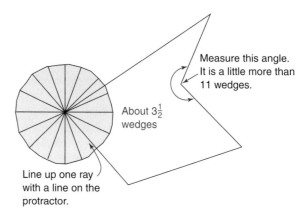

Measure this angle. It is a little more than 11 wedges.

About $3\frac{1}{2}$ wedges

Line up one ray with a line on the protractor.

FIGURE 19.14 **Measuring angles in a polygon using a waxed-paper protractor.**

be very close to 24 wedges. There are two possible ways to get the measure of the angle indicated with the arrow. How would you measure that angle if your protractor was only a half circle instead of a full circle?

The waxed-paper protractor makes it quite clear how a protractor fits unit angles into an angle for measurement. When measuring angles, students can easily estimate halves, thirds, or fourths of a "wedge," a possible name for this informal unit angle. This is sufficiently accurate to measure, for example, the interior angles of a polygon and discover the usual relationship between number of sides and sum of the interior angles. For a triangle, the sum is 8 wedges, recorded as 8^w. For a quadrilateral, the sum is 16^w. And in general, the sum for an n-sided polygon is $(n - 2) \times 8^w$. The superscript w is a forerunner of the degree symbol (°).

Figure 19.15 illustrates how a tagboard semicircle can be made into a protractor to measure angles in wedges. This tagboard version is a bit closer to a standard protractor, since the rays do not extend down to the vertex and the markings are

FIGURE 19.15 **Comparisons of protractors and unit angles.**

Waxed-paper wedges

Degrees

Tagboard protractor

Standard protractor

The marks on the tagboard wedge protractor are the rays on the waxed-paper version.
The marks on a plastic protractor are the rays of <u>degrees</u>. A degree is just a very small angle.
A large picture of 180 degrees can be found in Blackline Masters.

numbered in two directions. The only difference between this protractor and a standard one is the size of the unit angle. The standard unit angle is the *degree,* which is simply a very small angle. A standard protractor is not very helpful in teaching the meaning of a degree. But an analogy between wedges and degrees and between these two protractors is a very effective approach. (See the Blackline Masters)

Introducing Standard Units

As pointed out earlier, there are a number of reasons for teaching measurement using nonstandard units. However, measurement sense demands that children be familiar with the common measurement units and that they be able to make estimates in terms of these units and meaningfully interpret measures depicted with standard units.

Perhaps the biggest error in measurement instruction is the failure to recognize and separate two types of objectives: first, understanding the meaning and technique of measuring a particular attribute and, second, learning about the standard units commonly used to measure that attribute. These two objectives can be developed separately; when both objectives are attempted together, confusion is likely.

STOP How many of the five reasons why you might use informal units can you recall? Which of these seem most important to you and why?

Reread the list of reasons for using informal units on p. 319. Not all reasons apply to every situation you may face. To avoid wasting time in your measurement program it is important to know why you are or are not using informal or nonstandard units. It is only when students are comfortable with measurement of an attribute that they can focus on things like cups and quarts or the number of inches in a foot or feet in a yard or have a feel for grams and kilograms.

Instructional Goals

Three broad goals relative to standard units of measure can be identified:

1. *Familiarity with the unit.* Familiarity means that students should have a basic idea of the size of commonly used units and what they measure. Without this familiarity, measurement sense is impossible. It is more important to know about how much 1 liter of water is or to be able to estimate a shelf as 5 feet long than to have the ability to measure either of these accurately.
2. *Ability to select an appropriate unit.* Related to unit familiarity is knowing what is a reasonable unit of measure in a given situation. The choice of an appropriate unit is also a matter of required precision. (Would you measure your lawn to purchase grass seed with the same precision as you would use in measuring a window to buy a pane of glass?) Students need practice in using common sense in the selection of appropriate standard units.
3. *Knowledge of a few important relationships between units.* The emphasis should be kept to those relationships that are commonly used, such as inches, feet, and yards or milliliters and liters. Tedious conversion exercises do little to enhance measurement sense. The goal of unit relationships is the least important of all measurement objectives.

Developing Unit Familiarity

The importance of familiarity with standard units of measure can be seen in the reluctance (even fear) on the part of a majority of U.S. citizens to adopt the metric system. The average adult develops a "feel" for units used throughout life: inch, foot, mile, pound, cup, gallon. These *customary* units are not easier to use than metric units, but they are familiar, whereas *metric* units are not. Helping students develop familiarity with the most frequently used units of measure in both systems is, thus, an important goal of instruction.

Two types of activities can help develop familiarity with standard units: (1) comparisons that focus on a single unit and (2) activities that develop personal referents or benchmarks for single units or easy multiples of units.

ACTIVITY 19.16

About One Unit

Give students a model of a standard unit, and have them search for things that measure about the same as that one unit. For example, to develop familiarity with the meter, give students a piece of rope 1 meter long. Have them make lists of things that are about 1 meter. Keep separate lists for things that are a little less (or more) or twice as long (or half as long). Encourage students to find familiar items in their daily lives. In the case of lengths, be sure to include circular lengths. Later, students can try to predict if a given object is more than, less than, or close to 1 meter.

The same activity can be done with other unit lengths. Parents can be enlisted to help students find familiar distances that are about 1 mile or about 1 kilometer. Suggest in a letter that they check the distances around the neighborhood, to the school or shopping center, or along other frequently traveled paths.

For capacity units such as cup, quart, and liter, students need a container that holds or has a marking for a single unit. They should then find other containers at home and at school that hold about as much, more, and less. Remember that the shapes of containers can be very deceptive when estimating their capacity.

For the standard weights of gram, kilogram, ounce, and pound, students can compare objects on a two-pan balance with single copies of these units. It may be more effective to work with 10 grams or 5 ounces. Students can be encouraged to bring in familiar objects from home to compare on the classroom scale.

Standard area units are in terms of lengths such as square inches or square feet, so familiarity with lengths is important. Familiarity with a single degree is not as important as some idea of 30, 45, 60, and 90 degrees.

The second approach to unit familiarity is to begin with very familiar items and use their measures as references or benchmarks. A doorway is a bit more than 2 meters. A bag of flour is a good reference for 5 pounds. Your bedroom may be about 10 feet long. A paper clip weighs about a gram and is about 1 centimeter wide. A gallon of milk weighs a little less than 4 kilograms.

ACTIVITY 19.17
Familiar References

For each unit of measure you wish to focus on, have students make a list of at least five familiar things and measure those things using that unit. For lengths, encourage them to include long and short things; for weight, to find both light and heavy things; and so on. The measures should be rounded off to nice whole numbers. Discuss lists in class so that different ideas are shared.

Of special interest for length are benchmarks found on our bodies. These become quite familiar over time and can be used as approximate rulers in many situations. Even though young children grow quite rapidly, it is useful for them to know the approximate lengths that they carry around with them.

ACTIVITY 19.18
Personal Benchmarks

Measure your body. About how long is your foot, your stride, your hand span (stretched and with fingers together), the width of your finger, your arm span (finger to finger and finger to nose), the distance around your wrist and around your waist, and your height to waist, to shoulder, and to head? Perhaps you cannot remember all of these, but some may prove to be useful benchmarks, and some may be excellent models for single units. (The average child's fingernail width is about 1 cm, and most people can find a 10-cm length somewhere on their hands.)

To help remember these references, they must be used in activities where lengths, volumes, and so on are compared to the benchmarks to estimate measurements.

Choosing Appropriate Units

Should the room be measured in feet or inches? Should the concrete blocks be weighed in grams or kilograms? The answers to questions such as these involve more than simply knowing how big the units are, although that is certainly required. Another consideration involves the need for precision. If you were measuring your wall in order to cut a piece of molding or woodwork to fit, you would need to measure it very precisely. The smallest unit would be an inch or a centimeter, and you would also use small fractional parts. But if you were determining how many 8-foot molding strips to buy, the nearest foot would probably be sufficient.

ACTIVITY 19.19
Guess the Unit

Find examples of measurements of all types in newspapers, on signs, or in other everyday situations. Present the context and measures but without units. The task is to predict what units of measure were used. Have students discuss their choices.

Developing Relationships Between Units

The number of inches in a foot or a yard or the number of cups in a quart is the type of information that must eventually be committed to memory. Practice with conversions is something that lends itself well to pencil-and-paper work. This procedural aspect of unit familiarity has been overworked in the curriculum largely due to the ease of testing rather than the need to know.

Many students may know that there are 16 ounces in 1 pound, but when they try to determine how many pounds are in 90 ounces, they get confused over which operation to use. This is partly a matter of understanding the meanings of operations. However, simple common sense can help. In this example, since pounds are heavier than ounces, it is reasonable to end up with fewer pounds than ounces.

The customary system involves an unfortunate variety of conversion factors, and as long as the United States continues to use it, teachers will have to deal with helping children commit the most commonly used factors to memory.

Exact conversions between the metric and the customary system should never be done. From the standpoint of familiarity with these systems, "soft" or "friendly" conversions are useful as long as we live in a country that seems bent on having two systems of measurement. For example, a liter is "a gulp more" than a quart, and a meter is "a bit longer" than a yard. The same is true for benchmarks. One hundred meters is about one football field plus one end zone, or about 110 yards.

Important Standard Units

Both the customary and metric systems include many units that are not used in everyday living. Table 19.2 lists the units that are most common.

TABLE 19.2
Commonly Encountered Units of Measure

	Metric System	Customary System
Length	millimeter	inch
	centimeter	foot
	meter	yard
	kilometer	mile
Area	square centimeter	square inch
	square meter	square foot
		square yard
Volume	cubic centimeter	cubic inch
	cubic meter	cubic foot
		cubic yard
Capacity	millimeter	ounce*
	liter	cup
		quart
		gallon
Weight	gram	ounce*
	kilogram	pound
	metric ton	ton

*In the U.S. customary system, the term *ounce* refers to a weight or *avoirdupois* unit, 16 of which make a pound, and also a volume or capacity unit, 8 of which make a cup. Though the two units have the same name, they are not related.

The Metric System

Unit familiarity with the popularly used units should be the principal focus of almost all instruction with standard units.

Before students have developed a full understanding of decimal notation, there is little advantage in teaching the very nice relationships in the metric system. Whereas the customary system frequently mixes units (3 pounds 6 ounces, or 6 feet 2 inches), the metric system uses a single unit for each measure. To adhere to this "rule" would mean that primary-grade children, who do not understand decimal numbers, should report a measure in the smallest unit used. For example, a length would be recorded as "235 cm" instead of "2.35 m" or "2 m and 35 cm." How important this rule is for the second grade may be open to debate.

Perhaps one of the worst errors in the metric measurement curriculum is having students "move decimal points" to convert from one metric unit to another prior to a complete development of decimal notation. Confused, children memorize rules about moving decimals so many places this way or that, and the focus becomes rules and right answers.

As children begin to appreciate the structure of decimal notation, the metric system can and should be developed with all seven places: three prefixes for smaller units (*deci-, centi-, milli-*) and three for larger units (*deka-, hecto-, kilo-*). With decimal knowledge and familiarity with the basic

and popularly used units, the complete metric system is easy to learn.

Making conversions within the metric system can be approached in two related ways. As we saw in Figure 17.6 in Chapter 17 (p. 283), a place-value chart gives a metric name to each of seven consecutive places. If it is understood that the decimal point always identifies the units position, then given any metric measurement, each digit is in a position with a metric name. The decimal point can be repositioned if the name of the unit is changed. In the measure 17.238 kg, the decimal indicates that the 7 is in the units position. The label "kg" indicates that the name of the position is kilograms. Therefore, the 2 is in the hectogram position, the 3 in the dekagram position, and the 8 in the gram position. Repositioning the decimal to indicate grams as the units makes the same measure read 17,238 g or 17,238.0 g.

An alternate rationale is to think of decimal point shifting as multiplying or dividing by powers of 10. In our example, since there are 1000 grams in a kilogram, change to grams by multiplying by 1000, or shift the decimal three places to the right.

It should be emphasized once again that unit conversion is perhaps the least important part of learning the metric system or any standard system. It is a skill that is not used frequently in daily life.

The Customary System

The "familiar" system of units is technically known as the U.S. customary system. After an attempt in the 1970s to go completely metric, most schools and textbooks have resigned themselves to teaching both metric and customary systems.

Conversion of units within the customary system is difficult for children for two reasons: There are more conversion ratios to memorize, and they are not conveniently related to the decimal system. For example, many children will add 3 feet 8 inches to 5 feet 6 inches and get 9 feet 4 inches instead of 9 feet 2 inches. (Why?) Similar difficulties occur with all conversions in the customary system. Once again, while it is important to know how many inches in a foot and a few other common relationships, overemphasis on conversions in the customary system is unwarranted.

ESTIMATING MEASURES

Measurement estimation is the process of using mental and visual information to measure or make comparisons without the use of measuring instruments. It is a practical skill. Almost every day, we make estimates of measures. Do I have enough sugar to make the cookies? Can you throw the ball 50 feet? Is this suitcase over the weight limit? About how long is the fence?

Besides its value outside the classroom, estimation in measurement activities helps students focus on the attribute being measured, adds intrinsic motivation, and helps develop familiarity with standard units. Therefore, measurement estimation both improves measurement instruction and develops a valuable life skill.

Techniques of Measurement Estimation

Just as for computational estimation, specific strategies exist for estimating measures. Four strategies can be taught specifically:

1. *Develop and use benchmarks or referents for important units.* (This strategy was also mentioned as a way to develop familiarity with units.) Students should have a good referent for single units and also useful multiples of standard units. Referents or benchmarks for 1, 5, 10, and perhaps 100 pounds might be useful. A referent for 500 milliliters is very useful. These benchmarks can then be compared mentally to objects being estimated: "That tree is about as tall as four doorways, or between 8 and 9 meters tall."

2. *Use "chunking" when appropriate.* Figure 19.16 is an example. It may be easier to estimate the shorter chunks along the wall than to estimate the whole length as one. The weight of a stack of books is easier if some estimate is given to an "average" book.

3. *Use subdivisions.* This is a similar strategy to chunking, with the chunks imposed on the object by the estimator. For example, if the wall length to be estimated has no useful chunks, it can be mentally divided in half and then in fourths or even eighths by repeated halving until a more manageable length is arrived at. Length, volume, and area measurements all lend themselves to this technique.

4. *Iterate a unit mentally or physically.* For length, area, and volume, it is sometimes easy to mark off single units visually. You might use your hands or make marks or folds to keep track as you go. For length, it is especially useful to use a body measure as a unit and iterate with that. If you know, for ex-

ample, that your stride is about $\frac{3}{4}$ meter, you can walk off a length and then multiply to get an estimate. Hand and finger widths are useful for shorter measures.

Tips for Teaching Estimation

Each of the four strategies just listed should be taught directly and discussed with students. But the best approach to improving estimation skills is to have students do a lot of estimating. Keep the following tips in mind:

1. Help students learn strategies by having them use a specified approach. Later activities should permit students to choose whatever techniques they wish.

2. Periodically discuss how different students made their estimates. This will help students understand that there is no single right way to estimate and also remind them of different approaches that are useful.

3. Accept a range of estimates. Think in relative terms about what is a good estimate. Within 10 percent for length is quite good. Even 30 percent off may be reasonable for weights or volumes.

4. Sometimes have students give a range of measures that they believe includes the actual measure. This not only is a practical approach in real life but also helps focus on the approximate nature of estimation.

5. Make measurement estimation an ongoing activity. A daily measurement to estimate can be posted on the bulletin board. Students can turn in their estimates on paper and discuss them in a 5-minute period. Older students can even be given the task of making up the things to estimate, with a team assigned this task each week.

6. Make an effort to include estimations of all attributes. It is easy to get carried away with length and forget about area, volume, weight, and angles.

FIGURE 19.16 Estimating measures by chunking.

Estimate the room length.
Use: windows, bulletin board, and spaces between as "chunks."
Use: cabinet length—looks like about three cabinets will fit into the room—plus a little bit.

Measurement Estimation Activities

Estimation activities need not be elaborate. Any measurement activity can have an "estimate first" component. For more emphasis on the process of estimation itself, simply think of things that can be estimated, and have students estimate. Here are a few suggestions.

ACTIVITY 19.20

Estimation Quickie

Select a single object such as a box, a watermelon, a jar, or even the principal. Each day, select a different attribute or dimension to estimate. For a watermelon, for example, students can estimate its length, girth, weight, volume, and surface area.

ACTIVITY 19.21

Estimation Scavenger Hunt

Conduct measurement scavenger hunts. Give teams a list of measurements, and have them find things that are close to having those measurements. Permit no measuring instruments. A list might include the following items:

A length of 3.5 m

Something that weighs more than 1 kg but less than 2 kg

A container that holds about 200 ml

Let students suggest how to judge results in terms of accuracy.

ACTIVITY 19.22

E-M-E Sequences

Use estimate-measure-estimate sequences (Lindquist, 1987a). Select pairs of objects to estimate that are somehow related or close in measure but not the same. Have students estimate the measure of the first and check by measuring. Then have them estimate the second. Here are some examples of pairs:

Width of a window, width of a wall

Volume of a coffee mug, volume of a pitcher

Distance between the eyes, width of the head

Weight of a handful of marbles, weight of a bag of marbles

Activity 19.22 can help students understand how benchmarks are used in estimation.

In the 3–5 grade band, the *Principles and Standards* document suggests several estimation strategies that are similar to those you have just read about. It points out that the techniques of estimation will vary with the situation at hand. The authors encourage teachers to have students share both their estimates and their strategies for estimation as well.

DEVELOPING FORMULAS

The relationship between measurement and geometry is most evident in the development of formulas for measures of geometric figures. Formulas help us use easily made measures to determine indirectly some other measure that is not so easily found. For example, it is easy to measure the three dimensions of a box with a ruler, but it is not easy to actually measure the volume of the same box. By using a formula, the volume can be determined from the length measures.

Children should never use formulas without participating in the development of those formulas. Formulas for area and volume should all be developed by children. Developing the formulas and seeing how they are connected and interrelated is significantly more important than blindly plugging numbers into formulas, which is primarily computational tedium.

Common Difficulties

Many children become so encumbered with the use of formulas and rules that an understanding of what these formulas are all about is completely lost.

Overemphasizing Formulas

In the sixth National Assessment of Educational Progress, students were asked to draw on a square grid a rectangle with an area of 12 square units. Correct responses were given by 42 percent of fourth-grade and 66 percent of eighth-grade students. When asked for the area of a carpet 9 feet long and 6 feet wide, correct responses for these grades were given 19 percent and 65 percent of the time, respectively. Most fourth-grade students selected the sum of the dimensions (15) as their answer. The eighth-grade performance is consistent with that of drawing the 12-square-unit rectangle but is not a strong performance (Kenney & Kouba, 1997).

Many such items from this assessment and earlier NAEP studies indicate that children often have difficulty applying area measurement formulas and that formulas for area and perimeter are often confused.

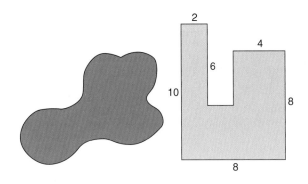

"How would you determine the areas of these shapes?"

Note: Many children believe that such shapes do not have areas or that the areas are impossible to determine because there are no formulas.

FIGURE 19.17 **Understanding the attribute of area.**

The tasks in Figure 19.17 cannot be solved with simple formulas; they require an understanding of concepts and how formulas work. "Length times width" is not a definition of area.

Height or Side

Another common error when students use formulas comes from failure to conceptualize the meaning of height in geometric figures, both two- and three-dimensional. The shapes in Figure 19.18 each have a slanted side and a height given. Students tend to confuse these two. Any side or flat surface of a figure can be called a *base* of the figure. For each base that a figure has, there is a corresponding height. If the figure were to slide into a room on its base, the *height* would be the height of the shortest door it could pass through without bending over—that is, the perpendicular distance to the base. Children have a lot of early experiences with the length-times-width formula for rectangles, in which the height is exactly the same as the length of a side. Perhaps this is the source of the confusion.

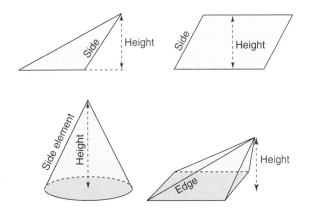

FIGURE 19.18 **Heights of figures are not always measured along an edge or a surface.**

Before formulas involving heights are discussed, children should be able to identify where a height could be measured for any base that a figure has.

The Area of Rectangles, Parallelograms, Triangles, and Trapezoids

The development of area formulas is a fantastic opportunity to follow the spirit of the NCTM *Principles and Standards*. First, a problem-solving approach can meaningfully involve students and help them see that mathematics is a sense-making endeavor. Second, the connectedness of mathematics is evident. Here you will see that all of the standard area formulas are intimately related and can be developed and learned as an integrated whole rather than as a collection of isolated facts.

Rectangles

The formula for the area of a rectangle is one of the first that is developed and is usually given as $A = L \times W$, "area equals length times width." Looking forward to other area formulas, an equivalent but more unifying idea might be $A = b \times h$, "area equals *base* times *height*." The base-times-height formulation can be generalized to all parallelograms and is useful in developing the area formulas for triangles and trapezoids. Furthermore, the same approach can be extended to three dimensions, where volumes of cylinders are given in terms of the *area of the base* times the height. Base times height, then, helps connect a large family of formulas that otherwise must be mastered independently.

The following sequence of activities to develop the area formula for a rectangle is illustrated in Figure 19.19. Approach each step of this sequence with a problem-solving spirit: How can we figure this out?

1. Have students determine the areas of rectangles drawn on square grids or geoboards. Or have students draw rectangles that have specified areas (but do not give the dimensions). Some may count every square; others may multiply to find the total number of squares.

2. Examine rectangles not on a grid but with whole-number dimensions. Provide students with a single square and a ruler. Challenge students to find a way to determine the area with just these two tools but without drawing in all of the squares or moving the square from place to place. Require justifications and share different ideas.

3. Give students rectangles with only the dimensions provided, and have them determine the area. Require them to justify their results.

4. Examine rectangles with dimensions that are not whole numbers. If the base is $4\frac{1}{2}$ units, then $4\frac{1}{2}$ unit squares will fit along the base. If the height is $2\frac{1}{3}$ units, then there are $2\frac{1}{3}$ rows with $4\frac{1}{2}$ squares in each, or $2\frac{1}{3}$ sets of $4\frac{1}{2}$.

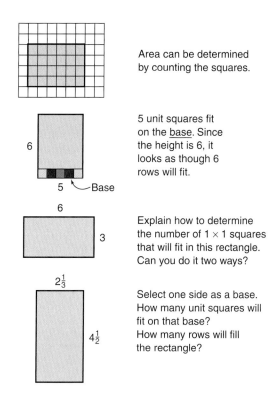

Area can be determined by counting the squares.

5 unit squares fit on the <u>base</u>. Since the height is 6, it looks as though 6 rows will fit.

Explain how to determine the number of 1 × 1 squares that will fit in this rectangle. Can you do it two ways?

Select one side as a base. How many unit squares will fit on that base? How many rows will fill the rectangle?

FIGURE 19.19 **Determining the area of a rectangle.**

STOP Before reading further, return to step 2 in the preceding sequence. How would you solve this task, assuming that you did not know a formula for the area of a rectangle?

Step 2 in the preceding sequence is the critical point in the development. As students discuss their various approaches, focus on those ideas that are closest to this idea: *The length of a side will determine the number of squares that can be fit on the side. The length of the other side will determine how many rows of these squares will fit in the rectangle all together. Multiply the length of a row by the number of rows.* When this concept is well understood, introduce the vocabulary of *base* and *height*. Students should be able to explain why any side of the rectangle can be called the base and the length of the adjoining side can be called the height.

From Rectangles to Other Parallelograms

Once students understand the base-times-height formula for rectangles, the next challenge is to determine the areas of parallelograms. Do not provide a formula or other explanation. Rather, give students several parallelograms drawn on a grid or on a plain sheet of paper. Their task is to develop a method for finding the area of a parallelogram that they can use with any parallelogram, not just those they are working with. If students are stuck, ask them to examine ways that the parallelogram is like a rectangle or how it can be changed into

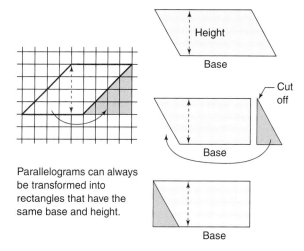

Parallelograms can always be transformed into rectangles that have the same base and height.

FIGURE 19.20 **Area of a parallelogram.**

a rectangle. As shown in Figure 19.20, a parallelogram can always be transformed into a rectangle with the same base, the same height, and the same area. Thus, the formula for the area of a parallelogram is exactly the same as for a rectangle: base times height.

From Parallelograms to Triangles

It is very important for students to understand the parallelogram formula before exploring triangle area. With that background, the area of a triangle is relatively simple.

As with parallelograms, students should be challenged to figure the area of a triangle in such a manner that the method applies to all triangles. Have students fold a piece of paper in half, draw a triangle on the folded paper, and cut it out, making two identical copies. Suggest that they try using the two triangles to construct a figure for which they have an area formula.

As shown in Figure 19.21, two congruent triangles can always be arranged to form a parallelogram with the same base and the same height as the triangle. The area of the triangle will, therefore, be one-half as much as the parallelogram. Have students further explore all three possible parallelograms, one for each triangle side serving as base. Will the computed areas always be the same?

A = base × height

Two copies of any triangle will always form a parallelogram with the same base and height; therefore, the triangle has an area of half of the parallelogram, $A = \frac{1}{2}$ (base × height).

FIGURE 19.21 **Two triangles always make a parallelogram.**

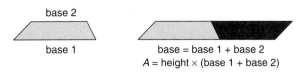

base = base 1 + base 2
A = height × (base 1 + base 2)

Two trapezoids always make a parallelogram with the same height and a base equal to the sum of the bases in the trapezoid. Therefore,

$$A = \tfrac{1}{2} \times \text{height} \times (\text{base 1} + \text{base 2})$$

FIGURE 19.22 Two trapezoids always form a parallelogram.

From Parallelograms to Trapezoids

After developing formulas for parallelograms and triangles, your students may be interested in tackling trapezoids without any further assistance. (See Figure 4.1, p. 40, for an example of a completely open challenge.) There are at least ten different methods of arriving at a formula for trapezoids, each related to the area of parallelograms or triangles. One of the nicest methods uses the same general approach that was used for triangles. Suggest that students try working with two trapezoids that are identical, just as they did with triangles. Figure 19.22 shows how this method results in the formula. Now, not only are all of these formulas connected, but similar methods were used to develop them.

Here are a few hints, each leading to a different approach to finding the area of a trapezoid.

- Make a parallelogram inside the given trapezoid using three of the sides.
- Make a parallelogram using three sides that surround the trapezoid.
- Draw a diagonal forming two triangles.
- Draw a line through the midpoints of the nonparallel sides. The length of that line is the average of the lengths of the two parallel sides.
- Draw a rectangle inside the trapezoid leaving two triangles and then put those two triangles together.

Do you think that students should learn special formulas for the area of a square? Why or why not? Do you think students need formulas for the perimeters of squares and rectangles?

![laptop] TECHNOLOGY NOTE

The relationship among the areas of rectangles, parallelograms, and triangles can be dramatically illustrated using a dynamic geometry program such as *The Geometer's Sketchpad* (Key Curriculum Press) or *Geometry Inventor* (Riverdeep). Draw two congruent segments on two parallel lines, as shown in Figure 19.23. Then connect the endpoints of the segments to form a parallelogram and two triangles. A segment between the parallel lines and perpendicular to each indi-

Explore the area of parallelograms and triangles.

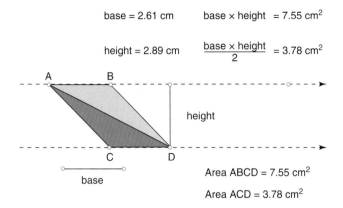

Drag A or C to sheer the parallelogram left or right.
Drag D to change the height.

FIGURE 19.23 Dynamic geometry software shows that figures with the same base and height maintain the same area.

cates the height. Either of the two line segments can be dragged left or right to "sheer" the parallelogram and triangle but without changing the base or height. All area measures remain fixed! ∎

Circle Formulas

The relationship between the *circumference* of a circle (the distance around or the perimeter) and the length of the *diameter* (a line through the center joining two points on the circle) is one of the most interesting that children can discover. The circumference of every circle is about 3.14 times as long as the diameter. The exact ratio is an irrational number close to 3.14 and is represented by the Greek letter π. So $\pi = C/D$, the circumference divided by the diameter. In a slightly different form, $C = \pi D$. Half the diameter is the radius (r), so the same equation can be written $C = 2\pi r$. (Chapter 20 will discuss in detail the concept of π and how students can discover this important ratio.)

Figure 19.24 presents an argument for the area formula $A = \pi r^2$. This development is one commonly found in textbooks.

Regardless of the approach you use to develop the area formula, students should be challenged to figure it out on their own. For example, show students how to arrange 8 or 12 sectors of a circle into an approximate parallelogram. Their task should be to use this as a hint toward development of an area formula for the circle. You may need to help them notice that the arrangement of sectors is an approximate parallelogram and that the smaller the sectors, the closer the arrangement gets to a rectangle. But the complete argument for the formula should come from your students.

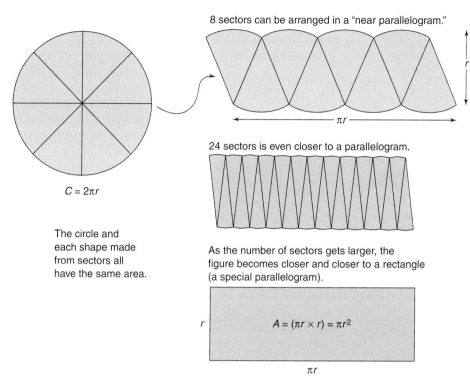

8 sectors can be arranged in a "near parallelogram."

FIGURE 19.24 Development of the circle area formula.

$C = 2\pi r$

The circle and each shape made from sectors all have the same area.

24 sectors is even closer to a parallelogram.

As the number of sectors gets larger, the figure becomes closer and closer to a rectangle (a special parallelogram).

$$A = (\pi r \times r) = \pi r^2$$

Students can cut a circle into eight sectors or perhaps even more and rearrange them to form a near rectangle with dimensions of half the circumference by the radius.

Volumes of Common Solid Shapes

The relationships between the formulas for volume are completely analogous to those for area. As you read, notice the similarities between rectangles and prisms, between parallelograms and "sheered" (oblique) prisms, and between triangles and pyramids. Not only are the formulas related, but the process for development of the formulas is similar.

Volumes of Cylinders

A *cylinder* is a solid with two congruent parallel bases and sides with parallel elements that join corresponding points on the bases. There are several special classes of cylinders, including *prisms* (with polygons for bases), *right prisms, rectangular prisms,* and *cubes* (see Chapter 20). Interestingly, all of these solids have the same volume formula, and that one formula is analogous to the area formula for parallelograms.

Provide students with some cardboard shoe boxes or similar cardboard boxes, a few cubes, and a ruler. As was done with rectangles, the task is to determine how many cubes will fit inside the box. Most likely your boxes will not have whole-number dimensions, so tell students to ignore any fractional parts of cubes. Although they may have seen or used a volume formula before, for this task they may not rely on a formula. Rather, they must come up with a method or formula that they can explain or justify. If a hint is required, suggest that they begin by finding out how many cubes will fit on the bottom of the box.

The development of the volume formula from this box exploration is exactly parallel to the development of the formula for the area of a rectangle. Figure 19.25 shows the development as if the grid paper were on the bottom of the box.

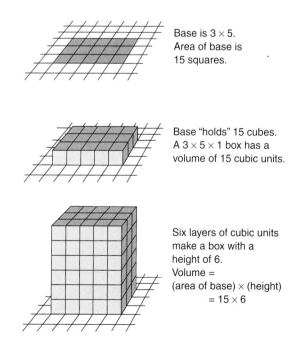

Base is 3×5.
Area of base is 15 squares.

Base "holds" 15 cubes.
A $3 \times 5 \times 1$ box has a volume of 15 cubic units.

Six layers of cubic units make a box with a height of 6.
Volume =
(area of base) $\times$ (height)
$= 15 \times 6$

FIGURE 19.25 Volume of a prism.

FIGURE 19.26 **Two cylinders with the same base and height have the same volume.**

Recall how the area formula for rectangles was developed (see Figure 19.19, p. 337), and notice how that development is like the one for volume. Instead of *length* of the base × height (for *area* of rectangles), in three dimensions, the *volume* formula for the corresponding figure is *area* of the base × height.

Recall that a parallelogram can be thought of as a "sheered" rectangle, as was illustrated with the dynamic geometry software (Figure 19.23). Show students a stack of three or four decks of playing cards (or a stack of books or paper). When stacked straight, they form a rectangular solid. The volume, as just discussed, is $V = A \times h$, with A equal to the area of one card. Now if the stack is sheered or slanted to one side as shown in Figure 19.26, what will the volume of this new figure be? Students should be able to argue that this figure has the same volume (and same volume formula) as the original stack.

What if the cards in this activity were some other shape? If they were circular, the volume would still be the area of the base times the height; if they were triangular, still the same. The conclusion is that the volume of *any* cylinder is equal to the *area of the base* times the *height*.

Volumes of Cones and Pyramids

Just as there is a nice relationship between the areas of parallelograms and triangles, there is a similar relationship between the volumes of cylinders and cones.

Help students make a poster board prism and a pyramid with the same height and base. (Plastic models of these related shapes such as Power Solids can be purchased.) Leave the base of each open. Score fold lines for accurate folds. Dimensions for a square pyramid and prism are given in Figure 19.27. Have students estimate the number of times the pyramid will fit into the prism. Then have them test their prediction by filling the pyramid with beans or rice and emptying it into the prism. They will discover that exactly three pyramids will fill a prism with the same base and height. (An alternative method is carefully to make models from clay and compare the weights.)

The 3-to-1 ratio of volumes is true of all cylinders and cones with the same base and height regardless of the shape of the base or the position of the vertex. That is, for any cone or pyramid, $V = \frac{1}{3}(A \times h)$. Recall that for parallelograms and triangles that have the same base and height, the areas are in a 2-to-1 ratio. *Area* is to *two*-dimensional figures what *volume* is to *three*-dimensional figures. Further, triangles are to parallelograms as pyramids are to prisms.

NCTM Standards The *Standards* points out that the development of area and volume formulas is a "particularly accessible and rich domain" for investigation at the sixth- to eighth-grade level (p. 244) and that middle school students should connect their study of length, area, and volume measures to the study of similarity and proportions. This includes examining the ratios of measures of similar figures and looking for relationships. On page 246 of the *Standards,* you will find the poem "One Inch Tall" by Shel Silverstein along with suggestions for posing problems relating to scale measurement and proportionality.

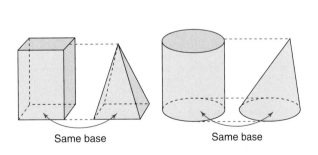

The volume of a pyramid or cone is one-third the volume of a prism or cylinder with the same base and same height.

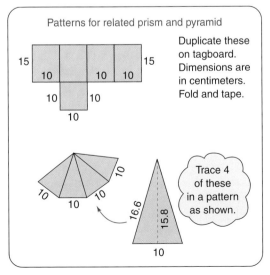

FIGURE 19.27 **Comparing volumes of prisms to pyramids and cones to cylinders.**

Measuring Time

Time is measured in the same way that other attributes are measured: A unit of time is selected and used to "fill" the time to be measured. *Time* can be thought of as the duration of an event from its beginning to its end. An informal unit of time might be the duration of a pendulum swing, the steady drip of a water faucet, or the movement of the sun's shadow between two fixed points (as on a sundial). To measure time, the units of time are started at the same time as the activity being measured ("timed") and counted until the activity is finished. Thus the pendulum swings, for example, are "fitted into" the duration of time that it takes the child to print his or her name. Young children enjoy timing events with informal units. Older children can appreciate the measurement of time as a process similar to the measurement of other attributes and thus see commonality in all measuring.

Clock Reading

Telling time has little to do conceptually with the measurement of time. The skills of clock reading are related to the skills of reading any meter that uses pointers on a numbered scale. Clock reading is a difficult skill to teach in the early grades, yet nearly everyone learns to tell time by middle school.

Some Difficulties

Young children's problems with clock reading may be due to the curriculum. Children are usually taught first to read clocks to the hour, then the half and quarter hours, and finally to 5- and 1-minute intervals. In the early stages of this sequence, children are shown clocks set exactly to the hour or half hour. Many children who can read a clock at 7:00 or 2:30 have no idea what time it is at 6:58 or 2:33.

Digital clocks permit students to read times easily but do not relate times very well. To know that a digital reading of 7:58 is nearly 8 o'clock, the child must know that there are 60 minutes in an hour, that 58 is close to 60, and that 2 minutes is not a very long time. These concepts have not been developed by most first-grade and many second-grade children. The analog clock (with hands) shows "close to" times without the need for understanding big numbers or even how many minutes in an hour.

Further, the standard approach to clock reading ignores the distinctly different actions and functions of the two hands. The little hand indicates broad, approximate time (nearest hour), and the big hand indicates time (minutes) before or beyond an hour. When we look at the hour hand, we focus on where it is pointing. With the minute hand, the focus is on the distance that it has gone around the clock or the distance yet to go for the hand to get back to the top.

Suggested Approach

The following suggestions can help students understand and read analog clocks.

1. Begin with a one-handed clock. A clock with only an hour hand can be read with reasonable accuracy. Use lots of approximate language: "It's about 7 o'clock." "It's a little past 9 o'clock." "It's halfway between 2 o'clock and 3 o'clock" (see Figure 19.28).

2. Discuss what happens to the big hand as the little hand goes from one hour to the next. When the big hand is at 12, the hour hand is pointing exactly to a number. If the hour hand is about halfway between numbers, about where would the minute hand be? If the hour hand is a little past or before an hour (10 to 15 minutes), about where would the minute hand be?

3. Use two real clocks, one with only an hour hand and one with two hands. (Break off the minute hand from an old clock.) Cover the two-handed clock. Periodically during the day, direct attention to the one-handed clock. Discuss the time in approximate language. Have students predict where the minute hand should be. Uncover the other clock and check.

4. Teach time after the hour in 5-minute intervals. After step 3 has begun, count by fives going around the clock. Instead of predicting that the minute hand is pointing at the 4, encourage students to say it is about 20 minutes after the hour. As skills develop, suggest that students always look first at the little or hour hand to learn approximately what time it is and then focus on the minute hand for precision.

5. Predict the reading on a digital clock when shown an analog clock, and vice versa; set an analog clock when shown a digital clock. This can be done with both one-handed and two-handed clocks.

"About 7 o'clock"

"Halfway between 2 o'clock and 3 o'clock"

"A little bit past 9 o'clock"

FIGURE 19.28 Approximate time with one-handed clocks.

A Teaching Clock

A simple clock for use on the overhead projector can be made easily with three sheets of acetate. On one, draw a simple clock face but leave off the hands. Cut a small hole in the center, and insert a brass fastener from the back side. Leave the fastener sticking straight up; do not spread the prongs. Cut two circles from the other sheets. The radius of the circles should be the same as the minute and hour hands of the clock. Cut small holes in the center of these circles, and draw a clock hand on each that extends from the center to the edge of the circle. If you slip just the smaller hour hand over the brass fastener, you have a very nice one-handed clock. For a clock with two hands, place the larger circle on first.

Use your overhead clock to practice one-handed clock reading, emphasizing approximate language. Set the little hand at various places on the clock, and have children suggest how to read it. Let students set the hour hand at times like half-past 5 or a little before 8 o'clock.

Related Concepts

Students also need to learn about seconds, minutes, and hours and to develop some concept of how long these units are. You can help by making a conscious effort to note the duration of short and long events during the day. Timing small events of $\frac{1}{2}$ minute to 2 minutes is fun and useful. TV shows and commercials are a good standard. Have students time familiar events in their daily lives: brushing teeth, eating dinner, riding to school, spending time in the reading group.

As students learn more about two-digit numbers, the time after the hours can also be related to the time left before the hour. This is helpful not only for telling time but for number sense as well. Note that in the sequence suggested, time after the hour is stressed almost exclusively. Time before or till the hour can come later.

Problem-solving exercises such as "If it was 7:30 when Bill left home and the trip took 8 hours, what time did he arrive?" are important. Even middle school students have difficulty with these ideas. Adding and subtracting time involve understanding the relationships between minutes and hours and also the two cycles of 12 hours in the day.

 ASSESSMENT NOTES

Gathering useful assessment data in the area of measurement requires open-ended activities that permit students to show how they understand measurement concepts. Traditional textbook tests tend to focus on prescriptive, procedural skills such as conversion of units from feet to inches or the use of a formula. Examine these test items, and ask yourself if they really tell you what you want to know about your students and measurement.

Focus on Ideas

As you progress through your measurement unit, think about what students really need to know to develop an understanding of measurement of any given attribute.

How well do students understand the attribute being measured? Observing how students do comparison activities ("Which of these regions is the largest? How can you tell?") will tell you what you need to know. Be wary of overly directing students; make sure that the ideas you observe are theirs, not yours. Rather than direct a student to measure something the way you prescribe, have students select their own methods and explain what they did and why they made the choices they made. If reasonable, ask them to find more than one way to measure the same object.

Do students use measuring tools meaningfully? Rulers, protractors, and clocks are often poorly understood. Ask students to find two different ways to measure with a ruler, or have them react to the technique used by another student. ("Monique measured the width of her locker. She lined up the 10 cm mark on one side. The other side of the locker was lined up between the 42 and 43 cm marks. Monique was confused. Without measuring the locker again, how would you help Monique?") Another technique is to have students explain how a ruler or protractor works to make a measurement. To help with their explanations, have them compare a student-made device, such as the waxed-paper protractor, with the standard device.

Standard Units

Again, the danger is the traditional focus on conversions of units rather than familiarity with the units. Consider these two tasks:

1. 427 centimeters = _____ meters
2. Estimate the length of this rope in centimeters and in meters. What ideas did you use to help make your estimate?

Both tasks relate centimeters to meters. The second task requires a student to have unit familiarity as well. Does the child use a meter-centimeter relationship or make two independent estimates? How are the estimates made? Are familiar benchmarks for the unit being used? Feedback related to these questions is available as children do the second task but not the first. As with all assessment, the information can be used to guide your instruction or for evaluation purposes.

Formulas

Plugging numbers into formulas, even requiring students to memorize the formulas, does very little to develop measurement understanding. Spend time in conceptual development of formulas and less time on practice with their use. ■

LITERATURE CONNECTIONS

Various fantasy books about giants, or strange lands, and unusual occurrences prompt comparisons of measures with our everyday world. There are also a large number of "concept books" for measurement, books that are designed to help children explore interesting aspects of measurement. The selections here are offered as examples.

How Big Is a Foot?
Myller, 1990

The story in this concept book is very attractive to younger children. The king measures his queen (crown included) using his feet and orders a bed made that is 6 feet long and 3 feet wide. The chief carpenter's apprentice, who is very small, makes the bed according to his own feet. The problems give rise to the need for standard units. But children are also motivated to use their own measuring methods for different purposes. Lubinski and Thiessen (1996) show how students create a "ruler" with footprints linked together and share activities conducted in a first-grade class.

Jim and the Beanstalk
Briggs, 1970

A variation on the classic tale of *Jack and the Beanstalk,* Jim helps the giant, who is growing quite old. Jim makes him a giant-sized pair of glasses and eventually measures the giant for false teeth and a wig. As with the books for ratio concepts discussed in Chapter 18, children are intrigued with the notion of how big these giant things would be and with discussing other large things that would fit in the story.

A similar story is Jonathan Swift's classic, *Gulliver's Travels.* A fourth-grade unit titled *My Travels with Gulliver* (Education Development Center, 1991) guides students to create drawings and use measurements to explore the lands in Gulliver's journey. The land of the Brobdingnag is a place where objects are about ten times normal size.

Counting on Frank
Clement, 1991

The dog, Frank, and his young master, the narrator of the story, engage in a series of estimations of everyday things: the length of a line that can be drawn by the average ballpoint pen, the number of Franks that would fit in the bedroom, or the time it would take to fill the entire bathroom with water if the tap were left on. These fanciful ideas and hilarious drawings easily motivate students to make their own estimates. Younger children may not be able to go further than a guess of one of their own ideas. By third grade, students can investigate how well their estimate agrees with reality. This book can lead children to investigate length, weight, volume, area, and time and connect each to their personal world. "If I filled my room with stuffed duffel bags, I estimate it would take 3000 bags. Altogether these bags would weigh over 15,000 pounds. If the duffel bags were each as big as my dad's car, they would take a space as big as the football stadium." Ideas such as this are fun to imagine but can also be tested against reality through measurement and calculations. One idea is to have class members contribute to their very own Frank book and provide an appendix that explains their estimates.

8,000 Stones
Wolkstein, 1972

This is an interesting folktale concerning the Supreme Governor of China, who wishes to find a method of weighing an elephant that has been received as a gift. The emperor's son solves the problem by putting the elephant in a boat and noticing the water level on the side. The amount of weight to produce the same effect is that of the elephant. This is a wonderful introduction to indirect methods of measurement for middle grade students. Not only can the same weighing method be explored, but students can research other measurements and find out how they are made. For example, how do we measure temperature with a mercury thermometer, and how is it done with a bimetal thermometer, the kind that causes a dial to rotate? ■

REFLECTIONS ON CHAPTER 19

Writing to Learn

1. Explain what it means to measure something. Does your explanation work equally well for length, area, weight, volume, and time?
2. A general instructional plan for measurement has three steps. Explain how the type of activity to use at each step accomplishes the instructional goal.
3. Five reasons were offered for using informal units instead of standard units in instructional activities. Which of these seem most important to you, and why?

4. For each of the following attributes, describe a comparison activity, one or two possible informal units, and a group activity that includes an estimation component:
   a. Length   d. Weight
   b. Area   e. Capacity
   c. Volume
5. With a straightedge, draw a triangle, a quadrilateral, and a five-sided figure. Make each about as large as a sheet of notebook paper. Make a waxed-paper protractor, and measure each interior

angle. Did the sum of the angles for each figure come close to what is predicted?

6. What is a degree? How would you help children learn what a degree is?

7. What do students need to know about standard units? Of these, which is the most and least important?

8. Develop in a connected way the area formulas for rectangles, parallelograms, triangles, and trapezoids. Draw pictures and provide explanations.

9. Explain how the volume formula for a right rectangular prism can be developed in an analogous manner to the area formula for a rectangle.

10. Explain how the area of a circle can be determined using the basic formula for the area of a parallelogram. (If you have a set of fraction "pie pieces," these can be used as sectors of a circle.)

11. Describe the differences between the typical approach for teaching clock reading and the one-handed approach discussed in this chapter.

For Discussion and Exploration

1. Make your own measuring instrument for an informal unit of measure. Use your instrument to measure, and then make the same measurement directly with a unit model. What are the values and limitations of each method? Can you see the importance of having children do this both ways?

2. Frequently, a textbook chapter on measurement will cover length, area, volume, and capacity with both metric and customary units. This means a very light treatment of each. An alternative for the publisher is to focus on one area of measurement in each grade and risk not matching the curriculum guides for many states and districts. Get a teacher's edition of a basal textbook for any grade level, and look at the chapters on measurement. How well does the book cover measurement ideas? How would you modify or expand on the lessons found there?

Recommendations for Further Reading

Highly Recommended

Nitabach, E., & Lehrer, R. (1996). Developing spatial sense through area measurement. *Teaching Children Mathematics, 2,* 473–476. This is a superb article. The authors describe six principles of measurement, giving special attention to area measurement. They then proceed to describe some nice activities with first and second graders and the children's responses. Too often we take simple measurement ideas for granted. This article provides a research-based view of reality.

Rubenstein, R. N., Lappan, G., Phillips, E., & Fitzgerald, W. (1993). Angle sense: A valuable connector. *Arithmetic Teacher, 40,* 352–358. This is an important article for the middle school teacher. The authors describe a series of investigations of angles in various polygons using pattern blocks and an angle-measuring device called a *goniometer.* Among other interesting ideas is a discussion

of the question "Why are there 360° in a circle?" and a graphical exposition of the interior angles of polygons that goes beyond the usual.

Wilson, P. S., & Rowland, R. E. (1993). Teaching measurement. In R. J. Jensen (Ed.), *Research ideas for the classroom: Early childhood mathematics* (pp. 171–194). Old Tappan, NJ: Macmillan. There is an interesting, research-based idea for every teacher in this well-written review of measurement in the classroom. All areas of measurement are discussed, with clear descriptions of some of the difficulties children experience. The chapter contains great activities as well.

Other Suggestions

Battista, M. T. (1999). Fifth graders' enumeration of cubes in 3D arrays: Conceptual progress in an inquiry-based classroom. *Journal for Research in Mathematics Education, 30,* 417–448.

Ferrer, B., Hunter, B., Irwin, K., Sheldon, M., Thompson, C., & Vistro-Yu, C. (2001). By the unit or square unit. *Mathematics Teaching in the Middle School, 7,* 132–137.

Friederwitzer, F. J., & Berman, B. (1999). The language of time. *Teaching Children Mathematics, 6,* 254–259.

Karp, K. S., & Brown, T. E. (2001). Geo-dolls: Traveling in a mathematical world. *Teaching Children Mathematics, 8,* 132–137.

Martin, G., & Strutchens, M. E. (2000). Geometry and measurement. In E. A. Silver & P. A. Kenney (Eds.), *Results from the seventh mathematics assessment of the National Assessment of Educational Progress* (pp. 193–234). Reston, VA: National Council of Teachers of Mathematics.

McClain, K., Cobb, P., Gravemeijer, K., & Estes, B. (1999). Developing mathematical reasoning within the context of measurement. In L. V. Stiff (Ed.), *Developing mathematical reasoning in grades K–12* (pp. 93–106). Reston, VA: National Council of Teachers of Mathematics.

Rectanus, C. (1997). *Math by all means: Area and perimeter, grades 5–6.* Sausalito, CA: Math Solutions Publications.

Reynolds, A., & Wheatley, G. H. (1997). Third-grade students engage in a playground measuring activity. *Teaching Children Mathematics, 4,* 166–170.

Rhone, L. (1995). Measurement in a primary-grade integrated curriculum. In P. A. House (Ed.), *Connecting mathematics across the curriculum* (pp. 124–133). Reston, VA: National Council of Teachers of Mathematics.

Richardson, K. (1997). Too easy for kindergarten and just right for first grade. *Teaching Children Mathematics, 3,* 432–437.

Stephan, M., Cobb, P., Gravemeijer, K., & Estes, B. (2001). The role of tools in supporting children's development of measuring conceptions. In A. A. Cuoco (Ed.), *The roles of representation in school mathematics* (pp. 63–76). Reston, VA: National Council of Teachers of Mathematics.

Strutchens, M. E., Harris, K. A., & Martin, W. G. (2001). Assessing geometric and measurement understanding using manipulatives. *Mathematics Teaching in the Middle School, 6,* 402–405.

Szetela, W., & Owens, D. T. (1986). Finding the area of a circle: Use a cake pan and leave out the pi. *Arithmetic Teacher, 33*(9), 12–18.

C H A P T E R

20

GEOMETRIC THINKING AND GEOMETRIC CONCEPTS

Geometry in K–8 is finally being taken seriously. Geometry used to be the chapter that was skipped or put off until late in the year. Many teachers were not comfortable with geometry, associating it with high school and proofs. Nor was geometry seen as important because it was only minimally tested on standardized tests. Now geometry is a strand of the curriculum in nearly every state and district.

This change is due in large part to the influence of the NCTM standards movement beginning in 1989. A second significant influence is an attention to a theoretical perspective that has helped us understand how students reason about spatial concepts.

 ## Big Ideas

1. What makes shapes alike and different can be determined by an array of geometric properties. For example, shapes have sides that are parallel, perpendicular, or neither; they have line symmetry, rotational symmetry, or neither; they are similar, congruent, or neither.

2. Shapes can be described in terms of their location in a plane or in space. Coordinate systems can be used to describe these locations precisely. In turn, the coordinate view of shape offers another way to understand certain properties of shapes, changes in position (transformations), and how they appear or change size (visualization).

3. Shapes can be moved in a plane or in space. These changes can be described in terms of translations (slides), reflections (flips), and rotations (turns).

4. Shapes can be seen from different perspectives. The ability to perceive shapes from different viewpoints helps us understand relationships between two- and three-dimensional figures and mentally change the position and size of shapes.

 ## CONTENT CONNECTIONS

A rich understanding of geometry has clear and important implications for other areas of the curriculum. Take advantage of these connections whenever possible.

■ **Measurement** (Chapter 19): Measurement and geometry are clearly aligned in the development of area and volume formulas and in an understanding of area/perimeter and surface/volume relationships. Coordinate geometry provides new ways to determine lengths, areas, and volumes. The Pythagorean relationship is at once an algebraic, geometric, and metric relationship.

■ **Proportional Reasoning** (Chapter 18): Similar geometric objects have proportional dimensions and provide visual representation of proportionality.

■ **Algebra** (Chapter 23): Coordinate graphing provides an analytic view of the concept of slope, and in turn, of perpendicular and parallel relationships. The Pythagorean relationship gives us an algebraic approach to the distance between points in a plane. Transformations of shapes (slides, flips, and turns) can be described in terms of coordinates, allowing for the digital manipulation of shapes. The entire world of computer animation is based on a marriage of geometry and algebra.

■ **Integers** (Chapter 24): The coordinate plane provides a connection because both positive and negative numbers are used in the description of position in the plane and in space.

Since children study fractional parts of shapes, fractions have a relationship to geometry. This connection is probably more pedagogical than mathematical.

THREE EXPLORATORY ACTIVITIES

To provide some common view of the nature of elementary and middle school geometry and how young children approach geometric concepts, three simple activities are offered here for you to do. The activities will provide some idea of the spirit of informal geometry as well as background for a discussion of children's geometric thinking. All you will need is a pencil, several pieces of paper, scissors, and 15 to 20 minutes.

DIFFERENT TRIANGLES

Draw a series of at least five triangles. After the first triangle, each new one should be different in some way from those already drawn. Write down why you think each is different.

SHAPES WITH TRIANGLES

Make a few copies of the 2-cm isometric grid found in the Blackline Masters, or simply place a sheet of paper over the grid. Draw three or four different figures by following the grid lines. Make each figure so that it has an area of ten triangles. Count to find the distance around each figure (the perimeter), and record this next to each drawing. Did you find shapes with different perimeters? What about a shape would make it have a larger or smaller perimeter?

A TILING PATTERN

First make at least eight copies of any shape in Figure 20.1. An easy way to do this is to fold a piece of paper so that there are eight thicknesses. Trace the shape on an outside section, and cut through all eight thicknesses at once.

Think of the shapes you cut out as tiles. The task is to use the tiles to make a "regular tiling pattern" with two properties: First, the tiles must fit together without overlapping and without leaving any spaces. Second, if you were to tile an endless floor with your pattern, the design in one section of the floor would be the same as that in any other section. Several different tiling patterns are possible for each of the three tiles. Experiment to decide on a pattern that you like.

Notice that each of the tile shapes is made up of triangles and can be drawn on an isometric dot grid found in the Blackline Masters. When you have decided on a tiling pattern, place a piece of paper over the grid, and draw your tiling pattern using the grid as a guide. Cover most of the grid with your pattern. Then shade in some of the tiles to make a regular pattern in two colors.

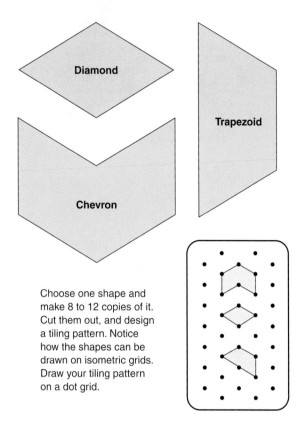

Choose one shape and make 8 to 12 copies of it. Cut them out, and design a tiling pattern. Notice how the shapes can be drawn on isometric grids. Draw your tiling pattern on a dot grid.

FIGURE 20.1 **Three tile patterns.**

Reflections on the Activities

The following observations apply to all geometry activities in school as well as the activities you have just completed.

- Different people think about geometric ideas in different ways. The way you approached and completed these activities is probably different than your peers. School-aged students may also do them differently than you. Research suggests that geometric experiences are the major influence on geometric thinking—not age.
- Explorations help develop relationships. The more you play around with the ideas in any of these activities, the more relationships you will discover. Try drawing different quadrilaterals instead of triangles. What discoveries about area and perimeter can you find in the "Shapes with Triangles" task? How many different tiling patterns are there for each of these shapes? Students need to learn how to explore ideas in geometry and play around with the relationships in order for ideas to develop and become meaningful.
- The best geometry activities involve hands-on materials. Try to imagine the "Tiling Pattern" problem without having the tiles to play around with. Activities on dot grids are a second-best alternative to real objects. Virtually *every activity* that is appropriate for K–8 geometry should involve some form of hands-on materials or at least paper for drawing.

Spatial Sense

Just as a good definition of number sense is an intuition about numbers and their relationships, *spatial sense* can be defined as an intuition about shapes and the relationships among shapes. Individuals with spatial sense have a feel for the geometric aspects of their surroundings and the shapes formed by objects in the environment.

Spatial sense includes the ability to visualize mentally objects and spatial relationships—to turn things around in your mind. It includes a comfort with geometric descriptions of objects and position. People with spatial sense appreciate geometric form in art, nature, and architecture. They are able to use geometric ideas to describe and analyze their world.

Many people say they aren't very good with shape or that they have poor spatial sense. The typical belief is that you are either born with spatial sense or not. This simply is not true! We now know that rich experiences with shape and spatial relationships, when provided consistently over time, can and do develop spatial sense. Without geometric experiences, most people do not grow in their spatial sense or spatial reasoning. Between 1990 and 1996, NAEP data indicated a steady, continuing improvement in students' geometric reasoning at all three grades tested, 4, 8, and 12 (Martin & Strutchens, 2000). Students did not just get smarter. More likely there has been an increasing emphasis on geometry at all grades. Still, much more needs to be done if U.S. children are to rise to the same level as their European and Asian counterparts.

 STOP Reflect for a moment about your own beliefs concerning an individual's abilities in the area of spatial sense. What do you think causes some people to have better spatial sense than others?

 The *Standards* supports the notion that all students can grow in their geometric skills and understandings. "The notion of building understanding in geometry across the grades, from informal to more formal thinking, is consistent with the thinking of theorists and researchers" (p. 41).

THE DEVELOPMENT OF GEOMETRIC THINKING

Not all people think about geometric ideas in the same manner. Certainly, we are not all alike, but we are all capable of growing and developing in our ability to think and reason in geometric contexts. The research of two Dutch educators, Pierre van Hiele and Dina van Hiele-Geldof, has provided insight into the differences in geometric thinking and how the differences come to be.

The van Hieles' work began in 1959 and immediately attracted a lot of attention in the Soviet Union but for nearly two decades got little notice in this country (Hoffer, 1983; Hoffer & Hoffer, 1992). But today, the van Hiele theory has become the most influential factor in the American geometry curriculum.

The van Hiele Levels of Geometric Thought

The most prominent feature of the model is a five-level hierarchy of ways of understanding spatial ideas. Each of the five levels describes the thinking processes used in geometric contexts. The levels describe how we think and what types of geometric ideas we think about, rather than how much knowledge we have. A significant difference from one level to the next is the objects of thought—what we are able to think about geometrically.

Level 0: Visualization

The objects of thought at level 0 are shapes and what they "look like."

Students recognize and name figures based on the global, visual characteristics of the figure—a gestaltlike approach to shape. Students operating at this level are able to make measurements and even talk about properties of shapes, but these properties are not abstracted from the shapes at hand. It is the appearance of the shape that defines it for the student. A square is a square "because it looks like a square." Because appearance is dominant at this level, appearances can overpower properties of a shape. For example, a square that has been rotated so that all sides are at a 45-degree angle to the vertical may now be a diamond and no longer a square. Students at this level will sort and classify shapes based on their appearances—"I put these together because they are all pointy" (or "fat," or "look like a house," or are "dented in sort of," and so on). With a focus on the appearances of shapes, students are able to see how shapes are alike and different. As a result, students at this level can create and begin to understand classifications of shapes.

The products of thought at level 0 are classes or groupings of shapes that seem to be "alike."

Level 1: Analysis

The objects of thought at level 1 are classes of shapes rather than individual shapes.

Students at the analysis level are able to consider all shapes within a class rather than a single shape. Instead of talking about *this* rectangle, it is possible to talk about *all* rectangles. By focusing on a class of shapes, students are able to think about what makes a rectangle a rectangle (four sides, opposite sides parallel, opposite sides same length, four right angles, congruent diagonals, etc.). The irrelevant features (e.g., size or orientation) fade into the background. At this level, students begin to appreciate that a collection of shapes goes together because of properties. Ideas about an individual shape can now be generalized to all shapes that fit that class. If a shape belongs to a particular class such as cubes, it has the corresponding properties of that class. "All cubes have six congruent faces, and each of those faces is a square." These properties were only implicit at level 0. Students operating at level 1 may be able to list all the properties of squares, rectangles, and parallelograms but not see that these are subclasses of one another, that all squares are rectangles and all rectangles are parallelograms.

In defining a shape, level 1 thinkers are likely to list as many properties of a shape as they know.

The products of thought at level 1 are the properties of shapes.

Level 2: Informal Deduction

The objects of thought at level 2 are the properties of shapes.

As students begin to be able to think about properties of geometric objects without the constraints of a particular object, they are able to develop relationships between and among these properties. "If all four angles are right angles, the shape must be a rectangle. If it is a square, all angles are right angles. If it is a square, it must be a rectangle." With greater ability to engage in "if-then" reasoning, shapes can be classified using only minimum characteristics. For example, four congruent sides and at least one right angle can be sufficient to define a square. Rectangles are parallelograms with a right angle. Observations go beyond properties themselves and begin to focus on logical arguments *about* the properties. Students at level 2 will be able to follow and appreciate an informal deductive argument about shapes and their properties. "Proofs" may be more intuitive than rigorously deductive. However, there is an appreciation that a logical argument is compelling. An appreciation of the axiomatic structure of a formal deductive system, however, remains under the surface.

The products of thought at level 2 are relationships among properties of geometric objects.

Level 3: Deduction

The objects of thought at level 3 are relationships among properties of geometric objects.

At level 3, students are able to examine more than just the properties of shapes. Their earlier thinking has produced conjectures concerning relationships among properties. Are these conjectures correct? Are they "true"? As this analysis of the informal arguments takes place, the structure of a system complete with axioms, definitions, theorems, corollaries, and postulates begins to develop and can be appreciated as the necessary means of establishing geometric truth. At this level, students begin to appreciate the need for a system of logic that rests on a minimum set of assumptions and from which other truths can be derived. The student at this level is able to work with abstract statements about geometric properties and make conclusions based more on logic than intuition. This is the level of the traditional high school geometry course. A student operating at level 3 can clearly observe that the diagonals of a rectangle bisect each other, just as a student at a lower level of thought can. However, at level 3, there is an appreciation of the need to prove this from a series of deductive arguments. The level 2 thinker, by contrast, follows the argument but fails to appreciate the need.

The products of thought at level 3 are deductive axiomatic systems for geometry.

Level 4: Rigor

The objects of thought at level 4 are deductive axiomatic systems for geometry.

At the highest level of the van Hiele hierarchy, the objects of attention are axiomatic systems themselves, not just the deductions within a system. There is an appreciation of the distinctions and relationships between different axiomatic systems. For example, spherical geometry is based on lines drawn on a sphere rather than in a plane or ordinary space. This geometry has its own set of axioms and theorems. This is generally the level of a college mathematics major who is studying geometry as a branch of mathematical science.

The products of thought at level 4 are comparisons and contrasts among different axiomatic systems of geometry.

Characteristics of the van Hiele Levels

You no doubt noticed that the products of thought at each level are the same as the objects of thought at the next. This object-product relationship between levels of the van Hiele theory is illustrated in Figure 20.2. The objects (ideas) must be created at one level so that relationships among these objects can become the focus of the next level. In addition to this key concept of the theory, four related characteristics of the levels of thought merit special attention.

1. The levels are sequential. To arrive at any level above level 0, students must move through all prior levels. To move through a level means that one has experienced geometric thinking appropriate for that level and has created in one's own mind the types of objects or relationships that are the focus of thought at the next level.

2. The levels are not age-dependent in the sense of the developmental stages of Piaget. A third grader or a high school student could be at level 0. Indeed, some students and adults remain forever at level 0, and a significant number of adults never reach level 2. But age is certainly related to the amount and types of geometric experiences that we have. Therefore, it is reasonable for all children in the K–2 range to be at level 0, as well as the majority of children in grades 3 and 4.

3. Geometric experience is the greatest single factor influencing advancement through the levels. Activities that permit children to explore, talk about, and interact with content at the next level, while increasing their experiences at their current level, have the best chance of advancing the level of thought for those children.

4. When instruction or language is at a level higher than that of the student, there will be a lack of communication. Students required to wrestle with objects of thought that have not been constructed at the earlier level may be forced into rote learning and achieve only temporary and superficial success. A student can, for example, memorize that all squares are rectangles without having constructed that relationship. A student may memorize a geometric proof but fail to create the steps or understand the rationale involved (Fuys, Geddes, & Tischler, 1988; Geddes & Fortunato, 1993).

The van Hiele Theory of Geometric Thought

FIGURE 20.2 At each level of geometric thought, the ideas created become the focus or object of thought at the next level.

Instructional Goals: Thought and Content

The van Hiele theory does not tell us what content to teach, but it does provide the thoughtful teacher with a framework in which to conduct geometric activities. The district or state in which you teach will prescribe the specific content of your geometry curriculum. You should be clear about both content goals and the goals implicit in the van Hiele theory.

Content Goals for Geometry

For too long, the geometry curriculum in the United States has been somewhat of an eclectic mix of activities and lists of "bold print words"—too much emphasis has been placed on learning terminology. At the same time, the growing emphasis placed on geometry has spawned a huge assortment of wonderful tasks for students. Fortunately, the authors of *Principles and Standards for School Mathematics* have provided a content framework for the pre-K–12 curriculum. As with each of the content standards, the geometry standard has a number of goals that apply to all grade levels. (In Appendix A, the goals are the statements found in the left-hand column under the word "Standard.") The four goals for geometry can be loosely summarized with these headings: *Shapes and Properties*, *Location*, *Transformation*, and *Visualization*. A very brief description of these headings is offered next.

- *Shapes and Properties* includes a study of the properties of shapes in both two and three dimensions, as well as a study of the relationships built on properties.
- *Location* refers primarily to coordinate geometry or other ways of specifying how objects are located in the plane or in space.
- *Transformation* includes a study of translations, reflections, and rotations (slides, flips, and turns) and the study of symmetries.
- *Visualization* includes the recognition of shapes in the environment, developing relationships between two- and three-dimensional objects, and the ability to draw and recognize objects from different perspectives.

The value of these content goals is that a content framework finally exists that cuts across grades so that both teachers and curriculum planners can examine growth from year to year.

Goals of Geometric Thinking and Spatial Sense

If the van Hiele theory is correct—and there is much evidence to support it—then a major goal of the K–8 curriculum must be to advance students' level of geometric thought. If students are to be adequately prepared for the deductive geometry curriculum of high school, then it is important for their thinking to have grown to level 2 by the end of the eighth grade.

Not every teacher will be able to move children to the next level. However, all teachers should be aware that the experiences they provide are the single most important factor in moving children up this developmental ladder. Every teacher should be able to see some growth in geometric thinking over the course of the year.

Implications for Classroom Strategies

The van Hiele theory and the developmental perspective of this book highlight the necessity of teaching at the child's level of thought. However, almost any activity can be modified to span two levels of thinking, even within the same classroom. For many activities, how we interact with individual children will adapt the activity to their levels and encourage them or challenge them to operate at the next higher level.

The following sections contain descriptions of the types of activity and questioning that are appropriate for each of the first three levels. Apply these descriptors to the tasks that you pose to students, and use them to guide your interaction with students. The use of physical materials, drawings, and computer models is a must at every level.

Instruction at Level 0

Instructional activities in geometry appropriate for level 0 should:

- Involve lots of sorting and classifying. Seeing how shapes are alike and different is the primary focus of level 0. As students learn more content, the types of things that they notice will become more sophisticated. At an early stage they may talk about very non-geometric-sounding attributes of shape such as "fat" or even the color of the pieces. When properties such as symmetry and numbers of sides and corners are introduced, students should be challenged to use these features to classify shapes.

● Include a sufficient variety of examples of shapes so that irrelevant features do not become important. Students need ample opportunities to draw, build, make, put together, and take apart shapes in both two and three dimensions. These activities should be built around specific characteristics or properties so that students develop an understanding of geometric properties and begin to use them naturally.

To help students move from level 0 to level 1, students should be challenged to test ideas about shapes for a variety of examples from a particular category. Say to them, "Let's see if that is true for other rectangles," or "Can you draw a triangle that does *not* have a right angle?" In general, students should be challenged to see if observations made about a particular shape apply to other shapes of a similar kind.

Instruction at Level 1

Instructional activities in geometry appropriate for level 1 should:

● Focus more on the properties of figures rather than on simple identification. As new geometric concepts are learned, the number of properties that figures have can be expanded.

● Apply ideas to entire classes of figures (e.g., *all* rectangles, *all* prisms) rather than on individual models. Analyze classes of figures to determine new properties. For example, find ways to sort all possible triangles into groups. From these groups, define types of triangles. Dynamic geometry software such as *The Geometer's Sketchpad* (Key Curriculum Press) is especially useful for exploring many examples of a class of shapes.

To assist students in moving from level 1 to level 2, challenge them with questions such as "Why?" and those that involve some reasoning. For example, "If the sides of a four-sided shape are all congruent, will you always have a square?" and "Can you find a counterexample?"

Instruction at Level 2

Instructional activities in geometry appropriate for level 2 should:

● Encourage the making and testing of hypotheses or conjectures. "Do you think that will work all the time?" "Is that true for all triangles or just equilateral ones?"

● Examine properties of shapes to determine necessary and sufficient conditions for different shapes or concepts. "What properties of diagonals do you think will guarantee that you will have a square?"

● Use the language of informal deduction: *all, some, none, if . . . then, what if,* and so on.

● Encourage students to attempt informal proofs. As an alternative, require them to make sense of informal proofs that other students or you have suggested.

Task Selection and Levels of Thought

If you teach at the K–3 level, nearly all of your students will be at level 0. However, by at least grade 3 you certainly want to begin to challenge students who seem able. In the upper grades you may have children at two or even all three levels within the same classroom. How do you discover the level of each student? Once you know, how will you select the right activities to match your students' levels?

No simple test exists to pigeonhole students at a certain level. However, examine the descriptors for the first two levels. As you conduct an activity, listen to the types of observations that students make. Can they talk about shapes as classes? Do they refer, for example, to "rectangles" rather than basing discussion around a particular rectangle? Do they generalize that certain properties are attributable to a type of shape or simply the shape at hand? Do they understand that shapes do not change when the orientation changes? With simple observations such as these, you will soon be able to distinguish between levels 0 and 1.

At the upper grades, attempt to push students from level 1 to level 2. If students are not able to follow or appreciate logical arguments and are not comfortable with conjectures and if-then reasoning, these students are likely still at level 1 or below.

The remainder of this chapter offers a sampling of activities organized broadly around the first three van Hiele levels. To aid you with content, each of the three large sections of the chapter is further subdivided according to the four content goals of the NCTM standards: Shapes and Properties, Location, Transformations, and Visualization. Understand that all of these subdivisions are quite fluid. An activity found at one level can easily be adapted to an adjacent level simply by the way it is presented to the students. As you will see, even the content subdivisions overlap.

The activities that most clearly reflect the van Hiele levels are found in the Shapes and Properties sections. As you explore some of the activities in each section, you should begin to get a feeling for why an activity is appropriate for one level or the other. Do not become so concerned about matching levels and activities that you agonize over task selection. As a rough guide, if you teach K–2, begin with level 0; for 3–5, look at levels 0 and 1; at the 6–8 level, look at level 1 and level 2 activities.

ACTIVITIES FOR LEVEL 0

The emphasis at level 0 is on the shapes that students can observe, feel, build, take apart, and perceive in many ways. The general goal is to explore how shapes are alike and different and use these ideas to create classes of shapes (both physically and mentally). Some of these classes of shapes have names—rectangles, triangles, prisms, cylinders, and so on. Properties of shapes, such as parallel sides, symmetry, right angles, and so on, are included at this level but only in an informal, observational manner.

Remember that *level 0* is not a synonym for *primary*. If you teach in the upper grades, you will almost certainly have students who need to begin with activities similar to these.

Shapes and Properties

Children need experience with a rich variety of both two- and three-dimensional shapes. Triangles should be more than just equilateral. Shapes should have curved sides, straight sides, and combinations of these. Along the way, the names of shapes and their properties can be introduced casually.

Sorting and Classifying

As young students work at classification of shapes, be prepared for them to notice features that you do not consider to be "real" geometric attributes, such as "curvy" or "looks like a rocket." Children at this level will also attribute to shapes ideas that are not part of the shape, such as "points up" or "has a side that is the same as the edge of the board."

For variety in two-dimensional shapes, create your own materials. A good set found in the Blackline Masters is called 2-D Shapes. Make multiple copies so that groups of children can all work with the same shapes. The shapes in Figure 20.3 are similar to those in the Blackline Masters, but you will want

many more. Once you have your sets constructed, the following activities provide several ideas.

ACTIVITY 20.1

Shape Sorts

Have students work in groups of four with a set of 2-D Shapes similar to those in Figure 20.3. Here are several related activities that might be done in order:

- Each child randomly selects a shape. In turn, the students tell one or two things they find interesting about their shape. There are no right or wrong responses.
- Children each randomly select two shapes. The task is to find something that is alike about their two shapes and something that is different. (Have them select their shapes before they know the task.)
- The group selects one shape at random and places it in the center of the workspace. Their task is to find all other shapes that are like the target shape, but all according to the same rule. For example, if they say "This one is like our shape because it has a curved side and a straight side," then all other shapes that they put in the collection must have these properties. Challenge them to do a second sort with the same target shape but using a different property.
- Have students share their sorting rules with the class and show examples. All students then draw a new shape that will also fit in the group according to the same rule. They should write about their new shape and why it fits the rule.
- Do a "secret sort." You or one of the students creates a small collection of about five shapes that fit a secret rule. Leave others that belong in your group in the pile. The other students try to find additional pieces that belong to the set and/or guess the secret rule.

FIGURE 20.3 An assortment of shapes for sorting.

⊗ STOP Why do you think that the teacher should not say things such as, "Find all the pieces with straight sides," or "Find the triangles," and instead have students choose how to sort?

In any sorting activity, the students should decide how to sort, not the teacher. This allows the students to do the activity using ideas *they* own and understand. By listening to the kinds of attributes that they use in their sorting, you will be able to tell what properties they know and use and how they think about shapes. Figure 20.4 illustrates a few of the many possible ways a set might be sorted.

Shapes with curved edges

Opposite sides "go the same way"—parallelograms

Three sides—triangles

Shapes with a "square corner"—right angle

These all "dent in"—concave

FIGURE 20.4 By sorting shapes, students begin to recognize properties.

The secret sorting activity is one option for introducing a new property. For example, sort the shapes so that all have at least one right angle or "square corner." When students discover your rule, you have an opportunity to talk more about that property.

The following activity is also done with the 2-D Shapes.

ACTIVITY 20.2

What's My Shape?

From the Blackline Masters, make a set of 2-D Shapes on paper. Cut out about a third of the shapes and paste each inside a folded half-sheet of construction paper to make "secret shape" folders.

In a group, one student is designated the leader and given a secret-shape folder. The other students are to find the shape that matches the shape in the folder. To this end, they ask questions to which the leader can answer only "yes" or "no." The group can sort the shapes as they ask questions to help narrow down the possibilities. They are not allowed to point to a piece and ask, "Is it this one?" Rather, they must continue to ask questions that reduce the choices to one shape. The final piece is tested against the one in the leader's folder.

The difficulty of Activity 20.2 is largely dependent on the shape in the folder. The more shapes in the collection that resemble the secret shape, the more difficult the task.

Most of the activities in Shape Sorts can and should be done with three-dimensional shapes as well. The difficulty is finding or making a collection that has sufficient variability. Geoblocks are a large set of wooden blocks available through various distributors. The variety is good, but no blocks have curved surfaces. Check catalogs for other collections. Consider combining several different sets to get variation. Another option is to collect real objects such as cans, boxes, balls, and Styrofoam shapes. Figure 20.5 illustrates some classifications of solids.

FIGURE 20.5 Early classifications of three-dimensional shapes.

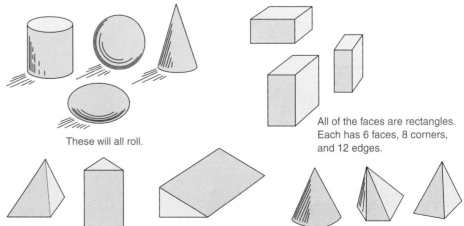

These will all roll.

All of the faces are rectangles. Each has 6 faces, 8 corners, and 12 edges.

These all have a triangle.

These all have a "point."

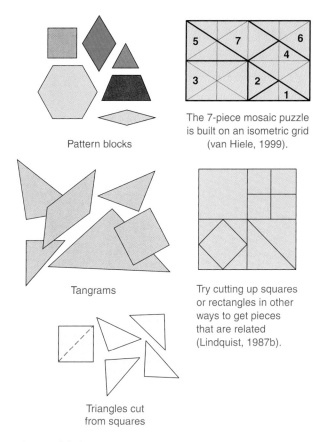

Pattern blocks

The 7-piece mosaic puzzle is built on an isometric grid (van Hiele, 1999).

Tangrams

Try cutting up squares or rectangles in other ways to get pieces that are related (Lindquist, 1987b).

Triangles cut from squares

FIGURE 20.6 **Activities with tiles can involve an assortment of shapes or can be designed with just one shape.**

Constructing and Dissecting Shapes

Children need to freely explore how shapes fit together to form larger shapes and how larger shapes can be made of smaller shapes. Among two-dimensional shapes for these activities, pattern blocks and tangrams are the best known. In a 1999 article, Pierre van Hiele describes an interesting set of tiles he calls the mosaic puzzle (see Figure 20.6). Another excellent tile set for building is a set of triangles cut from squares (isosceles right triangles). Patterns for the mosaic puzzle and tangrams can be found in the Blackline Masters.

Figure 20.7 shows four different types of tangram puzzles in increasing order of difficulty. Numerous resource books are available devoted entirely to tangrams and NCTM's *e-Standards* includes a tangram applet (Example 4.4). One form of the applet includes eight figures that can be made using all seven of the pieces. The e-version of tangrams has the advantage of motivation and the fact that you must be much more deliberate in arranging the shapes. *Investigations in Number, Data, and Space* uses pattern blocks in first grade in an activity similar to tangrams. As you can see in the excerpt on p. 354, pattern blocks, like the mosaic puzzle, offer considerable flexibility for young children in this type of activity.

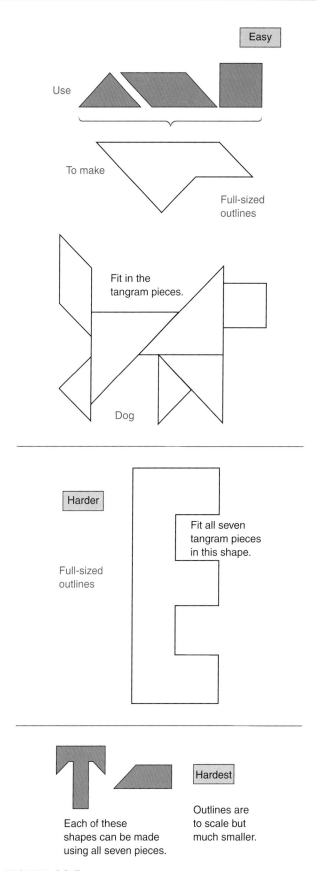

Easy

Use

To make

Full-sized outlines

Fit in the tangram pieces.

Dog

Harder

Full-sized outlines

Fit all seven tangram pieces in this shape.

Hardest

Each of these shapes can be made using all seven pieces.

Outlines are to scale but much smaller.

FIGURE 20.7 **Four types of tangram puzzles illustrate a range of difficulty levels.**

INVESTIGATIONS in NUMBER, DATA, and SPACE

Grade 1, *Quilt Squares and Block Towns*
Investigation 1: 2-D Shapes and Patterns

Context

The activity is designed for the seventh class period of this investigation. The earlier sessions and some that follow are involved, as is this one, in finding different ways to fill an outline with pattern blocks. The *Investigations* program also has a computer component that uses the *Shapes* program (Clements & Sarama, 1995) described in the Technology Note on p. 356. Most of the work prior to this lesson is done individually at stations. At this point, the computer program is also used in a free-play mode, in which students create their own designs on the screen. Other materials used in this unit include geoblocks and a set of shape cards for sorting.

Task Description

By this time, students are accustomed to filling in shapes with pattern blocks. They also have been recording their work in one of several possible ways: pasting in construction paper or sticker versions of pattern blocks or coloring in their designs freehand. In previous activities they recorded the number of times each type of block is used. In this activity they fill in the same shape at least three times, each time trying to use a different number of blocks. Students work in pairs, with one of the worksheets (shown here) for each pair of children. As the teacher interacts with the students, she or he focuses on what approach students take. Some children use the obvious shapes (the hexagon and trapezoid) and have difficulty finding other methods. Others use only triangles or only trapezoids.

Number is an added focus of the activity. Students are encouraged to try to find another way to fill in the design with *more* or *fewer* blocks or a number of blocks that is between two different totals. This focus on number has the potential to encourage students to substitute smaller blocks for an equivalent larger block (decompose shapes) or larger blocks for smaller ones (combine shapes).

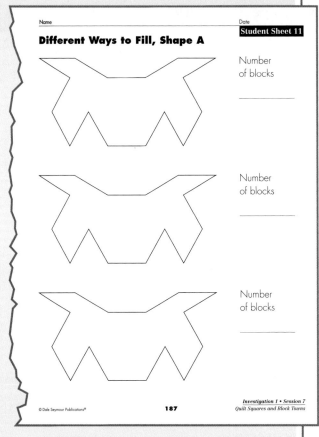

Page 187 from *2-D and 3-D Geometry: Quilt Squares and Block Towns* by S. J. Russell, D. H. Clements, & J. Sarama. *Investigations in Number, Data, and Space.* Copyright © 1998 by Dale Seymour Publications. Reprinted by permission of Pearson Education, Inc.

In the full class discussion, students list all of the different totals that they found. (There are eight different solutions.) Questions revolve around the possibility of a solution with even more blocks, or fewer blocks, or some additional solutions in between. The teacher is looking for students' comfort with reasoning and with manipulation of the shapes in making substitutions.

The value of van Hiele's mosaic puzzle is partly due to the fact that the set contains five different angles (see Figure 20.8). If appropriate, you can use the pieces to talk about square corners (*right* angles) and angles that are more and less than a right angle (*obtuse* and *acute* angles).

The geoboard is one of the best devices for "drawing" two-dimensional shapes. Here are just three of many possible activities appropriate for level 0.

ACTIVITY 20.3

Geoboard Copy

Copy shapes, designs, and patterns from prepared cards as in Figure 20.9. Begin with designs shown with dots as on a geoboard, and later have students copy designs drawn without dots.

Make this house with two pieces. Now do it a different way. Can you make it with 3 pieces? How many ways? What about 4 pieces?

This is a long parallelogram. What other parallelograms can you make?

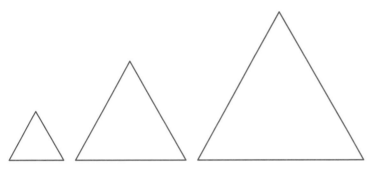

Build enlargements of the equilateral triangle.

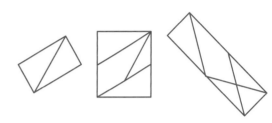

How many different rectangles can you make? Can you make any in more than one way?

How many different sized angles can you find in the set of pieces? Put them in order from smallest to largest.

FIGURE 20.8   A sample of activities with the mosaic puzzle.

Based on van Hiele, P. M. (1999). Developing geometric thinking through activities that begin with play. *Teaching Children Mathematics, 5,* 310–316.

Have children copy shapes from pattern cards onto a geoboard.

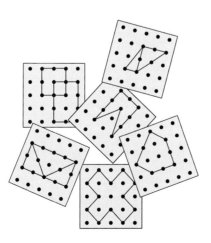

Besides pattern cards with and without dots, have children copy <u>real</u> shapes—tables, houses, letters of the alphabet, etc.

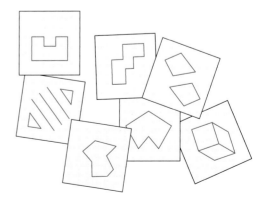

FIGURE 20.9   Shapes on geoboards.

ACTIVITY 20.4

Congruent Parts

Copy a shape from a card, and have students subdivide or cut it into smaller shapes on their geoboards. Specify the number of smaller shapes. Also specify whether they are all to be congruent or simply of the same type as shown in Figure 20.10. Depending on the shapes involved, this activity can be made quite easy or relatively challenging.

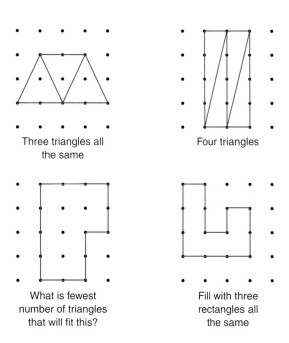

Three triangles all the same

Four triangles

What is fewest number of triangles that will fit this?

Fill with three rectangles all the same

Start with a shape, and cut it into smaller shapes.
Add special conditions to make the activity challenging.

FIGURE 20.10 **Subdividing shapes.**

Have lots of geoboards available in the classroom. It is better for two or three children to have 10 or 12 boards at a station than for each to have only one. That way, a variety of shapes can be made and compared before they are changed.

Teach students from the very beginning to copy their geoboard designs. Paper copies permit students to create complete sets of drawings that fulfill a particular task. Drawings can be placed on the bulletin board for classification and discussion, made into booklets illustrating a new idea that is being discussed, and sent home to show parents what is happening in geometry.

Younger students can use paper with a single large geoboard on each sheet. Later, a paper board about 10 cm square is adequate. Older children can use centimeter dot grids. All are found in the Blackline Masters.

To help children in the very early grades copy geoboard designs, suggest that they first mark the dots for the corners of their shape ("second row, end peg"). With the corners identified, it is much easier for them to draw lines to make the shape.

 ## Technology Note

The *e-Standards* provides a very good electronic geoboard. Although found in the K–2 section and entitled "Investigating the Concept of a Triangle," this is actually a great geoboard applet for any grade. It allows you to select and delete bands, and select and delete vertices. The *Geoboard* applet from the National Library of Virtual Manipulatives (http://matti.usu.edu/nlvm/nav/vlibrary.html) is essentially the same but with instant calculation of perimeter and area with the click of a button and without vertex removal (other than to move a vertex to coincide with another). *Mighty Math: Number Heroes* (Edmark, 1996) also has a powerful electronic geoboard in the *GeoComputer* component. Students can move an entire shape to any part of the geoboard without changes. The shapes can be colored and flipped over or rotated 90 degrees—moves that are not simple to accomplish on a physical board. ■

 STOP If you have never used a geoboard, play around with the electronic geoboard in the *e-Standards*. If you know about geoboards but have never used an e-geoboard, now would be a good time to try one.

Assorted dot and grid papers provide an alternative to geoboards. Virtually all of the activities suggested for tiles and geoboards can also be done on dot or grid paper. Changing the type of paper changes the activity and provides new opportunity for insight and discovery. The Blackline Masters have a variety of dot and grid paper.

Building three-dimensional shapes is a little more difficult compared with two-dimensional shapes. A variety of commercial materials permit fairly creative construction of geometric solids (for example, 3D Geoshapes, Polydron, and the Zome System). The 3D Geoshapes and Polydron are examples of materials consisting of plastic polygons that snap together to make three-dimensional models. The Zome System is a stick and connector set; skeletal models can be created with a great deal of variation. Zome is probably too difficult to use below the third grade. The following are three highly recommended homemade approaches to skeletal models.

● *Plastic coffee stirs with modeling clay.* Plastic stirs can be easily cut to different lengths. Use small chunks of clay (about 1 to 2 cm in diameter) to connect the corners.

This is a good model as long as the structures are not too elaborate.

- *Plastic drinking straws with flexible joints.* Cut the straws lengthwise with scissors from the top down to the flexible joint. These slit ends can then be inserted into the uncut bottom ends of other straws, making a strong but flexible joint. Three or more straws are joined in this fashion to form two-dimensional polygons. To make skeletal solids, use tape or wire twist ties to join polygons side to side.
- *Rolled newspaper rods.* Fantastic superlarge skeletons can be built using newspaper and masking tape. Roll three large sheets of newspaper on the diagonal to form a rod. The more tightly the paper is rolled, the less likely the rod is to bend. Secure the roll at the center with a bit of masking tape. The ends of the rods are thin and flexible for about 6 inches where there is less paper. Connect rods by bunching this thin part together and fastening with tape. Use masking tape freely, wrapping it several times around each joint. Additional rods can be joined after two or three are already taped (see Figure 20.11).

With these homemade models, students should compare the rigidity of a triangle with the lack of rigidity of polygons with more than three sides. Point out that triangles are used in many bridges, in the long booms of construction cranes, in gates, and in the structural parts of buildings. Discuss why this may be so. As children build large skeleton structures, they will find that they need to add diagonal members to form triangles. The more triangles, the less likely their structure will collapse.

The newspaper rod method is exciting because the structures quickly become large. Let students work in groups of four or five. They will soon discover what makes a structure rigid and ideas of balance and form. Primary-grade students can benefit from creating free-form structures. Older students can be challenged to make more well-defined shapes.

Tessellations

A *tessellation* is a tiling of the plane using one or more shapes in a repeated pattern with no holes or gaps. Making tessellations is an artistic way for level 0 students from first grade to eighth grade to explore patterns in shapes and to see how shapes combine to form other shapes. One-shape or two-shape tessellation activities can vary considerably in difficulty.

Some shapes are easier to tessellate than others (see Figure 20.12). When the shapes can be put together in more than one pattern, both the problem-solving level and the creativity increase. Literally hundreds of shapes can be used as tiles for tessellations.

Most children will benefit from using actual tiles to create patterns. Simple construction paper tiles can be cut quickly on a paper cutter. Other tiles can be traced onto construction paper and several thicknesses cut at once with scissors. Older children may be able to use dot or line grids and plan their tessellations with pencil and paper. To plan a tessellation, use only one color so that the focus is on the spatial relationships. To complete an artistic-looking tessellation, add a color design. Use only two colors with younger children and never more than four. Color designs are also repeated regularly all over the tessellation.

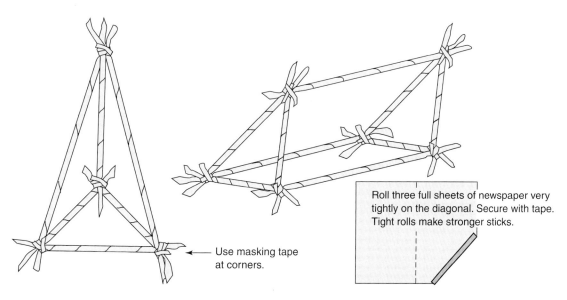

Use masking tape at corners.

Roll three full sheets of newspaper very tightly on the diagonal. Secure with tape. Tight rolls make stronger sticks.

FIGURE 20.11 **Large skeletal structures and special shapes can be built with tightly rolled newspaper. Young children can build free-form sculptures. Older children can be challenged to build shapes with specific properties. Overlap the ends about 6 inches to ensure strength.**

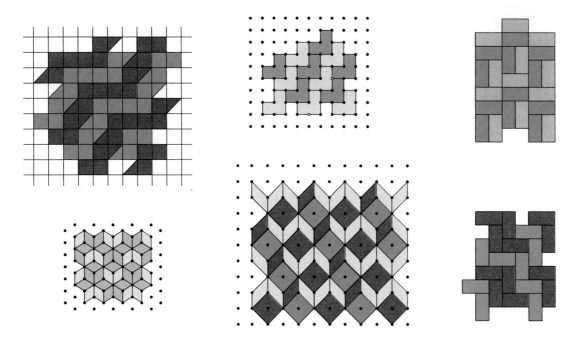

Tessellations can be drawn on grids or made of construction paper tiles. They are challenging and provide an opportunity for both artistic creativity and spatial reasoning.

FIGURE 20.12 **Tessellations.**

Tessellations can be made by gluing paper tiles to large sheets of paper, by drawing them on dot or line grids, or by tracing around a poster board tile. Work from the center out, leaving ragged edges to indicate that the pattern goes on and on.

 Look at the top-left tessellation in Figure 20.12. What single tile (a combination of squares and half squares) made this pattern?

sections of the grid. He then tells the other player where to put blocks on her grid to match his own. When all four pieces are positioned, the two grids are checked to see if they are alike. Then the players switch roles. Model the game once by taking the part of the first student. Use words such as *top row, middle, left,* and *right.* Students can play in pairs as a station activity.

Location

In kindergarten children learn about everyday positional descriptions—*over, under, near, far, between, left,* and *right.* These are the beginnings of the *Standards'* goal of specifying locations. Eventually, a need for a coordinate system will develop.

The activities at this level prepare students for coordinates and build on students' use of positional language.

ACTIVITY 20.5

Hidden Positions

For the game boards, draw an 8-inch square on tagboard. Subdivide the squares into a 3 × 3 grid. Two students sit with a "screen" separating their desktop space so that neither student can see the other's grid (see Figure 20.13.) Each student has four different pattern blocks. The first player places a block on four different

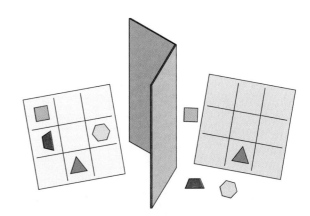

FIGURE 20.13 **The Hidden Position game. Players must communicate verbally the positions of their blocks on the grid.**

Students can begin to use a simple coordinate system as early as the first grade. Draw a coordinate grid on the board

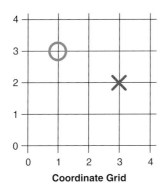

FIGURE 20.14 A simple coordinate grid. The X is at (3,2) and the O is at (1,3). Use the grid to play Three in a Row (like Tic-Tac-Toe). Put marks on intersections, not spaces.

FIGURE 20.15 Coloring in different paths on a grid. What is the fewest number of turns needed to get from A to B? The most?

or on the overhead projector like the one shown in Figure 20.14. Explain how to use two numbers to designate an intersection point on the grid. The first number tells how far to move to the right. The second number tells how far to move up. For younger children use the words along with the numbers: 3 right and 0 up. Be sure to include 0 in your introduction. Select a point on the grid and have students decide what two numbers name that point. If your point is at $(2,4)$ and students incorrectly say "four, two," then simply indicate where the point is that they named. Emphasize that when they say or write the two numbers, the first number is the number of steps to the right and the second is the number of steps up.

The next activity explores the notion of different paths on a grid.

ACTIVITY 20.6

Paths

On a sheet of 2-cm grid paper, mark two different points A and B as shown in Figure 20.15. Using the overhead or the chalkboard, demonstrate how to describe a path from A to B. For the points in the figure, one path is "up 5 and right 6." Another path might be "right 2, up 2, right 2, up 3, right 2." Count the length of each path. As long as you always move toward the target point (in this case either right or up), the path lengths will always be the same. Here they are 11 units long. Students draw three paths on their papers from A to B using different colored crayons. For each path they write directions that describe their paths. They should check the lengths of each path. Ask, "What is the greatest number of turns that you can make in your path?" "What is the smallest number?" "Where would A and B have to be in order to get there with no turns?"

If you add a coordinate system on the grid in "Paths," students can describe their paths with coordinates: For example: $(2,3) \longrightarrow (2,5) \longrightarrow (5,5) \longrightarrow (5,8) \longrightarrow (8,8)$.

 TECHNOLOGY NOTE

The NCTM *e-Standards* contains a nice applet (Applet 4.3) that is similar to the previous activity but offers some additional challenges. Students move a ladybug by issuing directions. The task is to make a list of directions to hide the ladybug beneath a leaf. When the directions are complete, the ladybug is set in motion to follow them. The ladybug is also used to draw shapes such as a rectangle in a tilted position or to travel through mazes. This applet is a very minimal version of the powerful computer programming language Logo.

Logo is technically a computer programming language. Versions developed in recent years such as *Turtle Math* (Clements & Meredith, 1994) make programming easy enough for third graders. Briefly, in Logo's graphics mode, a "turtle" (a small triangle or a picture of a turtle) can be made to go forward or backward any distance and to turn left or right any number of degrees. The turtle draws a line in its path. The string of commands **fd 50 rt 90 fd 30 rt 90** will cause the turtle to draw a long and a short segment at right angles to each other. The Command **rt 30 repeat 2[fd 60 rt 90 fd 30 rt 90]** will create a 60 × 30 rectangle tilted 30 degrees.

Logo brings a completely different perspective on geometric shapes and, thus, on geometric explorations and spatial development. Because students are required to draw shapes by issuing precise commands, Logo requires that a drawing be conceptualized in terms of its component parts—dimensions of sides, angle sizes, turn directions, and orientation in the plane. *Turtle Math* is used in the *Investigations in Number, Data, and Space* curriculum. (For a detailed discussion of Logo, see Clements & Battista, 2001.) ■

Transformations

Transformations are also called "rigid motions"—movements that do not change the size or shape of the object moved. Usually, three transformations are discussed: *translations* or slides, *reflections* or flips, and *rotations* or turns. Interestingly, the study of symmetry is also included under the study of transformations. Do you know why?

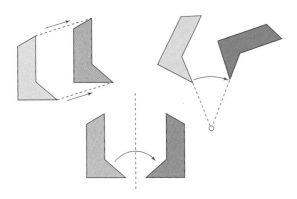

FIGURE 20.16 Translation (slide), reflection (flip), rotation (turn).

Slides, Flips, and Turns

At the beginning level, the terms *slide*, *flip*, and *turn* are adequate. The goal is to help students recognize and apply these transformations. You can use a nonsymmetric shape on the overhead to introduce these terms (see Figure 20.16).

In the following activity, rotations are restricted to $\frac{1}{4}$, $\frac{1}{2}$, and $\frac{3}{4}$ turns in a clockwise direction. The center of the turn will be the center of the figure. Reflections will be flips over vertical or horizontal lines. These restrictions are for simplicity. In the general case, the center of rotation can be anywhere on or off of the figure. Lines of reflection can also be anywhere.

ACTIVITY 20.7

Motion Man

Draw the Motion Man on an 9 × 9 square of 2-cm grid paper. On a second 9 × 9 square, draw the exact mirror image of Motion Man (see Figure 20.17). Make copies of the first Motion Man and then copy the mirror image on the backs of these copies. Experiment first. You want the back image to match the front image when held to the light. Cut off the excess paper to leave a square. Give each student a Motion Man.

Demonstrate each of the possible motions. A slide is simply that. The figure does not rotate or turn over. Demonstrate $\frac{1}{4}$, $\frac{1}{2}$, and $\frac{3}{4}$ turns. Emphasize that only clockwise turns will be used for this activity. Similarly, demonstrate a horizontal flip (top goes to bottom) and a vertical flip (left goes to right). Practice by having everyone start with his or her Motion Man in the same orientation. As you announce one of the moves, students slide, flip, or turn Motion Man accordingly.

Then display two Motion Men side by side in any orientation. The task is to decide what motion or combination of motions will get the man on the left to match the man on the right. Students use their own man to work out a solution. Test the solutions that students offer. If both men are in the same position, call that a slide. (If you allow for each of the two diagonal flips as well, the Motion Man can assume any new position in one move.)

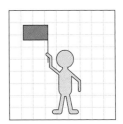

FIGURE 20.17 **The Motion Man is printed back to back. Use to show slides, flips, and turns. (See Blackline Masters.)**

If a shape can be folded on a line so that the two halves match, then it is said to have *line symmetry* (or mirror symmetry). Notice that the fold line is actually a line of reflection—the portion of the shape on one side of the line is reflected onto the other side. That is the connection between line symmetry and transformations.

To explain line symmetry to children, you can show examples and nonexamples. Another approach is to have students fold a sheet of paper in half and cut out a shape of their choosing. When they open the paper, the fold line will be a line of symmetry. A third way is to use mirrors. When you place a mirror on a picture or design so that the mirror is perpendicular to the table, you see a shape with symmetry when you look in the mirror.

Here is an activity with line symmetry.

ACTIVITY 20.8

Pattern Block Mirror Symmetry

Students need a plain sheet of paper with a straight line through the middle. Using about six to eight pattern blocks, students make a design completely on one side of the line that touches the line in some way. The task is to make the mirror image of their design on the other side of the line. When finished, they use a mirror to check their work. They place the mirror on the line and look into it from the side of the original design. With the mirror in place they should see exactly the same image as they see when they lift the mirror. You can also challenge them to make designs with more than one line of symmetry.

Building symmetrical designs with pattern blocks tends to be easier if the line is "pointing" at the student, that is, with a left and a right side. With the line oriented horizontally or diagonally, the task is harder.

The same task can be done with a geoboard. First, stretch a band down the center or from corner to corner. Make a design on one side of the line and its mirror image on the other. Check with a mirror. This can also be done on either isometric or rectangular dot grids as shown in Figure 20.18.

A shape has *rotational symmetry* if it can be rotated about a point and land in a position exactly matching the one in

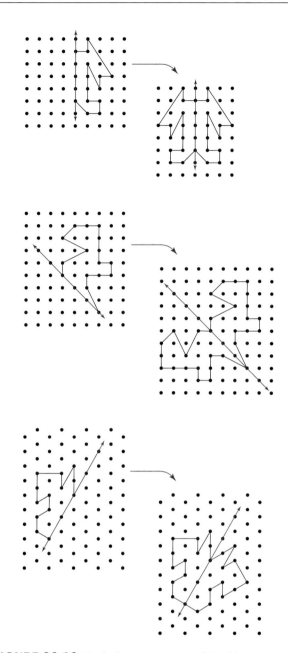

FIGURE 20.18 Exploring symmetry on dot grids.

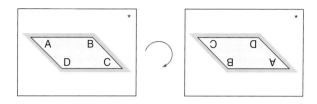

FIGURE 20.19 This parallelogram fits in its box two ways without flipping it over. Therefore, it has rotational symmetry of order 2.

which it began. A square has rotational symmetry as does an equilateral triangle.

A good way to understand rotational symmetry is to take a shape with rotational symmetry, such as a square, and trace around it on a piece of paper. Call this tracing the shape's "box." The order of rotational symmetry will be the number of ways that the shape can fit into its box without flipping it over. A square has rotational symmetry of *order* 4, whereas an equilateral triangle has rotational symmetry of *order* 3. The parallelogram in Figure 20.19 has rotational symmetry of order 2. Some books would call order 2 symmetry "180-degree symmetry." The degrees refer to the smallest angle of rotation required before the shape matches itself or fits into its box. A square has 90-degree rotational symmetry.

ACTIVITY 20.9

Pattern Block Rotational Symmetry

Have students construct designs with pattern blocks with different rotational symmetries. They should be able to make designs with order 2, 3, 4, 6, or 12 rotational symmetry. Which of the designs have mirror symmetry as well?

Visualization

Visualization activities involve seeing and understanding shapes from different perspectives.

Finding out how many different shapes can be made with a given number of simple tiles demands that students mentally flip and turn shapes in their minds and find ways to decide if they have found them all. That is the focus of the next activity.

ACTIVITY 20.10

Pentominoes

A pentomino is a shape formed by joining five squares as if cut from a square grid. Each square must have at least one side in common with another. Provide students with five square tiles and a sheet of square grid paper for recording. Challenge them to see how many different pentomino shapes they can find. Shapes that are flips or turns of other shapes are not considered different. Do not tell students how many pentomino shapes there are. Good discussions will come from deciding if some shapes are really different and if all shapes have been found.

Once students have decided that there are just 12 pentominoes (see Figure 20.20), the 12 pieces can then be used in a variety of activities. Paste the grids with the children's pentominoes onto tagboard, and let them cut out the 12 shapes. These can be used in the next two activities.

It is also fun to explore the number of shapes that can be made from six equilateral triangles or from four 45-degree right triangles (halves of squares). With the right triangles, sides that touch must be the same length. How many of each of these "ominoes" do you think there are?

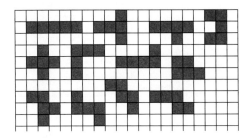

There are 12 pentominoes.

Finding all possible shapes made with five squares—or six squares (called "hexominoes") or six equilateral triangles and so on—is a good exercise in spatial problem solving.

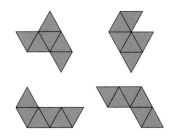

Four of the different shapes that six equilateral triangles will make.

Four of the different shapes that four "half-square" triangles will make.

FIGURE 20.20 Pentominoes and related shape challenges.

Lots of activities can be done with pentominoes. For example, try to fit all 12 pieces into a 6 × 10 or 5 × 12 rectangle. Also, each of the 12 shapes can be used as a tessellation tile. Another task is to examine each of the 12 pentominoes and decide which will fold up to make an open box. For those that are "box makers," which square is the bottom?

Another aspect of visualization for young children is to be able to think about solid shapes in terms of their faces or sides. For these activities you will need to make "face cards" by tracing around the different faces of a shape, making either all faces on one card or a set of separate cards with one face per card (see Figure 20.21).

ACTIVITY 20.11

Face Matching

There are two versions of the task: Given a face card, find the corresponding solid, or given a solid, find the face card. With a collection of single-face cards, students can select the cards that go with a particular block. For another variation, stack all of the single-face cards for one block face down. Turn them up one at a time as clues to finding the block.

The ability to discern shapes in the environment is part of the visualization agenda. A search for shapes can be modified to accommodate both level 0 and level 1 students at the same time by altering what is being searched for.

ACTIVITY 20.12

Shape Hunts

Have students search (inside and outside, or as a homework assignment) not just for triangles, circles, squares, and rectangles but also for properties of shapes. A shape hunt will be much more successful if you let students look for either one thing or for a specific list. Different groups can hunt for different things. For example:

- Parallel lines (lines "going in the same direction")
- Right angles ("square corners")
- Curved surfaces or curved lines
- Two or more shapes that make another shape
- Circles inside each other (concentric)
- Shapes with "dents" (concave) or without "dents" (convex)
- Solids that are like a box, a cylinder, a pyramid, a cone
- Five shapes that are alike in some way
- Shapes that have line or rotational symmetry

NCTM Standards The *Standards* contains lots of activity suggestions. A "quick image" activity is suggested for visualization at the K–2 level. A simple drawing like the one to the right is shown briefly on the overhead projector and students try to draw from memory what they saw (p. 101).

 ## Technology Note

Geometry is one area of the curriculum for which a variety of fascinating computer programs exist. Many programs allow students to "stamp" geometric shapes such as tangrams or pattern blocks onto the screen and then manipulate them. We have already discussed e-geoboards, e-tangrams, and the computer program Logo. Here are some more examples.

Shape Up (Sunburst, 1995) and *Shapes* (Clements & Sarama, 1995) are two good examples of computer versions of physical tiles. Both programs include a pattern block and tangram format in which students can stamp pieces onto a blank screen. Pieces are easily moved around, rotated, or flipped through either a vertical or horizontal line. In *Shapes*, two or more pieces can be "glued together" to create new shapes. The

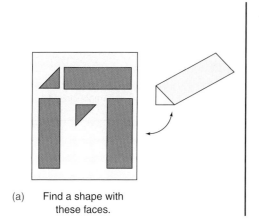

(a)   Find a shape with
these faces.

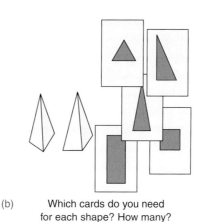

FIGURE 20.21 **Matching face
cards with solid shapes.**

(b)   Which cards do you need
for each shape? How many?

pattern blocks include a quarter circle that adds to the variability. Both programs allow shapes to be enlarged or reduced in size. Some puzzles are included with the packages, and new puzzles are easily created. *Shape Up* has a third mode in which six regular shapes can be manipulated and each can be cut into many smaller shapes and rearranged in endless ways.

It is not clear that any greater geometric benefit is gained with the virtual versions of these blocks. However, the environment and the variability are sufficiently different to warrant the use of this type of program along with physical models. Students who have difficulty with fine motor control are often unable to produce drawings or cut-and-paste recordings of their geometry activities. Since the computer permits students to print colorful copies of their work and include written journal entries, these students take real pride in the products they produce. ■

Activities for Level 1

A significant difference between level 1 and level 0 is the object of students' thought. While students will continue to use models and drawings of shapes, they begin to see these as representatives of classes of shapes. Their understanding of the properties of shapes—such as symmetry, perpendicular and parallel lines, and so on—continues to be refined.

Shapes and Properties

For the sake of clarity, the important definitions of two- and three-dimensional shapes are provided here. You will notice that shape definitions include relationships between and among shapes.

Special Categories of Two-Dimensional Shapes

Table 20.1 lists some important categories of two-dimensional shapes. Examples of these shapes can be found in Figure 20.22.

TABLE 20.1

Categories of Two-Dimensional Shapes

Shape	Description
Simple Closed Curves	
Concave, convex	An intuitive definition of *concave* might be "having a dent in it." If a simple closed curve is not concave, it is *convex*. A more precise definition of *concave* may be interesting to explore with older students.
Symmetrical, nonsymmetrical	Shapes may have one or more lines of symmetry and may or may not have rotational symmetry. These concepts will require more detailed investigation.
Polygons Concave, convex Symmetrical, nonsymmetrical	Simple closed curves with all straight sides.
Regular	All sides and all angles are congruent.
Triangles	
Triangles	Polygons with exactly three sides.
Classified by sides	
Equilateral	All sides are congruent.
Isosceles	At least two sides are congruent.
Scalene	No two sides are congruent.
Classified by angles	
Right	Has a right angle.
Acute	All angles are smaller than a right angle.
Obtuse	One angle is larger than a right angle.
Convex Quadrilaterals	
Convex quadrilaterals	Convex polygons with exactly four sides.
Kite	Two opposing pairs of congruent adjacent sides.
Trapezoid	At least one pair of parallel sides.
Isosceles trapezoid	A pair of opposite sides is congruent.
Parallelogram	Two pairs of parallel sides.
Rectangle	Parallelogram with a right angle.
Rhombus	Parallelogram with all sides congruent.
Square	Parallelogram with a right angle and all sides congruent.

FIGURE 20.22 Classification of two-dimensional shapes.

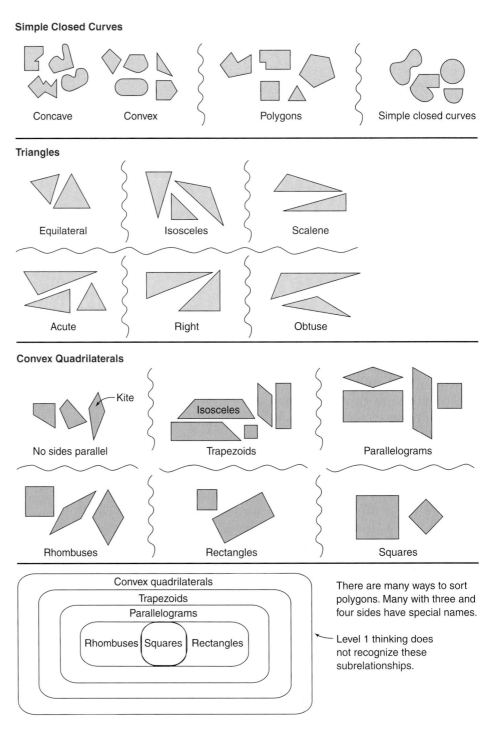

In the classification of quadrilaterals and parallelograms, the subsets are not all disjoint. For example, a square is a rectangle and a rhombus. All parallelograms are trapezoids, but not all trapezoids are parallelograms.* Children at level 1 have difficulty seeing this type of subrelationship. They may quite correctly list all the properties of a square, a rhombus, and a rectangle and still identify a square as a "nonrhombus" or a "nonrectangle." Is it wrong for students to refer to subgroups as disjoint sets? By fourth or fifth grade, it is only wrong to encourage such thinking. Burger (1985) points out that upper

---

*Some definitions of trapezoid specify *only one* pair of parallel sides, in which case parallelograms would not be trapezoids. The University of Chicago School Mathematics Project (UCSMP) uses the "at least one pair" definition, meaning that parallelograms and rectangles are trapezoids.

TABLE 20.2

Categories of Three-Dimensional Shapes

Shape	Description	Shape	Description
Sorted by Edges and Vertices		**Cylinders**	
Spheres and "egglike" shapes	Shapes with no *edges* and no *vertices* (corners). Shapes with *edges* but no *vertices* (e.g., a flying saucer). Shapes with *vertices* but no *edges* (e.g., a football).	Cylinder	Two congruent, parallel faces called *bases*. Lines joining corresponding points on the two bases are always parallel. These parallel lines are called *elements* of the cylinder.
Sorted by Faces and Surfaces		Right cylinder	A cylinder with elements perpendicular to the bases. A cylinder that is not a right cylinder is an *oblique cylinder*.
Polyhedron	Shapes made of all faces (a *face* is a flat surface of a solid). If all surfaces are faces, all the edges will be straight lines. Some combination of faces and rounded surfaces (cylinders are examples, but this is not a definition of a cylinder). Shapes with all curved surfaces. Shapes with and without edges and with and without vertices. Faces can be parallel. Parallel faces lie in planes that never intersect.	Prism	A cylinder with polygons for bases. All prisms are special cases of cylinders.
		Rectangular prism	A cylinder with rectangles for bases.
		Cube	A square prism with square sides.
		Cones	
		Cone	A solid with exactly one face and a vertex that is not on the face. Straight lines (elements) can be drawn from any point on the edge of the base to the vertex. The base may be any shape at all. The vertex need not be directly over the base.
		Circular cone	Cone with a circular base.
		Pyramid	Cone with a polygon for a base. All faces joining the vertex are triangles. Pyramids are named by the shape of the base: *triangular* pyramid, *square* pyramid, *octagonal* pyramid, and so on. All pyramids are special cases of cones.

elementary students correctly use such classification schemes in other contexts. For example, individual students in a class can belong to more than one club. A square is an example of a quadrilateral that belongs to two other clubs.

Special Categories of Three-Dimensional Shapes

Important and interesting shapes and relationships also exist in three dimensions. Table 20.2 describes classifications of solids. Figure 20.23 shows examples of cylinders and prisms.

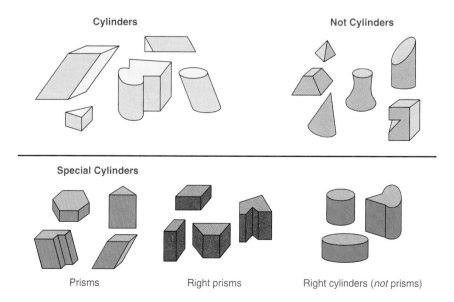

FIGURE 20.23 Cylinders and prisms.

Cylinders have two parallel faces, and parallel lines join corresponding points on these faces. If the parallel faces are polygons, the cylinder can be called a prism.

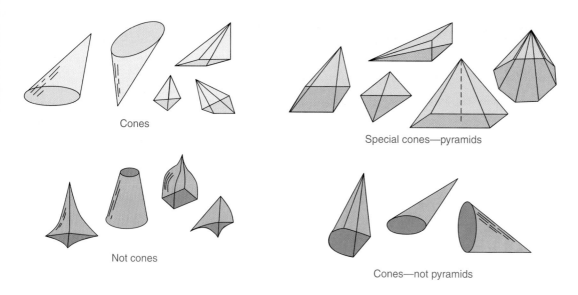

Cones

Special cones—pyramids

Not cones

Cones—not pyramids

Cones and cones with a polygon base (pyramids) all have straight-line elements joining every point of the base with the vertex. (Yes, a pyramid is just a special type of cone.)

FIGURE 20.24 Cones and pyramids.

Note that prisms are defined here as a special category of cylinder—a cylinder with a polygon for a base. Figure 20.24 shows a similar grouping of cones and pyramids.

⊗ STOP Explain the following: Prisms are to cylinders as pyramids are to cones. How is this relationship helpful in learning volume formulas?

Many textbooks define cylinders strictly as circular cylinders. These books do not have special names for other cylinders. Under that definition, the prism is not a special case of a cylinder. This points to the fact that definitions are conventions, and not all conventions are universally agreed upon. If you return to the volume formulas in Chapter 19, you will see that the more inclusive definition of cylinders and cones given here allows one formula for any type of cylinder—hence, prisms—with a similar statement that is true for cones and pyramids.

Sorting and Classifying Activities

The next activity provides a good method when you want to introduce a category of shapes.

ACTIVITY 20.13

Mystery Definition

Use the overhead or chalkboard to conduct activities such as the example in Figure 20.25. For your first collection be certain that you have allowed for all possible variables. In Figure 20.25, for example, a square is included in the set of rhombi. Similarly, choose nonexamples to be as close to the positive examples as is

necessary to help with an accurate definition. The third or mixed set should also include those nonexamples with which students are most likely to be confused.

Rather than confirm the choice of shapes in the third set, students should write an explanation for their choice.

All of these have something in common.

None of these has it.

Which of these have it?

The name of a property is not necessary for it to be understood. It requires more careful observation of properties to discover what shapes have in common.

FIGURE 20.25 All of these, none of these: a mystery definition.

The value of the "Mystery Definition" approach is that students develop ideas and definitions based on their own concept development. After their definitions have been discussed and compared, you can offer the usual "book" definition for the sake of clarity.

For defining types or categories of triangles, the next activity is especially good and uses a different approach.

ACTIVITY 20.14

Triangle Sort

Make copies of the Assorted Triangles sheet found in the Blackline Masters. Note the examples of right, acute, and obtuse triangles; examples of equilateral, isosceles, and scalene triangles; and triangles that represent every possible combination of these categories. Have students cut them out. The task is to sort the entire collection into three groups so that no triangle belongs to two groups. When this is done and descriptions of the groupings have been written, students should then find a second criterion for creating three different groupings. Students may need a hint to look only at angle sizes or only at the issue of congruent sides, but hold these hints if you can.

"Triangle Sort" results in definitions of the six different types of triangles without having to list these definitions on the board and have students memorize them. As a follow-up activity, make a chart such as the one shown here. Challenge students to sketch a triangle in each of the nine cells.

 Of the nine cells in the chart, two of them are impossible to **STOP** fill. Can you tell which ones and why?

Quadrilaterals (polygons with four sides) are an especially rich source of investigations. For the following activity, students should be familiar with the concepts of right, obtuse, and acute angles, congruence of line segments, and symmetry (line and rotational).

ACTIVITY 20.15

Property Lists for Quadrilaterals

Prepare worksheets for parallelograms, rhombi, rectangles, and squares. (See the Blackline Masters.) On each sheet are three or four examples of that category of shape. Examples are illustrated in Figure 20.26.

Assign students working in groups of three or four to one type of quadrilateral. Their task is to list as many properties as they can. Each property listed must be applicable to all of the shapes on their sheet. They will need a simple index card to check right angles, to compare side lengths, and to draw straight lines. Mirrors (to check line symmetry) and tracing paper (for angle congruence and rotational symmetry) are also useful tools. Encourage students to use the words "at least" when describing how many of something: for example, "rectangles have at least two lines of symmetry," since squares—included in the rectangles—have four.

Have students prepare their property lists under these headings: Sides, Angles, Diagonals, and Symmetries. Groups then share their lists with the class and eventually a class list for each shape will be developed.

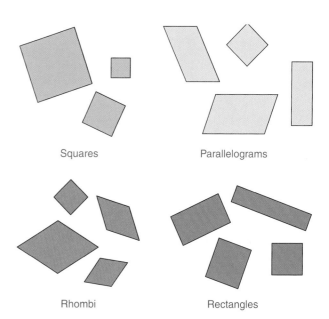

FIGURE 20.26 Shapes for "Property Lists for Quadrilaterals" worksheets can be found in the Blackline Masters.

This last activity may take two or three periods. Share lists beginning with parallelograms, then rhombi, then rectangles, and finally squares. Have one group present its list. Then others who worked on the same shape should add to or subtract from it. The class must agree with everything that is put on the list. As new relationships come up in this presentation-and-discussion period, you can introduce proper terminology. For example, if two diagonals intersect in a square corner, then they are *perpendicular.* Other terms such as *parallel, congruent, bisect, midpoint,* and so on can be clarified as you help students write their descriptions. This is also a good time to introduce symbols such as ≅ for "congruent" or || for "parallel."

As an extension, repeat Activity 20.15 using kites and trapezoids. "Property Lists for Quadrilaterals" has some important follow-ups that are described in the section on level 2 activities (see p. 376). Furthermore, similar activities can be used to introduce three-dimensional shape definitions.

Construction Activities

Students building or drawing shapes continues to be important at level 1. Dynamic geometry software (*Geometer's Sketchpad, The Geometry Inventor,* and *Cabri*) dramatically enhances the exploration of shapes at this level.

In the "Property Lists" activity (Activity 20.15), students examine the diagonals of various classes of quadrilaterals. If that activity has not been done already, the following exploration is very interesting. Rather than beginning with the shapes, it begins with the diagonals.

ACTIVITY 20.16

Diagonal Strips

For this activity, students need three strips of tagboard about 2 cm wide. Two should be the same length (about 30 cm) and the third somewhat shorter (about 20 cm). Punch nine holes equally spaced along the strip. (Punch a hole near each end. Divide the distance between the holes by 8. This will be the distance between the remaining holes.) Use a brass fastener to join two strips. A quadrilateral is formed by joining the four end holes as shown in Figure 20.27. Provide students with the list of possible relationships for angles, lengths, and ratios of parts. Their task is to use the strips to determine the properties of diagonals that will produce different quadrilaterals. The strips are there to help in the exploration. Students may want to make drawings on dot grids to test the various hypotheses.

Every type of quadrilateral can be uniquely described in terms of its diagonals using only the conditions of length, ratio of parts, and whether or not they are perpendicular. Some students will work with the diagonal relationships to see what shapes can be made. Others will begin with examples of the shapes and observe the diagonal relationships. A dynamic geometry program such as *The Geometer's Sketchpad* is an excellent vehicle for this investigation.

Similar Figures and Proportional Reasoning

In Chapter 18 on proportional reasoning, we saw a good first definition of similar figures as shapes that "look alike but are different sizes" (see Activity 18.1, p. 301). More precisely, two figures are *similar* if all of their corresponding angles are congruent and the corresponding sides are proportional. Other proportional reasoning activities are also good connections to geometry. Activities 18.7, 18.8, and 18.9 involve scale drawings and proportional relationships in three-dimensional figures that are similar.

A *dilation* is a nonrigid transformation that produces similar figures. Figure 20.28 shows how a given figure can be *dilated* to make larger or smaller figures. If different groups of students dilate the same figure using the same scale factor, they will find that the resulting figures are all congruent, even with each group using different dilation points. Dynamic geometry software makes the results of this exercise quite dramatic. The software allows for the scale factors to be set at any value. Once a dilation is made, the dilation point can be dragged around the screen and the size and shape of the image clearly stay unchanged. Scale factors less than 1 produce smaller figures.

Circles

Many interesting relationships can be observed between measures of different parts of the circle. Among the most astounding and important is the ratio between measures of the circumference and the diameter.

FIGURE 20.27   **Diagonals of quadrilaterals.**

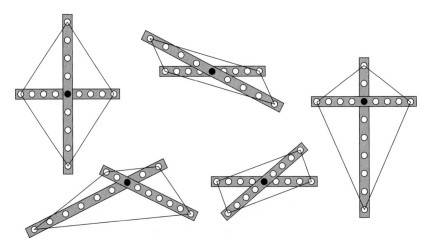

Quadrilaterals can be determined by their diagonals. Consider the length of each, where they cross, and the angles between them. What conditions will produce parallelograms? Rectangles? Rhombi? Challenge: What properties will produce a nonisosceles trapezoid?

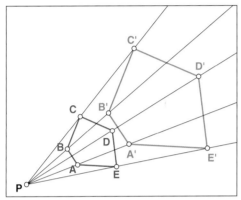

FIGURE 20.28 Begin with figure ABCDE and place point P anywhere at all. Draw lines from P through each vertex. Place point A' twice as far from P as A is from P (scale factor of 2). Do similarly for the other points. In this drawing, ABCDE is the same in both figures and the images are congruent.

 True or False: All circles are similar. Explain.
STOP

ACTIVITY 20.17

Discovering Pi

Have groups of students carefully measure the circumference and diameter of many different circles. Each group measures different circles.

Measure both the circumference and diameter of circular items such as jar lids, tubes, cans, and wastebaskets. To measure circumference, wrap string once around the object and then measure that length of string.

Also measure large circles marked on gym floors and playgrounds. Use a trundle wheel or rope to measure the circumference.

Collect measures of circumference and diameter from all groups and enter them in a table. Ratios of the circumference to the diameter should also be computed for each circle. A scatter plot of the data should be made with the horizontal axis representing

diameters and the vertical axis circumferences. If the data are entered on a spreadsheet or in a graphing calculator, the scatter plot can be generated easily and all ratios computed at once.

Most ratios should be in the neighborhood of 3.1 or 3.2. The scatter plot should approximate a straight line through the origin. The slope of the line should also be close to 3.1. (Recall from Chapter 18 that graphs of equivalent ratios are always straight lines through the origin.) The exact ratio is an irrational number, about 3.14159, represented by the Greek letter π (pi).

What is most important in Activity 20.17 is that students develop a clear understanding of π as the ratio of circumference to diameter in any circle. The quantity π is not some strange number that appears in math formulas; it is a naturally occurring and universal ratio.

 ## Technology Note

As students begin to do more than build with geometric "blocks" (tangrams, pattern blocks, grid drawing, etc.), the computer begins to offer powerful tools for explorations.

Dynamic Geometry Software

In a dynamic geometry program, points, lines, and geometric figures are easily constructed on the computer using only the mouse. Once drawn, the geometric objects can be moved about and manipulated in endless variety. Distances, lengths, areas, angles, slopes, and perimeters can be measured. As the figures are changed, the measurements update instantly.

Lines can be drawn perpendicular or parallel to other lines or segments. Angles and segments can be drawn congruent to other angles and segments. A point can be placed at the midpoint of a segment. A figure can be produced that is a reflection, rotation, or dilation of another figure. The most significant thing is that when a geometric object is created with a particular relationship to another, that relationship is maintained no matter how either object is moved or changed.

Three of the best known dynamic geometry programs are *The Geometer's Sketchpad* (Key Curriculum Press), *Geometry Inventor* (Riverdeep), and *Cabri Geometry II* (Chartwell-Yorke). Although each operates somewhat differently, they are sufficiently alike that separate descriptions are not required here. Originally designed for high school students, all can be used profitably and should be used starting about grade 4.

Dynamic Geometry Examples

To appreciate the potential (and the fun) of dynamic geometry software, you really need to experience it on a computer. In the meantime, an example is offered here in an attempt to illustrate how these programs work.

FIGURE 20.29   A *Sketchpad* construction illustrating an interesting property of quadrilaterals.

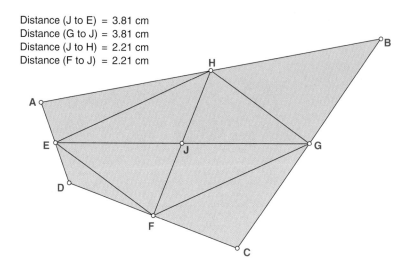

Distance (J to E) = 3.81 cm
Distance (G to J) = 3.81 cm
Distance (J to H) = 2.21 cm
Distance (F to J) = 2.21 cm

In Figure 20.29, the midpoints of a freely drawn quadrilateral ABCD have been joined. The diagonals of the resulting quadrilateral (EFGH) are also drawn and measured. No matter how the points A, B, C, and D are dragged around the screen, even inverting the quadrilateral, the other lines will maintain the same relationships (joining midpoints and diagonals), and the measurements will be instantly updated on the screen.

Remember that at level 1, the objects of thought are *classes* of shapes. In a dynamic geometry program, if a quadrilateral is drawn, only one shape is observed, as would be the case on paper or on a geoboard. But now that quadrilateral can be stretched and altered in endless ways. Students actually explore not one shape but an enormous number of examples from that class of shapes. If a property does not change when the figure changes, the property is attributable to the *class* of shapes rather than any particular shape.

As another example, suppose you draw a triangle with a segment joining the midpoints of two sides (called a *midsegment*). Measures of various lengths, angles, and areas are placed on the screen. Now you drag vertices and sides to change the specific shape of the triangle. All of the measures of the triangle are updated instantly as the figure is changed. Regardless of the angles in the triangle, certain pairs of angles always seem to be the same. The length of the midsegment is exactly half of the third side. It seems always to be parallel to it as well. You are experiencing a property of midsegments of *all* triangles, not just a few.

The symmetry investigations (both line symmetry and rotational symmetry), "Diagonal Strips" (Activity 20.16, p. 368), investigations of similarity, and "Discovering Pi" (Activity 20.17, p. 369) can all be explored profitably with dynamic geometry programs. In Chapter 19, the program was used to help develop the relationship between the areas of parallelograms and triangles. (See Figure 19.23, p. 338.) The publishers of these programs provide excellent activities that are appropriate for level 1 investigations. Many activities are included with the software, and others are found in supplementary publications. ∎

Location

At level 1, shapes and properties should be investigated on a full coordinate grid. Even fourth- and fifth-grade students can use negative integers so that all four quadrants of the plane can be represented. The activities here suggest how coordinates can be used to examine transformations.

ACTIVITY 20.18

Coordinate Reflections

Have students draw a five-sided shape in the first quadrant on coordinate grid paper using grid points for vertices. Label the Figure ABCDE and call it Figure 1. Use the *y*-axis as a line of symmetry and draw the reflection of the shape in the second quadrant. Call it Figure 2 (for second quadrant) and label the reflected points A'B'C'D'E'. Now use the *x*-axis as the line of symmetry. Reflect both Figure 2 and Figure 1 into the third and fourth quadrants, respectively, and call these Figures 3 and 4. Label the points of these figures with double and triple primes (A" and A‴, and so on). Write in the coordinates for each vertex of all four figures.

■ How is Figure 3 related to Figure 4? How else could you have gotten Figure 3? How else could you have found Figure 4?

■ How are the coordinates of Figure 1 related to its image in the *y*-axis, Figure 2? What can you say about the coordinates of Figure 4?

■ Make a conjecture about the coordinates of a shape reflected in the *y*-axis and a different conjecture about the coordinates of a shape reflected in the *x*-axis.

■ Draw lines from the vertices of Figure 1 to the corresponding vertices of Figure 2. What can you say about these lines? How is the *y*-axis related to each of these lines?

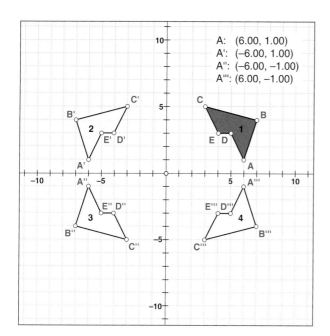

FIGURE 20.30 Figure 1 (ABCDE) is reflected across the
y-axis. Then both Figures 1 and 2 are reflected across the x-axis.

 STOP Use Figure 20.30 or a drawing of your own to answer the
questions in the last activity.

Rotations can be explored in a similar manner to Activity 20.18. Have students begin with a figure in the first quadrant, rotate it a quarter turn clockwise and a quarter turn counterclockwise into the second and fourth quadrants, using the origin as the center of rotation. Then have students rotate the original figure a half turn into the third quadrant. Similar questions can be asked about the coordinates. An interesting result can be seen in the figure in the third quadrant.

 STOP There is a relationship between a 180-degree turn and reflections through two perpendicular lines. Can you tell what that is?

In the activities just discussed, students perform a transformation on a figure and observe how the transformation affects the coordinates. In the next two activities, the coordinates will be changed and students observe the resulting change on the figure. Get a coordinate grid and follow along with the next activity.

--- **ACTIVITY 20.19** ---

Coordinate Translations

Students begin with a five-sided shape in the first quadrant. Make a list of the coordinates. Next, students make a new set of coordinates by adding 3 to all of the x-coordinates of the initial figure and then they draw this figure. They then create a third figure by subtracting 4 from each of the y-coordinates of the original figure. What happens? What will happen if you do both:

add 3 to the x-coordinates and subtract 4 from the y-coordinates? Try it. Students now have the original and three image figures on their paper. Now have them draw lines from the vertices of the original figure to the corresponding vertices of the last figure (the one in which both coordinates were changed). What do you notice about these lines? (They are parallel and the same length.) In general, what does adding or subtracting a fixed value to all coordinates do to a figure?

Students who have done the two preceding activities and the variation for rotational symmetry should have a general way to describe translations, reflections across an axis, and 90-degree rotations about the origin all in terms of coordinates. In the following activity, multiplying a constant times the coordinates makes a different type of change.

--- **ACTIVITY 20.20** ---

Coordinate Dilations

Students begin with a four-sided shape in the first quadrant. They then make a list of the coordinates, and make a new set of coordinates by multiplying each of the original coordinates by 2. They plot the resulting shape. What is the result? Now have students multiply each of the original coordinates by $\frac{1}{2}$ and plot that shape. What is the result? Next, students draw a line from the origin to a vertex of the largest shape on their paper. Repeat for one or two additional vertices and ask for observations. (An example is shown in Figure 20.31.)

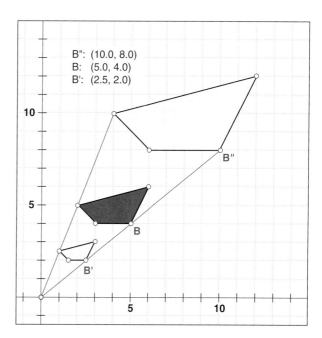

FIGURE 20.31 Dilations with coordinates. Coordinates of the center figure were multiplied by 2 and also by 0.5 to create the other two figures.

STOP How do the lengths of sides and the areas of the shapes compare when the coordinates are multiplied by 2? What if they are multiplied by 3 or by $\frac{1}{2}$?

It is impressive to see how an arithmetic operation can control a figure. Imagine being able to control slides, flips, turns, and dilations, not just in the plane but also for three-dimensional figures. The process is identical to and is the essence of computer animation techniques.

Transformations

Progression in transformation activities from van Hiele level 0 to level 1 is primarily a matter of increased sophistication. Students are still looking at particular transformations and describing them.

Symmetries

We have already seen how symmetries can be attributed to classes of shapes in the earlier "Property List" activity (Activity 20.15). The activities in this section are suggested for students at level 1 but do not necessarily require the attributes of level 1 thought.

The next activities connect line and rotational symmetry to the corresponding ideas in three dimensions.

A plane of symmetry in three dimensions is analogous to a line of symmetry in two dimensions. Figure 20.32 illustrates a shape built with cubes that has a plane of symmetry.

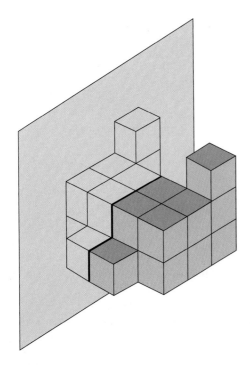

FIGURE 20.32 **A block building with one plane of symmetry.**

ACTIVITY 20.21

Plane Symmetry Buildings

With cubes, build a building that has a plane of symmetry. If the plane of symmetry goes between cubes, slice the shape by separating the building into two symmetrical parts. Try making buildings with two or three planes of symmetry. Build various prisms. Do not forget that a plane can slice diagonally through the blocks.

Rotational symmetry in the plane (also referred to as *point symmetry*) has an analogous counterpart in three dimensions. Whereas a figure in a plane is rotated about a point, a three-dimensional figure is rotated about a line. This line is called an *axis of symmetry*. As a solid with rotational symmetry revolves around an axis of symmetry, it will occupy the same position in space (its "box"), but in different orientations. A solid can have more than one axis of rotation. For each axis of symmetry, there is a corresponding order of rotational symmetry. A regular square pyramid has only one axis of symmetry that runs through the tip of the pyramid and the center of the square. A cube, by contrast, has a total of 13 axes of symmetry: three (through opposite faces) of order 4, four (through diagonally opposite vertices) of order 3, and six (through midpoints of diagonally opposite edges) of order 2.

ACTIVITY 20.22

Find the Spin Lines

Give students a solid shape that has one or more axes of rotational symmetry. Color or label each face of the solid to help keep track. The task is to find all axes of rotational symmetry (spin lines) and determine the order of rotational symmetry for each. Suggest that students use one finger of each hand to hold the solid at the two points where the axis of symmetry emerges. A partner can then slowly turn the solid, and both can decide when the solid is again "in its box"—that is, in the same space it was in originally (see Figure 20.33).

Composition of Transformations

One transformation can be followed by another. For example, a figure can be reflected over a line, and then that figure can be rotated about a point. A combination of two or more transformations is called a *composition*.

Have students experiment with compositions of two or even three transformations using a simple shape on a rectangular dot grid. For example, have students draw an L-shape on a dot grid and label it L_1. (Refer to Figure 20.34.) Reflect it through a line, and then rotate the image $\frac{1}{4}$ turn clockwise about a point not on the shape. Call this image L_2, the image of a composition of a reflection followed by a rotation. Notice that if L_1 is rotated $\frac{1}{4}$ turn clockwise about the same point used before to L_3 there is a relationship between L_1 and L_3. Continue to ex-

FIGURE 20.33 **Rotations of a cube.**

With A on top, the cube fits in its "box" four ways. Through this axis, the order of rotational symmetry is order 4.

These two axes also have rotational symmetry of order 4.

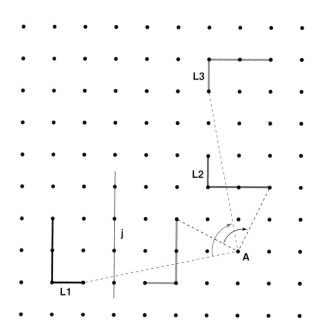

Edge-to-edge axes each have symmetry of order 2. How many are there?

If the axis is corner to opposite corner, what is the order of symmetry? How many of these axes are there?

plore different combinations of transformations. Don't forget to include translations (slides) in the compositions. Compositions do not have to involve different types of transformations. For example, a reflection can be followed by another reflection. When your students understand compositions of transformations on a grid, challenge them with the next task.

FIGURE 20.34 **Shape L₁ was reflected across line j and rotated $\frac{1}{4}$ turn about point A resulting in L₂. L₁ was also rotated $\frac{1}{4}$ turn about point A. How are L₂ and L₃ related? Will this always work?**

ACTIVITY 20.23

Mystery Transformations

Draw a small L-shaped figure near one corner of a rectangular dot grid. On this page, students draw a congruent L-shape somewhere near the center of the page. The second L can be flipped or turned in any orientation they wish. Then students trade papers with a partner. The task is to find some combination of slides, flips, and $\frac{1}{4}$ or $\frac{1}{2}$ turns that will take the shape in the corner onto the shape drawn by the students.

This is a challenging activity. To help students, ask if the L has been flipped over or not. If it is flipped over, then there will have to be one or three reflections. Regardless of how the two shapes are oriented, it can always be done in three or fewer transformations.

NCTM Standards

In NCTM's *e-Standards*, "Understanding Congruence, Similarity, and Symmetry" (Applet 6.4) is one of the best examples of a simple yet valuable interactive applet. In the first part of the applet, students develop an understanding of all three rigid motions. In the second part, a transformation is complete and the student uses a guess-and-check procedure to determine what exact transformation was done. In the last two parts, students can explore compositions of reflections and then other compositions up to three transformations. This applet is strongly recommended.

Tessellations Revisited

Either by using transformations or by combining compatible polygons, students at level 1 can create tessellations that are artistic and quite complex.

The Dutch artist M. C. Escher is well known for his tessellations, where the tiles are very intricate and often take the shape of things like birds, horses, angels, or lizards. Escher took a simple shape such as a triangle, parallelogram, or hexagon and performed transformations on the sides. For example, a curve drawn along one side might be translated (slid) to the opposite side. Another idea was to draw a curve from the midpoint of a side to the adjoining vertex. This curve was then rotated about the midpoint to form a totally new side of the tile. These two ideas are illustrated in part (a) of Figure 20.35. Dot paper is used to help draw the lines. *Escher-type tessellations,* as these have come to be called, are quite popular projects for students in grades 5 and up. Once a tile has been designed, it can be cut from two different colors of construction paper instead of drawing the tessellation on a dot grid.

A *regular tessellation* is made of a single tile that is a regular polygon (all sides and angles congruent). Each vertex of a regular tessellation has the same number of tiles meeting at that point. A checkerboard is a simple example of a regular tessellation. A *semiregular tessellation* is made of two or more tiles, each of which is a regular polygon. At each vertex of a semiregular tessellation, the same collection of regular polygons come together in the same order. A vertex (and therefore the complete semiregular tessellation) can be described by the series of shapes meeting at a vertex. Under each example of these tessellations in part (b) of Figure 20.35, the vertex numbers are given. Students can figure out what polygons are possible at a vertex and design their own semiregular tessellations.

Tessellations like these are very popular with teachers in grades 3 and above. A number of excellent resource books can be found in catalogs such as ETA Cuisenaire.

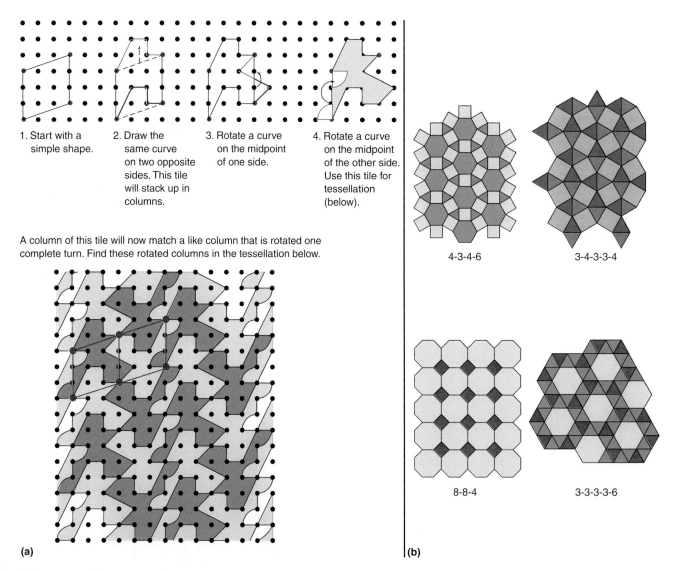

(a)
(b)

FIGURE 20.35 (a) One of many ways to create an Escher-type tessellation. (b) Examples of semiregular tessellations.

Technology Note

Several computer programs make it easy to create Escher-type tessellations. One example is *TesselMania!* (The Learning Company). Although exciting to use, these programs should be used with care. It is so easy to create intricate results with almost no understanding of the transformations being used. Planning on paper before using the computer is strongly recommended. Then the computer can be used to do the tedious work of creating a finished product complete with color and embellishments. ∎

Visualization

One of the main goals of the visualization strand of the Geometry Standard is to be able to identify and draw two-dimensional images of three-dimensional figures and to build three-dimensional figures from two-dimensional images. Activities aimed at this goal often involve drawings of small "buildings" made of one-inch cubes.

ACTIVITY 20.24

Viewpoints

a. In the first version, students begin with a building and draw the left, right, front, and back direct views. In Figure 20.36, the building plan shows a top view of the building and the number of blocks in each position. After students build a building from a plan like this, their task is to draw the front, right, left, and back direct views as shown in the figure.

b. In the reverse version of the task, students are given a right and front view. The task is to build

---

the building that has those views. To record their solution, they draw a building plan (top view with numbers).

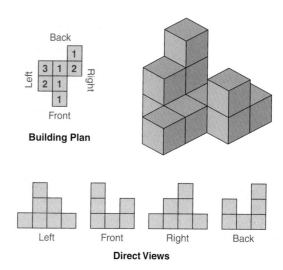

FIGURE 20.36 **Tasks can begin with the Building Plan, or with the Direct View, or even with the building. Students give the other representations.**

Notice that front and back direct views are symmetric, as are the left and right views. That is why only one of each is given in part b of the activity.

Another interesting connection between two and three dimensions is found in slicing solids in different ways. When a solid is sliced into two parts, a two-dimensional figure is formed on the slice faces. Figure 20.37 shows a cube being sliced off

FIGURE 20.37 **Predict the slice face before you cut a clay model with a piano wire.**

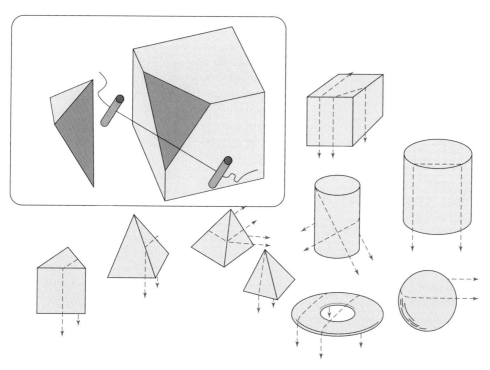

at the corner, leaving a triangular face. Slices can be explored with clay sliced with a potter's wire as shown in the figure. A niftier method is to partially fill a plastic solid with water. The surface of the water is the same as the face of a slice coinciding with the surface of the water. By tilting the shape in different ways, every possible "slice" can be observed. Small plastic solids such as *Power Solids* are excellent for this.

ACTIVITY 20.25

Water Slices

Students are given a solid and challenged to find out how to slice it to make a designated slice face. The list of challenges should include some that are impossible. Before water is poured into the solids, students must commit themselves on paper as to whether or not the slice is possible. If they think it is possible, they write and/or draw a description of where the slice must be made. Then water is put into the shape to test their predictions. If there are no plastic shapes available, clay models are the next best option. Here is a list of potential slice faces for a cube:

Square, nonsquare rectangle, nonrectangular parallelogram, isosceles trapezoid, nonisosceles trapezoid, equilateral triangle, isosceles right triangle, other isosceles triangle, scalene right triangle, other scalene triangle.

A tetrahedron, a square pyramid, and prisms offer similar challenges. For other solids, it may be more interesting to find out how many different types of slice faces can be found and to describe each.

Activities for Level 2

The hallmark of level 2 activities is the inclusion of informal logical reasoning. Students have developed an understanding of various properties of shapes. Now it is time to encourage conjecture and to wonder "Why?" or "What if?"

Shapes and Properties

The activities in this section mark a significant shift from simply learning about shapes. Students begin to engage in simple proofs and explore ideas that connect directly to algebra.

Definitions and Proofs

To really understand the difference between levels 1 and 2 of the van Hiele theory, contrast the required thinking in the level 1 activity "Property Lists for Quadrilaterals" (Activity 20.15, p. 367) and the following activity that is designed as a follow-up to that one.

ACTIVITY 20.26

Minimal Defining Lists

(This activity must be done as a follow-up to the "Property Lists" activity on p. 367.) Once property lists for the parallelogram, rhombus, rectangle, and square (and possibly the kite and trapezoid) have been agreed upon by the class, have these lists posted or type them up and duplicate them. In groups, the task is to find "minimal defining lists," or MDLs, for each shape. An MDL is a subset of the properties for a shape that is "defining" and "minimal." "Defining" here means that any shape that has all the properties on the MDL *must* be that shape. Thus, an MDL for a square will guarantee that you have a square. "Minimal" means that if any single property is removed from the list it is no longer defining. For example, one MDL for a square is a quadrilateral with four congruent sides and four right angles. Students should attempt to find at least two or three MDLs for their shape. A proposed list can be challenged as either not minimal or not defining. A list is not minimal if a property can be removed yet the list still defines the shape. A list is not defining if a counterexample—a shape other than one being described—can be produced using only the properties on the list.

The parallelogram, rhombus, rectangle, and square each have at least four MDLs. One of the most interesting MDLs for each shape consists only of the properties of its diagonals. For example, a quadrilateral with diagonals that bisect each other and are perpendicular (intersect at right angles) is a rhombus. Several MDLs have only one property. For example, a parallelogram is a quadrilateral with rotational symmetry of at least order 2.

The MDL activity is worth some further discussion. First, notice the logic component. "*If* a quadrilateral has these properties, *then* it must be a square." Logic is also involved in disproving a faulty list. A second feature is the opportunity to discuss what constitutes a definition. In fact, any MDL could be the definition of the shape. The definitions we usually use are MDLs that have been chosen probably due to the ease with which we can understand them. A quadrilateral with diagonals that bisect each other does not immediately call to mind a parallelogram. Recall that when students created their property lists, no definition was given, only a collection of shapes and a label. Theoretically, the lists could have been created without ever having heard of these shapes. Finally, notice that the object of students thinking in this activity is clearly on properties, not on shapes. The products of the activity are relationships among the properties.

The next activity is also a good follow-up to the "Property Lists" activity, although it is not restricted to quadrilaterals and can include three-dimensional shapes as well. Notice again the logic involved.

ACTIVITY 20.27

True or False?

Prepare statements of the following forms: "If it is a _____, then it is also a _____." "All _____ are _____." "Some _____ are _____."

A few examples are suggested here but numerous possibilities exist.

■ If it is a square, then it is a rhombus.
■ All squares are rectangles.
■ Some parallelograms are rectangles.
■ All parallelograms have congruent diagonals.
■ If it has exactly two lines of symmetry, it must be a quadrilateral.
■ If it is a cylinder, then it is a prism.
■ All prisms have a plane of symmetry.
■ All pyramids have square bases.
■ If a prism has a plane of symmetry, then it is a right prism.

The task is to decide if the statements are true or false and to present an argument to support the decision. Four or five true-or-false statements will make a good lesson. Once this format is understood, let students challenge their classmates by making their own lists of five statements. Each list should have at least one true statement and one false statement. Use the students' lists in subsequent lessons.

✕ STOP   Use the property list for squares and rectangles to prove "All squares are rectangles." Notice that you must use logical reasoning to understand this statement. It does little good to simply force it on students who are not ready to develop the relationship.

Although logic has been involved in the previous activities, you may have difficulty understanding how middle school students can actually do proofs. The following activity was designed by Sconyers (1995) to demonstrate that students can create proofs in geometry well before high school.

ACTIVITY 20.28

Two Polygons from One

Pose the following problem:

Begin with a convex polygon with a given number of sides. Connect two points on the polygon with a line segment forming two new polygons. How many sides do the two resulting polygons have together?

Demonstrate with a few examples (see Figure 20.38). Have students explore by drawing polygons and slicing them. Encourage students to make a table showing sides in original and resulting sides. Students should first make conjectures about a general rule. When groups are comfortable with their conjecture, they should try to reason why their statement is correct—that is, prove their conjecture.

Obviously, the number of resulting sides depends on where the slice is made. With the exception of triangles, there are three possibilities. For each case, a clear argument can be made. The appropriate conjecture and proof are left to you, but trust that students working together can do this task.

Notice that in this task, as in others we have explored, the statements to be proved come from students. If you write a theorem on the board and ask students to prove it, you have already told them that it is true. If, by contrast, a student makes a statement about a geometric situation the class is exploring, it can be written on the board with a question mark as a *conjecture*, a statement whose truth has not yet been determined. You can ask, "Is it true? Always? Can we prove it? Can we find a counterexample?" Reasonable deductive arguments can be forged out of discussions.

The Pythagorean Relationship

The *Pythagorean relationship* is so important that it deserves some special attention. In geometric terms, this relationship

FIGURE 20.38 Start with a polygon, and draw a segment to divide it into two polygons. How many sides will the two new polygons have?

Begin with: 3 sides
Two new shapes: 7 sides

Begin with: 4 sides
Two new shapes: 7 sides

Begin with: 6 sides
Two new shapes: 8 sides

Begin with: 5 sides
Two new shapes: 8 sides

Begin with: 5 sides
Two new shapes: 9 sides

states that if a square is constructed on each side of a right triangle, the areas of the two smaller squares will together equal the area of the square on the longest side, the hypotenuse. To discover this relationship, consider the following activity.

ACTIVITY 20.29

The Pythagorean Relationship

Have students draw a right triangle on half-centimeter grid paper. Assign each student a different triangle by specifying the lengths of the two legs. Students are to draw a square on each leg and the hypotenuse and find the area of all three squares. (For the square on the hypotenuse, the exact area can be found by making each of the sides the diagonal of a rectangle. See Figure 20.39.) Make a table of the area data (Sq. on leg 1, Sq. on leg 2, Sq. on hyp.), and ask students to look for a relationship between the squares.

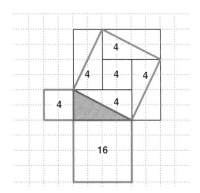

FIGURE 20.39 **The Pythagorean relationship. Note that if drawn on a grid, the area of all squares is easily determined. Here 4 + 16 = area of the square on the hypotenuse.**

As an extension to the last activity, students can explore drawing other figures on the legs of right triangles and computing areas. For example, draw semicircles or equilateral triangles instead of squares. The areas of any regular polygons drawn on the three sides of right triangles will have the same relationship.

Activity 20.29 establishes the Pythagorean relationship. What about a proof? Figure 20.40 shows two proofs that students can follow. The first consists of only the two drawings. It is taken from the book *Proofs without Words* (Nelson, 1993). An algebraic proof is shown below the drawings, based on the second square.

 Use the two drawings in Figure 20.40 to create a proof of the Pythagorean relationship.

 The *e-Standards* includes a dynamic proof without words that is worth sharing with your students (Applet 6.5). Because it requires knowing that parallelograms and rectangles with the same base and height have the same area (see Chapter 19), it is also a good review.

The area of the large square is $(a + b)^2 = a^2 + 2ab + b^2$

The same area is also c^2 plus 4 times the area of one triangle.
$$c^2 + 4\left(\tfrac{1}{2}ab\right) = c^2 + 2ab$$

So $c^2 + 2ab = a^2 + 2ab + b^2$
$$c^2 = a^2 + b^2$$

FIGURE 20.40 **Two proofs of the Pythagorean relationship. The two squares together are a "proof without words." Can you supply the words? The second proof is the algebraic proof based on the right-hand figure.**

Finding Versus Explaining Relationships

Dynamic geometry software such as *The Geometer's Sketchpad* allows students to explore an entire class of figures and observe properties or relationships that are attributable to that class. At level 2, however, the focus is on reasoning or deductive thinking. Can these computer programs help students develop deductive arguments to support the relationships they come to believe through inductive reasoning? Consider the following situation.

Suppose that you have students use a dynamic geometry program to draw a triangle, measure all of the angles, and add them up. As the triangle vertices are dragged around, the sum of the angles would remain steadfast at 180 degrees. Students can conjecture that the sum of the interior angles of a triangle is always 180 degrees, and they would be completely convinced of the truth of this conjecture based on this inductive experience. (Several noncomputer activities lead to the same conclusion.)

As Michael de Villiers notes in his excellent book *Rethinking Proof with the Geometer's Sketchpad* (1999), "The observation that the sun rises every morning does not explain why this is true" (p. 24). De Villiers points out that the experience leading to the conjecture or truth should also help students develop a rationale for the result. In the case of interior angles of a triangle, the experience just described fails to explain *why it is so*. Consider the following activity, which can be done easily with paper and scissors or quite dramatically with a dynamic geometry program.

ACTIVITY 20.30

Angle Sum in a Triangle

Have all students cut out three congruent triangles. (Stack three sheets of paper, and cut three shapes at one time.) Place one triangle on a line and the second directly next to it in the same orientation. Place the third triangle in the space between the triangles as shown in Figure 20.41(a). Based on this experience, what conjecture can you make about the sum of the angles in a triangle?

segment DE, as in Figure 20.42. Measure the length of DE and BC. Also measure angles ADE and ABC. Drag points A, B, and C. What conjectures can you make about the relationships between segment DE, the *midsegment* of ABC, and BC, the base of ABC?

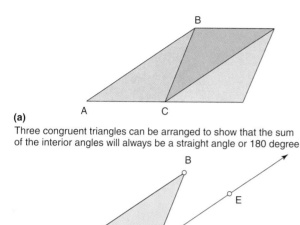

(a)
Three congruent triangles can be arranged to show that the sum of the interior angles will always be a straight angle or 180 degree

(b)
Draw CE parallel to AB. Why is angle BAC congruent to angle ECD? Why is angle ABC congruent to angle BCE?

FIGURE 20.41 Deductive, logical reasoning is necessary to *prove* **relationships that appear true from observations.**

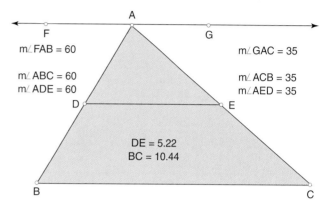

FIGURE 20.42 The midsegment of a triangle is always parallel to the base and half as long.

In a dynamic geometry program, the three triangles in Figure 20.41(a) can be drawn by starting with one triangle, translating it to the right the length of AC, and then rotating the same triangle about the midpoint of side BC. When vertices of the original triangle are dragged, the other triangles will change accordingly and remain congruent. We still do not know why the angle sum is always a straight angle, but this exploration allows students to see why it might be so. In the figure, there are lines parallel to each side of the original triangle. By using properties of angles formed by cutting parallel lines with a transverse line, it is easy to argue that the sum of the angles will always be a straight line [see Figure 20.41(b); the proof is left to you].

Dynamic geometry software can be enormously powerful for helping students observe geometric relationships and make conjectures. The truth of the conjectures will often be obvious. At level 2, however, we must begin to ask why. The following activity further illustrates the point.

It is very clear that the midsegment is half the length of the base and parallel to it, but why is this so? Students will need a bit more guidance, but you should not necessarily have to provide the argument for them. Suggest that they draw a line through A parallel to BC. List all pairs of angles that they know are congruent. Why are they congruent? Note that triangle ABC is similar to triangle ADE. Why is it similar? With hints such as these, many middle grade students can begin to make logical arguments for why the things they observe to be true are in fact true.

Location

Some of the explorations on the coordinate grid that were suggested for level 1 may also be appropriate for level 2 students. (See Activities 20.18, 20.19, and 20.20.) Note especially the conjecturing aspect of those activities. Students at level 2 should continue to explore ideas on the coordinate grid.

Applying the Pythagorean Relationship

The geometric version of the Pythagorean relationship is about areas. The following activity has students use the coordinate grid and the Pythagorean relationship to develop a formula for the distance between points.

ACTIVITY 20.31

Triangle Midsegments

Using a dynamic geometry program, draw a triangle, and label the vertices A, B, and C. Draw the segment joining the midpoints of AB and AC, and label this

---
ACTIVITY 20.32

The Distance Formula

Have students draw a line between two points in the first quadrant that are not on the same horizontal or vertical line. The task is to use only the coordinates of the endpoints to find the distance between them in terms of the units on the grid. To this end, suggest that they draw a right triangle using the line as the hypotenuse. The vertex at the right angle will share one coordinate from each endpoint. Students compute the areas of the squares on the legs and add to find the area of the square on the hypotenuse. Now the length of the original line segment (the distance between the points) is the number whose square is the area of the square on the hypotenuse. (This last sentence is a geometric interpretation of square root.) Have students follow these directions to compute the length of the line.

Next, have them look through all of their calculations and see how the coordinates of the two endpoints were used. Challenge students to use the same type of calculations to get the distance between two new points without drawing any pictures.

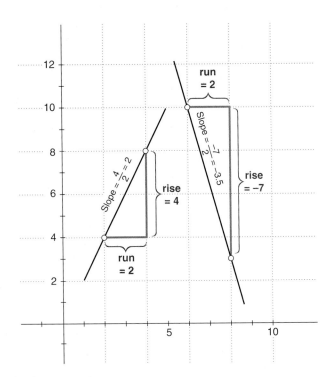

FIGURE 20.43 **The slope of a line is = rise ÷ run.**

Level 2 students do not necessarily construct proofs but should be able to follow the rationale if shown proofs. By leading students through the procedure of finding the length of one line (or the distance between the endpoints), you give them sufficient information to compute the lengths of other lines. Students will see that all they need are the coordinates of the two endpoints to compute the areas of all three squares and, hence, the length of the hypotenuse. If you then help them substitute letters for specific coordinates, a general distance formula results.

Slope

The topic of slope is another important connection between geometry and algebra. To begin a discussion of slope, draw several different slanted lines on the board. Discuss how they are different. Some are steeper than others. Some go up, others go down. If you agree that "up" means sloping upward from left to right, then you can agree which ones go up and which go down. This "steepness" of a line is an attribute that can be measured like other measurable attributes. To give slope a number requires a reference line. The coordinate grid provides a reference (the x-axis) and the numbers to use in the measurement. Spend some time having students invent their own methods for attaching a number to the concept of steepness.

The convention for measuring the steepness of a line or the *slope* is based on the ideas of the *rise* and *run* between any two points on the line. The *rise* is the vertical change from the left point to the right point—positive if up, negative if down. The *run* is the horizontal distance from the left point to the right point. Slope is then defined as *rise ÷ run* or the ratio of the vertical change to the horizontal change (see Figure 20.43). By agreement, vertical lines have no slope or the slope is said to be "undefined." Horizontal lines have a slope of 0 as a result of the definition.

Once students are given the definition, they should be able to compute the slopes of any nonvertical line drawn on

a coordinate grid without further assistance and *without formulas*. Once the convention of the slope definition is understood, nothing else is required.

A good problem-based task is to figure out what can be said about the slopes of parallel lines and perpendicular lines. (Is this geometry or algebra? Does it matter?)

Transformations

By the time students are nearing level 2, they will have developed an understanding of symmetries. The following activity is a challenge to use these ideas to establish an interesting relationship between symmetries and transformations.

ACTIVITY 20.33

Pentomino Positions

Have students cut out a set of 12 pentominoes from 2-cm grid paper. (See Figure 20.20, p. 362.) Mark one side of each piece to help remember if it has been flipped over. The first part of the task is to determine how many different positions on the grid each piece has. Call positions "different" if a reflection or a turn is required to make them match. Therefore, the cross-shaped piece has only one position. The strip of five squares has two positions. Some pieces have as many as eight positions. The second part of the task is to find a relationship between the line symmetries and rotational symmetries for each piece and the number of positions it can have on the grid.

CONNECTED MATHEMATICS

MIDDLE GRADES

Grade 8, *Kaleidoscopes, Hubcaps, and Mirrors*
Investigation 4: Symmetry and Algebra

Context

The interesting title of this unit comes from the first investigation, in which students examine symmetry in hubcap designs, designs made by kaleidoscopes (hexagonal), and those made by mirrors. Symmetry is actually *defined* in terms of transformations. "A geometric figure is *symmetric* if a reflection or rotation of the figure produces an image that matches the original figure exactly." A lot of the work in this unit is done with the coordinate grid.

Task Description

This lesson explores combinations of two symmetry transformations of an equilateral triangle and a square. Students make a table that resembles a multiplication table but represents the result of one transformation followed by another. The notation for reflections is related to which line of symmetry is used.

For example, L_1 is a reflection about line 1. Rotations are counterclockwise. R_{240} refers to a counterclockwise rotation of 240 degrees. By labeling the corners, students can keep track of each position of the triangle. The explanation above the table indicates how it is to be filled in.

After filling in the table, students are asked to look for patterns or other interesting results that may appear. They then complete an ordinary multiplication table for the numbers 1 to 6 and make comparisons of patterns found there and the patterns in the symmetry transformations table. Notice, for example, that R_{360} is placed in the same position as the number 1 in the multiplication table and behaves as an identity element. The commutative property works for some combinations but not others. None of the whole numbers in the multiplication table have a multiplicative inverse. However, recall that every rational number does. For example,

4.1 Transforming Triangles

The operations of arithmetic—addition, subtraction, multiplication, and division—define ways of putting two numbers together to get a single number. In a similar way, you can think of combining symmetry transformations as an operation that puts two transformations together to produce a single, equivalent transformation.

In this problem, you will explore combinations of symmetry transformations for an equilateral triangle. The notation L_n means a reflection over line n, and the notation R_n means a counterclockwise rotation of n degrees. The symbol $*$ represents the combining operation. You can read this symbol as "and then." For example, $L_1 * L_2 = R_{240}$ means that reflecting the triangle over line 1 "and then" reflecting it over line 2 is equivalent to rotating the triangle 240°.

Problem 4.1

The operation table below is reproduced on Labsheet 4.1B. Complete the table to show the results of combining symmetry transformations of an equilateral triangle. Each entry should be the result of performing the transformation in the left column followed by the transformation in the top row. The two entries already in the table represent the combinations you explored in the introduction:

$$L_1 * L_2 = R_{240} \qquad L_3 * R_{120} = L_2$$

$*$	R_{360}	R_{120}	R_{240}	L_1	L_2	L_3
R_{360}						
R_{120}						
R_{240}						
L_1					R_{240}	
L_2						
L_3		L_2				

Note that transformation R_{360}, a 360° rotation, carries every point back to where it started. As you combine transformations, you will discover that many combinations are equivalent to R_{360}.

■ Problem 4.1 Follow-Up
1. Look carefully at the entries in your table. Describe any interesting patterns in the rows, columns, or blocks of entries. What do these patterns tell you about the results of combining rotations and line reflections?

60   Kaleidoscopes, Hubcaps, and Mirrors

From *Connected Mathematics: Kaleidoscopes, Hubcaps, and Mirrors: Symmetry and Transformations.* © 2002 by Michigan State University, Glenda Lappan, James T. Fey, William M. Fitzgerald, Susan N. Friel, and Elizabeth Difanis Phillips. Published by Prentice Hall. Used by permission of Pearson Education, Inc.

3 and $\frac{1}{3}$ are inverses of each other because their product is 1. For the symmetries of the triangle, every transformation has an inverse.

In addition to continuing their study of symmetry, this lesson really is a connection to algebra. It reviews the properties of operations and makes it clear that they really depend on the system being used.

The first part of this activity was adapted from the classic book *Boxes, Squares, and Other Things* (Walter, 1970), which has many more excellent explorations. The second part of the problem is not hard if students make a table of what they know. The solutions to the task are left to you and your students. As a follow-up to Activity 20.33, examine the excerpt from the eighth grade *Connected Mathematics* curriculum on this page. Incidentally, a very similar exploration can be found in *Boxes, Squares, and Other Things.*

The next task challenges students to develop generalizations about certain compositions of transformations.

ACTIVITY 20.34

Double Reflections

There are two similar tasks in this activity:

1. Verify that the composition of two reflections across parallel lines (first across one and then the other) is the same as a translation. Make a drawing on a dot grid to illustrate. Challenge: If you know the distance between the two parallel lines, what can you say about the translation—both its direction and its distance? Does it matter where the shape begins (between the lines or outside) or which line is used as the first reflection? Explain your conclusions.

2. Verify that the composition of two reflections across intersecting lines is the same as a rotation about the point of intersection of the lines. Make a drawing on a dot grid to illustrate. Challenge: How is the angle of rotation related to the angle between the lines? Explain your conclusions.

In the first problem, the translation distance is always double the distance between the lines and is perpendicular to them. The direction is determined by which line is used for the first reflection in relation to the preimage. In the second problem, the angle of rotation is double the angle between the lines. It is possible to construct reasonable arguments for these conclusions by examining drawings.

Visualization

In "Viewpoints" (Activity 20.24, p. 375), students made "buildings" out of 1-inch cubes and coordinated these with direct views of the sides and top. A significantly more challenging activity is to draw perspective views of these block buildings or to match perspective drawings with a building. Isometric dot grids are used for the drawings. The next activity provides a glimpse at this form of visualization activity.

ACTIVITY 20.35

Perspective Drawings

a. In the first version, students begin with a perspective drawing of a building. The assumption is that there are no hidden blocks. From the drawing the students build the actual building with their blocks. To record the result, they draw a building plan indicating the number of blocks in each position.

b. In the second version, students are given either a block plan or the five direct views. They build the building accordingly and draw two or more of the perspective views. There are four possible perspectives from above the table: the front left and right, and the back left and right. It is useful to build the building on a sheet of paper with the words "front," "back," "left," and "right" written on the edges to keep from getting different viewpoints confused.

Figure 20.44 shows an example of this last activity. Some excellent resource books exist for this type of activity. It is not necessary to prepare these tasks yourself. Perhaps the best-known book is *Middle Grades Mathematics Project: Spatial Visualization* (Winter, Lappan, Phillips, & Fitzgerald, 1986). NCTM's *Navigating Though Geometry* books have similar activities in both the 3–5 and 6–8 grade books. (See Recommendations for Further Reading.)

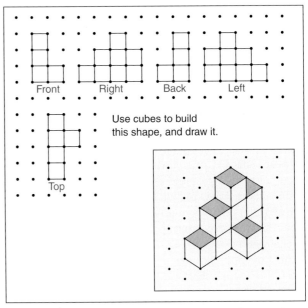

Use cubes to build this shape, and draw it.

FIGURE 20.44 **Develop perspective and visual perception with cubes and plain views. Draw block "buildings" on isometric grids.**

 Technology Note

An amazing computer tool for drawing perspective views of block buildings such as in Activity 20.35 is available on the *Illuminations* Web site (http://illuminations.nctm.org/imath/6-8/isometric.index.html). This applet requires only mouse clicks to draw either whole cubes, any single face of a cube, or just lines. The drawings, however, are actually "buildings"

and can be viewed as three-dimensional objects. They can be rotated in space so that they can be seen from any vantage. Prepared investigations are informative and also lead students through the features of the tool. ∎

A *polyhedron* is a three-dimensional shape with polygons for all faces. Among the various polyhedra, the Platonic solids are especially interesting. *Platonic Solids* is the name given to the set of completely regular polyhedrons. "Completely regular" means that each face is a regular polygon and every vertex has exactly the same number of faces joining at that point. An interesting visualization task appropriate for this level is to find and describe all of the Platonic solids.

ACTIVITY 20.36

Search for the Platonic Solids

Provide students with a supply of equilateral triangles, squares, regular pentagons, and regular hexagons from one of the plastic sets for building solids (e.g., *Polydron* or *Geofix*). Explain what a completely regular solid is. The task is to find as many different completely regular solids as possible.

One approach to conducting this activity is to leave it as stated and allow students to work with no additional guidance. Success will depend on their problem-solving skills. Alternatively, you might suggest a systematic approach as follows. Since the smallest number of sides a face can have is three, begin with triangles, then squares, then pentagons, and so on. Furthermore, since every vertex must have the same number of faces, try three faces at a point, then four, and so on. (It is clearly impossible to have only two faces at a point.)

With this plan, students will find that for triangles they can have three, four, or five triangles coming to a point. For each of these, they can begin with a "tent" of triangles and then add more triangles so that each vertex has the same number. With three at a point you get a four-sided solid called a *tetrahedron* (*tetra* = four). With four at each point you get an eight-sided solid called an *octahedron* (*octa* = eight). It is really exciting to build the shape with five triangles at each point. It will have 20 sides and is called an *icosahedron* (*icosa* = twenty).

In a similar manner, students will find that there is only one solid made of squares—three at each point and six in all—a *hexahedron* (*hex* = six), also called a cube. And there is only one solid with pentagons, three at each point, 12 in all. This is called a *dodecahedron* (*dodeca* = twelve).

STOP Why are there no regular polyhedra with six or more triangles or four or more squares? Why are there no regular polyhedra made with hexagons or with polygons with more than six sides? The best way to answer these questions is to experiment with the polygons and explain the answers in your own words. Students should do the same.

A fantastic skeletal icosahedron can be built out of the newspaper rods described earlier. (See Figure 20.11, p. 357.) Since five triangles converge at each point, there are also five edges at each point. Simply work at bringing five rods to each vertex and remember that each face is a triangle. This icosahedron will be about 4 feet across and will be amazingly sturdy.

 # ASSESSMENT NOTES

At the beginning of this chapter we talked about two kinds of goals for your students: goals of spatial sense and geometric thinking, and goals of geometric content. This chapter has been organized to help you gain some perspective of these two agendas. By planning your assessment of geometric thinking as well as and separately from content, you can avoid the trap of teaching to content objectives in a superficial way. Activities that do not appear to directly match a content objective should at least have a growth objective.

Clarifying Your Geometry Objectives
Spatial Sense and van Hiele Objectives

In the early grades, when you can expect your students to be level 0 thinkers, you want to be sure that their thinking is increasing in its sophistication and is moving toward level 1. Here are suggestions for things to look for:

- Child attends to a variety of characteristics of shapes in sorting and building activities.
- Child uses language that is descriptive of geometric shapes.
- Child shows evidence of geometric reasoning in solving puzzles, exploring shapes, creating designs, and analyzing shapes.
- Child recognizes shapes in the environment.
- Child solves spatial problems.

Each of these statements can be assessed as indicative of either a level 0 thinker or a level 1 thinker. For example, at level 0, the types of characteristics that students are likely to pay attention to are not properties of general classes of shapes ("pointy," "fat," "has five sides," "goes up," etc.). Properties such as "parallel" or "symmetrical" may be used by level 0 thinkers as well as those at level 1. The distinction is found in what the properties are attributed to. At level 0, students are restricted in thought to the shapes they are currently working with, while at level 1, students attribute properties to classes of shapes (*all* rectangles or *all* cylinders). Language, reasoning, shape recognition, and spatial problem solving can all be assessed as being appropriate for level 0 or level 1. By thinking in this manner, teachers can begin to get a sense of the geometric growth of their students beyond the specific content knowledge that may have been developed.

At the upper elementary and middle grades, teachers can begin to think in terms of students being at level 1 or level 2 in their geometric thought. Before grade 6 or 7, very few students will have achieved level 2 thinking, but teachers need to be aware of progress in that direction. The following general indicators are more indicative of level 2 thinkers rather than level 1:

- Child shows improvement in spatial visualization skills.
- Child has an inclination to make and test conjectures in geometric situations.
- Child makes use of logical explanations in geometric problem solving.
- Child justifies conclusions in geometric contexts.
- Child assesses the validity of logical arguments in geometric situations.

Most of these indicators or objectives include elements of reasoning and logical sophistication that are not generally present in a level 1 thinker. As noted in the discussions of dynamic geometry software, a level 1 thinker is using inductive reasoning to discover relationships in shapes, whereas a level 2 thinker is, with guidance, beginning to develop arguments that explain why a particular relationship exists.

Geometric Concept Objectives

Principles and Standards is extremely helpful for articulating growth in geometric content across the grades. For each of the

four goals articulated by the standards (shape and properties, location, transformations, and visualization) examine the grade-level expectations not only at your grade band but above and below as well. This chapter has been organized to help you obtain some sense of that growth across the K–8 span of grades.

Of course, you must attend to the content prescribed by your school system. That content may or may not align well with that outlined by the NCTM *Standards*. However, nearly all geometry taught in the K–8 span can be found within that standard. Try to include a sense of growth over time in your assessment of content. If you limit your assessment to a mastery of skills or definitions, the spirit of exploration that you want in your geometry program will be lost. We most often teach in a manner that reflects our assessment plans. Although mastery of some ideas is perhaps important, conceptual development is rarely reflected in memorizing definitions.

In deciding what to assess and how, it is best to take a long-term view of geometry rather than a more traditional mastery-oriented approach. Two major perspectives have been suggested:

- Growth in spatial sense and geometric thought
- Understanding of geometric concepts ■

Reflections on Chapter 20

Writing to Learn

1. Describe in your own words the first three van Hiele levels of geometric thought (levels 0, 1, and 2). Note in your description the object of thought and the product of thought. How do these ideas create a progression from one level to the next?
2. Describe the four characteristics of the van Hiele levels of thought. For each, reflect on why each characteristic might be important for teachers.
3. How would activities aimed at levels 0, 1, and 2 differ?
4. Briefly describe the nature of the content in each of the four geometric strands featured in this chapter and in the *Standards*: Shapes and Properties, Location, Transformations, and Visualization. In your description, note a progression across van Hiele levels (or across grade levels K–2, 3–5, and 6–8).
5. Rather than trying to become familiar with all of the activities in this chapter, pick a few activities for each of the four content areas within the levels at which your course is directed. Use these activities to illustrate how geometric thinking is different at each level. For this purpose, activities from the Shapes and Properties sections will be the most helpful.
6. What can you do when the students in your classroom are at different van Hiele levels of thought?
7. The use of computers was discussed at each of the three van Hiele levels. Describe at least one computer activity appropriate for each level, and explain why each is targeted at that level rather than a higher or lower level. If possible, try some geo-

metric software that you can access, and consider its usefulness in terms of the van Hiele levels of thought.
8. How can a teacher assess students in terms of general geometric growth or spatial sense? Assuming that the van Hiele theory is correct, why is it important to understand where your students are in terms of that theory?

For Discussion and Exploration

1. How important should geometry be in the primary grades, the intermediate grades, and the middle school grades? Consider, at each of these levels, the competing demands of other areas of the mathematics curriculum, and suggest how many of the roughly 36 weeks of the year should be spent on geometry. What justification can you give for your position?
2. Examine the teacher's edition of a basal textbook at any grade level. Select any lesson on geometry. Remember that the authors of the pupil's book are restricted to the printed page by the very nature of books. Teachers are not so restricted. How would you teach this lesson so that it was a *good* geometry lesson? Your lesson should include a hands-on activity and have a problem-solving spirit.
3. At the elementary and middle school levels, computer software should be an important component of your instructional tools. If you are not familiar with the types of software discussed in this chapter, find out what you have access to, and play around to learn what each program can do.

Recommendations for Further Reading

Highly Recommended

NCTM's *Navigations Series*

Findell, C. R., Small, M., Cavanagh, M., Dacey, L., Greenes, C. E., & Sheffield, L. J. (2001). *Navigating through geometry in prekindergarten–grade 2.* Reston, VA: National Council of Teachers of Mathematics.

Gavin, M. K., Sinelli, A. M., & St. Marie, J. (2001). *Navigating through geometry in grades 3–5.* Reston, VA: National Council of Teachers of Mathematics.

Pugalee, D. K., Frykholm, J., Johnson, A., Slovin, H., Malloy, C., & Preston, R. (2002). *Navigating through geometry in grades 6–8.* Reston, VA: National Council of Teachers of Mathematics.
Each of these three excellent books from the *Navigations Series* provides both a perspective on the geometry standard and also a collection of excellent activities appropriate for the grade band of the book. Activities are organized under the four strands of the Geometry Standard (as is this chapter). Each book includes a CD-ROM with the Blackline Masters, a small collection of excellent applets, plus the full text of selected articles. A great resource.

National Council of Teachers of Mathematics. (1999). Geometry and geometric thinking [Focus Issue]. *Teaching Children Mathematics, 5*(6).
One of the best focus issues in recent years, this issue of *TCM* is full of practical ideas and useful perspectives on geometry for the early grades. Of special note is a wonderful article by Pierre van Hiele, in which he describes a series of activities with a unique collection of shapes (the Mosaic Puzzle). For the small price, this focus issue is a very valuable resource for any teacher.

Wyat, K. W., Lawrence, A., & Foletta, G. M. (1998). *Geometry activities for middle school students with the Geometer's Sketchpad.* Berkeley, CA: Key Curriculum Press.
As noted in this chapter, dynamic geometry software belongs in the upper elementary and middle grades. This book of explorations for the *Geometer's Sketchpad* can be used to introduce students (and *you*) to the software even if you have never used *Sketchpad* before. The activities explore triangles, quadrilaterals, symmetry, transformations, and constructions. With this book you will be convinced of the value of dynamic geometry in grades 4 to 8. (Also see Battista's *Shape Makers* below.)

Other Suggestions

Battista, M. T. (1998). *Shape makers: Developing geometric reasoning with the Geometer's Sketchpad.* Berkeley, CA: Key Curriculum Press.

Bennet, D. (1999). *Exploring geometry with the Geometer's Sketchpad.* Berkeley, CA: Key Curriculum Press.

Brahier, D. J., & Speer, W. R. (1997). Worthwhile tasks: Exploring mathematical connections through geometric solids. *Mathematics Teaching in the Middle School, 3,* 20–28.

Carroll, W. M. (1998). Middle school students' reasoning about geometric situations. *Mathematics Teaching in the Middle School, 3,* 398–403.

Clements, D. H. (1999). Geometric and spatial thinking in young children. In J. V. Copley (Ed.), *Mathematics in the early years* (pp. 66–79). Reston, VA: National Council of Teachers of Mathematics.

Crowley, M. L. (1987). The van Hiele model of the development of geometric thought. In M. M. Lindquist (Ed.), *Learning and teaching geometry, K–12* (pp. 1–16). Reston, VA: National Council of Teachers of Mathematics.

DeGroot, C. (2001). From description to proof. *Mathematics Teaching in the Middle School, 7,* 244–248.

Del Grande, J. (1993). *Geometry and spatial sense: Addenda series, grades K–6.* Reston, VA: National Council of Teachers of Mathematics.

de Villiers, M. D. (1999). *Rethinking proof with the Geometer's Sketchpad.* Emeryville, CA: Key Curriculum Press.

Enderson, M. C., & Manouchehri, A. (1998). Technology-based geometric explorations for the middle grades. In L. Leutzinger (Ed.), *Mathematics in the middle* (pp. 193–200). Reston, VA: National Council of Teachers of Mathematics.

Fosnaugh, L. S., & Harrell, M. E. (1996). Covering the plane with rep-tiles. *Mathematics Teaching in the Middle School, 1,* 666–670.

Giganti, P., Jr., & Cittadino, M. J. (1990). The art of tessellation. *Arithmetic Teacher, 37*(7), 6–16.

Hannafin, R. D., Burruss, J. D., & Little, C. (2001). Learning with dynamic geometry software: Perspectives of teachers and learners. *Journal of Educational Research, 94,* 132–144.

Kleiman, G. M. (1995). Seeing and thinking mathematically in the middle school. In P. A. House (Ed.), *Connecting mathematics across the curriculum* (pp. 153–158). Reston, VA: National Council of Teachers of Mathematics.

Lehrer, R., & Curtis, C. L. (2000). Why are some solids perfect? Conjectures and experiments by third graders. *Teaching Children Mathematics, 6,* 324–329.

Malloy, C. (1999). Perimeter and area through the van Hiele model. *Mathematics Teaching in the Middle School, 5,* 87–90.

Manouchehri, A., Enderson, M. C., & Pugnucco, L. A. (1998). Exploring geometry with technology. *Mathematics Teaching in the Middle School, 3,* 436–442.

Martin, G., & Strutchens, M. E. (2000). Geometry and measurement. In E. A. Silver & P. A. Kenney (Eds.), *Results from the seventh mathematics assessment of the National Assessment of Educational Progress* (pp. 193–234). Reston, VA: National Council of Teachers of Mathematics.

Mercer, S., & Henningsen M. A. (1998). The pentomino project: Moving students from manipulatives to reasoning and thinking about mathematical ideas. In L. Leutzinger (Ed.), *Mathematics in the middle* (pp. 184–192). Reston, VA: National Council of Teachers of Mathematics.

Nakagomi, K. (2000). Gathering circles: An experience in creativity and variety. *The Mathematics Teacher, 93,* 746–751.

Peterson, B. (2000). From tessellations to polyhedra: Big polyhedra. *Mathematics Teaching in the Middle School, 5,* 348–356.

Sandberg, S. E. (1998). A plethora of polyhedra. *Mathematics Teaching in the Middle School, 3,* 388–391.

Seymour, D., & Britton, J. (1989). *Introduction to tessellations.* Palo Alto, CA: Dale Seymour Publications.

Walter, M. J. (1970). *Boxes, squares, and other things.* Reston, VA: National Council of Teachers of Mathematics.

Winter, J. J., Lappan, G., Phillips, E., & Fitzgerald, W. (1986). *Middle grades mathematics project: Spatial visualization.* Menlo Park, CA: AWL Supplemental.

CHAPTER

21

Exploring Concepts of Data Analysis and Probability

Graphs and statistics bombard the public in advertising, opinion polls, reliability estimates, population trends, health risks, and progress of students in schools, just to name a few areas. We hear about the probability of contracting this or that disease, having twins, winning the lottery, or living to be 90. Simulations of complex situations are frequently based on probabilities and are then used to design highways and storm sewers, plan for disasters, or design spacecraft.

To deal with this information, students should have ample opportunity throughout their school years to have informal yet meaningful experiences with the basic concepts involved. The emphasis from the primary level into high school should be placed on activities leading to intuitive understanding and conceptual knowledge rather than computations and formulas.

 ## Big Ideas

1. A collection of objects with various attributes can be classified or sorted in different ways. A single object can belong to more than one class. Classification is the first step in the organization of data.

2. Data are gathered and organized in order to answer questions about the populations from which the data come. With data from only a sample of the population, inferences are made about the population.

3. Data sets can be analyzed in various ways to provide a sense of the shape of the data, including how spread out they are (range, variance) and how they are centered (mean, median, mode). Measures that describe data with numbers are called statistics. Data can be organized in various graphical forms to visually convey information. The use of a particular graph or statistic can mediate what the data tell about the population.

4. The occurrence of a future event can be characterized along a continuum from impossible to certain. Assigning a number from 0 (impossible) to 1 (certain) to a future event is a measurement of the probability of that event.

5. Theoretical or exact probabilities can be computed when the occurrence of the event can be clearly determined as a fraction of all possible outcomes. By running experiments or otherwise gathering data, estimates of probabilities can be determined. The larger the size of the data set, the closer the experimental probability will be to the theoretical probability.

 ## Content Connections

The combined areas of data analysis and probability use numbers and graphs to describe the world in which we live. The numbers that are used as tools in these areas are important to the study of data analysis and probability. However, the clearest connection of this area of mathematics is to algebra.

- **Number Sense** (Chapter 9): Young children analyze graphs and use the graphs to talk about quantity. Graphs indicate numeric relationships of more, less, difference, and relative magnitude. Each bar of a graph is a part of the whole (part-part-whole relationships).

- **Fractions, Ratios, and Percents** (Chapters 15 and 18): Fractions, decimals, and percents are used to describe data and are also used as measures of probability.

- **Measurement** (Chapter 19): Much of the real-world data that are gathered consist of measurements. Pedagogically, measurement can be interwoven with data analysis as students make measurements to answer questions and create data to be analyzed.

■ **Algebra** (Chapters 22 and 23): Algebra is used to analyze and describe relationships. Whenever data are gathered on two related variables (e.g., height and arm span, age and growth), algebra can be used to describe the relationship between the variables. The resulting relationship can then be used to predict outcomes for which no data have yet been gathered. The better that the data are approximated by the algebraic relationship or function, the better the probability that the function has predictive value.

Data Analysis and Probability in the Curriculum

Data analysis is more than statistics. It includes both asking and answering questions about our world. To answer the questions, data must be gathered and organized and then an analysis made. Sometimes statistics are used to describe the data. In a similar way, probability is more than spinning spinners and flipping coins. It, too, helps us answer questions about our world in terms of the chances of future events occurring or not.

Principles and Standards for School Mathematics emphasizes the importance of these areas by making Data Analysis and Probability one of the five content strands across all grades. Topics that were at one time reserved for special classes in high school or college are now part of the K–12 curriculum. Students can begin even in kindergarten to use data to answer questions. As they progress through the K–8 years, they can begin to add to their conceptual understanding of the ways to represent and describe data. Various types of graphs and statistics can be added to their repertoire of ideas as better descriptions of data are required.

Similarly, concepts of chance can be developed long before sophisticated ideas of probability are introduced. The *Standards* recognizes that children need to begin these experiences in the earliest grades so that an intuitive understanding of probability is developed on which more traditional methods can be built.

Without this careful development of concepts and techniques over the elementary and middle school years, students attempting to learn more rigorous approaches in later years have no intuitive ideas to bring to the task.

Gathering Data to Answer Questions

The first goal in the Data Analysis and Probability standard of *Principles and Standards* says that students should "formulate questions that can be addressed with data and collect, organize, and display relevant data to answer them" (NCTM, 2000, p. 48). Notice that data collection should be for a purpose, to answer a question, just as in the real world. At all grades, the analysis of data should have the agenda of adding information about some aspect of our world. This is what political pollsters, advertising agencies, market researchers, census takers, wildlife managers, and hosts of others do: gather data to answer questions.

When students formulate the questions they want to ask, the data they gather become more and more meaningful. How they organize the data and the techniques for analyzing them have a purpose. For example, one class of students gathered data concerning which cafeteria foods were most often thrown in the garbage. As a result of these efforts, certain items were removed from the regular menu. The activity illustrated to students the power of organized data, and it helped them get food that they liked better.

Ideas for Questions and Data

Often the need to gather data will come from the class naturally in the course of discussion or from questions arising in other content areas. Science, of course, is full of measurements and thus abounds in data requiring analysis. Social studies is also full of opportunities to pose questions requiring data analysis. The next few sections suggest some additional ideas.

Classroom Questions

Young children can learn about themselves, their families and pets, the animals in their neighborhood, measures such as arm span or time to get to school, their likes and dislikes, and so on. At the K–2 level, the easiest questions to deal with are those that can be answered by each class member's contributing one piece of data. When there are lots of possibilities, suggest that students restrict the number of choices. Here are a few ideas:

> *Favorites:* TV show, fruit, season of the year, color, football team, pet, ice cream flavor
>
> *Numbers:* Number of pets, sisters, or brothers; hours watching TV or hours of sleep; birthdays (month or day of month); bedtime
>
> *Measures:* Height, arm span, area of foot, long-jump distance, letters in name, time to button a sweater, daily temperature, weather, shadow length, rainfall

Beyond the Classroom

As children get older, they can begin to think about various populations and differences between them. For example, how are fifth graders similar or different from middle school students? Students might examine questions concerning boys versus girls, adults or teachers versus students, or categories of workers or college graduates. These situations involve issues of sampling and making generalizations and comparisons.

INVESTIGATIONS in NUMBER, DATA, and SPACE

Grade 5, *Data: Kids, Cats, and Ads*
Investigation 3: Sampling Ourselves

Context

In the first two investigations of this last unit of the fifth grade, students learn about a variety of different graphing techniques with an emphasis on line plots. No attention is given to measures of center (median or mean). Instead, students use both fractions and percents to compare data sets. Throughout the unit a clear effort is made to connect "nice" fractions (halves, thirds, fourths, etc.) to percents. This third investigation takes about four days. It is followed by two more units on sampling—one involving the percent of ad space in newspapers and one concerning play injuries on playgrounds. The data are very true to life.

Task Description

After a review of fractions, decimals, and percents (a one-hour activity), the next two days are devoted to exploring the implications of small samples to tell about a larger population. Using a list of six fun questions (e.g., Do you squeeze the toothpaste tube from the bottom or the middle? Do you put your ketchup to the side of the fries or on top of them?), students compare the results of samples of four students to the results for the full class. In addition to sampling issues, students must compare simple fractions such as $\frac{3}{4}$ to fractions such as $\frac{19}{26}$. Strips of paper are used to graphically show the part-whole relationships. The proportion issue of different-sized wholes (the sample of four versus the full class) is also revisited.

Next, class data are gathered for the seven questions shown here. The percentages given are from a national survey done in 1994. To make comparisons, students must convert their fractions to percents. Discussion concerns why the data from the class may be different from the national sample. Students are given information about the sample. It included children from ages 8 to 12 with equal numbers of each age. They came from all parts of the na-

---

Survey Results

Name _____   Date _____

Student Sheet 15

	Responses	National sample	Our class
1. When your family eats dinner, do you all eat together at the same time?	yes	82%	
	sometimes	8%	
	no	9%	
2. Do you watch television while you are eating dinner?	yes	29%	
	sometimes	19%	
	no	53%	
3. What's your favorite meal of the day—breakfast, lunch, or dinner?	breakfast	24%	
	lunch	33%	
	dinner	43%	
4. Do you get to choose what you eat for dinner?	yes	27%	
	sometimes	34%	
	no	40%	
5. Do you help set the table?	yes	57%	
	sometimes	19%	
	no	24%	
6. Do you help cook?	yes	26%	
	sometimes	37%	
	no	37%	
7. If you had a choice of cooking dinner, setting the table, or cleaning the dishes, which would you choose?	cook dinner	37%	
	set table	44%	
	clean dishes	18%	

Data (rounded to nearest percent) from "America's Children Talk About Family Time, Values, and Chores," 1994, Massachusetts Mutual Life Insurance Co.

© Dale Seymour Publications®   **139**   *Investigation 3 • Session 4*
                                                                              Data: Kids, Cats, and Ads

Page 139 from *Statistics: Data: Kids, Cats, and Ads* by A. Rubin and J. Mokros. *Investigations in Number, Data, and Space.* Copyright © 1998 by Dale Seymour Publications. Reprinted by permission of Pearson Education, Inc.

tion. About 80 percent lived with their parents, and so on. Students can both see how they are alike and different and can also make judgments about their class as a suitable sample for the nation.

The combination of this activity with the earlier samples of four students to represent the whole classroom provides students with a good look at sampling, an approach that can be found every day in the newspaper and on the nightly news.

The news media frequently report what the latest survey reveals about the "typical" family, business, teenager, drug addict, or member of some other population or group. How did they survey everyone, and what does "typical" mean? Do the students in your classroom believe they are typical? Are they like those in the next classroom or the next grade level? To describe a group usually involves asking a variety of questions, and deciding on which questions to ask is not nearly as easy as it may sound. How many questions should be asked? Should they be multiple choice? If not, how

will the answers be handled? To describe a large group (say, the school), how many people should be surveyed? How should they be selected? Students should be involved in making these decisions as they formulate their questions and design surveys.

Much of the fifth-grade statistics unit in *Investigations in Number, Data, and Space* explores the issue of sampling. In the excerpt described on this page, students first compare small samples from the class to the full class data. They also compare classroom data to national data.

Other Sources of Information

Do not restrict students from asking questions that can be answered by gathering the data themselves. Gathering data can mean using data that have been collected by others. For example, newspapers, almanacs, sports record books, maps, and various government publications are sources of data that may be used to answer student questions. Students may be interested in facts about another country as a result of a social studies unit. Olympic records in various events over the years or data related to space flight are other examples of topics around which student questions may be formulated. For these and hundreds of other questions, data can be found on the World Wide Web. (See Chapter 8.)

The Shape of Data

A big conceptual idea in data analysis can be referred to as the *shape of data:* a sense of how data are spread or grouped, what characteristics they have, and what they tell us in a global way about the population from which they are taken.

Each of the graphical techniques we will discuss gives a visual picture of the shape of data. Students should learn that different graphs provide different snapshots of the data. For the particular question being answered, the choice of graphs is made around the notion of the shape of the data.

Statistical techniques provide a numeric picture of the shape of the data. The numbers can be thought of as measures of the shape. For example, the median tells us where the center is. The range tells about the spread of the data.

CLASSIFICATION AND DATA ANALYSIS

Classification involves making decisions about how to categorize things. This basic activity is fundamental to data analysis. In order to formulate questions and decide how to represent data that have been gathered, decisions must be made about how things might be categorized. Farm animals, for example, might be grouped by number of legs; by type of product they provide; by those that work, provide food, or are pets; by size or color; by the type of food they eat; and so on. Each of these groupings is based on a different attribute of the animals.

Young children need experiences with categorizing things in different ways in order to learn to make sense of real-world data. Attribute activities are explicitly designed to develop this flexible reasoning about the characteristics of data.

Attribute Materials

Attribute materials are sets of objects that lend themselves to being sorted and classified in different ways. *Unstructured* attribute materials include such things as seashells, leaves, the children themselves, or the set of the children's shoes. The *attributes* are the ways that the materials can be sorted. For example, hair color, height, and gender are attributes of children. Each attribute has a number of different *values:* for example, blond, brown, or red (for the attribute of hair color); tall or short (for height); male or female (for gender).

A *structured* set of attribute pieces has exactly one piece for every possible combination of values for each attribute. For example, several commercial sets of plastic attribute materials have four attributes: color (red, yellow, blue), shape (circle, triangle, rectangle, square, hexagon), size (big, little), and thickness (thick, thin). The specific values, number of values, or number of attributes that a set may have is not important. Two teacher-made sets of structured attribute pieces are illustrated in Figure 21.1 on page 390.

The value of using structured attribute materials is that the attributes and values are clearly identified and easily described by students. There is no confusion about what values a particular piece possesses, so you can focus your attention on the reasoning skills that the activities are meant to serve.

NCTM Standards "Organizing data into categories should begin with informal sorting experiences, such as helping to put away groceries. . . . Young children should continue activities that focus on attributes of objects and data so that by the second grade, they can sort and classify simultaneously, using more than one attribute" (pp. 109–110).

Activities with Attribute Materials

Most attribute activities are best done with young children sitting on the floor in a large circle where all can see and have access to the materials. All activities should be conducted in an easygoing manner that encourages risk taking, clear thinking, attentiveness, and discussion of ideas.

Most of the activities here will be described using the geometric shapes in Figure 21.1. However, each could be done with any structured set, and some could be done with nonstructured materials.

Learning Classification Schemes

Several attribute activities involve using overlapping loops, each containing a designated class of materials such as pieces that are "red" or "not square." Loops can be made of yarn or drawn on large sheets of paper. When two loops overlap, the area that is inside both loops is for the pieces that have both properties. Children as young as kindergarten can have fun with simple loop activities. With the use of words such as *and, or,* and *not,* the loop activities become quite challenging.

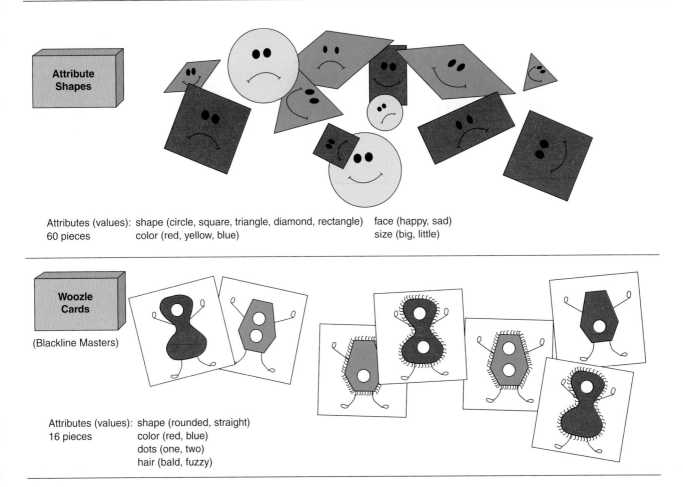

Attributes (values): shape (circle, square, triangle, diamond, rectangle) face (happy, sad)
60 pieces   color (red, yellow, blue)   size (big, little)

Attributes (values): shape (rounded, straight)
16 pieces   color (red, blue)
          dots (one, two)
          hair (bald, fuzzy)

FIGURE 21.1 Three teacher-made attribute sets. Attribute shapes are made in large sizes from poster board and laminated. Woozle Cards can be duplicated on card stock, quickly colored in two colors, laminated, and cut into cards (see Blackline Masters).

Before children can use loops in a problem-solving activity, the scheme itself must be understood. A good way to accomplish this is to do a few activities that involve the loops. Children find these interesting and fun. After several days of working with these initial activities, you can move on to problem-solving activities involving the same formats.

ACTIVITY 21.1

The First Loops

Give children two large loops of yarn or string. Direct them to put all the red pieces inside one string and all triangles inside the other. Let the children try to resolve the difficulty of what to do with the red triangles. When the notion of overlapping the strings to create an area common to both loops is clear, more challenging activities can be explored.

Later, "strings" or loops can be drawn on poster board or on large sheets of paper. If you happen to have a magnetic blackboard, try using small magnets on the backs of the pieces, and conduct full-class activities with the pieces on the board. Students can come to the board to place or arrange pieces inside loops drawn on the board with colored chalk.

Each loop can be given a label indicating a particular attribute. As shown in Figure 21.2, the labels need not be restricted to single attributes. Affix or draw labels on each loop and have students take turns placing pieces in the appropriate regions. If a piece does not fit in any region, it is placed outside of all of the loops.

It is important to introduce labels for negative attributes such as "not red" or "not small." Also important is the use of *and* and *or* connectives, as in "red and square" or "big or happy." This use of *and, or,* and *not* significantly widens children's classification schemes. It also will cause young children considerable difficulty as they attempt to place pieces in the correct regions of the loop diagrams.

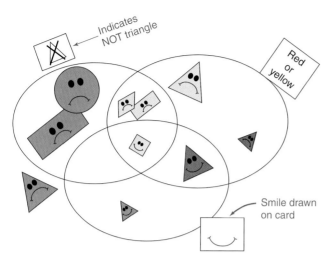

Indicates NOT triangle

Red or yellow

Smile drawn on card

FIGURE 21.2 **A three-loop activity with attribute pieces.**

Classification Problems

The activities described so far have students attempting to classify materials according to *our* schemes—the teacher creates a classification, and the children fit pieces into it. All that is required in these activities is an understanding of the loop method of classification and the ability to discriminate the attributes. Very limited logical reasoning is involved. A more significant activity is to infer how things have been classified when the scheme is not clearly articulated. The following activities require students to make and test conjectures about how things are being classified. These activities more directly prepare students to analyze their world, formulate questions, and do data analysis.

ACTIVITY 21.2

Guess My Rule

For this activity, try using students instead of shapes as attribute "pieces." Decide on an attribute of your students such as "blue jeans" or "stripes on clothing," but do not tell your rule to the class. Silently look at one child at a time and move the child to the left or right according to this attribute rule. After a number of students have been sorted, have the next child come up and ask students to predict which group he or she belongs in. Before the rule is articulated, continue the activity for a while so that others in the class will have an opportunity to determine the rule. This same activity can be done with virtually any materials that can be sorted. When unstructured materials such as students, students' shoes, shells, or buttons are used, the classifications may be quite obscure, providing an interesting challenge.

ACTIVITY 21.3

Hidden Labels

Select label cards for the loops of string, and place the cards face down. Begin to sort pieces according to the turned-down labels. As you sort, have students try to determine what the labels are for each of the loops. Let students who think they have guessed the labels try to place a piece in the proper loop, but avoid having them guess the labels aloud. Students who think they know the labels can be asked to "play teacher" and respond to the guesses of the others. Point out that one way to test an idea about the labels is to select pieces that you think might go in a particular section. Do not turn the cards up until most students have figured out the rule. With simple, one-value labels and only two loops, this activity can easily be played in kindergarten.

Connections to Data Analysis

"Guess My Rule" can and should be repeated with real-world materials connected to students' current explorations. For example, if you were doing a unit on animals in the backyard, you can use pictures of animals. The loops used with the attribute materials provide a first form of data presentation. The class can "graph" data about themselves by placing information in loops with labels. A graph of "Our Pets" might consist of a picture of each student's pet or favorite stuffed animal (in lieu of a pet) and be affixed to a wall display showing how the pets were classified. Different classifications would produce different graphs. For example, the graphs could show pets by the number of legs; by fur, feathers, or scales; by how long they have been with the family; and so on.

Numerous resource books contain exciting and challenging activities involving attribute materials. These are aimed primarily at logical reasoning and less at the skills of classification. These logic activities were first made popular in the 1960s and 1970s. The idea was that young children would learn reasoning skills by playing these games. But reasoning should not be a strand of the curriculum. Rather, it should pervade all of the mathematics that occurs in the classroom. Furthermore, research has not supported the hoped-for claims of logic activities. They have persisted in the early childhood curriculum primarily because they are fun and involve thinking. No harm is done by these activities, but they do not really fit into any of the content strands of the curriculum.

 TECHNOLOGY NOTE

A popular program that encourages creation of classification schemes and using loop diagrams is *Tabletop, Jr.* (Brøderbund, 1995b). This program can be used by individuals or the full class. The program provides a wide variety of objects that can each be constructed with varying attributes. Various sorting choices are available, including the loop diagrams seen here. Objects can also be sorted according to a hidden rule specified by a user, a computer version of "Guess My Rule" with a lot of variation. Picture graphs can be constructed with the objects providing a direct link to data graphing.

One of the most challenging and most interesting programs in this area is *Zoombinis Logical Journey*, EEV (The Learning Company). Zoombinis are little creatures with variations in hair, eyes, nose, and feet. The program has 12 problems of increasing difficulty to solve, each in an adventure context involving the Zoombini creatures. These are more logic tasks than classification. ∎

Graphical Representations

How data are organized should be directly related to the question that caused you to collect the data in the first place. For example, suppose that students want to know how many pockets they have on their clothing, an idea suggested by Marilyn Burns (1996). Each student in the room counts his or her pockets and the data are collected.

❌ **STOP** If your second grade class had collected these data, what are some ways that you might suggest they organize and graph them? Is one of your ideas better than others for answering the question about how many pockets? Think about this before reading on.

If a large bar graph is made with a bar for every student, that will certainly tell how many pockets each student has. However, is it the best way to answer the question? If the data were categorized by number of pockets, then a graph showing the number of students with two pockets, three pockets, and so on will easily show which number of pockets is most common and how the number of pockets varies across the class.

Students should be involved in deciding how they want to represent their data. However, children with little experience with the various methods of picturing data will not be aware of the many options that are available. Sometimes you can suggest a new way of displaying data and have children learn to construct that type of graph or chart. Once they have made the display, they can discuss its value. Did this graph (or chart or picture) tell about our data in a clear way? Compared to other ways of displaying data, how is this better?

The emphasis or goal of this instruction should be to help children see that graphs and charts tell about information, that different types of representations tell different things about the same data. The value of having students actually construct their own graphs is not so much that they learn the techniques but that they are personally invested in the data and that they learn how a graph conveys information. Once a graph is constructed, the most important activity is discussing what it tells the people who see it, especially those who were not involved in making the graph. Discussions about graphs of real data that the children have themselves been involved in gathering will help them interpret other graphs and charts that they see in newspapers and on TV.

What we should *not* do is get overly anxious about the tedious details of graph construction. The issues of analysis and communication are your agendas and are much more important than the technique! In the real world, technology will take care of details.

There are two equally good possibilities you may consider when planning to have your students construct graphs or charts. First, you can simply encourage students to do their best and make charts and graphs that make sense to them and that they feel communicate the information they wish to convey. This is not to say that children do not need guidance. They should have seen and been involved in group constructions of various types of graphs and charts. This provides them with some ideas from which to choose for their own graphs. This informal approach may be best with younger students because they will be more personally invested in their work and not distracted by the techniques of technology. Care should be taken not to worry about fancy labeling or nice, neat pictures. The intent is to get the students involved in communicating a message about their data.

The second option is to use technology. The computer and graphing calculators have provided us with many tools for constructing simple yet powerful representations. With the help of technology, it is possible to construct several different pictures of the same data with very little effort. The discussion can then focus on the message or information that each format provides. Students can make their own selections of various graphs and can justify their choice based on their own intended purposes. As just one example, Figure 21.3 shows four graphs produced by *The Graph Club* (Tom Snyder, 1993). When two or more graphs are being created from the same data, it is possible to see all graphs change accordingly. How does a pie graph show information differently than a picture graph?

Bar Graphs

Bar graphs and tally charts are among the first ways to group and present data and are especially useful in grades K–3. At this early level, bar graphs should be made so that each bar consists of countable parts such as squares, objects, tallies, or pictures of objects. No numeric scale is necessary. Graphs

Fruits We Like Best

Title	
What	How Many?
🍌	6
🍎	4
🍊	3
🍑	9
🍐	5

FIGURE 21.3 **Four graphs produced with *Graph Club* software.**

0 1 2 3 4 5 6 7 8 9 10

should be simple and quickly constructed. Figure 21.4 on page 394 illustrates a few techniques that can be used to make a graph quickly with the whole class.

A "real graph" uses the actual objects being graphed. Examples include types of shoes, seashells, and books. Each item can be placed in a square so that comparisons and counts are easily made.

Picture graphs use a drawing of some sort that represents what is being graphed. Students can make their own drawings, or you can duplicate drawings to be colored or cut out to suit particular needs.

Symbolic graphs use something like squares, blocks, tallies, or Xs to represent the things being counted in the graph. An easy idea is to use sticky notes as elements of a graph. These can be stuck directly to the chalkboard or other chart and rearranged if needed.

To make a quick graph of class data, follow these steps:

1. Decide on what groups of data will make up the different bars. It is good to have two to six different bars in a graph.
2. Have each participant prepare a contribution to the graph before you begin. For real or picture graphs, the object or picture should be ready to be placed on the graph. For symbolic graphs, students should write down or mark their choice.
3. Have students, in small groups, quickly place or mark their entry on the graph. A graph mat can be placed on the floor, or a chart can be prepared on the wall or chalkboard. If tape or pins are to be used, have these items ready.

A class of 25 to 30 students can make a graph in less than 10 minutes, leaving ample time to use it for questions and observations.

Clip paper pictures or symbols on a chart that
has a paper clip prepared in each square.

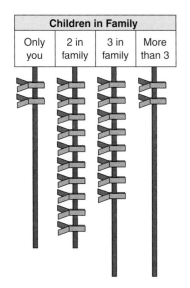

Hang ribbons, and students
clip on pinch-style clothespins

A graph mat can be
made on a sheet of
plastic about 8 to 10
feet long and used
on the floor. Make
5 or 6 columns with
12 to 15 squares in
each column. Students
place real objects in
the columns to show
the number of each.

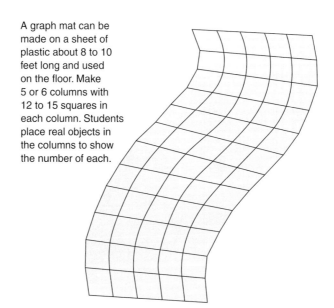

FIGURE 21.4 Some ideas for quick graphs that can be used again and again.

Once a graph has been constructed, engage the class in a discussion of what information the graph tells or conveys. "What can you tell about our class by looking at this shoe graph?" Graphs convey factual information (more people wear sneakers than any other kind of shoe) and also provide opportunities to make inferences that are not directly observable in the graph (kids in this class do not like to wear leather shoes). The difference between actual facts and inferences is an important idea in graph construction and is also an important idea in science. Older students can examine graphs found in newspapers or magazines and discuss the *facts* in the graphs and the *message* that may have been intended by the person who made the graph.

As children begin to see different types of graphs, they can begin to make their own graphs of information gathered independently or by a group. A simple way to move graphing from the entire class to a small group is to assign different data collection tasks to different groups of children. The task is to gather the data and decide on and make

a graph that displays as clearly as possible the information found.

Stem-and-Leaf Plots

Stem-and-leaf plots are a popular form of bar graph in which numeric data are plotted by using the actual numerals in the data to form the graph. By way of example, suppose that the American League baseball teams had posted the following record of wins over the past season:

Baltimore	45	Milwaukee	91
Boston	94	Minnesota	98
California	85	New York	100
Chicago	72	Oakland	101
Cleveland	91	Seattle	48
Detroit	102	Toronto	64
Kansas City	96	Texas	65

If the data are to be grouped by tens, list the tens digits in order and draw a line to the right, as in Figure 21.5(a). These form the "stem" of the graph. Next, go through the list of scores, and write the ones digits next to the appropriate tens digit, as in Figure 21.5(b). These are the "leaves." The process of making the graph groups the data for you. Furthermore, every piece of data can be retrieved from the graph. (Notice that stem-and-leaf plots are best made on graph paper so that each digit takes up the same amount of space.)

To provide more information, the graph can be quickly rewritten, ordering each leaf from least to most, as in Figure 21.5(c). In this form, it may be useful to identify the number that belongs to a particular team, indicating its relative place within the grouped listing.

Stem-and-leaf graphs are not limited to two-digit data. For example, if the data ranged from 600 to 1300, the stem could be the numerals from 6 to 13 and the leaves made of two-digit numbers separated by commas.

Figure 21.6 illustrates two additional variations. When two sets of data are to be compared, the leaves can extend in opposite directions from the same stem. In the same example, notice that the data are grouped by fives instead of tens. When plotting 62, the 2 is written next to the 6; for 67, the 7 is written next to the dot below the 6.

(a) First make the stem.

(b) Write in the leaves directly from the data.

(c) It is easy to rewrite each leaf in numeric order. This puts all of the data in order.

FIGURE 21.5 **Making a stem-and-leaf plot.**

FIGURE 21.6 **Stem-and-leaf plots can be used to compare two sets of data.**

Stem-and-leaf plots are significantly easier for students to make than bar graphs, all of the data are maintained, they provide an efficient method of ordering data, and individual elements of data can be identified.

Continuous Data Graphs

Bar graphs or picture graphs are useful for illustrating categories of data that have no numeric ordering—for example, colors or TV shows. When data are grouped along a continuous scale, they should be ordered along a number line. Examples of such information include temperatures that occur over time, height or weight over age, and percentages of test takers scoring in different intervals along the scale of possible scores.

Line Plots

Line plots are useful *counts* of things along a numeric scale. To make a line plot, a number line is drawn and an X is made above the corresponding value on the line for every corresponding data element. One advantage of a line plot is that every piece of data is shown on the graph. It is also a very easy type of graph for students to make. It is essentially a bar graph with a potential bar for every possible value. A simple example is shown in Figure 21.7.

Histograms

A *histogram* is a form of bar graph in which the categories are consecutive equal intervals along a numeric scale. The height or length of each bar is determined by the number of data elements falling into that particular interval. Histograms are not difficult in concept but can cause problems for the students constructing them. What is the appropriate interval to use for the bar width? What is a good scale to use for the length of the bars? That all of the data must be grouped and counted within each

Line Plot

Test scores, Period 6

Histogram (TI-83)

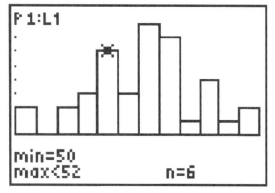

Age of U.S. presidents at inauguration

Line Graph

Temperature change over 24 hours

FIGURE 21.7 **Three approaches to graphing data over continuous intervals. Notice that the horizontal scale must show some progression and is not just a grouping, as in a bar graph.**

interval causes further difficulty. Technology helps us with all of these decisions, allowing children to focus on the graph and its message. Graphing calculators, for example, produce histograms without much difficulty. They allow for the size of the interval to be specified and easily changed. By connecting the calculator to a computer, the graphs can be printed out or pasted into a word processor for inclusion in a student report. Figure 21.7 shows an example of a histogram produced on a TI-83.

The little figure that looks like a bug on top of one of the bars is the trace indicator. It can be moved from bar to bar.

For each bar, the trace indicates the number of data points in that interval. On this bar, there are six data points indicated by "$n = 6$" in the lower part of the screen.

Line Graphs

A *line graph* is used when there is a numeric value associated with equally spaced points along a continuous number scale. Points are plotted to represent two related pieces of data, and a line is drawn to connect the points. For example, a line graph might be used to show how the length of a flagpole shadow changed from one hour to the next during the day. The horizontal scale would be time, and the vertical scale would be the length of the shadow. Discrete points can be plotted and straight lines drawn connecting them. In the example of the shadow, a shadow did exist at all times, but its length did not jump or drop from one plotted value to the other. It changed continuously as suggested by the graph. See the example in Figure 21.7.

Circle Graphs

A circle or pie graph is used when data have been partitioned into parts and interest is in the ratio of each part to the whole. In Figure 21.8, each of two graphs shows the percentages of students with different numbers of siblings. One graph is based on classroom data and the other on schoolwide data.

Fifth Grade: Mrs. Jones
30 students

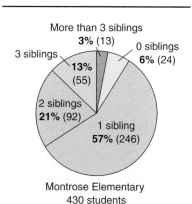

Montrose Elementary
430 students

FIGURE 21.8 **Circle graphs show ratios of part to whole and can be used to compare ratios.**

Because pie graphs display ratios rather than quantities, the small set of class data can be compared to the large set of school data. That could not be done with bar graphs.

Easily Made Circle Graphs

You have already seen (in Figure 21.3) a computer-generated circle graph (or pie graph) that can be used by children as early as the second grade. Nearly every spreadsheet program has circle graph capabilities.

Even without technology, there are a variety of ways that circle graphs can be made easily. Circle graphs of the students in your room can be made quickly and quite dramatically. Suppose, for example, that each student picked his or her favorite basketball team in the NCAA tournament's "Final Four." Line up all of the students in the room so that students favoring the same team are together. Now form the entire group into a circle of students. Tape the ends of four long strings to the floor in the center of the circle, and extend them to the circle at each point where the teams change. Voilà! A very nice pie graph with no measuring and no percentages. If you copy and cut out a hundredths disk (one is in the Blackline Masters) and place it on the center of the circle, the strings will show approximate percentages for each part of your graph (see Figure 21.9).

Another easy approach to circle graphs is similar to the human pie graph. Begin by having students make a bar graph of the data. Once complete, cut out the bars themselves, and tape them together end to end. Next, tape the two ends together to form a circle. Estimate where the center of the circle is, draw lines to the points where different bars meet, and trace around the full loop. You can estimate percentages using the hundredths disk as before.

From Percentages to Pie Graphs

If students have experienced either of the two methods just described, using their own calculations to make pie graphs will make more sense. The numbers in each category are added to form the total or whole. (That's the same as taping all of the strips together or lining up the students.) By dividing each of the parts by the whole with a calculator, numbers between 0 and 1 result—fractional parts of the whole. If rounded to hundredths, these numbers are now percentages of the whole. Rounding may cause some error. With a copy of the hundredths disk, students can easily make a pie chart and never have to mess with degrees and protractors. Trace around the disk to make the outline of the pie. Mark the center through a small hole in the disk, and draw a line to the circle. Start from that point, and use the disk to measure hundredths around the outside.

DESCRIPTIVE STATISTICS

Although graphs provide visual images of data, measures of the data are a different and important way to describe data. Numbers that describe data are *statistics,* measures of the data that quantify some attribute of them. The things that are most often described numerically about a set of data are the distance between the highest and lowest data values (the *range*), some measure of where the center of the data is (an *average*), and how dispersed the data are within the range (the *variance* or *dispersion*). Students can get an idea of the importance of these statistics by exploring the ideas informally.

Averages

The term *average* is heard quite frequently in everyday usage. Sometimes it refers to an exact arithmetic average, as in "the average daily rainfall." Sometimes it is used quite loosely, as in "She is about average height." In either situation, an average is a single number or measure that is descriptive of a larger collection of numbers. If your test average is 92, it is assumed that somehow all of your test scores are reflected by this number.

The *mean, median,* and *mode* are specific types of averages or *measures of central tendency.* The *mode* is the value that occurs most frequently in the data set. Of these three statistics, the mode is the least useful and could perhaps be ignored completely. Consider the following set of numbers:

$$1, 1, 3, 5, 6, 7, 8, 9$$

The mode of this set is 1 and not a very good description of this set. If the 8 in this string of numbers were a 9, there would be two modes. If one of the ones were changed to a 2, there would be no mode at all. In short, the mode is a statistic that does not always exist, does not necessarily reflect the center of the data, and can be highly unstable, changeable with very small changes in the data.

The *mean* is computed by adding all of the numbers in the set and dividing the sum by the number of elements added. This is the statistic that is sometimes referred to as the *average,* although the terms are not synonymous. The mean

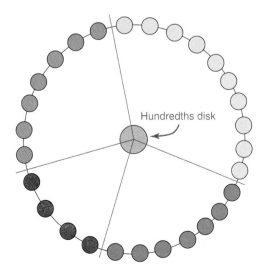

FIGURE 21.9 A human pie graph: Students are arranged in a circle, with string stretched between them to show the divisions.

Hundredths disk

FIGURE 21.10 Ordered stem-and-leaf plots grouped by fives. Medians and upper and lower quartiles are found on the stem-and-leaf plots. Medians and quartiles are circled or are represented by a bar (I) if they fall between two elements.

The following numbers represent the ages in months of a class of sixth-grade students.

Boys		Girls	
132	122	140	131
140	130	129	128
133	134	141	131
142	125	134	132
134 *Joe B.*	147	124	130
(137)	131	129 *Whitney*	127
139	129	(125)	

All students

```
12 | 2, 4
 • | 5, 5, 7, 8, (9,) 9, 9,
13 | 0, 0, 1, 1, (1,) 2, 2, 3, 4, 4, 4
 • | (7,) 9
14 | 0, 0, 1, 2
 • | 7
```

Boys

```
12 | 2
 • | 5, 9
13 | (0,) 1, 2, 3, |4, 4
 • | 7, (9)
14 | 0, 2
 • | 7
```

Girls

```
12 | 4
 • | 5, 7,|8, 9, 9
13 | (0,) 1, 1, 2,|4
 • |
14 | 0, 1
 • |
```

of our sample set is 5 (40 ÷ 8). The mean is discussed in more detail later in the chapter.

The *median* is the middle value in an ordered set of data. Half of all values lie at or above the median and half below. For the eight numbers in our sample set, the median is between 5 and 6, or 5.5. The median is easier to understand and to compute and is not affected, as the mean is, by one or two extremely large or extremely small values outside the range of the rest of the data.

Box-and-Whisker Plots

Box-and-whisker plots (or just *box plots*) are an easy method for visually displaying not only the median statistic but also information about the range and distribution or variance of data. In Figure 21.10, the ages in months for 27 sixth-grade students are given, along with stem-and-leaf plots for the full class and the boys and girls separately. Box-and-whisker plots are shown in Figure 21.11.

Each box-and-whisker plot has these three features:

1. A box that contains the "middle half" of the data, one-fourth to the left and right of the median. The ends of the box are at the *lower quartile,* the median of the lower half of the data, and the *upper quartile,* the median of the upper half of the data.
2. A line inside the box at the median of the data.
3. A line extending from the end of each box to the *lower extreme* and *upper extreme* of the data. Each line therefore covers the upper and lower fourths of the data.

Look at the information these box plots provide at a glance! The box and the lengths of the lines provide a quick indication of how the data are spread out or bunched together. Since the median is shown, this spreading or bunching can be determined for each quarter of the data. The entire class in this example is much more spread out in the upper half than the lower half. The girls are much more closely grouped in age than either the boys or the class as a whole. It is immediately obvious that at least three-fourths of the girls are younger than the median age of the boys. The *range* of the data (difference between upper and lower extremes) is represented by the length of the plot, and the extreme values can be read directly.

FIGURE 21.11 Box-and-whisker plots show a lot of information.

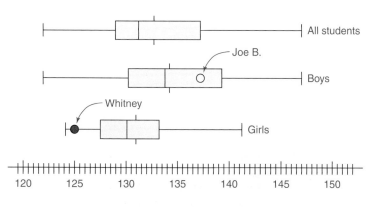

Age (months) of 27 sixth-grade students

It is easy to mark and label entries of particular interest. For example, Joe B. and Whitney might be the class officers.

Making box-and-whisker plots is quite simple. First, put the data in order. An easy and valuable method is to make a stem-and-leaf plot and order the leaves, providing another visual image as well. Next, find the median. Simply count the number of values and determine the middle one. This can be done directly on the stem-and-leaf plots as was done in Figure 21.10. To find the two quartiles, ignore the median itself, and find the medians of the upper and lower halves of the data. Mark the two extremes, the two quartiles, and the median above an appropriate number line. Draw the box and the lines. Box plots can also be drawn vertically.

Note that the means for the data in our example are each just slightly higher than the medians (class = 132.4; boys = 133.9; girls = 130.8). For this example, the means themselves do not provide nearly as much information as the box plots. In Figure 21.11, the means are shown with small marks extending above and below each box.

Graphing calculators and several computer programs draw box-and-whisker plots, making this relatively simple process even more accessible. The TI-73 and TI-83 calculators can draw box plots for up to three sets of data on the same axis. In Figure 21.12, the data for the top box plot are based on 23 items. The second plot has 122 items. The third plot has 48 items of data. When you compare both large and small sets of data in this manner, the spread or lack of spread of the data becomes much more obvious.

❌ **STOP**   Notice that in Figure 21.11 the box for the boys is actually a bit longer than the box for the whole class. How can that be when there are clearly more students in the full class than there are boys? How would you explain this apparent discrepancy to a class of seventh graders?

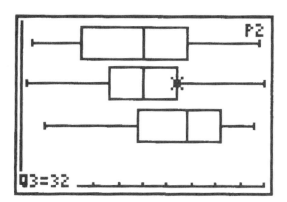

FIGURE 21.12 **Three box plots of data falling between the values of 0 and 50. Twenty-three items are represented by the top plot, 122 by the middle plot, and 48 by the bottom plot. The cursor on the middle plot shows that the third quartile is 32. What other information can be determined from this plot?**

Understanding the Mean: Two Concepts

Due to ease of computation and stability, the median when compared to the mean has some advantages as a practical average. However, the mean will continue to be used in popular media and in books. For smaller sets of data such as your test scores, the mean is perhaps a more meaningful statistic. Finally, the mean is used in the computation of other statistics such as the standard deviation. Therefore, it remains important that students have a good concept of what the mean tells them about a set of numbers.

There are actually two different ways to think about the mean. First, it is a number that represents what all of the data items would be if they were leveled out. In this sense, the mean represents all of the data items. Statisticians prefer to think of the mean as a central balance point. This concept of the mean is more in keeping with the notion of a measure of the "center" of the data or a measure of central tendency. Both concepts are discussed in the following sections.

A Leveling Concept of the Mean

Suppose that the average number of family members for the students in your class is 5. One way to interpret this is to think about distributing the entire collection of moms, dads, sisters, and brothers to each of the students so that each would have a "family" of the same size. To say that you have an average of 93 for the four tests in your class is like spreading the total of all of your points evenly across the four tests. It is as if each student had the same family size and each test score were the same, but the totals matched the actual distributions. This concept of the mean is easy to understand and explain and has the added benefit that it leads directly to the algorithm for computing the mean.

ACTIVITY 21.4

Leveling the Bars

Have students make a bar graph of some data using plastic connecting cubes such as Unifix. Choose a situation with 5 or 6 bars with no more than 10 or 12 cubes in each. For example, the graph in Figure 21.13 shows prices for six toys. The task for students is to use the graph itself to determine what the price would be if all of the toys were the same price, assuming that the total for all the toys remained the same. Students will use various techniques to rearrange the cubes in the graph but will eventually create six equal bars, possibly with some leftovers that could mentally be distributed in fractional amounts. (In the example, the total number of cubes is a multiple of six.) Do not tell students they are finding the average or mean, only that they are to find equal-length bars.

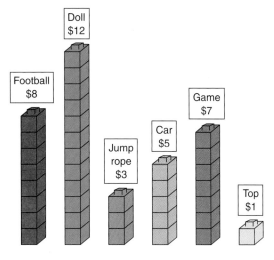

Bar graph made with plastic snap cubes

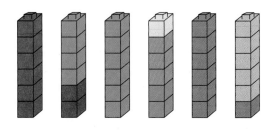

The same cubes rearranged into equal stacks.
Their height is the <u>mean</u> value of the bars above.

FIGURE 21.13 Understanding the mean as a leveling of the data.

Explain to students that the size of the leveled bars is the *mean* of the data—the amount that each item would cost if all items cost the same amount but the total of the prices remained fixed.

Follow "Leveling the Bars" with the next activity to help students develop an algorithm for finding the mean.

ACTIVITY 21.5

The Mean Foot

Pose the following question: What is the mean length of our feet in inches? Have each student cut a strip of adding machine tape that matches the length of his or her foot. Students record their names and the length of their feet in inches on the strips. Suggest that before finding a mean for the class, you will first get means for smaller groups. Put students into groups of four, six, or eight students. (Groups of five or seven will prove to be problematic.) In each group, have the students tape their foot strips end to end. The task for each group is to come up with a method of finding the mean without using any of the lengths

written on the strips. They can only use the combined strip. Each group will share their method with the class. From this work, they will devise a method for determining the mean for the whole class.

 STOP Before reading on, what is a method that the students could use in "The Mean Foot"?

To evenly distribute the inches for each student's foot among the members of the group, they can fold the strip into equal parts so that there are as many sections as students in the group. Then they can measure the length of any one part.

How can you find the mean for the whole class? Suppose there are 23 students in the class. Using the strips already taped together, make one very long strip for the whole class. It is not reasonable to fold this long strip into 23 equal sections. But if you wanted to know how long the resulting strip would be, how could that be done? The total length of the strip is the sum of the lengths of the 23 individual foot strips. To find the length of one section if the strip were actually folded in 23 parts, simply divide by 23. In fact, students can mark off "mean feet" along the strip. There should be very close to 23 equal-length "feet." This dramatically illustrates the usual add-up-and-divide algorithm for finding the mean.

A Balance Point Concept of the Mean

Statisticians think about the mean as a point on a number line where the data on either side of the point are balanced. To help think about the mean in this way, it is useful to think about the data placed on a line plot rather than as bar graphs. What is important is not how many pieces of data are on either side of the mean or balance point but the distances of data from the mean that must balance.

To illustrate, draw a number line on the board, and arrange eight sticky notes above the number 3 as shown in Figure 21.14(a). Each sticky note represents one family. The notes are positioned on the line to indicate how many pets are owned by the family. Stacked up like this would indicate that all families have the same number of pets. The mean is three pets. But different families are likely to have different numbers of pets. So we could think of eight families with a range of numbers of pets. Some may have zero pets, and some may have as many as ten or even more. How could you change the number of pets for these eight families so that the mean remains at 3? Students will suggest moving the sticky notes in opposite directions, probably in pairs. This will result in a symmetrical arrangement. But what if one of the families has eight pets, a move of five spaces from the 3? This might be balanced by moving two families to the left, one three spaces to the 0 and one two spaces to the 1. Figure 21.14(b) shows one way the families could be rearranged to maintain a mean

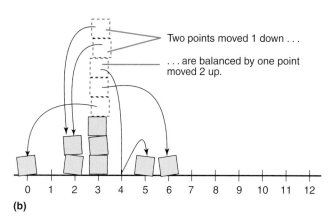

Two points moved 1 down . . .

. . . are balanced by one point moved 2 up.

(a)

(b)

FIGURE 21.14 **(a) If all data points are the same, the mean is that value. (b) By moving data points away from the mean in a balanced manner, different distributions can be found that have the same mean.**

of 3. You should stop here and find at least two other distributions of the families, each having a mean of 3.

Use the next activity to find the mean or balance point given the data.

ACTIVITY 21.6

Finding the Balance Point

Have students draw a number line from 0 to 12 with about an inch between the numbers. Use six small sticky notes to represent the prices of six toys as shown in Figure 21.15. Have them place a light pencil mark on the line where they think the mean might be. For the moment, avoid the add-up-and-divide computation. The task is to determine the actual mean by moving the sticky notes in toward the "center." That is, the students are finding out what price or point on the number line balances out the six prices on the line. For each move of a sticky one space to the left (a toy with a lower price), a different sticky must be moved one space to the right (a toy with a higher price). Eventually, all stickies should be stacked above the same number, the balance point or mean.

FIGURE 21.15 **Move data points in toward the center or balance point without changing the balance around that point. When you have all points at the same value, that is the balance or the mean.**

STOP Stop now and try this exercise yourself. Notice that after any pair of moves that keep the distribution balanced, you actually have a new distribution of prices with the same mean. The same was true when you moved the stickies out from the mean when they were all stacked on the same point.

The balance concept does not lead to the add-up-and-divide algorithm for computing the mean. However, it is useful to do the following side-by-side approach. Make bars of cubes for the original data in Figure 21.15. Level the bars by moving only one cube at a time from a longer bar to a shorter bar. Each time you move a cube off of a bar, the sticky note for that bar must be moved one space to the left. At the same time, the sticky note for the bar to which the cube was added must be moved one space to the right. As you continue to move cubes one at a time, adjust the sticky notes accordingly.

Changes in the Mean

Notice that the mean only defines the center of a set of data and so by itself is not a very useful description of the shape of the data. The balance approach to the mean clearly illustrates that many different distributions can have the same mean.*

Especially for small sets of data, the mean is significantly affected by extreme values. For example, suppose that another toy with a price of $20 is added to the six we have been using in the examples. How will the mean change? If the $1 toy were removed, how would the mean be affected? Suppose that one new toy is added that increases the mean from $6 to $7. How much does the new toy cost? Students should be

---

*The balance concept of the mean is the one developed in the Connected Math Project, one of the three reform programs for the middle grades. It is also developed in the *Used Numbers* book *Statistics: Middles, Means, and In-Betweens* (Friel, Mokros, & Russell, 1992).

challenged with questions such as these using small sets of data and either the balance or the leveling concept.

 In NCTM's *e-Standards,* the applet "Comparing Properties of the Mean and the Median" shows seven data points that can dragged back and forth along a number line with the mean and median updated instantly. The applet allows students to see how stable the median is and how changing one point can affect the mean.

Scatter Plots and Relationships

Data are often analyzed to search for or demonstrate relationships between two sets of data or phenomena. For example, what are the relationships, if any, between time spent watching television and overall grades? Does the size of a college have anything to do with the cost of attending?

All sorts of real situations exist where we are interested in relationships between two variables or two numeric phenomena. The world of science abounds with experimental data. How far does a toy car roll down an inclined plane as compared to the angle of the plane? How tall do beans grow over a 21-day period from the day they sprout? Such data are generally gathered from some sort of experiment that is set up and observed, with measurements taken. The experiment defines the various variables to look at.

Data that may be related are gathered in pairs. For example, if you were going to examine the possible relationship between hours of TV watched and grades, each person in the survey or sample would produce a pair of numbers, one for TV time and one for grade point average.

Scatter Plots

Regardless of the source of the data, a good first attempt at examining them for possible relationships is to create a *scatter plot* of the two variables involved, a graph of points on a co-

ordinate grid with each axis representing one of the two variables. Each pair of numbers from the two sets of data, when plotted, produces a visual image of the data as well as a hint concerning any possible relationships. Suppose that the following information was gathered from 25 eighth-grade boys: height in inches, weight in pounds, and number of letters in their last name. The two graphs in Figure 21.16 show two possibilities. Graph (a) is a scatter plot of height to weight, and graph (b) is a plot of name length to weight. Both were made with a graphing calculator.

As you would expect, the boys' weights seem to increase as their heights increase. However, the relationship is far from perfect. There is no reason to expect any relationship between name length and weight, and indeed the dots appear to be almost randomly distributed.

 "Teachers should encourage students to plot many data sets and look for relationships in the [scatter]plots; computer graphing software and graphing calculators can be very helpful in this work. Students should see a range of examples in which plotting data sets suggests linear relationships, and no apparent relationships at all" (p. 253).

Best-Fit Lines

If your scatter plot indicates a relationship, it can be simply described in words. "As boys get taller, they tend to get heavier." This is correct but not particularly useful. What exactly is the relationship? If I knew the height of a boy, could I predict what his weight might be based on this information? Like much of statistical analysis, the value of a statistic is to predict what has not yet been observed. We poll a small sample of voters before an election to predict how the full population will vote. Here, can a sample of 30 students predict the weights of other students?

The relationship in these cases is not a number like a mean or a standard deviation but rather a line or curve. Is there a line that can be drawn through the scatter plot that

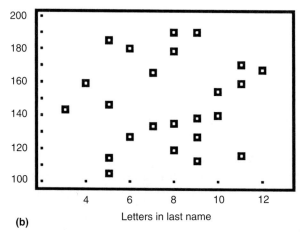

(a)   Height in inches   (b)   Letters in last name

FIGURE 21.16 Scatter plots show potential relationships or lack of relationships.

represents the "best" approximation of all of the dots and reflects the observed trend? If the scatter plot seems to indicate a steadily increasing or steadily decreasing relationship (as in the height–weight graph), you would probably try to find a straight line that approximates the dots. Sometimes the plot will indicate a curved relationship, in which case you might try to draw a smooth curve like a parabola to approximate the dots.

What Determines Best Fit?

From a strictly visual standpoint, the line you select defines the observed relationship and could be used to predict other values not in the data set. The more closely the dots in the scatter plot hug the line you select, the greater the confidence you would have in the predictive value of the line. Certainly you could draw a straight line somewhere in the name length–weight graph, but you would not have much faith in its predictive capability because the dots would be quite dispersed from any line you might draw.

ACTIVITY 21.7

Best-Fit Line

Once students have collected related data and prepared a scatter plot, duplicate an accurate version of the plot for each group of students. Provide the groups with a piece of spaghetti to use as a line. The task is to tape the line on the plot so that it is the "best" line to represent the relationship in the dots. Further, the students are to develop a rationale for why they positioned the line as they did.

Using an overhead transparency of the plot, compare the lines chosen by various groups and their rationales.

STOP Before reading further, return to the height–weight plot in Figure 21.16, graph (a), and draw a straight line that you think would make a good line of best fit. (You may want to make a photo enlargement of that figure to use with your class.) What reason would you offer for why you drew the line where you did?

Many of the reasons students will give for their best-fit line will be rather subjective: "It just looks right" or "There are just as many points above as below." Others will see how many points they can make the line touch. Most intuitive ideas fail to consider all of the points. Two different people using the same criteria might well come up with very different lines. There is a need for a better definition of a best-fit line.

Encourage students to use a more "mathematical" reason for why a line might be best. Since a good line is one around which most dots cluster, a good-fitting line is one where the distances from all of the dots to the line is minimal. This general notion of least distance to the line for all points can lead to an algorithm that will always produce a unique line for a given set of points. Two such algorithms are well known and

used in statistics. The more complicated approach is called the *least squares regression* line. It is an algebraic procedure that is not accessible to middle grade students and is also rather tedious to compute. The second algorithm produces what is called the *median-median* line and is quite easy to determine.

Median-Median Line

The median-median line can be determined either directly from the graph or from the data. It is based on the simple median statistic. The method for determining the median-median line essentially consists of these steps:

1. Separate the data into three "equal" sets of points along the horizontal axis. (In the example of Figure 21.17, since there are 25 points, put the extra point into the middle third.)
2. Find the *median point* in each third of the points. (This is described in the text that follows.)
3. Connect the median points in the first and third sets of data. This line takes into consideration all points in these two sections but ignores the points in the middle third.
4. Draw a parallel line one-third of the distance from this first line to the center median point. This gives the center collection of points a proportional influence on the position of the line.

A *median point* in a scattered collection of points is the point with its first coordinate equal to the median of all the first coordinates and its second coordinate equal to the median of all the second coordinates. Another way of saying this is that the median point is one that is midway vertically and midway horizontally. Using this second formulation, the median point can be found by counting points from the bottom up until you have half the points below and half above. With an odd number of points, draw a horizontal line through the middle point. With an even number of points, draw the line halfway between the two middle points. The median point will fall on this horizontal line. Repeat the process, moving from left to right. The vertical line you find this way

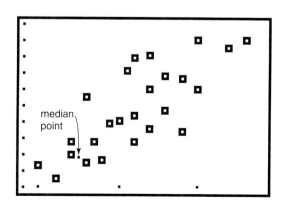

FIGURE 21.17 A height-versus-weight scatter plot. Use the graph to find the median-median line. The single pixel in the lower left is the median point for the left third of the points.

will intersect the horizontal line at the median point. Note that it is not necessary for the median point to be a data point.

In Figure 21.17, the median point in the left-hand third of the data (the first eight points counting left to right) is shown as a single pixel.

 Find the other two median points on your own, and complete steps 3 and 4. Use Figure 21.17.

Median-Median Lines with a Calculator

The TI-73 and TI-83 calculators will compute the median-median line for you. Figure 21.18 shows the calculator plot of the median-median line for the same height-versus-weight data.

Thinking About Functional Relationships

It is worth noting that the median-median line is a graphical representation of a function relating the variable on the horizontal axis to the variable on the vertical axis. Using the height–weight example, it is appropriate to say that *the weight of a boy is a function of his height.* The best-fit line is a mathematical method of determining what the function might be. Different methods of finding the best-fit line will likely develop slightly different lines.

Note that if the function (line) that we found accurately predicted the weight of a boy based on his height, all of the data points would fall along a perfectly straight line. That they do not is a vivid picture of the difference between data found in the world (the points on the graph) and a mathematical model of the real world (the line).

Scatter plots and best-fit lines are discussed again in Chapter 23 on functions. The connection among the real world, statistics, and algebraic ideas is a valuable one to make.

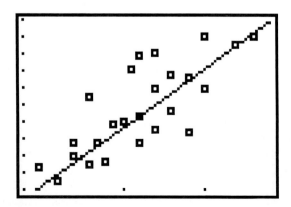

FIGURE 21.18 The median-median line for the points plotted in Figure 21.17.

 ## Technology Note

Data analysis is an area of the curriculum in which technology really changes the way we teach. In the past, the emphasis was on *how* to create the graph and *how* to compute the statistic. Students had to labor over graph paper, drawing scales, labeling axes, coloring the graphs, and so on. Today, every graphical technique and every statistic mentioned in this chapter is readily available in a variety of technologies. An exception may be stem-and-leaf plots. With the help of technology, the focus of instruction in data analysis can and should shift to the big ideas of using graphs and statistics: to describe data, to get a sense of the shape of data, to answer questions with data, and to communicate this information to others.

At the primary level, it is useful to have a software program into which children can enter data and select from a variety of graphical representations. *The Graph Club* (Tom Snyder, 1993), though not new, is an excellent example of software in this category (see Figure 21.3). *The Cruncher* 2.0 (Sunburst) is a slightly simplified spreadsheet designed for grades 3 and up. Every popular spreadsheet will compute any statistic for columns or rows of data. If the data are changed, the statistics change instantly. Spreadsheets also make very nice bar graphs, line graphs, and circle graphs. Teachers should also check to see if the publisher of their textbook offers graphing software.

On the NCTM *Illuminations* Web site, there is a fully functioning spreadsheet that can be downloaded for free or used on-line. Look under Math-lets.

The graphing calculator puts data analysis technology in the hands of every student. The TI-73 calculator is designed for middle grade students. It will produce eight different kinds of plots or graphs, including pie charts, bar graphs, and picture graphs that are not available on the TI-83. All graphing calculators will compute and graph best-fit lines using either the median-median method or the regression method.

An argument can be made for having students do some graphing and computing of statistics without technology. Appropriate methods have been suggested in this chapter. However, the intent of by-hand methods should always be to help understand the graphs or the statistics. Given today's readily available technology, there is no reason for repetitious exercises with tedious by-hand methods. ■

 ## Assessment Notes

Care should be taken in assessment of statistical ideas to distinguish between the use of related algorithms and techniques and the quite different kind of knowledge that involves judgment and interpretation.

Of course, you want your students to know how to make a stem-and-leaf plot and a box plot or find the mean and the median. But many students can learn to do these things without interpreting them. Choice and interpretation of graphs and statistics are more important than the ability to construct and compute.

Choice

Computers and calculators will make graphs even when they are inappropriate to your needs. Students must be able to select appropriate graphs and statistics to suit their purposes. It is important to pose situations that include a real context and have students decide what statistics and what graphs would best serve the purposes. Is a bar graph or a line graph more appropriate? Why? Which statistic is better in this situation, the mean or the median?

Interpretation

In a similar manner, making the graph or computing the best-fit line does not help me understand what it tells me about the data. There are a number of ways to get at interpretation. For example, several graphs and statistics for the same situation and data can be presented. "Suppose you were a newspaper editor. Which of these statistics and graphs should you use in your story? Explain your selection. Are any of these statistics of no value to the message?" In this type of interpretation, several options are provided, and the choice is based on the intended audience and purpose. There is no need actually to compute the statistics or create the graphs.

Another idea is to provide graphs and statistics for two related situations: your class and the rest of the school, your state and the rest of the country, hamburgers at McDonald's and hamburgers at Burger King. What can be determined for sure from these data? What inferences can be made? What would help you make a decision about _____ that you cannot determine from the information gathered? How could you use this information to argue in favor of _____? How could you use the same information to argue on the reverse side of the issue? ■

INTRODUCTION TO PROBABILITY

Let's first experiment with some basic ideas of probability before considering how to help children develop these ideas.

Two Experiments

Consider answering the following two questions by actually performing the experiments enough times to make a reasonable guess at the results.

TOSSING A CUP

Toss a small "portion" cup or other small cup once or twice, letting it land on the floor. Notice that there are three possible ways for the cup to land: upside down, right side up, or on its side. If the cup were tossed this way 100 times, about how many times do you think it would land in each position?

FLIPPING TWO COINS

If you were to flip one coin 100 times, you would expect that it would come up heads about as many times as tails. If two coins were tossed 100 times, about how many times do you think that they would both come up heads?

A quick way to conduct these experiments is to work in groups. If ten people each do ten trials and pool their data, the time needed for 100 trials is not long. Twenty cups can be placed on a tray and tossed at one time.

 Even if you do not actually do the experiments, jot down your predictions to each of these experiments now before reading on.

Theoretical Versus Experimental Probability

In the cup toss, there is no practical way to determine the results before you start. However, once you had results for 100 flips, you would undoubtedly feel more confident in predicting the results of the next 100 flips. If you gathered data on that same cup for 1000 trials, you would feel even more confident. Say that your cup lands on its side 78 times out of 100. You might choose a round figure of 75 or 80 for the 100 tosses. If, after 200 flips, there were 163 sideways landings, you would feel even more confident of the 4-out-of-5 ratio and predict about 800 sideways landings for 1000 tosses. The more flips that are made, the more confident you become. You have determined an *experimental probability* of $\frac{4}{5}$ or 80 percent for the cup to land on its side. It is experimental because it is based on the results of an experiment rather than a theoretical analysis of the cup.

In a one-coin toss, the prediction of about 50 percent heads could confidently be made before you flipped the coin, based on your understanding of a fair coin. Your prediction for two heads in the two-coin version may be more difficult. It is quite common for people to observe that there are three types of outcomes: both heads, both tails, and one of each;

First Coin	Second Coin
Head	Head
Head	Tail
Tail	Head
Tail	Tail

FIGURE 21.19 Four possible outcomes of flipping two coins.

so they predict that two heads will come up about one-third of the time. (What did you predict?) After conducting the experiment, however, they are surprised to find that two heads come up only about one-fourth of the time. This experience might cause them to return to their original analysis and look for an error in their thinking.

There is only one way for two heads to occur and one way for two tails to occur, but there are *two* ways that a head and a tail could result: Either the first coin is heads and the second tails, or vice versa. As shown in Figure 21.19, that makes a total of four possible outcomes, not three. The assumption that each outcome is equally likely was correct. Therefore, the correct probability of two heads is 1 out of 4, or $\frac{1}{4}$, not $\frac{1}{3}$. This *theoretical probability* is based on a logical analysis of the experiment, not on experimental results.

When we talk about probabilities, we are assigning some measure of chance to an experiment. An *experiment* is any activity that has two or more clearly discernible results or *outcomes*. Both tossing the cup and tossing the two coins were experiments. Observing tomorrow's weather and shooting ten free throws on the basketball court are also experiments. An organized listing of all possible outcomes is generally referred to as the *sample space*. As you have already seen, the toss of two coins has four outcomes in the sample space. Tomorrow's weather can be described in many ways: precipitation or no precipitation, or dry, rain, sleet, or snow. An *event* is any subset of the outcomes or any subset of the sample space. For the two-coin experiment, the event we were concerned with was getting two heads. For the free-throw shoot, we might be interested in the event of getting five or more baskets out of the ten tosses.

When all possible outcomes of a simple experiment are equally likely, the *theoretical probability* of an event is

$$\frac{\text{Number of outcomes in the event}}{\text{Number of possible outcomes}}$$

In real-world situations, outcomes are often not equally likely, as they are for coin flips or dice rolls. The cup-tossing experiment, though not a practical situation, is "muddy" and

real. The outcomes are difficult to predict, and they are not equally likely. In situations like these, we can determine the observed relative frequency of the event by performing the experiment a lot of times. The *relative frequency* of an event is

$$\frac{\text{Number of observed occurrences of the event}}{\text{Total number of trials}}$$

It should be clear that the relative frequency is not a good predictor of the chance of the event's happening unless the number of trials is very large. The *experimental probability* of an event is the ratio that the relative frequency approaches as the number of trials gets infinitely large. Because it is impossible to perform an infinite number of trials, we must be satisfied with some large number of trials. The more trials, the more confident we might be that the relative frequency is close to the actual probability.

Implications for Instruction

There are many reasons why an experimental approach to probability, actually conducting experiments and examining outcomes, is important in the classroom.

- It is significantly more intuitive. Results begin to make sense and do not result from some abstract rule.
- It eliminates guessing at probabilities and wondering, "Did I get it right?" Counting or trying to determine the number of elements in a sample space can be very difficult without some intuitive background information.
- It provides an experiential background for examining the theoretical model. When you begin to sense that the probability of two heads is $\frac{1}{4}$ instead of $\frac{1}{3}$, the analysis in Figure 21.19 seems more reasonable.
- It helps students see how the ratio of a particular outcome to the total number of trials begins to converge to (get closer and closer to) a fixed number. For an infinite number of trials, the relative frequency and theoretical probability would be the same.
- It develops an appreciation for a simulation approach to solving problems. Many real-world problems are actually solved by conducting experiments or simulations.
- It is a lot more fun and interesting! Even searching for a correct explanation in the theoretical model is more interesting.

Whenever possible, then, try to use an experimental approach in the classroom. If a theoretical analysis (such as with the two-coin experiment) is possible, it should also be examined, and the results should be compared. Rather than correcting a student error in an initial analysis, we can let experimental results guide and correct student thinking.

NCTM Standards

The *Standards* makes the following suggestion for students at the 3–5 grade level: "Students should also explore probability through experiments that have only a few outcomes, such as using game spinners. . . . Through these experiences, students encounter the idea that although they cannot determine an individual outcome, such as which color the spinner will land on next, they can predict the frequency of various outcomes" (p. 181).

Developing Probability Concepts

Informal ideas about chance and probability, when developed early, provide necessary background for concepts to be constructed at the middle and secondary levels.

Early Concepts of Chance

Children in kindergarten and the primary grades need to develop an intuitive concept of chance: the idea that some events, when compared with others, have a better or worse likelihood or an approximately equal likelihood of happening.

Many young children believe that an event will happen "because it's my favorite color" or "because it's lucky" or "because it did it that way last time." Many games such as Candy-Land or Chutes and Ladders are very exciting for young children who do not comprehend that the outcomes are entirely random. When they finally learn that they have no control over the outcome, children begin to look for other games where there is some element of player determination.

ACTIVITY 21.8

Is It Likely?

Ask students to judge various events as *certain*, *impossible*, or *possible* ("might happen"). Consider these examples:

It will rain tomorrow.

Drop a rock in water, and it will sink.

Trees will talk to us in the afternoon.

The sun will rise tomorrow morning.

Three students will be absent tomorrow.

George will go to bed before 8:30 tonight.

You will have two birthdays this year.

Children describe or make up events that are certain, impossible, or possible. For each event, they should justify their estimate of likelihood.

ACTIVITY 21.9

Who Will Win?

Play simple games where the chance of one side's winning can be controlled. Before playing the games, have students predict who will win and why. Afterward, discuss why they think things turned out as they did. For example, the hockey game in Figure 21.20 starts with a counter in the center. Two players take turns spinning a spinner. The counter moves one space toward the goal that comes up on the spinner. Play the game with different spinners. As a variation, let students choose a spinner on each turn. Ask them to explain their choices.

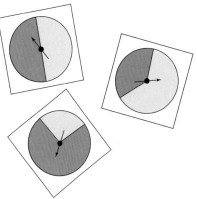

FIGURE 21.20 A simple game of chance played with different spinners helps young children with basic concepts of chance.

Determining Probabilities for Simple Events

From a basic understanding that one event can be more or less likely than another, students can begin to predict specific ratios of outcomes of simple events. Before students have worked with part-to-whole ratios, use language such as "65 out of 100" instead of using fractions. A discussion of reasons for students' predictions is always important. The experiment should then be conducted and the results compared with expected outcomes.

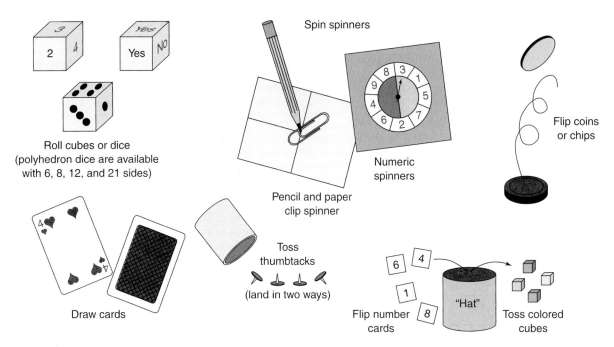

FIGURE 21.21 **There are many simple ways to produce random outcomes.**

Figure 21.21 illustrates a number of simple random devices that can be used for experiments. To get large numbers, let groups of students conduct the same experiment and combine results. Ask students to notice that the results for smaller numbers of trials are all different and that they are frequently quite different from what might be expected.

Occasionally, have students list the outcomes of their experiments in a row, to show the order of the outcomes. Interestingly, truly random events do not alternate. They frequently appear in clusters or runs. If eight odd numbers in a row come up on a die roll, the chance remains exactly $\frac{1}{2}$ (3 out of 6) that the next roll will be odd. The die has no memory. The previous roll of a die cannot affect the next roll. It is very unlikely that even numbers will come up seven times in a row (1 chance in 128). However, if that does happen, the chance for an even number on the next roll is still $\frac{1}{2}$.

Experiments with Two or More Independent Events

Flipping two coins and observing the result of each is an example of an experiment with two independent events. The flip of one coin has no effect on the other. The events are *independent.* Another example is that of drawing a card and spinning a spinner. Many interesting experiments involve two or more separate, independent events.

Determining the experimental probability of compound events is no different than for simple events. The experiment is performed numerous times, and the number of favorable

results is compared to the total trials as before. The challenge comes in trying to reconcile experimental results with theoretical ones.

Suppose that a class is conducting an experiment to determine the probability of rolling a 7 with two dice. They might tally their results in a chart showing each sum from 2 to 12 as a single event, as in part (a) of Figure 21.22.

The results of their experiment will show clearly that these events are not equally likely and that in fact the sum of 7 has the best chance of occurring. To explain this, they might look for the combinations that make 7: 1 and 6, 2 and 5, and 3 and 4. But there are also three combinations for 8. It seems as though 8 should be just as likely as 7, and yet it is not.

Now suppose that the experiment is repeated. This time, for the sake of clarity, suggest that students roll two different-colored dice and that they keep the tallies in a chart like the one in part (b) of Figure 21.22.

The results of a large number of dice rolls indicate what one would expect, namely, that all 36 cells of this chart are equally likely. But there are more cells with a sum of 7 than any other number. Therefore, students were really looking for the event that consists of any of the six ways, not three ways, that two dice can add to 7. There are six outcomes in the desired event out of a total of 36, for a probability of $\frac{6}{36}$, or $\frac{1}{6}$.

To create the sample space for a compound event, it is helpful to use a chart or diagram that keeps the two independent events separate and illustrates the combinations. The matrix in Figure 21.22(b) is one good suggestion when there are only two events. A tree diagram (Figure 21.23) is another method of creating sample spaces that can be used with any number of events.

Sum of Two Dice

2	𝍇 |
3	𝍇 𝍇
4	𝍇 𝍇 𝍇 ||||
5	𝍇 𝍇 𝍇 ||||
6	𝍇 𝍇 𝍇 𝍇 𝍇 ||||
7	𝍇 𝍇 𝍇 𝍇 𝍇 𝍇 𝍇 ||||
8	𝍇 𝍇 𝍇 𝍇 𝍇 𝍇 ||||
9	𝍇 𝍇 𝍇 𝍇 𝍇
10	𝍇 𝍇 𝍇 |
11	𝍇 ||
12	𝍇 𝍇

(a)

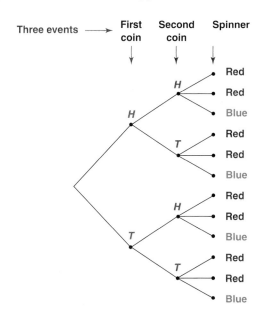

There are six ways to get 7.

(b)

FIGURE 21.22 Tallies can account only for the total (a) or keep track of the individual dice (b).

Three events ⟶ First coin   Second coin   Spinner

FIGURE 21.23 A tree diagram showing all possible outcomes for two coins and a spinner that is $\frac{2}{3}$ red.

ACTIVITY 21.10

Compound Outcomes

The following are examples of compound events composed of independent events.

> Rolling an even sum with two dice
>
> Spinning blue and flipping a cup on end
>
> Getting two blues out of three spins (depends on spinner)
>
> Having a tack or a cup land up if each is tossed once
>
> Getting *at least* two heads from a toss of four coins

Have students first make and defend a prediction of the probability of the event. Then they should conduct an experiment with a large number of trials, comparing their results to their predicted probabilities. Finally, they should reconcile differences. Where appropriate, students can try to determine the theoretical probability as part of their final analysis of the experiment.

Words and phrases such as *and, or, at least,* and *no more than* can also cause children some trouble. Of special note is the word *or,* since its everyday usage is generally not the same as its strict logical use in mathematics. In mathematics, *or* includes the case of *both.* So in the tack-and-cup example, the event includes tack up, cup up, and *both* tack *and* cup up.

Theoretical Probabilities with an Area Model

One way to determine the theoretical probability of a compound event is to list all possible outcomes and count those that are favorable, that is, those that make up the event. This is useful and intuitive as a first approach. However, it has some limitations. First, what if the events are not all equally likely? For example, the spinner may be only $\frac{1}{4}$ blue. Second, it is difficult to move from that approach to even slightly more sophisticated methods. An area model approach has been used successfully with fifth-grade students and is quite helpful for some reasonably difficult problems.

Suppose that after many experiences, you have decided that your cup lands on its side 82 percent of the time. The experiment is to toss the cup and then draw a card from a deck. What is the probability that the cup will land on its side *and* you will draw a spade? Draw a square to represent one whole. First partition the square to represent the cup toss,

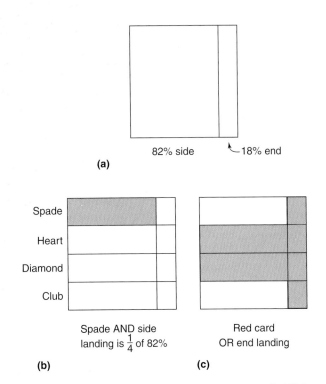

(a)

82% side   18% end

(b)

Spade AND side
landing is $\frac{1}{4}$ of 82%

(c)

Red card
OR end landing

FIGURE 21.24 An area model for determining probabilities.

82 percent and 18 percent, as in Figure 21.24(a). Now partition the square in the other direction to represent the four equal card suits. As shown in Figure 21.24(b), one region is the proportion of time that both events, sideways and spades, happen. The area of this region is $\frac{1}{4}$ of 82 percent, or 20.5 percent.

You can use the same drawing to determine the probability of other events in the same experiment. For example, what is the probability of the cup landing on either end *or* drawing a red card? As shown in Figure 21.4(c), half of the area of the square corresponds to drawing a red card. This section includes the case of drawing a red card *and* an end landing. The other half of the 18 percent end landings happen when a red card is not drawn. Half of 18 percent is 9 percent of the area. The total area for a red card *or* an end landing is 59 percent.

The area approach is easy for students to use and understand for experiments involving two independent events when the probability of each is known. For more than two independent events, further subdivision of each region is required but is still quite reasonable. The use of *and* and *or* connectives is easily dealt with. It is quite clear to students, without memorization of formulas, how probabilities should be combined.

Exploring Dependent Events

The next level of difficulty occurs when the probability of one event depends on the result of the first. For example, suppose that there are two identical boxes. In one box is a dollar bill

and two counterfeit bills. In the other box is one of each. You may choose one box and from that box select one bill without looking. What are your chances of getting a genuine dollar? Here there are two events: selecting a box and selecting a bill. The probability of getting a dollar in the second event depends on which box is chosen in the first event. These events are *dependent*, not independent.

As another example, suppose that you are a prisoner in a faraway land. The king has pity on you and gives you a chance to leave. He shows you the maze in Figure 21.25. At the start and at each fork in the path, you must spin the spinner and follow the path that it points to. You may request that the key to freedom be placed in one of the two rooms. In which room should you place the key to have the best chance of freedom? Notice that the probability of ending the maze in any one room is dependent on the result of the first spin.

Either of these two problems could be explored with an experimental approach, a simulation. Remember, that approach should always be used first. A second approach to both problems is to use the area model to determine the theoretical probabilities. An area model solution to the prisoner problem is shown in Figure 21.26. How would the area model for the prisoner problem be different if the spinner at Fork II were a $\frac{1}{3}$ versus $\frac{2}{3}$ spinner?

STOP It would be good to stop at this point and try the area approach for the problem of the counterfeit bills. The chance of getting a dollar is $\frac{5}{12}$. Can you get this result?

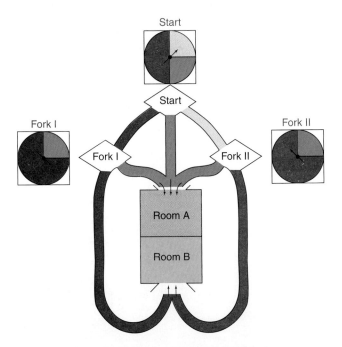

FIGURE 21.25 Should you place your key to freedom in Room A or Room B? At each fork, the spinner determines your path.

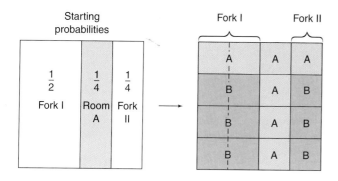

At Fork I, $\frac{3}{4}$ of the time you will go to Room B. (<u>Note</u>: Not $\frac{3}{4}$ of the square but $\frac{3}{4}$ of the times you go to Fork I.)

At Fork II, $\frac{3}{4}$ of <u>these</u> times (or $\frac{3}{16}$ of <u>total</u> time) you will go to Room B.

Therefore, you will end up in Room A $\frac{7}{16}$ of the time and Room B $\frac{9}{16}$ of the time.

FIGURE 21.26 Using the area model to solve the maze problem.

The area model will not solve all probability problems. However, it fits very well into a developmental approach to the subject because it is conceptual, it is based on existing knowledge of fractions, and more symbolic approaches can be derived from it. Figure 21.27 shows a tree diagram for the same problem, with the probability of each path of the tree written in. After some experience with probability situations, the tree diagram model is probably easier to use and adapts to a wider range of situations. You should be able to match up each branch of the tree diagram in Figure 21.27 with a section of the square in Figure 21.26. Use the area model to explain why the probability for each complete branch of the tree is determined by multiplying the probabilities along the branch.

SIMULATIONS

Simulation is a technique used for answering real-world questions or making decisions in complex situations where an element of chance is involved. To see what is likely to happen in the real event, a model must be designed that has the same probabilities as the real situation. For example, in designing a rocket, a large number of related systems all have some chance of failure. Various combinations of failures might cause serious problems with the rocket. Knowing the probability of serious failures will help determine if redesign or backup systems are required. It is not reasonable to make repeated tests of the actual rocket. Instead, a model that simulates all of the chance situations is designed and run repeatedly with the help of a computer. The computer model can simulate thousands of flights, and an estimate of the chance of failure can be made.

Many real-world situations lend themselves to simulation analysis. In a business venture, the probability of selling a product might depend on a variety of chance factors, some of which can be controlled or changed and others not. Will advertising help? Should high-cost materials be used? What location provides the best chance of sales? If a reasonable model can be set up that simulates these factors, an experiment can be run before actually entering into the venture to determine the best choices.

The following problem and model are adapted from the excellent materials developed by the Quantitative Literacy Project (Gnanadesikan, Schaeffer, & Swift, 1987). In Figure 21.28, a diagram shows water pipes for a pumping system connecting A to B. The five pumps are aging, and it is estimated that at any given time, the probability of pump failure is $\frac{1}{2}$. If a pump fails, water cannot pass that station. For example, if pumps 1, 2, and 5 fail, water can flow only

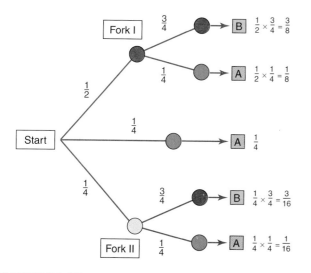

FIGURE 21.27 A tree diagram is another way to model the outcomes of two or more dependent events.

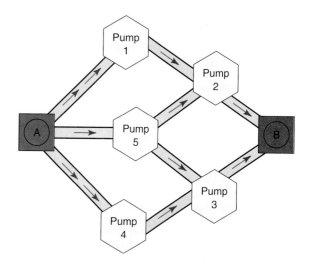

FIGURE 21.28 Each of these five pumps has a 50 percent chance of failure. What is the probability that some path from A to B is working?

through 4 and 3. Consider the following questions that might well be asked about such a system:

What is the probability that water will flow at any time?

On the average, about how many stations need repair at any time?

What is the probability that the 1–2 path is working at any time?

For any simulation, a series of steps or a model can serve as a useful guide.

1. *Identify key components and assumptions of the problem.* The key component in the water problem is the condition of a pump. Each pump is either working or not. The assumption is that the probability that a pump is working is $\frac{1}{2}$.

2. *Select a random device for the key components.* Any random device can be selected that has outcomes with the same probability as the key component—in this case, the pumps. Here a simple choice might be tossing a coin, with heads representing a working pump.

3. *Define a trial.* A trial consists of simulating a series of key components until the situation has been completely modeled one time. In this problem, a trial could consist of tossing a coin five times, each toss representing a different pump.

4. *Conduct a large number of trials, and record the information.* For this problem, it would be good to keep the record of heads and tails in groups of five because each set of five is one trial and represents all of the pumps.

5. *Use the data to draw conclusions.* There are four possible paths for the water, each flowing through two of the five pumps. As they are numbered in the drawing, if any one of the pairs 1–2, 5–2, 5–3, and 4–3 is open, it makes no difference whether the other pumps are working. By counting the trials in which at least one of these four pairs of coins both came up heads, we can estimate the probability of water flowing. To answer the second question, the number of tails per trial can be averaged.

 How would you answer the third question concerning the 1–2 path's being open?

Steps 4 and 5 are the same as solving a probability problem by experimental means. The interesting problem-solving aspects of simulation activities are in the first three steps, where the real-world situation is translated into a model. Translation of real-world information into models is the essence of applied mathematics.

Here are a few more examples of problems that can be solved by simulation and are easy enough to be tackled by middle school students.

In a true-or-false test, what is the probability of getting 7 out of 10 questions correct by guessing alone? (*Key component:* answering a question. *Assumption:* Chance of getting it correct is $\frac{1}{2}$.) What if the test were multiple-choice with 4 choices?

In a group of five people, what is the chance that two were born in the same month? (*Key component:* month of birth. *Assumption:* All 12 months are equally likely.)

Casey's batting average is .350. What is the chance he will go hitless in a complete nine-inning game? (*Key component:* getting a hit. *Assumptions:* Probability of a hit for each at-bat is .35. Casey will get to bat four times in the average game.)

Krunch-a-Munch cereal packs one of five games in each box. About how many boxes should you expect to buy before you get a complete set? (*Key component:* getting one game. *Assumption:* Each game has a $\frac{1}{5}$ chance. *Trial:* Use a $\frac{1}{5}$ random device repeatedly until all five outcomes appear; the average length of a trial answers the question.) What is the chance of getting a set in eight or fewer boxes?

 TECHNOLOGY NOTE

Truly random events often occur in unexpected groups; a fair coin may turn up heads five times in a row. A 100-year flood may hit a town twice in ten years. Hands-on random devices such as spinners, dice, or cubes drawn from a bag give students an intuitive feel for the imperfect distribution of randomness. Students believe in the unbiased outcomes of these devices. The downside is that hand-on devices require a lot of time to produce a large number of trials. This is where technology can help enormously.

Electronic devices, including some relatively simple calculators and graphing calculators, are designed to produce random outcomes at the press of a button. Computer software is available that flips coins, spins spinners, or draws numbers from a hat. Calculators produce random numbers that can then be interpreted in terms of the desired device. As long as students accept the results generated by the technology as truly random or equivalent to the hands-on device, they offer significant advantages for performing experiments.

Probability Software

Software for exploring probability concepts can generally be described as computer-animated random devices. Graphics show students the coins being flipped or the spinner being spun. Most allow different speeds. In a slow version, students may watch each spin of a spinner or coin flip. Faster speeds show the recording of each trial but omit the graphics. An even quicker mode simply shows the cumulative results. The number of trials can be set by the user. Volume 1 of *MathKeys: Unlocking Probability* (MECC, 1995c) includes options for a single coin, a single die, a choice of six different two-color spinners, or two colors of marbles drawn from a bag. In Volume 2, compound experiments using multiple spinners, dice, or marble bags can be designed and run. As is typical of these programs, results are not only tallied but also shown on a bar graph for a visual display of outcome ratios. Both volumes include some interesting games that are problem-based and permit students to apply their understanding of probability.

Tangible Math: Probability Constructor (Riverdeep, 2002), designed for students at the middle grades, is more sophisticated and offers many more options. Within each of six devices, the probability of the outcomes is adjustable. An area model allows for the exploration of compound events, and outcomes can be displayed in a variety of ways. The support materials include a complete series of lessons and teacher notes that are quite well done. For younger students (grades 3 to 6) *Mighty Math: Number Heroes* (Edmark, 1996) has a probability component that also allows the user to explore a variety of compound experiments.

Even with only one computer in the room, a good probability program is a worthwhile investment.

Probability with Calculators

Many relatively simple calculators include a key that will produce a random number. Usually, the random numbers generated are between 0 and 1. Students who are going to use these random number generators will need some direction in using them to their advantage. Each number generated will likely have eight or more decimal places. A list of five numbers might look like this:

0.8904433368

0.0232028877

0.1669322714

0.1841957303

0.5523714952

How could a list of decimals like this replace flipping a coin or spinning a spinner? Suppose each was multiplied by 2. The results would be between 0 and 2. If you ignore the decimal part, you would have a series of zeros and ones that could stand for heads and tails, boys and girls, true and false, or any other pair of equally likely outcomes. For three outcomes, the same as a $\frac{1}{4}$-$\frac{1}{4}$-$\frac{1}{2}$ spinner, you might decide to look at the first two digits of the number and assign values from 0 to 24 and 25 to 49 to the two quarter portions and values 50 to 99 for the one-half portion. Alternatively, each number could be multiplied by 4, the decimal part ignored, resulting in random numbers 0, 1, 2, and 3. These could then be assigned to the desired outcomes. In effect, random numbers can simulate any simple random device.

With graphing calculators, the random number generator can be used inside of a simple program that produces the numbers and stores them in a list. The list can then be displayed graphically. The program in Figure 21.29 is for a TI-82 or TI-83 calculator. It will "roll" as many dice as you request. At the end of the program, a histogram displays the

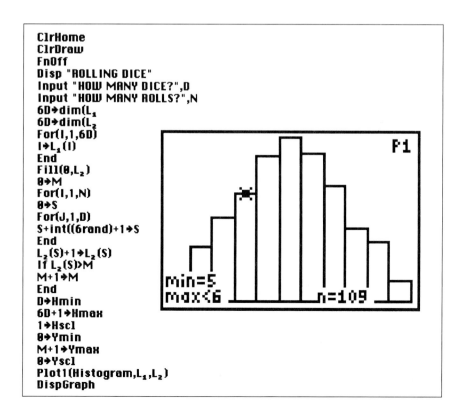

```
ClrHome
ClrDraw
FnOff
Disp "ROLLING DICE"
Input "HOW MANY DICE?",D
Input "HOW MANY ROLLS?",N
6D→dim(L₁
6D→dim(L₂
For(I,1,6D)
I→L₁(I)
End
Fill(0,L₂)
0→M
For(I,1,N)
0→S
For(J,1,D)
S+int((6rand)+1→S
End
L₂(S)+1→L₂(S)
If L₂(S)>M
M+1→M
End
D→Hmin
6D+1→Hmax
1→Hscl
0→Ymin
M+1→Ymax
0→Yscl
Plot1(Histogram,L₁,L₂)
DispGraph
```

FIGURE 21.29 This TI-82 or TI-83 program can be used to simulate thousands of dice rolls and accumulate the results.

totals for each sum. With the TRACE feature, the value for each bar in the graph is displayed. The figure shows the result of rolling two dice 1000 times. It took about $2\frac{1}{2}$ minutes to run the program and produce the graph. (Computer programs produce the result almost instantly.) The TI-73 calculator designed for middle school has a built-in coin and dice function.

Although computer programs are much faster, allow for more variation, and include attractive graphics, the advantage of calculator approaches is availability. Every student can design and run an experiment individually. When computers are at a premium, this is a significant advantage. ■

ASSESSMENT NOTES

As with data and statistics, in your assessment of probability, it is important to distinguish between skills and an understanding of big ideas.

The skills that are easy to assess involve the computation of probabilities. Even young children should be able to tell if an event is possible or impossible or is very likely or not very likely. Older children should be able to determine probabilities in well-designed experiments such as those discussed in this chapter.

You also want to be aware of students' understanding of chance and probability. What does it mean that an event has a probability of 89 percent or $\frac{2}{3}$? How many times should a simulation or an experiment be conducted before you can have confidence in the results? What does "confidence in the results" mean? Can knowing the probability of an event ever predict what will happen on the next trial? How are probability ideas used in the real world?

These more subtle ideas can be determined by having class discussions and listening for the reasoning of students and making efforts to check students' understanding of the key ideas you are looking for. You might use a four-point rubric to rate students quickly on their understanding. Middle school students can write short reports about a situation that includes your main ideas, and you can have them specifically address the issues you want to assess. ■

LITERATURE CONNECTIONS

It may be difficult to find books that specifically address the concept of probability or data analysis. The books suggested here will provide springboards for discussions of chance, classification, and comparisons.

Do You Wanna Bet? Your Chance to Find Out About Probability
Cushman, 1991

The two characters in this book, Danny and Brian, become involved in everyday situations both in and out of school.

Each situation has an element of probability involved. For example, two invitations to birthday parties are for the same day. What is the chance that two friends would have the same birthday? In another situation, Brian wonders if he should do his homework because the weather forecaster predicts a 60 percent chance that there will be enough snow to close schools. When it doesn't snow at all, the question is, was the forecaster wrong? Secret notes passed in class lead to the discussion of letter frequencies in our language. These and other situations woven into an interesting story can each lead to a probability experiment or discussion. Students might create simulations to examine some of the same ideas, or the story may provoke similar questions for exploration.

Frog and Toad Are Friends
Lobal, 1970

When Frog and Toad go walking, Frog loses a button. As they search to find the button, they find many buttons. Whenever one of Frog's friends asks, "Is this your button?" Frog responds (with a touch of anger), "No, that is not my button! That button is _____, but my button was _____." The phrase is repeated with each newly found button. It turns out that Frog did not lose the button on the walk but in his own home before they left. This provides another value to the story as Frog must find a way to make up for being so angry with his friends.

The approach to finding the button is very much like the game "One of These Things Is Not like the Others." It is also a perfect lead-in to secret sorting activities as described in this chapter. Young students can model the story directly with sets of buttons, shells, attribute blocks, Woozle Cards, or other objects with a variety of attributes. With a highly varied set of geometric shapes, the children could play the game and explore their geometric language and perceptions of geometric attributes.

Incredible Comparisons
Ash, 1996

Not a story but an amazing collection of facts and comparisons, Ash's book includes 23 topics for comparison, each graphically displayed. For example, different-sized squares are used to compare the size of the continents. Maps of major countries are layered on top of each other to indicate relative areas. Data about area and distances are also provided in different units of measure. The amount of time needed to travel the widths of countries is demonstrated as well. Data and drawings such as these can prompt students to find clever but acceptable ways to display the information or to research similar information in other resources. Other topics include big buildings, animal speeds, growth and age, and population. ■

Reflections on Chapter 21

Writing to Learn

1. Explain why attribute activities are important in the development of data analysis skills. Why would you use structured attribute materials for these activities instead of informal or unstructured materials such as buttons?

2. In initial loop activities, the teacher tells the students how to sort the attribute pieces. What is the purpose of these not so problem-based activities? What are students learning in activities where the loop labels are not shown or the sorting rule is a secret?

3. Draw a picture of a line plot, a histogram, and a line graph. How are all of these alike?

4. Put at least 30 numbers in a stem-and-leaf plot, and use it to determine the median, the upper and lower quartiles, and the range and to draw a box-and-whisker plot.

5. What are three ways to make a circle graph? What does a circle graph tell you that a bar graph does not? What does it not tell?

6. What are three different forms of averages? Which is the most stable? Explain.

7. Describe two different concepts of the mean. How can each be developed? Which idea leads to the method of computing the mean?

8. Describe what is meant by a best-fit line. When would you want to find such a line?

9. On a grid, make a scatter plot of about 30 points that appear to have a negative linear relationship or correlation. Use these points to draw the median-median line. Suppose that your points represented number of yearly visits to the mall as related to miles between home and mall. How could your best-fit line be used to predict the number of visits to the mall for a person who was not included in your data set? How much potential error would you assign to your prediction based solely on the scatter plot that you drew?

10. Describe the difference between theoretical probability, relative frequency, and experimental probability.

11. Why is it a good idea to have students conduct experiments before trying to figure out probabilities?

12. What are the first ideas that young students should develop about the concept of chance? How can this be done?

13. Describe how you could use a random-number generator on a computer or calculator to produce a simulation of a three-part spinner with all parts equal.

14. What is the purpose of a simulation? Set up a simulation for at least one of the examples on page 412. Conduct a few trials.

15. Use an area model and a tree diagram to determine the theoretical probability for the following experiment:

    Dad puts a $5 bill and three $1 bills in the first box. In a second box, he puts another $5 bill but just one $1 bill. Junior, for washing the car, gets to take one bill from the first box without looking and put it in the second box. After these have been well mixed, he then gets to take one from the second box without looking. What is the probability that he will get $5?

    Design a simulation for the problem, and try it out. Does it agree with your theoretical probability?

For Discussion and Exploration

1. Examine one of six books from the Used Numbers Project or the two *Teach-Stat Activities* books (see Recommendations for Further Reading). These books have some of the best statistics activities for elementary students. You might share an activity or idea in the book that excited you, react to a lesson described in the book, or share an idea in the book with a teacher and get his or her reaction.

2. How important is it, in your opinion, to teach probability concepts in the early grades (K–4)? What about in the middle grades? Does your answer change if you substitute statistics for probability? Explain your position. Some experts have argued that the ability to understand probability and statistical ideas is so much more important than the related skills that being able to compute probabilities and statistics or to make graphs are skills that we could skip in favor of increased reasoning in this area. What position would you take on this issue?

Recommendations for Further Reading

Highly Recommended

Curcio, F. R. (2001). *Developing data-graph comprehension in grades K–8* (2nd ed.). Reston, VA: National Council of Teachers of Mathematics.

Curcio has updated this valuable book, originally published in 1989. Here you will find useful discussion of graphs and how to help students understand and construct them. Every form of graph found in this chapter is discussed in Curcio's book. Most of the book consists of activities, each carefully coded by grade level and objective.

National Council of Teachers of Mathematics. (1999). Data & chance in the middle school curriculum [Focus Issue]. *Mathematics Teaching in the Middle School, 4*(6).

In keeping with the overall quality of this journal, this focus issue is a valuable resource for the twin topics of data and probability. The first article describes a fascinating activity involving killer bees with a solid connection to biology. Other articles are equally useful.

University of North Carolina Mathematics and Science Education Network. (1997). *Teach-stat activities: Statistics investigations for grades 1–3.* Palo Alto, CA: Dale Seymour Publications.

University of North Carolina Mathematics and Science Education Network. (1997). *Teach-stat activities: Statistics investigations for grades 3–6.* Palo Alto, CA: Dale Seymour Publications.

These two books contain a wealth of superb data activities developed through a National Science Foundation Grant under the direction of some of North Carolina's top mathematics educators. The activities are each designed to follow a four-stage model: pose the question, collect the data, analyze the data, interpret the results. That is, data are collected with the purpose of answering a question. The activities are each described in detail with all necessary blacklines included. A companion professional development manual is also available.

Zawojewski, J. S. (1991). *Dealing with data and chance: Addenda series, grades 5–8.* Reston, VA: National Council of Teachers of Mathematics.

Middle school teachers interested in teaching probability and statistics must have this book. It is not timid in its suggestions for demanding activity, yet all activities are appropriate for middle grade students. The book is organized around the four theme standards of the Curriculum Standards.

Other Suggestions

Bolster, C. H., Scheaffer, R., Bereska, L., & Bolster, L. C. (1998). *Exploring statistics in the elementary grades: Book one (K–6), Book two (4–8).* White Plains, NY: Dale Seymour Publications.

Burns, M. (1995). *Math by all means: Probability, grades 3–4.* Sausalito, CA: Math Solutions Publications.

Corwin, R. B., & Friel, S. N. (1990). *Statistics: Prediction and sampling.* (A unit of study for grades 5–6 from *Used numbers: Real data in the classroom.*) Palo Alto, CA: Dale Seymour.

Curcio, F. R., & Artzt, A. F. (1996). Assessing students' ability to analyze data: Reaching beyond computation. *Mathematics Teacher, 89,* 668–673.

Curcio, F. R., Nimerofsky, B., Perez, R., & Yaloz-Femia, S. (1998). Developing concepts in probability: Designing and analyzing games. In L. Leutzinger (Ed.), *Mathematics in the middle* (pp. 206–211). Reston, VA: National Council of Teachers of Mathematics.

Elementary Quantitative Literacy Project. (1998). *Exploring statistics in the elementary grades: Book one (K–6).* White Plains, NY: Dale Seymour Publications.

Friel, S. N., Mokros, J. R., & Russell, S. J. (1992). *Middles, means, and in-between.* (A unit of study for grades 5–6 from *Used numbers: Real data in the classroom.*) Palo Alto, CA: Dale Seymour.

Frykholm, J. A. (2001). Eenie, meenie, minie, moe . . . building on intuitive notions of chance. *Teaching Children Mathematics, 8,* 112–118.

Haruta, M. E., Flaherty, M., McGivney, J., & McGivney, R. J. (1996). Coin tossing. *Mathematics Teacher, 89,* 642–645.

Jones, G. A., Thornton, C. A., Langrall, C. W., & Tarr, J. E. (1999). Understanding students' probabilistic reasoning. In L. V. Stiff (Ed.), *Developing mathematical reasoning in grades K–12* (pp. 146–155). Reston, VA: National Council of Teachers of Mathematics.

Karp, K. S. (1994). Telling tales: Creating graphs using multicultural literature. *Teaching Children Mathematics, 1,* 87–91.

Lindquist, M. M. (1992). *Making sense of data: Addenda series, grades K–6.* Reston, VA: National Council of Teachers of Mathematics.

Masse, L. N. (2001). The possibility of perfection. *Mathematics Teaching in the Middle School, 6,* 500–505.

McClain, K., Cobb, P., & Gravemeijer, K. (2000). Supporting students' ways of reasoning about data. In M. J. Burke (Ed.), *Learning mathematics for a new century* (pp. 174–187). Reston, VA: National Council of Teachers of Mathematics.

Russell, S. J., & Corwin, R. B. (1989). *Statistics: The shape of the data.* (A unit of study for grades 4–6 from *Used numbers: Real data in the classroom.*) Palo Alto, CA: Dale Seymour.

Russell, S. J., & Corwin, R. B. (1990). *Sorting: Groups and graphs.* (A unit of study for grades 2–3 from *Used numbers: Real data in the classroom.*) Palo Alto, CA: Dale Seymour.

Russell, S. J., & Stone, A. (1990). *Counting: Ourselves and our families.* (A unit of study for grades K–1 from *Used numbers: Real data in the classroom.*) Palo Alto, CA: Dale Seymour.

Uccellini, J. C. (1996). Teaching the mean meaningfully. *Mathematics Teaching in the Middle School, 2,* 112–115.

Usnick, V., McCarthy, J., & Alexander, S. (2001). Mrs. Whatsit "socks" it to probability. *Teaching Children Mathematics, 8,* 246–249.

Zawojewski, J. S., & Shaughnessy, J. M. (2000). Data and chance. In E. A. Silver & P. A. Kenney (Eds.), *Results from the seventh mathematics assessment of the National Assessment of Educational Progress* (pp. 235–268). Reston, VA: National Council of Teachers of Mathematics.

22

Algebraic Reasoning

When the authors of *Principles and Standards for School Mathematics* chose Algebra as one of the five content standards to span all grades, pre-K–12, they were not thinking about the typical algebra of the eighth grade or high school. Rather, the algebra described in the *Principles and Standards* is about the development of algebraic thinking and algebraic concepts. The focus is on patterns, functions, and the ability to analyze situations with the help of symbols.

Algebraic reasoning involves representing, generalizing, and formalizing patterns and regularity in all aspects of mathematics. In this chapter, we will look specifically at activities that focus on this thinking and reasoning throughout the grades. As algebraic reasoning develops, so must the language and symbolism that have been developed to support and communicate that thinking, specifically equations, variables, and functions. Function and functional notation, significant components of algebraic reasoning, are such important ideas in mathematics that a separate chapter has been devoted to them.

Big Ideas

1. Logical patterns exist and are a regular occurrence in mathematics. They can be recognized, extended, and generalized with both words and symbols. The same pattern can be found in many different forms. Patterns are found in physical and geometric situations as well as in numbers.

2. Symbolism, especially that involving equations and variables, is used to express generalizations of patterns and relationships.

3. Variables are symbols that take the place of numbers or ranges of numbers. They have different meanings depending on whether they are being used as representations of quantities that vary or change, representations of specific unknown values, or placeholders in a generalized expression or formula.

4. Equations and inequalities are used to express relationships between two quantities. Symbolism on either side of an equation or inequality represents a quantity. Thus, $3 + 8$ and $5n + 2$ are both expressions for numbers, not something "to do."

Content Connections

As Kaput (1998) notes, it is difficult to find an area of mathematics that does not involve generalizing and formalizing in some central way. In fact, this type of reasoning is at the heart of mathematics as a science of pattern and order. Many instances of algebraic reasoning have been addressed in earlier chapters.

■ **Number and Place Value** (Chapters 9 and 12): Number forms the core of early mathematics development. All of the patterns and relationships that help students make sense of number, basic facts, and computation can be formalized with symbols. For example, odd numbers are always one more than even numbers and so can be expressed in the form $2n + 1$ because $2n$ is any even number.

■ **Operation Concepts** (Chapter 10): As children learn about the operations, they also learn that there are regularities in the way they work. For example, the order properties say that $a + b = b + a$, and $a \times b = b \times a$. How the operations are related one to another (addition to subtraction and multiplication to division) are also general patterns that are used to solve algebraic equations.

■ **Geometry** (Chapter 20): Geometric patterns help young students see regularities in nonnumeric ways. Growing geometric patterns give rise to functional relationships. Coordinates are used to describe and define geometric shapes and relationships. And, of course, coordinates are used to graph algebraic relationships.

The broad topics of proportional reasoning, data analysis, and measurement also have direct ties to algebra, primarily as they each include important functional relationships. More will be said about these connections in the following chapter on functions.

REPEATING PATTERNS

Identifying and extending patterns is an important process in algebraic thinking. Simple repetitive patterns can be explored as early as kindergarten.

Using Materials in Patterning

When possible, patterning activities should involve some form of physical materials. This is especially true of repeating patterns in grades K–3. When patterns are built with materials, children are able to test the extension of a pattern and make changes without fear of being wrong.

Many kindergarten and first-grade textbooks have pages where students are given a pattern such as a string of colored beads. The task may be to color the last bead or two in the string. There are two differences between this and the same activity done with actual materials. First, by coloring on the page, the activity takes on an aura of right versus wrong. If a mistake is made, correction on the page is difficult and can cause feelings of inadequacy. Materials allow a trial-and-error approach to be used. Second, pattern activities on worksheets prevent children from extending patterns beyond the few spaces provided by the page. Most children enjoy using materials such as colored blocks, buttons, and connecting cubes to extend their patterns well beyond the printed page. Children are frequently observed continuing a pattern with materials halfway across the classroom floor.

Repeating-Pattern Activities

The concept of a repeating pattern and how a pattern is extended or continued can be introduced to the full class in several ways. One possibility is to draw simple shape patterns on the board and extend them in a class discussion. Oral patterns can be joined in by all children. For example, "do, mi, mi, do, mi, mi, . . . " is a simple singing pattern. Up, down, and sideways arm positions provide three elements with which to make patterns: up, side, side, down, up, side, side, down, . . . Boy-girl patterns or stand-sit patterns are also fun. From these ideas, the youngest children learn quickly the concept of patterns. Students can begin to work more profitably in small groups or even independently once a general notion of patterns is developed.

ACTIVITY 22.1

Pattern Strips

Students can work independently or in groups of two or three to extend patterns made from simple materials: buttons, colored blocks, connecting cubes,

---

toothpicks, geometric shapes—items you can gather easily. For each set of materials, draw two or three complete repetitions of a pattern on strips of tagboard about 5 cm by 30 cm. The students' task is to use actual materials, copy the pattern shown, and extend it as far as they wish. Figure 22.1 illustrates possible patterns for a variety of materials. Make 10 to 15 different pattern strips for each set of materials. With six to eight sets, your entire class can work at the same time, in small groups working with different patterns and different materials.

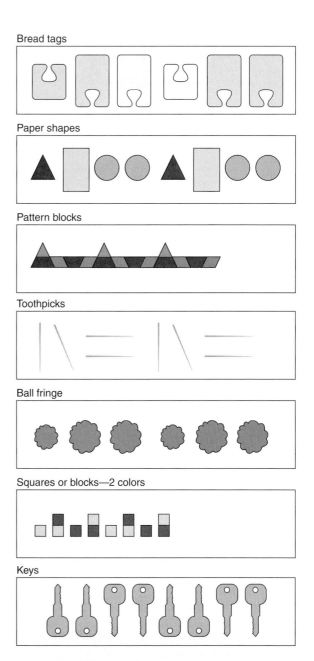

Bread tags

Paper shapes

Pattern blocks

Toothpicks

Ball fringe

Squares or blocks—2 colors

Keys

FIGURE 22.1 Examples of pattern cards drawn on tagboard. Each pattern repeats completely and does not split in the middle of a core.

FIGURE 22.2 **More examples of repeating patterns.**

The *core* of a repeating pattern is the shortest string of elements that repeats. Notice in Figure 22.1 that the core is always fully repeated and never only partially shown. If the core of a pattern is –oo, a card might have –oo–oo (two repetitions of the core), but it would be ambiguous if the card showed –oo–oo– or –oo–.

A significant step forward mathematically is to see that two patterns constructed with different materials are actually the same pattern. For example, the first pattern in Figure 22.1 and the first pattern in Figure 22.2 can both be "read" A-B-B-A-B-B-, and the pattern below those in both figures is A-B-C-C-A-B-C-C-.

NCTM Standards

". . . students should recognize that the color pattern 'blue, blue, red, blue, blue, red' is the same in form as 'clap, clap, step, clap, clap, step.' This recognition lays the foundation for the idea that two very different situations can have the same mathematical features and thus are the same in some important ways. Knowing that each pattern above could be described as hav-

ing the form AABAAB is for students an early introduction to the power of algebra" (pp. 91–92).

The following activities reflect the powerful algebraic concept of repeating patterns just described in the quotation from *Principles and Standards*.

ACTIVITY 22.2

Pattern Match

Using the chalkboard or overhead projector, show six or seven patterns with different materials or pictures. Teach students to use an A, B, C method of reading a pattern. Half of the class can close their eyes while the other half uses the A, B, C scheme to read a pattern that you point to. After hearing the pattern, the students who had their eyes closed examine the patterns and try to decide which pattern was read. If two of the patterns in the list have the same structure, the discussion can be very interesting.

The following independent activity involves translation of a pattern from one medium to another, which is another way of helping students separate the relationship in a pattern from the materials used to build it.

ACTIVITY 22.3

Same Pattern, Different Stuff

Have students make a pattern with one set of materials given a pattern strip showing a different set. This activity can easily be set up by simply switching the pattern strips from one set of materials to another. A similar idea is to mix up the pattern strips for four or five different sets of materials and have students find strips that have the same pattern. To test if two patterns are the same, children can translate each of the strips into a third set of materials or can write down the A, B, C pattern for each.

The challenge in the next activity is a forerunner to looking at the function aspect of patterns.

ACTIVITY 22.4

Predict Down the Line

For most repeating patterns, the elements of the pattern can be numbered 1, 2, 3, and so on. Provide students with a pattern to extend. Before students begin to extend the pattern, have them predict exactly what element will be in, say, the fifteenth position. Students should be required to provide a reason for their prediction, preferably in writing. Students should then extend the pattern as before and check their prediction. If their prediction is incorrect, have them examine their reasoning and try to figure out why the prediction was off.

The prediction activity may be quite challenging before the second grade. Eventually, students will figure out that the length of the core of the pattern plays a significant role. If you ask for a prediction of the hundredth element or even the three-hundredth element, students will not be able to check the prediction by extending the pattern. Verification focuses on the rationale for the prediction. Students may need to use a calculator to skip-count or multiply. But it is always the reasoning that is most important.

GROWING PATTERNS

Beginning at about the fourth grade and extending through the middle school years, students can explore patterns that involve a progression from step to step. In technical terms, these are called *sequences*; we will simply call them *growing patterns*. With these patterns, students not only extend patterns but also look for a generalization or an algebraic relationship that will tell them what the pattern will be at any point along the way. Growing patterns also demonstrate the concept of function and can be used as an entry point to this very important mathematical idea.

Figure 22.3 illustrates some growing patterns that are built with various materials or drawings. The patterns consist of a series of separate steps, each new step related to the previous one according to the pattern.

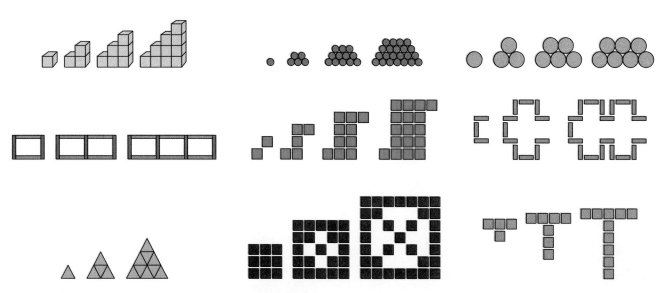

FIGURE 22.3 Growing patterns with materials or drawings.

The first thing to do with patterns in the upper and middle grades is to get students comfortable with building patterns and talking about how they can be extended in a logical manner. Building the patterns with physical materials such as tiles, counters, or flat toothpicks allows students to make changes if necessary and to build on to one step to make a new step. It is also more fun! The following activity will introduce growing patterns.

ACTIVITY 22.5

Extend and Explain

Show students the first three or four steps of a pattern. Provide them with appropriate materials or grid paper, have them extend the patterns, and explain why their extension indeed follows the pattern.

When discussing a pattern, students should try to determine how each step in the pattern differs from the preceding step. If each new step can be built by adding on to or changing the previous step, the discussion should include how this can be done. For example, each stairstep in Figure 22.3 can be made by adding a column of blocks to the preceding stairsteps. In contrast, the pattern of red tiles involves a form of expansion rather than adding on.

Growing patterns also have a numeric component, the number of objects in each step. As shown in Figure 22.4, a table can be made for any growing pattern. One row of the table or chart is always the number of steps, and the other is for recording how many objects are in that step.

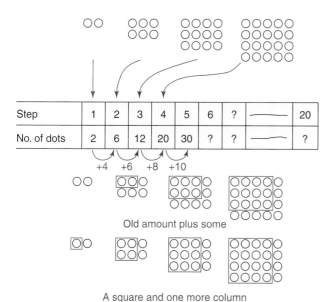

FIGURE 22.4 **Two different relationships in a visual pattern.**

Frequently, a pattern grows so quickly and requires so many blocks or spaces to draw it that it is only reasonable to build or draw the first five or six steps. This leads to the following activity.

ACTIVITY 22.6

Predict How Many

Have students begin to extend a growing pattern you provide. They should also make a table showing how many items are needed to make each step of the pattern. The task is to predict the number of items in the twentieth step of the pattern. The challenge is to see if there is a way to do this without filling in the first 19 entries of the table. Predictions should also be accompanied by an explanation.

Activity 22.6 is a natural progression from the earlier prediction activity with repeating patterns. Finding a way to determine the twentieth or even the hundredth entry in the table gets at the heart of finding a relationship that later students will understand is an example of a function. We next look at how to help students find these relationships.

Searching for Relationships

Once a table or chart is developed, students have two representations of the pattern: the one created with the drawing or materials and the numeric version that is in the table. When looking for relationships, some students will focus on the table and others will focus on the physical pattern. It is important for students to see that whatever relationships they discover, they exist in both forms. So if a relationship is found in a table, challenge students to see how that plays out in the physical version.

Patterns from Step to Step: Recursive Relationships

For most students, it is easier to see the patterns from one step to the next. When you have a chart constructed, the differences from one step to the next can be written next to or below it, as in Figure 22.4. In that example, the number in each step can be determined from the previous step by adding successive even numbers. The description that tells how a pattern changes from step to step is known as a *recursive relationship*.

Whenever there is a pattern in the table, see if students can find that same pattern in the physical version. In Figure 22.4, notice that in each step, the previous step has been outlined. That lets you examine the amount added and see how it creates the pattern of adding on even numbers. The picture or physical pattern and the table should be as closely connected as possible.

Patterns from Step Number to Step: Functional Relationships

The recursive step-to-step pattern is almost certainly the first that your students will observe. However, to find the table entry for the hundredth step, the only way a recursive pattern can help is to find all of the prior 99 entries in the table. If a rule or relationship can be discovered that connects the number of objects in a step to the number of the step, any table entry can be determined without building or calculating all of the intermediate entries. A rule that determines the number of elements in a step from the step number is an example of a *functional relationship*.

There is no single best method for finding this relationship between step number and step. Some students may get insight by simply "playing around" with the numbers and asking, "How can I operate on the number of the step to get the corresponding number in the table?" Most will benefit from examining the physical pattern for regularities. At the bottom of Figure 22.4, a square array is outlined for each step. Each successive square is one larger on a side. What relationship might exist between this subset of the pattern and the step numbers? In this example, the side of each square is the same as the step number. The row to the right of each square is also the step number.

![STOP] With that information, how would you describe the twentieth step? Can you determine how many elements will be in it without drawing the picture?

At this point, a significant activity is to write a numeric expression for each step number using the same pattern. For example, the first four steps in Figure 22.4 are $1^2 + 1$, $2^2 + 2$, $3^2 + 3$, and $4^2 + 4$.

It may take much searching and experimenting for students in groups or as a class to come up with an expression that is similar for each step. Do not be upset if students have difficulty. Encourage the search for relationships to continue, even if it takes more than one day. The search for relationships is the most significant portion of these activities.

Moving from Patterns to Function and Variable

When students have discovered numeric expressions for each step using step numbers, write them with brackets around the step numbers as shown in Figure 22.5. If this results in a pattern, the bracketed numbers will change from step to step, while the other numbers in the expressions remain the same. Now the bracketed numbers can be replaced by a letter or variable, resulting in a general formula. The formula defines the functional relationship between step numbers and step values.

![STOP] Before reading on, explore some of the patterns in Figure 22.3 to see if you can find formulas (functional relationships) for each. You should be able to "plug in" the step numbers in your formulas and get the value for that step. Some are a bit harder than others.

The discussion to this point is summarized in the following activity, an elaboration of "Predict How Many." It is best to do this in groups so that ideas can be generated more freely.

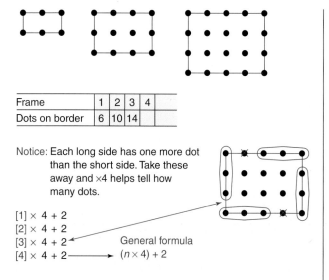

Frame	1	2	3	4	
Dots on border	6	10	14		

Notice: Each long side has one more dot than the short side. Take these away and ×4 helps tell how many dots.

[1] × 4 + 2
[2] × 4 + 2
[3] × 4 + 2   General formula
[4] × 4 + 2 → $(n \times 4) + 2$

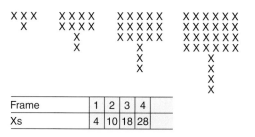

Frame	1	2	3	4	
Xs	4	10	18	28	

Notice: If the tail part is added to the side of the top part, there is always a square and three more columns.

[1] × [1] + (3 × [1])
[2] × [2] + (3 × [2])
[3] × [3] + (3 × [3])
        General formula
$n \times n + 3n = n^2 + 3n$

FIGURE 22.5 **Finding functional relationships in patterns.**

ACTIVITY 22.7

Find the Function in the Pattern

Give students the first three or four steps of a pattern. Their tasks are as follows:

1. Extend the pattern several more steps until they are sure they understand the pattern. They should always look backward to the beginning of the pattern to see that their idea works for all steps. Record this in a drawing.
2. Make a table that shows the number of elements in each step they have constructed.
3. Find and describe in writing as many patterns as possible, both from the table and from the physical pattern. For each pattern found in the table, they should see how that idea can be found in the physical pattern. The most important pattern to look for is the one from steps to number of elements, the functional relationship.
4. Write the functional relationship as a formula in terms of the step number. Show how the formula works for each part of the table already constructed. Use the formula to predict the next entry in the table, and check this with an actual construction of the pattern, if possible. Use the formula to predict the twentieth entry in the table.

Graphing the Patterns

So far, growing patterns are represented by the physical materials or drawings, by a chart, and by a symbolic rule.

A graph adds a fourth representation. The individual points in a pattern can be plotted even if the physical pattern has not been discovered. Figure 22.6 shows the graph for each of the two patterns in Figure 22.5. Notice that the first is a straight-line (linear) relationship and the other is a curved line that would make half of a parabola if the points were joined.

Do not forget how easy it is both to plot points and to draw curves on the graphing calculator. The second graph in Figure 22.6 is also shown on a graphing calculator with the function $y = x^2 + 3x$ (same as $n^2 + 3n$) drawn through it.

NCTM Standards

"In grades 3–5, students should investigate numerical and geometric patterns and express them mathematically in words or symbols. They should analyze the structure of the pattern and how it grows or changes, organize this information systematically, and use their analysis to develop generalizations about the mathematical relationships in the pattern" (p. 159).

Returning for a moment to the recursive relationships for growing patterns, notice that when the recursive pattern is constant, as it is for the "Dots on the Border" pattern (Figure 22.5), the graph is a straight line or is *linear*. If the recursive pattern is not constant, the graph is a curve. For the "Ts of Xs" pattern (Figure 22.5) the recursive pattern is +6, +8, +10, ... The amount of change from step to step is increasing and the graph in Figure 22.6 reflects this as it curves upward in a steeper and steeper manner. Now look at the changes *in the*

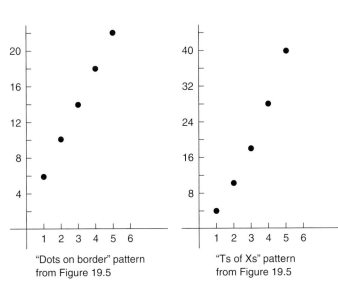

"Dots on border" pattern from Figure 19.5

"Ts of Xs" pattern from Figure 19.5

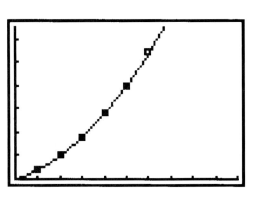

TI-83 graph of $y = x^2 + 3x$

FIGURE 22.6 Graphs of growing patterns.

INVESTIGATIONS in NUMBER, DATA, and SPACE

Grade 5, *Patterns of Change*
Investigation 1: Number Patterns in Changing Shapes

Context

This unit occurs in the second half of the fifth grade. In this first investigation, students explore growing block patterns and graph them. For most of the remainder of the unit, instead of geometric patterns, students look at graphs of distance traveled away from a starting point with the steps being intervals of time. Nowhere in the unit are students asked to find general formulas. However, they do learn about rates of change.

Task Description

During the first two days of this investigation, students make tables and plot the graphs of growing patterns made with square tiles. The patterns grow from one step to the next by adding on to the previous step. When students add on to their patterns, they change the color of tile they are using.

By using the change-of-color approach, students need only draw one picture to show all of the steps of the tile pattern. This is recorded in the upper left portion of the worksheet shown here where the first three steps of the pattern are given. Based on the pattern, students fill in the table for the first eight steps. These tables have three columns, not just two. The middle column, labeled "New tiles (step size)," is actually the recursive relationship or the slope of the graph for that step. Next, students make two graphs: one of the steps and the step size, and the second of the step and the number of tiles. For a pattern such as this one in which two new tiles are added at each step, the first graph is a horizontal line two units up. The graph of the total tiles is a straight line increasing upward, always with a slope of 2. For the student page shown here, the first graph is a straight line going up with a slope of 1. The graph of the total is a curve.

When students begin graphing distances from a starting point, they explore a full variety of curves, including

Page 114 from *Tables and Graphs: Patterns of Change* by C. Tierney, R. Nemirovsky, T. Noble, & D. Clements. *Investigations in Number, Data, and Space.* Copyright © 1998 by Dale Seymour Publications. Reprinted by permission of Pearson Education, Inc.

those that decrease and are horizontal. For example, in one activity, students look at walking rates and positions from the start point. Not only can walking speed (step size) be fast, slow, or even zero, but it can also be negative (walking backward or toward the start). Therefore, graphs of step sizes are both above and below the horizontal axis, and the corresponding position graphs go up or down with differing rates of change.

changes (the recursive relationship *in the recursive relationship*). For straight lines, there is no change in the changes. The *rate* of change is 0. The slope remains the same. For the "Ts of Xs," however, the change in the changes, or the rate of change, is increasing with each step.

In the fifth grade of *Investigations in Number, Data, and Space,* an entire unit focuses specifically on this rate of change aspect in functional relationships. As you can see in the excerpt on this page, the recursive relationship is recorded on a third line of the table.

Other Patterns to Explore

It would be an error to leave the impression that repeated patterns and growing patterns as discussed so far are all that students need to know about patterns. Mathematicians continue to search for and discover new patterns and relationships. Applications of mathematical patterns have led to solutions of real-world problems that were once thought to be unsolvable. Patterns are powerful ideas.

Patterns on the Hundreds Chart

The hundreds chart is a rich field for exploring number relationships and should not be thought of solely as a device for teaching numeration.

In Chapter 12, children colored skip-counts on the hundreds chart and looked for patterns (see Activity 12.11, p. 191). Here are some additional tasks you might explore in a similar manner.

Which numbers make diagonal patterns? Which make column patterns?

Can you find two skip-count patterns with one "on top of" the other? That is, all of the squares for one pattern are part of the pattern for the other. How are these two skip-count numbers related? Are there other patterns that are on top of each other?

What patterns only have some squares in common but not all? On what numbers do the patterns cross? Can you tell without looking at the charts?

ACTIVITY 22.8

Change the Charts, Change the Patterns

Have students make number charts with fewer than ten numbers in a row. Color the skip-count patterns as before. The challenge is to discover which skip counts will form diagonal patterns and which will form column patterns. The answer will vary, depending on the width of the chart. (See Figure 22.7 for two examples.) Have students look for relationships involving the skip-count number, the width of the chart, and whether the pattern is diagonal or makes columns.

Students will find that the same patterns are on top of each other as with the regular chart. However, patterns go in columns only when skip-counting by a factor or a multiple of the chart width. For example, on a chart of width 9, the threes make columns but the twos make diagonals. What will sixes do on a 9-wide chart? What if the width of the chart is a prime number? You can also explore charts that are wider than 10.

Fours on a 5-wide chart

Threes and fives on a 4-wide chart

FIGURE 22.7 **Patterns on hundreds charts of different widths.**

Number Patterns

Many worthwhile patterns can be observed with numbers alone. These can be simple repeating patterns such as 1, 2, 1, 2, ... Even very young children can use numbers in patterns like these. Generally, however, numeric patterns involve some form of progression. The pattern 1, 2, 1, 3, 1, 4, 1, 5, . . . is a simple example that even young students can discover. Here are some more numeric patterns:

2, 4, 6, 8, 10, . . .	(even numbers; add 2 each time)
1, 4, 7, 10, 13, . . .	(start with 1; add 3 each time)
1, 4, 9, 16, . . .	(squares: 1^2, 2^2, 3^2, etc.)
0, 1, 5, 14, 30, . . .	(add the next square number)
2, 5, 11, 23, . . .	(double the number and add 1)
2, 6, 12, 20, 30, . . .	(multiply successive pairs)
3, 3, 6, 9, 15, 24, . . .	(add the two preceding numbers—an example of a Fibonacci sequence)

The challenge in these patterns or sequences of numbers is not only to find and extend the pattern but also to try to determine a general rule to produce the nth number in the sequence. Informal or exploratory approaches are similar to those described for growing patterns.

The calculator provides a powerful approach to patterns. For a good example, see the discussion of "Start and Jump Numbers" in Chapter 2 (p. 14).

Another form of number pattern is found in function machines as in the next activity.

ACTIVITY 22.9

Guess My Rule

A simple in-out box is drawn on the board as in Figure 22.8. The machine "operator" knows the secret that is "stored" in the machine. For example, a rule might be $2n + 1$ (double the input number and add 1). Students try to guess the rule by putting numbers into the machine and observing what comes out. Students tell the operator what number to put in. The operator tells what number comes out. A list of "in-out" pairs are kept on the board. Students who think they have guessed the rule raise their hands. As more numbers are "put into the machine," those who think they know the rule tell what comes out. Continue until most have guessed the rule.

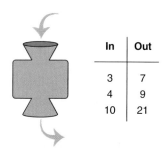

In	Out
3	7
4	9
10	21

FIGURE 22.8 A simple function machine is used to play "Guess My Rule." Students suggest input numbers and the operator records the output value.

Students can play "Guess My Rule" in small groups. Provide a collection of rules on cards or let students make up their own rules. The rule should be in writing before the guessing begins.

 A graphing calculator can easily be made into a true function machine to play "Guess My Rule."

On the TI-73 or TI-83, the following simple program will take an entry, display the output, and continue to accept inputs until you press Quit.

```
Prgm 1: GUESS
:Lbl 1
:Disp "ENTER X"
:Input X
:2x+5⇒A   (This line stores the secret function.)
:Disp A
:Goto 1
```

Students using the program will see only

```
Prgm 1: GUESS
"ENTER X"
?3
                          11
ENTER X
?5
                          15
```

The function line of the program is easily changed.

The following activities also explore patterns with a calculator.

ACTIVITY 22.10

Amazing Digits

Enter 9 ⊠ n, where n is any number from 1 to 9. Press =. Now press other numbers followed by =. Even if students know their nines facts, this step will serve to clarify the process and illustrate that each new press of = multiplies the display by 9. Now enter 99 ⊠ n =. Try other values of n followed by =. What is the pattern? Try 999 ⊠ n and even 9999 or 99999 ⊠ n. Students should play with and explore this idea as long as they wish. Next try using repeating digits for n (3333 or 66). Instead of using nines for the multiplier, try using 0.009 or 99.9. Also experiment with other repeat-digit multipliers. If students are interested, the patterns with nines might be analyzed by looking at 999 as $1000 - 1$ or as 9×111.

ACTIVITY 22.11

More Amazing Digits

Especially if students have shown interest in "Amazing Digits," try division by 9. Begin by just dividing single-digit numbers by 9. (The calculator remembers the last divisor, so after the first division, just enter the new number and press =.) After this, there are all sorts of variations to try:

a. Divide by 99, 999, . . .
b. Divide by 0.9, 0.09, 0.009, . . .
c. Divide by 9, but use two-digit dividends. Can you predict the results?
d. Try three-digit dividends and a divisor of 9.
e. Combine (a) or (b) with (c) or (d).

The patterns in "More Amazing Digits" are spectacular and interesting by themselves, but you may want to also try using a digit other than 9 in that exercise.

For more activities with number patterns and patterns in general, see the NCTM *Addenda Series* books on patterns. Both the K–6 book (Coburn, 1993) and the middle school book (Phillips, Gardella, Kelly, & Stewart, 1991) have excellent ideas. (See Recommendations for Further Reading.)

The Fibonacci Sequence

For a growing pattern that is just a little bit different, see Figure 22.9. It begins with a little square. Each successive frame is formed by building a new and larger square onto the previous design. (Can you see how to continue drawing this pattern?) If the side of the first two little squares is 1 each, then the sides of each new square are the numbers of most interest in this pattern. For those squares shown in the figure, the sides are 1, 1, 2, 3, 5, 8, and 13. What would the side of the next square be? This series of numbers, known as the *Fibonacci sequence,* is named for the Italian mathematician Leonardo Fibonacci (c. 1180–1250). The sequence occurs in a variety of living things. For example, if you count the sets of spirals that go in opposite directions on a pineapple or the seeds of a sunflower, the two numbers will be adjacent numbers in the Fibonacci sequence, usually 8 and 13 for a pineapple and 55 and 89 for sunflowers.

Another interesting fact about the Fibonacci sequence is that the ratio of adjacent numbers in the sequence gets closer and closer to a single fixed number known as the *golden ratio,* a number very close to 1.618. Each larger rectangle in Figure 22.9 has sides in ratio a little closer to the golden ratio. A rectangle in that ratio is called a *golden rectangle,* examples of which can be found in most of the prominent examples of ancient Greek architecture as well as in much art and architecture through the ages. The spiral that is drawn in the last rectangle

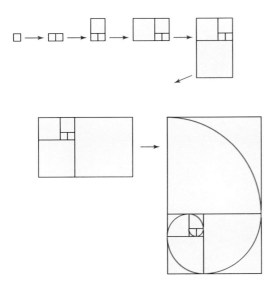

FIGURE 22.9 A growing pattern of squares: Each new rectangle is a little closer to a "golden rectangle."

shown (made from quarter circles drawn in each square) is the same spiral found in the shell of the chambered nautilus.

The Fibonacci sequence and the golden ratio are fascinating phenomena of mathematics. For those who would like to learn more about the connections of this sequence with nature, art, and mathematics, books by Runion (1990) and by Garland (1987) are highly recommended.

VARIABLES AND EQUATIONS

Variables constitute an extremely powerful method of expressing the regularities found in mathematics. Variables enable us to use mathematical symbolism as a tool to think and help better understand mathematical ideas in the same way physical objects and drawings are used. But if variables are to be included with these other "thinker toys," it is important to help students develop an understanding of the various ways they are used.

Variables

A *variable* is a symbol that can stand for any one of a set of numbers or other objects. Although correct, this simple-sounding definition has a variety of interpretations, depending on how the variables are used. A less than clear understanding can lead to a host of misinterpretations.

Misunderstandings About Variables

Even though students are exposed throughout the elementary years to boxes and letters in arithmetic expressions, studies indicate that most children have a very narrow understanding of the concept of "variable" (Booth, 1988; Chalouh & Herscovics, 1988; Lodholz, 1990).

Some students believe that $7w + 22 = 109$ and $7n + 22 = 109$ will have different solutions. Letters are sometimes taken to represent objects rather than numeric values.

> **⊗ STOP** We all know there are 3 feet in a yard. Using *F* for feet and *Y* for yards, which of these equations correctly expresses this relationship: $3F = Y$ or $F = 3Y$? Make your choice before reading on.

Translating real relationships into symbolic equations is often difficult for students. Most students will pick the first equation, $3F = Y.$ Perhaps you did also. Try putting some numbers in $3F = Y.$ For example, if *F* is 3, then *Y* should be 1. But that does not work in $3F = Y.$ The difficulty is in the syntax. Compare the statement "There are three feet in one yard" with "The *number* of feet is three times the *number* of yards." *F* stands for the *number* of feet and *Y*, the *number* of yards. And so, the correct equation is $F = 3Y.$

Conventions of notation also compound the difficulty. For example, we use *ab* to mean $a \times b,$ but $3 \times 5 \neq 35.$ Similarly, $ab = ba,$ but $35 \neq 53;$ and $4 + 0.75 = 4.75,$ but $2x + y \neq 2xy.$

Different Uses of Variables

Meanings of variables change with the way they are used. Usiskin (1988) identified three uses of variables that are commonly encountered in school mathematics:

1. *As a specific unknown.* In the early grades, this is the use found in equations such as 8 + ❑ = 12. Later, we see exercises such as this: If $3x + 2 = 4x - 1$, solve for x.
2. *As a pattern generalizer.* Variables are used in statements that are true for all numbers. For example, $a \times b = b \times a$ for all real numbers. Formulas such as $A = L \times W$ also show a pattern.
3. *As quantities that vary in joint variation.* Joint variation occurs when change in one variable determines a change in another. In $y = 3x + 5$, as x changes or varies, so does y. Formulas are also an example of joint variation. In $C = 2\pi r$, as r, the radius, changes, so does C, the circumference.

Variables as Unknowns

The following activity is a reasonable way for students to experience the meaning of a variable as a placeholder for a specific unknown.

ACTIVITY 22.12

Story Translations

Read a simple story problem to students, but omit the question. Their task is to write an equation that means the same thing. For example: *There are 3 full boxes of pencils and 5 extra pencils. There are 41 pencils in all.* (3 × ❑ + 5 = 41) Be sure to include all meanings of all four operations as described in Chapter 10. The activity can be reversed by providing an equation with an unknown and letting students make up a story to go with it. Once equations are agreed on, students should use whatever means they wish to find values that make the sentences true. Trial and error is a reasonable first strategy.

Sometimes students will write what may look like different equations. For example, *If Yolanda has 12 cards and Karl has 5, write the equation that tells how many more cards Yolanda has.* Both of these equations might be written: 12 − 5 = ❑ and 5 + ❑ = 12. Students should decide how these equations are alike and how they are different.

ACTIVITY 22.13

Number Tricks

Have students do the following sequence of operations:

Write down any number.

Add to it the number that comes after it.

Add 9.

Divide by 2.

Subtract the number you began with.

Now you can "magically" read their minds. Everyone ended up with 5!

The challenge is to see if students can discover how the trick works. If students need a hint, suggest that instead of using an actual number, they use a box or a letter to begin with. Start with N. Add the next number: $N + (N + 1) = 2N + 1$. Adding 9 gives $2N + 10$. Dividing by 2 leaves $N + 5$. Now subtract the number you began with, leaving 5.

There are endless trick sequences like the one in this activity. Here are two more:

> Pick a number between 1 and 9, multiply by 5, add 3, multiply by 2, add another number between 1 and 9, subtract 6. What do you see?

> Pick a number, multiply by 6, add 12, take half of the result, subtract 6, divide by 3. What happens?

These tricks can also be explored with models by using a small box or a cube for the unknown. Figure 22.10 shows how the first of the two tricks above might be modeled. Notice the place-value component required to understand the result.

Variables as Pattern Generators

Variables are often used to illustrate rules or regularities that exist in our number system. We often write down these rules using variables without giving much thought to the fact that students may not understand the variables involved.

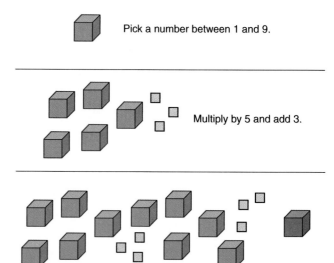

Pick a number between 1 and 9.

Multiply by 5 and add 3.

Multiply by 2 and add another 1-digit number.

Subtract 6, and then . . .

10 × ❑ + ❑ = ❑❑ (a 2-digit number)

FIGURE 22.10 Number tricks can be modeled using a block or a box for the unknown. Additional numbers are shown with counters or base-ten pieces.

ACTIVITY 22.14

What's True for All Numbers?

Ask students how they know that 465 + 137 = 137 + 465 without doing the computation. Students' explanations should show evidence of understanding the commutative property for addition, although the name of the property is not important. How can this be written to show that it's a rule that is true for every number, even fractions and decimals? If students do not suggest it, offer the idea that letters or shapes could be used like this:

$$\Delta + \square = \square + \Delta \qquad \text{or} \qquad n + m = m + n$$

Be sure students understand that the choice of letter or shape is totally arbitrary as long as it is understood that each stands for any number and that when the same letter or shape appears in the same equation, it must represent the same value.

With this introduction, challenge students to find other statements that are true for all numbers.

Students may need some prodding to think about things that are always true, but it is best that they come up with the ideas themselves. One way to provide hints is to explore some specific examples. For example, draw a divided rectangle as shown in Figure 22.11. What are two ways to calculate the area? This can lead to the generalized version of the distributive property: $a(b + c) = (a \times b) + (a \times c)$. In addition to properties of the number system, also think about definitions of exponents or rules for negative numbers, all of which can be expressed in a general form using variables.

FIGURE 22.11 The distributive property is just one of many ideas that can be generalized using variables.

ACTIVITY 22.15

Special Quantities

What numeric expression would tell the number of chair legs on 376 chairs? (376 × 4) What about 195 chairs? (195 × 4) How would you write the number of legs on any number of chairs? (N × 4) Using this as an example, challenge students to write expressions for other types of quantities: fingers on students, eggs in cartons, crayons in boxes, wheels on tractor trailers, hours in days, inches in feet, quarts in gallons, and so on. Similarly, use variables to express these special numbers: any odd number, any even number, any multiple of 7, a multiple of 3 plus a different multiple of 5, any two-digit number, any power of 2. Once students get the idea, have them make up their own special quantities and see if others can describe them verbally.

The way that variables are used in the "Special Quantities" activity is essentially the way variables are used in spreadsheets. In Figure 22.12, odd and even numbers are generated

	A	B	C	D	E	F	G	H	I
1	**Exploring Odd and Even Numbers**								
2									
3	N	Even	Odd	E + E	E + O	O + O	E × E	E × O	O × O
4	1	2	3	4	5	6	4	6	9
5	2	4	5	8	9	10	16	20	25
6	7	14	15	28	29	30	196	210	225
7	10	20	21	40	41	42	400	420	441
8	15	30	31	60	61	62	900	930	961

FIGURE 22.12 A spreadsheet formula uses variables to represent values in other cells. The expression in a cell is a pattern generalizer for that cell. The same spreadsheet is shown twice here, once with the formula in each cell and once with the cell values calculated. Note that any change in column A will produce changes in the entire row.

	A	B	C	D	E	F	G	H	I
1	**Exploring Odd and Even Numbers**								
2									
3	N	Even	Odd	E + E	E + O	O + O	E × E	E × O	O × O
4	1	=2*A4	=2*A4+1	=B4+B4	=B4+C4	=C4+C4	=B4*B4	=B4*C4	=C4*C4
5	2	=2*A5	=2*A5+1	=B5+B5	=B5+C5	=C5+C5	=B5*B5	=B5*C5	=C5*C5
6	7	=2*A6	=2*A6+1	=B6+B6	=B6+C6	=C6+C6	=B6*B6	=B6*C6	=C6*C6
7	10	=2*A7	=2*A7+1	=B7+B7	=B7+C7	=C7+C7	=B7*B7	=B7*C7	=C7*C7
8	15	=2*A8	=2*A8+1	=B8+B8	=B8+C8	=C8+C8	=B8*B8	=B8*C8	=C8*C8

from the numbers in column A. These values are then used in the sums and products columns.

Variables as Quantities That Vary

"Joint variation is at the heart of understanding patterns and functions. As students grow in their ability to derive meaning for variables in contexts, they encounter variables that are changing in relation to each other" (Lappan, 1998, p. 57). Whenever students develop charts that list the corresponding values of two related quantities, they are exploring the idea of *joint variation;* the value in one row varies according to the value in the other row. Young children make charts showing the number of eyes for different numbers of kids. In the study of ratio and proportion, students make charts relating cost to the number of units purchased or relating miles driven to gallons of gasoline used. In measurement, charts are made that relate circumference to diameter or volume to the area of the base of a cylinder. In data analysis, best-fit lines produce generalizations of the way two variables are approximately related, for example, height and arm span. In this chapter, we have seen that the study of growing patterns results in formulas that connect the step number to the number of elements in that step of the pattern.

All of these are examples of joint variation—one value changing in relation to another. They are also examples of functions, the rule that determines the way that the two variables are related. Chapter 23 is devoted to helping children understand and analyze functions. There we will examine ways to help students explore joint variation of variables expressed in contextual situations, in equations, in charts, in graphs, and in words.

 The *Standards* echoes this emphasis on variables. "In the elementary grades, students typically develop a notion of variables as a placeholder for a specific number, as in __ + 2 = 11. Later, they should learn that the variable x in the equation $3x + 2 = 11$ has a very different use from the variable in the identity $0 \times x = 0$ and that both uses are quite different from the use of r in the formula $A = \pi r^2$" (p. 39).

Equations and Inequalities

In the expression $3B + 7 = B - C,$ the equal sign means that the quantity on the left *is the same as* the quantity on the right. To understand expressions in this way, students must interpret simple arithmetic expressions such as $3 + 5$ or 4×87 as *single quantities.*

Unfortunately, students tend to look on expressions such as $3 + 5$ and 4×87 as commands or things to do. The = tells you to add, and students think of *add* as a verb or an operator button, like pressing ⊟ on a calculator. As students read left to right in an equation, the = tells them, "Now give the answer."

Because of this "get an answer" view of operations and equal signs, students fail to think of $5 + 2$ as another way to write 7.

A Balance Pan Approach to Equality

The following activities are ways to help students with the basic concepts needed to understand equations.

ACTIVITY 22.16

Names for Numbers

Challenge students to find different ways to express a particular number, say, 10. Give a few simple examples, such as $5 + 5$ or $12 - 2$. Encourage the use of two or more different operations. "How many names for 8 can you find using only numbers less than 10 and at least three operations?" In your discussion, emphasize that each expression is a way of representing or writing a number.

Notice that there are no equal signs used in Activity 22.16. The next activity develops the concept of the equal sign. It begins with numbers only but is quickly extended to include variables.

ACTIVITY 22.17

Tilt or Balance

On the board, draw a simple two-pan balance. In each pan, write a numeric expression, and ask which pan will go down or whether the two will balance (see Figure 22.13). Challenge students to write expressions for each side of the scale to make it balance. For each, write a corresponding equation to illustrate the meaning of =. Note that when the scale "tilts," either a "greater than" or "less than" symbol (> or <) is used.

After a short time, add variables to the two-pan balance activity.

In Figure 22.14, a series of examples shows scale problems in which each shape on the scales represents a different value. Two or more scales for a single problem provide different information about the shapes or variables. Problems of this type can be adjusted in difficulty for children throughout first to eighth grades. (See the books and article by Greenes and Findell in the Recommendations for Further Reading.)

When no numbers are involved, as in the top two examples of Figure 22.14, students can find combinations of numbers for the shapes that make all of the balances balance. If an arbitrary value is given to one of the shapes, then values for the other shapes can be found accordingly. In the second

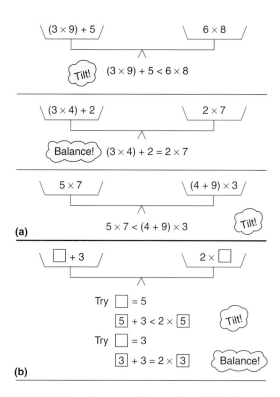

(a)

(b)

FIGURE 22.13 Using expressions and variables in equations and inequalities. The two-pan balance helps develop the meaning of =, <, and >.

example, if the sphere = 2, then the cylinder must be 4 and the cube = 8. If a different value is given to the sphere, the other shapes will change accordingly.

The scale problems (with a number for each scale) are to be solved for a unique value for each shape. There are usually several paths to finding a solution.

 STOP How would you solve the last problem in Figure 22.14? Can you solve it in two ways?

You (and students) can tell if you are correct by checking your solutions with the original scale positions. Believe it or not, you have just solved a series of simultaneous equations, a skill generally left to a formal algebra class.

Solving Equations

To *solve an equation* means to find values of the variable that make the equation true. To help students develop skills of solving equations in one variable, it is advisable to maintain the image of the balance pans. The balance makes it reasonably clear to students that if you add or subtract value from one side, you must add or subtract like values from the other side to keep the scales balanced.

Which shape weighs the most? Explain.
Which shape weighs the least? Explain.

What will balance 2 spheres? Explain.

How much does each shape weigh? Explain.

How much does each shape weigh? Explain.

How much does each shape weigh? Explain.

FIGURE 22.14 Examples of problems with multiple scales (equations).

ACTIVITY 22.18

Adjust the Balance

Show a balance with variable expressions in each side. Use only one variable. Make the tasks such that a solution by trial and error is not reasonable. For example, the solution to $3x + 2 = 11 - x$ is not a whole number. Suggest that adjustments can be made to the quantities in each pan as long as the balance is maintained. If you begin with simple equations such as $x - 17 = 31 - x$, students should be able to develop skills and explain their rationale. Students should also be challenged to devise a method of proving that their solutions are correct. (Solutions can be tested by substitution in the original equation.)

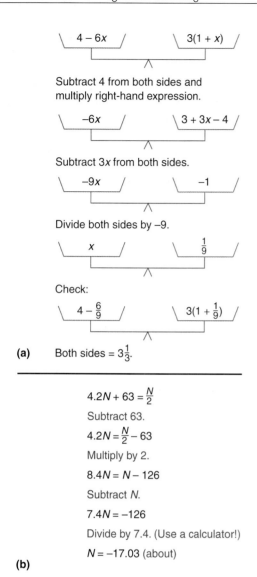

(a) Both sides = $3\frac{1}{3}$.

$$4.2N + 63 = \frac{N}{2}$$

Subtract 63.

$$4.2N = \frac{N}{2} - 63$$

Multiply by 2.

$$8.4N = N - 126$$

Subtract N.

$$7.4N = -126$$

Divide by 7.4. (Use a calculator!)

$$N = -17.03 \text{ (about)}$$

(b)

FIGURE 22.15 Using a balance scale to think about solving equations.

Figure 22.15 shows solutions for two equations, one in a balance and the other without. Even after you have stopped using the balance, it is a good idea to refer to the scale or balance pan concept of equality and the idea of keeping the scales balanced.

As students begin to develop equations they wish to graph, the equations will often be in a form in which neither variable is isolated. For example, in the equation $3A - B = 2A$, they may want A in terms of B or B in terms of A. The same technique of solving for one variable can be used to solve for one variable in terms of the other by adjusting the expressions on both sides while keeping the equation in balance.

 ## LITERATURE CONNECTIONS

Many teachers find pattern explorations sufficiently interesting that they may not think of using literature to provide a springboard for student explorations. However, here are three examples of books that are excellent beginnings for patterns and chart building.

Pattern
Pluckrose, 1988

This book brings pattern from the real world to the classroom in the form of brilliantly colored photographs. Pattern is seen in the soles of tennis shoes, dishes, butterflies, leaves, and flowers. The book provides a jumping-off point for an exploration of pattern in the world around us. A photo collage could be made of patterns found by the children. Drawings of patterns with explanations of the source and descriptions of the patterns can be assembled into a book. A display of patterns from your class activities and those found in nature, in the home, and in the neighborhood would make an excellent show for parents.

Anno's Mysterious Multiplying Jar
Anno & Anno, 1983

Like all of the books illustrated by Mitsumasa Anno, this one is beautiful. It tells an imaginative story of a mysterious jar that contains a sea. On the sea is one island. The island has two mountains. Each mountain has three countries. Within each country are four walled kingdoms. . . . Finally, each of nine boxes contains ten jars. The illustrations help develop the quickly expanding numbers of factorials. After the story, the authors help conceptualize the size of each factorial with arrays of tiny stars and suggest other ways to explore this fascinating number pattern.

Children of almost any age are likely to be interested in exploring the factorial concept due to the large numbers. A simple idea is to create a multiplying story and illustrate it or collect objects to show how many items are involved. Another idea is to examine nested situations in the real world even if they are not factorials. For example, talk to a grocery store about how small items such as chewing gum are shipped to the store. There will likely be cartons in which there are smaller boxes. In each box there may possibly be packages. Each package might contain several packs of gum and then finally single sticks. How many in all is determined by the same multiplication process.

Anno's Magic Seeds
Anno, 1994

Another wonderful book by Mitsumasa Anno, *Magic Seeds* develops a pattern that changes throughout, becoming a bit more elaborate with each change. A wise man gives Jack two magic seeds. He is told to eat one and plant the other. The seed he eats will keep him from hunger for a whole year, and the planted seed will produce two new seeds by the following year. Several years later, Jack decides to plant both seeds rather than eating one. This new pattern continues until he marries, has a child, and starts to sell seeds.

At each stage of the story, there is an opportunity to develop a chart and extend the current pattern into the future. Austin and Thompson (1997) outline in considerable detail how they used the story to develop patterns and charts with sixth- and seventh-grade students. Their article is worth looking up. However, you will have no problem developing good pattern lessons from this book without any assistance. ■

ASSESSMENT NOTES

The main content of this chapter is found in the ideas related to patterns (repeating, number, and growing) and the related ideas of variables and equations. At any particular grade level, your particular curriculum will likely specify particular skills in these areas. To assess this particular knowledge is straightforward. Can your students recognize and extend patterns of the appropriate type for their grade level? Do they use variables in ways that suggest an understanding of the various uses and meanings of *variable*—again, commensurate with their grade level? And do they solve equations appropriate for their grade level? Answers to these questions should be found in the way students respond to the activities you conduct in class or in end-of-unit tests that assess these ideas directly.

More pervasive than these specific ideas, however, is the general notion of algebraic reasoning. It is appropriate to gather data that indicate the degree to which students make generalizations based on their mathematical experiences and use appropriate language and symbolism to represent these generalizations. Since pattern and regularity can be found in nearly all areas of mathematics, algebraic reasoning should be developed and assessed throughout the curriculum. Students who ask questions like "Will that work for any numbers?" or who observe similarities from one area of mathematics to another are using algebraic reasoning. Students who have difficulty seeing and expressing relationships such as the way two patterns are alike or who have difficulty expressing rules and formulas are not as strong in their algebraic reasoning.

Make a conscious effort to observe and keep anecdotal records of behaviors that are indicative of algebraic reasoning. It is quite likely that such records over time will give you useful insights into the mathematical talents of your students. ■

REFLECTIONS ON CHAPTER 22

Writing to Learn

1. Describe in your own words what algebraic reasoning means. At what grade level should algebraic reasoning begin?
2. Make up three pattern strips showing repeating patterns for some common objects that might be found in the classroom. Label each using an A, B, C scheme. No two schemes should be alike, but all should use the same materials. What is the core of each pattern? What will be the twenty-fifth element of each?
3. What is a recursive relationship? Where in a growing pattern would you look for a recursive relationship? In terms of growing patterns, what is a functional relationship?
4. How can you tell from the recursive relationship whether the graph will be linear (in a straight line) or will be a curve? Explain the recursive relationship in terms of rate of change or slope of the line.
5. The following growing pattern consists of square borders. The elements of each step are the number of squares or tiles that make up the border. Draw the fifth border and the tenth border in the sequence. Make a chart showing the number of tiles in each of the first ten borders. Find a recursive relationship that permits you to get from one step to the next. With attention to the drawings of this growing pattern, try to find one or more ways to express the general functional relationship that the pattern defines.

6. How can a hundreds chart be used to develop pattern ideas?
7. Give an example of each of the three different uses of variables. For each use, describe at least one activity that addresses students' understanding of variables used in that manner.
8. Make up a scales problem involving three different variables. After you have made it up, show at least one way that it can be solved other than by trial and error.
9. What misconceptions do children have about expressions such as $4 + 8$ and the equal sign that can cause difficulty working with equations?
10. Explain how to solve the equation $4x + 3 = x + 12$ using a pan balance.

For Discussion and Exploration

1. The Reasoning standard in *Principles and Standards for School Mathematics* is meant to permeate all content areas. However, it has special significance for the types of activities found in this chapter. Read the Reasoning standard, either the overview found in Chapter 3 of *Principles and Standards* or the corresponding elaboration found in the grade band of most interest to you. Discuss how the inclusion of algebraic reasoning throughout the elementary and middle school grades emphasizes the use of reasoning for all students.

2. Explorations of patterns such as the number and calculator patterns or the Fibonacci sequence are not presented in typical textbooks except as enrichment or extras, especially in the upper grades. (Repeat patterns are quite popular in grades K and 1.) Is it reasonable to spend time in the fourth through eighth grades on explorations of this sort? Take a position and defend it.

3. The Disney film *Donald in Mathmagic Land* is a classic from the 1940s that is now available on videotape and occasionally aired on the Disney Channel. The film explores pattern and several related beauties of mathematics in a timeless manner. Your mathematics education is not quite complete if you haven't seen it. It will intrigue children from third grade to high school, and a creative teacher can find many ways to follow up with explorations. View it if you can, and share an idea for using the film with children.

Recommendations for Further Reading

Highly Recommended

Coburn, T. G. (1993). *Patterns: Addenda series, grades K–6*. Reston, VA: National Council of Teachers of Mathematics.

This is one of the best resource books on patterns for the K–6 grades. Examples of virtually every type of pattern activity are included. The *Addenda Series* books were to the 1989 *Standards* what the *Navigations Series* is to the 2000 *Standards*. As with other elementary *Addenda* books, the same activities are found in each of the grade-level books. What you get in this book are not only good activities but also a view of how pattern can easily progress from kindergarten to grade 6.

NCTM's *Navigations Series*

Greenes, C., Cavanagh, M., Dacey, L., Findell, C., & Small, M. (2001). *Navigating through algebra in prekindergarten–grade 2*. Reston, VA: National Council of Teachers of Mathematics.

Cuevas, G. J., & Yeatts, K. (2001). *Navigating through algebra in grades 3–5*. Reston, VA: National Council of Teachers of Mathematics.

Friel, S., Rachlin, S., & Doyle, D. (2001). *Navigating through algebra in grades 6–8*. Reston, VA: National Council of Teachers of Mathematics.

If you want some good algebra activities that are directly reflective of *Principles and Standards*, it would be hard to go wrong with these books. As with all of the *Addenda Series* books, the authors discuss the standards in the introductory portion of the book and then follow with representative activities presented with just the right level of detail. Each book includes a CD-ROM that includes the blackline masters for the activities, several

very nice applets, and the full text of selected articles related to the topic.

National Council of Teachers of Mathematics. (1997). Algebraic thinking [Focus Issue]. *Teaching Children Mathematics, 3*(6).

National Council of Teachers of Mathematics. (1997). Algebraic thinking: Opening the gates [Focus Issue]. *Mathematics Teaching in the Middle School, 2*(4).

In 1997, NCTM responded to the growing interest in algebraic reasoning by publishing focus issues on the topic in all three of its school-based journals. Together, these journals provide teachers not only with algebraic activities at all levels but also a long-range perspective on the growth of algebraic reasoning across the grades. These are especially valuable issues.

Other Suggestions

Bay-Williams, J. M. (2001). What is algebra in elementary school? *Teaching Children Mathematics, 8*, 196–200.

Bishop, J. W., Otto, A. D., & Lubinski, C. A. (2001). Promoting algebraic reasoning using students' thinking. *Mathematics Teaching in the Middle School, 6*, 509–514.

Chappell, M. F., & Strutchens M. E. (2001). Creating connections: Promoting algebraic thinking with concrete models. *Mathematics Teaching in the Middle School, 7*, 20–25.

Cramer, K. (2001). Using models to build and understanding of functions. *Mathematics Teaching in the Middle School, 6*, 310–318.

Driscoll, M. J. (1999). *Fostering algebraic thinking: A guide for teachers, grades 6–10*. Portsmouth, NH: Heinemann.

Driscoll, M., & Moyer, J. (2001). Using students' work as a lens on algebraic thinking. *Mathematics Teaching in the Middle School, 6*, 283–287.

English, L. D., & Warren, E. A. (1998). Introducing the variable through pattern exploration. *Mathematics Teacher, 91*, 166–172.

Esty, W. W., & Teppo, A. R. (1996). Algebraic thinking, language, and word problems. In P. C. Elliott (Ed.), *Communication in mathematics, K–12 and beyond* (pp. 45–53). Reston, VA: National Council of Teachers of Mathematics.

Falkner, K. P., Levi, L., & Carpenter, T. P. (1999). Chilren's understanding of equality: A foundation for algebra. *Teaching Children Mathematics, 6*, 232–236.

Greenes, C., & Findell, C. (1999). Developing students' algebraic reasoning abilities. In L. V. Stiff (Ed.), *Developing mathematical reasoning in grades K–12* (pp. 127–137). Reston, VA: National Council of Teachers of Mathematics.

Greenes, C., & Findell, C. (1999). *Groundworks: Algebra puzzles and problems* (separate books for grades 4 to 7). Chicago: Creative Publications.

Greenes, C., & Findell, C. (1999). *Groundworks: Algebraic thinking* (Separate books for grades 1, 2, and 3). Chicago: Creative Publications.

MacGregor, M., & Stacey, K. (1999). A flying start to algebra. *Teaching Children Mathematics, 6*, 78–85.

Moses, B. (Ed.) (1999). *Algebraic thinking, grades K–12: Readings from NCTM's school-based journals and other publications*. Reston, VA: National Council of Teachers of Mathematics.

National Council of Teachers of Mathematics, & Mathematical Sciences Education Board. (1998). *The nature and role of algebra in the K–14 curriculum: Proceedings of a national symposium, May 27 and 28, 1997*. Washington, DC: National Academy Press.

Phillips, E., Gardella, T., Kelly, C., & Stewart, J. (1991). *Patterns and functions: Addenda series, grades 5–8.* Reston, VA: National Council of Teachers of Mathematics.

Quinn, A. L., Koca, R. M. Jr., & Weening, F. (1999). Developing mathematical reasoning using attribute games. *Mathematics Teacher, 92,* 768–775.

Rubenstein, R. N. (2002). Building explicit and recursive forms of patterns with the function game. *Mathematics Teaching in the Middle School, 7,* 426–431.

Schifter, D. (1999). Reasoning about operations: Early algebraic thinking in Grades K–6. In L. V. Stiff (Ed.), *Developing mathematical reasoning in grades K–12* (pp. 62–81). Reston, VA: National Council of Teachers of Mathematics.

Speer, W. R., & Brahier, D. J. (1995). What comes nex__? *Teaching Children Mathematics, 1,* 100–108.

Swafford, J. O., & Langrall, C. W. (2000). Grade 6 students' preinstructional use of equations to describe and represent problem situations. *Journal for Research in Mathematics Education, 13,* 89–112.

Vance, J. H. (1998). Number operations from an algebraic perspective. *Teaching Children Mathematics, 4,* 282–285.

Williams, S. E., & Copley, J. V. (1994). Promoting classroom dialogue: Using calculators to discover patterns in dividing decimals. *Mathematics Teaching in the Middle School, 1,* 72–75.

Exploring Functions

The concept of function is one of the big ideas in all of mathematics. Functions are the tool used for mathematically modeling all types of real-world change. Functions can be represented in ways that lead to analysis and understanding of that change. Students experience the function concept whenever they consider how a change in one variable can cause or have a corresponding effect on another. The study of functions should focus on change relationships in contexts that are meaningful and interesting to students. An informal study of change relationships can begin as early as the third grade and continue through high school. Students should develop an understanding of the multiple methods of expressing real-world functional relationships using words, graphs, equations, and tables.

Big Ideas

1. Functions are relationships or rules that uniquely associate members of one set with members of another set.

2. Functional relationships can be expressed in real contexts, graphs, algebraic equations, tables, and words. Each representation for a given function is simply a different way of expressing the same idea. Each representation provides a different view of the function. The value of a particular representation depends on its purpose.

Content Connections

Algebraic reasoning involves a search for regularity in all of mathematics. Functions are one of the most powerful tools in this endeavor. Functions allow us to see, generalize, and represent relationships between variables in every area of mathematics in which there are variables to be related.

■ **Proportional Reasoning** (Chapter 18): Every proportional situation gives rise to a linear or straight-line function. The constant ratio between proportional objects is the slope of the line.

■ **Data Analysis** (Chapter 21): Whenever data are collected involving two numeric variables (e.g., years of smoking and death rates), functions are used to describe the relationship in mathematical terms.

■ **Measurement** (Chapter 19): In the real world, all sorts of measures are related to some other quantity or idea that is also measurable. Measurement produces the data that are explored for regularities. These regularities or relationships in turn are expressed as functions. Measurement formulas are themselves functions.

Function Concepts and Representations

A study of functions is a study of the way change in one variable affects change in another; it is a study of *joint variation* of variables. A *function* is a rule that uniquely defines how the first or independent variable affects the second or dependent variable.

There are five different ways to interpret or represent a function. Each is a different way of communicating the same rule of correspondence or relationship. It is important to see that each representation expresses the same idea yet provides a different way of looking at or thinking about the relationship. We will use the context of a hot-dog vendor to illustrate all five representations.

Brian is trying to make money to help pay for college by selling hot dogs from a hot-dog cart at the coliseum during major performances and ball games. He pays the cart owner $35 per night for the use of the cart. He sells hot dogs for $1.25 each. His costs for the hot dogs, condiments, napkins, and other paper products are about 60 cents per hot dog on average. The profit from a single hot dog is therefore 65 cents.

Contextual Representations of Functions

This function begins with a context: selling hot dogs and the resulting profit. We are interested in Brian's profit in terms of the number of hot dogs sold: The more hot dogs Brian sells, the more profit he will make. Brian does not begin to make a profit immediately because he must pay the $35 rent on the vending cart. Nonetheless, Brian's profit is dependent on—is *a function of*—the number of hot dogs he sells.

Not every function has a real-world context, but at the middle school level, it is useful to place functions in contexts that make sense to students. Here are some other contexts in which functional relationships are to be found:

- Suppose that the value of a new car depreciates at the rate of 20 percent each year. There is a definite relationship between the age of the car and its current value.
- If you measure the height and arm span of a lot of different people, from very short to very tall, you will likely find that there is a predictable relationship between these two measures. Arm span is related to height.
- A ride on a roller coaster has several possible relationships. As time passes from the beginning of the ride to the end of the ride, the height of the cars above the ground changes. It increases slowly at first, then most likely has a fast decrease followed by a series of lesser increases and decreases. The speed of the cars on the roller coaster is also a function of time. The speed of the cars has an effect on how loud the passengers scream, and so it is reasonable to say that speed and screams are related, although perhaps not as precisely as the height is related to the time.
- If you build rectangles so that all have the same fixed perimeter, the length of the rectangles will decrease as the widths increase. If you begin with a very small width and a longer length, the area of the rectangles first increases as the width increases from zero and then decreases.

These are all contexts in which there is a functional relationship. For the height versus arm span and the loudness of roller coaster passengers, a relationship is not easy to determine precisely. Riders will not always scream at exactly the same decibel level, nor will everyone's height-to-arm span ratio be the same. However, all of these situations illustrate functions in meaningful contexts. Each has at least two values that vary jointly, with one being dependent on or related to the other.

Table Representations of Functions

Brian the hot-dog vendor might well sit down and calculate some possible income figures based on hypothetical sales. This will give him some idea of how many franks he must sell to break even and what his profit might be for an evening. For example, if he sells no hot dogs, he will be $35 in the hole, or his profit will be negative $35. Selling 70 hot dogs would yield a profit of $70 \times 0.65 - 35 = 45.50 - 35$, or $10.50. A table of similar values might look like this:

Hot Dogs	Profit
0	−35.00
70	10.50
100	30.00
150	62.50

The number of hot dogs shown in the table is purely a matter of choice. One could calculate the profit for 10,000 hot dogs ($10,000 \times 0.65 - 35$), even though it is not reasonable to expect Brian to sell that many. One of the values of contexts in thinking about functions is to see how mathematical representations can ignore reality. The person who interprets the table must take the context into consideration.

 STOP When a set of data such as the height and arm span is organized in a table, it does not yet create a function. Why not?

A function must *uniquely* define the value of one variable in terms of the other. Heights can predict arm span but not precisely. There may be many different persons in the data set with the same height who have different arm spans. As you saw in Chapter 21, a line can be drawn to approximate data that are not perfectly organized. A best-fit line for the height–arm span data would define a functional relationship that approximates reality to the degree that the line fits or represents the data.

Language Expressions for Functions

Functional relationships are dependent relationships or rules of correspondence. In the hot-dog vendor situation, Brian's profit depends on the number of hot dogs that are sold. In functional language, we can say, "Profit *is a function of* the number of hot dogs sold." The phrase "is a function of" expresses the dependent relationship. The profit *depends on*—is a function of—the hot-dog sales.

Looking at the other examples, we would say that the current value of a car is a function of its age or its value depends on its age. If someone were to ask what speed the roller coaster is going, you might respond, "It depends on the time since the ride began," or, in functional terms, "That depends. The speed is a function of the time since the ride began."

 See if you can express the relationships in the other examples in functional terms.

Graphical Representations of Functions

They say that a picture is worth a thousand words. This is certainly true of functions. In the case of a function the picture is a graph. In Figure 23.1, six different values of hot-dog sales are plotted on a graph. The horizontal axis represents the number of hot dogs sold, and the vertical axis, the profit. As we have already established, the profit goes up as the sales go up. There is, in this situation, a very clear pattern to the six values.

The graph shows that the relationship between sales and profits is *linear*—a straight line—and is increasing. It also allows us easily to answer questions about Brian's profits. How many hot dogs must be sold to break even? The graph shows zero profit (the break-even point) where the line crosses the horizontal axis. (Why?) It looks to be near 53 or 54. What is Brian's profit for 130 hot dogs? How many hot dogs must be sold to make a profit of $100? The context gives meaning to the graph, and the graph adds understanding to the context.

The graph is another mathematical model that, in terms of the context, does not make sense for all portions of the picture. If the line is extended indefinitely, there would be values where Brian's sales were negative (to the left of the vertical axis). This clearly does not make sense. Nor is it reasonable

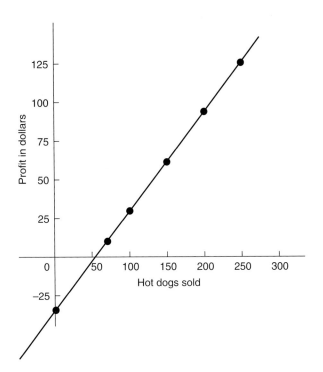

FIGURE 23.1 **A graph showing profit as a function of hot-dog sales.**

to talk about sales of millions of hot dogs even though the graph can extend as far as is wished.

Not all functions have straight-line graphs. If you start with a rectangle that has a fixed perimeter of 24 inches and increase the length beginning at 1 inch, both the width and the area will vary accordingly (see Figure 23.2). The width graph is linear. It decreases at a constant rate. By contrast, the area graph rises in a curve, reaches a maximum value, and then goes back down.

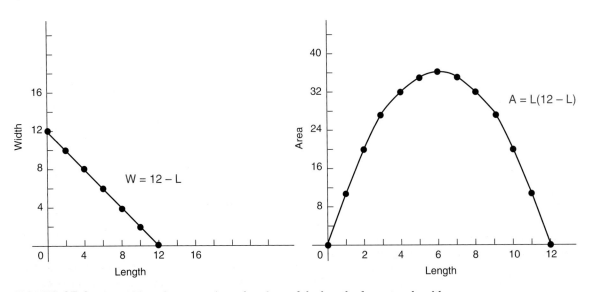

FIGURE 23.2 **The width and area graphs as functions of the length of a rectangle with a fixed perimeter of 24 units.**

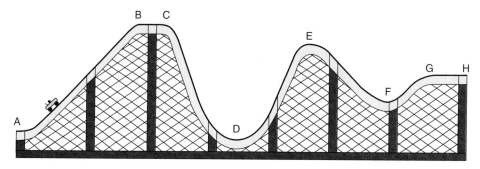

FIGURE 23.3 If it takes 120 seconds to ride this roller coaster, sketch a graph of the height of the car as a function of time. How should the points A through H be spaced along the time line? Sketch a second graph of the speed as a function of time. The time axis with points A to H should be the same. What would a graph of "scream decibels" look like?

Figure 23.3 shows a simple roller coaster. Suppose that it takes just 120 seconds to ride.

STOP Try to sketch a graph that shows the *height* of the roller coaster throughout the ride. Why will your graph not be exactly the same as the path of the roller coaster? Now make another graph that shows the *speed* of the car over the 120 seconds of the ride. Share your sketches with a friend. How are these two graphs related to each other?

Equations to Represent Functions

Suppose that we pick a letter, say, H, to represent the number of hot dogs Brian sells. For each hot dog sold, his income is $1.25 \times H$ dollars. But to determine his profit, we have to subtract from his income the rental cost of the cart and 60 cents cost per hot dog. Therefore, Brian's profit is represented by $(1.25 \times H) - (0.60 \times H) - 35$, or $(0.65 \times H) - 35$. To make an equation, we can assign another letter to stand for profit: $P = (0.65 \times H) - 35$. This equation defines a mathematical relationship between two values or two variables, profit and hot dogs. Taken out of context, it is simply a relationship between P and H. It is the same as the relationship between x and y in the equation $y = 0.65x - 35$.

By expressing a function as an equation, it can be examined in its most abstract form. Different types of equations have different properties. When the properties are understood, they can be applied to the context as well. In our hot-dog example, the equation has the general form of a linear equation, $Y = mX + b$. In this form, the value of m tells us how quickly or steeply the line goes up or down moving from left to right. The value of b tells where the graph will cross the vertical axis.

In the rectangle context, the following two equations represent the width and area, respectively, as functions of the length (assuming that the perimeter is fixed at 24 units):

$$W(L) = \frac{24 - 2L}{2} = 12 - L$$

$$A(L) = L(12 - L) = 12L - L^2$$

Expressing functions in an equation can make it easier to see what is happening. In this example, the function notations $W(L)$ and $A(L)$ were used instead of a single letter for each. $W(L)$ stands for the width. Within this efficient notation is an indication that the width is a function of the length L. "The width when the length is 3" can now be represented symbolically as $W(3)$. The symbolic name for the function itself—the relationship between the length and width—is represented by the letter W. Similarly for the area function A: $A(L)$ is the area for any given value of L; $A(4)$ is the area when the length is 4. The area is a function of the length.

Equations also make it easier to calculate values of the function. The equation can be entered into a graphing calculator, and the calculator can do the calculations to produce a table or draw a graph. Without the equation representation of the function, the graphing calculator is much less useful. Figure 23.4 shows the screen of a TI-83 calculator with both the width and the area graphs drawn. The table to the right computes the area for every length in steps of one-half. It requires very little expertise to do this on the calculator and allows the middle school child the chance to see and explore graphs without the tedium of having to plot points.

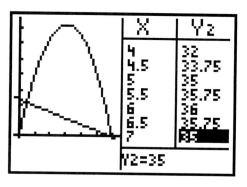

FIGURE 23.4 This graphing calculator shows graphs of both the width and the area of a rectangle of fixed perimeter as functions of the length. The table can show all possible length and area values.

Sometimes equations come from selecting a curve (and its corresponding equation) that seems to "fit" the data available. That is how an equation for the height–arm span relationship would be determined. A "best-fit curve" would be determined to fit the data. You may recall finding a median-median line for height and weight data in Chapter 21.

Developing Function Concepts in the Classroom

If the discussion so far had focused only on Brian the hot-dog vendor, the development would be similar to the approach in a middle school classroom. Begin with a context, explore the relationships, and develop different representations to show what has been found.

Begin with Meaningful Contexts

Today, algebra is dominated by the study of functions and should begin with meaningful situations in which functions can be found. Numerous contexts contain functional relationships that are completely accessible to students, even as early as fifth grade. By exploring a context and making sense of it, the function relationship is already developed.

In the context of Brian's sales, a discussion can involve finding the number of hot dogs that need to be sold to make a given amount of money and how much profit is made by selling a particular number of hot dogs. By examining and explaining these questions, students are working with the joint variation between hot dogs sold and profit made. They are actually using a function before they have been asked to worry about symbols and definitions.

Our lives abound with situations that involve functional relationships. Making money and the ideas related to profit and loss are both realistic and interesting. Social studies provides many relationships. For example, populations of various regions may be related to health, income, production levels, education levels, death rates, and so on. Science offers another area of investigations. Pendulums can be swung to investigate period as a function of length. The distance a toy car will roll down a ramp can be compared to the angle of the ramp. Plant growth can be related to quantities of fertilizer or to the number of days since germination. These are just a few real contexts that can make the study of functions meaningful.

Connect Different Representations

Figure 23.5 illustrates the five representations of functions that we explored earlier. The most important idea is to see that for a given function, each of these representations illustrates

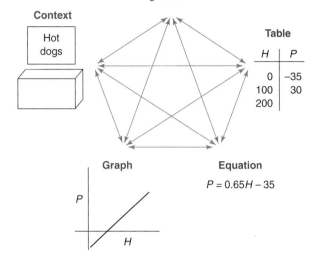

FIGURE 23.5 **Five different representations of a function. For any given function, students should see that all these representations are connected and illustrate the same relationship. Each representation provides a different perspective on the function.**

the same relationship. The *context* provides an embodiment of the relationship outside the world of mathematics. *Language* helps express the relationship in a meaningful and useful manner. *Tables* explicitly match up selected elements that are paired by the function. The joint variation is implicit in the pairings of numbers. The *graph* translates the number pairs into a picture. Any point on the graph of a function has two coordinates. The function is the rule that relates the first coordinate to the second. The *equation* expresses the same functional relationship with the economy and power of mathematical symbolism.

Use Technology

In the past, when students had to plot points and do by hand all the computations that were involved, functions were limited to very simple examples. Eighth-grade students would probably never see a function with an equation much more complicated than $y = 3x + 2$. The tedium of computing and plotting function values meant that examples had to use numbers that were small and relatively easy to work with, making the link to real contexts almost impossible. Thanks to technology, we can now explore realistic contexts involving not-so-nice numbers. Students can investigate all sorts of functions as long as a relationship can be identified.

Consider the examples in the first part of this chapter. The profit example is the easiest to work with and could probably be examined without technology. The car depreciation is an exponential function. The area for a fixed perimeter is a quadratic function. If students can come up with an equation to go with a function rule, technology can be used to make a graph and do the necessary number crunching to make a table. The technology is not "thinking" for the students; on the contrary, student effort is focused on the thinking and not on the mechanics of computation and plotting points.

Students who have talked about exponents and about percents—both middle grades topics—are equipped to develop an equation for the car depreciation situation. That exploration might go like this: If the car loses 20 percent of its value in 1 year, then it must be worth 80 percent of its value after a year. So after 1 year, the $15,000 car is worth $15,000 × 0.8. In the second year, it loses 20 percent of that value, so it will be worth only 80 percent of its value at the end of year one: ($15,000 × 0.8) × 0.8 = $15,000 × 0.8^2. At the end of the third year, the value will be $15,000 × 0.8^3, and so on. In general, at the end of n years, the value of the car can be expressed in this equation: $V = \$15,000 \times 0.8^n$. Figure 23.6 shows the graph and the table of values on a graphing calculator. This equation is no more difficult to enter into a graphing calculator or a computer graphing utility than $y = 3x + 2$. The idea is to see that there are functional relationships and that these can be expressed in different ways.

NCTM Standards

"By the middle grades, students should be able to understand the relationships among tables, graphs, and symbols and to judge the advantages and disadvantages of each way of representing relationships for practical purposes. As they work with multiple representations of functions—including numeric, graphic, and symbolic—they will develop a more comprehensive understanding of functions" (p. 38).

STOP

The NCTM *Standards* quotation you just read refers to "numeric, graphic, and symbolic" representations of functions. Match these three representations with three of the five representations illustrated in Figure 23.5. Why might the *Standards* authors not have mentioned the other two representations?

FUNCTIONS FROM PATTERNS

Growing patterns are often used to introduce the idea of function rules connected to a context. Growing patterns or sequences developed from physical or pictorial drawings were discussed at length in Chapter 22. Now that we have a more complete view of the function concept and the various representations of functions, let's explore one more example of a growing pattern and see how all of these ideas fit together in that context.

ACTIVITY 23.1

Perimeter Patterns

In this activity, students explore the perimeters of strings of regular polygons. Each string is made up of tiles of the same shape. Adjoining tiles share one side, as shown in Figure 23.7. For a given shape, the task is to develop a rule or formula for the perimeter of strings of any number of tiles. For example, if the tiles are square, the perimeter for one square is 4, for two squares is 6, for three squares is 8, and so on. What is a formula for the perimeter of a string of N squares? Figure 23.7 shows strings for three different shapes. Pattern blocks are an excellent manipulative for this task because all edges are 1 inch long except for the trapezoid, which has a long side of 2 inches.

FIGURE 23.6 The graph and table for $V = 15,000 \times 0.8^n$. The graph shows n for values 0 to 15. The vertical axis runs from 0 to 15,000.

FIGURE 23.7 What is the perimeter of a string of N pattern blocks?

Students working at "Perimeter Patterns" should first develop a table by adding tiles to their string one at a time and recording the perimeters in a table as they go. A recursive relationship is easy to determine. For hexagons, it is "add 4 to the preceding perimeter." A table for hexagons looks like this:

1	2	3	4	5	6	7	8	...	N
6	10	14	18	22	26	30	34	...	?

So now we have a table and a contextual situation. The next challenge is the most interesting: Find a rule or equation that tells the perimeter for N hexagons. What students come up with depends on whether they focus on the table of numbers or the string of tiles. In either case, they are likely to have a variety of ideas.

 STOP Before reading further, see if you can come up with at least two different formulas for the perimeter of N hexagons.

Here are five different-looking formulas:

$4N + 2$

$2(2N + 1)$

$6 + (N - 1)4$

$(N - 2)4 + (2 \times 5)$

$2N + 2N + 2$

Are your formulas in this list? Perhaps you found a different one. When students share different formulas for the same pattern, others might be challenged to see how they arrived at the patterns. The following three ideas generate three of the five formulas given:

- *The first tile has a perimeter of 6. Each new tile adds 4 more.* (This idea can be found in the table as well as the block pattern.)
- *Each tile has two edges on the top. Include the one extra edge on the left along with the top edges. The bottom edges plus the right edge are the same as this.*
- *Each tile has two edges on the top and two on the bottom plus the two end edges.*

 STOP Match these three ways of thinking of the perimeter with three of the formulas. Then try to figure how one may have been thinking to generate the other two. Of course, all of these "different" formulas are equivalent, with the simplest form being $4N + 2$.

To add language to our representations, we can say, "The perimeter of a string of hexagons is a function of the number of hexagons in the string."

Next, a graph of the perimeter relationship provides the fifth representation. The points on the graph will lie along a straight line and go up 4 units for every added tile. The graphs for each of the other tile shapes will go up at different rates or with different *slopes* (see Figure 23.8).

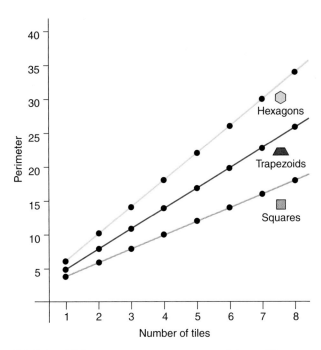

FIGURE 23.8 Graphs of the perimeters of three different pattern-block strings.

The perimeter problem has an interesting extension. If different groups of students have been working on strings of shapes using different polygons, the resulting formulas will be similar. See if students can find an even more general formula with two variables: N representing the number of tiles and S representing the number of sides per tile. (This challenge is left to you.)

Functions from the Real World

Patterns are but one way to get students into an investigation of functions. Here are some other ideas that develop the same concepts.

Relationships Found in the Real World

Real-world situations, such as the example of Brian selling hot dogs, can be explored with children by having them make tables of data using the information given. By computing several entries in the table, students will begin to see a pattern develop. Consider the following activity.

ACTIVITY 23.2

How Many Gallons Left?

Present this situation to students: A car gets 23 miles per gallon of gas. It has a gas tank that holds 20 gallons. Suppose that you were on a trip and had filled

the tank at the outset. Make a table showing the number of gallons remaining in the tank for at least three different points in a trip of 350 miles. Plot the data on a graph. Show how you calculated each entry in your table, and be prepared to discuss with the class what you did.

Notice that very little direction is given in this activity. However, the situation presented to the students is fairly clear. Some teachers may prefer to use numbers that would be easier to compute, but that takes much of the realism out of the situation. If a student decides to make a table entry for 50 miles, he or she will first have to figure out what to do. On a calculator, $50 \div 23 = 2.173913$. This amount should be subtracted from 20 to find out how many gallons remain in the tank. Should you subtract 2 or 2.17 or 2.173913? This is a good example to use to discuss numbers in real contexts. Avoid being prescriptive so that students will do their own thinking and not rely on your directions. Students are bound to make errors in reasoning as well as in computation. Class discussion will sort things out.

As part of the discussion, help students develop functional language to represent the situation. Here the number of gallons in the tank is dependent on how far the car has been driven. Thus the number of gallons remaining *is a function of* the miles driven. In addition to the language, work toward student development of an equation that represents the relationship in the situation. In this case, one possible equation is $g = 20 - \frac{m}{23}$. Or, using functional notation, you might say $G(m) = 20 - \frac{m}{23}$.

Students can draw a line through their plotted points, or with a computer or graphing calculator they can enter the equation and have technology do the graphing. In either case, use the graph to answer questions about the situation: "How can you tell from the graph how much gas will be left after driving 300 miles?" "How many miles can you drive before the gas tank has only 3 gallons left?" "What will happen to the graph if the driver stops to fill the tank after driving 350 miles?" The *trace* feature on a graphing calculator is a great help for getting values from a graph.

Here are a few suggestions for similar explorations.

Mr. Calloway wants to build a fenced pen against one side of his shed. The shed is 15 feet long, and he wants to use the full side of the shed. The pen is to be in the shape of a rectangle with two sides 15 feet long. How much fence will he have to buy if he knows how long the other two sides of the pen will be (side versus fence length)? Add in a gate that is 3 feet long and costs $32. If fencing is $4.25 per foot, rethink the problem in terms of side versus cost. You can also discuss area and side length.

Mark is an avid cyclist. He can average 17 miles per hour for about 4 hours. He leaves home and travels for $2\frac{1}{2}$ hours at this rate, stops for lunch for $\frac{1}{2}$ hour, and then starts home. What is his distance from home at any given time? Suppose he goes faster for 1 hour and slower for 2 more hours and then returns home. Suppose he has a flat tire and has to stop for 15 minutes to repair it. How fast will he have to go in order to return home at the same time as scheduled, including the same lunch break? Does it make any difference where the breakdown occurs?

Pleasant's Hardware buys widgets for $4.17 each, marks them up 35 percent over wholesale, and sells them at that price. Relate widgets sold to total income. Consider profit instead of income. Incorporate a sale using a reduced price.

NCTM Standards The *e-Standards* has two applets that demonstrate the connection between a real-world context and graphs, tables, and equations. In Applet 5.2 students can adjust the speed, direction, and starting position of two runners. As the runners are set in motion, a time–distance graph is generated dynamically for each runner (see Figure 23.9). In Applet 6.2, when the cost per minute of a phone call is adjusted, a graph and equation of the total cost are adjusted accordingly. Two rates on the same graph help illustrate rate (slope) visually.

The seventh-grade *Connected Mathematics* curriculum has an entire unit in which students explore and use both graphs and tables to represent functions found in real contexts. As you

FIGURE 23.9 Applet 6.2, "Understanding Distance, Speed, and Time Relationships Using Simulation Software."

Used with permission from NCTM *e-Standards*. Copyright © 2003 by the National Council of Teachers of Mathematics, Inc. All rights reserved. The presence of the screenshot from NCTM *e-Standards*, http://standards.nctm.org/document/eexamples/chap5/5.2/index.htm, does not constitute or imply an endorsement by NCTM.

CONNECTED MATHEMATICS

Grade 7, *Variables and Patterns*
Investigation 3: Analyzing Graphs and Tables

Context

Much of this unit is built on the context of a group of students who take a multiday bike trip from Philadelphia to Williamsburg, Virginia, and who then decide to set up a bike tour business of their own. Students explore a variety of functional relationships between time, distance, speed, expenses, profits, and so on. When data are plotted as discrete points, students consider what the graph might look like between points. For example, what interpretations could be given to each of these five graphs showing speed change from 0 to 15 mph in the first 10 minutes of a trip?

Task Description

In this investigation, the fictional students in the unit are gathering data in preparation for setting up their tour business. For the first task, data are given from two different bike rental companies as shown here—from one company in the form of a table and from the other in the form of a graph. The task is interesting because of the firsthand way in which students experience the value of one representation over another, depending on the need of the situation. In this unit students are frequently asked whether a graph or a table is the better source of information.

In the tasks that follow, students are given a table of data showing results of a phone poll that asked at which price former tour riders would take a bike tour. Students must find the best way to graph this data. After a price for a bike tour is established, graphs for estimated profits are created with corresponding questions about profits depending on different numbers of customers.

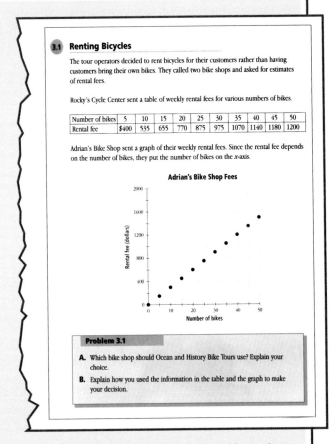

From *Connected Mathematics: Variables and Patterns: Introducing Algebra.* © 2002 by Michigan State University, Glenda Lappan, James T. Fey, William M. Fitzgerald, Susan N. Friel, and Elizabeth Difanis Phillips. Published by Prentice Hall. Used by permission of Pearson Education, Inc.

The investigations use no formulas to this point. The subsequent investigation is called "Patterns and Rules" and begins the exploration of connecting equations or rules to the representations of graphs and tables. In the final investigation, students use graphing calculators to explore how graphs change in appearance when the rules that produce the graphs change.

can see from the excerpt on this page, the initial focus is on these two representations with almost no concern for equations.

Proportional Situations

Many relationships involving rates or proportions offer a valuable opportunity for examining functions. The following is a typical proportion problem.

Two out of every three students who eat in the cafeteria drink a pint of white milk. If 450 students eat in the cafeteria, how many gallons of milk are consumed?

As the problem is stated, there is a fixed number of students (450) and a single answer to the problem. Students would be expected to set up a proportion and solve for the unknown. But if only the first sentence of the problem is provided, students can be asked to create a table showing the number of pints (or gallons) of milk consumed for four or five different numbers of students, plot the data on a graph, and create an equation that shows the relationship between students in the cafeteria and milk consumed. Functional language can be discussed: The number of pints of milk consumed in the cafeteria *is a function of* the number of students who eat there. The graph can be used to answer the question about milk for 450 students. Students can be challenged to find an equation that gives the amount of milk in terms of the number of students.

The following problem has been converted to a function investigation by asking for an answer in terms of an unknown instead of a specific number.

If each lemonade recipe will serve 20 people, how many recipes are needed to serve n people? If it takes three cans of concentrate to make one recipe, how many cans should be purchased to serve n people?

This example has two questions. One equation can be written to relate the number of recipes as a function of the number of people [$R = f(p)$], and a second equation to give the number of cans of concentrate as a function of the number of recipes [$C = g(R)$]. Using these equations you can find an equation that gives cans of concentrate as a function of the number of people.

Notice that the graphs of all proportional situations are straight lines that pass through the origin. Students will find that the slope of these lines is also the rate between the two variables.

Functions from Formulas

Geometric formulas relate various dimensions, areas, and volumes of shapes. Each of these formulas involves at least one functional relationship.

Consider any familiar formula for measuring a geometric shape. For example, $V = \frac{1}{3}\pi r^2 h$ is the formula for the volume of a circular cone. Here the volume is related to both the height of the cone and the radius. If the radius is held constant, the volume is a function of the height. Similarly, for a fixed height, the volume is a function of the radius. Figure 23.10 shows how both of these ideas might be illustrated and the graph that would be associated with each.

The following activity is an example of using functions in a practical way.

FIGURE 23.10 Volume as a function of height or radius. If the radius is fixed, changes in height produce a straight-line graph, but if the height is fixed, changes in the radius produce a curved line.

ACTIVITY 23.3

Designing the Largest Box

Begin with a rectangular sheet of cardboard, and from each corner, cut a square. Fold up the four resulting flaps, and tape them together to form an open box. The volume of the box will vary, depending on the size of the squares. (The sheet in Figure 23.11 measures 9 by 12 inches.) Write a formula that gives the volume of the box as a function of the size of the cutout squares. Use the function to determine what size the squares should be to create the box with the largest volume.

FIGURE 23.12 A graphing calculator plot of the volume function for the problem in Figure 23.11.

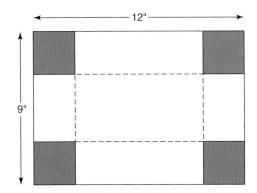

FIGURE 23.11 If squares are cut from a 9-by-12-inch piece of cardboard so that the four flaps can be folded up, what size squares should be cut so that the volume of the box is the largest possible?

In "Designing the Largest Box," the resulting equation is a cubic or third-power polynomial. However, any seventh-grade student who knows that the volume of a box is the product of the three dimensions could develop this formula. A table of values and a graph are easily produced on a graphing calculator.

As with some other contexts we have looked at, this function is defined for values that do not make sense in the context. The largest square that could be cut out is 4.5 inches on a side, in which case the squares from adjacent corners would touch and there would be no flap to turn up. But the function will produce "negative volumes" for values between 4.5 and 6 and positive volumes for values of the variable greater than 6. The equation representation of the function makes sense in this context *only* for values between 0 and 4.5. This is a useful discussion for students to help them realize that a mathematical model cannot be completely divorced from the context. Figure 23.12 shows the graph on a calculator. The tracer is near the point at which a maximum volume will occur.

Functions from Scatter Plot Data

Often in the real world, phenomena are observed that seem to suggest a functional relationship but not necessarily as clean or as well defined as the situations we have observed so far. In these cases, the data are generally plotted on a graph to produce a scatter plot of points. A visual inspection of the graphed data may suggest what kind of relationship, if any, exists. When a functional relationship seems to be suggested, an equation can be sought that defines a function approximating the data.

A situation like this was explored in Chapter 21. Data representing the heights and weights of people in a sample were plotted on a graph as a set of points, one for each person in the sample. The plot suggested a straight-line relationship between the heights and weights. A median-median line was found. In that case, the median-median line was the function (in graphical form) that approximated the data and was used to define the observed relationship between height and weight. In functional language, we could say that weight appeared to be a function of height. (See pp. 402–404.)

Students in the middle grades might easily gather data found in an interesting context and perform this same type of analysis—that is, plot the data, look for a possible relationship, and find a best-fit line. When a line is drawn on the scatter plot, all representations of the function are present—the context produced the data. The graph of the best-fit line is a graphical representation of the function, and functional language can easily be used. A table can be made from points on the best-fit line. (Why would the table be made from the line or the equation and not from the actual data?) The equation can be found using the method described in Chapter 21, or the graphing calculator can be used to generate the equation.

The position in this chapter is that functional relationships can be explored as early as the sixth grade. In cases where a simple equation is not readily accessible technology can be used to produce the equation. There seems little reason to stop students from using graphing calculators or curve-fitting software to see that methods do exist for finding best-fit curves. The calculator permits students to see what these best-fit curves and equations may look like, even though the techniques of finding the equations without technology will have to wait.

ACTIVITY 23.4

Pendulum Swings

Give pairs of students string and a small weight that can be tied to the string (a large washer or a tennis ball, for example). Assign each pair a different length for their pendulum, from about 30 cm to 3 m (if the room is tall enough). The pendulum should be measured from the suspension point to the bottom of the weight. Have students carefully time the swing of the pendulum through ten full (back-and-forth) swings. If time permits, they can perform the experiment several times and take an average of their times to report to the class.

In the pendulum experiment, the data will form a surprisingly accurate curve. Students can use their hand-drawn curve to predict the times for other pendulum lengths. The curve is the top half of a parabola that opens to the right. It can be found on the graphing calculator by experimenting with the equation $y = a\sqrt{x}$ for different values of a until a curve is found that fits nicely. What is most important at this level is seeing how a physical law can be expressed as a function and represented in table and graphical form.

Electronic Data Gathering

Technology now offers students a way to gather physical data that has exciting implications for connecting function concepts to the real world. The Calculator-Based Laboratory (CBL) is a device that interfaces between the graphing calculator and data sensors to gather and record real data directly into the calculator. Experiments that measure things such as temperature of a liquid, motion of a rolling car or a bouncing ball, light intensity, pH, and force can be conducted, with no pencil-and-paper record keeping. Theories of science that before could only be described can now be observed with real data gathered and analyzed.

Figure 23.13 shows a simple experiment using two different sensors connected through the CBL to a graphing calculator. The motion detector senses the motion back and forth as the hand stretches the rubber bands. The force sensor is connected to the rubber bands and measures the force applied and transmitted through them. A program available with Texas Instruments' manual (Brueningsen, Bower, Anti-

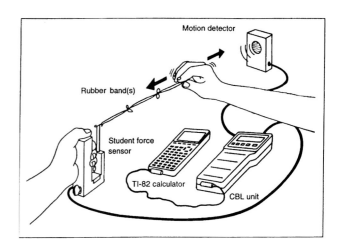

FIGURE 23.13 Two data probes are used to deliver force and motion data directly to a graphing calculator.

Source: "Real-World Math with the CBL System." Copyright Texas Instruments Inc., Dallas, TX. Reprinted by permission of Texas Instruments Inc.

---

none, & Brueningsen, 1994) is loaded into the calculator. The program directs the CBL to collect data at regular intervals and store them in the calculator. Like any other data, these can then be plotted and a best-fit line determined. Figure 23.14 shows a scatter plot of data from running this experiment. It is fairly clear that there is a linear relationship and that a best-fit line would likely go through the origin. It is appropriate to say that the force applied to the rubber band is directly proportional to the distance the rubber band is stretched. In functional language, the force *is a function of* the amount the rubber band is stretched.

Other Scatter Plot Ideas

Consider gathering information that may be of personal interest to students. For example, do grades earned in social

FIGURE 23.14 A graphing calculator scatter plot of data gathered in a rubber-band-stretching experiment as depicted in **Figure 23.13.**

studies predict grades earned in mathematics? What about science and mathematics? What would the functional relationships be here? Even if a scatter plot of some information that was gathered showed no particular trend, functional language could still be employed—for example, "The grades on last week's mathematics test do *not* appear to be a function of the number of hours' sleep students got the night before the test."

Data can also be obtained from sports records, census reports, the business section of the newspaper, and many other sources. As noted toward the end of Chapter 8, the Internet has lots of sites where data can be found.

 "When doing experiments or dealing with real data, students may encounter 'messy data,' for which a line or a curve may not be an exact fit. They will need experience with such situations and assistance from the teacher to develop their ability to find a function that fits the data well enough to be useful as a prediction tool" (p. 228).

Fun Experiments

There are all sorts of experiments that students can invent to see what functional relationships, if any, exist between two variables.

ACTIVITY 23.5

Fun-Function Experiments

The task is to try to develop a functional relationship between two variables by conducting an experiment. Data should be entered in a table and plotted on a graph. The goal is to determine an equation (function) that can be used to make predictions. A graphing calculator or computer will be a useful tool for curve fitting, although for some experiments that may not be necessary. Students should explain which is the independent variable and which the dependent. Here are some ideas for experiments:*

- How long would it take for 100 students standing in a row to complete a wave like the ones done at football games? Experiment with different numbers of students from 5 to 25. Can the relationship predict how many students it would take for a given wave time?
- How far will a Matchbox car roll off of a ramp, based on the height the ramp is raised?

---

*Most of these experiments were inspired by the article "Algebra: Real-Life Investigations in a Lab Setting" (McCoy, 1997), which contains additional ideas and useful suggestions.

- How is the flight time of a paper airplane affected by the number of paper clips attached to the nose of the plane?
- What is the relationship between the number of dominoes in a row and the time required for them to fall over? (Use multiples of 100 dominoes.)
- Make wadded newspaper balls using different numbers of sheets of newspaper. Rubber bands help hold the paper in a ball. What is the relationship between the number of sheets and the distance the ball can be thrown?
- If colored water is dropped on a paper towel, what is the relationship between the number of drops and the diameter of the spot? Is the relationship different for different brands of towels?
- How much weight can a toothpick bridge hold? Lay toothpicks in a bunch to span a 2-inch gap between two boards. From the toothpicks, hang a bag or other container into which weights can be added until the toothpicks break. Begin with only one toothpick.

Experiments like these are fun. They also provide an opportunity for students to engage in experimental design. Students need practice in identifying independent and dependent variables, controlling experiments for other variables, measuring and recording results, and analyzing data. This is a perfect blend of mathematics and science.

Graphs Without Equations

The graph is one of the most powerful representations of a function. It is both fun and profitable to interpret and construct graphs related to real situations but without using any specific data, equations, or numbers. The advantage of activities such as these is the focus on how a graph can express the relationships involved.

ACTIVITY 23.6

Sketch a Graph

Sketch a graph for each of these situations. No numbers or formulas are to be used.

a. The temperature of a frozen dinner from 30 minutes before it is removed from the freezer until it is removed from the microwave and placed on the table. (Consider time 0 to be the moment the dinner is removed from the freezer.)
b. The value of a 1970 Volkswagen Beetle from the time it was purchased to the present. (It was kept by a loving owner and is in top condition.)

c. The level of water in the bathtub from the time you begin to fill it to the time it is completely empty after your bath.
d. Profit in terms of number of items sold.
e. The height of a baseball in terms of time from when it is thrown straight up to the time it hits the ground.
f. The speed of the baseball in the situation in (e).

 STOP Stop for a moment and sketch graphs for each of the situations in the last activity.

In a classroom, it is fun to have students sketch their graphs on transparencies without identifying which situation is being graphed (no labels on the graphs). Let students examine the graphs to see if they can determine which situation goes with each graph that is presented. Examine the graphs for one situation drawn by several students to decide which graph represents a situation best and why. Figure 23.15 contains six graphs that match the six situations described in the "Sketch a Graph" activity. Can you match these graphs with the six situations? How do these graphs compare to the graphs that you sketched?

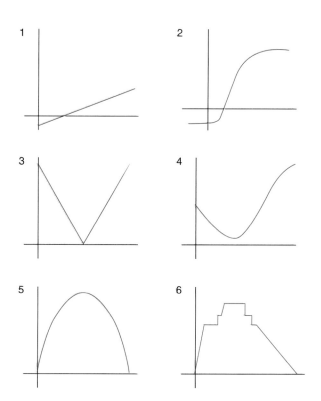

FIGURE 23.15 Match each graph with the situations described in Activity 23.6. Talk about what is happening in each case.

A similar example of rates is found in situations involving time and distance. Consider the following:

A car is traveling along a road at about 45 mph and comes to a stop sign. It stops for the sign and then accelerates to the same 45-mph speed.

Sketch a graph of the *distance* the car has traveled from the beginning of the story to the end. The horizontal axis should be *time*. In other words, the graph should show distance as a function of time. How would a graph of the *speed* of the car look over the same interval?

The following activity could be done after children have sketched graphs for a variety of time and distance situations.

ACTIVITY 23.7

Create a Journey Story

Suppose that a student has created the time-distance graphs shown in Figure 23.16. Each is supposed to represent the journey of a single vehicle or person. Some of them are impossible and could not represent any journey. First identify the impossible graphs. Then make up a plausible journey story for each of the remaining graphs.

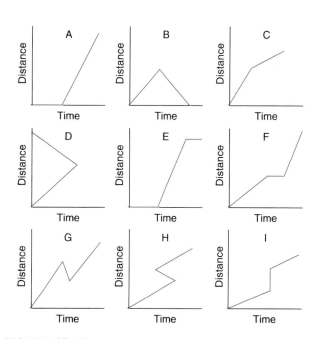

FIGURE 23.16 Which graphs could not possibly describe a journey? Why? Invent a journey story for each of the possible graphs.

Students could share their stories without telling which graph each story was supposed to match. The class could then discuss which graph best fits each tale.

The next activity is similar but begins to develop the idea of rate of change—how rapidly or slowly something changes.

ACTIVITY 23.8

Bottles and Volume Graphs

Figure 23.17 shows six bottles and six graphs. Assume that the bottles are filled at a constant rate. Because of their shapes, the height of the liquid in the bottles will increase either more slowly or more quickly as the bottle gets wider or narrower. Match the graphs with the bottles.

Find some bottles or glasses that have different shapes. One place to look is in the science lab. Using a small container such as a medicine cup, pour water into each bottle. Measure the height after each small containerful is poured. Make a graph of the heights as a function of the volume. If students do an actual experiment, the discussion of which graph fits which bottle and why will be much more meaningful.

"A major goal in the middle grades is to develop students' facility with using patterns and functions to represent, model, and analyze a variety of phenomena and relationships in mathematics problems or in the real world. With graphing calculators to produce graphical representations and perform complex cal-culations, students can focus on using functions to model patterns of quantitative change" (p. 227).

ASSESSMENT NOTES

The main thrust of the ideas in this chapter is that students should begin to see functional relationships in a variety of sit-uations—relationships where the change in one quantity has a predictable effect on the change in another.

An equally important idea is communication of these functional relationships. Functions can be expressed in terms of context, language, tables, graphs, and equations. What is most important is that students see these representations as different but related methods of telling about a function.

If you keep these big ideas in mind, your assessment plans should be focused accordingly.

- What kinds of strategies do students use to search for patterns and generalizations? (Do they use the differ-ences from one frame to the next, look for regularities in the physical patterns, coordinate frame numbers with different aspects of the physical pattern, exhibit flexible thinking in the search for patterns?)
- Do students distinguish between a recursive relationship in a pattern and a functional rule that will produce the frame value for any frame?
- Do students effectively translate real situations into func-tional language, graphs, symbols, tables?
- Are students able to demonstrate the way these various representations of a function are connected?
- When gathered data only approximate a function rule (scatter plots), do students indicate an understanding of the difference between the real data and the best-fit line or the constructed function rule? ■

FIGURE 23.17 If the bottles are filled at a constant rate, match the graphs with the bottles.

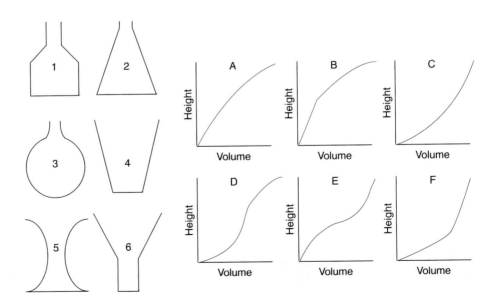

Reflections on Chapter 23

Writing to Learn

1. Describe in your own words the five different representations of a function and how they are related or actually represent the same thing. Use an example of your own (not one from the book) to explain.
2. Describe in general terms how you might develop function concepts through the use of growing patterns, a real-world situation, and an experiment. Indicate how the five representations are used in each method.
3. Make up a real-world situation that defines a functional relationship. Use your example to do the following:
   a. Sketch a graph illustrating the relationship.
   b. State the relationship using the language of functions.
   c. Build a chart with numbers that might go with your relationship.
   d. Explain the graph and the chart as ways of presenting the same information in different forms.
   e. Explain how your example meets the formal definition of a function.
4. The table of values used to create a scatter plot, as in the height versus–arm span example, is not a function table. Explain why not. How do you get a function out of a scatter plot?
5. Regarding graphs without equations, one activity in the text has students sketch graphs for situations, another has students match graphs to a collection of situations, and a third has them make up stories to go with graph sketches. What is the value of these exercises? Are there any differences in what students learn or think about in these different exercises?

For Discussion and Exploration

1. Some people feel that graphing calculators are too expensive for use in the middle grades. Others argue that students need to know the "basics" before they should be allowed to use these devices. What is your position? Can you defend it?
2. As a part of the Third International Mathematics and Science Study (TIMSS), a video study was done at grade 8. Tapes are available that show algebra lessons from an eighth-grade class in the United States, Japan, and Germany. The lessons show marked differences in the focus and methods of instruction. If at all possible, view the tapes and discuss your reactions.

Recommendations for Further Reading

Highly Recommended

Fey, J. T., & Heid, M. K. (1995). *Concepts in algebra: A technological approach*. Dedham, MA: Janson.

This is a full-year text for beginning algebra that was originally developed under a National Science Foundation grant to illustrate how technology could be used to teach algebra. The authors strongly believe that algebra should be tightly connected to real-world examples, not simply as applications at the ends of a unit but as the springboard of every idea. The emphasis is on functions and graphs. Symbol manipulation is minimal. Factoring is not included as a skill anywhere in the book. Many of the ideas in this book are embedded in the current chapter. This is a highly recommended resource for teachers if not a text for a middle grade algebra course.

Fulton, B. S., & Lombard, B. (2001). *The pattern and function connection*. Emeryville, CA: Key Curriculum Press.

The authors of this resource provide the teacher with clear lesson plans and Blackline Masters for a complete development of functions. Each new idea is developed from a pattern. After learning how to graph functions, students learn about slopes and intercepts, and nonlinear functions. Most of the book is accessible to middle school. This is an extremely practical and innovative approach to the topic. Call this a must resource.

Phillips, E., Gardella, T., Kelly, C., & Stewart, J. (1991). *Patterns and functions: Addenda series, grades 5–8*. Reston, VA: National Council of Teachers of Mathematics.

It is hard to improve on this book for ideas related to function development. The first section involves students with a wide variety of functions in real contexts, including exponential decay, linear, quadratic, and cubic functions. Throughout the book, the concept of function grows out of pattern development in a variety of creative and interesting activities that connect many middle school mathematics topics to a development of functions. This is an important contribution to the development of function concepts prior to algebra.

Other Suggestions

Arcidiacono, M. J., & Maier, E. (1993). *Picturing algebra: Unit 9, Math in the mind's eye*. Salem, OR: Math Learning Center.

Blume, G. W., & Heckman, D. S. (2000). Algebra and functions. In E. A. Silver, & P. A. Kenney (Eds.), *Results from the seventh mathematics assessment of the National Assessment of Educational Progress* (pp. 269–306). Reston, VA: National Council of Teachers of Mathematics.

Browning, C. A., & Channell, D. E. (1997). *Graphing calculator activities for enriching middle school mathematics*. Austin, TX: Texas Instruments.

Day, R. P. (1995). Using functions to make mathematical connections. In P. A. House (Ed.), *Connecting mathematics across the curriculum* (pp. 54–64). Reston, VA: National Council of Teachers of Mathematics.

Day, R., & Jones, G. (1997). Building bridges to algebraic thinking. *Mathematics Teaching in the Middle School, 2,* 209–212.

Dixon, J., Glickman, C, Wright, T., & Nimer, M. (2000). Functioning in a world of motion. *The Mathematics Teacher, 93,* 180–185.

Essex, N. K., Lambdin, D. V., & McGraw, R. H. (2002). Racing against time: Using technology to explore distance, rate, and time. *Teaching Children Mathematics, 8,* 322–326, 347.

Heid, M. K. (1995). *Algebra in a technological world: Addenda series, grades 9–12*. Reston, VA: National Council of Teachers of Mathematics.

Johnston, E. C., & Young, D. A. (1999). *Data collection activities for the middle grades with the TI-73, CBL, and CBR.* Austin, TX: Texas Instruments.

Lobato, J., & Thanheiser, E. (2002). Developing understanding of ratio and measure as foundation for slope. In B. Litwiller (Ed.), *Making sense of fractions, ratios, and proportions* (pp. 162–175). Reston, VA: National Council of Teachers of Mathematics.

McCoy, L. (1997). Algebra: Real-life investigations in a lab setting. *Mathematics Teaching in the Middle School, 2,* 220–224.

McCoy, L. P., Baker, T. H., & Little, L. S. (1996). Using multiple representations to communicate: An algebra challenge. In P. C. Elliott (Ed.), *Communication in mathematics, K–12 and beyond* (pp. 40–44). Reston, VA: National Council of Teachers of Mathematics.

National Council of Teachers of Mathematics. (2002). Learning and teaching mathematics with technology [Focus Issue]. *Teaching Children Mathematics, 8*(6).

Patterson, A. C. (1999). Grasping graphing. *Mathematics Teacher, 92,* 758–762.

Rubenstein, R. (1996). The function game. *Mathematics Teaching in the Middle School, 2,* 74–78.

Shell Centre for Mathematical Education, University of Nottingham. (1985). *The language of functions and graphs.* Nottingham, England: Author.

Specht, J. (2000). *More than graphs: Mathematics explorations for TI-73, TI-82, TI-83, and TI-83 Plus graphing calculators.* Emeryville, CA: Key Curriculum Press.

The Graphing Technology in Mathematics Project. (1995). *Graphing power: Middle school activities for the TI-81 and TI-82.* Palo Alto, CA: Dale Seymour Publications.

Yerushalmy, M., & Shternberg, B. (2001). Charting a visual course to the concept of function. In A. A. Cuoco (Ed.), *The roles of representation in school mathematics* (pp. 251–268). Reston, VA: National Council of Teachers of Mathematics.

24

Developing Concepts of Exponents, Integers, and Real Numbers

Much of the middle grades curriculum has been discussed in other chapters, including decimals, ratio and proportion, percent, measurement, geometry, probability, statistics, and algebraic reasoning. Each of those topics has its initial development in earlier grades but continues in the middle school. Specifically, students in the middle grades need to develop a more complete understanding of the number system, extend whole numbers to integers, start to think of fractions as rational numbers (both positive and negative), and begin to appreciate the completeness of the real number system.

Big Ideas

1. Exponential notation is a powerful way to express repeated products of the same number. Specifically, powers of 10 express very large and very small numbers in an economical manner.

2. Integers add to number the idea of opposite, so that every number has both size and a positive or negative relationship to other numbers. A negative number is the opposite of the positive number of the same size.

3. Every fraction, both positive and negative, is a rational number. Furthermore, every rational number can be expressed as a fraction.

4. Many numbers are not rational and can be expressed only symbolically or approximately using a close rational number. Examples include $\sqrt{2} \approx 1.41421\ldots$ and $\pi \approx 3.14159\ldots$

Content Connections

The ideas in this chapter represent an expansion of the ways in which we represent numbers. These representations expand or enhance earlier ideas of whole numbers, fractions, and decimals.

■ **Whole-Number Place Value, Fractions, and Decimals** (Chapters 12, 15, and 17): When exponential notation is combined with decimal notation, very small and very large numbers can be written efficiently. Decimals and fractions help to describe the difference between rational and irrational numbers. Negative numbers extend the number line in both directions.

■ **Algebra** (Chapters 22 and 23): The symbolic manipulation of numbers, including the rules for order of operations, is exactly the same as is used with variables. An ease with manipulation and representations of numbers will translate to algebraic manipulations. The study of integers helps with the notion of "opposite," represented by a negative sign: $^-6$ is the opposite of $^+6$ and ^-x is the opposite of ^+x, regardless of whether x is negative or positive. Exponents can also be variables, giving rise to exponential functions.

Large Numbers, Small Numbers, and Exponents

As numbers in our technological world get very small or very large, expressing them in standard form is cumbersome. Exponential notation is much more efficient for conveying numeric or quantitative information.

Exponents

In algebra classes, students get confused trying to remember the rules of exponents. For example, when you raise numbers to powers, do you add or multiply the exponents? Here is an example of procedural knowledge that is often learned without supporting conceptual knowledge. Before algebra, students should have ample opportunity to explore working with exponents on whole numbers rather than with letters or variables. By doing so, they are able to deal directly with the concept and actually generate the rules themselves.

A *whole-number exponent* is simply shorthand for repeated multiplication of a number times itself; for example, $3^4 = 3 \times 3 \times 3 \times 3$. That is the only conceptual knowledge required.

Conventions of symbolism must also be learned. These are arbitrary rules with no conceptual basis. The first is that *an exponent applies to its immediate base.* For example, in the expression $2 + 5^3$, the exponent 3 applies only to the 5, so the expression is equal to $2 + (5 \times 5 \times 5)$. However, in the expression $(2 + 5)^3$, the 3 is an exponent of the quantity $2 + 5$ and is evaluated as $(2 + 5) \times (2 + 5) \times (2 + 5)$, or $7 \times 7 \times 7$.

The other convention involves the *order of operations:* Multiplication and division are always done before addition and subtraction. Since exponentiation is repeated multiplication, it also is done before addition and subtraction. In the expression $5 + 4 \times 2 - 6 \div 3$, 4×2 and $6 \div 3$ are done first. Therefore, the expression is evaluated as $5 + 8 - 2 = 13 - 2 = 11$.

 STOP   Try evaluating the same expression in left-to-right order. Do you get 4?

Parentheses are used to group operations that are to be done first. Therefore, in $(5 + 4) \times 2 - 6 \div 3$, the addition can be done inside the parentheses first, or the distributive property can be used, and the final result is 16. The phrase "*P*lease *e*xcuse *m*y *d*ear *A*unt *S*ally" is sometimes used to help students recall that operations inside *p*arentheses are done first, then *e*xponentiation, and then *m*ultiplication and *d*ivision before *a*ddition and *s*ubtraction.

Calculators and Notation

Most scientific calculators employ "algebraic logic" that will evaluate expressions correctly and also allow grouping with parentheses. However, with the exception of the TI-Math-Mate, simple four-function calculators generally do not use algebraic logic. Operations are processed as they are entered. On calculators without algebraic logic, the following two keying sequences produce the same results:

Key: →   3 [+] 2 [×] 7 [=]
Display → 3   2   5   7   35

Key: →   3 [+] 2 [=] [×] 7 [=]
Display → 3   2   5   7   35

Whenever an operation sign is pressed, the effect is the same as pressing [=] and then the operation. Of course, neither result is correct for the expressions $3 + 2 \times 7$, which should be evaluated as $3 + 14$, or 17. Calculators designed for middle grades do use algebraic logic and include parenthesis keys so that both $3 + 2 \times 7$ and $(3 + 2) \times 7$ can be keyed in the order that the symbols appear. Now all of the

major manufacturers offer calculators that show an entire expression in the window, including parentheses, as do graphing calculators. Results are shown only after pressing the [Enter] key. With the Explorer Plus and most scientific calculators, the display shows only one number at a time, as illustrated here.

Key: →   3 [+] 2 [×] 7 [=]
Display → 3   2   7   17

Notice that the display does not change when [×] is pressed: A right parenthesis is never displayed. Instead, the expression that the right parenthesis encloses is calculated and that result displayed.

Key: →   [(] 3 [+] 2 [)] [×] 7 [=]
Display → [3   2   5   7   35

The graphing calculator offers the best solution to these problems. When the expression $3 + 2 \times (6^2 - 4)$ is keyed in, the display shows the full expression. Nothing is evaluated until you press [Enter] or [EXE]. Then the result appears on the next line to the right of the screen:

$$3 + 2 * (6^2 - 4)$$
$$67$$

Moreover, the last expression entered can be recalled and edited so that students can see how different expressions are evaluated. Only minimum key presses are required.

$3 + 2 * (6^2 - 4)$	67
$(3 + 2) * (6^2 - 4)$	160
$(3 + 2) * 6^2 - 4$	176
$3 + 2 * 6^2 - 4$	71

Nevertheless, the simple four-function calculator remains a powerful tool regardless of its limitations. For example, to evaluate 3^8, press 3 [×] [=] [=] [=] [=] [=] [=]. (The first press of [=] will result in 9, or 3×3.) Students will be fascinated by how quickly numbers grow. Enter any number, press [×], and then repeatedly press [=]. Try two-digit numbers. Try 0.2.

Give students ample opportunity to explore expressions involving mixed operations and exponents with only the conventions and the meaning of exponents to guide them. No rules for exponents should be promoted. When experience has provided a firm background, the rules of exponents will make sense and should not require rote memorization.

ACTIVITY 24.1

What's in an Expression?

Provide students with numeric expressions to evaluate with simple four-function calculators. Here are some examples of the types of expressions that can be valuable:

| $3 + 4 \times 8$ $4 \times 8 + 3$ | $3^6 + 2^6$ $(3 + 2)^6$ | $3^4 \times 7 - 5^2$ $(3 \times 7)^4 - 5 \times 2$ | $3^4 \times 5^2$ $(3 \times 5)^6$ |

| $\dfrac{5^3 \times 5^2}{5^6}$ | $4 \times 3 - 2^3 \times 5 + 23 \times 9$ | $\dfrac{4 \times 3^5}{2}$ $\quad 4 + \dfrac{3^5}{2}$ |

When experiencing difficulty, students should write equivalent expressions without exponents or include parentheses to indicate explicit groupings. For example:

$$(7 \times 2^3 - 5)^3 = (7 \times (2 \times 2 \times 2) - 5) \times$$
$$(7 \times (2 \times 2 \times 2) - 5) \times$$
$$(7 \times (2 \times 2 \times 2) - 5)$$
$$= ((7 \times 8) - 5) \times$$
$$((7 \times 8) - 5) \times$$
$$((7 \times 8) - 5)$$
$$= (56 - 5) \times (56 - 5) \times (56 - 5)$$
$$= 51 \times 51 \times 51$$

When discussing results, place all of the emphasis on the procedures rather than the answer. The fact that two groups got the same result does not help a group that got a different result. For many expressions, there is more than one way to proceed, and one may be easier to do or to understand than another.

Of course, calculators with algebraic logic will automatically produce correct results. Yet it remains important for students to know the correct order of operations. The calculator should not replace an understanding of the rules. The order-of-operation rules apply to symbolic manipulation in algebra and must also be understood if a calculator without algebraic logic is used.

Very Large Numbers

The real world is full of very large quantities and measures. We see references to huge numbers in the media all the time. Unfortunately, most of us have not developed an appreciation for extremely large numbers. Here are a few examples:

- A state lottery with 44 numbers from which to pick 6 has over 7 million possible combinations of 6 numbers. There are $44 \times 43 \times 42 \times 41 \times 40 \times 39$ possible ways that the balls could come out of the hopper (5,082,517,440). But generally the order in which they are picked is not important. Since there are $6 \times 5 \times 4 \times 3 \times 2 \times 1 = 720$ different arrangements of 6 numbers, each collection appears 720 times. Therefore, there are *only* $5,082,517,440 \div 720$ possible lottery numbers, or in other words, 1 out of 7,059,052 chances to win.
- An estimate of the size of the universe is 40 billion light-years. One light-year is the number of miles light travels in *one year*. The speed of light is 186,281.7 miles per *second*, or 16,094,738,880 miles in a single day.
- The human body has about 100 billion cells.

- The distance to the sun is about 150 million kilometers.
- The population of the world has surpassed 6 billion.

Representation of Large Numbers: Scientific Notation

The more common it becomes to find very large numbers in our daily lives, the more important it is to have convenient ways to represent them. One option is to say and write numbers in their common form. However, this practice can at times be cumbersome. Another option is to use exponential notation and our base-ten place-value system.

Students in elementary school learn how to multiply by 10, by 100, and by 1000 by simply adding the appropriate number of zeros. Help students expand this idea by examining powers of 10 on a calculator that handles exponents. A graphing calculator is best but not the only option.

ACTIVITY 24.2

Exploring Powers of 10

Have students use any calculator that permits entering exponents to explore some of the following:

a. Explore 10^N for various values of N. What patterns do you notice. What does 1E15 mean? (1E15 is the typical calculator form of 1×10^{15}.)
b. Find out the easiest expressions for one thousand, one million, one billion, one trillion. What patterns are there in these numbers?
c. Enter 45 followed by a string of zeros. How many will your calculator permit? What happens when you press ⏎ Enter? What does 4.5E10 mean?
d. What does 5.689E6 mean? Can you enter this another way?
e. Try sums like $(4.5 \times 10^N) + (27 \times 10^K)$ for different values of N and K. What can you find out?
f. What happens with products of numbers like those in item (e)?

It is useful to become comfortable with the power-of-10 expressions in Activity 24.2. Students should eventually discover that when scientific or graphing calculators display numbers with more digits than the display will hold, they use *scientific notation*—a decimal number between 1 and 10 times a power of 10. For example, on a TI-73, the product of $45,000,000 \times 8,000,000$ is displayed as 3.6E14, meaning 3.6×10^{14}, or 360,000,000,000,000 (360 trillion).

Ask students why there are only 13 zeros. What happens when the numbers in the computation do not involve a lot of zeros?

STOP With each factor in the product expressed in scientific notation: $(4.5 \times 10^7) \times (8 \times 10^6)$, or 4.5E7 × 8.0E6, can you compute the result mentally?

CONNECTED MATHEMATICS

MIDDLE GRADES

Grade 8, *Growing, Growing, Growing: Exponential Relationships*
Investigation 3: Growth Factors

Context

This entire unit, comprising approximately 20 days, is devoted to the concept of exponential growth as seen in real contexts. The unit begins with some fun examples to review the meaning of exponents. In the second investigation, the examples include the growth of single-celled organisms and the area covered by the growth of mold. The base of the exponent is called the *growth factor*. Through the first two units, growth factors are always small whole numbers. This and the next investigation explore growth factors that are not whole numbers.

Task Description

As a lead-in to this first task, students learn of the problem rabbit population in Australia. (Rabbits were introduced to Australia in 1859. In one year, a female rabbit can have as many as seven litters with five rabbits each.) The table provides hypothetical data that might have been collected during the first four years after the rabbits were introduced.

Time (years)	Rabbit population
0	100
1	180
2	325
3	580
4	1050

In the problem box shown here, notice how a recursive relationship is used to define the growth factor. This method of determining the growth factor was introduced

---

Problem 3.1

A. The table above shows that the rabbit population grows exponentially. What is the growth factor for this rabbit population? The growth factor from one year to the next is the fraction:

$$\frac{\text{population for year } n}{\text{population for year } n-1}$$

To find an approximate overall growth factor, compute the growth factors between several pairs of consecutive years and average your results.

B. If this growth pattern had continued, how many rabbits would there have been after 10 years? After 25 years? After 50 years?

C. How many years would it have taken the rabbit population to exceed 1 million?

D. Assume this growth pattern continued. Write an equation you could use to predict the rabbit population, *P*, for any year, *n*, after the rabbits were first counted.

From *Connected Mathematics: Growing, Growing, Growing: Exponential Mathematics.* © 2002 by Michigan State University, Glenda Lappan, James T. Fey, William M. Fitzgerald, Susan N. Friel, and Elizabeth Difanis Phillips. Published by Prentice Hall. Used by permission of Pearson Education, Inc.

earlier in the unit. The growth factor is a bit different for each year, as would be expected. Thus, the formula will be an approximation of the actual population of rabbits. This is a good example of the way that mathematical models often approximate real data.

As follow-up, students are asked related questions that involve changes in the basic formula developed in the initial problem, providing practice with the main idea.

In the fourth and final investigation of this unit, the growth factors are less than 1. These relationships are examples of "exponential decay" rather than of growth. One example from the text involves the rate at which water cools over time.

Notice the advantages of scientific notation, especially for multiplication and division. Here the significant digits can be multiplied mentally (4.5 × 8 = 36) and the exponents added to produce almost instantly 36×10^{13} or 3.6×10^{14}.

Different notations have different purposes and values. Consider this fact: In 1990, the population of the world was more than 5,050,700,000 persons, about 1 billion fewer than in the year 2000. This can be expressed in various ways:

5 billion 50 million 700 thousand

5,050,700,000

5.0507×10^9

Less than 5.1 billion

A little more than 5 billion

Each way of stating the number has value and purpose in different contexts. Rather than spend time with exercises

converting numbers from standard form to scientific notation, consider large numbers found in newspapers, magazines, and atlases. How are they written? How are they said aloud? When are they rounded? When not and why? What forms of the numbers seem best for the purposes?

The *Standards* reminds us that large numbers and scientific notation are used in various contexts. "A newspaper headline may proclaim, 'Clean-Up Costs from Oil Spill Exceed $2 Billion!' or a science textbook may indicate that the number of red blood cells in the human body is about 1.9×10^{13}" (p. 217).

In the eighth grade, the *Connected Mathematics* program looks at exponents as a particular type of function—exponential functions. The program uses real contexts throughout the development. An example is explored on this page.

Negative Exponents

When students begin to explore exponents and have also experienced negative integers, it is interesting to consider what it might mean to raise a number to a negative power. For example, what does 2^{-4} mean, if anything? Two related options for exploring the possibilities of negative exponents seem reasonable. First, in the spirit of patterns in mathematics, examine a pattern of numbers, and see how it might best be expanded. As with large numbers, the powers of 10 seem the most profitable to explore because they are directly related to place value. Have students consider 10^N as follows:

$$10^4 = 10,000$$
$$10^3 = 1000$$
$$10^2 = 100$$
$$10^1 = 10$$
$$10^0 = ?$$
$$10^{-1} = ?$$

In this sequence, the most obvious entry for 10^0 is 1, and that is the *definition* of 10^0. That is, it is a convention that 10 or any other nonzero number raised to the power 0 is 1. So what is 10^{-1}? If the pattern is to continue, the 1 should move to the right of the decimal:

$$10^0 = 1$$
$$10^{-1} = 0.1$$
$$10^{-2} = 0.01$$
$$10^{-3} = 0.001$$

and so on. Notice how each of these numbers is written as a fraction:

$$10^{-3} = 0.001 = \frac{1}{1000} = \frac{1}{10^3}$$

Students should be encouraged to explore these numbers on a calculator. That leads to the second way to explore negative exponents: Use a calculator to see if you can figure out what things like 4^{-3} or 2^{-5} mean. The calculator should, of course, never be seen as the *reason* for anything in mathematics, but here you are searching for a notation convention. Assuming that one exists, it is reasonable to believe that the calculator will have the correct convention incorporated. If the calculator has decimal-to-fraction conversion, suggest that students use that feature to help develop the meaning of negative exponents. Figure 24.1 gives an example of how this might look on a graphing calculator.

Very Small Numbers

As with large numbers, it is extremely important to use real examples of very small numbers. Without real contexts, you may be tempted to resort to drill exercises that have little meaning for students. Here are a few examples of real-world values to explore:

- The length of a DNA strand in a cell is about 10^{-7} m. This is also measured as 1000 *angstroms*. (Based on

FIGURE 24.1 Graphing calculators routinely evaluate expressions as decimals. However, they also provide a way to convert decimals to fractions. This figure shows the screen of a TI-73 calculator. The F↔D **key converts fractions to decimals and also decimals to fractions as shown here.**

this information, how long is an angstrom?) How large is a cell?
- Human hair grows at the rate of 10^{-8} miles per hour.
- The chances of winning the Virginia lottery, based on selecting six numbers from 1 to 44, is 1 in 7.059 million. That is a probability of less than 1.4×10^{-10}.
- The mass of one atom of hydrogen is 0.000 000 000 000 000 000 000 001 675 g.
- It takes sound 0.28 second (2.8×10^{-1}) to travel the length of a football field. In contrast, a TV signal travels a full mile in about 0.000005368 second, or 5.3×10^{-6} second. A TV viewer at home hears the football being kicked before the receiver on the field does.

INTEGER CONCEPTS

Students almost daily have some interaction with negative numbers or experience phenomena that negative numbers can model. Some examples:

A loss of money is a negative cash flow.

Slowing down the car is negative acceleration, and driving in reverse is negative velocity.

Below-zero temperature and below-ground level are negatives relative to a scale.

In fact, almost any concept that is quantified and has direction probably has both a positive and a negative value.

Generally, negative values are introduced with *integers*—the whole numbers and their negatives or opposites—instead of with fractions or decimals.

Intuitive Models of Signed Quantities

As with any new types of numbers that students encounter, real models or examples are useful. Negative numbers or situations that model them do exist. It is a good idea to discuss some of these with your class before jumping directly into computation with signed numbers.

Debits and Credits

Suppose that you are the bookkeeper for a small business. At any time, your records show how many dollars the company has in its account. There are always so many dollars in cash (credits or receipts) and so many dollars in accounts payable (debits). The difference between the debit and credit totals tells the value of the account. If there are more credits than debits, the account is positive, or "in the black." If there are more debits than credits, the account is in debt, shows a negative cash value, or is "in the red." Suppose further that all transactions are handled by mail. The mail carrier can bring mail, a positive action, or take mail away, a negative action.

With this scenario, it is easy to discuss addition and subtraction of signed quantities. An example is illustrated in Figure 24.2.

Integer Football

An integer football field might have the center as the 0-yard line with one goal the +50 goal and the other the −50 goal. Any position on the field is determined by a signed number between +50 and −50. Gains or losses are like positive and negative quantities. A positive team moves toward the positive goal, and a negative team toward the negative goal. If the negative team starts on the −15-yard line and has a loss of 20 yards, it will be on the +5-yard line.

> **✕ STOP** You should sketch a picture of this example and convince yourself that it is numerically the same as the one in Figure 24.2 using the debit-credit model.

Contrived situations such as mailing debits and credits and the football field are suggested as introductory discussion models. They can help students think intuitively about what happens to quantities when an action causes them to be less than 0. They also provide examples of a joining or positive action and a removal or negative action of both positive and negative quantities.

The calculator is another model that might be explored early in the discussion of signed numbers. It gives correct and immediate results that students seem to believe. The major drawback is that no rationale for the result is provided.

Have students explore subtraction problems such as 5 − 8 = ?, and discuss the results. (Be aware that the negative sign appears in different places on different calculators.)

Students can benefit by using the calculator along with the intuitive models and questions mentioned earlier. For example, how can you get from −5 to −17 by addition? 13 minus *what* is 15?

Mathematical Definition of Negative Numbers

The mathematician defines a negative number in terms of whole numbers. Therefore, the definition of negative 3 is the solution to the equation 3 + ? = 0. In general, the *opposite of n* is the solution to n + ? = 0. If n is a positive number, the *opposite of n* is a negative number. The set of integers, therefore, consists of the positive whole numbers, the opposites of the whole numbers, or negative numbers, and 0, which is neither positive nor negative. This is the definition found in student textbooks. Like many things in mathematics, abstract or symbolic definitions are best when there is some intuitive or conceptual framework with which to link the idea.

OPERATIONS WITH INTEGERS

Until students encounter integers, the plus and minus signs are used only for the operations of addition and subtraction. Notation for signed numbers represents a real problem for many students. For example, the sum of 3 and negative 7 can be written as 3 + (−7) or as 3 + ⁻7. The latter form might be clear in a printed book but may be obscure in handwritten form. The use of parentheses is awkward, especially in expressions already involving parentheses. On graphing calculators, the distinction is forced on the user: One key is used for subtraction and another for negatives. They do not work interchangeably.

Two Models for Integer Operations

Two models are popular for helping students understand how the four operations (+, −, ×, and ÷) work with the integers. One model consists of counters in two different colors, one for positive counts and one for negative counts. Two counters, one of each type, cancel each other out. Thus if yellows are positive and reds are negative, 5 yellows and 7 reds is the same as 2 reds, each representing −2 (see Figure 24.3). It is important with this model that students understand that it is always possible to add to or remove from a pile any number of pairs consisting of one positive and one negative counter without changing the value of the pile. (Intuitively, this is like

Credits		Debits		Balance
In	Out	In	Out	Begin 0
50				+50
		30		+20
	10			+10
			50	−40
25				−15
			(20)	+5

FIGURE 24.2 **A ledger sheet model for integers.**

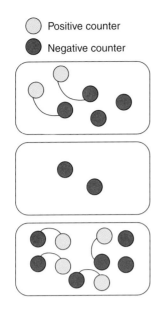

FIGURE 24.3 Each collection is a model of negative 2.

adding equal quantities of debits and credits.) The actions of addition and subtraction are the same as for whole numbers; addition is joining or adding counters, and subtraction is removing or taking away counters.

The other commonly used model is the number line. It is a bit more traditional and mathematical, yet many students find it confusing. The football field model provides an intuitive background. Positive and negative numbers are measured distances to the right and left of 0. It is important to remember that signed values are *directed distances* and not points on a line. The points on the number line are not models of integers; the directed distances are. To emphasize this for students, represent all integers with arrows, and avoid referring to the number line coordinates as "numbers." Poster board arrows of different whole-number lengths can be made in two colors, yellow pointing to the right for positive quantities and red to the left for negative quantities (see Figure 24.4). The arrows help students think of integer quantities as directed distances. A positive arrow never points left, and a negative arrow never points right. Furthermore, each arrow is a quantity with both length (magnitude or absolute value) and direction (sign). These properties remain for each arrow regardless of its position on the number line. Small versions

of the arrows can easily be cut from poster board for individual students to work with.

It is no doubt easier simply to give students the rules for integers than to develop them with arrows and counters. The conceptual explanations do not make the rules easier to use, and it is never intended that students continue to think in terms of these models as they practice integer arithmetic. Rather, it is important that students not view the procedural rules for manipulating integers as arbitrary and mysterious. Here is a case where we must make students responsible for the conceptual knowledge. If we emphasize only the procedural rules, there is little reason for students to attend to the conceptual justifications. Do not be content with right answers; always demand explanations.

Which Model to Use

Although the two models appear quite different, they are alike mathematically. Integers involve two concepts—*quantity* and *opposite*. Quantity is modeled by the number of counters or the length of the arrows. Opposite is represented as different colors or different directions.

Many teachers who have tried both models with their students report that students find one model easy and the other hard. (The counter model seems to be the favorite.) As a result, they decide to use only the model that students like or understand better. This is a mistake! Remember that the dual concepts of integers are not in the models but rather must be constructed by the students and imposed on the models. It may be that students find the operations easier when they use counters. This is not the same thing as understanding integer operations. Students should experience both models and, perhaps even more important, discuss how the two are alike. A parallel development using both models at the same time may be the most conceptual approach.

A Problem-Solving Approach for Integers

The following discussion is more a quick explanation of how counters and arrows can be used to model operations with integers than a suggested pedagogical approach. Once your students understand how integers are represented by each of the models, you can present the operations for the integers in the form of problems. In other words, rather than explaining how addition of integers works and showing students how to solve exercises with the models, you pose an integer computation and let students use their models to find a solution. It may be useful to assign half of the class the arrow model and the other half the counters. When solutions have been reached, the groups can compare and justify their results. Many incorrect ideas will surface, but the learning that will come from the discussion and clarification will be far superior to an expository approach.

FIGURE 24.4 Number-line model for integers.

Addition and Subtraction

Since middle school students will not have used counters or number lines for some time, it would be good to begin work with either of these models using positive whole numbers. After a few examples to help students become familiar with the model for addition or subtraction with whole numbers, have them work through an example with integers using exactly the same reasoning. Remember, the emphasis should be on the rationale and not on how quickly students can get correct answers.

Several examples of addition are modeled in Figure 24.5, each in two ways: with positive and negative counters and with the number-line-and-arrow model. First examine the counter model. After the two quantities are joined, any pairs of positive and negative counters cancel each other out, and students can remove these, making it easier to see the result.

To add using the arrow model, note that each added arrow begins at the point end of the previous arrow. Help students with the analogy between these arrows and the football situation: Players always face their own goal. They may go forward or backward, but they never face the opponents' goal. Addition is the advance of a team from the previous position. In the $^+3 + {}^-5$ example, the positive arrow (+ team) starts at 0 and ends at positive 3. From that point, the negative arrow begins (the negative team takes over and *advances* in the negative direction). The result, then, is an arrow beginning at 0 and ending where the second arrow ended.

Subtraction is represented as "remove" in terms of the counter model and "back up" in terms of the arrow model. In Figure 24.6, for $^-5 - {}^+2$, both models begin with a representation of $^-5$. To remove two positive counters from a set that has none, a different representation of $^-5$ must first be

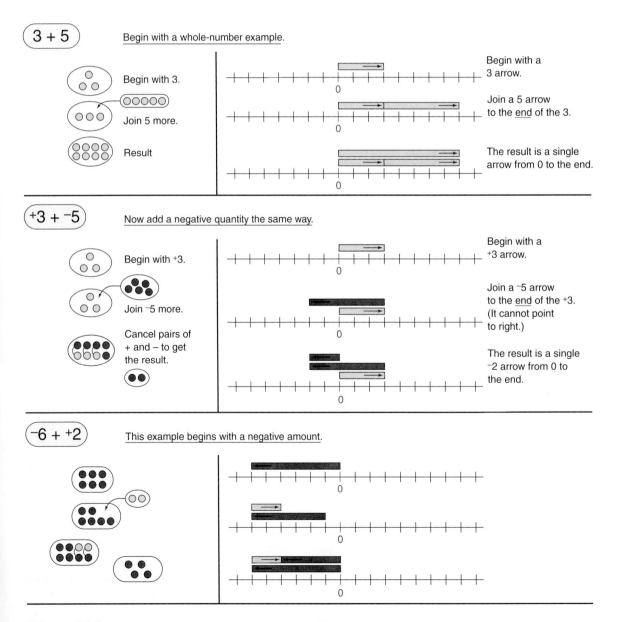

FIGURE 24.5 **Relate integer addition to whole-number addition.**

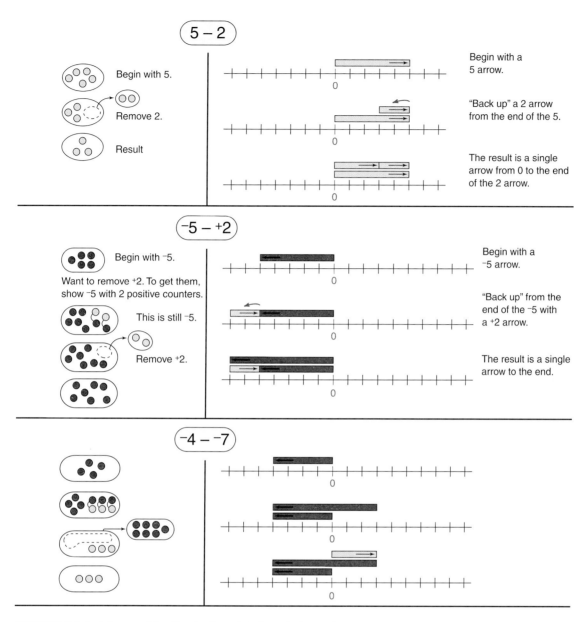

FIGURE 24.6 Integer subtraction is also related to whole numbers.

made. Since any number of neutral pairs (one positive, one negative) can be added without changing the value of the set, two pairs are added so that two positive counters can be removed. The net effect is to have more negative counters.

With the number-line-and-arrow model, subtraction means to back up or to move in the opposite direction. Using the football field analogy, teams move backward when penalized or they lose yardage. In the example of ⁻5 − ⁺2, the first arrow ends at ⁻5. Since a positive quantity is subtracted, use a positive arrow. To subtract it, move it in its opposite direction (left). The forward movement ends at ⁻8. The result of the operation is an arrow from 0 to the back end of the ⁺2 arrow.

 Before reading further, go through each example in Figures 24.5 and 24.6. Solve the problems without examining

the figure and then compare your results with those in the figures. You should feel comfortable with both models.

Have your students draw pictures to accompany integer computations. Set pictures are easy enough; they may consist of Xs and Os, for example. For the arrow model, there is no need for anything elaborate either. Figure 24.7 illustrates how a student might draw arrows for simple addition and subtraction exercises without even sketching the number line. Directions are shown by the arrows, and magnitudes are written on the arrows. For your initial modeling, however, the poster board arrows in two colors will help students see that negative arrows always point left and that addition is a forward movement and subtraction is a backward movement for either type of arrow.

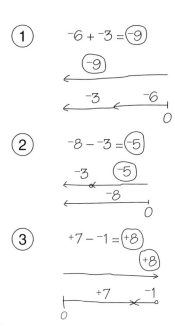

FIGURE 24.7 Students do not need elaborate drawings to think through the number-line model.

It is important for students to see that ⁺3 + ⁻5 is the same as ⁺3 − ⁺5 and that ⁺2 − ⁻6 is the same as ⁺2 + ⁺6. With the method of modeling addition and subtraction described here, these expressions are quite discernible and yet have the same result as they should have.

On graphing calculators, these expressions are entered using the "negative" key and the "subtraction" key. The difference is also evident in the display. The redundant superscript plus signs are not shown. Students can see that 3 + ⁻5 and 3 − 5 each results in ⁻2 and that 3 − ⁻5 and 3 + 5 are also alike.

Multiplication and Division

Multiplication of integers should be a direct extension of multiplication for whole numbers, just as addition and subtraction were connected to whole-number concepts. We frequently refer to whole-number multiplication as repeated addition. The first factor tells how many sets there are or how many are added in all, beginning with 0. This translates to integer multiplication quite readily when the first factor is positive, regardless of the sign of the second factor. The first example in Figure 24.8 illustrates a positive first factor and a negative second factor.

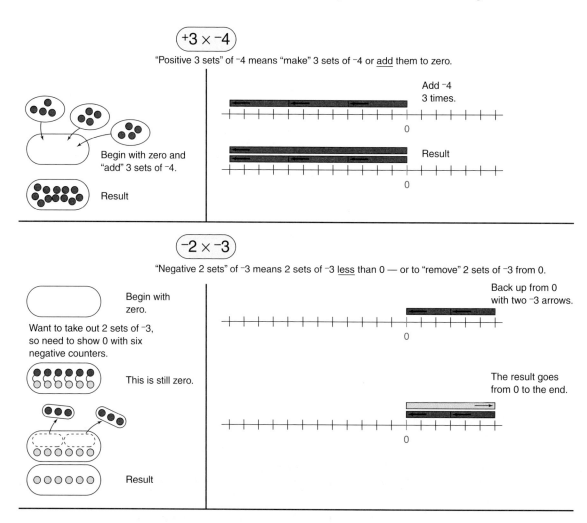

FIGURE 24.8 Multiplication by a positive first factor is repeated addition. Multiplication by a negative first factor is repeated subtraction.

What could the meaning be when the first factor is negative, as in ⁻2 × ⁻3? If a positive first factor means repeated addition (how many times added to 0), a negative first factor should mean repeated subtraction (how many times subtracted from 0). The second example in Figure 24.8 illustrates how multiplication with the first factor negative can be modeled.

The deceptively simple rules of "like signs yield positive products" and "unlike signs yield negative products" are quickly established. However, once more, it is not as important that your students be able to produce answers correctly and skillfully as that they be able to supply a rationale.

With division of integers, again explore the whole-number case first. Recall that 8 ÷ 4 with whole numbers has two possible meanings corresponding to two missing-factor expressions: 4 × ? = 8 asks, "Four sets of *what* make eight?"

whereas ? × 4 = 8 asks, "How many fours make eight?" Generally, the measurement approach (? × 4) is the one used with integers, although both concepts can be exhibited with either model. It is helpful to think of building the dividend with the divisor from 0, or repeated addition—to find the missing factor.

The first example in Figure 24.9 illustrates how the two models work for whole numbers. Following that is an example where the divisor is positive but the dividend is negative.

> ⊗ **STOP** Try using both models to compute ⁻8 ÷ ⁺2. Draw pictures using Xs and Os and also arrows. Check your understanding with the examples in Figure 24.9. Once you understand that example, try ⁺9 ÷ ⁻3 and also ⁻12 ÷ ⁻4.

FIGURE 24.9
Division of integers following a measurement approach.

The entire understanding of integer division rests on a good concept of a negative first factor for multiplication and a knowledge of the relationship between multiplication and division.

There is no need to rush your students on to some mastery of use of the models. It is much better that they first think about how to model the whole-number situation and then figure out, with some guidance from you, how to deal with integers.

"Positive and negative integers should be seen as useful for noting relative changes or values. Students can also appreciate the utility of negative integers when they work with equations whose solution requires them, such as $2x + 7 = 1$" (p. 218).

Rational Numbers

Several number ideas that students have been exposed to in earlier grades, coupled with the ideas of the integers, need to come together in the middle grades. A complete understanding of the rational numbers as positive and negative decimals and equivalently as positive and negative fractions is an important development.

Fractions as Indicated Division

If four people were to share three pizzas, the amount that each would get can be expressed as $3 \div 4$; that is, three things divided four ways. Each person would receive three-fourths of a pizza. So $\frac{3}{4}$ and $3 \div 4$ are both expressions for the same idea: 3 things divided by 4.

In Chapter 15, we saw that this sharing idea is in fact compatible with the part-whole meaning of fractions. With $\frac{3}{4}$ of a pizza, each pizza can be divided into four parts (the denominator) and then each person gets 3 of these $\frac{1}{4}$ pieces (the numerator). And so any fraction $\frac{k}{n}$ can be thought of as $k \div n$ or as k parts of $\frac{1}{n}$ pieces. These ideas appear quite different but in fact are not.

Students will likely find this division interpretation meaning of fractions unusual. Fractions are commonly thought of as parts of wholes, not as operations. Similarly, expressions such as $7 \div 3$ are thought of as operations (things to be done), not numbers. However, 4, $2 + 2$, $12 \div 3$, and $\frac{8}{2}$ are all symbolic expressions for the same number: $12 \div 3$ is not the question and 4 the answer; both are expressions for 4.

Here is one possible way to help students develop the idea that a fraction is another way of expressing division.

ACTIVITY 24.3

How Do You Write It?

Present students with a simple word problem similar to the following: *Zach has 18 meters of rope. He cuts off one-fifth of the rope to make a leash for his dog, Sam.*

How much rope did he use for the leash? Three students have solved this problem.

Student A: Zach cut off 3.6 meters because $18 \div 5 = 3.6$.

Student B: I did $\frac{1}{5} \times 18$ like this: $\frac{1}{5} \times \frac{18}{1} = \frac{18}{5} = 3\frac{3}{5}$. So the answer is 3 and $\frac{3}{5}$ meters.

Student C: I did the same thing, but I just said the answer was $\frac{18}{5}$ meters.

Which student is correct? Which one has the "best" answer?

  How would you respond to the questions in Activity 24.3?

In the discussion of a problem situation like the one in Activity 24.3, you can lead students to see that $18 \div 5$ and $\frac{18}{5}$ mean exactly the same thing. All three students are correct.

Similarly, discuss the difference between these three expressions:

$$\frac{1}{4} \text{ of } 24 \qquad \frac{24}{4} \qquad 24 \div 4$$

This discussion can lead to a general development of the idea that a fraction can be thought of as division of the numerator by the denominator or that $\frac{a}{b}$ is the same as $a \div b$.

Fractions as Rational Numbers

Because children tend to think of fractions as parts of sets or objects, they remain, in the minds of children, more physical object than number. This is one reason that children have such a difficult time placing fractions on a number line. A significant leap toward thinking about fractions as numbers is made when students begin to understand that a decimal is a representation of a fraction. In Chapter 17, we explored the idea of the "friendly" fractions (halves, thirds, fourths, fifths, eighths) in terms of their decimal equivalents.

In the middle grades, it is time to combine all of these ideas:

- $4\frac{3}{5}$ is 4.6 because $\frac{3}{5}$ is six-tenths of a whole, so 4 wholes and six-tenths is 4.6.
- $4\frac{3}{5}$ is $\frac{23}{5}$, and that is the same as $23 \div 5$, or 4.6 if I use decimals.
- 4.6 is read "four and six-tenths," so I can write that as $4\frac{6}{10} = 4\frac{3}{5}$.

What becomes clear in a discussion building on students' existing ideas is that any number, positive or negative, that can be written as a fraction can also be written as a decimal number. You can also reverse this idea and convert decimal numbers to fractions. Keep in mind that the purpose is to see that there are different symbolic notations for the same quantities—not to become skilled at conversions.

The result of this discussion is a reasonable definition of rational numbers: A *rational number* is any number that can be expressed as a fraction. Equivalently, a *rational number* is any number that can be written as either a terminating or repeating decimal number.

ACTIVITY 24.4

How Close Is Close?

Have students select any two fractions or any two decimals that they think are "really close." It makes no difference what numbers students pick or even how close together they really are. Now challenge them to find at least ten more numbers (fractions or decimals) that are between these two numbers. Do not be tempted to show students any clever methods for finding the numbers.

"How Close Is Close?" is an opportunity to find out how your students understand fractions and decimals. (The activity should be done in both forms eventually.) If students haven't been told a method, they must rely on their own ideas to come up with a solution. The activity offers a great opportunity for discussion, assessment of individual students' fraction and decimal concepts, and the introduction of perhaps the most interesting feature of the rational number system: density. The rational numbers are said to be *dense* because between any two rational numbers there exists an *infinite* number of other rational numbers.

The density of the rationals makes the irrationals even more amazing.

Real Numbers

As just noted, there are *irrational* numbers, numbers that are not rational. The irrationals together with the rational numbers make up the *real* numbers. The real numbers fill in all the holes on the number line even though the holes are infinitesimally small. Students' first experience with irrational numbers typically occurs when exploring roots of whole numbers.

Introducing the Concept of Roots

The following activity provides a good introduction to square roots and cube roots. From this beginning, the notion of roots of any degree is easily developed.

ACTIVITY 24.5

Edges of Squares and Cubes

Show students pictures of three squares (or three cubes) as in Figure 24.10. The edges of the first and last figure are consecutive whole numbers. The areas

---

(volumes) of all three figures are provided. The students' task is to use a calculator to find the edge of the figure in the center. Use of the square root key is not permitted. Solutions will satisfy these equations:

❏ × ❏ = 45,   or   ❏² = 45

and

❏ × ❏ × ❏ = 30,   or   ❏³ = 30

In "Edges of Squares and Cubes," the calculator permits students to test a possible edge length to see if it is too long or too short. For example, to solve the cube problem, students might start with 3.5 and find that 3.5^3 is 42.875, much too large. Quickly, they will find that the solution is between 3.1 and 3.2. But where?

 STOP   Use a calculator to continue getting a better approximation of the cube root of 30 to two decimal places.

From this simple introduction, students can be challenged to find solutions to equations such as ❏⁶ = 8. These students are now prepared to understand the general definition of the *nth root* of a number N as the number that when raised to the *n*th power equals N. The *square* and *cube roots* are simply other names for the second and third roots. The notational convention of the radical sign comes last. It should then be clear that $\sqrt{6}$ is a number and not an exercise to be done. The cube root of eight is the same as $\sqrt[3]{8}$ which is just another way of writing 2.

 NCTM Standards   "In grades 6–8, students frequently encounter squares and square roots when they use the Pythagorean relationship. They can use the inverse relationship to determine the approximate location of square roots between whole numbers on a number line" (p. 220). As examples, the authors note that $\sqrt{27}$ is

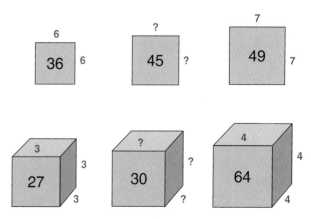

FIGURE 24.10 **A geometric interpretation of square roots and cube roots.**

a little more than 5 because $5^2 = 25$ and $\sqrt{99}$ is a little less than 10 since $10^2 = 100$.

Discussing Real Numbers

Eighth-grade students probably do not need a very sophisticated knowledge of the real number system. A few powerful ideas, however, deserve to be explored informally.

Irrational Numbers

One characterization of a rational number is that it can be written as a decimal where the decimal part is either finite or repeats infinitely. Thus, both 3.45 and 87.19363636 . . . are rational numbers and can each be converted to fractional form. But what about a decimal number that just goes on and on, with no repetition? Or what about the number 3.101001000100001000001 . . . ? These never repeat and are not finite and, therefore, are not rational. A real number that is not rational is called *irrational*.

The numbers π and $\sqrt{2}$ are both irrational numbers. The number π is a ratio of two measures in a circle, the circumference and the diameter. Although it is not possible to prove the irrationality of π at this level, the fact that it is irrational implies that it is impossible to have a circle with the lengths of both the circumference and the diameter rational. (Why?) A proof that $\sqrt{2}$ is irrational is generally explored at the junior high level. The usual argument assumes that $\sqrt{2}$ is rational, which then leads to a contradiction.

Density of the Real Numbers

If the density of the rationals is impressive, even more astounding is that the irrationals are also dense. And the irrationals and the rationals are all mixed up together. The density of the irrationals is not as easy to demonstrate and is not within the scope of the middle school.

Rational Roots

One reason it is difficult to comprehend irrational numbers is that we have very little firsthand experience with them. The ones we are most familiar with are roots of numbers. For example, we just noted that students are frequently shown a proof for the irrationality of $\sqrt{2}$. An intuitive notion of that fact is difficult to come by. Most calculators will show only eight to ten digits, requiring a leap of faith to accept that the decimal representation is infinitely long and nonrepeating.

Unfortunately, what can happen is that whenever students see the radical sign, they think the number is irrational. A possible approach is to consider roots from the opposite direction. Rather than ask what is the square root of 64 or the cube root of 27, we might suggest that *every* number is the square root, the cube root, the fourth root, and so on, of some number (3 is the second root of 9, the third root of 27, etc.). From this vantage point, students can see that "square root" is just a way of indicating a relationship between two numbers. That the cube root of 27 is 3 indicates a special relationship between 3 and 27.

 LITERATURE CONNECTIONS

Some topics in this chapter present opportunities for "playing around" with ideas and numbers. Although most teachers in the middle grades do not think of using literature as a springboard for mathematics, here are a few ideas that offer a change of pace in the upper grades.

The Phantom Tollbooth
Juster, 1961

Milo's remarkable journey through the lands beyond the magic tollbooth are so full of wonderful words and ideas that the story is a must to read and discuss with adolescents regardless of the potential mathematical content. But the first page of Chapter 14, with its road sign indicating three directions to Digitopolis, is worthy of time in your mathematics class. The sign reads:

DIGITOPOLIS

5	Miles
1600	Rods
8800	Yards
26,400	Feet
316,800	Inches
633,600	Half inches

AND THEN SOME

The discussion about which road is shorter or quicker is just great. Three pages later, Milo is told, "Why, did you know that if a beaver two feet long with a tail a foot and a half long can build a dam twelve feet high and six feet wide in two days, all you would need to build Boulder Dam is a beaver sixty-eight feet long with a fifty-one foot tail?" (p. 175). In the next chapter is an equally humorous discussion of infinity. That is followed by the chapter in which Milo meets the 0.58 boy.

Not only are these fanciful ideas in a story filled with excellent language, but there are also opportunities to wonder what if or to create similar fantasies based on numbers. For example, students could write a new chapter for the book in which Milo journeys to a world in outer space where the distances are enormous and everyone uses scientific notation.

In One Day
Parker, 1984

This is not literature but an amazing book of 365 facts concerning things that occur in one day in the United States. For example, in one day, Americans "fill in, or at least try to, 50 acres of crossword puzzles" and "buy at least 5 million things that are shaped like Mickey Mouse, or have a picture of Mickey Mouse on them." (That has probably increased since the book was published in 1984.)

It is difficult not to wonder at the amazing numbers in the book. Students may want to test the facts in some way or perhaps do a bit of research to add new facts that interest them. For example, how many footballs are thrown on an average fall day? If there is any interest in finding real-world numbers through some simple research, sharing this book with the class is probably worth the time.

Math Curse
Scieszka and Smith, 1995

This book was an instant hit probably because there are so many people out there who have math phobias. The first page sets the tone: "On Monday in math class Mrs. Fibonacci says, 'You know, you can think of almost everything as a math problem.' On Tuesday I start to have problems." Some may argue that this book is so antimathematics that it has no place in the middle grades. But it does provide an opportunity to show your human side as you discuss a wide range of mathematical ideas. ■

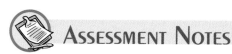

ASSESSMENT NOTES

Middle school teachers frequently get bogged down in the minutiae of their curriculum. Many books emphasize rules and exercises at the expense of opportunities for explorations.

The content of this chapter focuses on your students' mathematical power rather than their acquisition of skills.

For example, the discussion of exponents provides good opportunities to see how students reason, communicate ideas, go beyond the answer to generate their own ideas, and generally do mathematics. Once students have learned the relatively simple definition of what an exponent is, the search for easy tricks for multiplying and dividing should be left to students' discovery and their own reasoning. The discussions that ensue will be better than drilling rules about adding exponents when you multiply numbers with like bases. These are good opportunities to assess mathematical power.

With respect to integers, you have already been warned not to focus on the rules for operations. Certainly, the rules are important. However, if the rules for operating on the integers are developed by the students themselves, not only will students have a deeper understanding, but you will have an opportunity to observe and assess their mathematical power.

Similar comments can be made about fractions and decimal relationships and rational numbers. The development of reasoning ability and students' belief that they can do mathematics is far more important than drilling rules. ■

REfLECTIONS ON CHAPTER 24

Writing to Learn

1. Explain the value of the graphing calculator's ability to display a complete arithmetic expression (with or without a variable) on a single line and to evaluate it on another line.
2. How can a calculator be used to explore the order-of-operations convention? Why is this rule something you must simply tell students?
3. Explain how powers of 10 are used to write very small and very large numbers. What is the particular form of the power-of-10 symbolism used in scientific notation and on calculators? What is the value of this notation?
4. Why is it probably better to use two different models for the integers even if one of the two seems to cause students some confusion?
5. Use both the arrow model and the counter model to demonstrate the following:

   $^-10 + {^+13} = {^+3}$ $^-4 - {^-9} = {^+5}$ $^+6 - {^-7} = {^+13}$

   $^-4 \times {^-3} = {^+12}$ $^+15 \div {^-5} = {^-3}$ $^-12 \div {^-3} = {^+4}$

6. How can you help students understand that a fraction such as $\frac{7}{8}$ means the same thing as $7 \div 8$?
7. How would you explain the difference between a rational and an irrational number to a middle school student?
8. What does $\sqrt{6}$ mean? How is $\sqrt{6}$ different from $\sqrt{4}$? How are they the same?
9. What does it mean to say that the rational numbers are dense?

For Discussion and Exploration

1. A traditional self-contained Algebra I course also groups the content of this chapter with an additional focus on factoring polynomials and other symbolic manipulations. Does your local school system have an Algebra I course in grade 8? Do you think it should? What are some of the pros and cons of a special course?
2. Examine the table of contents in sixth-, seventh-, and eighth-grade books from two or three different publishers or books specifically intended for middle school mathematics. Using these books as a guide, how would you define "prealgebra"? How much of the curriculum of these three grade levels seems repetitious? Is this the same for all publishers?
3. Use a calculator for the following exercises:
   a. What do you think will happen if you enter 1000 in your calculator and then press ⊟ 2 ⊟ ⊟ . . . ? Try it.
   b. What do you think will happen if you enter 1000 in your calculator and then repeatedly press the √ key? Before you try it, try to explain why you think it will happen.

Recommendations for Further Reading
Highly Recommended

Fitzgerald, W., Winter, M. J., Lappan, G., & Phillips, E. (1986). *Middle grades mathematics project: Factors and multiples.* Menlo Park, CA: AWL Supplemental.

This book is one in a series of five that has stood the test of time. The related topics of prime, factor, composite, prime factorization, divisor, multiple, common multiple, common factor, and relatively prime number are all developed in a series of interesting games and activities for the middle grades. The focus is on pattern development and logical connections. This is a good way to involve students in good mathematics without overwhelming them with tedious algebraic ideas.

Graeber, A. O., & Baker, K. M. (1992). Little into big is the way it always is. *Arithmetic Teacher, 39*(8), 18–21.

This is one of the few articles that discuss the issue of a fraction as an indicated division. The authors look at practices in the elementary school that suggest why the difficulty exists and make practical suggestions for working with middle school students.

Phillips, E., Gardella, T., Kelly, C., & Stewart, J. (1991). *Patterns and functions: Addenda series, grades 5–8.* Reston, VA: National Council of Teachers of Mathematics.

Again, the *Addenda Series* is the place to go for excellent activities. In this volume, you will find sections on exponents and growth patterns, number theory and counting patterns, and rational number patterns. Other topics in the book are related more to the concepts of function and variable.

Other Suggestions

Bennett, A., Jr., Maier, E., & Nelson, L. T. (1989). *Modeling integers: Unit 6, Math in the mind's eye.* Salem, OR: Math Learning Center.

Borlaug, V. (1997). Building equations using M&M's. *Mathematics Teaching in the Middle School, 2,* 290–292.

Chalouh, L., & Herscovics, N. (1988). Teaching algebraic expression in a meaningful way. In A. F. Coxford (Ed.), *The ideas of algebra,* K–12 (pp. 33–42). Reston, VA: National Council of Teachers of Mathematics.

Eisen, A. P. (1999). Exploring factor sets with a graphing calculator. *Mathematics Teaching in the Middle School, 5,* 78–82.

Kieran, C., & Chalouh, L. (1993). Prealgebra: The transition from arithmetic to algebra. In D. T. Owens (Ed.), *Research ideas for the classroom: Middle grades mathematics* (pp. 179–198). Old Tappan, NJ: Macmillan.

Martinez, J. G. R. (1988). Helping students understand factors and terms. *Mathematics Teacher, 81,* 747–751.

Martinez, J. G. (2002). Building conceptual bridges from arithmetic to algebra. *Mathematics Teaching in the Middle School, 7,* 326–331.

Patterson, A. C. (1997). Building algebraic expressions: A physical model. *Mathematics Teaching in the Middle School, 2,* 238–242.

Paulos, J. A. (1988). *Innumeracy: Mathematical illiteracy and its consequences.* New York: Hill & Wang.

Rubenstein, R. N. (1996). The function game. *Mathematics Teaching in the Middle School, 2,* 74–78.

Sherard, H. (2000). How big is Bill Gates's fortune? *Mathematics Teaching in the Middle School, 6,* 250–252.

Slavit, D. (2001). Revisiting a difference of squares. *Mathematics Teaching in the Middle School, 6,* 378–381.

Sobel, M. A., & Maletsky, E. M. (1995). *Teaching mathematics: A sourcebook of aids, activities, and strategies* (3rd ed.). Upper Saddle River, NJ: Prentice Hall.

Stacey, K., & MacGregor, M. (1997). Building foundations for algebra. *Mathematics Teaching in the Middle School, 2,* 253–260.

Steinberg, R. M., Sleeman, D. H., & Ktorza, D. (1990). Algebra students' knowledge of equivalence of equations. *Journal for Research in Mathematics Education, 22,* 112–121.

appendix

A

Content Standards and Grade Level Expectations

Principles and Standards for School Mathematics

Source: Reprinted with permission from *Principles and Standards for School Mathematics*. Copyright ©2000 by the National Council of Teachers of Mathematics. All rights reserved.

Number and Operations

STANDARD

Instructional programs from prekindergarten through grade 12 should enable all students to—

	Pre-K–2	Grades 3–5
	Expectations In prekindergarten through grade 2 all students should—	**Expectations** In grades 3–5 all students should—
Understand numbers, ways of representing numbers, relationships among numbers, and number systems	• count with understanding and recognize "how many" in sets of objects; • use multiple models to develop initial understandings of place value and the base-ten number system; • develop understanding of the relative position and magnitude of whole numbers and of ordinal and cardinal numbers and their connections; • develop a sense of whole numbers and represent and use them in flexible ways, including relating, composing, and decomposing numbers; • connect number words and numerals to the quantities they represent, using various physical models and representations; • understand and represent commonly used fractions, such as 1/4, 1/3, and 1/2.	• understand the place-value structure of the base-ten number system and be able to represent and compare whole numbers and decimals; • recognize equivalent representations for the same number and generate them by decomposing and composing numbers; • develop understanding of fractions as parts of unit wholes, as parts of a collection, as locations on number lines, and as divisions of whole numbers; • use models, benchmarks, and equivalent forms to judge the size of fractions; • recognize and generate equivalent forms of commonly used fractions, decimals, and percents; • explore numbers less than 0 by extending the number line and through familiar applications; • describe classes of numbers according to characteristics such as the nature of their factors.
Understand meanings of operations and how they relate to one another	• understand various meanings of addition and subtraction of whole numbers and the relationship between the two operations; • understand the effects of adding and subtracting whole numbers; • understand situations that entail multiplication and division, such as equal groupings of objects and sharing equally.	• understand various meanings of multiplication and division; • understand the effects of multiplying and dividing whole numbers; • identify and use relationships between operations, such as division as the inverse of multiplication, to solve problems; • understand and use properties of operations, such as the distributivity of multiplication over addition.
Compute fluently and make reasonable estimates	• develop and use strategies for whole-number computations, with a focus on addition and subtraction; • develop fluency with basic number combinations for addition and subtraction; • use a variety of methods and tools to compute, including objects, mental computation, estimation, paper and pencil, and calculators.	• develop fluency with basic number combinations for multiplication and division and use these combinations to mentally compute related problems, such as 30 × 50; • develop fluency in adding, subtracting, multiplying, and dividing whole numbers; • develop and use strategies to estimate the results of whole-number computations and to judge the reasonableness of such results; • develop and use strategies to estimate computations involving fractions and decimals in situations relevant to students' experience; • use visual models, benchmarks, and equivalent forms to add and subtract commonly used fractions and decimals; • select appropriate methods and tools for computing with whole numbers from among mental computation, estimation, calculators, and paper and pencil according to the context and nature of the computation and use the selected method or tool.

Number and Operations

STANDARD

Instructional programs from prekindergarten through grade 12 should enable all students to—

	Grades 6–8	Grades 9–12
	Expectations	**Expectations**
	In grades 6–8 all students should—	In grades 9–12 all students should—
Understand numbers, ways of representing numbers, relationships among numbers, and number systems	• work flexibly with fractions, decimals, and percents to solve problems; • compare and order fractions, decimals, and percents efficiently and find their approximate locations on a number line; • develop meaning for percents greater than 100 and less than 1; • understand and use ratios and proportions to represent quantitative relationships; • develop an understanding of large numbers and recognize and appropriately use exponential, scientific, and calculator notation; • use factors, multiples, prime factorization, and relatively prime numbers to solve problems; • develop meaning for integers and represent and compare quantities with them.	• develop a deeper understanding of very large and very small numbers and of various representations of them; • compare and contrast the properties of numbers and number systems, including the rational and real numbers, and understand complex numbers as solutions to quadratic equations that do not have real solutions; • understand vectors and matrices as systems that have some of the properties of the real-number system; • use number-theory arguments to justify relationships involving whole numbers.
Understand meanings of operations and how they relate to one another	• understand the meaning and effects of arithmetic operations with fractions, decimals, and integers; • use the associative and commutative properties of addition and multiplication and the distributive property of multiplication over addition to simplify computations with integers, fractions, and decimals; • understand and use the inverse relationships of addition and subtraction, multiplication and division, and squaring and finding square roots to simplify computations and solve problems.	• judge the effects of such operations as multiplication, division, and computing powers and roots on the magnitudes of quantities; • develop an understanding of properties of, and representations for, the addition and multiplication of vectors and matrices; • develop an understanding of permutations and combinations as counting techniques.
Compute fluently and make reasonable estimates	• select appropriate methods and tools for computing with fractions and decimals from among mental computation, estimation, calculators or computers, and paper and pencil, depending on the situation, and apply the selected methods; • develop and analyze algorithms for computing with fractions, decimals, and integers and develop fluency in their use; • develop and use strategies to estimate the results of rational-number computations and judge the reasonableness of the results; • develop, analyze, and explain methods for solving problems involving proportions, such as scaling and finding equivalent ratios.	• develop fluency in operations with real numbers, vectors, and matrices, using mental computation or paper-and-pencil calculations for simple cases and technology for more-complicated cases; • judge the reasonableness of numerical computations and their results.

Algebra

STANDARD

Instructional programs from prekindergarten through grade 12 should enable all students to—

	Pre-K–2	Grades 3–5
	Expectations	**Expectations**
	In prekindergarten through grade 2 all students should—	In grades 3–5 all students should—
Understand patterns, relations, and functions	• sort, classify, and order objects by size, number, and other properties; • recognize, describe, and extend patterns such as sequences of sounds and shapes or simple numeric patterns and translate from one representation to another; • analyze how both repeating and growing patterns are generated.	• describe, extend, and make generalizations about geometric and numeric patterns; • represent and analyze patterns and functions, using words, tables, and graphs.
Represent and analyze mathematical situations and structures using algebraic symbols	• illustrate general principles and properties of operations, such as commutativity, using specific numbers; • use concrete, pictorial, and verbal representations to develop an understanding of invented and conventional symbolic notations.	• identify such properties as commutativity, associativity, and distributivity and use them to compute with whole numbers; • represent the idea of a variable as an unknown quantity using a letter or a symbol; • express mathematical relationships using equations.
Use mathematical models to represent and understand quantitative relationships	• model situations that involve the addition and subtraction of whole numbers, using objects, pictures, and symbols.	• model problem situations with objects and use representations such as graphs, tables, and equations to draw conclusions.
Analyze change in various contexts	• describe qualitative change, such as a student's growing taller; • describe quantitative change, such as a student's growing two inches in one year.	• investigate how a change in one variable relates to a change in a second variable; • identify and describe situations with constant or varying rates of change and compare them.

Algebra

STANDARD

Instructional programs from prekindergarten through grade 12 should enable all students to—

	Grades 6–8	Grades 9–12
	Expectations	**Expectations**
	In grades 6–8 all students should—	In grades 9–12 all students should—
Understand patterns, relations, and functions	• represent, analyze, and generalize a variety of patterns with tables, graphs, words, and, when possible, symbolic rules; • relate and compare different forms of representation for a relationship; • identify functions as linear or nonlinear and contrast their properties from tables, graphs, or equations.	• generalize patterns using explicitly defined and recursively defined functions; • understand relations and functions and select, convert flexibly among, and use various representations for them; • analyze functions of one variable by investigating rates of change, intercepts, zeros, asymptotes, and local and global behavior; • understand and perform transformations such as arithmetically combining, composing, and inverting commonly used functions, using technology to perform such operations on more-complicated symbolic expressions; • understand and compare the properties of classes of functions, including exponential, polynomial, rational, logarithmic, and periodic functions; • interpret representations of functions of two variables.
Represent and analyze mathematical situations and structures using algebraic symbols	• develop an initial conceptual understanding of different uses of variables; • explore relationships between symbolic expressions and graphs of lines, paying particular attention to the meaning of intercept and slope; • use symbolic algebra to represent situations and to solve problems, especially those that involve linear relationships; • recognize and generate equivalent forms for simple algebraic expressions and solve linear equations.	• understand the meaning of equivalent forms of expressions, equations, inequalities, and relations; • write equivalent forms of equations, inequalities, and systems of equations and solve them with fluency—mentally or with paper and pencil in simple cases and using technology in all cases; • use symbolic algebra to represent and explain mathematical relationships; • use a variety of symbolic representations, including recursive and parametric equations, for functions and relations; • judge the meaning, utility, and reasonableness of the results of symbol manipulations, including those carried out by technology.
Use mathematical models to represent and understand quantitative relationships	• model and solve contextualized problems using various representations, such as graphs, tables, and equations.	• identify essential quantitative relationships in a situation and determine the class or classes of functions that might model the relationships; • use symbolic expressions, including iterative and recursive forms, to represent relationships arising from various contexts; • draw reasonable conclusions about a situation being modeled.
Analyze change in various contexts	• use graphs to analyze the nature of changes in quantities in linear relationships.	• approximate and interpret rates of change from graphical and numerical data.

Geometry

STANDARD

Instructional programs from prekindergarten through grade 12 should enable all students to—

	Pre-K–2	Grades 3–5
	Expectations	**Expectations**
	In prekindergarten through grade 2 all students should—	In grades 3–5 all students should—
Analyze characteristics and properties of two- and three-dimensional geometric shapes and develop mathematical arguments about geometric relationships	• recognize, name, build, draw, compare, and sort two- and three-dimensional shapes; • describe attributes and parts of two- and three-dimensional shapes; • investigate and predict the results of putting together and taking apart two- and three-dimensional shapes.	• identify, compare, and analyze attributes of two- and three-dimensional shapes and develop vocabulary to describe the attributes; • classify two- and three-dimensional shapes according to their properties and develop definitions of classes of shapes such as triangles and pyramids; • investigate, describe, and reason about the results of subdividing, combining, and transforming shapes; • explore congruence and similarity; • make and test conjectures about geometric properties and relationships and develop logical arguments to justify conclusions.
Specify locations and describe spatial relationships using coordinate geometry and other representational systems	• describe, name, and interpret relative positions in space and apply ideas about relative position; • describe, name, and interpret direction and distance in navigating space and apply ideas about direction and distance; • find and name locations with simple relationships such as "near to" and in coordinate systems such as maps.	• describe location and movement using common language and geometric vocabulary; • make and use coordinate systems to specify locations and to describe paths; • find the distance between points along horizontal and vertical lines of a coordinate system.
Apply transformations and use symmetry to analyze mathematical situations	• recognize and apply slides, flips, and turns; • recognize and create shapes that have symmetry.	• predict and describe the results of sliding, flipping, and turning two-dimensional shapes; • describe a motion or a series of motions that will show that two shapes are congruent; • identify and describe line and rotational symmetry in two- and three-dimensional shapes and designs.
Use visualization, spatial reasoning, and geometric modeling to solve problems	• create mental images of geometric shapes using spatial memory and spatial visualization; • recognize and represent shapes from different perspectives; • relate ideas in geometry to ideas in number and measurement; • recognize geometric shapes and structures in the environment and specify their location.	• build and draw geometric objects; • create and describe mental images of objects, patterns, and paths; • identify and build a three-dimensional object from two-dimensional representations of that object; • identify and build a two-dimensional representation of a three-dimensional object; • use geometric models to solve problems in other areas of mathematics, such as number and measurement; • recognize geometric ideas and relationships and apply them to other disciplines and to problems that arise in the classroom or in everyday life.

Geometry

STANDARD

Instructional programs from prekindergarten through grade 12 should enable all students to—

	Grades 6–8	Grades 9–12
	Expectations	**Expectations**
	In grades 6–8 all students should—	In grades 9–12 all students should—
Analyze characteristics and properties of two- and three-dimensional geometric shapes and develop mathematical arguments about geometric relationships	• precisely describe, classify, and understand relationships among types of two- and three-dimensional objects using their defining properties; • understand relationships among the angles, side lengths, perimeters, areas, and volumes of similar objects; • create and critique inductive and deductive arguments concerning geometric ideas and relationships, such as congruence, similarity, and the Pythagorean relationship.	• analyze properties and determine attributes of two- and three-dimensional objects; • explore relationships (including congruence and similarity) among classes of two- and three-dimensional geometric objects, make and test conjectures about them, and solve problems involving them; • establish the validity of geometric conjectures using deduction, prove theorems, and critique arguments made by others; • use trigonometric relationships to determine lengths and angle measures.
Specify locations and describe spatial relationships using coordinate geometry and other representational systems	• use coordinate geometry to represent and examine the properties of geometric shapes; • use coordinate geometry to examine special geometric shapes, such as regular polygons or those with pairs of parallel or perpendicular sides.	• use Cartesian coordinates and other coordinate systems, such as navigational, polar, or spherical systems, to analyze geometric situations; • investigate conjectures and solve problems involving two- and three-dimensional objects represented with Cartesian coordinates.
Apply transformations and use symmetry to analyze mathematical situations	• describe sizes, positions, and orientations of shapes under informal transformations such as flips, turns, slides, and scaling; • examine the congruence, similarity, and line or rotational symmetry of objects using transformations.	• understand and represent translations, reflections, rotations, and dilations of objects in the plane by using sketches, coordinates, vectors, function notation, and matrices; • use various representations to help understand the effects of simple transformations and their compositions.
Use visualization, spatial reasoning, and geometric modeling to solve problems	• draw geometric objects with specified properties, such as side lengths or angle measures; • use two-dimensional representations of three-dimensional objects to visualize and solve problems such as those involving surface area and volume; • use visual tools such as networks to represent and solve problems; • use geometric models to represent and explain numerical and algebraic relationships; • recognize and apply geometric ideas and relationships in areas outside the mathematics classroom, such as art, science, and everyday life.	• draw and construct representations of two- and three-dimensional geometric objects using a variety of tools; • visualize three-dimensional objects from different perspectives and analyze their cross sections; • use vertex-edge graphs to model and solve problems; • use geometric models to gain insights into, and answer questions in, other areas of mathematics; • use geometric ideas to solve problems in, and gain insights into, other disciplines and other areas of interest such as art and architecture.

Measurement

STANDARD

Instructional programs from prekindergarten through grade 12 should enable all students to—

Understand measurable attributes of objects and the units, systems, and processes of measurement

Apply appropriate techniques, tools, and formulas to determine measurements

Pre-K–2

Expectations

In prekindergarten through grade 2 all students should—

- recognize the attributes of length, volume, weight, area, and time;
- compare and order objects according to these attributes;
- understand how to measure using nonstandard and standard units;
- select an appropriate unit and tool for the attribute being measured.

- measure with multiple copies of units of the same size, such as paper clips laid end to end;
- use repetition of a single unit to measure something larger than the unit, for instance, measuring the length of a room with a single meterstick;
- use tools to measure;
- develop common referents for measures to make comparisons and estimates.

Grades 3–5

Expectations

In grades 3–5 all students should—

- understand such attributes as length, area, weight, volume, and size of angle and select the appropriate type of unit for measuring each attribute;
- understand the need for measuring with standard units and become familiar with standard units in the customary and metric systems;
- carry out simple unit conversions, such as from centimeters to meters, within a system of measurement;
- understand that measurements are approximations and understand how differences in units affect precision;
- explore what happens to measurements of a two-dimensional shape such as its perimeter and area when the shape is changed in some way.

- develop strategies for estimating the perimeters, areas, and volumes of irregular shapes;
- select and apply appropriate standard units and tools to measure length, area, volume, weight, time, temperature, and the size of angles;
- select and use benchmarks to estimate measurements;
- develop, understand, and use formulas to find the area of rectangles and related triangles and parallelograms;
- develop strategies to determine the surface areas and volumes of rectangular solids.

Measurement

STANDARD

Instructional programs from prekindergarten through grade 12 should enable all students to—

	Grades 6–8	Grades 9–12
	Expectations	**Expectations**
	In grades 6–8 all students should—	In grades 9–12 all students should—
Understand measurable attributes of objects and the units, systems, and processes of measurement	• understand both metric and customary systems of measurement; • understand relationships among units and convert from one unit to another within the same system; • understand, select, and use units of appropriate size and type to measure angles, perimeter, area, surface area, and volume.	• make decisions about units and scales that are appropriate for problem situations involving measurement.
Apply appropriate techniques, tools, and formulas to determine measurements	• use common benchmarks to select appropriate methods for estimating measurements; • select and apply techniques and tools to accurately find length, area, volume, and angle measures to appropriate levels of precision; • develop and use formulas to determine the circumference of circles and the area of triangles, parallelograms, trapezoids, and circles and develop strategies to find the area of more-complex shapes; • develop strategies to determine the surface area and volume of selected prisms, pyramids, and cylinders; • solve problems involving scale factors, using ratio and proportion; • solve simple problems involving rates and derived measurements for such attributes as velocity and density.	• analyze precision, accuracy, and approximate error in measurement situations; • understand and use formulas for the area, surface area, and volume of geometric figures, including cones, spheres, and cylinders; • apply informal concepts of successive approximation, upper and lower bounds, and limit in measurement situations; • use unit analysis to check measurement computations.

Data Analysis and Probability

STANDARD

Instructional programs from prekindergarten through grade 12 should enable all students to—

Pre-K–2

Expectations

In prekindergarten through grade 2 all students should—

Grades 3–5

Expectations

In grades 3–5 all students should—

STANDARD	Pre-K–2 Expectations	Grades 3–5 Expectations
Formulate questions that can be addressed with data and collect, organize, and display relevant data to answer them	• pose questions and gather data about themselves and their surroundings; • sort and classify objects according to their attributes and organize data about the objects; • represent data using concrete objects, pictures, and graphs.	• design investigations to address a question and consider how data-collection methods affect the nature of the data set; • collect data using observations, surveys, and experiments; • represent data using tables and graphs such as line plots, bar graphs, and line graphs; • recognize the differences in representing categorical and numerical data.
Select and use appropriate statistical methods to analyze data	• describe parts of the data and the set of data as a whole to determine what the data show.	• describe the shape and important features of a set of data and compare related data sets, with an emphasis on how the data are distributed; • use measures of center, focusing on the median, and understand what each does and does not indicate about the data set; • compare different representations of the same data and evaluate how well each representation shows important aspects of the data.
Develop and evaluate inferences and predictions that are based on data	• discuss events related to students' experiences as likely or unlikely.	• propose and justify conclusions and predictions that are based on data and design studies to further investigate the conclusions or predictions.
Understand and apply basic concepts of probability		• describe events as likely or unlikely and discuss the degree of likelihood using such words as certain, equally likely, and impossible; • predict the probability of outcomes of simple experiments and test the predictions; • understand that the measure of the likelihood of an event can be represented by a number from 0 to 1.

Data Analysis and Probability

STANDARD

Instructional programs from prekindergarten through grade 12 should enable all students to—

	Grades 6–8	Grades 9–12
	Expectations	**Expectations**
	In grades 6–8 all students should—	In grades 9–12 all students should—
Formulate questions that can be addressed with data and collect, organize, and display relevant data to answer them	• formulate questions, design studies, and collect data about a characteristic shared by two populations or different characteristics within one population; • select, create, and use appropriate graphical representations of data, including histograms, box plots, and scatterplots.	• understand the differences among various kinds of studies and which types of inferences can legitimately be drawn from each; • know the characteristics of well-designed studies, including the role of randomization in surveys and experiments; • understand the meaning of measurement data and categorical data, of univariate and bivariate data, and of the term variable; • understand histograms, parallel box plots, and scatterplots and use them to display data; • compute basic statistics and understand the distinction between a statistic and a parameter.
Select and use appropriate statistical methods to analyze data	• find, use, and interpret measures of center and spread, including mean and interquartile range; • discuss and understand the correspondence between data sets and their graphical representations, especially histograms, stem-and-leaf plots, box plots, and scatterplots.	• for univariate measurement data, be able to display the distribution, describe its shape, and select and calculate summary statistics; • for bivariate measurement data, be able to display a scatterplot, describe its shape, and determine regression coefficients, regression equations, and correlation coefficients using technological tools; • display and discuss bivariate data where at least one variable is categorical; • recognize how linear transformations of univariate data affect shape, center, and spread; • identify trends in bivariate data and find functions that model the data or transform the data so that they can be modeled.
Develop and evaluate inferences and predictions that are based on data	• use observations about differences between two or more samples to make conjectures about the populations from which the samples were taken; • make conjectures about possible relationships between two characteristics of a sample on the basis of scatterplots of the data and approximate lines of fit; • use conjectures to formulate new questions and plan new studies to answer them.	• use simulations to explore the variability of sample statistics from a known population and to construct sampling distributions; • understand how sample statistics reflect the values of population parameters and use sampling distributions as the basis for informal inference; • evaluate published reports that are based on data by examining the design of the study, the appropriateness of the data analysis, and the validity of conclusions; • understand how basic statistical techniques are used to monitor process characteristics in the workplace.
Understand and apply basic concepts of probability	• understand and use appropriate terminology to describe complementary and mutually exclusive events; • use proportionality and a basic understanding of probability to make and test conjectures about the results of experiments and simulations; • compute probabilities for simple compound events, using such methods as organized lists, tree diagrams, and area models.	• understand the concepts of sample space and probability distribution and construct sample spaces and distributions in simple cases; • use simulations to construct empirical probability distributions; • compute and interpret the expected value of random variables in simple cases; • understand the concepts of conditional probability and independent events; • understand how to compute the probability of a compound event.

Professional Standards for Teaching Mathematics

Teaching Standards

Source: From *Professional Standards for Teaching Mathematics.* Copyright ©1991 by the National Council of Teachers of Mathematics. Used by permission.

Teaching Standards

1. Worthwhile Mathematical Tasks

The teacher of mathematics should pose tasks that are based on

- Sound and significant mathematics
- Knowledge of students' understandings, interests, and experiences
- Knowledge of the range of ways that diverse students learn mathematics

and that

- Engage students' intellect
- Develop students' mathematical understandings and skills
- Stimulate students to make connections and develop a coherent framework for mathematical ideas
- Call for problem formulation, problem solving, and mathematical reasoning
- Promote communication about mathematics
- Represent mathematics as an ongoing human activity
- Display sensitivity to, and draw on, students' diverse background experiences and dispositions
- Promote the development of all students' dispositions to do mathematics

2. Teacher's Role in Discourse

The teacher of mathematics should orchestrate discourse by

- Posing questions and tasks that elicit, engage, and challenge each student's thinking
- Listening carefully to students' ideas
- Asking students to clarify and justify their ideas orally and in writing
- Deciding what to pursue in depth from among the ideas that students bring up during a discussion
- Deciding when and how to attach mathematical notation and language to students' ideas
- Deciding when to provide information, when to clarify an issue, when to model, when to lead, and when to let a student struggle with a difficulty
- Monitoring students' participation in discussions and deciding when and how to encourage each student to participate

3. Students' Role in Discourse

The teacher of mathematics should promote classroom discourse in which students

- Listen to, respond to, and question the teacher and one another
- Use a variety of tools to reason, make connections, solve problems, and communicate
- Initiate problems and questions
- Make conjectures and present solutions
- Explore examples and counterexamples to investigate a conjecture
- Try to convince themselves and one another of the validity of particular representations, solutions, conjectures, and answers
- Rely on mathematical evidence and argument to determine validity

4. Tools for Enhancing Discourse

The teacher of mathematics, in order to enhance discourse, should encourage and accept the use of

- Computers, calculators, and other technology
- Concrete materials used as models
- Pictures, diagrams, tables, and graphs
- Invented and conventional terms and symbols
- Metaphors, analogies, and stories
- Written hypotheses, explanations, and arguments
- Oral presentations and dramatizations

5. Learning Environment

The teacher of mathematics should create a learning environment that fosters the development of each student's mathematical power by

- Providing and structuring the time necessary to explore sound mathematics and grapple with significant ideas and problems
- Using the physical space and materials in ways that facilitate students' learning of mathematics
- Providing a context that encourages the development of mathematical skill and proficiency
- Respecting and valuing students' ideas, ways of thinking, and mathematical dispositions

and by consistently expecting and encouraging students to

- Work independently or collaboratively to make sense of mathematics
- Take intellectual risks by raising questions and formulating conjectures
- Display a sense of mathematical competence by validating and supporting ideas with mathematical argument

6. Analysis of Teaching and Learning

The teacher of mathematics should engage in ongoing analysis of teaching and learning by

- Observing, listening to, and gathering other information about students to assess what they are learning
- Examining effects of the tasks, discourse, and learning environment on students' mathematical knowledge, skills, and dispositions

in order to

- Ensure that every student is learning sound and significant mathematics and is developing a positive disposition toward mathematics
- Challenge and extend students' ideas
- Adapt or change activities while teaching
- Make plans, both short- and long-range
- Describe and comment on each student's learning to parents and administrators, as well as to the students themselves

Guide to Blackline Masters

This Appendix contains images of all of the Blackline Masters that are listed below. The actual masters can be found in either of two places:

- In hard copy at the end of the Field Experience Guide
- On the Companion Web Site (www.ablongman.com/vandewalle5e)

Dot cards   1–6
Five-frame   7
Ten-frame   8
Double ten-frame   9
10 × 10 multiplication array   10
Missing-part blanks   11
Base-ten materials grid   12
Hundreds master for bean stick base-ten pieces   13
Little ten-frames   14–15
Place-value mat (with ten-frames)   16
Base-ten grid paper   17
Addition and subtraction record blanks   18
Multiplication and division record blanks   19
Blank hundreds chart (10 × 10 square)   20
Hundreds chart   21
Four small hundreds charts   22
Circular fraction pieces   23–25
10 × 10 grids   26
Hundredths disk   27
10,000 grid   28
Degrees and wedges   29
2-cm square grid   30
1-cm square grid   31
0.5-cm square grid   32
1-cm square dot grid   33
2-cm isometric grid   34
1-cm isometric dot grid   35
1-cm square/diagonal grid   36
Assorted shapes   37–43
Coordinate grid   44
Geoboard pattern   45
Geoboard recording sheets   46
Tangrams and Mosaic Puzzle   47
Motion Man   48–49
Property lists for quadrilaterals   50–53
Assorted triangles   54
Woozle Cards   55

Suggestions for Use and Construction of Materials

Card Stock Materials

A good way to have many materials made quickly and easily for students is to have them duplicated on card stock at a photocopy store. Card stock is a heavy paper that comes in a variety of colors. It is also called *cover stock* or *index stock*. The price is about twice that of paper.

Card stock can be laminated and then cut into smaller pieces, if desired. The laminate adheres very well. Laminate first, and then cut into pieces afterward. Otherwise you will need to cut each piece twice.

Materials are best kept in plastic bags with zip-type closures. Freezer bags are recommended for durability. Punch a hole near the top of the bag so that you do not store air. Lots of small bags can be stuffed into the largest bags. You can always see what you have stored in the bags.

The following list is a suggestion for materials that can be made from card stock using the masters in this section. Quantity suggestions are also given.

Dot Cards

One complete set of cards will serve four to six children. Duplicate each set in a different color so that mixed sets can be separated easily. Laminate and then cut with a paper cutter.

Five-Frames and Ten-Frames

Five-frames and ten-frames are best duplicated on light-colored card stock. Do not laminate; if you do, the mats will curl and counters will slide around.

10 × 10 Multiplication Array

Make one per student in any color. Lamination is suggested. Provide each student with an L-shaped piece of tagboard.

Base-Ten Pieces (Centimeter Grid)

Use the grid (number 11) to make a master as directed. Run copies on white card stock. One sheet will make 4 hundreds and 10 tens or 4 hundreds and a lot of ones. Mount the printed card stock on white poster board using either a dry-mount press or permanent spray adhesive. (Spray adhesive can be purchased in art supply stores. It is very effective but messy to handle.) Cut into pieces with a paper cutter. For the tens and ones pieces, it is recommended that you mount the index stock onto *mount board* or *illustration board,* also available in art supply stores. This material is thicker and will make the pieces easier to handle. It is recommended that you *not* laminate the base-ten pieces. A kit consisting of 10 hundreds, 30 tens, and 30 ones is adequate for each student or pair of students.

Bean Stick Base-Ten Pieces

Use dried beans (great northern, pinto, etc.) to make bean sticks. Craft sticks can be purchased in craft stores in boxes of 500. Use white glue (such as Elmer's) or a glue gun. Also dribble a row of glue over the beans to keep them from splitting off the sticks. (The white glue dries clear.) For hundreds, use the master mounted on poster board.

Little Ten-Frames

There are two masters for these materials. One has full ten-frames and the other has 1 to 9 dots, including two with 5 dots. Copy the 1-to-9 master on one color of card stock and the full ten-frames on another. Cut off most of the excess stock (do not trim) and then laminate. Cut into little ten-frames. Each set consists of 20 pieces: 10 full ten-frames and 10 of the 1-to-9 pieces, including 2 fives. Make a set for each child.

Place-Value Mat (with Ten-Frames)

Mats can be duplicated on any pastel card stock. It is recommended that you not laminate these because they tend to curl and counters slide around too much. Make one for every child.

Circular Fraction Pieces

First make three copies of each page of the master. Cut the disks apart and tape onto blank pages with three of the same type on a page. You will then have a separate master for each size with three full circles per master. Duplicate each master on a different color card stock. Laminate and then cut the circles out. A kit for one or two students should have two circles of each size piece.

Hundredths Disk

These disks can be made on paper but are much more satisfying on card stock. Duplicate the master on two contrasting colors. Laminate and cut the circles and also the slot on the dotted line. Make a set for each student. It's easy and worthwhile.

Tangrams and Mosaic Puzzle

Both tangrams and the Mosaic Puzzle should be copied on card stock. For younger children, the card stock should first be mounted on poster board to make the pieces a bit thicker and easier to put together in puzzles. You will want one set of each per student.

Woozle Cards

Copy the Woozle Card master on white or off-white card stock. You need two copies per set. Before laminating, color one set one color and the other a different color. An easy way to color the cards is to make one pass around the inside of each Woozle, leaving the rest of the creature white. If you color the entire Woozle, the dots may not show up. Make one set for every four students.

Transparencies and Overhead Models

A copy of any page can be made into a transparency with a photocopier.

Some masters make fine transparency mats to use for demonstration purposes on the overhead. The 10 × 10 array, the blank hundreds board, and the large geoboard are examples. The five-frame and ten-frame work well with counters. The place-value mat can be used with strips and squares or with counters and cups directly on the overhead. The missing-part blank and the record blanks for the four algorithms are pages that you may wish to use as write-on transparencies.

A transparency of the 10,000 grid is the easiest way there is to show 10,000 or to model four-place decimal numbers.

A transparency of the degrees and wedges page is the very best way to illustrate what a degree is and also to help explain protractors.

All of the line and dot grids are useful to have available as transparencies. You may find it a good idea to make several copies of each and keep them in a folder where you can get to them easily.

For the Woozle Cards, dot cards, little ten-frames, and assorted shapes, make a reduction of the master on a photocopy machine. Then make transparencies of the small cards, cut them apart, and use them on the overhead.

Dot cards—1

Dot cards—2

Dot cards—3

Dot cards—4

Dot cards—5

Dot cards—6

Five-frame—7

Ten-frame—8

Double ten-frame—9

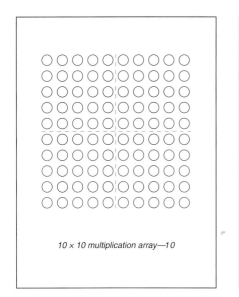

10 × 10 multiplication array—10

Missing-part blanks—11

Base-ten materials grid—12

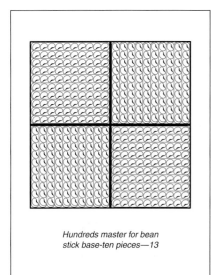

Hundreds master for bean stick base-ten pieces—13

Little ten-frames—14

Little ten-frames—15

Place-value mat (with ten-frames)—16

Base-ten grid paper—17

Addition and subtraction record blanks—18

Multiplication and division record blanks—19

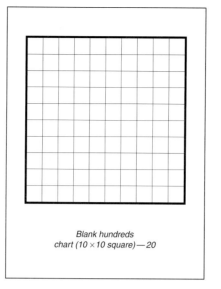

Blank hundreds chart (10 × 10 square)—20

Hundreds chart—21

Four small hundreds charts—22

Circular fraction pieces—23

Circular fraction pieces—24

Circular fraction pieces—25

10 × 10 grids—26

Hundredths disk—27

10,000 grid—28

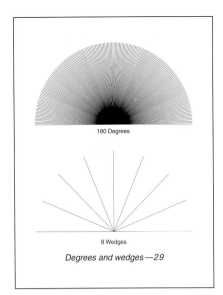

180 Degrees

8 Wedges

Degrees and wedges—29

2-cm square grid—30

1-cm square grid—31

0.5-cm square grid—32

1-cm square dot grid—33

2-cm isometric grid—34

1-cm isometric dot grid—35

1-cm square/diagonal grid—36

Assorted shapes—37 through 43

Coordinate grid—44

Geoboard pattern—45

Geoboard recording sheets—46

Tangrams and Mosaic Puzzle—47

Motion Man—48

Motion Man—49

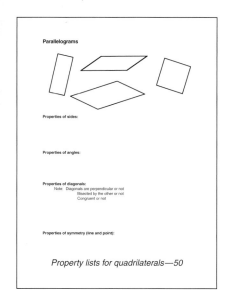

Parallelograms

Properties of sides:

Properties of angles:

Properties of diagonals:
Note: Diagonals are perpendicular or not
Bisected by the other or not
Congruent or not

Properties of symmetry (line and point):

Property lists for quadrilaterals—50

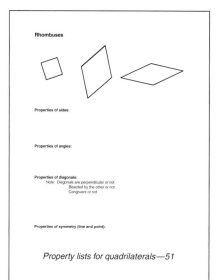

Rhombuses

Properties of sides:

Properties of angles:

Properties of diagonals:
Note: Diagonals are perpendicular or not
Bisected by the other or not
Congruent or not

Properties of symmetry (line and point):

Property lists for quadrilaterals—51

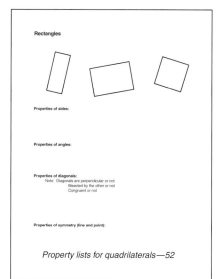

Rectangles

Properties of sides:

Properties of angles:

Properties of diagonals:
Note: Diagonals are perpendicular or not
Bisected by the other or not
Congruent or not

Properties of symmetry (line and point):

Property lists for quadrilaterals—52

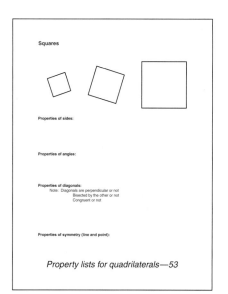

Squares

Properties of sides:

Properties of angles:

Properties of diagonals:
Note: Diagonals are perpendicular or not
Bisected by the other or not
Congruent or not

Properties of symmetry (line and point):

Property lists for quadrilaterals—53

Assorted triangles—54

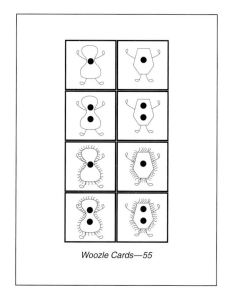

Woozle Cards—55

References

Anderson, B. J. (1990). Minorities and mathematics: The new frontier and challenge of the nineties. *Journal of Negro Education, 59*(3), 260–271.

Ann Arbor Public Schools. (1993). *Alternative assessment: Evaluating student performance in elementary mathematics.* Palo Alto, CA: Dale Seymour.

Ansell, E., & Doerr, H. M. (2000). NAEP findings regarding gender: Achievement, affect, and instructional experiences. In E. A. Silver & P. A Kenney (Eds.), *Results from the seventh mathematics assessment of the National Assessment of Educational Progress* (pp. 73–106). Reston, VA: National Council of Teachers of Mathematics.

ARC Center (2002). *The ARC tri-state student achievement study* [on-line]. Available: www.comap/elementary/projects/arc/

Ashcraft, M. H., & Christy, K. S. (1995). The frequency of arithmetic facts in elementary texts: Addition and multiplication in grades 1–6. *Journal for Research in Mathematics Education, 26,* 396–421.

Austin, R., & Thompson, D. (1997). Exploring algebraic patterns through literature. *Mathematics Teaching in the Middle School, 2,* 274–281.

Babcock, J. E. (1998). *U.S. TIMSS Report No. 8.* East Lansing, MI: TIMSS U.S. National Research Center, Michigan State University.

Backhouse, J., Haggarty, L., Pirie, S., & Stratton, J. (1992). *Improving the learning of mathematics.* Portsmouth, NH: Heinemann.

Baek, J. (1998). Children's invented algorithms for multidigit multiplication problems. In L. J. Morrow (Ed.), *The teaching and learning of algorithms in school mathematics* (pp. 151–160). Reston, VA: National Council of Teachers of Mathematics.

Baker, A., & Baker, J. (1991). *Maths in the mind: A process approach to mental strategies.* Portsmouth, NH: Heinemann.

Baker, J., & Baker, A. (1990). *Mathematics in process.* Portsmouth, NH: Heinemann.

Ball, D. L. (1992). Magical hopes: Manipulatives and the reform of math education. *American Educator 16*(2), 14–18, 46–47.

Baratta-Lorton, M. (1976). *Mathematics their way.* Menlo Park, CA: AWL Supplemental.

Baroody, A. J. (1985). Mastery of the basic number combinations: Internalization of relationships or facts? *Journal for Research in Mathematics Education, 16,* 83–98.

Baroody, A. J. (1987). *Children's mathematical thinking: A developmental framework for preschool, primary, and special education teachers.* New York: Teachers College Press.

Baroody, A. J., & Hume, J. (1991). Meaningful mathematics instruction: The case of fractions. *Remedial and Special Education, 12,* 54–68.

Battista, M. C. (1999). The mathematical miseducation of America's youth: Ignoring research and scientific study in education. *Phi Delta Kappan, 80,* 424–433.

Becker, J. R., & Jacobs, J. E. (2001). Introduction. In J. E. Jacobs, J. R. Becker, & G. F. Gilmer (Eds.) *Changing the faces of mathematics: Perspectives on gender* (pp. 1–8). Reston, VA: National Council of Teachers of Mathematics.

Becker, J. P., & Shimada, S. (Eds.). (1997). *The open-ended approach: A new proposal for teaching mathematics.* Reston, VA: National Council of Teachers of Mathematics.

Bell, M. (1998–1999, Winter). Problems with implementing new curricula: The example of the K–6 *Everyday Mathematics* Curriculum. *UCSMP Newsletter, 24,* 1–2.

Bley, N. S. (1994). Accommodating special needs. In C. A. Thornton & N. S. Bley (Eds.), *Windows of opportunity: Mathematics for students with special needs* (pp. 137–163). Reston, VA: National Council of Teachers of Mathematics.

Bley, N. S., & Thornton, C. A. (1995). *Teaching mathematics to students with learning disabilities* (3rd ed.). Austin, TX: Pro-Ed.

Boaler, J. (1998). Open and closed mathematics: Student experiences and understandings. *Journal for Research in Mathematics Education, 29,* 41–62.

Booth, L. R. (1988). Children's difficulties in beginning algebra. In A. F. Coxford (Ed.), *The ideas of algebra, K–12* (pp. 20–32). Reston, VA: National Council of Teachers of Mathematics.

Borasi, R. (1994, April). Implementing the NCTM *Standards* in "inclusive" mainstream classrooms. Presented at the annual meeting of the National Council of Teachers of Mathematics, Indianapolis, IN.

Bresser, R. (1995). *Math and literature (grades 4–6).* White Plains, NY: Cuisenaire (distributor).

Bright, G. W., Behr, M. J., Post, T. R., & Wachsmuth, I. (1988). Identifying fractions on number lines. *Journal for Research in Mathematics Education, 19,* 215–232.

Brooks, J. G., & Brooks, M. G. (1993). *In search of understanding: The case for the constructivist classroom.* Alexandria, VA: Association for Supervision and Curriculum Development.

Brownell, W., & Chazal, C. (1935). The effects of premature drill in third grade arithmetic. *Journal of Educational Research, 29,* 17–28.

Brueningsen, C., Bower, B., Antinone, L., & Brueningsen, E. (1994). *Real-world math with the CBL system: 25 activities using the CBL and TI-82.* Dallas: Texas Instruments.

Burger, W. F. (1985). Geometry. *Arithmetic Teacher, 32*(6), 52–56.

Burns, M. (1982). *Math for smarty pants.* New York: Little, Brown.

Burns, M. (1995a). Timed tests. *Teaching Children Mathematics, 1,* 408–409.

Burns, M. (1995b). *Writing in math class*. White Plains, NY: Cuisenaire (distributor).

Burns, M. (1996). *50 problem-solving lessons: Grades 1–6*. White Plains, NY: Cuisenaire (distributor).

Burns, M. (1999). *Making sense of mathematics: A look toward the twenty-first century*. Presentation at the annual meeting of the National Council of Teachers of Mathematics, San Francisco.

Burns, M. (2000). *About teaching mathematics: A K–8 resource* (2nd ed.). Sausalito, CA: Math Solutions Publications.

Burton, N. (1995). Trends in mathematics achievement for young men and women. In I. M. Carl (Ed.), *Prospects for school mathematics* (pp. 115–130). Reston, VA: National Council of Teachers of Mathematics.

Campbell, P. B. (1995). Redefining the "girl problem in mathematics." In W. G. Secada, E. Fennema, & L. B. Adajian (Eds.), *New directions for equity in mathematics education* (pp. 225–241). New York: Cambridge University Press.

Campbell, P. F. (1996). Empowering children and teachers in the elementary mathematics classrooms of urban schools. *Urban Education, 30,* 449–475.

Campbell, P. F. (1997, April). Children's invented algorithms: Their meaning and place in instruction. Presented at the annual meeting of the National Council of Teachers of Mathematics, Minneapolis, MN.

Campbell, P. F., & Johnson, M. L. (1995). How primary students think and learn. In I. M. Carl (Ed.), *Prospects for school mathematics* (pp. 21–42). Reston, VA: National Council of Teachers of Mathematics.

Campbell, P. F., Rowan, T. E., & Suarez, A. R. (1998). What criteria for student-invented algorithms? In L. J. Morrow (Ed.), *The teaching and learning of algorithms in school mathematics* (pp. 49–55). Reston, VA: National Council of Teachers of Mathematics.

Campione, J. C., Brown, A. L., & Connell, M. L. (1989). Metacognition: On the importance of understanding what you are doing. In R. I. Charles & E. A. Silver (Eds.), *The teaching and assessing of mathematical problem solving* (pp. 93–114). Reston, VA: National Council of Teachers of Mathematics.

Carey, D. A., Fennema, E., Carpenter, T. P., & Franke, M. L. (1995). Equity and mathematics education. In W. G. Secada, E. Fennema, & L. B. Adajian (Eds.), *New directions for equity in mathematics education* (pp. 93–125). New York: Cambridge University Press.

Carpenter, T. P. (1985). Learning to add and subtract: An exercise in problem solving. In E. A. Silver (Ed.), *Teaching and learning mathematical problem solving: Multiple research perspectives* (pp. 17–40). Hillsdale, NJ: Lawrence Erlbaum.

Carpenter, T. P., Ansell, E., Franke, M. L., Fennema, E., & Weisbeck, L. (1993). A study of kindergarten children's problem-solving processes. *Journal for Research in Mathematics Education, 24,* 428–441.

Carpenter, T. P., Carey, D. A., & Kouba, V. L. (1990). A problem-solving approach to the operations. In J. N. Payne (Ed.), *Mathematics for the young child* (pp. 111–131). Reston, VA: National Council of Teachers of Mathematics.

Carpenter, T. P., Fennema, E., Franke, M. L., Levi, L., & Empson, S. B. (1999). *Children's mathematics: Cognitively guided instruction*. Portsmouth, NH: Heinemann.

Carpenter, T. P., Franke, M. L., Jacobs, V. R., Fennema, E., & Empson, S. B. (1998). A longitudinal study of invention and understanding in children's multidigit addition and subtraction. *Journal for Research in Mathematics Education, 29,* 3–20.

Carpenter, T. P., & Moser, J. M. (1983). The acquisition of addition and subtraction concepts. In R. A. Lesh & M. Landau (Eds.), *Acquisition of mathematics concepts and processes* (pp. 7–44). Orlando, FL: Academic Press.

Carroll, W. M. (1996). Use of invented algorithms by second graders in a reform mathematics curriculum. *Journal of Mathematical Behaviour, 15,* 137–150.

Carroll, W. M. (1997). Results of third-grade students in a reform curriculum on the Illinois State Mathematics Test. *Journal for Research in Mathematics Education, 28,* 237–242.

Carroll, W. M., & Porter, D. (1997). Invented strategies can develop meaningful mathematical procedures. *Teaching Children Mathematics, 3,* 370–374.

Chalouh, L., & Herscovics, N. (1988). Teaching algebraic expressions in a meaningful way. In A. F. Coxford (Ed.), *The ideas of algebra, K–12* (pp. 33–42). Reston, VA: National Council of Teachers of Mathematics.

Chambers, D. (1996). Direct modeling and invented procedures: Building on students' informal strategies. *Teaching Children Mathematics, 3,* 92–95.

Charles, R. I., Chancellor, D., Harcourt, L., Moore, D., Schielack, J. F., Van de Walle, J., & Wortzman, R. (1998). *Scott Foresman—Addison Wesley MATH* (Grades K to 5), Glenview, IL: Addison Wesley Longman, Inc.

Charles, R. I., Lester, F. K., Jr., & O'Daffer, P. (1987). *How to evaluate progress in problem solving*. Reston, VA: National Council of Teachers of Mathematics.

Clark, F. B., & Kamii, C. (1996). Identification of multiplicative thinking in children in grades 1–5. *Journal for Research in Mathematics Education, 27,* 41–51.

Clements, D. H., & Battista, M. T. (1990). Constructivist learning and teaching. *Arithmetic Teacher, 38*(1), 34–35.

Clements, D. H., & Battista, M. T. (2001). *Logo and geometry*. Reston, VA: National Council of Teachers of Mathematics.

Cobb, P. (1988). The tension between theories of learning and instruction in mathematics education. *Educational Psychologist, 23,* 87–103.

Coburn, T. G. (1993). *Patterns: Addenda series, grades K–6*. Reston, VA: National Council of Teachers of Mathematics.

Corwin, R. B. (1996). *Talking mathematics: Supporting children's voices*. Portsmouth, NH: Heinemann.

Countryman, J. (1992). *Writing to learn mathematics: Strategies that work, K–12*. Portsmouth, NH: Heinemann.

Cramer, K., & Henry, A. (2002). Using manipulative models to build number sense for addition of fractions. In B. Litwiller, (Ed.), *Making sense of fractions, ratios, and proportions* (pp. 41–48). Reston, VA: National Council of Teachers of Mathematics.

Cuisenaire/Dale Seymour Pub. (1995). *Investigations in Number, Data, and Space*. White Plains, NY: Author.

Curcio, F. R., & Bezuk, N. S. (1994). *Understanding rational numbers and proportions: Addenda Series, grades 5–8*. Reston, VA: National Council of Teachers of Mathematics.

Damarin, S. K. (1995). Gender and mathematics from a feminist standpoint. In W. G. Secada, E. Fennema, & L. B. Adajian (Eds.), *New directions for equity in mathematics education* (pp. 242–257). New York: Cambridge University Press.

D'Ambrosio, U. (1985). Ethnomathematics and its place in the history and pedagogy of mathematics. *For the Learning of Mathematics, 5*(1), 44–48.

Davidson, E., & Hammerman, J. (1993). Homogenized is only better for milk. In G. Cuevas & M. Driscol (Eds.), *Reaching all students with mathematics* (pp. 197–212). Reston, VA: National Council of Teachers of Mathematics.

Davis, R. B. (1986). *Learning mathematics: The cognitive science approach to mathematics education.* Norwood, NJ: Ablex.

De Villiers, M. D. (1999). *Rethinking proof with the Geometer's Sketchpad.* Emeryville, CA: Key Curriculum Press.

Elliott, P., & Garnett, C. (1994). Mathematics power for all. In C. A. Thornton, & N. S. Bley (Eds.), *Windows of opportunity: Mathematics for students with special needs* (pp. 3–17). Reston, VA: National Council of Teachers of Mathematics.

Empson, S. B. (2002). Organizing diversity in early fraction thinking. In Litwiller, B. (Ed.), *Making sense of fractions, ratios, and proportions* (pp. 29–40). Reston, VA: National Council of Teachers of Mathematics.

Fennema, E., Carpenter, T. P., Franke, M. L., & Carey, D. A. (1993). Learning to use children's mathematics thinking: A case study. In R. B. Davis & C. A. Maher (Eds.), *School, mathematics, and the world of reality* (pp. 93–117). Boston: Allyn & Bacon.

Fennema, E., Carpenter, T., Levi, L., Franke, M. L., & Empson, S. (1997). *Cognitively guided instruction: Professional development in primary mathematics.* Madison, WI: Wisconsin Center for Education Research.

Fischer, F. E. (1990). A part-part-whole curriculum for teaching number in the kindergarten. *Journal for Research in Mathematics Education, 21,* 207–215.

Fosnot, C. T. (1996). Constructivism: A psychological theory of learning. In C. T. Fosnot (Ed.), *Constructivism: Theory, perspectives, and practice* (pp. 8–33). New York: Teachers College Press.

Fosnot, C. T., & Dolk, M. (2001). *Young mathematicians at work: Constructing number sense, addition, and subtraction.* Portsmouth, NH: Heinemann.

Friel, S. N., Mokros, J. R., & Russell, S. J. (1992). *Statistics: Middles, means, and in-betweens.* A unit of study for grades 5–6 from *Used numbers: Real data in the classroom.* White Plains, NY: Cuisenaire—Dale Seymour.

Fuson, K. C. (1984). More complexities in subtraction. *Journal for Research in Mathematics Education, 15,* 214–225.

Fuson, K. C. (1992). Research on whole number addition and subtraction. In D. A. Grouws (Ed.), *Handbook of research on teaching and learning* (pp. 243–275). Old Tappan, NJ: Macmillan.

Fuson, K. C. (1988). *Children's counting and concepts of number.* New York: Springer-Verlag.

Fuson, K. C., Carroll, W. M., & Drueck, J. V. (2000). Achievement results for second and third graders using the *Standards*-based curriculum *Everyday Mathematics. Journal for Research in Mathematics Education, 31,* 277–295.

Fuson, K. C., & Hall, J. W. (1983). The acquisition of early number word meanings: A conceptual analysis and review. In H. P. Ginsburg (Ed.), *The development of mathematical thinking* (pp. 49–107). Orlando, FL: Academic Press.

Fuys, D., Geddes, D., & Tischler, R. (1988). The van Hiele model of thinking in geometry among adolescents. *Journal for Research in Mathematics Education Monograph, 3.*

Gable, R. A., & Hendrickson, J. M. (1997). Teaching all students: A mandate for educators. In J. S. Choate (Ed.), *Successful inclusive teaching: Proven ways to detect and correct special needs* (2nd ed.) (pp. 2–17). Needham Heights, MA: Allyn & Bacon.

Gamoran, A., & Weinstein, M. (1998). Differentiation and opportunity in restructured schools. *American Journal of Education, 106,* 385–415.

Garland, T. H. (1987). *Fascinating Fibonaccis: Mystery and magic in numbers.* Palo Alto, CA: Dale Seymour.

Garofalo, J. (1987). Metacognition and school mathematics. *Arithmetic Teacher, 34*(9), 22–23.

Geddes, D., & Fortunato, I. (1993). Geometry: Research and classroom activities. In D. T. Owens (Ed.), *Research ideas for the classroom: Middle grades mathematics* (pp. 199–222). New York: Macmillan.

Gelman, R., & Gallistel, C. R. (1978). *The child's understanding of number.* Cambridge, MA: Harvard University Press.

Gelman, R., & Meck, E. (1986). The notion of principle: The case of counting. In J. Hiebert (Ed.), *Conceptual and procedural knowledge: The case of mathematics* (pp. 29–57). Hillsdale, NJ: Erlbaum.

Ginsburg, H. P. (1977). *Children's arithmetic: The learning process.* New York: Van Nostrand.

Gnanadesikan, M., Schaeffer, R. L., & Swift, J. (1987). *The art and techniques of simulation: Quantitative literacy series.* Palo Alto, CA: Dale Seymour.

Goldin, G. A. (1985). Thinking scientifically and thinking mathematically: A discussion of the paper by Heller and Hungate. In E. A. Silver (Ed.), *Teaching and learning mathematical problem solving: Multiple research perspectives* (pp. 113–122). Hillsdale, NJ: Lawrence Erlbaum.

Greenes, C., Garfunkel, F., & De Bussey, M. (1994). Planning for instruction: The individualized education plan and the mathematics individualized learning plan. In C. A. Thornton & N. S. Bley (Eds.), *Windows of opportunity: Mathematics for students with special needs* (pp. 115–135). Reston, VA: National Council of Teachers of Mathematics.

Greer, B. (1992). Multiplication and division as models of situations. In D. A. Grouws (Ed.), *Handbook of research on mathematics teaching and learning* (pp. 276–295). Old Tappan, NJ: Macmillan.

Groff, P. (1996). It is time to question fraction teaching. *Mathematics Teaching in the Middle School, 1,* 604–607.

Gutstein, E., & Romberg, T. A. (1995). Teaching children to add and subtract. *Journal of Mathematical Behavior, 14,* 283–324.

Hankes, J. E. (1996). An alternative to basic-skills remediation. *Teaching Children Mathematics, 2,* 452–457.

Hashimoto, Y., & Becker, J. (1999). The open approach to teaching mathematics—Creating a culture of mathematics in the classroom: Japan. In L. J. Sheffield (Ed.), *Developing mathematically promising students* (pp. 101–119). Reston, VA: National Council of Teachers of Mathematics.

Hembree, R., & Dessart, D. D. (1986). Effects of hand-held calculators in precollege mathematics education: A meta-analysis. *Journal for Research in Mathematics Education, 17,* 83–99.

Hiebert, J. (1990). The role of routine procedures in the development of mathematical competence. In T. J. Cooney (Ed.), *Teaching and learning mathematics in the 1990s* (pp. 31–40). Reston, VA: National Council of Teachers of Mathematics.

Hiebert, J., & Carpenter, T. P. (1992). Learning and teaching with understanding. In D. A. Grouws (Ed.), *Handbook of research* on mathematics teaching and learning (pp. 65–97). Old Tappan, NJ: Macmillan.

Hiebert, J., Carpenter, T. P., Fennema, E., Fuson, K., Human, P., Murray, H., Olivier, A., & Wearne, D. (1996). Problem solving as a basis for reform in curriculum and instruction: The case of mathematics. *Educational Researcher, 25* (May), 12–21.

Hiebert, J., Carpenter, T. P., Fennema, E., Fuson, K., Wearne, D., Murray, H., Olivier, A., & Human, P. (1997). *Making sense: Teaching and learning mathematics with understanding.* Portsmouth, NH: Heinemann.

Hiebert, J., & Lindquist, M. M. (1990). Developing mathematical knowledge in the young child. In J. N. Payne (Ed.), *Mathematics for the young child* (pp. 17–36). Reston, VA: National Council of Teachers of Mathematics.

Hiebert, J., & Wearne, D. (1996). Instruction, understanding, and skill in multidigit addition and subtraction. *Cognition and Instruction, 14,* 251–283.

Hilliard, A. G., III. (1995). Mathematics excellence for cultural "minority" students: What is the problem? In I. M. Carl (Ed.), *Prospects for school mathematics* (pp. 99–114). Reston, VA: National Council of Teachers of Mathematics.

Hoffer, A. R. (1983). Van Hiele–based research. In R. A. Lesh & M. Landau (Eds.), *Acquisition of mathematics concepts and processes* (pp. 205–227). Orlando, FL: Academic Press.

Hoffer, A. R., & Hoffer, S. A. K. (1992). Ratios and proportional thinking. In T. R. Post (Ed.), *Teaching mathematics in grades K–8: Research-based methods* (2nd ed.) (pp. 303–330). Needham Heights, MA: Allyn & Bacon.

Hope, J. A., Leutzinger, L. P., Reys, B. J., & Reys, R. E. (1988). *Mental math in the primary grades.* Palo Alto, CA: Dale Seymour.

Hope, J. A., Reys, B. J., & Reys, R. E. (1987). *Mental math in the middle grades.* Palo Alto, CA: Dale Seymour.

Hope, J. A., Reys, B. J., & Reys, R. E. (1988). *Mental math in the junior high school.* Palo Alto, CA: Dale Seymour.

House, P. A. (1999). Promises, promises, promises. In L. J. Sheffield (Ed.), *Developing mathematically promising students* (pp. 1–7). Reston, VA: National Council of Teachers of Mathematics.

Howden, H. (1989). Teaching number sense. *Arithmetic Teacher, 36*(6), 6–11.

Huinker, D. (1994, April). Multi-step word problems: A strategy for empowering students. Presented at the annual meeting of the National Council of Teachers of Mathematics, Indianapolis, IN.

Huinker, D. (1998). Letting fraction algorithms emerge through problem solving. In L. J. Morrow (Ed.), *The teaching and learning of algorithms in school mathematics* (pp. 170–182). Reston, VA: National Council of Teachers of Mathematics.

Isaacs, A. C., & Carroll, W. M. (1999). Strategies for basic-facts instruction. *Teaching Children Mathematics, 5,* 508–515.

Janvier, C. (Ed.). (1987). *Problems of representation in the teaching and learning of mathematics.* Hillsdale, NJ: Erlbaum.

Johnson, G. M. (1999). Inclusive education: Fundamental instructional strategies and considerations. *Preventing School Failure, 43*(2), 72–78.

Kamii, C. K. (1985). *Young children reinvent arithmetic.* New York: Teachers College Press.

Kamii, C. K. (1989). *Young children continue to reinvent arithmetic: 2nd grade.* New York: Teachers College Press.

Kamii, C. K., & Clark, F. B. (1995). Equivalent fractions: Their difficulty and educational implications. *The Journal of Mathematical Behavior, 14,* 365–378.

Kamii, C. K., & Dominick, A. (1997). To teach or not to teach the algorithms. *Journal of Mathematical Behavior, 16,* 51–62.

Kamii, C. K., & Dominick, A. (1998). The harmful effects of algorithms in grades 1–4. In L. J. Morrow (Ed.), *The teaching and learning of algorithms in school mathematics* (pp. 130–140). Reston, VA: National Council of Teachers of Mathematics.

Kaput, J. J. (1998). Transforming algebra from an engine of inequity to an engine of mathematical power by "algebrafying" the K–12 curriculum. In *The nature and role of algebra in the K–14 curriculum: Proceedings of national symposium* (pp. 25–26). Washington, DC: National Academy Press.

Karplus, R., Pulos, S., & Stage, E. K. (1983). Proportional reasoning of early adolescents. In R. A. Lesh & M. Landau (Eds.), *Acquisition of mathematics concepts and processes* (pp. 45–90). Orlando, FL: Academic Press.

Kenney, P. A., & Kouba, V. L. (1997). What do students know about measurement? In P. A. Kenney & E. Silver (Eds.), *Results from the sixth mathematics assessment of the national assessment of educational progress* (pp. 141–163). Reston, VA: National Council of Teachers of Mathematics.

Kenney, P. A., & Silver, E. (Eds.) (1997). *Results from the sixth mathematics assessment of the national assessment of educational progress.* Reston, VA: National Council of Teachers of Mathematics.

Kliman, M., & Russell, S. J. (1998). *The number system: Building number sense (Grade 1).* Glenview, IL: Scott Foresman.

Kouba, V. L. (1989). Children's solution strategies for equivalent set multiplication and division word problems. *Journal for Research in Mathematics Education, 20,* 147–158.

Kouba, V. L., Brown, C. A., Carpenter, T. P., Lindquist, M. M., Silver, E. A., & Swafford, J. O. (1988a). Results of the fourth NAEP assessment of mathematics: Number, operations, and word problems. *Arithmetic Teacher, 35*(8), 14–19.

Kouba, V. L., Zawojewski, J. S., & Strutchens, M. E. (1997). What do students know about numbers and operations. In P. A. Kenney & E. Silver (Eds.), *Results from the sixth mathematics assessment of the national assessment of educational progress* (pp. 87–140). Reston, VA: National Council of Teachers of Mathematics.

Kulm, G. (1994). *Mathematics and assessment: What works in the classroom.* San Francisco: Jossey-Bass.

Kuske, C. T. (2001). It all fits together: Number patterns that foster number sense in K–2 students—A brain based model. Unpublished Masters Thesis, Antioch University Seattle.

Labinowicz, E. (1985). *Learning from children: New beginnings for teaching numerical thinking.* Menlo Park, CA: AWL Supplemental.

Labinowicz, E. (1987). Assessing for learning: The interview method. *Arithmetic Teacher, 35*(3), 22–24.

Ladson-Billings, G. (1995). Making mathematics meaningful in multicultural contexts. In W. G. Secada, E. Fennema, & L. B. Adajian (Eds.), *New directions for equity in mathematics education* (pp. 126–145). New York: Cambridge University Press.

Ladson-Billings, G. (1997). It doesn't add up: African American students' mathematics achiement. *Journal for Research in Mathematics Education, 28,* 697–708.

Lamon, S. J. (1993). Ratio and proportion: Connecting content and children's thinking. *Journal for Research in Mathematics Education, 24,* 41–61.

Lamon, S. J. (1996) The development of unitizing: Its role in children's partitioning strategies. *Journal for Research in Mathematics Education, 27,* 170–193.

Lamon, S. J. (1999b). *Teaching fractions and ratios for understanding: Essential content knowledge and instructional strategies for teachers.* Mahwah, NJ: Lawrence Erlbaum.

Lamon, S. J. (1999a). *More: In-depth discussion of the reasoning activities in "Teaching fractions and ratios for understanding."* Mahwah, NJ: Lawrence Erlbaum.

Lamon, S. J. (2002). Part-whole comparisons with unitizing. In B. Litwiller, (Ed.), *Making sense of fractions, ratios, and proportions* (pp. 79–86). Reston, VA: National Council of Teachers of Mathematics.

Lampert, M. (1990). When the problem is not the question and the solution is not the answer: Mathematical knowing and teaching. *American Educational Research Journal, 27,* 29–63.

Landwehr, J. M., & Watkins, A. E. (1987). *Exploring data: Quantitative literacy series.* Palo Alto, CA: Dale Seymour.

Lappan, G. (1998). Capturing patterns and functions: Variables and joint variation. In *The nature and role of algebra in the K–14 curriculum: Proceedings of national symposium* (pp. 57–59). Washington, DC: National Academy Press.

Lappan, G., & Briars, D. (1995). How should mathematics be taught? In I. M. Carl (Ed.), *Prospects for school mathematics* (pp. 115–156). Reston, VA: National Council of Teachers of Mathematics.

Lappan, G. & Even, R. (1989). *Learning to teach: Constructing meaningful understanding of mathematical content* (Craft Paper 89–3). East Lansing: Michigan State University.

Lappan, G., & Mouck, M. K. (1998). Developing algorithms for adding and subtracting fractions. In L. J. Morrow (Ed.), *The teaching and learning of algorithms in school mathematics* (pp. 183–197). Reston, VA: National Council of Teachers of Mathematics.

Leder, G. C. (1995). Equity inside the mathematics classroom: Fact or artifact? In W. G. Secada, E. Fennema, & L. B. Adajian (Eds.), *New directions for equity in mathematics education* (pp. 209–224). New York: Cambridge University Press.

Lesh, R. A., Post, T. R., & Behr, M. J. (1987). Representations and translations among representations in mathematics learning and problem solving. In C. Janvier (Ed.), *Problems of representation in the teaching and learning of mathematics* (pp. 33–40). Hillsdale, NJ: Erlbaum.

Lesh, R. A., Post, T. A., & Behr, M. (1988). Proportional reasoning. In J. Hiebert & M. Behr (Eds.), *Number concepts and operation in the middle grades* (pp. 93–118). Reston, VA: National Council of Teachers of Mathematics.

Lester, F. K., Jr. (1989). Reflections about mathematical problem-solving research. In R. I. Charles & E. A. Silver (Eds.), *The teaching and assessing of mathematical problem solving* (pp. 115–124). Reston, VA: National Council of Teachers of Mathematics.

Lester, F. K., Jr. (1994). Musings about mathematical problem-solving research, 1970–1994. *Journal for Research in Mathematics Education, 25,* 660–675.

Liedtke, W. (1988). Diagnosis in mathematics: The advantages of an interview. *Arithmetic Teacher, 36*(3), 26–29.

Lindquist, M. M. (1987a). Estimation and mental computation: Measurement. *Arithmetic Teacher, 34*(5), 16–17.

Lo, J., & Watanabe, T. (1997). Developing ratio and proportion schemes: A story of a fifth grader. *Journal for Research in Mathematics Education, 28,* 216–236.

Lodholz, R. D. (1990). The transition from arithmetic to algebra. In E. L. Edwards, Jr. (Ed.), *Algebra for everyone* (pp. 24–33). Reston, VA: National Council of Teachers of Mathematics.

Lubinski, C. A., & Thiessen, D. (1996). Exploring measurement through literature. *Teaching Children Mathematics, 2,* 260–263.

Ma, L. (1999). *Knowing and teaching elementary mathematics: Teachers' understanding of fundamental mathematics in China and the United States.* Mahwah, NJ: Lawrence Erlbaum.

Mack, N. K. (1995). Confounding whole-number and fraction concepts when building on informal knowledge. *Journal for Research in Mathematics Education, 26,* 422–441.

Mack, N. K. (2001). Building on informal knowledge through instruction in a complex content domain: Partitioning, units, and understanding multiplication of fractions. *Journal for Research in Mathematics Education, 32,* 267–295.

Madell, R. (1985). Children's natural processes. *Arithmetic Teacher, 32*(7), 20–22.

Martin, G., & Strutchens, M. E. (2000). Geometry and measurement. In E. A. Silver & P. A. Kenney (Eds.), *Results from the seventh mathematics assessment of the National Assessment of Educational Progress* (pp. 193–234). Reston, VA: National Council of Teachers of Mathematics.

Martin, R., Sexton, C., Wagner, K., & Gerlovich, J. (1997). *Teaching science for all children.* Boston: Allyn & Bacon.

Mathematical Sciences Education Board, National Research Council. (1989). *Everybody counts: A report to the nation on the future of mathematics education.* Washington, DC: National Academy of Sciences Press.

Mather, J. R. C., & Chiodo, J. J. (1994). A mathematical problem: How do we teach mathematics to LEP elementary students? *The Journal of Educational Issues of Language Minority Students, 13,* 1–12.

Mau, T. S., & Leitze, A. R. (2001). Powerless gender or genderless power? The promise of constructivism for females in the mathematics classroom. In J. E. Jacobs, J. R. Becker, & G. F. Gilmer (Eds.) *Changing the faces of mathematics: Perspectives on gender* (pp. 37–41). Reston, VA: National Council of Teachers of Mathematics.

McCoy, L. (1997). Algebra: Real-life investigations in a lab setting. *Mathematics Teaching in the Middle School, 2,* 220–224.

Mokros, J., Russell, S. J., & Economopoulos, K. (1995). *Beyond arithmetic: Changing mathematics in the elementary classroom.* Palo Alto, CA: Dale Seymour Publications.

Mulligan, J. T., & Mitchelmore, M. C. (1997). Young children's intuitive models of multiplication and division. *Journal for Research in Mathematics Education, 28,* 309–330.

National Council of Teachers of Mathematics. (1989). *Curriculum and evaluation standards for school mathematics.* Reston, VA: Author.

National Council of Teachers of Mathematics. (1991). *Professional standards for teaching mathematics.* Reston, VA: Author.

National Council of Teachers of Mathematics. (1995). *Assessment standards for school mathematics.* Reston, VA: Author.

National Council of Teachers of Mathematics. (2000). *Principles and standards for school mathematics.* Reston, VA: Author.

National Research Council. (2001). *Adding it up: Helping children learn mathematics.* J. Kilpatrick, J. Swafford, & B. Findell

(Eds.). Mathematics Learning Study Committee, Center for Education Division of Behavioral and Social Sciences and Education. Washington, DC: National Academy Press.

Nelson, R. B. (1993). *Proofs without words: Exercises in visual thinking.* Washington, DC: MAA.

Noddings, N. (1993). Constructivism and caring. In R. B. Davis & C. A. Maher (Eds.), *Schools, mathematics, and the world of reality* (pp. 35–50). Needham Heights, MA: Allyn & Bacon.

Noelting, G. (1980). The development of proportional reasoning and the ratio concept: 1. Differentiation of stages. *Educational Studies in Mathematics, 11,* 217–253.

Oakes, J. (1990). *Multiplying inequalities: The effects of race, social class, and tracking opportunities to learn mathematics and science.* Santa Monica, CA: Rand.

Oakes, J. (1995). Opportunity to learn: Can standards-based reform be equity-based reform? In I. M. Carl (Ed.), *Prospects for school mathematics* (pp. 78–98). Reston, VA: National Council of Teachers of Mathematics.

O'Brien, T. C. (1999). Parrot math. *Phi Delta Kappan, 80,* 434–438.

Oppedal, D. C. (1995). Mathematics is something good. *Teaching Children Mathematics, 2,* 36–40.

Papert, S. (1980). *Mindstorms: Children, computers, and powerful ideas.* New York: Basic Books.

Phillips, E., Gardella, T., Kelly, C., & Stewart, J. (1991). *Patterns and functions: Addenda series, grades 5–8.* Reston, VA: National Council of Teachers of Mathematics.

Poplin, M. S. (1988a). Holistic/constructivist principles of the teaching/learning process: Implications for the field of learning disabilities. *Journal of Learning Disabilities, 21,* 401–416.

Poplin, M. S. (1988b). The reductionistic fallacy in learning disabilities: Replicating the past by reducing the present. *Journal of Learning Disabilities, 21,* 389–398.

Post, T. R. (1981). Fractions: Results and implications from the national assessment. *Arithmetic Teacher, 28*(9), 26–31.

Post, T. R., Behr, M. J., & Lesh, R. A. (1988). Proportionality and the development of prealgebra understandings. In A. F. Coxford (Ed.), *The ideas of algebra, K–12* (pp. 78–90). Reston, VA: National Council of Teachers of Mathematics.

Post, T. R., Wachsmuth, I., Lesh, R. A., & Behr, M. J. (1985). Order and equivalence of rational numbers: A cognitive analysis. *Journal for Research in Mathematics Education, 16,* 18–36.

Pothier, Y., & Sawada, D. (1983). Partitioning: The emergence of rational number ideas in young children. *Journal for Research in Mathematics Education, 14,* 307–317.

Rathmell, E. C. (1978). Using thinking strategies to teach the basic skills. In M. N. Suydam (Ed.), *Developing computational skills* (pp. 13–38). Reston, VA: National Council of Teachers of Mathematics.

Rectanus, C. (1997). *Math by all means: Area and perimeter, grades 5–6.* Sausalito, CA: Math Solutions Publications.

Reese, C., M., Miller, K. E., Mazzeo, J., & Dossey, J. A. (1997). *NAEP 1996 mathematics report card for the nation and the states: Findings from the National Assessment of Educational Progress.* Washington, DC: National Center for Education Statistics.

Resnick, L. B. (1983). A developmental theory of number understanding. In H. P. Ginsburg (Ed.), *The development of mathematical thinking* (pp. 109–151). New York: Academic Press.

Reys, B. J., & Reys, R. E. (1987). Calculators in the classroom: How can we make it happen? *Arithmetic Teacher, 34*(6), 12–14.

Reys, B. J., & Reys, R. E. (1995). Japanese mathematics education: What makes it work. *Teaching Children Mathematics, 1,* 474–475.

Reys, B. J., Robinson, E., Sconiers, S., & Mark, J. (1999). Mathematics curricula based on rigorous national standards: What, why, and how? *Phi Delta Kappan, 80,* 454–456.

Reys, R. E. (1998). Computation versus number sense. *Mathematics Teaching in the Middle School, 4,* 110–113.

Reys, R. E., & Reys, B. J. (1983). *Guide to using estimation skills and strategies (GUESS)* (Boxes I and II). Palo Alto, CA: Dale Seymour.

Riordin, J. E. & Noyce, P. E. (2001). The impact of two *Standards*-based mathematics curricula on student achievement in Massachusetts. *Journal for Research in Mathematics Education, 32,* 368–398.

Ross, S. H. (1986). *The development of children's place-value numeration concepts in grades two through five.* Presented at the annual meeting of the American Educational Research Association, San Francisco. (ERIC Document Reproduction Service No. ED 2773 482)

Ross, S. H. (1989). Parts, wholes, and place value: A developmental perspective. *Arithmetic Teacher, 36*(6), 47–51.

Rowan, T. E. (1995, March). Helping children construct mathematical understanding with IMPACT. Presented at the regional meeting of the National Council of Teachers of Mathematics, Chicago, IL.

Rowan, T. E., & Bourne, B. (1994). *Thinking like mathematicians: Putting the K–4 standards into practice.* Portsmouth, NH: Heinemann.

Runion, G. E. (1990). *The golden section.* Palo Alto, CA: Dale Seymour.

Russell, S. J. (1997, April). *Using video to study students' strategies for whole-number operations.* Paper presented at the annual meeting of the National Council of Teachers of Mathematics, Minneapolis, MN.

Russell, S. J., & Corwin, R. B. (1990). *Sorting: Groups and graphs. A unit of study for grades 2–3 from Used numbers: Real data in the classroom.* White Plains, NY: Cuisenaire—Dale Seymour.

Scheer, J. K. (1980). The etiquette of diagnosis. *Arithmetic Teacher, 27*(9), 18–19.

Schifter, D., Bastable, V., & Russell, S. J. (1999a). *Developing mathematical understanding: Numbers and operations, Part 1, Building a system of tens (Casebook).* Parsippany, NJ: Dale Seymour Publications.

Schifter, D., Bastable, V., & Russell, S. J. (1999b). *Developing mathematical understanding: Numbers and operations, Part 2, Making meaning for operations (Casebook).* Parsippany, NJ: Dale Seymour Publications.

Schifter, D., Bastable, V., & Russell, S. J. (1999c). *Developing mathematical understanding: Numbers and operations, Part 2, Making meaning for operations (Facilitator's Guide).* Parsippany, NJ: Dale Seymour Publications.

Schifter, D., & Fosnot, C. T. (1993). *Reconstructing mathematics education: Stories of teachers meeting the challenge of reform.* New York: Teachers College Press.

Schmidt, W. H., McKnight, C. C., & Raizen, S. A. (1996). *Executive summary of a splintered vision: An investigation of U.S. science and mathematics education.* Boston: Kluwer.

Schoenfeld, A. H. (1988). What's all the fuss about metacognition? In A. H. Schoenfeld (Ed.), *Cognitive science and mathematics education* (pp. 189–215). Hillsdale, NJ: Erlbaum.

Schoenfeld, A. H. (1992). Learning to think mathematically: Problem solving, metacognition, and sense making in mathematics. In D. A. Grouws (Ed.), *Handbook of research on teaching and learning* (pp. 334–370). Old Tappan, NJ: Macmillan.

Schoenfeld, A. H. (1994). Reflections on doing and teaching mathematics. In A. H. Schoenfeld (Ed.), *Mathematical thinking and problem solving* (pp. 53–70). Hillsdale, NJ: Erlbaum.

Schroeder, T. L., & Lester, F. K., Jr. (1989). Developing understanding in mathematics via problem solving. In P. R. Trafton (Ed.), *New directions for elementary school mathematics* (pp. 31–42). Reston, VA: National Council of Teachers of Mathematics.

Schwartz, S. L. (1996). Hidden messages in teacher talk: Praise and empowerment. *Teaching Children Mathematics, 2,* 396–401.

Sconyers, J. M. (1995). Proof and the middle school mathematics student. *Mathematics Teaching in the Middle School, 1,* 516–518.

Seymour, D. (1971). *Tangramath.* Palo Alto, CA: Creative Publications.

Sheffield, L. J. (1999). Serving the needs of the mathematically promising. In L. J. Sheffield (Ed.), *Developing mathematically promising students* (pp. 43–55). Reston, VA: National Council of Teachers of Mathematics.

Sheffield, S. (1995). *Math and literature (K–3)* (Vol. 2). Sausalito, CA: Math Solutions Publications.

Shroyer, J., & Fitzgerald, W. (1986). *Mouse and elephant: Measuring growth.* Menlo Park, CA: AWL Supplemental.

Silver, E. A., & Kenney, P. A. (Eds.) (2000). *Results from the seventh mathematics assessment of the National Assessment of Educational Progress.* Reston, VA: National Council of Teachers of Mathematics.

Silver, E. A., Smith, M. S., & Nelson, B. S. (1995). The QUASAR project: Equity concerns meet mathematics education reform in the middle school. In W. G. Secada, E. Fennema, & L. B. Adajian (Eds.), *New directions for equity in mathematics education* (pp. 9–56). New York: Cambridge University Press.

Silver, E. A., & Stein, M. K. (1996). The QUASAR project: The "revolution of the possible" in mathematics instructional reform in urban middle schools. *Urban Education, 30,* 476–521.

Simon, M. A. (1995). Reconstructing mathematics pedagogy from a constructivist perspective. *Journal for Research in Mathematics Education, 26,* 114–145.

Skemp, R. (1978). Relational understanding and instrumental understanding. *Arithmetic Teacher, 26*(3), 9–15.

Smith, J. P., III. (1996). Efficacy and teaching mathematics by telling: A challenge for reform. *Journal for Research in Mathematics Education, 27,* 387–402.

Smith, J. P., III. (2002). The development of students' knowledge of fractions and ratios. In B. Litwiller, (Ed.), *Making sense of fractions, ratios, and proportions* (pp. 3–17). Reston, VA: National Council of Teachers of Mathematics.

Steffe, L. (1988). Children's construction of number sequences and multiplying schemes. In J. Hiebert & M. J. Behr (Eds.), *Number concepts and operations in the middle grades* (pp. 119–140). Hillsdale, NJ: Erlbaum.

Stein, M. K., Grover, B. W., & Henningsen, M. (1996). Building student capacity for mathematical thinking and reasoning: An analysis of mathematical tasks used in reform classrooms. *American Educational Research Journal, 33,* 455–488.

Stein, M. K., & Lane, S. (1996). Instructional tasks and the development of student capacity to think and reason: An analysis of the relationship between teaching and learning in a reform mathematics project. *Educational Research and Evaluation, 2*(1), 50–58.

Steinberg, R. M. (1985). Instruction on derived facts strategies in addition and subtraction. *Journal for Research in Mathematics Education, 16,* 337–355.

Stenmark, J. K. (1989). *Assessment alternatives in mathematics: An overview of assessment techniques that promote learning.* Berkeley: EQUALS, University of California.

Stenmark, J. K. (Ed.). (1991). *Mathematics assessment: Myths, models, good questions, and practical suggestions.* Reston, VA: National Council of Teachers of Mathematics.

Stoessiger, R., & Edmunds, J. (1992). *Natural learning and mathematics.* Portsmouth, NH: Heinemann.

Taber, S. B. (2002). Go ask Alice about multiplication of fractions. In Litwiller, B. (Ed.) *Making sense of fractions, ratios, and proportions* (pp. 61–71). Reston, VA: National Council of Teachers of Mathematics.

Theissen, D., Matthias, M., & Smith, J. (1998). *The wonderful world of mathematics: A critically annotated list of children's books in mathematics* (2nd ed.). Reston, VA: National Council of Teachers of Mathematics.

Thompson, C. S. (1990). Place value and larger numbers. In J. N. Payne (Ed.), *Mathematics for the young child* (pp. 89–108). Reston, VA: National Council of Teachers of Mathematics.

Thompson, C. S., & Hendrickson, A. D. (1986). Verbal addition and subtraction problems: Some difficulties and some solutions. *Arithmetic Teacher, 33*(7), 21–25.

Thompson, C. S., & Van de Walle, J. A. (1984). The power of 10. *Arithmetic Teacher, 32*(3), 6–11.

Thompson, P. W. (1994). Concrete materials and teaching for mathematical understanding. *Arithmetic Teacher, 41,* 556–558.

Thornton, C. A. (1982). Doubles up—easy! *Arithmetic Teacher, 29*(8), 20.

Thornton, C. A. (1990). Strategies for the basic facts. In J. N. Payne (Ed.), *Mathematics for the young child* (pp. 133–151). Reston, VA: National Council of Teachers of Mathematics.

Thornton, C. A., & Bley, N. S. (Eds.). (1994). *Windows of opportunity: Mathematics for students with special needs.* Reston, VA: National Council of Teachers of Mathematics.

Thornton, C. A., & Noxon, C. (1977). *Look into the facts: (Addition, subtraction, multiplication, division).* Palo Alto, CA: Creative Publications.

Thornton, C. A., & Toohey, M. A. (1984). *A matter of facts: (Addition, subtraction, multiplication, division).* Palo Alto, CA: Creative Publications.

Trafton, P. R., & Claus, A. S. (1994). A changing curriculum for a changing age. In C. A. Thornton & N. S. Bley (Eds.), *Windows of opportunity: Mathematics for students with special needs* (pp. 19–39). Reston, VA: National Council of Teachers of Mathematics.

Tsuruda, G. (1994). *Putting it together: Middle school math in transition.* Portsmouth, NH: Heinemann.

Tzur, R. (1999). An integrated study of children's construction of improper fractions and the teacher's role in promoting learning. *Journal for Research in Mathematics Education, 30,* 390–416.

U.S. Dept. of Education, Office of Educational Research and Improvement. (1996). *Pursuing excellence: A study of U.S.*

eighth-grade mathematics and science teaching, learning, curriculum, and achievement in international context. NCES 97-198, by L. Peak. Washington, DC: U.S. Government Printing Office.

U.S. Dept. of Education, Office of Educational Research and Improvement. (1997a). *Introduction to TIMSS*. Washington, DC: U.S. Government Printing Office.

U.S. Dept. of Education, Office of Educational Research and Improvement. (1997b). *Moderator's guide to eighth-grade mathematics lessons: United States, Japan, and Germany*. Washington, DC: U.S. Government Printing Office.

U.S. Dept. of Education, Office of Educational Research and Improvement. (1997c). *Pursuing excellence: A study of U.S. fourth-grade mathematics and science achievement in international context*. NCES 97-255. Washington, DC: U.S. Government Printing Office.

Usiskin, Z. (1988). Conceptions of school algebra and uses of variables. In A. F. Coxford (Ed.), *The ideas of algebra, K–12* (pp. 8–19). Reston, VA: National Council of Teachers of Mathematics.

Usiskin, Z. (1993). If everybody counts, why do so few survive? In G. Cuevas & M. Driscol (Eds.), *Reaching all students with mathematics* (pp. 7–22). Reston, VA: National Council of Teachers of Mathematics.

van Hiele, P. M. (1999). Developing geometric thinking through activities that begin with play. *Teaching Children Mathematics, 5*, 310–316.

von Glasersfeld, E., (1990). An exposition of constructivism: Why some like it radical. In R. B. Davis, C. A. Maher, & N. Noddings (Eds.), *Constructivist views on the teaching and learning of mathematics* (pp. 19–29). Reston, VA: National Council of Teachers of Mathematics.

von Glasersfeld, E. (1996). Introduction: Aspects of constructivism. In C. T. Fosnot (Ed.), *Constructivism: Theory, perspectives, and practice* (pp. 3–7). New York: Teachers College Press.

Wakefield, D. V. (2000). Math as a second language. *The Educational Forum, 64*, 272–279.

Walter, M. I. (1970). *Boxes, squares and other things: A teacher's guide for a unit in informal geometry*. Reston, VA: National Council of Teachers of Mathematics.

Wearne, D., & Kouba, V. L. (2000). Rational numbers. In E. A. Silver & P. A Kenney (Eds.), *Results from the seventh mathematics assessment of the National Assessment of Educational Progress* (pp. 163–191). Reston, VA: National Council of Teachers of Mathematics.

Wheatley, G. H., & Hersberger, J. (1986). A calculator estimation activity. In H. Schoen (Ed.), *Estimation and mental computation* (pp. 182–185). Reston, VA: National Council of Teachers of Mathematics.

Whitin, D. J., & Wilde, S. (1992). *Read any good math lately? Children's books for mathematical learning, K–6*. Portsmouth, NH: Heinemann.

Whitin, D. J., & Wilde, S. (1995). *It's the story that counts: More children's books for mathematical learning, K–6*. Portsmouth, NH: Heinemann.

Winter, M. J., Lappan, G., Phillips, E., & Fitzgerald, W. (1986). *Middle grades mathematics project: Spatial visualization*. Menlo Park, CA: AWL Supplemental.

Wirtz, R. (1974). *Mathematics for everyone*. Washington, DC: Curriculum Development Associates.

Wood, T., Cobb, P., Yackel, E., & Dillon, D. (Eds.). (1993). *Rethinking elementary school mathematics: Insights and issues* (*Journal for Research in Mathematics Education* Monograph No. 6). Reston, VA: National Council of Teachers of Mathematics.

Wood, T., & Sellers, P. (1996). Assessment of a problem-centered mathematics program: Third grade. *Journal for Research in Mathematics Education, 27*, 337–353.

Wood, T., & Sellers, P. (1997). Deepening the analysis: Longitudinal assessment of a problem-centered mathematics program. *Journal for Research in Mathematics Education, 28*, 163–168.

Yackel, E., Cobb, P., Wood, T., Wheatley, G. H., & Merkel, G. (1990). The importance of social interaction in children's construction of mathematical knowledge. In T. J. Cooney (Ed.), *Teaching and learning mathematics in the 1990s* (pp. 12–21). Reston, VA: National Council of Teachers of Mathematics.

Zaslavasky, C. (1996). *The multicultural classroom: Bringing in the world*. Portsmouth, NH: Heinemann.

Children's Literature

Anno, M. (1982). *Anno's counting house*. New York: Philomel Books.

Anno, M. (1994). *Anno's magic seeds*. New York: Philomel Books.

Anno, M., & Anno, M. (1983). *Anno's mysterious multiplying jar*. New York: Philomel Books.

Ash, R. (1996). *Incredible comparisons*. New York: Dorling Kindersley.

Briggs, R. (1970). *Jim and the beanstalk*. New York: Coward-McCann.

Carle, E. (1969). *The very hungry caterpillar*. New York: Putnam.

Chalmers, M. (1986). *Six dogs, twenty-three cats, forty-five mice, and one hundred sixteen spiders*. New York: HarperCollins.

Chwast, S. (1993). *The twelve circus rings*. San Diego, CA: Gulliver Books, Harcourt Brace Jovanovich.

Clement, R. (1991). *Counting on Frank*. Milwaukee: Gareth Stevens Children's Books.

Cushman, R. (1991). *Do you wanna bet? Your chance to find out about probability*. New York: Clarion Books.

Dee, R. (1988). *Two ways to count to ten*. New York: Holt.

Friedman, A. (1994). *The king's commissioners*. New York: Scholastic.

Gag, W. (1928). *Millions of cats*. New York: Coward-McCann.

Giganti, P. (1988). *How many snails? A counting book*. New York: Greenwillow.

Giganti, P. (1992). *Each orange had 8 slices*. New York: Greenwillow.

Hoban, T. (1981). *More than one*. New York: Greenwillow.

Hutchins, P. (1986). *The doorbell rang*. New York: Greenwillow.

Jaspersohn, W. (1993). *Cookies*. Old Tappan, NJ: Macmillan.

Juster, N. (1961). *The phantom tollbooth*. New York: Random House.

Lobal, A. (1970). *Frog and Toad are friends*. New York: HarperCollins.

Mathews, L. (1979). *Gator pie*. New York: Dodd, Mead.

McKissack, P. C. (1992). *A million fish . . . more or less*. New York: Knopf.

Munsch, R. (1987). *Moira's birthday*. Toronto: Annick Press.

Myller, R. (1990). *How big is a foot?* New York: Dell.

Norton, M. (1953). *The borrowers.* New York: Harcourt Brace.

Parker, T. (1984). *In one day.* Boston: Houghton Mifflin.

Pluckrose, H. (1988). *Pattern.* New York: Franklin Watts.

St. John, G. (1975). *How to count like a Martian.* New York: Walck.

Schwartz, D. (1985). *How much is a million?* New York: Lothrop, Lee & Shepard.

Schwartz, D. (1989). *If you made a million.* New York: Lothrop, Lee & Shepard.

Schwartz, D. M. (1999). *If you hopped like a frog.* New York: Scholastic Press.

Scieszka, J., & Smith, L. (1995). *Math curse.* New York: Viking Penguin.

Sharmat, M. W. (1979). *The 329th friend.* New York: Four Winds Press.

Silverstein, S. (1974). One inch tall. In *Where the sidewalk ends* (p. 55). New York: Harper & Row.

Tahan, M. (1993). *The man who counted: A collection of mathematical adventures* (Trans. L. Clark & A. Reid). New York: Norton.

Wells, R. E. (1993). *Is a blue whale the biggest thing there is?* Morton Grove, IL: Whitman.

Wolkstein, D. (1972). *8,000 stones.* New York: Doubleday.

COMPUTER SOFTWARE

Broderbund. (1995a). *James discovers math.* Novato, CA: Author.

Broderbund. (1995b) *Tabletop, Jr.* . Novato, CA: Author.

Broderbund. (1996a). *Kid pix.* Novato, CA: Author.

Broderbund. (1996b). *The zoombinis' logical adventure.* Novato, CA: Author.

Clements, D. H., & Meredith, J. S. (1994). *Turtle math.* Highgate Springs, VT: Logo Computer Systems.

Clements, D. H., & Sarama, J. (1995). *Shapes—Mathematical Thinking.* Highgate Springs, VT: Logo Computer Systems Inc. (LCSI).

Davidson & Associates. (n.d.). *Math for the real world.* Torrence, CA: Author.

Davidson & Associates. (n.d.). *Mega Math Blaster.* Torrence, CA: Author.

Edmark Corp. (1993). *Millie's math house.* Redmond, WA: Author.

Edmark Corp.(1996a). *GeoComputer.* Redmond, WA: Author.

Edmark Corp. (1996b). *Mighty math: Number heroes.* Redmond, WA: Author.

Education Development Center. (1991). *My travels with Gulliver.* Scotts Valley, CA: Wings for Learning.

EduQuest. (1994). *Math and more 3: Patterns on lattices.* Atlanta: IBM Corp.

EdVenture Software. (1997). *Gold Medal Mathematics.* Norwalk, CT: EdVenture Software.

Gamco Education Software. (1994). *Word problem square off.* Clayton, MO: Siboney Learning Group.

Hickey, A. (1996). *Unifix Software.*Rowley, MA: Didax Educational Resources.

Jazz Interactive. *Performance Math.* Glenview, IL: Scott Foresman–Addison Wesley.

Key Curriculum Press. (2001). *The geometer's sketchpad* (Version 4.0). Berkeley, CA: Key Curriculum Press.

Knowledge Adventure. (n.d.). *Math for the real world.* Pleasantville, NY: Author.

Learning Co. (1994). *TesselMania!* Mahwah, NJ: Author.

Learning Co. (1995). *Math munchers deluxe.* Mahway, NJ: Author.

Learning Co. (1996). *The new adventures of Jasper Woodbury.* Mahwah, NJ: Author.

Learning Co. (1999). *Kid pix.* Mahwah, NJ: Author.

Learning Co. (n.d.) *CornerStone ATS 3.2.* Mahwah, NJ: Author.

MECC. (1994). *TesselMania!* [Computer software]. Minneapolis, MN: Author.

MECC. (1995a). *MathKeys: Geometry, Vol. 1* [Computer Software]. Minneapolis, MN: Author.

MECC. (1995b). *MathKeys: Unlocking probability, Vols. 2 & 3* [Computer Software]. Minneapolis, MN: Author.

MECC. (1995c). *MathKeys: Unlocking whole numbers grades 3–5* [Computer Software]. Minneapolis, MN: Author.

MECC. (1996a). *MathKeys: Unlocking whole numbers grades K–2* [Computer Software]. Minneapolis, MN: Author.

MECC. (1996b). *MathKeys: Unlocking Fractions and Decimals grades 3–5* [Computer Software]. Minneapolis, MN: Author.

O'Brien, T. C. *Teasers by Tobbs: Numbers and operations* [Computer Software]. Pleasantville, NY: Sunburst Communications.

Pierian Spring Software. (1996). *CampOS Math* [Computer Software]. Portland, OR: Author.

Riverdeep. (1994a). *Tangible math: The geometry inventor.* Cambridge, MA: Author.

Riverdeep. (1994b). *Tangible math: The probability constructor.* Cambridge, MA: Author.

Sunburst Communications. (1995). *Shape up.* Pleasantville, NY: Author.

Sunburst Communications. (n.d.). *Factory deluxe.* Pleasantville, NY: Author.

Sunburst Communications. (n.d.). *Math arena.* Pleasantville, NY: Author.

Sunburst Communications. (n.d.). *Splish splash math.* Pleasantville, NY: Author.

Sunburst Communications. (n.d.). *The cruncher 2.0.* Pleasantville, NY: Author.

Sunburst Communications. (n.d.) *The king's rule.* Pleasantville, NY: Author.

Tenth Planet. (1997) *Grouping and place value.* Pleasantville, NY: Sunburst Communications.

Tenth Planet. (1998a) *Combining and Breaking Apart Numbers.* Pleasantville, NY: Sunburst Communications.

Tenth Planet. (1998b). *Fraction Operations.* Pleasantville, NY: Sunburst Communications.

Tenth Planet. (1998c). *Number Meanings and Counting* [Computer Software]. Pleasantville, NY: Sunburst Communications.

Tenth Planet. (1998d). *Representing Fractions* [Computer Software]. Pleasantville, NY:

Texas Instruments. (1994). *Cabri geometry II* [Computer Software]. Dallas: Author.

Tom Snyder. (1993). *The graph club* [Computer Software]. Watertown, MA: Author.

Tom Snyder Productions. (1998). *Fizz & Martina's math adventures: Lights, camera, fractions* [Computer Software]. Watertown, MA: Author.

Tom Snyder Productions. (1999). *Prime time math.* Watertown, MA: Author.

Index

Acceleration, for gifted and talented students, 99–100
Access, 95
Accommodation, 23
Accountability, 8
Acute angles, 354
Addenda Series (NCTM), 427
Addition, 135–143
  comparison models, 140–141
  computational estimation in, 234–235
  contextual problems, 138–139
  of decimals, 293
  of fractions, 265–269
  invented strategies for, 205–206, 208
  model-based problems, 139–140, 211–212
  order property, 141
  in problem-solving approach with integers, 460–462
  problem structures, 135–138
  proportional reasoning and, 300–301
  strategies for mastery of basic facts, 159–165
  symbolism in, 139
  technology and, 143
  traditional algorithms for, 211–213, 267–268
  zero property, 141–142, 161
Affective factors, tests and, 73
African Americans. *See* Cultural diversity
Algebraic reasoning, 417–433
  assessment and, 433
  children's literature and, 432–433
  equations and inequalities, 430–432
  Fibonacci sequence, 427
  number patterns, 425–427
  patterns on hundreds chart, 425
  repeating patterns, 418–420
  sequences, 420–424, 427
  variables, 427–430
Algebra standard, 4, 417
Algorithmic procedures, 28
Alignment, grading and, 78
Alternative assessment, 62
American Association for the Advancement of Science, 112
Analysis, in geometry, 347–348, 350, 363–376
Analytic scale, 66–67
Anchoring numbers to 5 and 10, 120, 122–123
Anecdotal notes, 67
Angles
  measurement of, 329–331
  types of, 354
  units of, 329

Annenberg/CPB Projects, 112
Anno's Counting House (Anno), 132
Anno's Magic Seeds (Anno), 432–433
Anno's Mysterious Multiplying Jar (Anno), 432
Applets, 107, 112–113, 184, 193, 224, 356, 359
Appropriate assessment, 62–64
  nature of, 62
  tasks in, 62–64
Approximation
  in fraction computation, 286–287
  in measurement, 319–320
Arcytech, 113
Area
  measuring, 323–327, 336–338
  perimeter and, 326–327
  units of, 325–326
Area model, 216–217, 244, 260–261, 409–410
Arrays, 147
Assessment, 59–78
  of algebraic reasoning, 433
  appropriate, 62–64
  changing beliefs about, 92
  computational estimation and, 240
  of conceptual mathematics, 61
  contextual problems in, 153
  of data analysis, 404–405, 415
  decimals and, 296
  diagnostic interviews in, 76–77
  disposition in, 62
  functions and, 450
  in geometry, 383–384
  grading in, 64, 77–78
  homogeneous grouping and, 96
  of mathematical processes, 61–62
  of measurement concepts, 322, 342
  models and, 31
  nature of, 59
  of number relationships, 127–129
  observation in, 67–68, 225
  percents and, 296
  of place-value development, 198–199
  portfolios in, 74–76
  of probability, 414
  of procedural mathematics, 61
  of proportional reasoning, 314
  purposes of, 60–61
  rubrics in, 64–68
  tests in, 72–74

Assessment (continued)
  tracking and, 96
  of whole-number computation, 211, 224–225
  writing and journals in, 69–72
Assessment Principle (NCTM), 3, 59
Assessment Standards for School Mathematics (NCTM), 2, 6, 59,
    60–61
Assimilation, 23
Association for Supervision and Curriculum Development, 112
At-risk students, 96
Attention deficits, adaptations for, 94
Attitude inventories, 71–72
Attitudes, 55
  calculators and student, 104
  in problem solving, 55, 56
  relational understanding and, 26–27
Attribute materials, 389–391
Authentic assessment, 64
Automaticity, 86–87
Averages, 397–398
Averaging technique, 236
Axis of symmetry, 372

Bar graphs, 392–394
Base-ten concepts. See Place-value development
Basic facts, 156. See also Mastery of basic facts
Basic skills, 7, 14, 53–54, 104–105
Beliefs in mathematics, 55
  challenging traditional, 92
  gender and, 98
  relational understanding and, 26–27
Best-fit lines, 402–404, 446
Big ideas, 48, 74
Blocks and tiles software, 108
Borrowers, The (Norton), 314
Box-and-whisker plots, 398–399
Brainstorming, 43, 71
Bridging, 208

Cabri Geometry II (Chartwell Yorke), 368, 369
Calculator/computer-based laboratory (CBL), 106, 447
Calculators
  benefits of using, 103–104, 176
  computational estimation activities, 237–238
  counting and, 118
  developmental approach and, 33
  for every student, every day, 105
  fractions and, 249–250, 285
  graphing, 105–107, 109, 405, 426, 443
  myths and fears concerning, 104–105
  notation and, 454–456
  number patterns and, 425–427
  numeral recognition and, 117
  probability with, 413–414
  tests and, 72
CampOS Math, 313
Capacity, measurement of, 327–328, 339–340
Cardinality principle, 117
CBL (calculator/computer-based laboratory), 106, 447
Chance. See Probability

Charts, in problem solving, 55
Checklists
  for full classes, 68
  for individuals, 68
Children's literature, 50–51
  algebraic reasoning and, 432–433
  computational estimation and, 239–240
  decimals and, 295–296
  early number sense and, 132
  for exponents, integers, and real numbers, 466–467
  fractions in, 261–262
  mathematical operations and, 153–154
  measurement and, 343
  percents and, 295–296
  place-value development and, 197–198
  probability and, 414
  proportional reasoning and, 313–314
  whole-number computation and, 224
Children with learning problems, 92–95
  mental disabilities, 94–95
  specific learning disabilities, 92–94
Chunking, 334
Circle graphs, 396–397
Circles
  formulas for, 338–339
  relationships within, 368–369
Circumference of circle, 338–339
Clock reading, 341–342
Cluster problems, 232
Cognitively Guided Instruction (CGI) (Fennema et al.), 153
Cognitive schemas, 23
Coherence Standard (NCTM), 60
Combination (Cartesian product) problems, 143, 145–146
Combining and Breaking Apart Numbers (Tenth Planet), 126
Common denominators, 248–249, 266–268, 277
Communication standard, 4–5, 61
Commutative property
  in addition, 141
  in multiplication, 149
Comparisons, 137, 144–145
  in addition, 140–141
  fractions and, 252–254
  measurements and, 318, 320, 323–325, 327, 328, 329
  ratios and, 302–303, 308
  in subtraction, 140–141
Compatible numbers, 235–237
Compensation strategies, 215–216
Complete-number strategies, 215
Composition of transformations, 372–373
Computation, 25
  with decimals, 292–295
  fluency in, 202
  with fractions. See Fraction computation
  mental, 43, 132–133, 228
  whole-number. See Whole-number computation
Computational estimation, 228–240
  addition in, 234–235
  assessment and, 240
  children's literature and, 239–240
  choosing form of, 229

with decimals, 239, 292
division in, 234, 235, 236
without estimates, 230–231
exercises for, 237–238
with fractions, 239, 256–257, 268–269, 273
from invented strategies, 231–232
multiplication in, 234, 235
with percents, 239, 290–292
real-world applications of, 229, 230
strategies for, 233–237
subtraction in, 234–235
suggestions for teaching, 229–230
technology in, 238–239
understanding, 229
Computational forms of equations, 138
Computers in mathematics, 107–111. *See also* Internet
    resources; Software; Technology in mathematics
Conceptual mathematics, 27. *See also* Early number concepts
assessment of, 61
calculators in, 104
examples of problem-based tasks in, 38–39
instructional software for, 109
Cones, volume of, 340
Connected Mathematics, 8
Grade 6: Bits and Pieces II, 269, 295
Grade 7: Comparing and Scaling, 308
Grade 7: Variables and Patterns, 444
Grade 8: Growing, Growing, Growing, 456
Grade 8: Kaleidoscopes, Hubcaps, and Mirrors, 381
Connections standard, 5
Constructivism, 22–27
developmental approach and, 31–32
examples of constructed learning, 23–24
models and, 30
nature of, 22–24
rote learning and, 24
teaching approach for, 54
understanding and, 24–27
Content standards (NCTM), 4, 417
Contextual problems. *See also* Children's literature
in addition, 138–139
analyzing, 150–152
difficulty of, 138
in division, 146–147, 150–153
to encourage invented strategy use, 205
key word strategy in, 152
in multiplication, 146–147, 150–153
representations of functions, 437, 440
in subtraction, 138–139
two-step, 152–153
Continuous data graphs, 395–396
Cookies (Jaspersohn), 224
Cooperative learning groups, 33
Coordinate grids, 370–372
CornerStone ATS 3.2: Mathematics (The Learning Company),
    238–239
Counting on Frank (Clement), 314, 343
Counting skills, 116–117, 118–119, 164
fractional-parts counting, 247–248
money, 194

place-value development and, 179–180, 199
Count On, 113
Credits, 458
Cruncher, 2.0, The (Sunburst), 404
Cubes, 339
Cultural diversity, 95–98
access and, 95
at-risk students, 96
ethnomathematics, 96–97
expectations and, 95–96
teaching second language learners, 97–98
Curriculum
changing beliefs about, 92
modifications for mental disabilities, 95
reform, 8
traditional, 8
Curriculum and Evaluation Standards for School Mathematics
    (NCTM), 1–2, 36, 60
Curriculum Principle (NCTM), 3
Customary system, 333
Cylinders, volume of, 339–340

Data analysis, 387–405
assessment and, 404–405
attribute materials, 389–391
children's literature and, 414
classification and, 389–392
descriptive statistics, 397–402
functional relationships, 404, 422–423
gathering data, 387–389
graphical representations, 392–397
scatter plots, 402–404
shape of data, 389
technology and, 391–392, 404
Data analysis and probability standard, 4, 387
Debits, 458
Decimals, 280–296. *See also* Percents
addition of, 293
assessment and, 296
children's literature and, 295–296
computation with, 292–295
connections with fractions, 280–288
decimal point, 282–283
estimation with, 239, 292
number sense, 285–288
ordering decimal numbers, 287–288
technology and, 288
Deduction, in geometry, 348, 350, 376–383
Denominators, 248–249, 266–268, 277
Dependent events, 410–411
Depth, for gifted and talented students, 100
Descriptive statistics, 397–402
averages, 397–398
box-and-whisker plots, 398–399
mean, 397–402
Developmental approach, 31–33
foundations of, 31–32
strategies for effective teaching, 32–33
Diagnostic interviews, 76–77
in assessment of whole-number computation, 225

Diagnostic interviews (*continued*)
  planning, 76–77
  reasons for using, 76
  suggestions for effective, 77
Diameter of circle, 338–339
Differentiated tasks, 84–85
Direct modeling, in whole-number computation, 202–203, 205
Discipline problems, 38
Discourse
  developmental approach and, 33
  in problem solving, 46–47, 52
Disposition
  in assessment, 62
  nature of, 55
Distributive property, in multiplication, 150
Diversity, 84–85, 91–100
  challenging traditional beliefs, 92
  children with learning problems, 92–95
  children with mental disabilities, 94–95
  cultural and social, 95–98
  differentiated tasks and, 84–85
  drill and practice, 87
  gender, 98–99
  gifted and talented students, 99–100
  heterogeneous groupings and, 85
  listening to students, 85
  multiple entry points and, 84
Division, 143–154
  computational estimation in, 234, 235, 236
  contextual problems, 146–147, 150–153
  of decimals, 294–295
  of fractions, 273–278
  fractions as indicated, 464
  invented strategies for, 220
  model-based problems, 147–149, 221
  by one-digit divisors, 221–223
  in problem-solving approach with integers, 462–464
  problem structures, 143–146
  strategies for mastery of facts, 173–174
  symbolism in, 146–147, 223
  traditional algorithms for, 220–224, 277–278
  by two-digit divisors, 223–224
  zero in, 150
Divisors
  fractional, 275
  one-digit, 221–223
  two-digit, 223–224
  whole-number, 274–275
Dodecahedron, 383
Doing mathematics, 12–20
  basics in, 7, 14, 53–54
  environment for, 14
  helping students with, 20
  mathematics as science of pattern and order, 13
  sample problems for, 14–20
  traditional views in, 12–13
  verbs of, 13–14
Doorbell Rang, The (Hutchins), 262
Dot card activities, 127

Double relationships, 129–130, 161, 164, 169, 172
Do You Wanna Bet? Your Chance to Find Out About Probability (Cushman), 414
Drawings
  in journals, 71
  tests and, 72
Drawing software, 108
Drill and practice, 24, 54, 85–87
  appropriateness of, 86–87
  avoiding premature drill, 158
  calculators in, 104
  deciding to use, 174–175
  as homework, 87, 88
  individualization of drills, 159, 174
  instructional software and, 110, 238–239
  new definitions of, 85–86
  outcomes of, 86
  in remediation with upper-grade students, 176
  as strategy for mastery of basic facts, 158, 159, 174–175
Dynamic geometry software, 108, 308, 338, 368, 369–370, 378–379

Each Orange Had 8 Slices (Giganti), 153–154
Early number concepts, 115–119. *See also* Early number sense
  counting, 116–117, 118–119, 164
  numeral writing and recognition, 117–118
  relationships of *more, less,* and *same,* 116, 119, 121–122, 129, 132
  technology and, 118
Early number sense, 119–133. *See also* Early number concepts
  anchors or "benchmarks" of 5 and 10, 120, 122–123
  assessment and, 127–128
  children's literature and, 132
  defined, 119
  dot card activities, 127
  extensions to early mental mathematics, 132–133
  one and two more, one and two less, 119, 121–122, 160
  part-part-whole relationships, 120, 123–126, 127–128
  real world and, 130–132
  relationships among numbers 1 through 10, 119–128
  relationships among numbers 10 to 20, 129–130
  spatial relationships, 119, 120–121
  technology and, 126
EdWeb Home Page, 112
Effective teaching
  at-risk students and, 96
  nature of, 32
  strategies for, 32–33
8,000 Stones (Wolkstein), 343
Eisenhower National Clearinghouse, 111
Engaging students, in problem solving, 47
Enrichment, for gifted and talented students, 99–100
Environment
  creating mathematical, 32
  for doing mathematics, 14
  for problem solving, 56
  shifts in classroom, 6, 20
Equal-group problems, 143, 144

EQUALS and Family Math, 112
Equations, 430–432
 balance pan approach to equality, 430–431
 graphical representations without, 448–450
 to represent functions, 439–440
 solving, 431–432
Equity
 gender, 98–99
 multicultural and social, 95–98
Equity Principle (NCTM), 3, 41, 95
Equity Standard (NCTM), 60
Equivalent fractions, 254, 257–261, 312
Equivalent ratios, 301–302
e-Standards (NCTM), 5–6, 84, 108, 113, 193, 356, 359, 373, 402
Estimation, 43, 130
 with decimals, 239, 292
 with fractions, 239, 256–257, 268–269, 273
 in measurement process, 229, 319, 333–335
 with percents, 290–292
 with whole numbers. *See* Computational estimation
Ethnomathematics, 96–97
Evaluation
 defined, 60
 portfolio, 76
 of programs, 61
 of student achievement, 60–61
Everybody Counts (MSEB), 13
Expectations
 impact of tracking on, 96
 of teachers, 44–45, 95–96
Experimental probability, 405–407
Exponents, 453–457
 negative, 457–458
 in scientific notation, 455–456
 in very large numbers, 455–456
 in very small numbers, 457–458
Extensions, in problem solving, 46

Factor-of-change method of solving proportions, 310
Factors, 143, 148, 273
Fair-sharing problems, 143, 144
Fibonacci sequence, 427
Five-frames, 122
Fives facts, 169
Fizz & Martina series (Tom Snyder Productions), 143, 150, 239, 256
Flexible strategies for computation, 87, 208, 211, 230
Flips, 359–361
Formulas, 335–340, 342
 for area of parallelograms triangles, and trapezoids, 336–338
 for circles, 338
 functions from, 445–446
 problems with, 335–336
 for volume, 339–340
Four-point rubric, 64, 65, 66
Fraction computation, 264–278
 addition, 265–269
 approximation, 286–287

 connections with decimals, 280–288
 division, 273–278, 464
 estimation, 239, 256–257, 268–269, 273
 multiplication, 261, 270–273
 number sense and, 251–254, 264–265
 subtraction, 265–269
 technology and, 278, 285
 traditional algorithms in, 260–261, 264–265, 267–268, 272–273, 277–278
Fraction Operations (Tenth Planet), 278
Fractions, 242–262. *See also* Fraction computation
 addition of, 265–269
 children's literature and, 261–262
 division of, 273–278
 equivalent fractions, 254, 257–261, 312
 improper, 249–250
 as indicated division, 464
 language of, 244, 246–247
 mixed numbers, 249–250, 268
 models for, 244–246, 260–261
 number sense and, 251–254, 264–265
 percents and, 289
 as rational numbers, 464–465
 sharing tasks and, 243–244, 246–247
 symbols for, 247–251
 technology and, 249–250, 254–257, 261, 278, 285
Frog and Toad Are Friends (Lobal), 414
Front-end methods, 234
Functional relationships, 404, 422–423
Function graphers, 109
Functions, 436–450
 assessment and, 450
 contextual representations of, 437, 440
 defined, 436
 developing function concepts in classroom, 440–441
 equations to represent, 439–440
 from formulas, 445–446
 fun experiments, 448
 graphical representations of, 438–439, 440, 448–450
 graphs without equations, 448–450
 language expressions for, 437–438
 from patterns, 441–442
 proportional situations, 444–445
 from the real world, 442–450
 from scatter plot data, 446–448
 table representations of, 437, 440
 technology and, 440–441, 447

Games, 83–84
Gator Pie (Mathews), 262
Gender equity
 possible causes of inequity, 98
 remedies for inequity, 98–99
Generalizations, in problem solving, 46
Geometer's Sketchpad, The (Key Curriculum Press), 308, 338, 368, 369, 378–379
Geometry, 345–384
 assessment in, 383–384
 classroom strategies for, 349–350
 content goals for, 349

Geometry (continued)
    development of thinking in, 347–348
    exploratory activities, 346–347
    measurement and, 335–338
    proportional reasoning and, 300, 368
    spatial sense, 347, 349, 383–384
    task selection in, 350
    technology in, 356, 359, 362–363, 369–370, 375, 382–383
    tool software for, 108, 356, 362–363, 368
    van Hiele levels of thought, 347–384
Geometry Inventor (Riverdeep), 338, 368, 369
Geometry standard, 4, 384
Giant journal, 70
Gifted and talented students, 99–100
    acceleration and enrichment for, 99–100
    depth for, 100
    identification of, 99
Golden ratio, 427
Golden rectangle, 427
Gold Medal Mathematics (EdVenture Software), 175, 224
Grading, 64, 77–78
    alignment in, 78
    myth of, 77–78
    values in, 78
Graph Club, The (Tom Snyder Productions), 392, 404
Graphical representations, 131–132, 306, 392–397
    bar graphs, 392–394
    circle graphs, 396–397
    continuous data graphs, 395–396
    without equations, 448–450
    of functions, 438–439, 440, 448–450
    of patterns, 423–424
    stem-and-leaf plots, 394–395
Graphing calculators, 105–107, 109, 405, 426, 443
    advantages of using, 105–106
    electronic data collection with, 106–107
Grids, 18, 326
Group discussion, engaging all class members in, 47
Grouping and Place Value (Tenth Planet), 187
Groupings in mathematics, place-value development, 180–181, 183–188, 199
Groupings of students
    heterogeneous, 85
    homogeneous, 96
GUESS boxes, 240
Guessing, 229

Height, measurement of, 336
Heterogeneous groupings, 85
Hexahedron, 383
High-stakes testing, 73–74
    improving performance in, 73–74
    teaching state-mandated standards, 73
Hints, in problem solving, 45
Hispanics. See Cultural diversity
Histograms, 395–396
Home Page for New Math Teachers, 112
Homework, 87–88
    drill as, 88
    practice as, 87

Homogeneous grouping, 96
How Big Is a Foot? (Myller), 343
How Many Snails? (Giganti), 153
How to Count Like a Martian (St. John), 197
Hundreds chart, 190–192, 425
Hypotheses, in problem solving, 47–48

Icosahedron, 383
If You Hopped Like a Frog (Schwartz), 313–314
Illuminations Web site (NCTM), 110, 112, 113, 382, 404
Improper fractions, 249–250
Incredible Comparisons (Ash), 414
Independent events, 408–409
Inferences Standard (NCTM), 60
Informal deduction, in geometry, 348, 350, 376–383
Informal units, 319
In One Day (Parker), 466–467
Instructional scaffolding, 96
Instructional software, 109–110, 126
    concept instruction, 109
    drill, 110, 238–239
    problem solving, 110
    selecting and using, 110–111
Instructional strategies
    for effective teaching, 32–33
    in geometry, 349–350
    looking-back, 56
    modifications for mental disabilities, 94–95
    plan-and-carry-out, 55–56
    problem-analysis skills, 55
    problem solving. See Problem solving
Instrumental understanding, 25
Integers
    operations with, 458–459
    problem-solving approach for, 459–464
Integrative deficits, adaptations for, 94
Internet resources, 111–113
    applets, 107, 112–113, 184, 193, 224, 356, 359
    professional information, 111–112
    for selecting software, 110
    for teachers, 112
Interviews. See Diagnostic interviews
Invented strategies
    activities for flexible thinking, 208–211
    for addition, 205–206, 208
    benefits of, 204
    contextual problems and, 205
    direct modeling and, 205
    for division, 220
    estimations for, 231–232
    mental computation strategy, 204
    for multiplication, 214–217
    nature of, 203
    for subtraction, 205–208
    three-part lesson format and, 205
    traditional algorithms versus, 203
    in whole-number computation, 203–211, 214–217, 220
Investigations in Number, Data, and Space, 8
    Grade K: How Many in All?, 128
    Grade 1: Number Games and Story Problems, 182

Grade 1: Quilt Squares and Block Towns, 354
Grade 2: Coins, Coupons, and Combinations, 142
Grade 3: From Paces to Feet, 323
Grade 3: Things That Come in Groups, 173
Grade 4: Different Shapes, Equal Pieces, 255
Grade 4: Packages and Groups, 217
Grade 5: Building on Numbers You Know, 233
Grade 5: Data, 388
Grade 5: Patterns of Change, 424
Irrational numbers, 465, 466
Is a Blue Whale the Biggest Thing There Is? (Wells), 224

Jim and the Beanstalk (Briggs), 343
Join problems, 136
Joint variation, 430, 436
Journals
    for early learners, 70–71
    nature of, 69–70
    tool software and, 107
Justification for responses, developmental approach and, 33

Kid Pix (Bröderbund), 143
King's Commissioners, The (Friedman), 197

Language
    base-ten, 180
    of doing mathematics, 13–14
    of estimation, 230
    of fractions, 244, 246–247
    for functions, 437–438
    names for numbers, 188–190, 192–193
    second language learners, 97–98
Large numbers
    conceptualizing, 196–197
    estimating, 197
    place-value development for, 195–196
    whole-number computation with, 208
Learning disabilities. *See* Mental disabilities; Specific learning
        disabilities
Learning Principle (NCTM), 3, 27
Learning Standard (NCTM), 60
Least-squares regression line, 403–404
Length
    fractions and, 244–246, 321
    measuring, 320–323
    units of, 320–321
Lesson format
    for problem solving, 41–48
    textbook, 88–89
Limited English proficiency (LEP) students, 97–98
Line graphs, 396
Line plots, 395
Line symmetry, 360
Listening
    developmental approach and, 33
    diversity of students and, 85
    in problem solving, 45, 56
Lists, in problem solving, 56
Literature. *See* Children's literature
Location, in geometry, 358–359, 370–372, 379–380

Logic problems, 110
Logo, 359
Long-term memory deficits, adaptations for, 93–94
Looking-back strategies, 56

Make-ten facts, 162–163, 164
Manipulatives. *See also* Models
    electronic, 107, 118, 184, 193
    tests and, 72
Man Who Counted: A Collection of Mathematical Adventures
        (Tahan), 262
Mass
    measuring, 328–329
    units of, 328
Mastery of basic facts, 156–176
    addition facts, 159–165
    division facts, 173–174
    drill in, 174–175
    multiplication facts, 168–172
    reasoning skills and, 176
    remediation with upper-grade students, 176
    subtraction facts, 165–168
    three-stage approach to, 156–159
    timed tests in, 175
Materials
    attribute, 389–391
    nonproportional, 184
    in patterning, 418
Math Blaster (Knowledge Adventure), 175, 238–239
Math Curse (Scieska and Smith), 467
Mathematically Sane, 112
Mathematical power, 37–38
Mathematics Archives: K12 Internet Sites, 112
Mathematics Assessment (NCTM), 74–76
Mathematics Standard (NCTM), 60
Mathematics Teaching in the Middle School (journal), 51
Math for the Real World (Kaplan/Knowledge Adventure), 150
Math Forum, The (web site), 110, 112
MathKeys (MECC), 143, 224, 261, 413
Math Munchers Deluxe (The Learning Company), 175
Mean, 397–402
    balance point concept of, 400–401
    changes in, 401–402
    leveling concept of, 399–400
Measurement, 130, 275–277, 316–343
    of angles, 329–331
    of area, 323–327, 336–338
    assessment of, 322, 342
    of capacity, 327–328, 339–340
    children's literature and, 343
    comparisons in, 318, 320, 323–325, 327, 328, 329
    decimal with, 283–284
    developing concepts and skills in, 318–323
    estimation in, 229, 319, 333–335
    formulas for, 335–338, 340, 342
    informal units in, 319
    instruments in, 318–319, 321–322, 327–328, 329–331,
        341–342
    of length, 320–323
    of mass, 328–329

Measurement (continued)
  meaning and process of, 317
  models for fractions, 244–246
  proportional reasoning and, 303–309
  standard units in, 319, 331–333, 342
  technology and, 338
  of time, 341–342
  of volume, 327–328, 339–340
  of weight, 328–329
Measurement division problems, 143, 144
  and fractions, 275–277
Measurement standard, 4, 316, 320
Measures of central tendency, 397–402
Measuring cups, 327–328
Median, 397, 398
Median-median lines, 403–404, 446
Median point, 403–404
MegaMath!, 112
Memory, relational understanding and, 26
Memory deficits, adaptations for, 93–94
Mental computation, 43, 132–133, 204, 228. See also Computational estimation
Mental disabilities, 94–95
  modifications in curriculum, 95
  modifications in instruction, 94–95
Metacognition
  developing habit of, 56
  nature of, 54–55
Metric system, 333
Mid-segment, 370
Mighty Math (Edmark), 356, 413
Million Fish . . . More or Less, A (McKissack), 197–198
Minilessons, 83
Missing-part activities, 125–126
Mixed numbers, 249–250, 268
Mode, 397
Model-based problems. See also Direct modeling
  in addition, 139–140, 211–212
  in division, 147–149, 221
  for fractions, 244–246, 260–261
  in multiplication, 147–149, 217–218
  for percents, 289
  for place value, 183–184, 192–193
  in subtraction, 140, 213
Models, 17, 28–31
  classroom use of, 30–31
  developmental approach and, 33
  examples of, 28–30
  for fractions, 244–246, 260–261
  incorrect use of, 31
  instructional software and, 109
  for measurement, 318
  in problem solving, 55
Moira's Birthday (Munsch), 197
Money
  counting, 194
  decimal with, 283–284
More Than One (Hoban), 153
Multicultural mathematics, 96–97
Multiple entry points, 38, 40–41, 84

Multiplicand, 143
Multiplication, 143–154
  computational estimation in, 234, 235
  contextual problems, 146–147, 150–153
  of decimals, 293–294
  distributive property, 150
  of fractions, 261, 270–273
  invented strategies for, 214–217
  model-based problems, 147–149, 217–218
  multiplicative identity, 261
  order property, 149
  in problem-solving approach with integers, 462–464
  problem structures, 143–146
  proportional reasoning and, 300–301
  by single-digit multiplier, 215–216, 217–218
  strategies for mastery of facts, 168–172
  symbolism in, 146–147
  traditional algorithms for, 217–219, 272–273
  by two-digit multiplier, 216–217, 218–219
  using multiples of 10 and 100, 216
  zero and one in, 149–150, 170
Multiplicative comparison problems, 143, 144–145
Multipliers, 143
  single-digit, 215–216, 217–218
  two-digit, 216–217, 218–219
Multistep problems, 152

Names for numbers
  in place-value development, 188–190, 192–193
  three-digit, 189–190
  two-digit, 188–189
National Assessment of Educational Progress (NAEP), 7, 26, 98, 249, 286, 287, 288, 318, 347
National Council of Teachers of Mathematics (NCTM), 1–9
  Addenda Series books, 51
  Assessment Standards for School Mathematics, 2, 6, 59, 60–61
  Curriculum and Evaluation Standards for School Mathematics, 1–2, 36, 60
  e-Standards, 5–6, 84, 108, 113, 193, 356, 359, 373, 402
  "Every Child" statement, 91
  growth and, 8–9
  Illuminations Web site, 110, 112, 113, 382, 404
  journals, 51
  Navigations series, 107
  News Bulletin, 111
  other influences and pressures on reform, 6–8
  Principles and Standards for School Mathematics, 1, 2–6, 13, 36, 37–38, 59, 61, 73, 103, 107, 228, 316, 387
  Professional Standards for Teaching Mathematics, 2, 6, 20
  Task Force on the Mathematically Promising, 99–100
  web site, 111, 261
National Library of Virtual Manipulatives (NLVM), 113, 184, 193, 261, 356
National Science Foundation (NSF), 8
Native Americans. See Cultural diversity
Navigations series (NCTM), 107
Near-double relationships, 129–130, 162
Negative exponents, 457–458
Negative numbers, 457–458
New Standards Project, 64

Nines in multiplication, 170–171
No Child Left Behind Act (2001), 73
Nonproportional materials, in place-value development, 184
Notation
    calculators and, 454–456
    scientific, 455–456
Number and operations standard, 4
Number concepts
    early, 25
    in mastery of basic facts, 157
    models for, 28–31
    problem solving examples, 38–39
    relational understanding and, 26
Number patterns, 425–427
Number relationships, 119–130
    anchoring numbers to 5 and 10, 120, 122–123
    assessment and, 127–129
    double and near-double relationships, 129–130, 161–162, 164, 169, 172
    extending *more* and *less* relationships, 129
    one and two more, one and two less, 119, 121–122
    part-part-whole relationships, 120, 123–126, 127–128
    pre-place-value relationship with 10, 129
    searching for, 421–423
    spatial, 119, 120–121
    technology and, 126
Number sense
    approximate numbers, 194
    decimal, 285–288
    early. *See* Early number sense
    fraction, 251–254, 264–265
    place-value development in, 193–195
    real-world ideas and, 130–132, 194
    rounding, 194, 234–235, 288
Numerals, recognition and writing of, 117–118
Numerators, 248–249

Observation, 67–68, 225
    anecdotal notes in, 67
    checklists for, 68
    rubrics in, 67–68
Obtuse angles, 354
Octahedron, 383
One and two more, one and two less, 119, 121–122, 160
Open-ended problem solving, 100
Openness Standard (NCTM), 60
Operations in mathematics, 135–154. *See also names of specific operations*
    addition, 135–143
    children's literature and, 153–154
    division, 143–154
    with integers, 458–459
    in mastery of basic facts, 157
    multiplication, 143–154
    subtraction, 135–143
Order property
    in addition, 141
    in multiplication, 149

Parallelograms, area of, 336–337
Partial product, 218
Partition division problems, 274–275
    and fractions, 274–275
Partitioning strategies, 215
Partition problems, 143, 144
Part-part-whole relationships, 120, 123–126, 127–129
    activities, 124–126
    basic ingredients, 123–124
    problems in, 137
    technology and, 126
Parts of numbers
    activities for flexible thinking, 209–211
    parts-and-whole-tasks, 250–251
Part-to-part ratios, 299
Part-to-whole ratios, 299
Patterned set recognition, 119, 120–121
Pattern (Pluckrose), 432
Patterns
    functions from, 441–442
    graphing, 423–424
    on hundreds chart, 425
    number, 425–427
    in problem solving, 55
    relationships in, 421–423
    repeating, 418–420
    sequences, 420–424, 427
    variables as generators of, 428–430
Percents, 288–292
    assessment and, 296
    children's literature and, 295–296
    computational estimation with, 239, 290–292
    estimation with, 290–292
    fractions and, 289
    hundredths in, 288–289
    proportional reasoning and, 312–313
    realistic problems with, 289–292
Perceptual deficits, adaptations for, 93
Performance assessment, 62
Performance indicators, 64–66
Perimeter, 326–327
Personal digital assistants (PDAs), 106–107
Phantom Tollbooth, The (Juster), 296, 466
Physical models, 17
Pie charts, 396–397
Place-value development, 178–199
    activities for flexible thinking, 209
    assessment and, 198–199
    base-ten fraction models, 281–282
    basic ideas in, 179–182
    children's literature and, 197–198
    counting in, 179–180, 199
    extension to decimals, 282–284
    grouping in, 180–181, 183–188, 199
    hundreds chart, 190–192
    integration of groupings in, 179–181
    models for place value, 183–184, 192–193
    numbers beyond 1000, 195–197
    number sense development and, 193–195
    oral names for numbers in, 188–190, 192–193

Place-value development (*continued*)
  pre-base-10 concepts, 129, 178–179
  relational understandings in, 181
  symbols in, 180–181, 190, 192–193
  technology in, 184, 187, 193
  thousands chart, 192
Place-value mats, 190
Platonic solids, 383
Point symmetry, 372
Polyhedron, 383
Portfolios, 74–76
  content suggestions, 74–76
  defined, 74
  management of, 76
Practice. *See* Drill and practice
Practice tests, 73–74
Praise, in problem solving, 47, 56
Principles and Standards for School Mathematics (NCTM),
    1, 2–6, 13, 36, 37–38, 61, 73, 103, 107, 228,
    316, 387
  content standards in, 4
  drills and, 13
  goals for students, 2
  principles in, 3–4, 27, 59
  process standards in, 4–6
Prisms, 339, 340
Probability, 405–414. *See also* Data analysis and probability
    standard
  assessment issues, 414
  children's literature and, 414
  developing concepts of, 407–411
  simulations and, 411–414
  technology and, 109, 412–414
  theoretical versus experimental, 405–407
Probability software, 109, 412–413
Problem solving, 36–56
  analytic scale for, 66–67
  assessment of, 61
  calculators in, 104
  description of tasks or problems, 38
  designing and selecting tasks for, 48–52
  differentiated tasks in, 84–85
  examples of problem-based tasks, 38–40
  fractions and, 265
  frequently asked questions and, 53–54
  goals of, 54, 55–56
  instructional software and, 110
  multiple entry points for, 38, 40–41, 84
  open-ended, 100
  operations in, 459–464. *See also* Addition; Division;
    Multiplication; Subtraction
  as principal instructional strategy, 36–38
  relational understanding and, 26
  strategies for, 54–55
  teaching about, 54–55
  teaching tips and questions for, 52–54
  three-part lesson format, 41–48, 81–84, 205
  value of, 37–38
  worthwhile tasks and, 32–33

Problem solving standard, 4, 5, 61
Procedural mathematics, 27–28
  assessment of, 61
  examples of problem-based tasks in, 39–40
Process standards (NCTM), 4–6
Product-of-measures problems, 143, 146
Professional Standards for Teaching Mathematics (NCTM), 2
  shifts in classroom environment, 6, 20
  teaching standards, 6
Proportional reasoning, 298–314
  activities to develop, 301–309, 311–313
  additive, 300–301
  assessment of, 314
  characteristics of, 300
  children and, 300
  children's literature and, 313–314
  functions in, 444–445
  geometry and, 300, 368
  multiplicative, 300–301
  percent problems in, 312–313
  proportions in, 300, 309–313
  ratios in, 299–300, 301–305, 309
  solving proportions, 309–313
  technology and, 313
Protractor, 329–331
Pyramids, volume of, 340
Pythagorean relationship, 377–378, 379–380

Quantity estimation, 229
Quartiles, 398

Ramp problems, 38, 40–41
Range, 398–399
Rates, as ratios, 299–300
Rational numbers, 464–465, 466
Ratios, 25–26
  within and between, 309
  comparing, 302–303, 308
  equivalent, 301–302
  ratio tables, 303–305
  types of, 299–300
Real numbers, 465–466
Real-world situations
  computational estimation in, 229, 230
  functions in, 442–450
  number sense and, 130–132, 194
  percents in, 289–292
Reasoning and proof standard, 4, 5, 61
Rectangles, area of, 336–337
Recursive relationships, 421–422, 424
Reflections, 359–361
Reflective thinking, 23, 32
Region models, for fractions, 244
Relational understanding, 25, 26–27, 181
Relative magnitude, 193
Remainders, in division, 147
Repeated-addition problems, 143, 144
Repeated-subtraction problems, 143, 144
Repeating patterns, 418–420

Representations
    equivalent, in place-value development, 187–188
    useful, in invented strategies for multiplication, 214–215
Representation standard, 5
Representing Fractions (Tenth Planet), 254–256
Review and practice, 74
Right angles, 354
Rigor, in geometry, 348
Roots, 465–466
Rotational symmetry, 360–361
Rotations, 359–361, 370–372
Rote learning, 24
Rounding, 194, 234–235, 288
Rubrics, 64–68
    analytic scale, 66–67
    four-point scale, 64, 65, 66
    nature of, 64
    observation, 67–68
    performance indicators, 64–66
    simple, 64
    student involvement with, 66
Rulers, 321–322
Rules, in problem solving, 47–48

Sample space, 406
Scaffolding, 96
Scales, 329
Scaling, with ratio tables, 303–305, 308
Scatter plots, 402–404
    best-fit lines, 402–404, 446
    functions from, 446–448
Scientific notation, 455–456
Second language learners, 97–98
Second method, in problem solving, 46
Self-assessment, 71–72
    attitude inventories in, 71–72
    nature of, 71
Self-generativity, relational understanding and, 26
Semantic forms of equations, 138
Separate problems, 136–137
Sequences, 420–424, 427
Set models, for fractions, 246
Shape of data, 389
Shapes
    circles, 338–339, 368–369, 396–397
    constructing and dissecting, 353–357, 368
    definitions and proofs, 376–377
    parallelograms, 376–377
    Pythagorean relationship, 377–378, 379–380
    sorting and classifying, 351–352, 366–368, 370
    three-dimensional, 356–357, 365–366
    two-dimensional, 363–365
Shapes (Clements & Sarama), 362–363
Shape Up (Sunburst), 362–363
Sharing tasks, fractions and, 243–244, 246–247
Shodo Education Foundation, Inc.: Project Interaction, 113
Short-term memory deficits, adaptations for, 93–94
Simulations, 411–414
Skip counting, 191, 194

Slides, 359–361
Slope, 380
Socioeconomic status (SES), 95
Software, 107–111
    instructional, 109–110, 126, 238–239
    probability, 109, 412–413
    selecting and using, 110–111
    tool, 107–109
Spatial relationships, 119, 120–121
Spatial sense, 347, 349, 383–384
Special children, problem solving and, 56
Specific learning disabilities, 92–94
    adaptations for, 93–94
    perspective on, 93
Spreadsheets, 109, 306, 313
Standard units, 319, 331–333, 342
    choosing appropriate, 332
    familiarity with, 331–332
    important, 332–333
State-mandated standards, 73
State standards, 7–8
Stem-and-leaf plots, 394–395
Story problems. *See* Contextual problems
Strategies for computational estimation, 233–237
    compatible numbers, 235–237
    front-end methods, 234
    rounding methods, 234–235
Strategies for mastery of basic facts, 156–176
    addition, 159–165
    development of, 157–158
    division, 173–174
    drill-based, 158, 159, 174–175
    fact remediation with upper-grade students, 176
    multiplication, 168–172
    selection or retrieval of, 158, 159, 174–175
    subtraction, 165–168
    timed tests, 175
Structural set, 389
Subdivisions, 334
Subtraction, 135–143
    comparison models, 140–141
    computational estimation in, 234–235
    contextual problems, 138–139
    of decimals, 293
    of fractions, 265–269
    invented strategies for, 205–208
    model-based problems, 140, 213
    order property, 141
    in problem-solving approach with integers, 460–462
    problem structures, 135–138
    strategies for mastery of basic facts, 165–168
    symbolism in, 139
    technology and, 143
    as think-addition, 140, 165–168
    traditional algorithms for, 213–214, 267–268
    zero property, 141–142, 213
Success, in problem solving, 56
Suggestions, in problem solving, 45
Sums greater than 10, 166–168

Sums to 10, 165–166
Symbolism
    in addition, 139
    calculators and notation, 454–456
    in division, 146–147, 223
    for fractions, 247–251
    models and, 31
    in multiplication, 146–147
    in place-value development, 180–181, 190, 192–193
    in subtraction, 139
Symmetry
    axis of, 372
    line, 360
    point, 372
    rotational, 360–361, 370–372

Tables
    in problem solving, 55
    representations of functions, 437, 440
Tabletop, Jr. (Bröderbund), 391–392
Take-away subtraction, 207–208
Tangible Math (Riverdeep), 413
Tangrams, 324
Tape measures, 322
Tasks
    for appropriate assessment, 62–64
    for problem solving, 38–40, 48–52, 82, 84–85
    selection of geometry, 350
Teachers
    expectations for students, 44–45, 95–96
    gender issues and, 98
    role in problem solving, 41–48
Teacher's editions, 88
Teaching Children Mathematics (journal), 51
Teaching Principle (NCTM), 3, 41
Teaching standards, 6
Technology in mathematics, 103–113. See also Calculators; Internet resources; Software
    addition and subtraction problems, 143
    calculators, 103–107
    computational estimation and, 238–239
    computers and software, 107–111
    data analysis and probability standard, 391–392, 404
    decimals and, 288
    drill and practice, 175
    early number concepts, 118
    early number sense, 126
    fractions and, 249–250, 254–257, 261, 278, 285
    functions and, 440–441, 447
    geometry and, 356, 359, 362–363, 369–370, 375, 382–383
    Internet resources, 111–113
    measurement and, 338
    multiplication and division problems, 150
    place-value development, 184, 187, 193
    proportional reasoning and, 313
    whole-number computation, 224
Technology Principle (NCTM), 3–4, 103
Ten-frame facts, 164–165
Ten-frames, 122

Tessellations, in geometry, 357–358, 374
TesselMania! (The Learning Company), 375
Testing of ideas, in problem solving, 46
Tests, 72–74
Test-taking strategies, 74
Tetrahedron, 383
Textbooks
    development of, 88
    in problem-based classroom, 48–50, 88–89
    reform-oriented, 50
    suggestions for using, 89
    in task design and selection, 48–50
    teacher's editions, 88
    traditional, 48–50
    two-page lesson format, 88–89
Theoretical probability, 405–407
Think-addition, subtraction as, 140, 165–168
Third International Mathematics and Science Study (TIMSS), 7, 87
Thousands chart, 192
3D Geoshapes, 356–357
329th Friend, The (Sharmat), 239–240
Three-dimensional shapes, 356–357, 365–366
Three-part lesson format, 41–48, 81–84, 205
    to encourage invented strategy use, 205
    after phase, 42, 46–48, 83
    before phase, 41, 42–45, 83
    during phase, 41, 45–46, 83
    planning, 81–84
    variations on, 83
Time, measurement of, 341–342
Timed tests, 175
Tool software, 107–109
    electronic manipulatives, 107, 118
    function graphers, 109
    geometry, 108, 356, 362–363, 368
    probability and data analysis, 109
    selecting and using, 110–111
Trace feature, 443
Tracking, expectations and, 96
Traditional algorithms
    for addition, 211–213, 267–268
    for division, 220–224, 277–278
    for fractions, 260–261, 264–265, 267–268, 272–273, 277–278
    invented strategies versus, 203
    for multiplication, 217–219, 272–273
    for proportions, 310–311
    for subtraction, 213–214, 267–268
    timing of use, 204–205, 265
Transformations, in geometry, 359–361, 372–374, 380–382
Translations, 359–361
Trapezoids, area of, 338
Tree diagrams, 18
Triangles, area of, 337
Turns, 359–361
Turtle Math (Clements & Meredith), 359
Twelve Circus Rings, The (Chwast), 239
Two-dimensional shapes, 363–365
Two Ways to Count to Ten (Dee), 132

Understanding in mathematics, 22–33
  checking for, 43–44
  constructivism in, 22–27
  defined, 24
  developmental approach to, 31–33
  examples of, 25–26
  instrumental, 25
  relational, 25, 26–27
  role of models in developing, 28–31
  types of mathematical knowledge, 27–28
Unifix Software (Hickey), 118, 126, 187
U.S. Census Data, 113
U.S. customary system, 333
Unit fractions, 250–251
Unit perspective, 48
Unit-rate method of solving proportions, 310
Unknowns, variables as, 428

Values, grading and, 78
van Hiele levels of thought, 347–384
  characteristics of, 348
  Level 0: Visualization, 347, 349–363
  Level 1: Analysis, 347–348, 350, 363–376
  Level 2: Informal deduction, 348, 350, 376–383
  Level 3: Deduction, 348
  Level 4: Rigor, 348
Variables, 427–430
  different uses of, 428
  misunderstandings about, 427
  as pattern generators, 428–430
  as quantities that vary, 430
  as unknowns, 428
Verbs, of doing mathematics, 13–14
Very Hungry Caterpillar, The (Carle), 132
Very large numbers, 455–456
Very small numbers, 457–458
Visualization, in geometry, 347, 361–363, 375–376, 382–383

Volume
  of cylinders, 339–340
  measurement of, 327–328, 339–340
  units of, 327

Web of ideas, 25–26
Weight
  measuring, 328–329
  units of, 328
Whole-number computation, 201–225
  assessment and, 211, 224–225
  children's literature and, 224
  direct modeling in, 202–203, 205
  estimation in. *See* Computational estimation
  invented strategies in, 203–211, 214–217, 220
  place values in. *See* Place value-development
  technology in, 224
  traditional algorithms in, 203, 204–205, 211–214, 217–219, 220–224
Whole-number exponents, 454
Word Problem Square Off (Gamco), 150
Workstations, 83–84
World Fact Book, The, 113
Writing
  developmental approach and, 33
  of journals, 69–71
  prompts and ideas for, 70
  student self-assessment of, 71–72
  value of, 69

Zero property
  in addition, 141–142, 161
  in division, 150
  fraction number sense and, 251–252
  in multiplication, 149–150, 170
  in subtraction, 141–142, 213
Zome System, 356–357
Zoombinis Logical Journey, EEV (The Learning Company), 392